MEANS
ILLUSTRATED
CONSTRUCTION
DICTIONARY *Third Edition, Unabridged*

RSMeans
CMDGROUP

MEANS
ILLUSTRATED
CONSTRUCTION
DICTIONARY

Third Edition, Unabridged

Includes CD-ROM!

RSMeans
CMDGROUP

Copyright 2000

R.S. Means Company, Inc.
Construction Publishers & Consultants
Construction Plaza
63 Smiths Lane
Kingston, MA 02364-0800
(781) 585-7880

The editor of this book was John Marchetti. The managing editor was Mary Greene. The production manager was Michael Kokernak. The production coordinator was Marion Schofield. The book and cover were designed by Norman R. Forgit.

Printed in the United States of America

10 9 8 7 6 5 4 3

Library of Congress Catalog Number Pending

ISBN 0-87629-538-3

TABLE OF CONTENTS

ABOUT THE CD-ROM

Searching for a Term Electronically: The CD-ROM (found in the sleeve on the inside back cover of this book) contains the complete text of the print dictionary, plus some extra features. Using the CD, you can search for a specific term or browse through the book's pages on-screen.

Expanded information is available for many terms on the CD. Some terms have larger-scale, more detailed graphics than those that appear in the printed book. Other terms are expanded with in-depth discussion of a concept or practice.

The CD-ROM also provides a live link to a special Internet "home port," dedicated to this dictionary. This site will present regular updates of new construction terms as they become recognized in the industry. The home port also offers users an opportunity to suggest new terms that might be suitable for web updates and/or a future edition of the print book.

FOREWORD

This latest edition of the *Means Illustrated Construction Dictionary* is a great step forward. With nearly 1,000 additional terms and 200 new illustrations, it covers an even wider range of construction specialties than its highly praised predecessor. It addresses all of the recent developments in building materials and processes, from engineered lumber products to the newest seismic technologies. The companion CD-ROM that comes with this new edition adds more features: large detailed graphics, expanded definitions, and links to applicable CSI MasterFormat numbers. It also provides the gateway to a *Construction Dictionary* web site where users can get updates on the industry's latest terms and trends. Finally, the dictionary's reference section, already extensive, has been updated and includes a valuable listing of key professional organizations.

The *Means Illustrated Construction Dictionary* is written in the language used by the construction trades and professions today, and includes many slang, regional, and colloquial terms. Whenever possible, words or phrases are explained in non-technical language. Technical terms that are used in definitions are themselves defined as separate entries. Archaic architectural terms are purposely omitted, as this is intended to be a current construction dictionary with up-to-date terminology.

Areas that that have been significantly expanded and updated include building automation, energy and environmental issues, and historic preservation. To identify and define these terms, the editors obtained the assistance of industry groups, associations, societies, and manufacturers, as well as published authors who are nationally recognized authorities. A list of contributors appears in the acknowledgments on the following page.

ACKNOWLEDGMENTS

Many groups, associations, societies, manufacturers, and individuals have assisted in the production of this book by granting permission to reproduce specific text and graphics from their publications. The following is a list of these contributors and publications.

American Association of Cost Engineers (AACE)

American Ceramic Society (ACS)

American Concrete Institute (ACI), *Cement and Concrete Terminology*

American Institute of Steel Construction, Inc. (AISC)

American Society of Plumbing Engineers (ASPE)

The Asphalt Institute

Brick Industry Association

Builders' Hardware Manufacturers Association, Inc.

Deep Foundations Institute

The Gypsum Association

International Institute of Lath and Plaster

International Masonry Institute

The Lincoln Electric Company

New England Environmental Expo

North Castle Books, publishers of *Moving the Earth*

Portland Cement Association

Random Lengths, publishers of *Terms of the Trade*

United States League of Savings Institutions (USL)

Kweku K. Bentil, *Fundamentals of the Construction Process*

Harold R. Colen, *HVAC Systems Evaluation*

Paul J. Cook, *Bidding for Contractors*

Wayne J. DelPico, *Plan Reading & Material Takeoff*

Peter H. Emmons, *Concrete Repair and Maintenance Illustrated*

Carol E. Farren, *Planning & Managing Interior Projects*

Sylvia H. Fee, *Landscape Estimating Methods, 3rd Ed.*

Joseph J. Galeno and Sheldon T. Greene, *Means Plumbing Estimating Methods, 2nd Ed.*

R.D. Hebert, *Roofing: Design Criteria, Options, Selection*

Charles R. Heuer, *Means Legal Reference for Design & Construction*

Francis J. Hopcroft, David L. Vitale, and Donald L. Anglehart,
Hazardous Material and Hazardous Waste: A Construction Reference Manual

Deborah S. Kearney, *The ADA in Practice*

Michael S. Milliner, *Contractor's Business Handbook*

Waller S. Poage, *The Building Professional's Guide to Contract Documents*

Richard R. Rast, *Environmental Remediation Estimating Methods*

Richard C. Ringwald, *Means Heavy Construction Handbook*

William H. Rowe, *HVAC: Design Criteria, Options, Selection, 2nd Ed.*

Richard W. Sievert, *Total Productive Facilities Management*

Scot Simpson, *Basics for Builders: Framing & Rough Carpentry*

Theodore J. Trauner, Jr., and Michael H. Payne, *Bidding & Managing
Government Construction*

Timothy R. Twomey, *Understanding the Legal Aspects of Design/Build*

We are also grateful to members of the Department of Building Science at Clemson University who, under the direction of Roger Liska, P.E., assisted in reviewing these construction terms and definitions in the second edition.

The cover design of this book includes a floor plan prepared by Kaestle Boos Associates, Inc. Architects of New Britain, Connecticut and Frankin, Massachusetts.

ABBREVIATIONS

The abbreviations listed below are those most commonly used in the construction industry. Alternative forms (usually nonstandard) are shown in parentheses.

a acre, ampere

A area, area square feet, ampere

A&E architect-engineer

AAMA Architectural Aluminum Manufacturers Association

AASHTO American Association of State Highway and Transportation Officials

ABC aggregate base course, Associated Builders and Contractors

ABS acrylonitrile butadiene styrene, asbestos-bonded steel

ABT air blast transformer, about

ac, a-c, a.c. alternating current

a.c. asphaltic concrete (a.c. paving)

AC air-conditioning, alternating current (on drawings), armored cable (on drawings), asbestos cement

ACB asbestos-cement board, air circuit breaker

ACC accumulator

Access. accessory

ACD automatic closing device

ACEC American Consulting Engineers Council

ACGIH American Conference of Governmental Industrial Hygienists

ACI American Concrete Institute, Association of Construction Inspectors

ACM asbestos-containing material, asbestos-covered metal

ACS American Ceramic Society

ACSR aluminum cable steel reinforced, aluminum conductor steel reinforced

Acst acoustic

Actl actual

a.d. air-dried

AD access door, air-dried, area drain, as drawn

ADA Americans with Disabilities Act

ADAAG Americans with Disabilities Act Accessibility Guidelines

ADD addendum (on drawings), addition (on drawings)

Addit. additional

ADF after deducting freight (used in lumber industry)

ADH adhesive

ADI after date of invoice

adj adjacent, adjoining, adjust, adjustable

ADS automatic door seal

af audio frequency

AFE Association for Facilities Engineering (formerly the American Institute of Plant Engineers)

AFL-CIO American Federation of Labor and the Committee for Industrial Organization.

AG above grade

AGA American Gas Association

AGC Associated General Contractors

Agg., Aggr aggregate

AGL above ground level

AH, A HR, amp hr ampere-hour

AHERA Asbestos Hazard Emergency Response Act

AHU air-handling unit

AI Asphalt Institute

AIA American Institute of Architects, Asbestos Information Association

AIC ampere interrupting capacity

AIEE American Institute of Electrical Engineers

AIMA Acoustical and Insulating Materials Association

AISC American Institute of Steel Construction

AISE Association of Iron and Steel Engineers

AISI American Iron and Steel Institute

AITC American Institute of Timber Construction

AL, alum aluminum

Allow., ALLOW allowance

ALM alarm

ALS American Lumber Standards

alt altitude

ALT alternate

ALTN alteration

ALY alloy

a.m. ante meridiem

AMB asbestos millboard

AMD air-moving device

amp, Amp. ampere

ANFO ammonium nitrate fuel oil mix

ANL anneal

Anod. anodized

ANSI American National Standards Institute

AP access panel

APA The Engineered Wood Association (formerly the American Plywood Association)

APC acoustical plaster ceiling, American Plastics Council

APF acid-proof floor

API American Petroleum Institute

APPA The Association of Higher Education Facilities Officers (formerly the Association of Physical Plant Administrators)

Appd approved

Approx approximate

APR air-purifying respirator

Apt apartment

APW Architectural Projected Window

AR as required, as rolled

ARC W, ARC/W arc weld

ARS asbestos roof shingles

ART. artificial

AS automatic sprinkler

ASA American Standards Association

asb asbestos

ASBC American Standard Building Code

asbe asbestos worker

ASC asphalt surface course

ASCE American Society of Civil Engineers

ASCII American Standard Code for Information Interchange

ASEC American Standard Elevator Codes

ASHRAE American Society of Heating, Refrigeration, and Air-Conditioning Engineers

ASIS American Society for Industrial Security

ASME American Society of Mechanical Engineers

asph asphalt

ASR automatic sprinkler riser

ASSE American Society of Sanitary Engineering

ASTM American Society for Testing and Materials

AT asphalt tile, airtight

ATB asphalt-tile base

ATC acoustical tile ceiling; architectural terra-cotta, automatic temperature control

ATF asphalt-tile floor

atm atmosphere, atmospheric

aux auxiliary

av, ave, avg average

A/W all-weather

AW actual weight

AW&L All widths and lengths

AWG American wire gauge

AWI Architectural Woodwork Institute

AWPI American Wood Preservers Institute

AWS American Welding Society

AWWI American Wood Window Institute

FIRE EXTINGUISHER

(A)(B)(C)
WOOD, PAPER, ETC.,
BURNING LIQUIDS,
ELECTRICAL

ABC extinguisher

A-block

abaciscus, abaculus (1) A tessara used in mosaic tile. (2) A small abacus.

abacus The top component of a column capital.

abamurus A masonry buttress for the support of a wall.

abandon catch basin To destroy or fill in an existing catch basin.

abate (1) To cut away in stone or to beat down on metal in order to create figures or a pattern in relief. (2) To decrease concentrations of pollutants in an outfall.

abatement (1) The encapsulation or removal of building materials containing asbestos to prevent the release of and exposure to asbestos fibers. (2) In lumber industry, the amount of wood lost as waste during the process of sawing or planing.

abat-jour A sloped opening in a roof or wall designed to direct daylight downward.

abatsons Acoustical reflectors for directing sound waves.

abatvent A wall louver that restricts wind from entering a building, but admits light and air.

abatvoix An acoustical reflector for a single voice, such as behind and over a church pulpit.

ABC extinguisher A fire extinguisher suitable for use on type A, B, and C fires.

A-block A hollow masonry unit with one closed end commonly used at wall openings.

Abney level A hand-held level used for measuring vertical angles.

above-grade subfloors A floor above ground level, but with no headroom below.

abrade To scrape or wear away a surface by friction or striking.

Abrams' law The rule stating that with given materials, curing, and testing conditions, concrete strength is inversely related to the ratio of water to cement. Low water-to-cement ratios produce high strengths.

abrasion The process of wearing away a surface by friction.

abrasion resistance index A comparison of the abrasion resistance of a given material to that of rubber. The index is applied principally to aggregate handling equipment.

abrasive (1) A hard material used for wearing away or polishing a surface by friction. (2) The material that is adhered to or embedded in a surface such as sandpaper or a whetstone.

abrasive aggregate The aggregate used to increase the abrasiveness of the surface of a concrete slab.

abrasive blasting A method of cleaning surfaces with a high-pressure stream of air and an abrasive material such as sand or steel grit.

abrasive floor A floor with an abrasive adhered to or embedded in the surface to provide traction and prevent slipping.

abrasive floor tile Floor tile with an abrasive adhered to the surface.

abrasive nosing A strip of anti-skid abrasive adhered to or attached to the nosing of a stair tread.

abrasive stair tread A stair tread with an abrasive surface.

absorber plate

abrasive terrazzo A terrazzo floor with an abrasive surface rather than a high polish.

abreuvoir The mortar joint between masonry units.

absolute humidity *See* **humidity.**

absolute pressure *See* **pressure.**

absorbed moisture Moisture that has been absorbed by a solid such as masonry.

absorbent (1) A material that has an affinity for certain substances and attracts these substances from a liquid or gas with which it is in contact, thus changing the physical and/or chemical properties of the material. (2) A substance that attracts and holds large quantities of liquid.

absorber (1) A device containing liquid for the absorption of vapors. (2) In a refrigeration system, the component on the low-pressure side used for absorbing refrigerant vapors.

absorber plate That part of a solar energy system that collects the solar energy.

absorbing well *See* **dry well.**

absorption (1) The process by which a liquid is drawn into the pores of a permeable material. (2) The process by which solar energy is collected on a surface. (3) The increase in weight of a porous object resulting from immersion in water for a given time, expressed as a percent of the dry weight.

absorption air-conditioning An air cooling and dehumidifying system powered by solar or other energy collected on absorbing plates.

absorption bed or field (disposal field, drain field) A network of trenches that may contain coarse aggregate and

distribution pipe, and is used to distribute septic tank effluent into the surrounding soil.

absorption chiller Heat-operated refrigeration unit that uses an absorbent (lithium bromide) as a secondary fluid to absorb the primary fluid (water), which is a gaseous refrigerant in the evaporator. The evaporative process absorbs heat, thereby cooling the refrigerant (water) which in turn cools the chilled water circulating through the heat exchanger.

absorption loss (1) Water losses that occur until soil particles are sufficiently saturated, such as in filling a reservoir for the first time. (2) Water losses that occur until the aggregate in a concrete mix is saturated.

absorption rate (initial rate of absorption) The weight of water absorbed by a brick or concrete masonry unit that is partially immersed in water for one minute, expressed in grams or ounces per minute.

absorption refrigeration system (1) A cooling system in which the refrigerant vapors that enter an absorber are released into a generator by the application of heat. (2) A cooling system powered by heat from solar absorbers.

absorption trench *See* **absorption bed.**

absorption-type liquid chiller A system using an absorber, condenser, and associated accessories to cool a secondary liquid.

absorptive lens A filter lens designed to mitigate the effects of glare and reflected light.

abutment piece

access door

ABS plastic pipe Acrylonitrile-butadiene-styrene plastic pipe, which is resistant to heat, impact, and chemicals.

abstract of bids A list of the bidders for a sealed bid procurement indicating the significant portions of their bids.

abstract of title A deed for a parcel of land showing encumbrances and a history of ownership.

abut To join or touch at one edge or end without overlapping.

abutment (butment) (1) The structure that supports the end of a bridge or that anchors the cables of a suspension bridge. (2) The surface at which one member abuts another.

abutment piece In structural framing, the horizontal member that distributes the load of vertical members and is thus the sole plate of a partition.

abuttals The properties adjacent to a parcel of land or body of water and which mark the boundaries of that land or water body.

abutting joint A joint between two pieces of wood in which the grain of one is at an angle to the grain of the other (usually 90°).

abutting tenon In carpentry, one of two wood members that meet in a common mortise.

Abyssinian well *See* **wellpoint**.

accelerated life test A test at elevated levels of environmental stress to determine deterioration or failure more rapidly.

acceleration (1) An increase in velocity or rate of change. (2) The ordered or voluntarily expedited performance of construction work at a faster rate than anticipated in the original schedule, the purpose of which is to recapture project delay. This is accomplished by increasing labor hours and other resources. (3) The speeding up of the setting or hardening process of concrete by using an additive in the mix. The process of acceleration allows forms to be stripped sooner or floors finished earlier.

accelerator An additive which, when added to paint, concrete, mortar, or grout mix, speeds the rate of hydration and thereby causes it to set or harden sooner.

accelograph An instrument used to measure displacement during an earthquake. Often installed in buildings to measure movement.

accent lighting Fixtures or directional beams of light arranged so as to bring attention to an object or area.

acceptance Compliance by an offeree with the terms and conditions of an offer.

accepted bid The proposal or bid a contractor and an owner or owner's representative use as the basis for entering into a construction contract.

access (1) The means of entry into a building, area, or room. (2) A port or opening through which equipment may be inspected or repaired.

access connection A ramp or roadway for entering or exiting an arterial highway.

access control system Computerized building security equipment, such as badge readers, designed to protect against unauthorized entry into buildings or building zones.

access door or panel A means of access for the inspection, repair, or service of concealed systems, such as air-conditioning equipment.

accordion partition

acetylene torch

AC generator

access eye A fitting provided at drainpipe bends for rodding.

access flooring A raised flooring system with removable panels to allow access to the area below. This type of flooring is frequently used in computer rooms because it provides easy access to cables.

accessible That which is easily removed, repaired, or serviced without damaging the finish of a building.

accessories In the placing of concrete, the items used to assemble scaffolding, shoring, and forms, other than the wales, frames, and the forms themselves.

accessory building A secondary building on the same lot adjacent to the main building.

accident On construction sites, a sudden unexpected event, identifiable in terms of time and place, that results in personal injury or property damage.

accolade Ornamental treatment over an arch, doorway, or window formed by two ogee curves meeting in the middle.

accord and satisfaction A legal term referring to an agreement between parties to a contract whereby one accepts payment in the compromise of a dispute, claim, or change proposal. Typically this term is used concerning a mutual release of responsibility for a claim.
See also **settlement**.

accordion door A retractable door, usually fabric-faced, hung from an overhead track and folding like the bellows of an accordion.

accordion partition A retractable partition having the same features as an accordion door.

accouple To join, tie, or couple together.

accouplement (1) In architecture, the pairing of pilasters or columns, as in a colonnade or buttress. (2) In carpentry, a tie or brace between timbers.

accrued depreciation The total reduction of the value of property as stated on a balance sheet for accounting or tax purposes.

accumulator (surge drum, surge header) (1) A pressure vessel whose volume is used to maintain a constant pressure. (2) In refrigeration, a storage chamber for low-side refrigerant.

acetone A highly flammable organic solvent used with lacquers, paint thinners, paint removers, and resins.

acetylene A carbon gas which, when combined with pure oxygen and ignited, produces an extremely hot flame used in gas welding and metal cutting.

acetylene torch The torch used for welding and cutting. Contains compressed acetylene and oxygen.

AC generator A generator that produces alternating current.

achromatic color White, colorless light.

acid A liquid that has a pH of less than 7.0.

acid- and alkali-resistant grout or mortar A grout or mortar that is highly resistant to prolonged exposure to alkaline compounds, acid liquids, or gases.

acid etch (aciding) A method of cleaning the latence from concrete by washing it with an acid solution and rinsing with water.

aciding *See* **acid etch**.

acid polishing The polishing of a surface, particularly glass, by acid treatment.

acoustical metal deck

acid-proof floor A floor that resists deterioration when exposed to acid.

acid resistance A measurement of a surface's ability to resist the corrosive effect of acids.

acid-resistant brick Brick that resists deterioration caused by exposure to acid. This type of brick should be laid with acid-resistant mortar.

acid soil Soil with a pH value of less than 6.6.

acid steel Steel made with a silica flux or in a silica-lined furnace.

acorn nut Nut with hexagonal base and rounded top that encases the end of the screw.

acoustical A term used to define systems incorporating sound control.

acoustical barrier A building system that restricts sound transmission.

acoustical block (acoustic block) A masonry block with sound-absorbing qualities, usually defined in terms of its NRC (noise reduction coefficient) rating.

acoustical board A construction material in board form that restricts or controls the transmission of sound.

acoustical booth *See* **acoustical enclosure**.

acoustical ceiling A ceiling system constructed of sound-control materials. The system may include lighting fixtures and air diffusers.

acoustical correction Special planning, shaping, and equipping of a space to produce the optimum reception of sound for an audience.

acoustical door A door constructed of sound-absorbing materials and installed with gaskets around the edges.

acoustical enclosure (acoustical booth, acoustical room) An enclosure constructed of acoustical materials for privacy in speaking, listening, and recording, as in a recording studio or a telephone booth.

acoustical glass A pane of glass composed of two lites with dead air space between them for sound absorption. This type of glass is frequently used for borrow lights and other interior applications.

acoustic insulation *See* **sound insulation**.

acoustical lining Insulating material secured to the inside of ducts to limit sound and provide thermal insulation.

acoustical material A material fabricated for the sole purpose of absorbing sound.

acoustical metal deck A metal decking that includes a sound-absorbing material installed at a small additional cost per square foot.

acoustical panel Modular units composed of a variety of sound-absorbing materials for ceiling or wall mounting.

acoustical partition A term applied particularly to movable, demountable, and operable partitions with sound-absorbing characteristics.

acoustical plaster Wall and ceiling plaster that has sound-absorbing characteristics.

acoustical reduction factor A value, expressed in decibels, that defines the reduction in sound intensity that occurs when sound passes through a material.

acoustical room *See* **acoustical enclosure**.

acoustical tile

acoustical wallboard

acoustical sealant A caulking or joint sealant with acoustical characteristics.

acoustical sprayed-on material A fibrous material with acoustical properties applied to a surface by spraying through a nozzle.

acoustical tile A term applied to modular ceiling panels in board form with sound-absorbing properties. This type of tile is sometimes adapted for use on walls.

acoustical transmission factor The reciprocal of the sound reduction factor. A measure of sound intensity as it passes through a material, expressed in decibles.

acoustical wallboard Wallboard with sound-absorbing properties.

acoustical window wall Double-glazed window walls with acoustical framing. This type of wall system is used particularly at airports.

acoustic block *See* **acoustical block**.

acoustic lining Insulating material secured to the inside of ducts to attenuate sound and provide thermal insulation.

acoustics (1) The science of sound transmission, absorption, generation, and reflection. (2) In construction, the effects of these properties on the acoustical characteristics of an enclosure.

acquiescence A term frequently used when owners of adjacent properties agree on a boundary between their properties, if the original boundary is difficult or impossible to establish.

acre A common unit of land-area measurement equal to 160 square rods, or 43,560 square feet.

acre foot A unit of volume measurement equal to one acre times one foot thick. The acre foot is used to measure the volume of water or ore deposits.

acropodium An elevated pedestal or plinth bearing a statue.

acropolis The citadel of an ancient Greek city, usually surrounding the temple to the patron deity.

acrylate resin *See* **acrylic resin**.

acrylic *See* **acrylic resin**.

acrylic fiber Fiber produced from polymerized acrylonitrile, a liquid derivative of natural gas. A tough economical fiber commonly used in commercial and residential carpets and draperies.

acrylic plastic glaze A clear plastic sheet that is bonded to glass and that increases the ability of the glass to resist breaking and shattering.

acrylic resin (acrylate resin) In construction, clear, tough, thermoplastic resin manufactured in sheet and corrugated form, used as an adhesive, and as the main ingredient in some caulking and sealing compounds.

acrylonitrile-butadiene-styrene Copolymer with great strength and rigidity that is used in pipe and fittings for sanitary and storm drainage. Commonly used in drain waste vent piping.

actinic glass Glass that filters out radiation from sunlight.

action level The point when a concentration of hazardous materials reaches a level where OSHA regulations dictate protective steps be taken.

activated alumina A form of aluminum oxide that readily absorbs moisture and is therefore used as a drying agent.

activated carbon *See* **activated charcoal**.

activity

activity arrow

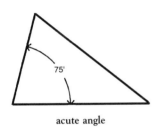

acute angle

adapter

activated charcoal (activated carbon) A material obtained principally as a by-product of the paper industry and used in filters for absorbing smoke, odors, and vapors.

activated rosin flux Flux with a base that enhances the rosin flow of solder.

activated sludge Sludge that has settled out of oxygenated sewage.

activated sludge process A sewage treatment method involving the introduction of oxygen and bacteria into sewage. The by-products are water and activated sludge.

active earth pressure The horizontal component of pressure exerted on a wall by earth.

active leaf In a double-leaf door, the leaf to which the latching or locking mechanism is attached.

active solar energy system A system that primarily collects and transfers solar energy using mechanical means that are not powered by solar energy.

activity In CPM (Critical Path Method) scheduling, a task or item of work required to complete a project.

activity arrow In CPM (Critical Path Method) scheduling, a graphic representation of an activity.

activity duration In CPM (Critical Path Method) scheduling, the estimated time required to complete an activity.

act of God An unforeseeable, inevitable event caused by natural forces over which an insurance policyholder has little or no control. Examples are windstorms, floods, earthquakes, and lightning strikes.

actual dimension The real dimensional measurement of a piece of lumber, masonry unit, or other construction material. *See also* **nominal dimension**.

actuator In hydraulics, a motor or cylinder designed to convert hydraulic energy into mechanical energy.

acute angle An angle less than 90°.

acute toxic chemical A substance that has immediate, but not necessarily permanent, adverse effects on health.

ADA Standards for Accessible Design As an adjunct to the Americans with Disabilites Act, a set of standards that establish minimum technical requirements for the design and construction of buildings and facilities. Their intent is to increase the level of accessibility in the built environment, in existing facilities as well as new construction and alterations.

adamant plaster A quick setting gypsum plaster usually applied over a base coat of plaster.

adapter Any device designed to match the size or characteristics of one item to those of another, particularly in the plumbing, air-conditioning, and electrical trades.

addenda Plural form of **addendum**.

addendum A document describing an addition, change, correction, or modification to contract documents. An addendum is issued by the design professional during the bidding period or prior to the award of contract, and is the primary method of informing bidders of modifications to the work during the bidding process. Addenda become part of the contract documents.

addition

adjustable wrench

addition (1) An expansion to an existing structure, generally in the form of a room, floor, or wing. An increase in the floor area or volume of a structure. (2) A chemical added to cement at the time of its manufacture to help the process or to alter the cement's characteristics.

additional services Professional services provided by the architect or engineer of a project which were not included in the original owner-architect agreement.

additive A substance that is added to a material to enhance or modify its characteristics, such as curing time, plasticity, color, or volatility.

additive alternate A specific alternate option for construction specifications or plans that results in a net increase in the base bid.

additive constant In stadia surveying, a correctional constant to be added to each calculated distance.

address system An electronic audio system with a microphone and speakers installed for either fixed (permanent) or mobile use. Wiring for a permanent system should be done prior to any finish work.

addressable system An advanced fire alarm or security system that provides for easy monitoring, remote testing, and quick location of an alarm condition.

adherend A material or part that is held to another by an adhesive.

adhesion The binding together of two surfaces by an adhesive.

adhesion-type ceramic veneer Ceramic tile or veneer attached to a backing by mortar, grout, or adhesive only. No anchors are used.

adhesive Generally, any substance that binds two surfaces together. In construction, the term is used principally in the wallboard and roofing trades.

adiabatic A condition in which there is no heat gain or heat loss.

adiabatic curing The curing of concrete or mortar, particularly a test cylinder, in a controlled environment with no heat gain or heat loss.

adiabatic process A thermodynamic process occurring in the absence of heat gain or heat loss.

adit (1) The entrance or approach to a building. (2) The entrance to a mine.

adjustable base anchor An attachment to the base of a door frame above a finished floor.

adjustable clamp A temporary clamping device that can be adjusted for position or size.

adjustable door frame A door frame with a jamb that can be adjusted to accommodate different wall thicknesses.

adjustable square (double square) A carpenter's tool used for marking and scribing lumber. An adjustable square usually incorporates a level bubble.

adjustable wrench A wrench with a jaw that can be adjusted to fit different size nuts or bolt heads.

adjusted base cost The total estimated cost of a project after adding or deducting addenda or alternatives.

adjuster A representative of the insurance company who negotiates with all parties involved in a loss in order to settle the claim equitably. An adjuster deals with the policyholder, repair contractor(s), witnesses, and police (if necessary), and acts as a middleman between these parties and the insurance company.

adjusting nut

adjusting nut A threaded nut used for alignment of an object. Often coupled with a locking nut to secure it in position.

adjusting screw A screw used for alignment of an object. Often coupled with a locking nut to secure it in position.

adjustment The determination of: (a) the cause of a loss, (b) whether it is covered by the policy, (c) the dollar value of the loss, and (d) the amount of money to which the claimant is entitled after all allowances and deductions have been made.

adjustment factor A constant (usually a multiplier) used in any calculation.

adjuvant (1) Any agent added to another substance to increase its effectiveness. (2) A nonpesticidal substance added to a pesticide to enhance its physical or chemical properties.

administrative remedy A nonjudicial remedy provided by an agency, board, commission, or the like.

admixture An ingredient other than cement, aggregate, or water that is added to a concrete or mortar mix to affect the physical or chemical characteristics of the concrete or mortar. The most common admixtures affect plasticity, air entrainment, and curing time.

adobe An aluminous clay used to make unfired brick.

adobe blasting *See* **mud-capping**.

adobe brick A large, roughly formed, unfired brick made from adobe and straw.

adsorbed water Water that is held on the surface of materials by electrochemical forces. This water, such as that on the surfaces of aggregate in a concrete mix, has a higher density and thus different physical properties from those of the free water in the mix.

adsorbent A material that has the ability to extract certain substances from gases, liquids, or solids by causing them to adhere to its surface without changing the physical properties of the adsorbent. Activated carbon, silica gel, and activated alumina are materials frequently used for this application.

adsorption The process of extracting specific substances from the atmosphere or from gases, liquids, or solids by causing them to adhere to the surface of an adsorbent without changing the physical properties of the adsorbent.

advanced slope grouting A method of grouting in which the grout is forced horizontally through preplaced aggregate.

advance slope method A method of placing concrete in which the sloped face of the fresh concrete moves forward as the concrete is placed.

adverse possession Ownership of real property without having purchased it and without having done anything more than openly and physically possessing it for a long time in the contravention of the rights of the true owner. Although state laws differ, 20 years is the typical length of time that must pass before the person in possession of the land becomes the owner.

advertisement for bids Published notice of an owner's intention to award a contract for construction to a constructor who submits a proposal according to instructions to bidders. In its usual form, the

adz

aerofilter

A-frame

advertisement is published in a convenient form of news media in order to attract constructors who are willing to prepare and submit proposals for the performance of the work. *See also* **bid call**.

adz A long-handled tool with a curved blade set perpendicular to the handle. Used for dressing lumber.

adz-eye hammer A claw hammer with a long eye for receiving the handle.

aeolian Windblown or transported by the wind.

aerate To introduce air into soil or water, for example, by natural or mechanical means.

aerated concrete *See* **cellular concrete**.

aeration The process of introducing air into a substance or area by natural or mechanical means.

aeration plant A sewage treatment plant in which air is introduced into the sewage to accelerate the decomposition process.

aerator A mechanical device that introduces air into a material such as soil, water, or sewage.

aerator fitting A pipe fitting used to introduce air into a flow of water.

aerial Pertaining to, caused by, or present in the air.

aerial ladder An extension ladder capable of reaching high places and often mounted on a vehicle such as a fire truck.

aerial lift A term commonly applied to mobile working platforms that are elevated hydraulically or mechanically.

aerial photography Photography performed from a vehicle in flight.

aerial sewer A sewer pipe or line supported above grade on bents or pedestals.

aerial survey A survey of the earth's surface based on aerial photographs and ground control points.

aerial tramway A cable and tower system used for transporting materials and personnel. Tramways are used in mining and dam building operations to transport great volumes of material over rough terrain.

aerodynamic instability A harmonic motion occurring in a structure during high winds and endangering structural integrity. The term was used to define the failure of the Tacoma Narrows Bridge.

aerofilter A bed of coarse aggregate used for filtering sewage.

aerograph A paint spray gun.

aerosol paints Paints packaged in a pressurized can with a spray nozzle attached.

affidavit of noncollusion A sworn statement by the bidders on a project that the prices on their proposals were arrived at independently without consultation between or among them.

affinity A tendency for two substances to unite chemically or physically.

A-frame (1) A structural system or hoisting system with three members erected in the shape of an upright capital letter "A." (2) A building with a steep gable roof that extends to the ground.

after-cooler A system that removes the heat from compressed gas after compression in a refrigeration system.

afterfilter (final filter) In air-conditioning, a filter located at the outlet end of the system.

aggregate

after-flush The water that drains from a water closet after flushing and before the valve is closed by the incoming water pressure.

after-sheathing window A window installed after the wall sheathing is in place.

aftertack (residual tack) A defect in paint that causes the painted surface to become tacky under certain environmental conditions.

age hardening A term used to describe a hardening process of metals at room temperature.

agency law Rules, regulations, and procedures promulgated by an agency.

agent Under agency law, an agent is authorized by the principal to act on the principal's behalf. (For example, an architect is frequently the owner's agent. The owner, then, is the principal.) Generally, an agent's acts bind the principal as though the principal had acted directly. *See also* **principal**.

agglomeration The gathering together of small particles to form into larger particles, particularly to accelerate settlement in suspensions.

aggregate Granular material such as sand, gravel, crushed gravel, crushed stone, slag, and cinders. Aggregate is used in construction for the manufacturing of concrete, mortar, grout, asphaltic concrete, and roofing shingles. It is also used in leaching fields, drainage systems, roof ballast, landscaping, and as a base course for pavement and grade slabs. Aggregate is classified by size and gradation.

aggregate, abrasive An antiskid aggregate worked into the surface of a concrete floor.

aggregate bin A structure designed for storing and dispensing aggregate.

It is loaded from the top and emptied from the bottom.

aggregate, coarse Aggregate that is larger than 1/8″ and is retained on the No. 8 sieve.

aggregate, coarse-graded Aggregate with a continuous grading from coarse to fine, with a predominance of coarse particles.

aggregrate, concrete The fine and course aggregate used in manufacturing concrete. Both are usually washed and graded.

aggregrate, exposed A concrete surface with the aggregate exposed, formed by applying a retarder to the surface before the concrete has set, and subsequently removing the cement paste to the desired depth.

aggregrate, fine Aggregate smaller than 1/8″. Fine aggregate passes through the No. 8 sieve.

aggregate gun A tool used to apply textured materials to gypsum drywall.

aggregrate, heavyweight The aggregate produced from materials with high specific gravity, such as linomite, iron ore tailings, and magnetite.

aggregate interlock The term applied to a situation in which the aggregate from one side of a concrete joint projects between the aggregate of the other side of the joint, thus resisting shear.

aggregate, lightweight One of several materials used to decrease the unit weight of concrete, thereby reducing the structural load and the cost of the building. The materials most commonly used are perlite and vermiculite. The use of lightweight aggregate is costly, but sometimes necessary in construction.

aggregate, macadam A crushed aggregate of uniform size, placed to

aggregate panel

aggregate roof

agitator

a specified depth, and covered over with hot asphalt.

aggregate, marble A material produced from crushed marble of varying colors. It is used extensively in decorative landscaping, highway shoulders, and built-up roofing.

aggregate, masonry Washed sand used in a mortar mix.

aggregate, open-graded An aggregate in which a skip between the sieve gradations has been deliberately achieved so that the voids are not filled with intermediate-size particles.

aggregate panel A precast concrete panel with exposed aggregate.

aggregate, plaster Natural or manufactured washed sand used in a plaster mixture.

aggregate, roof (1) The aggregate used for a tar-and-gravel application. (2) The ballast used for membrane-type roofing.

aggregate seal The application of emulsified asphalt followed by a layer of uniform-size aggregate. Used to form a wearing and weather-resistant course.

aggregate spreader A piece of equipment used for placing aggregate to a desired depth on a roadway or parking lot.

aggregrate, stone An aggregate consisting of crushed stone.

aggregrate testing Any of a number of tests performed to determine the physical and chemical characteristics of an aggregate. Common tests are for abrasion, absorption, specific gravity, and soundness.

aggregate, well-graded An aggregate that incorporates sizes from the maximum to the minimum specified so as to fill most of the voids. This type of aggregate is used for asphaltic concrete mixes and for base courses.

aggressive sampling During removal of hazardous materials, the agitation of air to test success of remediation effort.

aging (1) A method of classifying individual receivables by age groups, according to the time elapsed from the date due. (2) A process used to make building materials appear old or ancient. (3) The chemical and physical changes in a material incurred by the passage of time. Concrete generally increases in strength with age, whereas rubber deteriorates with prolonged oxidation.

agitating speed The rate at which a concrete or mortar mixer rotates the drum or blades in order to agitate mixed materials to prevent segregation or setting.

agitation The rotation of, or moving of blades through, a drum containing concrete or mortar to prevent segregation or setting of mixture.

agitator A mechanical device used to maintain plasticity and to prevent segregation, particularly in concrete and mortar.

aglite A lightweight aggregate produced from expanded clay and used in concrete mixes.

A-grade wood (1) A plywood surface that is smooth and paintable, and considered the best standard veneer. May be composed of more than one piece well jointed together. (2) Plywood designation A-face, best veneer grade.

agreement (1) A promise to perform, made between signatories to a document. (2) In construction, the specific documents setting forth the terms of the contracts between architect, owner, engineer, construction manager, contractor, and others.

air chamber

air compressor

agreement form A standard printed form used by the signatories to an agreement, with blank spaces to fill in information pertinent to a particular contract.

agricultural lime A granular hydrated lime used for soil conditioning.

agricultural pipe drain A drainage system consisting of porous, perforated, or open-jointed pipe laid in a trench with porous fill.

aiguille (1) A drill used for boring holes in masonry or cut stone. (2) A drill used for boring blast holes in rock.

air (1) In construction, shortened term for air-conditioning. (2) Sometimes used to refer to the oxygen used in an oxygen/acetylene torch system.

air alternator A system that switches air from one side of an ice chest to the other.

air balancing The process of adjusting a heating or air-conditioning duct system to provide equal distribution to all areas.

air base In aerial surveying, the distance between control stations in overlapping photographs.

air-blown mortar *See* **shotcrete**.

airborne transmission A term that refers to sound traveling through air in a structure.

air break A piping arrangement in which a drain from a fixture appliance or device discharges through an open connection into a receptacle or interceptor. Used to prevent backflow or back siphonage.

air brick Brick manufactured with perforations to ventilate a masonry structure.

airbrush A device with a nozzle for applying paint with compressed air.

air chamber In water piping, a vertical pipe containing entrapped air to absorb the pressure shock when a valve is closed suddenly.

air change The volume of air in an enclosure that is being replaced by new air. The number of air changes per hour is a measure of ventilation.

air circuit breaker A breaker that discontinues current flow in air.

air cleaner A device, often hung from the ceiling, for removing impurities from the air. The device may have a mechanical or electrostatic filter.

air compressor A machine that extracts air from the atmosphere and compresses it into a holding chamber. The most common use of compressed air is for the operation of pneumatic tools. Air compressors are classified by the number of CFM (cubic feet per minute) compressed air they can produce.

air-conditioner A mechanism that controls temperature, humidity, and/or the cleanliness of air within an enclosure.

air-conditioning The process of controlling the temperature, humidity, and cleanliness of air, then distributing it within an enclosure.

air-conditioning system An air treatment system designed to control the temperature, humidity, and cleanliness of air and to provide for its distribution throughout the structure.

air content The volume of air present in a concrete or mortar mix, expressed as a percentage of the total volume. A controlled air content prevents concrete from cracking during the freeze/thaw cycle.

air diffuser

air grating

air hammer

air-cooled slag Slag that is poured into beds and slowly cooled under ambient conditions.

air curtain (air wall) A narrow stream of air directed across an opening to deter the transfer of hot or cold air, contaminants, and insects from one side to the other. Air curtains are commonly used on grocery store refrigerator cases, mall storefronts, and loading platforms.

air density The weight per unit volume of air, expressed in pounds per cubic foot.

air diffuser An outlet in an air-supply duct for distributing and blending air in an enclosure. Usually, a round, square, or rectangular unit mounted in a suspended ceiling.

air-distributing ceiling A suspended ceiling system with small perforations in the tiles for controlled distribution of the air from a pressurized plenum above.

air drain An empty space left between a foundation wall and a parallel wall to prevent the fill from laying directly against the foundation wall.

air-entrained agent An additive to hydraulic cement or an admixture for concrete or mortar that causes air to be incorporated in the form of minute bubbles on the concrete or mortar during mixing, usually to increase its workability and frost resistance.

air entrained concrete *See* **concrete, air-entrained**.

air-entraining agent An admixture for concrete or mortar mixes that causes minute air bubbles to form within the mix. Air entrainment is desirable for workability of the mix and prevention of cracking in the freeze/thaw cycle.

air-entraining hydraulic cement Hydraulic cement containing an air-entraining addition in such amount to cause the product to entrain air in mortar within specified limits.

air escape In plumbing, a valve for automatically discharging excess air from a water line.

air filter A device for removing undesirable gaseous or solid particles from ambient air. All HVAC systems include some type of air filter.

air flue *See* **flue**.

airfoil fan A backward-curved fan with blades of airfoil design.

air-fuel ratio In combustion, the ratio of the air volume or weight to the fuel volume or weight.

air gap In plumbing, the distance between the outlet of a faucet and the overflow level of the fixture.

air grating A fixed metal grating, particularly in masonry foundation walls, for ventilation.

air hammer A portable, pneumatic percussion tool used for breaking and hammering.

air-handling troffer A ceiling lighting unit that incorporates an air diffuser.

air-handling unit (AHU) The traditional method of heating, cooling, and ventilating a building by which single- or variable-speed fans push air over hot or cold coils, then through dampers and ducts and into one or more rooms.

air lance A device that directs a high pressure stream of compressed air to heat or clear away debris from a surface.

air leakage The air that escapes from a system or enclosure through cracks, joints, and couplings.

airlock (1) An airtight chamber such as that used in tunnel and caisson excavation. (2) A system of double doorways permitting entry and exit while preventing airflow from one area to another, as from a contaminated area to an uncontaminated area. (3) An entrance room between areas of different pressures, such as the entrance to an air-supported structure. (4) In plumbing, air trapped in a system and preventing flow.

air makeup unit A system for introducing fresh, conditioned air into an enclosure from which air is being exhausted.

air meter A device for measuring the air content of a concrete or mortar mix.

air-mixing plenum In an air-conditioning system, a chamber in which fresh air is mixed with re-circulated air.

air monitoring In asbestos abatement, a procedure used to determine the fiber content in a volume of air over a measurable period of time.

air permeability test A procedure for determining the fineness of powdered material such as cement.

air pocket A void filled with air, such as in a water piping system or in a concrete form when placing concrete.

air-powered pump A water pump that uses compressed air to create suction.

air purge valve A device for eliminating trapped air from a piping system.

air-purifying respirator A device that removes pollutants from a contaminated atmosphere as a person breathes.

air receiver The air storage tank on a compressor.

air regulator An instrument for regulating the flow or pressure of air in a system.

air release valve A valve that releases air from a water pipe or fitting.

air rights The exclusive right of real property owners to possess the airspace above their land, as long as they comply with building and zoning laws.

air ring In a shotcrete nozzle, the perforated manifold that introduces air into the concrete.

air separator A pneumatic device that uses air to sort materials by size.

air shaft (air well) A roofless enclosed area within a building, admitting light and ventilation.

air slacking The absorption of moisture and carbon dioxide from the air by lime or cement.

air splitter Device inside an air duct that divides a single air stream into several streams.

air stripping A process by which volatile compounds are removed from soil or water by blowing clean air through the soil or water.

air-supported storage tank cover A nonrigid tank cover, usually for domestic water supplies, supported by atmospheric pressure that is slightly higher inside the tank than outside.

air-supported structure A nonrigid structure supported by atmospheric pressure that is slightly higher inside the tank than outside. The difference in pressure is created by fans.

air terminal The top of a lightning protection system on a building.

airway

air test A test for leaks in ductwork and in drainage and pipe systems where compressed air is forced into a sealed system and leaks are detected with a pressure gauge.

air transformer Attachment to a compressor that removes moisture and debris from the compressor's line.

air tool Any of a number of percussion tools that use pneumatic pressure to operate.

air tube system A tubular conveying system that uses air pressure to move capsules containing paperwork from one station to another.

air void The space occupied by entrained air in concrete or mortar.

air wall *See* **air curtain.**

air washer A water spraying mechanism for cleaning and humidifying air in a ventilation system.

airway The air space between the thermal insulation and sheathing on a roof.

air well *See* **air shaft.**

aisle A long passageway between sections of seats.

aisleway Any open passageway permitting access and traffic flow between sections within a building.

Alabama marble A fine-grained, white- or cream-colored marble.

alabaster A fine-grained translucent gypsum in white or pale hues.

albarium A white lime used for stucco.

alclad A product having an aluminum or aluminum alloy coating metallurgically bonded to the surface. The coating is anodic to the core, thus protecting it physically and electrolytically against corrosion.

alcove A recess or partly enclosed extension opening into a larger room.

alder A light-colored, lightweight hardwood often stained to simulate cherry or walnut, or used as plywood core.

algicide A chemical for preventing the growth of algae.

algorithm A set of mathematical instructions, or a computer program, used to produce a control output.

alidade A sighting apparatus often used with a plane table for determining and plotting horizontal and/or vertical angles.

alienation The act of transferring title of real property from one owner to another.

aliform Any object shaped like a wing.

aligning punch A tool used for aligning holes in structural steel. Often referred to as a spud wrench.

alignment (1) The adjustment of elements in a plane such as structural steel. (2) The plane or horizontal orientation of a structure or roadway.

aliphatic resin glue Thermoplastic adhesive used to bond wood and other porous materials.

alite The primary constituent of Portland cement clinker. Alite is composed of tricalcium silicate and small amounts of magnesium oxide, aluminum oxide, ferric oxide, and other materials.

alkali (1) A liquid that has a pH greater than 7.0. (2) Water soluble salts of alkali metals, such as sodium and potassium, which occur in concrete and mortar mixes. The presence of alkaline substances may cause expansion and subsequent cracking.

Allen wrench

alkali resistance The ability, particularly of paint, to resist attack by alkaline materials.

alkali soil Soil that has a pH value of 8.5 or higher, and is thus harmful to some plant life.

alkirk tunneler A tunnel-boring machine that drills a small pilot hole to serve as a center guide for the larger diameter tunneler.

alkyd paint A paint, with an alkyd resin base, that produces a quick drying, hard surface.

alkyd plastics Thermoset plastics with good heat and electrical insulation properties. Commonly used in paints, lacquers, and molded electrical parts where temperatures will not exceed 400°F.

alkyd resin A synthetic resin used as a binder in lacquers, adhesives, paints, and varnishes.

Allen head A screw or bolt with a hexagonal recess to receive an Allen wrench.

Allen wrench A section of hexagonal stock used to turn an Allen head screw or bolt.

alligatoring Rough cracking of a painted surface, usually caused by applying another coat before the first is dry, or by exposing a painted surface to extreme heat.

alligator shears (lever shears) A shop tool used for shearing sheet metal.

alligator wrench *See* **pipe wrench**.

all-in aggregate *See* **bank-run gravel**.

allocable cost A cost that is assignable to a particular contract or other cost objective.

allover A term used to describe a repeating pattern on a surface.

allowable bearing value (allowable soil pressure) The bearing capacity of a soil, in pounds per square foot (psf), determined by its characteristics, such as shear, compressibility, water content, and cohesion. The higher the allowable bearing value of a soil, the smaller the footing required to support a structural member.

allowable cost Any reasonable cost that may be recovered under the contract to which it is allocable.

allowable load The ultimate load divided by a safety factor.

allowable pile-bearing load The allowable load used to design a pile cluster to support a structure.

allowable soil pressure *See* **allowable bearing value**.

allowable stress The maximum stress allowed by code for members of a structure, depending upon the material and the anticipated use of the structure.

allowance (1) A stated requirement of the contract documents whereby a specified sum of money is incorporated, or allowed, into the contract sum in order to sustain the cost of a stipulated material, assembly, piece of equipment, or other part of a construction contract. This device is convenient in cases where the particular item cannot be fully described in the contract documents. (2) In bidding, an amount budgeted for an item for which no exact dollar amount is available. (3) A contingency for unforeseen costs. (4) The classification of connected parts or members according to their tightness or looseness.

alloy A homogeneous mixture of two or more metals developed and used because of its lower cost and/or the certain desirable properties it exhibits.

alloy steel Steel with one or more added materials (other than carbon

aluminum door

and the allowed impurities) which give it desired physical or chemical characteristics.

all risk insurance   An insurance policy that can be written separately to add coverage against certain specific risks of damage or loss from any number of potential events. These risks represent potential losses in excess of coverage provided by other forms of insurance purchased for the purpose of protecting the owner, design professional, and contractor during and after the construction process.

alluvium   Any material, such as gravel, sand, silt, or stone, that has been deposited by running water.

alphaduct   Flexible, nonmetal conduit used in electrical wiring configurations that require unusual bends.

alpha gypsum   A specially processed calcined gypsum with an extremely high compressive strength.

alteration   Construction within a structure or to its exterior closure that does not change the overall dimensions of the structure. Alteration includes remodeling and retrofitting.

alternate   A specified item of construction that is set apart by a separate sum. An alternate may or may not be incorporated into the contract sum at the discretion and approval of the owner at the time of contract award.

alternate bid   An amount stated in a bid which can be added or deducted by an owner if the defined changes are made to the plans or specifications of the base bid.

alternate dispute resolution   A method of settling a dispute without going to court or arbitration.

alternating current   An electric current that reverses direction at regular intervals. In the U.S., most current for domestic use reverses direction at 60 cycles per second.

alternator   A machine that develops alternating current by mechanical rotation of its rotor.

all-thread nipple   Pipe fitting with a thread running its entire length.

altitude   In surveying or astronomy, the angular distance of a celestial body above the horizon.

alum   A double sulfate added to plaster as a hardener and accelerator.

alumina   Aluminum oxide found in the clay used to make brick and clay tile.

aluminous cement   *See* **cement**.

aluminum   A silver-colored, nonmagnetic, lightweight metal used extensively in the construction industry. It is used in sheets, extrusions, foils, and castings. Sheets are often anodized for greater corrosion resistance and surface hardness. Because of its light weight and good electrical conductivity, aluminum is used extensively for electrical cables. Aluminum is usually used in alloy form for greater strength.

aluminum brass   Brass with an aluminum alloy to increase corrosion resistance.

aluminum bronze
A copper- aluminum alloy that is used in castings. Can also be cold-worked.

aluminum-coated steel   Steel coated with aluminum to inhibit corrosion.

aluminum door   A glazed door with aluminum stiles and rails.

aluminum foil   A very thin aluminum sheet used extensively for thermal reflection and moisture protection.

aluminum window

American standard beam

American standard channel

aluminum nitrate fuel oil mix (ANFO) An inexpensive explosive used in blasting and mining operations.

aluminum oxide *See* **alumina**.

aluminum paint A paint containing aluminum paste, which gives the paint good heat-, light-, and corrosion-resistant properties.

aluminum window A glazed window with an aluminum sash and muntins.

amalgam (1) A combination or mixture of different elements. (2) An alloy that includes mercury and one or more other metals.

ambient lighting The general background lighting, whether natural or artificial, of an area.

ambient noise The total noise level from all sources in a given area, either within a building or in an outside environment.

ambient temperature The temperature of the environment surrounding an object.

amended water Water to which a surfactant (a surface-active substance) has been added. Used in asbestos abatement operations.

American basement (walk-out basement) The floor of a building partly above and partly below grade.

American black walnut A close-grained, dark-colored hardwood often used for carving and furniture making.

American bond *See* **common bond**.

American Conference of Governmental Industrial Hygienists (ACGIH) An organization of professionals skilled in the science of industrial hygiene.

American Federation of Labor (AFL) A labor organization or union formed in the United States under the leadership of Samuel Gompers in 1886. The American Federation of Labor provided an "umbrella" organization, the purpose of which was to represent to management the interests of workers in various trades, crafts, and other skilled disciplines related to manufacturing and construction.

American Federation of Labor and the Committee for Industrial Organizations (AFL-CIO) A major union formed by the merger of the two organizations listed above under the leadership of John L. Lewis in 1955. The AFL-CIO represents the interests of various types of member workers in industry and other endeavors (including construction) for the purpose of negotiating with management for acceptable wages, benefits, and other material interests of worker-employees.

American Lumber Standards Committee (ALSC) The committee that maintains standards for hardwoood and softwood grading, including those for size and nomenclature. Rules for grading are established by the U.S. Department of Commerce and enforced by regional organizations.

American National Standards Institute (ANSI) Publisher of the American National Standards, a reference book outlining the approved standards and specifications for all facets of building construction.

American standard beam A hot-rolled steel I-beam designated by the prefix S before the size and weight.

American standard channel A hot-rolled steel channel designated by the prefix C before the size and weight.

American Standard Code for Information Interchange (ASCII) An accepted standard for computerized data transmission.

American standard pipe threads (Briggs standard) The thread size and pitch commonly used in the U.S. for connecting pipe and fittings.

American standard wire gauge *See* **American wire gauge**.

American table of distances A code for the safe storage of explosives, giving distances from cap storage, dwellings, and other buildings and materials.

American wire gauge (American standard wire gauge, Brown and Sharpe gauge) The standard in the U.S. for specifying and manufacturing wire and sheet metal sizes, particularly electrical wire and metal flashing.

Americans with Disabilities Act (ADA) A federal civil rights act prohibiting discrimination against people with disabilities. There are five sections that cover different aspects of discrimination: employment, state and local government, public accommodations and commercial facilities, telecommunications, and miscellaneous provisions.

Americans with Disabilities Act Accessibility Guidelines (ADAAG) The minimum guidelines that must be followed to meet ADA Standards for Accessible Design. *See also* **ADA Standards for Accessible Design**.

amino plastic A group of thermoset plastics derived from ammonia and often used in making electrical insulators.

ammeter An instrument for measuring the rate of ampere flow through an electric circuit.

ammonal An inexpensive explosive used for heavy blasting in dry holes.

ammonia A highly efficient, inexpensive gas used in manufacturing fertilizers and as a coolant in large refrigeration systems such as ice rinks.

ammonium chloride A white, crystalline compound used as a soldering flux and in the manufacture of iron cement.

ammonium nitrate fuel oil mix An inexpensive explosion used in blasting.

amorphous A type of rock that has no crystalline structure.

amortization The process of paying off stock, bonds, a mortgage, or other indebtedness through installments, or by a sinking fund.

amount of mixing The mixing action employed to combine the ingredients of concrete or mortar, measured in time or number of revolutions.

ampacity A designation of the current-carrying capacity of an electrical wire, expressed in amperes.

ampere The electromotive force required to move one volt of electricity across one ohm of resistance. A measure of electrical current.

amplifier An electronic device used to increase the magnitude of an electrical signal without changing the quality of the signal.

amplitude In sound or vibration, the maximum variation from the mean position.

amyl acetate (banana oil) A solvent for paints and lacquers that has an odor resembling that of bananas.

amylin A starch-like, water-soluable compound used as a wallpaper adhesive.

anchor (anchorage)

anchor bolt

analog point   In Building Automation Systems, a sensor, such as a damper or temperature sensor, which has a continuous range of settings that can be monitored or controlled by the system.

analog signal   A signal in the form of a fluctuating quantity (such as voltage or current strength) that reflects variations, such as loudness. It is not limited to discrete units.

anchor (anchorage)   (1) A device to prevent movement when in tension, such as a tie-back for sheet piling. (2) In masonry composite wall construction, the tension connection between components. (3) In prestressed or posttensioned concrete, the end connection for the tendons. (4) A timber connector. (5) The metal devices that secure metal door and window frames to masonry. (6) In piping systems, a device that secures piping to a structure.

anchorage   *See* **anchor.**

anchorage bond stress (development bond stress)   The forces on a deformed reinforcing steel bar divided by the product of the perimeter times the embedded length.

anchorage deformation (anchorage loss, anchorage slip)   In prestressing concrete members, the deformation of an anchor or slippage of tendons when the prestressing device is released.

anchorage loss   *See* **anchorage deformation.**

anchorage slip   *See* **anchorage deformation.**

anchorage zone   (1) In pretensioning, the area of the member in which the stresses in the tendon anchor are developed. (2) In posttensioning, the area adjacent to the anchorage which develops secondary stresses.

anchor block   A block of wood in a masonry wall that provides a means of attaching other wood members.

anchor bolt (foundation bolt, hold-down bolt)   A threaded bolt, usually embedded in a foundation, for securing a sill, framework, or machinery.

anchor bolt plan   A plan view showing size and location of all anchor bolts for a building's systems components. May be included in structural steel and shop drawings.

anchored-type ceramic veneer   Ceramic veneer that is attached to a backing by nonferrous anchors and grout. The minimum thickness of veneer and grout is 1″.

anchor log   A log buried in the ground to act as a deadman.

anchor plate   A plate attached to an object to which accessories or structural members may be attached by welding, screwing, nailing, or bolting.

anchor rod   A threaded metal rod attached to hangers and used to support pipe and ductwork.

ancillary   One of a group of buildings having a secondary or dependent use, such as an annex.

ancon   (1) Scrolled bracket or corbel that supports a cornice or entablature. (2) A projecting boss on a concrete masonry unit.

anechoic room   An enclosure whose interior surfaces do not reflect sound.

anemometer   An instrument that measures the velocity of airflow.

angle   (1) The figure or measurement of a figure formed when two planes diverge from a

angle cleat

angle float

angle framing

angle iron

common line. (2) In construction, a common name for an L-shaped metal member.

angle bar *See* **angle iron**.

angle bead (angle staff, staff angle) A metal or wood strip set at the corner of a wallboard or plaster wall to serve as a guide and to provide protection. Angle beads are most commonly made of nonferrous or galvanized perforated sheet metal.

angle beam Another term for angle iron. Usually, the term refers to one of heavier stock.

angle block (glue block) A small block of wood used to fasten or stiffen the joint of two adjacent wood members, usually at right angles.

angle board A board cut at an angle and used as a jig for erecting masonry or cutting other members at a constant angle.

angle bond A metal tie that projects into each wall at a corner and is used to bond masonry.

angle brace (angle tie) A piece of material temporarily or permanently secured across an angle to make it rigid, such as a strip of wood nailed across the corners of a window frame to keep it square during installation.

angle brick A brick cast with an oblique angle on one of its corners.

angle buttress One of two buttresses forming a right angle at the corner of a structure.

angle cleat (angle clip) A short section of angle iron used to attach structural members, such as precast panels, to structural steel.

angle clip *See* **angle cleat**.

angle closer A special brick or a portion of a brick used to close the bond on the outside corner of a brick wall.

angle collar (bevel collar) A cast-iron pipe angle fitting with a bell-type connection at each end.

angle divider A square with an adjustable hinged blade used for setting or bisecting angles.

angle dozer A bulldozer whose blade can be set at an angle so as to push the excess material to one side.

angle fillet (angle stile) A strip of triangular cross section used to cover the joint of two surfaces meeting at an angle less than 180°.

angle float (angle trowel) A trowel with two surfaces meeting at right angles. An angle float is used for finishing plaster or concrete in an inside corner.

angle framing Light-gauge framing with an angle iron.

angle gauge A template used to set or maintain an angle during construction.

angle hip tile *See* **arris hip tile**.

angle iron (angle bar, angle section) An L-shaped steel structural member classified by the thickness of the stock and the length of the legs. Sometimes referred to simply as angle.

angle lacing A system of connecting two structural components with angle irons.

angle of repose The maximum angle above horizontal at which a material of given density and moisture content will remain in place without sliding. This measurement is used specifically for earth cuts, fills, and stockpiled aggregates.

angle paddle A hand tool used to finish plaster.

annular ring nail

angle plane A hand tool used to remove projections and smooth inside corners on a plaster brown coat covering once it has set.

angle post *See* **corner post.**

angle rafter *See* **hip rafter.**

angle rage *See* **hip rafter.**

angle section *See* **angle iron.**

angle staff *See* **angle bead.**

angle stile *See* **angle fillet.**

angle strut An angle iron erected to carry a compression load.

anglet A groove in a material or structure, most often containing a right angle.

angle tie *See* **angle brace.**

angle trowel *See* **angle float.**

angle valve A valve with the inlet at right angles to the outlet for controlling flow in a pipe.

angular aggregate An aggregate made of crushed material with sharp edges, as opposed to screened gravel with rounded edges.

angular measure The deviation between two lines that meet at a point, measured in degrees, minutes and seconds.

anhydrite An additive used in the manufacture of Portland cement to control the set.

anhydrous calcium sulfate (dead-burnt gypsum) Gypsum from which all the water of crystallization has been removed.

anhydrous gypsum plaster A high-grade finish plaster with most of the water of crystallization removed.

anhydrous lime *See* **lime.**

animal glue A strong adhesive with poor water resistance made from bones and hides of animals. Often used in furniture manufacture.

anionic surfactant A negatively-charged adjuvant with limited compatibility used in asbestos abatement.

anisotropic In construction, a term to describe materials like wood that exhibit different properties when measured along different axes.

annealed wire A pliable wire used in construction primarily for reinforcing steel tie wires.

annealing The process of subjecting a material, particularly glass or metal, to heat and then slow cooling to relieve internal stress. This process reduces brittleness and increases toughness.

annex A secondary structure either near or adjoining a primary structure.

Annual Report of Carcinogens A list of those substances determined by the National Toxicology Program to be carcinogenic to humans.

annular ring nail A nail with a series of thread-like rings on its shank to give it good holding power. This type of nail is used for attaching gypsum board to wood studs.

annunciator An electrical signaling device that identifies when a circuit is engaged.

anode The conductor rod used in an electrical system to protect underground tanks and pipes from electrochemical action.

anodic coating The surface finish resulting from anodizing aluminum. The finish may be clear or colored.

anodize The process of creating electrolytically a hard, noncorrosive film of aluminum oxide on the surface of a metal. This film can be either clear or colored.

apex stone

anodized aluminum Aluminum coated by an electrolytic process to produce an oxide film that is corrosion-resistant.

antechamber An entrance, vestibule, or foyer.

antichecking iron A flat piece of iron, most often bent into a C, S or Z shape, that is driven into a timber end to prevent splitting.

anticorrosive paint A paint containing corrosive-resistant pigments such as zinc chromate, lead chromate, or red lead. This type of paint is used as a primer on iron and steel products.

antifloatation pads Concrete pads secured to underground tanks to add sufficient weight to the tank to overcome buoyancy when empty.

antimonial lead (hard lead, regulus metal) A lead alloy containing antimony that is used in sheet form for roofing, cladding, and tank lining. This alloy is harder than pure lead.

antimony oxide A white pigment added to plastics and paints to give them flame-retardant properties.

antioxidant Any substance that inhibits oxidation, which deteriorates plastics and other materials.

antiquing (broken-color work) A method of applying paint in which a second color is exposed from underneath. Used on trim and furniture to give the wood an older appearance.

antisiphon trap (deep-seal trap) In a drainage system, a plumbing trap that provides a water seat to prevent siphonage.

antislip paint A paint with coarse particles mixed in to roughen the surface to which it is applied. This type of paint is used on steps, ramps, walkways, and porches.

antismudge ring The frame around a ceiling-mounted air diffuser that reduces the formation of rings of dirt around the diffuser.

antistatic agent An additive that reduces the development of static electricity on the surface of plastics or on carpeting.

anvil The part of a pile hammer that transmits the driving force to a pile.

aperture In construction, any opening left in a wall for a door, window, or for ventilation.

apex The peak, or highest point of any structure.

apex stone (keystone, saddle stone) The highest stone or block in an arch, gable, dome, or vault. Apex stones are often decorative.

apparent candlepower The measure of a light source at a specified distance expressed as the candle power that produces the same illumination at that same distance.

appeal notice A notice to a board of contract appeals that a contracting officer's final decision or failure to issue a decision will be appealed.

appentice (pent, pentice) A subordinate structure, like a shed, built against another structure.

appliance panel An electrical service panel with circuit breakers or fuses specifically designed for service to appliances.

application bond The measurement of the strength of adhesion between two adhered surfaces.

application butyl An adhesive with a butyl base used in caulking and sealants.

application cement A common term for mastics used in flooring and roofing applications.

application failure The separation by chemical or physical means of two adhered surfaces.

applied trim

apron

application for payment A formal written request for payment by a contractor for work completed on a contract and, if allowed for in the contract, materials stored on the job site or in a warehouse.

application mortar A mixture with an adhesive additive used for affixing ceramic wall or ceiling tile.

application neoprene A liquid neoprene compound applied to concrete foundation walls for waterproofing.

application spreader A trowel with notched edges used for applying adhesive.

application wall clips Special clips used for installing wallboard with adhesive in lieu of nails or screws.

applied trim Strips or moldings applied to, as opposed to manufactured with, door and window frames and wood paneling.

applique A nonstructural decorative object attached to a member or structure for decorative purposes.

appraisal A dollar estimate of the value of a certain item of property, or the assessment of the value of a loss. The estimate is developed from market value, replacement cost, income produced, or a combination of these factors. Appraisals are usually made by qualified professional appraisers.

appraisal clause A clause included in some property insurance policies stating that if the policyholder and the insurance company disagree over the dollar value of the loss, then both parties may hire their own independent appraiser. If these two appraisers do not agree, a third appraiser, acting as "umpire," is hired (the expense is shared by the policyholder and the insurance company), and his word is considered final.

apprentice A person who works with a skilled craftsman for a number of years in order to learn the trade. An apprentice is generally rated by the number of years served.

approach ramp (1) An access for vehicles to a highway. (2) A sloped access for the handicapped to a building, in lieu of stairs.

approach-zone district An area defined by a zoning ordinance or bylaw to be within the flight path of an airport. Building height and the type of industry allowed are often restricted within such an area.

approved In construction, materials, equipment, and workmanship in a system, or a measurable portion thereof, which have been accepted by an authority having jurisdiction. Usually the term refers to approval for payment, approval for continuation of work, or approval for occupancy.

approved equal Material, equipment, or method of construction that has been approved by the owner or the owner's representative as an acceptable alternative to that specified in the contract documents.

appurtenance (1) Something added on to a main structure or system. (2) A condition added to a property deed, such as a right-of-way.

apron (1) A piece of finished trim placed under a window stool. (2) A slab of concrete extending beyond the entrance to a building, particularly at an entrance for vehicular traffic. (3) The piece of flat wood under the base of a cabinet. (4) Weather protection paneling on the exterior of a building. (5) A splashboard at the back of a sink. (6) At an airport, the pavement adjacent to hangars and appurtenant buildings.

apron flashing

arch

apron flashing (1) The flashing that diverts water from a vertical surface on a building to a sloped roof, such as that around a chimney. (2) Flashing that leads water from a roof into a gutter.

apron lining A board or veneer that covers the apron piece of a stair case.

apron molding The piece of flat wood under the base of a cabinet.

apron piece (pitching piece) A piece of lumber protruding from a wall to support the rough stringers at the top or at a landing of a wooden staircase.

apron rail A horizontal rail attached to a door at the height of the lock.

apron wall A distinct exterior wall panel extending from a window sill to the window below.

aquastat An electrical control activated by changes in water temperature.

aqueduct A water-conveying system that relies on gravity to maintain water flow. An aqueduct may be underground or elevated; an elevated aqueduct may be covered or open.

aquifer A geological water-bearing formation that can provide water for wells.

arbitration The process by which parties agree to submit their disputes to the determination of a third, impartial party (referred to as the arbitrator), rather than pursuing their claims before a judge and jury in a court of law. Parties often agree in advance to binding arbitration of disputes, either as a clause in the contract or at the occurrence of a dispute. This method of avoiding litigation can save both time and money.

arbor (1) An enclosure of closely planted trees, vines, or shrubs which are either self-supporting or supported on a framework. (2) The rotating shaft of a circular saw or shaper.

arc (1) The electrical discharge between two electrodes. When the electrodes are surrounded by gas in a lamp, they become a bright, economical light source. (2) Any portion of a circle or the angle that it makes.

arcade A covered passageway between buildings, often with shops and offices on one or both sides.

arc blow The phenomenon that occurs when an electric arc loses stability. It is caused by magnetic forces created during welding.

arc cutting A method of cutting metal with an electric welding machine. The metal melts from the heat produced by the arc between the electrode and the metal.

arc discharge An electric discharge that produces light and is often used in lamps.

arc gouging A shaping or grooving of metal by arc cutting.

arch A curved or flat structure spanning an opening. The shape and size of arches are limited by the materials used and the support provided.

arch band The visible ribs in a vaulted ceiling.

arch bar A metal strap or beam that supports an arch.

arch beam A beam whose upper surface is arched.

arch brace A curved brace in a wooden roof truss that gives the roof an arched appearance from the inside.

architectural concrete

architectural millwork

arch brick (compass brick, feather edge brick, radial brick, radiating brick, radius brick, voussoir brick) (1) One of a number of types of brick manufactured to construct curved surfaces such as arches and round manholes. (2) Extremely hard-burned brick from an arch of a scove kiln.

arch buttress *See* **flying buttress**.

arch center The falsework used to support masonry during construction of an arch.

arch corner bead A job-cut corner bead used to finish an arch.

arching The bridging of shear stresses in a soil mass across an area of low shear strength to adjacent areas of higher shear strength.

architect A professionally qualified and licensed person who prepares plans and specifications for a building or structure. Architectural services include such duties as project analysis, development of the project design, and the preparation of construction documents (including drawings, specifications, bidding requirements, and general administration of the construction contract).

architect-engineer A person or company providing services as both architect and engineer.

architect's approval Permission granted by the architect, acting as the owner's representative, for actions and decisions involving materials, equipment, installation, change orders, substitution of materials, or payment for completed work.

architectural Pertaining to a class of construction, particularly in home building, of higher-than-average quality. The term often pertains to the ornamental features of a structure.

architectural area of buildings The total of all stories of a building, after adjustments, computed according to AIA standards, measured from the exterior faces of exterior walls and from the center line of walls between buildings.

architectural bronze An alloy consisting of 57% copper, 40% zinc, 2.75% lead, and 0.25% tin, used for ornamental forgings and extrusions.

architectural concrete Structural or nonstructural concrete that will be permanently exposed to view and therefore requires special attention to uniformity of materials, forming, placing, and finishing. This type of concrete is frequently cast in a mold and has a pattern on the surface.

architectural door A grade classification of door which designates higher-than-standard specifications for material and appearance.

architectural fee The cost of architectural services to an owner, usually a percentage of the total contract amount. The fee varies according to the services provided and the complexity of the project.

architectural glass Glass with a configurated surface to obscure vision or diffuse light.

architectural millwork (custom millwork) Millwork manufactured to meet the specifications of a particular job, as distinguished from stock millwork.

architectural terra-cotta Hard-burned, glazed, or unglazed clay building units, plain or ornamental, machine extruded or hand molded, and generally larger in size than brick or facing tile.

architectural volume The total architectural areas of a building (repeating the area of a story for

areaway

additional floors) including the measurement from beneath the lowest floor to the average height of the roof surface for each various building height.

architecture The art and science of designing and building structures.

architrave In classical architecture, (1) the bottom-most beam that spans from column to column resting directly upon the capitals. (2) Ornamental moldings around door or window openings.

arch stone The wedge-shaped masonry units used in building an arch.

arch truss A roof truss having a curved upper chord and a straight lower chord.

archway A passageway through an arch, particularly a long one.

arc light A light produced by an arc across two electrodes.

arc voltage The reaction of a circuit's inductance to the rate of current change in the circuit.

arc welding The joining of metal parts by fusion. Heat is produced by the electricity passing between an electrode and the metal, and is usually accompanied by a filler metal and/or pressure.

are An area equal to 100 square meters.

area (1) A measurement of a given planar region or of the surface of a solid. (2) A particular part of a building that has been set aside for a specific purpose.

area drain A catch basin or other device designed to collect surface water.

area light A light source used to illuminate a significant area, either indoors or outdoors.

area method A construction cost estimating system employing unit square foot costs multiplied by the adjusted gross floor area of a building.

area wall A masonry wall surrounding or partly surrounding an open area, particularly one below grade, such as an areaway at the entrance to a basement.

areaway An open area located below grade and adjacent to a building to provide light, air, or access to a basement or crawl space.

areaway grating A steel or cast-iron grating placed over an areaway, usually at grade level.

arenaceous In classifying soil, a term referring to material that is composed mostly of sand.

argillaceous In classifying soil, a term referring to material that is composed mostly of clay or shale.

argillite A shale composed mostly of clay and silt.

Arizona marble A stone mined in a variety of colors, the best known of which are Apache Gold, Geronimo, and Navajo Black.

Arkansas marble A stone mined in a variety of colors, the best known of which are Ozark Famosa, Ozark Fleuri, and Ozark Rouge.

arkose A sandstone containing a high percentage of feldspar and used as a building stone.

armature The rotating part of a motor or generator consisting of copper wire wound around an iron core.

arm conveyor A belt with protruding arms or angles to carry materials into a building.

armor coat Durable pavement comprised of two or more thin layers of aggregate and asphalt.

armored cable

armoured faceplate

armored cable (metal-clad cable) An electrical conduit of flexible steel cable wrapped around insulated wires.

armored concrete Concrete with a surface treatment containing steel or iron and used in areas with heavy, steel-wheeled traffic.

armored faceplate A metal faceplate mortised into the edge of a door to protect the lock mechanism.

armored front A tamperproof metal plate that covers the set screws of a mortise lock.

armored plywood Plywood that is faced on one or both sides with metal cladding.

armor plate (kick plate) A metal plate that is installed on the lower part of a door to protect it from kicks and scratches.

aromatic red cedar A highly aromatic, fine-textured wood with a distinctive red and white color used for fence posts and rails and for mothproofing closets.

arrester (1) A wire screen at the top of a chimney or incinerator to prevent burning material from flying out. (2) In electrical equipment, a protective device that limits surge voltages by diverting current.

arris fillet (doubling piece, tilting fillet) A triangular piece of wood used under roofing to tilt it away from a vertical surface, such as a parapet or chimney. *See also* **cant strip**.

arris gutter An archaic term used to describe a V-shaped wooden gutter fixed to the eaves of a building.

arris hip tile (angle hip tile) An L-shaped roof tile manufactured to fit over the hip of a roof.

arris rail A triangular wooden rail with the broadest section used as a base.

arrissing tool A special float used to round the edges of freshly placed concrete.

arrow diagram A CPM (Critical Path Method) diagram in which arrows represent activities in a project.

Art Deco A popular decorative style of the 1920s and 1930s, characterized by vivid colors, bold outlines, zigzag forms, and new building materials like plastics.

article A subdivision of a document such as a contract document.

artificial intelligence Computer systems that solve problems symbolically rather than algorithmically. Similar to the warning, decision-making, and problem-solving process in the human brain.

artificial turf A synthetic material designed to simulate a natural surface, and used to form playing surfaces for indoor or outdoor sports arenas, such as football fields.

asbestine A fine, powdered talc used in mixing paint.

asbestos (asbestos fiber) A flexible, noncombustible, inorganic fiber used primarily in construction as a fireproofing and insulating material. Because airborne asbestos fibers have been demonstrated to constitute a health hazard, the use of asbestos for new construction is heavily regulated and generally banned for all practical purposes.

asbestos blanket Asbestos fibers woven or bonded into a flexible blanket that at one time was used as a fire or heat barrier.

asbestos-cement pipe

asbestos-cement board (asbestos cement wallboard, asbesto sheeting wallboard, asbestos sheeting)
A dense, rigid board made from asbestos fibers bonded together with Portland cement and used formerly in building construction where fire or heat protection was required.

asbestos-cement pipe A strong, light, noncorrosive pipe made from asbestos fibers and Portland cement and formerly used in construction for water pipe drainage and air ducts.

asbestos-cement wallboard
See **asbestos-cement board**.

asbestos-containing material Any material containing more than one percent asbestos.

asbestos duct Asbestos-cement pipe used as an air duct.

asbestos encapsulation An airtight enclosure of asbestos fibers with sealant or film that prevent fibers from becoming airborne and creating a potential health hazard.

asbestos felt A building product used extensively in roofing and sheathing systems that was made by saturating asbestos felt material with asphalt or some other binder.

asbestos fiber *See* **asbestos**.

asbestos formboard Rigid asbestos cement shaped into formboard, formerly used in cementitious decks.

asbestosis Chronic inflammation of the lungs caused by inhalation of airborne asbestos fibers.

asbestos joint runner (pouring rope)
Asbestos fibers woven into a rope and formerly used to wrap around a bell joint as a retainer for molten lead caulking.

asbestos plaster A fireproof plaster with high insulating properties made from asbestos fibers and bentonite.

asbestos removal A special trade that has developed since the health hazards of airborne asbestos have been revealed. Applies principally to ceiling tile, fireproofing, and pipe insulation.

asbestos roofing
Rigid asbestos-cement sheets, either flat or corrugated, with good insulating and fireproofing qualities.

asbestos roof shingle Roofing shingle containing asbestos fibers.

asbestos runner
See **asbestos joint runner**.

asbestos sheeting
See **asbestos-cement board**.

asbestos sheeting wallboard
See **asbestos-cement board**.

asbestos waterproofing
A foundation waterproofing in sheet form consisting of PVC with an asbestos sheet backing.

asbestos work A classification system designed by OSHA that rates the level of training needed to perform asbestos-related tasks. Class I involves the removal or abatement of thermal insulation or surfacing asbestos-containing materials (ACM); Class II involves removing asbestos floor or ceiling tiles, siding, roofing or piping; Class III involves repair and maintenance operations where employees may disturb ACM; and Class IV involves custodial activities during which employees contact ACM.

asbo *See* **asbestos**.

as-built drawings Record drawings made during construction. As-built drawings record the locations, sizes, and nature of concealed items such as structural elements, accessories, equipment, devices, plumbing lines, valves, mechanical equipment, and

ash dump and pit

ashlar masonry

asphalt base course

the like. These records (with dimensions) form a permanent record for future reference.

as-built schedule A time-scaled graphic depiction of the historical record of events, activities, and progress of a given project.

ash A sturdy, long-grained hardwood with excellent bending qualities. This wood is used in veneers, trim, and flooring.

ash dump An opening in the bottom of a firebox or fireplace into which ashes are swept, falling into an ashpit below.

ashlar (1) Any squared building stone. The term usually refers to thin stone used as facing. If the horizontal courses are level, it is called coursed ashlar, if they are broken, it is called random ashlar. (2) Short vertical studs between the ceiling joists and the rafters.

ashlar brick (rock-faced brick) A brick with a broken face resembling stone.

ashlar line A horizontal line on the exterior face of a masonry wall.

ashlar masonry A stone masonry wall or veneer composed of rectangular units bonded with mortar. *See also* **ashlar.**

ashlar veneer A nonstructural wall facing composed of ashlar masonry.

ashpit A cleanout under a fireplace, usually at the base of a chimney, where ashes are removed.

aspect The orientation of a building with respect to the points of a compass.

aspect ratio (1) In any configuration, the ratio of the long dimension to the short dimension. (2) The ratio of the width of a duct to its height.

aspen A smooth-grained, white hardwood used for trim and veneer.

asphalt A dark brown to black bitumen pitch that melts readily. It appears in nature in asphalt beds and is also produced as a by-product of the petroleum industry.

asphalt base course A bottom paving course consisting of coarse aggregate and asphalt.

asphalt block A manufactured paving block made from asphaltic concrete and aggregate. The block is typically manufactured in squares, rectangles, and hexagons, and comes in dark gray or black colors.

asphalt, blown Asphalt that has had air blown through it at high temperatures to give it workability for roofing, pipe coating, foundation waterproofing, and other purposes.

asphalt cement Asphalt that has been refined to meet the specifications for use in paving and other special uses. It is classified by penetration. *See also* **penetration.**

asphalt coating (asphalt-lined pipe) The asphaltic coating of corrugated metal pipe. Coatings can be inside, outside, or just on the invert.

asphalt color coat An asphalt surface treatment that has been impregnated with aggregate of a specified color.

asphalt concrete *See* **asphaltic concrete.**

asphalt curb An extruded or hand-formed berm made from asphaltic concrete.

asphalt cutback An asphalt that has been liquefied by an additive for a specific use.

asphalt cutter Any of a variety of machines designed to cut asphalt pavement.

asphalt expansion joint

asphalt dampproofing
The application of asphalt to the surface of a concrete or masonry wall to prevent passage of absorption of water or moisture.

asphalt emulsion Liquid asphalt in which water has been suspended. When the water evaporates, the asphalt hardens. Asphalt emulsion is used in paving as a tack coat to bind one course to another.

asphalt expansion joint Premolded felt or fiberboard impregnated with asphalt and used extensively as an expansion joint for cast-in-place concrete.

asphalt felt Felt impregnated with asphalt and used in roofing and sheathing systems. *See also* **asphalt-prepared roofing**.

asphalt filler (asphalt joint filler)
A liquid asphalt used for filling joints and cracks in pavement and floors.

asphalt flashing cement A semisolid asphaltic material used to apply flashing.

asphalt floor tile Any of a number of economical, resilient floor tiles with an asphalt base. These tiles are particularly well-suited for application to concrete floors on grade, as they are not affected by moisture. For wood subfloors, they are usually laid on a felt underlayment.

asphaltic A term used to describe materials containing asphalt. While sometimes used interchangeably with asphalt in the construction industry, it is usually more correct to use asphaltic.

asphaltic concrete (asphalt paving, bituminous concrete, blacktop)
A mixture of liquid asphalt and graded aggregate used as a paving material for roadways and parking lots. It is usually spread and compacted in layers over a prepared base while still hot.

asphaltic macadam A term generally referring to a penetration method of paving whereby the aggregate is placed first, then liquid asphalt is sprayed into the voids, followed by the addition of a finer-graded aggregate. Penetration macadam usually needs a seal coat to prevent damage caused by water infiltration.

asphaltic mastic (mastic asphalt)
A viscous asphaltic material used as an adhesive, a waterproofing material, and a joint sealant.

asphalt joint filler *See* **asphalt filler**.

asphalt lamination A lamination of sheet material, such as paper or felt, using asphalt as the adhesive.

asphalt leveling course A course of asphaltic concrete pavement of varying thickness spread on an existing pavement to compensate for irregularities prior to placing the next course.

asphalt-lined pipe
See **asphalt coating**.

asphalt, liquid An asphaltic material having a fluid consistency at normal temperatures. The common types specified for pavements are cutback, rapid curing (RC), medium curing (MC), and slow curing (SC), which are blended with petroleum solvents and emulsion, which is blended with water.

asphalt overlay One or more courses of asphaltic concrete placed over existing pavement. The process of overlaying usually includes cleaning, and application of a tack coat, followed by a leveling course.

asphalt paint An economical, liquid-asphaltic product used principally for weatherproofing.

asphalt shingles

asphalt surface course

asphalt paper A paper that has been coated or saturated with asphalt for use as a moisture barrier.

asphalt pavement Any pavement made from one or more layers of asphaltic concrete.

asphalt pavement sealer A material applied to asphalt pavement after compaction to protect it from deterioration caused by exposure to weather or petroleum products.

asphalt pavement structure
All the successive courses of asphalt products placed above the subgrade in a section of pavement.

asphalt paving
See **asphaltic concrete.**

asphalt penetration A measure of the hardness or consistency of asphalt, expressed as the distance a needle of standard diameter will penetrate a sample under given time, load, and temperature conditions.

asphalt plank A reinforced, premolded, structural plank made of asphalt-impregnated fibers and mineral filler. The material comes in 3′ to 8′ lengths, 6″ to 12″ wide.

asphalt-prepared roofing (asphaltic felt, bituminous felt, cold-process roofing, prepared roofing, rolled roofing, rolled strip roofing, roofing felt, sanded bituminous felt, saturated felt, self-finished roofing felt) A roof covering manufactured in rolls and made from asphalt-impregnated felt with a harder layer of asphalt applied to the surface of the felt. All or part of the "weather" side may be covered with aggregate of various sizes and colors.

asphalt prime coat A tack coat, usually an emulsion, to increase the adhesion of one course to another in pavement construction.

asphalt primer A liquid asphalt of low viscosity that is applied to a nonbituminous surface such as concrete to prepare the surface for an asphalt course.

asphalt seal coat A thin asphalt surface treatment used to waterproof and improve the wearing surface texture of pavement, particularly that of an asphaltic macadam. Depending on the intended purpose for the pavement, a seal coat may or may not include aggregate.

asphalt shingles (composition shingles, strip slates) Roofing felt saturated with asphalt, coated on the weather side with a harder asphalt and aggregate particles, and cut into shingles for application to a sloped roof.

asphalt soil stabilization Treatment of existing soil with asphalt penetration, mixing, and compaction. Often used as a base for asphaltic concrete pavement.

asphalt spray mulch Emulsified asphalt sprayed on a freshly seeded area to prevent erosion and reduce evaporation.

asphalt surface course The top or wearing course of asphaltic concrete pavement.

asphalt surface treatment The application of liquid asphalt to any asphaltic pavement, with or without adding aggregate.

asphalt tack coat A light coat of asphalt, usually an emulsion, added to an existing pavement to create a bond between the pavement and another course.

asphyxiant A substance that interferes with the normal function of the lungs.

aspiration In an air-conditioning system, the introduction of room air into the flow of air from a diffuser.

astragals

attic ventilator

aspirator A device that draws a stream of gas or liquid into it by means of the suction created by liquid or gas passing through an orifice. An aspirator is used for mixing air with a stream of water or for mixing a controlled amount of a chemical with water.

as-planned schedule A project schedule prepared by the contractor to indicate the intended progress and method of performance.

assembled occupancy For design purposes, the maximum number of people who will occupy a room or hall at one time.

assembling bolt A threaded bolt used for temporarily holding structural steel members together during welding.

assembly adhesive A powerful adhesive used to bond parts together, as in the manufacture of furniture or marine equipment.

assembly drawing A drawing showing all parts of a machine or structure in operating position.

assessed valuation The value of a property assigned by a municipality for real estate tax purposes. The valuation may be higher or lower than the market value of the property.

assessment (1) A tax on property. (2) A charge for specific services, such as sewer or water, by a government agency.

assessment ratio The ratio between the market value and assessed valuation of a property, expressed as a percent.

assignment (1) A transfer of rights, frequently involving rights arising under a contract. (2) With respect to a contract, a document stating that payment for work completed or materials delivered must be made to someone other than the company or person specified in the contract.

associate dimensioning A feature of a computer-aided design and drafting system that dynamically recalculates all dimensions affected by a change the operator has made.

asymmetric A term used to describe the offset current waveform that can accompany an electric fault.

astragal (1) A molding attached to one of a pair of doors or casement windows to cover up the joint between two stiles. (2) A bead molding, most often half-round and ornate, with a narrow flat band, or fillet, on at least one side.

athley wagon Large trailer used in heavy construction to transport soil and rock.

atmospheric pressure The pressure (14.7 psi) exerted by the earth's atmosphere at sea level under standard conditions.

attenuation The sound reduction process utilizing a sound-absorbing system.

Atterberg limits Terms defining the properties of soils at different water contents.

Atterberg test Laboratory tests to determine the Atterberg limits.

attic tank A domestic water storage tank installed above the highest plumbing fixture in a building to provide water pressure by gravity.

attic ventilator An electric fan, frequently thermostatically controlled, to push hot air out of an attic.

audible signage Signage with the ability to transmit a voice message to the visually impaired.

audio frequencies Frequencies between 15 and 20,000 cycles per second (Hz), which is within hearing range of the human ear.

auger

automatic fire vent

automatic sprinkler

audit The examination of records, documents, and other evidence for the purpose of determining the propriety of transactions and assessing fiscal compliance with relevant cost and accounting requirements.

auger (1) A carpenter's hand tool used for boring holes in wood. (2) A hand-held or rotary-powered tool with a helical cutting edge used for drilling holes in soil. Augers are used for taking soil samples, drilling for caissons, or drilling for cast-in-place piles.

autoclave A chamber in which steam at high pressure is used to cure precast concrete members.

autogenous healing The natural tendency of concrete or mortar to repair surface hairline cracks when kept in contact with water.

automatic Descriptive of any device activated by the environment or a predetermined condition, such as a ventilator that opens at a given temperature.

automatic air vent A vent that opens and closes at a predetermined temperature.

automatic batcher A batcher that blends all the ingredients of a mixture at predetermined weights upon receiving a single command.

automatic circuit breaker See **circuit breaker.**

automatic closing device See **closing device.**

automatic door A power-operated door that opens at the approach of a person or vehicle and closes when the person or vehicle has passed.

automatic door bottom (drop-bottom seal) An attachment to the bottom of a door that is actuated when the door is closed to seal the bottom of the door at the threshold.

automatic fire pump A pump in a standpipe or sprinkler system that turns on when the water pressure drops below a predetermined level.

automatic fire vent (automatic smoke vent) A device in the roof of a building that operates automatically to control fire or smoke.

automatic iris An optical device, much like the iris in the eye, containing a diaphragm that expands and contracts to control the amount of light that passes through the lens.

automatic operator A remote-control operating device. The term usually refers to the opening and closing of doors by electronically actuated switches.

automatic smoke vent See **automatic fire vent.**

automatic sprinkler system A fire safety system designed to provide instant and continuous spraying of water over large areas in the case of fire.

automatic temperature control Electromechanical temperature-regulating equipment. ATC equipment is usually not integrated with other components of a Building Automation System because it is not digital.

automatic transfer switch In an electrical system, a switch that automatically transfers the load to another circuit when the voltage drops below a predetermined level.

auxiliary contact An additional contact not normally associated with operation of a switching device such as a contact or circuit breaker.

awning

awning window

ax hammer

axial fan

auxiliary rafter (cushion rafter)
A rafter used to strengthen the main rafter, usually at the area of greatest load.

auxiliary reinforcement In a prestressed concrete member, refers to all reinforcing steel other than the prestressing steel.

auxiliary rim lock
A surface-mounted lock installed in addition to the main lock on a door.

average bond stress The force exerted on a steel reinforcing bar divided by the product of the perimeter multiplied by the embedded length.

average grade The average of ground surface elevations within a building site.

average haul The average distance material is transported from where it originates to where it is deposited, such as from cut to fill in roadway construction.

aviation snips *See* **tin snips.**

avodire (white mahogany)
A light-colored wood used for interior trim, plywood, and paneling.

award A party's formal communication of their acceptance of a bid or proposal for services, construction, materials, or equipment.

awl A hand tool used for piercing holes, particularly in leather. Often fitted with a needle for sewing heavy materials.

awning A projection over a door or window, often retractable, for protection against rain and sun.

awning blind A blind that is hinged at the top.

awning window A window that is hinged at the top.

ax (axe) A sharp-edged hand tool for splitting wood and hewing timber.

axe *See* **ax.**

axed brick (rough axed brick)
Brick shaped by an ax so as to create rough surfaces.

ax hammer A hand tool for dressing stone.

axial fan A fan that produces pressure from the velocity of gas passing through the impeller, with no pressure being produced by centrifugal force.

axial flow fan
See **centrifugal fan.**

axial force
See **axial load.**

axial force diagram In statics, a graphic representation of the axial loads acting at each section of a structural member.

axial load (axial force)
The longitudinal force acting on a structural member.

axis A straight line representing the center of symmetry of a plane or solid object.

azimuth The horizontal angle measured clockwise from north to an object.

B

B ABBREVIATIONS

The abbreviations listed below are those most commonly used in the construction industry. Alternative forms (usually nonstandard) are shown in parentheses.

B beam, boron, brightness

BA bright annealed

BAS building automation system

bat. batten

B&B in the lumber industry, grade B and better; balled and burlapped

bbl, Bbl., brl barrel

BC building code

b&cb beaded on the edge and center

b.c.c. body-centered cubic

BCM broken cubic meter

BCY broken cubic yard

bd. in the lumber industry, board

bdl bundle

BE in the piping industry, beveled end

BET between

Beth. B Bethlehem beam

bev beveled

bev sid beveled siding

BF, bd. ft. board foot

BFP backflow preventer

bg bag

BG below ground or below grade

Bg cem bag of cement

Bh Brinell hardness

Bhn Brinell hardness number

BHP brake horsepower, boiler horsepower

BI black iron

BICSI Building Industry Consulting Service International

Bit., Bitum. bituminous

Bk. backed

Bkrs. breakers

B/L bill of lading

BL building line

bldg, Bldg. building

blk, blk. block, black

BLKG blocking

BLO blower

BLR boiler

blt built, borrowed light

b.m. board measure

BM. beam

BM bench mark

B/M, BOM bill of materials

BMEP brake mean effective measure

B&O back-out punch

BOCA Building Officials and Code Administrators International

b of b back of board

boil. boilermaker

BP blueprint, baseplate, bearing pile, building paper

bpd barrels per day

BPG beveled plate glass

B.P.M. blows per minute

BR bedroom

BRI building-related illness

brc brace

brcg bracing

BRG bearing

BRK brick

BRKT, bkt bracket

BRS brass

Br Std, BS British Standard

BRZ bronze

BRZG brazing

B&S beams and stringers, bell and spigot, Brown and Sharpe gauge

BSMT basement

BSR building space requirements

BTB bituminous treated base**

btr, Btr. better

Btu British thermal unit

BTUH Btu per hour

but. buttress

BW butt weld

B&W black and white

BX interlocked armored cable

B1S banded one side, bead one side

B2E banded two ends

B2S banded two sides, bead two sides, bright two sides

B2S1E banded two sides and one end

B3E beveled on three edges

B4E beveled on four edges

B DEFINITIONS

back check

backfill

backfilling

babbitt An antifriction alloy composed of tin and lesser amounts of copper and antimony. Babbitt is used in bushings and bearings.

back (1) That part, area, or surface that is farthest from the front. (2) The portion behind or opposite that is intended for use or view. (3) The reverse (scale). (4) That portion which offers strength or support from the rear. (5) The extrados of an arch or vault sometimes concealed in the surrounding masonry. (6) In slate or tile, the side opposite the bed. (7) The surface of wallboard that receives the plaster. (8) The side of a piece of lumber or plywood opposite the face. The back is the side with the lower overall quality or appearance.

back arch A concealed arch that supports the inner part (or backing) of a wall where a lintel carries the exterior facing.

backband A rabbeted molding used to surround the outside edge of a casing in an opening such as a door or window.

backbone subsystem In a premises distribution system, the cable that runs from the equipment room to the various floors in a building. In a single-floor building, the subsystem is the main trunk of the communications system.

back boxing Thin boards used in construction of double-hung windows to enclose the channel in which the sash weights hang, and to keep the channel free of mortar. *See also* **back lining.**

back-brush To paint over a freshly painted surface with a finishing return stroke.

back check The mechanism in a hydraulic door closer or door check that reduces the speed with which the door can be opened.

back clip A special clip used on the hydraulic door closer or door check which reduces the speed with which the door can be opened.

back coating Asphalt coating applied to the back of shingles or rolled roofing.

back-draft damper A damper, the blades of which are gravity-controlled and allow the passage of air in one direction only.

back edging A process by which glazed ceramic pipe is cut by first chipping away the glaze and then chipping the underlying pipe until it is cut through.

backer rod foam Foam rope used to seal wide gaps and joints before caulk is applied, reducing unwanted air leakage.

backfill Earth, soil, or other material used to replace previously excavated material, as around a newly constructed foundation wall.

back fillet The return of a fillet molding.

backfilling (1) The process of placing backfill. (2) Rough masonry laid behind a facing or between two faces. (3) Brickwork laid in spaces between structural timbers. *See also* **nogging.**

back flap (back fold, back shutter) That leaf of a folding window shutter which falls behind the exposed leaf, sometimes in a recess in the casing.

backflap hinge (flap hinge) A hinge with a flat plate or strap to fasten to

backflow preventer

backhoe

back-mop

the face of a door or shutter. This type of hinge is used especially when the stile is too thin to accept a butt hinge.

backflow (1) The unintentional reversal of the normal and intended direction of flow. Backflow is sometimes caused by back siphonage. (2) The flow of water or other liquids, mixtures, or substances into the distributing pipes of a potable water supply system from a source other than the intended source. *See also* **back siphonage**.

backflow preventer A device or means to prevent backflow into the potable water system.

backflow valve *See* **backwater valve**.

back fold *See* **back flap**.

back gutter A shallow gutter installed on the upslope side of a chimney on a sloping roof. A back gutter is used to divert water around the chimney.

backhoe A powered excavating machine used to cut trenches by drawing a boom-mounted bucket through the ground toward the machine. The bucket is raised and swung to either side to deposit the excavated material.

backing (1) The bevel applied to the upper edge of a hip rafter. (2) Positioning furring onto joists to create a level surface on which to lay floorboards. (3) Furring applied to the inside angles of walls or partitions to provide solid corners for securing wallboard. (4) The first coat of plaster on lath. (5) The unseen or unfinished inner face of a wall. (6) Coursed masonry applied over an extrados of an arch. (7) Interior wall bricks concealed by the facing bricks. (8) The wainscoting between a floor and a

window. (9) The material under the pile or facing of a carpet. (10) The stone used for random rubble walls.

backing board (1) In a suspended acoustical ceiling, gypsum board to which acoustical tiles are secured. (2) Gypsum wallboard or other material secured to wall studs prior to paneling to provide rigidity, sound insulation, and fire resistance.

backing brick A lower quality of brick used in places where it will be concealed by face brick or other masonry.

backing ring (chill ring) A metal ring used to prevent melted metal from entering a pipe when making a butt-weld joint, and to provide a uniform gap for welding.

back iron Reinforcing steel plate on a wood plane.

back jamb *See* **back lining**.

backjoint A rabbet in masonry such as that over a fireplace to receive a wood nailer.

backlight To illuminate from behind (and often above) an object.

back lining (back jamb) (1) In a weighted sash window, the thin wood strip that closes the jamb of a cased frame to provide a smooth surface for the operation of the sash and, where applicable, prevents abrasion of brickwork by the sash weights. (2) The framing piece that constitutes the back recess for box shutters.

back lintel A lintel used to support the backing of a masonry wall, and therefore, not visible on the face.

back-mop To apply hot bituminous material, either by mop or mechanical applicator, to the underside of roofing felt during the construction of a built-up roof.

backset

backup

back-nailing Nailing the layers, or plies, of a built-up roof to the substrate to help prevent slippage. Performed in addition to hot mopping.

back nut (1) A threaded nut that helps to create a watertight joint, as on the long thread of a pipe connector, and whose one dished side accepts a grommet. (2) A locknut.

back-paint To apply paint to the reverse or unseen side of an object, not for appearance but for protection against weather.

backplastering Plaster applied to one face of a lath system following the application and subsequent hardening of plaster that has been applied to the opposite face.

backplate A wood or metal plate that functions as backing for a structural member.

back pressure Hydraulic or pneumatic pressure in a direction opposite the normal and intended direction of flow through a pipe, conduit, or duct. Usually caused by a restriction to the flow.

back-pressure valve
See **check valve.**

back primed Back-painted woodwork. Used primarily for exterior shingles, siding, or trim.

back putty (bed glazing) The glazing compound applied between the glass and its sash or frame.

backsaw A handsaw used in finish carpentry work. The back (noncutting) edge of the saw is stiffened with a steel or brass strip. A backsaw is used for cutting mitered joints and other joinery work.

backset The offset or horizontal distance between the face or front of a door back to the center of the keyhole or central axis of the knob.

backshoring Reinsertion of shores beneath a stripped concrete slab after the original formwork and shoring has been removed from a small section. Unlike reshoring, backshoring keeps the slab from supporting its own weight or the weight of existing loads above it until the slab attains full strength.

back shutter *See* **back flap.**

back sight In surveying, a sight on an established survey point or line.

back siphonage The backward flow of used, contaminated, or polluted water from a plumbing fixture or vessel into the potable water supply, often due to negative pressure in a pipe. *See also* **backflow.**

backsplash A protective panel, apron, or sheet of waterproof material positioned on a wall behind a sink, counter, or lavatory.

backstamp A stamp that appears on all plywood panels manufactured by American Plywood Association member mills.

backup (1) That part of a masonry wall behind the exterior facing. (2) Any substance placed into a joint to seal the joint and reduce its depth, and/or to inhibit sagging of the sealant. (3) Overflow due to blockage in a piping system.

backup figures The detailed calculations that produce unit prices.

backup strip (lathing board)
A narrow strip of wood secured to the corner of a wall or partition to provide a base on which to nail the ends of the lathing.

back veneer The ply on veneer plywood opposite the face veneer and usually of lesser quality.

balanced earthwork

back vent In plumbing, a venting device installed on the downstream side of a trap to protect it from siphonage.

backward curved fan Centrifugal fan with blades that curve backward away from the direction of the rotation.

backwater valve (backflow valve) A check valve in a drainage pipe that prevents reversal of flow.

badger A tool used to remove excess mortar or other deposits from the inside of pipes or culverts after they have been laid. *See also* **badger plane**.

badger plane A large, wooden hand plane for rabbeting, whose mouth is fashioned obliquely from side to side to allow its use close to corners.

badigeon (1) A cement for filling holes or covering defects in masonry and woodwork. (2) A plaster and powdered stone mixture applied to walls to give them texture.

baffle (1) A tray or partition employed on conveying equipment to direct or change the direction of flow. (2) An opaque or translucent plate-like protective shield used against direct observation of a light source; a light baffle. (3) A plate-like device for reducing sound transmission. (4) Any construction intended to change the direction of flow of a liquid.

bag (sack) A quantity of Portland cement; 94 pounds in the United States, 87.5 pounds in Canada, 112 pounds in the United Kingdom, and 50 kilograms in most other countries. Different weights per bag are commonly used for other types of cement.

bag plug An inflatable drain stopper usually placed at the lowest point in a piping system; used during testing of the system's integrity.

bag trap A plumbing trap, shaped like an S, whose inlet and outlet are in alignment.

baked finish A film of paint or varnish baked at temperatures above 150°F to produce a tough, durable finish.

bakelite A plastic developed for use in electrical fittings, door handles, pulls, etc. Bakelite has high chemical and electrical resistance.

balance arm A supporting arm at the side of a projected window which allows the sash to be opened without an appreciable change in its center of gravity.

balance bar *See* **balance beam**.

balance beam (balance bar) A counterbalance consisting of a long beam attached to a moveable structure, such as a drawbridge or gate, whose weight it offsets during opening and closing.

balanced circuit A three-wire electric power circuit whose main conductors all carry substantially equal currents, either alternating or direct, and in which there exists substantially equal voltages between each main conductor and neutral.

balanced door A door that is installed using double-pivoted hardware, which allows it to swing open in a semi-counterbalanced manner.

balanced earthwork Cutting and filling in which the amount of one is equal to the amount of the other after swelling and compaction factors are applied.

balanced load (1) In an electric circuit, such as a three-wire system, a load connected such that the currents on each side are equal. (2) In reinforced concrete beam

balanced sash

balancing valve

design, a load that would cause crushing of concrete and yielding of tensile steel simultaneously.

balanced moment Moment capacity at simultaneous crushing of concrete and yielding of tensile steel. *See also* **balanced load**.

balanced reinforcement An amount and distribution of reinforcement in a flexural member such that the allowable tensile stress in the steel and allowable compressive stress in the concrete are attained simultaneously.

balanced sash A sash in a double-hung window that requires very little effort to raise or lower because its weight is counterbalanced with weights or pretensioned springs.

balanced step (dancing step, dancing winder) One of a series of winders which are balanced (as opposed to radiating from a common center). Their narrow ends are nearly equal in width to that of the straight portion of the adjacent stair flight to provide the line of traffic with a relatively even tread width.

balancing (1) Adjusting the mass distribution of a rotor to diminish journal vibrations and control the forces on the bearings from eccentric loading. (2) In an HVAC system, adjusting the system to produce the desired level of heating and cooling in each area of a building.

balancing damper A plate or adjustable vane installed in a duct branch to regulate the flow of air in the duct.

balancing plug cock *See* **balancing valve**.

balancing valve (balancing plug cock) A pipe valve used to control the flow rather than to shut it off.

balata (1) A rubber-like, nonelastic latex gum used to make industrial belting and gaskets. (2) A tropical American tree that yields a latex-like sap.

balaustre (canary wood) A heavy, hard, and glossy South American wood. May be yellowish brown, purplish brown, or orange in color.

balcony (1) A platform that protrudes from a building. It can be cantilevered or supported from below, and is usually protected by a railing or balustrade. (2) A gallery protruding over the main floor of an auditorium; usually provides additional seating. (3) In a theater, an elevated platform used as part of a permanent stage setting.

balk (baulk) In building construction, a squared timber whose dimensions are at least 4″ x 4-1/2″.

ballast (1) A layer of coarse stone, gravel, slag, etc., over which concrete is placed. (2) The crushed rock or gravel of a railroad bed on which ties are set. (3) The transformer-like device that limits the electric current flowing through the gas within a fluorescent lamp. (4) A high-intensity discharge that provides a lamp with the proper starting voltage. (5) Material placed in a vessel to provide temporary stability.

ballast cycling The undesirable condition that occurs when the ballast turns lamps on and off because of an overheated thermal switch.

ballast factor The ratio of the luminous output of a lamp when functioning on a ballast to its luminous output when functioning under standardized rating conditions.

ball-check valve

ballast noise rating The degree of noise created by a fluorescent lamp ballast, represented by the letters A (the quietest) to F (the loudest).

ballast-tamper A portable machine used to compact the ballast under railroad ties. Usually powered by electricity or compressed air.

ball-bearing hinge A butt hinge having ball bearings positioned between the knuckles to reduce friction.

ball catch A door fastener in which a spring-tensioned metal ball engages the striking plate to keep the door closed until force is applied.

ball-check valve A device used to stop the flow of liquid in one direction while allowing flow in an opposite direction. The pressure against a spring-loaded ball opens the valve in one direction of flow. Pressure from the other direction forces the ball against a seat, closing the valve and preventing flow.

ball cock A float valve incorporating a spherical float; used to control the height of water, as in a toilet tank. *See also* **float valve**.

ball float The somewhat spherical floating device by which a ball valve is controlled.

balling up In welding, the globules of flux or molten brazing filler metal that result from inadequate wetting of the metal being welded.

ball joint A flexible mechanical joint that allows the axis of one part to be set at an angle to the other by virtue of the design of the two components. One possesses a fixed spherical shell to accommodate the ball-shaped end of the other.

balloon frame *See* **balloon framing.**

balloon framing (balloon frame) A style of wood framing in which the vertical structural members (the posts and studs) are single, continuous pieces from sill to roof plate. The intermediate floor joists are supported by ledger boards spiked to or let into the studs. The elimination of cross grains in the studding reduces differential shrinkage.

balloon-payment loan An installment loan demanding a final payment significantly larger than any of the previous annuity payments. Often employed temporarily, until long-term financing arrangements are finalized.

ballpark figure A rough estimate.

ball peen hammer A hammer having a hemispherical peen on one end and used by metal workers, stonemasons, and mechanics.

ball test (1) A test to determine the consistency of freshly mixed concrete by measuring the depth of penetration of a cylindrical metal weight or plunger that has been dropped into it. (2) A test to determine whether or not a drain is circular and unobstructed, performed by rolling a certain size ball through the drain. *See also* **Kelley ball**.

ball valve A spherically shaped gate valve that provides a very tight shut-off for fluids in a high-pressure piping system.

balsa (corkwood) A soft, porous wood which, at a density of 7-10 pounds per cubic foot, makes it lighter in weight than any other wood. Balsa is used for models and as the core material in lightweight sandwich panels.

baluster (banister) (1) One of a series of short, vertical supporting elements for a handrail or a coping. (2) Any vase-shaped supporting

49

balustrade

band clamp

band saw

member or column. (3) The roll on the side of an Ionic capital.

balustrade A complete railing system, including a top rail, balusters, and sometimes a bottom rail.

banana oil *See* **amyl acetate**.

band (1) A group of small bars or the wire encircling the main reinforcement in a concrete structural member to form a peripheral tie. A band is also a group of bars distributed in a slab, wall, or footing. (2) A horizontal ornamental feature of a wall, such as a flat frieze or fascia, usually having some kind of projecting molding at its upper and lower edges. (3) Frequencies that occur in a range between two set limits.

band board Perimeter floor joist that sits atop the sill in a wood floor framing system.

band clamp A metal clamp consisting of two pieces that are bolted at their ends to hold riser pipes.

banding Wood strips or veneer attached to the exposed edges of plywood or particleboard in the construction of furniture or shelves.

band iron A thin, metal strip used as a form tie or form hanger.

band joist A vertical member that forms the perimeter of a floor system.

band saw A power saw consisting of a continuous piece of flexible steel that runs around two pulleys and has teeth on one or both sides. A band saw is used to cut logs into cants, to rip lumber, and to cut curved shapes.

bandwidth A range of frequencies expressed in cycles per second (Hertz). The greater the bandwidth,

the more information that can be transmitted.

banister (1) A handrail. (2) A balustrade, especially one on the side of a staircase. *See also* **baluster.**

banjo vanity A bathroom vanity top shaped like a banjo, usually with the "handle" extending over the toilet for added storage.

bank A mass of soil rising above a digging or trucking level. Excavation and loading are done at the face of a bank.

bank cubic yard A unit designating one cubic yard of earth or rock, measured or calculated before removal from the bank.

banker A table or bench on which stonemasons or bricklayers shape their materials before setting them.

bank gravel *See* **bank-run gravel**.

bank material Soil or rock in its natural state before excavation or blasting.

bank measure A determination of the volume of a mass of soil or rock in its natural state before excavation or blasting.

bank plug Wooden stake used by surveyors to measure grade.

bank-run gravel (bank gravel, run-of-bank gravel, all-in aggregate) Granular material excavated without screening, scalping, or crushing. This type of gravel is a naturally occurring aggregate comprised of cobbles, gravel, sand, and fines.

bank sand Sand which is unlike lake sand in that it has sharp edges that provide a better bond and more strength when used in plastering.

bar (1) A deformed steel member used to reinforce concrete. (2) A solid piece of metal whose length is substantially greater than its width.

barbed wire (barbwire)

bar joist

barb bolt (rag bolt) A bolt with jagged edges that prevent it from being easily removed from any object into which it has been driven.

barbed wire (barbwire) Two or more wires twisted together with intermittent barbs incorporated during manufacture. Used for security and livestock fencing.

bar bending The process of bending reinforcing steel into shapes required for reinforced concrete construction.

barbwire *See* **barbed wire**.

bar chair *See* **bar support**.

bar chart (Gantt chart) A chart that graphically describes activities on a work-versus-time scale, illustrating planned start and completion dates for the various project activities.

bar clamp A carpenter's clamping device consisting of a long bar with adjustable clamping jaws. A bar clamp is used to hold joinery components during gluing.

bare (1) Descriptive of a piece of building material whose actual dimensions are smaller than those specified. (2) Scant.

bare cost The estimated cost of an item of work or a project before the bidder's markup for overhead and profit.

barefaced tenon (bareface tenon) A tenon that has a "shoulder" on one side only, and is used in the construction of wood doors.

bargain and sale deed A deed in which the grantor admits that he has some interest in, though not necessarily a clear and unencumbered title to, the property being conveyed. This kind of deed often contains a warranty that the grantor did not encumber the property or convey away any part of the title during his period of ownership.

bargeboard A board that hangs from the projecting end of a gable roof, often ornamental.

barge spike (boat spike) A long, square spike with a chisel point, used primarily in heavy timber construction.

bar graph A graphical representation of simultaneous events charted with reference to time. A bar graph is a simplified method of charting events, such as the processes of building construction. The horizontal axis of the chart is scaled to increments of time; the various events are charted vertically. The duration of the event is charted by a horizontal line or bar beginning at the time the event is scheduled to begin and ending at the time the event is scheduled to be completed. At any point in time, the reader can observe the number of events that are occurring simultaneously.

bar handle A horizontal rod used to open a door.

barite (barytes) A mineral of barium sulfate often used as an aggregate for concrete in the construction of high-density radiation shielding.

barium plaster A gypsum plaster to which barium salts have been added during manufacturing. Used on walls of x-ray rooms.

barium sulfate *See* **barite**.

bar joist A light steel joist of open-web construction with a single zigzag bar welded to upper and lower chords at the points of contact. Used as floor and roof supports.

bar mat An assembly of steel reinforcement composed of two or more layers of bars placed at right angles to each other and tied together by welding or wire ties.

bar sash lift

bar support (bar chair)

bar-type grating

bar molding (bar-rail molding)
A rabbeted molding that serves as a nosing when fixed to the edge of a countertop or bar.

barn-door hanger A type of hanger used for heavy exterior sliding or rolling doors. Consisting of two pulleys secured in tandem to the top of the door and connected by a heavy metal strap. The door moves by rolling along a horizontal track that either hangs from the lintel or is anchored to a parallel member projecting slightly from it.

barn-door stay One of at least a pair of small pulleys that facilitate and direct the movement of a sliding barn (or other) door by rolling along a horizontal track or rail.

barometer A device that measures atmospheric pressure.

Baroque A style of architecture and decoration developed in the late 17th century and characterized by the elaborate use of scrolls, curves, and other symmetrical ornamentation.

barracks A usually simple, unadorned building or group of buildings that provide temporary housing, often for military personnel.

bar-rail molding *See* **bar molding**.

barrel (1) A unit of weight measure for Portland cement, equivalent to four bags or 376 pounds. (2) A standard cylindrical vessel with a liquid capacity of 31-1/2 gallons. (3) That part of a pipe where the bore and wall thickness remain uniform.

barrel bolt (tower bolt)
A cylindrical bolt mounted on a plate that has a case projecting from its surface to contain and guide the bolt.

barreling (tumbling) A process in which small articles are placed in a cylindrical case and painted by being tumbled in a barrel of paint.

barricade An obstruction used to deter the passage of persons or vehicles. Any of several devices used to detour or restrict passage.

barrier-free environment A building or area that is fully accessible and usable by disabled people.

barrow (1) A wheelbarrow. (2) A large mound of earth or pile of rocks intentionally placed on top of an ancient burial site for protection.

barrow run A temporary smooth ramp of planks or plywood for wheeled transport of materials at a construction site.

bar sash lift A handle on the bottom rail of a sash for raising and lowering the sash.

bar screen A coarse screening device made from equally spaced parallel bars or rods, used to separate large stones from gravel or crushed stone. *See also* **bar strainer.**

bar size section A hot-rolled bar, angle, channel tee, or zee whose largest cross-sectional dimension does not exceed 3″.

bar spacing The distance between parallel reinforcing bars, measured center to center.

bar strainer (1) A screening device, fabricated from parallel bars or rods, used over a drain to prevent the entrance of foreign objects. (2) A bar screen.

bar support (bar chair) A rigid device of formed wire, plastic, or concrete, used to support or hold reinforcing bars in proper position during concrete operations.

bar-type grating An open grate with parallel bearing bars evenly spaced and attached to a frame.

base angle

base flashing

The grating may be cast or welded and may have crossbars.

barway A gate with one or more sliding bars that act as large latch bolts.

barytes *See* **barite.**

BAS *See* **Building Automation System.**

basalt A dark, fine-grained igneous rock of high density widely used for paving aggregate.

bascule A structure that rotates like a saw around a horizontal axis, and that has a counterbalance at one end. The most common use is for a bascule bridge.

bascule bridge A bridge designed with counterbalances so that as one end is lowered, the other end is raised.

base (scrubboard, skirting board, washboard) (1) The lowest part of anything upon which the whole rests. (2) A subfloor slab or "working mat," either previously placed and hardened or freshly placed, on which floor topping is placed. (3) The underlying stratum on which a concrete slab, such as pavement, is placed. (4) A board or molding used against the bottom of walls to cover their joint with the floor and to protect them from kicks and scuffs. (5) The protection covering the unfinished edge of plaster or gypsum board. (6) The lowest visible part of a building.

base anchor A fixed or adjustable metal device attached to the base of a door frame to secure it to the floor.

base angle Angle iron stock attached to the perimeter of a foundation for supporting and aligning tilt-up wall panels.

base bid The amount of money stated in the bid as the sum for which the bidder offers to perform the work described in the bidding documents, prior to the adjustments for alternate bids that have been submitted.

base bid specifications The specifications that list or describe those specific materials, equipment, and construction methods which comprise the base bid exclusive of any alternate bids.

base block A usually unadorned, squared block that terminates a molded baseboard at an opening or serves as a base when attached to the foot of a door or the bottom of window trim.

baseboard *See* **base (4).**

baseboard heater A heating system in which the heating elements are housed in special panels placed horizontally along the baseboard of a wall.

baseboard radiator unit A heating device designed to be positioned in a room so as to replace a baseboard. The heat source is commonly from hot water, steam, or electricity.

base coat (1) The plaster beneath the finish coat. (2) The initial coat of paint or stain applied to a surface.

base course (1) A layer of material of specified thickness constructed on the subgrade or sub-base of a pavement to serve one or more functions, such as distributing loads, providing drainage, or minimizing frost action. (2) The lowest course of masonry in a wall, pier, foundation, or footing course.

base elbow A cast-iron pipe elbow with a flange or baseplate for placement on a floor or block.

base flashing (1) In roofing, the flashing supplied by the upturned edges of a watertight membrane. (2) The metal or composition

baseplate

basin wrench

flashing used with any roofing material at the joint between the roofing surface and a vertical surface, such as a parapet or wall.

base line (1) The meticulously established reference line used in surveying or timber cruising. (2) In construction, the center or reference line of location of a highway, railway, building, or bridge.

base light Uniform and diffuse illumination without accent.

base map A map employed in urban planning to indicate the principal outstanding physical characteristics of an area and which is thereafter used as a reference for subsequent mapping.

basement The bottom full story of a building below the first floor. A basement may be partially or completely below grade.

basement soil *See* **subgrade**.

base metal In joining two metal pieces, the parent metal that is actually welded, brazed, or soldered, and remains unmelted after the joining process, as opposed to the filler metal deposited during the joining operation.

base molding Trim molding applied to the upper edge of interior baseboard.

baseplate A plate used to distribute vertical loads from structural columns or machinery.

base screed A galvanized metal screed with perforated or expanded flanges to provide ground for plaster and to separate areas of dissimilar materials.

base sheet The saturated and/or coated felt sheeting laid as the first ply in a built-up roof system.

base shoe (base shoe molding, carpet strip, carpet stripmolding, floor molding, shoe molding) The molding or carpet strip covering the joint between a floor and a baseboard, often a quarter-round bead.

base shoe corner A block or a piece of molding installed in the corner of a room so as to eliminate the need to miter the base shoe.

base shoe molding *See* **base shoe**.

base tee A pipe tee that has an attached supporting baseplate.

base tile The bottom course of tile in a tiled wall.

base trim Any decorative molding at the base of a wall, column, or pedestal.

basic insulation level The measure of the insulation capability of a piece of electrical equipment; the equipment's ability to withstand very high voltage surges.

basic module (1) A unit of dimension used when coordinating the sizes of building elements and other components. (2) The fundamental unit of size in the systems of coordination in metric building, or 100 mm.

basin (1) A somewhat circular natural or excavated hollow or depression having sloping sides and usually used for holding water. (2) A similarly shaped plumbing fixture, such as a sink.

basin wrench A wrench with a long shank and ratcheted jaws used in plumbing for difficult-to-reach areas, as when installing a faucet behind a sink.

basket crib A construction of interlocking timbers which can be arranged to function as a shaft liner, a protective device around a

basket weave

batch mixer

batten

concrete pier in water, or a temporary floating foundation.

basket weave A pattern of bricks placed flat or on edge and arranged in a checkerboard layout.

bas-relief (basso-riviero, basso rilievo) Sculpture, carving, or embossing that protrudes slightly from its background.

basso-riviero *See* **bas-relief.**

basso rilievo *See* **bas-relief.**

basswood (American linden) A fine-textured softwood used for carving, cabinet work, and paneling. Basswood is also the primary source of excelsior.

bastard Any nonstandard item deviating from normal size, slope, fabrication, or quality.

bastard file A flat file whose grain is somewhat less than coarse and which is primarily used to smooth metal surfaces.

bastard granite A gneissic rock whose formation resembles that of true granite. Bastard granite is used mostly in wall construction but is not a true granite.

bastard joint *See* **blind joint.**

bastard masonry (1) Thin blocks of facing stones used to face brick or rubble walls. Bastard masonry is dressed and built to resemble ashlar. (2) Rough, quarry-dressed ashlar stones.

bastard pointing In masonry, a type of pointing that emphasizes the joint by forming a small ridge projecting along its center.

bastard-sawn (1) Lumber that has been sawn so that the annual rings make angles of 30°-60° to the surface of the piece. (2) Any lumber that has been flat-sawn, plain-sawn, or slash-sawn.

bastard spruce *See* **Douglas fir.**

bastard tuckpointing *See* **bastard pointing.**

bat (1) A burned brick or shape that, because it is broken, has only one good end. (2) A piece of brick. (3) A single unit of batt insulation. (4) A piece of wood that serves as a brace.

Bataan mahogany *See* **tanguile.**

bat bolt A bolt whose butt or tang has been provided with barbs or similar protrusions to increase its grip.

batch The quantity produced as the result of one mixing operation, as in a batch of concrete.

batch box A container of known volume used to measure the constituents of concrete or mortar in proper proportions.

batch mixer A machine that mixes concrete, grout, or mortar in batches in accordance to a design mix. Each batch is used completely before a second batch is started.

batch plant An installation of equipment including batchers and mixers as required for batching and mixing concrete materials. Called a *mixing plant* when mixing equipment is included.

batement light A window constructed with an angular bottom to fit a curved or sloping member.

bathroom A room usually equipped with a water closet, a lavatory, a bathtub and/or a shower.

batted work (broad tooled) Stone whose surface has been scored downward from the top by administering 8 to 10 narrow, parallel strikes per inch with a batting tool.

batten (1) A narrow strip of wood used as siding to cover the joints of

batten seam

batter boards

battered wall

parallel boards or plywood. The resultant pattern is referred to as *board and batten.* (2) A strip of wood placed perpendicular to several parallel pieces of wood to hold them together. (3) A furring strip fastened to a wall to provide a base for lathing or plastering. (4) In roofing, a strip of wood placed over boards or roof structural members to provide a base for the application of wood or slate shingles, or clay tiles. (5) The steel strip that fastens the metal flooring on a fire escape.

battenboard *See* **coreboard.**

batten door (ledged door, unframed door) A door in which stiles are absent and which consists of vertical boards or sheathing secured on the back side by horizontal battens.

battened column A column composed of two longitudinal shafts fastened securely to each other by batten plates.

battened wall (strapped wall) A wall to which battens have been secured.

batten plate (stay plate) A steel plate connecting two parallel components (such as flanges or angles) of a built-up structural column, girder, or strut, and transmitting the shear between them.

batten roll (conical roll) In metal roofing, a roll joint fabricated over a triangular wood piece.

batten seam In metal roofing, a seam fabricated around a wood strip.

batter (1) To incline from the vertical. (2) A slope, such as that of the outer side of a wall, that is wider at the bottom than at the top.

batter boards Pairs of horizontal boards nailed to wood stakes adjoining an excavation. Used with strings as a guide to elevation and

to outline a proposed building. The strings strung between boards can be left in place during excavation.

batter brace (batter post) (1) A bracing member positioned diagonally so as to reinforce an end of a truss. (2) An inclined timber that forms a side support to a tunnel roof.

battered wall A wall that slopes backward, as by recessing or sloping masonry in successive courses.

batter level An instrument used to measure the inclination of a slope.

batter pile (brace pile, raking pile, spur pile) (1) A pile driven somewhat diagonally so as to resist horizontal forces. (2) Any pile installed at an angle to the vertical.

batter post *See* **batter brace.**

batter rule An instrument used to adjust the inclination of a battered wall during its construction. A batter rule incorporates a rule or frame and a plumb line and bob.

batter stick A tapered board hung vertically by its wide end or used in conjunction with a level to check the batter of a wall surface.

battery A device in which electrochemical action is employed to store and provide direct electric current.

batting tool A mason's dressing chisel used to apply a striated surface to stone.

batt insulation Thermal or sound-insulating material, such as fiberglass or expanded shale, which has been fashioned into a flexible, blanket-like form, often with a vapor barrier on one side. Batt insulation is manufactured in dimensions that facilitate its installation between the studs or joists of a frame construction. *See also* **blanket insulation.**

bay window

beam-and-girder
construction
(concrete)

battleships *See* **Madison clips**.

baud In data transmission, a unit of measure equal to one bit per second.

Bauhaus A school of art, design, and architecture established by Walter Gropius in Weimar, Germany, 1919.

baulk *See* **balk**.

bay (1) In construction, the space between two main trusses or beams. (2) The space between two adjacent piers or mullions, or between two adjacent lines of columns. (3) A small, well-defined area of concrete laid in the course of placing larger areas, such as floors, pavements, or runways. (4) The projecting structure of a bay window.

bayonet saw *See* **jigsaw**.

bay stall A built-in window seat at the opening of a bay window.

bay window A usually large window or group of windows that projects from a wall of a building forming a recess within the building.

beacon (1) A light that indicates a location by directing its powerful beam slightly above the horizontal and rotating it so that to a stationary observer, it appears to be flashing. A beacon is used at airports, on lighthouses, etc. (2) A transmitter that broadcasts warning or guiding signals.

bead (1) Any molding, stop, or caulking used around a glass panel to hold it in position. (2) A stop or strip of wood against which a door or window sash closes. (3) A strip of sheet metal that has been fabricated so as to have a projecting nosing and two perforated or expanded flanges. A bead is used as a stop at the perimeter of a plastered surface or as reinforcement at the corners.

(4) A narrow, half-round molding, either attached to or milled on a larger piece. (5) A square or rectangular trim less than 1″ in width and thickness. (6) A choker ferrule; the knob on the end of a choker.

bead and butt *See* **bead butt**.

bead-and-real Half-round molding into which are incorporated alternating patterns of discs and elongated beads.

bead butt (bead and butt) Thick, framed panelwork, as on a door, having one face flush with the frame and decorated with moldings (beads) on the adjoining edges, running with the grain and butting against the rail. The other side is recessed and without moldings.

bead butt and square Door paneling comprising one flush face and one bead butt.

bead molding Small, half-round, convex molding, either continuous or divided, that resembles a succession of beads.

bead plane A special plane with a curved cutting edge employed in the cutting of beads in wood.

beam (1) A horizontal structural member, such as a girder, rafter, or purlin, which transversely supports a load and transfers the load to vertical members, such as columns and walls. (2) The graduated horizontal bar of a weighing scale.

beam anchor (joist anchor, wall anchor) A metal tie used to secure a beam, joist, or floor firmly to a wall.

beam-and-girder construction A type of floor construction in which slabs are used to distribute the load to evenly spaced beams and girders.

beam-and-slab floor A type of floor construction in which reinforced

beam bolster

beam form

beam pocket

bearing

concrete beams are used to support a monolithic concrete floor slab.

beam bearing plate A metal plate positioned under the end of a beam to distribute the reaction load over a larger area. When used under a column, it is called a *loose plate*.

beam blocking Covering or enclosing a beam, joist, or girder to make it appear larger than it really is.

beam bolster A rod or heavy wire device used to support steel reinforcement in the formwork for a reinforced concrete beam.

beam bottom The soffit of a beam.

beam box *See* **wall box**.

beam brick A lintel made of brick courses, often held together by metal straps.

beam ceiling A type of construction in which the structural and/or ornamental overhead beams are left exposed to view from the room below.

beam column A structural member that transmits an axial load as well as a transverse load.

beam compass An instrument comprising a small horizontal bar with two vertical components that can slide along it. One carries a sharp-pointed tip and is held by the user in a stationary position. The other carries a pencil tip and is moved around the first to draw circles or arcs of circles for full-size working drawings.

beam fill (beam filling) Masonry, brickwork, or concrete placed between floor or ceiling joists to stiffen the joists and provide fire resistance.

beam filling *See* **beam fill**.

beam form A retainer or mold constructed to give the necessary

shape, support, and finish to a concrete beam.

beam hanger (beam saddle) (1) A wire, strap, or other hardware device used to hang beam forms from another structural member. (2) In timber construction, a strap, wire, or stirrup used to support a beam.

beam haunch A poured concrete section that continues beyond a beam to support the sill.

beam pocket (1) A space left open in a vertical structural member to receive a beam. (2) An opening in the column or girder form where forms for an intersecting beam will be framed.

beam saddle *See* **beam hanger**.

beam side The side panels of a form for a concrete beam.

beam spread A measure of the dispersion of a beam of light. Expressed as the angle between two directions in the plane in which the candlepower is equal to a specified percent (usually 10%) of the maximum candlepower in the beam.

beam test A method of measuring the flexural strength (modulus of rupture) of concrete by testing a standard unreinforced beam.

bearer (1) A horizontal member of a scaffold on which the platform rests and which may be supported by ledgers. (2) Any load-supporting horizontal structural member. (3) Any device that provides support for a landing or window in a stair. (4) In balloon framing, the ribbon board on which the joists for the second floor rest.

bearing (1) That section of a structural member, such as a column, beam, or truss, which rests on the supports. (2) A device used to support or steady a shaft, axle, or trunnion. (3) In surveying, the

bearing pile

bearing plate

horizontal angle between a reference direction, such as true north, and a given line. (4) Descriptive of any wall that provides support to the floor and/or roof of a building.

bearing bar (1) A wrought-iron bar used on masonry to offer a level support for floor joists. (2) A supporting bar for a grating.

bearing capacity The maximum unit pressure that soil or other material can withstand without failure or excessive settlement.

bearing pile A pile that supports a vertical load.

bearing plate A steel plate positioned under a beam, column, girder, or truss to distribute a load to a support member.

bearing pressure The existing load on a bearing surface, divided by the area of the bearing surface.

bearing stratum The soil or rock stratum on which a footing or mat bears or carries the load transferred to it by a pile, caisson, or similar deep foundation unit.

bearing wall Any wall that supports a vertical load as well as its own weight.

Beaufort scale A numerical scale used to indicate the successive range of wind velocity (0 for calm, 12 for hurricane force).

bed (1) The mortar into which masonry units are set. (2) Sand or other aggregate on which pipe or conduit is laid in a trench. (3) To set in place with putty or similar compound, as might be performed in glazing. (4) A supporting base for engines or machinery. (5) To level or smooth a path onto which a tree will be felled. (6) To set glass in place using putty.

bed coat See **bedding coat.**

bedding (1) A prepared base for masonry or concrete. (2) The lath or other support(s) on which pipe is laid. See also **bed (2)** and **(3).**

bedding coat (bed coat) Ordinarily, the initial coat of joint compound on gypsum board applied over tape, bead, and other fastener heads.

bedding course The initial layer of mortar at the bottom of a masonry construction.

bedding dot A small area of plaster built out of the face of a finished wall or ceiling that acts as a screed for leveling and plumbing in a plastering operation.

bedding stone A flat slab of marble with which bricklayers and masons check the flatness of rubbed bricks.

bed dowel A dowel placed in the mortar bed for a stone to prevent settlement before the mortar has set.

bed glazing See **back putty.**

bed joint (1) The horizontal layer of mortar on which a masonry unit is laid. (2) In an arch, a horizontal joint or one that radiates between adjacent voussoirs. (3) A horizontal fault in a rock formation.

bed molding (1) A molding placed at the angle between a vertical surface and an overhanging horizontal surface, such as between a side wall and the eaves of a building. (2) The lowest molding in a band of moldings. (3) In classical architecture, a molding of a cornice of an entablature, located between the corona and the frieze.

bedplate A baseplate, frame, or platform that supports a structural element, furnace, or heavy machine.

bedrock Solid rock that underlies the earth's surface soil and which can provide, by its very existence,

bell (hub)

bell-and-spigot joint

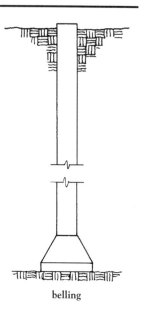

belling

the foundation on which a heavy structure may be erected.

bed timber A large wood member set perpendicular to trusses that serves as a foundation or support element.

beech (beechwood) Any of a number of hardwoods of the genus *fagus*, having characteristics of straight, close grain and good workability. Beech is often used in furniture, turnings, tools, and similar products.

beechwood *See* **beech**.

beetle (maul) A heavy mallet with a large wooden head used for driving pegs or wedges or in other applications where material might sustain damage if struck with a conventional sledgehammer.

before-sheathing window A window installed before the wall sheathing is in place.

Belgian block A paving stone shaped like a truncated pyramid and laid with the largest face down.

bell (hub) A portion of a pipe that, for a short distance, is sufficiently enlarged to receive the end of another pipe of the same diameter for the purpose of making a joint.

bell-and-spigot joint (bell joint, spigot-and-socket joint) The most commonly used joint in cast-iron pipe. Each length is made with an enlarged diameter or bell at one end into which the plain or spigot end of another piece is inserted. The joint is sealed by cement, oakum, lead, or rubber caulked into the bell around the spigot.

belled caisson A caisson with an enlarged, bell-shaped base.

belled excavation The bell-shaped lower portion of a shaft or footing excavation frequently used in caisson construction.

belling In pier, caisson, or pile construction, the process of enlarging the base of a foundation element at the bearing stratum to provide more bearing area.

bell joint *See* **bell-and-spigot joint**.

bell loop The circuit that provides notification of a fire condition in a fire alarm system.

bellows expansion joint In a run of piping, a joint accomplished with flexible metal bellows that can expand and/or contract linearly to allow for thermally induced linear fluctuations of the run itself.

bell transformer A very small transformer that supplies low voltage power on demand to doorbells or similar devices.

bell trap A bell-shaped trap sometimes used in floor drains. Its installation for residential use is prohibited by the National Plumbing Code.

bell wire Small-diameter wire of low current-carrying capacity whose insulation is rated at 30 volts or less.

belt (1) A flexible continuous loop that conveys power (or materials) between the pulleys or rollers around which it passes. (2) A course of brick or stone which protrudes from a wall of similar material and is usually positioned in line with the windowsills.

belt conveyor A power-driven apparatus comprising a single continuous belt and the idler wheels around which it passes to transport materials or products placed on the upper surface of the belt.

belt course (1) In masonry, a continuous layer of stone or brick that protrudes from the face of a stone or brick wall. (2) In carpentry, a horizontal band around a building, usually made of a flat board member and molding.

belt sander

benched foundation

bench vise

belt loader An excavating machine comprising an auger or other cutting edge that digs away the earth, and a conveyer belt that elevates the excavated material for loading onto a truck or depositing elsewhere.

belt sander An electrically powered, portable sanding tool with a continuous abrasive belt driven in one direction only. A belt sander is used to smooth surfaces, usually wood.

belt tightener A device incorporated into the construction of a conveyer belt for adjusting the belt tension by repositioning the counterweight and pulley.

belvedere A rooftop pavillion or a small structure, like a gazebo, for enjoying a vista.

bench (1) A long seat, with or without a back, made in any of several materials, such as wood, metal, or fiberglass, and usually accommodating more than one person. (2) One step, level, or shelf in a cut or excavation that is performed in several layers. (3) A pretensioning bed.

bench brake A large, heavy, bench-mounted device for bending sheet metal.

bench dog A peg or pin partially inserted into a hole at an edge or end of a workbench to help secure a piece of work or prevent it from sliding off the bench.

benched foundation (stepped foundation) A foundation cut as a series of horizontal steps in an inclined bearing stratum to prevent sliding when loaded.

bench hook (side hook) In carpentry, any device used to protect the top surface of a workbench from being scarred or damaged by any slipping or sliding of the work. It usually keeps the work positioned toward the front of the bench.

benching (1) A half-round channel cast in the concrete in the bottom of a manhole to direct discharge when the flow is low. (2) Concrete placed in horizontal steps on steeply sloping fill to prevent sliding. (3) Concrete laid on the side slopes of drainage channels where the slopes are interrupted by manholes, etc. (4) Concrete laid in a pipeline trench to provide firmer support.

bench mark (1) A marked reference point on a permanent object, such as a metal disc set in concrete, whose elevation as referenced to a datum is known. (2) A mark made by a surveyor or general contractor to be used as a reference point when measuring the elevation or location of other points.

bench plane A plane, such as a block plane or a jack plane, used primarily in bench work on flat surfaces.

bench sander An electrically powered, bench-mounted sanding machine that uses a rotating abrasive disk or grinder, or a continuous abrasive belt, to smooth the surface of objects held against it.

bench stop A usually notched, adjustable metal apparatus fastened close to an end of a workbench to hold a piece of wood securely during planing.

bench table A course of masonry, wide enough to form a seat, which protrudes from the foot of an interior wall or column.

bench vise An ordinary vise attached to a workbench to hold a material or component in place while it is being worked on.

bent

bent bar

bench work All work performed on a bench rather than on machines or in the field.

bend (1) An elbow fitting or other short length of bent conduit used to join two lengths of straight adjacent conduit. (2) A pipe fitting used to achieve a change in direction.

bending beam *See* **tie beam**.

bending extra A charge (an extra) by the fabricator for bending reinforcing bars. Extras are charged by the ton according to bar sizes.

bending iron A tool used to shape or expand pipe.

bending moment The bending effect at any section of a beam. The bending moment is equal to the algebraic sum of moments taken about the center of gravity of that section.

bending moment diagram A graphic representation of the variation of bending moment along the length of the member for a given stationary system of loads.

bending schedule A list of reinforcement prepared by the designer or detailer of a reinforced concrete structure which shows the shapes, dimensions, and location of every bar, and the number of bars required.

bend test Subjecting a flat bar to a 180° cold bend in order to test its weld or steel and to check its ductility, which is verified if no cracking occurs during the test.

beneficiation The process used to increase the iron content of ores.

benefits, mandatory and customary The employee benefits required by law (such as social security, workers' compensation, and disability insurance) and by custom (such as vacation, sick leave) as well as those that are optional, depending on the individual firm (such as pension plans, life insurance).

bent (1) A structural framework, transverse to the length of a structure, designed to carry lateral as well as vertical loads. (2) Any of several grasses of the genus *agrostis* which are used where a resilient, velvety texture is required.

bent approach The arrangement of a driveway such that it turns sharply through two out-of-line gateways. The bent approach is used for privacy and security.

bent bar A reinforcing bar bent to a prescribed shape, such as a truss, straight bar with hook, stirrup, or column tie. A bent bar is bent to pass from one face of a member to the other.

bentonite A clay composed principally of minerals in the montmorillonite group and characterized by high absorption and very large volume change with wetting or drying.

benzene A flammable liquid used in dyes and as a solvent and cleaning fluid.

Berea sandstone A fine-grain sandstone quarried in Amherst, Ohio.

berm (1) An artificially placed continuous ridge or bank of earth, usually along a roadside. Also called a *shoulder*. (2) A ridge or bank of earth placed against a masonry wall. (3) A ledge or strip of earth placed so as to support pipes or beams. (4) Earthen dikes or embankments constructed to retain water on land that will be flood-irrigated. (5) Earthen or paved dike-like embankments for diverting runoff water. (6) A raised wall enclosing a liquid waste storage or spill area. (7) An asphaltic concrete or concrete curb.

bevel chisel

beveled end

bibcock

berth A docking facility where a vessel can tie up and load or discharge cargo, fuel, etc.

Bethell process A method of pressure-impregnating wood with a creosote preservative.

bevel (1) Any angle (except a right angle) or inclination of any line or surface that joins another. (2)An adjustable instrument used for determining, measuring, or reproducing angles. (3) In welding, preparation on the edges to be welded.

bevel angle In welding, the angle created by the prepared edge of a member and a plane perpendicular to the surface of the member.

bevel board (pitch board) A board that has been cut to a predetermined desired, or required, angle and employed in any angular wood construction, including roof and stair framing.

bevel chisel A wood-cutting chisel whose cutting edge is angled between its sides.

bevel collar *See* **angle collar**.

bevel cut Any cut made at an angle other than a right angle.

beveled edge (1) A vertical front edge on a door, cut so as to have a slope of 1/8″ in 2″ from a plane perpendicular to the face of the door. (2) The factory-applied angle on the edge of gypsum board which creates a "vee" grooved joint when two pieces are installed together. (3) A chamfer strip incorporated into concrete forms for columns or beams so as to eliminate sharp corners on the finished product.

beveled end The end of a pipe or fitting that has been prepared for welding.

beveled washer A washer with a bevel on one side, and used mostly in structural steel work to provide a flat surface for the nut wherever a threaded rod or bolt passes through a beam at an angle.

bevel joint A carpentry joint in which two wood pieces meet at any angle except a right angle.

bevel protractor A graduated semicircular drafting device incorporating an adjustable pivoted arm and used for measuring and plotting angles.

bevel siding *See* **clapboard**.

bevel square A tool similar to a try square except that it has an adjustable blade that can be set at any angle.

B-grade wood The classification of a somewhat inferior grade of solid surface veneer that contains visible repair plugs and tight knots.

biannual report A report of the waste reduction and recycling activities of all hazardous waste generators. This report is published twice a year and is required by most states.

bias The fixed voltage applied to an electrode.

bib *See* **bibcock**.

bibb *See* **bibcock**.

bibcock (bib, bibb, bib tap) (1) Any faucet or stopcock that has its nozzle directed downward. (2) Any tap supplied by a horizontal pipe.

bib tap *See* **bibcock**.

bib valve Any standard bibcock or faucet equipped with a handle that is turned in one direction to initiate the flow of water, and turned in the opposite direction (screwed down) to shut off the flow by closing a washer disk onto a seating within the valve.

bidet

bid A complete signed proposal to perform work (or a designated portion) for a stipulated sum. A bid is submitted in accordance with the bidding documents.

bid abstract (summary) On a given project, a compilation of bidders and their respective bids, usually separated into individual items.

bid assembly The compiling of all estimates, prices, and sub-bids to produce a bid.

bid bond A form of security executed by the bidder or principal in conjunction with a surety to guarantee that the bidder will enter into a contract within a specified period of time and will furnish the required bonds for performance and labor and materials payment.

bid call A published announcement that bids for a specific construction project will be accepted at a designated time and place. *See also* **advertisement for bids**.

bid date A predetermined date for the receipt of bids, usually set by the architect and owner.

bidder An entity or person who submits a bid for a prime contract with the owner. A bidder is not a contractor on a specific project until a contract is signed between the bidder and the owner.

bidders mailing list A list of contractors to whom an owner or his representative sends invitations for bids for a particular project.

bidding documents Documents usually including advertisement or invitation to bidders, instructions to bidders, bid form, form of contract, forms of bonds, conditions of contract, specifications, drawings, addenda, and any other information needed to completely describe the work so that constructors can

adequately prepare proposals or bids for the owner's consideration.

bidding period The period of time beginning with the issuance of bidding documents, and ending at the *bid time*.

bidding requirements Those instructions included in the bidding documents, such as the invitation or advertisement for bids, instructions to bidders, bid form, and bid bond.

bidet A low, basin-like bathroom fixture used for washing the lower part of the body.

bid form A form, furnished to the bidder, on which to submit his bid.

bid guarantee *See* **bid security**.

bid letting *See* **bid opening**.

bid opening (bid letting) A formal meeting held at a specified time and place at which sealed bids are opened, tabulated, and read aloud.

bid package All drawings, specifications, documents, estimates, paperwork, bid forms, and bid bonds relevant to a construction project. A contract is based on the bid package.

bid price The amount for which a bidder offers to perform work. (This sum is stated in the bid.)

bid protest A challenge by a disappointed bidder. On a government contract, this is submitted to the Contracting Officer or the GAO.

bid results The display of all the bids on a project.

bid security (bid guarantee) A bid bond or deposit submitted with a bid to guarantee to the owner that the bidder, if awarded the contract, will execute the contract within a specified period of time and will furnish any bonds or other requirements of the bid documents.

bid time The exact date and time for submission of bids, established by

bifolding door

binder course

binding post

the owner or architect. *See also* **bid date**.

bifolding door A door that has two leaves, each consisting of two panels hinged together so that they fold on each other when the door is opened. One free edge of each leaf, or pair of panels, is hinged at a door jamb; the other edge is supported from and guided by an overhead track.

bilateral contract A contract in which both contracting parties are bound to fulfill obligations towards each other.

billet (1) A steel bar forged or rolled from an iron ingot. (2) A timber milled on three sides and left rounded on the fourth.

billet steel *See* **billet (1)**.

bill of materials *See* **quantity survey**.

bin A storage container, usually for loose materials such as sand, stone, or crushed rock.

binary code In computer technology, a system of representing numbers or letters using the base-2 (binary) number system.

binder (1) Almost any cementing material, either hydrated cement or a product of cement or lime and reactive siliceous materials. The kinds of cement and the curing conditions determine the general type of binder formed. (2) Any material, such as asphalt or resin, that forms the matrix of concretes, mortars, and sanded grouts. (3) That ingredient of an adhesive composition which is principally responsible for the adhesive properties that actually hold the two bodies together. (4) In paint, that nonvolatile ingredient, such as oil, varnish, protein, or size, which serves to hold the pigment particles together in a coherent film.

(5)A stirrup or other similar contrivance, usually of small-diameter rod, which functions to hold together the main steel in a reinforced concrete beam or column.

binder course (binding course) (1) A succession of masonry units between an inner and outer wall which serve to bind them. (2) In asphaltic concrete paving, an intermediate course between the base and the surfacing material comprised of bituminously bound aggregate of intermediate size.

binder warp *See* **binding yarn**.

binding agent *See* **binder (4)**.

binding beam (1) A timber or steel beam that carries the common joists in a double or framed elbow. (2) Any timber that ties together various components of a frame.

binding course *See* **binder course**.

binding joist *See* **binding beam (1)**.

binding piece A piece of lumber nailed between two parallel joists or beams to control lateral deflection.

binding post (1) A set screw that holds a conductor against the terminal of a device or on equipment. (2) A post attached to an electric wire, cable, or apparatus to facilitate a connection to it.

binding rafter *See* **purlin**.

binding yarn (binder warp, crimp warp) In carpeting, the natural or synthetic yarn incorporated lengthwise into the woven fabric to "bind" the tufts of pile securely.

bin-wall A retaining, supporting, or protective structure made from a group of connected bins filled with gravel or sand. May serve as an abutment, a pier, a retaining wall, or as a shield against gunfire or explosion.

biparting door

bird's mouth

bioaccumulative A substance that enters the body but is not removed through normal bodily functions.

biological remediation The process of degrading a contaminant through a bioremediation process.

bioremediation The use of naturally occurring biological agents to degrade hazardous waste to a non-hazardous state.

bioventing A process that intentionally stimulates in-situ biological degradation; also called soil venting.

biparting door A sliding door with two leaves that slide in the same plane and meet at the door opening.

birch A strong, fine-grained hardwood commonly used in veneer, furniture, flooring, and turned wood products.

birdbath Slang for a depression in a driveway that catches water.

bird screen Wire mesh used to cover chimneys, ventilators, and louvers to prevent birds from entering buildings through these accesses.

bird's-eye maple Lumber from a sugar maple tree that has been cut to exhibit a wavy grain with many small circular or elliptical markings.

bird's mouth An L-shaped cut made in a diagonal timber, such as a rafter, so that it snugly fits against another timber, such as a wall plate.

bit (1) The tool that fits into a brace or drill and is rotated to bore a hole. (2) On a soldering iron, the (usually copper) tip that heats the joint and melts the solder. (3) That part of a key which is inserted into a lock and engages the tumblers or bolt. (4) A binary digit; the smallest unit of computerized data.

bit brace *See* **handbrace**.

bite In glazing, the overlap between the innermost edge of the stop or frame and the outer edge of the light or panel.

bit extension A length of rod held at one end by the chuck of a brace and equipped at the other end for holding a bit. A bit extension permits the drilling of holes whose required depth is greater than the length of an ordinary bit.

bit gauge (bit stop) A piece of metal projecting outward from a bit to limit its depth of penetration.

bit key (wing key) Any key which has a bit.

bits per second A unit of measurement for data transmission. May be expressed as kilobits (Kbps) for thousands of bits per second; megabits (Mbps) for millions of bits per second; or gigabits (Gbps) for billions of bits per second.

bit stop *See* **bit gauge**.

bitumen Any of several mixtures of naturally occurring or synthetically rendered hydrocarbons and other substances obtained from coal or petroleum by distillation. Bitumen is incorporated in asphalt and tar and is used in road surfacing and waterproofing operations.

bituminous Composed of, similar to, derived from, relating to, or containing bitumen. The term bituminous is descriptive of asphalt and tar products.

bituminous base course (black base) Bituminously bound aggregate serving as a foundation for binder courses and surface courses in asphalt paving operations.

bituminous binder course *See* **binder course (2)**.

bituminous cement A class of dark substances composed of intermediate hydrocarbons.

bituminous coating

bituminous distributor

B-labeled door

Bituminous cement is available in solid, semisolid, or liquid states at normal temperatures.

bituminous coating Any waterproof or protective coating whose base is a compound of asphalt or tar.

bituminous concrete See **asphaltic concrete**.

bituminous distributor A tank truck equipped with a perforated spray bar through which heated bituminous material, such as tar or road oil, is pumped onto the surface of a road.

bituminous emulsion
(1) A suspension of any globules of a bituminous substance in water or an aqueous solution. (2) An invert emulsion of the above, i.e., a suspension of tiny globules of water or an aqueous solution in a liquid bituminous substance. This type of bituminous emulsion is applied to surfaces to provide a weatherproof coating. See also **emulsified asphalt**.

bituminous felt See **asphalt-prepared roofing**.

bituminous fiber pipe Drainage pipe made from a combination of coal tar and cellulose fiber.

bituminous grout A mixture of bituminous material and fine sand or other aggregate which, when heated, becomes liquid enough to flow into place without mechanical assistance. Bituminous grout will air-cure after being poured into cracks or joints as a filler and/or sealer.

bituminous leveling course In paving operations, a course consisting of a mixture of asphalt and sand and used to level or crown a base course or existing deteriorating pavement prior to the application of a surface.

bituminous macadam A paving material comprising bituminously coated coarse aggregate.

bituminous paint A thick black waterproofing paint containing substantial amounts of coal tar or asphalt.

B-labeled door A door carrying a certification from Underwriters' Laboratories that it is of a construction that will pass the standard fire door test required for a Class B opening, and that it has been prepared (with cuts and reinforcement) to receive the hardware required for a Class B opening.

black base See **bituminous base course**.

black japan A black, high-quality bituminous paint or varnish.

black-light (1) A fluorescent lamp with a phosphor that emits black light. (2) Electron-magnetic energy of the ultraviolet spectrum. Black light is used to excite fluorescent paints and dyes so that they become visible.

black plate Uncoated cold-rolled steel in 12″ to 32″ wide sheets.

black steel pipe Steel pipe that has not been galvanized.

blacktop See **asphaltic concrete**.

Blaine apparatus Air-permeability apparatus for measuring the surface area of a finely ground cement.

Blaine test A method for determining the fineness of cement or other material based on the permeability to air of a sample prepared under specified conditions.

blank door (1) A recess in a wall fitted with a fixed door, and used for architectural effect. (2) A door that has been fixed in position to seal an opening.

blanket (1) Soil or pieces of rock remaining or intentionally placed over a blast area to contain or to

blanket insulation

blank flange (blind flange)

blank jamb

direct the throw of fragments. (2) Insulation sandwiched between sheets of fabric, plaster, or paper facing, used for protecting fresh concrete during curing.

blanket encumbrance A lien or mortgage levied proportionately on every lot in a given subdivision.

blanket insulation Faced or unfaced thermal or sound insulation, usually made of fiberglass, available in densities and thicknesses that allow it to conform to the various-shaped spaces it encounters in its many applications. Blanket insulation is the same as batt insulation, except that it is supplied in continuous rolls instead of sheets. *See also* **insulation blanket**.

blank flange (blind flange) (1) A flange in which the bolt holes are not drilled. (2) A solid plate fitting used to seal off flow in a pipe.

blank jamb A vertical component of a door frame as installed without any preparation for hardware installation.

blank-off A blank plate sealing off a sector of a diffuser to prevent airflow in the direction of the blank-off plate.

blank wall (blind wall, dead wall) A wall with no openings on its entire surface.

blank window (blind window, false window) (1) A recess in a wall, having the appearance of a window. (2) A window that has been sealed off but is still visible.

blast To loosen, crack, or move rock or hard-packed soil by the detonation of explosives.

blast area The area in which explosives loading and blasting operations are being conducted.

blast cleaning Any cleaning method in which air, liquid, abrasive, or some combination of these is applied under pressure.

blast freezer A freezer room in which air at subfreezing temperature is circulated by blower for the purpose of freezing foods quickly.

blast-furnace slag The nonmetallic waste that develops simultaneously with iron in a blast furnace. Consists essentially of silicates and aluminosilicates of calcium and other bases.

blast heater A unit heater containing a set of heat-transfer coils through which air is forced or drawn at high velocities.

blast hole A vertical hole with a diameter of at least 4″ and drilled to accept a charge of blasting explosives.

blasthole drill A device that bores blast holes.

blasting The process of loosening rock or hard-packed material with explosives.

blasting agent A material or mixture consisting of a fuel and oxidizer used for blasting, but not classified as an explosive and in which none of the ingredients is classified as an explosive, provided the finished product cannot be detonated with a No. 8 blasting cap when confined. An example is a mixture of ammonium nitrate and fuel oil or coal.

blasting cap A metallic tube closed at one end, containing a charge of one or more detonating compounds, designed for and capable of detonation from the sparks or flame of a safety fuse inserted and crimped into the open end.

blasting mat A blanket of interwoven steel cable or interlocking steel rings placed over a blast to contain the resultant fragments.

blind

blind door

blast-resistant door A steel door designed and fabricated to resist dynamic pressures of short duration up to 3,000 psi (21 MPA).

bleaching Lightening, whitening, or removing color, either by chemical means, such as chlorine or oxalic acid, or by exposure to certain kinds of light.

bleeder A small valve used to drain fluid from a pipe, radiator, or small tank.

bleeder pipe (bleeder tile) A pipe (usually clay) placed to allow water from outside a basement retaining wall to pass through the foundation into drains within the building.

bleeder tile *See* **bleeder pipe.**

bleeding (1) The autogenous flow of mixing water within, or its emergence from, freshly placed concrete or mortar. Bleeding is caused by the settlement of the solid materials within the mass. Also called *water grain.* (2) In painting, seepage of resin or an undercoating of paint through the finish coat. (3) In lumber, the exuding of sap or resin.

bleeding rate The ratio of the volume of water which is released by bleeding to the original volume of the paste. *See* **bleeding (1).**

bleed-through (strike-through) Discoloration in the face plies of wood veneer caused by seepage of cement through the veneer.

blended cement A hydraulic cement consisting of an intimate and uniform blend of (a) granulated blast-furnace slag and hydrated lime, (b) Portland cement and granulated blast-furnace slag, (c) Portland cement and pozzolan, or (d) Portland-blast-furnace slag, cement, and pozzolan. Blended cement is produced by intergrinding Portland cement clinker with the other materials or by a combination of intergrinding and blending.

blending valve A three-way valve that permits the mixing required to obtain a desired liquid temperature.

blind (1) Any panel, shade, screen, or similar contrivance used to block light or inhibit viewing. (2) An assembly of wood stiles, rail and wood slats, or louvers used in conjunction with doors and windows.

blind alley (cul-de-sac) Any alley, road, or passageway that has only one end open for access or exit, and is closed at the other end so as to prohibit through traffic.

blind attic An attic that is rough-floored but unfinished.

blind casing The rough window frame or subcasing to which the trim is added.

blind door A door with a louver instead of glass.

blind dovetail *See* **secret dovetail.**

blind drain (1) A trench filled with pervious materials such as crushed stone through which water flows toward an outlet. (2) A drain that is not connected to a sewage system.

blind flange *See* **blank flange (2).**

blind header (1) A brick or other masonry unit which, when laid, gives the appearance of a header while in reality is somewhat less than a whole unit. A blind header can also be a half-brick laid where only one end is visible. (2) A header brick concealed within a wall and functioning to bond adjacent tiers of bricks.

blinding (1) Applying a layer of weak concrete or other suitable material to reduce surface voids or

blind mortise and tenon joint

blind nailing

block

provide a clean, dry working surface. (2) The clogging of the openings in a screen or sieve by the material being separated. (3) Applying small chips of stone to a freshly tarred surface.

blind joint (bastard joint) (1) A masonry joint, such as that of a *blind header*, which is entirely concealed. (2) In a double Flemish masonry bond, a thin joint between the adjacent ends of two stretchers. This joint bisects a header in the course directly below it.

blind miter A joint fastened with dovetails and concealed pins.

blind mortise (stopped mortise) A mortise in, but not through, a member.

blind mortise and tenon joint A joint between a blind mortise and a stub tenon.

blind nailing (concealed nailing, secret nailing) Nailing performed so that the nailhead cannot be seen on the face of the work.

blind pocket A pocket in the ceiling at a window head. A blind pocket is used to conceal an object when not in use, such as a venetian blind in the raised position.

blind rivet A small-headed pin with an expandable shank used for joining light gauge metal.

blind stop A rectangular molding nailed between the outside trim and the outside sash of a window frame, which serves as a stop for storm sashes or screens.

blind tenon A tenon that fits a blind mortise.

blind wall *See* **blank wall**.

blind window *See* **blank window**.

blister (1) Usually an undesirable moisture and/or air-induced bubble or bulge which often indicates that some kind of delamination has taken place. Blisters can occur between finish plaster and the base coat, between paint or varnish and the surface to which it has been applied, between roofing membranes or between membrane and substrate, between reinforcing tape and the gypsum board to which it has been adhered, etc. (2) A tree disease characterized by the seepage of pitch onto the bark surface.

bloated clay *See* **expanded clay**.

block (1) A usually hollow concrete masonry unit or other building unit, such as *glass block*. (2) A solid, often squared, piece of wood or other material. (3) A piece of wood nailed between joists to stiffen a floor. (4) Any small piece of wood secured to the interior angle joint to strengthen and stiffen it. (5) A pulley and its enclosure. (6) A solid piece of wood or other material used to fill spaces between formwork members. (7) One of several small rectangular divisions within a city, bounded on each side by successive streets.

block and tackle A mechanical device comprised of pulley blocks and ropes or cables, and used to hoist or move heavy objects or loads.

block beam In structural design, a flexural member composed of individual blocks joined together by prestressing.

block bridging (solid bridging, solid strutting) Short boards fixed between floor joists to stiffen the joists and distribute the load.

blockholing The breaking up of boulders by detonating a charge of explosives that has been loaded in a hole drilled into the rocks.

block-in-course A kind of masonry employed in heavy construction

blocking

blockwork

blow count

which consists of squared, hammer-dressed stones laid so that the joints are close and the course is not higher than 12″.

blocking (1) Small pieces of wood used to secure, join, or reinforce members, or to fill spaces between members. (2) Small wood blocks used for shimming. (3) A method of bonding two parallel or intersecting walls built at different times by means of offsets whose vertical dimensions are not less than 8″ (20 centimeters). (4) The sticking together of two painted surfaces when pressed together. (5) An undesired adhesion between touching layers of material, such as occurs during storage. (6) A situation in which all possible paths between two lines in a telephone network are in use, thereby preventing the lines from being interconnected.

blocking chisel Any rugged, broad-edged stonemason's chisel.

blocking course In masonry, a finishing course, usually of stones, placed on top of a cornice.

block plane A plane with a low-angle cutting blade (about 20°) and designed to be held in one hand. A block plane is used primarily to clean end grain and miters.

blockwork Masonry of concrete block and mortar.

bloom (1) A thin, hazy film on old paint, usually caused by weathering. (2) A similar film on glass, resulting from general atmospheric deposition of impurities, or caused more by smoke, vapor, etc. (3) Efflorescence on brickwork. (4) A hazy or other kind of discoloration which sometimes occurs on the surface of rubber products. (5) The term given to

steel that has been reduced from an ingot by being rolled in a blooming mill to a dimension of at least 6″ square; if further reduced, it becomes a *billet*.

blowback The difference between the pressure at which a safety valve opens and the pressure at which it closes automatically after the release of excess pressure has occurred.

blow count (1) The number of times that an object must be struck to be driven into the soil to a desired or specified depth. (2) In soil borings, the number of times a sample spoon must be struck to be driven 6″ or 12″. (3) In pile driving operations, the number of times a pile must be struck to be driven 12″. (4) The number of blows per unit distance of advance.

blower A fan, especially one for heavy-duty use such as forcing air through ducts to an underground excavation.

blowhole (gas pocket) In concrete, a bug hole or small regular or irregular cavity, not exceeding 15 mm in diameter, resulting from entrapment of air bubbles in the surface of formed concrete during placement and compaction.

blowing *See* **popping**.

blow joint *See* **blown joint**.

blown asphalt *See* **asphalt, blown**.

blown-in insulation Insulation that is pumped or injected into walls, roofs, and other areas.

blown joint (blow joint) A plumbing joint sealed with the use of a blowtorch.

blow-off (1) A discharge outlet on a boiler to allow for expulsion of undesirable accumulations of sediment and/or for drainage. (2) In a sewer system, an outlet pipe

board and batten

board insulation

for expelling sediment or water or for draining a low sewer.

blowout *See* **blow up.**

blows (boils) In dewatering, small springs that bubble up on the floor of an excavated pit caused by unrelieved aquifers. Blows can cause large soil movement if not attended to properly.

blowtorch A small, portable, gas-fired burner that generates a flame hot enough to melt soft metals. A blowtorch is used to melt lead in plumbing operations, heat soldering irons, and burn off paint.

blow up (blowout) Localized buckling or breaking up of rigid pavement as a result of excessive longitudinal pressure.

blueboard A water-resistant wall board finished with veneer plaster. Also used as a base for ceramic tile.

blueprint A negative image reproduction having white lines on a blue background and made either from an original or from a positive intermediate print. Today the term almost always refers to *diazo* prints, which are architectural or working drawings having blue or black lines on a white background.

blue stain A discoloration in the sapwood of some trees resulting from fungus growth. Does not affect the strength of the wood.

bluestone A hard, fine-grained sandstone or siltstone of dark green to bluish-gray color that splits readily to form thin slabs. A type of flagstone, bluestone is commonly used for paving walkways.

blue top A grade stake driven into the ground that indicates the finished grade level.

board (1) Lumber ranging from 4″ to 12″(10 x 30 cm) wide and less than 2″ (5 cm) thick. (2) A box office seating chart or ticket board.

board and batten A type of siding in which the joints between vertically placed boards or plywood are covered by narrow strips of wood. *See also* **batten.**

board and brace A type of carpentry work consisting of boards grooved on both edges with thinner boards inserted between them and fitted into the grooves.

board butt joint A joint in shotcrete construction achieved by sloping the gunned surface to meet a 1″ board laid flat.

board foot The basic unit of measurement for lumber. One board foot is equal to a 1″ thick board, 12″ in width and 1′ in length. Thus, a 10′ long, 12″ wide, 1″ thick piece contains 10 board feet. When calculating board feet, nominal sizes are assumed.

board insulation (insulating board, insulation board) Lightweight thermal insulation, such as polystyrene, manufactured in rigid or semi-rigid form, whose thickness is very small relative to its other dimensions. Board insulation offers little structural strength and is usually applied under a finish material, although some types are surface-finished on one side.

board knife A knife with a replaceable blade that has a straight cutting edge. Used to secure or trim gypsum products.

board measure A system of measuring quantities of lumber, using one board foot as the basic unit of measurement.

board rule A measuring device used to find the number of board feet in a given board.

boatswain's chair

boiler

board sheathing A sheathing made of boards, usually tightly spaced, although open spacing may be used in some roofs.

boardwalk A walkway made of boards or planks, often used as a promenade along a beach or shore.

boast To roughly dress stone in preparation for carving.

boasted work A dressed stone surface with roughly parallel narrow chisel grooves of varying widths that do not extend across the entire face of the stone.

boaster A flat, steel, mason's chisel used to dress stone.

boat spike *See* **barge spike**.

boatswain's chair A seat supported by slings and attached to a suspended rope. Designed to accommodate one worker in a sitting position.

bob *See* **plumb bob**.

bobbin A tool used to shape lead pipe.

bodily injury Any form of physical injury, sickness, or disease that is experienced by a person.

body (1) The principal volume of a building, such as the nave of a church. (2) The load-carrying part of a truck.

body coat In painting, an intermediate coat of paint applied after the priming coat but before the finishing coat.

bogie (tandem) (1) A two-axial driving unit in a truck. (2) A stage hanger for an overhead track from which scenery or flats are suspended.

boil (1) A wet run of material at the bottom of an excavation. (2) A swelling in the bottom of an excavation due to seepage. *See also* **blows**.

boiled linseed oil Linseed oil to which manganese, lead, or cobalt salts have been added so that it will harden rapidly when applied in thin layers.

boiler A closed vessel in which a liquid is heated or vaporized, either by application of heat to the outside of the vessel, by circulation of heat through tubes within the vessel, or by circulating heat around liquid-filled tubes in the vessel.

boiler compound A clear, concentrated liquid added to water in boilers to control hardness, corrosion and to reduce the formation of boiler scale.

boiler economizer The last pass of boiler tubes or a heat exchanger located in the flue pipe that extracts some of the heat from the flue gases before they are vented to the atmosphere.

boiler horsepower (1) Boiler horsepower is equal to the evaporation of 34.5 lbs of water per hour from and at 212° F, 33, 475 Btu/hour. (2) The largest rating obtained by dividing the square feet of a boiler's surface by 10.

boiler jacket The thermal insulation surrounding a boiler. A more aesthetically acceptable enclosure, often made of metal, usually covers the jacket.

boiler plate (1) Medium-hard steel from which boilers are fabricated. The steel is rolled into plates whose thicknesses may vary from 0.25″ to 1.5″. (2) Standard text used in documents such as contract agreements.

boiler rating The heating capacity of a boiler, expressed in Btus per hour. The boiler rating should not be confused with the horsepower rating. *See also* **boiler horsepower**.

bolster

bolt

bolt sleeve

boiler scale Disintegrated bits of steel plate from a boiler's interior lining, which flake and fall to the boiler floor and should be removed periodically.

boiler steel A medium-hard steel that is rolled to become boiler plate.

boiserie Floor-to-ceiling interior wood paneling, usually enhanced by carving, gilding, or painting, but seldom by inlaying.

bollard (1) A series of short posts set to prevent vehicular access or to protect property from damage by vehicular encroachment. A bollard is sometimes used to direct traffic. (2) A post on a slip or wharf for securing mooring or docking lines.

bolster (1) In concrete, an individual or continuous support used to hold reinforcing bars in position. Usually used in slab work. (2) A short wood or steel member positioned horizontally on top of a column to support beams or girders. (3) A mason's blocking chisel. (4) A piece of wood, generally a nominal 4″ in cross section, placed between stickered packages of lumber or other wood products to provide space for the entry and exit of the forks of a lift truck.

bolt (1) An externally threaded, cylindrical fastening device fabricated from a rod, pin, or wire, with a round, square, or hexagonal head that projects beyond the circumference of the shank to facilitate gripping and turning. A threaded nut fits onto the end of a bolt and is tightened by the application of torque. (2) The protruding part of a lock which prevents a door from opening. (3) Raw material used in the manufacture of shingles and shakes. A wedge-shaped split from a short length of log that is taken to a mill

for manufacturing. (4) Short logs to be sawn for lumber or peeled for veneer. (5) Wood sections from which barrel staves are made. (6) A large roll of cloth or textile. (7) A single package containing two or more rolls of wallpaper.

bolted pressure switch A switch that uses movable blades and stationary contacts with arcing contacts to make and break switching action.

bolt sleeve A tube surrounding a bolt in a concrete wall to prevent the concrete from sticking to the bolt and acting as a spreader for the formwork.

bona fide bid A good faith bid that is essentially complete and complies with the bidding documents. Must be signed by a properly empowered party.

bond (1) The adhesion and grip of concrete or mortar to reinforcement or to other surfaces against which it is placed, including friction due to shrinkage and longitudinal shear in the concrete engaged by the bar deformations. (2) The adhesion of cement paste to aggregate. (3) Adherence between plaster coat or between plaster and a substratum produced by adhesive or cohesive properties of plaster or supplemental materials. (4) In masonry, the connection between stones, bricks, or other materials formed by laying them in an overlapping arrangement, one on top of another, to form a single wall mass. (5) The arrangement of, or pattern formed by, the exposed faces of laid masonry units. (6) The layer of glue in a plywood joint. (7) A written document, given by a surety in the name of a principal to an obligee to guarantee a specific obligation. *See also* **bid bond, completion bond, fidelity bond, labor and materials**

bond beam

bond course

bonded posttensioning

bonded tendon

payment bond, performance bond, statutory bond, *and* surety bond.

bond area The area of interface between two elements across which adhesion develops or may develop, as between concrete and reinforcing steel.

bond beam A horizontally reinforced concrete or concrete masonry beam built to strengthen and tie a masonry wall together. A bond beam is often placed at the top of a masonry wall with continuous reinforcing around the entire perimeter.

bond blister A blister that sometimes forms between the base material and the coating, particularly on metal-clad products.

bond breaker A material used to prevent adhesion between freshly placed concrete and the substrate.

bond coat (1) That coat of plaster which is applied over masonry and is bonded to it. (2) A primer coat of paint or sealer.

bond course In masonry, the course consisting of units that overlap more than one wythe of masonry.

bonded member A prestressed concrete member in which the tendons are bonded to the concrete either directly (pretensioned) or by grouting (posttensioned).

bonded posttensioning A process in posttensioned construction whereby the annular spaces around the tendons are grouted after stressing in such a way that the tendons become bonded to the concrete section.

bonded roof A type of roofing guarantee offered by the manufacturer which may or may not be purchased by the owner and which covers materials and/or workmanship for a stated length of time.

bonded tendon A prestressing tendon that is bonded to the concrete either directly or through grouting.

bonder (header) A masonry unit that ties two or more wythes of a wall together by overlapping.

bonderizing A process that improves the paintability of steel by forming a film of zinc phosphate on its surface.

bond face That face of a joint to which a field-molded sealant is bonded.

bond header (throughstone) A bondstone or masonry unit that extends through the entire thickness of a wall.

bonding In electrical circuitry, the connecting or joining of metal parts to form an electrical conductive path. Prevents the accumulation of static electricity and assures the safe conduction of electrical current.

bonding agent A substance applied to a suitable substrate to create a bond between it and a succeeding layer, as between a subsurface and a terrazzo topping or subsequent application of plaster.

bonding capacity The maximum total contract value a bonding company will extend to a contractor in performance bonds. The total bonding capacity is the sum of all contracts being bonded.

bonding company A firm providing a surety bond for work to be performed by a contractor, payable to the owner in case of default of the contractor. The bond can be for work performance or for payment for materials and labor.

bonding conductor *See* **bonding jumper.**

bonding jumper (bonding conductor) In a circuit, the connection

boom

between parts of a conductor to maintain the ampacity requirements of the circuit.

bonding layer A thin layer of mortar that is often used when a new concrete slab is placed over an existing hardened concrete surface. The bonding layer is spread before placing concrete for the new slab.

bond length (development length) The length of embedment of reinforcing steel in concrete required to develop the design strength.

bond plaster A thin coat of specially formulated gypsum plaster applied as a bonding coat to a concrete surface before applying succeeding coats of plaster.

bond prevention (1) Procedures whereby specific tendons in pretensioned construction are prevented from becoming bonded to the concrete for a predetermined distance from the ends of flexural members. (2) Measures taken to prevent adhesion of concrete or mortar to surfaces against which it is placed.

bondstone In stone facing, a stone that extends into the backing to tie the facing wall with the backing wall. *See also* **bonder**.

bond strength (1) Resistance to separation of mortar and concrete reinforcing steel and other materials with which it comes in contact. (2) Collective expression of all forces, such as adhesion, friction due to shrinkage, and longitudinal shear in the concrete engaged by the bar deformations that resist separation.

bond stress (1) The force of adhesion per unit area of contact between two bonded surfaces. (2) Shear stress at the surface of a reinforcing bar, preventing relative movement between the bar and the surrounding concrete.

bond timber Horizontal timbers placed in a masonry wall to bond it together and provide a base to which lath, battens, and other wood members can be nailed.

bonnet A wire mesh cover over the top of a chimney or vent. *See also* **chimney cap**.

bonus and penalty clause A contract clause assigning payment of a bonus to the contractor when completing the work before a stipulated date. Also contains provision for a charge against the contractor should it fail to complete the work by this date.

bonus provisions Provisions in the contract between the owner and the contractor for granting monetary rewards to the contractor for achieving some savings that benefit the owner. For example, a stipulated bonus may be offered for early completion of the work, or the achievement of some savings in construction cost.

book matching (herringbone matching) Consecutive flitches of veneer from the same log, laid side by side so that the pattern formed is almost symmetrical from the common center line. Book matching is used in decorative paneling and cabinetry.

book value (carrying value, undepreciated value) The net amount at which an asset is carried on the books or reported in the financial statements; the asset's cost at acquisition, reduced by the amount of accumulated depreciation on the asset.

boom A long, straight member, hinged at one end, and used for lifting heavy objects by means of cables and/or hydraulics. Booms

boom crane

boot

can be of lattice construction or heavy tubular material.

boom crane A crane with a long slender boom, usually of lattice construction.

boom hoist A lifting device with a vertical mast and an inclined boom commonly used to hoist materials in multistory building construction.

boom jack A short member on which sheaves are mounted to guide cables to a working boom on a crane or derrick.

boost-buck transformer A device that raises or lowers the voltage of a supply line.

booster Any device that increases the power, force, or pressure produced by a system.

booster compressor A compressor that increases the productivity of the primary compressor by discharging into its suction line.

booster fan An auxiliary fan that increases the air pressure in a system, such as an HVAC system, during certain peak requirement times.

booster heater In plumbing, an auxiliary heater installed in a hot water piping system to increase the heat in one section.

booster pump An auxiliary pump installed in a system to increase or maintain the pressure or flow.

booster transformer A transformer installed to increase the voltage in an electric circuit.

boot A term used to describe sleeves or coverings in many construction trades, such as a boot for pile driving, a boot for passing a pipe through a roof, and a boot for cold air return to a furnace casing.

bore (1) The inside diameter of a pipe, valve, fitting, or other hollow tubular object. (2) The circular hole left by boring.

bored latch A door latch manufactured to fit into a circular hole in a door.

bored lock A lock manufactured to fit into a circular hole in a door.

bored pile *See* **cast-in-place pile**.

bored well A water well constructed by drilling a hole with an auger and then inserting a casing.

borehole *See* **boring**.

borescope A fiber optic device that allows for non-destructive investigation of an area with restricted access, such as a housed mechanical assembly or a cavity inside a wall. Often used with a still or video camera.

boring (borehole) A hole drilled in the ground to obtain samples for subsoil investigation. Borings are important in determining the load-bearing capacity of the soil and the depth of the water table.

borrow (borrow fill material) In earth moving, fill acquired from an excavation source outside the required cut area.

borrowed light A glazed unit in an interior partition to allow light to enter from an adjoining room or passageway.

borrow fill material *See* **borrow**.

borrow pit An excavation site, other than a designated cut area, from which material is taken for use nearby.

boss (1) A projecting block, usually ornamental, placed at the exposed intersection or termination of ribs or beams of a structure. (2) The enlarged portion of a shaft. (3) In masonry, a stone that is left protruding from the surface for carving in place at a later time.

bottle brick

bottom rail

bowstring truss

bow window

(4) A projection left on a cast pipe fitting for alignment or for gripping with tools.

Boston hip (Boston ridge, shingle ridge finish) (1) A method of finishing a ridge or hip on a flexible shingled roof in which a final row of shingles is bent over the ridge or hip with a lateral overlap. (2) A method of finishing a ridge or hip on a rigid-shingled slate or a tile roof in which the last rows on either side overlap at the hip or ridge. Alternate courses overlap in opposite directions.

Boston ridge *See* **Boston hip.**

bottle brick A hollow brick shaped so that it can be mechanically connected to adjoining bricks. In each brick there is also a void available for inserting reinforcing steel, if required.

bottom arm A long strap secured to the bottom rail of a door to attach it to a floor closer or pivot hinge.

bottom bolt A vertically mounted bolt on the bottom of a door which slides into a socket in the floor.

bottom car clearance The vertical distance between the lowest point of any mechanism attached to the underside of an elevator car and the floor of the elevator pit.

bottom chord The lowest longitudinal member of a truss. It is usually horizontal, but may be at an incline depending on truss design.

bottom dump A type of trailer with gates on the bottom, used to haul heavy materials such as sand, gravel, and crushed stone. A bottom dump is best used when material is to be distributed in layers on an embankment.

bottom lateral bracing In truss framing, the members interconnecting the bottom chords.

bottom rail The lowest bottom member of a door. The bottom rail connects the stiles.

boundary survey A closed diagram (mathematically) depicting the complete outer boundary of a site. Shows dimensions, compass bearings, and angles. A licensed land surveyor's signed certification is required, and a *metes and bounds* or other written description may be included.

bow The longitudinal deflection of a piece of lumber, pipe, rod, or the like, usually measured at its center.

bowled floor A floor that slopes downward toward a central point, as in an amphitheater.

bow saw A hand tool with a thin saw blade held in place between the two ends of a bow-shaped piece of metal.

bowstring beam *See* **bowstring truss.**

bowstring girder *See* **bowstring truss.**

bowstring roof A roof supported by bowstring trusses and fabricated in the shape of a bow.

bowstring truss (bowstring beam, bowstring girder) A structural roof truss having a bow-shaped top cord and a straight or cambered bottom cord.

bow window (1) A window that projects from a wall in the shape of an arc. (2) A rounded bay window.

box bolt A short piece of rectangular stock that slides inside a casing mounted on the edge of a door. The stock slides into a recess in the door frame to secure the door.

box casing In finished carpentry, the inner lining, as in a cabinet.

box chisel A special chisel used to pry open wooden boxes.

box column A built-up, hollow column, usually square in shape, used in porch construction.

box wrench

brace

box culvert A rectangular-shaped, reinforced concrete drainage structure either cast in place or precast in sections.

box drain A small rectangular-shaped drainage structure usually constructed of brick or concrete. It may be covered or have an open grate on top.

boxed mullion A hollow mullion in a window frame built up from boards so as to appear solid; houses sash weights.

box frame A window frame containing hollow sections on either side in which the sash weights are suspended.

box gutter A rectangular-shaped wooden roof gutter recessed in the eaves to conceal them and to protect them from falling foliage.

box-head window A window framed with a pocket in the head so that the sash can slide into it to provide maximum ventilation.

boxing (1) Enclosing or casing, as in window frame construction. (2) In welding, continuing a principle fillet weld around a corner of the member. (3) Pouring paint back and forth from one pail to another to ensure a uniform consistency.

box lewis A device used for hoisting heavy masonry units. Consists of metal components, some or all of which taper upward, and are inserted into a downward flaring hole (lewis hole) cut in the top of the masonry.

box nail A nail with a head similar to a common nail of the same penny designation, but having a shank smaller in diameter.

box out To make a form that will create a void in a concrete wall or slab when the concrete is placed.

box scarf A joint in a rectangular-shaped roof gutter formed by beveling the ends of the two pieces to be joined.

box sill A common method of frame construction using a header nailed across the ends of floor joists where they rest on the sill.

box stair An interior staircase in which the edges of the treads and risers are not revealed but closed in with a closed stringer. A box stair typically has a partition on both sides.

box stoop An elevated platform at the entrance to a building with stairs running parallel to the building. The underside of the platform and stairs is enclosed.

box strike A fastening on a door frame (a strike) with an enclosed recess to receive a lock bolt.

boxwood A hard, dense, light-colored wood used for turned work and inlay.

box wrench A mechanic's hand tool with a closed socket, usually at each end, that fits over the head of a bolt or a nut.

brace (bracing) (1) A diagonal tie that interconnects scaffold members. (2) A temporary support for aligning vertical concrete formwork. (3) A horizontal or inclined member used to hold sheeting in place. (4) A hand tool with a handle, crank, and chuck used for turning a bit or auger.

braced excavation Excavation in which the perimeter is supported by sheeting.

braced frame (brace frame, brace framing) A wooden structural framing system in which all vertical members, except for corner posts, extend for one floor only. The corner posts are braced to the sill and plates.

brad awl

branch duct

brace frame *See* **braced frame**.

brace framing *See* **braced frame**.

brace pile *See* **batter pile**.

brace rod A round steel member used as a tension brace, especially to transfer wind or seismic loads.

brace scale *See* **brace table**.

brace table (brace scale) (1) The markings on a carpenter's square indicating the length of the hypotenuse for right triangles with various length legs. (2) A brace table used by carpenters to determine the length to cut braces.

bracing *See* **brace**.

bracket An attachment projecting from a wall or column used to support a weight or a structural member. Brackets are frequently used under a cornice, a bay window, or a canopy.

bracket pile A steel H pile driven next to an existing foundation. A steel bracket is welded to the pile and extends under and supports the foundation.

bracket saw A handsaw with a narrow blade attached to the open ends of a three-sided rectangular holder. Used for cutting curved shapes.

bracket scaffold (bracket staging) Scaffolding supported by brackets that are temporarily attached to the side of a building or column. Bolts or inserts are usually left in the previous construction to attach the brackets. This method saves the expense of shoring from the ground up.

bracket staging *See* **bracket scaffold**.

brad A slender, smooth, wire nail with a small deep head. Used for finish carpentry work.

brad awl A carpenter's tool that looks like an ice pick and is used to make holes for brads and wood screws.

brad pusher A special tool used to grip and insert a brad in an inaccessible location.

brake (1) A device for slowing, stopping, and holding an object. (2) A machine used to bend sheet metal.

brake drum A rotating cylinder with a machined surface (either internal or external) on which a brake band or shoe presses in order to slow, stop, or hold an object.

brake horsepower The horsepower output of an engine or other mechanical device, as measured at the flywheel or belt by applying a mechanical brake and measuring the work per unit time.

branch In plumbing, an inlet or outlet from the main pipeline, usually at an angle to the main pipeline. The pipe may be a water supply, drain, vent stack, or any other pipe used in a mechanical piping system.

branch circuit A portion of the electric system which extends wiring beyond the fuse or other device that is protecting that circuit.

branch drain A drainpipe from the plumbing fixtures or soil line of a building which runs into a main line.

branch duct In HVAC, a smaller duct that branches from the main duct. At each branch duct, the cross-sectional area of the main duct is reduced.

branch ell A sharply bent pipe fitting with its back outlet in line with a run outlet.

branch interval A length of soil stack or waste stack, usually one story high, within which all

break joints

branches from one floor are connected.

branch sewer A sewer that receives sewage from a relatively small area and is connected to a main sewer or manhole.

branch vent (1) A vent connecting one or more individual vents to a vent stack or stack vent. (2) A vent pipe to which are connected two or more pipes that vent plumbing fixtures.

brand name or equal A product description that identifies one or more commercial products by brand name and sets forth those characteristics of the named product that are essential to the owner's needs.

brander To nail furring strips to girders, joists, or walls in preparation for installing plaster or another finish material.

brashy A condition of wood characterized by coarse, conspicuous annual rings. Such wood has a low resistance to shock and has a tendency to fail abruptly across the grain without splintering.

brass (1) A copper alloy with zinc as the principal alloying element. (2) Slang for plumbing fittings and faucets, regardless of their actual material of composition.

braze To join two pieces of metal by soldering them together with a nonferrous metal such as brass.

brazed joint In plumbing, a fitting made watertight and gas-tight by brazing.

Brazilian rosewood A dark-colored hardwood used for turned articles, paneling, and veneers.

breach of contract The failure, without legal cause, to perform some contractually described obligation in accordance with the terms of the contract.

breakdown A term used to define the separation of a project or an estimate into parts.

breakdown voltage Voltage that causes the failure of existing insulation, permitting the flow of electric current.

breaker *See* **crusher.**

breaker ball (wrecking ball) *See* **headache ball.**

break-in In brick masonry, a void or socket to accept a timber.

breaking load The smallest load, determined by test, that would cause the failure of a structural system.

breaking radius The limiting radius of curvature to which a material can be bent without breaking.

break joints (staggered joints) The arrangement of modular structural units, such as masonry or plywood sheathing, so that the vertical joints of adjacent units do not line up.

break lines Lines used in drafting to omit part of an object so that the representation will fit on a drawing.

breast (1) The part of a wall that extends from the window stool to the floor level. (2) A projecting part of a wall, such as at a chimney.

breast board A system of movable sheeting used to retain the face of an excavation, especially in tunnel work.

breast drill A hand-operated rotary drill that has an attachment for applying pressure with the chest. Carpenters use a breast drill for drilling horizontal holes in wood.

breast lining Interior wooden paneling applied between the window stool and the baseboard.

breast molding (1) The molding at a windowsill. (2) A Paneling between the windowsill and the floor.

breeching

breezeway

brick anchor

brick hammer

breastsummer (1) A large supporting horizontal timber that spans a wide opening in an external wall, usually the breast of the wall.

breast timber *See* **wale.**

breast work (1) The masonry work of a chimney breast. (2) The parapet of a building.

breather A mechanism that allows air to move in and out of a container to maintain even atmospheric pressure.

breech fitting A Y-shaped fitting in ductwork or pipework.

breeching The exhaust duct or pipe that leads from a furnace or boiler to the stack or chimney.

breeze brick A brick made from pan breeze and Portland cement, often laid into a brick wall because of its good nail-holding properties.

breezeway A covered passageway open at both ends, which connects two buildings or two portions of a building.

brick A solid masonry unit of clay or shale, formed into a rectangular prism while plastic, and then burned or fired in a kiln. *See also* **adobe brick, arch brick, beam brick, bottle brick, breeze brick, buff standard brick, building brick, economy brick, engineered brick, facing brick, fire brick, floor brick, gauged brick, jumbo brick, Norman brick, paving brick, Roman brick, salmon brick, salt-glazed brick, SCR brick, sewer brick, soft-mud brick,** *and* **stiff-mud brick.**

brick anchor Corrugated fasteners designed to secure a brick veneer to a structural concrete wall. *See also* **reglet** *and* **dovetail anchor.**

brick and brick A method of laying brick so that units touch each other with only enough mortar to fill surface irregularities.

brick-and-half wall A brick wall that has the thickness of one header plus one stretcher.

brick-and-stud work *See* **nogging.**

brickbat *See* **bat (1).**

brick beam A lintel made of bricks held in place with iron straps.

brick cement A waterproofed compound used in masonry and stucco work.

brick closure Short pieces of brick used in corners or jambs to maintain the pattern.

brick facing *See* **brick veneer.**

brick gauge A standard height for brick courses when laid, such as four courses in a height of 12″.

brick grade A durability rating given to brick. SW, MW, and NW ratings refer to a brick's ability to withstand severe weathering, moderate weathering, and negligible weathering, respectively.

brick hammer A hand tool used by masons for breaking and dressing brick. One end of the head is square and flat and the other end is shaped like a chisel.

bricklayer's square scaffold A scaffold composed of framed wood squares which support a platform. A bricklayer's square scaffold is limited to light- and medium-duty.

brick molding The wood molding covering between the brick masonry and a door or window frame.

brick nogging *See* **nogging.**

brick set A chisel-like tool used with a brick hammer to make exact cuts in brick.

brick trimmer A brick arch supporting a fireplace hearth or shielding a wood trimming joist from flames in front of a fireplace.

brick trowel A hand trowel with a pointed handle used to pick up

brick veneer

bridged floor

bridging

mortar from a mortar tub and place and spread it in the joints.

brick type A rating given to facing brick based on its tolerance, chippage, and distortion. FBS, FBX, and FBA are designations for solid brick; HBS, HBX, and HBB are for hollow brick.

brick veneer A facing of brick laid against a structural wall but not bonded to the wall, and which bears no load other than its own weight.

brick whistle (1) A weep hole in a brick wall. (2) A small hole in a mortar joint at the base of a wall for draining any moisture that penetrates the wall.

bridge (1) A structure built to span an obstruction or depression and capable of carrying pedestrians and/or vehicles. (2) In an electric blasting cap, the wire that heats with current and ignites the charge. (3) The temporary structure built over a sidewalk or roadway adjacent to a building to protect pedestrians and vehicles from falling objects.

bridgeboard A notched or cut stringer that supports the treads and risers of wooden stairs.

bridge crane A crane often used in manufacturing or assembling heavy objects. A bridge crane requires a bridge spanning two overhead rails. A hoisting device moves laterally along the bridge while the bridge moves longitudinally along the rails.

bridge deck The load-carrying floor of a bridge that transmits the load to the beams.

bridged floor A floor supported by common joists.

bridge joint *See* **bridle joint**.

bridge plank The subfloor on a bridge which supports the wearing surface. Usually made of corrugated steel.

bridge thrust The horizontal thrust from vertical loads on an arched bridge.

bridging A method of lateral bracing between joists for stiffness, stability, and load distribution.

bridle joint (bridge joint) A type of mortise and tenon joint used when two timbers are joined at an angle less than 90°.

Briggs standard *See* American standard pipe threads.

brine In a refrigeration system, a liquid used as a heat transfer agent that remains a liquid and has a flashpoint above 150°. The liquid is usually a salt solution.

Brinell hardness A measure of the hardness of a metal determined in the laboratory by measuring the indentation made by a steel ball in the surface of the metal.

brissance The crack pattern that forms milliseconds after detonation, but before blasted rock dislodgement.

British thermal unit (Btu) A standard measurement of the heat energy required to raise the temperature of one pound of water one degree Fahrenheit.

brittle A characteristic of a material which makes it fracture easily without bending or deforming.

broach (1) To free stone block from a quarry ledge by cutting out the webbing between holes drilled close together in a row. (2) To cut wide parallel grooves in a diagonal pattern across a stone surface using the point of a chisel, finishing it for architectural use. (3) Any pointed structure, such as a steeple or spire, that is built for ornamental purposes. (4) A spire that rises directly from a tower, often without an intervening parapet. (5) A half

broached spire

broken joints

broken joint tile

pyramid constructed above the corners of a square tower, serving as an architectural transition from the slat of the tower to an octagonal spire.

broached spire An octagonal spire set above a square tower, with broaches braced against it at the four corners of the tower to effect a visually appealing transition.

broaching (1) A method of quarrying stone in which close holes are drilled around the breakline. A chisel, called a *broach*, is used to break the remaining material. The stone is then removed with wedges. (2) A method of making shaped holes in metal by removing small pieces in succession with a reaming tool.

broad ax A broad-bladed ax used to rough dress timber.

broad knife (stripping knife) A square-edged knife with a blade shaped like a wedge, used chiefly for scraping off old paint or wallpaper.

broadloom A seamless carpet woven on a wide loom, usually 6′ to 18′ (1.8 to 5.5 meters) wide.

broadscope A term describing the content of a section of the specifications, as established by the Construction Specifications Institute. A broadscope section covers a wide variety of related materials and workmanship requirements. (*Narrowscope* specifications denote a section describing a single material; *mediumscope* denotes a section dealing with a family of materials.)

broad stone *See* **ashlar (1)**.

broad tool A wide steel chisel used in the finish dressing of stone.

broad-tooled *See* **batted work**.

brob A wedge-shaped spike that is used to brace and secure the end of

one timber butting against the side of another.

broken arch A segmented arch, used largely as door or window entablature, from which the center of the arch is cut out and replaced with an ornamental figure or design.

broken ashlar *See* **random work**.

broken-color work *See* **antiquing**.

broken-flight stair *See* **dogleg stair**.

broken joints Vertical joints of masonry arranged in a staggered structure with no unit placed directly on top of another. Provides a more solid bond and increases structural strength.

broken joint tile A roofing tile that overlaps only the tile directly below it.

broken rangework A form of stone masonry with horizontal courses of different heights, some of which are broken at intervals into multiple courses.

brokered project A project completely sublet by the general contractor or construction manager.

bronze (1) An alloy composed of copper and tin. (2) A bronze-colored alloy that uses a sizable measure of copper to alter the properties of its chief elements, as in aluminum bronze or magnesium bronze.

bronzing (1) The application of metal bronze provider to an object or substance. (2) The powdery decomposition of a paint film caused by exposure to the elements and natural wear.

broom (1) To press a layer of roofing material against freshly applied bitumen in order to create a tight, thorough bond. (2) To flatten or spread the head of a timber pile by pounding forcefully on it. (3) To brush fresh plaster or concrete with a broom.

broom finish concrete

brown coat

brush rake

buck

broom finish concrete Concrete that has been brushed with a broom when fresh in order to improve its traction or to create a distinctive texture.

brothers A two- or four-leg chain or rope sling.

Brown and Sharpe gauge *See* **American wire gauge.**

brown coat (floating coat) (1) In two-coat wet-wall construction, the first rough coat of plaster applied as a base coat over lath or masonry. (2) In three-coat work, the second coat of plaster applied over a scratch coat to serve as a base for the finish coat.

brown-glazed brick *See* **salt-glazed brick.**

brown millerite An oxide of calcium, aluminum, and iron commonly formed in Portland cement and high alumina cement mixtures.

brown-out (1) To apply a base coat of plaster. (2) The setting process of base-coat plaster, which darkens to a brown hue as it dries. (3) A partial loss of electrical power that dims lights. A brown-out is less severe than a blackout.

brown rot A fungus that attacks the cellulose of wood, so called for the residual brown powder it leaves behind on the destroyed matter.

brown stain A deep brown discoloration in the sapwood of some pines, caused by fungus.

brownstone (1) Arko sandstone, dark brown or reddish-brown in hue, which was used widely throughout the eastern United States in the nineteenth century for building homes and offices. (2) A house faced with brownstone.

browpiece A beam installed above a door.

brow post *See* **crossbeam.**

brush (brushed) finish A finish created by applying a rotating wire brush to a surface.

brushed plywood Plywood abraded to remove softer wood and reveal a more textured surface.

brush graining A process in which a dark, liquid stain is drawn across a light-colored, dry base coat to produce an imitation effect of a wood grain.

brush rake A large apparatus that is attached to the front of a tractor to clear land of brush and debris.

Brussels carpet (1) A carpet of worsted yarn in multiple colors, attached to a backing of tough linen thread in a pattern of uncut loops. (2) A less costly substitute for actual Brussels carpet, made in a single color of yarn.

bubble (1) Either the air bubble in a leveling tube or the tube itself. (2) A large void in gypsum board caused by air entrapment during manufacturing.

bubble diagram A diagram that shows the functional relationships in a building or firm.

bubble tube A tube containing an air bubble, used to level a tool or an instrument.

bubbling Trapped bubbles of air or vapors that erupt on a painted surface during application or drying.

buck (1) The wood or metal subframe of a door, installed in a wall to accommodate the finished frame. (2) One of a pair of four-legged supporting devices used to hold wood as it is being sawed. *See also* **sawbuck** *and* **doorbuck.**

bucket A scoop-shaped attachment for an excavating machine that digs and transports loose earthen materials. Often outfitted with

buggy (concrete cart)

opening and closing mechanisms to facilitate unloading.

bucket trap A mechanical steam trap that operates on buoyancy and is designed with an inverted or upright cup that prevents the passage of steam through the system it protects.

bucket-wheel excavator A machine that digs earth and loads it onto a conveyor belt as it moves across a site, functioning by means of a rotating wheel and a number of tooth-edged buckets. Used principally for trenching.

buck frame (core frame, subframe) A wood frame built into the wall studs of a partition to accommodate a door lining.

buckle (1) The distortion of a structural member such as a beam or girder under load. This condition is brought on by lack of uniform texture or by irregular distribution of weight, moisture, or temperature. (2) A flaw or distortion on the surface of a sheet of material, particularly asphalt roofing. (3) A thin tree branch bent in the shape of a U to fasten thatch onto roofs.

buckling load In a compression member or compression portion of a member, the load at which bending progresses without an increase in the load.

buck opening A rough door opening.

bucksaw A wood-cutting saw consisting of a blade set in an H-shaped frame.

budget A rough estimate of the value of a portion of, or total cost of, a construction project.

buff (1) To clean and polish a surface to a high luster. (2) To grind and polish a floor of terrazzo or other exposed aggregate concrete.

buffalo box (1) A vertical sleeve buried in the ground which provides access to a curb cock. (2) A large hopper mounted on the front of a bulldozer into which aggregate is dumped, permitting the aggregate to be spread evenly over a previously graded area.

buffer (1) Blasted rock left at a face to improve fragmentation and reduce scatter during a subsequent blast. (2) A loose metal mat used to control scattering of blast rock. *See also* **spring buffer** *and* **oil buffer**.

buff standard brick A buff-colored brick that may be either 2-1/4″ x 3-3/4″ x 7-3/4″ or 2″ x 4″ x 8″, nominal.

buggy (concrete cart) A two- or four-wheeled cart, with or without a motor, used to transport small amounts of concrete from hoppers or mixers to forms.

bug holes Small cavities, usually not exceeding 5/8″ (15 mm) in diameter, at the surface of formed concrete. Bug holes are caused by air bubbles trapped during placing and compacting of wet concrete.

bugle head screw A flat-headed screw commonly used in drywall installation.

builder's acid A mixture of hydrochloric acid and water used to remove mortar stains from brick.

builder's jack A temporary bracket, attached to a windowsill, which projects outward and supports scaffolding.

builder's level (1) A spirit level set in a wood or metal straightedge. (2) A tilting or dumpy level not made to the accuracy of one used in surveying.

builder's risk insurance A special form of property insurance to cover work under construction.

building block

building brick

building main

builder's staging A heavy scaffold made from square timbers, usually used where heavy materials are handled.

building area The sum of the horizontal projected area of all buildings on a site. Terraces and uncovered porches are excluded, unless the stipulations of a mortgage lender or governmental program require their inclusion.

Building Automation System A network of integrated computer components that automatically control a wide range of building operations such as HVAC, security/access control, lighting, energy management, maintenance management, and fire safety control.

building block Any rectangular masonry unit (except brick) used in building construction. Typical materials are burnt clay, concrete, glass, gypsum, etc.

building board Any board of building material, usually with a facing, which can be used as a finished surface on walls or ceilings.

building brick (common brick) Brick that has not been treated for color or texture. Used as an all-purpose building material.

building codes The minimum legal requirements established or adopted by a government such as a municipality. Building codes are established by ordinance, and govern the design and construction of buildings.

building drain That part of the lowest piping of a drainage system that receives the discharge from soil, waste, and other drainage pipes inside the walls of the building and conveys it to the building sewer.

building envelope The elements of a building that enclose conditioned areas and through which thermal energy may be transferred to or from the outside environment.

building grade *See* **grade (3)**.

building gravity drainage system A drainage system that employs gravity to lead waste into the building house sewer.

building height Generally, the greatest vertical distance measured from curb or grade level to the highest level of a flat or mansard roof, or to the average height of a pitched, gabled, hip, or gambrel roof. Penthouses and the like are usually excluded if they do not exceed a specified height or their projected area is less than a specified percentage of the main roof.

building inspector An official employed by a municipal building department to review plans and inspect construction to determine if they conform to the requirements of applicable codes and ordinances, and to inspect occupied buildings for violations of the same codes and ordinances. *See also* **building official**.

building insulation *See* **thermal insulation**.

building line (1) The line, established by law, beyond which a building shall not extend, except as specifically provided by law. Exceptions may be made for terraces or uncovered porches. (2) The outermost dimension of a building, generally used for building placement in relation to zoning or plot restrictions. *See also* **building restriction line**.

building main The water supply pipe (including fittings) that extends from the water main or other source of supply to the first distribution branch of a building.

building paper

built-up roofing

building material Any material used in construction, such as sand, brick, lumber, or steel.

building official (building inspector) An appointed government official who is responsible for enforcing building codes. The building official may approve the issuance of a building permit, review the contract documents, inspect the construction, and approve issuance of a certificate of occupancy.

building paper A heavy, asphalt-impregnated paper used as a lining and/or vapor barrier between sheathing and an outside wall covering, or as a lining between rough and finish flooring.

building permit A written authorization required by ordinance before construction on a specific project can begin. A building permit allows construction to proceed in accordance with construction documents approved by the building official.

building restriction Any restriction, statutory or contractual, imposed on construction of a building or use of land.

building restriction line A line, defined by local ordinances, beyond which a structure may not project. The line is usually parallel to the street line or other property line. *See also* **building line**.

building section Any portion of a building, whether a single room, a group of rooms, a floor, or a group of floors, that is within the limits of a fire division.

building services The utilities, including electricity, gas, steam, telephone, and water, supplied to and used within a building.

building sewer The pipe that carries sewage from the outside wall of the building to the public sewer.

building storm drain A drain in a building which conveys rainwater, surface water, condensate, and similar discharge to a building storm sewer that, in turn, extends to a specified point outside the building.

building trades The skilled and semiskilled crafts employed in building construction, such as carpentry, masonry, or plumbing.

building trap (main trap) A fitting installed on the outlet side of a building to prevent odors and gases from passing from a sewer to the plumbing system of the building.

build up To create a mass by applying successive layers.

built-up (1) Fabricated of two or more pieces or sheets that are laminated. (2) Assembled by fastening a number of pieces or parts to each other.

built-up air casing A field-fabricated enclosure for an air-handling system, with base, curbs, and drains.

built-up beam (1) A metal beam made of beam shapes, plates, and/or angles that are welded or bolted together. (2) A concrete beam made of precast units connected through shear connectors. (3) A timber beam made of smaller pieces that are fastened together.

built-up girder *See* **built-up beam**.

built-up rib A rib made of laminations of various size timbers.

built-up roofing (composition roofing, felt-and-gravel roofing, gravel roofing) A continuous roof covering made up of various plies or sheets of saturated or coated felts cemented together with asphalt. The felt sheets are topped with a cap sheet or a flood coat of asphalt or pitch, which may have a surfacing of applied gravel or slag.

bulb tee

bulkhead

bulldozer

bull float

built-up section In metal building systems, a structural member made from individual plates welded together.

built-up string A curved stair string constructed of wood members fastened together with counter clamps.

built-up timber *See* **built-up beam (3).**

bulb angle A hot-rolled angle with a formed bulb on the end of one leg.

bulb bar A rolled steel bar with a formed bulb on one edge.

bulb pile *See* **pedestal pile.**

bulb pressure *See* **pressure bulb.**

bulb tee A rolled steel tee with a formed bulb on the edge of the web.

bulk density The weight of a material per unit volume, including voids, solid particles, and any contained water.

bulkhead (1) A horizontal or inclined door providing outside access to a cellar or shaft. (2) A partition in concrete forms to separate placings. (3) A structure on the roof of a building to provide headroom over a stairwell or other opening. (4) A low structure on a roof covering a shaft or protruding service equipment. (5) A retaining structure that protects a dredged area from earth movement.

bulking (moisture expansion) An increase in the volume of a quantity of granular material when moist, over the volume of the same quantity when dry.

bulking factor A ratio comparing the volume of a quantity of moist granular material to the volume of the same quantity when dry.

bulking value In mixing paint, the specific gravity of a pigment, usually expressed as gallons per 100 pounds, or liters per kilograms.

bulk liquid A pumpable material that has a moisture content greater than 70%.

bulk modulus of elasticity (modulus of volume) The volumetric relationship between stress and strain within the elastic limit of a material. This quantity is expressed as the ratio between a pressure acting on a material and the fractional change in volume due to that pressure.

bulk sludge A material with a moisture content of between 30% and 70%.

bulk solid A material with a moisture content less than 30%.

bulk strain (volume strain) The ratio of the change in volume of a mass, due to an applied pressure, to the original volume.

bulldog grip A U-bolt threaded at each end.

bulldozer (1) A tractor with a large, blunt blade attached to its front end by hydraulic-controlled arms. A bulldozer is used to push, shape, or move earth or rock short distances. (2) A machine used to bend reinforcing bars into U-shapes.

bullet catch A type of door latch consisting of a spring-loaded steel ball. The loaded ball holds the door closed but rolls free when the door is pulled.

bulletproof glass *See* **bullet-resisting glass.**

bullet-resisting glass (bulletproof glass) A laminated assembly of glass, usually at least four sheets, alternated with transparent resin sheets, all bonded under heat and pressure. Bullet-resisting glass is also made of laminations of special plastics.

bull float A board of wood, aluminum, or magnesium mounted

bullnose stretcher

burner

on a pole and used to spread and smooth freshly placed, horizontal concrete surfaces.

bull gear The largest- or strongest-toothed driving gear.

bullhead tee (bullheaded tee) A piping tee in which the outlet opening on the branch is larger than the openings on the run.

bull header (bull head) A brick with one rounded corner used to form a corner at a door jamb or laid on edge to form a windowsill.

bullnose (bull's nose) (1) A rounded outside corner or edge. (2) A metal bead used in forming a rounded corner on plaster walls.

bullnose block A concrete masonry unit with one or more rounded corners.

bullnose plane A small, hand-held carpenter's plane with the blade set forward.

bullnose step (bull stretcher) A step, usually the bottom one in a flight, with a semicircular end that projects beyond the railing.

bullnose stretcher (1) A masonry stretcher with one of the corners rounded. (2) Any stretcher that is laid on edge, as at a windowsill.

bullnose trim A structural member or piece of trim that has a rounded edge, such as a stair tread, windowsill, or door sill.

bull pin A tapered steel pin used to align holes in steel members so bolts can be inserted.

bull-point A pointed steel hand drill that is struck with a hammer to chip off small pieces of rock or other masonry.

bull's nose See **bullnose**.

bull stretcher See **bullnose step**.

bulwark A low wall used as a defensive shield.

bumper (1) A device, other than a spring or oil buffer, used to absorb impact from an elevator or counterweight. (2) The rubber silencer on a door frame.

bundle of lath A quantity of lath for plastering, usually 50 pieces of wood lath, 5/16″ x 1-1/2″ x 48″ (0.79 x 3.8 x 122 cm) or 6 sheets of gypsum lath, 16″ x 48″ (41 by 122 cm).

bundler bars An assembly of up to four parallel reinforcing bars connected to one another and enclosed in stirrups or ties. Used as a unit in reinforced concrete, particularly in columns.

bungalow siding Clapboard siding that has a minimum width of 8″ (20 cm).

bunker (1) A compartmentalized storage container for aggregate or ore. (2) Space in a refrigerator for ice storage and for the cooling element. (3) A protective shelter usually constructed of reinforced concrete and located partially or fully below ground. (4) A metal shield in a crushing or screening operation used to direct raw material to the feed belt.

buoyant foundation A reinforced concrete foundation designed and located such that its weight and superimposed permanent load is approximately equal to the weight of displaced soil and/or ground water.

burden (1) The loose material that overlays bedrock. (2) The depth of material to be moved or loosened in a blast.

burned joint In plumbing, a joint formed with heat that fuses two lead pipes together.

burner That part of a boiler or furnace in which combustion takes place.

bus duct (busway)

bush hammer

Burnett's process A process of preserving wood that involves infusing the wood with a hot solution of chloride of zinc.

burning (1) Flame-cutting metal plates to a desired shape. (2) A method of repairing lead roofs by replacing damaged sections.

burning-brand test A standard test to determine the resistance of a roof covering to exposure from flying brands.

burnish To polish to a smooth, glossy finish.

burnt lime *See* **lime**.

burnt sienna Sienna that has been calcined to obtain a rich brown pigment. Used for coloring paint and stain.

burnt umber Umber that has been calcined to obtain a red to reddish-brown pigment. Used for coloring paint and stain.

burr (1) An uneven or jagged edge left on metal by certain cutting tools. (2) Partially fused brick. (3) A batch of bricks that were accidentally fused together. (4) A curly figure in lumber that was cut from an enlarged trunk of certain trees, such as walnut.

bursting strength The ability of sheet material to resist rupture under pressure, as measured by one of several tests.

bus (bus bar) An electric conductor, often a metal bar, that serves as a common connection for two or more circuits. A bus usually carries a large current.

bus bar *See* **bus**.

bus duct (busway) A prefabricated unit containing one or more protected busses.

bush hammer A hand or power hammer that has a serrated face

with many pyramidal points. A bush hammer is used to dress concrete or stone.

bush-hammered concrete Concrete with an exposed aggregate finish that has been obtained by removing the surface cement using a percussive hammer with a serrated face.

bush-hammer finish A stone or concrete finish obtained through use of a percussive hammer with a serrated face. Used for decorative purposes or to provide a rough surface for better traction or adhesion.

bushing (1) A threaded or smooth (for soldered tubing) pipe or tube fitting used to connect pipes or tubes of different diameters. (2) A metal sleeve screwed or fitted into an opening to protect and/or support a shaft, rod, or cable passing through the opening. Usually the inside surface of the bushing is machined to close tolerance to reduce friction and abrasion. (3) An insulating structure for a conductor, with provision for an insulated mounting.

business agent An official of a trade union who represents the union in negotiations and disputes and checks jobs for compliance with union regulations and union contracts.

busway *See* **bus duct**.

bus wire The wire(s) to which the leg wires of blasting caps are connected.

butcher block A kitchen work surface made from a single slab of hardwood or a composite of rectangular pieces that have been bonded together.

butment *See* **abutment**.

butt

butterfly valve

butt hinge

buttonhead

butt (1) A short length of roofing material. (2) The thick end of a shingle.

butt and break The staggering of joints in lath or on alternating studs in order to reduce cracking of plaster.

butt casement hinge A type of toe-plate hinge intended for use on casement sashes.

butt chisel A carpenter's chisel with a short blade used to shape recesses for hinges.

butted frame A door frame with a depth equal to or less than the thickness of the wall in which the frame is mounted.

butt end The thicker end of a handle, tapered pole, pile, or other rod-shaped object.

butt-end joint *See* **butt joint**.

butt-end treatment The process of protecting that part of a timber or post which will be exposed to soil and/or water by treating it with a preservative chemical.

butter (buttering) (1) To apply mortar to a masonry unit with a trowel. (2) To spread roofing cement smoothly with a trowel. (3) To apply putty or compound sealant to a flat surface of a member before setting the member, such as buttering a stop before installing it.

butterfly hinge A decorative hinge.

butterfly nut A wing nut.

butterfly roof A roof shape in which two surfaces rise from a control valley to the eaves.

butterfly spring A formed piece of spring metal set over the pin of a hinge to serve as a door closer.

butterfly valve A valve that contains a disk that rotates 90° within the valve body. Has excellent throttling characteristics.

butterfly wall tie A masonry wall tie made from heavy wire in the shape of a figure eight.

buttering *See* **butter**.

buttering trowel A small trowel used to apply mortar to a brick before laying the brick.

butternut (white walnut) A moderately soft, medium-textured wood of light to pale brown color. Butternut is used particularly for decorative veneer.

butt fusion A method of joining thermoplastic resin pipe or sheets in which the ends to be joined are heated to the molten state, pressed together, and held until the material sets.

butt hinge The common form of hinge consisting of two plates, each with one meshing knuckle edge, connected by means of a removable or fixed pin through the knuckles.

butt-hung door A swing door hung with butt hinges.

butt joint (1) A square joint between two members at right angles to each other. The contact surface of the outstanding member is cut square and fits flush to the surface of the other member. (2) A joint in which the ends of two members butt each other so that only tensile or compressive loads are transferred.

buttonhead The head of a bolt, rivet, or screw that is shaped like a segment of a sphere and has a flat bearing surface.

button punching Crimping the interlocking lap of metal ducting panels with a dull punching tool. Button punching has been largely replaced by spot welding overlapping edges.

buttonwood North American sycamore.

butt weld joint

buttress (1) An exterior pier of masonry construction, often sloped, which is used to strengthen or support a wall or absorb lateral thrusts from roof vaults. (2) An A-shaped formwork of timber or steel used to strengthen or support a wall.

butt splice A butt joint secured by fastening a short piece of wood or steel to each side of the butted members.

butt strap The short pieces used in a butt splice.

butt weld joint (1) A joint made by welding two butted pieces or sheets together. (2) A welded pipe joint made with the ends of the two pipes butting each other.

butt weld pipe Pipe that is welded along the seam, not lapped.

buttwood Lumber milled from the lower part of a tree.

butyl stearate A colorless, oily liquid used for dampproofing concrete.

buy a job Accept a construction contract at bare cost or below.

buy-in A bidder's attempt to win a contract by submitting a price that will result in a loss, with the hope of making the contract profitable through change orders or follow-on contracts.

buzz saw A power saw with a circular blade.

BX Flexible metal conduit armored with spirals of galvanized steel and containing multiple insulated electric wires.

bypass (1) A pipe or duct used to divert flow around an element. (2) A pipe used to divert flow around another pipe or piping system.

bypass valve A valve located to control a bypass.

bypass vent A vent stack parallel to a soil or waste stack and connected together at branch intervals.

byre A stable or barn for housing livestock.

C

C ABBREVIATIONS

The abbreviations listed below are those most commonly used in the construction industry. Alternative forms (usually nonstandard) are shown in parentheses.

c candle, cathode, channel, conductivity, cycle

C carbon, Celsius, centigrade, hundred

CAA Clean Air Act

Cab. cabinet

CAB cabinet, cement-asbestos board

CAD computer-aided design

CADD computer-aided design and drafting

CAFM computer-aided facility management

Cair air tool laborer

cal calorie

calc calculated

cap., Cap. capacity

Carp. carpenter

CAT. catalog (catalogue)

CATV community antenna television

CATW catwalk

CB catch basin, center beaded

C.B. circuit breaker

CB1S center beam one side

CB2S center beam two sides

CBMA Certified Ballast Manufacturers Association

CBR California bearing ratio

C&Btr. grade C and better (used in lumber industry)

cc cubic centimeter

C/C center to center

C.C.A. chromate copper arsenate

C.C.F. hundred cubic feet

CCTV closed-circuit television

CCW counterclockwise

cd candela

CD grade of plywood face and back

cd/sf candela per square foot

CDX plywood, grade C and D, exterior glue

Cefi cement finisher

ceil ceiling

Cem. cement

cem. fin. cement finish

cem. m cement mortar

cent. central

cer ceramic

CERCLA Comprehensive Environmental Response, Compensation, and Liability Act

CF centrifugal force, cooling fan, cost and freight, hundred feet

C.F. cubic feet

CFCs Chlorofluorocarbons

CFL compact fluorescent lamp

cfm, CFM cubic feet per minute

CFR Code of Federal Regulations

CFS cubic feet per second

c.g. center of gravity

CG ceiling grille, center of gravity, coarse gram, corner guard

CG2E center groove two edges

chfr chamfer

chkd checked

CHIM chimney

CHRIS Chemical Hazard Response Information System

CHU centigrade heat unit

CHW chilled water

CI cast iron, certificate of insurance

C.I. cast iron

CIF cost, insurance and freight

CIFE cost, insurance, freight and exchange

CII Construction Industry Institute

cin bl cinder block

CIP cast-iron pipe

C.I.P. cast in place

CIR circle, circuit, circular

Circ. circuit

CIRC circumference

cl closet

CL center line

C.L. carload lot

Clab. common laborer

C.L.F. hundred linear feet

CLF current-limiting fuse

clg ceiling

clk caulk

CLP cross-linked polyethylene

clr clear

cm centimeter

CM center matched, construction management

CMMS computerized maintenance management software

CMP corrugated metal pipe

CMPA corrupted metal pipe arch

C.M.U. concrete masonry unit

CND conduit

c-o cleanout

Co company

CO certificate of occupancy, change order, cleanout, cutout

CO$_2$ carbon dioxide

coef coefficient

col, col. column

com common

COMB., Comb. combination

comp compartment, compensate, component, composition

COMPF composition floor

COMPR, compr. composition roof, compress, compressor

conc, Conc. concrete

conc b concrete block

conc clg concrete ceiling

conc fl concrete floor

cond conductivity

const constant, construction

constr construction

Cont. continuous, continued

CONTR contractor

conv convector

cop. coping, copper

corb corbeled

corn. cornice

corr corrugated

Cos cosine

cot cotangent

Cov. cover

CP candlepower, cesspool

CPA control point adjustment

CPFF cost plus fixed fee

cplg. coupling

CPM, C.P.M. Critical Path Method, cycles per minute

C.Pr. hundred pair

CPU central processing unit

CPVC chlorinated polyvinyl chloride

CRC cold-rolled channel

Creos. creosote

CRI color rendering index

crib. cribbing

CRN cost of reproduction/replacement new

CRP controlled rate of penetration

cr pl chromium plate

Crpt. carpet and linoleum layer

CRSI Concrete Reinforcing Steel Institute

CRT cathode ray tube

c/s cycles per second

CS cast stone, carbon steel, commercial standard, caulking seam

CSA Canadian Standards Association (CSA International)

CSC cosecant

C.S.F. hundred square feet

csg casing

CSI Construction Specifications Institute

CSK countersink

ct coat (coats)

C.T. current transformer

CTB cement-treated base

c to c center to center

ctr center, counter

CTS copper tube size

cu cubic

cu. ft. cubic feet

cu. in. cubic inch

cur. current

cu. yd. cubic yard (27 cubic feet)

CV center vee

CV1S center vee one side

CV2S center vee two sides

cw clockwise, continuous wave

C.W. cool white, cold water

C.W. pt. cold water point

cwt hundred weight

C.W.X. cool white deluxe

CY cycle

C.Y. cubic yard (27 cubic feet)

C.Y./Hr. cubic yards per hour

cyl, cyl. cylinder

CYL L cylinder lock

cyp cypress ·

1/C single conductor

2/C two conductors

C

DEFINITIONS

cabin

cabinet

cabinet heater

cable

cabana A small shelter of open, tent, or wood-frame construction placed near swimming pools or the shoreline.

Cabba (1) A small cube-shaped building. (2) The small stone building in the court of the Great Mosque at Mecca, the sacred shrine of the Muslims.

cabin (1) A small, simple hut or house. (2) A rustic shelter often made of logs.

cabinet (1) A small room or private apartment, especially for study or consultations. (2) A suite of rooms for exhibiting articles and curiosities. (3) A case, box, or piece of furniture with sets of drawers or shelves and doors, used primarily for storage. (4) An enclosure with doors for housing electrical devices and wiring connections.

cabinet file A single-cut hand file that is half round on one side and flat on the other.

cabinet filler The wood piece that closes the space between cabinets and adjacent walls or the ceiling.

cabinet finish A varnished, oiled, or polished wood surface finish, as distinguished from a painted surface finish.

cabinet head A decorative molding along the top of a door frame.

cabinet heater A metal housing enclosing a heating element, with openings to facilitate air flow. The heater frequently contains a fan for controlling the air flow.

cabinet lock A spring bolt or magnetic latch.

cabinet scraper A flat steel blade used for smoothing wood or

removing a finish, such as paint or varnish, from a surface.

cabinet units Small air-handling units that house an air filter, heating coil, and a centrifugal blower.

cabinet window A projecting window or type of bay window popular during the nineteenth century for the display of shop goods.

cabinet work Wood joinery used in the construction of built-in cabinets and shelves.

cable (1) A rope or wire comprised of many smaller fibers or strands wound or twisted together. (2) A group of electric conductors insulated from each other but contained in a common protective cover.

cable assembly A cable and its accompanying connectors to be used for a specific purpose.

cable ceiling heat A radiant heating system, installed in a ceiling, that sends current through encased conductors to produce heat.

cable conduit See **cable duct** and **conduit**.

cable duct (cable conduit) A rigid, metal, protective enclosure through which electrical conductors are run. For underground installations, concrete or plastic pipes are usually used.

cable length A standard surveying measurement equal to 720 feet.

cable molding See **cabling**.

cable pulling compound A lubricant used to facilitate the pulling of wires through a cable duct or conduit.

cable tray

caisson

caisson pile

cable roof A system comprised of a roof deck and covering that are supported by cables.

cable sheath The protective cover that surrounds a cable.

cable support box An electrical box that is mounted on a wall and provides support for the weight of cables within a vertically installed conduit.

cable-supported construction A structure that is supported by a system of cables. This system is used for long-span roofs and for suspension bridges.

cable tray An open, metal framework used to support electrical conductors. Similar to cable duct except that the cable tray has a lattice-type construction and an open top.

cable vault An underground structure utilized in the pulling and joining of underground electric cables.

cableway A cable that bridges a gap between two points and permits materials to be pulled across the gap between the points.

cabling (cable molding) An ornament or molding of spiral design, similar to the twists of a cable.

cadastral survey A large-scale land survey conducted to define boundaries, areas, and ownership of real estate for purposes of subdivision or apportioning taxes.

cadmium plating A coating of cadmium metal applied over a base metal, usually for corrosion protection.

cadmium yellow A yellow pigment of cadmium sulfide valued in paint manufacturing for its quality and permanence.

cage (1) The box or enclosed platform of an elevator or lift. (2) An enclosure for electrical lights or signals. (3) Any rigid open box or enclosure.

caisson (1) A drilled, cylindrical foundation shaft used to transfer a load through soft strata to firm strata or bedrock. The shaft is filled with either reinforced or unreinforced concrete. (2) A watertight box or chamber used for construction work below water level.

caisson drill A piece of boring equipment used to excavate a shaft (usually vertical) in the earth for construction of a building footing.

caisson pile A cast-in-place pile formed by driving a hollow tube into the ground and filling it with concrete.

caking The undesirable mass of pigment that collects in the bottom of paint cans.

calcareous A term referring to any material containing calcite, calcium carbonate, or calcium, as in *calcareous soils*.

calcimine (kalsomine) A low-cost wash, white or colored, used on ceilings, interior plaster, or other masonry-type surfaces.

calcine The process of heating a substance to a point just below its melting temperature in order to remove chemically combined water.

calcined gypsum Gypsum that has been partially dehydrated. In this form it is used as a base material to which mineral aggregate, fiber, or other material may be added to produce the desired plaster.

calcite The main raw material used in the manufacture of Portland cement. Calcite is a crystallized form of calcium carbonate and is the

caliper

principal component in limestone, chalk, and marble.

calcite streak A break or fault in a mineral limestone deposit that has been filled in by calcite sedimentation.

calcium aluminate cement A combination of calcium carbonate and aluminates that have been thermally fused or sintered and ground to make cement.

calcium chloride A saltwater solution added to concrete and mortar during mixing. Acts as a drying agent and decreases setting time.

calcium silicate brick A concrete product made primarily from sand and lime that is hardened by autoclave curing.

calcium silicate insulation Hydrated calcium silicate that has been molded into rigid shapes and forms. The material is commonly used for pipe insulation where service temperatures reach 1,200° F. Particularly well-suited for pipe insulation because it is not appreciably affected by moisture.

calcs An engineer's formal mathematical analysis of loads.

calculate To do mathematical work; to seek a numerical value.

calculated live load The useful load-supporting capability above the weight of the structural members, usually specified in the applicable building code.

calculation The product or result of mathematical work.

calf's-tongue molding (calves-tongue molding) A molding with repeating semi-oval shapes, half pointing in the same direction or, when surrounding an arch, pointing to a common center.

caliber The internal diameter of a pipe. In construction, most pipe is specified by outside diameter, with a further designation for wall thickness.

caliche A term used to describe gravel or sand loosely cemented together by calcium carbonate or other salts.

caliduct A conduit for conveying hot air, hot water, or steam for heating.

California bearing ratio A ratio used to determine the bearing capacity of a foundation. It is a ratio of the force per unit area per minute required to penetrate a soil mass, to the force required for a similar penetration of a standard crushed rock material.

California brass ring A sampler used to collect soil samples during well installation. Samples are tested for volatile organic compounds.

caliper (calliper) An instrument with two hinged legs used to determine the thickness or diameter of objects.

calk *See* **caulk.**

calked rivet A rivet that has not been properly driven, but has been tightened to fit its hole by having the edge of its head driven under with a cold chisel.

calking *See* **caulking.**

calliper *See* **caliper.**

call loan A loan that is payable on formal notice of demand by the lender.

calorie The amount of heat required, at a pressure of one atmosphere, to raise the temperature of one gram of water 1 °C.

calorific value The amount of heat liberated by the oxidation or combustion of the unit weight of a solid material, or the unit volume of a gas or liquid.

canopy

calves-tongue molding
See **calf's-tongue molding**.

cam (1) An eccentric wheel mounted on a rotating shaft and used to produce reciprocal or variable motion in an engaged or contacted part. (2) In a lock, the rotating piece attached to the cylinder that actuates the locking mechanism.

camber A slightly convex curvature built into a beam or truss to compensate for deflection under a load. Camber is also built into structural components, roadways, or bridges to facilitate run off of water.

camber arch A flat arch with a very small upward curve of the undersurface. The upper surface may or may not be curved.

camber beam A beam constructed with a slight upward curve in the center.

camber diagram A construction drawing that shows the desired design camber along the beam, truss, or structural component.

camber piece The temporary wood support or template used to lay a slightly curved brick arch.

camber window A window constructed with a slightly arched head.

cambium The thin layer of tissue that lies between a tree's bark and its wood.

came A flexible, cast-lead rod used in stained glass windows to hold together panes or pieces of glass.

camelback truss A truss whose upper chord is comprised of a series of straight segments so that the assembly looks like the hump of a camel's back.

camelhair mop A high-quality, soft-haired brush used for varnishing, gilding, or painting.

cameo window A fixed oval window, often highly decorative.

cames H-shaped lead strips that hold glass in place in leaded windows.

cam handle (locking handle) On a hinged window, the handle that rotates against its keeper plate, thus pulling the window tight and locking it.

campaniform A term used to describe a structure in the shape of a bell.

Canadian Standards Association A non-governmental body established in Canada for the purpose of developing uniform standards on products, processes and procedures.

canal (canalis) (1) Any watercourse or channel. (2) A channel or groove fluting in carved ornamentation.

canalis *See* **canal**.

candela A unit of luminous intensity; formerly called *candle*.

candle *See* **candela**.

candlepower The luminous intensity of a light source expressed in *candelas*.

candle wicking In plumbing, a pipe thread tape used to make watertight seals.

canopy (1) An overhanging shelter or shade covering. (2) An ornamental roof-like structure over a pulpit.

cant (1) To slope, tilt, or angle from the vertical or horizontal. (2) A log that has been slabbed on one or more sides.

cant brick *See* **splay brick**.

cantilever (1) A structural member supported at one end only. (2) A beam, girder, or supporting member that projects beyond its support at one end.

cantilever
retaining wall

cant strip

cantilever footing (1) A footing with a tie beam connected to another footing to counterbalance an asymmetrical load. (2) In retaining wall construction, a wide, reinforced footing with reinforcing steel extending into the retaining wall to resist the overturning moment.

cantilever form In concrete construction, a form that is jacked up slowly and supported by the hardened concrete of the wall previously poured. *See also* **slip form**.

cantilever retaining wall A retaining wall that has a wide footing to resist its overturning moment.

cantilever steps Steps supported at one end by a wall and at the other end by the next lower step.

cantilever truss A truss that is anchored at one end and overhangs a support at the other end.

cantilever wall A wall that resists its overturning moment with a cantilever footing.

canting strip A horizontal ledge near the bottom of an exterior wall sloped to conduct water away from the face of a building or its foundation.

cant molding A molding with one beveled face.

cant strip (chamfer strip) A three-sided piece of wood, one angle of which is square, used under the roofing on a flat roof where the horizontal surface abuts a vertical wall or parapet. The sloped transition facilitates roofing and waterproofing. *See also* **chamfer**.

canvas A closely woven cloth, usually made of cotton, used for tarpaulins, awnings, sun covers, and temporary canopies.

canvas ceiling A ceiling made of tightly stretched canvas.

canvas wall A plaster wall with a canvas covering, that may be painted or wallpapered.

cap (1) The top piece, often overhanging, of any vertical architectural feature or wall. A cap may be external, as on an outside wall or doorway; or it may be internal, as on the top of a column, pilaster, molding, or trim. (2) A layered system of cover—whether natural soils, rock, synthetics, pavement, and/or polymeric liners—that controls hydrogeologic processes.

capacitance The property of a system that permits the storage of electronically separated charges when potential differences exist between the conductors. Expressed as a ratio of the quantity of electricity to the potential difference, usually measured in *farads* or *microfarads*.

capacitor A device used to introduce capacitance into an electric circuit. The device consists of conducting plates insulated from each other by a layer of dielectric material.

capacitor motor A single-phase induction motor with a main winding arranged for direct connection to a source of power and an auxiliary winding connected in series with a capacitor. The capacitor may be directly in the auxiliary circuit or connected to it through a transformer.

capacity insulation The properties of masonry that enable it to store heat: its mass, density, and specific heat.

Cape Cod house (cape) A simple frame house with a shingled, steeply-pitched roof, central chimney, and one or one-and-a-half floors. The style originated in

capital

cap plate

colonial Cape Cod, Massachusetts, and has evolved over hundreds of years into several popular variations.

capillary action In subsurface soil conditions, the rising of water above the horizontal plane of the water table.

capillary break A space that is intentionally made large enough to prevent moisture flow by capillary action.

capillary flow The flow of moisture through any form, shape, or porous solid by means of capillary action.

capillary joint A pipe or fitting connection made by melting a solder material at the edge of a slip fit so that it is drawn into the joint by capillary action and, on cooling, makes a tight joint.

capillary space A term used to describe air bubbles that have become embedded in cement paste.

capillary tube (1) A small-diameter tube used in refrigeration to restrict the flow of refrigerant from the condenser to the evaporator. (2) The small-diameter tubing used to connect temperature- and pressure-sensing bulbs to a control mechanism.

capillary water Water which, by virtue of capillary action, is either above the surrounding water level or has penetrated where a body of water would not normally go.

capital The top member of a column, pier, pillar, post, or pilaster; usually decorative.

capitalization The total value of a corporation's equity.

capitalize To increase the total value of a corporation's equity through expenditures that increase the evaluation of property, plant, and equipment.

cap load The lumber supplies needed for construction of the first floor deck of a structure.

cap molding (cap trim) The molding or trim above a door or window casing.

cap piece *See* **capping piece**.

capping The top component of an assembly after covering and weatherproofing a joint.

capping brick Brick that is used to cap off the top of a wall.

capping piece (cap piece, cap plate) The timber used to cover the top of a series of uprights or other vertical members.

cap plate The plate on top of a column or post that supports the load. *See also* **capping piece**.

cap screw A threaded fastener that screws into a threaded hole rather than into a nut. Cap screws are specified by diameter, length, and thread pitch.

cap sheet The top ply of mineral-coated felt sheet used on a built-up roof.

capstone A stone segment in a coping.

captain's walk A walk or platform, with a view of the sea, on the roof of early New England-style houses.

cap trim *See* **cap molding**.

caracole (1) A zigzag course or path. (2) A spiral staircase.

car annunciator The floor indicator panel or dial in an elevator.

carbolineum A wood preservative made of antracene oil and zinc chloride.

carbonaceous Material containing or composed of carbon, such as organic matter.

carbon-arc cutting A metal cutting process in which arc heat melts a

carcass roofing

path through metal. The arc is established between an electrode, which forms one terminal of an electric circuit, and the workpiece, which forms the other terminal.

carbon-arc lamp
An electric-discharge lamp employing an arc discharge between carbon electrodes. One or more of the electrodes may have a core of special chemicals to enhance the discharge.

carbon-arc welding An arc-welding process in which the heat for fusion is generated by an electric arc between a carbon electrode and the workpiece.

carbonation The process of burning or converting a substance through chemical reaction into a carbonate. For example, the reaction between carbon dioxide and the calcium compounds in cement paste or mortar to produce calcium carbonate.

carbon black A fine carbon in the form of soot obtained by the direct impingement of a flame on a metal surface. Carbon black is used as a pigment to color paints and other materials.

carbon steel Steel that owes its distinctive properties (primarily its strength) to the carbon it contains, as opposed to the characteristics imparted by other alloying elements.

carborundum An combination of carbon and silicon that is used for woodworking and metalworking tools, blades, and abrasives.

carcase *See* **carcass.**

carcass (carcase) (1) A body or shell without adornment or life. (2) The structural framework of a building without walls, trim carpentry, masonry, etc.

carcass flooring The joists and associated structures that support the floorboards above and the ceiling below.

carcass roofing The roofing framework before the decking, membrane, shingles, etc., have been applied.

carcinogen A cancer-causing substance.

card frame (card plate)
The small frame that attaches to a door surface for insertion of a name card or plate.

cardinal change A series of changes in the work that are so extensive and significant as to change the entire character of the work required by the contract, thereby constituting a breach of contract.

card plate *See* **card frame.**

care, custody, and control A feature of construction liability insurance policies that excludes damage to property in the care, custody, or control of the insured.

carillon A set of fixed bells sounded by striking with hammers operated either mechanically or from a keyboard. By extension, a bell tower or campanile.

carnauba wax A wax made from the leaves of the Brazilian wax palm. The wax is hard and is used in wood polishes and protective coatings.

carpenter Gothic Gothic-style architecture and ornamentation constructed of wood.

carpenter's brace (bit brace)
A crank-shaped tool with a chuck on one end to hold a drill bit or auger. A hole is bored by rotating the crank.

carpenter's bracket scaffold
A scaffold that supports a platform using wood or metal brackets.

carpenter's square

car platform

carport

carriage bolt

carpenter's level A hand tool used by carpenters to determine a horizontal or vertical plane or line. The level is a wood or metal bar about 2′ long with four spirit levels set into it.

carpenter's punch A hand tool similar to a nail set, but with a long, slender neck. The punch removes nails by driving them through a piece of wood, rather than by pulling them out.

carpenter's square (framing square) A flat, metal, L-shaped tool that constitutes an accurate right angle and is engraved with divisions and markings useful to a carpenter laying out and erecting framing.

carpet backing The base material on the back of a carpet. The backing is usually made of jute, cotton, or carpet rayon, and may have a coating of latex.

carpet bedding Beds of low-growing plants, which may be used in ornamental design or as an erosion-preventing ground cover.

carpet cushion (carpet underlayment) A padding made of hair, felt, jute, foam, or sponge rubber that is placed on the floor before a carpet is laid. The cushion helps to provide resilience and extends the life of a carpet.

carpet density The number of pile rows per inch, for the length of the carpet.

carpet float A tool used by plasterers to give texture to a sand finish. The tool consists of a wood float covered with a piece of carpeting. The density of the carpet determines the type of finish.

carpet pitch The number of yarns across the width of the carpet, expressed in yarn ends per 27″ of width.

carpet strip (1) A flat strip of molding used to fasten the edge of carpeting. (2) A piece of wood or metal, approximately the same thickness as the carpet, installed at the edge of a carpet, as at a threshold.

carpet underlayment *See* **carpet cushion**.

car platform The structural floor of an elevator car that supports the load.

carport A roofed shelter for automobiles, usually attached along the side of a dwelling, with one or more sides open.

carreau A square or diamond-shaped piece of glass or tile used in ornamental glazing.

carrel (cubicle) A small alcove, as in a cloister or a library, for individual study.

carrelage Decorative tiling used particularly in terra-cotta flooring.

carriage The sloping beam that is installed between the stringers to support the steps of a wooden staircase.

carriage bolt A threaded bolt with a round, smooth head. The bolt is prevented from rotating in its hole by a square neck directly under the head.

carriage clamp A clamp used in carpentry and cabinetry.

carriage house *See* **coach house**.

carriage porch A canopy structure that extends from the doorway of a building over a driveway.

carrier angle A metal angle attached to stair carriers or stringers to support the tread or riser.

carrier bar A flat metal bar used to support stair treads or risers in a manner similar to carrier angles.

cartridge fuse

cased opening

carrier fitting A support for a plumbing fixture that is also an integral part of the soil piping system.

carryover In a steam system, water that produces water hammer and may lead to pipe rupture.

carrying channel A three-sided metal molding used in the construction of a suspended ceiling.

cartridge fuse A low-voltage fuse consisting of a current-responsive element inside a cylindrical tube with a terminal on each end.

cartridge heater An electric heater in the shape of a cylindrical cartridge, with the heating coils at one end and a fan at the other.

carvel joint A flush, longitudinal joint between boards or planks with no tongues, grooves, or laps.

cascade refrigerating system Two or more refrigerating systems connected in series. The cooling coil of one system is used to cool the condenser of the next system. This type of system is an efficient way to produce and maintain ultra-low temperatures.

case (1) A box, sheath, or covering. (2) The process of covering one material with another; to encase. (3) A product or food display counter, such as a refrigerated case for displaying ice cream or frozen produce. (4) A lock housing.

case bay The area of a building floor or roof between two beams or girders.

cased beam An exposed interior beam encased in finished millwork.

cased frame (box frame, boxed frame, cased sash-frame) The hollow frame for double-hung windows with sash weights. The weights travel in the hollow frame.

cased glass (case glass, overlay glass) Ornamental glass made of two or more layers with cuts so that sublayers may show.

cased opening (trimmed opening) An interior doorway or opening with all the trim and molding installed, but without a door or closure.

cased post An exposed interior post or column encased in finished millwork.

cased sash-frame *See* **cased frame**.

case glass *See* **cased glass**.

case-hardened (1) Term used to describe a steel or iron alloy with a hard surface developed by a special heat-treatment process. (2) Timber whose outer fibers have dried too rapidly, thus causing checking and cracking.

case-hardened glass Glass that has been heated and quenched, thus giving it a hardness and strength several times greater than it originally possessed.

casein glue Glue made from the white amorphous phosphoprotein occurring naturally in milk. The glue is frequently used in carpentry and joinery.

casein paint A paint using the white amorphous phosphoprotein emulsion from milk as a base adhesive and binder.

casement (1) A window sash that opens on hinges that are fixed on either side. (2) A ventilation panel that opens on vertical hinges like a door. (3) A casing.

casement door (1) A door consisting of a wooden frame around glass panels, which make up a major portion of the area of the door. (2) A French door.

casement window

casework

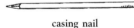

casing nail

casement molding A deeply concave, curved molding. *See also* **scotia**.

casement stay The brace or bar used to hold a casement window open in any of several positions.

casement ventilator A ventilation panel that opens on hinges along one side.

casement window A window assembly that has at least one casement or vertically hinged sash.

case mold A frame support, usually made of plaster, that holds smaller plaster pieces in position in a mold.

case steel *See* **case-hardened**.

casework A term for assembled cabinetry or millwork.

cash allowance A sum included in the contract for construction that covers required items not specifically described. Any differences in cost between the total charges for these items and the cash allowance amount are handled through change orders.

casing (1) The exposed millwork enclosure of cased beams, posts, pipes, etc. (2) The exposed trim molding or lining around doors and windows. (3) The pipe liner of a hole in the ground, such as that used for a well, caisson, or pile.

casing bead A metal molding or wood strip that acts as a stop, an edge, or a separation between different materials.

casing-bead door frame A metal door frame used in plaster walls that includes a strip or molding along its outer edges as a ground or guide for the plaster.

casing knife A knife used to trim wallpaper around casing, molding, or other edges.

casing nail (1) A nail with a very small head. (2) A finishing nail.

cassoon A deep panel in a ceiling or soffit.

castable refractory A dry-prepared mixture that, when reconstituted with water, becomes a concrete or mortar suitable for refractory use.

casting Any object that has been cast in a mold. The object may be made of iron, steel, plaster, concrete, plastic, or any other castable material.

casting plaster A plaster mixture with additives to provide properties desirable for casting work.

cast-in-place concrete (in situ concrete) Concrete poured into forms at its final location.

cast-in-place pile (bored pile) A concrete pile cast or formed at its permanent location. Such a pile can be cast with or without a casing.

cast iron An iron alloy cast in sand molds and machined to make many building products such as ornamentation, pipe and pipe fittings, and fencing.

cast-iron boiler A boiler made of cast-iron sections. Large cast-iron boilers may be transported in sections and assembled in place. Provides long-lasting, heavy-duty service.

cast molding A molding or molding component that has been cast, removed from the mold, and then fastened in place. The molding may be made of plaster, concrete, plastic, or some similar material.

cast stone A mixture of paste or mortar, with an aggregate of stone chips or fragments. Has the appearance of stone when cast into the desired form or structural shape.

catalyst (1) A substance that accelerates or retards chemical

catch basin

Catherine-wheel window

reactions. (2) The hardener that accelerates the curing of adhesives, such as synthetic resins.

catalytically blown asphalt
Asphalt that has had air with a catalyst blown through it while hot to give it the desired characteristics for a special use.

catch The fitting that mates with a latch or cam to lock a door, gate, or window.

catch basin (catch pit) A receptacle or reservoir that receives surface water runoff or drainage. Typically made of precast concrete, brick, or concrete masonry units, with a cast-iron frame and grate on top.

catch drain A long drain installed across or along a slope to collect and convey surface water.

catch pit *See* **catch basin**.

category One of the divisions of the breakdown in construction specifications, smaller than a trade.

catenary The curve formed by a flexible cord hanging between two points of support, as in power lines strung between poles.

catenary arch An arch constructed on the curve of an inverted catenary.

catface A rough flaw in a finish coat of plaster.

cathead The top piece of a hoist tower to which pulleys or sheaves are attached.

Catherine-wheel window (1) A round window with mullions like wheel spokes. (2) A rose window.

cathodic corrosion
See **electrochemical corrosion**.

cathodic protection A form of protection against electrolytic corrosion of fuel tanks and water pipes submerged in water or embedded in earth. Protection is

obtained by providing a sacrificial anode that will corrode in lieu of the structural component, or by introducing a counteracting current into the water or soil. This type of protection is also used for aluminum swimming pools, cast-iron water mains, and metal storage tanks.

cat ladder (gang boarding roof ladder) A board with a series of cross pieces nailed to it, used to provide footing on steep surfaces like a slope of a roof.

cat's eye In a piece of lumber, a small knot 1/4″ or less in diameter.

cat short A colloquial term for the bracing lumber used to strengthen wall construction. Cat shorts are placed horizontally between wall studs about halfway up the wall. *See also* **blocking (1)**.

catslide (1) The term used in the southern United States for a *saltbox* home. (2) The long pitched roof at the rear of a saltbox, which often sweeps down to the ground.

catwalk A small, permanent walkway, usually elevated, to provide access to a work area or service/ maintenance access to lighting units, stage draperies, etc.

caul A sheet of metal or plywood used to protect the surface of a sheet of plywood, particle board, or fiberboard from the presses during molding.

caulk (calk) (1) To fill a joint, crack, or opening with a sealer material. (2) The filling of joints in bell-and-spigot pipe with lead and oakum.

caulking (calking) A resilient silicone- or rubber-based compound used to prevent infiltration of water or outside air.

caulking ferrule A metal ring, usually brass, that is sealed with caulk.

caulking gun

cavity fill

cavity wall

C-clamp

caulking gun A hand or power tool that extrudes caulking material through a nozzle.

caulking recess In plumbing, the space between the bell or hub of one piece of pipe and the spigot that is inserted into it. The space is filled with caulking.

causeway A passage or roadway that has been raised above wet ground.

caustic An alkaline material that has a corrosive or irritating effect on living tissue.

caustic dip A strong cleaning solution into which materials are immersed.

caustic etch (frosted finish) A finish or decorative design produced on glass or other materials by a corrosive chemical.

caustic lime A material, white when pure, that is obtained by calcining limestone, shells, or other forms of calcium carbonate. Caustic lime is also called *quicklime* or *burnt lime* and is used in mortars and cements.

cavil *See* **kevel**.

cavitation The formation of a cavity or hollow in a fluid, as in the partial vacuum in water around a rapidly revolving propeller.

cavitation damage (1) The pitting damage done to propellers, turbine wheels, or other rotating equipment. (2) The pitting of concrete due to the collapse of bubbles in flowing water.

cavity The empty space between studs and joists.

cavity batten A length of wood placed in a cavity wall to catch mortar droppings during construction.

cavity fill Material placed in the hollow of a wall, ceiling, or floor to provide insulation or sound deadening.

cavity flashing The continuous waterproof barrier that covers the longitudinal opening in a cavity wall.

cavity wall (hollow masonry wall, hollow wall) An exterior masonry wall in which the inner and outer wythes are separated by an air space, but tied together with wires or metal stays.

C/B ratio saturation coefficient The ratio of the weight of water absorbed by a masonry brick or block immersed in cold water to the weight absorbed when immersed in boiling water. This is a measure of the resistance of the masonry to spalling due to freezing and thawing.

C-clamp A C-shaped clamp frequently used in carpentry and joinery. Force is applied by rotating a threaded shaft through one jaw of the C to force the work against the other jaw.

cedar A softwood with reddish heartwood and white sapwood noted for decay resistance and used for shingles, shakes, posts, and gutters.

ceiling (1) The overhead inside lining or finish of a room or area. (2) Any overhanging surface viewed from below.

ceiling area lighting A lighting system in which the entire ceiling functions as a single large luminaire. This lighting includes luminous and louvered ceilings.

ceiling cornice The molding installed at the intersection of the wall and ceiling planes.

ceiling diffuser Any air diffuser, located in a ceiling, through which warm or cold air is blown into an enclosure. The diffuser is designed to distribute the conditioned air over a given area.

ceiling strap

ceiling suspension system

cellar

ceiling fitting A fitting, usually electrical, that is attached to a ceiling, such as the attaching part of a ceiling light fixture.

ceiling flange An escutcheon or cover placed around holes in ceilings through which pipes pass or sprinkler heads protrude.

ceiling floor Framing intended to support a ceiling, but not a floor.

ceiling outlet In a ceiling, a metal or plastic junction box that supports a light fixture and encloses the connecting fixture wires.

ceiling plenum In air conditioning systems, the air space between a hung ceiling and the underside of the floor or roof above. Acts as a return to the air handling unit.

ceiling sound transmission The transmission of sound between adjacent rooms through the ceiling plenum above.

ceiling strap Wood strips nailed to the bottom of roof rafters or floor joists for the support or suspension of a ceiling.

ceiling strut A temporary brace suspended from an overhead structure or framing and used to hold door frames in place while the adjacent walls are being constructed.

ceiling suspension system A gridwork of metal rails and hangers erected for the support of a suspended ceiling and ceiling-mounted items, e.g., air diffusers, lights, fire detectors, etc.

ceiling switch A chain pull switch.

cellar A room or set of rooms below or predominantly below grade, usually under a building.

cellar hole The excavation for a cellar.

cellular concrete (aerated concrete) Concrete that has had gas-forming chemicals mixed with the basic ingredients, so that the final set material is lighter than ordinary concrete, due to its porosity. This type of concrete is often used as insulation when it is placed over a roof slab.

cellular construction Construction with concrete components that have been cast with voids for sound and thermal insulation and for decreased weight.

cellular-core door A hollow-core door filled with a lightweight, honeycomb-shaped, expanded material to provide rigidity and support.

cellular floor A flooring system that incorporates prefabricated raceways for telecommunications and electrical wiring.

cellular framing A method of framing in which the walls are composed of cells, with the cross walls transmitting the bearing loads to the foundation.

cellular material Material that contains voids or air pockets.

cellular plastic Plastic molding or extrusion with a pattern of cells that give it rigidity and reduce its weight.

cellular raceway A channel in a modular floor or wall that may be used as a raceway for electrical conductors.

cellular striation A pattern in a material that contains an integral layer of cells or voids.

celluloid A thermoplastic material often used in thin sheets because of its good molding properties.

cellulose A naturally occurring substance made up of glucose units.

Constitutes the main ingredient in wood, hemp, and cotton, and is used in many construction products.

cellulose acetate Any of several water-insoluble compounds formed by the action of acetic acid, anhydride of acetic acid, and sulfuric acid on cellulose. Used for making lacquers, varnishes, rayon, and packaging sheets.

cellulose enamel A lacquer paint made with a cellulose base.

cellulose fiber insulation A loose-fill insulation of recycled wood-based fiber with chemicals introduced to provide properties such as flame resistance.

cellulose fiber tile A sound-absorbing acoustical tile made from cellulose fiber.

Celsius scale A thermometer in which the interval between the freezing point and boiling point of water is divided into one hundred parts or degrees. Named after Aners Celsius, a Swedish astronomer. Also called a *centigrade thermometer*.

Celtic cross A cross formed from a long vertical column, a shorter horizontal bar, and a circle about their intersection.

cement Any chemical binder that makes bodies adhere to it or to each other, such as glue, paste, or Portland cement.

cement-aggregate ratio The ratio of cement to aggregate in a mixture, as determined by weight or volume.

cement-asbestos board A hard, noncombustible board fabricated from asbestos fibers impregnated and bonded with cement. Formerly used as roofing slates and wall shingles.

cementation The firming and hardening of a cementitious material.

cement board (cement backer board) A water-resistant wallboard made of concrete faced with fiberglass on both sides. Commonly used as an underlayment in wet areas like bathtub surrounds and as a backer for ceramic tile. Brand names include Durock® and Wonder Board®.

cement block An inaccurate term, usually in reference to concrete block or to a hollow or solid-cast masonry unit.

cement clinker A lump or ball of fused material, usually 1/8″ to 1″ in diameter, formed by heating cement slurry in a kiln. When cool, the clinker is interground with gypsum to form cement.

cement-coated nail A nail coated with cement to increase its friction and holding power.

cement content (cement factor) The quantity of cement per unit volume of concrete or mortar, expressed in pounds or bags per cubic yard.

cement factor *See* **cement content**.

cement fillet (weather fillet) A mortar bead or caulk used in place of flashing to provide a watertight seal in the joint between roofing and a wall.

cement gravel Gravel bound together in nature by clay or some other natural binding agent.

cement grout (1) A thin, watery mortar or plaster that is pumped or forced into joints, cracks, and spaces as an adhesive sealer. (2) A mixture that is pumped into the soil around a foundation to firm it up and provide better load-bearing characteristics.

cement gun A tool used for spraying or injecting cement grout or mortar material.

cementitious Capable of setting like a cement.

cement mixer

cement stucco

cement mixer (1) A concrete mixer. (2) A container used to mix concrete ingredients by means of paddles or a rotary motion. The container may be manually or power-operated.

cement mortar A plastic building material made by mixing lime, cement, sand, and water. Cement mortar is used to bind masonry blocks together or to plaster over masonry.

cement paint (concrete paint) Paint containing white Portland cement and usually applied over masonry surfaces as a waterproofing.

cement paste A mixture of cement and water.

cement plaster Plaster containing Portland cement as the binder and commonly used on exterior surfaces or in damp areas.

cement, Portland A fine gray powder made from three main ingredients: silica, alumina and lime. May also include slag or flue dust. Used as a base material for mortar and concrete.

cement rendering A wash of Portland cement and sand applied over a surface.

cement rock (cement stone) A natural, impure limestone that contains the ingredients for the manufacture of Portland cement.

cement screed *See* **screed**.

cement slurry A thin, watery cement mixture for pumping or for use as a wash over a surface.

cement stone *See* **cement rock**.

cement stucco (1) A mixture of Portland cement, sand, and a small percentage of lime. Used to form a hard covering for textured exterior walls. (2) A fine plaster used for interior decorations and moldings.

cement temper The addition of Portland cement to lime plaster to improve its strength and durability.

cement-wood floor The addition of sawdust to a mixture of Portland cement and sand for use as a poured floor.

center (1) A point that is exactly halfway between two other points or surfaces. (2) A point equidistant from all points on the circumference of a circle. (3) The internal core of a built-up construction.

center bit A cutter used for boring holes in wood. The cutting end consists of a sharp, threaded screw for guidance and for pulling the tool deeper into the work piece. The bit also has a scorer for marking the outline of the hole and a lip for cutting away the wood inside the hole. The other end of the bit is usually a tapered rectangular block that is clamped in the chuck of a brace.

center-hung door (center-pivoted door) A door that is supported by, and swings about, pivot pins. The pins are inserted into or attached to the door on the center line of its thickness.

center-hung sash A window sash hung so that it rotates horizontally about hinge pins at its center. To open, the top part of the window swings into the room and the bottom part projects outside the building.

centering (1) The temporary support for a masonry arch while the arch is being built. (2) The temporary forms for all supported concrete work.

center of gravity (center of mass) The location of a point in a body or shape about which all the parts of the body balance each other.

centrifugal pump

center of mass *See* **center of gravity**.

center pivot (1) The pins of a window sash that are centrally located in the frame so that the window rotates horizontally about its center line. (2) The pivot pins of a door that support the door on the center line of its thickness.

center-pivoted door *See* **center-hung door**.

center punch A tool for making starter indentations in metal where a hole is to be drilled. The punch has a sharp conical point on one end and is hit by a hammer on the other end.

center rail The horizontal portion or member that separates the upper and lower sections of a recessed panel door.

center stringer The structural member of a stair system that supports the treads and risers at the midpoint of the treads.

center-to-center (on center) The distance from the center line of one beam, part, or component of a structure to the corresponding center line of the next similar unit (for example, center-to-center of rafters or joists).

centimeter A metric unit of length equal to one one-hundredth of a meter. One inch equals 2.54 cm.

central-mixed concrete Concrete that is mixed in a stationary mixer and then transported to the site, as opposed to *transit-mixed concrete*.

central system A system that utilizes a single source and distribution system for an area. Examples are central heating and/or air-conditioning systems, central power systems, and central water systems.

centric load (concentric load) A load applied perpendicular to the neutral axis of a beam or column. The load acts through the geometric center (centroid) of gravity.

centrifugal chiller A gas compressor used for chilling in which the compression is obtained by centrifugal force.

centrifugal compressor An air or gas compressor in which the compression is obtained by centrifugal force.

centrifugal force The force away from the center of a rapidly spinning impeller.

centrifugal pump A pump that draws fluid into the center of a rapidly spinning impeller and uses the force of the spin (centrifugal force) to impart pressure and velocity to the fluid as it leaves the periphery.

ceramic Items made of clay or similar materials that are baked in a kiln to a permanent hardness. Ceramic products include pottery, tile, and stoneware.

ceramic coating A coating made of a nonmetallic mineral, such as clay, and compounded to provide the desired properties when baked or cured. A coating is usually applied to metals to provide heat or abrasive-wear protection.

ceramic-faced glass Glass that has had ceramic material fused to it during the heating and tempering process.

ceramic glaze A material that is applied over a clay product and then baked to produce a hard, vitreous, glassy surface. The glaze may be transparent or colored.

ceramic granules A coating applied to asphalt roof shingles to reflect heat, increase durability and provide color.

ceramic mosaic tile Small, unglazed tiles commonly used for flooring and

chain

walls. Patterns of various colors and shapes are first placed on sheets for ease in laying.

certificate A written document appropriately signed by responsible parties testifying to a matter of fact in accordance with a requirement of the contract documents.

certificate for insurance A document prepared by an insurance company or its agent that states the period of time for which the policy is in effect, along with the types and amounts of coverage for the insured.

certificate of occupancy A written document issued by the governing authority in accordance with the provisions of the building permit. The certificate of occupancy indicates that, in the opinion of the building official, the project has been completed in accordance with the building code. This document gives the owner permission from the authorities to occupy and use the premises for the intended purpose.

certificate of payment A statement issued by a design professional notifying the owner of the amount due to a contractor for work completed and/or the delivery or storage of building materials.

certified ballast Fluorescent lighting manufactured to meet standards set by the Certified Ballast Manufacturer's Association.

certified construction specifier A construction professional who, by experience and examination by the Construction Specifications Institute, has been certified as proficient in the knowledge and art of preparing technical specifications for the construction process.

certified output rating The output capacity of a piece of equipment or machinery that is accepted as meeting the standards of the government regulatory body or trade organization.

cesspool A lined excavation in the ground that receives the discharge of a drainage system, especially from sinks and water closets, and is designed to retain the organic matter and solids, while permitting the liquids to seep through the bottom and sides.

chain (1) A unit of length used by land surveyors (*Gunter's Chain*): 7.92″ = 1 link; 100 links = 66′ = 4 rods = 1 chain; 80 chains = 1 mile. (2) An engineer's chain is equal to 100′. (3) A series of rings or links of metal connected to each other to form useful lengths.

chain block (chain hoist) A grooved pulley or sheave suitable for chain. Typically, a chain hook is provided for hoisting or hauling.

chain bolt A spring bolt at the top of a door that is operated by pulling an attached chain.

chain course A bond course formed by masonry headers and held in place by cramps.

chain door fastener A chain that can be secured by a slide bolt between a door stile and a door jamb to allow the door to be opened slightly while remaining securely fastened.

chain fall An assembly of chain with blocks or pulleys for hoisting or pulling a heavy load.

chain hoist *See* **chain block**.

chaining The process of measuring a distance using a surveyor's chain.

chaining pin A metal pin used for marking measurements on the ground.

chain intermittent fillet weld An interrupted fillet weld on both sides of a joint. The weld segments are opposite one another.

chain link fence

chamfer

chain link fence A fence made of steel wire fabric supported by metal posts.

chain molding A molding carved to simulate the appearance of a chain.

chain-pipe vise A pipe vise that uses a chain to restrain a pipe.

chain-pipe wrench (chain tongs) A wrench for turning or restraining pipe. The wrench consists of a lever handle with a serrated jaw. The jaw is held in contact with the pipe by a roller chain that wraps around the pipe.

chain pull switch An electrical switch that is operated by pulling a bead chain. Frequently, this type of switch is an integral part of a light bulb socket.

chain pump A pump in which an endless chain with disks mounted on it is pulled through a pipe to move viscous material.

chain riveting A type of riveting in which the rivets are placed in parallel adjacent rows. Chain riveting is not as strong as the staggered riveting pattern, which has more tear material between rivets.

chain saw A gas- or electric-powered saw having cutting teeth running around a bar of flat steel. Used for cross-cutting logs, etc.

chain scale An engineer's scale on which the inch divisions are subdivided into 10 parts, or multiples of 10, such as 20, 30, 40, 50, etc.

chain timber Large beams built horizontally into a masonry wall to provide support and a tie-in during construction.

chain tones *See* **chain-pipe wrench**.

chain trencher A machine that uses a chain belt to excavate a trench.

chair (1) A frame built into a wall to provide support for a sink, lavatory, urinal, or toilet. Also called a *carrier*. (2) In concrete construction, a small metal or plastic support for reinforcing steel. The support is used to maintain proper positioning during concrete placement.

chair rail A horizontal piece of wood attached to walls to prevent damage to plaster or paneling from the backs of chairs.

chalk A soft limestone, white, gray, or buff-colored, composed of the remains of small marine organisms. In construction, chalk is commonly dyed blue and used with a chalk line or snap line for marking lines.

chalked A term for porcelain enamel that has lost its hard, glossy surface and is powdery when rubbed.

chalking A surface condition in which the binder of a coating breaks down so that the pigment comes off on anything touching it, or is washed away by rain, as can happen, for example, with self-cleaning white paint.

chalk line (1) A light cord that has been surface-coated with chalk (usually blue) and is used for marking. (2) The line left by a chalked string.

chamber test A test developed and conducted by Underwriters' Laboratories to determine the fire-hazard classification of building materials.

chamfer The beveled edge formed at the right-angle corner of a construction member. *See also* **cant strip**.

chamfer bit A tool bit for beveling the upper edge of a hole in wood so that a flat-head wood screw can be driven flush with the wood surface.

channel

channel block

chamfered rustication Masonry work in which the corner edge around the exposed face of each block is deeply chamfered, and the joint mortar is recessed, so that between two adjacent blocks an internal right angle is formed.

chamfer plane A carpenter's plane designed for cutting chamfers.

chamfer stop Any ornamentation or construction piece that ends or blocks the continuation of a chamfer.

chamfer strip *See* **cant strip**.

chancel An area in the front of a church that is reserved for use by the clergy and choir.

chancel aisle The side aisle of a chancel.

chancel arch An arch employed in some church designs to indicate the separation of the church body (*nave*) from the chancel or sanctuary.

chancel rail A railing or barrier used in place of a screen to separate the church body (*nave*) from the chancel.

chancel screen The screen that separates the church body from the chancel.

chancery (1) A room, suite of rooms, or building used as a court of record or office of records. (2) A chancellor's court or office; a secretariat.

chandelier A branched light fixture that is often ornate, and usually suspended from a ceiling.

chandlery (chandry) A place where lamps, candles, and other lighting supplies were kept before electricity was available.

chandry *See* **chandlery**.

change In construction, a deviation in the design or scope of the work as defined in the plans and specifications which are the basis for the original contract.

change order Written authorization provided to a contractor approving a change from the original plans, specifications, or other contract documents, as well as a change in the cost. With the proper signatures, a change order is considered a legal document.

changeover point That temperature and time at which a building requires neither heating nor cooling.

changes in the work Changes to the original design, specifications, or scope of work as requested by the owner. All changes in the work should be documented on change orders. *See also* **change order**.

channel (1) A structural steel member shaped like a "U." (2) In glazing, a U-shaped member used to hold a pane or panel. (3) A watercourse, usually manmade. (4) The suspension system for a suspended ceiling. (5) A path for the transmission and reception of electromagnetic signals between two or more points.

channel bar *See* **channel iron**.

channel beam A construction member with a U-shaped cross section.

channel block A hollow concrete masonry block with a groove or furrow in it to provide a continuous recess for reinforcing steel and grout.

channel clip A metal spring clip used to support perforated metal pans in a suspended ceiling system.

channel cutter A hand tool used to cut light-gauge metal framing.

channel glazing A window glazing system in which glass panels are set

charging door

in a U-shaped channel using removable beads or glazing stops.

channeling Decorative fluting or grooving, as in the grooves in a vertical column.

channel iron (channel bar) A U-shaped, rolled, structural steel member, the web of which is always deeper than the width of the flanges. The web depth is the size of the channel.

channel pipe A section of pipe with the top quarter or half removed. Channel pipe is used for directing flow in a manhole.

channel runner A primary horizontal support in a suspended ceiling system.

channel section A U-shaped section. *See also* **channel**.

chantlate The piece of wood across the rafters at the eaves and projecting so as to prevent rainwater from running straight down the wall.

charcoal filter (1) A filter containing pulverized charcoal for removing odors, smoke, and vapors from the air. (2) A filter for purifying and cleaning water.

charette The push or effort to complete an architectural problem within a specified time.

charge (1) A quantity of explosives set in place. (2) A load of refrigerant in a refrigeration or air-conditioning system.

charging (1) The insertion of refrigerant into a refrigeration or air-conditioning system. (2) The insertion of a predetermined mixture or quantity of materials into a concrete mixer, furnace, or other piece of processing equipment.

charging chute An enclosed slide in which waste material is dumped and subsequently fed into an incinerator.

charging door The door of a furnace or incinerator through which loads or charges are inserted.

Charpy test A measurement of material strength at impact. A specimen, usually notched, is struck by a pendulum at a velocity of 17.5 feet per second. The energy absorbed in the fracture is then measured.

chase A continuous enclosure in a structure that acts as a housing for pipe, wiring conduits, ducts, etc. A chase is usually located in or adjacent to a column, which provides some physical protection.

chase bonding The continuous vertical joint bond by which new masonry is joined to an older existing wall.

chase mortise (pulley mortise) A mortise or recess cut into a beam or structural member that has one side elongated and sloped to allow the tenon to be rotated in place from the side when space will not permit a direct perpendicular insertion.

chase wedge A wedge-shaped hand tool used for bossing and forming soft materials, such as lead and copper.

chat A stony material used as a base in asphalt paving.

chattel Any item of property, movable or immovable, except real estate or a freehold.

chattel mortgage A mortgage or security interest in personal property as collateral for a loan.

chatter marks The marks left on a work piece by a vibrating tool.

cheapener An additive in paint that is used to impart desirable characteristics to or extend

check

checkered plate

cheek

cheek cut

coverage of the paint. Cheapener does not necessarily make the paint cheaper in cost.

check (1) A flapper or valve that permits fluid to flow in one direction only. (2) An attachment that regulates movement, such as a door check. (3) A small split in wood that runs parallel to the grain. Caused by shrinking during drying.

check cracks *See* **check (3)** *and* **checking**.

checkered plate A metal plate with a waffle-like pattern of squared projections cast or rolled into its surface.

check fillet A water-control barrier or curb used on roofs.

checking (alligatoring, check cracks, map cracks, shelling) (1) Small cracks that appear in paint or varnish, but which usually do not expose the base material. (2) Small, closely spaced, irregular surface cracks in concrete, mortar, or plaster. *See also* **crazing**.

checking floor hinge A mechanism fixed on or in the floor that acts both as a door hinge and a closing speed controller.

check lock A small, supplementary lock designed to control the bolt or action of a larger lock.

check nut (locknut) A second nut, usually thin, that is installed on a bolt or shaft and tightened against the first nut to prevent it from vibrating or shaking loose.

check rail The horizontal meeting rail of a double-hung window.

check stop A molding strip or bead used to restrain a sliding unit such as a window sash.

check strip A bead or molding used for parting.

check throat The groove cut longitudinally along the underside of window and door sills to prevent rainwater from running back to the building wall.

check valve (back-pressure valve, clack valve, reflux valve) A valve designed to limit the flow of fluid to one direction only.

cheek In general, the side of any feature, such as the side of a dormer.

cheek boards The vertical stops or bulkheads placed at the ends of a concrete wall form. (2) Trim applied to the side of a dormer.

cheek cut (side cut) The oblique cut made in a rafter or jack rafter to permit a tight fit against a hip or valley rafter or to square the lower end of a jack rafter.

cheesiness A term used to describe the property of paint that has partially dried and can be torn and shredded.

chemical bond A bond between similar materials caused by the interlocking of their crystalline structures. Once formed, there is no defined parting line in the bond that would permit a clean separation.

chemical brown stain The brown stain that appears during kiln- or air-drying of lumber due to changes in the concentration of moisture in the wood.

chemical closet (chemical toilet) A toilet that contains or recirculates a chemical that breaks wastes down while serving as a disinfectant and deodorant. It does not use water to flush and carry away sanitary waste to a public septic system.

chemical flux cutting The use of a chemical compound or flux to expedite oxygen torch cutting.

chimney

chimney arch

chimney back

Chemical Hazard Response Information System (CHRIS) A series of monographs prepared for the U.S. Coast Guard, each of which provides detailed information on the hazards of a particular chemical.

chemically foamed plastic Spongy or cellular plastic material formed by the gas-producing action of its component chemical compounds.

chemical membrane A material applied to fresh concrete to aid curing by inhibiting evaporation.

chemical oxidation A chemical process that causes the loss of electrons from an element or ion.

chemical stability The tendency of a substance to remain unchanged over a wide range of physical, environmental, and chemical conditions.

chemical stabilization The introduction of chemicals into soil to increase its bearing strength and decrease its permeability.

chemical toilet *See* **chemical closet**.

cherry picker A powered lift for raising workers or materials. Consists of a basket or a lift attached to the end of a telescoping boom, and may be either self-propelled or mounted on a truck.

chert An impure, flintlike rock, usually dark in color. Some of its common impurities react with cement, making its use as an aggregate undesirable for certain applications.

chevron (1) A V-shaped stripe that may point up or down. Used as a distinguishing mark to indicate rank or service. Architecturally, it may be used as an ornamental repeating pattern on molding or trim. (2) On a gable roof, the place where the rafters meet at the ridge.

chevron slat A V-shaped configuration used in fences and other architectural elements to provide privacy while permitting ventilation.

Chicago window A large fixed sash flanked with narrow sashes on either side.

chicken ladder A board with wood strips or cleats nailed across it at regular intervals to provide safe footing across a void or on an inclined surface like a roof.

chilled-water refrigeration system A cooling system in which cold water is circulated to remote cooling coils/blower units.

chiller A piece of equipment that utilizes a refrigeration cycle to produce cold (chilled) water for circulation to the desired location or use. *See also* **absorption chiller** *and* **compression chiller**.

chilling The process of applying refrigeration in moderation so as to achieve cooling without freezing.

chimbley A regional term for chimney.

chimney A vertical, noncombustible structure with one or more flues to carry smoke and other gases of combustion into the atmosphere.

chimney apron The metal flashing built into the chimney and roof at the point of penetration. Serves as a moisture barrier.

chimney arch The upper structure over a fireplace.

chimney back The inside back wall of a fireplace, which may be made of fire-brick masonry or ornamental metal, and is intended to reflect heat out into the room.

chimney bar (turning bar) A lintel bar of iron or steel that bridges the fireplace opening. It is supported by the side masonry, and in turn

chimney cap

chimney jamb

supports the masonry above the opening.

chimney block Solid concrete blocks cast as segments of a circle for laying up or building round flues.

chimney board A board or screen used to cover or block the opening of a fireplace when it is not being used.

chimney bond A pattern of stretcher bond used in laying up the internal brickwork in masonry chimneys.

chimney breast (chimney piece) That part of the front of a fireplace that projects out into the room.

chimney can (chimney pot) A cylindrical extension placed on top of a chimney to improve the draft. It can be masonry or metal.

chimney cap (bonnet, chimney head) (1) The slab or masonry top piece on a chimney. (2) A metal top piece designed to minimize rainfall down the flue while improving the draft.

chimney cheek The masonry on either side of a fireplace opening that supports the mantel and the upper chimney construction.

chimney connector The smokepipe or metal breeching that connects the top of a stove, furnace, water heater, or boiler to a chimney flue.

chimney corner (inglenook, roofed ingle) A small area or alcove beside a fireplace, frequently with built-in benches.

chimney cowl An elaborate chimney pot for improving drafts.

chimney crane A swinging iron arm attached to the inside of a fireplace to support cooking pots over the fire.

chimney cricket (saddle) A small false roof built behind a chimney on the main roof to divert rainwater away from the chimney.

chimney crook (chimney hook) An extension bar that hangs on the chimney crane and supports cooking pots, letting smaller pots hang lower and closer to the fire. It can usually be adjusted for height.

chimney effect (flue effect, stack effect) The process by which air, when heated, becomes less dense and rises. The rising gases in a chimney create a draft that draws in cooler gases or air from below. Stairwells, elevator shafts, and chases in a building often draw in cold air from lower floors or outside through this same process.

chimney flue The vertical passageway in a chimney through which the hot gases flow. A chimney may contain one or several flues. Flues are typically lined with fired clay pipes to resist corrosion and facilitate cleaning.

chimney gutter The flashing placed around a chimney for waterproofing the roof penetration.

chimney head *See* **chimney cap**.

chimney hood A covering top or cap that blocks rain from entering the flue.

chimney hook *See* **chimney crook**.

chimney jamb The vertical sides of a fireplace opening.

chimney lining The noncombustible, heat-resisting material that lines the flue inside the chimney. Typically, the lining consists of round or rectangular fired clay material.

chimney piece Ornamentation around a fireplace, such as a mantelpiece. *See also* **chimney breast**.

chimney pot (chimney can) A metal, masonry, or ceramic extension placed on top of a chimney to improve draft, appearance, or to block rain.

chimney throat

chisel

chimney shaft The segment of a chimney that projects above the roof.

chimney stack (chimney stalk) A very large and tall chimney used by utilities, commercial and industrial installations, and large apartment houses. There may be several flues in a single chimney stack.

chimney stalk *See* **chimney stack**.

chimney throat (chimney waist) (1) The narrowest part of a flue. (2) The area above a fireplace and below the smoke shelf, where the damper is usually located.

chimney waist *See* **chimney throat**.

chimney wing The sides of a fireplace chimney above the opening that close into the throat of the damper opening.

china sanitary ware Water closets, lavatories, or other items made of vitrified china with a glazed finish.

China white (Chinese white) A white paint pigment containing white lead.

china wood oil A drying oil used in paints and varnishes.

chinbeak molding A molding that features a concave section intersecting with a convex section, creating a beak.

Chinese blue A blue paint pigment that is created from a cyanogen compound of iron.

Chinese lacquer (Japanese lacquer, lacquer) A natural varnish, originating in China or Japan, and extracted from the sap of a sumac tree. This lacquer forms a high-quality surface.

Chinese white A dense white pigment of zinc oxide. *See also* **china white**.

chink A small, elongated cleft, rent, or fissure, such as the openings between logs in a log cabin wall.

chinking Any material used to fill in voids, such as those in stone walls or between the timbers of a log cabin.

chip (1) A small piece of semiconducting substrate material, such as silicon, on which miniaturized electronic circuitry (LSI or VLSI circuits) is fabricated. (2) A small fragment of metal, wood, stone, or marble that has been chopped, cut, or broken from its parent piece.

chip ax A hand tool used for chipping and shaping wood or stone.

chipboard A flat panel manufactured to various thicknesses by bonding flakes of wood with a binder. Chipboard is an economical, strong material used for sheathing, subflooring, and cabinetry.

chip carving Ornamental work created by cutting away chips of material in various patterns.

chip cracks (eggshelling) Similar to alligatoring or checking except that the edges of the cracks are raised up from the base surface.

chipped grain On a wood surface, the depressions or voids occurring where the wood has been torn out as the result of dull planing or machining against the direction of growth.

chipper (1) A small pneumatic or electric reciprocating tool for cutting or breaking concrete. (2) Gasoline- or diesel-powered machine featuring a system of blades used to shred or chip logs or brush.

chipping The removal of weld spatter, rust, or old paint from ironwork using a hammer and cold chisel.

chisel A metal tool with a cutting edge at one end, used in dressing, shaping, or working wood, stone, or

chopping block

chord

chuck

metal. A chisel is usually tapped with a hammer or mallet.

chisel bar A heavy metal bar with a sharp edge at one end.

chisel knife A sharp, narrow, square-edged knife used to remove paint or wallpaper.

chloracne A skin rash caused by exposure to chlorine. Characterized by small pimples and inflammation of skin pores.

chlorinated paraffin wax A thick, viscous material used in flame-retardant paints.

chlorinated rubber A rubber-based product used in paints, plastics, and adhesives.

chlorinated solvent A material that dissolves greases and oils. Contains one or more chlorine atoms in its chemical structure.

chlorine A highly corrosive elemental gas.

chlorofluorocarbons (CFCs) Compounds consisting of chlorine, fluorine, and carbon atoms that are degraded only by the sun's radiation in the stratosphere, where released chlorine may contribute to ozone depletion. They can persist in the troposphere for 100 years or longer.

chock A wedge-shaped block used to prevent the movement of a wheeled vehicle or other object. Chocks are usually used in pairs.

chopping block *See* **butcher block**.

chord (1) The top or bottom members of a truss (typically horizontal), as distinguished from the web members. (2) A straight line between two points on a curve.

CHRIS *See* **Chemical Hazard Response Information System**.

chrismatory A font in a church that contains a basin of consecrated oil for baptism, confirmation, ordination, etc.

chromacity A measure of the color quality of a light, as defined by its dominant wavelength and purity.

chromate A greenish-yellow primer applied to steel members to inhibit corrosion. Chromate is a salt of chromic acid, frequently referred to as lead or zinc chromate.

chrome green A green pigment made from a blend of chromate salts and used to color paint. The pigment has rust-inhibiting properties.

chrome steel Carbon steel to which chromium has been added (in proportions of 0.5% to 2.0%) to increase the steel's hardness and yield strength.

chrome yellow (Leipzig yellow) A yellow pigment made from lead chromate and used to color paint. The pigment also has rust-inhibiting properties.

chromium A grayish-white metallic element added to steel to enhance its strength and hardness. It is also used as a plating medium because of the rust-resisting surface that results. Chromium plating produces a highly polished finish.

chromium plating The application, by electroplating, of a thin coat of chromium to provide a hard, protective wearing surface or a surface that can take a decorative high polish.

chronic toxic chemical A substance that causes adverse health effects that may be delayed in their appearance, but usually cause permanent damage.

chuck An adjustable device with teeth that holds a cutting or drill bit in place.

churn molding A molding with a repeating wavy or chevron pattern.

circuit breakers

circular stair

chute An inclined plane or trough for sliding various items or bulk materials to a lower level, with the help of gravity.

cima *See* **cyma**.

cimbia A decorative band or fillet encircling the shaft of a column.

cinder block (clinker block) A masonry block made of crushed cinders and Portland cement. This type of block is lighter and has a higher insulating value than concrete. Because moisture causes deterioration of cinder block, it is used primarily for interior rather than exterior walls.

cinder concrete A lightweight concrete that uses cinders for coarse aggregate.

cinders (1) A partly burned combustible material. (2) Slag from a metal furnace. (3) Ashes, especially from the burning of soft coal. (4) A form of volcanic lava.

circle trowel A trowel with a curved blade used for plastering a curved surface.

circline lamp A fluorescent lamp with a circular tube.

circuit (1) A closed path followed by an electric current. (2) A piping loop for a liquid or gas. *See also* **channel (5)**.

circuit breaker (automatic circuit breaker) An electrical device for discontinuing current flow during an abnormal condition. Unlike a fuse, a circuit breaker becomes reusable by resetting a switch.

circuit vent A vent designed to prevent pressure build-up or to eliminate air in a closed circuit system, as in a heating system or a solar heat-exchanger system.

circular arch An arch whose inner surface, and occasionally a portion of its outer surface, describe a circle.

circular cutting and waste The cutting of material such as flooring, roofing, or decking to create a curved surface or to go around a curved intersection. Also, a measure of the resulting waste material.

circular face A surface that, in plan view, is the outside or convex side of a circle.

circular mil An electrical term for the cross-sectional area of a wire. A conductor with a diameter of one mil (0.001″) has a cross-sectional area of one circular mil.

circular mil-foot A unit of measure for an electrical conductor that is one circular mil in diameter and 1′ long.

circular plane A carpenter's wood-planing tool that has a curved baseplate for finishing curved surfaces.

circular saw A circular steel blade fitted with cutting teeth and mounted on an arbor.

circular spike A metal timber connector with teeth set in a ring. The teeth grip the wood as a central axial bolt is tightened.

circular stair (spiral stair) A cylindrical stairway in which the staircase is built in the shape of a corkscrew.

circular sunk face A surface that, in plan view, is the inside or concave side of a circle; the opposite of a circular face.

circular work *See* **compass work**.

circulating head (circulating pressure) The pump-induced pressure in a piping system, such as one for hydronic heat, chilled water, or domestic hot water.

circulation (1) The flow of a liquid or a gas within a closed series of pipes. (2) The flow of air (fresh,

cladding

clamping screw

heated, or cooled) in a building. (3) The flow of people through a building. (4) Any pipe forming a part of a liquid or gas circuit.

cissing (sissing, random surface cracks) A mild form of alligatoring.

cistern A catch basin on a roof or an enlargement at the end of a gutter for catching and storing rainwater.

city plan A large-scale map of a city showing the streets, important buildings, parks, and other features.

city planning (town planning, community planning) The conscious control of growth or change in a city, town, or community, taking into account aesthetics, industry, utilities, transportation, and many other factors that affect the quality of life.

civic center In an urban area, a group of government or public service buildings, which may include a city hall, a library, a museum, an art center, a parking garage, a court house, etc.

civil engineer An engineer specializing in the design of public works, such as roads, buildings, dams, bridges, and other structures, as well as water distribution, drainage, and sanitary sewer systems.

Civil Rights Act Legislation enacted by Congress in 1964 prohibiting any act that discriminates against an individual for any reason, but particularly because of sex, race, age, ethnic origin, or religion.

C-label A door certified by Underwriters' Laboratories as meeting their class C level requirements.

clack valve See **check valve**.

clad alloy A metal to which a molecular-bonded surface coat has been applied to provide an improved wearing surface, a better appearance, or corrosion protection. See also **cladding**.

clad brazing sheet A sheet of metal that has brazing filler material prebonded to one or both sides. Intended for use in a brazing operation.

cladding A covering or sheathing applied to provide desirable surface properties, such as durability, weathering, and corrosion or impact resistance. See also **clad alloy**.

claim (1) A contractor's request for additional compensation or an extension of time pursuant to the contract terms. (2) A request to be paid for the cost of damages when an insured loss occurs.

claims examiner Relative to insurance claims, the supervisor who oversees the paperwork submitted by the field adjuster.

clairecolle See **clearcole**.

clamp A mechanical device used to hold items together or firmly in place while other operations are being performed. The clamping force may be applied by screws, wedges, cams, or a pneumatic/hydraulic piston.

clamp brick A brick that was retained in a clamp while being fired in a kiln.

clamping plate A metal splice plate that is bolted across a joint in a wooden frame to increase its strength.

clamping screw A screw used with wood or metal jaws to provide a clamping force for temporary or permanent fastening.

clamping time The amount of time a bonded joint must remain immobile in a clamp in order for the glue to set.

clapboard

clamp nail A mechanical fastener designed to bridge a joint and pull the two pieces tightly together as it is driven in place.

clamshell (1) A bucket used on a derrick or crane for handling loose granular material. The bucket's two halves are hinged at the top, thus resembling a clamshell. (2) A wood molding with a cross section that resembles a clamshell.

clapboard (bevel siding, lap siding) A wood siding used as exterior covering in frame construction. It is applied horizontally, overlapped with the grain running lengthwise. The thickest section of the board is on the bottom.

clapboard gauge (siding gauge) A spacing tool used to maintain a uniform overlap when applying clapboards.

clapper valve A swing check valve that permits fluid flow in one direction only.

clarification drawing An illustration provided by an architect or engineer to explain in more detail some area or item on the contract documents, or as a part of a job change order or modification.

clarifier A tank or other device used to remove suspended solids from a liquid.

Clarke beam A composite beam consisting of planks bolted with their flat sides together and then strengthened with a board nailed across the joint.

clasp nail *See* **cut nail**.

class (1) A group of items ranked together on the basis of common characteristics or requirements. (2) A division grouping or distinction based on grade or quality. (3) The opening into which a door or window will be fitted.

Class A, B, C, D, E Fire-resistance ratings applied to building components such as doors or windows. Class A is an Underwriters' Laboratories classification for a component having a 3-hour fire endurance rating; Class B, a 1 or 1-1/2-hour rating; Class C, a 3/4-hour rating; Class D, a 1-1/2-hour rating; and Class E, a 3/4-hour rating.

Class A fire A fire involving ordinary combustibles, such as wood, paper, some plastics and textiles.

Class B fire A fire involving oil, gas, paint, or other flammable liquids.

Class C fire A fire involving live electrical equipment that requires the use of electrically nonconductive extinguishing agents.

Class D fire A fire involving combustible metals such as magnesium, titanium, and sodium that require an extinguishing medium that does not react with the burning metal.

Class I – IV asbestos work *See* **asbestos work**.

Class Ia flammable liquid A liquid having a flash point below 73°F (22.8 °C) and a boiling point below 100°F (37.8 °C).

Class Ib flammable liquid A liquid having a flash point below 73°F (22.8 °C) and a boiling point at or above 100°F (37.8 °C).

Class Ic flammable liquid A liquid having a flash point at or above 73°F (22.8 °C) and below 100°F (37.8 °C).

Class II combustible liquid A liquid having a flash point at or above 100°F (37.8 °C).

Class IIIa combustible liquid A liquid having a flash point at or

classical architecture

clay pipe

clay spade

clay tile

above 140°F (60 °C) and below 200°F (93.4 °C).

Class IIIb combustible liquid A liquid having a flash point at or above 200°F (93.4 °C).

classical architecture Characteristic of or pertaining to the styles, types, and modes of structural construction and decoration practiced by the Greeks and Romans.

classicism An architectural style derived from the basic principles and design of Greco-Roman or Italian Renaissance buildings.

classroom window (awning window) A wide window, the upper portion of which is a fixed light, while the lower portion has two or more tilt-in panels positioned side by side.

clause A subdivision of a paragraph or subparagraph within a legal document such as a contract. A clause is usually numbered or lettered for easy reference.

clavel (clavis) A voussoir or keystone of an arch.

clavis *See* **clavel**.

claw bar A steel bar that is straight at one end and bent at the other. The straight end has a chisel point, while the bent end has a notch for pulling out nails. A claw bar is used for general demolition work.

claw chisel A hand tool with a notched edge for cutting stone.

claw hammer A hammer with a hardened face on one end of the head for driving nails, and curved, forked tines on the other end for pulling out nails.

claw hatchet A hatchet on which one end of the head is cleft.

claw plate A round timber connector that has raised prongs to bite into the wood.

clay A fine-grained material, consisting mainly of hydrated silicates of aluminum, that is soft and cohesive when moist, but becomes hard when baked or fired. Clay is used to make bricks, tiles, pipe, earthenware, etc.

clay binder A material, consisting of fine clay particles, that has good holding or fixing properties in a soil mass.

clay cable cover A fired-clay half pipe that is placed over underground electric cables as a protective cover.

clay content In any mixture of soil or earth, the percentage of clay by weight.

clay-mortar mix A mixture consisting of pulverized clay that is added to masonry mortar to act as a plasticizer.

clay pipe Pipe made of earthenware and glazed to eliminate porosity. Clay pipe is used for drainage systems and sanitary sewers.

clay puddle A mixture of clay and water used to prevent or retard the passage of water.

clay spade A wide, flat, chisel-like cutting tool used in a pneumatic hammer to cut into tightly compacted materials like clays.

clay tile A fired earthenware tile used on roofs. Called *quarry tile* when used for flooring.

Clayton Act Legislation enacted by Congress in 1914 to lessen the negative effects of the Sherman Anti-Trust Act by allowing labor to organize for purposes of negotiating with a single employer.

clean aggregate Sand or gravel aggregate that is free of clay, dirt, or organic material.

clean back The end of a bondstone that shows in masonry work.

cleanout

cleanout door

clean closure A land cover cap used to cover a site where environmental remediation has occurred.

cleaning eye An access plug in a cleanout pipe fitting, used for inspection and cleaning purposes.

cleaning sash A window sash that is normally inoperable, but may be opened with a special tool.

cleanout (1) A pipe fitting with a removable threaded plug that permits access for inspection and cleaning of the run. (2) A door in the base of a chimney that permits access for cleaning. (3) A small door in a ventilation duct to permit access for removal of grease, dust, and dirt blockages.

cleanout door The door in a cleanout frame. *See also* **cleanout**.

clean power Power that is relatively free of electrical noise and harmonic distortion.

clean room A special-purpose room that meets requirements for the absence of lint, dust, or other particulate matter. In a clean room, the filter systems are high efficiency and the air exchange is one-directional laminar flow.

clean timber (clear lumber, clear stuff, clear timber, clears, free stuff) Wood that is free of knots, splits, blemishes, or other defects.

clear The distance between any two points without interruptions, obstructions, or discontinuations, as in a clear span. *See also* **clearance**.

clearage *See* **clearance**.

clearance (clearage) (1) The distance by which one item is separated, or clear, from another; the empty space between them. (2) An intentional gap left to allow for minor dimensional variations of a component or a part.

clearcole (clairecolle) (1) A primer and sealer composed of water, glue, and a whitening pigment. (2) A clear coating used in the application of gold leaf.

clear glaze A transparent glaze for ceramic applications.

clearing The removal of trees, vegetation, or other obstructions from an area of land.

clearing arm A branch on a pipe to provide access for cleaning.

clear lumber *See* **clean timber**.

clears *See* **clean timber**.

clear span The distance between the inside surfaces of the two supports of a structural member. *See also* **clear**.

clearstory (clerestory) That part of a church or building which rises above the roofs of the other parts of the building, with windows for admitting light to the central interior area.

clear stuff *See* **clean timber**.

clear timber *See* **clean timber**.

cleat A small block of wood nailed to the surface of a wood member to stop or support another member.

cleat wiring Electrical wiring that is exposed and supported on standoff insulators.

cleavage A natural parting or splitting plane found in slate, mica, and some types of wood.

cleavage plane In crystalline material, the plane along which splitting can easily be performed.

cleft timber A wooden beam that has been split to the desired size or shape.

clench *See* **clinch**.

clench bolt (clinch bolt) A bolt designed to have one end bent over to retain it in place.

clevis

climbing crane

climbing form

clench nail (clinch nail) A nail made to have the protruding point bent over after being driven.

clerestory *See* **clearstory**.

clerk of the works A representative of the architect or owner who oversees construction, handles administrative matters, and ensures that construction is in accordance with the contract documents.

clevis A U-shaped bar of metal with holes drilled through the ends to receive a pin or bolt. A type of shackle.

climbing crane A hoisting device with a vertical portion that is attached to the structure of a building so that as the construction is built higher and higher, the crane rises along with it.

climbing form Vertical concrete formwork that is successively raised after each pour has hardened. The formwork is anchored to the concrete below. *See also* **slipform**.

clinch (clench) To secure a nail in place by bending the protruding point at a right angle.

clinch bolt *See* **clench bolt**.

clinch nail *See* **clench nail**.

clink (1) The sealed edge between sheets of metal roofing. (2) A pointed steel bar used to break up concrete.

clinker A vitrified residue of burnt coal sometimes used as the aggregate in cinder block. *See also* **cement clinker**.

clinker block *See* **cinder block**.

clinker brick A hard brick that is frequently formed with a distorted shape and is used for paving.

clinometer An instrument for measuring angles of elevation or inclination.

clip (1) To cut off, as with shears. (2) A short piece of brick that has been cut. (3) A small metal fastening device.

clip angle (lug angle) A small piece of angle iron attached to a structural member to accept or retain some structural load.

clip bond A style of decorative masonry for walls in which the corners of stretchers are cut, forming a V-notch to receive the corner of a diagonal header.

clip joint A thicker-than-usual mortar joint used to raise the height of a masonry course.

clipped gable A gable roof with a shortened ridge pole creating a short hip roof at the gable.

clipped header (false header) In masonry, a half-brick placed in a wall to look like a header.

clipped lintel A lintel connected to another structural member to help carry the load.

cloak rail A board attached to a wall and containing pegs or hooks for hanging clothes.

cloakroom *See* **coatroom**.

cloister (1) A monastic establishment such as a monastery or convent. (2) A covered passageway on the side of an open courtyard, usually having one side walled and the other an open arcade or colonnade.

cloistered arch (cloistered vault) A structure whose sides have the appearance of four quarter rounds fitted together so that the corner joints appear as an "X" when viewed from above.

cloistered vault *See* **cloistered arch**.

cloister garth An open courtyard surrounded by a cloister.

close-coupled tank and bowl

cloistral Of or pertaining to a cloister.

clone The reproduction of plant varieties by vegetative means, such as cuttings.

close (1) An enclosed place, such as the area around a cathedral. (2) A passage from a street to a court and the houses facing it. (3) The common stairway of an apartment building.

close-boarded (close-sheeted) (1) Sheathing with boards fitted tight against one another. (2) Privacy fencing in which adjacent boards are fitted tight against one another.

close-contact glue A glue that requires a tight contact between the surfaces that are to be bonded.

close couple Opposite rafters fastened at the peak and strengthened by a horizontal tie partway down their lengths.

close-coupled tank and bowl A toilet in which the bowl and water tank are manufactured separately and then bolted tightly together with only a gasket at the joint.

close-cut The trimming of a roof covering (shingle, tile, or slate) where adjacent surfaces of a hip or valley meet.

closed bidding *See* **closed competitive selection.**

closed-cell A type of foamed material in which each cell is totally enclosed and separate so that the bulk of the material will not soak up liquid like a sponge. Closed-cell material is characteristic of certain types or insulation board and flexible glazing gaskets.

closed-cell foam *See* **closed-cell.**

closed-circuit grouting A system of injection that fills all voids to be grouted at each hole and returns excess grout to the grouting apparatus.

closed-circuit television A television circuit with no broadcasting facilities and a limited number of reception stations. Transmission is typically between two points. Can be integrated into a Building Automation System and used for building security purposes.

closed competitive selection (closed bidding) A process of competitive bidding whereby the private owner limits the list of bidders to persons he has selected and invited to bid. *See also* **closed list of bidders.**

closed cornice A cornice that projects only slightly beyond a vertical wall so that there is no soffit. The overhang is filled by a crown molding.

closed eaves Projecting roof rafters that are boxed in.

closed list of bidders A list of those contractors who have been approved by the architect and owner as the only ones from whom bid prices will be accepted. *See also* **closed competitive selection.**

closed loop control An instrument that measures the changes in a controlled variable (temperature, pressure) and actuates the control device (valve, damper) to bring about a change.

closed loop system In Building Automation Systems, the arrangement of heating, ventilating, and air-conditioning components so that each component affects and can respond to the other, allowing system feedback.

closed newel The continuous central or inside wall of a circular staircase.

closed sheathing

closed valley

close nipple

closer

closed shaft A vertical opening in a building that is covered over or roofed at the top.

closed sheathing (closed sheeting) A continuous framework with boards or planks placed side by side to support or retain the sides of an excavation.

closed sheeting *See* **closed sheathing**.

closed shelving Shelving that can be concealed by closing a door or panel.

closed shop A term applied to a trade or skill that requires membership in a particular union to the exclusion of nonunion members.

closed specifications Specifications that require certain trade name products or proprietary processes. Provisions for alternatives are not included. *See also* **base bid specifications**.

closed stair (closed stair string, closed string) A stairway with covered strings on both sides so that the ends of the treads and risers are not visible. *See also* **box stair** *and* **close string**.

closed stair string *See* **closed stair**.

closed string *See* **closed stair**.

closed stringer *See* **close string**.

closed system Any heating or cooling system in which the circulating medium is not expended, but is recirculated through the system.

closed valley A roof covering in a roof valley laid so that the flashing is not visible.

close-grained Wood in which the annual growth rings are close together, thus indicating slow growth.

close nipple A short piece of pipe that is threaded from both ends, leaving no smooth outside surface.

closer (1) A mechanism for automatically closing a door. (2) The final masonry unit (brick, stone, or block) that completes a horizontal course. The unit may be whole or trimmed to size.

closer mold A wooden guide or jig for cutting closer bricks. *See also* **closer (2)**.

closer reinforcement A metal plate attached to a door and/or a frame to reinforce the area where a door closer is installed.

closer reinforcing sleeve A plate used to reinforce the corner joints of a metal door frame.

close-sheeted *See* **close-boarded**.

close string (close stringer, closed stringer, curb string, housed string) A stair string that has concealed tread and riser supports on its inside surface. The top and bottom edges of the string are straight and parallel. *See also* **closed stair**.

close stringer *See* **close string**.

close studding A method of construction in which studs are spaced close together and the intervening spaces are filled with plaster.

closet (1) A small room or recess for storing utensils or clothing. (2) A water closet.

closet bend The 90° soil pipe fitting installed beneath a toilet.

closet bolt A special bolt for securing a floor-mounted toilet to the floor and soil pipe flange.

closet lining Thin cedar boards with tongue-and-groove or lap edges, used to cover the inner surface of a closet in order to repel moths.

closing device

closing stile

coach bolt

close tolerance A term describing smaller allowable dimension deviation than would normally be allowed.

closet pole (closet rod) A strong rod mounted horizontally in a closet to support coat hangers.

closet rod *See* **closet pole**.

closet screw A screw used to hold a toilet floor flange to the floor.

closet stop valve The valve underneath a tank-type water closet. The valve is used to shut the water off so that repairs can be made to the flushing mechanism inside the tank.

close-up casement hinge A casement window support hinge with its pivot point placed so that when the window is open, there is a minimum space between the sash and the frame.

closing costs The costs associated with the sale/purchase of real estate property, such as legal fees, recording fees, and title search and insurance, but not including the cost of the property itself.

closing device (automatic closing device, self-closing device) (1) A mechanism that closes a door automatically and slowly after it has been opened. (2) A mechanism, usually fused, that releases and closes a fire door, damper, or shutter in the event of a fire.

closing stile The vertical side of a door or casement sash that seats against the jamb or frame when the door or window is closed.

closure bar A flat metal bar that is attached to a stair string next to a wall. The bar bridges or covers the opening between the string and the wall.

closure strip In metal building systems, a resilient strip used to cover openings between metal panels and flashing.

clothes chute (dirty linen chute) A vertical shaft commonly used in hospitals to drop dirty clothes and linens from one floor to another.

cloudiness A haziness or lack of transparency in a protective film such as in a varnish or urethane.

clout (1) A metal sheathing or protection plate on a moving wood member to protect it from wear. (2) A type of nail.

clout nail A nail with a large, flat head, a round shank, and a long, flattened point used on sheet metal and dry wallboard.

clustered column Two or more columns, joined together at the top and/or bottom, which share the structural load equally.

clustered pier A pier consisting of several shafts grouped together as a single unit, frequently surrounding a heavier central member.

cluster housing A planned residential development with dwelling units built close to one another and common open space for use by all residents.

clutch A friction or hydraulic coupling between a power source and a drive train.

coach bolt A bolt with a smooth, circular head. Rotation of the bolt in its hole during tightening is prevented by the square shoulder or neck under the head.

coach house (carriage house) A garage-like structure for the protection and storage of carriages.

coach screw A screw with a square head and a coarse pitched thread. *See also* **lag bolt**.

coak (1) A projection from the end of a piece of wood and used as a

coated base sheet

coat rack

tenon for inserting into a mating hole in another piece to form a joint. (2) A wooden pin used to hold beams together.

coal-tar pitch (tar) A black bituminous material made from the distillation of coal and used as a waterproofing material on built-up roofing and around elements that protrude through a roof.

coaming A raised frame or curb around a roof hatchway or skylight to prevent water from flowing in.

coarse aggregate Aggregate that will not pass through a 1/4″ sieve screen.

coarse filter A prefilter used in air-conditioning systems to remove large particles such as dust and lint. This type of filter is usually reusable after being vacuumed or washed.

coarse-grained (1) A term used to describe wood in which the annual growth rings are widely separated, thus indicating fast growth. *See also* **coarse-textured**. (2) The "pebbly" effect that sometimes occurs on a photographic enlargement.

coarse stuff A thick plaster intended for use as a base coat. Usually contains lime, sand, putty, and a fibrous material.

coarse-textured (coarse-grained) A term referring to a porous, open-grained wood that usually requires priming and filling to produce a smooth surface.

coat A single covering layer of any type of material, such as paint, plaster, stain, or surface sealant.

coated base felt *See* **coated base sheet**.

coated base sheet (coated base felt) The underlying sheet of asphalt-impregnated felt used in built-up roofing.

coated glass Insulating glass that has been treated to help retain building heat. Coated glass also blocks ultraviolet and infrared light.

coated nail A nail with a coating on it. The coating may be cement, copper, zinc, or enamel.

coat rack A piece of furniture that supports several coats (with or without hangers) and that may include a stand for umbrellas and a tray for galoshes.

coatroom (cloakroom) (1) A room for checking or storing outer garments, such as coats and hats, and usually located near the main entrance of a building.

coaxial cable A cable consisting of a tube of conducting material surrounding a central conductor. The tube is separated from contact with the cable by insulation. Coaxial cable is used to transmit telephone, telegraph, television, and computer signals.

cob A lump or piece of anything, such as coal, ore, or stone.

cobble *See* **cobblestone**.

cobblestone (cobble) (1) A stone, usually between 6″ and 10″ in diameter, used for paving roads and constructing foundations and walls. (2) A rough-cut, rectangular-shaped stone used for paving.

cob wall A wall formed of cob material, e.g., a mixture of clay, straw, and gravel.

cobwebbing In painting, the expulsion of fibrous strands of dried or partially dried paint from a spray gun.

cochlea (1) A spiral staircase. (2) The enclosure or tower for a spiral staircase.

cochleated Shaped like a spiral-shelled snail.

cock (1) A valve having a hole in a tapered plug. The plug is rotated to provide a passageway for fluid. (2) Any device that controls the flow of liquid or gas through a pipe. *See also* **sill cock** *and* **bibcock**.

cock bead A bead that projects higher than the adjacent surface.

cocking (cogging) The fitting together of notched timbers, beams, or pieces of wood to form a joint.

cocking piece A board attached to rafters at the eaves of a roof to give a slight upward tilt in order to break the straight roof line.

cockle stair A circular or spiral staircase.

cockloft An upper attic or loft.

cockscomb A piece of metal with a serrated edge used to scratch plaster and create a rough gripping surface for the next coat.

cockspur fastener A casement window catch.

coctile Building units made in an oven, such as brick or porcelain.

co-cumbustion The simultaneous combustion of two or more fuel types to produce useful energy.

code The legal requirements of local and other governing bodies concerning construction and occupancy. The enactment and enforcement of codes is intended to safeguard the public's health, safety, and welfare.

Code of Federal Regulations A uniform system of listing all the regulations promulgated by any federal agency.

code of practice A publication of an agreement by any trade or group of manufacturers of similar products, that lists minimum quality standards for material, workmanship, or conduct to be followed by group members.

coefficient of conductivity The measure of the rate at which a material will conduct thermal energy, or heat.

coefficient of discharge The measure of how efficiently a passage will allow air or water to flow through it.

coefficient of expansion For building materials, the increase in dimension per unit of length caused by a rise in temperature of one degree Fahrenheit, expressed in decimal form.

coefficient of friction A ratio of the force causing an object to slide to the total force perpendicular to the sliding plane. The ratio is a measure of the resistance to sliding.

coefficient of heat transmission *See* **coefficient of thermal transmission**.

coefficient of performance (1) In a heat pump, the ratio of heat produced to energy expended. (2) In a refrigeration system, the ratio of heat removed to energy expended.

coefficient of runoff The measure of gross storm water in a drainage system that is lost to evaporation, infiltration, and runoff.

coefficient of static friction The coefficient of friction required to make an object start sliding.

coefficient of subgrade reaction The ratio of load per unit area on soil to the correspondin deformation.

coefficient of thermal expansion *See* **coefficient of thermal transmission**.

coefficient of thermal transmission (coefficient of thermal expansion) The amount of heat passing through a partition per unit of area per degree difference in air temperature between the two sides of the partition. For example: Btu per square foot per hour per degree Fahrenheit.

cofferdam

coil

coffer (lacunar) (1) An ornamental recessed panel in the ceiling of a vault or dome. (2) A cofferdam; a caisson.

cofferdam A watertight enclosure used for foundation construction in waterfront areas. Water is pumped out of the cofferdam allowing free access to the work area.

coffering A ceiling with ornamental recessed panels.

cog (1) In a cogged joint, the portion of wood left where a beam has been notched. (2) A nib on roofing tiles.

cogeneration The simultaneous production of power and another form of useful thermal energy in a single process. A common example is the use of combustion or co-combustion processes to produce both electricity and steam or hot water.

cogged joint A joining of two pieces of wood, each of which has been notched to fit into the other.

cogging (cocking) The assembly of two pieces of wood that have been notched or cogged.

cohesion (1) In soils, the sticking together of particles. (2) In adhesives or sealants, the ability to stick together without cracking.

cohesionless soil A sod, such as clean sand, with no cohesive properties.

cohesive failure The internal shearing of a joint sealant that is weaker cohesively than the adhesion bond to the adjacent joint surfaces. The possible causes for failure include insufficient curing, excessive joint movement, improper joint dimensions, or improper selection of the sealant itself.

cohesive soil Soil that tends to hold together in a comparatively stable clump or mass, such as clay.

coil A term applied to a heat exchanger that uses connected pipes or tubing in rows, layers, or windings, as in steam heating, water heating, and refrigeration condensers and evaporators.

coiled expansion loop A gradual bend, loop, or coil of pipe or tube intended to absorb expansion and contraction caused by temperature changes. By flexing like a spring, undesirable stresses on the piping system are relieved or minimized.

coinsurance penalty The penalty against a policyholder for not carrying enough insurance on his or her property. In these cases, the full cost of the claim will not be paid by the insurance company. Repair contractors should be aware that the policyholder will have to pay a substantial part of the repair bill.

cold-air return In a heating system, the return air duct that transports cool air back into the system to be heated.

cold bending (cold gagging) The bending of any material without the application of heat to soften it. Some ductile materials can be bent in this manner without fracturing.

cold-cathode lamp An electric-discharge lamp that operates with low current, high voltage, and low temperature. The color of the light depends on the vapor used in the lamp.

cold cellar An underground storage area where fruit and vegetables are stored during the winter. The constant ground temperature keeps the contents from freezing and retards rotting.

cold check Fine cracks that appear in some wood finishes, such as paint and varnish, after being subjected to alternating warm and cold temperatures.

cold chisel A steel chisel with a tempered edge for cutting cold steel.

cold cutter A cold chisel with an offset handle like a hammer for holding it during striking with a maul.

cold deck (cold duct) In an HVAC system, the source of cold air for cooling interior zones.

cold-drawn A process in which metal is formed in shape and size by being pulled through dies while cold. This type of metal forming has an effect on final surface finish and hardness and is often used in the manufacture of wire, tubing, and rods.

cold-driven rivet A rivet that is driven and formed without being preheated.

cold-finished bar A metal bar that has been drawn or rolled to its final dimensions while cold. The process of cold finishing produces a hard, smooth, surface finish.

cold-finished steel Any steel shape that is rolled, drawn, or forged to its final shape and size when cold. The resulting finish is hard and smooth.

cold flow The continuing permanent change in slope of a structural system under constant load.

cold gagging See **cold bending**.

cold glue A glue that flows and bonds without being heated.

cold joint The joint between two consecutive pours of concrete if the time elapsed between the first and second pours is such that the first pour has started to set.

cold-laid mixture Any mixture that may spread at ambient temperatures without being preheated.

cold mix (cold patch) An asphaltic concrete made with slow-curing asphalts and used primarily as a temporary patching material when hot mix plants are closed. Cold mix is used to repair potholes, but is less durable than hot mix.

cold molding (1) Material that is shaped at ambient temperature and hardened by baking. (2) The material that is used in the cold-molding process.

cold patch See **cold mix**.

cold pie Mortar left over after laying a masonry unit.

cold-process roofing Built-up roofing consisting of layers of asphalt-impregnated felts that are bonded and sealed with a cold application of asphalt-based roof cement.

cold riveting Riveting done without preheating the rivets.

cold-rolled Descriptive of a metal shape that has been formed by rolling at room temperature, thus giving a dense, smooth, surface finish and high tensile strength.

cold room A walk-in refrigerator for storage of perishable materials.

cold saw A saw for cutting metal at room temperature. A cold saw may be either circular or reciprocating.

cold set A hardened hand tool used to flatten sheet metal seams.

cold-setting adhesive A glue that sets at ambient room temperature.

cold solder A soft-metal, air-hardening material used for bonding two metals at ambient temperatures. Cold solder, unlike a true solder, does not require a hot bond.

cold-solder joint An electrical wiring joint in which the metals to be joined have not been heated enough for the solder to bond.

cold-start lamp A fluorescent lamp that is started with high voltage

collar

collar tie

colonial casing

without having to preheat the electrodes.

cold strength The compressive or flexural strength of refractory concrete prior to firing.

cold-water paint Paint in which the pigment and binder are mixed in cold water.

cold welding The process of fusing together two pieces of metal that have had their common faces well cleaned and are then held in contact under high pressure. No heat is applied in cold welding.

cold-worked steel Steel that has been rolled, drawn, or formed to achieve permanent deformation at room temperature.

collar (1) A flashing for a metal vent or chimney where it passes through a roof. (2) A trim piece to cover the hole where a vent goes through a wall or ceiling. (3) A metal band that encircles a metal or wooden shaft.

collar beam The horizontal board that joins the approximate midpoints of two opposite rafters in order to increase rigidity.

collar beam roof (collar roof) A roof with rafters connected by collar beams.

collaring The pointing of masonry or tile joints under overhangs.

collar joint The joint between the collar beam and roof rafters.

collar roof *See* **collar beam roof.**

collar tie A horizontal tie connecting pairs of opposite rafters near the ridge of the roof.

collected plants Plantings that have been gathered from locations other than nursery stock.

collimator A surveyor's tool used to align lines along a parallel plane.

colloid Any substance divided into fine particles that range in diameter from 0.2 to 0.005 microns. When the substance is mixed in a liquid, it remains in suspension.

colloidal concrete Concrete that is a mix of aggregate and colloidal grout.

colloidal grout A mortar mix grout whose solid particles are in a fixed suspension.

colloidal mixer A mixing machine for making colloidal grout.

collusion A secret agreement or action of a fraudulent, illegal, or deceitful nature.

colombage Timber construction using half timbers, that is, members measuring not less than 5″ x 10″ in cross section.

colonial architecture (1) An architectural style from a mother country that has been incorporated into the buildings of settlements or colonies in distant locations. (2) 18th-century English Georgian architecture as reproduced in the original colonies of the United States.

colonial casing A style of door and window trim molding.

colonial panel door A type of door with recessed panels.

colonial revival An architectural style popular in the United States during the end of the 19th century. The style copied designs and details from 18th-century English Georgian colonist buildings.

colonial siding Exterior siding material consisting of wide, square-edged boards applied as clapboards.

colonnade A row of evenly spaced columns that usually support one side or end of a roof.

column

column baseplate

column clamp

color chart A standardized card or folder showing a display of colors or finishes.

colored aggregate Aggregate material that has been selected for use because of its natural color.

colored cement Cement that contains a colored pigment.

colored concrete Concrete mixed with colored cement or to which pigment has been added during mixing.

colored finishes A finish obtained by adding pigment or colored aggregate to plaster for a final coat so that the color goes through the full depth of the coat.

colorimetric test A diagnostic test undertaken to determine the amount of inorganic matter in a substance, such as in a concrete aggregate.

color pigment Any substance that can be mixed with a suitable liquid (vehicle), to color paints or stains.

color rendering index (CRI) A measure of the quality of a light, where the ability of the light to render an object's true color(s) is compared to that of a reference light. Under a lamp with a low CRI rating, colors will appear unnatural.

color retention The capability of a surface finish to maintain its original shade and intensity over a period of time and/or exposure to sunlight or weather.

color temperature The actual degree measurement, in Kelvin, of the color of a light source.

column A long, relatively slender, supporting pillar. A column is usually loaded axially in compression.

column baseplate A bearing plate beneath a column that distributes

the load coming down through the column over a wider area.

column capital (column head) The enlarged cross-sectional area at the top of a column.

column clamp A latching device for holding the sections of a concrete column form together while the concrete is being placed.

column footing The foundation under a column that spreads the load out to an area large enough so that the bearing capacity of the soil is not exceeded and differential settling does not occur.

column head *See* **column capital**.

column schedule A production plan outlining the construction of columns in a structure. Provides column sizes, elevations (top and bottom), and type and size of reinforcement required.

column ties Steel reinforcement surrounding the vertical reinforcement in a concrete column to align the bars and provide additional strength. May be rectangular or ring-shaped.

comb (1) A tool used to produce a rough surface or pattern in plaster or concrete. (2) A comb board.

comb board A board with notches on its upper edge, used to cover the joint at the ridge of a pitched roof.

comb cut A vertical cut similar to the cut on the end of a rafter where it is joined to a ridgeboard.

combed Descriptive of a surface that has been raked with a comb to produce a rough or patterned finish.

combed-finish tile Tile with a serrated rear face to provide a stronger grip with the bonding mastic.

combed joint A joint made by fitting together the ends of two

combination door

combination faucet

combined footing

pieces of wood that have been cut with a deep V-pattern, thus giving the joint a zigzag appearance.

comb-grained A term used to describe a piece of wood that has been sawn so that the growth rings are at a 45° angle to the wide face viewed from the end.

combination blade A circular saw blade suitable for both rip and cross cuts.

combination column A column of structural steel encased in concrete and designed so that each material carries a portion of the total load.

combination door An exterior door that has interchangeable panels of glazing and screening—one for summer and the other for winter use.

combination faucet A faucet that is connected to both hot- and cold-water supply pipes so that the water it dispenses can be of the desired temperature.

combination fixture (1) A combination kitchen and laundry sink in a single unit, with both deep and shallow bowls side by side. (2) An institutional or prison fixture that combines the functions of a sink and toilet into a single fixture.

combination plane A carpenter's or joiner's hand tool that has interchangeable blades or guides so that it can be used for various shaping operations.

combination pliers Any of several styles of pliers that can be used for cutting, swaging, or hammering, as well as for gripping.

combination square A carpenter's hand tool with a head that slides along a metal rule and may be locked at any location. The head has 90° and 45° angle surfaces, a bubble level, and a scribe pin.

combination waste and vent system A plumbing system with an oversized waste pipe that also serves as a vent pipe.

combination window A window with replaceable screen and glass inserts for summer and winter use.

combination wrench A wrench with open-end jaws on one end and closed-end jaws on the other.

combined aggregate A mixture of both fine and coarse aggregate used in concrete.

combined-aggregate grading The proportions of fine and coarse aggregate in a mix design.

combined building sewer A sewer system that handles both sewage and storm water.

combined footing A footing that receives loading from more than one column or load-supporting element.

combined frame A doorway with a fixed panel of glass on either or both sides of the door.

combined load The total of all the loads (live, dead, wind, snow, etc.) on a structure.

combined sewer A sewer that receives both storm water and sewage.

combined stresses A condition of stress loading that cannot be represented by a single resultant stress.

combing (1) The act of dressing a stone surface. (2) The use of a serrated comb or brush to create a surface pattern or roughness in paint, plaster, or concrete. (3) Those shingles on a roof that project above the ridge line. (4) The top ridge on a roof.

combplate The fixed floor plate at either end of an escalator or moving

common bond

walkway that has fingers that project into the serrations of the moving segments to prevent an object from wedging into the seam.

combustible   Descriptive of a substance that will burn in the air, pressure, and temperature conditions of a burning building.

combustion   A rapid chemical process, such as oxidation, that produces significant thermal energy (heat), and usually light as well.

come-along   A portable ratcheting winch consisting of a fastening device on one end and a hook attached to a cable at the other end. Operating a lever turns a drum, which tightens up the cable and exerts a pulling force on the hook.

comfort chart   A chart showing the limits of human comfort for various combinations of temperature, relative humidity, and circulating air velocity.

comfort station   A building or area with toilet and sink fixtures available for public use.

comfort zone   The range of effective temperatures over which a majority of adults will feel comfortable.

commercial bronze   A corrosion-resistant weatherstripping material made from an alloy of copper and zinc.

commercial projected window   A type of steel window used in commercial and industrial applications where decorative trims and moldings are not used. A projected window has one or more panels that rotate either inward or outward on a horizontal axis.

commercial tolerances   Allowable variations in the dimensions of items mass-produced for the commercial market.

comminution   To reduce to minute particles, as in the grinding of coal or the screening of sewage.

commissioning   The process of ensuring that the complex array of equipment that provides lighting, heating, cooling, ventilation and other amenities in facilities works together effectively and efficiently. Commissioning typically begins during the facility's conceptual design phase and ideally continues throughout the life of the facility.

Committee for Industrial Organizations (CIO)   A labor union organized in 1935 for the purpose of representing industrial workers. The CIO was created as a result of a dispute with the American Federation of Labor (AFL). John L. Lewis, president of United Mine Workers and a member of the CIO, was instrumental in merging the AFL and CIO in 1955.

commode step   On a staircase, the bottom step or steps that curve out around the newel post and are wider than the other steps.

common area   An area in or adjacent to a building or group of buildings for the use of tenants, such as a courtyard, entry area, lounge, or recreation area.

common ashlar   A rough-dressed block of stonemasonry.

common bond (American bond)   A brick masonry wall pattern in which a header course of brick is laid after every five or six stretcher courses.

common brass   A copper-zinc alloy of which 30% to 40% is zinc. It is relatively inexpensive, very ductile, and readily worked.

common brick   Brick not selected for color or texture, but instead used as filler or backing. Though usually not less durable nor of lower quality than face brick, common brick

common joist

common nail

compactor

typically costs less. Greater dimensional variations are also permitted. *See also* **building brick**.

common dovetail (box dovetail, through dovetail) A corner joint of interlacing wedge-shaped fingers of wood. The ends of each finger show through at the edge.

common ground A strip of wood recessed in a masonry or concrete wall to provide a surface to which something else can be nailed.

common joist (bridging joist) One of a series of parallel beams laid on edge to support a floor or ceiling.

common lap In roofing, an offset of one-half a shingle width for alternate rows of shingles.

common lime Hydrated lime or quick lime used in plaster or mortar.

common lumber Lumber with a number of knots, splits, blemishes, or other defects.

common nail A general-purpose, headed nail with a diamond-shaped point used where appearance is not important, as in framing.

common rafter (intermediate rafter, spar) A wood framing member that reaches from the rafter plate at the eaves to the ridge board.

common vent (dual vent) A plumbing vent that connects at the junction of two fixture drains and serves as a vent for both fixtures.

common wall (1) A wall built on the boundary between separate lots of land so that it does not belong completely to either owner. (2) A party wall between dwellings in a condominium or row house.

communicating frame A frame for two side-by-side, single-swing doors that open in opposite directions.

community antenna television (CATV) A single source of television signals transmitted to multiple receivers. Used in buildings that have television cables. Can be integrated in the building's communications system.

community planning *See* **city planning**.

compacted volume The volume of any mass of material after it has been compressed, particularly soil in an embankment or fill area.

compact fluorescent lamp A small fluorescent lamp with a life about ten times longer than incandescent lamps. Brand names include "Biax" (GE®), "Dulux" (Osram®), and "PL" (Phillips®).

compacting factor The ratio of the weight of concrete that has been gravity-filled in a cylinder to the weight of compacted concrete in a similar cylinder.

compaction (1) The compression of any material into a smaller volume; for example, waste compaction. In specifying compaction of embankment or fill, a percent compaction at optimum moisture content is often used. Another method is to specify the equipment, height of lift, and number of passes. (2) The elimination of voids in construction materials, as in concrete, plaster, or soil, by vibration, tamping, rolling, or some other method or combination of methods.

compaction tests Tests employed to determine the density of a soil.

compaction pile A pile driven into the ground to compact soil and increase its bearing capacity.

compactor A machine that compresses or compacts materials by using hydraulic force, weight, or vibration.

companion flange A flat, plate-like pipe connection device that is

141

compass

drilled and machined to match another flange on a pipe or fitting.

compartment One of the parts, divisions, or sections into which an enclosed space is divided.

compartmentation The containment of smoke within a building by using a system of barriers and compartments.

compartment ceiling A ceiling that has been divided into decorative panels, usually surrounded by moldings.

compass (1) An instrument for locating the magnetic north pole of the earth. (2) A mechanical drawing device used to draw circles.

compass brick A curved brick used in circular patterns or to form an arch.

compass-headed arch A semicircular arch.

compass plane A carpenter's plane with a curved baseplate and/or blade for finishing curved wood pieces.

compass rafter A rafter with one or both sides curved.

compass roof A roof built out of curved rafters.

compass saw (keyhole saw) A small tapering handsaw used to cut rounded shapes or circles.

compass survey A surveyor's traverse using bearings determined by a compass, as opposed to bearings determined by recording the angles turned by the instrument.

compass window A window that projects outward from the face of a wall. Similar to a *bow window*.

compass work (circular work) Carpentry or joinery based on a circular or curved motif.

compatibility agent A substance that, when added to another

substance, improves the stability and even distribution of that substance. For example, compatibility agents allow the simultaneous application of a pesticide and fertilizer, or two or more pesticides.

compatible wastes Wastes that, when mixed together, will not cause an adverse chemical reaction.

compensation (1) The amount paid for goods, labor, or services provided. (2) An amount paid to settle a claim for damages.

compensatory damages An award for damages intended to compensate the plaintiff by granting a monetary amount equal to the loss or injury suffered.

completed operations An insurance term referring to coverage for personal injuries or damage to property that occurs after construction has been completed. At least one of the following conditions must be met: all activities governed by the contract are finished; all activities at one project site are finished; or that part of the project which precipitated the claim is in use by the owner. This insurance does not cover the actual finished project itself.

complete fusion In welding, a total merging of the welded surfaces, including all of the weld filler material.

completion bond (construction bond, contract bond) The guarantee by a bonding company that a contract will be completed and will be clear of all liens and encumbrances.

completion date The date certified by the architect when the work in a building, or a designated portion thereof, is sufficiently complete, in accordance with the contract documents, so that the owner can

composite beam

composite construction

composite door

composition roofing

occupy the work or a designated portion thereof for the use for which it is intended.

completion list (punch list) The final list of items of work to be completed or corrected by the contractor.

complimentary bid A bid that is intentionally high. May be illegal if collusion is intended.

compo A slang term referring to any type of composition material.

composite arch An arch formed from three or four centers of curvature.

composite beam A beam combining different materials to work as a single unit, such as structural steel and concrete or cast-in-place and precast concrete.

composite board See **composition board**.

composite column A column designed to combine two different materials or two different grades of material to form a structural member. A structural steel shape may be filled with concrete, or a structural steel member for reinforcing may be encased in concrete.

composite construction A building constructed of various building materials, or by using more than one construction method, such as a structural steel frame with a precast roof, or a masonry structure with a laminated wood beam roof.

composite door A door with a wooden or metal shell over a lightweight core. The core is usually made of foam or a material that is shaped like a honeycomb cell.

composite fire door A door made of metal or chemically treated wood surrounding a core material. The

door is rated as resistant to fire for some specified period of time.

composite girder A girder assembled from component parts of similar or different materials; for example, a plate girder or a bar joist with wooden flanges.

composite joint (1) A joint that is secured by using more than one method, such as riveting and welding. (2) In plumbing, a general reference to joining bell-and-spigot pipe with packing materials such as rope and rosin, or cement and hemp.

composite panel See **composition board**.

composite pile A pile consisting of more than one member or material, but designed to act as one unit.

composite truss A load-supporting framework of several members. Those members in compression are made of wood; the tension members are usually made of steel.

composite wall A wall composed of multiple vertical layers of masonry, each one unit thick, in which one layer is different from the others in type or grade of stone/brick or mortar used.

composition board (composite board) A manufactured board consisting of any of several materials, usually pressed together with a binder. Composition board is frequently used as sheathing, wall board, or as an insulation or acoustical barrier.

composition joint A bell and spigot pipe joint that is sealed with a combination of materials, such as oakum and rosin or cement.

composition roofing (built-up roofing) A roof consisting of several layers, thicknesses, or pieces.

composition shingles

compound wall

composition shingles (asphalt shingles) Shingles made from felt impregnated and covered with asphalt, and then coated on the exposed side with colored granules.

compost A mixture of organic materials that have decomposed in a humus or earthen material. Used as a lightener and fertilizer when added to soil.

compound action snips A hand tool similar to tin snips used to cut sheet metal.

compound arch A built-up arch, or one having the appearance of several concentric arches.

compound beam (built-up beam) A beam consisting of smaller components that have been assembled and fastened together to function as a single unit.

compound pier (compound pillar) A column usually consisting of one central shaft surrounded by secondary shafts, or by two or more equal shafts working in conjunction with one another.

compound pillar *See* **compound pier.**

compound wall A wall constructed of more than one material.

compreg *See* **compregnated wood.**

compregnated wood (compressed wood, densified impregnated wood, resin-treated wood) Wood that has been impregnated with a resin under pressure and then cured. This process improves the strength and rot resistance of the wood.

Comprehensive Environmental Response, Compensation, and Liability Act (CERCLA) A federal law defining the government actions in the event of an uncontrolled release of hazardous materials into the environment.

comprehensive general liability insurance A type of insurance that provides blanket coverage for all types of liability with the exception of those specifically excluded. It covers contractural liability as well as unforeseen future hazards, and may also include automobile coverage. Completed operations liability, more extensive contractural coverage, and product liability insurance can be added to this type of policy.

comprehensive services Those services provided by an engineer or architect that encompass both the usual duties, and other professional services, such as project analysis and management, land use and feasibility studies, and financial and other consulting services.

compressed cork Cork that has been ground up and then pressed with a binder into a desired shape or sheet. Compressed cork is used as a vibration or sound absorber, as a wall covering, and for many other commercial and industrial applications.

compressed fiberboard Wood fiber that has been compressed into sheets and is commonly used as a paneling material.

compressed straw slab A board manufactured from straw compressed with a binder and cured.

compressed wood (compregnated wood, densified impregnated wood, resin-treated wood) Wood that has been impregnated with resin or other materials and then compressed under high pressure to increase its strength, density, and rot resistance.

compressibility The ease with which a fluid is reduced in volume by the application of pressure.

compression bearing joint

compressor

compression Structurally, it is the force that pushes together or crushes, as opposed to tension, which is the force that pulls apart.

compression bearing joint A joint consisting of a structural member in compression, pressing or bearing against another member also in compression.

compression chiller A system in which water is cooled by liquid refrigerant that vaporizes at a low pressure and proceeds into a compressor. The compressor increases the gas pressure so that it may be condensed in the condenser.

compression faucet A faucet that controls flow by compressing a washer against a valve seat. Compression facuets usually have two handles and a single spout.

compression flange The upper flange of a beam. If loaded as a simple span, the top flange will be in compression, and the bottom flange will be in tension.

compression joint (1) A bell and spigot joint that becomes watertight when the spigot is pressed into a compression gasket in the bell. (2) Any joint that is engineered to employ pressure as a seal.

compression molding A method of molding plastic in which the plastic material is injected into a metal mold under heat and pressure.

compression set (1) The permanent shortened or flattened condition of any material that has been compressed beyond its yield point, and thus cannot return to its original size and shape. (2) The permanent imprint in a compression gasket.

compression tank In a hot water heating system, a tank that absorbs the water pressure exerted.

compression test (1) A test of any material by compression to determine its useful strength characteristics. The test is most often performed in accordance with standards published by the American Society for Testing and Materials, or some other professional or industrial organization. (2) A determination of the compression developed in each cylinder of an internal combustion engine.

compression valve A valve that controls flow by compressing a washer against a valve seat.

compressive strength The resistance capacity of any material, but especially structural members, to crushing force. Compressive strength is usually expressed as the maximum number of pounds per square inch that can be resisted without failure.

compressive stress The resistance of a material to an external pushing or shortening force.

compressor (1) A machine that compresses air or gases. (2) In refrigeration/air conditioning, a machine that compresses a refrigerant gas, which then goes to an evaporator. (3) A truck- or trailer-mounted apparatus, usually diesel-driven, that generates compressed air for demolition hammers, sandblasting and similar needs on a construction site.

computation Same as calculation, but more formal.

computer-aided design (computer-aided design and drafting) The use of computer technology to analyze, design or model a building or system. Allows for greater efficiency and consistency, faster reproduction, and easier alteration than traditional methods.

concave joint

(plan)

(elevation)

concrete (symbols)

concrete block

computer-aided facilities management (CAFM) *See* **computerized maintenance management software**.

computerized maintenance management software (CMMS) The use of computer technology to schedule plant and equipment maintenance, track assets, and efficiently carry out overall facility management. The purpose of CMMS is to simplify the planning and administrative functions of maintenance, purchasing, and inventory management.

concave joint A masonry joint formed by a curved pointing tool and used particularly on exterior masonry walls.

concealed hinge A hinge mortised into both the jamb and edge of a door so that it is hidden when the door is closed.

concentric load *See* **centric load**.

concentric tendon One of several steel cables or rods that run through the center of gravity of a prestressed concrete member, thus placing it in compression.

concourse An open area for the circulation of large crowds within a building, as in an airport terminal or shopping mall.

concrete A composite material consisting of sand, coarse aggregate (gravel, stone, or slag), cement, and water. When mixed and allowed to harden, it forms a stone-like material.

concrete admixture A special substance or chemical added to a concrete mix. Typically, an admixture is used to control setting, entrain air, impart color, control workability, or to waterproof.

concrete aggregate Granular mineral material that is mixed with cement and water to form concrete.

concrete, air-entrained Concrete containing minute air bubbles that improve its workability and frost resistance.

concrete block A masonry building unit of concrete that has been cast into a standard shape, size, and style.

concrete bond (bond plaster) A thin gypsum plaster coat applied to a concrete face as a base for subsequent coats of plaster.

concrete collar (doughnut) A ring of reinforced concrete cast around an existing column and used to jack up the column.

concrete, confined Reinforced concrete with restraints implemented that are perpendicular to the applied strength.

concrete containment structure A structure made of reinforced concrete to safely contain hazardous materials.

concrete contraction The shrinkage of concrete that occurs as it cures and dries.

concrete curing compound A chemical applied to the surface of fresh concrete to minimize the loss of moisture during the first stages of setting and hardening.

concrete, cyclopean A mass concrete placement into which large stones weighing 100 pounds or more are placed.

concrete cylinder test A compression test for concrete strength. Wet samples of concrete are carefully placed in specially made containers 6″ in diameter and 12″ high. The cylinders are sent to a laboratory where a compression test is performed. This is done by putting the concrete in a hydraulic machine that measures the pressure(s) needed to crush it. Cylinder tests are usually

concrete
finishing machine

concrete insert

performed for each pour on a project that requires concrete strength control.

concrete, derated Concrete that has had a gas-forming chemical added to it so that when it sets it contains many air holes and is lightweight. *See also* **concrete, foamed.**

concrete, dry-packed Concrete with only a small amount of moisture, so that it must be rammed in place in order to be compacted.

concrete, fibrous Concrete into which fibrous material, such as glass fibers, has been mixed to increase tensile strength while reducing weight. *See also* **fibrous concrete.**

concrete finish The smoothness, texture, or hardness of a concrete surface. Floors are trowelled with steel blades to compress the surface into a dense protective coat. Walls that are exposed to the weather are often ground with a carborundum stone or wheel, with cement then added to fill the small voids. A smooth surface is desired so that water cannot enter the small holes, freeze, and deteriorate the surface.

concrete finishing machine (1) A portable machine with large paddles like fan blades used to float and finish concrete floors and slabs. (2) A large power-driven machine mounted on wheels that ride on steel pavement forms. Used to finish concrete pavements.

concrete floor hardener An additive used to impart extra wear and chip resistance to concrete floors. The additive may be placed in the mix before the floor is cast, or it may be applied to the surface in liquid or granular form.

concrete, foamed Concrete to which a chemical foaming agent has been added. The result is a light, porous material, full of air holes, with low

strength and good thermal properties. *See also* **foamed concrete.**

concrete gun A hand-controlled tool at the end of a hose for injecting or spraying concrete by pneumatic pressure.

concrete insert A device, such as a pipe sleeve, a threaded bolt, or a nailing block, that is attached to a concrete form before placing concrete. When the concrete forms are removed, the insert remains embedded in the concrete.

concrete, in-situ (cast-in-place) Concrete cast in its final location in the finished structure. *See also* **cast-in-place concrete** *and* **in-situ concrete.**

concrete masonry (1) Concrete blocks laid with mortar or grout in a manner similar to bricks. (2) Concrete that may be poured in place or as special tilt-up building walls.

concrete mixer (cement mixer) A machine that mixes cement, aggregate, and water to make concrete. The components are loaded into a rotating drum.

concrete nail A steel nail that has been hardened and fitted with a diamond point so that it can be driven into concrete without bending.

concrete, normal weight Concrete made with the standard mix of component materials and weighing approximately 148 lbs. per cu. ft. *See also* **normal weight concrete.**

concrete paint *See* **cement paint.**

concrete paver (1) A machine used to pave roads with concrete. A paver is equipped with a loading skip, a rotating drum, and a discharge boom. (2) A precast paving block used in landscaping for walks and patios.

147

concrete pile

concrete pump

concrete saw

condenser

concrete pile A slender, precast concrete-reinforced member that is embedded in the soil by driving, jetting, or insertion into a predrilled hole. May or may not be prestressed.

concrete planer A machine with cutters or grinders used to level and refinish old concrete pavement.

concrete plank A hollow-core or solid, flat beam used for floor or roof decking. Concrete planks are usually precast and prestressed.

concrete, preplaced-aggregate Coarse aggregate placed in a form, with Portland cement grout injected later. *See also* **preplaced-aggregate concrete**.

concrete, prestressed Concrete members with internal tendons that have been tensioned to put a compressive load on the members. When a load is applied to a prestressed member, compression is decreased where tension would normally occur. *See also* **prestressed concrete**.

concrete pump A pump that forces premixed concrete through a hose to a desired location.

concrete, ready-mixed (transit-mixed) Concrete delivered to a site, mixed and ready for placement. *See also* **ready-mixed concrete** *and* **transit-mixed concrete**.

concrete reinforcement Metal bars, rods, or wires placed within formwork before concrete is added. The concrete and the reinforcement are designed to act as a single unit in resisting forces.

concrete saw A power saw used, for example, to cut concrete in order to remove damaged sections of pavement or to groove the surface to create a control joint.

concrete slump test A test to determine the plasticity of concrete. A sample of wet concrete is placed in a cone-shaped container 12" high. The cone is removed by slowly pulling it upward. If the concrete flattens out into a pile only 4" high, it is said to have an 8" slump. This test is done on the job site. If more water is added to the concrete mix, the strength of the concrete decreases and the slump increases.

concurrent delay The occurrence of more than one delay in the same period of time.

concurrent insurance Insurance under two or more policies that are exactly alike in their terms and conditions, even though they might be different in the dollar amounts of coverage or the dates the policies begin. (Nonconcurrent insurance differs in the terms and conditions as well.) This condition can complicate the collection process for contractors.

condemnation (1) A declaration by the appropriate local governing authority that a structure is no longer fit or safe to use. (2) The seizure of private property by a governmental authority in order to use that property for some public purpose, as in the exercise of eminent domain.

condensation The conversion of moisture in the air to water, as in the formation of water droplets on the outside of cold pipes.

condenser The heat exchanger in a refrigeration system that removes heat from the high pressure refrigerant gas and transforms it into a cool liquid.

condensing unit In a refrigeration system, the mechanism that pumps vaporized refrigerant from the

conductor

conduit

evaporator, compresses and liquifies it, and returns it to the refrigerant control. Includes the compressor, condenser, condenser fan motor, and controls.

conditions of the contract A document detailing the rights, responsibilities, and relationships of the parties to the contract for construction.

condominium A legal system by which individual units of real property, such as apartments, stores, or offices, may be owned separately. Each unit owner obtains all the rights incidental to ownership of real property, and shares with the other owners rights to the common areas in the building, facilities, or land of the condominium.

conduction *See* **thermal conduction**.

conductive flooring Flooring designed to prevent electrostatic buildup and sparking. Typical uses include floors in computer areas and hospital operating rooms.

conductive mortar A tile mortar to which electric-conductive material has been added.

conductive rubber An abrasion-resistant, highly conductive rubber with great anti-static properties. Used in switches, keypads, and telecommunications assemblies.

conductor (1) Any substance that can serve as a medium for transmitting light, heat, or sound. (2) In electricity, a wire or cable that can carry an electric current. (3) A pipe that leads rainwater to a drain.

conduit (cable conduit) (1) A pipe, tube, or channel used to direct the flow of a fluid. (2) A pipe or tube used to enclose electric wires to protect them from damage.

conduit body The portion of a conduit or tubing system that makes the interior of the system accessible at a junction or terminal point.

cone crusher An aggregate crusher that employs the action of a revolving cone on an eccentric bearing, inside a concave bowl with crusher plates.

cone of depression The area surrounding and impacted by an extraction well. Groundwater flow, volume and pressure are all affected.

cone of recharge The area surrounding and impacted by an injection well. Injected water flow, volume and pressure are all affected.

confidentiality agreement A legal document that allows the release of trade secret information to physicians and others who may need this information to protect workers from danger or to treat an exposed worker.

configurated glass (figured glass) Glass that has a surface pattern impressed into it during manufacture to diffuse light or to obscure vision (for example, the glazing found on bathroom windows).

conglomerate A rock deposit consisting of stones of varying sizes naturally cemented together as a natural concretion.

conifer Any of an order of mostly evergreen trees and shrubs, including those with true cones, such as pines, and those with arillate fruit, such as yews.

connected load The total load, as measured in watts, that is connected to an electric supply system if all lights and equipment are turned on.

connector A device that will hold two or more electrical wires in close contact and can be quickly and easily removed.

consequential damages Losses that do not flow directly from the actions of the defendant, but rather are the result of special or remote circumstances relating to those actions.

conservation In the context of historic buildings, efforts to bring old building finishes and features to a condition as close as possible to their original state when new. Conservation also involves planning and carrying out maintenance practices that will ensure the best appearance and condition of the building and its features for as long as possible.

consideration The price, motive, or benefit that induces parties to form a contract. A contract is not legally enforceable without consideration.

consistency A reference to the relative mobility or plasticity of freshly mixed concrete or mortar, as measured by a slump test for concrete, and by a flow test for mortar and grout.

consistometer A device for measuring the firmness or consistency of concrete, mortar, grout, plaster, etc.

console (1) A control station with switches and gauges to govern the operation of mechanical, electrical, or electromechanical equipment. (2) An ornamental bracket-like member used to support a cornice.

consolidated formation Soil strata that may have been subjected to glacial or other consolidating loads in the geological past.

consolidation (1) Compaction of freshly poured concrete by tamping, rodding, or vibrating to eliminate voids and to ensure total envelopment of aggregate and reinforcement. (2) Compaction of soil in an embankment to achieve a higher bearing strength.

constant-voltage transformer A transformer designed to minimize or eliminate the variations in standard line voltage and to produce an unchanging voltage, as required by computers and some instrumentation.

constant volume reheat An HVAC system in which the volume of the supply air is unchanged, while the supply air temperature is raised as the local zone cooling load decreases.

constant-wattage ballast An efficient lamp ballast that provides high power factor by minimizing the effects of voltage variations.

construction administrator One who oversees the fulfillment of the responsibilities of all parties to the contract for construction, for the primary benefit of the owner. In the typical project, construction administration is usually provided by the design professional. However, the owner may employ a separate professional entity for this purpose.

Construction Advisory Committee A special committee established by Congress to advise the Secretary of Labor on matters affecting the health and safety of construction workers.

construction bond *See* **completion bond**.

construction documents The written specifications and drawings that provide the requirements of a construction project.

construction drawings The portion of the contract documents that gives a graphic representation of the work to be done in the construction of a project.

construction joint

construction wrench

contact ceiling

construction-grade lumber
Good quality lumber that is generally free of defects.

construction joint The interface or meeting surface between two successive pours of concrete.

construction manager One who directs the process of construction, either as the agent of the owner, as the agent of the contractor, or as one who, for a fee, directs and coordinates construction activity carried out under separate or multiple prime contracts.

constructive acceleration
A requirement that the contractor complete his work earlier than the contract time, including time extensions to which he is entitled because of excusable delays.

construction wrench A wrench with a handle and jaw at one end for holding or turning fasteners, pipes and fittings. The other end is pointed and is used to align mating holes in steel construction.

constructive change A change to a contract resulting from conduct by the owner that has the effect of requiring the contractor to perform work different from that presented in the contract.

constructive eviction An unlawful act by a landlord that makes a rented property uninhabitable.

constructor One who is in the business of managing the construction process. A contractor is a constructor who is acting under the terms of a contract for construction.

consultant A person (or organization) with an area of expertise or professional training who contracts to perform a service.

consulting engineer A licensed engineer, employed to perform specific engineering tasks.

Consumer Products Safety Act
A federal law passed in 1972 that establishes standards of safety for consumer products.

contact adhesive (dry-bond adhesive)
A bonding agent that is applied to two surfaces and allowed to dry before being pressed together.

contact ceiling A ceiling that is attached directly to the construction above, with no intermediate furring strips.

contact pressure The pressure or force that a footing and the structure it supports exerts on the soil below.

contact splice A connection between concrete reinforcing bars where the bars are lapped and in direct contact with each other.

containment box A temporary container for hazardous liquid spills.

containment berm A physical barrier used to keep liquids from running outside of a protected area.

continental seating Seats placed in an auditorium in continuous rows having no aisles or crossovers. Access is from either a wall aisle or though the doors in the side walls.

contingency An amount included in the construction budget to cover the cost of unforeseen factors related to construction.

contingency allowance A specified sum included in the contract sum to be used at the owner's discretion, and with his approval, to pay for any element or service that was unforeseen or that is desirable but not specifically required of the contractor by the construction documents.

continuous footing

contingent agreement An agreement in which a part of an individuals compensation is payable only if a particular condition is met, such as the securing of financial backing. This type of agreement is usually between an architect and an owner who may be seeking to raise funds through passage of a tax referendum, selling bonds, or some other means.

contingent closure A land-cover cap used to cover a hazardous waste site before environmental remediation of the soil.

continuing education A term applied to a regimen of attendance and application of special study toward a specific subject matter. Continuing education may be pursued through accredited professional seminars, college curriculum, and other forms of organized study that promote knowledge of the "state of the art" of professional endeavors.

continuous beam A beam supported at three or more points, and thus having two or more spans.

continuous flow plant An asphaltic concrete mixing plant that mixes liquid asphalt and aggregate in a continuous flow, as opposed to a batch mixer.

continuous footing A concrete footing supporting a wall or two or more columns. The footing may vary in depth and width.

continuous girder A girder supported at three or more points.

continuous header Wood frame construction in which the top plate is replaced by a double member, such as a 2″ x 8″ on edge, that acts as a lintel over all wall openings.

continuous hinge (piano hinge) A hinge that extends the full length of the moving part to which it is attached.

continuous load A load in which the maximum current is expected to continue for at least three hours.

continuous rating The constant load that a device can carry at rated primary voltage and frequency without damaging or adversely affecting it.

continuously reinforced pavement A longitudinally reinforced concrete pavement with no intermediate transverse expansion or contraction joints.

continuous span A rigid span extending over three or more supports so that bending movements are transmitted from one segment to the next.

continuous vent A vertical plumbing vent that is a continuation of the drain to which it connects.

continuous waste and vent A single pipe, the upper portion of which is a vent, while the lower portion functions as a waste drain.

contour line A line on a map or drawing indicating a horizontal plane of constant elevation. All points on a contour line are at the same elevation.

contract An agreement between two parties to perform work or provide goods, including an agreement or order for the procurement of supplies or services.

contract bond *See* **completion bond**.

contract change A change to the contract requirements within the general and contract clauses.

Contract Disputes Act of 1978 A federal law providing for methods of prosecuting contract claims against the federal government.

contract documents All the written and graphic documents concerning execution of a particular construction contract. These

contraction joints

include the agreement between the owner and contractor, all conditions of the contract including general and supplementary conditions, the specifications and drawings, any changes to the specifications and drawings, any changes to the original contract, and any other items specifically itemized as being part of the contract documents.

contract for construction An agreement between owner and contractor whereby the contractor agrees to construct the owner's project in accordance with the contract documents, within a specified amount of time, and for consideration to be paid by the owner as mutually agreed.

contracting officer The representative of a government agency with authority to bind the government in contract matters.

contracting officer's decision The contracting officer's final ruling regarding a properly submitted claim.

contraction joint (control joint) A formed, sawed, or tooled groove in a concrete structure. The purpose of the joint is to create a weakened plane and to regulate the location of cracking resulting from the dimensional change of different parts of the structure.

contract modification Any unilateral or bilateral written alteration of the contract in accordance with the governing regulations and contract clauses.

contractor A constructor who is a party to the contract for construction, pledged to the owner to perform the work of construction in accordance with the contract documents.

contractor's option As laid out in the contract documents, the ability of the contractor to select predetermined materials, methods, or systems, at his or her option, with no change in the contract sum.

contractor's qualification statement A statement of the contractor's qualifications, experience, financial condition, business history, and staff composition. This statement, together with listed business and professional references, provides evidence of the contractor's competence to perform the work and assume the responsibilities required by the contract documents.

contract sum An amount representing the total consideration in money to be paid the contractor for services performed under the contract for construction.

contract type The specific pricing arrangements employed for the performance of work under contracts. These arrangements include firm fixed-price, fixed-price incentive, cost-plus-fixed fee, cost-plus-incentive fee, and several others.

contraflexure point *See* **point of inflection**.

contributory negligence A term used to describe legal responsibility for an error or fault by one or more parties who have allegedly contributed in whole or in part to a loss or damage suffered by another party as a result of a specific occurrence.

control factor The ratio of the minimum to the average compressive strength of a material.

control joint *See* **contraction joint**.

controlled fill A backfilling or embankment operation in which the moisture content, depth of lift, and compaction equipment are closely regulated by specification and inspection.

cooling tower

controlled-flow roof drainage
A system of roof drainage that significantly slows the rate at which rainwater drains.

controlled low-strength material (CLSM) A building material, often used in beddings, encasements, and as flowable backfill, that results in a compressive strength of no more than 1200 pounds per square inch.

controller An electrical, electronic, pneumatic, or mechanical device designed to regulate an operation or function.

control station In surveying, a point whose location serves as a reference for other surveying operations.

convection The movement of a gas or liquid upward as it is heated and downward as it is cooled. The movement is caused by a change in density.

conversion (1) The change in use of a building, as from a warehouse to residential units, that may require changes in the mechanical, electrical, and structural systems. (2) The sawing or milling of lumber into smaller units.

conversion factor Any factor used to change from one unit of measurement to another. For example, yards are converted to feet by multiplying by three.

converter A device that changes electrical energy from one form to another, as in coverting alternating current to direct current.

conveyance An instrument or deed by which a title of property is transferred.

coolant A fluid used to transfer heat from a heat source to a heat exchanger, where the heat is removed and the coolant is usually recycled.

cooling plant The machinery that produces chilled water or cool refrigerant gas, such as the condenser, cooling tower, and condenser water pumps for watershed plants; air-cooled condensers for air-cooled systems; and chilled water pumps and expansion tanks for chilled water systems.

cooling tower An outdoor structure, frequently placed on a roof, over which warm water is circulated for cooling by evaporation and exposure to the air. A *natural draft cooling tower* is one in which the airflow through the tower is due to its natural chimney effect. A *mechanical draft tower* employs fans to force or induce a draft.

co-op *See* **cooperative.**

cooperative (co-op) A type of participant ownership in a building or complex. Actual ownership is by a nonprofit corporation. Individuals are part owners of the corporation and pay monthly fees for use or occupancy of part of the building.

coopered joint A joint made on a curved surface similar to the joints made between the staves of a barrel.

coordinator The device on a pair of double doors that permits the doors to close in the correct sequence. If the door with the overlapping astragal closed first, the other door would strike the astragal and not close properly.

cope (1) To cut the end of a molding to match the contour of the adjacent piece. (2) To cut structural steel beams so that they fit tightly together.

coped joint (scribed joint) The intersection of two pieces of molding, where one is cut to fit the contour of the other.

coping

copper roofing

corbel

coping The protective top member of any vertical construction such as a wall or chimney. A coping may be masonry, metal, or wood, and is usually sloped or beveled to shed water in such a way that it does not run down the vertical face of the wall. Copings often project out from a wall with a drip groove on the underside.

coping saw A light hand saw with a narrow blade mounted in a U-shaped frame with a handle. A coping saw is used to cut curves in wood. The blade may be rotated to keep the frame away from the work.

copper fitting In piping, an elbow, tee, reducer, or other fitting made of wrought copper, cast brass, or bronze.

copper roofing A roof covering made of copper sheets joined by weatherproof seams.

corbel A course or unit of masonry that projects beyond the course below. A corbel may be used entirely for decoration or for a ledge to support a load from above.

corded door A suspended door or divider made of plastic, vinyl, or wooden slats interconnected with cord or tapes. When opened, the door slides in tracks folding back flat in accordion pleats.

core (1) The interior structure of a hollow-core door. (2) A cylindrical sample of concrete or rock extracted by a core drill. (3) The void in a concrete masonry unit. (4) The center layer of a sheet of plywood. (5) The vertical stack of service areas in a multistory building. (6) The central part of an electrical winding. (7) Metal support for a handrail. (8) The rubble filling in a thick masonry wall. (9) The center material between facing papers in gypsum wallboard.

coreboard (battenboard) A manufactured board with a wood fiber or wood chip center and bonded veneer faces on both sides.

cored beam (1) A precast concrete beam with longitudinal holes through it. (2) A beam that has had core samples removed for testing.

core drill (1) A drill used to remove a core of rock or earth material for analysis. (2) The drilling of a hole through a concrete floor, wall, or ceiling for running pipe or conduit.

core frame *See* **buck frame**.

core gap An open joint extending through, or partly through, a plywood panel, that occurs when core veneers are not tightly butted. When center veneers are involved, the condition is referred to as a *center gap*.

core test A compression test on a sample of hardened concrete cut out with a core drill.

coring The core drilling of a sample of rock, soil, or concrete to obtain a test sample.

corkboard Compressed and baked granulated cork used in flooring and sound conditioning and as a vibration absorber.

cork tile Tile made from cork particles bound and pressed into sheets and covered with a protective wearing finish.

corner bead An L-shaped, light gauge metal strip used to finish drywall and plaster wall angles and corners.

corner bead clincher A hand tool used to set corner beads in place on walls without nails or screws.

corner board The vertical boards that are butted together to form the outside corner of a wood-frame

corner brace

cornice

corrugated metal

building. The siding or shingles butt up against it.

corner brace The diagonal braces let into the studs of wood frame structures for reinforcement.

corner bracket A fitting attached to a door frame at the upper hinge corner, used for mounting an exposed overhead door closer.

corner finisher A hand tool used to smooth and feather joint compound evenly over wallboard corner joints.

Cornerite® In plaster walls, strips of metal mesh bent at right angles and embedded in corners of ceilings and walls to prevent the plaster from cracking.

corner post (angle post, corner stud) (1) A glazing mullion in the corner of a structure that retains glazing in both walls. (2) A vertical member located at the corner of a timber structure.

corner reinforcement (1) The reinforcement in the upper corners of a metal door frame. (2) The metal angle strip used at the corners of plaster or gypsum board construction. (3) The bent reinforcing rods embedded at the corners of a cast-in-place concrete wall.

corner return block A concrete masonry block with solid faces on its sides and on one end. Used at the end of a run of blocks.

corner stud *See* **corner post.**

cornice (1) An ornamental molding of wood or plaster that encircles a room just below the ceiling. (2) An ornamental topping that crowns a structure. (3) An exterior ornamental trim at the meeting of the roof and wall. This type of cornice usually includes a bed molding, a soffit, a fascia, and a crown molding.

cornice lighting Accent lighting that is positioned high on a wall behind a shield and distributes light along the wall.

corporation An association of individuals established under certain legal requirements. A corporation exists independently of its members, and has powers and liabilities distinct and apart from its members.

corridor A long, interior passageway, usually with doors opening to rooms, apartments, or offices and leading to an exit.

corrosion The oxidation or eating away of a metal or other material by exposure to chemical or electrochemical action such as rust.

corrosion inhibitor A protective layer or coating of material, paint, or other surface finish applied to prevent oxidation of, or chemical attack on, the base material.

corrosive Descriptive of a substance that causes corrosion.

corrugated aluminum Sheet aluminum that has been rolled into a parallel wave pattern to impart stiffness.

corrugated fastener A small, wavy, steel fastener with one edge sharpened. The fastener is driven into two pieces of wood, bridging the joint in order to hold them together.

corrugated metal Sheet metal that has been rolled into a parallel wave pattern for stiffness and rigidity.

corrugated roofing Corrugated metal or fiberglass mounted on rafters as sheet roofing.

corrugated siding Siding made of sheet metal or asbestos-cement composition board and used for siding on factories and other nondecorative buildings. By corrugating the material, the structural strength is increased.

cost The total expenditure in dollars approved after the completion of a project.

cost breakdown *See* **schedule of values**.

cost-plus-fee agreement An agreement between an owner and the contractor or a design professional that provides for payment of all costs associated with completion of their duties. This includes direct and indirect costs as well as a fee for services, which may be a fixed amount or a percentage of costs.

cost-reimbursement contract A type of contract in which the pricing arrangement involves the payment of allowable costs incurred by the contractor during performance.

cotter pin A split metal pin which, when pushed through a hole in a shaft or a bolt (and having the ends bent), prevents parts or nuts from vibrating loose.

cotton mats Water-retaining quilts used in the curing of concrete. *See also* **curing blanket**.

counter (1) A person or device that keeps a tally of the occurrences of some event, such as the number of loads of fill. (2) A long, flat surface over which sales are transacted at a store or business. (3) A flat work surface in a kitchen.

counterbalanced window A double-hung window in which a system of weights and pulleys balances the weight of the sash, thus making it relatively easy to open and close.

counterbatten A strip of wood attached to the backs of boards to stiffen them.

counterbrace A diagonal brace that balances the force from another brace as part of a web network in a truss.

counterflashing A thin strip of metal frequently inserted into masonry construction and bent down over other flashing to prevent water from running down the masonry and behind the upturned edge of the base flashing.

counterfort In masonry construction, a pier, buttress, or pilaster on the inner side of a wall to resist thrust.

counterlathing *See* **cross-furring**.

counteroffer An offeree's response to an offer which neither accepts as offered nor rejects completely, but proposes modifications to the original offer.

countersink (1) A conical depression cut to receive the head of a flat-head bolt or screw for driving it flush with the surrounding surface. (2) A bit used to cut a conical depression.

countersunk bolt A flat-head bolt that tapers to the shank diameter so that it can be driven flush with the top of a countersunk hole.

countersunk rivet A rivet used in countersunk holes.

counterweight A weight that balances another weight; for example, a sash weight that balances a window sash, or a large weight that balances a lift bridge.

counterweight system A permanent system of weights mounted, for example, on a theatre stage to balance curtains, scenery, or lighting equipment.

couple Two equal, opposite, and parallel forces that tend to produce rotation. The movement equals the

course

coursed masonry

coursed rubble

product of one force times the perpendicular distance between the two.

coupled roof *See* **couple roof.**

coupled window A pair of independent windows separated by a mullion.

coupler A metal clamp-like device used to join and extend tubular frames and braces in barricades or scaffolding.

couple roof (coupled roof) A narrow-span, double-pitched roof in which opposite rafters are not tied together, thus leaving the outward forces to be resisted by the walls.

coupling A fitting for joining two pieces of pipe.

coupling pin In modular scaffolding erection, a pin used to connect scaffolding sections or lifts vertically.

course (1) A horizontal layer of bricks or blocks in a masonry wall. (2) A row or layer of any type of building material, such as siding, shingles, etc.

coursed masonry Any masonry units laid in regular courses, as opposed to rough or random rubble.

coursed rubble Masonry construction consisting of roughly dressed stones of mixed sizes and shapes, with small stones used to fill irregular voids.

coursing joint (1) The horizontal mortar joint between two courses of masonry. (2) In an arch, the arched joint between two curving courses.

cove A concave-shaped surface where a ceiling and wall meet.

coved vault An enclosure whose sides are like four quarter cylinders intersecting so that the joints look like an "X" in plane view.

cove lighting Indirect lighting in which the fixtures are behind a molding or valance, and thus out of sight.

cove molding A triangular-shaped piece of molding with one concave face used to cover interior angles, such as that between the ceiling and a wall.

covenant A term used to describe one or more specific points of agreement that may be set forth in a contract.

cover (1) That which envelops or hides, such as a protecting cover of paint. (2) That part of a tile or shingle that is overlapped by the next course. (3) The minimum thickness of concrete between the reinforcing steel and the outer surface of the concrete.

coverage (1) The nominal square feet of area that a can of stain or paint can be expected to cover. (2) The amount of surface that may be covered by a unit, such as a bundle, square, or ton of building material. (3) An insurance policy, or the dollar protection that policy provides. The amount of protection depends on many factors, including the type of insurance, amount of insurance purchased, policy limits, and exclusions. (4) Dependable estimates or firm bids for portions of a construction project.

coverstone A flat stone laid on a steel beam or girder to act as the foundation for the masonry above.

coving (1) Concave molding such as that used at the intersection of a wall and the ceiling. (2) The outward curve of an exterior wall to meet the eaves. (3) The curving sides of a fireplace that narrows at the back.

crane

crawler tractor

cowl (1) An elaborate chimney pot for improving drafts. (2) A covering over vent pipes to block rain and snow.

crack-control reinforcement The use of steel reinforcing rods in concrete and masonry to minimize crack size and occurrence.

cracking load The load that imposes a tensile stress in concrete in excess of its tensile strength, causing it to crack.

cradle (1) A scaffold that is suspended outside the roof or top of a structure. (2) A U-shaped support for pipe or conduit.

cradle-to-grave analysis A methodology used to determine the energy, environmental and waste implications of a product, material or system. The analysis begins at the point of raw material extraction includes refinement or fabrication, transportation, use, and eventual reuse or disposal.

cradling The framework on a vaulted ceiling that supports lath and plaster.

craft Synonymous with trade, but implies a trade requiring above-average skill.

cramp (1) A device for supporting a frame in place during construction. (2) A U-shaped metal bar used to lock adjacent blocks of masonry together, as in a parapet wall.

crandall A hand tool used for dressing stone. Consists of several sharp, pointed bars fixed to the end of a handle in a hammerlike configuration.

crane A machine for raising, shifting, or lowering heavy weights, commonly by means of a projecting swinging arm.

craneway Steel or concrete column and beam supports and rails on which a crane travels.

crank A twist or bend in a reinforcing bar.

crawler tractor A powered earthmoving vehicle that moves on continuous, segmented, cleated treads or tracks. The tracks provide low ground-bearing pressure and a high level of mobility and power.

crawling A defect in the application of paint whereby the paint film raises, separates, or breaks apart. Usually caused by painting over a slippery or glassy surface, or from applying heavy or elastic coatings over a hard or brittle surface.

crawl space (1) In a building or portion of a building without a basement, the accessible space between the surface of the ground and the bottom of the first floor joists, with less-than-normal headroom. (2) Any interior space of limited height designed to permit access to components such as ductwork, wiring, and pipe fittings.

crawl space vents A system of openings in a crawl space to allow for an air exchange that will reduce moisture and harmful gas buildup.

crazing Surface cracks that appear randomly, usually due to shrinkage in paints, plaster, concrete, varnish, etc. *See also* **checking**.

creasing One or more courses of masonry units laid on the top of a wall, chimney, or other vertical surface and overhanging the course below so that water will drip off and not run down the wall below. Coping is placed above the creasing if it is used.

creep (1) The slow but continual permanent deformation of a material under sustained stress. (2) The very slow movement of rock or soil under pressure. (3) Gradual deformation of a roofing membrane due to thermal stress.

crib

cricket

creep strength The maximum stress that can be applied to a material at a certain temperature without causing more than a specified percentage increase in dimension in a given time.

cremone bolt (cremorne bolt) A bolt system for windows and doors that features a long sliding rod that is engaged by the turn of a handle. Commonly used with French doors.

creosote An oily liquid obtained from tar and used to prevent wood from decaying. Creosote is used extensively for preserving railroad ties, wood piles, posts, and wood foundations.

crescent truss A truss in which the upper and lower chords are curved in the same direction, but with different radii of curvature, so that they meet at the ends, thus giving the assembly a crescent-shaped appearance.

crib (1) A boxed-in area, the sides of which may be an open lattice, often filled with stone, and used as a retaining wall or support for construction above. (2) A retaining framework lining in a shaft or tunnel.

cribbing A system of open boxes built with heavy timbers and filled with rocks or pervious fill. Used as a retaining wall.

cribwork An open construction of beams, at the face of an embankment, the alternate layers of which project to provide lateral stability, prevent erosion, and resist thrust or overturning.

cricket *See* **chimney cricket.**

crimp A sharp bend in a metal sheet, as in the joint in metal roofing.

crimped wire Wire that has been deformed or bent to improve its bonding effectiveness when used to reinforce concrete.

cripple (1) In construction framing, members that are less than full length; for example, studs above a door or below a window. (2) In roofing, a bracket secured at the ridge of a pitched roof to carry the scaffold for roofers.

cripple jack rafter A short supporting beam that extends from a valley rafter to a hip rafter.

critical angle The maximum angle or rise of a stair or ramp before it becomes unsafe for public use. For stairs the angle is 50°; for ramps, it is 20°.

critical load The load at which a member of structure is likely to fail.

critical path A term used to describe the order of events (each of a particular duration) that results in the least amount of time required to complete a project.

critical path method (CPM) A system of construction management that involves the complete planning and scheduling of a project, and the development of an arrow diagram showing each activity, its appropriate place in the timetable, and its importance relative to other tasks, and the complete project.

crocus cloth A fine abrasive used as a polishing medium for metal surfaces.

crook The warp in a board or a natural curve created by tension within the fibers of the piece.

crossband (crossbanding) (1) Any ornamental strip or band whose grain pattern is perpendicular to the main surface. (2) In plywood, a layer whose grain direction is perpendicular to the surface veneer.

crossbanding *See* **crossband.**

cross bar In a grating or grill, one of the bars perpendicular to the primary bar.

cross bracing

cross-furring

cross runner

crown

cross beam (brow post) (1) A large beam that spans two walls or sides of a structure, frequently holding them together. (2) A brace between opposite whalings or sheeting in an excavation. (3) In bridge construction, a beam that spans the trusses and supports the stringers or deck.

cross bracing (cross bridging) Diagonal braces placed in pairs that cross each other.

cross connection (1) A piping connection between two otherwise separate piping systems, one of which contains potable water, and the other water of unknown or questionable safety. (2) In a fire protection system, a connection from a siamese fitting to a standpipe or sprinkler system.

crosscut saw A saw with its teeth filed and set to cut across the grain of a piece of wood.

cross-furring (brandering, counterlathing) Strips or slats attached to the lower edge of joists to which plastering lathing is nailed.

cross-garnet hinge (T-hinge) A hinge that is shaped like the letter T, with the head attached to the door frame and the long part fastened to the door.

cross-laminated Laminated wood members in which the grain of some layers is at a right angle to the grain of other layers.

crosslap joint A wood joint in which two pieces are each cut to half their thickness at the overlap, so that the total thickness of the system does not change.

cross lighting Illumination from two sources on opposite sides of a subject.

crossover (1) In an auditorium, a walkway that is parallel to the stage and connects with the aisles. (2) A pipe fitting used to bypass a section of pipe. (3) A connection between two piping systems.

cross peen hammer A hammer with one face flat and the other a wedge. Used to break or work hard surfaces.

cross runner In a suspended or T-bar ceiling, one of a series of short pieces that span between the long runners.

cross section A diagram or illustration showing the internal construction of a part or assembly if the front portion were removed.

cross tongue A piece of wood, usually plywood, glued at a joint between two wood members for reinforcement.

cross ventilation The circulation or flow of air through openings, such as doors, windows, or grilles, that are on opposite sides of a room.

cross welt (transverse seam) On sheet metal roofing, a seam or joint that runs parallel to the ridge or across the flow of storm water down the roof.

crotch The area of a tree where the branches meet the trunk.

crotch veneer A veneer with an unusual grain milled from the crotch of a tree.

crow bar A steel bar with one end flattened for use as a lever and the other curved and clawed for pulling nails.

crown (1) An ornamental architectural topping. (2) The central top section of an arch or vault. (3) The high point in the center of a road that causes water to flow to the edges. (4) The top of a tree or flowering plant. (5) In plumbing, the section of a trap that

culvert

cupola

changes direction from vertical to horizontal. (6) The convex curvature or camber in a beam.

crown course (1) The top row of a roofing material. (2) The row that actually covers the ridge.

crown rafter The central common rafter in a hip roof.

crown saw A saw with a hollow rotating cylinder that has teeth around the edge for drilling round holes in wood.

crushed gravel Gravel that has been crushed and screened so that substantially one face of each particle is a fractured face.

crushed stone Stone crushed and screened so that substantially all faces result from fracturing.

crusher (breaker) A machine for reducing gravel, rocks, boulders, or blasted rock to smaller sizes.

crusher-run aggregate Aggregate that has been ground in a crusher, but has not been sorted for particle size.

crushing strength The greatest compressive load a material can withstand without fracturing.

crush plate A replaceable strip of wood attached to the edge of a concrete form to take the abuse of stripping or prying operations.

crystallization As applied to absorption chillers, the precipitation of salt crystals from the absorbent. This causes a slush-like mixture that plugs fluid passages within the chiller and renders it inoperable.

crystallized finish A random pattern of wrinkles in the finish of paint or varnish.

cube strength An analytical strength test of Portland cement in which a standard-size concrete cube is loaded to failure.

cubicle *See* **carrel.**

cul-de-sac A dead-end street that ends in an enlarged turn-around area.

cull Building materials, especially bricks, that are discarded because of defects.

cullet Raw glass or pieces of broken glass from a cut or a cooled melt.

culvert A transverse drain under a roadway, canal, or embankment other than a bridge. Most culverts are fabricated with materials such as corrugated metal and precast concrete pipe.

cumulative batching The weighing of a batch of material by adding the components successively to the same container and balancing the scale at each new total weight.

cup A distortion of a board, usually caused by exposure to moisture, where the width of the board curves upward at one or both ends.

cup joint A straight joint used in copper tubing. A swaging tool is driven into one of the ends to be joined, enlarging it so that it will fit over the other tube for a soldered connection.

cupola A dome-like structure, often ornamental, located on the top of a building at the ridge of a roof.

curb cock (curb stop) A control valve that is placed in the water supply pipe that runs from a water main in a street to a building.

curb form (1) A form used with a curb machine for extruding concrete curbs to produce a desired shape and finish on the curb. (2) A reusable metal form for cast-in-place concrete curbs.

curb level The elevation of the curb grade in front of a building, as measured at the center of its street frontage.

curtain wall

curb machine A self-propelled, hand-operated machine for extruding bituminous or concrete curbs.

curb plate (1) The wall plate at the top of a circular or elliptical structure. (2) The plate on which the upper rafters of a curb roof rest.

curb roof (gambrel roof, mansard roof) A roof with the slope divided into two pitches on each side.

curb stop *See* **curb cock**.

curb string *See* **close string**.

cure (1) A change in the physical and/or chemical properties of an adhesive or sealant when mixed with a catalyst or subjected to heat or pressure. (2) To maintain the proper moisture and temperature after placing or finishing concrete to assure proper hydration and hardening.

curing blanket A layer of straw, burlap, sawdust, or other suitable material placed over fresh concrete and moistened to help maintain humidity and temperature for proper hydration. *See also* **cotton mats**.

curing membrane Any of several kinds of sheet material or spray-on coatings used to temporarily retard the evaporation of water from the exposed surface of fresh concrete, thus ensuring a proper cure.

curling A change in the shape of wood, such as straightness or flatness, due to drying or temperature differences.

current The movement of electrons through a conductor. Measured in amperes.

current assets Cash and other assets that will be consumed or converted into cash within one year.

current-carrying capacity (ampacity) The maximum rated current, measured in amperes, that an electrical device is allowed to carry. Exceeding this limit could lead to early failure of the device or create a fire hazard.

current density The current flowing to or from a unit area of an electrode surface.

current liabilities Liabilities to be paid within one year.

current-limiting fuse A fuse that acts as a protective device by interrupting currents in its current-limiting range and guarding against overcurrents in an electrical system.

current transformer A transformer generally used to convert a current supplied at one current rate to another current rate.

curtain board (draft curtain) A heavy fireproof fabric hung from a roof or ceiling to isolate a hazardous area and act as a shield against the spread of a fire by containing heat and smoke for direct venting.

curtained doorway A doorway consisting of two overlapping sheets of plastic over a door frame, each attached to the frame at the top and down one side. Allows worker entry into and from an area while minimizing the air movement between rooms.

curtain grouting The injection of grout into the ground in a broad line to act as a barrier to subsurface water flow.

curtain wall The exterior closure or skin of a building. A curtain wall is nonbearing and is not supported by beams or girders.

cushion (1) Wood placed so as to absorb a force by acting as a buffer or by transmitting it over a larger

cut and fill

cut nail

area. (2) A stone placed to accept and spread out a vertical load. (3) An isolating pad against shock and vibration for glass, machinery, equipment, etc.

cut (1) Material excavated from a construction site. (2) A term for the area after the excavated material has been removed. (3) The depth of material to be removed, as in a 5′ cut. (4) To reduce a cost item.

cut-and-cover An operation for the laying of pipe or conduit, or for constructing a tunnel, in which a trench is dug, the pipe, conduit, or tunnel liner is placed, and the trench is covered by the excavated material.

cut and fill An operation commonly used in road building and other rock and earthmoving operations in which the material excavated and removed from one location is used as fill material at another location.

cutaway drawing A drawing of an area or object that shows what would be seen if a slice could be made into the area or object and a piece removed. *See also* **cross section**.

cutback asphalt A bituminous roof coating or cement that has been thinned with a solvent so that it may be applied without heat to roofs or other areas that need sealing or cementing. Also used for dampproofing concrete and masonry.

cut nail (clasp nail) A hard, wedge-shaped nail used for nailing hardwoods such as oak flooring.

cutoff (1) A wall or barrier placed to minimize underground water percolation or flow. A cutoff is often used at the inlet and outlet of culverts. (2) The design elevation

at which the tops of driven piles are cut.

cutout (1) A mechanical or electrical device used to stop a machine when its safe limits have been exceeded. (2) An opening in a wall or surface for access or other purposes. (3) A piece stamped out of sheet metal or other sheet material.

cutout box A metal box used in electrical wiring to house circuit breakers, fuses, or a disconnect switch.

cutting in A painting technique used to paint around the edges of an object or area, such as trim or a light fixture.

cycle The flow of alternating current as it travels in one direction, then reverses itself and travels in the opposite direction. A 60-cycle circuit completes 60 cycles per second.

cycle time The time required to complete a repetitive operation such as a batch mix or the refill of a toilet tank after flushing.

cyclopean concrete *See* **concrete, cyclopean**.

cylinder lock A lock in which the keyhole and tumbler mechanism are contained in a cylinder or escutcheon separate from the lock case.

cylinder unloaders Automatic devices used to hold open the reciprocating compressor valves of a number of cylinders in order to reduce compressor pumping capacity when not being used to full capacity.

cyma (cima) A molding with an S-curve section.

cypress A wood of average strength and very good decay resistance and durability.

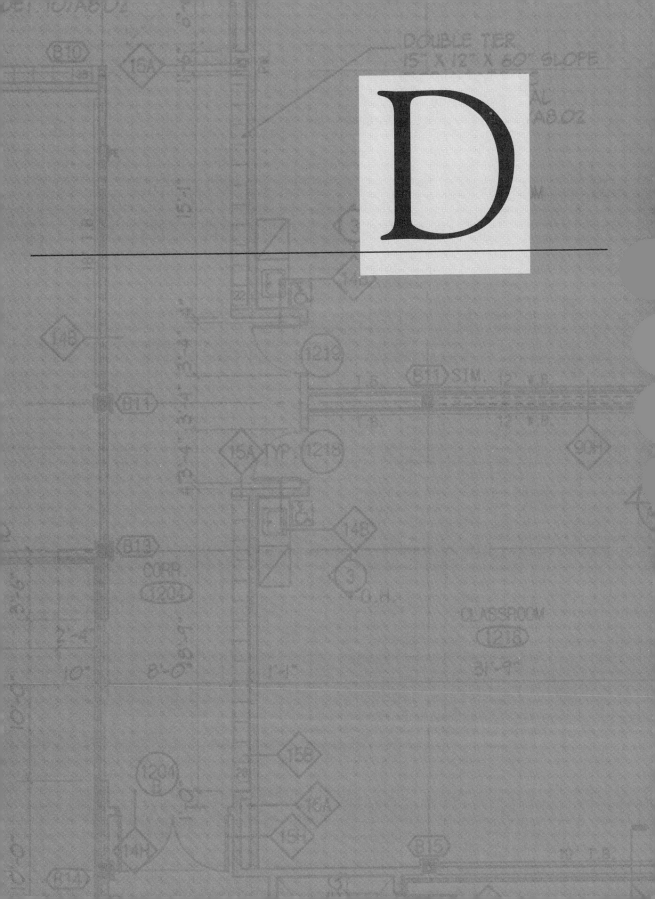

D ABBREVIATIONS

The abbreviations listed below are those most commonly used in the construction industry. Alternative forms (usually nonstandard) are shown in parentheses.

d degree, density, penny (nail size)

D deep, depth, diameter, dimensional, discharge

D&CM dressed and center matched

D&M dressed and matched

D&MB dressed and matched beaded

D&SM dressed and standard matched

D1S dressed one side

D2S dressed two sides

D2S&CM dressed two sides and center matched

D2S&SM dressed two sides and standard matched

D4S dressed four sides

DAD double acting door

db decibel

DBA a unit of sound level (as from the A-scale of a sound-level meter), doing business as

DB Clg double-headed ceiling

DBG distance between guides

Dbl. double

DBT dry-bulb temperature

DC direct current

DDC direct digital controller

DEC decimal

DEG degree, degrees

DEL delineation

Demo demolition

Demob demobilization

DEPT department

DET detached, detail, double end trimmed

DF damage free, direction finder, drainage free, drinking fountain, Douglas fir

dfl Douglas Fir-Larch

dflct deflection

d.f.u. drainage fixture unit

D.H. double-hung

DHW domestic hot water, double-hung window

DIA diameter

Diag diagonal

DIM dimension

DIN Dutch industry normal (German industry standard)

Dis., Disch discharge

Distrib. distribution

DIV division

Dk deck

dkg decking

DL dead load, deadlight, diesel

DN down

Do ditto

DOC delivery order contract

DOT Department of Transportation

DOZ dozen

Dp depth

DP degree of polymerization, dew point, double pitched

DPC dampproof course

DPST double pole, single throw

Dr, DR dining room, drain, dressing room, driver

DRG drawing

Drink drinking

drn drain, drainage

drwl drywall

DS double strength, downspout, drop siding

DSA double strength A grade

DSB double strength B grade

DSGN design

DT drum trap

DT&G double tongue and groove

Dty duty

DU disposal unit

DUP duplicate

DVTL dovetail

dwg, DWG drawing

DWV drain waste vent

DX deluxe white, direct expansion

dyn dyne

D Definitions

damper

dampproofing

darby

dabber A soft, round-tipped brush for applying varnish or for polishing and finishing gilding.

dabbing (daubing) Dressing a stone face with a sharp tool to give it a pitted appearance.

dado (1) The flat-bottomed groove cut into one board (usually across the grain) to receive the end of another. If the groove is cut at the edge of a board, it is called a *rabbet*. (2) An ornamental paneling above the baseboard of a room finish. (3) Part of a column between the base and the cap or cornice.

dado cap A cornice or chair rail along the highest part of a framed dado.

dado head A power saw blade designed specifically to produce dados or flat-bottomed grooves.

dado joint A joint created by fitting the end of one piece of wood at a right angle into a groove cut across the width of another, to a depth of half its thickness.

dado rail *See* **chair rail**.

dais A raised platform at one end of a hall, usually reserved for officers, dignitaries, or speakers.

dam The barrier built into the trapway of a toilet that controls the water level in the toilet bowl.

damages A measure of monetary compensation that a court or arbitrator awards to a plaintiff for loss or injury suffered by the plaintiff's person, property, or other legally recognizable rights. *See also* **liquidated damages**.

damp check *See* **damp course**.

damp course (damp check, dampproof course) In masonry construction, an impervious course or any material that prevents moisture from passing through to the next course (usually a horizontal layer of material such as metal, tile, or dense limestone).

damper (1) A blade or louver within an air duct, inlet, or outlet that can be adjusted to regulate the flow of air. (2) A pivotal cast-iron plate positioned just below the smoke chamber of a fireplace to regulate drafts.

damping (1) The force that acts to reduce vibrations in the same way that friction acts to reduce ordinary motion. (2) The gradual dissipation of energy over a period of time.

damping material Viscous material applied to the surface of a vibrating plate to subdue the vibrations and noise.

dampproof course *See* **damp course**.

dampproofing An application of a water-resisting treatment or material to the surface of a concrete or masonry wall to prevent passage or absorption of water or moisture. Can also be accomplished by using an admixture in the concrete mix.

dancers *See* **stairs**.

dancing step *See* **balanced step**.

dancing winder *See* **balanced step**.

dao (paldao) A moderately hard, heavy wood indigenous to the Philippines and New Guinea. The wood is variegated in color and used mostly for cabinets, plywood, and interior finishes.

dap A notch made in one timber to fit the end of another.

darby (derby, derby float, derby slicker) A hand float or trowel, about 4′ long, used by concrete finishers and plasterers in preliminary floating and leveling operations. The float is usually made of wood or aluminum and has either one or two handles.

dash-bond coat A thick slurry of Portland cement, sand, and water applied to a concrete wall with a brush or whiskbroom to act as a bond for a subsequent plaster coat.

database Part of a computer's software program that contains files and lists of related information organized for quick access. In Building Automation Systems, the database consists of digital and analog point names; descriptions such as temperature set points; and operating information such as programs and passwords.

date of agreement The date shown on the face of an agreement, or the date the agreement is signed (usually the date of the award).

date of commencement of the work The date established in the *notice to proceed* or, in the absence of such notice, the date of the agreement established by the parties for the work to begin.

date of substantial completion The date on which the work (or a portion of the work) is certified by the architect to be sufficiently complete as specified in the contract documents. The owner should be able to occupy the work fully or partially.

datum A base elevation to which other elevations are referred.

datum line An elevation reference line.

daub (1) To rough-coat with plaster. (2) To rough-coat a stone surface by striking it with a special hammer.

daubing *See* **dabbing.**

Davis-Bacon Act A federal labor law enacted in 1931 that requires laborers and mechanics (those who do physical work) on federally funded construction projects be paid no less than the local prevailing wages. The Davis-Bacon Act applies to all federally funded contracts over a specified value.

day In glazing, one division of a window, particularly in large church windows.

day gate In a bank, the metal grille door used when the main vault door is open.

daylight compensation An energy-saving lighting system controlled by a photocell that decreases lamp intensity as daylight increases.

daylight glass A blue-colored glass used with incandescent lamps to produce the optical characteristics of daylight.

daylight lamp A lamp manufactured with daylight glass. The output is generally 35% less than that from an incandescent lamp.

daylight width (sight size width) The width of that portion of a window which admits light.

db *See* **decibel.**

D-crack *See* **D-line crack.**

D-cracking The progressive formation of fine hairline cracks in concrete surfaces. In highway pavement these cracks run parallel to joints and edges and cut diagonally across corners. *See also* **D-line crack.**

DDC *See* **direct digital control.**

deactivator A tank containing iron filings, through which hot water is passed to be purged of its active oxygen and other corrosive elements.

dead Refers to a conductor that is not connected to an electrical source.

dead air space

dead end

deadman

dead air space   Unventilated air space between structural elements. The space is used for thermal and sound insulation.

deadband   In HVAC, a temperature range in which neither the heating nor cooling systems are activated.

dead bolt   The bolt on a type of door lock that must be operated positively in both directions by turning a key or a thumb bolt.

dead-burnt gypsum (anhydrous calcium sulfate)   Gypsum from which all the water of crystallization has been removed.

dead end   (1) In stressing a tendon, the end opposite the one to which stress is applied. (2) In plumbing, a drain line or vent that has been purposely terminated by a cap, plug, or other fitting.

dead-end anchorage   The anchorage for the stressing steel in a tendon opposite the jacking end.

deadening   The use of insulating and dampening materials to restrict the passage of sound.

dead-front   Refers to an electrical device in which the front part is insulated from voltage and can be touched without receiving an electric shock.

dead knot   A knot in cut lumber that is no longer connected to the surrounding wood.

deadlatch   *See* **night latch**.

dead level   (1) The state of being absolutely level, with no pitch or slope. (2) A grade of asphalt used on a level or nearly level roof.

deadlight   A fixed window sash.

dead load   A calculation of the weight of a building's structural components, fixtures, and permanently attached equipment (used in designing a building and its foundations).

deadlock   A type of door lock employing a dead bolt.

deadman   A heavy anchor, such as a concrete block or a log, usually buried underground and used for securing the end of a tie or guy. This device is frequently used with sheeting and retaining walls.

dead parking   Long-term, unattended parking of vehicles.

dead-piled   Freshly pressed plywood piled flat without spacers and weighted down while it attains normal temperature and moisture levels.

dead room   A room designed to have high sound-absorption properties.

dead sand   An unwashed, ungraded sand used for fill.

dead shore   An upright timber used as a temporary support for the dead load of a building during structural alterations. This type of shore is commonly used in pairs to support a needle.

dead-soft temper   A term describing the temper of sheet copper used for flashing.

deadwood   Dead tree limbs or the timber cut from dead trees.

deal   In the lumber industry, boards or planks usually more than 9″ wide and 3″ to 5″ thick.

debarment   The formal sanction by the government prohibiting a contractor from receiving contracts as a result of certain proscribed actions including crimes, fraud, etc.

debt service   The periodic repayment of loans including interest and a portion of the principal.

decal   A design that can be transferred from a special paper onto any of a number of different surfaces.

deck

deck curb

decking

decorative block

decay In wood, disintegration caused by the action of fungi.

decayed knot A knot that is softer than its surrounding wood.

decay rate (1) The rate at which sound reverberations decrease in an enclosure, expressed in decibels per second. (2) The rate at which vibrations in a mechanism decrease over a specific time period.

decenter To lower or remove shoring or centering.

decibel (1) The standard unit of measurement for the loudness of sound. (2) In closed-circuit television, a numerical unit used to express the difference in power levels, usually between acoustic or electric signals, equal to 10 times the common logarithm of the ratio of those two levels.

deciduous A term used to describe those trees that shed their leaves annually. Includes most hardwoods and some softwoods.

deck (1) An uncovered wood platform usually attached to or on the roof of a structure. (2) The flooring of a building. (3) The structural system to which a roof covering is applied.

deck clip (1) The H-shaped accessory placed between plywood sheets used as roof decking to prevent uneven deflection. This allows a thinner sheet of plywood to be used with no blocking beneath the joints. (2) A metal fastener used to attach roof deck units to the structural frame. (3) An accessory made for attaching rigid insulation material to a roof deck.

deck curb A curb around the edge of a roof deck or around roof-mounted equipment.

decking (1) Light-gauge, corrugated metal sheets used in constructing roofs or floors. (2) Heavy planking used on roofs or floors. (3) Another name for slab forms that are left in place to save stripping costs. (4) The use of inert material to separate explosive charges.

deck-on-hip A flat roof constructed over a hip roof.

deck paint A special hard-surface paint that is resistant to abrasive wear and used particularly on decks and porches.

decontamination chamber A series of rooms separated from one another and from the work area by airlocks. Prevents contamination of sensitive work areas and/or the spread of dangerous substances used in the work area. Commonly used in asbestos abatement.

decor A combination of materials and furnishings that creates a particular style of interior decorating.

decorative block A concrete masonry unit manufactured or treated to have a desired architectural effect. The particular effect may be in color, texture, or both.

dedicated street A street whose ownership has been relinquished and which has been accepted by a governmental agency for public use and maintenance.

deductible The dollar amount that the policyholder agrees to pay in the event of a loss. The insurance company pays the amount over the deductible, up to the limit of the policy. A homeowners policy usually has a deductible of $250. Commercial buildings may have much higher deductibles, commonly ranging from $5,000 to $10,000.

deduction The amount of money deducted from the contract sum by a change order.

deep-seal trap

deformed bar

deductive alternate An alternative bid that is lower than that bidder's base bid.

deductive change A change resulting in a reduction in the contract price.

deed (1) A legal document giving an individual rights or ownership to a property. (2) A document that forms part of a contract and which, when signed by both parties, legally commits the contractor to perform the work according to the contract documents, and commits the client to pay for the work.

deed restriction A restriction on the use of a property as set forth in the deed.

deep bead *See* **draft bead.**

deep cutting (deeping) (1) The resawing of timber parallel to its face. (2) The cutting out of a structural member to a depth relatively far below its surface.

deeping *See* **deep cutting.**

deep-seal trap (antisiphon trap) A U-shaped plumbing trap having a seal of 4″ or more.

default An omission of, or failure to perform, a contractual duty.

defect Any condition or characteristic that detracts from the appearance, strength, or durability of an object.

defective work (deficiencies) Work that does not comply with the requirements of a contract.

defendant An individual against whom a claim or action is brought. *See also* **plaintiff.**

defense An explanation or reason why a person or entity should not be held legally responsible (liable) as a result of claims made against them by another party.

deficiencies *See* **defective work.**

deflagration The rapid combustion of a material.

deflected tendons (draped tenon) Tendons in a concrete member that have a curved trajectory with respect to the gravity axis of the member.

deflection (1) The bending of a structural member as a result of its own weight or an applied load. (2) The amount of displacement resulting from this bending.

deflection angle In surveying, a horizontal angle as measured from the prolongation of the preceding transit line to the next line.

deflectometer An instrument for measuring the degree to which a transverse load causes a beam or other structure to bend.

deformation A change in the shape or form of a structural member that does not cause its failure or rupture.

deformed bar (deformed reinforcing bar) A reinforcing bar manufactured with surface deformations to provide bonding strength when embedded in concrete.

deformed metal plate A corrugated or otherwise horizontally deformed metal plate used at vertical joints to provide a mechanical interlock between sections.

deformed reinforcement In reinforced concrete, reinforcement comprising bars, rods, deformed wire, welded wire fabric, and welded deformed wire fabric. *See also* **deformed bar.**

degradation Deterioration of a painted surface by heat, light, moisture, or other elements.

degree 1/360th of the circumference of a circle or a round angle.

degree-day A unit of measure for heating-fuel consumption. The unit

delivery hose

deluge sprinkler system

demountable partition

is used to specify the nominal heating load of a building in winter. One degree-day is equal to the number of degrees, during a 24-hour day, that the mean temperature is below 65° F, which is the *base temperature* in the United States.

degree of compaction The measure of density of a soil sample, estimated by using a standard formula.

degree of density A measure of compaction.

degree of saturation The ratio of the volume of water in a given soil mass to the volume of intergranular voids, expressed as a percentage.

dehumidification The removal of moisture from the ambient air by physical or chemical means.

dehumidifier A device for removing water vapor from the air.

dehydration The removal of water vapor from the air by means of absorption or adsorption.

delamination Separation of plies of materials, usually due to failure of the adhesive. May occur, for example, in veneers, roofing, and laminated wood beams.

delay An event or condition that results in work activity starting, or the project being completed, later than originally planned.

delime To remove the scale that builds up on the inside of hot water heaters and boilers.

deliquescence The absorption of moisture from the air by certain salts in plaster or brick, resulting in damp spots that appear darker than the surrounding material.

delivery hose The hose through which concrete, mortar, grout, or shotcrete is pumped.

delivery order contract (DOC) A comprehensive procurement system for organizations to obtain construction services that is designed to lessen construction response time, reduce in-house workload and enhance quality control.

delta connection A configuration in a three-phase electrical transformer where the three windings form a triangular shape like the Greek letter delta. *See also* **wye connection**.

deluge sprinkler system A dry-pipe sprinkler system particularly well- suited for areas that may experience temperatures below freezing. The system is actuated by a heat- or smoke-detection device, which then turns a valve to admit the water.

demand The electric load integrated over a specific interval of time, usually expressed in watts or kilowatts.

demand factor In an electrical system, the ratio of the maximum demand to the connected load.

demand load The actual amount of electrical load on a circuit on any given time.

demand mortgage loan A mortgage loan that may be called at any time by the mortgagee.

demarcation In masonry, a fixed line for making a boundary limit.

demising partition *See* **party wall**.

demising wall *See* **party wall**.

demolition The intentional destruction of all or part of a structure.

demountable partition (relocatable partition) A non-load-bearing wall made of prefabricated sections that can be readily disassembled and relocated. These partitions may be full height or partial height.

dentils

deposited metal

demurrage (1) A late charge for detaining a cargo-carrying vehicle beyond the agreed-upon time for its return. (2) A late charge for oxygen and acetylene cylinder rentals and electrical cable reels.

den A small room in a home for work or leisure.

dense concrete Concrete containing a minimum number of voids.

dense-graded aggregate Aggregate sized so as to contain a minimum of voids, and therefore to have the maximum weight when compacted.

densified impregnated wood (compregnated wood, compressed wood, resin-treated wood) Laminated wood that has been impregnated with resins and compressed to greatly increase its density and strength.

density (1) In urban planning, the number of people dwelling upon an acre (or sometimes a square mile) of land. (2) The ratio of the mass of a specimen of a substance to the volume of the specimen; the mass per unit volume of a substance. (3) The closeness of pile yarn; the amount of pile packed into a given area of carpet, usually measured in ounces per square yard.

density control The testing of concrete used in a structure to maintain the specified density.

dentil band A wood molding installed to create the effect of a series of dentils.

dentils Square, toothlike blocks used as ornaments under a cornice.

Department of Health and Human Services The federal agency responsible for establishing health and safety standards for the protection of persons.

Department of Labor The federal agency that oversees all laws associated with hiring, employing, and protecting workers.

Department of Transportation (D.O.T.) The federal agency responsible for regulating the safe transportation of goods and materials within the United States.

depolished glass Glass whose surface has been diffused by sandblasting, etching, or some other surface treatment.

deposited metal The filler metal placed during welding.

deposit for bidding documents A deposit required from the bidder for each set of the plans, specifications, and other bidding documents for a contract. Normally the deposit is returned to the bidder upon return of the documents in good condition and within a specified time.

deposition A formal method of obtaining information relevant to a lawsuit by verbally asking an individual questions under oath prior to trial.

depository A location where bids are received by an awarding authority. *See also* **bank depository**.

depot (1) A storehouse, warehouse, or transfer station. (2) A railroad or bus station for ticketing, sheltering, transferring, and shipping passengers and freight.

depreciation The allocation of a part of the cost of a property, plant, or equipment item (that has a limited useful life) over its estimated useful life.

depreciation factor The ratio of initial illumination on an area to the present illumination of the same area, used in lighting calculations to account for depreciation of lamp intensity and reflective surfaces.

depressed arch An arch with a pitch less than that of an equilateral triangle.

derrick

depreter A form of stucco with rock dash finish, made by embedding aggregate in the plaster.

depth gauge An instrument for measuring or testing the depth of dados, grooves, drilled holes, and various other recessed portions of any structural work.

derated concrete *See* **concrete, derated**.

derby *See* **darby**.

derby float *See* **darby**.

derby slicker *See* **darby**.

dermatitis An inflammation of the skin.

derrick A device consisting of a vertical mast and a horizontal or sloping boom operated by cables attached to a separate engine or motor. The device is used for hoisting and moving heavy loads or objects.

descriptive specification A type of specification that provides a detailed description of the required properties of a product, material, or piece of equipment, and the workmanship required for its proper installation.

desiccant An absorbent material that removes water or vapors from another material or from the air. Used in the glazing and refrigeration industries.

desiccate To dry thoroughly or to make dry by removing the moisture content, as in the seasoning of timber by exposing it in an oven to a current of hot air.

desiccator An apparatus in which a substance is dried.

design (1) To create a graphic representation of a structure. (2) The graphic architectural concept of a structure. (3) To make a preliminary sketch, drawing, or outline.

design/build (design-construct) A method of construction in which the contractor provides both design and construction services to an owner.

design-construct *See* **design/build**.

design development phase The second phase of a designer's basic services, which includes developing structural, mechanical, and electrical drawings, specifying materials, and estimating the probable cost of construction.

design factor *See* **design load (1)**.

design for recycling A design concept that seeks to remove hazardous and non-recyclable materials from the production process through careful planning and design.

design load (1) In structural analysis, the total load on a structural system under the worst possible loading conditions. (2) In air conditioning, the maximum heat load a system is designed to withstand.

design pressure The highest pressure expected during operation of a system, device, or piece of equipment.

design professional A term used generally to refer to architects; civil, structural, mechanical, electrical, plumbing, and heating, ventilating, and air-conditioning engineers; interior designers; landscape architects; and others whose services have either traditionally been considered "professional" activities, require licensing or registration by the state, or otherwise require the knowledge and application of design principles appropriate to the problem at hand.

design specification A type of specification that prescribes the materials and methods to be used for contract performance.

detached garage

design strength (1) The assumed value for the strength of concrete and yield stress of steel, used to develop the ultimate strength of a section. (2) The load-bearing capacity of a structural member, determined by the allowable stresses assumed in the design.

design ultimate load (factored load) The working load multiplied by the load factor.

dessicate To dry thoroughly or to make dry by removing the moisture content, as in the seasoning of timber by exposing it in an oven to a current of hot air.

dessicator An apparaturs in which a substance is dried.

de-superheaters Heat exchangers that remove only some of the sensible heat from the hot, high-pressure refrigerant gas.

detachable bit In rock drilling, the cutting bit that is screwed into the end of the drill. The bit contains holes for blowing out the rock dust.

detached dwelling A structure intended for habitation that is surrounded by open space.

detached garage A parking structure whose exterior walls are surrounded by open space.

detail A large-scale architectural or engineering drawing indicating specific configurations and dimensions of construction elements. If the large-scale drawing differs from the general drawing, it is the architect's or engineer's intention that the large-scale drawing be used to clarify the general drawing.

detailed estimate of construction cost A forecast of the cost to construct a project, based on unit prices of materials, labor, and equipment, in contrast to a parameter estimate or square-foot estimate.

detailer A draftsman who prepares shop drawings and lists of materials.

detector *See* **sensor**.

detention door A special steel door with fixed lights and steel bars, used to restrict passage in prisons and mental institutions.

detention window A narrow, metal awning window manufactured especially for the security of prisons and mental institutions.

detergent A chemical compound that cleans surfaces and keeps foreign matter in solution or suspension.

detergent oil A heavy duty oil, commonly used in combustion engines, that contains a detergent additive.

detonating cord A flexible cord attached to a highly explosive core, used for setting off the explosive to which it is attached.

detonator Any of a number of devices, such as blasting caps, for detonating explosives.

detritus Loose material formed from disintegrating rock.

detritus tank A settling tank in a sewage-treatment system for collecting sediment without interrupting the flow of sewage.

detrusion The shearing of wood fibers along the grain.

developed area An area or site upon which improvements have been made.

developed length The length of a pipeline, including fittings, measured along its center line.

developed surface A curved or angular surface graphically represented as flattened out on a plane.

device

dewater

diagonal brace

development A tract of land that has been subdivided for housing and/or commercial usage and includes streets and all necessary utilities.

development bond stress *See* **anchorage bond stress**.

device In an electrical system, a component that carries but does not consume electricity, such as a switch or a receptacle.

devil A fire grate used to heat asphalt-spreading tools. *See also* **devil float**.

devil float (devil, nail float) A flat, hand-held tool with nails in each edge, used to scratch a coat of plaster prior to applying the next coat.

deviling The act of scratching a plaster coat prior to applying another coat.

dewater To remove water from a job site by pumps, wellpoints, or drainage systems.

dewpoint (1) The temperature at which air of a given moisture content becomes saturated with water vapor. (2) The temperature at which the relative humidity of the air is 100%.

dextrin (amylin, starch gum) A starch compound used for wall sizing and wallpaper adhesive.

D-grade wood Used only for interior wood applications, such as for inner plies and backs, where specified.

diabase (traprock) An igneous rock used extensively in construction materials such as asphaltic concrete, concrete, and pavement base courses. The rock crushes into sharp, angular fragments that interlock well with one another.

diaglyph A relief sculptured below the general surface.

diagonal A straight structural member forming the hypotenuse of a right triangle, as in the diagonal bracing of a stud wall.

diagonal bond A pattern of bricklaying in which every sixth course is a header course, with the bricks placed diagonally to the face of the wall to form a decorative herringbone pattern.

diagonal brace A member installed at an angle to make a rectangular frame more rigid.

diagonal bridging Crossing pairs of diagonal bracing that extend between the top of one floor joist and the bottom of the adjacent joist. The bracing is used to distribute the load and to decrease deflection.

diagonal buttress A support structure constructed at a 45° angle to the right-angle corner extension of two exterior walls.

diagonal crack A crack forming at about a 45° angle to the longitudinal dimension of a concrete member, beginning at the tension surface of the member.

diagonal grain In lumber, a deviation of the grain from a line parallel to the longitudinal edges, caused by improper sawing.

diagonal pitch The distance between one rivet or bolt in one row to the nearest rivet or bolt in the next row of a structural member with two or more rows of bolts.

diagonal rib A structural member that crosses the bay of a vault in a diagonal direction.

diagonal sheathing A covering of wooden boards placed diagonally over an exterior stud wall. Although slightly more expensive to install, this method provides a more rigid frame than horizontally-installed boards, and may be more architecturally pleasing.

diamond lath

diaphragm

diagonal slating (drop-point slating) A method of applying diamond-shaped roofing slates with one diagonal laid horizontally.

diagonal tension In concrete structural members, the tensile stress resulting from shearing stresses within the member.

dial saw An attachment used with a power drill to cut holes.

diameter The line in a circle passing through its center.

diamond blade A high strength circular saw blade used to cut brick, concrete, tile, and other hard surfaces.

diamond drill A high-strength rotary rock drill that cuts a core in rock to create blasting holes.

diamond fret (lozenge fret, lozenge molding) A molding with a diamond pattern.

diamond lath (diamond mesh) A type of expanded metal strip used as a base for plaster. Manufactured by slitting and expanding metal sheets.

diamond matching A method of laying up veneers in which four pieces are used, each with the grain running perpendicular to a line drawn diagonally across the whole panel. The resulting design is diamond-shaped.

diamond mesh *See* **diamond lath**.

diamond slate An asbestos-cement roofing shingle shaped like a diamond and used in diagonal slating; no longer used.

diamondwork Masonry laid up so as to incorporate diamond shapes, usually every sixth course.

diaphragm (1) A stiffening member between two structural steel members, used to increase rigidity. (2) The web across a hollow masonry unit. (3) An instrument to measure the flow of water in pipes.

diaphragm pump (mud sucker) A reciprocating water pump with a flexible diaphragm used for continuous dewatering of excavations containing mud and small stones.

diaphragm valve A valve that is actuated by fluid pressure on a diaphragm.

diazo A group of chemical compounds, such as benzenediazo hydroxide or diazomethene, generally used as a light-sensitive emulsion on a support such as paper or plastic. When this material is exposed, as in a photographic process, by the passage of light through an original drawing, and developed by reaction of a coupler (either an acid compound or alkaline agent), an image called a *whiteprint* is produced.

dichroic reflector lamp An incandescent lamp with a filter for correcting the lamp's light color to make it approximate daylight.

die A tool for cutting threads on pipe and bolts.

die-cast A method of casting by forcing molten metal into a mold.

differential leveling A method for determining the difference in elevation between two points using a level and rod.

differential settlement Uneven, downward movement of the foundation of a structure, usually caused by varying soil or loading conditions and resulting in cracks and distortions in the foundation.

differing site conditions Unanticipated physical conditions at the site that differ materially from those set forth in the contract or ordinarily encountered in work of the same nature.

diffuser

dimension stone

dimmer

diffused light Light reflecting from a surface rather than radiating directly from a light source.

diffuser (1) Any device or surface that scatters light or sound from a source. (2) A circular, square, or rectangular air distribution outlet, generally located in the ceiling, and comprised of deflecting members to discharge supply air in various directions.

diffusing glass A glass with an irregular surface, such as ground glass or sandblasted glass. Irregular surfaces can also be produced by grinding, sandblasting, or by rolling the glass during manufacturing. This type of glass provides a softer light for greater eye comfort.

diffusing panel A translucent material, usually plastic, used as a cover over a light source such as a luminaire to distribute the light more evenly.

diffusing surface A reflecting surface, usually rough-textured, used to scatter light or sound.

digital Refers to communications equipment and procedures in which information is represented in binary form (1 or 0), as opposed to analog form (variable, continuous wave forms).

dike (dyke) (1) An earth embankment for retaining water. (2) A large ditch.

dilation The expansion of concrete during cooling or freezing.

diluent Any agent used as a thinner.

dimension A distance between two points, lines, or planes.

dimensionally stable Refers to any building material whose shape does not alter appreciably with changes in temperature, moisture, and loading conditions.

dimension lumber (dimension stuff) Lumber that is cut from 2″ to less than 5″ thick, and 2″ or more wide.

dimension shingles Shingles cut to a uniform size, usually 5″ or 6″ wide, and used for special architectural effects.

dimension stock Hardwood plywood that has been manufactured to specific dimensions for a particular user.

dimension stone Stone that has been trimmed or cut to specifications for a particular use, such as for curbs, building stone, paving blocks, and the like.

dimension stuff *See* **dimension lumber**.

diminished arch (skeen arch, skene arch) An arch with less rise than a semicircle.

diminished stile (diminishing stile, gunstock stile) A door stile that has a narrower dimension at a panel, particularly at a glazed panel.

diminishing course *See* **graduated course**.

diminishing pipe (taper pipe) A pipe reducer.

diminishing stile *See* **diminished stile**.

dimmer An electrical device that varies the amount of light given off by an electrical lamp by varying the current.

dimples A colloquial term used to describe the round depressions left in wall board by a hammer driving nails. Dimples are beneficial as they provide a bed to hold the joint compound applied to hide nail heads.

dinging A rough stucco coat applied to a wall and sometimes scored to imitate masonry joints.

dipper stick

direct-fired air heater

diorama A three-dimensional scene constructed to scale, usually with a painted background.

diorite A granular, igneous rock composed of feldspar and hornblende.

dip (1) In geology, the slope of a fault or vein. (2) In plumbing, the lowest point of the inside top of a trap.

dipcoat A covering of paint or other coating applied by immersing an object in a liquid. Usually applied as an anticorrosive.

dipper The digging bucket attached to the stick or arm of a power shovel or backhoe.

dipper dredge A bucket used as part of a dredging operation for excavating under water.

dipper stick The straight arm that connects the dipper with the boom of a power shovel.

dipper trip The mechanism that releases the latch to the bucket door of a power shovel to discharge the load.

dip solution The solution used to produce a specific finish or color on copper or copper-alloy products.

direct-acting controllers Increase control pressure as the control variable (temperature or pressure) increases.

direct-acting thermostat A device that activates a control circuit within a predetermined temperature range.

direct component The portion of light from a lamp or luminaire that arrives at the workplane without being reflected.

direct costs The labor, material, subcontractor, and heavy equipment costs directly incorporated into the construction of physical improvements.

direct cross-connection A connection between two systems for maintaining equal water pressure.

direct current A term applied to an electrical circuit in which the current flows in one direction only.

direct damages Damages that can be expected to arise as a matter of course from a breach.

direct digital control (DDC) A system that receives electronic signals from sensors, converts those signals to numbers, and performs mathematical operations on the numbers inside a computer. The computer output (in the form of a number) is converted to a voltage or pneumatic signal to operate an actuator.

direct drive A system in which the driver and the driven element (motor and fan) are positively connected in line to operate at the same speed.

direct dumping The placing of concrete using a chute or bucket directly into open forms at or near its final position.

direct expansion (DX) Refrigeration systems that employ expansion valves or capillary tubes to meter liquid refrigerant into the evaporator.

direct expense All cost items that are directly incurred by or chargeable to a project, assignment, or task.

direct-fired air heater An air heating system in which the heat of combustion is applied directly to the intake air so that no heat exchanger is needed.

direct heating The heating of a space by means of exposed heated surfaces or a heat source such as a stove, a radiator, or fire.

direct-indirect lighting A lighting system employing diffused light

disappearing stair

luminaires that emit little or no light horizontal to the lighting unit.

directional drill rig A drill rig that can drill holes in directions other than vertical.

direct lighting A lighting system, usually emitting light in a downward direction, that distributes 90% to 100% of its light in the direction of the surface to be lit.

directional lighting The lighting of an object or workplace from a desirable source location.

direct leveling The determination of the difference in elevation of two or more points using a surveyor's level and a graduated rod.

direct luminaire A luminaire that directs 90% to 100% of its light downward.

direct nailing *See* **face nailing**.

directory board An informational panel with changeable letters, such as those located in an office building lobby.

direct personnel expense Salaries and wages, including fringe benefits, of all principals and employees attributable to a particular project or task.

direct return system A heating or cooling system in which the heating or cooling fluid is returned from the heat exchanger to the boiler or evaporator by the shortest, most direct route.

direct selection A process whereby the owner selects a contractor to construct a project. The selection is made at the owner's discretion based on the contractor's experience, availability, and capability. The terms of the contract for construction are reached by

negotiation rather than through the process of competitive bidding.

direct stress Tensile or compressive force applied without shear or bending.

direct system A heating, air conditioning, or refrigerating system that employs no intermediate heat exchanger to heat or cool a space.

dirt-depreciation factor A measurement of the reduction of light emitted by a luminaire as a result of accumulated dirt.

disability glare An objectionable effect of brightness that hampers visibility and causes discomfort.

disappearing stair A hinged stair, usually folding, that is attached to a trap door in the ceiling and can be raised out of sight when not in use.

discharge head The pressure (in pounds per square inch or psi) measured at the center line of the discharge side of a pump and very close to the discharge flange converted into feet.

discharging arch An arch built above the lintel of a door or window to distribute the weight to each side of the wall above.

discoloration Any change in hue, shade, or color from the original or adjacent color.

discomfort glare An objectionable effect of brightness that does not necessarily hamper visibility.

disconnecting means A device or group of devices that can disconnect the conductors of a circuit from their supply source.

discontinuous construction A method of construction whereby structural members are staggered to reduce sound transmission through a wall or floor.

distribution board

discontinuous easement A right of accommodation (for a specific purpose) requiring action by one of the parties, such as a right-of-way.

discovery A pretrial procedure providing for the full disclosure of all facts and documents related to a contract dispute. The methods used include production of documents, depositions, interrogations, and requests for admission.

disintegration Deterioration or crumbling caused by oxidation, freezing, or exposure to other elements. The term is often applied to the deleterious effects suffered by exposed concrete.

disk sander A hand-held power tool that has a rotating, circular abrasive disk used for smoothing or polishing a surface.

dispatchability The ability of a generating unit or another source of power to vary its output.

dispersant A material capable of holding finely ground particles in suspension. Used as a slurry thinner or grinding compound.

dispersing agent An additive that increases the workability or fluidity of a paste, mortar, or concrete.

dispersion In painting, small particles of pigment or latex held in suspension in paint or varnish.

displacement (1) The volume displaced by a piston or ram moving to the top or bottom of its stroke. (2) In hydraulics, the volume of water displaced by a floating vessel.

displacement pile A pile that displaces soil as it is driven by either shifting or compacting it.

disposal field *See* **absorption field**.

disposal unit An electric motor-driven unit installed in a sink to grind food waste for disposal through the sanitary sewer system.

dispute procedure The administrative procedure for processing a contract dispute with the United States government. This procedure is provided for in the Contract Disputes Act.

disruption The result of actions or inactions that interfere with performance efficiency, thereby requiring additional effort in performance of the contract work.

distance separation The distance, as specified in fire-protection codes, from an exterior wall to an adjacent building, property line, or the centerline of an adjacent street.

distemper An interior wall paint whose colors are tempered in a glutinous base.

distemper brush A wide, flat, long-bristled brush used to apply distemper.

distributed load A load distributed evenly over the entire length of a structural member or the surface of a floor or roof, expressed in weight per length or weight per area.

distribution (1) The movement of heated or conditioned air to desired locations. (2) The delivery of electricity over a system from transmission points. (3) The placement of concrete from where it is discharged to its final location.

distribution board (distribution panel, distribution switchboard) An electric switchboard or panel used to distribute electricity within a building. The switchboard is enclosed in a box and contains circuit breakers, fuses, and switches.

distribution box A container located at the outlet of a septic tank to distribute the effluent evenly to the drain tiles in the absorption field.

ditch

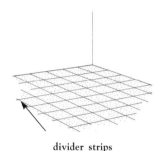

ditcher

divider strips

distribution cutout In a primary electrical circuit, a safety device that disconnects a circuit to prevent overload.

distribution line The main electrical feed line to which other circuits are connected.

distribution panel *See* **distribution board**.

distribution reinforcement The placement of small-diameter reinforcing steel at right angles to the main reinforcing steel in a slab. This method of reinforcement is used to distribute the load and prevent cracking.

distribution steel The small-diameter reinforcing steel used in distribution reinforcement.

distribution switchboard *See* **distribution board**.

distribution tile The tile laid in an absorption field to distribute effluent from a septic tank.

distribution transformer A device that transforms primary voltage into a lower secondary voltage for use within a building.

distributor truck A truck that is equipped with an insulated tank, heating units, and bars for applying liquid asphalt to a pavement area.

ditch A long, open trench used for drainage, irrigation, or for burying underground utilities.

ditcher (ditching machine) A device used for digging temporary ditches or trenches with vertical slopes. The device operates by means of buckets or teeth mounted on a continuously rotating wheel or chain.

ditching machine *See* **ditcher**.

diversion A pipe, trench, or channel, usually temporary, used to divert the flow of water from its usual course.

diversity factor In electrical systems, the sum of the individual demands of the subsystems divided by the maximum demand of the whole system.

diver's paralysis (the bends, caisson disease) Paralysis that may be fatal, caused by too-rapid decrease in air pressure after spending a period of time in a compressed atmosphere.

divided light door A French door with the glass divided into small panes.

divided tenon Two tenons side by side in the end of a member.

dividers A compass with both legs terminating in points. Used for transferring measurements from a plan or map to a scale, or vice versa.

divider strips The nonferrous metal or plastic strips used as screeds in terrazzo work. Also used to divide the panels.

division One of the standard sixteen major Uniform Construction Index classifications used in specifying, pricing, and filing construction data.

division bar *See* **muntin**.

division wall (fire wall) A regulation fire-resistant wall extending from the lowest floor of a building through the roof to prevent the spread of fire.

D-line crack (D-crack) (1) One of several fine, closely spaced, randomly patterned cracks in concrete surfaces. (2) Similar cracks parallel to the edges or joints in a slab. (3) Larger cracks in a highway slab that run diagonally across its corners.

dobying Blasting a boulder by mud-capping rather than drilling.

dock A raised platform for the loading and unloading of trucks. Often, the elevation of a portion of

dog

Dolly Varden siding

dome

dome light

the dock is adjustable to accommodate the differing heights of truck beds.

dock bumper A recoiling or resilient device attached to a dock to absorb the impact of a truck.

dog (1) In concrete forming, the hardware that holds the end of a snap tie. (2) Any device used for holding, gripping, or fastening an object. *See also* **dog anchor**.

dog anchor (dog iron) A short piece of iron with its two pointed ends bent at right angles, driven into two adjoining pieces of timber to hold them together.

dog bars Intermediate vertical members in the lower part of a gate, used to prevent animals from passing through.

dog-ear In roofing or flashing, an external corner formed by folding rather than cutting the metal.

dog house dormer *See* **gable dormer**.

dog iron *See* **dog anchor**.

dogleg stair A stair that forms a right angle turn at a landing.

dog's tooth A bricklaying pattern in which the corners of bricks project from the wall.

dolly (1) One of a variety of small, wheeled devices used to move heavy loads. (2) A block of wood placed on the upper end of a pile to cushion the blow of a hammer. (3) A steel bar with a shaped head to back up a rivet while the rivet is being driven.

Dolly Varden siding Beveled wood siding that is rabbeted along the bottom edge, such as on novelty siding.

dolomite A mineral containing calcium and magnesium carbonate, used primarily as an aggregate in making concrete. *See also* **dolomitic limestone**.

dolomitic lime A name commonly used for high-magnesium lime.

dolomitic limestone A form of cut limestone that contains dolomite and is used in building construction.

dome (1) A hemispherical roof such as that commonly seen on government structures. (2) A rectangular pan form used in two-way joist or waffle concrete floor construction.

dome light A dome-shaped skylight made of glass or plastic.

domestic hot-water heater A packaged unit that heats water for household purposes.

domestic sewage Household waste, including that originating from single- or multi-family housing.

dominant estate Pertaining to legal rights and benefits in property deeds. The property receiving the right or benefit is the *dominant estate*, whereas the property granting the right or benefit is the *servient estate*.

dook A wooden plug inserted into a wall and used for attaching finish trim to the wall.

door A movable member used to close the opening in a wall.

door area The total area of outside doors and facings. Used in computing heating and cooling requirements of a building.

door bolt A sliding bar or rod for locking a door.

door buck A rough wood or metal frame to which the finished door frame is aligned and attached.

door bumper A device placed on the wall or floor behind a door to limit its swing.

door butt A door hinge.

door casing The finished visible frame into which a door fits.

door closer

door frame

door catch A device for fastening a door, usually attached to one side of the door only.

door check An automatic door closer.

door cheek *See* **door jamb**.

door class A fire-rating classification for doors.

door clearance The distance or space between the bottom of a door and a finished floor, or between two double doors.

door closer A device that controls the speed and force of closure of a door.

door contact (door switch) A switch in an electrical circuit that is opened or closed by opening or closing a door.

door frame The surrounding assembly into which a door fits. Consists of two uprights, jambs, and a head over the top.

door frame anchor A device used to align and attach the door frame to the wall. The type of device used depends upon the type of wall and the material of the frame.

door guide A channel used to keep a sliding or rolling door on track during operation.

door hand (door swing) The direction of the swing of a door, expressed as either left-hand or right-hand.

door head (1) The horizontal upper member of a door frame. (2) A lintel.

door holder A device for holding a door open.

door jack A device for holding a wooden door in place while the hinges are being set or while the door is being planed to fit.

door jamb The vertical member on each side of a door frame.

door latch A device for holding a door closed. Usually a beveled bolt self-activated by a spring or by gravity when hitting the strike.

door mullion The vertical member in the middle of a double door frame that contains the strike of the two leaves.

door nail A large-headed nail against which a knocker strikes. Any large-headed, exposed nail in a wooden door.

door opening The size of a door frame opening measured between jambs and from the finished floor (or threshold) to the head.

door operator A power-operated mechanism for opening and closing an elevator door.

door pivot The pin on which a swinging door rotates.

door plate A nameplate on the outside of a door.

door pocket The opening in a wall or partition that receives a sliding door. The door is installed on tracks during the rough framing stage of construction.

door post *See* **door jamb**.

door rail Any of the horizontal members that connect the stiles of a door. In a flush door, the members are hidden. In a panel door, the members are exposed.

door roller The operational hardware used primarily on heavy doors, such as refrigeration doors, to allow them to roll.

door saddle A threshold or door sill.

door schedule A table in the contract documents listing all the doors by size, specifications, and location.

door sill *See* **threshold**.

door stile The outside, upright members of a door.

door stop

dormer

double-acting hinge

door stop The strip on the door frame against which the door closes.

door strip A weatherproofing material used around a door.

door swing *See* **door hand.**

door switch *See* **door contact.**

door trim The casing or molding around a door frame that covers the joint between the frame and the wall.

doorway Any opening in a wall that has a door.

dope (1) In plumbing, a material placed on pipe threads to make them waterproof. (2) An additive in mortar or plaster to accelerate or retard the set.

dormant beam Any large beam that supports smaller ones.

dormer A projection through the slope of a roof for a vertical window.

dormer cheek The side wall of a dormer.

dormer window A window on the front vertical face of a dormer.

dormitory A residential building that includes sleeping facilities. Most commonly found at an educational institution.

dosing tank A holding tank for raw or partially treated sewage that discharges automatically when a desired quantity has accumulated.

dot A small amount of plaster placed on a surface between grounds to aid the plasterer in maintaining a constant thickness.

dote (doze) An early form of decay in wood. Usually, the decay can be cut out and the remainder of the wood salvaged.

D.O.T. shipping name A material classification name assigned by the Department of Transportation to all transportable materials.

doty A term used to describe wood that shows an early form of decay.

double-acting butt A butt hinge that swings both ways.

double-acting door (swinging door) A door with double-acting hinges so that it can swing both ways.

double-acting frame A door frame without stops, which allows a double-acting door to swing both ways.

double-acting hinge A door hinge that allows the door to swing both ways.

double angle A structural member formed by using two L-shaped angle irons back to back.

double back (double up) A method of applying two coats of plaster in which the second coat is applied before the first coat has set.

double-bend fitting An S-shaped pipe fitting.

double-beveled edge The edge of a swinging door stile that is beveled from the center of the edge toward the two faces.

double-bitted ax An ax with two cutting edges.

double-break switch An electrical switch that opens and closes a conductor in two places.

double breasted A firm that operates or has ownership in both open shop and union companies.

double brick A masonry unit that measures 4″ by 5 1/3″ by 8″. The nominal measurement of standard bricks is 2″ x 4″ x 8″.

double bridging Bridging that breaks the span of joists into three sections.

double-center theodolite A precision instrument used in surveying to take repeated readings of the same angle. A standard procedure is to take the

double egress frame

sum of six readings and divide by six to minimize human error.

double cheek cut A two-sided cut that forms a "V" at the end of a rafter, especially in hip and gambrel roofs.

double-cleat ladder A wide, site-constructed ladder with a center rail to allow both ascending and descending traffic.

double corner block A concrete masonry unit that has flat, rectangular faces.

double course (doubling course) Two thicknesses of roofing or siding shingles laid one over the other so that there is complete coverage of at least two layers overall.

double-cut file A file with two sets of diagonal cutting ridges crossing each other on the face of the file.

double-cut saw A saw with teeth which cut both on the push and the pull stroke.

double door Two single doors or leaves hung in the same door frame.

double-dovetail key A hardwood wedge used to join two timbers. The wedge has a dovetail on each end, which is driven into a corresponding recess in each timber.

double drum hoist An engine for a material or personnel hoist. It has two drums that can be driven separately.

double eaves course A double course of roofing installed at the eaves of a sloping roof.

double egress frame A door frame designed for two doors, both of the same hand, swinging in opposite directions. The door that swings toward the viewer is called a *reverse-hand door*.

double-end tenoner A machine with a fixed and a movable cutter that is used by industrial woodworkers for the simultaneous double end trimming and shaping of panel type or lineal wood products.

double-end-trimmed Refers to wood that has been passed through saws and trimmed smoothly at both ends, commonly in length increments of 2′.

double-extra-strong pipe A specification for steel pipe that indicates the wall thickness has been increased to give the pipe double strength.

double-faced hammer A hammer whose head has two striking faces.

double-faced stock AA and AB grades of sanded plywood, both interior and exterior, having a good appearance on both sides.

double Flemish bond Brickwork laid up so that it has a pattern of headers and stretchers laid alternately on both faces.

double floor A floor constructed with a subfloor under a finished wood floor.

double-framed floor A floor system constructed with both binding joists and common joists. The ceiling is attached to the binding joists and the floor is laid on the common joists. The binding joists are framed by girders.

double-framed roof A roof framing system in which both longitudinal and lateral members are used, such as one that employs purlins.

double-fronted lot A lot bounded by a street on both the front and the back.

double-gable roof An M-shaped roof with a valley between two gables.

double glazing Window with two panes of glass with an air space between for increased thermal and sound insulation.

double-hung window

double L stair

double partition

doublehanded saw A crosscut saw with a handle on each end, designed to be used by two people.

double-headed nail (duplex-head nail, form nail, scaffold nail) A nail with two heads, one above the other, used for temporary construction such as concrete forms and scaffolds. The nail can secure the work but still be easily extracted.

double header A header joist for an opening made stronger by using two pieces of lumber.

double hem In sheet metal construction, the folding over of the sheet edge twice for greater rigidity and strength.

double-hung window A window that has two vertical sliding sashes, one above the other, mounted on separate guides so that either or both can be opened at one time. This is the type of window most commonly used on wood-frame houses.

double jack rafter A rafter that joins the roof hip to the valley.

double layer Two layers of gypsum board installed over each other to improve fire resistance or sound-suppression characteristics.

double-lock seam In metal roofing and ductwork, a seam formed by double-folding the edges of adjacent sheets and laying them down.

double L stair A stair with two landings turning 90° each, one near the top and one near the bottom.

double-margin door An extra-wide door constructed to look like two doors.

double nailing A method of applying drywall using two nails where one nail would ordinarily be used.

double offset In piping, a dogleg or two changes of direction near to each other.

double partition A partition constructed with two rows of studs to form a pocket door or a cavity for soundproofing.

double-pitched A roof with a second pitch or slope, such as a gambrel roof.

double-pole scaffold A scaffold erected with two rows of uprights independent of an adjacent wall.

double-pole switch An electrical switch that has two blades and contacts that open or close both sides of a circuit simultaneously.

double pour In built-up roofing, a second, final application of bitumen without adding another layer of felt.

double-rabbeted frame A door frame with a longitudinal groove cut on each edge so that a door can be hung on each side.

double rafter A pair of roof rafters installed alongside each other.

double return stair A stair with one flight to a landing, separating into two flights to the next floor.

double roof A roof-framing system in which the rafters rest on purlins.

double-shell tile A ceramic tile with two finished faces separated by a web.

double step In timber framing, a double notch cut into a tie beam supporting the rafters to reduce horizontal shear.

double-strength glass Plate or float glass that is 1/8″ thick.

double suction riser method The use of two pipes for the upward flow of refrigerant suction gas. During periods of low refrigeration load, the refrigerant flow of one of the risers is blocked by the

double T-beam

dovetail

accumulation of oil in the base of the riser, diverting refrigerant flow at a higher velocity to transport oil up the other riser.

double swing frame A frame for two matching doors, each of which swing in the same direction.

double T-beam A precast concrete member composed of two beams with a flat slab cast monolithically across and projecting beyond the top of the two beams.

double tenons Two tenons side by side in the end of a wood beam. *See also* **tenon**.

double-throw switch An electrical switch that can make connections in either of two circuits by changing its position.

double-tier partition A partition that is continuous through two stories of a building.

double up *See* **double back**.

double-wall cofferdam A cofferdam constructed from two rows of sheet piling with fill between them. Used principally for high cofferdams that require greater stability.

double-walled heat exchanger A heat exchanger with two walls between the collector fluid and the potable water.

double waste and vent In plumbing, a single vent that serves two fixtures.

double-welded joint A joint welded on both sides.

doubling course *See* **double course**.

doubling piece A cant strip or fillet.

doubly prestressed concrete A concrete member prestressed in two directions perpendicular to each other.

doubly reinforced concrete A concrete member cast with compression reinforcing steel as well as tension reinforcing steel.

doughnut (1) A large washer used as a concrete form accessory to increase the holding capacity of the forms. (2) A small, round concrete casting with a hole in the middle used to keep reinforcing steel the desired distance from the forms during the placement of concrete. (3) A concrete collar cast around a column and used to jack up the column. (4) A slang term for the wax ring used as a watertight seal in toilet installation.

Douglas fir *Pseudotsuga taxifolia*. A coniferous softwood found throughout the western United States and Canada and grown abundantly on the western slopes of the Cascade Mountains in Oregon. This tree produces a strong, durable timber that is widely used in general construction as well as in finish applications.

dovetail (dovetail joint) In finish carpentry, an interlocking joint that is wider at its end than at its base.

dovetail cramp A dovetail-shaped metal fastener used for lifting masonry units.

dovetail cutter A rotary power tool used to shape dovetail joints and mortises.

dovetail half-lap joint A dovetail joint and mortise cut halfway through adjoining pieces to give the appearance of a butt or miter joint on the opposite side.

dovetail hinge A strap hinge with both leaves shaped like a dove's tail (wider at the end than at the base).

dovetail joint *See* **dovetail**.

dovetail lath *See* **rib lath**.

dovetail miter A joint having a concealed dovetail so that it appears to be a miter joint.

dowel-bar reinforcement

downspout

draft hood

dovetail plane A wood-finishing tool used for preparing dovetail joints.

dovetail saw A small tenon saw or back saw with a stiffening strip along its back and fine teeth for preparing dovetails.

dowel A cylindrical piece of stock inserted into holes in adjacent pieces of material to align and/or attach the two pieces.

dowel-bar reinforcement Short sections of reinforcing steel that extend from one concrete pour into the next. Used to increase strength in the joint.

dowel bit (spoon bit) A carpenter's bit used with a brace for drilling dowel holes. The bit is shaped like a half-cylinder.

dowel lubricant A lubricant applied to dowels placed in adjoining concrete slabs to allow longitudinal movement in expansion joints.

dowel pin A special nail pointed at both ends and used to fasten mortise and tenon joints.

dowel plate A steel plate with holes through which dowels are driven to trim them to size.

dowel screw A threaded dowel.

downdraft A downward current of air, such as that which occurs in a chimney flue or a stairwell.

down-feed system A piping system in which the distribution lines are above the systems being supplied.

downlight A small direct-lighting unit, usually recessed in the ceiling and directing light downward only.

downspout (drainpipe, conductor, leader) A vertical pipe used to carry rainwater from the roof to either the ground or a drainage system.

downtime The amount of time a piece of equipment cannot be

used due to failure, repair, or maintenance.

doze *See* **dote**.

dozer *See* **bulldozer**.

dozer shovel A tractor-mounted unit that can be used for pushing, digging, or loading earth.

draft (1) The drawing power of air and gases through a chimney flue. (2) A note similar to a check except that banks will not cash it without certain preliminary processing. A draft takes 10 to 14 days to "clear," or be guaranteed by the bank. (During this period, the bank sends the draft back to the insurance company for validation.) (3) A smooth strip worked on a stone surface to be used as a guide for finishing the surface.

draft bead (deep bead, draft stop) A fillet or bead on the windowsill of a double-hung window that permits ventilation of the joint, but prevents a draft from entering the room.

draft curtain (curtain board) A noncombustible curtain surrounding a high-hazard area to contain and direct flame, smoke, and fumes.

draft fillet A narrow strip of material on which glass rests in glazing.

draft gauge An instrument used to measure differences in air pressure.

draft hood A cap that fits over a chimney flue to prevent downdrafts.

drafting chisel A tool used most commonly to cut a narrow border or line at the end of a stone.

drafting machine A device attached to a drafting table that combines the functions of a T-square, triangle, scale, and protractor.

drafting pen One of a variety of drawing instruments used for drafting.

drain

drapery track

draft stop *See* **draft bead.**

drag (1) A long, serrated plate used to level and score plaster in preparation for the next coat. (2) Any combination of logs, chains, or other materials dragged behind a tractor to fine-grade earth.

dragline A bucket attachment for a crane that digs by drawing the bucket towards itself using a cable. The attachment is most commonly used in soft, wet materials that must be excavated at some distance from the crane. This device is used extensively in marsh or marine work.

dragon beam A short, horizontal membrane that bisects the angle of the wall plate at the corner of a wood-frame building, and bisects the angle brace at its other end. The member supports a hip rafter at one end and is supported by the angle brace at the other end.

dragon tie An angle brace that supports a dragon beam.

drag saw A powered reciprocating saw used to cross-cut logs.

drag shovel *See* **backhoe.**

drag strut A structural member that transfers lateral force from one vertical member to another.

drain A pipe, ditch, or trench designed to carry away waste water.

drainage (1) Waste water. (2) The process by which waste water is carried away.

drainage fill (1) Granular material placed beneath a concrete floor slab to inhibit the capillary rise of moisture. (2) Lightweight concrete that is placed on a floor or roof to promote drainage.

drainage piping The piping comprising the plumbing of a drainage system.

drainage system All the components that convey the sewage and other waste water to a point of disposal.

drain cock A cock or spigot at the lowest point of a water system where the system can be drained.

drain field *See* **absorption field.**

drainpipe *See* **downspout.**

drain tile Short-length sections of tile laid with open joints, usually surrounded with aggregate and covered with asphaltic paper or straw. Used to drain the water from an area.

drain trap *See* **trap.**

draped tenon *See* **deflected tendon.**

drapery track A system of tracks or bars that support draperies and allow them to be drawn.

drawbar The bar attached to the back of a tractor for pulling equipment.

drawbore A hole in a tenon that is out of line with the holes in the mortise of a mortise-and-tenon joint, so that the joint is tightened when a pin is driven into the hole.

drawdown The distance by which the groundwater level is lowered by excavation, dewatering, or pumping.

drawer dovetail A dovetail joint in which the tenons of one member do not pass completely through the other member, such as the joint used on the front of a drawer.

drawer kicker A block that prevents a drawer from tilting downward when open.

drawer roller Prefabricated sliding drawer hardware employing rollers to facilitate the opening of a drawer.

drawer runner (drawer slip) The strips on which a drawer slides.

dressed and matched

drawer slide The hardware on which a drawer slides.

drawer slip *See* **drawer runner.**

drawer stop A device that prevents a drawer from sliding all the way out.

drawings (1) Graphic illustrations depicting the dimensions, design, and location of a project. Generally including plans, elevations, details, diagrams, schedules, and sections. (2) The term, when capitalized, refers to the graphic portions of a project's contract documents.

draw-in system An electrical wiring system in which all cables are pulled through conduits, ducts, and raceways.

drawknife (drawshave) A two-handled, curved, woodworking knife used by pulling it toward the user.

drawn finish A smooth, bright finish on longitudinal stock obtained by drawing the stock through a die.

draw pin A pin that attaches a tongue to a drawbar.

drawshave *See* **drawknife.**

draw tongue The bar attached to a machine so that it can be pulled by another machine.

dredge (1) To excavate under water. (2) The equipment used for excavating under water, such as a clamshell, dragline, or suction line.

drencher system A fire-protection sprinkler system that protects the outside of a building.

dressed Building material that has been prepared, shaped, or finished on at least one side or edge.

dressed and matched (tongued and grooved) Refers to boards or planks that have been machined so that each piece has a tongue on one edge and a groove on the other.

dressed lumber (dressed stuff) Lumber that has been processed through a planing machine in order to attain a smooth surface and uniformity of size on at least one side or edge.

dressed size The true dimensions of lumber after sawing and planing, as opposed to the nominal size.

dressed stuff *See* **dressed lumber.**

dresser A plumber's tool for flattening sheet lead and straightening lead pipe.

dresser coupling A device for connecting unthreaded pipe.

dressing compound Liquid bituminous material used to cover and protect the exposed surfaces of roofing felt.

dress up To fasten and fabricate structural members on the ground before erection.

drier (1) A unit containing a desiccant that is installed in a refrigeration circuit to collect excess water in the system. (2) An additive to paints and varnishes that speeds the drying process.

drift (1) In a water-spraying system, the entrained, unevaporated water picked up by the air movement through it. (2) In aerial surveying, the angle at which a plane must crab, or turn its nose into the wind, in order to fly a predetermined line. (3) A natural deposit of loose material such as rock or sand. (4) The lateral movement or deflection of a structure.

driftbolt A short rod or bar, 1 to 2 feet long, driven into prebored holes in timber to secure them to each other. The driftbolt is usually of square stock and slightly larger than the hole.

drill

drilled-in caisson

drill press

drift control agent An additive used in spray mixtures to ensure a cohesive spray solution and reduce spray drift.

drift eliminators Baffles in a cooling tower through which air passes before exiting the tower, the purpose of which is to remove entrained water droplets from the exhaust air.

drifter A pneumatic drill used for drilling horizontal or sloped blastholes.

driftpin (drift punch) A tapered pin used in steel erection to align holes for bolting or riveting.

drift plug A hardwood plug that is driven into a lead pipe to straighten it or to flare the end.

drift punch *See* **driftpin.**

drill (1) A hand-held, manually operated or power-driven rotary tool for boring holes in construction materials. (2) A large machine capable of drilling 4″ diameter blast holes 100′ deep in rock cuts or quarries. (3) A machine capable of taking core samples in rock or earth.

drill bit The part of a drill that does the cutting.

drilled-in caisson A caisson that is socketed into rock. *See also* **caisson.**

drill press A rotary drill, mounted on a permanent stand, that operates along a vertical shaft.

drill steel Hollow steel sections that connect the percussion drill with the bit. Air is blown through the steel to clean out the drill hole.

drip (1) A groove in the underside of a projection, such as a windowsill, that prevents water from running back into the building wall. (2) A condensation drain in a steam heating system.

drip cap (drip mold, drip molding) A horizontal molding placed over exterior door or window frames to divert rainwater.

drip channel *See* **drip (1).**

drip edge (1) The edge of a roof from which rainwater drips into a gutter or away from the structure. (2) The metal or wood strip that stiffens and protects this edge.

drip mold *See* **drip cap.**

drip molding *See* **drip cap.**

drip pan A device for catching and containing drips and leaks from liquid storage drums.

dripstone A drip cap made of stone.

dripstone course A course of stone projecting out beyond the face of a wall to shed water away from the wall.

drive band (driving band) A steel band placed around the top of a wooden pile to protect it during driving.

drive cap A steel covering placed atop a pile to protect it during driving.

driven pile A pile that is driven into place by striking it with a pile-driving hammer.

driven well A pipe fitted with a well point that has been driven into water-bearing soil.

drivepoint *See* **well point.**

drivescrew (screw nail) A screw that is driven with a hammer and removed with a screwdriver.

drive shoe A cap placed over the bottom of a pile to protect the pile during driving.

driveway A private access for vehicular traffic.

driving band *See* **drive band.**

drop ceiling
(dropped ceiling)

dropped girder

drop siding

driving cap A steel cap placed over the top of a pile to protect the pile during driving.

driving resistance The number of blows required to drive a pile a given distance.

drop In air conditioning, the vertical distance that a horizontally projected air stream has fallen when it reaches the end of its throw.

drop apron A metal strip that is bent downward at the edge of a metal roof to act as a drip.

drop-bottom bucket A concrete bucket whose bottom opens when it touches the surface where the concrete is to be deposited.

drop-bottom seal *See* **automatic door bottom.**

drop box An electrical outlet box hung from above, as from a ceiling.

drop ceiling (dropped ceiling) A nonstructural ceiling suspended below the structural system, usually in a modular grid pattern. A drop ceiling usually contains a lighting system.

drop chute A device, much like an elephant's trunk, used to place concrete with a minimum amount of segregation.

drop elbow A pipe fitting, at a 90° angle, with one or more flanges for attachment to a wall or stud.

drop hammer A pile-driving hammer which gains impact by free-falling after being lifted by a cable in the leads.

dropout An event where voltage decreases to zero for at least five miliseconds.

dropout ceiling A suspended ceiling with heat-sensitive tiles that are designed to drop out in the event of a fire and sprinkler discharge. A dropout ceiling is aesthetically

pleasing, as it does not require that sprinklers be extended below the ceiling.

drop panel The part of a cast-in-place flat slab that has been thickened on the underside at the location of the columns.

dropped ceiling *See* **drop ceiling.**

dropped girder (dropped girt) A girder that runs below the floor joists and supports them.

dropped girt *See* **dropped girder.**

drop-point slating *See* **diagonal slating.**

drop siding A type of siding that is tongued and grooved or ship-lapped so that the edge of each board fits into the edge of the adjoining board.

drop tee A pipe tee with lugs in the sides for attachment to a support.

drop vent In plumbing, a vent that is connected at a point below the fixture.

drop window A vertically sliding window that slides into a recess below the window stool so that the entire opening can be used for ventilation.

drop wire An electrical conductor dropped from a pole to a building to supply electric power to the building.

drove A mason's broad, blunt chisel used for facing stone.

drum (1) One of the stone cylinders forming a column. (2) The wall supporting a dome. (3) The rotating cylinder used to wind up cable on a hoist. (4) The cylinder in which transit-mixed concrete is transported, mixed, and agitated.

drum paneling A door panel that is covered with leather.

drum rasp A cylindrical abrasive device used with a power drill to

dry glazing

smooth or contour wood, plastic and soft metals.

drum sander A power tool with a cylindrical abrasive sleeve used to smooth or contour wood, plastic and soft metals. Usually mounted on a stand.

drum trap A cylindrical plumbing trap usually set flush with a floor so that easy access can be gained by unscrewing the top.

drunken saw (wobble saw) A type of circular saw designed to operate with a built-in wobble so that the kerf it makes is greater than the thickness of the saw. This type of saw is used for grooving and for other special purposes in carpentry.

dry area A narrow roofed area between a basement wall and a retaining wall, constructed to keep the basement wall dry.

dry basin systems Condenser water systems in which the cooling tower basin is located indoors, and away from the cooling tower.

dry batch weight The weight of the materials, excluding water, used to make a batch of concrete.

dry-bond adhesive (contact adhesive) An adhesive that seems dry but that adheres on contact.

dry-bulb temperature The ambient temperature indicated by an ordinary thermometer with an unmoistened bulb.

dry clamping The practice of piecing together all parts of an assembly, such as a table, before fastening to confirm that all joints fit.

dry concrete Concrete that has a low water content, making it relatively stiff. The effects are a lower water-cement ratio, less pressure on forms, lower heat of hydration, and a consistency that allows for placement on a sloping surface.

dry construction Building construction without the use of plaster or mortar. The use of dry materials speeds the construction process and allows earlier occupancy.

dry course The first course of a built-up roof, which lies directly on the insulation without bitumen.

dry density The weight of a soil sample that has been heated to 105° centigrade (Celsius) to remove the moisture.

dry filter A device for removing pollutants from the air in a system by passing the air through various screens and dry, porous materials. Most dry filters in HVAC systems today are made of spun fiberglass.

dry glazing The installation of glass using dry, preformed gaskets in place of glazing compound.

dry hydrate *See* **hydrated lime**.

dry ice A substance made of solid carbon dioxide that is used in refrigeration applications. Dry ice sublimates, or changes directly from a solid to a gas.

drying inhibitor A substance added to paint to prevent the surface from drying too rapidly, causing wrinkling or cracking.

drying oil An oil used in paints to promote quick, smooth, hard, and elastic drying qualities.

drying shrinkage Contraction caused by the loss of moisture, particularly in concrete, mortar, and plaster.

dry joint A masonry joint without mortar.

dry kiln A chamber in which wood products are seasoned by applying heat and withdrawing moist air.

dry-pipe sprinkler system

dry-pipe valve

dry masonry Masonry laid without mortar.

dry mix A concrete or mortar mixture that contains little water in proportion to its other ingredients.

dry-mix shotcrete Concrete or mortar that is pumped through a hose and to which water is added at the nozzle during application.

dry mortar Mortar mixed to a very dry consistency, but still wet enough for hydration. This type of mortar is used to prevent compaction in the joints of high, narrow lifts.

dryout In plywood manufacturing, an unsatisfactory glue bond that can occur if the glue becomes too dry to adhere properly when pressure is applied in the hot press.

dry-packing (dry-tamp process) The forceful injection of a damp concrete mixture into a confined space where high strength and little shrinkage is desired, such as under a bearing plate.

dry-packed concrete *See* **concrete, dry-packed.**

dry-pipe sprinkler system (dry sprinkler) A sprinkler system whose pipes remain empty of water until the system is activated. This type of system is particularly useful where there is danger of freezing.

dry-pipe valve The valve that activates a dry-pipe sprinkler system.

dry-powder fire extinguisher A hand-held fire extinguisher that discharges a dry powder by means of a compressed gas. This type of extinguisher is effective for Class B and Class C fires.

dry press A mechanical device for molding masonry units from a very dry mixture.

dry-press brick Bricks made in a dry press.

dry return In a steam heating system, a return pipe above the water level.

dry-rodded volume A standard method of compacting aggregate when designing a concrete mix.

dry-rodded weight The unit weight of aggregate compacted under standard conditions and used when designing a concrete mix.

dry rodding Compaction of aggregate in a container under standard conditions for determining the unit weight in a concrete mix design.

dry rot A type of decomposition in seasoned wood caused by fungi.

dry rubble construction A method of construction using stone rubble but no mortar.

dry sampling In soil testing, the practice of obtaining an undisturbed sample of earth with a boring tool.

dry shake (dry topping) A concrete surface treatment, such as color, hardening, or antiskid, which is applied to a concrete slab by shaking on a dry, granular material before the concrete has set and then troweling it in.

dry sheet The nonbituminous felt or light roofing paper laid between the roof deck and the roofing material to prevent adherence and to allow for independent motion of the two systems.

dry sprinkler *See* **dry-pipe sprinkler system.**

dry stone wall A stone wall constructed without mortar.

dry strength The strength of an adhesive joint determined under standard laboratory testing conditions.

dry-tamp process *See* **dry packing.**

dry tape The application of joint tape to gypsum board using an

dry rubble construction

drywall construction

drywall frame

duct

duct system

adhesive other than the standard joint compound.

dry topping *See* **dry shake.**

dry-type transformer A transformer whose core and coils are not immersed in an oil bath.

dry-volume measurement Measurement of the ingredients of a concrete or mortar mix by using their bulk volume. This method is used principally in mix design.

drywall Interior finish construction materials that are manufactured and installed in preformed sheets, such as gypsum wallboard. Drywall is an alternative to plaster.

drywall construction Interior construction using drywall rather than plaster.

drywall frame A door frame specifically designed to be used with drywall construction.

drywall router A small power tool for making cutouts for electrical boxes, windows, and other openings in drywall and panelling.

dry well A pit or well that is filled or lined with coarse aggregate or rocks and designed to contain drainage water until it can be absorbed into the surrounding ground.

dual bed system A gas-phase or liquid adsorption treatment system with two carbon adsorbers, a pump, and associated piping, that can be configured in series or in parallel, depending on facility requirements.

dual duct In electrical wiring, a duct that has two individual raceways.

dual-duct system An HVAC system using two ducts, one for hot air and one for cold air. The air from these ducts is blended in mixing boxes before distribution to each location.

dual-fuel system A heating unit that can use either of two types of fuel.

dual glazing *See* **double glazing.**

dual-head nail *See* **double-headed nail.**

dual vent (common vent) A single plumbing vent that serves two fixtures.

dubbing (dubbing out) (1) Filling in irregularities in a plaster wall before applying the final coat. (2) Roughing in a plaster cornice before forming it with the final coat.

dubbing out *See* **dubbing.**

duckboard A wooden walkway across a wet area.

duct (1) In electrical systems, an enclosure for wires or cables, often embedded in concrete floors or encased in concrete underground. (2) In HVAC systems, the conduit used to distribute the air. (3) In posttensioning, the hole through which the cable is pulled.

duct liner Fiberglass sound and thermal insulation material used inside the sheet metal ducts of air conditioning systems.

duct sheet The metal used in fabricating HVAC ducts.

duct silencer *See* **sound attenuator.**

duct static pressure (1) The pressure acting on the walls of a duct. (2) The total pressure less the velocity pressure. (3) The pressure existing by virtue of the air density and its degree of compression.

duct system The connected elements of an air-distribution system through ductwork.

ductwork The ducts of an HVAC system.

due care A legal term defining the standards of performance that can be expected, either by contract or by implication, in the execution of a particular task.

dumbwaiter

duplex

duplex receptacle

duration

dug well A hand-excavated water well that was cased either during or after excavation.

dumbwaiter A small hoisting mechanism or elevator in a building used for hoisting materials only. The dumbwaiter was originally developed by Thomas Jefferson for use in his home at Monticello.

dummy In CPM (Critical Path Method) scheduling, a restraint with no activity and no time.

dummy joint A groove formed on the surface of a concrete slab or wall for appearance and crack control.

dumpcrete A term applied to concrete that has been batched on site and delivered to placing location by agitator vehicle.

dumped fill Soil that has been deposited, usually by truck, but has not yet been spread or compacted.

dumpling Unexcavated soil, left in the middle of an excavation, which can be used for bracing against sheeting and forms during construction of the subgrade walls.

dumpster Portable container box normally placed on a construction site for the disposal of job-generated refuse.

dumpy level A surveying instrument consisting of a telescope rigidly attached to a vertical spindle. Used to determine relative elevation.

dunnage (1) Waste lumber. (2) Temporary timber decking. (3) Structural support for a system within a building that is independent of the building's structural frame. An example would be the supports for an air-conditioning cooling tower. (4) Strips of wood used in stowing cargo to provide air space between pieces or packages.

dunter A pneumatic machine for polishing stone surfaces.

duplex (duplex house, two-family house) A house with two separate dwelling units.

duplex apartment An apartment with rooms on two floors connected by a private staircase.

duplex burner A gas heating system with two burners that can either burn simultaneously for rapid heating or separately during lower heating demand.

duplex cable Two conductors, separately insulated, encased in a common insulated cover.

duplex-head nail *See* **double-headed nail**.

duplex house *See* **duplex**.

duplex outlet *See* **duplex receptacle**.

duplex receptacle (duplex outlet) Two electrical receptacles housed in the same outlet box.

duraluminum An aluminum alloy that has good anticorrosive properties, used principally in extrusions and rolled sheets.

duramen The hard inner portion, or heartwood, of a tree.

duration In CPM (Critical Path Method) scheduling, the estimated time to complete an activity.

Durham fitting A cast-iron, threaded, pitched fitting used on drainage pipes.

Durham system A waste-water system using all threaded pipes and pitched fittings.

durometer An instrument for determining the relative hardness of a material.

Dur-O-Wal® Trade name for horizontal reinforcement in masonry design.

Dutch hip roof

Dutch lap

dwelling

dust collector Any device used to collect the dust produced by a machine or tool, such as those required at all rock-drilling operations and those used with bench saws.

dust-free In paint and varnish drying, the stage in which dust will no longer stick to the surface.

dust-free time The time required for a paint or varnish application to become dust-free under given environmental conditions.

dusting The development of dust on the surface of a concrete floor. Dusting can result from troweling too soon, too much water in the mix, improper mix design, and other reasons.

dust-laying oil A petroleum distillate applied cold for dust control in unpaved areas.

dustproof strike A strike plate for a lock with a spring plunger that completely fills the bolt hole when the bolt is not in it.

Dutch door A door with two leaves, one above the other.

Dutch door bolt A bolt for locking together the upper and lower halves of a Dutch door.

Dutch hip roof A style of roof framing similar to that in a hip roof, but with a small gable at the top.

Dutch lap A method of applying shingles with a head lap and a side lap.

Dutch light A removable sash used in greenhouses.

dutchman In carpentry and joinery, a small piece inserted to cover a joint or a defect.

dwang A crowbar.

dwarf partition A partition that does not extend to the full ceiling height.

dwarf rafter *See* **jack rafter**.

dwarf wall Any wall less than one story in height, such as a subwall for a crawl space or a wall that supports sleepers for the floor above.

dwelling Any building designed for permanent living accommodations for one or more persons.

dwelling unit A room or rooms designed for permanent living accommodations for one or more persons.

dynamic Refers to information that will be updated and displayed automatically on a Building Automation System CRT or display panel when the status of the building equipment changes.

dynamic analysis The analysis of stresses in a framing system under dynamic loading conditions.

dynamic load A load on a structural system that is not constant, such as a moving live load or wind load.

dynamic loading Loading imposed by a piece of machinery through vibration, in addition to its dead load.

dynamic penetration test A test to determine the bearing capacity of soil where a testing device is delivered a series of blows to penetrate the soil.

dynamic resistance The resistance of a pile to blows from a pile hammer, expressed in blows per unit of penetration.

E

E ABBREVIATIONS

The abbreviations listed below are those most commonly used in the construction industry. Alternative forms (usually nonstandard) are shown in parentheses.

e eccentricity, erg

E east, engineer, equipment only, modulus of elasticity, 90° elbow

ea. each

EA exhaust air

EAM enterprise asset management

E and OE errors and omissions excepted

eastern S-P-F eastern spruce, pine, or fir

EB1S edge bead one side

E&CB2S edge and center bead two sides

ecol ecology

Econ. economy

EDA emergency declaration area

EDP electronic data processing

EDR equivalent direct radiation

EE eased edges, electrical engineer, errors excepted

EEO equal opportunity employer

eff efficiency

EG edge (vertical) grain

ehf extremely high frequency

EHP effective horsepower, electric horsepower

EIA Electronic Industries Association

EL elevation, elevator

elec electric, electrical

elec. electrician, electrical

elev elevation, elevator

Elev. elevating, elevator

EM end matched

EMF electromotive force

EMI electromagnetic interference

EMS energy management system

EMT electrical metallic conduit, thin wall conduit

emu electromagnetic unit

enam enameled

encl enclosure

eng engine

Eng. engine

engr engineer

EOL end of line termination

EPA Environmental Protection Agency

EPDM ethylene propylene diene monomer

EPS expanded polystyrene

eq equal

Eq. equation

Eqhv. equipment operator, heavy

Eqlt. equipment operator, light

Eqmd. equipment operator, medium

Eqmm. equipment operator, master mechanic

Eqol. equipment operator, oilers

equip equipment

equiv equivalent

erec erection

ERW electric resistance welding

est estimate

EST. estimated

esu electrostatic unit

ET ethyl

EV electron volt

evap evaporate

EV1S edge vee one side

EW each way

EWT entering water temperature

ex example, extra

exc excavation, except

excav excavation

Excav. excavation

exh exhaust

exp expansion

Exp. expansion

exp bt expansion bolt

ext exterior

Ext. exterior

extg extracting

extru, Extru. extrusion

exx examples

ear

E The rating of elasticity or stiffness of a material.

ear (shoulder) (1) A small decorative or structural projecting member or part of a structure or piece. (2) A small metal projection on a pipe by which it can be nailed to a wall.

ear lamp An incandescent lamp, part of whose envelope serves as an ellipsoidal reflector.

earliest event occurrence time In CPM (Critical Path Method) scheduling, the earliest completion of all the activities that precede the event.

early finish In CPM (Critical Path Method) scheduling, the first day on which no work is to be done for an activity, assuming work began on its early start time.

early start In CPM (Critical Path Method) scheduling, the first day of a project on which work on an activity can begin if all preceding activities are completed as early as possible.

early stiffening The premature development of rigidity in freshly mixed Portland cement paste, mortar, or concrete. Stiffening occurs when there is little heat generation from the batch, a condition that can be overcome by further mixing without adding water.

early strength The strength that has developed in concrete or mortar, usually within 72 hours after placement.

earlywood *See* **springwood**.

earth *See* **soil**.

earth auger (earth borer, earth drill) A screw-like drill (usually powered) for boring cylindrical holes in earth or rock.

earth berm A small, earthen, dike-like embankment, usually used for diverting runoff water.

earth borer *See* **earth auger**.

earth dam A water barrier composed of earth, clay, sand, gravel, or combinations of these materials.

earth drill *See* **earth auger**.

earth electrode A metal plate, water pipe, or other conductor of electricity, partially buried in the earth so as to constitute and provide a reliable conductive path to the ground.

earthing lead The conductor that makes the final connection to an earth electrode.

earth pigment Pigment derived from the processing of materials or substances mined directly from the earth.

earth plate A buried metal plate that serves as an earth electrode.

earth pressure The horizontal pressure exerted by retained earth.

earthquake load The total force that an earthquake exerts on a given structure.

earth station (ground station) The equipment set up on earth to communicate with satellites.

earthwork A general term encompassing all operations relative to the movement, shaping, or compacting of earth.

eased edge Any slightly rounded edge.

easement (1) The legal right afforded a party to cross or to make limited use of land owned by another. (2) A curve formed at the juncture of two members that otherwise would intersect on an angle.

eaves

eaves fascia (fascia board)

eccentric load

easing Excavation that allows an allotted space to accommodate a foreign piece or part.

eastern fir *See* **eastern S-P-F**.

eastern pine *See* **eastern S-P-F**.

eastern red cedar A distinctively red, fine-textured, aromatic wood often used for shingles and closet linings.

eastern S-P-F Eastern spruce, pine, or fir-softwoods whose primary uses include structural lumber as in posts, beams, framing, and sheathing.

eastern spruce *See* **eastern S-P-F**.

eaves (1) Those portions of a roof that project beyond the outside walls of a building. (2) The bottom edges of a sloping roof.

eaves board A thick, feather board nailed across rafters at the eaves of a building to slightly raise the first course of shingles.

eaves channel A long, shallow depression that serves to direct roof dripping along the top of a wall and into downspouts or gargoyles.

eaves course The first course of shingles or tiles at the eaves of a roof.

eaves fascia (fascia board) A board secured horizontally to, and covering the vertical ends of, roof rafters. The board may support a gutter.

eaves flashing A thin metal strip dressed into an eaves gutter from a roof in order to prevent overflowing water from running down the exterior siding.

eaves gutter (eaves trough) A long, shallow, wood or metal trough fitting installed under and parallel to the eaves in order to catch and direct water dripping from a roof.

eaves plate A wood beam installed horizontally at the eaves and used in the absence of a rafter-supporting wall to support the feet of roof

rafters between existing posts or piers.

eaves strut A structural piece spanning columns at the edge of a roof. The term is usually associated with pre-engineered steel buildings.

eaves tile A shorter-than-usual roofing tile used specifically in the eaves course.

eaves trough *See* **eaves gutter**.

eaves vent Vent openings under the eaves of a house to allow the exchange of air in the attic.

ebony Dark, durable, tropical hardwood used most often for ornamental work or carving.

eccentric Not having the same center or centerline.

eccentric fitting A fitting whose opening or centerline is offset from the run of pipe.

eccentric load A load or force upon a portion of a column or pile not symmetric with its central axis, thus producing bending.

eccentric tendon In prestressed concrete, a steel element or tendon that does not follow a trajectory coincidental with the gravity axis of the member.

echo The reflection of sound waves with a magnitude and time delay sufficient to be perceived by a listener as separate from sound communicated directly to the listener.

ecology The study of the relationship between living things and their environment.

economic life The term during which a structure is expected to be profitable. Generally shorter than the physical life of the structure.

economic obsolescence Loss in value due to unfavorable economic influences occurring from outside the structure.

economy brick

edger

edge strip

economic rent   Rent on a property that is sufficient to pay all operating costs exclusive of services and utilities.

economizer cycle   A system of dampers, temperature and humidity sensors, and actuators, which maximizes the use of outdoor air for cooling.

economy brick   A cored, modular brick with nominal dimensions of 4″ x 4″ x 8″ and intrinsic dimensions of about 3-1/2″ x 3-1/2″ x 7-1/2″.

economy wall   A 4″ thick, back-mortared brick wall strengthened at intervals with vertical pilasters. Designed to support roof framing or walls.

edge beam   A stiffening beam at the edge of a slab.

edge flange weld   A weld with both members flanged at the point of the weld.

edge form   Formwork used to limit the horizontal spread of fresh concrete on flat surfaces such as pavements or floors.

edge grain   Lumber sawn so as to reveal the annual rings intersecting the wide face or surface at an angle of at least 45°.

edge guide   An attachment to a router that ensures straight cuts by keeping the bit parallel to the work surface edge.

edge joint   (1) A joint between two veneers or laminations, formed in the direction of the grain. (2) A joint created by the edges of two boards or surfaces united so as to form an angle or corner.

edge molding   Any molding along the edge of a relatively thin member such as a door or a counter.

edge nailing   Nailing through the edges of successive boards, such as floorboards, so that each board conceals the nails in the board adjacent to it.

edge plate   An angle iron or channel-shaped guard to protect the edge of a door.

edge pull   Mortising in the edge of sliding doors or windows by which they can be pulled open or closed.

edger (edging trowel)   A tool used to fashion finishing edges or round corners on fresh concrete or plaster.

edge shot   Planed on the edges.

edge spacer   A spacer that positions and holds a pane of glass in place within a window frame.

edgestone   A stone used for curbing.

edge strip   A plain or molded strip of wood or metal used to protect the edges of panels.

edge tool   Any tool that has a sharp cutting edge, such as a chisel, plane, or hatchet.

edge treatment   The finish used to conceal the plies of a plywood edge. Finish may involve molding, wood strips, or wood putty.

edge vent   An opening at the perimeter of a roof for the relief of water vapor pressure within the roof system.

edge void   The gap that occurs on the edge of a plywood panel when an inner ply splits.

edging   (1) An edge molding. (2) An edging strip. (3) The process of rounding to reduce the possibility of chipping or spalling exposed edges of concrete slabs. (4) The process of grinding the edge of flat glass to fit an application.

edging trowel   *See* **edger**.

educated guess ("guesstimate")   The guess of an experienced person.

effective age   The estimated age of a structure based on observed physical condition determined by the degree of maintenance and repair.

effective area (1) The net area of an air inlet or outlet system through which air can pass. The effective area equals the free area of the device multiplied by the coefficient of discharge. (2) The cross-sectional area of a structural member, calculated to resist applied stress.

effective area of reinforcement In reinforced concrete, the product derived by multiplying the cross-sectional area of the steel reinforcement by the cosine of the angle between its direction and the direction for which its effectiveness is considered.

effective bond In brickwork, a bond that is completed at the ends with a 2-1/2″ closer.

effective depth The depth of a beam or slab section as measured from the top of the member to the centroid of the tensile reinforcement.

effective flange width The width of a slab poured monolithically with a stem acting as the compression flange of a T-section. This width is usually equal to one-half of the span on each side of the stem.

effective height The height of a brick.

effective height of a column In calculating the slenderness ratio, multiply a valve by the actual column length. The valve varies depending on whether the column is fully or partially restrained at both ends.

effective length The distance between inflection points in a column when it bends.

effective modulus of elasticity The combination of elastic and plastic effects in an overall stress-strain relationship in a service structure.

effective opening The minimal cross-sectional area of the opening at the point of water supply discharge, expressed in terms of the diameter of a circle. The diameter of a circle of equivalent cross-sectional area is given in instances where the opening is not circular.

effective prestress The stress remaining in concrete resulting from prestressing after *loss of prestress*. Effective prestress includes the effect of the weight of the member, but not the effects from any superimposed loads.

effective reinforcement The reinforcement assumed to be active in resisting applied stress.

effective span The center-to-center distance between the supports of a beam, girder, or other structural member.

effective stress In prestressed concrete, the remaining stress in the tendons after the loss of prestress.

effective temperature A single-figure index reflecting the combined effects of temperature, humidity, and air movement on the sensation of warmth and/or cold felt by the human body. Numerically equivalent to the temperature of still, saturated air, which produces an identical sensation.

effective thickness of a wall The thickness of a wall, used in calculating the slenderness ratio.

efficacy The ratio of light output to energy consumption, measured in lumens per watt.

efficiency The ratio of actual performance to theoretical maximum performance.

efflorescence A whitish, powdery deposit of soluble salts carried to the surface of stone, brick, plaster, concrete, or mortar by moisture.

effluent

ejector

The moisture evaporates, leaving the residue.

effluent (1) In sanitary engineering, the liquid sewage discharged as waste, as in the discharge from a septic tank. (2) Generally, the discharged gas, liquid, or dust by-product of a process.

egg and dart An ornamental convex molding with a tooled finish that alternates egg and arrow head shapes.

eggcrate louver A louver whose rectangular openings resemble the dividers used in some egg cartons.

eggshell A semimatte glaze or porcelain enamel surface that resembles the texture of an eggshell.

eggshell gloss (1) A low-gloss designation for a paint film that is glossier than flat or satin, but less glossy than semigloss or gloss. (2) A smooth matte face to building stone.

egress An exit or means of exiting.

Eichleay A method of calculating the contractor's recovery for home office overhead costs in the event of delays caused by the owner.

ejector (1) A pump for ejecting liquid. (2) In plumbing, a device used to pump sewage from a lower to a higher elevation.

ejector grill A ventilating grill with slots shaped so as to force out air in divergent streams.

E-lamp® An electrode-less induction lamp with a compact size and long life.

elastic Refers to any material that can return to its initial state after having been deformed by an outside force.

elastic arch An arch whose design is based on the elastic theory of materials.

elastic constant A constant or coefficient that expresses the degree to which a material possesses

elasticity. In an elastic material that has been subjected to a strain below its elastic limit, the elastic constant is the ratio of the unit stress to the corresponding unit strain.

elastic curve In structural analysis, the curve showing the deflected shape of a beam with an applied load.

elastic deformation A modification to the shape of an elastic material, but not its elasticity.

elastic design An analytical design method in which the design of a structural member is based on a linear stress-strain relationship that assumes that the active stresses are equal to only a fraction of the given material's limit of elasticity.

elasticity The ability of a material to return to its initial state after having been deformed by some outside force.

elastic knife A tool with a flexible steel blade used by plasterers to trim the brown coat.

elastic limit The maximum amount of deforming stress a material can sustain and still return to its initial shape without having incurred any permanent deformation.

elastic loss In pretensioned concrete, the condition resulting in the reduction of prestressing load due to the elastic shortening of a member.

elastic shortening (1) A linearly proportional decrease in the length of a structural member under an imposed load. (2) In prestressed concrete, the shortening of a member caused by, and occurring immediately upon, application of force induced by prestressing.

elastomer A term descriptive of various polymers which, after being temporarily but substantially deformed by stress, will return to their

elbow

electric baseboard heater

initial size and shape immediately upon the release of the stress.

elastomeric bearing An expansion bearing made from an elastomer. This type of bearing allows movement of the structure it supports.

elastomeric waterproofing A method of foundation moisture protection using impervious flexible sheet metal.

elbow A sharply bent or fabricated angle fitting, usually of pipe, conduit, or sheet metal. *See also* **knee**.

elbow board (1) A window board installed under a window on the interior side. (2) An elbow rail.

elbow catch A spring-loaded locking device having on one end a hook that engages a strike, and on the other end a right angle bend that provides a means for releasing the catch. This type of catch is commonly used to lock the inactive leaf of a pair of cabinet doors.

elbow rail A length of millwork or metal rail attached to a partition or under a window on the interior side and used as an armrest.

electric appliance A piece of equipment or a mechanism operated by electricity. Commonly found in a household or office.

electrical conductivity The ability to transmit an electrical current.

electrical insulator An electronics component which, because of the electrical resistance inherent in the material(s) from which it is fabricated, is itself considered to be a nonconductor of electric current. The component is sometimes designed so as to physically support a conductor while separating it electrically from another conductor or object.

electrically supervised Refers to a closed-circuit wiring system that utilizes a current-responsive device to indicate a failure within the circuit or an accidental grounding.

electrical metallic conduit Heavy-walled conduit that encloses and protects wiring.

electrical resistance The opposition to the flow of an electric current as manifested by a device, conductor, substance, or circuit element. Electrical resistance is measured in *ohms*.

electrical tape A tough, fibrous or thermoplastic adhesive tape used primarily to insulate electrical joints or conductors.

electric arc welding (electric welding) The joining of metal pieces by fusion, the heat for which is provided by an electric arc or the flow of electric current between the electrode and the base metal. The electrode is either a consumable, melting and bead-depositing, or nonconsumable metal rod. The base is the parent metal.

electric baseboard heater A heating system with electric heating elements installed in longitudinal panels, usually along the baseboards of exterior walls.

electric blasting cap A blasting cap that is detonated by an electric current.

electric cable (1) An electric conductor comprising several smaller-diameter strands that are twisted together. (2) A group of electric conductors that are insulated from one another.

electric delay blasting caps Electronically controlled blasting caps designed to detonate only after a predetermined length of time has elapsed after the ignition system has been electronically activated.

electric drill

electric fixture

electric panelboard

electric receptacle

electric-discharge lamp A lamp that emits light through a process where electric current flows through a vapor or gas.

electric drill A portable, hand-held, motor-driven tool used for boring holes in a material. Powered either by direct or alternating current.

electric duct An enclosed metal runway for electrical conductors or cables.

electric eye A photoelectric cell whose resistance varies in response to the amount of light that falls on the cell. An electric eye is often incorporated into electric circuits where it is used in measuring or control devices that depend on illumination levels or on the interruption of a light beam.

electric feeder In power distribution, a set of electric conductors that originate at a primary distribution center and supply power to one or more secondary distribution centers, branch-circuit distribution centers, or a combination of these.
See also **feeder**.

electric field A particular region or space characterized by the existence of a detectable electric intensity at every point within its perimeter.

electric fixture An electrical device that is fastened to a ceiling or wall and used to hold lamps.

electric generator A mechanism that transforms mechanical power into electrical power.

electric heat Heat resulting from the flow of electric current through resistance elements.

electric heating element A heat-producing device consisting of a length of resistance material, insulated supports, and terminals that connect to an electrical power source.

electric lock A locking mechanism in which the motion of a latch or bolt is controlled by applying voltage to the terminals of the mechanism.

electrical metallic tubing (EMT) *See* **thin-wall conduit**.

electric meter A device that measures the amount of electricity consumed over a certain period of time.

electric outlet A point in an electric wiring system at which current is delivered through receptacles equipped with sockets for plugs, making it available to supply lights, appliances, power tools, and other electrically powered devices.

electric panelboard A panel or group of individual panel units capable of being assembled as a single panel and designed to include fuses, switches, and circuit breakers. The units are housed in a cabinet or cutout box positioned in or against a wall or partition and accessible only from the front.

electric receptacle A contact device, usually installed in an outlet box, which provides the socket for the attachment of a plug to supply electric current to portable power equipment, appliances, and other electrically operated devices.

electric resistance welding (electric welding) A coalescence-producing set of welding processes whereby the required heat is derived from the application of pressure and from resistance of the work to the flow of electric current in a circuit, of which the work itself is an integral part.

electric space heater A portable, self-contained heating device in which electricity supplies the heat energy. The heat is blown into a given space or room by a powerful electric fan also contained within the unit.

electric squib An electronically activated mechanism used in blasting operations to ignite a charge.

electric strike An electrical mechanism that allows the release of a door at a remote location.

electric switch A device used for opening or closing electric circuits or for changing the connection of a circuit.

electric welding *See* **electric arc welding** *and/or* **electric resistance welding**.

electroacoustics The branch of electricity concerned with the transformation of acoustical energy into electrical energy, and vice versa.

electrode (1) A solid electric conductor through which an electric current enters or leaves an electrolyte, vacuum, gas, or other medium. (2) That component in an arc welding circuit through which electric current is conducted between the electrode holder and the arc itself. (3) In resistance welding, that component through which the electric current in the welding machine passes directly to the work and which is usually accompanied by pressure, such as from a clamp.

electrode boiler A boiler containing submerged electrodes that heat the surrounding water by passing electric current through it.

electrogalvanizing A method of coating iron or steel with zinc deposited by electroplating rather than by immersion.

electrogas welding A method of gas-metal arc welding or flux-cored arc welding that utilizes an externally supplied gas.

electrolier A hanging electric light fixture, such as a chandelier.

electrolysis The process of producing chemical changes or the breakdown of chemical compounds into their constituent parts by passing a current between electrodes and through an electrolyte.

electrolyte (1) A substance that separates into ions when in a solution or when fused, thereby becoming electrically conducting. (2) A conducting medium in which the flow of electric current occurs by the migration of ions.

electrolytic copper Copper refined through electrolytic deposition and used in the manufacturing of tough pitch copper and copper alloys.

electrolytic corrosion The deterioration of metal or concrete by the chemical or electrochemical reaction resulting from electrolysis.

electromagnet An iron-based object that becomes magnetic when a current is passed through the coils around it. The object loses its magnetism when the current is stopped.

electromagnetic interference (EMI) Radiation emission from a transmission medium caused by using high-frequency signal modulation. Can be reduced by shielding.

electromotive force (EMF) The force that moves electricity in a conductor. EMF, usually measured in volts, is the difference in electric potential, or voltage, between the terminals of a source of electricity.

electron acceptor An element or ion that accepts free electrons during a chemical treatment process.

electronic ballast A ballast that uses semiconductor components to increase the efficiency of a

211

elevator

elevator pit

fluorescent system by increasing the frequency (in kilohertz) of its lamp operation.

electronic controls In an HVAC system, the electronically operated sensors and controls.

electronic distance meter (EDM) A surveying device used to measure distance. Distance is determined from the time it takes transmitted electromagnetic waves to reach a target.

electroplating The deposition of a thin, sometimes decorative but usually protective metal coating onto another metal. Electroplating occurs by submerging the receiving metal into an electrolyte, where electrons from the anode (the coating metal) flow to and are deposited on the receiving metal (or cathode).

electrostatic air cleaner *See* **electrostatic precipitator**.

electrostatic precipitator (electrostatic air cleaner) A type of filtering device that prevents smoke and dust from escaping into the atmosphere by charging the particles electrically as they pass through a screen. The particles are attracted to one of two electrically charged plates and subsequently removed.

element The smallest division of a breakdown.

elephant trunk A long, cylindrical, device with a hopper-like top through which concrete is placed in deep shafts or forms. When in use, the device is kept filled with concrete to eliminate the free fall of material and the possible resultant segregation of its constituents.

elevated conduit An electrical conduit hung from structural floor members.

elevated floor Any floor system not supported by the subgrade.

elevated slab A floor or roof slab supported by structural members.

elevated water tank A domestic water tank supported on an elevated structural framework to obtain the required head of pressure.

elevation (1) A vertical distance relative to a reference point. (2) A view or drawing of the interior or exterior of a structure as if projected onto a vertical plane.

elevator A "car" or platform that moves within a shaft or guides and is used for the vertical hoisting and/or lowering of people or material between two or more floors of a structure. An elevator is usually electrically powered, although some short-distance elevators (serving fewer than six or seven floors) are powered hydraulically.

elevator car That part of an elevator that includes the platform, enclosure, car frame, and gate or door.

elevator car safety A mechanism attached to the car frame of an elevator or to the frame of the counterweight and whose function it is to slow, stop, and hold the car or counterweight in the event of integral equipment malfunction or failure, such as excessive speed or free-fall of the car.

elevator interlock A device on the door of each elevator landing that prevents movement of the elevator until the door is closed and locked.

elevator machine beam A steel beam that is usually positioned directly over the elevator in the elevator machinery room and is used to support elevator equipment.

elevator pit That part of an elevator shaft that extends from the threshold level of the lowest landing door down to the floor at the very bottom of the shaft.

elevator shaft

ell

embedded reinforcement

elevator recall The override of elevator operation by a building's fire safety system upon activation of a fire alarm. In a fire emergency, elevator cars automatically return to the ground floor and can be operated only by a fire department.

elevator shaft A hoistway through which one or more elevator cars may travel.

ell (el) (1) An extension, addition, or secondary wing that joins the principal dimension of a building at a right angle. (2) Same as *elbow*.

elliptical arch An arch in the shape of a semi-ellipse and whose intrados is in the form of an ellipse.

elm A strong, tough, dull brown, easily worked hardwood with moderately high density and a twisted, interlocking grain. Elm is used more for ornamental landscaping and shade purposes than for veneer, piles, or planks.

elongated bowl A toilet bowl with an extra few inches added to the front for added comfort and cleanliness.

elongated piece A particle of aggregate whose length-to-width ratio exceeds a specified value.

emarginate To notch a margin or perimeter of an object.

embankment A ridge constructed of earth, fill rocks, or gravel and used most commonly to retain water or to carry a roadway. The length of an embankment exceeds both its width and its height.

embedded length That length of embedded steel reinforcement that extends beyond a critical section.

embedded reinforcement In reinforced concrete, any slender steel members, such as rods, bars, or wires, that are embedded in concrete in such a way as to function together with the concrete in resisting forces.

embedment (1) The depth of a pile, measured from its deepest point to ground level. (2) The placing of one material into another so that the two become a single material.

embossed Describes a material whose surface is raised or indented.

emergency ballast A lighting system that uses a battery to function in the event of a power loss. When AC power fails, the emergency ballast senses the failure and immediately switches to the emergency mode to illuminate lamps at a reduced lumen output.

emergency declaration area (EDA) An area officially declared in need of hazardous waste or material cleanup.

emergency exit A door, hatch, or other device leading to the outside of the structure and usually kept closed and locked. The exit is used chiefly for the emergency evacuation of a building, airplane, or other occupied space when conventional exits fail, are insufficient, or are rendered inaccessible.

emergency lighting Temporary illumination provided by battery or generator and essential to safety during the failure or interruption of the conventional electric power supply.

emergency power Electricity temporarily produced and supplied by a standby power generator when the conventional electric power supply fails or is interrupted. Emergency power is essential in facilities like hospitals, where even relatively short power outages could be life-threatening to certain individuals.

emergency release On a door, a safety device that allows exit during emergency conditions. Unlike a panic exit device, an emergency release magnetic door holder that automatically releases in emergencies to close fire door, not necessarily preventing egress.

emergency stop switch A safety switch in the car of an elevator which can be manually operated to cut off electric power from the driving machine motor and brake of an electric elevator, or from the electrically operated valves and/or pump motor of a hydraulic elevation.

emery Bluish-grey or black, impure carborundum in granular form used as an abrasive for grinding and polishing the surfaces of materials such as metal, stone, glass, and other materials.

emery cloth A finely abrasive cloth manufactured by sprinkling powdered emery or aluminum oxide onto a thin cloth coated with glue. Used either wet or dry for polishing metallic surfaces.

emery wheel An abrasive wheel similar to a grinding wheel but composed primarily of emery (or aluminum oxide) and rotated at high speeds for fine grinding or polishing.

eminent domain The legal right or power of a government to take for public use privately owned property, usually with some degree of compensation to its owner.

emissivity The ratio of radiation intensity from a given body or surface to the radiation intensity at the same wavelength from a perfect blackbody at the same temperature and in the same ambience.

emittance A percentage of the energy absorbed by a solar energy collector.

employee's liability insurance Insurance protection against employee's claims for damages resulting from sickness or injury sustained during the course of work. Protection is based on negligence of common law (not under workers' compensation).

employee's quarterly federal tax return Form 941 on which employers must report the amount of federal income taxes and FICA taxes withheld and the dates and amounts deposited during each quarterly period.

employee's withholding allowance certificate The W-4 form prepared by each employee showing the number of withholding allowances currently claimed. This number establishes the amount of federal income tax that should be withheld by the employer from the employee's earnings.

empty-cell process A procedure in which wood is impregnated with liquid preservatives under pressure.

emulsified asphalt Asphalt cement that has been mixed with water containing a small amount of an emulsifying agent. *See also* **bituminous emulsion**.

emulsifier A substance that modifies the surface tension of colloidal droplets, inhibiting their coalescence and maintaining their suspension.

emulsion (1) A mixture of two liquids that are insoluble in one another and in which globules of one are suspended in the other (such as oil globules in water). (2) The mixture of solid particles and the liquid in which they are suspended but insoluble, as in a mixture of uniformly dispersed bitumen particles in water, in which the cementing action required in roofing

enameled brick

encase

encased beam

and waterproofing would occur as the water evaporates.

emulsion glue A usually cold-setting glue manufactured from emulsified synthetic polymers.

emulsion paint A paint comprising tiny beads of resin binder that, along with pigments, are dispersed in water. Evaporation of the water affects the coalescence of the resin particles, thus forming a film that adheres to the surface and binds the pigment particles. Vinyl, latex, or plastic paints are examples based on polyvinyl acetate emulsion.

emulsion sprayer An apparatus used in highway resurfacing to spray an emulsified asphalt tack coat on the existing surface.

enamel A type of paint composed of particles of finely ground pigments and a resin binder that dries to form a hard, glossy film with very little surface texture.

enameled brick In masonry, a brick or tile with a glazed ceramic finish.

encapsulant (sealant) A liquid applied to asbestos-containing material that prevents the release of fibers into the air either by forming a membrane over the material or by penetrating the material and binding the fibers together.

encapsulation A technique for trapping asbestos fibers in a dense chemical substance.

encase To cover with or enclose in a case or lining.

encased beam A metal beam usually enclosed in concrete or some other similar material.

encaustic (1) Descriptive of a process in which a material is covered with a mixture of paint solution and wax, then set by heat after application. (2) Relating to paint or pigment that has been applied to glass, tile, brick,

or porcelain and then set or fixed by the application of heat.

encaustic tile A decorative or pavement tile whose pattern is created by inlaying clay of one color in a background of a different-colored clay.

enchased Refers to hammered metalwork whose pattern in relief is created by hammering down the background or depressed portions of the design.

enclosed knot A wood knot that is invisible from the surface of a wood member because it is completely covered by surrounding wood.

enclosed stair An interior staircase that has a closed string on each side, often encased in walls or partitions. There are also door openings at various floor levels, thus making it accessible to hallways of living units.

enclosure The containment behind airtight, impenetrable, permanent barriers of sprayed-on or troweled-on asbestos-based materials.

enclosure system A contamination-control system consisting of a work area, a holding area, a washroom, and an uncontaminated area.

enclosure wall An interior or exterior non-load-bearing wall of skeleton construction, usually anchored to columns, piers, or floors.

encroachment The unauthorized intrusion or extension of a building or structure onto the property of another.

encumbrance (1) A liability attached to real property, such as a mortgage, a lien, and certain easements. (2) A restriction on the use of a piece of property.

end anchorage A mechanism designed to transmit prestressing

endless saw

force to the reinforced concrete of a posttensioned member.

end bearing pile A pile supported mainly by point resistance. The pile's point (toe) rests on or is embedded in a posttensioned member.

end block A member that has an enlarged end section designed to reduce anchorage stresses to allowable values.

end butt joint (end joint) (1) A joint formed when boards are connected square end to square end. (2) A joint between two veneers, formed perpendicular to the grain. (3) In masonry, a joint in which mortar connects the butt ends of two bricks.

end channel A metal stiffener welded horizontally into the tops and bottoms of hollow metal doors to supply strength and rigidity.

end checks Small cracks that develop in the end grain of drying lumber.

end-construction tile Tile that receives its principal stress parallel to the axes of the cells, and which is laid so that the axes of cells are vertical.

end distance The distance from an end of a member to the center of its nearest bolt hole, nail, or screw.

end grain The grain that is exposed when a piece of wood is cut perpendicular to the grain.

end-grain core Plywood or panel core made from wood blocks that are sawn and glued so that the grain is at right angles to the forces of the panels.

end-grain nailing The driving of nails into the end-grain surface of wood so that the resultant position of each nail shank is parallel to the grain.

end joint See **end butt joint**.

end lap The overlap in a lap joint, such as at the end of a ply of roofing felt.

end lap joint An angle joint involving two members, each having been cut to half its thickness and lapped over the other in such a way as to result in a change of direction.

endless saw A band saw.

end matched Descriptive of boards or strips that are tongued along one end and grooved along the other.

endorsement A document supplemental to an insurance policy covering a specified loss. An endorsement modifies the conditions of the contract terms stated on the face of the insurance policy.

endothermic Descriptive of a reaction occurring with the absorption of heat.

end post A post or other structural member in compression at the end of a truss.

end product specifications Embankment compaction specifications written to define the requirements rather than the method or equipment to obtain those requirements.

end rafter A common rafter positioned in line with the ridge of the roof.

end scarf A scarf joint between two timbers made by notching and lapping the ends and then inserting the end of one into an end of the other.

end section In a drainage system, the prefabricated, flared metal end attached at the inlet and outlet to prevent erosion.

end span In a continuous-span floor design, the exterior span, which is often more heavily reinforced.

engineer brick

end stiffener One of the vertical angles connected to the web of a beam or girder at its ends, to stiffen the beam and transfer the end shear to the shoe, baseplate, or supporting member.

end thrust The force that the end of a structural member exerts.

endurance limit The maximum stress that can be applied to a material during a specified number of stress cycles without causing failure of the material being stressed.

energized Electrically connected to a source of voltage.

energy The ability to do work.

energy audit A survey of heat loss through the components of a structure.

energy efficiency ratio In HVAC, the ratio of cooling capacity in Btu/hr to the electricity required in watts.

energy management system (EMS) A system that operates energy-consuming systems, in the most energy-efficient manner, through software programs.

Energy Star Program A rating program sponsored by the Department of Energy and the Environmental Protection Agency to encourage the use of energy-efficient products.

Energy Star Buildings A voluntary partnership between U.S. organizations and the U.S. Environmental Protection Agency (EPA) to promote energy efficiency in buildings.

enfilade The axial alignment of a series of doors through a sequence of rooms.

engaged Apparently or actually attached to a wall by virtue of being bonded to it or partially embedded in it.

engaged column A column that is apparently or actually attached to a wall by being bonded to it or partially embedded in it. The column is not actually freestanding; it is at least partially built into a wall.

engineer A design professional who, by education, experience, and examination, is duly licensed by one or more state governments for practice in the profession of engineering. This practice may be limited to one or more specific disciplines of engineering. Construction-related engineering disciplines include civil, structural, mechanical, or electrical systems design.

engineer brick Brick whose nominal dimensions are 3-1/5″ x 4″ x 8″.

engineered brick masonry Brick masonry whose design is the product of structural analysis.

engineering officer An engineer designated as having authority over specific operations or duties. Usually designated by a government agency or private corporation.

engineering survey A survey undertaken for the purpose of obtaining information essential to the planning of an engineering project.

engineer-in-training A person who is qualified to become a registered professional engineer in all respects but the necessary professional experience.

engineer's chain A chain-like device consisting of a series of one hundred links, each one foot long. The chain is used in land surveying for measuring distances.

engineer's level A precision leveling instrument used for establishing a horizontal line of sight and and to

engineer's scale

English garden wall bond

determining differences of elevation.

engineer's scale A straightedge on which each inch is divided into uniform multiples of ten, thus enabling drawings to be made with distances, loads, forces, and other calculations expressed in decimal values.

engineer's transit (1) An instrument used in surveying to measure and to lay out vertical and horizontal angles, distance, directions, and differences in elevation. (2) A theodolite, the directions of whose alidade and telescope are reversible.

English bond (1) Brickwork consisting of alternate courses of headers and stretchers. (2) A strong, easily laid bond.

English cross bond (St. Andrew's cross bond) Alternate courses of headers and stretchers on which the stretcher course breaks joints with the stretcher courses next to it.

English garden wall bond (American bond, common bond) Widely used brickwork that can be laid quickly because headers constitute only every fifth or sixth course, with all the other courses being stretchers.

English tile A smooth, flat, single-lap clay roofing tile with interlocking sides.

engrail To cut with a series of concave lines or curves.

enriched Adorned with ornate and/or decorative elements.

entablature In classical architecture, the total beam member spanning from column to column, including the architrave (bottom), frieze (middle), and cornice (top).

enterprise asset management Any software system designed to assist with facility management, including the maintenance of physical assets,

proper and safe plant operation, and warranty and leasing information.

enthalpy The total amount of heat in a system, measured in Btus per pound.

entitlement A claimant's right or grounds for recovering losses (as opposed to determining the amount of the losses).

entrained air Nearly spherical microscopic air bubbles that are purposely incorporated into mortar or concrete during mixing. Entrained air is added in order to lessen the effects of the freeze/thaw cycle on concrete that will be exposed to the weather.

entrainment The capture of part of the surrounding air by the air stream discharged from an air outlet.

entrance An exterior door, lobby, passage, or other designed point of entry into a building.

entrapped air Voids in concrete that are of at least one millimeter in diameter, and which are the result of air other than entrained air.

entry A passage hallway that affords entrance inside an exterior door.

envelope (1) A term used to denote the extreme outside surface and dimensions of a building. (2) An assembly of planes representing the limits of an area that may house a structure, i.e., a zoning envelope.

environmental design The adaptation of a building to its surroundings and the consequences of its incorporation into the setting.

environmental impact statement A detailed analysis, as required by the National Environmental Policy Act of 1969, of the probable significant environmental effects of either large-scale, federally funded construction or other proposed construction that may have

equalizing bed

equipment ground

potentially significant consequences on the environment.

environmental monitoring
A process of measuring physical and/or chemical properties of an environmental medium, such as air, soil or water.

Environmental Protection Agency (EPA) An independent federal agency, formed in 1970, that establishes and controls rules for protecting the environment.

environmental remediation The process of treatment, containment, or removal of hazardous or toxic wastes to protect human health and the environment.

EPA Identification Number
A number assigned to each generator of hazardous waste that notifies the EPA of its activity.

EPA Regional Administrator The senior EPA official in charge of EPA activities at a generation site.

EPDM roofing A single-ply roofing material manufactured of an elastomeric polymer synthesized from ethylene, propylene and a small amount of diene monomer. Because of its versatility in application methods, EPDM roofing may be used for any roof shape, slope, height, and climatic exposure.

epoxy Any of several synthetic, usually thermosetting, resins that provide superior adhesive power and hard, tough, chemical- and corrosion-resistant coatings.

epoxy joint In masonry, an unsealed joint in which epoxy resin is used in place of mortar.

epoxy resin A material containing an average of more than one epoxy group per molecule used in the preparation of special coatings or adhesives for concrete and as binders in epoxy resin mortars and concrete.

Equal Employment Opportunity Commission (EEOC) A government agency under the administration of the Department of Labor. This agency is dedicated to enforcing the provisions of Title IV of the Civil Rights Act of 1964, which forbids discrimination by an employer based on the race, color, religion, sex, or national origin of a potential employee.

equal friction method A way of sizing ductwork systems for a constant pressure loss per unit length of duct.

equalizer Any device that compensates for an undesired characteristic of a system or component.

equalizing bed A layer of sand, stone, or concrete laid in the bottom of a trench as a resting place for buried pipes.

equalizing grid A series of individual adjustable blades installed at the diffuser inlet to produce uniform velocity through the diffuser neck.

equipment All the machinery, tools, and apparatus necessary for the proper construction and acceptable completion of a project.

equipment ground (1) A connection that provides a path to ground a conductor within the equipment. (2) A ground connection to any metal part of a wiring system or equipment that does not carry current.

equipment room An area or room used to store contaminated clothing and equipment. Part of the worker decontamination enclosure system.

equitable adjustment An adjustment to the contract price or time resulting from a change, differing site condition, or the like, which compensates the contractor for reasonable costs, plus overhead and profit.

equity The residual value of a business or property, often calculated by subtracting the amount of outstanding liens or mortgages from the total value of the business or property.

equivalent direct radiation (EDR) A unit of heat delivery equal to 240 Btu per hour.

equivalent embedment length That longitudinal part of an embedded reinforcement which is capable of developing stress equivalent to that developed by a hook or mechanical anchorage.

equivalent length The resistance of a duct or pipe elbow, valve, damper, orifice, bend, fitting, or other obstruction to flow, expressed in the number of feet of straight duct or pipe of the same diameter that would have the same resistance.

equivalent round A term used to define the size of an oblong-shaped pipe. The equivalent round of the oblong pipe is equal to the diameter of a pipe with the same circumference.

erecting bill A list of structural building components prepared by the fabricator and indicating the tagging and location of each member.

equivalent thickness The solid thickness to which a hollow unit would be reduced if there were no voids and it had the same face dimensions.

erection The positioning and/or installation of structural components or preassembled structural members of a building, often with the assistance of powered equipment such as a hoist or crane.

erection bracing Temporary bracing used to hold framework in a safe condition during construction until enough permanent construction has been put in place to provide complete stability.

erection drawing A shop drawing that illustrates the constructional components of a project, with each one lettered or numbered to facilitate erection.

erection stress The stress effected by loads applied during erection.

erection wrench A wrench with an open end jaw on one side and a tapered point at the other. The pointed end is used to align bolt holes in adjoining members.

ergonomics The interaction between people and work, particularly the design of machines, chairs, tables, etc., to suit the body and to permit work with minimum fatigue.

erosion The gradual deterioration of metal or other material by the abrasive action of liquids, gases, and/or solids.

erratum An error in printing, writing, or editing, especially one included in a list of corrections appended to a book or publication in which the error appeared.

error of closure The measured difference between a theoretical angle or linear measurement and the actual value.

errors and omissions insurance Professional liability insurance protecting architects or engineers from claims for damages that may result from alleged professional negligence.

escalation An increase in the cost of performing construction work, resulting from performing the work in a later period of time and at a cost higher than originally anticipated in the bid.

escalator

escutcheon

escalator A continuously moving, power-driven, inclined stairway used to transport passengers between different floor levels of a building or into and out of underground stations.

escape The curved portion of a column shaft where it springs out from the base.

escape lighting *See* **emergency lighting**.

escheat The assumption of ownership by the state, of property whose owner cannot be determined.

escrow Property (such as money, a deed, stock, or a writing) that is delivered by a person (called a *grantor*) to a third party to be held until certain conditions are fulfilled. When the conditions are satisfied, the third party releases the property to another person (called a *grantee*).

escutcheon (1) The protective plate, usually metal or plastic, which surrounds a door keyhole or a light switch. (2) A pipe flange covering a floor hole through which the pipe passes. *See also* **faceplate**.

escutcheon pin A small nail, usually brass and often ornamental, used to fix an escutcheon.

esker A long, narrow deposit of coarse gravel left by a stream.

espagnolette A casement window lock that uses a long sliding rod with hooks to secure the window. *See also* **cremone bolt**.

espalier (1) A framework or trellis that directs branches of fruit trees or other decorative plantings to grow in a predesigned shape or to form on a single plane for improved air circulation and exposure to sun as well as for ornamental effect. (2) The trees or plants grown in this manner.

esplanade A flat, unobstructed stretch of grass or pavement, usually for strolling but sometimes for driving and observing a view.

esquisse A rough sketch demonstrating the general features of a project.

Essex board measure A chart appearing on a certain type of carpenter's steel square, listing the number of board feet contained in a board one inch thick and of several standard sizes.

estate A legal right, title, or interest in real property. Estates in real property fall into two broad categories: ownership, and rights to possess and use real property owned by another.

estimate The anticipated cost of materials, labor, equipment, or any combination of these for a proposed construction project.

estimated design load The sum of (a) the useful heat transfer, (b) the heat transfer to or from the connected piping, and (c) the heat transfer that occurs in any auxiliary apparatus connected to a heating or air-conditioning system.

estimated maximum load The calculated maximum heat transfer that a heating or air-conditioning system might have to provide.

estimating The process of determining the anticipated cost of materials, labor, and equipment of a proposed project.

estimator One who is capable of predicting the probable cost of a building project.

etching The process of using abrasion or corrosion (acid) to wear away the surface of glass or metal, often in a decorative pattern.

ethylene glycol (1) Antifreeze. (2) A water-miscible alcohol used to transfer heat in heating and cooling

event

excavation

provide stability in latex- and water-based paints during freezing conditions.

etiologic agent A substance that causes disease, such as the flu virus.

ettringite A naturally occurring mineral containing a large amount of sulfate calcium sulfoaluminate. Ettringite is also produced synthetically by sulfate attack on mortar and concrete.

eurythmy In architecture, orderliness or harmony of proportion.

evaporable water Water held by the surface forces or in the capillaries of set cement paste, measured as the water that can be removed by drying under specific conditions.

evaporation Loss, from a liquid, of moisture in vapor form.

evaporative cooling Cooling achieved by the evaporation of water in air, thus increasing humidity and decreasing dry-bulb temperature.

evaporator The part of a refrigeration system in which vaporization of the refrigerant occurs, absorbing heat from the surrounding fluid and producing cooling.

event In a CPM (Critical Path Method) arrow diagram, the starting point for an activity that cannot occur until all work preceding it has been performed. Indicated on the arrow diagram by a number enclosed in a circle.

eviction The lawful or unlawful removal of a tenant from a property.

excavation (1) The removal of earth, usually to allow the construction of a foundation or basement. (2) The hole resulting from such removal.

excavator (1) A company or individual who contracts to perform excavation. (2) Any of several types

of power-driven machines used in excavation.

excelsior Thin, curved wood shavings used for packing and stuffing.

Exception Report A report sent to the EPA by a generator of hazardous waste. The Exception Report is released when the generator does not receive copies of hazardous waste manifest forms from transporters or disposers of wastes that the generator has shipped off-site for disposal.

excess reprocurement costs Additional costs that the government incurs following a default termination to reprocure the defaulted quantity of supplies, services, or unfinished work.

exchange The centrally located arrangement of communications equipment governing the connection of incoming and outgoing lines, including signaling and supervisory tasks.

exchange, private branch (PBX) A telephone exchange system that provides manually operated private telephone service within an organization (a company, for example) as well as access to the public telephone network.

exclusionary provision A provision stated in an insurance policy covering potential loss where specific types or origins of loss are specifically excluded (by description) from the coverage provided.

excusable delay A delay to contract performance that is beyond the control, fault, or negligence of the contractor. If a delay is determined to be excusable, the government cannot initiate a termination for default.

executed (1) Under contract law, a contract that has been signed by

exhaust fan

exit device
(panic exit device)

both parties. (2) Work that has been completed.

exfiltration The flow of air outward through walls, joints, or other apertures.

exfoliated vermiculite Vermiculite whose original volume has been expanded several times by heat processing so as to render it suitable for lightweight aggregation, such as thermal insulation.

exfoliation (1) The flaking, scaling, or peeling of stone or other mineral surfaces usually caused by physical weathering, but sometimes by heating or chemical weathering. (2) The heat treatment of minerals for the purpose of expanding their original volume many times over.

exhaust fan A device used to draw unwanted, contaminated air away from a particular room or area of a building to the outside.

exhaust fume hood A prefabricated hood unit that serves to confine noxious or toxic fumes for subsequent exhausting or filtration.

exhaust grille A grate or louvers through which contaminated air exits to the atmosphere.

exhaust shaft A duct through which exhaust air is carried to the outside atmosphere.

exhaust ventilation A method of ventilation that allows fresh air to enter a space through available or controlled openings and employs mechanical means such as fans to remove foul air from the same space.

existing building In codes and regulations, an already completed building or one that prior laws or regulations allowed to be built.

exit That part of an exit system which, because of its separation from the rest of the building by devices such as walls, doors, and floors, provides a reasonably safe and protected emergency escape route from a building.

exit access The corridor or door leading to an exterior exit.

exit control alarm An electronic device that activates an alarm when a fire exit door is opened.

exit corridor An enclosed passageway or corridor that connects a required exit with direct or easy access to a street or alley.

exit device (panic exit device) An exit door locking device, consisting of a bar across the inside of a door which, when pushed, releases the door latch.

exit discharge That part of an exit system beginning at the termination of the exit at the exterior of a building and ending at ground level.

exit light An illuminating sign above an exit that identifies it as an exit.

exothermic Descriptive of a reaction during which heat is released.

expanded aluminum grating An aluminum grating manufactured by cutting and mechanically stretching a single piece of sheet aluminum.

expanded blast-furnace slag A cellular material, used as lightweight aggregate, derived from treating molten blast-furnace slag with water, steam, and/or other agents.

expanded cement *See* **expansive cement**.

expanded clay Clay expanded to several times its original volume by the formation of internal gas caused by heating it to a semiplastic state.

expanded glass (foam glass) A thermal insulation with a closed-cell structure, manufactured by foaming softened glass so as to produce a myriad of sealed bubbles, and then

expanded metal,
expanded metal partition

expansion anchor

molding the glass into boards and blocks.

expanded metal A type of open-mesh metal lath made by slitting and stretching sheet metal. Comes in different patterns and thicknesses.

expanded metal partition A partition constructed from thin framing or support members covered with heavy expanded metal lath and plastered on both sides to produce a solid finished product 1-1/2" to 2-1/2" thick.

expanded perlite A glassy, lightweight, naturally occurring, cellular volcanic material whose properties make it suitable for aggregate in concrete.

expanded plastic (cellular plastic) (1) A plastic containing a myriad of cells incorporated uniformly throughout its mass. (2) A plastic that has been expanded chemically, mechanically, or thermally to form a lightweight, closed-cell structure. This material is commonly used for thermal insulation.

expanded polystyrene (EPS) A type of foamed styrene plastic that has a high resistance to heat flow and a high strength-to-weight ratio. EPS is used as insulation, as an inexpensive glazing, and in formwork for concrete, among many other applications.

expanded rubber Closed-cell rubber manufactured from a solid rubber compound.

expanded shale A material manufactured by heat treating shale, which dramatically expands its volume. Suitable for use as a lightweight aggregate.

expanded slag A lightweight aggregate, manufactured by processing blast-furnace slag with water, that is used in concrete mix.

expanded slate Slate whose subjection to exfoliation results in a porous material suitable for use as a lightweight aggregate.

expanding bit (expansion bit) A drilling bit whose blade can be adjusted to bore holes of different diameters.

expanding cement *See* **expansive cement**.

expanding plug A drain stopper usually located at the lowest point of a piping system. When inflated, the plug seals the pipe.

expansion The increase in dimensions or volume of a body or material caused by thermal variations, moisture, or other environmental conditions. *See also* **expansion bend**.

expansion anchor *See* **expansion bolt**.

expansion attic In a completed house, an attic left unfinished to allow for future conversion into liveable space.

expansion bead In plastering, a metal strip placed between materials to allow for movement.

expansion bearing An end support of a span, which allows for the expansion or contraction of a structure.

expansion bend (expansion loop) In a pipe run, a usually horseshoe-shaped bend inserted to allow thermal expansion of the pipe.

expansion bit *See* **expanding bit**.

expansion bolt (expansion anchor, expansion fastener, expansion shield) An anchoring or fastening device used in masonry, which expands within a predrilled hole as a bolt is tightened.

expansion coil An evaporator fabricated from tubing or pipe.

expansion joint

expansion loop

expansion tank

expansion fastener *See* **expansion bolt.**

expansion joint In a building structure or concrete work, a joint or gap between adjacent parts which allows for safe and inconsequential relative movement of the parts, caused by thermal variations or other conditions.

expansion joint cover The prefabricated protective cover of an expansion joint, which also remains unaffected by the relative movement of the two joined surfaces.

expansion joint filler Material used to fill an expansion joint to keep it clean and dry. Materials commonly used are felt, rubber, and neoprene.

expansion loop (expansion bend) A large radius loop in a pipe line which absorbs the longitudinal expansion and contraction in the line due to temperature changes.

expansion pipe A pipe that directs hot water or steam from the relief valve of a water heater to a drain.

expansion shield *See* **expansion bolt.**

expansion sleeve A short length of metal or plastic pipe built into a wall or floor to allow for the inconsequential expansion and/or contraction of the element (usually another, smaller pipe) that passes through it.

expansion strip (1) The material used in an expansion joint. (2) Resilient insulating material used as a joint filler between a partition and a structural member.

expansion tank (1) In a hot-water system, the tank that provides for the increased volume of the water heated in the heating tank below it. (2) A device to control pressure in a fluid system by storing excess liquid.

expansion valve The valve that controls the flow of refrigerant to the cooling element in a refrigeration system.

expansive cement (expanded cement, expanding cement, sulfoaluminate cement) A type of cement whose set paste increases in volume substantially more than the set paste of Portland cement. Used in applications where the desired results include the compensation for volume decrease due to shrinkage, or the induction of tensile stress in reinforcement.

expansive-cement concrete A concrete made from expansive cement for the purpose of reducing or controlling volume changes that occur during curing.

expansive soil Soil that expands when water is added and shrinks when it dries out. This change in soil volume can cause shifting and cracking in structures.

expediter One who monitors and facilitates the arrival of building materials or equipment to meet a progress schedule.

expert witness In a court case or other legal or arbitration proceeding, an individual who, because of his/her exceptional knowledge, experience, or skill in a particular field or subject is accepted by the court (or by those presiding over other legal or arbitration proceedings) as being qualified to render an authoritative opinion in matters relating to his or her field of expertise.

expletive In masonry, the stone used to fill a cavity.

exploded view An illustration depicting the disassembled individual components in proper relationship to their assembled positions therein.

explosion-proof box

exposed aggregate

extended surface

explosion-proof box Electrical equipment housing designed in compliance with hazardous location requirements to withstand an explosion that could occur within it and to prevent ignition by the explosion of flammable material, liquid, or gas that might externally surround it.

explosion-proof fixture Electric lighting fixture that will not explode or ignite when in contact with a flammable gas or liquid.

explosion-proof lighting An electrical light system that will not explode or ignite flammable liquids or gases that surround it.

explosion welding The use of a controlled explosion to weld members together.

explosive Any device or chemical compound whose primary function is to produce an explosion.

explosive-actuated gun (stud gun) A stud driver in which the discharge of a blank cartridge provides the impact.

explosive rivet A rivet whose explosive-filled shank is exploded by striking it with a hammer after the rivet has been inserted.

exposed Refers to an unprotected or uninsulated "live" component of an electrical system whose location makes it susceptible to being inadvertently touched or approached by someone at an unsafe distance.

exposed aggregate The coarse aggregate in concrete work revealed when the surface layer of concrete paste is removed, usually before the full hardening of the concrete.

exposed area In roofing, the part of a shingle that is not covered by another shingle.

exposed joint In masonry, any masonry joint on the face of a wall that is above ground level.

exposed masonry Any masonry construction whose only surface finish is a coat of paint applied to the face of the wall.

exposed nailing A method of nailing that leaves the nails exposed to the weather.

exposed suspension system A method of installing a suspended acoustical ceiling in which the panel-supporting grid is left exposed in a room.

exposure hazard The probability of a building's exposure to fire from an adjoining or nearby property.

exposure level The level or concentration at which a person has been exposed to a hazardous material.

exposure limits *See* **permissable exposure limits**.

extended coverage insurance A form of property insurance protecting against loss or damage caused by wind, hail, aircraft, riot, land vehicles, explosion (except steam boiler explosion), or civil commotion.

extended overhead Overhead costs accumulated during compensable delay periods when full production was not achievable.

extended-service lamp (long-life lamp) A lamp designed to have a life substantially larger than others in its general class. Such an incandescent lamp provides an output of fewer lumens than a standard lamp of comparable voltage.

extended surface A fitting, usually composed of metal fins or ribs, that provides additional surface area on a

extension ladder

exterior stair

exterior trim

pipe or tube through which heat is transferred.

extender (1) An opaque, white, inert mineral pigment, such as calcium carbonate, silica, diatomaceous earth, talc, or clay, that is added to paint to provide texture, lower gloss, or reduce paint cost by providing bulk. (2) A volume-increasing, cost-reducing additive in synthetic resin adhesives.

extensibility The capability of a sealant to be stretched in tension.

extension (1) A wing, ell, or other addition to an existing building. (2) The product of a quantity multiplied by a unit price. (3) The completion of a mathematical equation.

extension bit A drill attachment used with a standard bit to increase the drill's reach.

extension bolt *See* **extension flush bolt**.

extension casement hinge An exterior hinge on a casement window whose sash swings outward. The hinge is located so as to provide enough clearance to allow the cleaning of the hinged side from the inside when the window is open.

extension device Any device, other than an adjustment screw, used for accomplishing vertical adjustment.

extension flush bolt (extension bolt) A type of flush bolt whose head connects to the operating mechanism via a rod, which is inserted through a hole bored in the door.

extension jamb *See* **jamb lining**.

extension ladder A ladder comprising more than one section, each of which slides within and locks on the other, thus allowing lengthening.

extension link That device which provides a long backset in the bored lock of a door.

extension rule A rule containing an extendable, calibrated, sliding insert.

exterior-glazed Descriptive of glazing that has been set from the outside of a building.

exterior paint Paint formulated with durable binder and pigment, making it suitable for exposure to weather.

exterior panel In a concrete slab, a panel with at least one of its edges not adjacent to another panel.

exterior plywood Plywood whose layers of veneer are bonded with a waterproof glue.

exterior stair An often legally required exit consisting of a series of flights of steps affixed to the structure but not enclosed.

exterior trim Any visible or exposed finish material on the outside of a building.

exterior wall An outer wall or vertical enclosure of a structure.

external vibration Brisk agitation of freshly mixed concrete by a vibrating device strategically positioned on concrete forms.

extra A work item performed in addition to the scope specified in the contract. Often involves an additional cost.

extraction procedure toxicity The propensity of a substance to emit toxins under a specific test procedure, defined by the EPA, which uses an acid to extract the toxins from the substance in question.

extrados The outer or upper surface of an arch.

extruded section

eye bolt

extranet A shared communications network that uses Internet technology to allow collaborating parties to share information. Especially useful with large, fast-track projects that require extensive documents.

extra-strong pipe The common designation for steel or wrought iron pipe having wall thickness greater than that of standard-weight pipe.

extra work Any work, desired or performed, but not included in the original contract.

extruded Descriptive of any item manufactured by forcing its hot constituent material through an orifice in a die.

extruded section Structural sections formed by extrusion and used in light construction.

extruded tile A tile formed by pushing clay through a die and cutting it into specified lengths.

extrusion coating A thin film of extruded molten resin, which is pressed onto a substrate to produce a coating with an adhesive.

exudation A substance that passes gradually through a pore or crack in a material, as in liquid oozing from a concrete surface.

eye (1) In architecture, the opening in the uppermost portion of a cupola. (2) The nearly circular center of the roll or volute of an Ionic capital. (3) The middle roundel of a pattern or ornament. (4) A hole through a member to provide access, such as for the passage of a pin. (5) In tools, the receiving orifice in the head of the implement.

eye bar A bar that functions as a tension member in a steel truss, as either or both of its ends contain an eye which provides for the passage of a pin, thus forming a joint.

eye bolt An anchoring device comprising a threaded shank with a lopped head, designed to accept a hook, cable, or rope.

eyebrow A window or ventilation opening though the surface of a roof. Unlike a dormer, it forms no sharp angles with the roof, but rather is incorporated into the general horizontal line of the continuous roof, which is carried over it in a wave line. *See also* **ventilating eyebrow**.

eye of a dome The opening at the very top of a dome.

F

F ABBREVIATIONS

The abbreviations listed below are those most commonly used in the construction industry. Alternative forms (usually nonstandard) are shown in parentheses.

f fine, focal length, force, frequency

F Fahrenheit, female, fill, fluorine

f. fiber stress

FA fresh air, fire alarm

fab fabricate, fabricated

fac facsimile

FAI fresh air intake

F.A.I.A. Fellow of the American Institute of Architects

FAO finish all over

FAR floor-area ratio

FAS free alongside ship, firsts and seconds

FBGS fiberglass

FBM foot board measure

f.c., F.C. footcandle, compressive stress in concrete, extreme compressive stress

FCC Federal Communications Commission

f.c.c face-centered cubic

FDB forced draft blower

FDC fire department connection

fdn, fdtn, fds, FDN foundation, foundations

fdry foundry

Fe ferrum (iron)

FE fire escape

F.E. front end

FEA Federal Energy Administration

FEMA Federal Emergency Management Agency

FEP Fluorinated Ethylene Propylene (Teflon)

FFA full freight allowance

FG fine grain, flat grain

F.G. finished grain, flat grain

FHA Federal Housing Administration

FHC fire hose cabinet

FHWA Federal Highway Administration

FID flame ionization detector.

Fig. figure

fill. filling

Fin. finish

Fixt fixture

fl floor, fluid

Fl floorline, floor, flashing

flash. flashing

FLG flooring

fl oz fluid ounce

Flr floor

FLUOR fluorescent

fm fathom

F.M. frequency modulation, Factory Mutual

Fmg. framing

FML flexible membrane liner

FMT flush metal threshold

FMV fair market value

fndtn. foundation

FOB free on board

FOC free of charge

FOHC free of heart centers

FOK free of knots

fount. fountain

fp fireplace, freezing point

f.pfg. fireproofing

fpm feet per minute

FPRF fireproof

fps feet per second

fr frame

F.R., Fr. fire rating

frmg framing, forming

FRP fiber reinforced plastic

frt freight

frwy freeway

FS federal specifications

FSES fire safety evaluation system

FST flat seam tin

ft foot, feet

ftc footcandle

ftg footing

fth fathom

ft lb foot pound

ft sm feet surface measure

Furn furnish, furnished

fus fusible

fv face velocity

FW flash welding

fwd forward, four wheel drive

F DEFINITIONS

face block

face brick

face frame cabinets

fabricate (1) To build, to construct, to manufacture. (2) To make by fitting together standardized parts. (3) To assemble in the shop, as to assemble a reinforced steel part.

façade The exterior face of a building, sometimes decorated with elaborate detail.

face (1) The surface of a wall, masonry unit, or sheet of material that is exposed to view or designed to be exposed in finish work. (2) To cover the surface layer of one material with another, as to *face* a wall with brick or fieldstone. (3) The surface area to be excavated during a construction project. (4) The side of a hammer head used to strike.

face block (faced block) A unit of concrete masonry with a plastic or ceramic face surface, often glazed or polished for special architectural uses.

face brick (facing brick) (1) Brick manufactured to present an attractive appearance. (2) Any brick that is exposed, such as on a fireplace.

face bushing A pipe fitting with both internal and external threads.

face cord A measurement of firewood. A face cord is 4' high x 8' long, but only as deep as the length of the pieces. A face cord may be 4' x 8', but only 16" deep, and thus contain only one-third of the wood volume of a standard cord.

faced insulation Any batt insulation with a moisture barrier on one or both sides. The barrier may be paper, plastic or foil.

faced plywood Plywood that is faced with plastic, metal, or any material other than wood.

faced wall A wall with facing and backing bonded so that both act together under load.

face edge (1) The best of the two narrow faces on a rectangular piece of lumber. (2) The edge from which other edges are measured or *trued*.

face feed The application of a filler metal in a brazed or soldered joint.

face frame cabinets Cabinets with a hardwood frame on the face of the cabinet that masks the raw edges of the sides, adds rigidity to the cabinet and provides a strong base for attaching hinges.

face glazing The compound applied with a glazing knife after a light has been bedded, set, and fastened in a rabbeted sash.

face grain The grain on the face of a plywood panel. The face grain should always be placed at right angles to the supports when applying it to a roof or subfloor.

face joint A visible joint on the surface of a masonry wall.

face line The reference line that a mason first sets and then follows when building walls.

face mark A mark made on the face of a piece of lumber, usually in pencil or crayon, near the edge or end of the piece that identifies the work face of a planed timber.

face measure The measurement of the area of a board or panel. Face measure is not the same as board measure, except when the piece being measured is 1" thick.

face milling Cutting done on the wide, exposed surface of a piece of lumber in order to produce a design.

face width

facing block

face mix A concrete mix bonded to the exposed surface of a cast stone building unit.

face mold (1) A template used in ornamental woodworking to mark the boards from which pieces will be cut. (2) A device used to examine the shape of wood and stone faces and surfaces.

face nailing Nailing perpendicular to the face of wood and through the face of the material.

face oiling A light coating of oil on the face of concrete panels to aid in removing the forms after the concrete sets.

faceplate Any protective and/or decorative plate such as an *escutcheon*.

face putty (front putty) Putty used on the exposed surface of window glass.

face side The better wide side of a rectangular piece of lumber.

face stock *See* **face veneer**.

face string (finish string) An exterior string, usually of better material or finish, placed over the rough string in the construction of a staircase.

face velocity The speed at which air passes through a forced-air system register.

face veneer Those veneers of higher grade and quality that are used for the faces of plywood panels, especially in the sanded grades. Face veneer is selected for decorative qualities rather than for strength.

face wall The front wall of a structure.

face width The width of the face of a piece of dressed lumber. In tongued or lapped lumber, the face width does not include the width of the tongue or lap.

facia *See* **fascia**.

facility audit (1) An assessment of the physical condition and functional performance of an organization's facilities. (2) A review of activities at a facility or location, the purpose of which is to identify the improper storage, handling, or disposal of hazardous materials or waste.

facility engineer An engineer who provides technical expertise to ensure the optimal operation of a facility's plants, grounds and offices. Responsibilities include maintaining and improving the efficiency of existing equipment and systems while overseeing the installation of new equipment and systems.

facility management system (FMS) An electronic control system that helps facility managers maximize a facility's performance.

facility manager A professional who coordinates the planning, design and management of a facility, including its systems, equipment, and furniture. A facility manager helps an organization meet its long-term strategic and operational objectives while daily maintaining a safe, efficient working environment.

facing (facework) Any material used to cover a rough or inferior surface, in order to provide a finished and more attractive appearance.

facing block A concrete masonry unit having a decorative exterior finish.

facing brick *See* **face brick**.

factored load *See* **design ultimate load**.

factor of safety (1) Stress factor of safety: the ratio of the ultimate strength, or yield point, of a material to the design working stress.

fairlead

(2) Load factor of safety: the ratio of ultimate load, moment, or shear of a structural member to the working load, moment, or shear, respectively, assumed in design.

factory-built A reference to a construction, usually a dwelling, that is built, or at least partially preassembled, in a factory rather than *on site*. Most factory-built units are constructed in two or more modules, often complete with plumbing, wiring, etc. The modules are delivered to a building site and assembled there. Finish work is then performed. Factory-built houses are generally less expensive to build and quicker to erect because of savings gained through mass production and factory efficiencies.

factory-filled particleboard Particleboard that has had its edges filled with plastic during manufacture.

factory finished A product that has been coated or stained as part of the manufacturing process.

factory lumber A broad category of lumber that includes stock of various grades and species intended for remanufacturing into items such as furniture, doors, windows, moldings, and boxes.

factory primed A product to which an initial undercoat of paint has been applied.

factory select A grade of shop lumber containing 70% or more of No. 1 door stock, but having other defects, such as pitch or bark pockets, beyond the restrictions allowed in the No. 1 grade of lumber.

failing wedge A V-shaped piece of steel, aluminum or plastic used by driving it into the back cut when felling a tree. The purpose is to keep the saw from binding, and to help control the direction of the fall.

fail soft A state of compromised operation, as opposed to complete disability, following equipment failure.

failure A deficiency of a structural element that makes it unable to continue the load-bearing function for which it was originally designed.

fair face concrete A concrete surface which, on completion of the forming process, requires no further (concrete) treatment other than curing. *See also* **architectural concrete**.

Fair Labor Standards Act (FLSA) An act of the Congress of the United States enacted in 1936, and the subject of numerous amendments to the present day. This act is commonly referred to as the Minimum Wage Law; it establishes a minimum wage for all workers with the exception of agricultural workers, and additionally provides a maximum of a 40-hour work week for straight time pay for employees earning hourly wages.

fairlead A device such as a ring or a block of wood with a hole in it, through which cable or rope is led for alignment.

fair market value A price that is fair and reasonable in light of current conditions in the marketplace.

fall The slope in a channel, conduit, or pipe, stated either as a percentage or in inches per feet.

falldown (1) Those lumber or plywood items of a lesser grade or quality that are produced as an adjunct to the processing of a higher quality stock. (2) A term used in waterborne shipments to indicate that a cargo was not ready for loading when a vessel called for it.

false joint

falsework

fan-coil unit

fanlight

fallout shelter A room or structure intended for shelter from the effects of radiation caused by nuclear explosions.

false attic An architectural addition, built above the main cornice of a structure, that conceals the roof rafters but has no rooms or windows.

false ceiling A ceiling suspended a foot or more below the actual ceiling to provide space for and easy access to wiring and ducts, or to alter the dimensions of a room. *See also* **suspended ceiling**.

false door A non-operable door placed in a wall for architectural appearance.

false front A front wall that extends beyond the sidewalls and/or above the roof of a building to create a more imposing facade.

false header In masonry, a header that does not connect two walls together; for example, when using half brick.

false heartwood Dark innerwood that has been colored by disease or fungi so that it resembles heartwood in color.

false joint A groove in a solid masonry block or stone, simulating the appearance of a joint.

false rafter A short extension added to a main rafter over a cornice.

false set The rapid development of rigidity in a freshly mixed Portland cement paste, mortar, or concrete without the evolution of much heat. Rigidity can be dispelled and plasticity regained by further mixing without addition of water. *Premature stiffening, hesitation set, early stiffening,* and *rubber set* are terms referring to the same phenomenon, but *false set* is the preferred designation.

falsework The temporary structure erected to support work in the process of construction. Falsework consists of shoring or vertical posting formwork or beams and slabs, and lateral bracing. *See also* **centering**.

fan brake horsepower (Bhp) The horsepower output of a fan as measured at the pulley or belt. Bhp includes losses due to turbulence and other inefficiencies.

fan-coil unit An air-conditioning unit that houses an air filter, heating or cooling coil, and a centrifugal fan, and operates by moving air through an opening in the unit and across the coils.

fancy butt A shingle with the butt end machined in a pattern. Fancy butt shingles are usually used on sidewalls to form geometric designs in the shingle pattern.

fan Fink truss A form of Fink truss with subdiagonals that extend outward from a central point.

fanlight A semi-circular or semi-elliptical window built above the opening of a door. A fanlight often has triangular panes of glass, in between radiating bars or leads, and resembles the form of an open fan.

fanlight catch The spring catch on a fanlight window or other hinged windows. The catch often has a cord attached for opening.

fan pressure curve The curve that represents the pressure developed by a fan operating at a fixed rpm at various air volumes.

fan suction box A specially designed 90° fitting installed at the fan inlet that reduces the inlet pressure loss created by system effect.

fan surge Turbulent flow caused when insufficient air enters the fan

fascia

wheel to completely fill the space between the blades. Some of the air reverses its direction over a portion of the fan blade.

fan truss   A truss with struts that radiate like the ribs of a fan, supported at their base by a common suspension member.

fascia (facia)   (1) A board used on the outside vertical face of a cornice. (2) The board connecting the top of the siding with the bottom of a soffit. (3) A board nailed across the ends of the rafters at the eaves. (4) The edge beam of a bridge. (5) A flat member or band at the surface of a building.

fascia board   *See* **eaves fascia**.

fascine   An assembly of live cuttings lashed together and allowed to set roots on banks to prevent surface erosion.

fastener   Any mechanical device used to hold together two or more pieces, parts, members, etc.

fast-pin hinge   A hinge with a pin fixed permanently in place.

fast-to-light   A material that will not fade when exposed to direct sunlight.

fast track construction   A building method in which construction is begun on a portion of the work for which the design is complete, while design on other portions of the work is underway.

fat   (1) Material accumulating on a trowel during smoothing. Fat is used to fill in small imperfections. (2) Descriptive of a mortar containing a relatively high proportion of cement.

fat area   *See* **fat spot**.

fat board   A bricklayer's mortarboard.

fat concrete   Concrete with a relatively large proportion of cement.

fat edge   A ridge of paint at the bottom edge of a surface when too much paint has been applied or because the paint runs too freely.

fatigue   The weakening of a material caused by repeated or alternating loads. Fatigue may result in cracks or complete failure.

fatigue failure   The phenomenon of rupture that occurs when a material is subjected to repeated loadings at a stress substantially less than the ultimate tensile strength.

fatigue life   (1) The number of cycles of a specified loading that a given specimen can be subjected to before failure occurs. (2) A measure of the useful life of similar specimens.

fatigue strength   The maximum stress that can be sustained for a number of stress cycles without failure.

fat lime (rich lime)   A quicklime or hydrated lime used in plastering and masonry obtained by burning a pure or nearly pure limestone source.

fat mix (rich mix)   A mortar or concrete mix with a relatively high cement content. Fat mix is more easily spread and worked than a mix with the minimum amount of cement required for strength.

fat mortar (rich mortar)   Mortar with a high percentage of cement. Fat mortar is sticky and adheres to a trowel.

fat spot (fat area)   A thick spot in an area paved with bituminous concrete.

fattening   The thickening of paint in a partially filled can that has been left standing over a period of time.

faucet ear   The projection on a pipe or fitting bell, used to bolt it to another pipe or fitting.

fault   (1) A defect in an electrical system caused by poor insulation,

feather edge

feeder

imperfect connections, grounding, or shorting. (2) A shifting along a plane in a rock formation that causes differential displacement.

faulting Differential vertical displacement of a slab or other member adjacent to a joint or crack.

faying surface The surface of a metal or wooden member joined closely to another member in such a way as to leave no space between them.

feasibility study A thorough study of a proposed construction project to evaluate its economic, financial, technical, functional, environmental, and cultural advisability.

feather To blend the edge or finish of new material smoothly into an existing surface.

featherboard A safety device used to prevent table saw kickback.

feather edge (featheredge) The beveling or tapering of the edge of one surface or surface coating where it meets another.

featheredge rule A straight-edged device used to shape and define angles in plastering.

feather joint A joint between two squared, closely butted boards made by plowing a groove along the length of each and fitting them with a common tongue.

feather tip A shingle or shake with an extra thin end.

Federal Communications Commission (FCC) A regulatory agency based in Washington, DC that was established by the Communications Act of 1934 to regulate broadcast communications (wire, radio, and television) in the United States.

Federal employer identification number A number assigned by the Internal Revenue Service to identify a business for tax purposes.

Federal Hazardous Substances Act The federal law that controls the use of hazardous constituents in consumer products.

Federal Home Loan Mortgage Corp. A government sponsored organization, nicknamed "Freddie Mac," that provides a secondary market for mortgages.

Federal Housing Administration (FHA) A division of the Department of Housing and Urban Development. The FHA works through lending agencies to provide mortgage insurance on private residences that meet the agency's minimum property standards. The FHA has also been charged with administering a number of special housing programs.

Federal Mediation and Conciliation Service An agency of the United States Department of Labor which acts as a mediator in the settlement of disputes as provided in the National Labor Relations Act of 1935 and the Labor Management Relations Act of 1947.

Federal National Mortgage Association A corporation that provides a secondary mortgage market for FHA-insured and VA-guaranteed home loans.

federal style The classic revival style of architecture in the U.S. from 1790 to 1830.

fee Remuneration for professional services.

feeder (1) An electrical cable or group of electrical conductors that runs power from a larger central source to one or more secondary or branch-circuit distribution centers.

felt

ferrule

(2) A tributary to a reservoir or canal. (3) A bolt or device that pushes material onto a crusher or conveyor.

feed rate The rate at which material can be fed to a machine, such as an edger or planer, without causing a jam.

feed wheel A material distributor or regulator in certain types of shotcrete equipment.

feeler gauge A gauge used to measure the thickness of a gap, consisting of a series of blades of graduated thicknesses.

fee owned timber Timber that is presently owned free and clear. The term *fee* comes from the legal phrases *fee simple* and *fee simple absolute*. A company's fee owned timber includes timber on land owned by the firm and also may include timber that is owned by the firm but is on land owned by another party.

fee simple An enduring, inheritable interest in land which may be legally honored until the death of all potential heirs of the original owner, and which the owner is free to convey at any time.

feldspar Any of a group of igneous minerals chemically composed of calcium silicates, potassium silicates, or sodium-aluminum silicates and having a consistency softer than quartz.

fell To cut down a tree. A faller fells a tree with a falling saw.

felt A fabric of matted compressed fibers, usually manufactured from cellulose fibers from wood, paper, or rags, or from glass fibers.

felt-and-gravel roofing See **built-up roofing**.

felt nail See **clout nail**.

felt paper Paper sheathing used to insulate walls and to prevent infiltration of moisture.

female coupling A coupling with internal threads on both ends.

female thread See **inside thread**.

femerell A ventilator, often louvered, used to draw smoke through a roof when a chimney is not provided.

fence A straight-edge guide mounted parallel to a saw blade to guide a cant as it passes through the saw.

fence pliers Heavy duty pliers used to cut thick wire. May also include a claw to remove pins and fasteners.

fender A protective bumper often of wood or old tires.

fenestration The layout and design of windows in a building.

feng shui An approach to interior design, based on Chinese ideals, that seeks to create harmonious surroundings, as in selecting light fixtures, arranging furniture or determining the siting of a house.

ferrocement A composite hydraulic structural material having thin sections consisting of cement mortar reinforced by a number of very closely spaced layers of steel wire mesh.

ferrous metal Metal in which the principal element is iron.

ferrule (1) A tube or metallic sleeve, fitted with a screwed cap to the side of a pipe to provide access for maintenance. (2) A metal sleeve or collar attached to the end of a short cable in making a choker. The ferrule fits into the bell of the choker. Also called a *nubbin*. (3) Spacer tube used in hanging metal gutter to prevent deforming of the gutter when attached.

fertilizer Any organic or inorganic material that acts as a nutrient.

fiber A thread-like structure of a plant that contributes to stiffness or strength.

fiberboard A general term referring to any of various panel products, such as particleboard, hardboard, chipboard, or other types formed by, bonding wood fillers by heat and pressure.

fibered plaster Gypsum plaster reinforced with fibers of hair, glass, nylon, or sisal.

fiberglass (fibrous glass, glass fiber) Filaments of glass formed by pulling molten glass into random lengths that are either gathered in a wool-like mass or formed as continuous threads. The wool-like form is used as thermal and acoustical insulation. The thread-like form is used as reinforcing material and in textiles, glass fabrics, and electrical insulation.

fiberglass reinforced plastic (FRP) A coating of glass fibers and resins applied as a protective layer to plywood. The resulting composite is tough and scuff resistant. It is used to manufacture containers, cooling towers, concrete forms, and shower stalls.

fiber optics The transmission of light pulses through bundles of fine, transparent fibers. *See also* **fiber optic waveguides** *and* **optic fiber cable**.

fiber optic waveguides Fine, transparent fibers, usually thin filaments of glass or plastic, through which a light beam can be transmitted.

fiber-reinforced concrete *See* **concrete, fibrous**.

fiber saturation point The point of wood moisture content when the cell walls are completely saturated with water, but there is no water in the cell lumens and intercellular spaces.

fiber stress The longitudinal compressive or tensile stress in a structural member.

fibrous Resembling or composed of fibers.

fibrous concrete Concrete with glass or other fibers added to increase tensile strength.

fibrous glass duct Ductwork constructed of fiberglass material.

fibrous plaster Cast plaster reinforced canvas, excelsior, or other fibrous material.

FICA A federal law which imposes a social security tax on employees, employers, and the self-employed.

fiddleback grain A rippling or undulating grain common to certain hardwoods, such as maple and sycamore. Pieces containing this grain pattern are often used on the backs of violins.

fiducial mark A standard reference point or line used as a base in surveying.

field (1) In masonry, an expanse of brickwork between two openings or corners. (2) A term used to designate a construction project site. (3) Occupation such as a trade, profession, or specialty. (4) An area of floor, wall or ceiling that is covered with tile or other preformed shapes that did not require cutting, as opposed to those areas along a border or edge.

field applied (1) The application of a material, such as paint, at a job site, as opposed to being applied at a factory. (2) The construction or assembly of components in the field.

field bending Bending of reinforcing bars on the job rather than in a fabricating shop.

field gluing

fieldstone

field chipping   The reduction to pulp chips of slash or small trees using a portable chipper in the woods.

field concrete   *See* **concrete, field.**

field-cured cylinders   Test cylinders cured nearly in the same manner as the concrete in the structure to indicate when supporting forms may be removed, additional construction loads may be imposed, or the structure may be placed in service.

field drain   *See* **agricultural drain pipe.**

field engineer   A representative of certain government agencies who oversees projects at the site. Also called a *project representative* or *field representative.*

field gluing   A method of gluing plywood floors in which specially developed glues are applied to the top edges of floor joists. Plywood is then laid on the joists and nailed in place. The combination of gluing and nailing results in a stiffer floor construction and tends to minimize squeaks and nail-popping.

field house   A long structure used for indoor athletic events.

field inspection   The reinspection of lumber or plywood in the field, usually at the buyer's location. A field inspection is requested by a buyer when he believes a delivered product to be inferior to that specified. *See also* **reinspection.**

field man   A representative of a trade association who is available to answer questions regarding grades, usage, and characteristics of various species (in the case of wood products), as well as the products produced by his association. The field man may also conduct clinics and demonstrations and otherwise promote the association's products.

field-molded sealant   A joint sealant in liquid or semi-solid form that can be molded to the desired shape as it is installed in the joint.

field order   In construction, a written order passed to the contractor from the architect to effect a minor change in work, requiring no further adjustment to the contract sum or expected date of completion.

field painting   The painting of structural steel or other metals after they have been erected and fastened.

field representative   *See* **field engineer** *and* **project representative.**

field rivet   A rivet driven in a field connection of structural steel.

field sound transmission class (FSTC)   An onsite measurement of the ability of a specific construction element, such as a wall partition, to block sound.

fieldstone   (1) Loose stone removed from the soil. (2) Flat slabs of stone suitable for use in dry wall masonry.

field supervision   The site supervisory work performed by a designated individual.

field welding   Welding performed at the construction site, usually with gasoline-powered equipment.

field work   Any work performed at a job site.

fifths   The lowest of the common lumber grades normally exported from Scandinavia and Eastern Europe.

fifth wheel   The swivel connection between highway-type tractors and semi-trailers.

figure   The natural wood pattern that is created by growth rings, knots and other deviations from regular grain.

figured glass   Translucent sheet glass rolled with a bas-relief pattern on

fill

fill insulation

one face, providing high but obscure, light transmission, with the degree of obscurity depending on the pattern.

filament A fine wire used in an incandescent lamp. The form is designated by a letter: S, straight wire; E, coil; CC, coiled coil.

file A hand-held steel tool with teeth or raised oblique ridges, used for scraping, redressing, or smoothing metal or wood.

filer (saw filer) The person in a sawmill or logging operation who keeps the saws sharp.

fill (1) The soil or other material used to raise the grade of a site area. (2) A subfloor leveling material.

filled particleboard Particleboard to which plastic material has been applied to fill gaps between particles on the edges or faces.

filler (1) Finely divided inert material, such as pulverized limestone, silica, or colloidal substances sometimes added to Portland cement, paint or other materials to reduce shrinkage, improve workability, or act as an extender. (2) Material used to fill an opening in a form.

filler block Concrete masonry units placed between joists or beams under a cast-in-place floor.

filler coat A coat of paint or varnish used as a primer.

filler metal Metal, added by a welding process, that has a melting point either approximately the same as or below the base metal.

filler plate A steel plate or shim used to fill any gap between columns or between a column and a roof member.

fillet (1) A narrow band of wood between two flutes in a wood

member. (2) A flat, square molding separating other moldings. (3) A concave junction formed where two surfaces meet. *See also* **chamfer strip**.

fillet weld A weld of approximate triangular cross section, used to join two surfaces at approximate right angles to each other. The weld metal may be deposited in one pass or built up with multiple passes.

filling piece A piece inserted into another to form a continuous surface.

fill insulation (1) Thermal insulation placed in prepared or natural cavities of a building. (2) Any variety of loose insulation that is poured into place.

fillister On a window, a rabbet on the outer edge of a muntin that holds the glass in place.

fillister head screw A common machine screw with a slightly domed head and straight body.

fill lighting Lighting used in addition to a primary light that will fill in shadows and reduce contrast.

fill packing The portion of a cooling tower that provides heat transfer surface.

fill-type insulation *See* **fill insulation**.

film glue A thin sheet of paper or scrim which has been impregnated with a thermosetting resin, used to bond expensive decorative veneers without bleed-through or in hot-pressing nonporous laminates.

film surfaced hardboard siding Hardboard to which a thin, dry sheet of paper, coated on both sides with a phenol-formaldehyde resin adhesive, has been applied. Such coatings are often printed with grain patterns in imitation of actual veneers, and are used as an

filter bed

filter block

inexpensive substitute for the higher priced veneer panels.

filter (1) A device to separate solids from air or liquids, such as a filter that removes dust from the air or impurities from water. (2) Granular matter placed on an area to provide drainage while preventing the entry and flow of sediment and silt.

filter bed A bed of granular material used to filter water or sewage.

filter block A hollow, vitrified clay masonry unit used for trickling filter floors in sewage treatment plants.

fin A narrow, linear projection on a formed concrete surface, resulting from mortar flowing out between spaces in the formwork.

final acceptance The formal acceptance of a contractor's completed construction project by the owner, upon notification from an architect that the job fulfills the contract requirements. Final acceptance is often accompanied by a final payment agreed upon in the contract.

final completion A term applied for a project that has been completed according to the terms and conditions set forth in the contract documents.

final inspection An architect's last review of a completed project before issuance of the final certificate for payment.

final payment The payment an owner awards to the contractor upon receipt of the final certificate for payment from the architect. Final payment usually covers the whole unpaid balance agreed to in the contract, plus or minus any amounts altered by change orders.

final prestress *See* **final stress**.

final set A degree of stiffening of a mixture of cement and water

greater than initial set, generally stated as an empirical value indicating the time in hours and minutes required for a cement paste to stiffen sufficiently to resist an established penetration of a weighted test needle. *See also* **initial set**.

final setting time The time required, for a freshly mixed cement paste, mortar, or concrete to achieve final set. *See also* **initial setting time**.

final stress (1) In prestressed concrete, the stress that remains in a member after substantially all losses in stress have occurred. (2) The stress in a member after all loads are applied.

fine aggregate (1) Aggregate passing the 3/8″ (9.5-mm) sieve and almost entirely passing the No.4 (4.75-mm) sieve and predominantly retained on the No. 200 (75-micrometer) sieve. (2) That portion of an aggregate passing the No. 4 (4.75-mm) sieve and predominantly retained on the No. 200 (75-micrometer) sieve. *See also* **aggregate** *and* **sand**.

fine grading The final grading of ground to prepare for seeding, planting, or paving.

fine-grained soil Soil in which the smaller grain sizes predominate, such as fine sand, silt, and clay.

fineness A measure of particle size.

fineness modulus A factor obtained by adding the total percentages by weight of an aggregate sample retained on each of a specified series of sieves, and dividing the sum by 100. In the United States the standard sieve sizes are No. 100 (150 micrometer), No.50 (300 micrometer), No.30 (600 micrometer), No.16 (1. 18 mm), No.8 (2.36 mm) and No.4 (4.75 mm), and 3/8″ (9.5 mm), 3/4″ (19

finial

finish carpentry (joinery)

mm), 1-1/2" (38.1 mm), 3" (75 mm), and 6" (150 mm).

fines (1) Soil which passes through a No. 200 sieve. (2) Fine-milled chips used in the production of particleboard. Fines are larger than sander dust or wood flour and are used on the faces of particleboard panels, with coarser chips used as the core of the board. (3) An undesirable by-product of cutting wafers and strands for waferboard and oriented strand board.

fine stuff A finish coat plaster made of pure lime and water.

finger guard A strip of soft rubber, vinyl, or neoprene applied to door frames to prevent injury to hands or fingers that get caught between the door and frame.

finger joint A method of joining two pieces of lumber end to end by sawing into the end of each piece a set of projecting "fingers" that interlock. When the pieces are pushed together, these form a strong glue joint.

finial A decoration on the point of a spire, pinnacle, or conical roof.

finish (1) The texture of a surface after compacting and finishing operations have been performed. (2) A high-quality piece of lumber graded for appearance and often used for interior trim or cabinet work.

finish builders' hardware Visible, functional hardware that has a finished appearance, including such features as hinges, locks, catches, pulls, and knobs.

finish carpentry Carpentry that involves the installation of finish woods, (and trim made of plastic or molded polyurethane materials) to provide a finished appearance to installed doors, windows, stairs, and other features of a building's interior. Elements include casing, baseboard, railings, mantels, louvers, paneling, and shelving.

finish carpentry (joinery) The wood finish to a building, such as moldings, doors, and windows.

finish casing The finish trim around a casing.

finish coat (1) Final thin coat of shotcrete preparatory to hand finishing. (2) An exposed coat of plaster and stucco.

finished grade The top surface of an area after construction is completed, such as the top of a road, lawn, or walk.

finished size The final size of any completed object including trim.

finisher A tradesman who applies the final treatment to a concrete surface, including patching voids and smoothing.

finish floor The wearing surface of a floor.

finish flooring The material used to make the wearing surface of a floor, such as hardwood, tile, or terrazzo.

finish grade *See* **finished grade**.

finish grinding (1) The final grinding of clinker into cement, with calcium sulfate in the form of gypsum or anhydrite generally being added. (2) The final grinding operation required for a finished concrete surface, such as bump cutting of pavement, fin removal from structural concrete, or terrazzo floor grinding.

finish hardware *See* **finish builders' hardware**.

finishing Leveling, smoothing, compacting, and otherwise treating surfaces of fresh or recently placed concrete or mortar to produce the desired appearance and service. *See also* **float** *and* **trowel**.

finishing machine

finishing nail

fire brick

finishing machine A power-operated machine used to give the desired surface texture to a concrete slab.

finishing nail A slender nail, with a narrow head, that may be driven entirely into a wood surface, leaving a small hole that can be filled with putty or a similar compound.

finish sag A defect in hardboard.

finish size *See* **finished size.**

finish skip A defect in hardboard.

finish string *See* **face string.**

finish work *See* **finish carpentry.**

Fink truss (Belgian truss, French truss) A symmetrical truss, formed by three triangles, commonly used in supporting large, sloping roofs.

fir (1) A form of softwood indigenous to temperate zones, used principally for interior trim and framing. Varieties include Douglas fir, silver fir, balsam fir, and white fir. (2) Although used most often to refer to Douglas fir, which is also a pseudo-fir, a general term for any of a number of species of conifers, including the true firs.

fire alarm system An electrical system, installed within a home, industrial plant, or office building that sounds a loud blast or bell when smoke and flames are detected. Certain alarms are engineered to trigger sprinkler systems for added protection.

fire area An area in a building enclosed by fire-resistant walls, fire- resistant floor/ceiling assemblies, and/or exterior walls with all penetrations properly protected.

fireback (chimney back) (1) The heat-resistant back wall of a fireplace, built of masonry, cast metal or wrought metal, that withstands flames and radiates heat into the area served. (2) A fire- resistant attachment to the back wall of a fireplace that keeps the masonry from absorbing too much heat.

fireblock *See* **fire stop.**

fireboard (chimney board, summer piece) A device used to close or cover the opening of a fireplace when it is not in service.

fire box In a chimney, the metal box that contains the fire.

firebreak (1) A strategic space between buildings, clusters of buildings, or sections of a city that helps to keep fires from leaping or spreading to surrounding areas before they can be contained. (2) Any doors, walls, floors, or other interior structures engineered to go inside a building.

fire brick A flame-resistant, refractory ceramic brick used in fireplaces, chimneys, and incinerators.

fire cement A cement, such as calcium aluminate cement, used in mortars for laying refractory brick.

fire clay An earthy or stony mineral aggregate having as the essential constituent hydrous silicates of aluminum with or without free silica. Fire clay is plastic when sufficiently pulverized and wetted, rigid when subsequently dried, and of suitable refractoriness for use in commercial refractory products.

fire control damper An automatic damper used to close a duct if a fire is detected.

fire cut A sloping cut on the end of a wood beam or joist supported on a masonry wall. If, somewhere along its length, the joist or beam burns through, injury to the wall is minimized.

fire damper *See* **fire control damper.**

fire extinguisher

fire-extinguishing system

fire hydrant

fire detection system A series of sensors and interconnected monitoring equipment which detect the effects of a fire and activate an alarm system.

fire division wall A wall that subdivides one or more floors of a building to discourage the spread of fire.

fire door (1) A highly fire-resistant door system, usually equipped with an automatic closing mechanism, that provides a certain designated degree of fire protection when it is closed. (2) The opening in a furnace or a boiler through which fuel is added.

fire-door rating A system of evaluating the endurance and fire resistance of door, window, or shutter assemblies, according to standards set by Underwriters' Laboratories, Inc., or other recognized safety authorities. Ratings of A through F are assigned in descending order of their effectiveness against fire.

fired strength The compressive or flexural strength of refractory concrete, determined upon cooling after first firing to a specified temperature for a specified time.

fired unit weight The unit weight of refractory concrete, upon cooling, after having been exposed to a specified firing temperature for a specified time.

fire endurance (1) The length of time a wall, floor/ceiling assembly, or roof/ceiling assembly will resist a standard fire without exceeding specified heat transmission, fire penetration, or limitations on structural components. (2) The length of time a structural member, such as a column or beam will resist a standard fire without exceeding specified temperature limits or

collapse. (3) The length of time a door, window, or shutter assembly will resist a standard fire without exceeding specified deformation limits.

fire escape A continuous, unobstructed route of escape from a building in case of fire, sometimes located on the outside of an exterior wall.

fire exit bolt *See* **panic exit device**.

fire extinguisher A portable device for immediate use in suppressing a fire. There are four classes of fires: A, B, C or D. A single device is designed for use on one or more classes.

fire-extinguishing system An installation of automatic sprinklers, foam distribution system, fire hoses, and/or portable fire extinguishers designed for extinguishing a fire in an area.

fire frame A cast-iron housing installed in a fireplace opening to reduce its size.

fire hazard The relative danger that a fire will start and spread, that smoke or toxic gases will be generated, or that an explosion will occur, endangering the occupants of a building or area.

fire-hazard classification A designation of high, ordinary, or low assigned to a building, based on its potential susceptibility to fire, judged by its contents, functions, and the flame-spread rating of its inner furnishings and finishes.

fire hydrant A supply outlet from a water main, for use in fire fighting.

fire limits The boundary of an area where the relative danger exists that a fire will start and spread or that an explosion will occur, endangering the lives of the occupants of the building.

fireproofing

fire load (fire loading) The amount of flammable contents or finishes within a building per unit of floor area, stated either in pounds per square foot or Btus per square foot.

fire management panel A fire alarm control unit consisting of multiple single zone fire alarm control modules, a telephone module, an HVAC module, and an audio communications module.

fire partition An interior partition that does not fully qualify as a fire wall, but has a fire endurance rating of not less than two hours.

fireproof (1) Descriptive of materials, devices, or structures with such high resistance to flame that they are practically unburnable. (2) To treat a material with chemicals in order to make it fire-resistant.

fireproofing The use of fire-resistant materials for the protection of structural members to insure structural integrity in the event of fire.

fireproof wood Chemically treated wood that is fire resistive. No wood can be completely fireproof, but wood can be treated so that it is highly resistant to heat and flame and very difficult to ignite under ordinary circumstances.

fire protection The practice of minimizing the probable loss of life or property resulting from fire, by fire-safe design and construction, the use of detection and suppression systems, establishment of adequate fire fighting services, and training building occupants in fire safety and emergency evacuation.

fire-protection rating *See* **fire endurance**.

fire-protection sprinkler system An automatic fire-suppression system, commonly heat-activated, that sounds an alarm and deluges an area with water from overhead sprinklers when the heat of a fire melts a fusible link.

fire-protection sprinkler valve A valve, normally open, that is used to control the flow of water in a sprinkler system.

fire-rated system Wall, floor, or roof construction using specific materials and designs that have been tested and rated for conformance to fire safety criteria, such as the flame spread rate.

fire resistance (1) The property of a material or assembly to withstand fire, characterized by the ability to confine a fire and/or to continue to perform a given structural function. (2) The property of a material or assembly that makes it so resistant to fire that, for a specified time and under conditions of a standard heat intensity, it will not fail structurally and will not permit the side away from the fire to become hotter than a specified temperature.

fire-resistance rating *See* **fire endurance**.

fire-resistant door A door designed to confine fire to one part of a structure, keeping it from spreading through an entire building. It may be a solid-core wooden door, or one sheathed in metal, depending on the intended location. Doors are rated for the projected time they could be expected to perform their function during a fire. Most building codes require that the door between living quarters and a garage be fire resistant.

fire-resistant material A material that will not ignite and burn when exposed to heat or flame; a noncombustible material.

fire-resistive Capable of resisting the effects of fire to some degree.

fire screen

firestop

fire wall

fire-resistive construction
Construction in which the floors, walls, roof, and other components are built exclusively of noncombustible materials, with fire-endurance ratings equal to or greater than those mandated by law.

fire-resistive wall A wall having the fire-resistance rating required by a building code or in accordance with underwriters' recommendations.

fire retardant (1) A chemical applied to lumber or other wood products to slow combustion and flame spread. (2) A chemical used to fight forest fires, often by dropping it from an airplane or helicopter.

fire-retardant finish Paint composed in part of noncombustible substances such as silicones, chlorinated waxes and resins, and antimony oxide, used to protect combustible surfaces, inhibiting the rapid spread of flames.

fire-retardant wood
Wood chemically impregnated or otherwise treated so that the fire hazard has been reduced.

fire-retarding glazing See **wire glass**.

fire road A road built to provide access to an area in case of fire.

fire screen A screen set in front of a fireplace to retain flying sparks or embers.

fire separation A floor or wall, with any penetrations properly protected, having the fire endurance required by authorities and acting to retard fire spread in a building.

fire shutter A complete metal shutter assembly with the fire endurance required by code. The rating depends on the location and nature of the opening.

firestat A fixed thermostat in an air-conditioning system, preset at a temperature required by code or other authorities, usually 125°F (52 °C).

firestop (1) A short piece of wood, usually a 2″ x 4″ or 2″ x 6″, placed horizontally between the studs of a wall. Firestops are equal in width to the studs. They are usually placed halfway up the height of the wall to slow the spread of fire by limiting drafts in space between the sheathing on the two sides of the wall. Building codes usually do not require firestops in walls that are less than 8′ high. (2) Masonry units placed in wood framed walls.

fire tower A vertical enclosure, with a stairway, having the fire endurance rating required by code and used for egress and as a base for fire fighting.

fire tube boiler Boilers in which flue gas flows through the tubes and water surrounds the tubes.

fire wall An interior or exterior wall that runs from the foundation of a building to the roof or above, constructed to stop the spread of fire.

fire window A window assembly with the fire endurance rating required by code for the location of the opening.

fir & larch A mixture of Douglas fir and western larch, sold as either individual species or as one species grouping. The two species are intermixed because they have similar characteristics and are used in similar ways.

fir fixed Unplaned lumber held in place by nails only.

firing The controlled-heat treatment in a kiln or furnace, of ceramic or brick ware.

fished joint

fittings

firmer chisel A long, narrow carpenter's chisel used for mortising.

firmer gouge A long, narrow carpenter's gouge used for cutting grooves.

firmwood The solid wood in a log suitable for manufacture into wood products or chips.

first coat The initial application of mortar, known as *base coat* in two-coat work, and *scratch coat* in three-coat work.

first floor (1) In the U.S., the floor of a building at or closest to grade. (2) In Europe, the floor of a building above the *ground floor*.

first in, first out (FIFO) A type of accounting for inventory in which items purchased first are assumed to be the first to be sold. An accountant will compute the cost and profit on the oldest or first in the inventory. *See also* **last in, first out (LIFO)**.

first mortgage The mortgage or security in a property that takes precedence over all other mortgages on the property.

firsts and seconds The highest standard grades of hardwood lumber.

fish beam Two beams attached end to end to form a single built-up beam with fishplates securing the opposite sides of the joint.

fish-bellied Descriptive of a beam or truss that has its bottom flange or chord convex and sagging downward.

fished joint A butted timber joint made using fishplates.

fisheye A spot, approximately 1/4″ (6.4 mm) in diameter, in a finish plaster coat caused by a piece of lumpy lime.

fishing wire *See* **snake** *and* **fish tape**.

fishplate A wood or metal plate fastened to the sides of two beams or rails to splice the two ends together.

fish scale A fancy-butt shingle pattern with the exposed portion of the shingle rounded. When used as siding, the overall effect is the pattern of fish scales.

fishtail A wedge-shaped piece of wood used as part of the support form between tapered pans in concrete joist construction.

fishtail bolt A bolt with a split end anchored in concrete.

fish tape *See* **snake**.

fitch A thin, long-handled paintbrush used especially for touching up recessed areas.

fitting (1) A standardized part of a piping system used for attaching sections of pipe together, such as a coupling, elbow, bend, cross, or tee. (2) The process of installing floor coverings around walks, doors, and other obstacles or projections. (3) In electrical wiring, a component, such as a bushing or locknut, that serves a mechanical purpose rather than an electrical function.

fitting-up Erecting a structure by partially bolting the members before aligning and completing the connections.

fitting-up bolt A temporary bolt used to secure structural members before they are permanently connected.

five-quarter (5/4) *See* **quarter measure**.

fixed assets Assets, such as real property, that are not readily converted to cash.

fixed-bar grille A grille with preset, nonadjustable bars, used to cover return and exhaust openings in air-conditioning systems.

fixed light

fixture

fixture supply

flagging

fixed beam A structural beam with fixed, as opposed to hinged, connections.

fixed costs These costs can be defined in two different ways. In total, fixed costs remain the same as volume changes. On a per unit basis, fixed costs decline as volume increases. Examples include office rent, administrative salaries, insurance, and office supplies.

fixed fee A fixed amount specified in a contract to compensate a contractor for all materials and services required to complete the project.

fixed light A window or portion of a window that does not open.

fixed limit of construction cost A maximum amount to be paid for a construction job as specified in the agreement between owner and architect.

fixed plate heat exchanger A static device that transfers sensible heat through plates separating a warm air stream from a cold air stream.

fixed-price contract A type of contract in which the contractor agrees to construct a project for an established price, agreed in advance.

fixed rate mortgage A mortgage on which the interest rate remains the same through the period of the loan.

fixed retaining wall A retaining wall supported both at its top and bottom.

fixed sash See **fixed light**.

fixed transom A glass light or panel that is built above a door and cannot be opened.

fixing The installation of glass panels in a ceiling, wall, or partition. Fixing is distinct from glazing, which covers most other uses, such as the installation of glass in windows, doors, and showcases.

fixture (1) An electrical device, such as a luminaire, attached to a wall or ceiling. (2) An article that becomes part of real property by virtue of being merged or affixed to it, although it was originally a distinct item of personal property.

fixture branch A pipe connecting and servicing two or more plumbing fixtures.

fixture drain A drain that leads from the trap of a fixture to another drainpipe.

fixture joint An electrical connection formed by twisting two conductors together and then folding them over.

fixtures Tangible goods that are permanently attached to, or embedded in, real property so that they are considered to be part of the real property.

fixture supply The pipe connecting a plumbing fixture to a supply line.

fixture unit A measure of the rate at which various plumbing fixtures discharge into a drainage system, stated in units of cubic volume per minute.

fixture-unit flow rate The total number of gallons discharged per minute from a single plumbing fixture, divided by 7.5 to provide the flow rate of that fixture in cubic feet per minute.

fixture whip A flexible wiring system used between the junction box and lighting fixture.

flagging (1) A walk or patio paved with flagstones. (2) The process of setting flagstones. *See also* **flagstone**.

flange

flap trap

flagman A person who directs vehicular traffic by means of flags or signs.

flagstone A flat, irregular-shaped stone, usually 1″ to 4″ thick, used as pedestrian paving or flooring. Flagstones are set in mortar or aggregate outdoors and in mortar indoors.

flake board (flakeboard) A building board composed of wood particles or flakes solidified with a binder. *See also* **particleboard** *and* **waferboard**.

flaking A peeling of paint caused by loss of adhesion and/or cohesion.

flame arrestor A mesh or perforated metal safety device used in a flammable storage can for protection from exterior ignition.

flame cleaning A method of cleaning mill scale, moisture, paint, and dirt from steel by applying a hot flame.

flame cutting Cutting metal with an oxyacetylene torch.

flame ionization detector An ionization detector that uses hydrogen flame to generate ions.

flameproof Able to resist the spread of flame and not easily ignited, but having less fire resistance than fire-retardant substances.

flame-retardant Treated to resist flame spread and ignition.

flame-spread rating A numerical value given to a material designating its resistance to flaming combustion. Materials can have a rating of 100, as in untreated lumber, to 0, as in asbestos sheets.

flame treating A process by which inert thermoplastic materials and objects are prepared to receive paints, adhesives, lacquers, and inks by immersion in open flame, causing surface oxidation.

flammability A material's capacity to burn.

flammable Capable of being ignited easily, burning intensely, or having a rapid rate of flame spread.

flanch (flaunch) To broaden the top of a chimney stack and to cant the edges to direct water away from the flue.

flange (1) A projecting ring, ridge, or collar placed on a pipe or shaft to strengthen, prevent sliding, or accommodate attachments. (2) The longitudinal part of a beam, or other structural member, that resists tension and compression.

flange angle An angle shape used as one of the parts making up the flange of a built-up girder.

flange cut A cut-out in a flange of a beam or girder to accommodate attachment or passage of another structural element.

flange union A method of connecting threaded pipe using a pair of flanges screwed onto the ends of the pipe and bolted together.

flanking transmission Transmission of sound by paths around, rather than through, a building component.

flapper The moving part of the flush valve in a toilet that allows water to leave the tank during the flush cycle.

flap trap (flap valve) A hinged flap within a plumbing system that restricts water flow to one direction, preventing backflow.

flare fitting A soft-tube connector made by flaring the end of the tube to provide a mechanical seal.

flare header In masonry, a header that is darker than the rest of the wall.

flaring tool

flashing

flat-chord truss

flaring tool A tool used to flare the end of a pipe for a fitting. *See also* **flare fitting**.

flash (1) To make a joint weathertight using flashing. (2) An intentional or accidental color variation on the surface of a brick. (3) A variation in paint color resulting from variable wall absorption. (4) The conversion of condensate into steam.

flash chamber A tank placed between the expansion valve and evaporator in a refrigeration system to separate and bypass any flash gas formed in the valve.

flash coat A light coat of shotcrete used to cover minor blemishes on a concrete surface.

flash cove A simple baseboard formed by running the edge of a resilient sheet flooring up the wall for several inches.

flashing A thin, impervious sheet of material placed in construction to prevent water penetration or direct the flow of water. Flashing is used especially at roof hips and valleys, roof penetrations, joints between a roof and a vertical wall, and in masonry walls to direct the flow of water and moisture.

flashing block A concrete masonry unit with a slot cast in one face to receive and hold one edge of a flashing.

flashing board A board to which one edge of a flashing is fastened.

flashing cement A mixture of solvent and bitumen, reinforced with inorganic glass or other fibers, and applied with a trowel.

flashing ring A collar encircling a pipe where it passes through a wall or floor, the purpose of which is to seal the opening.

flash point (1) The minimum temperature at which a combustible liquid will give off sufficient vapor to produce a combustible mixture when mixed with air and ignited. Defined flash points are for specific enclosure conditions and ignition energy. (2) The temperature at which a substance will spontaneously ignite.

flash set (quick set, grab set) The rapid development of rigidity in a freshly mixed Portland cement paste, mortar, or concrete, usually with the evolution of considerable heat. This rigidity cannot be dispelled, nor can the plasticity be regained, by further mixing without addition of water.

flash welding A welding process that joins metals with the heat produced by the resistance to an electric current between the surfaces of the metals, followed by application of pressure.

flat (1) Descriptive of a structural element having no slope, such as a flat roof. (2) One floor of a multilevel building, or full-floor apartment. (3) Descriptive of low gloss paint, used either as an undercoat or as a final coat. (4) A thin iron or steel bar with a rectangular cross section.

flat applicator A flat pad of sponge-like material with an attached handle used to paint shingles and other difficult surfaces.

flat arch An arch with slight curvature.

flat-chord truss A truss with the top and bottom chords nearly flat and parallel.

flat coat An intermediate coat of paint applied between the primer and finish coat.

flat plate

flat plate collector

flat enamel brush A brush used to apply smooth films of enamel on woodwork, about 2″ to 3″ (5 to 7.5 cm) wide with flagged and tapered bristles.

flat face Pipe flanges with the entire face of the flange faced straight across. These flanges use a full face gasket. Commonly employed for pressures less than 125 lbs.

flat glass See **window glass, late glass, float glass,** *and* **rolled glass.**

flathead (1) A screw or bolt with a flat top surface and a conical bearing surface. (2) A rivet with a flattened head.

flathead rivet See **flathead (2).**

flat jack A hydraulic jack made of light-gauge metal welded into a flat rectangular shape that expands under hydraulic pressure.

flat molding A thin, flat molding used only for interior and exterior finish work.

flat paint A paint that dries to a low gloss or flat finish.

flat piece of aggregate One in which the ratio of the width to the thickness of its circumscribing rectangular prism is greater than a specified value. *See also* **elongated piece of aggregate.**

flat plate A flat slab without column capitals or drop panels. *See* also **flat slab.**

flat plate collector A panel of metal or other suitable material used to convert sunlight into heat. Flat plate collectors are usually a flat black color and transfer the collected heat to circulating air or water.

flat pointing (flat joint pointing) (1) The process of finishing mortar in the joints of brickwork by applying it flush with the masonry surface, using a flat trowel. (2) A flush masonry joint with a narrow groove in the center of the joint for ornamentation.

flat rolled Steel plates, sheets or strips manufactured by rolling the steel through flat rollers.

flat roof A roof with only enough pitch to allow drainage.

flat sawing Sawing logs with parallel cuts, a conversion method that wastes less timber than others.

flat seam A seam between two joined sheets of metal, formed by turning up, folding, flattening, and finally soldering the edges.

flat skylight A skylight installed in a horizontal position, slanted only enough to permit rainwater runoff.

flat slab A concrete slab reinforced in two or more directions, generally with drop panels at supports, but without beams or girders. *See also* **flat plate.**

flat spot A spot on a glossy painted surface that fails to absorb the paint properly, usually because of a porous place on the undercoat, resulting in a flat finish that flaws the appearance of the surface.

flatting agent A paint or coating additive that reduces gloss.

flat varnish (matte varnish) A varnish that dries to a finish with low gloss or no gloss.

flat wall brush A paint brush, usually 4″ to 6″ (10 to 15 cm) wide, with long stiff bristles that are often synthetic.

flatwork A general term that refers to any concrete slab that requires finishing, such as a walkway or floor.

flaunch See **flanch.**

fleck A small spot or mark in wood, usually caused by wood rays or other irregular growth characteristics.

Flemish bond

flexible connector

Flemish bond A brick wall laid up with alternate headers and stretchers in each course. Headers in the next course are centered over the stretchers in the course below.

Flemish diagonal bond Alternating headers and stretchers in a course, followed by a course of stretchers.

Flemish double-stretcher bond A configuration of a header alternated with two stretchers.

Flemish garden bond A configuration of a header alternated with three stretchers.

fleur-de-lis The French royal lily adapted to ornamentation in late Gothic architecture.

flex (Greenfield) *See* **flexible metal conduit.**

flexible conduit *See* **flexible metal conduit, flexible metallic hose, flexible nonmetallic tubing,** *and* **flexible seamless tubing.**

flexible connector (1) In ductwork, an airtight connection of nonmetallic materials installed between ducts or between a duct and fan to isolate vibration and noise. (2) A connector in a piping system that reduces vibration along the pipes and compensates for misalignment. (3) An electrical connection that permits movement from expansion, contraction, vibration, and/or rotation.

flexible coupling A mechanical connection between rotating parts that adapts to misalignment, such as a universal joint.

flexible membrane liner (FML) A liner used to contain liquids or run-off in soil or on the soil surface.

flexible metal conduit A flexible raceway of circular cross section for pulling electric cables through.

flexible metallic hose Hose made from a continuous interlocking coil of metal with packing wound in the grooves, used for fluids at low pressure.

flexible-metal roofing Roof coverings of flat sheet metal, such as copper, galvanized iron, or aluminum.

flexible mounting A flexible support for machinery to reduce vibration between the machinery, its foundation or slab. Flexible mountings are usually made of rubber, neoprene, steel springs, or a combination of these.

flexible nonmetallic tubing (loom) A flexible tubing with a smooth interior and a wall of nonconducting, fibrous material, used as a mechanical protection for electric conductors.

flexible pavement A pavement structure that maintains intimate contact with and distributes loads to the subgrade and depends on aggregate interlock, particle friction, and cohesion for stability. Cementing agents, where used, are generally bituminous materials, as contrasted to Portland cement in the case of rigid pavement. *See also* **rigid pavement.**

flexible seamless tubing A seamless, welded, or soldered metal tube widely used for volatile gases and gases under pressure.

flexural bond In prestressed concrete, the stress between the concrete and the tendon that results from external loads.

flexural rigidity A measure of stiffness of a member, indicated by the product of the modulus of elasticity and moment of inertia divided by the length of the member.

float

floated coat

flexural strength A property of a material or structural member that indicates its ability to resist failure in bending. *See also* **modulus of rupture**.

flier A simple stair tread with parallel sides and a straight flight.

flight A run of steps without intermediate landings.

flight header A horizontal structural member used to support stair strings at a floor or platform.

flight rise The vertical distance between two levels connected by a flight of stairs.

flight run The horizontal distance between top and bottom risers in a flight of stairs.

flint A variety of chert. *See also* **chert**.

flitch (1) A log, sawn on two or more sides, from which veneer is sliced. (2) Thin layers of veneer sliced from a cross section of a log, as opposed to turning the log on a lathe and peeling from the outer edge in a continuous ribbon. Flitch veneers are often kept in order as they are sliced from a log. This provides a pattern to the veneer after it is laid up in panels. Panels that are laid up with matching flitches are said to have a flitch pattern. (3) A product cut from a log by sawing on two sides and leaving two rounded sides, often used for joinery.

flitch beam (flitch girder, sandwich beam) A beam built up by two or more pieces bolted together, sometimes with a steel plate in the middle. The pieces, or flitches, are cut from a squared log sawn up the middle. The outer faces of the log are placed together, with their ends reversed to equalize their strength.

flitch plate The steel plate pressed between components of a flitch beam.

float (1) A tool (not a darby), usually of wood, aluminum, magnesium, rubber, or sponge, used in concrete or tile finishing operations to impart a relatively even but still open texture to an unformed fresh concrete surface. (2) To rest by a dozer blade's own weight or to be held from digging by upward pressure of a load of dirt against its mold board. (3) A body floating on water, which opens a valve in a water tank when the water level falls. (4) A tool used to polish marble.

float ball *See* **float (3)**.

float coat A finish coat of cement paste applied with a float.

floated coat (topping coat) A layer of plaster applied to a surface with a float, usually the intermediate coat between the scratch coat and the finish coat.

float finish A rather rough concrete surface texture obtained by finishing with a float.

float glass A high quality, flat glass sheet with smooth surfaces, manufactured by floating molten glass on a bed of molten metal at a temperature high enough for the glass to flow smoothly.

floating The operation of finishing a fresh concrete or mortar surface by use of a float, preceding troweling when that is the final finish.

floating floor A floor used in sound-insulating construction. The finish floor assembly is isolated from the structural floor by a resilient underlayment or by resilient mounting devices for machinery. The construction isolates machinery from the building frame. *See also* **laminate flooring**.

float valve

floor beam

floating foundation A reinforced concrete slab designed to move with the surface of the ground without structural damage.

floating rule A long straightedge used as a float.

floating wood floor A floating floor constructed of wood flooring on a layer of resilient material that isolates it from the building structure.

float rod In a toilet, the threaded rod that links the ballcock and float.

float scaffold A large platform supported by ropes from overhead, used as a scaffold.

floatstone A stone used in bricklaying to rub the rough spots and ax marks from curved work.

float trap A steam trap regulated by a float in the condensate chamber.

float valve (float-controlled valve) A valve controlled by a float in a chamber, such as the float valve in a tank for a water closet.

floccuation A process used to remove extremely fine particles from water and wastewater.

flood coat (1) The top layer of bitumen poured over a built-up roof, which may have gravel or slag added as a protective layer. *See* **flow coat**.

flooding The stratification of different colored pigments in a film of paint.

flood-level rim The edge of a plumbing fixture or receptacle over which water will flow if the device is full.

floodlight (1) A projector type of luminaire designed to light an area or object to a level of illumination higher than the surrounding illumination. (2) A metal housing containing one or more lamps used to illuminate a stage uniformly.

floor (1) The surface within a room upon which one walks. (2) The horizontal division between two stories of a building, formed by assembled structural components or a continuous mass, such as a flat concrete slab.

floor arch A flat arch used as a floor.

floor/area ratio The ratio of the total floor area of a building to the area of the building lot.

floor batten A batten attached to a concrete subfloor, to be used as a nailer for a wood-finish floor.

floor beam Any beam that supports the floor of a building or the deck of a bridge.

floorboard One of the boards or planks used to form the finished floor.

floor box A metal electrical outlet box providing outlets from conduits in or under the floor.

floor brick A brick selected as a floor finish because of its smooth, dense texture and resistance to abrasion.

floor cavity In the science of lighting, the area formed by the workplane, the floor, and the walls between the two.

floor clamp A clamp used to force floor boards together while nailing them to joists.

floor clearance The distance between the bottom of a door and the finished floor or threshold.

floor clip *See* **sleeper clip**.

floor closer A device installed in a recess in the floor below a door used to regulate the opening and closing swing of the door.

floor drain

floor framing

floor pit

floor receptacle

floor drain A fixture set into a floor, used to drain water into a plumbing drainage system.

floor framing Structural supports for floor systems, including joists, bridging, and subflooring.

floor furring Wood furring used to raise a finished floor above the subfloor and provide a space for piping or conduit.

floor guide A groove in a floor or hardware mounted on a floor, used as a guide for a sliding door.

floor hanger See **stirrup (2)**.

floor hatch A unit with a hinged panel, providing access through a floor.

floor hole An opening in a floor, roof, or platform measuring less than 12″ in its least dimension, so that a person cannot fall through. See also **floor opening**.

flooring (1) A tongued and grooved piece of lumber used in constructing a floor. The basic size of flooring is 1″ x 4″, although other sizes are used. Flooring is sold mostly in superior and prime grades, and is produced either as vertical grain or flat grain. (2) Any finished floor material.

flooring cement See **Keene's cement**.

flooring nail A steel nail with a deformed shank, often helically threaded, having a countersunk head and a short diamond-shaped point.

flooring saw A handsaw with teeth on both edges and a blade that tapers to a narrow point, used to cut holes in wood floors.

floor joist Any light beam that supports a floor.

floor light A heavy glass pane in a floor that transmits light to the room below.

floor load The live load for which a floor has been designed, selected from a building code, or developed from an estimate of expected storage, equipment weights, and/or activity.

floor opening A hole or opening in a floor, roof, or platform that measures 12″ or more in its least dimension, wide enough to permit a person to fall through. See also **floor hole**.

floor panel A prefabricated section of floor, consisting of finish floor, subfloor, and joists.

floor pit Any deep recess in a floor used to provide access to machinery, such as an elevator pit.

floor plan A drawing showing the outline of a floor, or part of a floor, interior and exterior walls, doors, windows, and details such as floor openings and curbs. Each floor of a building has its own floor plan.

floor plate (1) A metal plate set into a floor, sometimes fitted with slots to which equipment may be fastened. (2) A steel plate with a raised pattern on the surface that helps prevent accidents due to slipping.

floor plug See **floor receptacle**.

floor receptacle An electric outlet set flush with the floor or mounted in a short pedestal at floor level.

floor register A register set flush with the floor that allows the passage of air.

floor sealer A liquid sealer applied with a brush, sprayer, or squeegee to seal floor surfaces, such as concrete or wood.

floor slab A structural slab, usually concrete, used as a floor or a subfloor.

floor sleeve A short tube set into and penetrating a floor.

floor span (1) The distance, in inches, between the centers of floor

floor underlayment

flow trough

joists in a floor system. (2) The span covered by floor joists between supports.

floor stilt A device attached to the bottom of a door frame to keep it above the finished floor.

floor stop A door stop mounted on the floor.

floor tile (1) Modular units used as finish flooring. Floor tile may be comprised of resilient (asphalt, vinyl, rubber, or cork), ceramic, or masonry materials. (2) Structural units used for floor or roof slab construction.

floor-type heater (floor furnace) An air-heating unit mounted below a floor grille or grate. Warm air rises from the center of the grille and cold air returns at the perimeter of the grille.

floor underlayment Particleboard, plywood, waferboard, or similar products used on a subfloor to provide a smooth surface on which to lay the finish floor. *See also* **carpet underlayment**.

floor varnish A tough, durable varnish used on floors.

flow (1) Time-dependent irrecoverable deformation. *See* **rheology**. (2) A measure of the consistency of freshly mixed concrete, mortar, or cement paste in terms of the increase in diameter of a molded, truncated cone specimen after liming a specified number of times. *See also* **flow table**.

flow brazing A brazing technique that brings metal to brazing temperature by pouring a molten filler metal over it.

flow coat A paint coating achieved by immersing an object in streams of paint and draining off the excess.

flow cone (flow factor) (1) A device for measurement of grout consistency in which a predetermined volume of grout is permitted to escape through a precisely sized orifice. The time of efflux (flow factor) is used to determine the consistency. (2) The mold used to prepare a specimen for the flow test.

flow control valve A cylindrical pressure-compensating valve that regulates the flow of water. Rated in gpm or gpd.

flow-downs Clauses from a prime contractor's contract with the government that are incorporated into the prime's subcontracts.

flow factor *See* **flow cone**.

flow pressure The pressure at or near an orifice during full fluid flow.

flow promoter A substance added to a surface coating, such as paint, to enhance the brushability, flow, and leveling properties.

flow table A jigging device used in making flow tests for consistency of cement paste, mortar, or concrete. *See also* **flow (2)**.

flow trough A sloping trough used to convey concrete by gravity flow from a transit mix truck, or a receiving hopper to the point of placement. *See also* **chute**.

flow welding A welding technique that brings metal to welding temperature by pouring a molten filler metal over it.

flue (1) A noncombustible and heat- resistant passage in a chimney used to convey products of combustion from a furnace fireplace or boiler to the atmosphere. (2) The chimney itself, if there is a single passage.

flue effect *See* **chimney effect**.

flue grouping The consolidation of multiple flues in one chimney or stack to limit the number of vertical shafts through a structure.

flue lining

flue pipe

fluorescent strip

flue lining (chimney lining) The lining of a chimney flue composed of heat-resistant firebrick or other fireclay materials, which prevents fire, smoke, and gases from escaping the flue to contaminate surroundings.

flue pipe A tight duct that conveys products of combustion to a chimney or flue.

fluid-filled column A hollow column, usually rectangular, filled with liquid to increase its fire endurance. A series of such columns may be connected to an expansion tank to increase circulation and endurance.

fluidifier An admixture employed in grout to decrease the flow factor without changing water content.

fluing Expanding or splaying, as in the construction of a window, by building the face of a jamb at an oblique angle to the wall in which it is set, enlarging the opening on one or both sides.

flume A channel made of wood, metal, or concrete and used for drainage purposes on a grade, trestle, or bridge.

fluorescence Visible light generated and emitted from a substance such as a phosphor by absorbing radiation of shorter wavelengths.

fluorescent lamp A low-pressure mercury electric-discharge lamp in which a phosphor coating on the inside of the tube transforms some of the ultraviolet energy generated by the discharge into visible light.

fluorescent lighting fixture A luminaire designed for fluorescent lamps.

fluorescent pigments Pigments that absorb ultraviolet radiant energy and convert it to brilliant, visible light.

fluorescent reflector lamp A fluorescent lamp with the coating on only a part of its cross section so that the light produced will be directed.

fluorescent snaking The visible twisting of the arc in a new fluorescent lamp, usually corrected by turning the appliance on and off several times.

fluorescent strip A luminaire in which fluorescent lamps are mounted on a wiring channel containing the ballast and lamp sockets. Usually reflectors or lenses are not used.

fluorescent U-lamp The tubular fluorescent lamp bent at 180° through its center, forming a U-shape.

Fluorinated Ethylene Propylene (FEP) A soft plastic copolymer with relatively low tensile strength, high chemical resistance, and low coefficient of friction. Applications include coatings and protective linings, chemical and medical equipment, extruded insulation and glazing film for solar panels. A common brand name is Teflon®.

fluosilicate Magnesium or zinc silica-fluoride used to prepare aqueous solutions sometimes applied to concrete as surface-hardening agents.

flush (1) Having a surface or face even with the adjacent surface. (2) To send a quantity of water down a pipe to clean, fill, or empty it.

flush ball See **flapper**.

flush bolt A door bolt or other bolt mounted on a surface.

flush bolt backset The distance between the center line of a door bolt and the vertical center line of the door's leading edge.

flush-cup pull

flush joint

flushometer

flush tank

flush bushing In plumbing, a bushing without a shoulder and engineered to fit flush into the fitting with which it connects.

flush-cup pull A door pull for a sliding door. The pull is mortised flush into the door and has a curved recess serving as a finger grip.

flush door A door with flush surfaces and concealed structural parts.

flush glazing Glazing in which glass is set in a channel, which may be formed by a rabbet and stops, in a frame. The glazing, formed or a compound, is flush with the frame at the top of the channel.

flush-head rivet A rivet with a countersunk head.

flush joint Any joint with its surface flush with the adjacent surfaces.

flush molding Any molding that is flush with the surface on which it sits.

flushometer (flushometer valve) A flushing valve, designed for use without a flush tank or cistern, that is activated by direct water pressure to deliver a certain quantity of water for flushing needs.

flush panel A panel in which the exposed surface is in the same plane as the exposed surfaces of the surrounding frame.

flush paneled door A door with one or both surfaces in the same planes as the surfaces of the rails and stiles.

flush pipe A straight pipe that carries flushing water from a cistern or other main source to plumbing fixtures, such as toilets, equipped with a flushing function.

flush plate In electricity, the metal or plastic cover that shields the flush wiring device in a wiring box and provides covering for an outlet or switch, with holes cut into its face

to accommodate switch handles and plugs.

flush ring A door pull mortised into a door, having a pulling ring that folds flat into a recess when not in use.

flush soffit The smooth, visible underside of a flight of spandrel steps.

flush switch An electrical switch installed in a flush wall box in such a way that only its front face is exposed to view.

flush tank A tank that holds water for flushing one or more plumbing fixtures.

flush valve A valve installed in the bottom of a toilet tank to discharge the water needed to flush the fixture.

flush wall box A wall box that houses an electric device and is embedded in a wall, floor, or ceiling with its exposed face in the same plane as the surrounding surface.

flush water *See* **wash water**.

flute In architecture, one of multiple grooves or channels of semi-circular to semi-elliptical sections, used to decorate and to embellish members, such as the shafts of columns.

flux (1) A substance that facilitates the fusion of metals and helps prevent surface oxidation during welding, brazing, and soldering. (2) A liquefied bituminous substance used to soften other bituminous materials.

flux-cored arc welding A welding process that produces coalescence by the heating of an arc between the materials being welded and a continuous electrode of filler metal.

fly ash The finely divided residue resulting from the combustion of coal which is transported from the fire box through the boiler by flue

flying scaffold

gases. Fly ash is a common additive to concrete to improve strength, workability, and waterproof qualities.

flying bond A masonry bond formed by laying occasional headers at random intervals.

flying buttress A masonry structure that transfers the horizontal thrust of a roof or vault to a detached pier or buttress, usually sloping slightly towards the pier or buttress.

flying form A system that can be used repetitively and moved in large sections not requiring disassembly.

flying scaffold Staging suspended by ropes or cables from outrigger beams attached at the top of a structure.

flying shore A horizontal member that provides temporary support between two walls.

flywheel effect The tendency of a building to retain heat due to its mass-thermal-inertia.

foam concrete A lightweight, cellular concrete made by infusing an unhardened concrete mixture with prepared foam or by generating gases within the mixture.

foam core The center of a plywood *sandwich panel*, consisting of plastic foam between wood veneers. The foam may be introduced in a liquid form that is forced under pressure into a space between the wood veneer skins, or the skins may be applied to a rigid plastic foam board.

foamed concrete (foam concrete) *See* **concrete, foamed**.

foamed polystyrene A foamed plastic, weighing about 1 lb. per cu. ft. (0.016 g/cc), which has a high insulation value, is low in cost, and is grease-resistant.

foam glass (cellular glass, expanded glass) A thermal insulation made by foaming glass with hydrogen sulfide. Foam glass has a closed cell structure and is a low fire hazard material. It is manufactured in the form of block or board with a density of 9 to 10 lb. per cu. ft. (14 to 16 kg per cu m).

foaming adjuvant A surfactant that forms a fast-draining foam to increase contact of the spray with plant surfaces, to insulate the plant surface, and to decrease the rate of evaporation.

foaming agent A substance incorporated into plastic mixtures of concrete, rubber, gypsum, or other materials that helps to produce a light foamy consistency by releasing gases into the mixture.

foam-in-place insulation A plastic foam employed for thermal insulation, prepared by mixing an insulation substance with a foaming agent just before it is poured or sprayed with a gun into the enclosed receptacle cavities.

foam suppressant In pesticides, an additive that suppresses surface foam and entrained air to allow for faster tank refilling while reducing the risk of exposure to toxic chemicals in the pesticidal foam.

fog The visibility and path of the effluent air stream exiting a cooling tower and remaining close to the ground.

fog curing (1) The storage of concrete in a moist room in which the desired high humidity is achieved by the atomization of fresh water. *See also* **moist room**. (2) The application of atomized fresh water to concrete, stucco, mortar, or plaster.

fog room *See* **moist room**.

folding door

folding partition

footing

footing beam

fog sealed Descriptive of surfaces lightly treated with asphalt without a mineral cover.

foil (1) In masonry, one of multiple circular or nearly circular holes, set tangent to the inside of a larger arc, that meet each other in pointed cusps around the arc's inner perimeter. (2) A metal formed into thin sheets by rolling.

foil-backed gypsum board A gypsum board with aluminum foil on one face. The foil acts as a vapor barrier.

folded plate (1) A framing assembly composed of sloping slabs in a hipped or gabled arrangement. (2) A prismatic shell with an open polygonal section.

folded-plate construction A type of construction used with span roofs. Thin, flat elements of concrete, steel, or timber are connected rigidly at angles to each other, similar to accordion folds, to form members with deep cross sections.

folded plate roof A roofing system consisting of sloping plates in a repetitive gable arrangement, usually a combination of plywood skins and lumber trusses. A folded plate roof permits a large, clear floor area.

folding casement (1) One of two casements with rabbeted masting stiles, installed in a single frame with a mullion. (2) One of several casements hinged together in a way that permits them to open and fold in a limited space.

folding door An assembly of two or more vertical panels hinged together so they can open or close in a confined space. A floor- or ceiling-mounted track is usually provided as a guide.

folding partition (1) Large panels hung from a ceiling track, sometimes supported also by a floor track, which form a solid partition when closed, but stack together when the partition is maneuvered into an open position. (2) A partition, faced with fabric and hung from a ceiling track, that folds up flexibly when opened like the pleated balloons of an accordion.

folding rule A rule made of lengths that are joined by pivots so it can be folded when not in use.

folding stair *See* **disappearing stair**.

foliated joint A joint made between two boards by fitting their rabbeted edges together, forming a continuous surface on either face.

follower A pile affixed member that allows the pile to be counterunk.

foot (1) The bottom or base of an object. (2) A unit of measurement of length in the English system. (3) A projection on a cylindrical roller used to compact a layer of earth fill.

foot block A mat of concrete, steel, or timber used to distribute a vertical load from a post or column over an area of supporting soil.

foot bolt A spring-operated bolt fastened to the lower part of a door and controlled with pressure of the foot.

footcandle The common U.S. unit of measurement of the illuminance on a surface. One footcandle is equal to one lumen per sq. ft. The international unit of measurement is the lux. One footcandle is equal to 10.76 lux.

footing That portion of the foundation of a structure that spreads and transmits the load directly to the soil.

footing beam (1) A reinforced concrete beam connecting pile caps or spread footings to distribute

footing step

forced-air furnace

horizontal loads caused by eccentric loading. (2) The tie beam in a roof system. *See also* **grade beam**.

footing course A broad course of masonry at the foot of a wall, which helps prevent the wall from settling.

footing step A change in elevation of a strip footing.

footing stop In concretework, a temporary board used to close up concrete until work can resume.

footlambert A quantitative unit for measuring the amount of reflected light. The footcandles striking a diffusing surface multiplied by the reflectance of the surface equals the luminance in footlamberts.

foot lift A simple device operated by foot to lift and position drywall for installation.

foot-meter rod A surveyor's rod graduated in feet and tenths on one side, and meters and hundredths on the other.

footpiece An item of ductwork in a heating, air-conditioning, or ventilating system that serves to change the direction of the airflow.

footplate A timber used in wood frame construction to disperse heavily concentrated structural loads among a number of supporting members, as a plate installed below a row of wall studs.

foot-pound A unit measure of work or energy in the English System, equal to the force in pounds multiplied by the distance in feet through which it acts.

footprint The area that falls directly beneath and shares the same perimeter as a structure.

footstall (plinth) The base of a pier or pillar, characterized by a particular architectural order or treatment.

force account Work ordered on a construction project without an existing agreement on its cost, and performed with the understanding that the contractor will bill the owner according to the cost of labor, materials, and equipment, plus a certain percentage for overhead and profit.

force, compression A force acting on a body, tending to compress the body. (Pushing action).

forced-air furnace A warm-air furnace, outfitted with a blower, that heats an area by transmitting air through the furnace and connecting ducts.

forced circulation The circulation of a fluid by mechanical means, as by a pump or fan.

forced convection Heat transfer produced by the forced circulation of air, water, etc.

forced draft A draft of air that is mixed with fuel before the mixture is fed into the combustion chamber of a furnace or boiler.

forced-draft boiler A boiler equipped with a power-driven fan that feeds air into the burner and boiler and expels smoke, gases, and ash through the chimney.

force, shear A force acting on a body which tends to slide one portion of the body against the other side of the body. (Sliding action).

force, tension A force acting on a body tending to elongate the body (Pulling action).

force, torsion A force acting on a body which tends to twist the body. (Twisting action).

foreclosure The legal transfer of a property deed or title to a bank or other creditor because of the owner's failure to pay the mortgage, whereupon the owner loses the right to the property.

form

form hanger

Formica®

foreclosure sale The optional right of the mortgagee or lending institution to sell mortgaged property if the mortgagor fails to make payment, applying proceeds from the sale toward the outstanding debt.

forest land As defined by the U.S. Forest Service, forest land is land at least 10% stocked with live trees, or land formerly having such a tree cover and not currently developed for nonforest use. The minimum area of forest land recognized is one acre.

forging A piece of metal worked into a desired shape by one or more processes, including pressing, rolling, hammering, and upsetting.

forked tenon A joint formed by a tenon cut into a long rail and inserted into an open mortise.

forklift truck A self-powered vehicle equipped with strong prongs, or forks, that can be raised or lowered. A forklift truck is used to move objects, especially material on pallets, from one location and/or level to another.

form A temporary structure or mold for the support of concrete while it is setting and gaining sufficient strength to be self-supporting. *See also* **formwork**.

form anchor A device used to secure formwork to previously placed concrete of adequate strength. The device is normally embedded in the concrete during placement.

format In construction, the standard arrangement of a project manual as set by the A.I.A. with bidding information, contract forms, conditions of the contract, and 16 subdivisions of specifications.

form board A board or sheet of wood used in formwork.

form coating A liquid applied to interior formwork surfaces for a specific purpose, usually to promote easy release from the concrete, to preserve the form material, or to retard the set of the near-surface matrix for preparation of exposed-aggregate finishes.

formed plywood Curved plywood, prepared by a special pressing technique using rigid forming dies. *See also* **molded plywood**.

form hanger A device used to support formwork from a structural framework. The dead load of forms, weight of concrete, and construction and impact must be supported.

Formica® The trade name for high-pressure laminated plastic material used where heat-, chemical-, and water-resistant surfaces are needed; for example, for wall coverings, as veneer for plywood panels, and for kitchen and bath cabinet and counter tops.

forming A process of shaping metal by a mechanical process other than machining, forging, or casting.

form insulation Thermal insulation, equipped with an airtight seal, that is applied to the exterior of concrete forms. Used to preserve the heat of hydration at required levels so that concrete can set properly in cold weather.

form lining Selected materials used to line the face of formwork in order to impart a smooth or patterned finish to the concrete surface, to absorb moisture from the concrete, or to apply a set-retarding chemical to the formed surface.

form nail *See* **double-headed nail**.

form oil Oil applied to the interior surface of formwork to promote easy release from the concrete when forms are removed.

form tie

foundation drainage tile

frame construction

form ply Plywood commonly used for constructing forms.

form pressure Lateral pressure acting on vertical or inclined formed surfaces, resulting from the fluid-like behavior of the unhardened concrete.

form release agent *See* **release agent**.

form scabbing The inadvertent removal of the surface of concrete as a result of adhesion to the form.

form spreader *See* **spreader**.

form stop A wooden piece used in concrete formwork to regulate or limit the flow of concrete at the end of a work day. Also used to create drops and special openings.

form stripping agent *See* **release agent**.

form tie A tensile unit adapted to prevent concrete forms from spreading due to the fluid pressure of freshly placed, unhardened concrete.

formwork The total system of support for freshly placed concrete, including the mold or sheathing which contacts the concrete, as well as all supporting members, hardware, and necessary bracing.

forty A standard unit of measurement used in surveying and describing units of forest land, equivalent to 40 acres, or 1/16th of a square mile.

forward-curved fan Centrifugal fan with blades that curve forward in the direction of the wheel rotation.

foundation The entire masonry substructure below the first floor or frame of a building, including the footing upon which the building rests.

foundation bolt *See* **anchor bolt**.

foundation drainage tile Tile or piping, either porous or set with open joints, used to collect subsurface water or for the dispersion of effluent.

foundation engineering The category of engineering concerned with evaluating the ability of a locus to support a given structural load, and with designing the substructure or transition member needed to support the construction.

foundation vent Vent openings in a foundation wall that allow for exchange of air and reduce moisture.

foundation wall That part of the foundation of a building forming a retaining wall for the portion of the building that is below grade.

fourths A common grade of lumber exported from Scandinavia and Eastern Europe.

four-way reinforcement *See* **reinforcement, four-way**.

four-way switch A switch used in a wiring layout to allow a circuit to be turned on or off from more than two places. Two three-way switches are used, and the remainder are four-way.

foxtail *See* **foxtail wedge**.

foxtail saw *See* **dovetail saw**.

foxtail wedge A small wedge used to spread the split end of a bolt in a hole or the split end of a tenon in a mortise to secure the bolt or tenon.

foyer A subordinate space between an entrance and the main interior of a theater, hotel, house or apartment.

fracture load *See* **breaking load**.

frame An assembly of vertical and horizontal structural members.

frame building *See* **framed building**.

frame clearance The clearance between a door and the door frame.

frame construction A construction system in which the structural parts

frame wall

framing

framing anchor

are wood or dependent on a wood framework for support. *See also* **framing**.

framed building A type of building construction in which vertical loads are carried to the ground on a frame.

framed door Any door with a stiff frame made up of a top rail, lock rail, bottom rail, lock stile, and hanging stile.

framed floor *See* **double floor**.

framed ground One of the vertical wood members fastened around an opening to which a door casing is attached, usually built with a tenon joint between the head and doorjambs.

framed joist A joist that is specially cut or notched in order to be joined securely with other joists or timbers.

framed partition (trussed partition) A partition made by covering framing of studs, braces, and struts that form a truss.

frame gasket A strip of flexible material applied to the stop of a door frame to ensure tight closure.

frame-high A term used in masonry to denote a height equal to the top of a door or window frame or to the lintel of an opening.

frame house A house of frame construction, usually with exterior walls sheathed and covered with wood siding.

frame pulley A pulley installed in a window frame to carry a sash chord.

frame wall A wall of frame construction.

framework A network of structural members or components joined to form a structure, such as a truss or multi-level building.

framing (1) Structural timbers assembled into a given construction system. (2) Any construction work involving and incorporating a frame, as around a window or door opening. (3) The unfinished structure, or underlying rough timbers of a building, including walls, roofs, and floors. *See also* **balloon framing** *and* **platform framing**.

framing anchor A sheet metal device used to join light wood members such as studs, joists, and rafters.

framing, balloon A system of framing a building in which all vertical structural elements of the bearing walls and partitions consist of single pieces extending from the top of the soleplate to the roofplate and to which all floor joists are fastened. *See also* **framing**.

framing plan A drawing of each floor of a building showing exact locations of framing members and their connections. May include wall elevations and details.

framing, platform A system of framing a building in which floor joists of each story rest on the top plates of the story below or on the foundation sill for the first story, and the bearing walls and partitions rest on the subfloor of each story. *See also* **framing**.

framing square *See* **carpenter's square**.

framing table *See* **rafter table**.

f rating The measurement of stress (symbolized by the letter f) in a piece of lumber. Generally, the higher the f rating, the stronger the piece of lumber.

free air Air that is at normal atmospheric pressure.

freeboard The distance between the design or normal water level and the top or overflow of a tank, dam or vessel.

freestanding

French roof

free cooling Cooling without the use of mechanical refrigeration.

free fall (1) Descent of freshly mixed concrete into forms without drop chutes or other means of confinement. (2) The distance the concrete falls.

free float A term used in project management, planning, and scheduling methods such as PERT and CPM. The free float of an activity is the amount by which the completion of that activity can be deferred without delaying the start of the following activities or affecting any other activity in the network.

free haul The distance a cubic yard of excavated material may be transported without incurring a hauling charge.

freehold A tenure of property that an owner may hold in fee simple, fee tail or for life. The term also refers to the property held under freehold.

free lime Calcium oxide (CaO) as in clinker and cement that has not combined with SiO_2, Al_2O_3 or Fe_2O_3 during the burning process, because of underburning, insufficient grinding of the raw mix, or the presence of traces of inhibitors.

free moisture Moisture having essentially the properties of pure water not absorbed by aggregate in a test sample or a stock pile. *See also* **surface moisture**.

free on board (FOB) Refers to the point to which the seller will deliver goods without charge to the buyer. Additional freight or other charges connected with transporting or handling the product become the responsibility of the buyer.

freestanding Said of a structural element that is fixed at its base and not braced at any upper level.

free water Water that is able to move freely through the soil by the force of gravity, as opposed to capillary or hygroscopic action. *See also* **free moisture** *and* **surface moisture**.

freezer A room or cabinet mechanically refrigerated to maintain a temperature of about 10°F (-12 °C) used for food storage.

freeze-stat A thermostat set to stop the fans before freezing air temperature is sensed.

freeze-thaw The cycle from freezing to thawing often detrimental to construction materials such as concrete. Air entrainment of concrete to be exposed to the elements is helpful in preventing damage from freeze-thaw cycles.

French door (casement door, door window) A door, or pair of doors, with glass panes constituting all or nearly all of its surface area. *See also* **French window**.

French drain A drainage ditch containing loose stone covered with earth.

Frenchman A kitchen knife with the end bent over, used with a jointing rule for pointing mortar joints.

French roof A mansard roof with nearly perpendicular sides.

French window A doorway with a single full-glazed door or a pair of such doors, hinged at the jamb. *See also* **French door**.

Freon® The trade name of a fluorocarbon refrigerant that is nontoxic but is being phased out because it is believed to deplete the stratospheric ozone layer.

frequency A measure of oscillations per second, applied to the current or

friction catch

friction pile

frontage

voltage of AC electrical circuits, sound waves or vibrating solid objects, and stated in hertz (HZ) or cycles per second (CPS).

frequency division multiplexing Splitting a channel's frequency band into narrower bands and allocating them to different sources.

frequency modulation A method of modifying a sound wave signal to relay information.

fresh-air inlet (1) A connection to a building drain, located above the drain trap and leading to the atmosphere. (2) An outside air vent for an HVAC system.

fret A form of architectural ornamentation, consisting of elongated rectangles that are painted, curved, or raised in an elaborate pattern of fillets, bands, and ringlets; frequently made up of continuous lines crafted in repeating rectangular shapes.

fretwork Ornamental openwork or relief consisting of bands of interlocking geometric patterns of contrasting light and dark elements.

friable Descriptive of a material that can be easily pulverized or crumbled in the hand.

friction The resistance to relative motion, sliding or rolling, between two surfaces in contact. May produce heat.

friction catch Any catch held in position by friction when engaged with its strike.

friction head In hydraulics, the energy lost by friction in a pipe. This may include losses at elbows and bends.

friction hinge A hinge that uses internal friction to hold a door or window in a selected position.

friction loss The stress loss in a prestressing tendon resulting from

friction between the tendon and duct or other device during stressing.

friction pile (floating pile foundation) A load-bearing pile that receives its principal vertical support from skin friction between the surface of the buried pile and the surrounding soil.

friction ring A seal component that employs friction to provide an airtight seal.

friction shoe A friction device used to hold a sash in any open position. The shoe position may be adjustable or preset.

friction tape An insulating tape used by electricians, made of a fibrous base impregnated with a moisture-resisting compound that will stick to itself but not to most other materials.

friction welding A process by which thermoplastic materials are softened and welded together with heat produced by friction.

frieze A horizontal exterior trim member positioned between the siding of a structure and its soffit.

fringe benefits Compensation paid to a worker in addition to his or her wages. Usually consists of paid vacation and sick time, pension, health insurance, and so forth.

frit A batch material of sand, soda, and limestone that is used in glass manufacture.

frog A depression in the bed surface of a masonry unit that is sometimes called a panel and provides a key for the mortar at the joint.

frontage The length of a property line or building line along the street or beachfront that forms its boundary line on one side.

front-end loader

fuel-fired boiler

front-end loader A machine with a bucket fixed to its front end, having a lift-arm assembly that raises and lowers the bucket. A front-end loader is used in earth moving and loading operations and in rehandling stockpiled materials.

front hearth (outer hearth) The part of a hearth that occupies the room served by a fireplace, skirting the front of the fireplace opening.

frontispiece The architecturally adorned front wall or bay of a building or edifice. Also, an ornamental porch or pediment.

front putty *See* **face putty.**

frost action (1) The loosening, spalling, and/or lifting process caused by alternate freezing and thawing of moisture in a material. (2) The effects of freezing and thawing on materials and the resultant structural damage.

frost boil (1) An imperfection on a concrete surface caused by the freezing of trapped moisture that swells and crumbles the affected concrete. (2) The softening of soil caused by melting and release of subsurface water during a thaw.

frost cracks Splits or cracks in the trunk of a tree, caused by extreme cold. Such cracks are defects in lumber manufactured from this timber.

frost heave The lifting of a soil surface or pavement due to the freezing of moisture in the underlying soil.

frost line The depth to which frost penetrates the ground. This depth varies from one part of the country to another. Footings should be placed below the frost line to prevent shifting.

frostproof closet A water-closet bowl that retains no standing water.

The trap and the valve for its water supply are located below the frost line.

fudge (slang) To depart from the design drawing for sake of appearance.

fuel-fired boiler An automatic, self-contained mechanical unit or system that produces heat by burning solid, liquid, or gaseous fuels.

fuel load The total amount of potential fuel for a fire in a given structure or area.

fugitive dye A dye whose color fades in a few days to neutral on exposure, usually to ultraviolet rays in sunlight. Fugitive dye is often used to temporarily color membrane-curing compounds so that coverage of the concrete surface can be observed.

full A reference to lumber that is slightly oversize.

full bond A masonry bond in which all bricks are laid as headers.

Fuller faucet A faucet in which a rubber ball is forced into the inlet to stop the flow.

Fuller's curve (Fuller-Thompson ideal grading curve) An empirical curve for gradation of aggregates. The curve is designed by fitting either a parabola or an ellipse to a tangent at the point where the aggregate fraction is one-tenth of the maximum size fraction. *See also* **grading curve.**

full-face respirator A respirator that covers the whole face with a protective shield.

full-flush door A door made of two sheets of steel assembled in hollow-metal construction with a top and bottom either flush or closed off with end panels, and seams that are visible only on the edge of the door.

full-louvered door

full-penetration butt weld

full-surface hinge

furring strip

full glass door A door with glass in the area between rails and stiles except for dividing mullions. The glass is usually heat treated or tempered.

full-louvered door A door with louvers filling the entire area between rails and stiles.

full mortar bedding Mortar applied to the entire thickness of a masonry unit. Used in foundations and other load-bearing construction.

full-penetration butt weld A butt weld with a depth equal to the thickness of the smaller of the two members between which it lies.

full pitch A roof pitch whose rise is equal to the width of the span of the roof.

full size Said of a drawing depicting an object at true size: not scaled.

full splice A splice that will transmit the full strength of the joined members.

full-surface hinge A hinge that may be installed on the surface of a door and jamb without need of mortising.

fully welded seamless door A door having all joints on its faces and edges fully welded and ground smooth, so as to conceal the joints.

functional obsolescence An inadequacy caused by outmoded design, dated construction materials or over or undersized areas, all of which cause excessive operating costs.

fungicide A substance poisonous to fungi, used to prevent or retard the growth of fungi.

furan A colorless liquid compound used in mortars and grouts for its chemical resistance.

furlong A unit of measure equal to 220 yards or 1/8 of a mile.

furnace (1) That part of a boiler or warm-air heating plant in which combustion takes place. (2) A complete heating unit that transfers heat from burning fuel to a heating system.

furnish The raw material used to make reconstituted wood-based nonveneer panel products.

furniture grade Lumber of a quality and size suitable for the manufacture of furniture.

furred Provided with furring to leave an air space, as between a structural wall and plaster or between a subfloor and wood flooring.

furring (1) Strips of wood or metal fastened to a wall or other surface to even it, to form an air space, to give the appearance of greater thickness, or for the application of an interior finish such as plaster. (2) Lumber 1″ in thickness (nominal) and less than 4″ in width, frequently the product of resawing a wider piece. The most common sizes of furring are 1″ x 2″ and 1″ x 3″. *See also* **strip**.

furring brick A hollow brick carrying no superimposed load and used as lining, furring, or as a key for plastering on an interior wall.

furring nail A galvanized, low-carbon steel nail, having a flat head and a diamond point. The shank is provided with a spacer for fastening wire lath and spacing it from the nailer.

furring strip Wood or metal channels used for attaching gypsum or metal lath to masonry walls as a finish or for leveling purposes. *See also* **furring**.

furring tile Tile designed for lining the inside of exterior masonry walls. It is not intended to support superimposed loads and has a scored face for the application of plaster.

fuse

fuse box

furrowing The process of making furrows in the mortar bed with the tip of a trowel to speed up bricklaying by better distributing mortar.

fuse A protective device, made of a metal strip, wire or ribbon that guards against overcurrent in an electrical system. The device melts if too much current is generated and breaks the circuit.

fuse box A metal box with a hinged cover which houses fuses for electric circuits.

fusetron A special fuse that will carry an overload of current for a short time without "blowing" or opening the circuit. A fusetron is used where a heavy load, such as the starting of a motor, may overload a circuit momentarily.

fusible link A metal link made of two parts held together by a low-melting-point alloy. When exposed to fire-condition temperatures, the link separates, allowing a door, damper, or device to be closed.

fusible metal An alloy with a low melting point used in high temperature detecting devices.

fusible solder An alloy, usually containing bismuth, having a melting point below that of tin-lead solder: 361°F (183 °C).

fusible tape *See* **joint tape**.

fusiform rust A type of blister rust disease, caused by the fungus, *Cronartium fusiform*. The disease attacks certain southern pine species. Similar rusts infect western pines.

fusion In welding, the melting and coalescence of a filler metal and base metal or two base metals.

FUTA A federal law that imposes an unemployment tax on employers.

fuzzy grain In surfacing lumber, a condition of the board surface in which some fibers are not completely severed in the surfacing process, giving it a fuzzy appearance.

G

G ABBREVIATIONS

The abbreviations listed below are those most commonly used in the construction industry. Alternative forms (usually nonstandard) are shown in parentheses.

g gram, gravity, gauge, girth

G gas

ga gauge

gal. gallon

galv galvanized

GAO The U.S. General Accounting Office

GATT General Agreement on Tariffs and Trade

GB glass block

GC general contractor

GCF greatest common factor

gen general

GFCI ground-fault circuit-interrupter

GI galvanized iron

gl glass, glazing

GM grade marked

GMV gram molecular volume

GOB general obligation bonds

Goth Gothic

gov/govt government

gpd gallons per day

gpf gallons per flush

gph gallons per hour

gpm gallons per minute

GPS global positioning system

gr grade, gravity, gross, grains

G/R grooved roofing

gran granular

gr.fl. ground floor

gr.fl.ar ground floor area

grnd ground

gr.wt gross weight

G/S grade-stamped

GT gross ton

gtd guaranteed

g.u.p. grading under pavement

GYP gypsum

G DEFINITIONS

gabion

gable

gable dormer

gabion A large compartmentalized container, usually cylindrical or rectangular, often fabricated from galvanized steel hexagonal wire mesh. When filled with stone it is used in the construction of foundations, dams, erosion breaks, etc.

gable The portion of the end of a building that extends from the eaves to the peak or ridge of the roof. The gable's shape is determined by the type of building on which it is used: triangular in a building with a simple ridged roof, or semi-octagonal in a building with a gambrel roof.

gableboard A board covering the timbers that extend over the gable end of a gable roof.

gable dormer A dormer that protrudes horizontally outward from a sloping roof and has its own gabled ends, whose base meets that of the sloping roof.

gable end An end wall with a gable.

gable molding The molding used as finish for a gable end of a roof.

gable post A short post into which the gableboards are fitted at the peak of a gable.

gable roof A ridged roof having one or two gabled ends.

gable shoulder The projection created by the gable springer at the foot of a gable.

gable springer The projecting stone under the loosest kneeler at the foot of a gable coping.

gable vents Vent openings mounted in the top of a gable of a house to allow the exchange of air in the attic.

gable wall A wall whose upper portion is a gable.

gable window A window built into or shaped like a gable.

gaffering *See* **galletting**.

gage *See* **gauge**.

gag process The use of a gag press to bend structural shapes.

gain (1) The mortise or notch in a piece of wood into a which a piece of wood, hinge, or other hardware fits. (2) An increase in transmission signal power from one point to another, expressed in decibels. (3) An increase in the volume of sound of a radio.

gaine A pedestal, square in shape but with one end tapered downward, used primarily for decoration.

gallery (1) A long enclosure that functions as a corridor inside or outside a building or between different buildings. (2) The elevated (usually the highest) designated seating section in an auditorium, theater, church, etc. (3) A room or building in which artistic works are exhibited.

gallery apartment house An apartment house whose individual units can be entered from an exterior corridor on each floor.

gallet A chip of rock, stone, or masonry.

galleting (gaffering) The use of chips of rock, stone, or masonry to fill the joints of rough masonry, either for appearance or to minimize the required amount of mortar.

gallon A standard liquid measure: The British imperial gallon contains 10 lbs. of water; the American gallon contains 8.33 lbs. of water.

gambrel roof

gang form

gallon per minute (gpm) A unit measure of flow. Equals a flow rate of one gallon in one minute.

gallows bracket A triangular wall bracket often used for the support of shelving.

galvanic corrosion The electrochemical action that occurs as a result of the contact of dissimilar metals in the presence of an electrolyte.

galvanize The process of protectively coating iron or steel with zinc, either by immersion or electroplating (electrogalvanizing).

galvanized iron Zinc-coated iron sheet metal.

galvanized pipe Zinc-coated steel or wrought-iron pipe.

gambrel roof A roof whose slope on each side is interrupted by an obtuse angle that forms two pitches on each side, the lower slope being steeper than the upper.

gandy dancer A slang term for a railroad worker who performs earth and tracklaying work.

gandy stick Railroad slang for a tamping rod.

gang A working technique in which several machines and/or apparatuses are controlled by a single force and combined in such a way as to function as a single unit.

gang boarding roof ladder *See* **cat ladder**.

gang form Prefabricated form panels connected together to produce large reusable units. Gang forms are usually lifted by crane or rolled to the next location.

Gang Nail® A multi-tooth connector made of steel that is used to fasten heavy timbers. Most commonly used in roof truss and flooring construction.

gang saw A number of toothed steel ribbons, fitted in a sash or frame, operating together.

gangway A temporary planked path that runs up to a building or over an unfinished portion thereof before the exterior steps are constructed. The gangway provides a passageway for men and materials on the construction site.

ganister A mixture of ground quartz and a bonding material, such as fire clay, used primarily for fireproofing, as around the hearths of furnaces.

gantry A framework or overhead structure of beams or timbers used as a working platform or as a means to support equipment.

gantry crane A revolving crane situated atop a heavy framework which moves along the ground on tracks.

GAO The U.S. General Accounting Office which, under the direction of the Comptroller General of the United States, has jurisdiction over bid protests. The GAO is an arm of the Congress.

gap-filling glue A type of glue used in applications where close-contact glue is inadequate because of the poor fit between the surfaces to be joined.

gap grading A particle-size distribution of aggregate which is practically or completely void of certain intermediate sizes.

garbage disposal unit An electrically motorized device that grinds waste food and mixes it with water before disposing of it through standard plumbing drainage pipes.

garden apartment (1) A two- or three-story suburban, multiple dwelling that emphasizes patios, balconies, walks, or even communal gardens to create or promote the

garden tie

garrison house

gas engine

illusion of privacy. (2) A ground-floor apartment having access to an adjacent outdoor space or garden.

garden city A residential development with significant plantings and trees composed largely of single-family, detached houses and providing vehicular parking.

garden house In a garden, a small gazebo or other shelter.

garden tie Usually, a railroad tie or similar timber used in landscaping.

garden tile Molded structural ceramic units used in a garden or on a patio as stepping stones.

garden wall bond Usually, ornamental brickwork that is only a single brick thick and is composed mostly of stretchers showing a fair face on each side.

gargoyle A waterspout, often with carvings of grotesque human or animal features, that projects from a roof gutter so as to drop rainwater clear of a wall, often through its open mouth.

garnet A silicate mineral with an isometric crystal structure. Garnet occurs in a variety of colors and is used as gemstones, abrasives, or gallers.

garnet hinge A T-shaped hinge with a longer leg that attaches to the door leaf and a shorter leg that attaches to the frame.

garnet paper A finishing and polishing paper covered with powdered garnet abrasive.

garrison house A style of house whose second story overhangs the face of the first story on one or more walls.

gas A fluid (in the form of air) with neither independent shapes nor

volume, that can expand indefinitely.

gas concrete A concrete whose light weight and insulating qualities are the result of cement alkalies and an aluminum powder admixture that reacts to generate hydrogen gas, and hence to produce voids in the unhardened mix.

gas engine An internal-combustion engine that uses a gas rather than gasoline as fuel.

gas filled lamp A type of incandescent lamp with a bulb atmosphere consisting a of an inert gas within which the filament operates.

gas-fired Heated by the burning of a gaseous fuel.

gas flow meter A device that measures the volume and/or velocity of flowing gases.

gas furnace A furnace that burns gas to produce heat.

gasket Any of a variety of seals made from resilient materials and placed between two joining parts (as between a door and its frame, an oil filter and its seat, pipe threads and their fitting, etc.) to prevent the leakage of air, water, gas, or fluid.

gaskin (1) A ring of rope placed into the socket of a stoneware pipe joint before it is sealed with cement mortar. (2) A type of inflatable ring for temporarily sealing a pipe joint.

gas main The public's gas supply as piped from the providing utility company into a community.

gas metal-arc welding A method of welding that achieves coalescence by arc-heating between the work and a consumable electrode.

gas meter A mechanical device that measures and records in cubic feet

gas vent

gate valve

gauge (gage)

the volume of gas passing a given point.

gas-phase absorption A natural process in which molecules of gas are physically attracted to and held at the surface of a solid.

gas pliers Rugged pliers having concave jaws with serrated faces for the efficient gripping of pipes.

gas pocket In a casting, a hole or void caused by the entrapment of air or gas that is produced during the solidification of the metal.

gas refrigeration A refrigeration system in which a gas flame is used to heat the refrigerant.

gas vent An exhaust pipe through which undesirable gaseous by-products of combustion are vented to the outside.

gas welding Any of several welding methods in which a gas flame provides the heat necessary for coalescence and in which pressure and/or a filler metal may or may not be employed.

gate A usually hinged device of solid or open construction that is installed as part of a fence, wall, or similar barrier and which, when opened (either by swinging, sliding, or lifting), provides access through that barrier.

gate hook (gudgeon) A metal bar (usually one of a pair, spaced one directly above the other) whose pointed or threaded end is driven or screwed into a wooden post or secured in a masonry or brick gate pier, with exposed upright pin engaging the gate hinge, thus hanging the gate.

gate house A building that accommodates the gateway to a castle, manor house, estate, or other important building or place.

gate operator An electronically operated mechanism which, when activated, serves to open or close a gate.

gate pier (gate post) A post of wood, brick, stone, or masonry on which a gate is hung or hinged, or against which it latches.

gate valve A valve utilizing a gate, usually wedge-shaped, which allows fluid flow when the gate is lifted from the seat. Gate valves have less resistance to flow than globe valves, and should always be used fully open or fully closed.

gathering The bringing together of flues within a single stack.

gauge (gage) (1) The numerically designated thickness of sheet metal. (2) The designated diameter of a screw or wire, or the thickness of the wall of tubing. (3) A measuring device for pressure or liquid level. (4) The distance between rows of bolt or rivet holes in the same member. (5) A wood or metal strip used as a thickness-control guide in bituminous or concrete paving operations. (6) In plastering, a screed. (7) The act of adding or the amount of gauging plaster needed to hasten the setting of common plaster. (8) In laid roofing, the exposed length of a shingle, slate, or tile.

gauge board (gauging board) A three-foot square on which plaster and tools are carried. (2) A board used for mixing plaster, cement, or mortar. (3) A carpenter's pitch board.

gauge box (gauging box) A container in which a batch of concrete, mortar, or plaster is measured and mixed.

gauged A term that refers to a material that has been ground so as to

gauged skim coat

gazebo

gear

produce particles of uniform shape and/or thickness.

gauged arch An arch constructed from bricks with a wedge shape that causes the joints to radiate from a common center.

gauged brick Brick that has been sawn, ground, or otherwise shaped to accurate dimensions for special applications.

gauged mortar (1) Mortar made of cement, sand, and lime in specific proportions. (2) Any plastering mortar that is mixed with plaster of paris to hasten setting.

gauged skim coat A mixture of gauging plaster and lime putty applied very thinly as a final coat in plastering. The mixture is troweled to produce a smooth, hard finish.

gauged stuff (1) A mixture of lime putty and gypsum plaster that is used as a finish coat in plastering. (2) Gauged mortar.

gauge glass A glass tubular device or vertical cylindrical device, often graduated, that indicates the level or amount of liquid in a tank or vessel.

gauge pile See **guide pile**.

gauge pressure The inherent pressure of a gas or liquid, exclusive of the value of atmospheric pressure.

gauge rod A stick used for measuring the gauge in brickwork. If used to mark floor and sill levels, the rod is termed a *story rod*, or *story pole*.

gauge stick (1) A dimensionally specific length of wood, metal, or other material used in measuring repetitive dimensions. (2) In roofing, a template used to measure tiles for accurate cutting.

gauging plaster Plaster of paris (gypsum plaster) that is usually

mixed with lime putty to produce a quick-drying finish coat.

gaul A hollow place in a coat of plaster or mortar, usually the finish coat, caused by poor troweling.

gazebo A small, round, octagonal, or similarly shaped structure, usually roofed but open-sided, built in parks or large gardens to provide shelter or a place to view the surrounding area.

G-clamp (G-cramp) A large G-shaped screw clamp often used in joining pieces of glued wood.

gear A toothed wheel, cone, cylinder, or other machined element that is designed to mesh with another similarly toothed element for purposes which include the transmission of power and the change of speed or direction.

gear jammer A slang term for a truck driver.

gefle standard A measure of roundwood volume equal to 100 cubic feet. The measure is used principally in the export trade.

gel The colloidal state of a material.

gelatin blasting The strongest and highest-velocity, commercially available explosive. The material is manufactured by dissolving nitrocotton in nitroglycerin.

gelatin molding A method of manufacturing that utilizes a semi-rigid mold composed primarily of gelatin to produce complicated undercut fibrous plaster coatings.

gel coat A relatively thin, often pigmented layer of resin which is usually sprayed onto a waxed mold to form the attractive exterior surface of a reinforced plastic molding, such as a fiberglass boat.

gemel (gimmer, gymmer, jammer) Any two structural elements that go together as a pair.

gemel window A two-bayed window.

General Agreement on Tariffs and Trade (GATT) A specialized agency of the United Nations that seeks to ease the barriers of international trade.

general conditions The portion of the contract document in which the rights, responsibilities, and relationships of the involved parties are itemized.

general contract In a single contract system, the documented agreement between the owner and the general contractor for all the construction for the entire job.

general contractor For an inclusive construction project, the primary contractor who oversees and is responsible for all the work performed on the site, and to whom any subcontractors on the same job are responsible.

general diffuse lighting Lighting from units that direct 40%–60% of their emitted light upward, and the remainder downward.

general drawing A drawing that illustrates structural cross-sections, main dimensions, elevation plans, substructural borings, and other basic details of a construction project.

general foreman The general contractor's on-site representative, often referred to as the *superintendent* on large construction projects. It is the responsibility of the general foreman to coordinate the work of various trades and to oversee all labor performed at the site.

general industrial occupancy The designation of a conventionally designed building that can be used for all but high-hazard types of manufacturing or production operations.

general lighting Lighting designed to produce a fairly consistent level of illumination over an entire area.

general obligation bonds Instruments of obligation which, by permission of the public through referendum, are issued to investors by a subdivision of government. These bonds promise incremental payment of principal and interest from revenues collected annually by the government. In return, funds are supplied by investors and are used to pay for the construction of publicly owned buildings or other public works projects.

general partnership An association of two or more people to conduct business for profit as co-owners. The participants in a general partnership, called *general partners*, share all aspects of the business including assets, profits/losses, liability, and management responsibility.

general-purpose branch circuit An electrical circuit that supplies a number of outlets.

general requirements The designation or title of Division 1 (the first of 16) in the Construction Specifications Institute's Uniform System. General requirements usually include overhead items and equipment rentals.

generator (1) A mechanical or electromechanical device that converts mechanical energy into electrical power, as an alternator producing alternating current or a dynamo producing direct current. (2) A person, firm, or entity whose activities create a hazardous waste.

generic A term used to generally describe a material, product, assembly, or piece of equipment, as in the descriptive specification, rather than naming it by a specific

German siding

gin block

trade name or source of manufacture or distribution.

geodesic dome A stable, dome-shaped structure fabricated from similar lightweight members connected to form a grid of interlocking polygons.

geodetic survey A land survey, usually of vast areas, whose calculations incorporate consideration of the earth's curvature and can accurately specify points from which surveys can be controlled.

geological map A map showing the character and distribution of outcrops of strata or igneous rocks, including faults, antidives, and other sizable formations. Some such maps show only the solid outcrops, excluding the overlying drift.

geometrical stair A stair, either winding or spiral, that is built around a stairwell and returns on itself as it ascends, but does not employ newels at the turns and has no landings between floors.

Georgian architecture Neoclassical style of architecture that prevailed in 18th-century Great Britain. Characterized by orderly design, rectangular shapes, and symmetrical window placement.

Georgia buggy A slang term for an on-site concrete-carrying hopper with heavy rubber wheels.

Georgia marble A general descriptive term applied to sparkling, crystal, light grey, or white marble.

Georgian siding Thick glass into which steel wire mesh is incorporated as reinforcement.

Georgian window A double-hung window.

geotextiles Synthetic fabrics that can be used to separate back filling

materials to promote proper drainage. Commonly used in conjuction with high retaining walls and landscape design.

German siding A type of drop siding installed so that the grooved bottom edge of the board above fits over the concave top edge of the board below.

gesso A plaster base coat, for gilding or decorative painting, consisting of gypsum plaster, calcium carbonate, and glue.

ghosting Descriptive of a thin coat of paint that leaves a skimpy appearance.

gib A metal strap used to fasten two members together.

gib-and-cotter joint A joint in which a gib, drawn tightly and wedged with cotters, secures the joined members together.

gig stick *See* **radius rod**.

gilding (1) The application of gilt (as gold leaf or flakes) to a surface. (2) A surface ornamented with gilt.

Gilmore needle A device used to determine the setting time of hydraulic cement.

gilsonite A naturally occurring, hard, brittle form of asphalt that is mined and used in the manufacturing of floor tile, paving, roofing, and paint.

gimlet A small hand tool, of ancient origin, whose handle is perpendicular to a screw point, and which is used for boring small holes (less than 1/4″) in wood.

gimmer *See* **gemel**.

gin A simple lifting device consisting of a vertical pole, tripod, or other frame.

gin block A simple tackle block, with a single pulley in a frame, having a hook on top for hanging.

girder casing

girt (girth)

glass block

gingerbread An ornate style of architecture, usually employed in exterior house trim, and common in the United States during the 19th century.

ginnywink A slang term for an A-frame derrick that has a fixed rear leg.

gin pole A cable-supported vertical pole used in conjunction with blocks and tackle for hoisting.

girandole A branched fixture or bracket for holding lamps or candles, either freestanding or protruding from a wall, often having a mirror behind it.

girder A large principal beam of steel, reinforced concrete, wood, or a combination of these, used to support other structural members at isolated points along its length.

girder casing Material that encloses and protects (as from fire) the part of a girder extending below ceiling level.

girder post Any support member, such as a post or column, for a girder.

girdle A horizontal band around the shaft of a column.

girt (girth) (1) A horizontal member used as a stiffener between studs, columns, or posts at intermediate level. (2) A rail or intermediate beam that receives the ends of floor joists on an outside wall.

girth (1) The circumference of any circular object. (2) The distance around a column.

girt strip A board secured horizontally to studding to carry floor joists. *See also* **ledgerboard**.

give-and-take lines Straight equalizing lines used in calculating band areas and their boundaries.

gland (1) In plumbing, a brass or copper ring that is compressed by a screwed fitting over a copper tube, and that deforms to become a seal between the two. (2) In electrical work, a seal used to prevent water from entering the end of a cable.

gland bolt A bolt used to tighten or loosen an unthreaded gland.

gland joint A joint on a metal soil pipe or hot water pipe which allows for thermal expansion.

glare Any unwanted brightness that brings discomfort or reduced visibility.

glass A hard, brittle, inorganic product, ordinarily transparent or translucent, made by the fusion of silica, flux, and a stabilizer, and cooled without crystallizing. Glass can be rolled, blown, cast, or pressed for a variety of uses.

glass bead *See* **glazing bead**.

glass block A hollow, translucent block of glass, often with molded patterns on either or both faces, which affords pleasantly diffused light when used in non-load-bearing walls or partitions.

glass cement Any glue or other adhesive material which serves to bind glass to glass, or glass to another material.

glass cloth A wall covering made from woven vegetable fibers, especially arrowroot bark, that are laminated onto a paper backing.

glass concrete A concrete panel or slab into which are set a pattern of translucent glass lenses that allow the passage of light.

glass cutter A small hand tool having a pointed diamond tip or a sharp, small, hardened steel wheel that scores glass.

glass door A door fabricated without stiles or rails and consisting entirely

glaze

glazed door

glazed structural unit

of thick, heat-strengthened, or tempered glass.

glass fiber (glass fibre)
See **fiberglass**.

glass, obscure Sheet glass that has been made translucent instead of transparent. It is sandblasted or molded to make the surfaces irregular.

glasspaper A fine sandpaper or polishing paper whose abrasive is powdered glass.

glass pipe A term defining both glass and glass-lined pipe used in process piping.

glass seam In limestone, a crack that has been cemented, annealled, and rendered structurally sound by the deposition of transparent calcite.

glass, shatter-proof *See* **bullet-proof glass**.

glass size The size to which a piece of glass is cut so as to glaze a given opening. Its length and width should be 1/8″ less than the distance between the outside edges of the rebates.

glass, stained *See* **stained glass**.

glass stop (1) A glazing bead. (2) A fitting at the lower end of a patent glazing bar to prevent the pane from sliding down.

glass, structural Cast glass in squares or rectangles, 1″-2″ thick, sometimes laid up between concrete ribs, frequently as tile. Larger units are made in hollow or vacuum blocks. The wide use of the product is in colored and polished sheets for interior wall surfacing.

glass tile Transparent or translucent units installed in a roof surface which allow light to enter the room below.

glass tower A slang term for any type of small crane.

glass, wire Glass in which wire mesh is embedded to prevent shattering.

glass wool Spun fiberglass used mostly for thermal and acoustical insulation and as a filtering medium in air and water filters.

glaze (1) To install glass panes in a window, door, or another part of a structure by applying putty or other material to hold the glass in place. (2) A hard, thin, glossy ceramic coating on the surface of pottery, earthenware, ceramics, and similar goods.

glaze coat (1) The smooth top layer of asphalt in built-up roofing. (2) A temporary, protective coat of bitumen applied to built-up roofing that is awaiting top-pouring and surfacing. (3) In painting, the application of a nearly transparent coat that enhances and protects the coat below it.

glazed brick Brick or tile with a surface produced by fusing it with a glazing material.

glazed door Any door with glass panes or panels and top and bottom rails.

glazed structural unit A hollow or solid unit with a smooth, glassy covering such as glazed tile.

glazed tile Ceramic or masonry tile with an impervious, glossy finish.

glazement A waterproof surfacing used on masonry that creates a smooth, durable finish.

glazier A person whose trade is to install glass in structures. The glazier removes old putty, cuts glass to fit the openings requiring it, and secures it there by whatever means are necessary or appropriate.

glazier's chisel A chisel-shaped putty knife used in setting glass.

glazing bead (glass stop)

globe valve

glazier's point (glazing brad, glazing point) A small, thin, flat, three- or four-cornered piece of metal which is sometimes pushed part way into the outside edges of the rebate, and buried in the face putty around a pane of glass to hold it in place.

glazier's putty A glazing compound often made from a mixture of linseed oil and plaster of paris, and sometimes including white lead.

glazing (1) Fixing glass in an opening. (2) The glass surface of an opening which has been glazed.

glazing bar A vertical or horizontal bar of wood or metal that subdivides a window and holds panes of glass.

glazing bead (glass stop) (1) A narrow strip of wood, plastic, or metal fastened around a rebate and used to hold glass in a sash. (2) At a glazed opening, removable trim that holds the glass in place.

glazing brad *See* **glazier's point.**

glazing channel A groove cut into a sash to hold glass.

glazing clip A metal clip used to hold glass in place in a metal frame during putty application.

glazing color A transparent wash applied over a ground coat of paint.

glazing compound Any putty or caulking compound used in glazing to seal the joint at the edges of the glass.

glazing fillet A narrow wood or plastic strip fastened to the rebate of a glazing bar and used instead of face putty to hold glass in place.

glazing gasket A narrow, sometimes grooved, prefabricated strip of material such as neoprene, which offers a dry alternative to glazing compound in glazing operations. The gasket is impervious to moisture and temperature and is often used with large panes or sheets of glass.

glazing molding (1) Molding that serves the same function as a *glazing fillet.* (2) A *glass stop.*

glazing point *See* **glaziers point.**

glazing size *See* **glass size.**

glazing spacer block One of several blocks which support glass in its frame.

glazing sprig A small headless nail that holds a pane of glass in its wooden frame while putty hardens.

glazing stop *See* **glass stop.**

glazing tape A resilient tape used to seal glass into a frame, sash, or opening.

global positioning system (GPS) A global system of U.S. navigational satellites that locates precise points and coordinates on earth.

globe (light globe) (1) A protective enclosure or covering over a light source. The globe is usually made of glass and can also serve to diffuse, redirect, or change the color of the light. (2) An incandescent lamp.

globe valve A valve with a rounded body utilizing a manually raised or lowered disc which, when closed, seats so as to prevent fluid flow. Globe valves are ideal for throttling in a semi-closed position.

glory hole (1) In mining, a slang expression for a vertical pit whose mined material drops into a shaft below the bottom of the pit. (2) A small shaft excavated to assess the quality of an ore.

gloss Surface luster, usually expressed in terms ranging from matte to high gloss.

glow lamp A type of low-consumption electric discharge lamp whose light is produced close to the electrodes within an ionized

gob bucket

gas. A glow lamp is often used as an indicating light.

glue A general term for any natural or synthetic viscous or gelatinous substance used as an adhesive to bind or join materials.

glue bleedthrough The seepage of glue through the face of open-pore wood.

glue bond A measure of how well articles are fastened together after being glued.

glued floor system A method of floor construction in which a plywood underlayment or other structural panel is both glued and nailed to the floor joists. This creates a stronger, stiffer floor less prone to squeaking than floors fastened only with nails.

glue gun A hand tool for the application of bulk or cartridge-type adhesives.

glue laminated (glu-lam) The result of a process in which individual pieces of lumber or veneer are bonded together with adhesives to make a single piece in which the grain of all the constituent pieces is parallel.

glue line The layer of glue or adhesive between two pieces of lumber or veneer.

glue nailed A term applying to plywood joints and connections that have been both glued and nailed to produce the stiffest possible construction.

glue-up The process of spreading glue on the surfaces of veneers of similar sizes and pressing them together to form a sheet of plywood.

glycol Liquid with a very low freezing point that is miscible with water.

glyph (1) An ornamental, usually vertical channel or groove, as in a column or freeze. (2) A sculptured pictograph.

gneiss A coarse-grained metamorphic rock similar to granite and containing quartz, mica, feldspar, or other minerals. In construction terms, gneiss is classed as *trade granite*.

gob bucket (concrete bucket) On a crane, the bucket that is used to carry concrete.

go-devil (1) A pipe-cleaning device inserted at the pump end of a pipeline and forced through the pipe by water pressure in order to clean it. (2) In lumbering, a sled or skid-pan designed to keep the leading end of a log off the ground when skidding.

going The horizontal distance between two consecutive risers or stairs. The horizontal distance between the first and last riser of an entire flight is called the *going of the flight* or the run.

going rod A rod used in planning the going of a flight of steps.

gold bronze Powdered copper or copper alloy used for bronzing, or in the manufacture of gold or bronze paint.

gold size An oleo-resinous varnish that becomes sticky upon application, but hardens slowly, thus making an appropriate adhesive for attaching gold leaf to a surface.

goliath crane A heavy but portable crane, usually about 50-ton capacity, used for jobs requiring heavy lifting and for shop fabrication involving heavy steel.

good one side (G1S) A grade of sanded plywood with a higher grade of veneer on the face than on the

goverment anchor

grab bar

gradall

grade beam

back. G1S is used in applications where the appearance of only one side is important.

good two sides (G2S) The highest grade of sanded plywood. G2S is allowed to have inlays or neat wood patches and is used in applications where the appearance of both sides is important.

gooseneck (1) In plumbing, a curved, sometimes flexible fitting connection or section of pipe. (2) In HVAC, a screened, U-shaped intake or exhaust duct. (3) The curved end of a handrail at the top of a stair. (4) The curved connector from a tractor to a trailer.

gothic In architecture, the prevalent style in Western Europe from the 12th through the 15th century, whose characteristic features included flying buttresses, ribbed vaulting, pointed arches, and lavishly fenestrated walls.

gothic arch A typically high, narrow arch with a pointed top and a jointed apex (as opposed to keystone).

gothic-arch window A window topped with a pointed arch.

gouge A cutting chisel having a long, curved blade and used for hollowing out wood, or for making holes, channels, or grooves in wood or stone.

government anchor A V-shaped anchoring device usually fabricated from 1/2″ round bar, and used in steelwork to secure a wall-bearing (or other) beam to masonry.

Gow caisson (Boston caisson, caisson pile) A series of steel cylinders from 8′–16′ high used to protect workers and equipment during deep excavation in soft earth. Each successive cylinder is 2′ in diameter smaller than its predecessor, through which it is dropped or driven deeper into the surrounding soft clay or silt to prevent excessive loss of ground and to facilitate deep excavation. When excavation and construction are complete, the cylinders are withdrawn.

grab bar A short length of metal, glass, or plastic bar attached to a wall in a bathroom, near a toilet, in a shower, or above a bathtub.

grab bucket A bucket-like device with hinged lower halves or "jaws" hydraulically or cable-operated from a crane or used for re-handling granular materials. *See also* **clamshell.**

grab crane A crane outfitted with a grab bucket.

gradall A trade name for a wheel-mounted, articulated, hydraulic backhoe often used with a wide bucket for dressing earth slopes.

gradation An assessment, as determined through sieve analysis, of the amounts of particles of different sizes in a given sample of soil or aggregate.

grade (1) The surface or level of the ground. (2) A classification of quality as, for instance, in lumber. (3) The existing or proposed ground level or elevation on a building site or around a building. (4) The slope or rate of incline or decline of a road, expressed as a percent. (5) A designation of a subfloor, either above grade, on grade, or below grade. (6) In plumbing, the slope of installed pipe, expressed in the fall in inches per foot length of pipe. (7) The classification of the durability of brick. (8) Any surface prepared to accept paving, conduit, or rails.

grade beam A horizontal end-supported (as opposed to ground-supported) load-bearing

grade course

grader

grading

foundation member that supports an exterior wall of a superstructure.

grade block A type of concrete masonry unit from which the top course of a foundation wall is constructed and above which a masonry wall is constructed.

grade boom That portion of the foundation system that directly supports the exterior walls of the building.

grade correction A distance measured on a slope and corrected to a horizontal distance between vertical lines through its end points.

grade course The first course of brick, block, or stone, at grade level, usually waterproofed.

graded aggregate (1) Aggregate having size ranging from coarse to graded sand. (2) A fine aggregate (under 1/4") having a uniformly graded particle size.

graded standard sand Ottawa sand that has been subjected to accurate grading between No. 30 and No. 100 sieves and is used in testing hydraulic cements.

grade line (1) A line of stakes with markings, each at an elevation relative to a common datum and from whose elevations a grade between their terminal points can be established. (2) A strong string used to establish the top of a concrete pour or masonry course.

grader A multipurpose earthworking machine used mostly for leveling and crowning. A grader has a single blade, centrally located, that can be lifted from either end and angled so as to cast to either side.

grade stamp (grade mark) A stamp on a manufactured piece of wood that designates it meets certain standards of quality as set forth by one of several standards organizations. Stamps for structural lumber, for instance, include information on species, moisture content and lumber grade.

grade stake In earthwork, a stake that designates the specified level.

grade strip A thin wooden strip fastened to the inside of a concrete form to indicate the level to which concrete should be placed.

gradient (1) The change in elevation of a surface, road, or pipe usually expressed in a percentage or in degrees. (2) The rate of change of a variable such as temperature, flow, or pressure.

gradienter A micrometer, attached to a transit's telescope, that allows the angle of incline to be measured in terms of the angle's tangent instead of in degrees and minutes.

grading (1) The act of altering the ground surface to a desired grade or contour by cutting, filling, leveling, and/or smoothing. (2) Sorting aggregate by particle size. (3) Classifying items by size, quality, or resistance.

grading curve A line on a graph illustrating the percentages of a given sample of material which pass through each of a specific series of sieves.

grading instrument A surveyor's level having a telescope that can be adjusted upward or downward to lay out a required gradient.

grading plan A plan showing contours and grade elevations for existing and proposed ground surface elevations at a given site.

grading rules Quality criteria that determine the classification of lumber, plywood, or other wood products.

gradual load The gradual application of a load to the supporting members of a structure.

granular fill insulation

graduated courses Courses of roofing slates having diminishing gauges from the eaves to the roof.

graffito A plaster surface applied over a colored undercoat for decorative effect. While still soft, the surface is scored with a pattern so as to expose the contrasting undercoat.

graft (1) The joining of a bud or scion of one plant or tree onto a part of a similar plant or tree. (2) Extortion by the unscrupulous leverage of one's position or knowledge.

grain (1) The directional arrangement of fibers in a piece of wood or woven fabric, or of the particulate constituents in stone or slate. (2) The texture of a substance or pattern as determined by the size of the constituent particles. (3) Any small, hard particle (like sand). (4) A metric unit of weight; 7,000 grains equal one pound.

graining The process of simulating grain on painted or manmade surfaces using special tools such as graining combs to manipulate an applied coat of translucent stain or *graining color*.

graining comb A painting tool with teeth used to simulate grain on a painted or manmade surface.

grain size (1) A size classification of mineral particles in soil or rock. (2) One of the physical characteristics of a particle of soil, which relates to its mechanical properties.

grain slope The angle of the grain in a piece of wood, as determined from a hypothetical line parallel to its length.

granatic finish A granite-like face mix on precast concrete.

grandmaster key (1) A key that not only operates all the locks within a given group having its own master key, but several such groups. (2) A master key of master keys.

granny bar A slang term for a large crowbar.

granolithic concrete A type of concrete made from a hard aggregate whose particle shape and surface texture render it conducive for wearing-surface finishes on floors.

granolithic finish A concrete wearing surface, placed over a concrete slab, containing aggregate chips to improve its longevity.

grantee (1) The party to whom a deed or similar document transfers property or property rights. (2) The buyer.

grantor (1) The party from whom a deed or similar document transfers property or property rights. (2) The seller.

granular (1) A technical term relating to the uniform size of grains or crystals in rock. (2) Composed of grains.

granular fill insulation An insulation material such as perlite or vermiculite that can be easily placed or poured because it comes in the form of chunks, pellets, or modules.

granular material A sandy type of soil whose particles are coarser than cohesive material and do not stick together.

graphics Engineering or architectural drawings created with attention to mathematical rules, such as perspective or projection.

graphite paint A type of paint made from boiled linseed oil, powdered graphite, and a drier. Graphite paint is used to inhibit corrosion on metal surfaces.

grass cloth

grate

gravel roofing

gravel stop

grapple An excavation or re-handling bucket on the end of a crane. *See also* **orangepeel bucket**.

grappler A pointed or wedge-shaped spike whose eye is left exposed after the spike is driven into a masonry joint, thus providing support for scaffold brackets.

grass cloth A wall covering made from woven vegetable fibers, especially arrowroot bark. The cloth is laminated onto a paper backing.

grate (1) A type of screen made from sets of parallel bars placed across each other at right angles in approximately the same plane. A grate allows water to flow to drainage, while covering the area for pedestrian or vehicular traffic. (2) A surface with openings to allow air to flow through while supporting a fuel bed, as in a coal furnace.

gravel Coarse particles of rock that result from naturally occurring disintegration or that are produced by crushing weakly bound conglomerate. Gravel is retained on a No. 4 sieve.

gravel, bank run Naturally occurring gravel deposits that are often located along rivers or lakes.

gravel board An easily replaceable board that is secured horizontally near the bottom edge of a wooden fence so as to prevent contact between the ground and the vertical boards, thus preventing rotting.

gravel roofing Roofing composed of several (built-up) layers of saturated or coated roofing felt, sealed and bonded with asphalt or coal-tar pitch which, for solar protection and insulation purposes, is then covered with a layer of gravel or slag.

Usually used on flat or nearly flat roofs.

gravel stop A metal strip or flange around the edge of a built-up roof. The stop prevents loose gravel or other surfacing material from falling off or being blown off a roof.

gravity dam A pyramid-shaped dam whose own weight resists the force of the water behind it.

gravity-operated toilet Any toilet that utilizes the natural downward pressure of water in the toilet tank to flush.

gravity separator A chamber in which oil rises and remains on the surface of wastewater until it is removed.

gravity wall A massive concrete retaining wall whose own weight prevents it from overturning.

gravity water supply (gravity water, gravity system) A water distribution system in which the supply source is located at an elevation higher than the use.

gray paper The rough textured, unsized paper that covers the back of regular gypsum board, or both face and back on backing board products.

gray scale A series of achromatic samples that vary discretely from white to black.

grazing iron (1) In plumbing, a tool for finishing soldered joints. (2) A glass-cutting device.

grease extractor A device installed in conjunction with a cooking exhaust system and employing grease-collecting baffles positioned so as to create a path of sharp turns through which the cooking exhaust is passed at high velocity. The grease, which is particulate and heavier than air, is collected on the baffles by centrifugal force, while

grease interceptor
(grease trap)

greenfield

greenhouse

grid

the carrying air continues around the sharp turns on its way to being exhausted, thus becoming cleaner at each baffle.

grease interceptor (grease trap) A device installed between the kitchen drain and the building sewer to trap and retain fats and grease from kitchen waste lines.

grease monkey (1) A slang expression for a person who lubricates, refuels, and/or repairs equipment. (2) A grease dauber who greases skids so that logs can be moved over them easily.

grease trap *See* **grease interceptor**.

green A term referring to unseasoned timber or to fresh, unhardened concrete, plaster, or paint.

greenbelt (1) An elongated section of trees or other plantings which serves as a boundary of, or divider within, a community. (2) Any large area of undeveloped land, including parks and farmland, that surrounds a community.

green board (moisture-resistant) Gypsum board distinguishable by the green color of its face paper. Green board is designed to be used in areas that are often damp, such as in bathrooms for tile backing.

green brick Molded clay block or brick before it has been fired in a kiln.

green concrete Concrete that has set but not hardened.

greenfield Flexible metal conduit for electrical wiring.

green glass A type of glass whose green color results from impurities in its raw materials.

greenhouse A glass-enclosed space with a controlled environment for growing plants, vegetables, and fruits out of season.

greenhouse effect (1) The conversion of the sun's rays into heat that is retained by the glass roof of a greenhouse. (2) The steady, gradual rise in temperature of the earth's atmosphere due to heat that is retained by layers of ozone, carbon dioxide, and water vapor.

Green Lights Program A government program sponsored by the Environmental Protection Agency that is aimed at promoting energy efficiency through investment in energy-saving lighting.

green lumber Undried, unseasoned lumber.

green manure (1) Crops (such as winter rye or alfalfa) which are plowed under to return nutrients into the soil. (2) The plowed-under remains of a crop from which a harvest has been reaped.

green mortar Mortar that has dried but not set.

grid (1) In surveying, a system of evenly spaced perpendicular reference lines with its intersections used to measure elevations. (2) The structural layout of a given building. (3) A system of crossed reinforcing bars used in concrete footings.

grid ceiling (1) A ceiling with apertures into which are built luminaries for lighting purposes. (2) Any ceiling hung on a grid framework.

grid foundation A foundation consisting of several intersecting continuous footings loaded at the intersections. A grid foundation covers less than 75% of the area within its outer limits.

gridiron (1) The plotting of city streets in rectangles. (2) The framework above a stage from which lights and scenery can be hung.

grille

grid line Any line that is part of a reference pattern for surveying or a layout.

griffe An ornamental form, somewhat like a claw, extending from the torus of a column base and lying on the four corners of the plinth.

grillage Steel or wooden beams used horizontally under a structure to distribute its load over its footing or underpinning.

grille (1) Any grating or openwork barrier used to cover an opening in a wall, floor, paving, etc., for decoration, protection, or concealment. (2) A louvered or perforated panel used to cover an air duct opening in a wall, ceiling, or floor. (3) Any screen or grating that allows air into a ventilating duct.

grillwork In construction, any heavy framework of timbers or beams used to support a load on soil instead of on a concrete foundation.

grind (1) To reduce in size by removing material by friction or crushing. (2) To sharpen (as a tool) by abrasion.

grinder (1) A device that sharpens or removes particles of material by abrasion. (2) A machine or tool for finishing concrete surfaces by abrasion.

grinder pump A sewage pump that reduces solids and grinds and pumps material.

grindstone A flat sandstone wheel which is rotated to sharpen implements or to reduce the size of a material by abrasion or grinding.

gringo blocks Nailing anchors made of wood and inserted in masonry walls to provide for fastening of door or window jambs.

grinning through (1) In plastering, a term to describe lathing that is discernable under plaster. (2) In painting, a term to describe an undercoat that is showing through a topcoat.

grip length (bond length) The minimum length, expressed in bar diameters, of rebar necessary for anchorage in concrete. *See also* **bond length**.

grisaille (1) A system of surface painting in various shades of gray so as to decorate or to suggest bas-relief. (2) Uncolored, nontransparent glass in a stained glass window.

grit (1) A granular abrasive used in making sandpaper or on grinding wheels to give a surface a nonslip finish. (2) Particles of sand or gravel contained in sewage.

grizzly (1) A screen or grate used to remove oversize particles during aggregate processing or loading. (2) A gate or similar device on a chute.

groin (1) In architecture, a ridge or curved line formed at the junction of two intersecting vaults. (2) A structure built outward from a shore into water to direct erosion or to protect against it.

groin centering (1) A method of supporting ribless groining during vaulting. (2) In ribbed vaulting, the support of the stone ribs by timbers until construction is complete.

grommet A metal or plastic eyelet that provides a reinforced hole in a material, such as cloth or leather, that might otherwise tear from the stress on the hole when a fastener or other device is passed through it or attached to it.

groove In carpentry, a narrow, longitudinal-channel cut in the edge or face of a wood member.

groove joint

groover

The groove is called a *dado* when cut across the grain, and a *plow* when cut parallel to it.

groove joint A joint formed by the intentional creation of a groove in the surface of a wall, pavement, or floor slab for the purpose of controlling the direction of random cracking.

groover A tool for creating grooved joints in unhardened concrete slabs.

groove weld A weld between the existing preformed grooves in members being joined.

gross area (1) The total area without deducting for holes or cut-outs. (2) The whole or entire area of a roof. (3) In shingles, the entire area of a shingle, including any parts which might have had to be cut out. (4) The total enclosed floor area of a building.

gross cross-sectional area The total area of that portion of a concrete masonry unit which is perpendicular to the load, inclusive of any areas within its cells and re-entrant spaces.

gross floor area The total area of all the floors of a building, including intermediately floored tiers, mezzanine, basements, etc., as measured from the exterior surfaces of the outside walls of the building.

gross load In heating, the net load to which allowances are added for pickup and piping losses.

gross margin The excess of net sales revenue over direct costs.

gross output The number of BTU's available at the outlet nozzle of a heating unit for continuously satisfying the gross load requirements of a boiler operating within code limitations.

gross section The total area of the cross section of a structural member as calculated without subtracting for any voids in that cross section.

gross volume (1) The total volume within the revolving part of a drum concrete mixer. (2) The total volume of the trough on an open-top concrete mixer.

grotto A natural or man-made cavern or cave.

ground (1) The conducting connection between electrical equipment or an electrical circuit and the earth. (2) A strip of wood that is fixed in a wall of concrete or masonry to provide a place for attaching wood trim or burring strips. (3) A screed, strip of wood, or bead of metal fastened around an opening in a wall and acting as a thickness guide for plastering or as a fastener for trim. (4) Any surface that is or will be plastered or painted. (5) Any electrical reference point.

ground area The area computed by the exterior dimensions of the structure.

ground beam (1) A reinforced concrete beam or heavy timber positioned horizontally at ground level to support a superstructure. (2) A ground sill.

ground brush A round or oval paintbrush used to carry large quantities of paint.

ground bus An electrical bus to which individual equipment grounds are connected and which itself is grounded at one or more points.

ground casing In carpentry, a term for the blind casing of a window.

ground coat The base or undercoat of paint or enamel, often designed to be seen through the topcoat or glaze coat.

ground-fault circuit-interrupter

grounding outlet

ground course A first horizontal course of masonry at ground level.

ground cover A planting of low plants that in time will spread to form a dense, often decorative mass. Ground cover is also used to prevent erosion.

grounded Descriptive of an object that is electrically connected to the earth or to another conducting body that is connected to the earth.

grounded conductor In an electrical system, a circuit conductor that is intentionally grounded, either solidly or through a device that limits current.

grounded system A system of electric conductors, at least one of which is intentionally grounded, either solidly or by means of a device that limits current.

grounded work Any joinery, such as a crown molding, attached to grounds. *See also* **ground (2)**.

ground-fault circuit-interrupter An electrical outlet fitted with code-required safety protection.

ground floor In a building, that floor closest to the level of the surrounding ground.

ground glass Glass having a light-diffusing surface produced by grinding with an abrasive.

grounding electrode A conductor that is firmly embedded in the earth, and can thus function to maintain ground potential on the conductors connected to it.

grounding outlet An electrical outlet whose polarity-type receptacle includes both the current-carrying contacts and a grounded contact that accepts an equipment- grounding conductor.

ground plan The plan of a structure at ground level.

grounding plug A receptacle plug comprising a male member which, when plugged into a live grounding outlet, provides a ground connection for an electric device.

ground joint (1) In masonry, a close-fitting joint, usually without mortar. (2) A closely fitted joint between machined metal surfaces.

ground joist Floor joists laid on sleepers, dwarf sills, or stones.

ground key valve A fluid-flow control valve containing a tapered plug with a hole bored into it. The keg-type handle requires only a one-quarter turn between its open and shut positions.

ground line The natural grade line or ground level from which excavation measurements are taken to determine excavation quantities.

ground plate *See* **ground sill**.

ground pressure (1) The weight of a machine or a piece of equipment divided by the area, in square inches, of the ground that supports it. (2) Pressure exerted on a structural member by the adjacent soil or fill.

ground sill (ground plate) The bottom horizontal structural member of a framed building on or near the ground level.

ground station *See* **earth station**.

groundwater (1) Naturally occurring water that moves through the earth's crust, usually at a depth of several feet to several hundred feet below the earth's surface. (2) Water contained in the soil below the level of standing water.

groundwater recharge The reintroduction of water into the ground, as from trenches beyond the construction area or through injection.

grouted masonry

grouting

groundwater table The top elevation of groundwater at a given location and at a given time.

ground wire (1) An electrical conductor leading directly or indirectly to the earth. (2) Strong, small-gauge wire used in establishing line and grade, as in shotcrete work.

groundwork Batters used in roofing and siding as a base over which slate, tiles, and shingles are applied.

group house (row house) A single dwelling unit contained in a long, unbroken line of vertically identical houses connected by common walls.

group vent In plumbing, a branch vent connected to two or more traps.

grouser The cleat on a track shoe, such as the shoe on a bulldozer track, that is used to improve traction.

grout (1) A hydrous mortar whose consistency allows it to be placed or pumped into small joints or cavities, as between pieces of ceramic clay, slate, and floor tile. (2) Various mortar mixes used in foundation work to fill voids in soils, usually through successive injections through drilled holes.

grout box A cone-shaped sleeve in a concrete slab into which an anchor bolt for machinery can be grouted.

grouted-aggregate concrete Concrete which is produced by injecting grout into prepositioned coarse aggregate.

grouted frame An originally hollow-metal door frame whose vacant interior has been filled with some type of cement or mortar mixture.

grouted masonry (1) Hollow masonry units with some or all of the cells filled with grout. (2) Masonry comprising two or more wythes, the spaces between which are filled solidly with grout.

grouting (1) The placing of grout so as to fill voids, as between tiles and under structural columns and machine bases. (2) The injection of grout to stabilize dams or mass fills, or to reinforce and strengthen decaying walls and foundations. (3) The injection of grout to fill faults and crevices in rock formations.

grout lift The height of grout placed in masonry wall voids during a single placement.

grout slope The naturally occurring slope of hydrous grout after its injection into preplaced aggregate concrete.

growth rate A measurement of wood growth taken from the number of growth rings and used to rate strength.

growth ring A ring that designates the amount of a tree's growth in a single year.

grub In site work, the clearing of stumps, roots, trees, bushes, and undergrowth.

grub axe (grub hoe, mattock) A hand tool for shallow digging or root pulling. One end of the head of the tool has a transverse cutting blade, while the other end has a cutting blade like an axe. *See also* **mattock**.

grub saw A hand-operated saw used for cutting stone (such as marble) into usable slabs.

grunt A slang term for a common laborer or an apprentice lineman.

guarantee (guaranty, warranty) A legally enforceable assurance of quality or performance of a product or work, or of the duration of satisfactory performance.

guaranteed maximum cost The maximum amount above which an owner and contractor agree that cost

guard board

guard rail

for work performed (as calculated on the basis of labor, materials, overhead, and profit) will not escalate.

guaranteed maximum cost contract A contract for construction wherein the contractor's compensation is stated as a combination of accountable cost plus a fee, with guarantee by the contractor that the total compensation will be limited to a specific amount. This type of contract may also have possible optional provisions for additional financial reward to the contractor for performance that causes total compensation to be less than the guaranteed maximum amount.

guaranty bond A type of bond which is given to secure payment and performance. Each of the following four bonds are types of guaranty bonds: (1) bid bond, (2) labor and material payment bond, (3) performance bond, and (4) surety bond.

guard (1) Any bars, railing, fence, or enclosure that serves as protection around moving parts of machinery or around an excavation, equipment, or materials. (2) A security guard hired to maintain safety and security at a construction site.

guard board A raised board around the edge of a scaffold or gantry crane to keep men and tools from falling off.

guarded front and strike A lock designed and constructed with the front and strike protected, thus preventing the latch bolt from being "jimmied" through the crevice between the door and the jamb.

guard rail (1) A horizontal rail of metal, wood, or cable fastened to intermittent uprights of metal, wood, or concrete around the edges of platforms or along the lane of a highway. (2) The rail that separates traffic entering or exiting through side-by-side automatic doors.

gudgeon (1) A metal pin or dowel used for joining two adjacent stones, blocks, or slabs. (2) A reinforced bushing or a block designated to absorb shock. (3) On a hinge, the leaf that is fastened to an immovable member. (4) The part of a gate hook fastened to the gate post.

guesstimate An educated guess or approximation of the cost of a project made by the cost estimator, without having performed a detailed quantity takeoff. *See also* **educated guess**.

guide bead *See* **inside stop**.

guide coat A very thin coat of paint that serves to identify, through emphasis, various imperfections on the surface under it.

guided-bend test A test to determine the strength of a weld and the ductility of metallic materials.

guide pile A heavy square timber driven vertically near sheet piles that support an excavation, so as to carry the full earth pressure from the waters, or sometimes simply to guide the sheet piles.

guide wire (1) A steel wire or cable used to guide the vertical movement of a stage curtain in a theater. (2) A line or wire that guides the movement of a counterweight arbor. (3) A wire placed along the edge of a roadway to be paved. A sensor on the pavement spreader adjusts the elevation of the pavement from the wire.

guillotine In woodworking or cabinetry, a trimming machine that can cut the two matching ends of a joint to any given angle.

gusset, gusset plate

gutter

guinea In surveying, a wooden marker that is first driven to grade, then topped with blue paint for identification during finish grading.

guinea chaser In surveying, a site worker who uncovers the blue-topped stakes and informs the blade operator whether fill should be added or removed.

gullet (1) The concave gap between the teeth of a file or saw. (2) The height of a saw tooth as measured from the base to the point. (3) The space between tabs on a standard asphalt strip shingle.

gum bloom A hazy or lusterless area on a painted surface that results from the use of the wrong reducer.

gumbo Soil composed of fine-grained clays. When wet, the soil is highly plastic, very sticky, and has a soapy appearance. When dried, it develops large shrinkage cracks.

gumwood Wood from a gum tree, especially eucalyptus, used mostly for interior trim.

gun (1) Equipment designed to deliver shotcrete. (2) A pressure cylinder for pneumatic delivery of freshly mixed concrete. (3) A spray gun. (4) A slang expression for a transit, as it is used to *shoot* grades.

gun consistency The degree of viscosity of caulking or glazing compound which renders it suitable for application by a caulking gun.

gun finish The finish on a layer of shotcrete left undisturbed after application.

gun grade *See* **gun consistency.**

gunite Concrete mixed with water at the nozzle end of a hose through which it has been pumped under pressure. Gunite is applied or placed pneumatically, as shot, onto a backing surface.

gunstock stile In joinery, a diminishing stile whose width is tapered.

Gunter's chain In surveying, a measuring device with 100 metal links and a total length of 66 feet.

gusset A metal or wood brace attached to structural members at their joints to add strength and stability.

gusset plate A plate fastened across a joint, as in wood or steel framework members. *See also* **chain.**

gutter (1) A shallow channel of wood, metal, or PVC positioned just below and following along the eaves of a building for the purpose of collecting and diverting water from a roof. (2) In electrical wiring, the rectangular space allowed around the interior of an electrical panel for the installation of feeder and branch wiring conductors.

gutter bed A strip of flexible metal over the wall side of a gutter which prohibits any gutter overflow from penetrating the wall.

gutter hook A bent metal strip used for securing or supporting a metal gutter.

gutter plate (1) A single side of a box or valley gutter, lined with flexible metal and carrying the feet of the rafters. (2) A beam that supports a lead gutter.

gutter spikes Long (6″ to 12″) aluminum or galvanized steel nails used to hang gutters.

guy A cable or rope anchored in the ground at one end and supporting or stabilizing an object at the other end.

guy derrick A derrick with a guyed mast and hinged boom at its base. This type of derrick is used for erecting and hoisting materials.

gummer *See* **gemel.**

gypsum board

gypsum concrete

gypsum-lath nail

gypsite Gypsum whose degree of purity is from 60% to 90%. Gypsite also contains sand, clay, and loam.

gypsum A naturally occurring, soft, whitish mineral (hydrous calcium sulfate) which, after processing, is used as a retarding agent in Portland cement and as the primary ingredient in plaster, gypsum board, and related products.

gypsum backerboard A type of gypsum board, not as smooth as wall- board, surfaced with gray paper, and manufactured specifically as a base onto which tile or gypsum wallboard is adhered.

gypsum block A lightweight, hollow or solid masonry unit made from gypsum and used to construct nonbearing partitions.

gypsum board A panel whose gypsum core is paperfaced on each side, and which is used to cover walls and ceilings while providing a smooth surface that is easy to finish. Used as a substitute for plaster.

gypsum cement *See* **Keene's cement.**

gypsum concrete A mixture of calcined gypsum binder, wood chips or other aggregate, and water. The mixture is poured to form gypsum roof decks.

gypsum fiber concrete A gypsum concrete whose aggregate is composed of wood shavings, fiber, or chips.

gypsum insulation A loose-fill thermal insulation made of gypsum.

gypsum-lath nail A low-carbon steel nail with a large flat head and long point. The characteristics make it especially suitable for fixing gypsum lath and plasterboard.

gypsum panel *See* **gypsum board.**

gypsum perlite plaster A base-coat plaster manufactured from gypsum and an aggregate of perlite.

gypsum plaster A plaster made from ground calcined gypsum. The set and workability of gypsum plaster are controlled by various additives. When mixed with aggregate and water, the resulting mixture is used for base-coat plaster.

gypsum sheathing A type of wallboard whose core is made from gypsum with which additives have been mixed to make it water-resistant. The sheathing is surfaced with a water-repellent paper to make it appropriate for exterior wall coverings.

gypsum trowel finish Factory-prepared plasters consisting primarily of calcined gypsum and used in finishing applications.

gypsum wallboard *See* **gypsum board.**

gyratory crusher A rock-crushing mechanism whose central conical member moves eccentrically within a circular chamber.

H

H ABBREVIATIONS

The abbreviations listed below are those most commonly used in the construction industry. Alternative forms (usually nonstandard) are shown in parentheses.

h harbor, hard, height, hours, house, hundred

H "head" on drawings, high, high strength bar joist, Henry, hydrogen

HA hour angle

H&M hit and miss

HASP health and safety plan

HAZMAT hazardous materials

HB hollow bark

HC, H.C. high capacity

HCFCs hydrochlorofluorocarbons

HD, H.D. heavy duty, high density

H.D.O. High Density Overlaid

HDPE high density polyethylene

Hdr header

hdwe, hdwr hardware

He. helium

HE. high explosive

Help. helper average

hem. hemlock

HEPA high efficiency particulate air

HEW Department of Health, Education, and Welfare

hex hexagon

hf half, high-frequency

H.F. hot finished

HFCs hydrofluorocarbons

hg hectogram

Hg mercury

hgt height

HI height of instrument

HID high intensity discharge

hip. hipped (roof)

HIPS high impact polystyrene

hl hectoliter

hm hectometer

HM hollow metal

HO high output

hor, horiz horizontal

H or M hit or miss

HOW. Home Owner's Warranty

hp, H.P. horsepower

HP high pressure, steel pile section

H.P.F. high power factor

hr hour

HRS hazard ranking system

H.S. high stength

HSC high short circuit

ht, Ht. height

HT high-tension

htg, Htg heating

Htrs. heaters

HTRW hazardous toxic radiological waste

HUD Department of Housing and Urban Development

hv, HV high voltage

HVAC heating, ventilating, and air-conditioning

hvy, Hvy. heavy

HW high-water, hot water

HWM high-water mark

hwy highway

hyd, hydraul hydraulic, hydrostatics

Hyd, Hydr. hydraulic

hyp, hypoth hypothesis; hypothetical

hz hertz (cycles)

H

DEFINITIONS

half-brick wall

half-landing

hachure One of the short parallel lines used on an architectural drawing for shading or for indicating a section of a drawn object, or on a topographic map for indicating the degree and direction of slopes and depressions.

hack (1) To cut or strike at something irregularly or carelessly, or to deal heavy blows. (2) A person who lacks, or does not apply, knowledge or skill in performing his job.

hacking (1) Striking a surface with a special tool so as to roughen it. (2) A style of brick-laying in which the bottom edge is set in from the plane surface of the wall. (3) In a stone wall, the breaking of a single course into two or more courses, sometimes for effect but usually because of the scarcity of larger stones.

hacking knife A glazier's tool used for removing old putty prior to reglazing.

hacksaw A lightweight, metal-cutting handsaw having a narrow, fine-toothed blade retained in an adjustable metal frame.

haft The handle of a cutting tool.

ha-ha (haw-haw) A trench or similar depression serving as a sunken fence or barrier for livestock.

hair interceptor In plumbing, a trap-like device installed in the waste drain side of a fixture's plumbing system to capture and collect hair on screens or in perforated steel baskets which are removable from the bottom of the device.

hairline cracks Very fine, barely visible random cracks appearing on, but not penetrating, the finish surface of materials such as paint and concrete.

hairpin (1) A type of wedge used in tightening some kinds of form ties. (2) Hairpin-shaped rebar sometimes used in beams, columns, and prefabricated column shear heads.

half baluster An engaged baluster having an outward protrusion equal to approximately half its diameter.

half bat (half brick) A half-brick produced by cutting a brick in two, across its length.

half-brick wall A brick wall having the thickness of a brick laid as a stretcher.

half by Slang term for any lumber with a half-inch thickness.

half column An engaged column protruding only slightly more than half its diameter.

half-face respirator A respirator that covers only the nose and mouth.

half hatchet A carpenter's hatchet similar to a plasterer's lath hammer but having a broader blade with a notched underpart for pulling nails.

half header Half of a brick or concrete block made by cutting the unit longitudinally through its faces. Half headers are used to close the work at the end of a course.

half-landing (halfpace landing, halfspace landing) A platform in a stairway, where the stairs change direction halfway between the floors of a building.

half-lapped joint (halved joint, halved splice) A transverse joint formed at the intersection of two equally thick pieces of wood, both having been notched to half their original depth, so as to form a joint with flush faces.

half mortise hinge

half-span roof

half story

halon fire extinguisher

half-life The period of time that the level of radioactivity for a substance decays by 50%.

half mortise hinge A door hinge with one plate surface-mounted on the jamb and the other plate mortised into the door stile.

half-pitch roof A roof with a pitch whose rise is equal to one half the width of the span.

half principal A roof rafter or similar member with the upper end not extending all the way to the ridgeboard, but instead supported by a purlin.

half rabbeted lock A type of mortise lock having a front turned into two perpendicular planes, used on a door with a rabbeted edge.

half-ripsaw A handsaw with teeth more closely spaced than those on a ripsaw.

half round (1) Molding having one flat side and one rounded side, making it semicircular in profile. (2) Veneer produced by slicing a flitch or log that has been sawn into two equal halves.

half-round file A file having one side in the shape of a segment of a circle and the other flat.

half slating See **open slating**.

halfspace landing See **half-landing**.

half-span roof (lean-to roof) A roof that slopes in only one plane and abuts a higher exterior wall.

half story An attic or story immediately below a sloping roof and usually having some partitions and a finished ceiling and floor.

half-surface hinge A door hinge having one plate surface-mounted onto the door leaf, and the other plate mortised into the jamb. A half-surface hinge is the opposite of a half-mortise hinge.

half timbered Descriptive of a building style common in the 16th and 17th centuries, with foundations, supports, knees, and studs all made of timbers. The wall spaces between the timbers are filled with masonry, brick, or lathed plaster.

half truss One side of a jack truss spanning from a main roof truss to a wall, usually at an angle to the main truss.

half turn Describes a stair making a 180° turn or two 90° turns at each landing.

halide lamp See **metal halide lamp**.

halide torch A device used to detect leaks of halocarbon refrigerant. The color of the sampling torch's normal, alcohol-produced, blue flame becomes a bright green when the refrigerant is detected.

hall (1) A large room in which people assemble for entertainment or meetings. (2) A small entrance room or corridor. (3) A term often used in the proper names of public or university buildings.

hallway A passageway providing access to various parts of a building.

halon fire extinguisher A suppressing system for use on all classes of fires. Its extinguishing agent is bromotrifluoromethane, a colorless, odorless, and electrically nonconductive gas of exceptionally low toxicity. Considered to be the safest of the compressed gas fire-suppressing agents. Although often used in computer equipment rooms, the use of halon is severely restricted because of its properties (which destroy the ozone layer).

hammer A hand tool with a handle perpendicular to its head, for driving nails or other applications involving pounding or striking.

① left hand
② right hand
③ left hand reverse
④ right hand reverse

hand

hand float

hammer ax (lath hammer)
A hammer having a head with a flattened end for driving nails and a notched, narrow hatchet end for pulling nails.

hammer beam (hammer-beam trusses) Either one of a pair of short horizontal members used in place of a tie beam in roof framing. A hammer beam is attached to the foot of a principal rafter and supported from below by a brace to the supporting column.

hammer-beam roof Timbered roof construction in which hammer beams carry the principal rafters and support the feet of arched ribs.

hammer brace The brace, often curved, between a hammer beam and pendant post.

hammer dressed Descriptive of stonemasonry having a finish created only by a hammer, sometimes at the quarry.

hammer drill A pneumatically powered mechanism using percussion to penetrate rock.

hammer finish A finish produced by the application of an enamel containing powdered metal and rendering an appearance similar to that of hammered metal.

hammerhead crane A heavy-duty crane with a swinging boom and counterbalance, giving it a "T" shape.

hammerhead key A hardwood key, dovetailed on both ends, and driven into similarly shaped recesses in the two timbers it serves to join.

hammer man The workman on a pile hammer who operates the hoist or controls the steam jet that, in turn, powers the hammer.

hammermill crusher An impact type crusher that breaks up and grinds materials to a finished size.

hammer post A pendant post at the foot of the truss in a hammer-beam roof.

hamm tip A nozzle, used to deliver shotcrete, having a larger diameter at midpoint than either inlet or outlet.

hance (1) A small arch or half arch connecting a larger arch or lintel to its jamb. (2) Light-concealing trim member at the top of a window.

hand (1) Prefaced by "left" or "right" to designate how a door is hinged and the direction it opens. (2) Preceded by "left" or "right" to designate the direction of turn one encounters when descending a spiral stair, with "right-hand" being clockwise.

hand brace A wood-boring hand tool made of a single frame of small diameter bar or rod bent to form a stationary bracing handle at one end and a bit-holding chuck at the other. A short distance from, but parallel to, the central axis, a handle repeatedly turns in wide circles, causing the bit to turn.

hand chisel A struck tool measuring 2" to 2-1/2", used to cut red hot steel. Should not be used to cut cold steel or rock.

hand drill A hand-operated boring device made up of a central steel tube containing a shaft. At one end is a handle and at the other a bit-holding chuck.

hand float A wooden tool used to lay on and to smooth or texture a finish coat of plaster or concrete.

handicap door opening system A door equipped with a knob or latch and handle located approximately 36" from the floor, and an auxiliary handle on the other side at the hinge edge, for convenience to persons in wheelchairs.

handrail

hanger

hanging gutter

hanging stile

handicap water cooler A water cooler set low and operated by push-bars or levers for convenience to persons in wheelchairs.

hand level In surveying, a hand-held sighting level having limited capability.

hand line (1) A line attached to a structural member or piece of building equipment being hoisted. Used to control the position of the item during erection or setting. (2) A line manipulated to control stage rigging in a theater.

handling tight A degree of tightness to which couplings are screwed onto a pipe causing their removal to necessitate the use of a wrench.

hand punch A struck tool designed for punching or marking metal, driving and removing pins, and aligning holes. Range in size from 1/4" to 1" in diameter, and 4-1/2" to 20" long.

handrail A bar of wood, metal, or PVC, or a length of wire, rope, or cable, supported at intervals by upright posts, balusters, or similar members or, as on a stairway, by brackets from a wall or partition, so as to provide persons with a handhold.

handrail scroll, handrail wreath The spiraled end of a handrail.

handsaw Any manual woodcutting saw having a handle at one end by which it is gripped and manipulated.

hand screw A woodworker's clamp made up of two parallel wooden jaws, connected by two parallel screws tightened from opposite sides.

hand split and resawn (HS and RS) A type of cedar shake. Handsplits are split from cedar bolts by a mallet and froe (a type of steel blade). The pieces are then ripped on a resaw to produce two shakes, each with a rough, split face and a smooth, sawn back.

hand tight Descriptive of couplings tightened by hand by the application of force roughly equal to the force an average man can exert.

hang To install a door or window within its respective frame and/or by its respective hardware.

hangar An enclosure, usually for housing and/or repairing aircraft.

hanger (1) A strip, strap, rod, or similar hardware for connecting pipe, metal gutter, or framework, such as for a hung ceiling, to its overhead support. (2) Any of a class of hardware used in supporting or connecting members of similar or different material as, for instance, a stirrup strap or beam hanger for supporting the end of a beam or joist at a masonry wall. (3) A person whose trade it is to install gypsum board products.

hanging gutter A metal gutter attached to the roof eaves with metal straps and sometimes further supported by the fascia.

hanging post The post from which a gate or door is hung.

hanging rail The horizontal section at the top and bottom of a door, to which the hinges are secured.

hanging sash See **hung sash**.

hanging shingling Shingling fixed to very steep or vertical surfaces.

hanging steps Cantilevered steps.

hanging stile (1) The vertical structural member on the side opposite the handle, to which the hinges are fastened. (2) That vertical section of a window frame to which the casements are hinged.

hard asphalt A solid form of asphalt having a normal penetration of less than 10.

hardback Molding and BTR lumber which is D-select graded from the good face only, which must be clear. The back may contain knots that do not extend through the piece.

hardboard Dense sheets of building material made from heated and compressed wood fibers.

hard-burnt (1) Descriptive of clay products, such as bricks or tiles, having been burnt or fired at high temperatures, resulting in their durability, high compressive strength, and low absorption. (2) A hard plaster, such as Keene's.

hard compact soil All earth materials not classified as running or unstable.

hard conversion The conversion from one system of measurement to another, with an inherent consequence being the necessity of changing the physical sizes of the products involved.

hard copy Information from a computer in printout form.

hard-dry The stage at which a paint film is sufficiently dry to resist thumb-inflicted mutilation, and therefore ready to accept a topcoat or other method of finishing.

hard edge A special preparation used in the core of gypsum board under the papered edges to provide extra resistance.

hardener (1) Any of several chemicals serving to reduce wear and dusting when applied to concrete sustaining heavy traffic, such as a floor. (2) The curing agent of a two-part synthetic resin, adhesive, or similar coating. (3) A substance used to harden plaster casts or gelatin molds.

hard facing Creating a hard, abrasion-resistant cutting edge on tools such as drill bits and saw blades, by welding tungsten carbide onto the steel or other metal.

hard finish A mixture of gypsum, plaster, and lime applied as a finish coat, usually over rough plastering, then troweled to provide a dense, hard, smooth finish.

hard lead *See* **antimonial lead**.

hard light Light creating well-defined shadows.

hard maple The sugar maple tree, *Asersaccharum*, or its wood.

hardness (1) The resistance of a substance, material, or surface, to cutting, scratching, denting, pressure, wear, or other deformation. (2) The degree, expressed as parts per million or grains per gallon of calcium carbonate in water, to which calcium and magnesium salts are dissolved in water.

hardpan Highly compacted soil, boulder clay, or other usually glacially deposited mixture, sometimes including sand, gravel, or boulders. The extreme density of hardpan makes its excavation difficult.

hard pine Any of the resinous pines, such as Loblolly or yellow pine.

hard plaster Quick-setting calcined gypsum, usually used in finishing, often requiring a retarding agent to be incorporated in the mix to help control the set.

hard solder Solder containing silver, copper, or aluminum, and thus requiring more intense heat for melting than does soft solder. Hard solder is usually applied with a brazing torch.

hard stopping A stiff paste having a calcined gypsum content, causing it to harden quickly. Hard stopping is used in painting operations to fill deep holes and wide cracks.

hardtop A road which has been hard-surfaced.

hardware

hatch

hardwall A base-coat plaster made from gypsum, often without aggregate.

hardware (1) A general term encompassing a vast array of metal and plastic fasteners and connectors used in or on a building and its inherent or extraneous parts. The term includes rough hardware, such as nuts, bolts, and nails, and finish hardware, such as latches and hinges. (2) The mechanical equipment associated with data processing. In Building Automation Systems, computer hardware includes the Central Processing Unit (CPU), hard disk drive, monitor (CRT), keyboard, controllers, and analog or digital point modules. Digital equipment such as controls, sensors, and actuators are considered field hardware.

hardware cloth Usually galvanized, thin screen made from wire welded or woven to produce a mesh size of 1/8″ to 3/4″.

hard water Water containing a concentration higher than 85.5 ppm of dissolved calcium carbonate and other mineral salts.

hard wired A communications link permanently joining two devices, nodes, or stations.

hardwood A general term referring to any of a variety of broad-leaved, deciduous trees, and the wood from those trees. The term does not designate the physical hardness of wood, as some hardwoods are actually softer than some softwood (coniferous) species.

harmonic The sinusoidal component of an arc voltage that is a multiple of the fundamental wave frequency.

harsh mixture A concrete mixture lacking mortar or aggregate fines, resulting in an undesirable consistency and workability.

harsh mortar A mortar that is difficult to spread due to an improper measure of materials.

Hartford loop The configuration of a steam boiler's return piping connections serving to equalize the pressure between the supply and return sides of the system, thus preventing water from backing out of the boiler and into the return line.

hashing over Discussing, debating, and revising estimates.

hasp A metal fastening device made up of a staple secured to and protruding from one member, and a hinge with a slotted plate fastened to another member. The slotted plate can be slipped over the staple and then locked with a tapered pin or a padlock.

hasp lock A device permanently secured to the hasp on a door which causes the hasp to be locked as soon as the door is closed. Hasp locks are often used in prisons.

hatbanding A defect in a painting job caused by uneven application. Hatbanding occurs when paint is brushed or rolled on too heavily in an area, or when a roller is used with an excessively long nap.

hatch An opening in a floor or roof of a building, as in a deck of a vessel, having a hinged or completely removable cover. When open, a hatch permits ventilation or the passage of persons or products.

hat channel furring A light gauge metal furring strip used on vertical concrete surfaces to provide for fastening of finish materials.

hatchet A wood-handled tool having a steel head flattened at one end and suitable for striking or driving, and formed at the other end into a wide, sharp blade suitable for chopping. The underpart of the blade may or may not be notched for pulling.

haunch

haunched floor

H-beam

hatchet iron The hatchet-shaped tip of a type of plumber's soldering iron.

haul *See* **haul distance.**

haul distance The distance that any material must be transported.

haul road A crude temporary road built to facilitate the movement of people, equipment, and/or materials along the route of a job.

haunch (1) A bracket built into a wall or column to support a load falling outside the wall or column, such as a hammer brace in a hammer-beam roof. (2) Either side of an arch between the crown, or centerstone, and the springing, or impost. (3) A thickening of a concrete slab to support an additional load, as under a wall.

haunched beam A beam or similar member broadened or thickened near the supports.

haunched floor A floor slab thickened around its perimeter.

haunched tenon A tenon narrower, at least in part, than the wood member from which it is fashioned.

haw-haw *See* **ha ha.**

hawk A flat, thin piece of wood or metal approximately one foot square and having a short, perpendicular handle centered on its underside. A hawk is used by plasterers for holding plaster from the time it is taken from the mixer to the time it is troweled.

hawk snip (hawkbill snips, duck bill snips) Tin snips with curved jaws for cutting along curves.

haydite Heated shale having an expanded cellular structure, making it a suitable lightweight aggregate for concrete.

hazard class A Department of Transportation shipping designation code.

hazard classes Nine classes established by the United Nations to categorize hazardous materials: flammable liquids, flammable solids, explosives, gases, oxidizers, radioactive materials, corrosives, poisonous and infectious substances, and dangerous substances.

hazardous area (1) The part of a building where highly toxic chemicals, poisons, explosives, or highly flammable substances are housed. (2) Any area containing fine dust particles subject to explosion or spontaneous combustion.

hazardous substance Any substance that, by virtue of its composition or capabilities, is likely to be harmful, injurious, or lethal.

hazardous waste A material defined by any of several statutes and regulations, usually characterized by a propensity to cause an adverse health effect to humans.

hazard rating system A system used to score a hazardous or toxic waste site's risk to human health and the environment.

H-bar A steel or aluminum bar used in structural systems, such as suspended ceilings, that has a cross section in the shape of an "H".

H-beam A misused designation for an HP pile section.

H-block A hollow masonry unit having no ends and opposite pairs of unconnected faces. The result is a block shaped like an "H".

H-brick Brick with horizontal perforations.

head (1) The top of almost anything, such as the head of a nail or a window head. (2) In roofing, a tile of normal width but only half the normal length, and used in constructing the eaves course.

header

header course

headlap

(3) The horizontal member across the top of a window or door between the jambs, sometimes offering structural support for construction above it. (4) The measure of the pressure of water, expressed in feet of water. One psi equals 2.31 feet of water.

headache ball (breaker ball) The rounded, heavy, metal or concrete demolition device swung on a cable from the boom of a crane to break through concrete or masonry construction.

head casing The horizontally placed board at the head or top of a door or window opening between the two vertical casings.

header (1) A rectangular masonry unit laid across the thickness of a wall, so as to expose its end(s). (2) A lintel. (3) A member extending horizontally between two joists to support tailpieces. (4) In piping, a chamber, pipe, or conduit having several openings through which it collects or distributes material from other pipes or conduits. *See also* **manifold.** (5) The wood surrounding an area of asphaltic concrete paving.

header block A concrete masonry unit from which part of one face shell has been removed to facilitate bonding with adjacent masonry, such as brick facing.

header bond A bond whose face shows only headers, the center of which is placed directly above the joint of the two adjacent headers below.

header course In masonry, a course comprising only headers.

header joist A beam or timber positioned horizontally between two longer beams so as to support the ends of tailpieces or to accept common joists in order to frame around an opening. *See also* **header (3).**

header pipe A pipe functioning as a central connection for two or more smaller pipes. *See also* **header(4).**

header tile In a masonry-faced wall, a tile having recesses to accept headers.

head flashing In a masonry wall, the flashing over a projection, protrusion, or window opening.

heading (1) In mining, the digging face and its immediate work area in a tunnel, drift, or gallery. (2) The increase of expansion of a localized cross-sectional area of metal bar due to hot-forging. (3) A general classification of a category of data, under which follow more specific classifications. (4) Pieces of lumber from which a keg, or barrel head, is cut. (5) Stock after it has been cut and assembled to form a barrel head.

heading bond *See* **header bond.**

heading course *See* **header course.**

heading joint (1) The joint formed between two pieces of timber connected end-to-end, in a straight line. (2) The joint between two adjacent masonry units in the same course.

head jamb The horizontal member which constitutes the doorhead or top of a door opening.

headlap That portion of a shingle not exposed to the weather, because it is covered by the shingle(s) in the course above it.

head mast The tower portion of a cable excavator, which carries the working lines.

head mold The molding over an opening such as a door or window.

head nailing Nailing shingles near the top instead of at the middle.

headstone

headwall

head piece The capping horizontal piece in a frame of vertical wood members.

head plate *See* **wall plate**.

head pressure The operating pressure in the discharge line of a refrigeration system.

head race A channel through which water is fed to a waterwheel, mill, or turbine.

head room (1) The vertical distance, or space, allowable for passage, as in a room or under a doorway. (2) The space between the top of one's head and the nearest obstacle above it, as inside a vehicle. (3) The unobstructed vertical space between a stair tread and the ceiling or stairs above. (4) The distance between the top of the finished floor to the bottom of the finished ceiling.

headstone Any principal stone in masonry construction, such as the keystone in an arch or the cornerstone of a building.

headwall The wall, usually of concrete or masonry, at the outlet side of a drain or culvert, serving as a retaining wall, as protection against the scouring or undermining of fill, or as a flow-diverting device.

heart The center portion of the cross-section of a log. The term usually refers to heartwood.

heart bond A masonry bond, used in walls too thick for through stones, in which a third header covers the joint of two headers meeting within a wall.

heart check Seasoning checks in the central core of a timber.

heart face The face side of a piece of lumber that is free of sapwood.

hearth The floor of a fireplace and the adjacent area of fireproof material.

hearthstone (1) A large stone used as the floor of a fireplace. (2) Other naturally occurring or synthetic materials used to construct a hearth. (3) Figuratively, the fireside.

hearting The interior of a masonry wall to whose face or faces finishing is subsequently applied.

heartshake A radial crack or split emanating from the center of a log or timber, usually as a result of uncontrolled or improper drying.

heart side The side of a piece of lumber that, if it were still part of the log, would be closest to the heart of the log. In flat grain lumber, it is the side on which the grain is more likely to rise or separate from the piece.

heartwood (heart wood) The core of a tree, which is no longer vital to the life growth of the tree and which is often darker and of a different consistency than the growing sapwood.

heat The form of energy inherent in the motion of atoms or molecules, measured in British thermal units, and transferred automatically (wherever temperature differences exist) from warmer to cooler bodies, areas, or elements by conduction, convection, or radiation.

heat absorbing glass Slightly blue-green tinted plate glass or float glass designed with the capacity to absorb 40% of the infrared solar rays and about 25% of the visible rays that pass through it. Cracking from uneven heating can occur if the glass is not exposed uniformly to sunlight.

heat-affected zone In welding or soldering, an area of metal that has been altered but has not yet melted.

heat balancing (1) An efficient procedure for determining a numerical degree of combustion by totaling all the heat losses, in

heater

heat exchanger

heating plant

percentages, and subtracting the result from 100%. (2) A condition of thermal equilibrium where heat gains equal heat losses.

heat capacity The amount of heat required to increase the temperature of a given mass by one degree. The capacity is arrived at numerically by multiplying the mass by the specific heat.

heated doorway See **air curtain**.

heater (1) A general term including stoves, appliances, and other heat-producing units. (2) A person who heats something, such as a steelworker who heats rivets on a small forge before passing them to the sticker.

heat exchanger A device designed to transfer heat between two physically separated fluids. The fluids are usually separated by the thin walls of tubing.

heat gain (1) The net increase in Btus, caused by heat transmission, within a given space. (2) A piece of resistance material connected between terminals to produce heat electrically. (3) That portion of a heating device, such as a stove or soldering gun, consisting of a wire or other metal piece heated by an electric current.

heating load The number of Btus per hour required to maintain a specified temperature within a given enclosed space.

heating medium The fluid or gas conveying the heat from a source, such as a stove or boiler, to an area or substance being heated. The heating medium may or may not be confined within carriers such as pipes.

heating plant The entire heating system of a building or complex, including either a boiler, piping,

and radiators, or a furnace, ducts, and air outlets.

heating rate The rate of temperature increase in degrees per hour, as in a kiln or autoclave.

heating system The method and its related necessary equipment used in a given heating application, such as a forced hot air system.

heat loss (1) The net decrease in Btus within a given space, by heat transmission through spaces around windows, doors, etc. (2) The loss by conduction, convection, or radiation from a solar collector after its initial absorption.

heat of fusion The amount of heat needed to melt a unit mass of a solid at a specified temperature.

heat of hydration (1) Heat resulting from chemical reactions with water, as in the curing of Portland cement. (2) The thermal difference between dry cement and partially hydrated cement.

heat pump A refrigeration system designed to utilize alternately or simultaneously the heat extracted at a low temperature and the heat rejected at a higher temperature.

heat recovery The extraction of heat from any source not primarily designed to produce heat, such as a chimney or lightbulb.

heat-reflective glass Window glass in which the exterior surface has been treated with a transparent metallic coating to reflect substantial portions of the light and radiant heat striking it.

heat-resistant concrete Concrete immune to disintegration when subjected to constant or cyclic heating to below ceramic-bonding temperature.

heat-resistant paint A paint, usually containing silicon resins, which is

heavy-duty scaffold

used on items such as stoves and radiators because of its stability at high temperatures.

heat sealing The use of heat and pressure to bond plastic sheets or films.

heat sink (1) The substance or environment into which heat is discharged after its removal from a heat source, as by a heat pump. (2) Any medium capable of accepting discharged heat.

heat source (1) Any area, environment, or device which supplies heat. (2) The area from which a refrigeration system removes heat.

heat tracing system A heating system with an externally applied heat source, usually a heating cable, that traces the object to be heated.

heat transfer fluid The liquid substance used to carry heat away from its source to be cooled, usually by another fluid, as in a heat exchanger.

heat transmission The rate at which heat passes through a material by the combination of conduction, convection, and radiation.

heat transmission coefficient Any of several coefficients used to calculate heat transmission by conduction, convection, and radiation through a variety of materials and structures.

heat treatment Subjecting any solid metal or alloy to heating and cooling to produce specific, desired changes in its physical condition or properties.

heave The localized upward bulging of the ground due to expansion or displacement caused by phenomena such as frost or moisture absorption.

heavy concrete High-density concrete. Concrete having a high

unit weight up to 300 pounds per cubic foot, primarily due to the types of aggregate employed and the density of their ultimate incorporation. Such diverse materials as trap rock, barite, magnetite, steel nuts, and bolts can be used as aggregate. The density makes heavy concrete especially suitable for protection from radiation.

heavy construction Construction requiring the use of large machinery, such as cranes or excavators.

heavy-duty scaffold A scaffold constructed to carry a working load not to exceed 75 lbs. per square foot.

heavy-edge reinforcement In highway pavement slabs, reinforcement made of wire fabric with up to four edge wires that are heavier than any of the other longitudinal wires.

heavy joist A timber at least 4″ thick and 8″ wide.

heavy metal A naturally occurring elemental metal with a high molecular weight.

heavy soil A fine-grained soil consisting primarily of clay and silt, which are damper, hence heavier, than sand.

heavy timber (1) A type of construction requiring noncombustible exterior walls with a minimal fire-resistance rating of two hours, solid or laminated interior members, and heavy plank or laminated wood floors and roofs. Also called *mill construction*. (2) Rough or surface pieces with a least dimension of 5″.

heavyweight aggregate Aggregate possessing a high specific gravity, such as barite, magnetite, limonite, ilmenite, iron, and steel, making it suitable for use in heavy concrete.

helical reinforcement

helical staircase
(spiral staircase)

helix

heck (1) A type of door having an upper section that swings independently of its lower section. (2) A gate of latticework.

heel (1) The lower end of a door's hanging stile or of a vertically placed timber, especially if it rests on a support. (2) A socket, floor brace, or similar device for wall-bracing timbers. (3) The bottom inside edge of a footing or a retaining wall. (4) The back end of a carpenter's plane.

heel bead A glazing compound used at the base of the channel after setting a pane but prior to the installation of the removable stop, so as to prohibit leakage past the stop.

heeling The temporary, severely angular planting of trees and shrubs, often in trenches, to facilitate their removal prior to permanent transplanting.

heel post (1) A post or stanchion at the open end of a stall partition. (2) The post, either of a gate or stairway, to which the gate hinges are secured.

heel strap A steel fastening device for connecting a rafter to its tie beam.

height (1) The distance between two points in vertical alignment or from the top to the bottom of any object, space, or enclosure. (2) The vertical distance between the average grade around a building, or the average street curb elevation, and the average level of its roof. (3) The rise of an arch.

height board A measuring device for setting the heights of stair risers.

height of instrument The height of a leveling instrument above the datum being used in the survey.

helical reinforcement Column reinforcement bent in the form of a helix. More commonly called *spiral reinforcement.*

helical rotary compressor (screw-type compressor) A device that compresses gas by trapping it in the space formed by the flutes of meshing screws, thus reducing the gas volume.

helical staircase (spiral staircase) A staircase built in the form of a helix.

helicline A helical ramp, as in a parking garage.

heliograph In surveying, a device to make a distant surveying station easily identifiable by reflecting sunlight in flashes.

heliostat An instrument having an automatically adjusting mirror that follows the apparent movement of the sun and continuously reflects its rays onto a collector.

heliport An airport or landing area specifically for helicopters.

helix (1) A reinforcing rod bent to form a spiral used for reinforcing the circumference of concrete columns. (2) A volute found on a Corinthian or Ionic capital. (3) Any spiral structure, ornament, or form.

helm roof A roof with four steeply-pitched faces rising diagonally from four gables to form a spire where they converge.

helve (1) A tool handle, such as that of an ax, hatchet, or hammer. (2) The handle of a wagon.

hem-bal A combination of western hemlock and balsam fir produced in British Columbia for overseas markets.

hem-fir A species combination used by grading agencies to designate any of various species, such as white fir and western hemlock, having common characteristics. The designation is used for identification and standardization of recommended

herringbone work

high-bay lighting

design values and because some species, in lumber form, cannot be visually distinguished.

hemihydrate Any hydrate having only half a molecule of water for every molecule of compound. The most common hemihydrate is partially hydrated gypsum, or plaster of paris.

hemlock A coniferous North American tree, the wood of which is used in general construction and for pulp.

hemlock spruce (eastern hemlock, eastern spruce) A coniferous tree of eastern North America having soft, coarse wood of uneven texture that is unusable in construction but widely used for pulp.

hemp A natural fiber once widely used in cordage, but now almost totally replaced by synthetic fibers, such as nylon and dacron. Hemp is still laminated to a paper backing to produce a type of wallcovering.

hem-tam A combination of eastern hemlock and tamarack produced in the northeastern United States and eastern Canada.

HEPA-filter *See* **high efficiency particulate air filter**.

HEPA-filtered vacuum A vacuum device fitted with a high efficiency particulate removal system.

hepatoxin A substance that causes liver damage.

herbicide A substance that kills plants on contact.

Herculite Trade name for a type of thick, tempered plate glass, commonly used for doors without framing.

hermaphrodite caliper A tool with two hinged legs used to lay out lines that are parallel with the edges of the workpiece. It can also be used to locate the center of cylindrical shaped workplaces.

herringbone bond In masonry, a type of raking bond in which a zigzag effect is created by laying rows of headers perpendicular to each other.

herringbone drain (chevron drain) A V-shaped drain.

herringbone work In masonry, the zigzag pattern created by laying consecutive courses of masonry units at alternating 45° angles to the general run of the course.

hertz A unit of measurement of frequency equal to one cycle per second.

hesitation set *See* **early stiffening**.

hession *See* **burlap**.

hewn Roughly cut, fabricated, shaped, or dressed.

hex roofing Hexagonally shaped asphalt roofing shingles.

hickey (hicky) (1) A threaded electrical fitting for connecting a light fixture to an outlet box. (2) An apparatus used to bend small pipe, conduit, or reinforcing bar.

hick joint In masonry, a mortar joint cut in any direction to be flush with the face of the wall, resulting in a hairline crack that render the joint no longer watertight.

hiding power The capacity of a paint film to completely obscure the surface, including flaws, to which it is applied.

high-alumina cement *See* **calcium aluminate cement**.

high-bay lighting Usually an industrial lighting system having direct or semidirect luminaires located high above floor or work level.

high-bond bar *See* **deformed bar**.

high-build coating A coating composed of a series of films that are

311

high chair

high hat

high-intensity
discharge lamp

thicker than those normally associated with paints (minimum 5 mls) and thinner than troweled material.

high-calcium lime A type of lime composed primarily of calcium oxide or calcium hydroxide and containing a maximum of 5% magnesium oxide or hydroxide.

high-carbon steel Steel having a carbon content between .6% and 1.5%.

high chair Slang for a heavy, wire, vaguely chair-shaped device used to hold steel reinforcement off the bottom of the slab during the placement of concrete.

high-density concrete See **heavy concrete.**

high-density foam Usually a type of synthetic rubber applied as a liquid foam to the back side of carpeting. When cured, the foam is an integral part of the whole.

high-density overlay A cellulose fiber sheet impregnated with a thermosetting resin and bonded to plywood, rendering a hard, smooth, waterproof, wear-resistant surface for use in concrete formwork and decking.

high-density plywood Plywood manufactured from resin-impregnated veneer and formed with heat at high pressures to render a product having at least twice the density of conventional plywood.

high density polyethylene An extensively polymerized plastic used for pipe. Polyethylene material is highly abrasion and corrosion resistant, and thereby able to handle a wide variety of slurries and abrasive materials as well as nearly all acids, caustics, salt solutions and other corrosive liquids and gases.

high-discharge mixer
See **inclined-axis mixer.**

high-early-strength concrete Concrete containing high-early-strength cement or admixtures causing it to attain a specified strength earlier than regular concrete.

high efficiency particulate air filter (HEPA filter) A high-efficiency (99.9%) dry filter made in an extended surface configuration of deep space folds on submicron glass fiber paper.

high-frequency gluing An extremely rapid gluing process in which high-frequency electronic waves are passed through the wood and glue to cause bonding, as in the construction of laminated beams.

high gloss Descriptive of a substantial degree of luster or of a paint which dries with a lustrous, enamel-like finish.

high hat (1) A recessed lighting fixture that sheds its light vertically downward. (2) A black circular tube attached to the front of a spotlight to contain the stray light around the perimeter of the beam.

high-hazard contents Those building contents that, in a fire, might explode, burn with such vigor as to approximate explosion, produce toxic fumes, or produce other dangerous effects.

high impact polystyrene A plastic with good toughness, moderately high heat resistance, and good resistance to stress cracking.

high-intensity discharge lamp A mercury, high-pressure sodium, or other electric discharge lamp requiring a ballast for starting and for controlling the arc, and in which light is produced by passing an electric current through a contained gas or vapor.

high rib lath

high rise

high-joint pointing Pointing in which a high joint is grooved on each side by scraping along the edges of the brick while the mortar is still soft.

high-lift grouting In masonry, a method of grouting in which each lift is raised at least 12′.

high line A high-tension electric power supply line.

high-magnesium lime The product resulting from calcining dolomitic limestone or dolomite and containing 37%-41% magnesium oxide or hydroxide, as compared to the 5% contained in high-calcium lime.

high-output fluorescent lamp A rapid-start fluorescent lamp with greater flux as a result of its operation on higher current.

high polymer (1) A substance consisting of a large molecule often made of repeat units of low molecular weight. (2) A polymer with a molecular weight greater than 10,000.

high-pressure laminate Laminate manufactured at pressures between 1,200 and 2,000 pounds per square inch during its molding and curing processes. Used in furniture, paneling, and cabinet manufacturing, high pressure laminate is also an ideal material for access flooring around sensitive equipment because of its excellent ability to dissipate static electricity.

high-pressure mercury lamp A mercury vapor lamp designed to function at a partial mercury vapor pressure of about one atmosphere or more (usually 2-4).

high-pressure overlay A plastic laminate consisting of layers of melamine sheet or phenolic-impregnated kraft paper onto which a melamine-impregnated printed pattern sheet and/or a translucent melamine overlay may have been impressed. The laminate is produced at a temperature above 300°F and a pressure of about 400 psi, resulting in a hard, smooth, wear-resistant surface that is often bonded to wood and used in doors and on tabletops.

high pressure side *See* **high side**.

high-pressure sodium lamp A sodium vapor lamp, operating at a partial vapor pressure of 0.1 atmosphere, that produces a wide-spectrum yellow light.

high-pressure steam curing (autoclave curing) The steam curing of products made from cement, sand-lime, concrete, or hydrous calcium silicate in an autoclave at temperatures of 340° to 420°F.

high-pressure steam heating system A steam heating system in which heat is transported from a boiler to a radiator by steam at pressures above 100 psi.

high relief Sculptured relief in which the modeled figures protrude from the background by at least half their thickness.

high rib lath An expanded metal lath used as a backup for wet wall plaster and as formwork for thin concrete slabs.

high rise (1) A building having many stories and serviced by elevators. (2) A building with upper floors higher than fire department aerial ladders, usually ten or more stories. (3) Slang for a traffic-control device consisting of a barricade with stationary flagged arms positioned at 10 o'clock, 12 o'clock, and 2 o'clock and located at each end of a construction zone.

hinge

hinge, electric

hinge, paumelle

high side (high pressure side)
(1) Those parts in a refrigeration system which are exposed to pressure at least as great as condenser pressure. (2) Slang for the *outside* of a pipe bend or conduit bend.

high-silicon bronze A copper alloy made of 96% copper, 3% silicon, and 1% zinc, manganese, aluminum, iron, and/or nickel.

high steel Steel containing a higher than normal amount of carbon.

high-strength bolts Bolts made from high-strength carbon steel or from alloy steel that has been quenched and tempered.

high-strength steel Steel with an inherent high yield point.

high-temperature sprinklers Automatic sprinklers normally set to operate at 212°F (boiling point of water).

high-tensile bolt (high-tension bolt) A bolt made from high-strength steel and tightened to a specified high tension. High-tensile bolts have replaced the use of steel rivets in steel-frame construction.

high transmission glass Glass that transmits an exceptionally high percentage of visible light.

high-velocity duct system A duct system carrying air at more than 2,400 feet per minute.

hinge A flexible piece or a pair of plates or leaves joined by a pin so as to allow swinging motion in a single plane of one of the members to which it is attached, such as a door or gate.

hinge backset The horizontal distance from the edge of a hinge to the face of the door that closes against a rabbet or stop.

hinge, brass A hinge made from or plated with brass, either for ornamental effect or because its imperviousness to corrosion is

desired or required, as in marine applications.

hinge, cabinet Any decorative hinge used in cabinetwork.

hinge, electric A hinge designed to pass electric wires from the frame to the door for use in an electric-controlled lock.

hinge, hospital *See* **hospital hinge**.

hinge jamb The doorjamb to which the hinges are fastened.

hinge joint Any joint allowing action similar to that permitted by a hinge and only a very slight separation between the adjacent members.

hinge, paumelle Usually a contemporary-designed pivot-type door hinge with a single joint.

hinge plate *See* **hinge strap**.

hinge reinforcement A metal plate secured to a door or its frame to supply a base to which a hinge is attached.

hinge, residential A lighter hinge than those designed for commercial and industrial use.

hinge, security (1) A hinge with a pin that cannot be removed. (2) A hinge with a stud in one leaf projecting into the other leaf when the door is closed so the door cannot be moved with the pin removed. (3) *See* **hinge, electric**.

hinge strap (hinge plate) A usually ornamental metal strap fastened to the surface of a door to render the appearance of a strap hinge.

hip (1) The exterior inclining angle created by the junction of the sides of adjacent sloping roofs, excluding the ridge angle. (2) The rafter at this angle. (3) In a truss, the joint at which the upper chord meets an inclined end post.

hip-and-valley roof A roof incorporating both hips and valleys.

hip rafter

hip roof

hip bevel (1) The angle between two adjacent sloping roofs separated only by a hip. (2) The angle at the end of a rafter which allows its conformation to the oblique construction at a hip.

hip capping The top layer of a hip's protective covering.

hip hook *See* **hip iron**.

hip iron (hip hook) A galvanized steel or wrought iron bar or strip secured to the foot of a hip rafter to hold the hip tiles in place.

hip jack In a hip roof, a rafter shorter in length than most of the other rafters used in the same construction, whose upper end is secured to a hip rafter.

hip knob An ornament, such as a finial, at the top hip of a roof or at the apex of a gable.

hip molding The molding on a hip rafter.

hipped end Either of the triangular ends of a hipped roof.

hipped gable (jerkin head) A modified gabled end that is gabled only about halfway to the ridge and then inclines backwards and forms hips where it meets the two principal slopes.

hipped-plate construction *See* **folded-plate construction**.

hip rafter The rafter which, in essence, is the hip of a roof, by virtue of its location at the junction of adjacent inclined planes of a roof.

hip roll The finish covering over the hip of a roof, fashioned from wood, metal, tile, or thin material.

hip roof A roof formed by several adjacent inclining planes, each rising from a different wall of building, and forming hips at their adjacent sloping sides.

hip tile Shaped tile, of material such as clay or concrete, covering the other roof tiles meeting at the hips.

The lowest tile is held by a hip hook. *See also* **hip iron**.

hip vertical The upright tension member in a truss, the lower end of which carries a floor beam, and the upper end of which joins an inclined end post and an upper cord at a hip.

historic preservation Any activity related to the identification, evaluation, protection, and preservation of the built environment, including historic buildings, neighborhoods and landscapes.

hit-and-miss window A two-part window with the lower sash containing movable ventilation panels. One panel slides in front of the other to permit air flow.

H-molding An H-shaped trim piece used in a butt joint assembly. The two channels of the "H" hold the members in place. *See also* **H-runner**.

hoarding A crude, temporary wall or fence on the site of a construction project.

hod In masonry construction, a V-shaped, trough-like container with a pole handle projecting vertically downward from the bottom to allow steadying with one hand while being carried on the shoulder of a laborer (hod carrier) at a construction site. A hod is used to transport bricks or mortar.

hoe (1) An implement similar to a garden hoe but having a larger blade to facilitate the mixing of cement, lime, and sand in a mortar tub at a construction site. (2) A backhoe.

hog (1) In masonry, a course which is not level, usually because the mason's line was incorrectly set and/or pulled. (2) A closer in the middle of a course. (3) A machine to grind waste wood into chips for fuel or other purposes.

hoist

hollow masonry unit
(hollow block)

hollow metal door

hollow metal frame

hog-backed Cambered. The term is often used in reference to a sagging roof.

hogging The sagging of the end extremities of a beam or timber supported only in the middle.

hogsback tile A slightly-less-than-half-round ridge tile.

hoist (1) Any mechanical device for lifting loads. (2) An elevator. (3) The apparatus providing the power drive to a drum, around which cable or rope is wound in lifting or pulling a load. Also called a *winch*. *See also* **chain hoist**.

hoistway *See* **elevator shaft**.

holdback A safety device on a conveyor to prevent reverse motion of the belt automatically.

hold-down bolt *See* **anchor bolt**.

hold-down clip A fastener used in an exposed suspension acoustical ceiling system or in roofing to join and anchor adjacent sections of capping.

holder-up A dolly bar used by an ironworker to back up a rivet while the driver forms a head on it.

hold harmless A clause of indemnification by which an insurance carrier agrees to assume his client's contractual obligation and to assume responsibility in certain situations which otherwise might be the obligation of the other party to the contract.

holding tank A tank used for temporary storage of chemicals or materials being processed.

hole saw *See* **crown saw**.

holiday A small area inadvertently missed during painting or other surfacing applications.

holing A process of punching holes in roofing slates to facilitate nailing during installation.

hollow-backed Descriptive of the unexposed surface of a piece of wood, stone, or other material, intentionally hollowed to render a snug fit against an irregular surface.

hollow bed In masonry, a bed joint in which mortar is placed so as to provide contact only along the edges.

hollow block *See* **hollow masonry unit**.

hollow brick A hollow clay masonry unit in which the net cross-sectional area is at least 60%.

hollow chamfer Any concave chamfer.

hollow-core door A flush door with plywood or hardwood faces secured over a skeletal framework, the interior remaining void or honeycombed.

hollow masonry unit (hollow block) A masonry unit in which the net cross-sectional area is less than 75% of the gross cross-sectional area when compared in any given plane parallel to the bearing surface.

hollow metal (1) Light-gauge metal fabricated into a door, window frame, or similar assembly. (2) Descriptive of an assembly thus produced.

hollow metal door A hollow-core door constructed of channel-reinforced sheet metal. The core may be filled with some type of lightweight material.

hollow metal frame A door frame constructed of sheet metal with reinforcing at hinges and strikes.

hollow partition A partition constructed of hollow blocks or in two separate sections between which a void is left for accepting a sliding door and/or acoustic or thermal insulation.

hood

hook bolt

hooked bar

hollow plane A woodworking plane with a convex blade for fashioning hollow or concave molding.

hollow roll A process of joining two flexible metal roofing sheets in the direction of the roof's maximum slope by lifting them at the joint and bending them there to create a cylindrical roll. The fastening of the roll sometimes requires a fastener or metal clip.

hollow tile *See* **structural clay tile**.

hollow wall A masonry wall designed to provide for airspace inside the wall.

homogeneous Similar in structure, composition, appearance, or texture.

hone A smooth, fine-grained stone against which a tool's cutting edge is worked to achieve a finish edge much sharper than that yielded by the coarser stone used in preliminary sharpening procedures. Usually an oil is used in the process to carry off minute particles of loose stone and metal to prevent them from clogging the pores on the stone's surface.

honed finish The very smooth surface of stone effected by manual or mechanical rubbing.

honeycomb (1) In concrete, a rough, pitted surface resulting from incomplete filling of the concrete against the formwork, often caused by using concrete that is too stiff or by not vibrating it sufficiently after it has been poured. (2) Voids in concrete resulting from the incomplete filling of the voids among the particles of coarse aggregate, often caused by using concrete that is too stiff. (3) In sandwich panel construction or in some hollow-cored doors, resin-impregnated paper is fabricated into a network of small, interconnected, open-ended, tubular hexagons laminated between two face panels to provide internal support.

honeycomb wall A brick wall whose face contains a pattern of openings created by missing units or gaps between stretchers, sometimes used under floors to provide ventilation and/or joist support.

hood (1) A protective cover over an object or opening. (2) A cover, sometimes including a fan, a light fixture, fire extinguishing system, and/or grease filtration/extraction system, and supported, hung, or secured to a wall such as above a cooking stove chimney, or to draw smoke, fumes, and odors away from the area and into a flue. (3) A curved baffle used to minimize scattering and separation of material discharged by a conveyor belt.

hoodmold The interior or exterior drop molding projecting over a door.

hook (1) Any bent or curved device for holding, pulling, catching, or attaching. (2) A terminal bend in a reinforcing bar. (3) Slang term for a *crane*.

hook-and-butt joint A scarf joint between timbers with their ends fashioned to lock together positively and resist tension.

hook bolt A bolt with an unthreaded end bent into an "L" shape.

hooked bar In reinforced concrete, a reinforcing bar which has a hooked end to facilitate its anchorage. *See also* **hook (2)**.

hook knife (hook bill knife, linoleum knife) A knife with a blade in which the cutting edge is bent back toward itself in the same plane, forming a hook shape.

hook strip A narrow board fastened horizontally to a closet wall to provide a surface to which clothes hooks are secured.

horizontal bridging

hoop iron Thin iron strips used to bond masonry, as in a chain bond.

hoop reinforcement Closely-spaced steel rings providing circumferential or lateral reinforcement to prevent buckling of vertical reinforcing bars in concrete columns.

hopper (1) A top-loading, bottom-discharging funnel or storage bin, as for crushed stone or sand. (2) One of a pair of draft barriers at the sides of a hopper light. (3) A toilet bowl, usually funnel-shaped.

hopper frame The bottom-hinged, inward-opening upper sash of a window frame.

hopper head A funnel-shaped enlargement at the top of a downspout where the gutter rainwater is received.

hopper lite (hopper light) (1) A bottom-hinged, inward-opening window sash which allows air to pass above it when open. (2) A side-hinged, inward opening window sash which, when open, allows most of the passing air over its top, but also allows the passage of some air through a narrow opening along its bottom.

hopper window (hospital window) A hopper light with hoppers along the sides to minimize draft. *See also* **hopper (2)**.

horizon (1) The apparent intersection of the earth and sky, as perceived from any given position. (2) The same illusion as it might be portrayed in a perspective drawing.

horizontal Parallel to the plane of the horizon and perpendicular to the direction of gravity.

horizontal application A method of installing gypsum board with its length perpendicular to the framing members.

horizontal auger A drilling machine with a horizontally mounted auger, used to drill blast holes in strip mining.

horizontal boring Soil-boring on the horizontal as opposed to the vertical.

horizontal bracing Any bracing lying in a horizontal plane.

horizontal branch A branch drain accepting waste products delivered to it vertically, by gravity, from one or more similar but usually smaller fixtures, and conducting them horizontally to the primary disposal drain.

horizontal bridging Perpendicular braces between joists or beams placed horizontally to stiffen the system and distribute the load.

horizontal cell tile Structural masonry ceramic tile with the cells installed horizontally in a wall.

horizontal circle In surveying, a device for measuring horizontal angles and consisting of a graduated circle on the lower plate of a transit or telescope.

horizontal control In surveying, a control system in which the relative positions of points has been established by traverse, triangulation, or another system.

horizontal diaphragm A metal plate serving to disperse forces in a horizontal plane.

horizontal distance The distance between points anywhere on a horizontal plane.

horizontal lock A lock in which the primary dimension is horizontal.

horizontal panel A wall panel in which the major dimension is horizontal.

horizontal pipe Any pipe placed or laid horizontally or at an angle to the horizontal of less than 45°.

horizontal sheeting

horizontal shoring

horn

hose bib
(hose cock)

horizontal sheeting In excavation, any type of earth-restraining sheeting placed horizontally between and supported by soldier piles.

horizontal shoring (1) Extendible beams or trusses capable of providing concrete form support over fairly long spans, thus reducing the number of vertical supports required. (2) The collective support provided by several horizontal shores in an application.

horizontal wiring subsystem (gray cable) In a premises distribution system, the cables that connect the satellite closet and an information outlet.

horn (1) The extension beyond a right-angled joint that is part of a stile, jamb, or sill. (2) The stub of a broken branch left on a log.

hornblende A mineral composed of iron, silicate of magnesium, calcium, and aluminum.

horse (1) Framework functioning as a temporary support, such as a sawhorse. (2) In a stair, one of the slanting supports or strings carrying the treads and risers.

horsehead (1) A frame-like device for supporting a pulley back over a pit so that people and materials may be lowered into it and raised out from it. (2) Forepole support when tunneling through soft material.

horse mold A template for a cornice mounted on a wooden frame, and used in plastering to shape a cornice.

horsepower A unit measurement of power or energy in the United States Customary System. Mechanically, a single horsepower represents 550 foot-pounds per second. Electrically, a single horsepower represents 746 watts.

horsepower hour A unit representing the amount of work performed by one horsepower in one hour.

horse scaffold A scaffold for light or medium duty, composed of horses supporting a work platform.

hose bib (hose cock) An outdoor water faucet protruding from a building at about sill height, which is usually threaded to accept a hose connection.

hose cabinet Identifiable cabinet to house folded hose and valve, partially recessed and wall-mounted.

hose cock *See* **hose bib**.

hose coupling A connection between hoses or between a hose and a pipe.

hose station In a fire safety system, a storage rack that includes a valve, hose, and nozzle.

hose stream test A test that measures an assembly's ability to withstand lateral impact from falling debris during a fire endurance period and before active fire suppression efforts begin.

hose thread A standard screw thread (12 threads per inch on 3/4″ pipe) used in garden hose connections.

hospital A building or institution in which 24-hour medical care and services are available and provided.

hospital arm pull A door handle having an extension to allow opening by hooking one's arm around it, thus leaving the hands free.

hospital door A flush door through an opening large enough to allow passage of beds and/or other large equipment.

hospital door hardware The special hardware with which hospital doors are often equipped, such as arm pulls, hinges, terminated stops, latches, and strategically placed protective metal strips or plates.

hospital frame A door frame incorporating terminated stops.

hospital hinge A fast pin hinge furnished with a special tip to eliminate the possibility of injuries caused by the projection of conventional hinge tips.

hospital partition A system of tracks and curtains used to provide a degree of privacy around beds commonly called *hospital cubicles.*

hospital window *See* **hopper window.**

hot-setting adhesive An adhesive whose proper setting necessitates a minimum temperature of 212°F.

hot Slang for a *live* or electrically charged wire or other electrical component.

hot-air furnace A heating unit in which air is warmed and from which the warmed air is drawn into ducts to be carried throughout a building or selected portion thereof.

hotbed A usually small, shallow (rarely larger than 5′ x 10′ x 18″) enclosure, usually of wood and often covered by glass, containing a plant-growing medium heated by electric cables buried in it or by fermenting manure. A hotbed is used to provide a controlled environment favorable to seed germination and maximum seedling and plant growth.

hot-cathode lamp A type of fluorescent, electric discharge lamp in which the electrodes operate at incandescent temperatures and in which the arc and/or circuit elements provide the energy required to maintain the cathodes at incandescence.

hot cement Cement having a high physical temperature resulting from improper cooling after manufacture.

hot chisel A type of chisel used to cut red hot steel. Has a sharp edge usually 2″ to 2-1/4″ wide.

hot deck (hot duct) In a heating system the source of hot air for interior heating.

hot-dip galvanized Descriptive of iron or steel immersed in molten zinc to provide it with a protective coating.

hot driven rivet Any rivet heated just prior to placement.

hot glue A glue requiring heating before being used.

hothouse A greenhouse in which the interior atmosphere is kept very warm.

hot line A telephone line serving two phone sets exclusively. Dialing is not necessary, as the system is designed so that one phone will ring simply by lifting the receiver of the other.

hotmelt A thermoplastic substance almost always heated before being applied as a coating, sealer, or adhesive.

hot mix Paving made of a combination of aggregate uniformly mixed and coated with asphalt cement. To dry the aggregate and obtain sufficient fluidity of asphalt cement for proper mixing and workability, both the aggregate and asphalt must be heated prior to mixing.

hot press The method of producing plywood, laminates, particleboard, or fiberboard, in which adhesion of layers in the panel is accomplished by the use of thermosetting resins and a heat process, under pressure, to cure the guidelines.

hot rolled Descriptive of structural steel members or sections shaped from steel fillets or plates, heated to a plastic state, by passing them through successive pairs of massive steel rollers, each of which serves to bring the product closer to its final, intended shape, such as an angle, channel, or plate.

hot water boiler

hot water supply

housed joint

hot-setting adhesive An adhesive whose proper setting necessitates a minimum temperature of 212°F.

hot spraying The spraying of paints or lacquers in which the viscosity has been reduced by heat rather than by thinners, allowing formation of a thicker coat, requiring less spraying pressure, hence less overspray.

hot surface (1) A highly alkaline or highly absorbent surface. (2) A surface having a high temperature.

hot water boiler Any heating unit in a hot water heating system in which or by which water is heated before being circulated through pipes to radiators or baseboards throughout a building or portion thereof.

hot water heating system One in which hot water is the heating medium. Flow is either gravity or forced circulation.

hot water supply The combination of equipment and its related plumbing supplying domestic hot water.

hot-wire anemometer An anemometer with a velocity-sensing device consisting of a temperature-sensitive wire resistor connected to an electrical circuit and placed directly in the path of the airflow.

hot wires An electrically charged or power-carrying wire.

house connection See **house sewer**.

housed (1) Descriptive of a piece or member fitted into another piece or member that has been modified, as by hollowing, gouging, or chiseling. (2) Enclosed.

housed joint A usually perpendicular joint formed where the full thickness of one member's edge or end is accepted into a corresponding housing, groove, or dado in another member.

house drain In any given plumbing system, as of a house or building, the major lowest horizontal pipe(s) connecting directly to the building sewer just outside the building wall.

house pump In a gravity supply system, the pump that is used to fill the gravity tank that supplies water to the building.

housed stair An entire stair between two walls. See also **box stair**.

housed string See **housed stair, close string**.

house sewer The exterior horizontal extension of a house drain outside the building wall leading to the main sewer, either public or private, and connecting directly to the sewer pipe.

house slant A pipe fitting connecting a house drainage system to a sewer.

Howe truss A truss with vertical and diagonal webs. The members of the vertical web absorb tension while those of the diagonal web absorb compression.

H-pile A type of steel beam driven into the earth by a pile driver.

HP-shape A typical pile section made from hot-rolled steel and used for a specific type of pile in which the size is prefaced by "HP."

H-runner A lightweight, H-shaped, metal member used on its side in a suspended ceiling system, so that its flat top fastens to a channel and the flat bottom fits into the kerfs in the ceiling tiles.

hub (1) The central core of a building, usually the area into which stairs and/or elevators are incorporated, and from which hallways or corridors emanate. (2) The usually strengthened central part of a wheel, gear, propeller, etc. (3) That end of a pipe enlarged into a bill or socket. (4) A rotating piece within a lock, through whose central aperture the

hung ceiling

hung window

hydrant

knob spindle passes to actuate the mechanism. (5) In surveying, a stake designating a theodolite position.

hudee rim A metal frame used to secure a sink in a countertop.

hue (1) The designation of color. (2) Characteristic by which one color differs from another.

human exposure The subjection of a human being, through inhalation, to levels of airborne contaminants, taking into consideration concentration of contamination and duration or exposure.

humidifier A mechanical apparatus to add moisture to the air or other material.

humidistat (hygrostat) The automatic regulating device of a humidifier or dehumidifier which is sensitive to and actuated by changes in humidity.

humidity The water vapor contained in a given space, area, or environment.

humus Soil-like organic substance composed of decayed or decaying organic matter.

hung ceiling A nonstructural ceiling having no bearing on walls, being entirely supported from above by the overhead structural element(s) from which it is suspended.

hungry Descriptive of a surface so absorbent that paint applied to it leaves a thin film revealing every detail of the background.

hung sash A sash hung from its sides by cords or chains, whose other ends are secured to counterweights to allow movement in the vertical plane.

hung slating (1) Slates installed to cover a vertical surface, rather than an inclining or horizontal surface.

(2) Slates secured by wire clips rather than nails.

hung window A window containing one or more hung sashes.

hurricane clips Metal anchor used in pole construction to fasten floor joists to a supporting beam or other structural member.

hurricane protection shield A durable guard that folds out accordion-style to protect windows and sliding glass doors from the high winds of hurricanes.

hybrid The result of breeding plants of two different varieties.

hybrid beam A fabricated beam having flanges made from steel with a specified minimum yield strength different from that of the steel used in the web plate.

hydrant A discharge connection to a water main, usually consisting of an upright pipe having one or more nozzles and controlled by a gate valve.

hydrargyrum medium arc-length iodide lamp (HMI lamp) A mercury-halide discharge lamp that approximates daylight with an approximate color temperature of 5600K.

hydrated lime A dry, relatively stable product derived from slaking quicklime.

hydration (1) Any chemical action occurring as the result of combining a material with water. (2) The chemical reaction that occurs when cement is mixed with water.

hydraulic Characterized or operated by fluid, especially under pressure.

hydraulic cement Cement whose constituents react with water in ways that allow it to set and harden under water.

hydraulic jack

hydraulic lift

hydraulic conductivity The rate at which a fluid flows through a porous substance, such as soil.

hydraulic dredge A floating dredge or pump by which water and soil, sediment, or seabed are pumped, either on board for sifting, as for clams or oysters before they are discharged overboard, or through a series of floating pipes for discharge on shore.

hydraulic ejector A pipe through which the working chamber of a pneumatic caisson is cleansed of sand, mud, or small gravel. *See also* **elephant trunk**.

hydraulic excavator A powered piece of excavating equipment having a hydraulically operated bucket.

hydraulic fill Fill composed of solids and liquid, usually water, and usually delivered by a dredge. After placement, the water eventually drains to leave only the solid fill.

hydraulic friction Resistance to flow, effected by roughness or obstructions in the pipe, channel, or similar conveying device.

hydraulic glue Glue unaffected by water.

hydraulic hydrated lime The dry, hydrated, cementitious product resulting from the process of calcining a limestone containing silica and alumina to a temperature just below incipient fusion. The resultant lime will harden under water.

hydraulic jack A mechanical lifting device incorporating an external lever to which force is applied to cause a small internal piston to pressurize the fluid, usually oil, in a chamber. The pressure exerts force on a larger piston, causing it to move vertically upward and raise the bearing plate above it.

hydraulic jump An abrupt increase in the depth of a fluid flowing in a channel as its velocity is slowed and kinetic energy is converted to potential energy.

hydraulic lift An elevator car or platform moved by a piston, or plunger, powered by a pressurized fluid, usually oil, in a cylinder.

hydraulic lime Lime composed of at least ten silicates and which will set and harden under water.

hydraulic mortar A mortar capable of hardening under water, hence used for foundations or underwater masonry construction.

hydraulic pile driving The employment of hydraulic force to drive sheet piles.

hydraulic pump The device causing the fluid to be forced through a hydraulic system.

hydraulic radius The ratio of the cross-sectional area of a stream of fluid within a conduit to the wetted perimeter of that conduit.

hydraulic splitter A concrete- or rock-cracking mechanism incorporating a wedge inserted into a predrilled hole and then expanded by hydraulic power to cause the cracking.

hydraulic spraying Paint spraying accomplished by high fluid pressure rather than by compressed air.

hydraulic test Employing pressurized water to test a plumbing line for pressure integrity.

hydrocarbons Class of chemical compounds consisting of hydrogen and carbon.

hydrochlorofluorocarbons (HCFCs) Compounds comprised of hydrogen, chlorine, fluorine, and carbon atoms. They do not persist to the same extent as chloroflourocarbons, and so do not pose as great a threat to the ozone layer.

hydrofluorocarbons (HFCs) Compounds comprised of hydrogen, fluorine, and carbon atoms. Because they do not contain chlorine, they are not involved in ozone depletion.

hydrogeologic testing A means of determining the structure and characteristics of subsurface soils and rocks, and the way water flows through them.

hydronic A term pertaining to water used for heating or cooling systems.

hydrophobic cement A treated cement with a reduced tendency to absorb moisture.

hydro-seeding The liquid application of a combined mixture of grass seed, fertilizer, pesticide, and a moisture-retaining binder sprayed under pressure over an area requiring lawn or grass cover.

hydrostatic head The pressure in a fluid, expressed as the height of a column of fluid, which will provide an equal pressure at the base of the column.

hydrostatic pressure Pressure exerted by water, or equivalent to that exerted on a surface by water in a column of specific height.

hydrostatic strength The capability of a pipe to resist internal pressure buildup, measured under specific conditions.

hydrostone A plaster of high strength and density suitable for casting and ornamental use.

hygrometer An instrument used for measuring the moisture content of air.

hygrometric expansion The expansion of a material as it takes on moisture.

hygroscopic Having the tendency to absorb and retain moisture from the air.

hygrostat *See* **humidistat**.

Hypalon® caulking *See* **Hypalon® roofing**.

Hypalon® roofing An elastomeric roof covering available commercially in liquid, sheet, or putty-like (caulking) consistency in several different colors. Hypalon roofing is more resistant to thermal movement and weathering than neoprene.

hypotenuse The side of a right triangle that faces the right angle.

I

I ABBREVIATIONS

The abbreviations listed below are those most commonly used in the construction industry. Alternative forms (usually nonstandard) are shown in parentheses.

I moment of inertia

IARC International Agency for Research on Cancer

IBI Intelligent Buildings Institute

IC interrupting capacity, ironclad, incense cedar

ICBO International Conference of Building Officials

ICC Interstate Commerce Commission, International Code Council

ID inside dimension, inside diameter, identification

IDHA International District Heating Association.

IDLH immediately dangerous to life and health

IEEE Institute of Electrical and Electronics Engineers, Inc.

IES Illuminating Engineering Society

IF inside frosted

IFB Invitation for Bids

Ihp indicated horsepower

IMC intermediate metal conduit

imp imperfect

in. inch

inc included, including, incorporated, increase, incoming

incan incandescent

incl included, including

Ins insulate, insurance

inst installation

insul insulation, insulate

int intake, interior, internal

IP iron pipe

IPS iron pipe size

IPT iron pipe threaded

IR inside radius at the start, or initiation, of an activity

IRS Internal Revenue Service

ISO Insurance Services Office, International Organization for Standardization

IWP Idaho white pine

I DEFINITIONS

I-beam

illuminated sign

i In the Critical Path Method, the symbol which represents the event at the start, or initiation, of an activity.

IARC Monograph A brief summary of the carcinogenic effects of a particular substance as determined by the International Agency for Cancer Research.

I-beam A structural member of rolled steel whose cross section resembles the capital letter "I."

ice dam An accumulation of ice and snow at the eaves of a sloping roof.

ichnography The graphic, geometrically scaled representation of a horizontal section.

idler A gear or wheel used to impart a reversal of direction or rotation of a shaft.

igneous rock A rock formed by the solidification of molten materials.

illuminated sign A sign that is illuminated by an internal or external source and used to mark a path of emergency exit.

illumination The luminous flux density on a surface exposed to incident light.

immersion heater A thermostatically controlled electric resistance heating device that is submerged in the fluid it heats.

impact The stress to which a structure is subjected from vibrating, falling, or shifting loads. Impact is a percentage of the structure's live load.

impact crusher A primary type crushing machine that utilizes a series of hammers to break up materials.

impact damages Losses that affect the overall performance and cost of the contract work, such as delay to the project, lost labor productivity, and acceleration. Distinguished from direct damages.

impact factor A number by which a static load is multiplied to approximate that load applied dynamically.

impact force Force resulting from the collision of two or more objects.

impact insulation class (IIC) A test method that gives single number ratings for the transmission of impact sound through various types of construction. A high rating number indicates better noise resistance.

impact isolation (1) The use, in buildings, of insulating material and structures that reduce the transmission of impact noise. (2) The degree of effective reduction of impact noise transmission accomplished by the structures and materials designed and used specifically for that purpose.

impact load The dynamic effect upon a stationary or mobile body as imparted by the short, forcible contact of another moving body.

impact noise The sound created when a body strikes a surface.

impact noise rating The single-number rating used to evaluate and compare the effectiveness of assemblies and floor/ceiling constructions in isolating impact noise. The higher the number, the greater the effectiveness in suppressing noise.

impact resistance The resistance of a member or assembly to dynamic loading.

impact wrench

in-and-out bond

impact test Any of a number of dynamic tests, usually a load striking a specimen in a specified manner, used to estimate the resistance of a material to shock.

impact transmission The transfer of sound waves through walls, floors, and other structures.

impact wrench An electric or pneumatic wrench with adjustable torque that is supplied to a nut or bolt in short, rapid impulses.

impedance Measured in ohms, the total opposition or resistance to the flow of current when voltage is applied to an alternating-current electric circuit.

impeller (1) The vaned member of a rotary pump that employs centrifugal force to convey fluids from intake to discharge. (2) A related device used to force pressurized gas in a given direction. (3) In ventilation, a device that rotates to move air.

impending slough The consistency of shotcrete such that no more water can be added without causing it to sag or flow after placement.

impermeable Descriptive of a material that does not allow the passage of liquid.

impervious Highly resistant to penetration by water.

impervious soil A very fine-grained soil, such as clay or compacted loam, that is so resistant to water penetration that slow capillary creep is the only means by which water can enter.

implied contract A contract not created by explicit agreement between the parties, but inferred by law from their acts or conduct.

imposed load Any load that a structure must bear, exclusive of dead load.

impost The often distinctively decorated uppermost member of a column, pillar, etc., that supports an end of an arch.

impoundment A water storage area or tank.

impregnated wood (impreg) Wood with cell walls impregnated with a synthetic resin to reduce shrinking and swelling.

impregnation (1) The penetration of a (timber) product under pressure with an oil, mineral, or chemical solution, usually for preservation. (2) Treating soil with a liquid waterproofing agent to reduce leakage.

improved land Land where water, sewers, sidewalks, and other basic facilities have been installed prior to residential or industrial development.

improvement A physical change or addition made on a property so as to increase its value or enhance its appearance.

inactive leaf (inactive door) In a pair of doors, the stationary leaf to which the strike plate is secured. It is usually bolted at the head and sill.

in-and-out bond A bond in which masonry units are arranged so that headers and stretchers alternate in successive courses. This arrangement is most often used when forming a corner.

inband A header stone used in a reveal.

inbark (bark pocket) Ingrown bark enclosed in the wood of a tree by growth and subsequently exposed by manufacture.

inbond A masonry bond across the entire thickness of a wall, and usually consisting of headers or bondstones.

inclination

increaser

incandescence The emission of visible light as a consequence of being heated.

incandescent lamp A lamp in which electricity heats a (tungsten) filament to incandescence, producing light.

incandescent lighting fixture A complete luminaire, comprising an incandescent lamp, socket, reflector, and often a diffusing apparatus.

incense cedar *Libocedrus decurrens*. A tree, indigenous to the area from northern Oregon to southern California, whose aromatic, durable wood is used in pencil manufacture and for many of the same applications as western red cedar. Incense cedar is highly resistant to moisture.

inch A measure of length equal to 1/12 of a foot (2.54 centimeters).

inch of water A unit of pressure which is equal to the pressure exerted by a one-inch high column of liquid water at a temperature of 39.2°F (4 °C).

inch-pounds (1) A unit of work derived by multiplying the force in pounds by the distance in inches through which it acts. (2) A unit of energy that will perform an equivalent amount of work.

inch stuff Descriptive of building materials having a nominal thickness of 1″, but in reality somewhat less (usually 7/8″).

incident radiation Solar energy, both direct and diffuse, upon its arrival at the surface of a solar collector or other surface.

incinerator A type of furnace in which combustible solid, semisolid, or gaseous wastes are burned.

incipient decay The early stage of decay in timber in which the disintegration has not proceeded far enough to affect the strength or hardness.

incising (1) Cutting in, carving, or engraving, usually for decorative purposes. (2) Cutting slits into the surface of a piece of wood prior to preservative treatment to improve absorption.

inclination (1) The deviation of a surface or line from the vertical or horizontal. (2) The angle produced by the deviation of a surface or line from the vertical or horizontal.

incline A slope, slant, or gradient.

inclined-axis mixer A truck-mounted concrete mixer. A revolving drum rotates around an axis that is inclined from the horizontal axis of the truck's chassis.

inclusive coverage A provision in an insurance policy for potential loss where specific types or origins of loss are included by description under the coverage provided.

incombustible (non-combustible) Incapable of burning.

incorporator A person who joins with others to form a corporation. The successors of those who actually sign the papers.

increaser In plumbing, a coupling with one end larger than the other. Generally the small end has outside threads and the large end has inside threads.

incrustation Mineral, chemical, or other deposits left in a pipe, vessel, or other equipment by the liquids that they convey.

indemnification An obligation contractually assumed or legally imposed on one party to protect another against loss or damage from stated liabilities. *See also* **insurance**.

indent In masonry, a gap left in a course by the omission of a masonry

indented bar

unit. An indent is used for bonding future masonry.

indented bar A deformed concrete reinforcing bar having indentations for improving the bond between the steel and the concrete.

indented bolt A type of anchor bolt comprising a plain bar into which indentations have been forged to increase its grip in concrete or grout.

indented joint A type of butt joint where a notched fish plate is fitted to notches in the timbers and the entire assembly is fastened with bolts.

indented wire Wire whose surface has been provided with indentations to increase its bond when used as concrete reinforcement or for pretensioning tendons.

indenture (1) An official agreement between a bond issuer and his bond holders. (2) Any deed or contract between two or more parties. (3) A document in duplicate, triplicate, etc., whose edges have been irregularly indented so that the copies can later be matched to corroborate authenticity.

index mark In surveying, a mark used as a sighting reference to take measurements.

index of plasticity The numerically expressed difference between the liquid and plastic limits (of a cohesive material).

Indiana limestone A durable, easily sawn, planed, carved, and lathed limestone quarried in, and exported from, the state of Indiana.

indicated horsepower The horsepower, determined by an indicator gauge, that is developed in the cylinders exclusive of losses sustained due to engine friction.

indicator bolt A type of door bolt used primarily on doors of bathrooms and toilets that indicates

occupancy when locked, and vacancy when unlocked.

indicator button An occupancy-indicating mechanism used mostly on the locks of hotel room doors.

indicator pile A pile driven to evaluate future pile.

indicator pollutant An easily measured pollutant that may or may not be hazardous in normally occuring concentrations, but which may indicate the presence of a more dangerous pollutant. (e.g., NO_3 levels resulting from sewerage infiltration to ground H_2O).

indicator valve A valve which includes some device indicating its open or closed condition.

indigenous Descriptive of any product, substance, growth, outcropping, characteristic, etc., that is geographically native to the area where it occurs, as opposed to having been introduced there.

indirect expense Overhead or other indirect costs incurred in achieving project completion, but not applicable to any specific task.

indirect gain/loss In passive solar design, heat gain or loss that occurs at the surface of a thermal storage wall. Typical materials include brick, concrete, and water.

indirect heating (1) A method of heating areas which are removed from the source of heat by steam, hot air, etc. (2) Central heating.

indirect lighting Lighting achieved by directing the light emitted from a luminaire toward a ceiling, wall, or other reflecting surface, rather than directly at the area to be illuminated.

indirect luminaire A luminaire that distributes 90-100% of its emitted light upward.

indirect system

induced draft boiler

indirect system A system of heating, air-conditioning, or refrigeration whereby the heating or cooling of an area is not accomplished directly. Rather, a fluid is heated or cooled, then circulated to the area requiring the conditioning, or used to heat or cool air which then is circulated to achieve the same end.

indirect waste pipe A waste pipe that discharges through an air break or air gap into a trapped receptacle or fixture, rather than directly into the building drainage system.

indirect water heater A water heater system that increases the temperature of the water via a remote heat exchanger.

individual vent A pipe which vents a fixture drain and which is connected to the main vent system at some point higher than the fixture.

indoor air quality (IAQ) The quality and general healthfulness of air within a building, as affected by temperature, humidity, and airborne contaminants.

indoor/outdoor carpet A carpet in which all the components have been designed or treated so as to remain essentially unaffected by water, sun, temperature, etc.

induced draft A process in which air is drawn through the cooling tower into the fan.

induced draft boiler A boiler that uses a fan at its discharge end to pull air through the burner and oiler, and transfer the exhaust products into the atmosphere through a chimney.

induced draft fan *See* **induced draft boiler**.

induced draft water-cooling tower A water-cooling tower incorporating one or more fans in the path of the saturated air stream leaving the tower.

inductance The process that occurs when one conductor is placed next to another carrying AC current. The ever-changing magnetic field that results will induce a current in the first conductor.

induction The entrainment of air in a room by the strong flow of primary air from an air outlet.

induction air terminal units A factory assembly consisting of a cooling coil and/or heating coil that receives preconditioned air under pressure that is mixed with recirculated air by the induction process.

induction brazing A brazing process whereby required heat is derived from the resistance of the work to an induced electric current.

induction heating A technique used to heat-treat completed welds in piping. The heat is generated by the use of induction coils around the piping.

induction motor A motor which operates on alternating current. Its primary winding is usually on the starter, which is connected to the electric power source. Its secondary winding, usually on the rotor, conveys the induced current.

induction soldering A soldering process whereby required heat is derived from the resistance of the work to an induced electric current.

induction welding A type of welding in which coalescence is achieved by heat derived from the work's resistance to an induced electric current, either with or without applied pressure.

inductive loads Loads whose voltage and current are out-of-phase. Most loads in modern electrical distribution systems are inductive.

infilling

industrial appearance grade
Structural glue-laminated timber produced for use where appearance is not a primary concern.

industrial hygienist In asbestos abatement, a professional hired by the building owner to sample and monitor the air, and for other safety-related tasks.

industrial tubular door A tubular steel door with locked seams and welded corners.

industrial waste Liquid waste from manufacturing, processing, or other industrial operations, which might include chemicals, but not rainwater or human waste.

industry specification A type of specification prepared by technical or industry associations that is approved for use by federal agencies.

industry standard Readily available information in the form of published specifications, technical reports and disclosures, test procedures and results, codes and other technical information and data. Such data should be verifiable and professionally endorsed, with general acceptance and proven use by the construction industry.

industry standard specification A published specification meeting the general definition of an *industry standard*.

inelastic behavior Deformation of a material that remains even after the force which caused it has been relieved or removed.

inert (1) Chemically inactive. (2) Resistant to motion or action.

inertia The tendency of a body at rest to remain at rest, or of a body in motion to remain in motion in a straight line unless directly influenced by an external force.

inertia block Usually a concrete block supported on some sort of resilient material and used as a base for heavy, vibrating mechanical equipment, such as pumps and forms, to reduce the transmission of vibration to the building structure.

inertial guidance system (1) A guidance system in which a predetermined course is used to heat-treat completed welds in piping. The heat is generated by the use of induction coils around the piping. (2) A guidance system in which a predetermined course is maintained by a computer utilizing gyroscopic and accelerometer data.

inert pigment A pigment or extender that does not react chemically with the materials with which it is being mixed.

infilling Fill material providing insulation, stiffness, and/or fire resistance. It is used in buildings to fill the void areas, within a frame, between structural members.

infiltration The leakage of air into a building through the small spaces around windows, doors, etc., caused by pressure differences between indoor and outdoor air.

inflammable Easily ignitable and highly combustible. The preferred term is *flammable*. *See also* **combustible**.

inflatable gasket A type of gasket whose effective seal results from inflation by compressed air.

inflatable structure An airtight structure of impervious fabric, supported from within by slightly greater than atmospheric pressure generated by fans.

inflection The bending of a straight line from concave to convex, or the converse.

inflecture point

inflecture point That point in a flexural structural member where reversal of curvature occurs and the bending moment is zero.

influence line A technique, useful in solving problems that involve moving loads, which indicates the effect at a given section of a unit load imposed at any point on the structure.

information stake A stake used on-site to convey surveying measurements to an excavation crew.

infrared Descriptive of invisible electromagnetic radiation which, when produced by a light source, is usually undesirable, except in certain industrial applications, such as drying and baking finished surfaces.

infrared drying Drying which is accomplished or accelerated by infrared lamps so as to decrease drying time.

infrared heater A source of heat-producing wavelengths, longer than visible light, which do not heat the air through which they pass, but only those objects in the line of sight.

infrared lamp A type of incandescent lamp that often has a red glass bulb to reduce its radiated visible light. Such a lamp emits more radiant power in the infrared region than does a standard incandescent lamp, and it has a lower filament temperature, which contributes to its longer life.

infrared photography Photography in which the film used is more sensitive to infrared rays than to visible light rays.

ingle (1) A fireplace. (2) A hearth.

inglenook A nook or part of a corner near a chimney or fireplace, often having built-in seats.

ingot A large mass of molten metal cast in a vertical mold but requiring further processing before becoming a finished product.

ingot iron An iron, primarily used in sheets, containing very small amounts of carbon, manganese, and other impurities.

inhibiting pigment Rust-, corrosion-, or mildew-resistant pigments, such as lead and zinc chromate or red lead, which are added to coatings to color it and to provide it with their protective qualities.

inhibitor Oxidants added to coatings to retard drying, skinning, and other undesirable effects or conditions.

initial drying shrinkage The difference between the length of a concrete specimen when first poured and the final, permanent length of the same specimen after it has dried, usually expressed as a percentage of the initial moist length.

initial graphics exchange specification A neutral file specification that allows for the transfer of data between CAD/CAM systems. Focuses primarily on 2D & 3D graphical information.

initial prestress The stress or force applied to prestressed concrete at the time of its stressing.

initial set That point in the setting of a concrete and water mixture when it has attained a certain degree of stiffness, but is not yet finally set. Initial set is usually expressed in terms of the time required for a cement paste to stiffen enough to resist a pre-established degree of penetration by a weighted test needle.

initial setting time The time it takes for a fresh mixture of cement paste, mortar, or concrete to attain *initial set*.

inserts

inside casing

initial stress The stress existing in a prestressed concrete member prior to the occurrence of any loss of stress.

initiating circuit A circuit in a fire safety system that contains sensors to detect a fire condition.

injecter The mechanism in a diesel engine that sprays the fuel into the combustion chamber.

injection burner A gas burner in which gas and air for combustion are forced into the burner by a gas jet.

injection molding The process of pouring heat-softened plastic into a cool mold to create a desired shape.

inlaid work Small pieces of material, different from that of the background, which are laid or set into a surface so as to produce a decorative pattern.

inlay (1) To decorate with inlaid work. (2) An ornamental design cut into the surface of linoleum, wood, or metal, and filled with a material of different color, often by gluing.

inlet (1) The surface connection to a closed drain or pipe. (2) The upstream end of any structure through which there is a flow.

inlet well An opening at the surface of the ground through which runoff water enters the drainage system.

inner court An outdoor area which is open above, but surrounded on four sides by the exterior walls of a building or structure.

inorganic material Substances of mineral composition, not carbon compounds of animals or vegetables.

input/output device Any piece of equipment used to communicate with the central host computer in a building automation system, for example, a telephone, keyboard, or annunciator command terminal.

input system A ventilating system utilizing a fan to draw air from a roof into rooms through ducts. An air cleaner or filter and an automatic air heater are usually included.

insecticide A substance toxic to insects.

insert (1) A patch, plug, or shim used to replace a defect in a plywood veneer. (2) A unit of hardware embedded in concrete or masonry to provide a means for attaching something. (3) A nonstructural patch in laminated timber, made for the sake of appearance.

insert grille A grille which is fabricated separately from the door and installed in the field.

inset staple To staple the paper flange of bat insulation to the inside portion of a stud or rafter.

inside-angle tool In masonry and plastering, a float designed especially for shaping inside (internal) angles.

inside caliper A caliper with pointed legs turned outward which is used for measuring inside diameters.

inside casing The interior trim around the frame of a door or window, which might consist of dressed boards, molding, and trim.

inside corner molding Concave or canted molding used to cover the joint at the internal angle of two intersecting surfaces.

inside glazing External glazing that is placed from within the frame or from inside the building.

inside lining (1) Inside casing. (2) Any part of a cased frame that has its face toward the building or structure.

inside micrometer An instrument used to accurately measure the inside diameters of relatively small cylinders or pipes.

inside stop Usually a beaded or molded strip of wood secured to the

inside thread

inspection eye

inspection manhole

casing along the inside edge of the inner sash to hold it in place and restrict its movement to the vertical plane.

inside thread The threaded inner surface of a pipe or fitting that accepts the outside threads of another pipe or fitting.

inside trim Any trim used inside a building. *See also* **inside casing**.

in situ (1) In place, as natural, undisturbed soil. (2) Descriptive of work accomplished on the site rather than in prefabrication elsewhere, as in cast-in-place concrete.

in situ biodegration A process used to degrade organic wastes through biological processes in the soil or groundwater.

in situ concrete Concrete placed where it will harden to become an integral part of the structure, as opposed to precast concrete.

in situ soil test Soil testing performed in a borehole, tunnel, or trial pit, as opposed to being performed elsewhere on a sample which has been removed.

in situ vitrification A process that electronically melts contaminated soil at temperatures well above the soil's initial melting range.

insoluble residue The part of an aggregate or cement that does not dissolve in diluted hydrochloric acid.

inspection (1) A visual survey of construction work–either completed or in progress–to ensure that it complies with the contract documents. (2) Examination of the work by a public official, owner's representative, or others.

inspection eye A pipe fitting equipped with a plug which can be removed to allow examination or cleaning of the pipe run.

inspection fitting *See* **inspection eye**.

inspection junction *See* **cleanout**.

inspection list A list of incomplete or incorrect work items that must be addressed by the contractor before final payment can be issued.

inspection manhole A covered shaft leading from the outside down to a sewer or duct, so constructed as to allow a person to enter it from the surface.

inspector A person authorized and/or assigned to perform a detailed examination of any or all portions of the work and/or materials. *See also* **building inspector, owner's inspector,** *and* **resident engineer**.

instancing A buzz word used in CADD technology to describe the copying of a part of a drawing for reuse somewhere else.

instant lock (instant locker) (1) An automatic lock that is actuated by the closing of the door. (2) A time lock or chromatic lock working on the same principle.

instant-start fluorescent lamp An electric discharge lamp that is started without the preheating of electrodes, but rather by application of a high enough voltage to eject electrons from the electrodes by field emission, initiate electron flow through the lamp, ionize the gases, and initiate a discharge through the lamp.

instructions to bidders A document, part of the bidding requirements, usually prepared by the design professional. Instructions to bidders set forth specific instructions to candidate constructors on procedures, expectations and disclaimers of the owner, and other necessary information for the preparation of proposals for consideration by the owner for a competitive bid.

insulating board

insulation batt

insulate To provide with special features and/or materials which afford protection against sound, moisture, heat, or heat loss.

insulated cavity wall A hollow masonry wall with a cavity containing some type of insulation.

insulated conductor An electrical conductor that is contained within an NEC-approved, non-conductive material.

insulated flange A coupling that interrupts the electrical transmission between two metal pipes.

insulated metal roofing A type of roofing panel made from mineral fiber, insular glass, foamed plastic, etc., and faced with light-gauge flexible metal.

insulating board A thin, lightweight, rigid or semi-rigid board, usually of processed plant fibers, which offers little structural strength but does provide thermal insulation. It is usually applied under a finish material.

insulating cement A putty-like mixture of hydraulic-setting cement or other bonding material and a loose-fill insulation. Used to fill voids, joints, cracks, etc.

insulating concrete Concrete possessing low thermal conductivity and used as thermal insulation.

insulating fiberboard Building board manufactured from processed plant fiber in a variety of sizes, thicknesses, densities, and strengths. *See also* **insulating board**.

insulating formboard Insulation board that serves as a permanent form for poured-in-place gypsum or lightweight concrete roof decks.

insulating glass Glazing comprising two or more panes of glass, between which there exist(s) a hermetically sealed airspace(s), joined around the edges.

insulating oil The oil contained and used within the enclosure of a transformer, switch, or other electric device for cooling and insulation.

insulating plasterboard Gypsum board with aluminum foil backing, which provides resistance to heat flow and moisture.

insulating resistance The measure of a material's ability to inhibit electric current flow.

insulating strip The soft, resilient material used in an expansion joint.

insulating varnish A varnish that is applied to wires or electric circuits as an insulator.

insulation (1) Material used to reduce the effects of heat, cold, or sound. (2) Any material, device, or technique that provides protection against fire or the transfer of electricity, heat, cold, moisture, or sound. (3) Thermal insulation is a material used for covering pipes, ducts, vessels, etc., to effect a reduction of heat loss or gain.

insulation batt Flexible insulation of loosely matted plant or glass fibers faced on one or both sides with kraft paper or aluminum foil and usually available in specifically sized sections.

insulation blanket Usually composed of the same materials and the same widths and thicknesses as batts, but is available in rolls.

insulation density The number of fibers per square inch in an insulation product. Denser insulation brings higher resistance to heat, cold and sound.

insulation lath Gypsum lath with an aluminum foil backing which provides resistance to heat flow and moisture.

insulation resistance The resistance of an insulator to a directly applied current.

insulator An insulating device designed and used to physically support a conductor and electrically separate it from other conductors or objects.

insurance A contract, typically referred to as an insurance policy, in which the insurer, in return for the premium stated in the policy, agrees to pay the insured up to the limits specified in the policy for losses or damages incurred by the insured.

insurance, bodily injury A form of insurance that covers physical injury, sickness, or disease sustained by a person. *See also* **personal injury**.

insurance, builder's risk A specialized form of property insurance that provides coverage for loss or damage to the work during the course of construction. *See also* **property insurance**.

insurance, care, custody, and control The term used to describe a standard exclusion in liability insurance policies. Under this exclusion, the liability insurance does not apply to damage to property over which the insured is for any purpose exercising physical control.

insurance, certificate of A document, issued by an authorized representative of an insurance company, stating the types, amounts, and effective dates of insurance in force for a designated insured.

insurance, completed operations Liability insurance coverage for injuries to persons or damage to property occurring (1) when all operations under the contract have been completed or abandoned; or (2) when all operations at one project site are completed; or (3) when the portion of the work out of which the injury or damage arises has been put to its intended use by the person or organization for whom that portion of the work was done. Completed operations insurance does not apply to damage to the completed work itself.

insurance, comprehensive general liability A broad form of liability insurance covering claims for bodily injury and property damage that combines, under one policy, coverage for all liability exposures, (except as specifically excluded), on a blanket basis and automatically covers new and unknown hazards that may develop. Comprehensive general liability insurance automatically includes contractual liability coverage for certain types of contracts. Products liability, completed operations liability, and broader contractual liability coverages are available on an optional basis. This policy may also be written to include automobile liability.

insurance, contractor's liability Insurance purchased and maintained by the contractor to protect the contractor from specified claims which may arise out of, or result from, the contractor's operations under the contract, whether such operations are by the contractor or by any subcontractor, or by anyone directly or indirectly employed by any of them, or by anyone for whose acts any of them may be liable.

insurance, employer's liability Insurance protection for the employer against claims by employees or employees' dependents for damages which arise out of injuries or diseases sustained in the course of their work, and which are based on common law negligence rather than on liability under workers' compensation acts.

337

insurance, errors and omissions
See **professional liability insurance**.

insurance, extended coverage An endorsement to a property insurance policy which extends the perils covered to include windstorm, hail, riot, civil commotion, explosion (except steam boiler), aircraft, vehicles, and smoke. *See also* **property insurance**.

insurance, liability Insurance which protects the insured against liability on account of injury to the person or property of another. *See also* **completed operations insurance, comprehensive general liability insurance, contractor's liability insurance, employer's liability insurance, owner's liability insurance, professional liability insurance, property damage insurance, public liability insurance,** *and* **special hazards insurance**.

insurance, loss of use Insurance protecting against financial loss during the time required to repair or replace property damaged or destroyed by an insured peril.

insurance, owner's liability
Insurance to protect the owner against claims arising out of the operations performed for the owner by the contractor and arising out of the owner's general supervision.

insurance, personal injury Bodily injury, and also injury or damage to the character or reputation of a person. Personal injury insurance includes coverage for injuries or damage to others caused by specified actions of the insured, such as false arrest, malicious prosecution, willful detention or imprisonment, libel, slander, defamation of character, wrongful eviction, invasion of privacy, or wrongful entry. *See also* **bodily injury**.

insurance, personal liability
See **personal injury**.

insurance policy A contract which provides insurance against specific loss. *See also* **insurance**.

insurance, professional liability
Insurance coverage for the insured professional's legal liability for claims for damages sustained by others allegedly as a result of negligent acts, errors, or omissions in the performance of professional services.

insurance, property Coverage for loss or damage to the work at the site caused by the perils of fire, lightning, extended coverage perils, vandalism and malicious mischief, and additional perils (as otherwise provided or requested). *See also* **builder's risk insurance, extended coverage insurance,** *and* **special hazards insurance**.

insurance, property damage
Insurance covering liability of the insured for claims for injury to or destruction of tangible property, including loss of use resulting therefrom, but usually not including coverage for injury to, or destruction of, property which is in the care, custody, and control of the insured. *See also* **care, custody, and control**.

insurance, public liability Insurance covering liability of the insured for negligent acts resulting in bodily injury, disease, or death of persons other than employees of the insured, and/or property damage. *See also* **comprehensive general liability insurance** *and* **contractor's liability insurance**.

insurance, special hazards Insurance coverage for damage caused by additional perils or risks to be included in the property insurance (at the request of the contractor, or at the option of the owner). Examples

integral frame

integral lock

interceptor

often included are sprinkler leakage, collapse, water damage, and coverage for materials in transit to the site or stored off the site. *See also* **property insurance**.

insurance, Workers' Compensation (workmen's compensation insurance) Insurance covering the liability of an employer to employees for compensation and other benefits required by workers' compensation laws with respect to injury, sickness, disease, or death arising from their employment.

insurance, work in progress *See* **insurance, builder's risk**.

intake The opening or device through which a gas or fluid enters a system.

intake belt course In building, a belt course whose molded face is cut so as to function as an intake between the varying thicknesses of two walls.

intarsia Mosaic accomplished with small pieces of wood inlaid in contrasting colors.

integral frame A metal door frame whose trim, backhands, rabbets, and stops are all fabricated from one piece of metal for each jamb and for each head.

integral lock A type of mortise lock in which the cylinder is contained in the knob.

integral waterproofing The waterproofing of concrete achieved by the addition of a suitable admixture.

integrated building system A building designed to efficiently use climatic resources for heating, cooling, lighting, and electric power generation.

integrated ceiling A suspended ceiling system in which the grid and individual acoustical, illumination, and air-handling elements are combined to form a single, integrated system.

intelligent building (smart building) A building that contains some degree of automation, such as centralized control over HVAC systems, fire safety and security access systems, and telecommunication systems.

Intelligent Buildings Institute A nonprofit professional organization formed in 1986 to promote the *intelligent building* industry through market information, government advocacy, regulatory action, and general education.

intercept In surveying, the length of the staff visible between the two stadia hairs of a transit's telescope.

intercepting drain A ditch, trench, or similar depression surrounding a subdrainage pipe and filled with a pervious filter material.

intercepting sewer A sewer into which empty the dry-weather flows from several branch sewers or outlets, and which may also receive a certain amount of storm water.

interceptor An apparatus which functions to trap, remove, and/or separate harmful, hazardous, or otherwise undesirable material from the normal waste which passes through it, allowing acceptable waste and sewage to discharge by gravity to the disposal terminal.

intercom A general term for an internal communication system, such as one employing telephones, or microphones and loudspeakers which function without a central switchboard.

interconnection Any arrangement of pipes whereby water may flow from one system to another as determined by the pressure differential between the two systems.

interior span

interior trim

interest expense A contractor's cost of borrowing funds or use of equity capital.

interface A common boundary shared by two adjacent parts of a system.

interface strength *See* **bond**.

interfenestration The area between windows in a facade consisting primarily of the windows and their ornamentation.

interference (1) Any obstruction that prevents planned or normal usage or operations. (2) Cooling tower effluent that enters the intake of an adjacent tower.

interior casing *See* **inside casing**.

interior door A door installed inside a building, as in a partition or wall, having two interior sides.

interior finish The interior exposed surfaces of a building, such as wood, plaster, and brick, or applied materials such as paint and wallpaper.

interior glazed Descriptive of glass that has been placed from inside a building.

interior hung scaffold A scaffold that is suspended from a ceiling or roof structure rather than being supported from below.

interior lot A lot bounded by a street either at its front or back, but not on either of its sides.

interior plywood Plywood in which the laminating glue is adversely affected by moisture; hence, it should be restricted to indoor or interior applications.

interior span An uninterrupted beam or slab that is continuous with neighboring spans.

interior stop In glazing, a removable bead or molding strip that serves to hold a light or panel in position when the stop is on the interior of

the building, as opposed to an exterior stop.

interior trim (1) Any trim, but especially that around door and window casings, baseboards, stairs, and on the inside of a building. (2) Inside finish.

interior wall A wall having two interior faces and existing entirely within the exterior walls.

interlaced fencing (interwoven fencing) Fencing that is constructed from very thin, flat boards which are woven together.

interlocked (1) Firmly joined. (2) Closely united. (3) Placed in close relative proximity, or in a specific relationship with another or others.

interlocking Software program in which an event or set of events triggers another event or sequence of events. For example, a temperature rise above a set point that activates a fan.

interlocking joint (1) In ashlar or other stonework, a joint accomplished by joggles in the joining units. (2) In sheet metal, a joint between two parts whose preformed edges engage to form a continuous locked splice.

interlocking tile Single-lap tiles designed so that a groove along the edge of one tile accommodates an edge of an adjacent tile in the same course.

interlock wiring Control wiring permitting a secondary sequence to be enabled by a primary action.

intermediate floor beam In floor framing, any other floor beams that are positioned between the end floor beams.

intermediate rafter *See* **common rafter**.

intermediate rail

intermediate rail In a door, any rail, one of which might be a lock rail, between the top and bottom rails.

intermediate sight In leveling, a staff reading that is neither a back sight nor a foresight.

intermediate stiffener On a beam or girder, any stiffener between the end stiffeners.

intermittent-flame-exposure test An ASTM test of roof covering that involves exposing a sample of the roof material to a gas flame for a specified interval.

intermittent weld A weld whose continuity is interrupted by recurrent unwelded spaces.

internal dormer A vertical window in a sloped roof that is set in a depression in the main roof. An internal dormer is the inverse of a standard dormer.

internal glazing Glazing placed in interior partitions or walls (different from inside glazing). *See also* **borrowed light**.

internal partition trap A plumbing trap that relies on an internal partition of some form, rather than the water used in a standard trap, for a seal.

internal pressure The pressure within a building. Dependent on outside conditions, such as wind velocity, and the number and location of openings in the building.

internal quality block A masonry block which is structurally sufficient, but whose inferior surfaces make it suitable only for concealed work.

internal thread *See* **inside thread**.

internal treatment The treatment of water by feeding chemicals into the boiler rather than into the preheated water itself.

internal vibration Rapid agitation of freshly mixed or placed concrete performed by mechanical vibrators inserted at strategic locations. *See also* **concrete vibration**.

intern architect An apprentice architect who works under the direction of registered architects.

interpier sheeting (interpile sheeting) Usually wooden sheeting placed horizontally between underpinning pits or piles, used in applications not requiring continuous underpinning.

interrogatories A formal method of obtaining information relevant to a lawsuit from a party by submitting written questions that must be answered under oath within a certain time period.

interrupting rating A designation given to an electrical device based on the highest current at rated voltage the device is designed to interrupt under standard testing conditions.

interstate commerce The buying, selling, or exchange of goods or property across state lines.

interstitial condensation Condensation that forms within an element of a building, such as within a wall.

intertie An intermediate member used horizontally between studs to strengthen them, especially at door heads or other places between floor heads.

intrados The under surface or interior curve of an arch or vault.

intumescent Descriptive of a material, like a paint or caulk, that forms a passive fire protection system when applied to another material, like steel or pipe. The intumescent material remains inactive until subjected to heat, when it swells and chars and creates a fire barrier.

invert

inventory control (1) A management plan designed to minimize the number and quantity of hazardous substances on a construction project. (2) A managerial process to control the quantity of items in storage.

invert The lowest inside surface or floor of a pipe, drain, sewer, culvert, or manhole.

invert block A wedge-shaped, hollow, masonry tile incorporated into the invert of a masonry sewer.

inverted asphalt emulsion A type of emulsified asphalt, anionic or cationic, in which asphalt (usually in liquid form) is the continuous phase, and whose discontinuous phase comprises minute globules of water in relatively small amounts.

inverted ballast A lamp ballast that operates on direct current.

inverted crown The fall or pitch from the sides to the center of a road, driveway, etc.

invert elevation The elevation of an invert (lowest inside point) of pipe or sewer at a given location in reference to a bench mark.

invisible hinge A door hinge designed, fabricated, and installed with no visible or exposed parts when the door is in the closed position.

invitation to bid A written notice of an owner's intention to receive competitive bids for a construction project wherein a select group of candidate constructors are invited to submit proposals.

invited bidders (preferred bid list) A group of bidders chosen by the owner to submit bids for a project.

involute (1) The locus of a fixed point on a string as the string is unwound from a fixed plane curve, such as a circle (the Spiral of Archimedes), generally used to generate cams. (2) Spirally curved, intricate, complex.

ion An atom with one or more electrons missing.

ion exchange The process of either gaining or losing electrons from compounds in a chemical exchange.

Ionic order An order of architecture characterized by a column that has spiral volutes at its capital.

ionization detector A device that indicates the presence of specific gaseous compounds in air by subjecting the compound to ultraviolet light or hydrogen flame, and recording the number of ions created.

Iowa curb A concrete curb that is relatively flat and mountable. Poured as part of the paved surface of a roadway.

iron A lustrous, malleable, magnetic, magnetizable, metallic element mined from the earth's crust as ore in hematite, magnetite, and lemonite. These minerals are heated together to 3,000°F in a blast furnace to produce pig iron, which emerges from the furnace as 95% iron, 4% carbon, and 1% other elements.

iron, cast An iron alloy usually containing 2-1/2% to 4% carbon and silicon, possessing high compressive but low tensile strength, and which, in its molten state, is poured into sand molds to produce castings.

iron-cement A type of cement that contains cast-iron boring or filings, sal-ammoniac sulfur, and other additives, and used for joining or repairing cast-iron parts.

iron, core The steel bar under the wooden handrail connecting the tops of balusters in a stair.

ironwork

irregular coursed rubble

island base kitchen cabinet

iron, malleable Cast iron that has undergone an annealing process to reduce its brittleness.

iron oxide A primary ingredient in a whole range of inorganic pigments. *See also* **rust (ferric oxide).**

ironwork A comprehensive term for iron fashioned to be used decoratively or ornamentally, as opposed to structurally.

iron, wrought The purest form of iron metal, which is fibrous, corrosion-resistant, easily forged or welded, and used in a wide variety of applications, including water pipes, rivets, stay bolts, and water tank plates.

irregular coursed rubble Rubble walls constructed in courses of various depths.

irregular pitch A type of roof whose slope does not have a constant rise per foot throughout.

irrigation (1) The process or system, and its related equipment, by which water is transported and supplied to otherwise dry land. (2) The use of water thus supplied for its intended purpose.

irritant A substance that causes discomfort, such as tearing, choking, vomiting, rashes, reddening of the skin, itching, or other topical responses.

island base kitchen cabinet A freestanding kitchen cabinet having exposed sides and a counter or work surface.

isobar A line drawn on a map to indicate the limits of equal contaminant or pressure concentrations.

isodomum An ancient, very regular masonry pattern with units of uniform length and height placed to form continuous horizontal joints, with vertical joints centered above

the blocks forming discontinuous straight lines.

isolated solar gain Passive solar heating in which heat to be used on one area is collected in another area.

isolated spread footing A footing that transmits a load from columns to the supporting soil. If the soil is weak or the column loads heavy, isolated spread footings must be larger.

isolating membrane An underlay.

isolating switch A switch that isolates a circuit from its power source.

isolation Sound privacy effected by reducing direct sound paths.

isolation joint A joint positioned so as to separate concrete from adjacent surfaces or into individual structural elements which are not in direct physical contact, such as an expansion joint.

isolator The device on a circuit that can be removed to break the circuit in the absence of flowing current.

isometric drawing A type of projection drawing showing three dimensions. The horizontal planes generally appear at 30° from the standard horizontal axis, while the vertical lines are drawn parallel to the actual vertical axis.

isotherm A line on a graph or map joining points of equal temperature.

isothermal Descriptive of a process or procedure that occurs at a constant temperature.

isotropic Exhibiting the same properties in all directions.

Italian tiling (pan-and-roll roofing tile) A roof covering with two different kinds of single-lap tiles, one being the curved and tapered overtile, and the other being the flanged, tapered, tray-shaped undertile.

item   A subdivision of the breakdown, smaller than a category, but larger than an element.

itemize   To list or state each item separately, as in an itemized bid.

ivorywood   A South American wood used mostly for cabinet and lathe work. White to pale yellow-brown in color, sometimes even with a tinge of green, it is heavy, hard, and strong, yet lacks durability.

Izod impact testing   A type of impact test, used to estimate the resistance of a material, in which a falling or swinging pendulum delivers energy in a single impact.

J

J ABBREVIATIONS

The abbreviations listed below are those most commonly used in the construction industry. Alternative forms (usually nonstandard) are shown in parentheses.

J & P joists and planks

jct junction

J.I.C. Joint Industrial Council

jour journeyman

JP jet propulsion

jt, jnt joint

jtd jointed

jsts joists

junc junction

J

DEFINITIONS

jack

jacket

jackhammer

j A symbol used to describe the event at the head of an activity arrow in a CPM schedule.

jack (1) A portable mechanism for moving loads short distances by means of force applied with a lever, screw, hydraulic press, or air pressure, as in applying the prestressing force to the tendons, or making small adjustments in the elevations of forms or form support, as in lift slab or slipform operations. (2) In electricity, a female connecting device or socket to which circuit wires are attached and into which a plug may be inserted (as on a telephone switchboard).

jack arch An arch whose intrados is flat or almost flat, instead of being curved or rounded.

jack beam A beam that is used to support another beam or truss, thereby eliminating the need for a column.

jack boom A boom that supports sheaves between the hoist and the main boom in a dredge or pull shovel.

jacked pile A pile which is forced into the ground by jacking against the building above it.

jacket (1) A covering, either of cloth or metal, applied to exposed heating pipes or ducts, to exposed or unexposed casing pipes, or over the insulation of such pipes. (2) A watertight outer housing around a pipe or vessel, the space between being occupied by a fluid for heating, cooling, or maintaining a specific temperature. (3) In wire and cable, the outer sheath or casing that protects the individual wires within from the elements and provides additional insulation properties.

jacketing The surrounding of a pipe or vessel by a confined bath or stream of fluid for temperature control or heat absorption. *See also* **jacket (2)**.

jackhammer A hand-held, pneumatically powered device that hammers and rotates a bit or chisel. A jackhammer is used for drilling rock or breaking up concrete, asphalt paving, etc.

jacking In plumbing, a method of providing drainage by forcing a pipe into a precut opening using horizontal jacks.

jacking device A mechanism used to stress the tendons for prestressed concrete, or to raise a vertical slipform. *See also* **jack**.

jacking dice Blocks, usually of concrete-filled steel cylinders or pipes, used as temporary fillers during the jacking operations, as in foundation work.

jacking force The temporary force applied to tendons by a jacking device to produce the tension in prestressing tendons.

jacking plate A steel bearing plate used during jacking operations to transmit the load of the jack to the pile.

jacking stress The maximum stress that occurs during the stressing of a precast concrete tendon.

jackknife (1) A tractor and trailer arriving at such an angle with each other that the tractor cannot move forward. (2) The unintentional raising of a boom on a derrick, as caused by the load.

jack lagging The timber-bearing members employed in building the forms for arches or for other unusual shapes.

jack shore

Jacob's ladder

jamb anchor

jackleg An outrigger post.

jack plane A medium-sized carpenter's plane used to do the coarse work on a piece of timber, such as truing up the edges in preparation for finish planing.

jack rafter Shortened rafter generally found in hip roofs. A hip jack rafter spans from the plate to the hip rafter. A hip-valley cripple jack spans between a hip rafter and a valley rafter. A valley jack spans from a valley rafter to the ridgeboard.

jack rib Any curved jack rafter used in a framed arch or small dome roof.

jack screw A screw-operated mechanical device equipped with a load-bearing plate and used for lifting or leveling heavy loads.

jack shaft A short drive shaft, as between a clutch and a transmission.

jack shore An adjustable, usually telescopic, single-post metal shore.

jack timber In framework, a timber that is shorter than the rest, because it has been intercepted by another member.

jack truss (1) A roof truss which is smaller than the main trusses, such as a truss in the end slopes of a hip roof. (2) A truss that provides for the elimination of a column support by supporting a beam or another truss.

Jacob's ladder A marine ladder of rope or chain with wooden or metal rungs.

jagger A toothed, stone-dressing chisel.

jalousie A window shutter or blind having stationary or adjustable slats angled so as to permit ventilation and provide shade and even some privacy, while simultaneously preventing the entrance of rain.

jalousie window See **louvered window**.

jamb An exposed upright member on each side of a window frame, door frame, or door lining. In a window, these jambs outside the frame are called *reveals*.

jamb anchor A metal anchoring device that secures the frame to the wall when inserted in the rear of the jamb of a door frame or window frame.

jamb block A concrete masonry unit that is slotted at one end and used as an opening to receive a window or door frame.

jamb depth The face-to-face depth of a door frame.

jamb horn In a window frame, that portion of the jamb which extends beyond the sill or head jamb.

jamb lining A wood facing at the inside edge of a window jamb for the purpose of increasing its width.

jamb post The vertical timber that serves as a jamb at the side of an opening.

jamb shaft A small shaft having a capital and a base, positioned against or incorporated into the jamb of a door or window (sometimes called *esconsons* when employed in the inside axis of a window jamb). Often seen in medieval architecture.

jambstone A stone that forms the jamb of a door.

jammer See **gemel**.

japan (1) A dark-colored, short-oil varnish used to provide a hard, glossy surface. (2) A type of resin varnish often used in paints as a drying agent.

japanned Painted with a black japan and then baked.

jaw One of a pair of opposing members of a device used for

jib boom

jigsaw

holding, crushing, or squeezing an object, as the jaws of a vise or a pair of pliers.

jaw crusher A rock-crushing device comprising one fixed inclined jaw and one movable inclined jaw. It is used to reduce rock to specific sizes.

J channel A plastic or metal channel, shaped like a "J," that is used to support building trim material.

jedding ax A stone mason's hand tool with two faces, one flat and the other pointed.

jemmy (jimmy) A short (less than 18″) pinch bar or crowbar, both ends of which are curved.

jenny (1) A machine that cleans surfaces by emitting a steady or pulsating jet of steam. (2) A British term for a gin block.

jerkinhead *See* **hipped gable**.

jerrybuilt Constructed in a shoddy or flimsy manner.

jesting beam Any beam employed strictly for decorative or ornamental, as opposed to structural, purposes.

jet (1) A high-velocity, pressurized stream of fluid or mixture of fluid and air, as emitted from a nozzle or other small orifice. (2) The nozzle or orifice that shapes the stream. (3) An orifice or other feature of a toilet that starts the siphon action by directing water into the trapway.

jetted pile A pile whose sinking has been accomplished by jetting.

jetting The process by which piles or well points are sunk with the aid of high pressure water or air. Jetting is the option usually employed in locations where nearby buildings might be adversely affected during pile-driving operations.

jetty (1) Any portion of a building that protrudes beyond the part immediately below it, such as a bay window or the second story of a garrison house. (2) A dike-like structure, usually of rock, that extends from a shore into water, usually to provide some kind of protection, but sometimes to induce scouring or bank-building. (3) A deck on pilings constructed for landing at the edge of a body of water.

jewel An ornamental glass protrusion in a leaded window.

jib (1) The hoisting arm of a crane or derrick, whose outer end is equipped with a pulley, over which the hoisting cable passes. (2) The arm that holds a drifter on a rock drill.

jib boom The hinged extension attached to the upper end of a cranes boom. Its purpose is to extend the reach of the crane or the height of the boom.

jib crane (1) A crane having a swinging jib, as opposed to an overhead traveling crane, which does not. (2) A cantilevered boom or horizontal beam with hoist and trolley capable of picking up loads in all or part of a radius around the column to which it is attached.

jib door A door constructed and installed so as to be flush with its surrounding wall and whose unobtrusiveness is furthered by the lack of hardware on its interior face.

jig A device that facilitates the fabrication or final assembly of parts by holding or guiding them in such a way as to insure their proper mechanical and relative alignment. A jig is especially useful in assuring that duplicate pieces are identical.

jigsaw An electrically-powered, table-mounted saw having a small, thin, narrow, vertically reciprocating blade which is capable of cutting a tighter radius than a band saw.

jimmer A hinge composed of two leaves that are permanently joined with a fixed pin. *See also* **gemel**.

jimmy (1) Slang for a General Motors Corporation motor, engine, or truck. (2) *See* **jemmy**.

jitterbug A grate tamper used to cause sand and cement grout to rise to the surface of wet concrete during placement of slabs. May be motorized or hand operated.

job (job site) (1) Term commonly used to indicate the location of a construction project. (2) An entire construction project or any component of a construction project.

jobber (1) A person reasonably knowledgeable and somewhat skilled in most of the more common construction operations, such as carpentry, masonry, or plumbing. (2) In construction, a jack-of-all-trades.

job condition Those portions of the contract documents that define the rights and responsibilities of the contracting parties and of others involved in the work. The conditions of the contract include general conditions, supplementary conditions, and other conditions.

job-made Made or constructed on the construction site, as a job-made ladder.

job site The area within the defined boundaries of a project.

jog An offset, such as an intentional change in direction or other unintentional irregularity in a line or surface.

joggle (1) A notch or protrusion in one piece or member that is fitted to a protrusion or notch in another piece to prevent slipping between the members. (2) A protrusion or shoulder that receives the thrust of a brace. (3) A horn or stub tenon at the end of a mortised piece to strengthen it and prevent its lateral movement. (4) The enlarged portion of a post by which a strut is supported. *See also* **key**.

joggle beam A built-up beam in which joggles are used to secure the components in their respective positions.

joggle joint In masonry or stonework, a joint that employs joggles in the adjacent members so as to prevent their lateral movement. *See also* **joggle**.

joggle post (1) A post constructed of two or more joggled timbers. (2) A king post whose lower end has been joggled to support the feet of struts. *See also* **joggle**.

joggle truss A roof truss comprising a single, centrally positioned post whose upper end is joggled to connect with the overhead chord, and whose lower end is supported by two braces that angle upward to join the ends of the chord.

joggle work Masonry or stonework in which the units of vertically adjacent courses are joggled on at least one side, resulting in a joggled horizontal joint.

joiner (1) A primarily British term for a craftsman who constructs joints in woodwork. (2) A carpenter who deals primarily with joining fitted parts, such as of a door.

joiner's chisel (paring chisel) A long-handled woodworking chisel whose cutting is accomplished without the aid of a striking tool, but by hand force only.

joiner's gauge *See* **marking gauge**.

joiner's hammer A hammer whose head has a flat end for striking and a clawed end for pulling nails.

joints

joinery (1) Woodworking that deals more with joining and finishing, such as that required by doors, cabinets, or trim. (2) A European designation for quality grades of lumber suitable for cabinetry, millwork, or interior trim.

joint (1) The point, area, position, or condition at which two or more things are jointed. (2) The space, however small, where two surfaces meet. (3) The mortar-filled space between adjacent masonry units. (4) The place where separate but adjacent timbers are connected, as by nails or screws, or by mortises and tenons, glue, etc.

joint bolt (handrail bolt) A threaded metal rod or bolt having a nut at each end, used to bring two ends of a handrail together, and also used in joinery to bolt two mating surfaces together, as in a butt joint.

joint box A cast-iron box constructed around a joint between the ends of two electric cables. The cables' protective lead (or other) sheathing is secured by bolted clamps on the exterior of the box which itself may be filled with insulation.

joint compound (joint cement) A premixed finishing material for embedding joint tape, and filling and finishing gypsum panel joints, corner bead, trim and fasteners. Sanded to a smooth finish.

joint efficiency The ratio of the strength of a welded joint to the strength of the base metal, expressed as a percentage.

jointer (joiner plane) (1) A power-driven woodworking tool or long, hand-operated, bench plane used to square the edges of lumber or panels. (2) An offset metal tool used to smooth or indent mortar joints in masonry. (3) A metal tool about 6″ long and 2″ to 4″ wide,

having interchangeable depth-regulating bits and used for cutting joints in fresh concrete. (4) In masonry, a bent strip of iron used in a wall to strengthen a joint.

jointer plane *See* **jointer.**

joint fastener A small strip of corrugated steel, having one sharpened edge and used to fasten (usually corner) pieces in rough carpentry. A joint fastener is positioned vertically, sharp edge down, over the joining edges of the two pieces, and then hammered down into them.

joint filler (1) A powder that is mixed with water and used to treat joints, as in plasterboard construction. (2) Any putty-like material similarly used. (3) A compressible strip of resilient material used between precast concrete units to provide for expansion and/or contraction.

jointing (1) Finishing the surface of mortar joints, as between units or courses, by tooling before the mortar has hardened. (2) The finishing, as by machining, of a squared, flat surface on one face or edge of a piece of wood. (3) The initial operation in sharpening a cutting tool, consisting of filing or grinding the teeth or knives to the desired cutting circle.

jointing compound (1) In plumbing, any material, such as paste, paint, or iron cement, used to ensure a tight seal at the joints of iron or steel pipes.

jointing material A sheet of rubber, asbestos, or synthetic compressible material from which gaskets or washers may be cut for use in joints of flanged pipes, pumps, etc.

jointing rule In masonry, a long straightedge used for drawing lines and pointing.

351

joint reinforcing

joist

joist anchor

joist hanger

joint knife A hand tool with a wide flexible blade used to apply and smooth joint compound to drywall.

jointless flooring Although often laid or poured without joints, magnesite or epoxy-based flooring is often best laid with joints which allow for shrinkage.

joint reinforcement Any steel reinforcement used in or on mortar joints, such as reinforcing bars or steel wire.

joint rule A metal rule having one end formed at a 45° angle. It is used in plastering to form and shape miters at the joints of cornice moldings.

joint runner In plumbing, an incombustible packing material, such as pouring rope, used around the outside of a pipe joint to contain the molten lead which is poured in the bell of a joint.

joint sealant An impervious substance used to fill joints or cracks in concrete or mortar, or to exclude water and solid matter from any joints.

joint tape Paper, paper-faced cotton tape, or plastic mesh fabric, used with mastic or plaster to cover the joints between adjacent sheets of wallboard. *See also* **fusible tape**.

joint tenancy A form of ownership in which two or more people own equal shares of the same real property. Each co-owner, called a *joint tenant*, has the right to occupy and use all of the property and, therefore, must share with the other owners. The most important distinguishing feature of a joint tenancy is the right of survivorship. This means that when one of the owners dies, his or her share of ownership is split among the surviving owners, thereby increasing the surviving owners' proportionate shares.

joint venture (contractual joint venture) The joining together of two or more parties to form an entity with the legal characteristics of a partnership, to achieve a specific objective.

joist (1) A piece of lumber two or four inches thick and six or more inches wide, used horizontally as a support for a ceiling or floor. Also, such a support made from steel, aluminum, or other material. *See also* **random lengths**. (2) Parallel beams of lumber, concrete, or steel used to support floor and ceiling systems.

joist anchor A beam, wall anchor, or metal tie used to anchor beams or joists to a wall. An example of a joist anchor is a metal strip with one end embedded in a concrete or masonry wall and the other end secured to a joist or rafter, so as to provide a lateral tie between the wall and a floor or roof. This type of anchor acts in shear and in tension. *See also* **beam anchor**.

joist bridging Lateral braces inserted between joists to evenly distribute loads.

joist chair A wire device used to support reinforcing steel in the formwork of a concrete beam, ensuring that the steel bars touch neither the bottom nor sides of the forms.

joist hanger A metal angle or strap used to support and fix the ends of wood joists or rafters to beams or girders. This type of anchor acts in shear and in tension.

joule The metric unit used to measure heat, work, and energy. One joule is the amount of work done or energy expended by a force of 1 newton acting through a distance of 1 meter.

jumbo brick

junction boxes

journal That section of a shaft or axle that rotates within a load-supporting bearing.

journeyman The second or intermediate level of development of proficiency in a particular trade or skill. As related to building construction, a journeyman's license, earned by a combination of education, supervised experience, and examination, is required in many areas for those employed as intermediate level mechanics in certain trades (e.g., plumbing, mechanical, and electrical work).

judas A small hole or opening in a door, as in a prison door, used for inspection or surveillance.

judgment A judicial decision rendered as a result of a course of action in a court of law.

jumbo (1) A mobile support for concrete forms. (2) An assortment of tunnel-drilling devices mounted on a carriage.

jumbo brick (1) A brick manufactured larger than standard size, measuring 8″ x 4″ x 4″, including mortar joints. (2) A brick accidentally larger than standard size.

jumper (1) The short length of wire or cable used to make a usually temporary electrical connection within, between, or around circuits and/or their related equipment. (2) A steel bar used manually as a drilling or boring tool. (3) A stretcher covering two or more vertical joints in snecked or square rubble. (4) The inverted mushroom-shaped component of a domestic water tap, on which the washer fits.

jumper wire A short length of conductor used to link two cross-connect termination points of a circuit, or to bypass a circuit.

junction box A metal box in which splices in conductors or joints in runs of raceways or cable are protectively enclosed, and which is equipped with an easy access cover.

junction chamber That section in a sewer system where the flow from one or more sewers joins or converges into a main sewer.

junction manhole A manhole located over the convergence of two or more sewers.

junior beam Lightweight, structural steel sections rolled to full I-beam shape.

junior channel An obsolete term for a lightweight structural channel.

jurisdiction The authority of a judicial or administrative forum to hear and resolve disputes.

jurisdictional dispute An argument between or among labor unions over which entity should perform certain work.

jut Any protruding part of a building or structure, such as a jut window. *See also* **jetty (1)**.

jute A plant fiber, from which a strong, durable yarn is made and used mostly for carpet backing, burlap, and rope.

jut window Any window that projects from an exterior wall, such as a bow window.

K

K ABBREVIATIONS

The abbreviations listed below are those most commonly used in the construction industry. Alternative forms (usually nonstandard) are shown in parentheses.

k kilo, knot

K Kalium

Ka cathode

kc kilocycle

kcal kilocalorie

kc/s kilocycles per second

KD kiln-dried

KDN knocked down

kg keg, kilogram

KIT. kitchen

kl kiloliter

KLF kips per lineal foot

km kilometer

kmps kilometers per second

kn knot

Kr krypton

kv kilovolt

kvar kilovar

kw kilowatt

kwhr/kwh kilowatt-hour

kalamein door

kalamein door A fire door whose solid wood core is usually covered with galvanized sheet metal.

kalsomine *See* **calcimine**.

kaolin A usually white mineral found in rock formations, composed primarily of low-iron hydrous aluminum silicate, and used as a basic ingredient in the manufacture of white cement and as a filler or coating for paper and textiles.

keel molding A molding having two ogee curves that meet at a point or fillet, forming a shape that resembles that of a ship's keel.

Keene's cement (1) A white cementitious material manufactured from gypsum which has been burned at a high temperature and ground to a fine powder. Alum is added to accelerate the set. The resulting plaster is hard and strong and accepts and maintains a high polish, hence it is used as finishing plaster. (2) Anhydrous calcined gypsum.

keeper *See* **strike plate**.

keeping the gauge In masonry, maintaining the proper spacing of courses of brick.

keeping the perpends In masonry, the accurate laying of the units so that the perpends (end joints) in alternating courses line up vertically.

kellastone A rough stucco finish.

kelly ball A round-bottomed metal plunger that is dropped into fresh concrete, the degree of penetration indicating the consistency of the concrete.

kerf (1) A saw-cut in wood, stone, etc., which is usually performed crosswise and usually not completely through the member. Cuts are usually made to allow for bending.

kerf

(2) A groove cut into the edges of acoustical tiles to accommodate the splines or supporting elements in a suspended acoustical ceiling system.

kerfed beam A beam in which several kerfs have been cut so as to permit bending.

kerfing The process of cutting grooves or notches (called *kerfs*) across a board to make it easier to bend. Kerfs are cut to about two-thirds the thickness of the board.

kettle (1) The storage container for asphalt to be used for "hot mopped" roof construction. (2) Any open vessel used to contain paint or in which glue is melted.

kevel An axe whose head has a flat face at one end and a pointed peen at the other. A kevel is used by stonemasons for removing angular projections or diminishing surfaces.

key (1) The removable actuating device of a lock. (2) A wedge of wood or metal inserted in a joint to limit movement. (3) A *keystone*. (4) A wedge or pin through the protruding part of a projecting tenon to secure its hold. (5) A back piece on a board to prevent warping. (6) The tapered last board in a sequence of floorboards, which, when driven into place, serves to hold the others in place. (7) The roughened underside of veneer or other similar material intended to aid in bonding. (8) In plastering, that portion of cementitious material which is forced into the openings of the backing lath. (9) A *joggle*. (10) A *keyway*. (11) A *cotter*. (12) A small, usually squared piece which simultaneously

keystone

keyway

fits into the keyways or grooves of a rotating shaft and the pulley.

key brick A brick whose proper fit in an arch is attained by tapering it toward one end.

key course A course of adjacent keystones as might be used in an archway too deep for a single keystone, or in the crown of a barrel vault.

key drop A pivoting cover of a keyhole, usually attached to the escutcheon above the hole and covering it when at rest.

keyed Fastened or fixed in position in a notch or other recess, as forms become keyed into the concrete they support.

keyed beam (1) A lap-jointed beam with joggles or slots cut into both components. Keys are driven into the joggles or slots to increase the bending strength of the joint. (2) A compound beam whose adjacent layers possess mating grooves to help resist horizontal shearing stress at the interfaces.

keyed brick A brick, one of whose faces has been supplied with a usually dovetail-shaped recess which serves as a mechanical key for plastering or rendering.

keyed joint (1) A joint between two timbers which employs a key to ensure its security. (2) The concave pointing of a mortar joint.

keyhole saw (hole saw) A thin, narrow-bladed saw used to cut holes in panels or other surfaces.

keying (1) A process used to add strength to mitered joints. (2) Fastening or fixing in position in a notch or other recess.

keying in The tying in or bonding of a brick or block wall to an existing one.

key plan A small plan which depicts the units in a layout.

key plate An escutcheon.

keystone The usually wedge-shaped uppermost, hence last, set stone or similar member of an arch, whose placement not only completes the arch but also binds or locks its other members together.

key switch An on-off switch in an electric circuit, which is actuated by a removable key rather than a toggle or button.

key valve A valve operated by a key rather than a handle or lever.

keyway (1) A recess or groove in one lift or placement of concrete which is filled with concrete of the next lift, giving shear strength to the joint. Also called a *key*. (2) In a cylindrical lock, the aperture that receives and closely engages the key for its entire length, unlike a keyhole of a common lock. (3) A key-accepting groove in a shaft, pulley, sprocket, wheel, etc.

keyword In Building Automation Systems, abbreviation used by system operators to communicate instructions in recognizable commands via a computer. For example, STA and STO are the commands for *start* and *stop*.

K factor The measure of a transformer's ability to withstand the heating effects of nonsinusoidal harmonic currents.

kibble A bucket-like device in which material, water, tools and/or men are raised from a shaft.

kick (1) In brick, a shallow depression, fray, or panel. (2) The raised fillet of a brick mold which forms the frog. (3) The pitch variation between patent glazing and the surrounding roof.

kicker

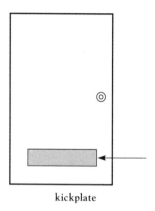

kickplate

kickback (1) When a rotating sawblade is pinched by the material it is cutting, momentarily stopping the blade and causing it to pull away from the material. (2) The illegal return of part of the purchase price by the seller to induce purchase or to improperly influence future purchase of goods or services.

kicker (1) A wood block or board attached to a formwork member in a building frame or formwork to make the structure more stable. In formwork, a kicker acts as a haunch to take the thrust of another member. Sometimes called a *cleat*. (2) A catalyst. (3) An activator, as the hardener for a polyester resin. (3) A luminaire used to accent or highlight a subject.

kicker plate A timber used to anchor a stair to concrete.

kicking piece A short timber attached to a wale for absorbing the thrust of a raking shore.

kickout (1) In excavation work, the accidental release or failure of a shore or brace. (2) In a downspout, the section (usually lowest) which directs the flow away from a wall.

kickpipe A short length of pipe that provides protection for an electric cable where it protrudes from a floor or deck.

kickplate (1) A metal strip or plate attached to the bottom rail of a door for protection against marring, as by shoes. (2) A plate, of any metal, used to create a ridge or lip at the open edge of a stair platform or floor, or at the back edge or open ends of a stair tread.

kick rail A usually short rail affixed near the bottom of a door to facilitate its opening by kicking. It is used primarily in institutions.

kick strip *See* **kicker**.

kill (1) To terminate electrical current from a circuit. (2) To shut off an engine. (3) To prevent resin from bleeding through paint on wood by the preliminary application to knots of a shellac or other resin-resistant coating.

killesse A grooved or channeled piece of wood, such as one in which a frame slides.

kiln A furnace, oven, or heated enclosure for drying (wood), charring, hardening, baking, calcining, sintering, or burning various materials.

kiln-dried (1) Control-dried or seasoned artificially in a kiln. (2) Lumber that has been seasoned in a kiln to a predetermined moisture content.

kiln run Descriptive of bricks or tiles from one kiln which have not been sorted or graded for size or color variation.

kiloampere A unit of electric current equal to 1,000 amperes.

kilocalorie The amount of heat needed to raise the temperature of one kilogram of water one degree Celsius.

kilovolt A unit of potential difference equal to 1,000 volts.

kilovolt-ampere A unit of apparent power equal to 1,000 volts or amperes.

kilowatt A measurement or unit of power equal to 1,000 watts or approximately 1.34 horsepower.

kilowatt consumption The amount of electrical power used over a specified time.

kilowatt demand The maximum electrical power usage required to operate a facility over a specified time.

kilowatt-hour A unit of measurement equal to the amount of energy

king closer

kitchen cabinet

knee brace

expended in one hour by one kilowatt of power.

king bolt A vertical tie rod which takes the place of the king post of a truss.

king closer A rectangular brick, one corner of which has been removed diagonally to leave a 2″ end, and which functions as a closer in brickwork.

king pile In strutted sheet pile excavation, a long guide pile driven at the strut spacing in the center of the trench before it is excavated.

kingpin A vertically mounted swivel, pivot, or hinge pin usually supported both above and below.

king post In a roof truss, a member placed vertically between the center of the horizontal tie beam at the lower end of the rafters and the ridge, or apex of the inclined rafters.

king stud In framing, a vertical support member that extends from the bottom to top plate alongside an opening for a door or window.

kiosk (1) A small gazebo. (2) A small, freestanding structure either open or partially enclosed, where merchandise is displayed, advertised, or sold.

kip (1) A unit of weight equal to 1,000 pounds. (2) Slang term for a bunkhouse on a construction site.

kiss mark Marks on the faces of bricks where they were in contact with one another during their firing in a kiln.

kitchen cabinet In a kitchen, a case or box-type assembly, or similar cupboard-like repository, having shelves, drawers, doors, and/or compartments, and used primarily for storing utensils, cutlery, food, linen, etc.

kitchenette A small kitchen.

kite A sheet of kraft paper applied to a sheet of coated roofing during manufacturing to measure the weight of the granules applied to the surface of the roofing.

kite winder The center tread on a staircase winder with three steps. A kite winder is so named because its shape resembles that of a kite.

knapping hammer A steel hammer whose head design may vary, but which is used for breaking and shaping stone, splitting cobbles, etc.

knee (1) A naturally or artificially bent piece of wood, as used for a brace or haunch. (2) A sharp, right-angled bend in a pipe. Also called an *elbow*. (3) A convex handrail.

kneeboards Support pads worn by workers during concrete finishing that distribute the finisher's weight and minimize marring of the concrete surface.

knee brace A brace between vertical and horizontal members in a building frame or formwork to make the structure more stable. In formwork, it acts as a haunch.

knee bracket A brace used to provide extra support under bow and angle bay projecting windows.

kneeler (1) The pattern-breaking stone or brick at the point where a normal masonry wall changes and begins to form the curve or angle of an arch or vault. (2) In a gable, the sloped-top, level-bedded stone which supports the inclined coping. (3) Ecclesiastical furnishing that may be provided for kneeling in a pew. May be attached to the frontal or to the back of the pew.

knee rafter A rafter whose lower end is bent downward to rest more firmly against a wall. Sometimes called a *knee piece*.

knife-blade fuse

knob rose

knockout

knee wall (1) A wall that shortens the span of the roof rafters by acting as a knee brace, in that it supports the rafters at some intermediate point along their length. (2) A short wall constructed to extend the height of an existing foundation or other wall system.

knife-blade fuse A type of cartridge fuse in which the metal blades at each end of the cylinder make contact with the fuse within.

knife consistency A compound whose degree of firmness makes it suitable for application with a putty knife.

knife switch A type of electric switch designed with a hinged or removable blade which enters or embraces the contact clips.

knife-type trencher A vibratory plow attachment used on a trenching machine to install telephone and power cable, television cable, irrigation systems or other light weight cable-type products in the ground without digging a trench.

knob (1) A usually round or somewhat spherical handle by which a latch, lock, or other device is operated. (2) Any similarly shaped ornament.

knob bolt A door lock whose bolt is operated not by a key, but by a knob or thumb piece on either or both sides of the door.

knob latch A door latch whose spring bolt is operated not by a key, but by a knob on one or both sides of the door.

knob lock A door lock whose spring bolt is operated by one or more knobs, but whose dead bolt is actuated by a key.

knob rose The usually raised round plate which is attached to a door face so as to surround a hole in the door and form a knob socket.

knob shank The stem of a doorknob, into whose hole or socket the spindle is received and fastened.

knob top The usually round or somewhat spherical terminal end of a knob which is grasped by the hand and turned.

knocked down Descriptive of precut, prefitted, and premeasured, but unassembled construction components, such as might be delivered to a job for on-site assembly.

knocked down frame A door frame which comes from the manufacturer in three or more parts.

knocker A hinged, usually metal fixture on the exterior face of a door, used for striking or knocking.

knockout A prestamped, usually circular section in an electrical junction box, panel box, etc., which can be easily removed to provide access for a fitting or raceway cable.

knot (1) The hard, cross-grained portion of a tree where a branch meets the trunk. (2) An architectural ornament of clusters of leaves or flowers at the base of intersecting vaulting ribs. (3) Intentional or accidental compact intersection(s) of rope(s) or similar material.

knot brush A rather thick brush whose bristles or fibers are bunched into one, two, or three round or oval knots.

knot cluster A compact grouping of two or more knots surrounded by deflected wood fibers or contorted grain.

knot sealer Any sealer, such as shellac, used to cover knots in new wood to prevent sap or resin bleed-through.

knotting *See* **knot sealer**.

knotty pine Pine wood sawn so as to expose firm knots as an appearance feature. Knotty pine is used for interior paneling and cabinets.

knuckle One of the enlarged, protruding, cylindrical parts of a hinge through which the pin is inserted.

knuckle joint A hinged joint by which two rods are connected.

knurling Very small ridges or beads as machined on a surface to facilitate gripping.

kraft paper A strong brown wrapping paper made from sulfate wood pulp that is sometimes impregnated with asphalt or resin for better moisture resistance when used in construction.

K truss A truss in which the arrangement of panels, chords, and web members resembles the letter "K".

k value The thermal conductivity of a substance or material.

kyanize Soaking or impregnating wood with a solution of mercuric chloride to preserve it against decay.

Kyoto protocol An international treaty adopted in 1997 that requires a number of nations, including the U.S., to reduce their greenhouse gas emissions to specific levels by the year 2012.

L

L ABBREVIATIONS

The abbreviations listed below are those most commonly used in the construction industry. Alternative forms (usually nonstandard) are shown in parentheses.

L Lambert, large

l labor only, left, length, liter, long, lumen

Lab. labor, laboratory

LAG lagging

LAM laminated

LAN local area network

LAT latitude, lattice

Lath lather

LAV lavatory

lb, lbs pound, pounds

lbf/sq in pound-force per square inch

lb/hr pounds per hour

lb/LF pounds per linear foot

Lbr lumber

LCL less-than-carload lot

LCM least common multiple, loose cubic meter

L&CM lime and cement mortar

LCY loose cubic yard

ld load

LDG landing

LDPE low-density polyethylene

LE leading edge

LECA light expanded clay aggregate

LED light emitting diode

LEMA Lighting Equipment Manufacturers' Association

lf lightface, light framing, lineal foot, linear foot, low frequency

lg large, length, long

LG liquid gas

lgr longer

lgt lighting

lgth length

L&H light and heat

LH left hand, long-span, high strength bar joist

LIC license

LIFO Last in, first out

lin linear, lineal

lin ft linear foot, lineal feet

lino linoleum

LJ obsolete designation for long-span, standard-strength bar joist

L&L latch and lock

LL&B latch, lock, and bolt

LL live load

LLD lamp lumen depreciation

lm lumen

LM lime mortar

lm/sf lumen per square foot

lm/W lumen per watt

lng, Lng lining

L&O lead and oil (paint)

LOA length over all

log logarithm

LP liquid petroleum, low pressure

L&P lath and plaster

LPF low power factor

LPG liquid petroleum gas

LR living room, law reports

LS left side, loudspeaker

LT long ton, light

Lt Ga light gauge

LTL less than truckload lot

Lt Wt lightweight

LUST leaking underground storage tank

LV low voltage

LVL laminated veneer lumber

LW low water

LWC lightweight concrete

LWM low water mark

L

Definitions

label A projecting molding along the sides or top of a window.

labeled Descriptive of doors, windows, frames, and other building components that carry certification of approval from a recognized testing laboratory based on fire tests conducted on identical materials and articles.

labeled door A door that carries a certified fire-rating issued by Underwriters' Laboratories, Inc. **3-hour fire doors (A)** are used in walls separating buildings or dividing a single building into fire areas. **1-1/2-hour (B and D)** fire doors are used in openings in 2-hour rated vertical enclosures such as stairs, elevators, etc., or in exterior walls subject to severe fire exposure from outside the building. **1-hour fire doors** are for use in openings in 1-hour rated vertical enclosures. **3/4-hour fire doors (C and E)** are for use in openings in corridor and room partitions or in exterior walls which are subject to moderate fire exposure from outside the building. **1/2-hour fire doors** and **1/3-hour fire doors** are used where smoke control is a primary consideration, and for the protection of openings between a habitable room and a corridor when the wall has a fire-resistance rating of not more than one hour.

labeled frame A door frame that conforms to standards and tests required by Underwriters' Laboratories, Inc., and has received its label of certification.

labeled window A fire-resistant window that conforms to the testing standards of Underwriters' Laboratories, Inc., and bears a label designating its fire rating.

labor Any work performed by an employee.

labor and material payment bond (payment bond) A bond procured by a contractor from a surety as a guarantee to the owner that the labor and materials applied to the project will be paid for by the contractor. Those who have direct contacts with the contractor may be considered claimants.

laborer Ordinarily denotes a construction worker who has no specific trade and whose function is to support the activity of the licensed trades.

labor union An organization or confederation of workers with the same or similar skills who are joined in a common cause (such as collective bargaining) with management or other employers for work place conditions, wage rates, and/or employee benefits.

labyrinth A maze of passageways or paths.

laced corner A method of laying shingles at interior and exterior corners on sidewalls. The corner shingles of each course are laid alternately on the faces of the two walls in order to overlap each other and eliminate the need for corner boards.

laced valley On a roof, the interweaving of shingles or tiles where two planes meet at a downward angle.

lacing A system of members used to connect the different elements of a composite column or girder in such a way that they structurally act in unison.

lag bolt

lally column

laminated beam

lacing course A continuous layer of brickwork built into a stone wall for the purpose of bonding and leveling.

lacquer A glossy enamel, composed of volatile solvents and dilutants, that evaporates and dries quickly upon application to a surface.

lacunar Having sunken or recessed panels, as in a soffit or ceiling panel.

ladder core A hollow structure of wood or insulation board used as the core of interior doors and built with strips running vertically or horizontally through the core area.

ladder ditcher Excavation equipment used in heavy construction to dig trenches. Rotating bucket-like shovels work to remove earth.

ladder jack scaffold A simple scaffolding system that uses ladders for support. The ladder jack is attached to the ladders to provide support for the staging plank.

ladder ties Long parallel reinforcing rods studded with cross rods so as to resemble a ladder. Used in masonry installations.

lag bolt (coach screw, lag screw) A threaded screw or bolt with a square head.

lagging (1) Heavy wood boards used to line the sides of excavations and prevent cave-ins. (2) Preformed insulation for pipes and tanks.

lag screw *See* **lag bolt.**

laitance In concrete, a weak, crumbly, and dusty surface layer caused by excessive water that has bled to the surface and subsequently weakened it. Over-working the surface during finishing can aggravate the problem. If laitance forms between pours, it must be brushed and washed away.

lally column A trade name for a pipe column from 3″ to 6″ in diameter, sometimes filled with concrete.

lambert A unit of measure for the brightness of reflective surfaces (1 lumen/sq. cm.).

lamb's tongue (1) A quarter round molding with a fillet. (2) A curve at the end of a handrail that resembles a tongue.

laminate (1) To form a product or material by bonding together several layers or sheets with adhesive under pressure and sometimes with nails or bolts. (2) Any material formed by such a method.

laminated beam (laminated veneer lumber) A straight or arched beam formed by built-up layers of wood. The method of lamination may be gluing under pressure, mechanical nailing or bolting, or a combination. *See also* **laminated wood.**

laminated glass (safety glass, shatterproof glass) A shatter-resistant safety glass made up of two or more layers of sheet glass, plate glass, or float glass bonded to a transparent plastic sheet.

laminated plastic Layers of synthetic resin-coated or resin-impregnated filler materials bonded together into a single piece by application of heat and pressure.

laminated wood (laminated veneer lumber) Any of several products formed by built-up layers (plies) of wood. Thin wood veneers may be laminated to a wood subsurface, several plies may be laminated together to form plywood, or thicker pieces may be used to form structural members such as beams or arches.

laminate floor A composite flooring product notable for its durability that is made of plastic resin and

lamp post

landing tread

cellulose paper with a decorative finish layer. Its core material is a high density fiberboard.

laminboard A compound board consisting of a core of small strips of wood glued together and covered by veneer faces.

lamp Any device that converts electric energy into light. Types include **incandescent, fluorescent, metal halide** and **high pressure sodium**.

lamp ballast *See* **ballast**.

lampblack A black pigment composed of carbon from the soot of burning oil.

lamp depreciation The loss of luminous output in a lamp over time due to the accumulation of dirt on lamps, reflectors, and room walls and ceilings.

lamp life A rating that provides the life expectancy of a lamp. Obtained by testing a sample of lights and noting when 50% are no longer operating.

lamp post A supporting device, for an external light or luminaire, with wiring attachments concealed inside and with outside attachments for the bracket.

lancet window A tall, narrow, window with a sharp arch.

land-clearing rake A device outfitted with blades and attached to the front of a tractor to cut, collect, and remove brush from the site of proposed construction.

land drain *See* **agricultural pipe drain**.

landfill An engineered disposal system characterized by the burial of waste material in alternating layers with an approved fill material.

landing An intermediate platform between flights of stairs, or the platform at the top or bottom of a staircase.

landing newel (angle newel) A newel positioned on a stair landing or at any point where stairs change direction.

landing tread That board or portion of a stair landing that is closest to the next step down. The tread has an appearance and dimensions similar to the other treads, but it is actually part of the landing, and not a true tread.

landmark In the context of historic properties, an historic property that is listed on a local, state or federal register.

land reclamation Gaining land from a submerged or partially submerged area by draining, filling, or a combination of these procedures.

Landrum-Griffin Act Enacted by Congress in 1959, this act requires labor union management to be subject to audit for the funds of union members for which they are responsible.

landscape architect A person whose professional specialty is designing and developing gardens and landscapes, especially one who is duly licensed and qualified to perform in the landscape architectural trade.

land survey *See* **boundary survey** *and* **survey**.

land surveyor A person (usually registered in the state where survey is being done) whose occupation is to establish the lengths and directions of existing boundary lines on landed property, or to establish any new boundaries resulting from division of a land parcel.

land tie *See* **deadman**.

land tile Clay tile laid with open joints and usually surrounded by

lane striping

lap joint

lapping

porous materials. *See also* **agricultural pipe drain.**

land treatment area A defined parcel of land on which wastes are deposited for the purpose of allowing natural cleansing actions to occur.

land-use analysis A systematic study of an area or region that documents existing conditions and patterns of use, identifies problem areas, and discusses future options and choices. A part of the general planning process, such an analysis might cover topics such as traffic flow, residential and commercial zoning, sewer services, water supply, solid-waste management, air and water pollution, or conservation areas. In short, any factors that could affect how particular areas of land should or should not be used.

lane striping The application of lines on pavement to define parking spaces, traffic lanes, etc.

lanyard A safety line tying a worker to a stable element of a structure to prevent a long fall in the event of an accident above ground level.

lap cement Asphalt used in roll roofing as an adhesive between the laps.

lap joint In construction, a type of joint in which two building elements are not butted up against each other, but are overlapped, with part of one covering part of the other. Typical examples include roof and wall shingles, clapboard siding, welded metal sheets or plates, and concrete reinforcing bars lapped together at their ends.

lapped dovetail A carpentry joint commonly used in constructing the front of a drawer, on which the pegged end of one member does not pass completely through the

thickness of the adjacent perpendicular members.

lapped joint A lapped joint, like a van stone joint, is a type of pipe joint made using loose flanges on lengths of pipe. The ends of this pipe are lapped over to give a bearing surface for a gasket or metal-to-metal joint.

lapped tenons Overlapping tenons that enter a mortise from opposite sides.

lapping (1) The overlapping of reinforcing bars or welded wire fabric for continuity of stress in the reinforcing when a load is applied. (2) The smoothing of a metal surface using a fine abrasive.

lap-riveted The riveting together of two metal members or plates where they have been deliberately overlapped, thus forming a lap joint.

lap seam The same as a lap joint, but typically used to refer to sheet metal, and sometimes plates, that are welded, soldered, or riveted at the overlapping joint.

lap siding Horizontal siding with each row covering part of the next, rather than butted up against each other.

lap splice In concrete construction, the simplest method for providing continuity of steel reinforcement. Ends of reinforcing bars are overlapped a specified number of diameters, usually no fewer than 30, and tied with wire.

lap weld A weld used to join two pieces of metal at their common joint.

lap weld pipe Pipe made by welding along a scarfed longitudinal seam in which one part is overlapped by another.

larch (tamarack) A heavier-than-average softwood from a coniferous

EARLY START	EARLY FINISH
Account No.	
ACTIVITY DESCRIPTION	
DURATION	FLOAT
LATE START	LATE FINISH

KEY

latest start date

tree, characterized by fine texture and hard, strong, straight-grained consistency.

large quantity generator A classification of the Resource Conservation and Recovery Act (RCRA).

larmier (corona, lorymer) A specific drip strip or molding that is part of a cornice. By projecting from the surrounding cornice, it catches rain and forces it to drip off away from the wall.

laser An acronym for light amplification by stimulated emission of radiation, a device that amplifies radiation in the visible or infrared parts of the spectrum.

laser level Surveying tool that employs a laser as a reference for measurements or verifying alignment.

last in, first out (LIFO) A method of accounting for inventory in which it is assumed that goods bought last are sold first. This allows automatic updating of inventory values.

latch A fastening device for a door or window, usually operable from both sides and built without a dead bolt or provisions for locking with a key.

latch bolt In a door or window, a bolt that is spring-loaded and beveled. As the door or window is closed, the bevel forces the bolt into the member, and is then released when in the fully closed position as the spring forces the bolt into a notch in the frame.

latchkey A key used to open or raise the latch on a door.

latchstring A string that is attached to the inside latch of a door and passed through a hole above the latch to the outside in order to operate the latch from the exterior.

latent defect A defect in materials or equipment that would not be revealed under reasonably careful observation. A patent defect, on the other hand, is one which may be discovered by reasonable observation.

lateral buckling The failure of any structural column, wall, or beam which has undergone excessive side-to-side (lateral) deflection, movement, or twist.

lateral load *See* **wind load** *and* **earthquake load**.

lateral reinforcement *See* **reinforcement, lateral**.

lateral sewer A sewer that discharges into another sewer or branch, but is engineered without any other common tributary to it.

lateral support Any bracing, temporary or permanent, that provides greater support in resisting side-to-side (lateral) forces and deflections. Floor and roof members typically provide lateral support for walls, columns, and beams. Vertical pilasters or secondary walls may also provide support.

lateral thrust Any force applied at a right angle to a member.

latest event occurrence time In the CPM (Critical Path Method) of construction scheduling, the final deadline by which a particular item of work must be completed in order to avoid delaying the entire project.

latest finish date In the Critical Path Method of scheduling, a completion deadline for a particular activity. Work performed after this deadline will result in project delay.

latest start date In the Critical Path Method of scheduling, the deadline for starting a particular activity. A late start will throw off the schedule and delay the project.

lattice

lavatory

latex (1) The sap of a rubber tree. (2) An emulsion in water of very fine particles of rubber or plastic.

latex foam Sponge rubber manufactured with a latex base.

latex paint A paint with a latex binder, usually a polymeric compound, characterized by its ability to be thinned or washed from applicators with water.

latex patching compound A compound used to fill voids, large gaps or penetrations in a floor, especially a subfloor before application of a floor covering.

lath Strips of wood or metal used as a base for plaster.

lathe A machine used to shape circular pieces of wood, metal, or other material. The stock is rotated on a horizontal axis while a stationary tool cuts away the unwanted material or creates ornamental turned work.

lath hammer A hammer used chiefly for cutting and nailing wood lath, designed with a nail-driving hammer head, as well as a hatchet blade with a lateral nick that is used for pulling out nails.

lathing The process of assembling or placing laths.

lathing hammer *See* **lath hammer**.

lath laid-and-set A two-coat method of plastering walls and ceilings. The first coat is called *laying* and is scratched so as to provide a rough bonding surface.

latrine A public toilet or privy.

latrobe A type of heater located inside a fireplace. Rooms above may be heated by hot air, but the room containing the stove is heated by direct radiation.

lattice Typically, a diagonal network or grid of strips of material. Lattice is often used as ornamental screening, or to provide privacy.

lattice truss (lattice beam, lattice girder) A structural truss in which the web is a latticework of diagonal members.

lattice window A window with diagonal glazing bars.

latticework Any item or member formed by the repetitive crossing of thin, diagonally placed strips, often of wood or metal.

lauan Philippine mahogany.

laundry chute A shaft running between the upper and lower floors of a building and used to convey soiled laundry to the lower level by gravity.

lavas Natural stone used in building as a facing, veneer, and decoration. Pink, purple, and black are typical shades.

lavatory (1) A basin, with running water and drainage facilities, used for washing the face and hands. (2) A room with a wash basin and a toilet, but no bathtub. (3) A room containing a toilet or water closet.

lay A term used to define the direction of twist of the strands or wires in wire rope. The strands or wires have either a right-hand or left-hand lay.

lay-in Describes tile or panels which are installed into metal channels in suspended ceiling systems.

laying line (laying guide) Lines printed on felt or roll roofing as a guide for the amount of lap required.

laying out (1) Marking of materials in preparation for work, showing where they are to be cut. (2) Marking the location for the placement of building members.

layout A design scheme or plan showing the proposed arrangement

L-beam

leader

of objects and spaces within and outside a structure.

lay the leads A slang expression that means to build up the corners in a brick wall.

lay-up (1) The reinforcing material that is placed into position in the mold during the manufacturing of reinforced plastics. Also, the resin-impregnated reinforcement. (2) The method or process of assembling veneers to manufacture plywood.

lazy susan A revolving circular shelf or tray, often used in cabinets to utilize space more efficiently at blind corners.

L-beam A beam whose section has the form of an inverted "L", usually occurring in the edge of a floor, of which a part forms the top flange of the beam.

L-column The portion of a precast concrete frame composed of the column, the haunch, and part of the girder.

L/D ratio The relationship of the span (L) of a beam, slab or truss to its depth (D).

leachate Liquid from rainfall, groundwater, or other sources that has percolated through a landfill mass and that contains biological and/or chemical wastes and dissolved or suspended materials. This waste is often hazardous and may need to be collected and treated to avoid groundwater contamination.

leaching The process of separating liquids from solid materials by allowing them to percolate into surrounding soil.

leaching cesspool An underground storage tank or chamber for domestic wastes. The sides are made porous with small holes so that solids are retained but liquids may leach out into the surrounding earth.

leaching field *See* **absorption field**.

leaching pit *See* **leaching well**.

leaching well (leaching pit) Like a cesspool, a pit with porous walls that retain solids but permit liquids to pass through.

lead (1) (Pb) A soft, dense heavy metal easily formed and cut. Historically, lead was used for flashing and for the joints in stained glass windows. (2) End sections of a masonry wall, usually at the corners, which are built up, in steps, before the main part of the wall is begun. Also, a string stretched between these end sections that serves as a guide for the rest of the wall. (3) In electricity, conduction of electric current from the electric source to point of contact such as a welding lead.

lead chromate One of a number of opaque pigments that range from orange to yellow in color and have strong tinting properties.

lead-covered cable (lead-sheathed cable) An electric cable protected from damage and excess moisture by a lead covering.

leaded glass *See* **leaded light**.

leaded light A window whose diamond-shaped or rectangular glass panes are set in lead frames called cames.

leader (1) In a hot-air heating system, a duct that conveys hot air to an outlet. (2) A downspout.

leader head That part of a drainpipe assembly that is placed at the top of a leader and serves as a catch basin to receive water from the gutter.

lead foil tape An acrylic, weather-resistant, highly malleable tape with good tack, bond and

leading edge

lead-lined door

lead shield

resistance to solvents and heat. Used as a moisture barrier, a maskant in electroplating and chemical milling, and in thermopane window sealing. Also used in alarm systems, with conductive tape attached to a window to detect breakage.

lead glazing *See* **leaded light**.

leading edge The vertical edge of a hinged swinging door or window which is opposite the hinged edge and in proximity to the knob or latch.

lead joint A joint in a water pipe, such as a bell-and-spigot joint, into which molten lead is poured.

lead-lag ballast A ballast that serves to cut down on the stroboscopic effect of two fluorescent lamps, one of which is on a leading current and the other on a lagging current.

lead-lined door A door with lead sheets lining its internal core to prevent the penetration of x-ray radiation.

lead-lined frame A frame that is used with lead-lined doors and is itself lined internally with lead sheets to prevent penetration of x-ray radiation.

lead-lined sheetrock Sheetrock internally lined with sheet lead to provide protection from x-ray radiation.

lead paint A paint having white lead as one of its pigments.

lead plug (1) A cylinder of lead placed inside a hole in a masonry, plaster, or concrete wall. A screw or nail driven into it will then be firmly held in place. (2) In stonemasonry, a piece of lead that holds adjacent stones together. Grooves are cut in both rock surfaces to be joined, and molten lead is poured into it.

lead roof A flat roof with a surface of sheet lead.

leads A collective term for short sections of electric conductors, generally insulated.

lead-sheathed cable *See* **lead-covered cable**.

lead shield A lead sleeve used to provide anchorage for expansion bolts or screws. Similar to a *lead plug*.

lead slate (copper slate, lead sleeve) A cylinder of sheet lead or sheet copper that surrounds a pipe at the point where it passes through a roof, ensuring a watertight intersection.

lead sleeve *See* **lead slate**.

lead soaker A piece of lead sheeting that forms a weathertight joint at the intersection of a roof and of any vertical wall that passes through the roof at a hip or valley.

lead spitter The tapered part of a drainpipe assembly that connects a lead gutter with a downpipe.

lead tack (1) A lead strip used to attach a lead pipe to some means of support. (2) A lead strip placed along the edge of metal flashing. One side of the strip is attached to the structure, while the other side is folded over the free edge of the flashing.

lead wool Fine strands of lead formed into a wool-like consistency, often used as caulking at the joints of pipes.

leaf *See* **wythe**.

leakage current Unwanted electric current that remains in a circuit or device. Can occur with improperly grounded electrical equipment. Leakage current can be observed by wire or semiconductor detectors.

lean concrete Concrete of lower than usual cement content.

lean-to

ledger

lean mix (lean mixture) (1) A mixture of concrete or mortar with a relatively low cement content. (2) A plaster with too much aggregate and not enough cement, which thus renders it unworkable. (3) A mixture of gasoline and oil in which the gasoline portion is on the high side in relation to the oil.

lean mortar A mortar with a low cement content, which makes it sticky, overly adherent to the trowel, and difficult to apply.

lean-to A small shed or building addition with a single pitched roof attached to the exterior wall of the main building.

lean-to roof A roof with one pitch, supported at one end by a wall extending higher than the roof.

learning curve A term applied to the time required for a new craftsman or crew to attain the productivity level of an experienced craftsman or crew.

lease A contract that transfers the right of possession and use of buildings, property, vehicles, or items of equipment for a time agreed upon in the contract, in return for rent as monetary compensation.

leasehold A tenure established by lease. Also, real estate that is held under a lease.

ledge (1) A molding that projects from the exterior wall of a building. (2) A piece of wood nailed across a number of boards to fasten them together. (3) An unframed structural member used to stiffen a board or a number of boards or battens. (4) Bedrock.

ledged-and-braced door A batten door outfitted with diagonal bracing for extra strength.

ledger (1) A horizontal framework member that carries joists and is supported by upright posts or by hangers. (2) A slab of stone laid flat, such as that over a grave. (3) A horizontal scaffold member, positioned between upright posts, on which the scaffold planks rest.

ledger board (1) One of multiple boards attached horizontally across a series of vertical supports, as in the construction of a fence. (2) A ribbon strip.

ledger plate *See* **ledger strip** *and* **ledger**.

ledger strip On a beam that carries joists flush with its upper edge, the strip of wood attached along the bottom edge of the beam that serves to seat the joists and to support them.

left-hand door *See* **hand**.

left-hand lock A lock designated for use on a left-hand door.

left-hand reverse door *See* **hand**.

left-hand stairway A stairway on which the handrail is positioned on the left-hand side in the direction of ascent.

left on the table The dollar difference between the low bid and the next bid above.

legal notice A covenant, often incorporated in the language of an agreement between two or more parties, that requires communication in writing, serving notice from one party to the other in accordance with terms of the agreement.

legitimate Ethical and legal.

length The longest dimension of an object.

lessee A person who receives use and possession of property by lease.

lessor The party who grants the use and possession of property by lease.

let-in brace

leveling plate

lewis bolt (lewis pin)

let in In joinery, to fasten a timber securely in place by inserting or embedding it in another.

let-in brace A diagonal brace inserted or let in to a stud.

let or sublet Issue a contract for a portion of the project.

letter chute *See* **mail chute**.

letter form of agreement (letter agreement) An agreement, in letter format, written by the sender, to be signed by the addressee, intended to be legally binding.

letter of intent A letter that states the intent to enter into a formal agreement. Terms of the anticipated agreement may be stated in a general way.

letting of bid *See* **bid opening**.

level (1) A term used to describe any horizontal surface that has all points at the same elevation and thus does not tilt or slope. (2) In surveying, an instrument that measures heights from an established reference. (3) A spirit level, consisting of small tubes of liquid with bubbles in each. The small tubes are positioned in a length of wood or metal which is hand-held and, by observing the position of the bubbles, used to find and check level surfaces.

level A-D clothing The EPA's classification of personal protective equipment. Level A clothing offers the greatest amount of protection and should be worn whenever there is a risk to skin, eyes and the respiratory system. It utilizes an encapsulated chemical protective suit. Level D offers little protection and should only be worn on a site with no hazards.

level control Bench marks or other devices used to identify points of known elevation on a project site.

leveling The procedure used in surveying to determine differences in elevation.

leveling course *See* **asphalt leveling course**.

leveling plate A bearing plate set to an elevation used for setting structural steel.

leveling rod (leveling staff) A graduated straight rod used in construction with a leveling instrument to determine differences in elevation. The rod is marked in feet and fractions of feet, and may be fitted with a movable target or sighting disc. *See also* **New York leveling rod** *and* **Philadelphia leveling rod**.

leveling rule A long level used by plasterers to detect irregularities in the height of horizontal surfaces measured at various points.

leveling staff *See* **leveling rod**.

leveraged buyout Any acquisition of a company where the buyer uses the company's internal assets and cash flows to provide the collateral for the loans required to make the acquisition.

lever arm In a structural member, the distance from the center of the tensile reinforcement to the center of action of the compression.

lever tumbler In a lock, a type of pivoted tumbler.

lewis (lifting pin) A metal device used to hoist heavy units of masonry. A lewis is equipped with a dovetailed tenon that is made in sections and fitted into a corresponding recess cut into the piece of masonry to be moved.

lewis bolt (lewis pin) (1) A bolt shaped into a wedge at its end, which is inserted into a prepared hole in a heavy unit or stone and secured in place with poured concrete or melted lead. (2) An eyebolt inserted into heavy stones and used in the manner of a lewis to lift and move the stones.

lewis hole A dovetailed hollow cut into a stone block, column, or heavy piece of masonry to receive a lewis.

L-head The top of a shore formed with a braced horizontal member projecting from one side and forming an inverted L-shaped assembly.

liability A situation in which one party is legally obligated to assume responsibility for another party's loss or burden. Liability is created when the law recognizes two elements: the existence of an enforceable legal duty to be performed by one party for the benefit of another, and the failure to perform the duty in accordance with applicable legal standards.

liability insurance Insurance designed to safeguard the insured from liability resulting from injury to another person or another person's property. *See also* **insurance**.

license The permission by competent authority to do an act which, without such permission, would be illegal.

licensed architect *See* **architect**.

licensed contractor An individual or a firm that has, where required by law, obtained certification from a government office, to practice construction contracting.

licensed engineer *See* **professional engineer**.

lid Slang term for ceiling.

lien A legal means of establishing or giving notice of a claim or an unsatisfied charge in the form of a debt, obligation, or duty. A lien is filed with government authorities against title to real property. Liens must be adjudicated or satisfied before title can be transferred. *See also* **mechanic's lien**.

lien waiver *See* **waiver of lien**.

life cycle A term often used to describe the period of time that a building can be expected to actively and adequately serve its intended function.

life-cycle assessment The determination of the environmental burdens associated with a product or process, including materials used and wastes released. The assessment considers the extraction and manufacturing of the materials, transportation and distribution, use and maintenance, and final disposal or reuse.

life-cycle costing The determination of the value of a system, such as roof covering, amortized over the projected life of the system, as opposed to the value determined by the initial cost only. Life-cycle costs include such costs as service and maintenance.

life safety code Developed by the NFPA Committee on Safety to Life, an international organization dedicated to saving lives from fire.

lift (1) The concrete placed between two consecutive horizontal construction joints, usually consisting of several layers or courses, such as in slip forming. (2) A metal handle or projection from the lower sash in a hung window, used as an aid in lifting the sash. (3) The amount of grout, mortar, or concrete placed in a single pour. (4) A British term for elevator. (5) Slang for an amount of material bound together for ease of handling, such as a lift of 2x4s or a lift of cement.

lifting block A combination of pulleys or sheaves that provide a

lift slab

light

mechanical advantage for lifting a heavy object.

lifting pin *See* **lewis.**

lift joint A surface at which two successive concrete lifts meet.

lifts (tiers) The number of frames of scaffolding erected one above each other in a vertical direction.

lift slab A method of concrete construction in which floor and roof slabs are cast at ground level and hoisted into position by jacking. Also, a slab that is a component of such construction.

ligger (1) A horizontal timber that supports floor boards or scaffolding. (2) In thatched roofs, a strip of wood placed along the ridge.

light (1) A man-made source of illumination, such as an electric light. (2) A pane of glass.

light bulb *See* **incandescent lamp.**

light dimmer *See* **dimmer.**

light framing Lumber that is 2″ to 4″ thick, 2″ to 4″ wide, and is graded Construction, Standard, or Utility No. 3.

lighting A system for providing illumination to an area.

lighting cost The total of the cost of a system's lamps, operating energy, and lamp replacement.

lighting fixture *See* **luminaire.**

lighting outlet An electrical outlet that serves to accommodate the direct connection of a lighting fixture or of a lamp holder and its pendant cord.

lighting panel An electric panel housing fuses and circuit breakers, that serve to protect the branch circuits of lighting fixtures.

lighting unit *See* **luminaire.**

light loss factor In illumination calculations, an adjustment factor

that estimates losses in light levels over time due to aging of the lamp, dirt on the room surfaces, and other causes. Losses corrected by lamp replacement or cleaning are termed recoverable. Non-recoverable losses would be due to deterioration of the fixture or voltage drops.

lightning arrester A device that connects to and protects an electrical system from lightning and other voltage surges.

lightning conductor (lightning rod) A cable or rod built of metal that protects a building from lightning by providing a direct link to ground.

light-reflective glass *See* **reflective glass.**

light source A *See* **standard source A.**

light source B *See* **standard source B.**

light source C *See* **standard source C.**

lightweight aggregate *See* **aggregate, lightweight.**

lightweight block A cement masonry unit manufactured using lightweight aggregate and often used to reduce the weight of partitions.

lightweight concrete Concrete of substantially lower unit weight than that made using gravel or crushed stone aggregate.

light well An inside shaft with an open top through which light and air are conveyed from the outdoors to windows opening on the shaft.

lignin (1) A substance that occurs naturally in wood and joins with cellulose to make up the chief constituents of wood tissue. (2) A crystalline by-product of paper pulp, used in manufacturing plastics, wood chipboard, and protective chemical coatings that prevent corrosion.

lime Specifically, calcium oxide (CaO). Also, a general term for the

linear diffuser

various chemical and physical forms of quicklime, hydrated lime, and hydraulic hydrated lime.

lime-and-cement mortar A lime, cement, and sand mortar used in masonry and cement plaster. In addition to imparting a favorable consistency to the mix, the lime also increases the flexibility of the dried mix, thus limiting cracks and minimizing water penetration.

lime concrete A lime, sand, gravel, and concrete mix made without Portland cement. Lime concrete is found in older structures, but is no longer in general use.

lime mortar An uncommon mix of lime putty and sand that is not often used because it hardens at a very slow rate.

lime putty A thick lime paste used in plastering, particularly for filling voids and repairing defects.

limestone A sedimentary rock composed mostly of calcium carbonate, calcium, or dolomite. Limestone can be used as a building stone, with its commercial grades being A. Statuary, B. Select, C. Standard, D. Rustic, E. Variegated, and F. Old Gothic. It is also crushed into aggregate, crushed for agricultural lime, or burned to produce lime.

limewash (whitewash, whiting) A milk-like mixture of water and lime used to coat the exterior or interior surfaces of a structure.

limit control A safety device for a variety of mechanical systems that detects unsafe conditions, sounds an alarm, and shuts off the system.

limit design Any of a number of structural design methods based on limits related to stability, elasticity, fatigue, deformation, and other structural criteria.

limited combustible material A material that is noncombustible, as defined by the National Fire Protection Agency, yet fails to meet the NFPA's definition of combustible material. Must not exceed a potential heat value of 3500 Btu per pound.

limited partners Partners in a limited partnership who contribute capital and share profits, but have no decision-making power and no control over the day-to-day operations of the limited partnership's business.

limited partnership A form of partnership that is a hybrid between a general partnership and a corporation, and which is composed of both general partners and limited partners.

limit of liability The greatest amount of money that an insurance company will pay in the event of damage, injury, or loss.

limit switch (1) An electrical switch that controls a particular function in a machine, often independently of other machine functions. (2) A safety device, such as a switch that automatically slows down and stops an elevator at or near the top or bottom terminal landing.

line A marked or defined limit or border.

lineal foot A straight-line measurement of one foot, as distinguished from a cubic foot volume or a square foot area.

linear diffuser An elongated diffuser with parallel slots with deflectors to divert airflow in various directions.

linear heat detector A cable-like component of a fire detection system that detects heat anywhere along its length.

line level

linear measurement (long measure)
A unit or system of units for
measuring length: 12″ = 1′, 3′ = 1
yard, 1 yard = 0.9144 meters,
1 mile = 5,280 feet.

linear prestressing Prestressing as
applied to linear structural members,
such as beams, columns, etc.

line drawing A graphic representation
made with lines and solids, as
opposed to one made with tone
gradations, such as a photograph
or rendering.

line drilling In the blasting of rock,
the boring of a series of holes along
the desired line of breakage. Holes
are spaced several inches apart to
create a plane of weakness.

line drop A decrease in voltage
caused by the resistance of
conductors in an electric circuit.

line item Any item specifically
called for on a plan or specification
price-out sheet and listed with all
of the quantities, unit prices, and
extensions.

line level A spirit level used in
excavation and pipe laying. Each
end of the level has a hook used to
hang it from a horizontal line.

linemen's pliers Pliers used to
work with heavy-gauge wire.

line of credit A fixed amount of
credit granted to cover a series
of transactions.

line of levels A series of differences
in elevation as measured and
recorded by surveyors.

line of sight (sight line) The line
extending from a telescope or other
long-distance sighting device, along
which distant objects can be
viewed.

line pin A metal pin used in masonry
work to support a horizontal string
or line. The mason positions the
line and then uses it as a guide
in maintaining proper alignment
of the work.

line pipe A welded or seamless pipe
typically used to convey gas, oil, or
water.

liner Extra stone bonded or
otherwise attached to the back face
of thin stone veneers. The purpose
is to add strength and to create a
deeper joint.

liner panel An interior finish panel.

lining Any sheet, plate, or layer of
material attached directly to the
inside face of formwork to improve
or alter the surface texture and
quality of the finished concrete.

lining panel A strip that secures the
lower edges of sheet metal roofing
sheets along the eaves of a roof.

lining paper A waterproof or
water-resistant building paper
placed under siding and roofing
shingles.

link (1) The circuit that connects two
points. (2) An enclosed connector
between two buildings.

link dormer A dormer that is formed
around a chimney. Also, a dormer
that connects one roof area to
another.

linked switch A series of
mechanically connected electrical
switches designed to act
simultaneously or sequentially.

link fuse A type of exposed fuse
attached to electrically insulated
supports.

linoleum An inexpensive form of
resilient floor covering that is
manufactured of ground cork and
oxidized linseed oil. Linoleum is
applied to a coarse fabric backing
and possesses a low resistance to
staining, dents, and abrasion.

linoleum knife *See* **hook knife.**

lintel

lintel block (U-block)

linseed oil A drying oil processed from flaxseed and used in many paints and varnishes.

lintel A horizontal supporting member, installed above an opening such as a window or a door, that serves to carry the weight of the wall above it.

lintel block (U-block) A special U-shaped concrete block used with other blocks to form a continuous-bond beam or lintel. Reinforcing steel is placed in the void followed by mortar or grout.

lintel course A course of stonemasonry set level to a lintel, but different from the rest of the wall by virtue of size or finish.

lip A rounded, overhanging edge or member.

lip union A pipe connection with a lip on the inside to keep the gasket from being forced into the pipe.

liquation The separation of metals based on their melting point.

liquefaction The sudden failure of a loose soil mass due to total loss of shearing resistance. Typical causes are shocks or strains that abruptly increase the water pressure between soil particles, causing the entire mass to behave similarly to a liquid.

liquid adsorption A natural process in which molecules of a liquid are physically attracted to and held at the surface of a solid.

liquid asphaltic material An asphaltic product too soft to be measured by a penetration test at normal temperatures. The material is principally used for cement surface treatments. *See also* **liquid roofing**.

liquidated damages An amount, specified in a contract for construction, to cover damages incurred by the owner as a result of the contractor's failure to complete the work within the time frame set forth in the contract.

liquid indicator A device located in the liquid line of a refrigerating system and having a sight port through which flow may be observed for the presence of bubbles.

liquid limit The water content at which soil passes from the plastic to the liquid state under standard test conditions. The limit is expressed as a percentage of the dry weight of the soil. *See also* **Atterberg limits**.

liquid line In a refrigeration system, the pipe transporting refrigerant away from the condenser.

liquid membrane forming compound A material sprayed or rolled on a fresh concrete surface to restrict the loss of moisture from the concrete.

liquid petroleum gas (LPG) A general term referring to propane, butane, and other similar hydrocarbons used as fuel.

liquid roofing Any of a number of different liquid or semi-liquid roofing materials used to create a seamless waterproof membrane.

liquid volume measurement A measurement of grout on the basis of the total volume of solid and liquid constituents.

liquid waste The discharge from any plumbing fixture, area, appliance, or component that does not contain fecal matter.

liter A metric measure of capacity equal to 61.022 cubic inches, or 2.113 American pints.

litharge A pipe thread sealant of lead powder mixed with glycerine.

lithium bromide A chemical compound (salt) with the ability to absorb water and cool it by evaporation.

First Floor Plan

living unit

load-bearing partition

load-bearing wall

loader

lithologic log A log of the structure and content of soils and rock recorded during a drilling or excavating operation.

litigation The process by which parties submit their disputes to the jurisdiction and procedures of federal or state courts for resolution.

litmus A piece of test paper containing a chemical indicator that changes color when exposed to liquids. Litmus paper is used to determine acidity or alkalinity values expressed as pH variations.

live (1) Descriptive of a wire or cable connected to a voltage source. (2) A descriptive term for a room with a very low level of sound absorption.

live-front Descriptive of an item of electrical equipment constructed so that one or more of its *live parts* can be touched from the front of the device.

live load The load superimposed on structural components by the use and occupancy of the building, not including the wind load, earthquake load, or dead load.

live part Any part or component of an electrical device or system that is engineered to function at a voltage level different from that of the earth.

live steam Steam that has not condensed and still retains its energy, such as steam issuing from a boiler or radiator.

living unit A dwelling place or any self-contained area or part thereof that comprises complete living facilities for a family, including space and fixtures for sleeping, cooking, eating, living, bathing, and sanitation.

load (1) The force, or combination of forces, that act upon a structural system or individual member. (2) The electrical power delivered to any device or piece of electrical equipment. (3) The placing of explosives in a hole.

load-bearing partition A partition that can support a load in addition to its own weight.

load-bearing tile A form of tile used in masonry walls that is capable of supporting loads superimposed on the wall structure.

load-bearing wall A wall specifically designed and built to support an imposed load in addition to its own weight.

load binder A device used to tighten chains that are holding loads in place on a truck bed.

load center *See* **panel box**.

loader A construction machine used to push or transport earth, crushed stone, or other construction materials. The bucket, or scoop, is located on the front of the vehicle and can be raised, lowered, or tilted.

load factor (1) In structural design, the factor applied to the working load to determine the designs ultimate load. (2) In a drainage system, the percentage of the total flow that occurs at a particular location in the system. (3) A ratio of the average air-conditioning load on a system to the maximum capacity.

load-indicating bolt A bolt that permits measurement of its tension. Upon tightening, a small projection on the bolt compresses and is measured by a feeler gauge.

loading cycles A calculation of the number of repetitions of load that a structure is expected to support in its lifetime. The calculation is used as a determining criterion in measuring the structure's fatigue strength.

location survey

loading dock leveler Typically, an adjustable mechanized platform built into the edge of a loading dock. The platform can be raised, lowered, or tilted to accommodate the handling of goods or material to or from trucks.

loading dock seal A flexible pad installed around the door of a loading dock to form a tight seal between the receiving doors and the opening of a truck that is backed into the dock.

loading hopper A hopper in which concrete or other free-flowing material is placed for loading by gravity into buggies or other conveyances.

loading platform (loading dock) A platform adjoining the shipping and receiving door of a building, usually built to the same height as the floor of the trucks or railway cars on which shipments are delivered to and from the dock.

loading ramp A fixed or adjustable inclined surface that adjoins a loading platform and is installed to ease the conveyance of goods between the platform and the trucks or railway cars that transport goods.

loam Soil consisting primarily of sand, clay, silt, and organic matter.

local area network (LAN) A type of distance-limited communications network used for data transfer, text, facsimile, and video applications.

local buckling In structures, the failure of a single compression member. The local failure may cause the failure of the whole structural member.

local lighting Lighting used to illuminate a limited area without significantly altering the illumination of its wider surroundings.

location plan *See* **site plan**.

location survey The establishment of the position of points and lines on an area of ground, based on information taken from deeds, maps, and documents of record, as well as from computation and graphic processes.

locator One who locates land, or sets boundaries of a mining claim.

lock bevel In a door lock, the angled surface of the latch bolt.

lock corner A corner held together by interlocking construction of adjacent members, such as the dovetail joint on the front panel of a drawer.

Locke level A *hand level*.

lock face The surface of a mortise lock, which remains visible in the edge of a door when the lock is installed.

lock front On a door lock or latch, the plate through which the lock or latch bolt projects.

lock front bevel A lock front that is installed flush with the beveled edge of a door.

locking device In scaffolding, a device used to secure a cross brace to the frame or panel.

locking pliers Pliers with clamping jaws that can be tightened with a screw attachment on one handle. A common brand name is Vise Grip®.

lock jamb *See* **strike jamb**.

lock joint *See* **lock seam**.

lock keeper The box on a door jamb that accommodates the extending bolt on a lock.

locknut (1) A special nut that locks when tightened so that it will not come loose. (2) A second nut used to prevent a primary nut from loosening.

lock rail

lock-strip gasket
(structural gasket)

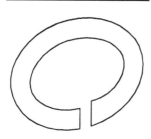

lock washer

lock plate *See* **strike plate** *and* **box strike plate**.

lock rail On a door, the horizontal structural member situated between the vertical stiles at the same height as the lock.

lock reinforcement A metal plate installed inside the lock stile or lock edge of a door and designed to receive a lock.

lock reinforcing unit In a metal door, a metal device that houses and supports a lock.

locksaw A saw used for cutting the seats for locks in doors. The saw is designed with a tapering blade that can be flexibly maneuvered. *See also* **compass saw**.

lock seam (lock joint) In sheet metal roofing, a joint or seam formed by bending the two adjoining edges over in the form of hooks, which are interlocked. The hooks are then pressed down tightly to form a seam.

lockset A complete system including all the mechanical parts and accessories of a lock, such as knobs, reinforcing plates, and protective escutcheons.

lock stile (closing stile, locking stile, striking stile) On a door or a casement sash, the vertical member that closes against the jamb of the frame that surrounds it. The stile is located on the side away from the hinges.

lock strike *See* **strike plate**.

lock-strip gasket (structural gasket) Typically, a thick and stiff black neoprene glazing gasket that holds and attaches panes of glass to each other or to the surrounding structure. During installation the gasket is tightened by the insertion of a wedge-like strip (the lock-strip) along the entire length of the gasket.

lock washer A circular washer with a break that helps it keep a nut tightly in position.

locust The coarse-grained wood of the locust tree, which is used in construction because of its strength, hardness, durability, and resistance to decay.

loess Silty material that is deposited by the wind, but maintains significant cohesion due to the presence of clay or other cementitious materials.

loft (1) Space beneath a roof of a building, most commonly used for storage of goods. (2) In a barn, the upper space at or near the ceiling with an elevated platform on which hay and grains are stored. (3) The upper space in a church or auditorium, sometimes enclosed and cantilevered, which accommodates a pipe organ or area for a choir. (4) The space between the grid and the upper part of the proscenium in a theatre stagehouse. (5) Within a loft building, the unpartitioned upper spaces visible from the floor immediately below. *See also* **attic** *and* **garret**.

loft building A commercial/industrial building containing large, open, unpartitioned floor areas.

loft ladder *See* **disappearing stair**.

logic panel Any electronic control panel that is designed to perform a specific control sequence.

long-and-short work In rubble masonry, quoins that are alternately placed horizontally and vertically.

long column In structural design, a column of sufficient slenderness to necessitate a reduction of its load-bearing capacity.

long float A concrete finishing float designed to be handled by two men.

longitudinal reinforcement

long-radius elbow

long span

long header A header that runs a wall's full depth.

longitudinal bar *See* **longitudinal reinforcement**.

longitudinal bond In masonry, a bond in which a number of courses are laid only with stretchers and used principally for thick walls.

longitudinal bracing Bracing that extends lengthwise or runs parallel to the center line of a structure.

longitudinal joint Any joint parallel to the long dimension of a structure or pavement.

longitudinal reinforcement Steel reinforcement placed parallel to the long axis of a concrete member.

long-life lamp An incandescent lamp that has a lower luminous output than standard lamps of equal wattage, but a longer design life than the value set for lamps of its general class.

long measure *See* **linear measurement**.

long nipple (space nipple) A nipple with a long unthreaded middle section.

long-radius elbow In plumbing, a pipe elbow with a larger radius than is standard. The elbow is designed to mitigate losses from friction and to facilitate the flow of liquids through the pipe.

long screw A nipple, usually measuring 6″ long, with one thread that is longer than average.

long span (1) The distance between supports in a structure, usually spanned by a truss or heavy timber. (2) A logging operation where logs are yarded over a long distance.

long span lintel A lintel used in light-gauge metal stud framing that has a steel channel for extra support over an opening.

long span steel joist A structural framing joist that provides large open areas within a building. It is usually a very deep beam due to the nature of the building system.

long span structure A building that uses long span roof joist systems in its design to create large unobstructed areas within the structure, e.g., a domed stadium.

long-term liabilities Debts of a business that are not due for at least one year.

long ton A unit of weight equal to 2,240 pounds (1,016 kilograms).

lookout A short wooden brace or block that supports an overhanging portion of a roof.

loop (1) Sometimes called a local line or subscriber loop, the local circuit between a subscriber station and the exchange. (2) *See* **loophole** *and* **circuit vent**.

loophole An aperture in a wall or parapet to provide air, light, and a view of the outside.

looping in In interior electrical wiring, the connection of an outlet by two conductor cables, one to and one from the outlet. Splices (junction boxes) are thus avoided, but more wire is used.

loop vent In plumbing, a venting configuration for multiple fixtures, as in a public restroom. The vent pipe is connected to the waste branch in only two places, before the first and last fixtures. The fixtures are not individually vented. The two vents are connected together in a loop, and the loop is then connected to the vent stack.

loose cubic yard (meter) A unit of measure with which to express the volume of loose soil, rock, or blasted earth material.

loose-fill insulation

loose-pin hinge

louver

loose estimate One allowing for contingencies, a "safe" or high estimate.

loose-fill insulation Any of several thermal insulation materials in the form of granules, fibers, or other types of pieces that can be poured, pumped, or placed by hand.

loose-joint hinge A door hinge that can be separated by lifting. The door can thus be removed without unscrewing the hinges.

loose knot A knot on a piece of lumber that is not fixed firmly and is likely to fall out.

loose lintel A lintel that is placed across a wall opening during construction to support the weight of the wall above, but which is not attached to another structural member.

loose material Soil, rock, or earth materials in loose form, whether blasted or broken by artificial or natural means.

loose-pin hinge A hinge, usually for a door, that can be separated by the removal of a vertical pin.

loose-tongue (cross tongue) In a timber joint, the piece of wood that extends into the opposite member, thus strengthening a tenoned frame.

loose yards A term defining the cubic measurement of earth or blasted rock after excavation, as when loaded on a truck. Equal to a volume of 27 cubic feet.

lorymer *See* **larmier**.

Los Angeles Abrasion Test A test for abrasion resistance on concrete aggregates.

loss of prestress In prestressed concrete, the reduction in prestressing force which results from the combined effects of strain in the concrete and steel, including slip at

anchorage, relaxation of steel stress, frictional loss due to curvature in the tendons, and the effects of elastic shortening, creep, and shrinkage of the concrete.

loss of use Insurance coverage for any financial loss that may be incurred while property, damaged or destroyed by an insured hazard, is being replaced or repaired.

loss on ignition The percentage loss in weight of an ignited sample to constant weight at a specified temperature, usually 900-1,000 °C.

loss payable clause A clause in insurance policies protecting the financial institution that holds the mortgage on the insured property. Any payment that the insurance company makes will be made payable to both the policyholder and the lender.

lot A parcel of land that is established by a survey or delineated on a recorded plot.

lot line The limit or boundary of a land parcel.

louver A framed opening in a wall, fitted with fixed or movable slanted slats. Though commonly used in doors and windows, louvers are especially useful in ventilating systems at air intake and exhaust locations.

louver board (luffer board) One of multiple narrow boards or slats on a louver door, window, or ventilator. The boards are installed at an angle.

louver door A door or louver, usually assembled with its blades in a horizontal position, which allows air to pass through the door when it is closed.

louver shielding angle The angle, measured from the horizontal, above which objects are concealed by a louver.

louver window

low bed

louver window A window composed of a series of sloping, overlapping blades or slats that may be adjusted to admit varying degrees of air or light.

louvre *See* **louver**.

low-alkali cement A cement containing smaller than usual amounts of sodium and/or potassium. Its use is necessary with certain types of aggregate which would otherwise react with high levels of alkali.

low-alloy steel Steel composed of less than 8% alloy.

low bed (low boy) A flatbed trailer used to carry heavy equipment.

low bid In bidding for construction work, the lowest price submitted for performance of the work in accordance with the plans and specifications.

low-carbon steel (mild steel) Steel with less than 0.20% carbon. This type of steel is not used for structural members, due to its ductility. It is good for boilers, tanks, and objects that must be formed.

low consumption toilet Any toilet designed to use 1.6 gallons of water or less per flush.

low-density concrete Any concrete with a unit weight lower than 50 pounds per cubic foot.

low-density polyethylene (LDPE) A widely used thermoplastic that is inexpensive and easy to process. Low density polyethylene is the softest and most flexible version of this material, and is commonly used in packaging and injection molding.

low emissivity glass (low e glass) Insulating glass with a coating or special component that keeps heat in during winter and out during summer. Low e glass reflects internal long wave radiation, like that from a heat source, back into a home while keeping the short wave radiation of the sun out.

lowest qualified bidder *See* **lowest responsible bidder**.

lowest responsible bidder (lowest qualified bidder) The bidder who has submitted the lowest legitimate bid. The owner and architect must agree that this person (or firm) is capable of performing the work covered by the bid proposal.

lowest responsive bid The lowest bid that meets the requirements set forth in the bid proposal.

low-hazard contents Building contents with such an exceptionally low level of combustibility that they are unable to propagate or sustain a fire in and of themselves.

low-heat cement (type IV cement) A special cement that minimizes the amount and rate of heat generation during hydration (setting). Strength is also achieved at a slower rate. Use is limited to structures involving large masses of concrete, such as dams, where the heat generated would be excessive if normal cement were used.

low-iron glass Glass with a low iron content that has a higher visible transmittance and thus a greater ability to collect solar energy.

low-lift grouting The common and simple method of unifying concrete masonry, in which the wall sections are built to a height of not more than 4′ (1.2 meters) before the cells of the masonry units are filled with grout.

low-pressure mercury lamp A mercury-vapor lamp, including germicidal and fluorescent lamps, whose partial pressure during operation is no more than 0.001 atmosphere.

lumber core (stave core)

low-pressure sodium lamp A lamp that produces light via radiation from sodium vapor. Because it renders most colors gray, it is considered a monochromatic light source.

low-pressure steam curing *See* **atmospheric-pressure steam curing.**

low steel A characteristically soft steel that contains less than 0.25% carbon.

low-temperature supply air Supply air below 50°F.

low-voltage lamp A lamp, typically compact halogen, that operates at 12V and requires a transformer. Popular lamps include MR11, MR16 and PAR36.

low-voltage lighting control A remote control system that controls a number of lighting circuits. Lights are turned on or off automatically by electronic controls located within the low-voltage lighting control panel.

L runner The fastener used at the base of solid gypsum lath.

L-shore A shore with an L-head. *See also* **L-head**.

lubricant A substance used to minimize friction between two areas.

Lucite The trade name for a strong, clear plastic material manufactured in sheets and other forms.

luffing boom (live boom) A crane boom with the ability to move vertically while slewing 360 degrees.

lug (1) Any of several types of projections on a piece of material or equipment. Such projections are used during handling and installation. (2) A connector for fastening the end of a wire to a terminal.

lug bolt A bolt with a flat iron bar welded to it.

lug sill A windowsill or doorsill with ends that extend beyond the window or doors, converging with and built into the masonry of the jambs.

lumber Timbers that have been split or processed into boards, beams, planks, or other stock that is to be used in construction and is generally smaller than heavy timber.

lumber core (stave core) Wood core made up of narrow strips of lumber glued together at the edges and commonly held together by a veneer, which is glued to both faces with its grain at 90° to that of the core wood.

lumber, matched Lumber whose side or end edges are cut to form tongue-and-groove joints that fit together when laid side by side or end to end.

lumen A unit of luminous flux that defines the quantity of light.

lumen-hour A measurement of light equal to one lumen for one hour.

lumen method A simple way to calculate the luminaires required to achieve a desired lighting intensity for an area.

luminaire A lighting fixture, with or without the lamps in it.

luminaire dirt depreciation *See* **lamp depreciation.**

luminaire efficiency In lighting calculations, a special ratio of the light emitted by a light fixture to the light emitted by the lamps inside the fixture.

luminaire shielding Any device such as a louver, lens or baffle that controls or directs light from a lamp.

luminous ceiling An area lighting system, mounted on a ceiling, that has a surface of light-transmitting materials with light sources installed above it.

luminous paint A phosphorescent or flourescent paint that glows in the dark after exposure to direct light. Has many safety applications, including use on light switch plates, exit signs, stair edges, and fuse boxes.

lump sum An item or category priced as a whole rather than broken down into its elements.

lump sum agreement *See* **stipulated sum agreement**.

lute (1) A long-handled scraper used to level asphalt or wet concrete. (2) A straightedge used to strike off clay from a brick mold.

lux A measure of illumination striking a surface. One lux is equal to one lumen per square meter.

M

ABBREVIATIONS

The abbreviations listed below are those most commonly used in the construction industry. Alternative forms (usually nonstandard) are shown in parentheses.

m meter

M thousand, bending moment (on drawings)

ma milliampere

MA mechanical advantage

mach machine, machinist

mag magazine, magneto

MAN manual

manuf manufacture

mas masonry

mat, matl material

max maximum

mb millibar

MBF one thousand board feet

MBH 1,000 BTU's per hour

MBM, M.b.m. thousand feet board measure

MBMA Metal Building Manufacturer's Association

MC moisture content, metal-clad, mail chute

MDF medium density fiberboard

MDO medium density overlay

me marbled edges

ME mechanical engineer

meas measure

mech mechanic, mechanical

med medium

memb member

mep mean effective pressure

MER mechanical equipment room

met metallurgy

mezz mezzanine

mf mill finish

mfg manufactured

Mg magnesium

MG motor generator, mixed grain

mgt management

MH manhole

MHW mean high water

mi mile

mid middle

min minimum, minor, minute

MIS Management Information System

misc miscellaneous

mix, mixt mixture

mks meter-kilogram-second

ml, ML material list

mldg, MLDG molding

MLW mean low water

MMF magnetomotive force

Mn manganese

MN magnetic North, main

Mo molybdenum

MO month

mod, modif modification

MOD model

MOE modulus of elasticity

MOL maximum overall length

MOT motor

mp melting point

mpg miles per gallon

mph miles per hour

mr moisture resistant

MRT mean radiant temperature

MSDS Material Safety Data Sheet

MSF per 1,000 square feet

msl mean sea level

MSR machine stress rated

mtg, mtge mortgage

mult multiple, multiplier

mun, munic municipal

mxd mixed (lumber industry)

M DEFINITIONS

machine bolt

machine excavation

machine room

macadam A method of paving in which layers of uniformly graded, coarse aggregate are spread and compacted to a desired grade. Next, the voids are completely filled by a finer aggregate, sometimes assisted by water (water-bound), and sometimes assisted by liquid asphalt (asphalt-bound). The top layers are usually bound and sealed by some specified asphaltic treatment.

machine bolt A threaded straight bolt usually specified by gauge, thread, and head type.

machine burn Any darkening or burning of a material during milling or other machining.

machined A term used to describe a smooth finish on a metal surface.

machine excavation Digging or scooping performed by a machine, as opposed to that performed by hand.

machine finish A finish on a stone surface produced by a smooth-edged planer.

machine rating A standard describing the power that an electric motor is designed to produce.

machine room The room in an elevator system that is designed to house an elevator-hoisting machine and control equipment.

machine stress-rated lumber Lumber that is rated mechanically by a machine that evaluates its structural properties.

made ground Land or ground created by filling in a low area with rubbish or other fill material. Often, such created land is not suitable for building without the use of a pile foundation.

Madison clips (battleships) In electrical work, thin metal clips used to fasten switches and receptacles. Common in old electrical work.

magazine A building for storage of explosives.

magnesia Finely processed magnesium oxide.

magnesite flooring A finished surface material consisting of magnesium oxide, sawdust, and sand combined in various proportions, and subsequently applied to integral concrete floors.

magnesium A lightweight silver-colored metal that is highly flammable and immune to alkalies and is usually used in an alloy. A scale-forming element found in some boiler feed water.

magnesium float A hand tool with a flat magnesium base used to finish concrete flatwork.

magnetic bearing The horizontal angle from magnetic north for a given survey line.

magnetic catch A door catch that uses a magnet to hold it in the closed position.

magnetic driver A tool, employing a magnet, used to hold and drive nails.

magnetic overload relay An overcurrent protection switch or fuse.

magnetic switch An electric switch using an electromagnet for operation.

magnetite A naturally occurring, black iron oxide used as an iron ore and as a high-density aggregate in concrete.

main beam

main runner

main tie

mahlstick (maulstick) A long wooden stick, often padded, that painters use to support and steady the hand while painting ornamental work.

mahogany A straight-grained, medium-density wood originating in the West Indies and Central and South America and used principally in interior plywoods and cabinetry.

mail chute A shaft for dropping mail from upper floors of a building to a central collection box.

mail slot A slot in a wall or door for receiving incoming mail. The slot usually has a cover to prevent draft.

main (1) In electricity, the circuit that feeds all sub-circuits. (2) In plumbing, the principal supply pipe that feeds all branches. (3) In HVAC, the main duct that feeds or collects air from the branches.

main bar (main reinforcement) A reinforcing bar in a concrete member designed to resist stresses from loads and moments, as opposed to those designed to resist secondary stresses.

main beam A structural beam that transmits its load directly to columns, rather than to another beam.

main contractor See **prime contractor**.

main couple The main truss in a timber roof.

main divisions (1) General contractor's work. (2) Each subcontractor's work.

main member See **primary member**.

main office expense A contractor's main office expense consists of the expense of doing business that is not charged directly to the job. Depending on the accounting system used, and the total volume, this can vary from 2 to 20 percent, with the median about 7.2 percent of the total volume.

main rafter A structural roofing member that extends from the plate to the ridge pole at right angles.

main reinforcement See **main bar**.

main runner In a suspended ceiling system, one of the main supporting members.

main sewer In a public sanitary sewer system, the trunk sewer into which branch sewers are connected.

main stack In plumbing, a vent that runs from the building drains up through the roof.

maintainer A small motor grader used for driveways and for repairing the fine grade inside buildings.

maintenance bond A contractor's bond in which a surety guarantees to the owner that defects of workmanship and materials will be rectified for a given period of time. A one-year bond is commonly included in the performance bond.

maintenance curve For a light source, a plot of lumens vs. time.

maintenance factor In lighting calculations, the ratio of illumination of a light source or lighted surface at a given time to that of the initial illumination. This factor is used to determine the depreciation of a lamp or a reflective surface over a period of time.

maintenance period The period after completion of a contract during which a contractor is obligated to repair any defects in workmanship and materials that may become evident. See also **maintenance bond**.

main tie In a roof truss, the bottom straight member that connects the two feet.

male thread

manhole

main vent *See* **vent stack**.

major diameter The largest diameter of a screw thread.

makeup air unit A unit to supply conditioned air to a building to replace air that has been removed by an exhaust system or by combustion.

makeup water Water that is added to a system to replace water that has been lost through evaporation or leaking.

malachite A copper-bearing ore also used as ornamental stone.

male connector An electrical connector with contacts that fit into a female connector.

male nipple A short length of pipe with threads on the outside of both ends.

male plug An electrical plug that inserts into a receptacle.

male thread A thread on the outside of a pipe or fitting.

mall (1) A shaded or covered walk for pedestrians that is often lined with shops. (2) The median strip dividing a highway.

malleability The property of a metal that enables it to be hammered, bent, and extruded without cracking.

malleable iron Cast iron that has been heat-treated to reduce its brittleness.

mallet A small wooden hammer used to drive another tool, such as a chisel or a gouge.

mallet-headed chisel A steel mason's chisel with a rounded head.

mall front A glazed store front facing an enclosed mall.

management host computer A computer that serves as a management-machine interface in a building automation system.

managing partner A partner who is responsible for a wide variety of day-to-day decisions on behalf of the partnership.

mandate A court-authorized command or direction that a person is bound by law to obey.

mandrel A retractable insert for driving a steel pile.

manganese An alloy that is added to most steels as a hardener and deoxidizer.

manhole A vertical access shaft from the ground surface to a sewer or underground utilities, usually at a junction, to allow cleaning, inspection, connections, and repairs.

manhole block Concrete block cast with curved faces and used to form a cylindrical manhole.

manhole cover A removable cast iron cover for a manhole. As many manholes are in paved areas, the cover must be strong enough to bear the weight of traffic.

manhole frame The cast iron frame into which a manhole cover fits.

manhole invert In a sewer manhole, the elevation or grade of the inlet or outlet pipes.

manhole removal An item of work in site preparation that includes demolition and/or filling in an existing manhole.

manhole step A preformed metal or fiberglass step that is permanently fixed to the inside of a manhole or catch basin.

man-hour A unit describing the work performed by one person in one hour.

manifest (1) A list of the contents or the cargo of any shipment. (2) A specific form used by a generator of hazardous waste to track the waste

manifold

mansard roof

mantel (mantelpiece)

from the site of generation to the site of final treatment or disposal.

manifold A distribution or collection pipe or chamber having one inlet and several outlets, or one outlet and several inlets.

manipulative joint A joint in copper tubing where the ends of the tubing are belled outwards.

man lock A chamber in which personnel pass from one environmental pressure to another, such as when entering or leaving a caisson.

manometer A U-shaped tube filled with a liquid used to measure the differential pressure of gasses.

mansard roof A roof with a double pitch on all four sides, the lower level having the steeper pitch. *See also* **curb roof**.

mansion An extremely large and imposing residence.

mantel (mantelpiece) The shelf above and the finished trim or facing around a fireplace.

manual A system of controls that can be operated by hand.

manual batcher A batcher with gates and scales that can be operated by hand.

manual fire pump A pump for water supply to a sprinkler or standpipe system that must be activated by hand.

manufactured homes (mobile homes) Manufactured homes are factory-finished inside and out, and usually have wheeled chassis.

manufactured sand A fine aggregate that is produced by crushing stone, gravel, or slag.

map cracking *See* **checking**.

maple A hardwood that grows in North America and Europe and has a dense uniform texture. Maple is used primarily in flooring and furniture.

marble A metamorphic rock, chiefly calcium carbonate, with various impurities that give it distinctive colors. Marble is used in the architectural facing of both interior and exterior walls.

marbling The application of paints to a surface to give it the appearance of marble.

marezzo A cast imitation of marble used extensively for commode tops and wall facing.

margin (1) The amount added to the cost of materials as a markup. (2) An edge projecting over the gable of a roof. *See also* **verge**. (3) The space between a door and the jambs. (4) The measurement of the exposure of overlapped shingles.

marginal bar A glazing bar that separates a large glazed area in the middle of a window from smaller panes around the outside.

margin draft In stonemasonry, a dressed border on the edge of the face of a hewn stone.

margin light *See* **side light**.

margin strip In wood flooring, a narrow strip that forms a border.

margin trowel A plasterer's hand trowel on which the edges are turned up to finish plaster in corners.

marigold window *See* **rose window**.

marine glue A waterproof glue used on exterior plywoods and other wood-gluing applications where water may be encountered.

marine paint A paint containing elements to withstand exposure to sunlight, salt, and fresh water.

marine plywood A high-grade plywood especially adaptable to

masonry (stone)

boat hull construction. All inner plies must be B grade or better.

marked face The front or veneer side of a wood building product.

market price The price at which both seller and buyer are ready and willing to commit to a sale in the ordinary course of trade.

marking gauge A carpenter's hand tool for scribing a line parallel to an edge. The gauge has a scribe on a rod whose distance is adjustable at the head , and rides along the edge of the material.

mark out To lay out the locations where cuts are to be made on lumber.

markup A percentage of other sums that may be added to the total of all direct costs to determine a final price or contract sum. In construction practice, the markup usually represents two factors important to the contractor. The first factor may be the estimated cost of indirect expense often referred to as *general overhead*. The second factor is an amount for the anticipated profit for the contractor.

marl A silty clay, found in the bottom of lake beds or swamps, with a high percentage of calcium carbonate.

marl brick A high-grade brick made from marl.

marquee A canopy extending out from an entrance for protection from the weather.

marquetry Mosaics of inlaid wood and sometimes ivory and mother of pearl.

martin lock A lock designed to be mortised into a door stile rather than mounted on the surface.

Martin's cement Similar to Keene's cement and used in plaster. This type of cement contains potassium carbonate as an additive in place of the alum used in Keene's cement.

mash hammer A heavy, short-handled mason's hammer with two striking faces. Used with a chisel to remove old mortar between bricks in preparation for repointing. This term is also used regionally as another name for a sledge hammer.

masking The temporary covering of areas adjacent to those to which paint is to be applied. Masking is applied either by sticking something on, as with masking tape, or by covering with a firm mask.

masking tape An adhesive-backed tape used for masking that comes in rolls and various widths. The tape is applied to the surface that is to be left unpainted and removed after the painting has been done, leaving a clean, straight line.

mason A workman skilled in the trade of masonry and/or the finishing of concrete floors.

Masonite® A trade name for a nonstructural building board about 1/4 inch thick, usually with one surface hard and smooth. Masonite can be either tempered or untempered, the tempered form being harder and more water-resistant.

masonry Construction composed of shaped or molded units, usually small enough to be handled by one man and composed of stone, ceramic brick, or tile, concrete, glass, adobe, or the like. The term *masonry* is sometimes used to designate *cast-in-place concrete*.

masonry anchor A metal device attached to a door or window frame that is used to secure it to masonry construction.

395

masonry reinforcing

masonry units

masonry block *See* **masonry unit**.

masonry bonded hollow wall A hollow masonry wall in which the inner and outer wythes (thicknesses) are tied together with masonry units rather than metal ties.

masonry cement A mill-mixed mortar to which sand and water must be added.

masonry drill *See* **star drill**.

masonry fill Insulation material used to fill the voids in masonry units.

masonry filler unit Masonry units that are placed between joists or beams prior to placing the concrete for a concrete slab. The filler unit is used to reduce the amount of concrete required and the weight of the slab.

masonry guard *See* **plaster guard**.

masonry insulation Sound and thermal insulation used in masonry walls. The material can be either rigid insulation, or an expanded aggregate such as perlite.

masonry nail A hard steel nail with a fluted shank that can be driven into masonry or concrete.

masonry panel A prefabricated masonry wall section that is constructed on the ground or in a shop and erected by crane.

masonry pointing Troweling mortar into a masonry joint after the masonry units have been laid.

masonry reinforcing Refers to both the lateral steel rods or mesh laid between the courses of masonry units and the vertical rods that are grouted into the voids.

masonry tie *See* **wall tie**.

masonry toothing Cutting or leaving out of alternate masonry units in a wall to provide a bond for new work.

masonry unit Natural or manufactured building units of burned clay, stone, glass, gypsum, concrete, etc.

masonry veneer A single wythe of masonry for facing purposes.

mason's adjustable multiple-point suspension scaffold A scaffold with a platform supported by bearers that are suspended from wire rope and overhead supports. This type of scaffolding is designed and operated in such a way as to permit the platform to be raised or lowered to any desired working position.

mason's ax *See* **ax hammer**.

mason's hammer A steel hammer having one square face for striking and one curved chisel face for trimming masonry units.

mason's joint A projecting V-shaped masonry joint.

mason's level Three separate levels set in a straight bar of wood or metal for determining level or plumb lines. The level is usually about 4 feet long.

mason's lime Lime used in preparing plaster or mortar.

mason's line A heavy string or cord used by masons to align courses of masonry.

mason's measure A method of making a quantity survey of masonry units required for a job that counts corners twice and does not deduct for small openings.

mason's miter A corner formed out of a solid masonry unit, the inside of which looks like a miter joint. The joints are actually butt joints away from the corner.

mason's putty A lime-based putty mixed with Portland cement and stone dust, and used in ashlar masonry construction.

mason's scaffold

mast arm

mason's scaffold A self-supporting scaffold for the erection of a masonry wall. The scaffold must be strong enough to support the weight of the masons, the masonry units, and the mortar tubs during construction.

mass concrete Any volume of concrete with dimensions large enough to require that measures be taken to cope with generation of heat from hydration of the cement and attendant volume change, to minimize cracking.

mass curing Adiabatic curing in sealed containers.

mass diagram A plotted diagram of the cumulative cuts and fills at any station in a highway job. The diagram is used in highway design and to determine haul distances and quantities.

mass foundation A foundation that is larger than that required for support of the structure and one that is designed to reduce the effects of impact or vibration.

mass haul curve A curve developed from the mass diagram to display haul distances and quantities in a highway job.

mass profile A road profile graphically showing volumes of cut and fill between stations.

mass shooting The simultaneous detonation of explosives in blast holes, as opposed to detonation in sequence with delay caps.

mast The vertical member of a tower crane that carries the load lines.

mast arm The bracket attached to an exterior lamp post that supports a light.

master A term applied to the third and highest level of achievement for a tradesman or mechanic, who by supervision, experience, and examination has earned a master's license attesting that he is a master of the trade and no longer requires supervision of his work, as is the case with the journeyman and apprentice levels.

Master Builder A term applied to one who performs the functions of both design and construction. The Master Builder approach to building construction has been a practice commonplace in much of the world for many centuries. In the United States, design and construction are traditionally seen as two separate and distinct functions.

master clock system An electrical system that synchronizes all the clocks in a building.

MasterFormat The name owned and created by the Construction Specifications Institute (CSI) of the United States and Construction Specifications Canada (CSC) denoting a numerical system of organization for construction-related information and data, based on a 16-division format.

master key A key that operates all the locks in a master-keyed series.

master-keyed lock A locking system intended for use in a series, each lock of which may be actuated by two different keys, one capable of operating every lock of the series, and the other capable of operating only one or a few of the locks.

master plan A zoning plan of a community classifying areas by use, or zoning code used as a guide for future development.

master plumber A plumber licensed to install and assume responsibility for contractual agreements pertaining to plumbing, and to secure needed permits. A journeyman plumber is licensed to

matched boards

install plumbing only under the supervision of a master plumber.

MASTERSPEC® A widely used master specification system, developed by the American Institute of Architects, for design professionals and members of the construction and building industries.

master switch An electrical switch that controls two or more circuits.

mastic (1) A thick bituminous-based adhesive used for applying floor and wall tiles. (2) A waterproof caulking compound used in roofing that retains some elasticity after setting.

mastic asphalt *See* **asphaltic mastic.**

mat (1) A heavy, flexible cover for retaining blasted rock fragments that is usually made of wire, chain, or cordage. (2) A grid of reinforcing bars.

matched boards Boards having been worked with a tongue on one edge and/or end, and a groove at the opposite edge and/or end to provide a tight joint when two pieces are fitted together.

matched lumber *See* **lumber, matched.**

matched siding *See* **drop siding.**

material Any product or substance specified for use in the construction of a project.

material hose *See* **delivery hose.**

materialman A term applied to a person through whom the contractor may obtain the materials of construction. The materialman may be a manufacturer's representative or he may be a distributor or salesman of the tools, products, materials, assemblies, and equipment vital to the process of construction.

material safety data sheet (MSDS) A form published by manufacturers of hazardous materials to describe the hazards thereof.

materials cage The platform on a hoist used for transporting materials to upper floors.

materials lock The chamber through which materials are passed from one environmental pressure to another.

mat foundation A continuous thick-slab foundation supporting an entire structure. This type of foundation may be thickened or have holes in some areas and is typically used to distribute a building's weight over as wide an area as possible, especially if soil conditions are poor.

Matheson joint A bell-and-spigot joint in wrought iron pipe.

matrix In concrete, the mortar in which the coarse aggregate is embedded. In mortar, the cement paste in which the fine aggregate is embedded.

mat sink The depression at an entrance door into which a floor mat is placed.

matte A dull surface finish with low reflectance.

matte dip A treatment given to metals to produce a matte finish. The dip is a mixture of sulfuric and nitric acid and zinc oxide or sulfate.

matte-surfaced glass Glass that has been etched, sandblasted, or ground to create a surface that will diffuse light.

mattock A heavy digging tool with a hoe blade on one side of the head and a pick or ax on the other. *See also* **grub axe.**

mattress A grade-level concrete slab used to support equipment, such as

mechanical drawing

mechanical joint

transformers and air conditioning units, outside a building.

maturing The curing and hardening of construction materials such as concrete, plaster, and mortar.

maul A long-handled heavy wooden mallet. *See also* **beetle**.

maximum demand (1) The greatest anticipated load on an electrical system during a given period of time. (2) The greatest anticipated load on a sanitary waste system during a given period of time.

maximum density The largest unit weight to which a material may be compressed.

maximum rated load The greatest live load, plus dead load, which a scaffold is designed to carry, including a safety factor.

maximum size of aggregates The maximum size of aggregate permitted in a concrete mix design determined by the thickness of slab, distance from the reinforcing steel to the face of the concrete, and the method of placement.

meager lime A low purity lime commonly used in plaster. Contains at least 15% impurities.

means of egress Any continuous exit path from a building to the outside.

measurement A quantity survey from plans or a field survey of work to be done.

measurement standard Any standard set to ensure that measurements are recorded in a reliable, uniform manner.

measuring chain *See* **chain**.

mechanic (1) A person skilled in the repair and maintenance of equipment. (2) Any person skilled in a particular trade or craft.

mechanical advantage The ratio of the weight lifted by a machine divided by the force applied.

mechanical analysis *See* **sieve analysis**.

mechanical application The placing of plaster or mortar by pumping or spraying, as opposed to placement by hand with a trowel.

mechanical bond (mechanical connection) A bond formed by keying or interlocking as opposed to a chemical bond by adhesion, as plaster bonding to lath or concrete bonding to deformed reinforcing rods.

mechanical draft The movement of air through a cooling tower by means of a fan or other mechanical device.

mechanical drawing (1) A graphic representation made with drafting instruments. (2) Plans showing the HVAC and plumbing layout of a building.

mechanical equivalent of heat A measure of mechanical energy that equates work (measured in Joules) and thermal energy (measured in calories). Equal to one Btu of heat and 778 foot-pounds.

mechanical joint A plumbing joint that uses a positive clamping device to secure the sections, such as a flanged joint using nuts and bolts.

mechanical plan In construction documents, the print that shows piping, ductwork, HVAC equipment, and fire safety systems.

mechanical properties The properties of a material defining its elasticity and its stress-strain relationships.

mechanical trowel A machine with interchangeable metal or rubber blades used to compact and smooth plaster.

medium duty scaffold

mechanic's lien A legislative attempt to provide leverage to help secure payments owed for work resulting in an improvement to real property. Generally, a mechanics lien entitles the party who provided the goods and services to place a lien on the property which, like a mortage, is a recognition of a debt that must be paid by the property owner within a prescribed time period. If it is not paid, the lien holder can sell the property and use the proceeds to pay the lien amount.

media filtration A physical process that removes suspended solids from an aqueous waste stream by forcing the fluid through a porous medium.

median The untraveled portion in the center of a divided highway which separates the traffic traveling in opposite directions. *See also* **mall (2)**.

mediation A method of trying to resolve a dispute by the use of an impartial intermediary to suggest ways to settle the dispute, rather than imposing a decision upon the parties.

medium (1) Any material used for the transmission of signals (radio, light, and sound waves). A medium could be cable or wire (radio); optical fiber (light); or water, air, or free space (sound). (2) In paint, the liquid in which the other ingredients are suspended or dissolved.

medium carbon steel Steel with a carbon content of from 0.3 to 0.6 percent.

medium curing asphalt Liquid asphalt composed of asphalt cement and a kerosene-type dilutent (thinner) of medium volatility.

medium curing cutback An asphalt that has been liquefied using a kerosene-based solvent.

medium density fiberboard (MDF) A fiberboard made of compressed wood fibers glued together. The smooth and stable surfaces of MDF provide an excellent substrate for painting or the application of decorative lamination or wood veneers. Commonly used to manufacture furniture, cabinets and flooring systems.

medium density overlay (MDO) An exterior-grade plywood or fiberboard with a fiber resin veneer on both sides. An ideal base for paint, MDO is commonly used for signs.

medium density polyethylene (MDPE) A widely used, inexpensive thermoplastic that is easy to process and has good to excellent chemical resistance. It is also soft and cannot be used in temperatures much above 150°F. MDPE combines the characteristics of low and high density polyethylene. It is less translucent than LDPE but more flexible than HDPE.

medium duty scaffold A scaffold designed and constructed to carry a working load not to exceed 50 psf.

mediumscope A term established by the Construction Specifications Institute (CSI) to denote a section of the specifications that describes a family of related or integrated materials and workmanship requirements. (Narrowscope specifications denote a single product; broadscope specifications denote a section describing differing materials used in a related manner.)

medium-temperature water-heating system A water heating system with a boiler that heats water to between 250° and 350°F before it is supplied to heating devices.

meeting of the minds A mutual agreement to the terms and conditions of a contract.

membrane roofing

membrane waterproofing

mercury vapor lamp

meeting posts With a double gate, the stiles which meet in the middle.

meeting rail With a double-hung window, the horizontal rails which meet in the middle.

meeting stile Any abutting stiles in a pair of doors or windows.

megabit Approximately one million bits.

megahertz One million hertz (Hz).

megalith A very large hewn or unhewn stone used in architecture or as a monument.

melamine A plastic laminate made by fusing a resin-impregnated surface material, under heat and pressure, into a dense, 5/8″ board. Has superior scratch and water resistance and is not prone to delamination.

member A general term for a structural component of a building, such as a beam or column.

membrane The impervious layer or layers of material used in constructing a flat roof.

membrane curing A process of controlling the curing of concrete by sealing in the moisture that would be lost to evaporation. The process is accomplished either by spraying a sealer on the surface or by covering the surface with a sheet film.

membrane fireproofing A lath and plaster layer applied as a fireproofing barrier.

membrane roofing A term that most commonly refers to a roof covering employing flexible elastomeric plastic materials from 35 to 60 mils thick, that is applied from rolls and has vulcanized joints. The initial cost of an elastomeric-membrane roof covering system is higher than a built-up roof, but the life cycle cost is lower.

membrane theory In thin-shell design, the assumption that a shell has no strength in bending because of deflection, and, that the only stresses in any section are in tension, compression, and shear.

membrane waterproofing The application of a layer of impervious material, such as felt and asphaltic cement, to a foundation wall.

mending plate A steel strap with predrilled screw holes used to span and strengthen wood joints.

mensuration The determination of length, area, and volume.

merchant pipe A lightweight pipe that is up to 8% lighter than standard pipe.

mercury switch An electrical switch that contains mercury in a vial to make a silent contact.

mercury vapor lamp A high intensity discharge (HID) lamp that produces a blue-white light by creating an arc in mercury vapor enclosed in a globe or tube.

mesh (1) A network of wire screening or welded wire fabric used in construction. (2) The number of openings per lineal inch in wire cloth.

mesh reinforcing *See* **welded wire fabric**.

mesothelioma A rare form of cancer linked in almost all cases to asbestos exposure.

metal-clad cable *See* **armored cable**.

metal-clad fire door A flush door with a wood core or stiles and rails and heat-insulating material covered with sheet metal.

metal crating Open metal flooring for pedestrian or vehicular traffic used to span openings in floors, walkways, and roadways.

metal deck

metal framing

metal lath

metal curtain wall A metal exterior building wall which is attached to the structural frame but does not support any roof or floor loads.

metal deck Formed sheet-metal sections used in flat-roof systems.

metal framing Metal framed partitions commonly used for fire-rated construction around columns and at beams.

metal gutter Typically, a preformed aluminum or galvanized steel trough attached at the eaves of a sloped roof.

metal halide lamp A high intensity discharge (HID) lamp that produces light from a metal vapor such as mercury or sodium.

metal lath Any of a variety of metal screening or deformed and expanded plate used as a base for plaster. The metal lath is attached to wall studs or ceiling joists.

metallic insulation A heat shield of thin metal applied over insulating board or sheething.

metallic paint A paint containing metal flakes that reflect light.

metallize To coat with a metal, usually by spraying with molten metal.

metal nosings Metal enclosures over the cut ends of acoustic lining sections in ductwork.

metal pan A form used for placing concrete in floors and roofs. A metal pan may also be made of molded fiberglass. *See also* **perforated metal pan**.

metal primer The first coat of paint on a metal surface. Primer usually contains rust inhibitors and/or agents to improve bonding.

metal sash block A concrete masonry unit with a groove in the end into which a metal sash can fit.

metal track In metal stud construction, a U-shaped channel member used along floors, ceilings and walls as a brace for metal studs.

metal trim Grounds, angle beads, picture rails, and other metal accessories that are attached prior to plastering.

metal valley A roof valley gutter lined with sheet metal flashing.

metal wall ties The prefabricated metal strips that secure a masonry veneer to a structural wall.

metal window A solid metal-framed window such as those used in factories.

metamorphic rock A rock mass whose crystalline structure, composition, or texture has been altered by great heat or pressure during its formation.

meter (1) The base unit of length in the metric system of measurement. A meter is equivalent to 39.37 inches. (2) A device for measuring the flow of liquid, gas, or electrical current. *See* **Table of Equivalents** *in Appendix*.

meter stop A valve in a water service line that cuts off the flow of water before it reaches the meter.

metes and bounds The limits or boundaries of property, as identified by measured distances and compass bearings.

methyl methacrylate (MMA) A rigid, transparent material widely used in the manufacture of acrylic resins and plastics, as well as in surface-coating resins, emulsion polymers, and impact modifiers.

metrication The process of converting to the metric system.

metric ton A weight equal to 1,000 kilograms or 2,205 pounds.

middle rail

mezzanine A suspended floor, usually between the first floor and the ceiling, that covers less area than the floor below.

mica A naturally occurring, clear silicate used in thermal and electrical insulation, paint suspensions, and composite roofing materials.

mica pellets *See* **exfoliated vermiculite**.

micrometer (1) Instrument used for accurately measuring extremely small distances. (2) Unit of linear distance equal to one-millionth of a meter.

micron A unit of measurement equal to 0.00004 inch, or one-millionth of a meter.

microwave A very short electromagnetic wave with a wavelength range from one millimeter to one meter.

microwave motion detector A device that detects motion by sending out a microwave signal and looking for a return. A moving object will reflect back some microwave energy, triggering a response. Applications include security, lighting and automatic door systems.

middle lap joint A T-shaped joint formed when the end of one member and the middle of another are joined. Each member is halved along the area of the joint to form a flush connection.

middle rail The intermediate horizontal rail between two door stiles that can be either exposed as in a panel door or concealed as in a flush door.

middle strip In flat-slab framing, the slab portion that occupies the middle half of the span between columns. *See also* **column strip**.

mil A lineal measurement equal to 0.001 inch. Used to measure wire and material thickness.

mildew A fungus that grows on damp fabric and other materials, particularly when there is a lack of air circulation.

mildewstat A mildew-inhibiting chemical.

mild steel A steel having a low carbon content, and therefore being relatively soft and ductile. This type of steel is sometimes used for the manufacture of boilers and tanks, but not for structural beams, columns, or lintels. Mild steel is not as resistant to corrosion as wrought or cast iron and corrodes faster if not regularly maintained.

mile A distance measure equal to 5,280 feet, 1760 yards, or 8 furlongs.

mileage A rate per mile established as an allowance for traveling expenses.

mileage tax A license tax levied on intrastate transportation business to compensate for use of the state's public roads.

milkiness A whitish haze caused by moisture and often occurring in a varnish finish.

milk of lime A hydrated lime slaked in water to form a lime putty.

mill To shape metal or wood to a desired dimension by a machine that removes excess material.

mill construction Historically, a type of construction used for factories and mills and consisting of masonry walls, heavy timbers, and plank floors. *See also* **heavy timber**.

Miller Act A federal labor law that requires general contractors working on federally funded construction projects to obtain performance bonds and labor and

millwork

mineral fiber tile

material payment bonds to protect the interests of subcontractors and suppliers. The Miller Act applies to all United States government construction contracts valued at more than $25,000.

mill finish The type of finish produced on metal by the extrusion or cold rolling of sections.

milling (1) In metal, the process of shaping an item by rotary cutting machines. (2) In stonework, the shaping of a stone to the desired dimensions.

mill length (random length) Refers to length of pipe, usually for power plant or oil field use, often made in double random lengths of 30 to 35 feet. (The usual run-of-the-mill pipe is 16 to 20 feet in length.)

mill run Products from a mill, such as a sawmill, which have not been graded or sized.

mill scale A thin, loose coat of iron oxide which forms on iron or steel when heated.

millwork All the building products made of wood that are produced in a planing mill, such as moldings, door and window frames, doors, windows, blinds, and stairs. Millwork does not include flooring, ceilings, and siding.

millwright A carpenter skilled in the layout, installation, and alignment of heavy equipment such as that used in manufacturing.

mineral admixture A substance added to concrete as both a filler, improving the physical structure by occupying the spaces between the cement particles, and as a "pozzolan," reacting chemically to impart far greater strength and durability.

mineral aggregate *See* **aggregate**.

mineral dust Aggregate passing the No. 200 screen, usually a by-product of crushed limestone or traprock.

mineral fiber A fibrous material produced from glass, rock or slag.

mineral fiber insulation Insulation primarily comprised of rock, slag, or glass fibers.

mineral fiber tile A preformed ceiling tile composed of mineral fiber and a binder with good acoustical and thermal properties.

mineral-filled asphalt Asphalt with mineral dust in suspension to improve its body and plasticity.

mineral filler *See* **mineral dust**.

mineral-insulated cable Seamless copper tubing carrying one or more conductors that is embedded in refractory minerals and used in areas that may be subjected to high heat.

mineral right A legal interest or right to the minerals in a parcel of land, with or without ownership of the surface of that land.

mineral spirits A liquid paint thinner and solvent obtained from a petroleum distillation process.

mineral-surfaced felt A roofing felt used on flat or sloped roofs which has a mineral-aggregate surface that improves its wearing and heat-reflecting properties.

mineral wool Fibers formed from mineral slag, the most common being glass wool, which is used in loose or batt form for thermal and sound insulation and for fireproofing.

miner's dip needle An instrument with a magnetic needle that indicates the presence of magnetic material in the ground.

minimum acceptable pressure The lowest pressure in an air and water

mission tile

distribution systems that still allows for safe and efficient operation.

Minimum Wage Law Common term used to describe the Fair Labor Standards Act enacted by Congress in 1938. This act established a minimum wage for workers and the 40-hour work week.

minor change A job change requiring field approval only. No change order is necessary.

minor diameter The smallest diameter of a screw thread.

minute An angle measurement equal to 1/60 of a degree.

mirror glazing quality A definable high standard of quality used in the glass industry.

misfire An explosive charge which has failed to detonate.

mission tile A clay roofing tile shaped like a longitudinal segment of a cylinder. The tile is used on sloped roofs with the concave side alternately up, then down.

mist coat A very thin sprayed coat of paint or lacquer.

miter *See* **miter joint**.

miter box A device used by a carpenter or cabinetmaker to cut the bevels for a mitered joint.

miter brad A corrugated fastener that spans a mitered joint.

miter clamp A clamping device that holds a mitered joint during fastening and gluing.

miter cut The beveled cut, usually 45°, made at the end of a piece of molding or board that is used to form a mitered joint.

miter dovetail A dovetail joint in which the pins do not project all the way through, so that it looks like a mitered joint.

mitered hip A roofing hip that has been close cut.

mitered valley A roofing valley that has been close cut.

miter gauge A gauge that measures the angle of a miter.

miter joint A joint, usually 90°, formed by joining two surfaces beveled at angles, usually 45° each.

miter knee The miter joint formed when the horizontal handrail at a landing is joined to the sloping handrail of the stairs.

miter plane A carpenter's planing tool used for preparing the surfaces for miter or butt joints.

miter rod A flat metal plate with on end cut at a 45° angle that plasterers use to finish inside corners.

miter saw *See* **tenon saw**.

miter square A carpenter's square with one edge having an angle of 45° for laying out miter joints.

miter valve A valve with a disk that sits at a 45° angle to the valve axis.

mitigation of damages A duty that the law imposes on an injured party to make a reasonable effort to minimize his or her damages after an injury.

mix A general term referring to the combined ingredients of concrete or mortar. Examples might be a five-bag mix, a lean mix, or a 3,000-psi mix.

mix design The selection of specific materials and their proportions for a concrete or mortar batch, with the goal of achieving the required properties with the most economical use of materials.

mixed glue A premixed synthetic resin glue including the hardener.

mixed in place An asphalt course of mineral aggregate and emulsified asphalt mixed at the site by special road-mixing equipment.

mixer

mixed occupancy Two or more classes of occupancy in a single structure.

mixer A machine for blending the ingredients of concrete, mortar, or grout. Mixers are divided into two categories: batch mixers and continuous mixers. Batch mixers blend and discharge one or more batches at a time, whereas continuous mixers are fed the ingredients and discharge the mix continuously.

mixer efficiency The ability of a mixer to produce a homogeneous mix within a given number of revolutions or a given period of time.

mixer truck *See* **transit mix concrete**.

mixing box In HVAC systems a chamber, usually located upstream of the filters, that collects outside air and return air.

mixing cycle The elapsed time between discharges of a batch mixer.

mixing plant *See* **batch plant**.

mixing speed In mixing a batch of concrete, the rate of rotation of a mixer drum or of the mixing paddles expressed in revolutions per minute (RPM). The rate can also be expressed as the distance traveled, in feet per minute (FPM), of a point on the circumference of a mixer drum at its maximum diameter.

mixing time The elapsed time for mixing a batch of concrete or mortar.

mixing valve A valve that mixes two liquids or a liquid and a gas, such as steam with water or hot water with cold water.

mixing water The water used in mixing a batch of concrete, mortar, or grout, exclusive of water

previously absorbed by the aggregates. As a general rule, the water should be clean enough to drink.

mix proportions The quantities of cement, coarse aggregate, fine aggregate, water, and other additives in a batch of concrete by weight or volume.

mobile crane Any crane mounted on wheels or tracks. They are classified by lifting capacity.

mobile gantry A movable framework housing a work platform or means to support equipment.

mobile hoist A personnel or material platform hoist that can be towed to and around the site on its own wheels.

mobile home A term commonly applied to any prefabricated dwelling, whether or not wheels are attached.

mobile scaffold A scaffold that can be moved on wheels or casters.

mock-up A model, either full size or to scale, of a construction system or assembly used to analyze construction details, strength, and appearance. Mock-ups are commonly used for masonry and exposed concrete construction projects.

model (1) A scale representation of an object, system, or building used for structural, mechanical, or aesthetic analysis. (2) A compilation of parameters used in developing a system.

model codes Professionally prepared building regulations and codes, regularly attended and revised, designed to be adopted by municipalities and appropriate political subdivisions by ordinance. Model codes are used to regulate building construction for the welfare and safety of the general public.

modem Short for *modulator/demodulator*. An electronic device that transmits data to or from a computer via telephone lines. A modem translates between digital signals (used by data processing equipment) and analog signals (used in voice switching equipment). Once the data is sent through the telephone lines, it is retranslated back into digital form in the computer at the receiving end.

modification (to construction contract documents) (1) A change to a contract which is made after the contract has been signed by both parties. (2) A change order.

modified bitumen A heavy roofing material employing multiple layers of asphalt and reinforcers around a core of plastic or rubber modifiers. Installed with a special torching apparatus, a cold adhesive or hot mopped into place using methods of asphalt application.

modified wood Wood processed by a chemicals, heat, compression, or other means to increase strength and resistance properties.

modular construction (1) Construction in which similar units or subcomponents are combined repeatedly to create a total system. (2) A construction system in which large prefabricated units are combined to create a finished structure. (3) A structural design which uses dimensions consistent with those of the uncut materials supplied. Common modular measurements are 4 inches to 4 feet.

modular masonry unit A brick or block manufactured to a modular dimension of 4″.

modular ratio The ratio of the modulus of elasticity of steel to that of elasticity of concrete, denoted by n in the formula: $n = Es/Ec$.

modulation The tendency of a control to adjust by increments and decrements, rather than in an "on/off" fashion.

module A unit representing a dimension or item used in planning, estimating, or recording the construction of a project.

modulus of compression The measure of a material's resistance to inward pressure.

modulus of elasticity The unit stress divided by the unit strain of a material that has been subjected to a strain below its elastic limit.

modulus of resilience The measure of the elastic energy absorbed by a unit volume of a material when it has reached its elastic limit in tension.

modulus of rigidity The measure of a material's resistance to shear. The ratio of unit shearing stress to unit shearing strain.

modulus of rupture The measure of a beam's maximum load-carrying capacity. The ratio of the rupture's bending moment to the beam's section modulus.

modulus of toughness The measure of energy per unit volume that is absorbed by a material when subject to impact, up to the point of fracture.

modulus of volume *See* **bulk modulus of elasticity**.

moellon Stone rubble used as fill placed inside a masonry wall.

mogul base A screw-in type base for a large incandescent lamp usually of 300 watts or more.

moisture proofing

molding

Mohs' scale An arbitrary scale devised to determine the relative hardness of a mineral by its resistance to scratching by another mineral. Talc is rated No. 1, and diamond is rated No. 10.

moist room An enclosure maintained at a given temperature and relative humidity and used for curing test cylinders of concrete or mortar.

moisture barrier A dampproof course or vapor barrier, but not necessarily waterproof. *See also* **vapor barrier**.

moisture content The weight of water in materials such as wood, soil, masonry units, or roofing materials, expressed as a percentage of the total dry weight.

moisture expansion The increase in dimensions of a material as a result of the absorption of water. *See also* **bulking**.

moisture gradient The difference in moisture content between the inside and the outside of an object, such as a wall or masonry unit.

moisture migration The movement of moisture through the components of a building system such as a floor or wall. The direction or the movement is always from high-humidity areas to low-humidity areas.

moisture movement *See* **moisture migration**.

moisture proofing The application of a vapor barrier.

mold The hollow form in which a casting or pressing is made.

moldboard The curved shape or blade of a plow, bulldozer, grader, or other earth-moving equipment.

molded brick Brick that has been cast rather than pressed or cut, often with a distinct design or shape.

molded-case circuit breaker An electrical circuit breaker manufactured in a molded insulated housing.

molded insulation Thermal insulation premolded to fit plumbing pipes and fittings. Common materials are fiberglass, calcium silicate, and urethane foams, with or without protective coverings.

molded plywood Plywood that has been permanently shaped to a desired curve during curing.

molding An ornamental strip of material used at joints, cornices, bases, door and window trim, and the like, and most commonly made of wood, plaster, plastic, or metal.

mold stone (jamb stone) A stone that serves as a window jamb.

mole A machine used to bore tunnels.

mole ball An egg-shaped ball pulled behind a special subsoil plow to provide a water course for drainage.

molecular sieve A device for selective collection, by adsorption, of a substance in a gas or a liquid.

mole drain A subsurface drain created by a mole ball.

moler brick Brick, made from moler earth or diatomite, that has better insulation properties than common brick.

molly A threaded insert for plaster, sheetrock, or concrete walls for receiving a bolt, screw, or nail.

moment An applied load or force which creates bending in a structural member. It is numerically expressed as the product of the force times the length of the lever arm, and given in units such as foot-pounds.

moment connection

mop sink

mortar

moment connection A rigid connection between structural members which transfers moment from one member to the other, and thus resists the moment force. A pinned connection cannot resist moment forces, only shear forces.

moment of inertia In a structural member, the product of each element of mass times the square of the distance from an axis.

momentum The mass times the velocity of a moving object.

Monel® The registered trademark name of a nickel alloy containing two-thirds nickel, one-third copper and small amounts of other metals. Monel®, which is ductile, stronger than mild steel and more resistant to corrosion than bronze, has been used for roofing, flashing and decorative elements. Excellent for making fasteners and anchors.

money damages A monetary award that a party who has breached a contract is ordered by a court to pay as compensation to the nonbreaching party.

monitor (1) A raised section of a roof, often along the ridge of a gable roof, with louvers or windows in the side for ventilation or light. (2) In closed-circuit television, a video display device used to check the quality of a picture or image transmitted by a camera.

monk bond A modified Flemish bond with two stretchers and a header.

monkey tail A vertical scroll at the bottom of a handrail.

monkey wrench A wrench with a fixed jaw and an adjustable jaw.

monolith A large architectural member or monument cut from one stone or cast as one unit from concrete.

monolithic In glazing, a window containing only one light or pane.

monolithic concrete Concrete that has been cast continuously with no joints other than construction joints.

monolithic construction The pouring of concrete grade beam and floor slab together to form a building foundation.

monolithic surface treatment A concrete finish obtained by shaking a dry mixture of cement and sand on a concrete slab after strike-off, then troweling it into the surface.

monolithic terrazzo Terrazzo applied directly over a concrete surface instead of over a mortar underbed.

monomer A molecule of low molecular weight capable of reacting with other molecules of low molecular weight to form a polymer.

Monotube® pile A cold-processed steel pile with a fluted cross section for use in deep foundations.

mopboard *See* **baseboard**.

mop plate A protective plate at the bottom of a door, such as a kickplate.

mop sink A low, deep sink used by janitors.

mopstick A wood handrail with a circular cross section, except for a small flat section on the bottom for attaching the supports.

mortar (1) A plastic mixture used in masonry construction that can be troweled and hardens in place. The most common materials that mortar may contain are Portland, hydraulic, or mortar cement, lime, fine aggregate, and water. (2) The mixture of cement paste and fine aggregate which fills the voids between the coarse aggregate in fresh concrete.

mortar box

Mortise and tenon joint

motor controller

mortar aggregate (mortar sand)
Natural or manufactured fine
aggregate, usually washed screened
sand.

mortar bed A layer of fresh mortar
into which a structural member or
flooring is set.

mortarboard A board about 3 feet
square on which mortar is placed
for use by a mason on a scaffold.

mortar box A shallow box in which
mortar or plaster is mixed by hand.

mortar cube A standard-sized cube
made of mortar for testing the
compressive strength of a mix.

mortar mill (mortar mixer) A
machine with paddles in a rotating
drum for mixing and stirring mortar.

mortar mixer See **mortar mill**.

mortar sand See **mortar aggregate**.

mortgage A loan in which property
is pledged as collateral.

mortgagee The lender in a
mortgage loan.

mortgage lien A filed charge using
property as security. Often mortgage
liens are obtained by contractors or
material suppliers for a particular
project.

mortgagor The borrower in a
mortgage loan.

mortise (1) A recess cut in one
member, usually wood, to receive
a tenon from another member.
(2) A recess such as one cut into a
door stile to receive a lock or hinge.

mortise and tenon joint A joint
between two members, usually
wood, which incorporates one or
more tenons on one member fitting
into mortises in the other member.
Used on joints such as door stiles,
door rails, window sashes, and
cabinetry.

mortise chisel A carpenter's tool
for cutting mortises.

mortised astragal A two-piece
astragal door with two leaves. One
piece of the astragal is mortised into
the edge of each door.

mortise gauge A carpenter's tool for
scribing the location on mortises. It
is similar to a marking gauge, but
scribes two parallel lines.

mortise machine A power-driven
machine for cutting rectangular or
round mortises in a wood member.

mortise pin A pin that secures a
mortise and tenon joint by being
driven through either the extension
of the tenon or through the whole
joint.

mosaic (1) An aerial photographic
map pasted up using the center
portion of overlapping vertical
photographs. (2) A design created
by inlaying pieces of stone, glass, or
tile in a mortar bed. (3) A design
of inlaid pieces of wood.

motion detection equipment
A device that detects motion by
sending out a fixed electromagnetic
or ultrasonic signal. A moving
object will disrupt the frequency
of the signal, triggering a response.
Applications include security,
lighting and automatic door
systems.

motor controller A device that
controls the power delivered to
a motor or motors.

motor grader See **grader**.

mottle A clouding, spotting, or
irregular grain appearing in stone
such as marble or in wood and
wood veneers.

mottler A thick paintbrush used for
creating a mottled or grained look.

mottling A defect in spray-painted
surfaces appearing as round marks.

mouse (1) A device with a piece of
curved lead and string for pulling a
sash cord over a pulley. (2) A hand-

movable form

multifolding door

held device that is moved around on a desk or surface to control the cursor in a computer and select functions.

movable form A large prefabricated concrete form of a standard size which can be moved and reused on the same project. The form is moved either by crane or on rollers to the next location.

movable partition A non-load-bearing demountable partition that can be relocated and can be either ceiling height or partial height.

moving ramp A continuously moving belt or other system designed for carrying passengers on a horizontal plane or up an incline.

moving stairs *See* **escalator.**

moving walk *See* **moving ramp.**

M-roof Any roof that incorporates two adjacent pitched roofs in resemblance to the letter "M."

muck (1) A soil high in organic material, often very moist. (2) Any soil to be excavated.

mud (1) Soil containing enough water to make it soft and plastic. (2) A slang expression for joint compound.

mudcapping The process of blasting boulders or rock surfaces by placing explosives in the surface and covering them with mud rather than placing the explosive in a blast hole.

mudjacking A method of raising a depressed concrete highway slab or slab-on-grade by boring holes at selected locations and pumping in grout or liquid asphalt.

mudroom An entrance, particularly to a rural residence, where muddy footwear can be removed and stored.

mud rotary drilling method A drilling method that uses mud as the lubricant for the drill.

mudsill A plank or beam laid directly on the ground, especially for posts or shores for formwork or scaffolding.

mud slab A base slab of low-strength concrete from 2″ to 6″ thick placed over a wet subbase before placing a concrete footing or grade slab.

mud sucker *See* **diaphragm pump.**

muffle A layer of grout over a plaster mold used to rough in the plaster. The muffle is chipped off when the final coat of plaster is applied.

mulch Organic material such as straw, leaves, or wood chips spread on the ground to prevent erosion, to control weeds, to minimize evaporation as well as temperature extremes, and to improve the soil.

mule A template used to form concrete curbs and gutters.

mullion The vertical member separating the panels or glass lights of a window or door system.

multiconductor An electrical cable containing multiple wires inside a single outer jacket.

multifolding door A large door or room divider composed of hinged, rigid panels supported on an overhead track. When the door is open, the panels fold against each other.

multimedia filter A water supply system filter that incorporates several different filtering elements or materials.

multiple dwelling A building that houses two or more independent residential dwelling units.

multiple glazing Any glazing that incorporates two or more sheets of glass, as in a thermal or sound insulating application.

multiple layer adhesive An adhesive film used as a bond between dissimilar materials.

multizone system

muntin

mushroom construction

multiple of direct personnel expense An accounting method used to pay for professional services. A factor (based on personnel cost) is applied to cover indirect and direct costs, as well as profit.

multiple of direct salary expense An accounting method used to pay for professional services. It is based on direct salary expenses multiplied by a factor that accounts for the cost of benefits that are linked to direct salary as well as indirect expenses, other direct expenses, and profit.

multiple ownership A form of ownership whereby two or more people or entities own interests in the same real property at the same time. There are three basic forms of multiple ownership of real property. *See also* **tenancy in common, joint tenancy,** *and* **tenancy by the entirety**.

multiple prime contract A contract used when one or more constructors are employed under separate contracts to perform work on the same project, either in a sequence or coincidentally.

multiple prime contracts A construction approach whereby the owner enters into separate contracts with different trade contractors, rather than one contract with a general construction contractor.

multiple surface treatments A term applied to successive pavement surface treatments of asphaltic materials and aggregate.

multiplex To send signals from more than one source simultaneously over a single channel. *See also* **frequency division multiplexing** *and* **time division multiplexing**.

multiplier A factor used to adjust costs for modifications, such as for location, time, or size of project.

multistage stressing The prestressing

of concrete members in stages as the construction progresses.

multistory A term commonly applied to buildings with five or more stories.

multiunit wall A masonry wall with two or more wythes.

multizone system (1) An air conditioning system that is capable of handling several individual zones simultaneously. (2) A heating or HVAC system having individual controls in two or more zones in a building.

multizone units Air-handling units with parallel heating and cooling air paths providing individual mixing of air-distribution circuits into a single duct for each zone.

municipality A political unit, legally incorporated for self-government or other public purposes.

municipal lien A claim or lien filed by a municipality against a property owner for collection of the property owner's proportionate share of a public improvement made by the municipality that also improves the property owner's land.

muntin A short vertical or horizontal bar used to separate panes of glass in a window or panels in a door. The muntin extends from a stile, rail, or bar to another bar. *See also* **vertical bar**.

muriatic acid An acid mixed with water to clean masonry. Muriatic acid is also commonly used to etch smooth concrete surfaces for painting.

mushroom construction A system of flat-slab concrete construction, with no beams, in which columns are flared at the top to resist shear stresses near the column head.

music wire (piano wire) Steel wire used for alignment.

mute A mortised rubber silencing device for a door.

mutual assent The agreement of two or more parties to be bound to the terms of a contract. A contract is not legally enforceable without mutual assent.

N

ABBREVIATIONS

The abbreviations listed below are those most commonly used in the construction industry. Alternative forms (usually nonstandard) are shown in parentheses.

n, N noon, number, North, nail, nitrogen, normal

Na sodium

NAAMM National Association of Architectural Metal Manufacturers

NAT natural

NBC National Building Code

nbm net board measure

NBS National Bureau of Standards

NC noise criterion

NCM noncorrosive metal

NCX fire-retardant treated wood

NDT nondestructive testing

NEC National Electrical Code

NECA National Electrical Contractors Association

NELMA Northeastern Lumber Manufacturers Association

NEMA National Electrical Manufacturers Association

NESC National Electrical Safety Commission

NESHAPS National Emission Standards for Hazardous Air Pollutants

NFC National Fire Code

NFIP National Flood Insurance Program

NFPA National Fire Protection Agency

NHLA National Hardwoods Lumber Association

NHPMA Northern Hardwood and Pine Manufacturers Association

Ni nickel

NIC not in contract

NIOSH National Institute of Occupational Safety and Health

NLRA National Labor Relations Act

NLRB National Labor Relations Board

NM nonmetallic sheathed

NOM nominal

NOP not otherwise provided for

norm normal

NPS nominal pipe size

nr near, noise reduction

NRC noise reduction coefficient

NS not specified

ntp normal temperature and pressure

NTS not to scale

nt. wt., n.wt. net weight

num numeral

NWWDA National Wood Window and Door Association

N1E nosed one edge (used in lumber industry)

N2E nosed two edges (used in lumber industry)

nail

nail puller

naked flooring

narrow light door

nagging *See* **nogging**.

nail A slender piece of metal with a point on one end which is driven into construction materials by impact. Nails are classified by size, shape, and usage.

nailable concrete Concrete, usually made with a suitable lightweight aggregate, with or without the addition of sawdust, into which nails can be driven.

nailer A strip of wood or other fitting attached to or set in concrete, or attached to steel to facilitate making nailed connections.

nail float *See* **devil float**.

nailing block (nog) A wood block set into masonry or steel and used to facilitate fastening other structural members by nailing.

nailing ground A nailing strip to which trim is attached.

nail puller One of a variety of hand tools for pulling nails. The shape and size depends on the nails to be pulled.

nail punch *See* **nail set**.

nail set A hand-held, tapered steel rod specifically designed to drive nail heads below the surface of wood. The rod is used specifically in finish carpentry work.

naked flooring The system of floor joists and beams over which flooring will be placed.

naked wall A wall or partition, with lath in place, ready for plastering.

NA number A classification code assigned to a particular material by the Department of Transportation.

naphtha-based oil Petroleum oil used as an additive in herbicides.

Naphtha oil alone has herbicidal properties on some weeds and grasses.

narrow light door A door with a narrow vertical light near the lock stile. *See also* **vertical vision light door**.

narrow ringed timber Lumber with fine-grained, closely spaced growth rings.

Narrowscope A term established by the Construction Specifications Institute to denote a section of the specifications that describes a single product. *See also* **Mediumscope** *and* **Broadscope**.

National Electric Code® (NEC) A nationally recognized code that addresses proper installation of electrical systems and equipment. Published by the National Fire Protection Association, the code is revised and reissued every three years. The revision process includes a proposal period when suggestions from the public are accepted. Code-making panels review all proposals and make recommendations that are then reviewed by a correlating committee.

National Emission Standards for Hazardous Air Pollutants (NESHAPS) Federal air pollution regulations instituted by the Clean Air Act and enforced by the Environmental Protection Agency (EPA).

National Fire Protection Agency A non-profit organization that publishes the National Electrical Code®, the Life Safety Code®, the Fire Prevention Code™, the National Fuel Gas Code®, and the National Fire Alarm Code®.

natural stone

National Historic Landmark
A property listed in the National Register of Historic Places. Properties are assigned this designation by the Secretary of the Interior based on their national (as compared to state or regional) importance. The National Parks Service administers the process of designating properties as NHLs through the National Historic Landmarks Program.

National Labor Relations Act
An act of Congress sometimes known as the Wagner Act, enacted in 1935. This act mandated a framework of procedure and regulation by which management-labor relations are to be conducted.

National Labor Relations Board
An organization established by the United States government to enforce the National Labor Relations Act.

National Lumber Grades Authority
One of seven regional grading agencies in North America that are authorized to write and publish grading rules for lumber. *See also* **grade stamp**.

natural asphalt Asphalt occurring in nature through natural evaporation of petroleum. This type of asphalt can be refined and used in paving materials.

natural attenuation
An environmental remediation process that is based on allowing naturally occurring processes to decompose or degrade wastes.

natural cement A hydraulic cement produced by heating a naturally occurring limestone at a temperature below the melting point, and then grinding the material into a fine powder.

natural convection The movement of air resulting from differences in density usually caused by differences in temperature.

natural draft Refers to the movement of air through a cooling tower by the force of air density differential.

natural finish A finish on wood that allows the grain to show; a clear finish.

natural gas A naturally occurring combustible gas used for industrial and domestic heating and power.

natural grade The undisturbed elevation of a property before any excavation operations.

natural resin Any naturally occurring thermoplastic substance. Used in paints and varnishes, among other applications.

natural seasoning In the lumber industry, a curing process using natural air convection.

natural stone Stone shaped and sized by nature as opposed to stone which has been quarried and cut.

NCX fire-retardant treated wood Treated wood generally used on exterior balconies, steps, and roof systems. Carries the Underwriters' Laboratories rating of FRS.

neat (1) Idiom for exact dimensions, i.e., excavation to the designed width of the footing. (2) A term referring to a process by which a material is prepared for use without addition of any other materials except water. Examples include neat cement or neat plaster.

neat cement A cement mortar or grout made without addition of sand or lime.

neat line The line or plane defining the limits of work, particularly in excavation of earth or rock. Excavation beyond the neat line is usually not a pay item in a unit price contract.

needle valve

neat plaster Plaster mixed with no aggregate.

neat size The final size after trimming, planing, or finishing.

needle (1) In underpinning, the horizontal beam that temporarily holds up the wall or column while a new foundation is being placed. (2) In forming or shoring, a short beam passing through a wall to support shores or forms during construction. (3) In repair or alteration work, a beam that temporarily supports the structure above the area being worked on.

needle bath A shower bath in which many water jets are sprayed horizontally onto the bather.

needle beam *See* **needle**.

needle nose pliers Pliers that are outfitted with long thin jaws for use in narrow spaces.

needle scaffold A scaffold that is supported by needles passing through a wall.

needle valve A type of globe valve in which a long pin or needle, tapered at the end, moves in and out of a conical seat to regulate the flow of liquid.

needling The placing of needles, or a support system using needles.

negative easement A right of accomodation that allows its holder to prevent the owner of the land from actions on his land. For example, a landowner may be unable to build a structure on his property because his neighbor owns a negative easement requiring an unobstructed view of an adjacent body of water.

negative friction The additional load placed on a pile by the settling of fill placed around it. The effect of negative friction is to pull the pile down.

negative pressure ventilation system A method of providing low-velocity airflow from uncontaminated areas into contaminated areas by means of a portable exhaust system equipped with HEPA filters.

negative reinforcing Steel reinforcing for negative moment in a reinforced concrete structural member.

negligence The failure of a party to conform its conduct to the standard of care required by law. The law requires that a person excercise that degree of care which a reasonable person would exercise under the same or similar circumstances. *See also* **due care**.

negotiated procurement A procedure used by the U.S. government for contracting whereby the government and potential contractor negotiate on both price and technical requirements after submission of proposals. Award is made to the contractor whose final proposal is most advantageous to the government.

negotiating Arriving at an agreement by bargaining.

negotiation A process used to determine a mutually satisfactory contract sum, and terms to be included in the contract for construction. In negotiations, the owner directly selects the constructor and the two, often with assistance of the design professional, derive by compromise and a meeting of the minds the scope of the project and its cost.

negotiation phase *See* **bidding**.

neon lamp A lamp that gains its illumination by electric current passing through neon gas.

neoprene A synthetic rubber with high resistance to petroleum

neoprene roof

neoprene vibration pads

products and sunlight. Neoprene is used in many construction applications, such as roofing and flashing, vibration absorption, and sound absorption.

neoprene roof A roof covering made of neoprene sheet material with heat-welded joints, which can be either ballasted or non-ballasted. This type of roof covering has good elastic and durability properties over a long time span.

neoprene vibration pad A vibration-absorbing device placed under permanently installed machinery.

neoprene waterproofing Sheet waterproofing material placed on the outside of a foundation wall with a mastic.

nephrotoxin A substance that causes kidney damage.

nestable joist Standard shape for a light gauge framing joist.

nested nails Nails having a crescent-shaped piece missing in the head to allow them to be fitted tightly together.

nested studs Two studs placed together for additional support in framing an opening.

net cross-sectional area In defining a masonry unit, the gross cross-sectional area minus the area of the ungrouted cores or cellular voids.

net cut In excavation, the total cut, minus the compacted fill required, between particular stations.

net fill In excavation, the compacted fill required, minus the cut material available, between particular stations.

net floor area The occupied area of a building not including hallways, elevator shafts, stairways, toilets, and wall thicknesses. The net floor area is used for determining rental space and fire-code requirements.

net load In heating calculations, the heating requirement, not considering heat losses, between the source and the terminal unit.

net mixing water *See* **mixing water**.

net price The lowest price, after all deductions, discounts, etc.

net site area The area of a building site less streets and roadways.

net weight The weight of an article, cargo, or other load minus the transporting vehicle.

network In CPM (Critical Path Method) terminology, a graphic representation of activities showing their interrelationships.

network schedule A method of scheduling the construction process where various related events are programmed into a sequential network on the basis of starting and finishing dates.

neurotoxin A substance that adversely affects the nervous system or brain.

neutral axis In structural design, an imaginary line in a structural member where no tension, compression, or deformation exist. If holes are to be drilled through a structural member for conduits or pipes, they should be drilled at the neutral axis.

neutral (1) An electrical conductor used as the primary return path for current during normal operation of an electrical device. (2) The center tap of a three- or four-wire transformer. Neutral cable will carry current when there is an unbalanced load between wires.

neutralize To reduce the pH of an alkali, or to raise the pH of an acid, to approximately 7.0.

newel

nibbed tile

neutralizing The treatment of concrete, plaster, or masonry surfaces with an acid solution in order to neutralize the lime before application of paint.

neutralizing basin In a building drainage system, a device that nutralizes acid-bearing wastes before their entry into the system.

newel The post supporting a handrail at the top and bottom of a flight of stairs. Also, the center post of a spiral staircase.

newel cap The often decorative top or cap of a newel.

newel drop A decorative downward projection of a newel through a soffit.

newel joint The joint between a newel and the handrail.

newel post See **newel**.

New Urbanism A movement in city planning that tries to recommit traditional town planning designs to a modern context. It seeks to lessen dependence on automobiles while encouraging a small-world lifestyle where jobs, shops, and homes are near each other.

New York rod A two-piece surveyor's rod with narrow markings and a movable target.

N-grade wood (1) In molding, stock intended for natural or clear finishes. The exposed face must be of one single piece. (2) In plywood, cabinet quality panels for natural finishes.

nib Any particle or piece projecting from a surface, particularly used to describe a defect on a painted or varnished surface.

nibbed tile A small lug at the upper end of a roofing tile that hooks over a batten.

nib grade (nib guide, nib rule) A wooden straight edge nailed on the ceiling's base plaster coat as a guide for a cornice molding.

niche A recess in a wall, usually intended for statuary. Often a base and a canopy project out from the wall around the recess.

nickel A silver-colored, hard ductile metal used in alloys, batteries, and electroplating. Nickel is used extensively on plumbing fixtures, where its anti-corrosive properties are important.

nickel steel A steel alloy with 3 to 5% nickel content, which gives it greater strength, ductility, and anti-corrosive properties.

nidge (nig) To dress or shape the edge of a masonry stone with the sharp point of a hammer, as opposed to doing so with a chisel and mallet.

nidged ashlar Ashlar stone that has been shaped with the sharp point of a hammer.

nig See **nidge**.

night cycle program In a building automation system, an energy-saving computer program that maintains a reduced temperature in the heating season and an elevated temperature during the cooling season during unoccupied periods.

night latch A door lock with a spring bolt that cannot be operated from the outside except by a key.

night purge program In a building automation system, a computer program that replaces building air with cooler outdoor air during the early morning hours of the cooling season.

night vent A small light with horizontal hinges that is mounted in an operable sash to allow ventilation without opening the entire sash.

nipple

noise insulation

nominal dimension

nippers A hand tool for cutting wire and small rods.

nipple A piece of pipe less than 12 inches long and threaded on both ends. Pipe over 12 inches long is regarded as a cut measure.

Nissen hut A semi-cylindrically shaped building made of corrugated metal. *See also* **Quonset hut**.

nobble The process of shaping building stones to the roughly desired dimensions while the stone is still at the quarry.

node (1) In CPM (Critical Path Method) scheduling, a junction of arrows containing the i-j number, early start, and late finish. (2) In electrical wiring, a junction of several conductors.

no-fines concrete A concrete mixture with little or no fine aggregate.

nog *See* **nailing block**.

nogging The process of filling the space between timber framing members with bricks.

nogging piece A horizontal timber fitted between vertical studs or beams to give lateral support, especially when nogging is used.

"no hazard" designation A designation that indicates a particular site or medium poses no hazard to human health or to the environment.

no-hub pipe Cast iron pipe that is fabricated without hubs for coupling.

noise In closed-circuit television, interference detected on a cable circuit that reduces or destroys the clarity of the signal. Sometimes called snow.

noise absorption The reduction of noise in an enclosure by introducing sound-absorbing materials or methods of

construction which restrict the transmission of sound.

noise criterion curve Defines the limits that the octave band spectrum of a noise source must not exceed if a certain level of occupant acceptance is to be achieved.

noise energy The total sound from all sources within a room at a given time, including reverberations and echos.

noise insulation Sound-absorbing materials installed in partitions, doors, windows, ceilings, and floors.

noise reduction (1) The difference, expressed in decibels, between the noise energy in two rooms when a noise is produced in one of the rooms. (2) The difference in noise energy from one side of a partition to another when a noise is produced on one side.

noise reduction coefficient The average sound absorption coefficient of a material to the nearest 0.05 at four frequencies: 250, 500, 1000, and 2000 cycles.

nominal Name given to standard pipe size designations through 12″ nominal O.D. For example, 2″ nominal is 2-3/8″ O.D.

nominal diameter The size designation that specifies the size of a pipe, bolt, reinforcing bar, or rive. The actual dimension may vary.

nominal dimension (1) The size designation for most lumber, plywood, and other panel products. In lumber, the nominal size is usually greater than the actual dimension, thus, a kiln-dried 2″x 4″ ordinarily is surfaced to 1-1/2″ x 3-1/2″. In panel products, the size is generally stated in feet for surface dimensions and increments of 1/16″ for thickness. Product standards permit various tolerances for the

nominal size

nonbearing wall

latter, varying according to the type and nominal thickness of the panel. (2) In masonry, a dimension larger than the one specified for the masonry unit by the thickness of a joint.

nominal mix The proportions of the constituents of a proposed concrete mix.

nominal size The dimensions of sawn lumber before it is surfaced and dried. *See also* **nominal dimension**.

nonagitating unit A truck-mounted container for transporting central-mixed concrete, not equipped to provide agitation (slow mixing) during delivery.

non-air-entrained concrete Concrete in which neither an air-entraining admixture nor air-entraining cement has been used. *See also* **air-entraining agent**.

nonbearing partition A partition which is not designed to support the weight of a floor, wall, or roof.

nonbearing wall A wall designed to carry no load other than its own weight.

noncohesive soil A soil in which the particles do not stick together, such as sand or gravel.

noncollusion affidavit A notarized statement by a bidder that the bid was prepared without any kind of secret agreement intended for a deceitful or fraudulent purpose.

noncombustible Any material which will neither ignite nor actively support combustion in air at a temperature of 1200°F when exposed to fire.

noncombustible construction Construction in which the walls, partitions, and the structural members are of noncombustible materials.

noncompensable delay A delay for which the contractor receives a time extension only, and may not recover its delay-related costs from the owner.

nonconcordant tendons In a statically indeterminate structure, tendons that are not coincident with the pressure line caused by the tendons.

nonconductor A material that does not easily conduct electric current. Such materials are used as insulators.

nonconforming A building, or the use of a building, that does not comply with existing laws, rules, regulations, or codes.

nonconforming uses Existing uses of land or structures which do not conform to local zoning ordinances.

nonconforming work Work that does not fulfill the contractually agreed upon requirements.

noncorrosive flux A flux used in soldering operations that does not chemically attack the base metal.

nondestructive testing The examination of an object with technology that does not affect the object's future usefulness. Applications include the evaluation of the strength of concrete or a weld using ultrasonic measures. *See also* **borescope**.

nondrying A term applied to a material containing oils that do not oxidize or evaporate, and therefore do not form a surface skin. The term is often applied to glazing compounds.

nonelectric delay blasting cap A detonating cap with a delay device built in so that it detonates at a designated time after receiving an impulse or signal from a detonating cord.

nonmetallic sheathed cable

nonprestressed
reinforcement

nonevaporable water The water that is chemically combined during cement hydration and which is not removable by specified drying.

nonexcusable delay A delay which is the fault of the contractor for which the contractor will receive neither a time extension nor compensation.

nonferrous A term referring to any metal or alloy that does not contain iron, such as brass or copper.

nonfibered Roofing materials, including coating and primer, that do not contain asbestos fibers.

nonflammable A material which will not burn with a flame.

nonfreeze sprinkler system A fire protection sprinkler system that is designed to operate in freezing temperatures. *See also* **dry-pipe sprinkler system** *and* **preaction sprinkler system**.

non-ionic surfactant An adjuvant with no electrical charge. Non-ionic surfactants are compatible with all types of pesticides.

non-load-bearing partition *See* **nonbearing partition**.

non-load-bearing tile Tile designated for use in masonry walls carrying no superimposed loads.

non-load-bearing wall *See* **nonbearing wall**.

nonmetallic sheathed cable Two or more electrical conductors enclosed in a nonmetallic, moisture-resistant, flame-retardant sheath.

nonnailable decks In built-up roofing, a deck or substrate requiring the base sheet to be adhered rather than mechanically fastened.

nonpressure pipe A pipe with no pressure rating, and therefore only suitable for conveying liquid by gravity.

nonpressure process A method of treating wood by allowing it to soak in a preservative and to absorb the preservative naturally.

nonprestressed reinforcement Reinforcing steel in a prestressed, concrete structural member which is not subjected to prestressing or posttensioning.

nonrestrictive specification A type of specification which is written so as not to restrict the product to a particular manufacturer or material supplier.

nonreturn valve A check valve that allows flow in only one direction.

nonsimultaneous prestressing The posttensioning of tendons individually rather than simultaneously.

nonsiphon trap A plumbing fixture that creates a water seal that cannot be siphoned, but still allows the free flow of liquids.

nonskid floor A concrete floor surface treated with carborundum powder, iron filings, or other material to improve its traction qualities, especially when wet. The surface may also be brushed before the concrete sets to create a rough finish.

nonslip concrete *See* **nonskid floor**.

nonstaining mortar A mortar, with low free-alkali content, that avoids efflorescence or staining of adjacent masonry units by migration of soluble materials.

nontilting mixer A rotating drum concrete mixer on a horizontal axis. Concrete is discharged by inserting a chute that catches the concrete from the rotating fins.

nonunion *See* **open shop**.

normal consistency (1) The degree of wetness exhibited by a freshly mixed concrete, mortar, or neat

Norman brick

nosing

cement grout when the workability of the mixture is considered acceptable for the purpose at hand. (2) The physical condition of neat cement paste determined with the Vicat apparatus in accordance with a standard method of testing.

normalizing The heating of steel or other ferrous alloys to a specified temperature above the transformation range, followed by cooling in ambient air. The process reduces the brittleness and strength of the metal, but increases its ductility.

normally closed valves Valve ports are closed to flow when external power or pressure is not being applied.

normally open valves Valve ports are open to flow when external power or pressure is not being applied.

normal weight concrete Concrete having a unit weight of approximately 150 pounds per cubic foot and made with aggregates of normal weight. *See also* **concrete, normal weight**.

Norman brick A brick with nominal dimensions of 2-3/4 "x 4 " x 12 ". Three courses of Norman brick lay up to 8 ".

Northeastern Lumber Manufacturers One of seven regional grading agencies in North America that are authorized to write and publish grading rules for lumber. *See also* **grade stamp**.

Northern Hardwood and Pine Manufacturersw Association One of seven regional grading agencies in North America that are authorized to write and publish grading rules for lumber. *See also* **grade stamp**.

nosing The horizontal projection of an edge from a vertical surface, such as the nosing on a stair tread.

nosing line The slope of a stair as defined by a line connecting the nosing of each stair tread.

no-slump concrete Fresh concrete with a slump of 1 " or less.

notch board A stair stringer with the notches cut in for the treads.

notched bar test An impact test for metals.

notching A timber joint in which one or both of the members have a section or notch cut out.

notch joist A joist with a section cut out to fit a ledger or girder.

notice to bidders A notice included in the bidding documents that informs prospective bidders of the bidding procedures and the opportunity to submit a bid.

notice to creditors During bankruptcy proceedings, the formal notification to creditors of a meeting, or the granting of an order for relief.

notice to proceed A written notice from the project owner to the contractor in which the contractor is authorized to proceed with the work on a specified date.

novation One party's agreement to release another party from a contract in exchange for a new party as substitute.

novelty siding *See* **drop siding**.

nozzle An attachment to the outlet of a pipe or hose that controls or regulates the flow.

nozzle liner A replaceable rubber insert for the inside of a nozzle. The liner is used to prevent wear to the metal parts, particularly to shotcrete nozzles.

nut

nozzle pattern The most efficient layout for spray heads in a lawn watering system.

N-truss A Pratt truss.

nurses call system An electrically operated system for use by patients or personnel for summoning a nurse.

nut A short metal block with a threaded hole in the center for receiving a bolt or threaded rod.

nylon fiber A synthetic fiber used extensively in floor coverings, wall coverings, drapery, and other furnishings.

ABBREVIATIONS

The abbreviations listed below are those most commonly used in the construction industry. Alternative forms (usually nonstandard) are shown in parentheses.

O oxygen

OA overall

O/A on approval

OAI outside air intake

O.B.M. ordinance bench mark

OBS obsolete, open back strike

OC, o.c. on center

OCT octagon

OD outside diameter

OEM original equipment manufacturer

OFF. office

OG, o.g. ogee

O/H, OVHD, OH overhead

OHS oval-headed screw

O.J.T. on-the-job-training

opp opposite

opt optional

OR. outside radius, owner's risk

ord order, ordinance

ORIG original

OS&Y outside screw and yoke

OSHA Occupational Safety and Health Administration, Occupational Safety and Health Act

OZ, oz ounce

O DEFINITIONS

oblique drawings

obscure glass

oak A hard, dense wood used for heavy framing, flooring, interior trim, plywood, and furniture. The two types available from the mill are white oak and red oak.

oakum A caulking material made from hemp fibers which are sometimes saturated with tar. Oakum is commonly used with a bell-and-spigot joint in cast iron pipe. Oakum is packed into the joint with a hammer and chisel before molten lead is poured into the joint to seal it.

obligation A result of custom, law, or agreement by which an individual is duty bound to fulfill an act or other responsibility.

oblique drawings One face of an object is drawn directly on the picture plane. Projected lines are drawn at a 30° or 45° angle.

oblique photograph An aerial photograph taken with the camera axis inclined away from the vertical. A high oblique photograph is one that shows the horizon; a low oblique does not include the horizon.

oblique section An architectural or mechanical drawing of a section through an object, at an angle other than 90° to its long axis.

obscure glass Glass that transmits light but does not allow a view of objects on the other side, such as ground glass or frosted glass; translucent glass.

obscuring window A window glazed with obscure glass, installed for privacy.

observation of the work The architect, during construction-phase visits to a project, observes the progress and quality of the work. The purpose of the visits is to verify that work is proceeding as specified in the contract documents.

occupancy The designed or intended use of a building. Also, the ratio of present space being used or rented to the designed full use, expressed as a percent.

occupancy permit
See **certificate of occupancy**.

occupancy rate The number of persons per building, unit, room, or floor.

occupancy sensor A heat-sensitive electronic sensor that reacts to moving heat sources within its monitored field. Used as a component of security and lighting systems.

occupant load The maximum number of persons in an area at a given peak period.

Occupational Safety and Health Act The federal law governing the safety of workers in the workplace.

Occupational Safety and Health Administration The federal agency responsible for worker health and safety.

occurrence In insurance terminology, a happening or event. Usually refers to an injury or damage that is neither expected nor intended.

occurrence form An agreement that covers insurance claims from both accidents and occurrences. (In contrast to the accident-only form.)

odorless mineral spirit A thinner used in interior paints because of its odorless qualities.

oderless paint

offset stakes

ogee molding

odorless paint A water-base paint, or a base using odorless mineral spirit, which produces very little odor.

off-center (out-of-center) A load that is applied off the geometric center of a structural member, or a structural member that is placed off the geometric center of an applied load.

off-count mesh Wire mesh in which the spacing or count is greater in one direction than in the other.

offer A proposal, as in a wage and benefits package, to be accepted, negotiated, or rejected.

offering list A list of items for sale, published by a mill or wholesaler and distributed to potential customers. The list usually includes a description of the item, shipping information, price, and terms of sale.

office occupancy The use of a building or space for business, as opposed to manufacturing, warehousing, or other uses.

Office of Federal Contract Compliance (OFCC) An agency of the U.S. Department of Labor charged with administration of Executive Order 11246, issued by President Lyndon B. Johnson. This agency requires contractors for federal projects to maintain affirmative action in providing equal rights for employees under the provisions of Title IV of the Civil Rights Act of 1964, which forbids discrimination by an employer on the basis of race, color, religion, sex, or national origin.

off-road hauler A heavy-duty rear dump truck or bottom dump wagon capable of routinely hauling over rough haul roads.

offset (1) In surveying, a line or point placed at a given distance from a control line or point used to reestablish the original location. (2) In plumbing, an assembly of fittings on a pipeline that takes one section of pipe out of line but parallel to a second section. (3) Any bend in a pipe.

offset bend An intentional distortion from the normal straightness of a steel reinforcing bar in order to move the center line of a segment of the bar to a position parallel to the original position of the center line. The offset bend is commonly applied to vertical bars that are used to reinforce concrete columns.

offset scale A scale used on a map or plan for plotting points which have been determined by field measurements.

offset screwdriver A screwdriver whose head is set at 90° to its shaft.

offset stakes Stakes placed by the excavator to mark the corners of a building after the surveyor's stakes have been removed.

ogee (1) A double curve much like the letter "S." (2) The union of concave and convex lines.

ogee molding Cornice molding (may be multiple moldings) utilizing ogee and/or reverse ogee curves to provide definition.

ohm A unit of electrical resistance in a conductor that produces a decrease in voltage of 1 volt with a constant current of 1 ampere.

ohmmeter An instrument for measuring the electrical resistance in a conductor or appliance in ohms.

Ohm's law A scientific law stating that the current in an electrical circuit is directly proportional to the voltage and inversely proportional to the resistance. Stated as an equation: I (current) E (voltage) / R (resistance).

oil burner

oil-filled transformer

olive knuckle hinge

oilborne preservative One of two general classifications for wood preservatives, the other being waterborne salts. Examples of oilborne preservatives include creosote and various chlorinated phenols, such as pentachlorophenol.

oil-bound distemper A distemper, or water-base paint, that contains some drying oils to enhance its spreading and drying characteristics.

oil burner A fuel-oil burning unit installed in a furnace or boiler.

oil canning (tin canning) The waving or buckling of formed sheet metal such as roofing or siding.

oiled and edge sealed A process used to resist moisture and preserve plywood concrete form panels. Oiling and sealing increases the number of times a panel can be used and makes the panel easier to release from the concrete.

oiler The second person assigned to a piece of equipment such as a crane. An oiler's principal job is to lubricate the equipment.

oil-filled transformer A transformer having its core and coils immersed in an insulating oil such as mineral oil.

oil-immersed transformer *See* **oil-filled transformer**.

oil paint A paint with drying oil as a base, as opposed to a water base or other base.

oil preservative *See* **oilborne preservative**.

oil separator In a refrigeration system, a device for purging the refrigerant of oil and oil vapor.

oil soak treatment A method of treating wood with preservative.

oil stain A stain, with an oil base containing dye or pigment, used to penetrate and permanently color wood or other porous materials.

oilstone A stone with a fine-grained, oil-lubricated surface used to sharpen the cutting edge of tools.

oilstone slip An oilstone used to sharpen gauges and chisels.

oil switch (oil-immersed switch) A switch immersed in oil or in another insulating fluid.

oil varnish A high-gloss varnish which contains a blend of drying oil and gum or resin, principally used for interior finishes.

oil/water separator A device that allows oils mixed with water to become trapped in a holding section for removal, while the water is allowed to pass through for disposal.

old bundling (full-length bundling) A method of packaging siding in which each piece is of equal length. Most shippers use "new bundling," in which pieces of various lengths are nested.

old English bond A brick pattern of alternating courses of headers and stretchers, with a closer placed at the corners of each header course. *See also* **English bond**.

old wood Reused wood that has previously been worked.

old work A general term for any electrical work that involves an existing wiring.

olive butt *See* **olive knuckle hinge**.

olive hinge *See* **olive knuckle hinge**.

olive knuckle hinge (olive butt, olive hinge) A single-pivot paumelle hinge with knuckles that join to form an oval shape.

on center (1) A measurement of the distance between the centers of two repeating members in a structure. (2) A term used for defining the spacing of studs, joists, and rafters.

one-way joist construction

one-way slab

one by A slang term for lumber with a nominal thickness of 1″, as in a 1″ by 3″ board.

one-hour rating A measure of fire resistance, indicating that an object can be exposed to flame for an hour without losing structural integrity or transmitting excessive heat.

one-line system A graphic representation of a power distribution system using lines and symbols to indicate its major components.

one-on-two (one-to-two) A slope in which the elevation rises one foot in two horizontal feet.

one-piece toilet A toilet whose tank and bowl were manufactured as a single fixture.

one-pipe system (1) In drainage systems, two vertical pipes, with waste and soil water flowing down the same pipe, and all the branches connected to the same anti-siphon pipe. (2) A heating circuit in which all the flow and return connections to the radiators come from the same pipe. The radiator at the far end is therefore much cooler than the radiator which is nearest the heat source.

one-way joist construction A concrete floor or a roof framing system with monolithic parallel joists cast with the slab. The joists are supported on girders, which in turn are supported by columns.

one-way slab A slab panel, bound on its two long sides by beams and on its two short sides by girders. The dead and live loads acting on the slab area may be considered to be entirely supported in the short or transverse direction by the beams; hence, the term *one-way*.

one-way system The arrangement of steel reinforcement within a slab that is designed to bend in only one direction.

on grade A concrete floor slab resting directly on the ground.

opacity In painting, the ability of a paint to cover or hide the original background.

on-off sprinkler A fire safety system sprinkler that activates like a traditional sprinkler but ceases operation when room temperature reaches a safe level. On/off sprinklers can reduce the amount of water discharged during a fire, thus reducing cleanup and water damage.

opalescent glaze A smooth surface with a milky appearance.

opaque ceramic-glazed tile A fire-bonded facing tile with an opaque, colored, ceramic glaze and a glassy or satin finish.

OPC relationship The relationship that normally exists between owner, (design) professional, and contractor during the construction process.

open assembly time The time required between the application of glue to veneer or to joints and the assembly of the pieces.

open bid An offer to perform a contract in which the bidder reserves the right to reduce his bid to compete with a lower bid.

open bidding A bidding procedure wherein bids or tenders are submitted by and received from all interested contractors, rather than from a select list of bidders privately invited to compete.

open boarding A system of laying boards on a roof, leaving a gap between adjacent boards.

open cell A cell that interconnects with other cells in foam rubber, cellular plastics, and similar materials.

open cut

open-end block

open floor

open-cell foam Cellular plastic with a great many open and interconnected cells.

open-cell process A process for fixing preservative in wood under pressure. The chemical used as a preservative is retained in the cell walls only, with the cells left empty.

open circuit The absence of a direct connection between two points in an electrical network.

open-circuit grouting A grouting system with no provision for recirculation of grout to the pump.

open construction A description of any building element that is temporarily left unfinished or exposed to allow for easy inspection.

open cornice (open eaves) Overhanging eaves with exposed rafters that are visible from below.

open cut An excavation in the ground that is open to the sky at its surface, as opposed to a tunnel or horizontal mine shaft.

open defect Any hole or gap in lumber, veneer, or plywood that has not been filled and repaired.

open eaves *See* **open cornice.**

open-end block (1) An A-block or H-block of concrete masonry. (2) A block of standard material and size built with recessed end webs.

open-end mortgage A mortgage arrangement wherein the mortgagor may borrow additional sums for the repair and upkeep of property after the original loan is granted. The mortgages are paid over an extended period.

open excavation Excavation in which no shores, piles, or sheeting are used to hold back the soil at the edge of the excavation.

open floor A floor in which joists are visible from the floor beneath.

open-frame girder An open-web girder or truss built with verticals connected rigidly to top and bottom chords, but with no diagonals.

open-graded aggregate (1) An aggregate that contains almost no mineral filler. (2) A compacted aggregate with relatively large void spaces.

open grain (1) Lumber that is not restricted by the number of rings per inch or rate of growth. (2) Timber with a coarse texture and open pores.

opening light An operable pane or sash in a window which may be open or shut, as opposed to a fixed light.

opening of bids *See* **bid opening.**

opening protective A device installed over an opening to guard it against the passage of smoke, flame, and heated gases.

opening size The size of a door opening as measured from jamb to jamb and from the threshold or floorline to the head of the frame, allowing for the size of the door and for the necessary clearance to open and close it freely. *See also* **door opening.**

open joint (1) A joint in which two pieces of material that are joined together are not entirely flush. (2) A joint that is not tight.

open loop control A hydraulic control system that does not have a direct link between the valve of the controlled variable (temperature, pressure) and the controller.

open mortise A mortise, or notch, that is open on three sides of the piece of timber into which it is cut. *See also* **slot mortise.**

open-riser stair

open shelving

open stairway

open-newel stair (hollow newel stair, open-well stair) (1) A stairway that is built around a wall and has open spaces between its strings. (2) A stair without newels.

open plan A building plan that has relatively few interior walls or partitions to subdivide areas for different uses.

open plumbing Plumbing that is exposed to view beneath its fixtures, with ventilated drains and traps readily accessible for inspection and repairs.

open riser The space between two successive treads of a staircase built without solid risers.

open-riser stair A stair built without solid risers.

open roof (open-timbered roof) A style of roof with exposed rafters, sheathing, and supporting timbers visible from beneath, and no ceiling.

open shaft A vertical duct or passage in a building that is used to ventilate interior spaces, drawing in outside air from its open top.

open sheathing See **open sheeting**.

open sheeting (open sheathing, open timbering) Vertical or horizontal supporting planks and timbers that are set along an excavated surface at intervals. Open sheeting is used whenever the ground is firm and dry enough to be effectively shored up without closed sheeting.

open shelving Shelving that is exposed to view, not concealed by doors or cabinets.

open shop (merit shop, nonunion shop) A term describing a firm whose employees are not covered by collective bargaining agreements.

open slating A method of installing roofing slates where a space is left between slates in each course.

open space A term used in urban planning for parks, woods, lawns, recreation spaces, and other areas on which no building stands.

open stair (open-string stair) A stairway with treads that are visible from one side or both sides.

open stairway A stairway with one side or both sides open to the room in which it is located.

open string (open stringer, cut string) A stairway string with its upper edge cut or notched to conform with the treads and risers of the stairs.

open-string stair See **open stair**.

open system A piping system for water or fuels in which the conduits that circulate the liquid are attached to an elevated tank or tower, with open vents to facilitate storage, access, and inspection.

open tank A tank for treating wood with preservative at atmospheric pressure.

open-timbered floor A style of floor construction in which the joists and other supporting timbers are exposed and visible from the underside.

open-timbered roof See **open roof**.

open-timbering Description of structures built with their timberwork or wooden framework exposed to view, or without plaster or another covering; exposed timberwork.

open time The time that is required for the completion of the bond after an adhesive has been spread.

open-top mixer A mixer consisting of a trough or a segment of a cylindrical mixing compartment within which paddles or blades

open-web steel joist

operable partition

operable window

rotate about the horizontal axis of the trough. *See also* **mixer** *and* **horizontal shaft**.

open valley A type of roof valley on which shingles and slates are not applied to the intersection of two roof surfaces, leaving the underlying metal or mineral-surfaced roofing material exposed along the length of the valley.

open web A form of construction on a truss or girder in which multiple members, arranged in zigzag or crisscross patterns, are used in place of solid plates to connect the chords or flanges.

open-web steel joist A steel truss with an open web, constructed of hot-rolled structural shapes or shapes of cold-formed, light-gauge steel.

open-web studs Light gauge steel framing construction of wire rods welded to flanges for use as backing lath.

open wiring A network of electrical wiring that is not concealed by the structure of a building, but is protected by cleats, flexible tubing, knots, and tubes, which also support its insulated conductors.

openwork (1) Ornamental work characterized by perforations. (2) A section of work on a fortress wall that is unprotected by a parapet or another defensive structure at the site of a gorge or bastion opening.

operable partition A partition made of two or more large panels suspended on a ceiling track, and sometimes also supported on a floor track, which may be opened by sliding the panels so that they overlap. The panels form a solid partition when closed.

operable transom A glass light or panel that is installed above a door and may be opened or shut for ventilation.

operable wall *See* **operable partition**.

operable window A window that may be opened and shut to accommodate ventilation needs, as opposed to a fixed light or fixed sash.

operating engineer The worker or technician who operates heavy machinery and construction equipment.

operating pressure The pressure registered on a gauge when a system is in normal operation.

opposed-blade damper A damper installed over an air passage to regulate the volume of air entering an enclosure. The damper is operated by means of two sets of blades linked so that adjacent blades can open and turn in opposite directions.

optical access control A security device, often featuring turnstiles, that allows only properly identified people to pass through an access port.

optical coatings Very thin coatings applied to glass or other transparent materials to increase the transmission of or reduce the reflection of sunlight. Coatings are also used to reflect infrared radiation back to the heat exchanger from which it was emitted.

optical fiber cable A medium over which light pulses are transmitted, consisting of a glass core surrounded by a protective sheath. Light pulses are introduced into the optical fiber by a laser or light-emitting diode.

orbital sander

optical losses Losses resulting from solar radiation reflecting from the surface of the cover plate.

optical plummet In surveying, a device used in place of a plumb bob to center transits and theodolites over a given point, preferred for its steadiness in strong winds.

optics (1) The study of light and vision. (2) A system of lenses, filters, prisms, or mirrors used in electronics to direct, disperse, reflect, or otherwise control light rays.

optimum moisture content The percentage or degree of moisture in soil at which the soil can be compacted to its greatest density. Optimum moisture content is used in specifications for compacting embankments.

optimum start program A building automation system that delays the startup of a heating or cooling system until the last possible moment while still maintaining building comfort levels during occupancy.

option A financial agreement between a property owner and user that grants the latter party, upon payment of a stated sum, the right to buy or to rent the property within a time limit specified on the contract.

opus quadratum Stonemasonry in which the stones are cut into squares and laid out in regular ashlar courses.

orangeburg (1) A standard paneling pattern used in decorative plywood. Orangeburg panels have random width grooving, with the width between each panel following a pattern of 4-8-4-7-9-6-4-6 inches. (2) A common term for bituminous fiber drainage pipe.

orange peel (orange peeling) (1) A surface flaw on paint, resulting from poor flow or application, that leaves the finish pocked with tiny holes like citrus skins. (2) A wavy surface defect on porcelain enamel. (3) A segmented hemispherical bucket that resembles a peel of half an orange, equipped with self-opening and closing capabilities and used to excavate earth. (4) A distinctive texture applied to drywall.

orange peel bucket *See* **orange peel (3)**.

orbital sander A hand-held electrical sander whose base, covered with sandpaper or abrasive material, moves rapidly in an elliptical pattern and is used chiefly for coarse work.

ordinance An authoritative rule of law, public decree, or regulation enacted by a municipality or other political subdivision fully enforceable through the court system of the municipality or other political subdivision.

ordinary construction Construction in which some interior materials and members are of smaller dimensions, composed wholly or in part of wood or other combustible materials, but in which exterior bearing walls and nonbearing exterior walls are of stable, noncombustible construction with a minimum fire endurance of two hours.

ordinary-hazard contents Building contents that burn at moderate speed and give off smoke, but release no poisonous fumes or gases that would cause an explosion under fire conditions.

ordinary Portland cement (Type 1 Portland cement) A basic formula for Portland cement used in general construction, containing none of

oriel window

orient

the distinctive properties or refinements of other cements.

ordnance Any chemical substance or physical item related to munitions that is designed to cause damage through explosive force, incendiary action or toxic effects.

Oregon cedar *See* **Port Orford cedar**.

Oregon larch (Pacific silver fir, and noble fir) Lumber from the latter two species shared the Oregon larch designation for many years in sales to the Orient.

Oregon maple (big leaf maple) A wood used in furniture, especially its burls, and as core veneer in some plywood.

Oregon pine (Douglas fir) Needled evergreen producing medium-hard, close-grained wood commonly used for frames, trim, and paneling.

Oregon spruce (Sitka spruce) Needled evergreen producing soft, close-grained wood commonly used for frames and trim.

Oregon white cedar (Port Orford cedar) Needled evergreen producing soft, close-grained wood commonly used for interior and exterior trim and paneling.

Oregon white pine (ponderosa pine) Needled evergreen producing soft, close-grained wood used for frames, trim, paneling, and cabinetry.

organic Descriptive of materials or compounds produced from vegetable or animal sources.

organic clay Clay containing a high volume of composted animal or vegetable materials.

organic silt Silt composed in large part of organic substances.

organic soil A highly compressible soil with heavy organic content, considered generally undesirable for construction because of its inability to bear sizable loads.

oriel In architecture, a projecting bay, frequently outfitted with one or more windows, that is corbeled out from the wall of a structure or supported by brackets and which serves both to expand interior space and to enhance the appearance of the building.

oriel window A window housed in an oriel. An oriel window's projection does not extend to the ground, differentiating it from a bay window.

orient (1) To locate a building by points of the compass. (2) To locate a church so the altar end is toward the east.

oriented-core barrel A surveying instrument that takes and marks a core to show its orientation, and at the same time records the bearing and slope of the test hole.

oriented strand board (OSB) Panels made of narrow strands of wood fiber oriented lengthwise and crosswise in layers, with a resin binder. Depending on the resin used, OSB can be suitable for interior or exterior applications.

orifice meter A device used to measure the amount of liquid or gas flowing through a pipe.

original equipment manufacturer (OEM) A company that uses components from one or more other companies to build a product that it sells under its own company name.

O ring A round gasket used as a sealant in pipe joints and valves.

orthographic projection A method of representing the exact shape of an object by dropping perpendiculars from two or more sides of the object to planes, generally at right angles to each other. Collectively, the views on these planes describe the object

oscillating saw

outlet box

completely. The term *orthogonal* is sometimes used for this system of drawing.

orthography The drafting procedure in which elevations or sections of buildings are geometrically represented.

orthotropic A contraction of the terms *orthogonal* and *anistropic* as in the phrase "orthogonal anistropic plate"; a hypothetical plate consisting of beams and a slab acting together with different flexural rigidities in the longitudinal and transverse directions, as in a composite beam bridge.

oscillating saw A power saw with a straight blade that oscillates in short strokes.

oscillator Any electronic component that generates alternating voltage.

oscilloscope An electronic device that uses a cathode ray tube or a fluorescent-coated tube to produce visual displays corresponding to changes in electrical signals.

Ottawa sand Silica sand produced by processing material obtained by hydraulic mining of massive orthoquartzite situated in deposits near Ottawa, Illinois. The sand is composed almost entirely of naturally rounded grains of nearly pure quartz and is used in mortars for testing of hydraulic cement. *See also* **standard sand** *and* **graded standard sand**.

outband A masonry jambstone that serves as a stretcher and is cut to accommodate a frame.

outbuilding A building that is separate from a main building but attendant on it or collateral to it in its function, such as a stable, a garage, or an outside lavatory.

outcrop A segment of an underground rock stratum or a formation that breaks through the surface of the earth and forms a visible protuberance.

outdoor-air intake *See* **outside-air intake**.

outer court An outdoor space that is bounded on three sides by property lines or building walls, but maintains a view of the sky and is open on one side to an adjacent street or public area.

outer string On a stairway, the string that stands away from the wall on the exposed outer edge of the stair.

outfall The final receptacle or depositing area for sewage and drainage water.

outfall sewer A sewer that receives the sewage from the collecting system and conducts it to a point of final discharge or to a disposal plant.

outgassing The driving out or freeing of gases from fabrics and building materials.

outlet (1) The point in an electrical wiring circuit at which the current is supplied to an appliance or device. (2) A vent or opening, principally in a parapet wall, through which rainwater is released. (3) In a piping system, the point at which a circulated liquid is discharged.

outlet box The metal box, located at the outlet of an electrical wiring system, that serves to house one or more receptacles.

outlet ventilator An opening covered with a louvered frame, serving as an outlet from an enclosed attic space to the outside.

outline lighting Gaseous tubes or incandescent lamps that are arranged around the outline of a building, a door, a window, or

outside-air intake

outside casing

outside studding plate

another part of a structure in order to emphasize its configuration.

outline specifications A listing of shortened specification requirements (normally part of schematic or design development documents).

outlooker In roof construction, a projecting member that supports the portion of the roof beyond the face of a gable.

out-of-center *See* **off-center**.

out-of-plumb Deviating from a true vertical line of descent, as determined by a plumb line.

out-of-sequence services Services performed in an order or sequence other than that in which they are normally carried out.

out-of-true Descriptive of a structural member that is twisted or otherwise out of alignment.

output (1) The net volume of work produced by a system. (2) The maximum capacity or performance which a system is capable of under normal conditions of operation.

outrigger (1) A beam that projects beyond a wall in order to support an overhanging roof or extended floor, built in a direction perpendicular to the joists of the structural member it serves. (2) An extended beam that supports scaffolds or hoisting tackle as work is being performed on or near a building's wall. (3) A beam that gives stability to a crane by widening its base.

outrigger scaffold A scaffold suspended from outrigger beams or brackets fixed to the outer wall of a building.

outrigger shore (horsing) A bracket installed temporarily to support an outrigger beam or another projecting member.

outside-air intake (fresh air intake, outdoor-air intake) An opening or inlet to the outside of a building, through which fresh air is introduced to the boiler room or to an air-conditioning system.

outside caliper A measuring instrument set on adjustable legs and used especially to measure the outside circumference and diameter of round or cylindrical objects and structures.

outside casing (outside architrave, outside facing, outside lining, outside trim) The supporting members of the jamb or head on a cased window that face the outside and have the appearance of trim.

outside corner molding A molding that covers and protects the projecting outside angle of two intersecting surfaces, as in wood veneer. *See also* **corner bead**.

outside facing *See* **outside casing**.

outside finish (exterior finish) Ornamental trim or surface treatment on the outside of a building.

outside foundation line A line that indicates where the outer side of a foundation wall is located.

outside glazing External windows or glass doors installed in a building from the outside.

outside screw and yoke A valve configuration where the valve stem, with exposed external threads supported by a yoke, indicates the open or closed position of the valve.

outside studding plate The soleplate or double top plate in the construction of a wood-frame wall or partition, usually built with stock of a size equal to the studding.

outstanding leg A leg of a structural angle member, generally unconnected to any other member.

out-to-out

outsulation (1) The placing of insulation to the exterior of a wall. (2) The elimination of all thermal bridges between the inner and outer surfaces of a wall.

out-to-out In measurements, a term meaning that the dimensions are overall.

ovals Marble chips that have been tumbled until a smooth oval shape has been obtained.

ovendry The condition resulting from having been dried to essentially constant weight in an oven at a temperature which has been fixed, usually 221°F and 230°F (105 °C and 115 °C).

ovendry wood (bone dry wood) Wood that gives off no moisture when subjected to a temperature of 212°F (100 °C).

overall (overall dimension) The total external dimension of any building material, including all projections.

overbreak Excavation performed beyond the work limits established by the neat line.

overburden (1) A mantle of soil, rock, gravel, or other earth material covering a given rock layer or bearing stratum. (2) An unwanted top layer of soil that must be stripped away to open access to useful construction materials buried beneath it.

overcloak The portion of a metal roofing sheet that overlaps the edge of an adjacent sheet set underneath it.

overconsolidated soil deposit A soil deposit that has been forced to withstand an effective pressure exceeding the pressure imposed by its present overburden.

overcurrent Electrical current of a magnitude beyond that rated for the equipment in use or the ampacity of a conductor. May result from a short circuit, ground fault, or electrical overload.

overcurrent protection Safety provisions within an electrical system, such as would be furnished by ground fault circuit interrupters, that guard against damage and injury resulting from excessive current by shutting off the flow of current when it reaches a certain level.

overdesign A term used to describe adherence to structural design requirements beyond service demands, as a means of compensating for statistical variation, anticipated deficiencies, or both.

overdig The amount of clean soil that is removed below or beyond the extent of contamination at a site to make sure all waste has been taken away.

overflow (overflow pipe) (1) A pipe installed to prevent flooding in storage tanks, fixtures, and plumbing fittings, or to remove excess water from buildings and systems. (2) An outlet fitted to a storage tank to set the proper level of liquid and to prevent flooding.

overgrainer A special brush with flat, thin, elongated bristles that is used to create imitations of natural wood grains.

overhand work The process by which bricklayers install brick in an external wall while standing on a scaffold or on the floor inside a building or structure.

overhang (1) A jetty. (2) The extension of a roof or an upper story of a building beyond the story situated directly beneath.

overhead door

overhung door

overlapping astragal

overlay flooring

over-haul The distance excavated material is transported beyond that given as the stated hauling distance.

overhead (indirect expense, overhead expense) The costs to conduct business other than direct job costs; included in bidder's markup.

overhead balance A tense steel coil or spring installed in the head jamb of a window frame to serve as a balance for the sash.

overhead concealed closer A door closer, installed out of view in the head of the door frame, designed with a hinged arm that connects the door with the top rail of the frame.

overhead door (overhead-type garage door) A door, constructed of a single leaf or of multiple leaves, that is swung up or rolled open from the ground level and assumes a horizontal position above the entrance way it serves when opened. Commonly used as a garage door.

overhead expense *See* **indirect expense and overhead.**

overhead service Electric service that is delivered to a structure by lines that are above the ground.

overhead shovel A tractor loader that digs at one end, swings the bucket overhead, and dumps at the other end.

overhead traveling crane A lifting machine generally power-operated at least in its hoisting operation. The crane is carried on a horizontal girder, reaching between rails above window level at each side of a shop, and consists of a hoisting cab that can travel from end to end on the girder. The whole area between the rails can thus be traversed by the cab.

overhung door A sliding door or multiple folding door that is suspended from an overhead track.

overlaid plywood (overlay) Plywood with a surfacing material added to one or both sides. The material usually provides a protective or decorative characteristic to the side, or a base for finishing. Materials used for overlays include resin-treated fiber, resin film, impregnated paper, plastics, and metal.

overlap In plywood manufacture, a defect in panel construction caused by one of two adjacent veneers overriding the other.

overlapping astragal (wraparound astragal) A molding that is attached lengthwise along the masting edge on one of a pair of doors to close the gap between them, providing a weather-resistant seal and stopping the transmission of light or smoke from one side of the doors to the other.

overlay (1) A layer of concrete or mortar, seldom thinner than 1″ (25 millimeters), placed on and usually bonded to the worn or cracked surface of a concrete slab either to restore or to improve the function of the original surface. (2) The surfacing of a plywood face with a solid material other than wood. *See also* **overlaid plywood.**

overlay flooring Finish flooring of maple, mahogany, oak, or other hardwood cut into narrow tongue-and-groove strips.

overlay glass Glass that is made up of two or more layers of different colors fused together, and which is often cut to permit a lower layer of glass to show on top for decorative effect.

oversailing course

ovolo

overlay technique A method of producing composition roofing in which a layer of asphalt is spread over an existing asphalt layer.

overload (1) A load exceeding that for which the bearing structure was designed. (2) Excess power, current, or voltage in an electrical device or circuit that is not designed to accommodate it.

overload capacity The limit of excess power, current, or voltage that an electrical device or circuit can accommodate before it is damaged.

overload relay A relay in a motor circuit that disconnects the motor from its power source if the current that feeds the motor surpasses a certain predetermined level.

overrun (1) The amount the cost of an item increases beyond the estimated cost. (2) The amount a quantity increases over the estimated quantity.

overrun brake (overriding brake) A brake fitted to a towed vehicle, such as a concrete mixer to a trailer. It operates as soon as the towing truck slows down and the towed vehicle tends to push into it. Movement of the towed vehicle applies the overrun brake, making safe high-speed towing possible.

oversailing course (1) A course of masonry that extends beyond the face of the wall in which it is set. (2) A string course.

oversanded Descriptive of mortar or concrete containing more sand than necessary to produce adequate workability and a satisfactory condition for finishing.

oversite concrete A layer of concrete that is laid below a slab or flooring to prevent the ground beneath from being disturbed, to block out air and moisture, and to provide a hard, level surface for subsequent flooring layers.

oversize brick A brick measuring greater than 2-1/2" x 3-1/2" x 7-1/2".

overstretching Stressing of tendons to a value higher than designed for the initial stress to: (a) overcome friction losses, (b) overstress the steel temporarily to reduce creep that occurs after anchorage, and (c) counteract loss of prestressing force that is caused by subsequent prestressing of other tendons.

overtime (1) A term applied to the number of hours worked in excess of the normal contract for one day or one week. (2) A term applied to the payment for this time, frequently 1-1/2 or double the normal rate of pay.

overturning The failure of a retaining wall as the result of hydraulic or earth pressure on one side. Overturning occurs when walls are built on a narrow base or with materials too light to withstand surrounding pressure.

overvibration Excessive use of vibrators during placement of freshly mixed concrete, causing segregation and excessive bleeding.

overvoltage A voltage above the normal rated voltage or the maximum operating voltage of a device or circuit.

ovolo A convex molding approximately the shape of a quarter circle.

owner The owner of a project, that is also party to the owner-contractor and owner-designer agreements.

owner-architect agreement Contract between owner and architect for professional design services.

owner-contractor agreement The contract formed between owner and contractor describing performance

oxyacetylene torch

of the construction work for a project (or a portion thereof).

owner's equity The owner's or owners' claims against the assets of a business. As used in this text, owner's equity implies that the business is a single proprietorship and, therefore, represents the proprietor's claims against assets of the single proprietorship.

owner's inspector A party hired by an owner to inspect the work. *See also* **clerk of the works**.

owner's liability insurance Insurance procured to protect the owner against claims originating from the work performed by the contractor.

owner's representative The designated official representative of the owner (may be an architect, engineer, or contractor) to oversee a project.

ox eye A slang term for any circular window.

oxidation (1) The reaction of a chemical compound mixed or exposed to oxygen. (2) Part of the asphalt refining process, wherein oxygen is incorporated in hot, bituminous liquids by blowing it through the melted substance. (3) The hardening of asphalt coating on a roof under exposure to sun and air.

oxidation stain A stain that occurs when a mineral in wood combines with oxygen.

oxidized asphalt Asphalt that has been specially treated by having air blown through it at high temperatures, making it suitable for use in roofing, hydraulics, pipe coating, membrane envelopes, and undersealing.

oxidizer An agent which, when acting on another substance, causes the attachment of an oxygen atom thereto.

oxter piece A vertical length of timber used in ashlaring.

oxyacetylene The mixture of oxygen and acetylene, forming a highly combustible gas used for cutting and welding metal.

oxyacetylene torch A welding or cutting torch that produces a superheated flame through combustion of oxygen and acetylene.

oxychloride cement (sorel cement) A hard, durable cement made up of calcined magnesia and magnesium chloride, occasionally blended with fillers.

oxygen cutting A process of metal cutting in which the separation of the metal is effected by its chemical reaction with oxygen at high temperatures.

oxygen starvation Areas of corrosion on metals exposed to an electrolyte, caused by a smothering effect or by the formation of a crevice between two areas of the metal or between the metal and any other adjacent material.

ozone Triatomic oxygen (O_3), an unstable form of oxygen that is produced by ultraviolet activity and electrical discharges and is used as an oxidizing agent, a deodorizer in air-conditioning and cold storage systems, and as an agent for stemming the growth of bacteria, fungus, and mildew. Excessive concentrations of ozone are poisonous to humans.

P

P ABBREVIATIONS

The abbreviations listed below are those most commonly used in the construction industry. Alternative forms (usually nonstandard) are shown in parentheses.

p part, per, pint, pipe, pitch, pole, post, port, power

P phosphorus, pressure, pole, page

P1E planed one edge

P1S planed one side

P1S2E planed one side and two edges

P4S planed four sides

P&T posts and timbers

PA particular average, power amplifier, preliminary assessment, professional association, purchasing agent

pan. panel

PAR. paragraph, part, partition, parabolic aluminized reflector

par. parapet

p.a.r planed all round

part, partn partition

PASS. passenger

Pat. pattern

pat. patent

PAX private automatic (telephone) exchange

Pb lead

PC Portland cement

pc piece

PCB polychlorinated biphenyl

PCE pyrometric cone equivalent

pcf pounds per cubic foot

pc/pct percent

pcs pieces

PD per diem, potential difference

pd paid

Pd palladium

P.E. professional engineer

PE professional engineer, probable error, plain end, polyethylene

p.e. plain edged

pecky cyp pecky cypress

PEP Public Employment Program

per. perimeter, by the, period

PERF perforate

PERM permanent

PERP perpendicular

PERT project evaluation and review technique

PET precision end trimmed

PF power factor

PFA pulverized fuel ash

PFD preferred

P&G post and girder

ph phase, phot

PH phase, Phillips head

Ph phenyl

PIB polyisobutylene

PID photoionization detector

pil pilaster

piv pivoted

pk park, peak, plank

pkfr. plank frame

pkwy parkway

P/L plastic laminate

PL pile, plate, plug, power line, pipe line, private line

pl place, plate

platf platform

PLG piling

plmb, plb, PLMB plumbing

PLYWD plywood

pmh production man-hour

PNEU pneumatic

PNL panel

PO purchase order

POL polish; petroleum, oil and lubricants
PORC porcelain
PORT. CEM Portland cement
pos, POS positive
pot. potential
pp ponderosa pine
PP-AC air-conditioning power panel
Ppd prepaid
PPE personal protective equipment
PPGL polished plate glass
ppm parts per million
ppt, pptn precipitate, precipitation
PR payroll, pair
prcst precast
preb prebend
prec preceding
prefab prefabricated
prelim preliminary
prin principal
prod. production
proj project, projection
prop. property
prov provisional
PRP potentially responsible party
prs pairs
PRV pressure-regulating valve
ps pieces, polystyrene
p.s.e. planed and square-edged
psf pounds per square foot
psi pounds per square inch
p.s.j. planed and square-jointed
P.T. pipe thread
PT part, point
pt paint, pint, payment, port, point
ptfe polytetrafluoroethylene

p.t.g. planed, tongued, and grooved
PTN partition
PU pickup
PUD pickup and delivery
pur purlins
PUR polyurethane
PVA polyvinyl acetate
PVC polyvinyl chloride
PW paper wrapped
PWA Public Works Administration
pwr power
pwt pennyweight
1PH single phase
3PH three phase

packaged air-conditioner

packaged boiler

pace A landing in a staircase.

pache Color coding used on drawings to aid in quantity takeoffs for estimating.

Pacific coast cypress *See* **Alaska yellow cedar**.

Pacific coast spruce *See* **Sitka spruce**.

Pacific coast yellow cedar *See* **Alaska yellow cedar**.

Pacific red cedar *See* **western red cedar**.

Pacific silver fir *Ables ammilis*. This species is found in British Columbia, Washington, and Oregon. The name comes from the silvery appearance of the underside of the tree's needles. Its wood is classed in the hem-fir group.

Pacific yew *Taxus brevifolia*. This species, generally small in size, is not a commercially important tree. Its wood is heavy and strong and is used for such purposes as archery bows. Yews are usually found growing in the shade of larger trees.

pack The bundling in which shakes and shingles are shipped. In shakes, the most prevalent pack is a 9/9. This describes a bundle packed on an 18″ wide frame with nine courses, or layers, at each end. The most common pack for shingles is 20/20. Because of their smoother edges, shingles can be packed tighter than shakes, a bundle of shakes usually contains a net of about 16″ of wood across the 18″ width of the frame.

packaged air-conditioner A factory-assembled air-conditioning unit ready for installation. The unit may be mounted in a window, an opening through a wall, or on the building roof. These units may serve an individual room, a zone, or multiple zones.

packaged boiler A factory-assembled water or steam heating unit ready for installation. All components, including the boiler, burner, controls, and auxiliary equipment, are shipped as a unit.

packaged concrete, mortar, grout Mixtures of dry ingredients in packages, requiring only the addition of water to produce concrete, mortar, or grout.

package dealer A contractor responsible for the design and construction of a project to specific end requirements, usually for a fixed sum.

packaged lumber Lumber strapped in standard units, usually milled to length and wrapped in paper or plastic.

package trim Prefabricated door and window moldings.

packer A device inserted into a hole in which grout is to be injected, which acts to prevent return of the grout around the injection pipe. A packer is usually an expandable device actuated mechanically, hydraulically, or pneumatically.

packer-head process A method of casting concrete pipe in a vertical position in which concrete of low water content is compacted with a revolving compaction tool.

packing (1) Stuffing of shaped elastic material to prevent fluid leakage at a shaft, valve stem, or joint. (2) Small stones, usually embedded in mortar, used to fill cracks between larger stones.

pad foundation

pale (paling)

palladian window

packing gland A protective sleeve used over cable or piping in applications where pressure or other factors pose a threat.

pack set The condition where stored cement will not flow from a container such as a rail car or silo. It is caused by interlaced particles or electrostatic charges on particles. *See also* **sticky cement**.

pad (1) A plate or block used to spread a concentrated load over an area, such as a concrete block placed between a girder and a loadbearing wall. (2) A shoe of a crawler-type track.

paddle A tool or implement with a wide blade at one end.

paddle wheel scraper A heavy duty excavation machine with a wheel that scrapes soil into a large bowl section.

paddock An enclosed area for animals, usually horses.

pad foundation A thick slab-type foundation used to support a structure or a piece of equipment.

padlock A unit lock with a U-shaped bar that is passed through a staple of a hasp or link in a chain, and the bar pressed into the body to lock.

pad saw A keyhole saw.

padstone A concrete or stone block used to spread a concentrated load over an area of wall.

pad support A wire grid to keep a sound-absorbing insert from contact with the perforated pan in a metal acoustical ceiling.

pailing Sheething constructed of vertical boards that is used in concrete formwork.

paint (1) A mixture of a solid pigment in a liquid vehicle which dries to a protective and decorative coating. (2) The resultant dry coating.

paint base The liquid vehicle into which a pigment is mixed to produce a paint.

painter A tradesperson experienced and trained in painting.

paint grade A description of a wood product that is more suitable for painting than for a clear finish.

paint kettle An open container with a wire handle used while painting.

paint remover A liquid solvent applied to dry paint to soften it for removal by scraping or brushing.

paint roller A tube with a fiber surface that is mounted on a roller and handle, and used to apply paint.

paint system A specific combination of paints applied in sequence. A paint system consists of a combination of some of the following coats: sealer or primer, stain, filler, undercoat, and one or more top coats.

paint thinner A liquid compatible with the vehicle of a paint, used to make a paint flow easier. Paint thinner lowers the viscosity of paints, adhesives, etc.

pairing veneers Matching full sheets of veneers (faces and backs) together to reduce handling when laying up panels at the glue spreader.

pale (paling) (1) One of the stakes in a palisade. (2) A picket in a fence.

palisade A fence of poles driven into the ground and pointed at the top.

palladiana terrazzo Randomly fractured marble slabs 3/8″ to 1″ thick with the largest dimension being 15″, with smaller chips filling the spaces between.

palladian window A tripartite, or three-light, window that features a

449

pan

panelboard

panel door

central arched window with balanced rectangular lights on each side.

pallet (1) A platform used for stacking material and arranged to be handled by a forklift truck. (2) A wood insert in a brick wall used for support of a surface system.

pallet brick A brick made with a groove, to hold a pallet.

palletized A term used frequently in the shingle and shake industry. Both items are often shipped on pallets from the mill for ease in handling while in transit. These shipments are referred to as palletized loads.

pallet stock Lumber used to make pallets.

palm sander A hand-held electrical sander with a vibrating or orbital base to which sandpaper is attached for finer sanding.

pan (1) A prefabricated form unit used in concrete joist floor construction. (2) A container that receives particles passing the finest sieve during mechanical analysis of granular materials. (3) A structural panel.

panache The triangular-like surface of a vault between a supported dome and two supporting arches.

pan and roll roofing tile A roofing tile system consisting of two types of tile: A flat or slightly curved tile with a flange on each side, and curved tile that fits the flanges and closes the joints.

pan construction A type of concrete floor or roof in which pan forms are used to create intersecting ribs and resulting in a waffle-like undersurface.

pane (1) A flat sheet of glass installed in a window or door. The installed sheet is also referred to as a light. (2) A British term for the

peen of a hammer. (3) One face or side of a building.

panel (1) A section of form sheathing, constructed from boards, plywood, metal sheets, etc., that can be erected and stripped as a unit. (2) A concrete member, usually precast, rectangular in shape, and relatively thin with respect to other dimensions. (3) A sheet of plywood, particle board, or other similar product, usually of a standard size, such as 4' x 8'. (4) See **frog**.

panelboard A board on which electric components and/or controls are mounted.

panel box A box in which electric switches and fuses are mounted.

panel clip A specially shaped metal device used in joining panels in roof construction. The clip substitutes for lumber blocking and helps to spread the load from one panel to the next one.

panel construction A general term used to describe construction where building components are assembled elsewhere before being brought to a site for placement.

panel divider Molding or trim used to fill or cover the joint between two surface sheets.

panel door A door constructed with panels, usually shaped to pattern, installed between the stiles and rails which form the outside frame of the door.

panel, drop See **drop panel**.

paneled door (Colonial door) A door which consists of raised or indented panels.

panel heating A method of heating a space using floor, wall, or roof panels in which are embedded electric elements or pipes for hot water, steam, or hot air.

paneling

panic hardware

paneling The material used to cover an interior wall. Paneling may be made from a 4'x4' *select* milled to a pattern and may be either hardwood or softwood plywood, often prefinished or overlaid with a decorative finish, or hardboard, and usually prefinished.

panel insert A metal unit used instead of glass in a panel door.

panel mold A mold in which plaster panels are cast.

panel molding A decorative molding, originally used to trim raised panel wall construction.

panel patch *See* **patch.**

panel pin A very thin nail used to fasten wood paneling to supports.

panel point Point of intersection of the members of a truss.

panel product Any of a variety of wood products such as plywood, particle board, hardboard, and waferboard, sold in sheets or panels. Although sizes vary, the board size for most panel products is 4'x8'.

panel saw A power saw held in a framework and used in cutting panels to size.

panel strip (1) A strip extending across the length or width of a flat slab for design purposes. (2) A narrow piece of wood or metal used to hide a joint between two sheathing boards forming a panel.

panel wall An exterior, non-load-bearing wall with individual panels hung from or supported by the framing of the building.

panel window A picture window with several sash or fixed glazings.

pan form stair A metal stair assembly with metal sheet pans at the treads to hold precast or cast-in-place masonry or stone treads.

pan formwork The support-work for the forms while a concrete pan construction floor or roof is being built.

pan fraction (1) The reported results of mechanical analysis of granular materials. (2) The weight of the material retained on any one sieve divided by the initial weight of the sample.

pan head A head of a screw or rivet shaped like a truncated cone.

panic bolt The bolt in panic hardware that is released by pressure on a horizontal bar.

panic exit hardware, mortise type Panic exit hardware in which the lock mechanism is concealed within the door or set into a rectangular cavity (called a *mortise*) that has been cut in the edge of the door.

panic exit hardware, rim type Panic exit hardware in which the lock mechanism is located on the inside face of the door.

panic exit hardware, vertical rod type Panic exit hardware with latches at the top and/or bottom of the door. The latches are connected to a vertical rod that, in turn, is connected to a crossbar. In an emergency, the latches are released simply by pressing the crossbar.

panic hardware A door-locking assembly that can be released quickly by pressure on a horizontal bar. Panic hardware is required by building codes on certain exits.

panier A corbel form for smoothing the angle between a beam and pilaster.

pan mixer *See* **mixer, pan.**

panopticon A building plan with corridors that radiate from a central point. All corridors can be observed from that location.

paper form

paper sheathing

pan steps   Prefabricated treads for a pan form stair.

pantile   A roofing tile shaped like an elongated "S." Joints are protected by the overlapping edges. In older buildings, galvanized roofing was sometimes used in the form of pantiles to imitate wood and slate shingles and terra-cotta tiles.

pantograph   A device for tracing drawings at different scales.

pants   Steel plates attached to the hammer of a pile driver to aid in driving sheet piling.

pan-type humidifier   A pan with water placed in a flow of air to increase humidity. A heating element may be placed in the pan for greater evaporation.

pan-type stairs   *See* **pan form stair**.

pap   The vertical outlet from a roof gutter.

paper and wire   Backing for tile installation that consists of tar paper and wire mesh or metal lath.

paper backed lath   Any lath with building paper attached. A paper backed lath serves as formwork and reinforcing for a concrete floor over open web joists.

paper birch   *Betula papyrifeya*. A North American birch with a tough bark.

paperboard (pasteboard, cardboard)   A stiff cardboard composed of layers of paper, or paper pulp, compressed into a sheet.

paper form   A heavy paper mold used for casting concrete columns and other structural shapes.

paper hanger   A tradesperson experienced and trained in preparing surfaces for and hanging wall coverings.

paper overlay   Paper prepared for application to the face of a panel after first being printed in four colors with the grain and color of a more valuable wood, or in a decorative design.

paper sheathing   Felt or heavy paper sheets used as an air and/or vapor barrier in walls.

paper wrap   A method of packaging wood products for shipment on a truck or railroad flatcar, with the paper designed to protect the product from dirt and the elements.

papreg   A paper product produced by impregnating sheets of high-strength paper with synthetic resin and then laminating the sheets to form a dense, moisture-resistant product.

parabolic aluminized reflector (PAR) lamp   A lamp that utilizes a light reflector shaped so as to project light from a small source in an approximately parallel beam, as in a spotlight.

parabolic luminaire   A fluorescent fixture with a louver of parabolic-shaped baffles that provide excellent light control and reduce glare.

paraffin-based oil   Petroleum oil used as summer oil, dormant spray, and as a vehicle for conveying pesticides. Also used as an additive to increase the effectiveness of pesticides.

paraform   Paraformaldehyde, an additive used with wood flour as a hardener in adhesives. *See also* **resorcinal resin adhesive**.

paragraph   In AIA and other contract documents, the first subdivision of an article. The next levels are subparagraphs and clauses.

paraline drawings   Projected pictorial drawings of an object or building that give a three-dimensional quality. Oblique, dimetric,

parapet

pargetting

isometric, and trimetric are examples of paraline drawings.

parallel (1) The condition in which two lines or planes are an equal distance apart at all points. (2) Electric blasting caps arranged so that the firing current passes through all of them at the same time.

parallel application An installation of gypsum board with the long dimension of the board in the same direction as the framing members.

parallel chord truss An engineered structural component, composed of a combination of members, with its top and bottom members positioned flat and parallel to each other.

parallel circuit An electrical circuit that has at least two paths for electricity to flow, with loads parallel to each other as a result.

parallel configuration An electrical configuration that provides more than one path for the flow of current.

parallel connection A connection at which a flow is diverted to two or more parallel conduits.

parallel flow An arrangement of a heat exchanger where the hot and cold materials enter at the same end and flow to the exit.

parallel gutter *See* **box gutter**.

parallel-laminated veneer A product in which the veneers have been laminated with their grains parallel to one another. Parallel laminated veneer is used in furniture and cabinetry to provide flexibility over curved surfaces, and in the production of laminated veneer structural products.

parallel series Two or more series of blasting caps arranged in parallel.

parallel siding (square-edged siding) (1) Siding that is not beveled.

(2) Siding having edges of the same thickness.

parallel welding The joining of metal parts by fusion, with the electric current that produces the weld divided and routed through the electrode and metal along similar paths.

parallel-wire unit A posttensioning tendon composed of a number of wires or strands which are approximately parallel.

parameter A variable in a mathematical expression.

parameter estimate A cost estimate based on an evaluation of the building's systems.

parapet (1) That part of a wall that extends above the roof level. (2) A low wall along the top of a dam.

parapet gutter A gutter built or placed behind a parapet.

parapet skirting Roofing felt turned up against a parapet.

parapet wall *See* **parapet**.

parcel A contiguous land area, subject to single ownership and legally recorded as a single unit.

paretta Cast masonry with a surface of protruding pebbles.

parge To coat with plaster, particularly foundation walls and rough masonry.

parge coat A coat of masonry cement applied to masonry for resistance to penetration of moisture.

pargetting (1) Lining of a flue to aid in smooth flow and increase fire resistance. (2) Application of a dampproofing masonry cement. (3) Ornamental, often elaborate, facing for plaster walls.

Parian cement A hard finish plaster, similar to Keene's cement plaster, except borax is used as an additive in place of alum.

parquet flooring

partition

paring Trimming wood by shaving small portions from the surface with a chisel.

paring chisel A long-handled chisel used to shape wood by hand without the use of a mallet.

paring gouge A long thin woodworking gouge, the cutting edge of which is beveled on the concave side.

parkerized Descriptive of steel products, such as fasteners, that have been given a zinc phosphate coating for corrosion protection.

parking garage A garage for short term storage of automobiles only.

parking lot A ground-level space for short term storage of automobiles.

parking space A marked-off area for short term storage of a single automobile.

PAR lamp *See* **parabolic aluminized reflector lamp**.

parliament hinge An H-shaped hinge.

parquet flooring A floor covering composed of small pieces of wood, usually forming a geometric design.

parquet strip A wood flooring composed of tongued and grooved hardwood boards.

parsing A thin coat of plaster or masonry cement.

partial cover plate A cover plate attached to the flange of a girder but not extending the full length of the girder.

partially air-dried (PAD) Wood seasoned to some extent by exposure to the atmosphere without artificial heat, but still considered green or unseasoned.

partial occupancy An owner's occupation and use of a project before final completion. *See also* **final completion**.

partial payment *See* **progress payment**.

partial prestressing Prestressing to a stress level such that, under design loads, tensile stresses exist in the precompressed tensile zone of the prestressed member.

partial release Release in a prestressed concrete member of a portion of the total prestress initially held wholly in the prestressed reinforcement.

particle board A generic term used to describe panel products made from discrete particles of wood or other ligno-cellulosic material rather than from fibers. The wood particles are mixed with resins and formed into a solid board under heat and pressure.

particle shape The shape of a particle. *See also* **cubical piece**, **elongated piece**, *and* **flat piece**.

particle size (1) Minimum particle diameter that will be removed by an air filter. (2) Diameter of a pigment particle in paint. (3) Diameter of a grain of sand in a mechanical analysis test.

particle size distribution A tabulation of the result of mechanical analysis expressed as the percentage by weight passing through each of a series of sieves.

parting bead A narrow strip between the upper and lower sashes in a double-hung window frame.

parting slip A thin piece of wood in the cased frame of a sash window separating the sash weights.

parting stop *See* **parting bead**.

parting tool A turning tool with a narrow blade and V-shaped gouge used for cutting recesses or grooves in wood.

partition A dividing wall within a building, usually non-load-bearing.

partition block

partition block Light concrete masonry unit with a nominal thickness of 4″ to 6″.

partition plate The top horizontal member of a partition, which may support joists or rafters.

partition stud A steel or wood upright in a partition.

partition tile A hollow, clay unit for use in interior partitions. The surface of a partition tile is often grooved for plastering.

partnership The joining of two or more individuals for a business purpose whereby profits and liabilities are shared.

party wall A common wall between two living units.

Pascal's law A principle that states that pressure applied to a confined fluid at any point is transmitted equally in all directions.

pass (1) Layer of shotcrete placed in one movement over the field of operation. (2) A single progression of a welding operation along a joint, resulting in a weld bead.

passage (passageway) A horizontal space for moving from one area of a building to another.

pass door A door through the wall separating a stage from the auditorium.

passenger elevator An elevator mainly used for people.

passings The dimension of the overlap between sheets of flashing.

passive design An approach to design that minimizes energy consumed by burning fuel or using power. *See also* **sustainable design**.

passive solar energy system A solar energy system that collects and distributes thermal energy through a structure via natural means, without using pumps or fans.

pass-through An opening in a partition for passing objects between adjacent areas.

paste board *See* **paper board**.

paste content (of concrete) Proportional volume of cement paste in concrete, mortar, or the like, expressed as volume percent of the entire mixture. *See also* **neat cement paste**.

paste filler A filler in paste form used in preparing wood surfaces for painting.

paste paint A paste-like mixture of pigment and solvent, usually requiring additional solvent for use.

paste volume (of concrete) *See* **paste content**.

pat A specimen of neat cement paste about 3″ (76 mm) in diameter and 1/2″ (13 mm) in thickness at the center, and tapering into a thin edge on a flat glass plate for indicating setting time.

patch (1) A piece of wood or synthetic material used to fill defects in the plies of plywood. Also called a *plug*. (2) A compound used in stonemasonry to replace chips and broken corners or edges in fabricated pieces of cut stone or to fill natural voids. The patch is applied in plastic form.

patch board (patch panel) A board with jacks and plugs for terminals of electric circuits. The circuits may be temporarily interconnected by patch cords.

patch gun (1) A hand tool that "shoots" a premixed material for patching and repairing exterior finishes like stucco. (2) A hand tool used to apply joint compound to drywall.

patching machine A machine that cuts out the defect in a piece of

paumelle

pavement, concrete

pavement saw

veneer and replaces the defect with a solid piece of veneer used as a patch. The machine is often referred to by the brand name of the machine.

patch panel *See* **patch board**.

patent defect A defect present in materials, equipment, or completed work detectable by reasonably careful observation. A patent defect is distinguished from a latent defect, which could not be discovered by reasonable observation. *See also* **latent defect**.

patent glazing Any of a number of devices, usually preformed neoprene gaskets, for securing glass in frames without putty.

patent hammer A hammer with chisel-like faces, used for dressing stone.

patent-hammered Stonework finish applied to the face of building stone.

patent knotting A solution of shellac and benzine or similar solvent used to seal knots in wood.

patent plaster A packaged hard plaster.

patent stone (artificial soil) Stone chips embedded in a binder of mortar, cement, or plaster. The surface may be ground and/or polished.

patina Color and texture added to a surface as a result of oxidation or use, such as the green coating on copper or its alloys.

patio An outdoor area, usually paved and sometimes shaded, adjoining a building.

patten The base of a column.

pattern (1) A plan or model to be a guide in making objects. (2) A form used to shape the interior of a mold.

pattern cracking Fine openings on concrete surfaces in the form of a pattern, resulting from a decrease in volume of the material near the surface and/or an increase in volume of the material below the surface.

patternmaker's saw A small hand saw with fine teeth used to make intricate cuts.

pattern staining Dark areas on finished plaster, particularly on the interior of external walls, which are caused by different thermal conductances of backings.

paumelle A door hinge with a single joint, usually of modern design.

paved invert In piping, the lower portion of a corrugated metal pipe whose corrugations have been filled with smooth bituminous material to resist scour and erosion and improve flow.

pavement base The layer of a pavement immediately below the surfacing material and above the subbase.

pavement, concrete A layer of concrete over roads, sidewalks, canals, playgrounds, and those areas used for storage or parking. *See also* **rigid pavement**.

pavement light Transparent or translucent inserts in a pavement to light a space below.

pavement saw A self-propelled machine with a circular saw blade for cutting control joints.

pavement sealer A bituminous coating used to seal and renew the surface of asphalt paving.

pavement structure The collection of courses of specified materials placed on a graded surface.

paver (1) A block or tile used as a wearing surface. (2) A machine that places concrete pavements.

paving stone

peak joint

pavilion roof (1) A roof composed of equally hipped areas. (2) A pyramid-shaped roof.

paving The hard surface covering of areas such as walks, roadways, ramps, waterways, parking areas, and airport runways.

paving aggregate The various solid materials, such as sand, gravel, or slag, used in construction of a pavement.

paving asphalt A sticky residue from the refining of crude oil. Paving asphalt is used in built-up roofing systems, as the binder in asphaltic concrete, or as a waterproofing agent.

paving breaker (chipper) A hand-held, pneumatic tool for cutting pavements.

paving brick A vitrified clay brick with good resistance to abrasion.

paving stone (rock) A block of natural stone shaped or selected for use in a pavement surface.

paving train An assemblage of equipment designed to place and finish a concrete pavement.

paving unit A fabricated or shaped unit used in a pavement surface.

payment bond A form of security purchased by the contractor from a surety, which is provided to guarantee that the contractor will pay all costs of labor, materials, and other services related to the project for which he is responsible under the contract for construction. *See also* **labor and material payment bond.**

payment request *See* **application for payment.**

payments withheld A provision of AIA document A201-General Conditions of the Contract for Construction, Paragraph 9.6, which provides that the owner may withhold payments to the contractor if, in the opinion of the design professional, the work falls behind the schedule of construction, or in the event that the work deviates from the provisions of the contract documents.

payroll deductions Amounts withheld from gross pay by the employer, including federal and state taxes, union dues, and medical insurance.

p bar A heavy steel bar, shaped like a chisel at one end, used for prying.

PCB A polychlorinated biphenon compound.

peacock's eye A circular marking in wood, such as bird's eye in maple, found particularly in sugar maple but also in other species.

pea gravel Screened gravel, most of the particles of which will pass a 3/8″ (9.5 mm) sieve and be retained on a No. 4 (4.75 mm) sieve.

pea gravel grout A grout with pea gravel added.

peaked roof A roof of two or more slopes that rises to a peak.

peak joint The joint of a roof truss that is at the ridge.

peak levels In measuring ambient air contamination, above average levels of ambient contamination due to the sudden release of a contaminant into the air. Usually occurs for a short period of time immediately following the release.

peak load The maximum demand or design load of a device, system, or structure over a designated time period.

peak-load controller An electrical controller used to limit the maximum power demands to a device or system.

pedestal

pedestal pile

pediment

peat Fibrous organic matter in various stages of decomposition, found in swamps and bogs, and used to enrich soil for plantings.

peat moss (1) A type of moss growing in wet areas. (2) The partially decomposed moss used as mulch.

peavey A long-shafted tool with a hook that is used by loggers to roll logs, break jams, pry rocks, tighten chains, and push over trees .

pebble dash (rock dash) An exterior finish in which crushed rock or pebbles are embedded in mortar, plaster or stucco.

pecan *Carya illinoensis.* One of the largest native hickories, its wood is used in furniture and flooring, while it is grown commercially for its nuts in the Mississippi River valley.

peck (1) Channeled or pitted areas or pockets sometimes found in cedar or cypress, the decay resulting from fungus in isolated spots. (2) A dry measure equal to two gallons.

pecky Characterized by peck, channeled, or pitted areas or pockets found in cedar and cypress.

pecky timber Decay-spotted timber. In cedar and cypress the decay stops when the wood is dried.

pedestal An upright compression member whose height does not exceed three times its average least lateral dimension, such as a short pier or plinth used as the base for a column.

pedestal floor A flooring system that is elevated from the subfloor to accommodate cabling, piping, ductwork, or other building systems.

pedestal lavatory Lavatory supported by a pedestal rather than wall hung. Supply and waste lines are enclosed by the pedestal.

pedestal pavers A paving system suitable for pedestrian traffic that features concrete or stone pavers on pedestals over an insulated base.

pedestal pile A cast-in-place concrete pile constructed so that concrete is forced out into a widened bulb or pedestal shape at the foot of the pipe which forms the pile.

pedestal urinal A urinal that is supported by a pedestal rather than wall-hung. Supply and waste lines are enclosed by the pedestal.

pedestrian control device Any device, especially turnstiles, but including gates, railings, or posts, used to control the movement of pedestrians.

pediment A decorative unit, often triangular in shape, above a doorway.

peel To produce veneer from a log through rotary cutting.

peeler A log from which veneer is peeled on a lathe, for the production of plywood. A peeler-grade log most frequently is from an old growth tree, with a high proportion of clear wood.

peeler core That portion of a peeler block that remains after the veneer has been taken. Peeler cores are often used as raw material for the production of studs.

peeling A process in which thin flakes of mortar are broken away from a concrete surface, such as by deterioration or by adherence of surface mortar to forms as they are removed.

peen The end of a hammer, other than a claw hammer, opposite the hammering face. A peen may be pointed or ball- or cone-shaped. A peen is used for chipping, indenting, and metalworking.

peen-coated nail A mechanically galvanized nail coated by tumbling

pendant luminaire

in a container with zinc dust and glass balls.

peening   To hammer, bend, or shape with a peen.

peg   (1) A pointed pin of wood used to fasten wood members together. (2) A short, pointed wooden stick used as a marker by surveyors.

peg-and-plank   A rustic wood floor of planks and exposed pegs.

pegboard   A hard fiberboard sheet, usually 1/4″ thick with regular rows of holes for attaching pegs or hooks.

pelmet   A valance or cornice, sometimes decorative, at the head of a window to conceal a drapery track or other fittings.

pelmet board   A board at the head of a window, acting as a pelmet.

pelmet lighting   Lighting furnished by sources that are concealed by a pelmet.

penal bond   A combined performance, and labor and material payment bond.

penal sum   An amount specified in a bond or contract designated as a penalty to be paid by a specific signatory if contractual obligations are not met.

penalty and bonus clause   *See* **bonus and penalty clause**.

penalty clause   A clause in a contract specifying a charge against the contractor for failure to complete the work by a pre-arranged date. *See also* **liquidated damages**.

pencil cedar   Eastern red cedar.

penciling   Painting mortar joints, usually white.

pencil rod   Plain metal rod of about 1/4″ (6 mm) diameter.

pencil rot   A type of decay found in cedar.

pencil stock   Pieces of eastern red cedar or incense cedar from which pencils are manufactured. Pencil stock consists of squares 8″ in length, or in multiples of 8″, and equal to the thickness of the piece in width.

pendant   (1) An electric device suspended from overhead. (2) A suspended ornament in Gothic architecture, used in vaults and timber roofs.

pendant luminaire   A suspended lighting unit.

pendant switch   An electric switch suspended by an electric cord and used to control lamps or other devices that are out of reach.

pendent sprinkler   A fire safety system sprinkler with a head that features a deflector plate that directs discharged water downward.

pendulum saw   *See* **swing saw**.

penetrant   An additive that increases a liquid's ability to penetrate a surface or enter the pores of a substrate. Penetrants are typically used as wetting agents.

penetrating finish   A low-viscosity oil or varnish that penetrates into wood with only a film of material at the surface.

penetration   (1) A test of the hardness of an asphalt utilizing a weighted needle at standard conditions. (2) The cut-off depth of piles or sheet piling. (3) The depth of a caisson below ground level. (4) The intersection of two surfaces of vaulting.

penetration macadam   Pavement made from layers of coarse, open-graded aggregate (crushed stone, slag, or gravel) followed by the spray application and penetration of emulsified asphalt.

pent roof

penetration probe A device for obtaining a measure of the resistance of concrete to penetration, customarily determined by the distance that a steel pin is driven into the concrete from a special gun by a precisely measured explosive charge.

penetration resistance The resistance, usually expressed in pounds per square inch (psi) or megapascals (MPa), of mortar or cement paste to penetration by a plunger or needle under standard conditions.

penetration test A test to estimate the bearing capacity of soil by recording the number of blows required to drive a standard tool into soil.

peninsula-base kitchen cabinet A kitchen cabinet or series of cabinets at right angles to a wall and having access from two sides.

penitent Variation of **pendant (2)**.

penitent post A short post placed against the wall and supporting an arch or tie beam.

penny A measure of the length of a nail. The larger the number is, the longer the nail is.

penta Short for *pentachlorophenol*, a wood preservative.

pentachlorophenol A chemical used in wood preserving, usually applied under pressure so that it will penetrate the wood.

penthouse A structure on the roof of a building, usually less than one-half the projected area of the roof, and housing mechanical and electrical equipment or residents.

pent roof A roof with a single plane surface sloping on one side only.

peppermint test A test for leaks in a drainpipe using oil of peppermint as a trace odor source.

percentage agreement A contractual agreement for which compensation will be based on a certain percentage of the total cost of construction.

percentage fee A fee paid to the contractor or the architect that is a percentage of the total construction cost. *See also* **fee** *and* **compensation**.

percentage humidity The ratio, expressed as a percentage, of the weight of water vapor in a pound of dry air to the weight of water vapor if the same weight of air were saturated.

percentage of reinforcement The ratio, expressed as a percentage, of the cross-sectional area of reinforcing steel to the effective cross-sectional area of a member.

percentage void The ratio, expressed as a percentage, of the volume of voids to the gross volume of material.

percent fines (1) Amount, expressed as a percentage, of material in aggregate finer than a given sieve, usually the No. 200 sieve. (2) The amount of fine aggregate in a concrete mixture expressed as a percent by absolute volume of the total amount of aggregate.

percent saturation The ratio, expressed as a percentage, of the volume of water in a soil sample to the volume of voids.

percent voids *See* **percentage void**.

perched water table A water table, of limited area, held above the normal water table by an intervening strata of impervious confining strata.

percolation The movement of a fluid through a soil.

percolation test A test to estimate the rate at which a soil will absorb waste fluids, performed by measuring the rate (percolation rate) at which the water level drops in a hole full of water.

percussion drill A pneumatic or electric tool that drills holes by applying a rapid series of blows.

pereletok The bottom of the active layer of permafrost that sometimes remains frozen throughout the year.

perennial A plant or shrub with a life cycle greater than two years.

perfections Shingles 18″ long and 0.45″ thick at the butt.

perforated drain A subsurface draining system that uses pipes with holes in the bottom to allow water or other liquid to percolate into the soil.

perforated facing A perforated sheet or board used as a finished surface and allowing a fraction of sound to penetrate the surface to an absorbent layer.

perforated hardboard *See* **pegboard**.

perforated metal pan A unit that forms the exposed surface of a type of acoustical ceiling. The perforated pan contains a sound-absorbent material, usually in pad form.

perforated tape A special paper tape used to reinforce the material covering joints between gypsum boards.

performance (1) A term meaning fulfillment of a promise made by one party to a contract or agreement in return for compensation. (2) The manner in which or the efficiency with which something acts or reacts in the manner in which it is intended.

performance bond (1) A guarantee that a contractor will perform a job according to the terms of the contract, or the bond will be forfeited. (2) A bond procured by the contractor which shows that a surety guarantees (to the owner) that the work will be performed

in accordance with the contract documents. Unless prohibited by statute, the performance bond can be combined with the labor and material payment bond. *See also* **surety bond**.

performance specification A description of the desired results or performance of a product, material, assembly, or piece of equipment with criteria for verifying compliance.

pergola An arbor or similar open-air structure with trelliswork supported on columns or posts. Vines or other plants are usually trained over pergolas.

periclase A crystalline mineral, magnesia (MgO), the equivalent of which may be present in Portland cement clinker, Portland cement, and other materials, such as open hearth slags, and certain basic refractories.

periderm The cork-producing tissue of a tree.

perimeter grouting Injection of grout, usually at relatively low pressure, around the periphery of an area which is subsequently to be grouted at greater pressure. Perimeter grouting is intended to confine subsequent grout injection within the perimeter.

perimeter heating system A system of warm-air heating in which outlets for air ducts are located near the outside walls of rooms and are close to the floor. The returns are near the ceiling.

perimeter installation A method of floor installation where adhesive is only used along the outside edges and seams of the flooring material, allowing for faster installations and easier repairs

perimeter isolation A method of installing a building material, such

perlite plaster

as concrete or wallboard, so that it is separated from structural elements. This isolation helps reduce the cracking that can result when structural members shift. Perimeter isolation is also used as a sound control measure.

periphery wall A wall on the exterior of a building.

perlite A volcanic glass having a perlitic structure, usually having a higher water content than obsidian when expanded by heating. Perlite is used as a lightweight aggregate in concretes, mortars, and plasters.

perlite composite board A rigid insulation board formed of expanded perlite, fibers, and a sizing material. Often recommended as a product for sustainable design because it is commonly manufactured with post-consumer paper.

perlite plaster A plaster using perlite as an aggregate instead of sand.

perlitic structure A structure produced in a homogeneous material, generally natural glass, by contraction during cooling, and consisting of a system of irregular convoluted and spheroidal cracks.

perm A unit of water vapor transmission through a material, expressed in grains of vapor per hour per inch of mercury pressure difference.

permafrost Permanently frozen soil or subsoil found in arctic or subarctic regions.

permanent bracing Bracing that forms part of a structure's resistance to horizontal loads. Permanent bracing may also function as erection bracing.

permanent form Any form that remains in place after the concrete has developed its design strength. A permanent form may or may not become an integral part of the structure.

permanent load The load, including a dead load or any fixed load, that is constant through the life of a structure.

permanent set Inelastic elongation or shortening.

permanent shore An upright used to support dead loads during alterations to a structure and left in place.

permeability (1) The property of a material that permits passage of water vapor. (2) The property of soil which permits the flow of water.

permeability to water, coefficient of The rate of discharge of water under laminar flow conditions through a unit cross-sectional area of a porous medium under a unit hydraulic gradient and standard temperature conditions, usually 20 °C.

permeameter An instrument to measure the coefficient of permeability of a soil sample.

permeance The resistance, measured in perms, to the flow of water vapor through a given thickness of material.

permit A document issued by a governing authority such as a building inspector approving specific construction.

permit, building *See* **building permit.**

permit, occupancy *See* **certificate of occupancy.**

permit, zoning *See* **zoning permit.**

perpend (1) A stone which extends completely through a wall and is exposed on each side of the wall. (2) A joint between masonry units.

personal injury (insurance terminology) Protection against claims for bodily or character injury, or damage to one's reputation. This

petcock

insurance protects against damage caused by specified actions of the insured. Includes false arrest, malicious prosecution, willful detention or imprisonment, libel, slander, defamation of character, wrongful eviction, invasion of privacy, or wrongful entry. *See also* **bodily injury.**

personal property Generally, all property that is not real property. Tangible goods, such as furniture, cars, books, and equipment, and intangible goods, such as money, notes, bonds, and stocks.

personal protective equipment (PPE) Special clothing, devices and equipment worn by workers for protection against documented or potential site hazards. Examples include respirators and eye, ear and skin protection. *See also* **level A-D clothing.**

perspective (1) The technique of preparing a perspective drawing. (2) The appearance of objects in depth.

perspective center A point of origin or termination of perspective rays used in preparing a perspective drawing.

perspective drawing A three-dimensional graphic presentment of a project (or part of a project).

PERT schedule *See* **project evaluation and review technique.**

pervious cesspool A tank in the ground which receives domestic sewage or other organic wastes. The walls and floor of the tank are designed to permit the liquids to seep through to the soil.

pervious soil A soil that allows relatively free passage of water.

petcock A small valve installed on equipment or piping for drainage of liquids or air.

petrifying liquid A penetrating solution used for waterproofing masonry surfaces.

petrography The branch of petrology dealing with description and systematic classification of rocks, aside from their geologic relations, mainly by laboratory methods, largely chemical and microscopical. Also, loosely referred to as *petrology* or *lithology*.

petroleum asphalt Asphalt refined directly from petroleum, as opposed to asphalt from natural deposits.

petroleum hydrocarbon Any of a number of solvents refined from cured petroleum and used to lower the viscosity of oils and resins.

petroleum oil A refined spray oil made from a flammable hydrocarbon-based mixture found beneath the earth's surface. Petroleum oils are categorized as unsaturates, aromatics, naphthenes, and paraffins.

petroleum spirit A thinner, for paints and varnishes, having a low-aromatic hydrocarbon content, obtained in petroleum distillation.

petrology The science of rocks, dealing with their origin, structure, composition, etc., from all aspects and in all relations. *See also* **petrography.**

pew A bench-like seat used in a church.

p-grade Molding stock intended to be covered with opaque finishes or overlays. P-grade stock can be finger-jointed and/or edge-glued.

pH A measure of the relative acidity or alkalinity of a liquid.

phantom line A broken line, usually fine, with alternating long and short dashes, in order to show details.

phase converter An electrical device that converts single-phase power to the smooth, continuous and universally adaptable three-phase power.

phased application The installation of built-up roofing plies in two or more applications, usually at least one day apart.

phenol A product of the petroleum industry used in the production of phenolic resin, epoxy resins, plasters, and exterior plywood glue. Phenol is made from benzene. It exists naturally in coal tar and wood tar. However, phenol from these sources is rarely used in the production of glue.

phenolic compounds Substances containing phenols.

phenolic insulation A rigid, closed cell foam insulation product made with phenolic plastics. No longer used in the roofing industry because when wet it will chemically attack steel decks. However, it has not posed problems when used over concrete or wood decks, or gypsum boards sealed with a vapor retarder.

phenolic resin A class of synthetic, oil-soluble resins (plastics) produced as condensation products of phenol, substituted phenols and formaldehyde, or some similar aldehyde that may be used in paints for concrete.

phenolic resin glue An adhesive used for bonding exterior plywood. Phenolic resin is produced in a reaction between phenol and formaldehyde. An extender is usually added to the phenolic resin prior to use in the plywood-manufacturing process.

phi factor Capacity reduction factor in structural design. The factor is expressed as a number less than 1.0 (usually 0.65-0.90) by which the strength of a structural member or element, in terms of load, moment, shear, or stress, is required to be multiplied in order to determine design strength or capacity. The magnitude of the factor is stipulated in applicable codes and construction specifications for respective types of members and cross sections.

Philadelphia leveling rod A leveling rod in two sliding parts with color-coded graduations. The rod can be used as a self-reading leveling rod.

Philippine mahogany The wood of several types of trees found in the Philippines. The wood resembles mahogany in grain. Density varies from very light to quite heavy. The heavier, darker woods are durable and strong and used like mahogany. The lighter weight, colored woods are used for interior plywood.

Phillips head screw A screw with a recessed head and an X-shaped driving indentation.

phosphor mercury-vapor lamp A high-pressure mercury-vapor lamp with a phosphor-coated glass cover over the lamp proper. The phosphor in the cover adds colors not generated by the lamp.

phot A measure of illumination equal to one lumen per square centimeter.

photoelectric cell An electronic device for measuring illumination level or detecting interruption of a light beam. The electric output or resistance of the device varies according to the illumination.

photoelectric control An electric control that responds to a change in incident light.

photogrammetry The practice of calculating measurements and drawing up surveys through the use

picture window

pierced louver

of photographs, especially aerial photographs.

photoionization detector An ionization detector that uses ultraviolet light to generate ions.

photometer A device that measures luminous intensity, light distribution, color, and other qualities of a luminaire.

piano hinge A continuous strip hinge used in falling doors, etc.

Picea The general botanical classification of the spruces.

pick A hand tool, consisting of a steel head pointed at one or both ends and mounted on a wooden handle, for loosening and breaking up compacted soil or rock.

pick and dip A method of laying brick in which the bricklayer picks up a brick in one hand and, with a trowel in the other hand, scoops enough mortar to lay the brick.

pickax *See* **pick**.

pick dressing The rough dressing of hard, quarried stone with a heavy pick or wedge-shaped hammer.

picked finish A surface finish for stonemasonry in which the surface is covered with small pits made by striking it perpendicularly with a pick or chisel.

picket A sharpened or pointed stake, post, or pale, usually used as fencing.

picket fence A fence consisting of vertical piles, often sharpened at the upper end, supported by horizontal rails.

pickled A metal surface that has been treated with strong oxidizing agents to remove scale and provide a tough oxide film.

pickling Slang for the preservative treatment of wood, metals, and piping systems.

pickup (1) The amount by which an estimate for an item is higher than the actual cost; savings; underrun. (2) Unwanted adherence of solids to the open surface of a sealant. (3) Common term for a small open-body truck with a 1/2 ton to 1 ton capacity.

pickup load The heat consumption required to bring piping and radiators to their operating temperature when a heating system is first turned on.

picture molding Molding designed to support picture hooks near the ceiling.

picture plane The plane on which rays are projected when making a perspective drawing.

picture window A large window, usually a fixed sheet of plate or insulating glass.

pieced timber (1) A timber made from two or more pieces of timber fitted together. (2) A damaged timber patched with a fitted piece of wood.

piece mark A mark given to one or more pieces in an assembly designating a location in the assembly, as shown on shop drawings.

pien check In a stair constructed of stone, a rabbet cut in the front edge of a tread that fits over the riser below it.

pier (1) A short column to support a concentrated load. (2) Isolated foundation member of plain or reinforced concrete.

pierced louver A louver set in the face sheets or panels of a door.

pierced wall An ornamented, nonbearing masonry wall laid with void spaces between the blocks.

pilaster

pile

pile cap

pier glass A mirror hung between two windows.

pigeonhole A small compartment for holding papers or small objects, usually one of an adjoining series.

piggyback (1) A method of transportation whereby truck trailers are carried on trains, or cars on trucks. (2) In staple application to gypsum wallboard, a second staple is driven directly on top of the first. The staple will spread to create a firm bond between the wallboard and the tile.

pigment A coloring matter, usually in the form of an insoluble fine powder, dispersed in a liquid vehicle to make paint.

pigment figure A natural pattern in woods, such as rosewood and zebra wood, consisting of variations in color rather than grain.

pig spout A sheet metal flashing system that directs water out through the face of a gutter instead of through a downspout.

pigtail (1) An anti-siphon piping device used to protect a pressure gauge. (2) A flexible conductor attached to an electric component for connecting the component to a circuit.

pigtail splice A connection of two electric conductors, made by placing the ends of the conductors side by side and twisting the ends about each other.

pig tin A metal alloy which is at least 99.80% tin.

pike pole A long pole, with a spear-type point and a hook on one end, used to move logs around in a mill pond.

pike staff Similar to a pike pole, but lighter.

pilaster A column built within a wall, usually projecting beyond the wall.

pilaster block Concrete masonry units designed to form plain or reinforced concrete masonry pilasters of the projecting type.

pilaster face The form for the front surface of a pilaster parallel to the wall.

pilaster side The form for the side surface of a pilaster perpendicular to the wall.

pile A slender timber, concrete, or steel structural element, driven, jetted, or otherwise embedded on end in the ground for the purpose of supporting a load.

pile-bearing capacity The load on a pile or group of piles that will theoretically produce failure if exceeded.

pile bent Two or more piles driven in a row transverse to the long dimension of the structure and fastened together by capping and (sometimes) bracing.

pile cap (1) A structural member placed on, and usually fastened to, the top of a pile or a group of piles and used to transmit loads into the pile or group of piles and, in the case of a group, to connect them into a bent. Also known as a *rider cap* or *girder*. (2) A masonry, timber, or concrete footing resting on a group of piles. (3) A metal cap or helmet temporarily fitted over the head of a precast pile to protect it during driving. Some form of shock-absorbing material is often incorporated.

pile core The mandrel used to drive the shell of a cast-in-place concrete pile.

pile driver A machine for driving piles, usually by repeated blows, from a free-falling or driven hammer. A pile driver consists of a framework for holding and guiding the pile, a

pile shoe

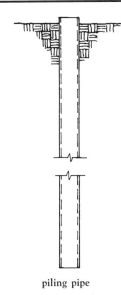

piling pipe

hammer, and a mobile plant to provide power.

pile eccentricity The amount that a pile deviates from its plan location, or from plumb.

pile extractor A machine for loosening piles in the ground by exerting upward striking blows. The actual removal is by a crane.

pile foundation The system of piles, and pile caps, that transfers structural loads to bearing soils or bedrock.

pile friction The friction forces on an embedded pile limited by the adhesion between soil and pile and/or the shear strength of the adjacent soil.

pile hammer A weight which strikes a pile to drive it into the ground. The weight may fall freely or be assisted by steam or air pressure.

pile head The top of a pile.

pile height The height of piles in a rug measured from the top surface of the backing to the top of the pile.

pile load test A static load test of a pile or group of piles used to establish an allowable load. The applied load is usually 150% to 200% of the allowable load.

pile shoe A pointed or rounded device on the foot of a pile to protect the pile while driving.

pile tolerance The permitted deviation of a pile in the horizontal and vertical planes.

piling The behavior of a quick-drying paint in which viscosity increases during application, resulting in uniform coverage.

piling pipe A pipe used as the shell or a section of shell for a cast-in-place concrete pile.

pillar (1) A post or column. (2) A column of ore left in a mine to support the ground overhead.

pilot boring A preliminary boring or series of borings to determine the nature of the soil in which a foundation will be dug or a tunnel driven.

pilot hole A guiding hole for a nail or screws, or for drilling a larger hole.

pilot lamp *See* **pilot light**.

pilot light (1) A small, constantly burning flame used as an ignition source in a gas burner. (2) A low-wattage light used to indicate that an electric circuit, control, or device is active.

pilot nail A temporary nail used to align boards until permanent nails are driven.

pilot punch A machine punch in which the punching tool is fitted with a small control plug to be inserted in a guide hole in the material to be punched.

pin A peg or bolt of some rigid material used to connect or fasten members.

pincers A joined tool with a pair of jaws and handles used to grip an object.

pinch bar A steel bar with a chisel point at one end used as a lever for lifting or moving heavy objects.

pin-connected truss A truss in which the main members are connected by pins.

pin connection In structural analysis, any member connection to a foundation. Designed to transfer axial and shear forces, but not moments.

pine Any of various softwoods of the genus *Pinus*.

pin hinge

pipe

pipe bend

pipe cutter

pine oil A high-boiling-point solvent, obtained from the resin of pine trees and used in paint to provide good flow properties and as an anti-skinning agent.

pine shingles Shingles made from pine wood.

pine tar A blackish-brown liquid distilled from pine wood. Pine tar is used as an antiseptic externally and an expectorant internally and also to make the grips of tools sticky.

pin hinge A butt hinge with a pin for the pivot.

pinhole (pin hole) (1) In wood, a small, round hole made by a beetle or worm in the standing timber. (2) In plaster, a surface defect caused by trapped air. (3) In painted surfaces, a defect usually caused by impurities or dirt. (4) In glazed ceramic surfaces, a small round hole.

pin joint A structural joint found in trusses and some girder seats.

pin knot A knot with a diameter no larger than 1/2″.

pinnacle (1) The highest point. (2) A turret or elevated portion of a building. (3) A small ornamental body or shaft terminated by a cone or pyramid.

pinner A small stone which supports a larger stone in masonry.

pinning Fastening or securing by means of a pin.

pinning in Filling in joints of masonry with chips of the stone.

pinning up The operation of driving wedges to bring an upper work to fully bear on shoring or underpinning.

pintle A vertical pin fastened at the bottom and serving as a center of rotation.

pin tumbler A lock mechanism having a series of small pins that must be properly aligned by a key to open.

pinyon pine (pinon pine, nut pine) *Pinus monophylla, P. cembroides, P. quadrifolia, P. edulis.* A group of small pines, 20′ to 40′ in height, occurring in scattered groves in the semi-arid areas of the west. They produce an edible seed, mostly used as topping for salad. Trees exposed to constant winds take on a sprawling form.

pipe (1) A hollow cylinder or tube for conveyance of a fluid. (2) From ASTM B 251–557: Seamless tube conforming to the particular dimensions commonly know as "standard pipe size."

pipe bend (pipe elbow) A pipe fitting used to change direction.

pipe bracket A shaped metal assembly used to support a pipe from a wall or floor.

pipe chase A vertical space in a building reserved for vertical runs of pipe.

pipe column A column made of steel pipe and often filled with concrete.

pipe coupling A fitting used to connect two lengths of pipe in a direct line.

pipe covering Any wrapping on a pipe which acts as thermal insulation and/or a vapor barrier.

pipe cross A fitting used to connect four lengths of pipe in the same plane with all lengths at right angles to each other.

pipe cutter A hand tool for cutting pipe or tubing, consisting of a frame with a cutting wheel and drive wheels. Cutting is accomplished by forcing the cutting wheel into the pipe material and rotating the tool around the pipe a number of times.

pipe tee

pipe die An adjustable tool for cutting threads on or in a pipe.

pipe elbow *See* **pipe bend**.

pipe expansion joint An assembly, other than a fabricated U-bend, designed to compensate for pipe contraction or expansion.

pipe fitting Ells, tees, and other connectors used in assembling pipe.

pipe gasket A fabricated packing to seal flanged joints in pipe.

pipe hanger A device or an assembly to support pipes from a slab, beam or other structural element.

pipe laser (1) A self-leveling instrument used in surveying that employs a laser as a reference for measurements or verifying alignment. (2) A plumber's tool used to simplify pipe alignment and installation. Once a hole is drilled in a stud or beam for pipe placement, the laser is directed through the hole to indicate where the hole in the next stud or beam should go.

pipelayer (1) A tradesperson skilled and trained in laying and joining pipes of glazed clay, concrete, iron, or steel in a trench. (2) An attachment for a tractor or other machine consisting of a winch and side boom for placing lengths of pipe in a trench.

pipeline heater A heater, usually a wrapping, with an electric element used to prevent the liquid in the pipe from freezing or to maintain the viscosity of the liquid.

pipeline refrigeration Refrigeration provided to a group of buildings by piping refrigerant from a central plant.

pipe pile A steel cylinder, usually 10″–24″ in diameter, generally driven with open ends to form a bearing pile. This pile may consist of several sections from 5′ to 40′ long joined by special fittings, such as cast-steel sleeves. A pipe pile is sometimes used with its lower end closed by a conical steel shoe.

pipe plug A pipe fitting with outside threads and a projecting head used to close the opening in another fitting.

pipe reamer A plumber's hand tool with a spinning cone that is used inside a pipe to remove burrs.

pipe reducer A pipe fitting used to connect two lengths of pipe of different diameters.

pipe ring A circular-shaped metal part used to support a pipe from a suspended rod.

pipe run Any path taken by pipe in a distribution or collection system.

pipe saddle An assembly to support a pipe from the underside.

pipe sleeve A cylindrical insert cast in a concrete wall or floor for later passage of a pipe.

pipe stock An assembly to hold a pipe die.

pipe stop A stopcock in a pipe.

pipe strap A thin metal strip used as a pipe hanger.

pipe tee A T-shaped fitting to connect three lengths of pipe in the same plane with one length at right angles to the other two.

pipe thread A V-cut screw thread cut on the inside or outside of a pipe or fitting. The diameter of the thread tapers.

pipe tongs A hand tool used to screw or unscrew lengths of pipe and/or fittings.

pipe vise A vise for holding pipe or tubing for cutting or threading. The pipe is held in curved, V-shaped, serrated jaws or, for larger pipes, by chains.

pipe wrench

pitched roof

pipe wrench (alligator wrench)
A heavy hand tool with adjustable serrated jaws for gripping, screwing, or unscrewing metal pipe.

piping (1) An assembly of lengths of pipe and fittings, i.e., a run of pipe. (2) Movement of soil particles by percolating water that produces erosion channels.

piping loss The heat lost from piping between the heat source and the radiators.

piston A solid cylinder that fits inside a larger cylinder and moves as a result of the power it receives from a connecting rod. Found in reciprocating engines, pumps, and compressors.

pit (1) An excavation, quarry, or mine made or worked by the open cut method. A pit seldom goes below the ground water level. (2) The area between the stage and the first row of seats in a theater. (3) A small hole or cavity on a surface.

pit boards Horizontal boards used as sheeting to retain the soil around a pit.

pitch (1) An accumulation of resin in the wood cells in a more or less irregular patch. Pitch is classified for grading purposes as light, medium, heavy, or massed. (2) The angle or inclination of a roof, which varies according to climate, architectural design, and roofing materials used, and is expressed as a ratio of rise per run. (3) The set, or projection, of teeth on alternate sides of a saw to provide clearance for its body. (4) The ratio of rise to run of stairs. (5) The reciprocal of the number of threads per inch.

pitch board A thin piece of board used as a guide in stair construction. The board is cut in the shape of a right triangle to the slope of the nosings of the treads. Usually, the two sides equal the tread length and rise of the stair.

pitch dimension The distance between the bases of the top and the bottom risers in a flight of stairs, measured parallel to the slope.

pitched roof A roof having one or more surfaces with a slope greater than 10° from the horizontal.

pitched stone A rough-faced stone having each edge of the exposed face pitched at a slight bevel from the plane of the face.

pitched truss A truss that ties sloping top chords to the bottom chord with angled struts.

pitching chisel A mason's chisel with a wide, thick edge used for rough dressing stone.

pitch pine *Pinus rigida.* This pine is found in a wide area, from Maine to northern Georgia. Lumber from it is graded under rules established by the Northeastern Lumber Manufacturers Association.

pitch pocket An opening between growth rings which usually contains or has contained resin, or bark, or both. A pitch pocket is classified for grading purposes as very small, small, medium, large, closed, open, or through.

pitch seam Shake or check filled with pitch.

pitch select D select or better, except that the grade admits any amount of medium to heavy pitch. Massed pitch is admissible but limited to half the area of an otherwise high line piece. Dimensions are 4″ and wider, 6′ and longer in multiples of one foot.

pitch streak A well-defined accumulation of pitch in a more or less regular streak. A pitch streak is

pivot hinge

classified for grading purposes as small, medium, or large.

pitch symbol A triangular symbol used on elevation drawings to indicate the incline of a roof.

pith The small, soft core in the center of a log.

pith fleck A narrow streak resembling pith on the surface of a piece of lumber, usually brownish and up to several inches in length, resulting from the burrowing of larvae in the growing tissue of the tree.

pith knot A minor defect in lumber, a pith knot is a knot whose only blemish is a small pith hole in the center.

pitot tube A device, used with a manometer or other pressure-reading device, to measure the velocity head of a flowing fluid.

pit prop A timber used as a support in an excavation or mine.

pit-run gravel Ungraded gravel used as taken from a pit.

pitting Development of relatively small cavities in a surface due to phenomena such as corrosion, cavitation, or, in concrete, localized disintegration. *See also* **popout**.

pivot A short shaft or pin about which a part rotates or swings.

pivoted door A door that swings on pivots, rather than a door hung on hinges.

pivoted window A window with a sash that rotates about fixed horizontal or vertical pivots.

pivot hinge A hinge with a short fixed shaft or pin upon which a part rotates or swings. Commonly used for cabinet doors.

placeability *See* **workability**.

placement (1) The process of placing and consolidating concrete. (2) A quantity of concrete placed and finished during a continuous operation. Also, inappropriately referred to as *pouring*.

placing The deposition, distribution, and consolidation of freshly mixed concrete in the place where it is to harden. Also, inappropriately referred to as *pouring*.

placing drawings Detailed drawings used to position steel reinforcement in concrete construction.

plain ashlar A rectangular block of stone, the face of which has been smoothed with a tool.

plain bar A reinforcing bar without surface deformations, or one having deformations that do not conform to the applicable requirements.

plain concrete (1) Concrete without reinforcement. (2) Reinforced concrete that does not conform to the definition of reinforced concrete. (3) Used loosely to designate concrete containing no admixture and prepared without special treatment.

plain end (P.E.) Used to describe the ends of pipe which are shipped from the mill with unfinished ends. These ends may eventually be threaded, beveled, or grooved in the field.

plain masonry Masonry with no reinforcement or with reinforcement only for shrinkage and temperature changes.

plain rail A meeting rail in a double-hung window that is the same thickness as the other members of the frame.

plain-sawn Wood sawn from logs so that the annual rings intersect the wide faces at an angle less than 45°.

plaintiff The party that initiates a claim or action against another party. *See also* **defendant**.

planking

plain tile A flat, rectangular tile of concrete or burnt clay.

plan A two-dimensional overview of the design, location, and dimensions of a project (or a portion of a project). *See also* **drawings**.

planar frame A structural frame with all members in the same plane.

plancier The wood or plaster soffit or underside of an overhanging eave.

plan deposit *See* **deposit for bidding documents**.

plane (1) A flat surface. (2) A tool used to smooth or shape wood. (3) To run sawn wood through a planer to smooth its surface.

planed all round A piece that has been surfaced on all four sides.

planed lumber Lumber which has been run through a planer to finish one or several sides.

plane iron The smoothing metal blade in plane.

plane of weakness The plane along which a body under stress will tend to fracture. The plane of weakness may exist by design, by accident, or because of the nature of the structure and its loading.

planer A machine used to surface rough lumber.

planer heads Sets of cutting knives mounted on cylindrical heads which revolve at high speed to dress lumber fed through them. Top and bottom heads surface or pattern the two faces, while side heads dress or pattern the two edges or sides.

planer knife One of the sharp blades used in a planer head.

plane surveying Surveying which neglects the curvature of the earth.

plane table A device, consisting of a drawing board on a tripod and a telescope attached to a ruler, for plotting lines of a survey directly from observations.

planimeter A mechanical device that measures plane areas on a map or drawing.

planing The process of smoothing a surface by shaving off small chips.

planing machine (1) Several types of a fixed machine for planing wood or steel. (2) A portable machine for planing a wood floor in place.

plank A piece of lumber two or more inches thick and six or more inches wide, designed to be laid flat as part of a load-bearing surface, such as a bridge deck.

plank-and-beam construction *See* **post-and-lintel construction**.

planking Material used for flooring, decking, or scaffolding.

planking and strutting The temporary timbers supporting the soil at the side of an excavation.

plank-on-edge floor A subfloor formed by joists in contact with each other to form a continuous surface.

plank-type grating An aluminum extrusion consisting of a tread plate reinforced by integral ribs. The tread plate is perforated between the ribs.

planning The process of developing a scheme of a building or group of buildings by studying the layout of spaces within each building, and of building and other installations in an open space.

planning grid A graph-like paper with the lines at right angles or other selected angles to each other, used by architects or engineers in modular planning.

plan room A service provided by construction industry organizations

plaster

plaster base
(gypsum lath)

or service companies, sometimes available to interested constructors, material men, vendors, and manufacturers. Plan rooms provide access to contract documents for projects currently in the process of receiving competitive or negotiated bids.

planted molding A molding which is nailed, tongued-in, or otherwise fastened to a base, as opposed to one cut into the base material.

planted stop A molding or strip nailed to a frame and used as a door or casement stop.

planting In masonry, laying the first courses of a foundation on a prepared bed.

plant mix (1) A mixture of aggregate and asphalt cement or liquid asphalt, prepared in a central or traveling mechanical mixer. (2) Any mixture produced at a mixing plant.

plan view A drawing that depicts an object, assembly, or floor plan from above.

plaster (1) A cementitious material or combination of cementitious material and aggregate that, when mixed with a suitable amount of water, forms a plastic mass or paste. When applied to a surface, the paste adheres to it and subsequently hardens, preserving in a rigid state the form or texture imposed during the period of elasticity. (2) The placed and hardened mixture created as in definition 1 above. *See also* **stucco.**

plaster aggregate Graded mineral particles and mineral, vegetable, or animal fibers to be used with gypsum or cement-base plasters to produce a plaster mix.

plaster base Any working ground to receive plaster, including wood,

metal, or gypsum lath, insulating board, or masonry.

plaster-base finish tile Ceramic tile with exposed surface, scored or roughened for an application of a plaster system.

plaster bead An edging, usually metal, to strengthen applied plaster at corners.

plasterboard (sheetrock, drywall) Any prefabricated board of plaster with paper facings. Plasterboard may be painted or used as a base for a finish coat of applied plaster.

plasterboard nail A nail for fastening plasterboard to a supporting system. The nails are galvanized with a flat head and a deformed shank.

plaster bond The mechanical or chemical adhesion of plaster to a surface.

plaster ceiling panel A raised or sunken section of a plaster ceiling, forming a panel.

plaster cornice A molding of plaster at the intersection of a wall and a ceiling.

plaster cove A concave molding of plaster at the intersection of a wall and a ceiling.

plasterer's putty A hydrated lime with just enough water added to make a thick paste for use as a hole or crack filler.

plaster ground A wood strip or metal bead used as a guide for application of a desired thickness of plaster or for attaching trim.

plaster guard A shield attached behind the hinge and strike reinforcement on a hollow metal door frame to prevent mortar or plaster from entering mounting holes.

plaster lath A supporting structure for plaster, such as a wood lath, metal lath, or lath board.

plaster mold A mold or form made from gypsum plaster, usually to permit concrete to be formed or cast in intricate shapes. *See also* **mold** *and* **form**.

plaster of paris Gypsum, from which three-quarters of the chemically bound water has been driven off by heating. When wetted, it recombines with water and hardens quickly. *See also* **hemihydrate**.

plaster ring A metal collar attached to a base and used as a guide for thickness of applied plaster and a fastener for trim.

plaster set The initial stiffening of a plaster mix that may be reworked without the addition of water.

plaster wainscot cap A horizontal wood strip which covers the joint between the wainscoting and the plaster surface.

plastic Possessing plasticity, or possessing adequate plasticity. *See also* **plasticity**.

plastic bond fire clay (1) A fire clay of sufficient natural plasticity to bond nonplastic material. (2) A fire clay used as a plasticizing agent in mortar.

plastic cement A synthetic cement used in the application of flashing.

plastic centroid Centroid of the resistance to load computed for the assumptions that the concrete is stressed uniformly to 85% its design strength and the steel is stressed uniformly to its specified yield point.

plastic consistency (1) Condition of freshly mixed cement paste, mortar, or concrete that allows that deformation to be sustained continuously in any direction without rupture. (2) In common usage, concrete with slump of 3″ to 4″ (80 to 100 mm).

plastic cracking Cracking that occurs in the surface of fresh concrete soon after it is placed and while it is still plastic.

plastic deformation Deformation that does not disappear when the force causing the deformation is removed.

plastic design *See* **ultimate-strength design**.

plastic flow *See* **creep**.

plastic glue Resin bonding materials used in joining wood pieces. These materials include: (1) Thermosetting resins such as phenol-formaldehyde, urea-formaldehyde, and melamine resin. (2) Thermoplastics such as acryl-polymers and vinyl-polymers. (3) Casein plastics. (4) Natural resin glues.

plastic-hinge Region where ultimate moment capacity in a member may be developed and maintained with corresponding significant inelastic rotation as main tensile steel elongates beyond yield strain.

plasticity (1) The capability of being molded, or being made to assume a desired form. (2) A property of wood that allows it to retain its form when bent. (3) A complex property of a material involving a combination of qualities of mobility and magnitude of yield value. (4) That property of freshly mixed cement paste, concrete, or mortar, which determines its resistance to deformation and ease of molding.

plasticity index (1) The range in water content through which a solid remains plastic. (2) Numerical adherence between the liquid limit and the plastic limit. *See also* **Atterberg limits**.

plasticizer (1) A material that increases plasticity of a cement paste, mortar, or concrete mixture. (2) Various substances added to organic

plastic skylight

plate girder

platform

compounds to create a more flexible finished product. These additives are frequently used in roofing materials and concrete.

plasticizing (1) Producing plasticity or becoming plastic. (2) Softening wood by hot water, steam or chemicals to increase its moldability.

plastic laminate A thin board used as a finished surfacing, made from layers of resin-impregnated paper fused together under heat and pressure.

plastic limit The water content at which a soil will just begin to crumble when rolled into a thread approximately 1/8″ (3 mm) in diameter. *See also* **Atterberg limits**.

plastic loss *See* **creep**.

plastic lumber An alternative building material that is usually manufactured with recycled plastics. In contrast to wood, it will not splinter, rot, or warp. Used in decking and pilings, among other applications.

plastic mortar A mortar of plastic consistency.

plastic shrinkage cracks *See* **plastic cracking**.

plastic skylight A molded unit of transparent or translucent plastic that is set in a frame for use as a skylight.

plastic soil Any soil that can be molded or deformed by moderate pressure without crumbling.

plastic wood A quick-drying putty of nitrocellulose, wood flour, resins, and solvents used as a filler for holes and cracks.

plate (1) In formwork for concrete, a flat, horizontal member at the top and/or bottom of studs or posts. If on the ground, a plate is called a *mudsill*. (2) In structural design, a member, the depth of which is substantially smaller than its length and width. (3) A flat rolled iron or steel product. *See also* **flat plate, load-transfer assembly**.

plate anchor An anchor bolt used to fasten a plate or sill to a foundation.

plate beam *See* **plate girder**.

plate bolt *See* **plate anchor**.

plate girder A girder fabricated from plates, angles, or other structural shapes, welded or riveted together.

plate glass High-quality glass of the same composition as window glass but thicker, up to 1-1/4″, with ground and polished faces, usually used for large areas in a single sheet.

platen A flat plate in a hot press, usually one of many in a multi-opening press used in the manufacture of panel products.

plate rail Decorative molding on the upper part of a wall and grooved to hold chinaware plates or decorations.

plate stock Component that makes up the bottom and top of a typical wood framed wall. Usually the same dimension as the wall framing stock but may be a lesser grade.

plate-type tread A stair tread fabricated from metal plate and/or floor plate. The riser may be integral.

plate vibrator A self-propelled, mechanical vibrator used to compact fill.

platform (1) A floor or surface raised above the adjacent level. (2) A landing in a stairway. (3) A working space for persons, elevated above the surrounding floor or ground level such as a balcony or platform for the operation of machinery or equipment.

plenum

plot

platform frame See **platform framing**.

platform framing A framing system in which the vertical members are only a single story high, with each finished floor acting as a platform upon which the succeeding floor is constructed. Platform framing is the common method of house construction in North America.

platform roof (1) A truncated roof. (2) A roof, the top of which is a horizontal plane.

plenishing nail A large nail used to fasten planks to joists.

plenum (1) A closed chamber used to distribute or collect warmed or cooled air in a forced air heating/cooling system. (2) The space between the suspended ceiling and the floor above.

plenum barrier A barrier, erected in a plenum ceiling, used to reduce sound transmission between rooms or over a large area.

plenum chamber See **plenum**.

plenum fans (plug fans) Single-inlet, single-width centrifugal fans without the scroll, permitting 360° air delivery from the fan wheel.

plen-wood system A system for distributing air for heating and cooling using the entire underfloor area of a building as a plenum chamber. The system eliminates the need for ductwork in some structures. Proponents of the system cite savings in both construction costs and in the costs of heating and cooling.

Plexiglass® The brand name, often used generically, for a clear and rigid plastic sheet product.

pliers A pincer-like hand tool with opposing jaws for gripping, cutting and bending.

plinth (1) A block or slab supporting a column or pedestal. (2) The base course of an external masonry wall when of different shape from the masonry in the wall proper. (3) The base of a monument or statue often with inscription.

plinth course (1) The masonry course that forms the plinth of a stone wall. (2) The final course of a brick plinth in a brick wall.

plot (1) A measured and defined area of land. (2) A ground plan of a building and adjacent land.

plough See **plow (2)**.

plow (1) In molding, a rectangular slot of three surfaces cut with the grain of the wood. (2) In carpentry, a tool that cuts grooves. (3) A drywall tool with a bent trowel used to finish corners.

plow and tongue joint See **tongue-and-groove joint**.

plucked finish A rough-textured stone surface, made by overcutting with a planer so that stone is removed by spalling rather than shaving.

plug (1) A wood peg driven into a wall for support of a fastener. (2) A stopper for a drain opening. (3) A male-threaded fitting used to seal the end of a pipe or fitting. (4) A fixture for connection of electric wires to an outlet socket. (5) A fibrous or resinous material used to fill a hole and close a surface. (6) Material that stops or seals the discharge line of a channel or pipe.

plug and feathers A heavy device consisting of a wedge and two tapered plates of metal used to split boulders.

plug center bit A plug-shaped bit used to enlarge a hole or counterbore around the hole.

plug cock

plumb bob

plumbing fixtures

plug cock A valve where full flow is through a hole in a tapered plug. Rotating the plug 90° completely stops the flow.

plug cutter A small bit used to cut a hole to receive a plug. A plug cutter is used to conceal recessed screwheads in hardwood floors.

plug fuse A fuse contained in an insulated container with a metal screwbase. There is a small window on the face of the container for checking the condition of the fuse element.

plugged lumber Lumber in which a defect has been filled by plastic material to provide a smooth paint surface.

plugging Drilling a hole in a masonry surface for a wood plug. The plug will later be used to support a fastener.

plugging chisel A steel rod, with a star-shaped point, used for drilling holes in masonry by striking with a hammer.

plug-in A temporary figure in an estimate price-out sheet to be used until a more dependable one is obtained.

plug tap See **plug cock**.

plug tenon A short tenon which projects from the material into which it is fitted, the free end fitting into a mortise. A plug tenon is used to provide lateral stability for a wood column.

plug valve See **plug cock**.

plug weld A weld made through a circular hole in one of the members to be connected.

plum (plum stone) A large randomly shaped stone dropped into freshly placed mass concrete to economize on the volume of concrete used. See also **cyclopean concrete**.

plumb Vertical, or to make vertical.

plumb bob A cone-shaped metal weight, hung from a string, used to establish a vertical line or as a sighting reference to a surveyor's transit.

plumb bond Any bond in masonry in which the vertical joints are in line.

plumb bond pole A pole used to insure that vertical masonry joints are in line.

plumb cut A vertical cut, as in the cuts in a rafter at the top ridge where it meets the ridge plate.

plumber's dope See **dope**.

plumber's friend See **plunger**.

plumber's furnace A portable, gas-fired furnace for melting solder, heating lead, or soldering iron.

plumber's rasp A coarse rasp used to file lead.

plumber's round iron A specially shaped soldering iron used to solder seams in tanks.

plumber's soil A mixture of lampblack and glue used to prevent solder from adhering where not wanted.

plumber's solder An alloy of lead and tin, with a melting point below that of lead, used for joining lead pipes.

plumbing (1) The work or practice of installing in buildings the pipes, fixtures and other apparatus required to bring in the water supplies and to remove water-borne wastes. (2) The process of setting a structure or object truly vertical.

plumbing fixture A receptacle in a plumbing system, other than a trap, in which water or wastes are collected or retained for use and ultimately discharged to drainage.

plumbing system Arrangements of pipes, fixtures, fittings, valves, and traps, in a building which supply water and remove liquid-borne wastes, including storm water.

plumb joint A sheet metal joint made by lapping the edges and soldering them together flat.

plumb level A level that is set in a horizontal position by placing it at a right angle to a plumb line.

plumb line The cord or line that supports a plumb bob.

plumb rule A board or metal rule, fitted with one or more leveling bubbles, used to establish horizontal and vertical lines.

plume (1) The effluent mixture of heated air and water vapor discharged from a cooling tower. (2) An identifiable and definable stream of pollutants in an otherwise clean volume of air or water.

plummet *See* **plumb bob**.

plunger (plumber's friend) A tool, consisting of a large rubber suction cup on a wood handle, for clearing plumbing traps of minor obstructions.

ply (1) A single layer or sheet of veneer. (2) One complete layer of veneer in a sheet of plywood.

Plyform The trademark owned by the American Plywood Association for concrete form panels produced by its association members.

plymetal Plywood covered on one or both sides with sheet metal.

plywood A flat panel made up of a number of thin sheets (veneers), of wood. The grain direction of each ply, or layer, is at right angles to the one adjacent to it. The veneer sheets are united under pressure by a bonding agent. Interior-grade plywood is suitable for indoor use or for outside use when subject only to occasional, temporary moisture, while exterior-grade plywood uses a weather-resistant adhesive.

plywood grade The widely-recognized grading system administered by the American Plywood Association that rates plywood on the quality of its veneer (from A to D) and on its exposure durability.

plywood, marine *See* **marine plywood**.

plywood squares Plywood fabricated for use as floor tile.

pneumatically applied mortar *See* **shotcrete**.

pneumatic caisson Method of caisson construction requiring that air pressure be controlled during the construction process.

pneumatic control system A system in which control is effected by pressurized air.

pneumatic drill A reciprocating rock or masonry drill actuated by compressed air.

pneumatic feed Shotcrete delivery equipment in which material is conveyed by a pressurized air stream.

pneumatic hammer An air-powered reciprocating drill fitted with a chisel or hammer.

pneumatic placement *See* **pneumatic feed**.

pneumatic structure A fabric envelope supported by an internal air pressure slightly above atmospheric pressure. The pressure is provided by a series of fans.

pneumatic water supply A water supply system for a building in which water is distributed from a tank containing water and compressed air.

point-bearing pile

point of support

pocket (1) A recess in a masonry wall to receive an end of a beam. (2) A recess in a wall to receive part or all of an architectural item, such as a curtain or folding door. (3) The slot on the pulley stile of a double-hung window through which the sash weight is placed in the sash weight channel.

pocket chisel A chisel with a wide blade that is sharpened on both sides.

pocket door A door that opens by sliding into and "hiding" in a wall recess.

pocket piece A small piece of wood that closes the *pocket* in the pulley stile of a double-hung window.

pocket rot A type of decay found in cedar.

pockmarking Undesirable depressions formed in a painted surface or varnish film.

podium (1) A stand for a speaker. (2) An elevated platform for a conductor. (3) The masonry platform on which a classical temple was built.

point (1) A fee equal to 1% of the principal amount of a loan. Charged by the lender when the loan is made. (2) A tooth for a saw. (3) A mason's tool. (4) A thin, triangular or diamond-shaped piece of metal used in glazing to hold glass in a wooden frame. (5) A piece of equipment that is monitored or controlled by a building automation system.

point-bearing pile A pile that transfers its load to the supporting stratum by point bearing as opposed to a friction pile.

point count Method for determination of the volumetric composition of a solid by observation of the frequency with which areas of each component coincide with a regular system of points in one or more planes intersecting a sample of the solid.

point count (modified) The point count method supplemented by a determination of the frequency with which areas of each component of a solid are intersected by regularly spaced lines in one or more planes intersecting a sample of the solid.

pointed ashlar Rectangular stonework with face markings made by a pointed tool.

pointed work The rough finish on the face of a stone that is made by a pointed tool.

pointing (1) The finishing of joints in a masonry wall. (2) The material with which joints in masonry are finished.

pointing trowel A diamond-shaped trowel used in pointing or repointing masonry joints.

point load A term used in structural analysis to define a concentrated load on a structural member.

point of contraflexure *See* **point of inflection.**

point of inflection (point of contraflexure) (1) The point on the length of a structural member subjected to flexure where the curvature changes from concave to convex or conversely, and at which the bending moment is zero. (2) Location of an abrupt bend in a plotted locus of points in a graph.

point of service (point of delivery) The location where a utility company's wires or pipes join a customer's electrical or piping system.

point of support A point on a member where part of its load is transferred to a support.

polarized receptacle

point source A light source, the dimensions of which are insignificant at viewing distance. A fluorescent lamp is a point source at a large distance.

Poisson's ratio The ratio of transverse (lateral) strain to the corresponding axial (longitudinal) strain resulting from uniformly distributed axial stress below the proportional limit of the material. The ratio will average about 0.2 for concrete and 0.25 for most metals.

polarity The direction of electric current flow in a DC circuit.

polarized receptacle An electric receptacle with contacts arranged so a mating plug must be inserted in only one orientation.

polarizing microscope A microscope equipped with elements permitting observations and determinations to be made using polarized light. *See also* **Nicol prism**.

pole (1) A long, usually round piece of wood, often a small diameter log with the bark removed, used to carry utility wires or for other purposes. A pole is often treated with preservative. (2) Either of two oppositely charged terminals as in an electric cell or battery. (3) Either extremity of an axis of a sphere.

pole-frame construction A construction system using vertical poles or timbers.

pole plate A horizontal board or timber that rests on the tie beams of a roof and supports the lower ends of the common rafters at the wall, and also raises the rafters above the top plate of the wall.

pole sander A sanding block on the end of a long pole that makes the sanding of drywall ceiling joints easier.

pole shore *See* **post shore**.

pole trailer A specially constructed log trailer designed to carry extremely long poles, usually employing a disconnected rear section with independent steering, much like a long-ladder fire truck.

polish (1) To give a sheen or gloss to a finish coat of plaster. (2) The operation in which fine abrasives are used to hone a finished surface to a desired smoothness.

polished finish A stonework finish so smooth that it forms a reflective surface, usually produced by mechanical buffing and chemical treatment of a surface with no voids.

polish grind (final grind) The final operation in which fine abrasives are used to hone a surface to its desired smoothness and appearance.

polishing varnish A hard varnish that can be polished by rubbing with abrasive and mineral oil without dissolving the resin.

poll The broad end or striking face of a hammer.

polycarbonate A transparent thermoplastic with a high impact strength and a high modulus of elasticity. Its excellent insulating qualities make it ideal for many electrical applications.

polychlorinated biphenyls (PCBs) A group of hydrocarbon-containing chlorine compounds that, before being banned as pollutants, were used in hundreds of industrial and commercial applications, including electrical and hydraulic equipment, sealants, rubber, paints, and plastics. PCBs are not readily biodegradable, and the United States stopped producing them in 1977.

polychloroprene (neoprene) An oil-resistant, synthetic rubber. In roofing, used for membranes and

polyethylene

flashing. The generic name for polychloroprene is neoprene.

polychromatic finish (1) A finish obtained by blending a number of colors. (2) A finish obtained by using a paint containing metallic flakes on transparent pigments. The resulting effect is the appearance of a variety of colors when viewed from different angles.

polyester resin A synthetic resin that polymerizes during curing and has excellent adhesive properties, high strength, and good chemical resistance.

polyethylene A thermoplastic high-molecular-weight organic compound. In sheet form, polyethylene is used as a protective cover for concrete surfaces during the curing period, a temporary enclosure for construction operations, and as a vapor barrier. It is also commonly used for culvert pipes and in other piping systems.

polyethylene vapor barrier A plastic film attached to insulation to prevent the passage of vapor or moisture into areas where it could collect and do damage.

polygonal masonry Masonry constructed of stones with multi-sided faces.

polyisobutylene (PIB) A synthetic rubber derived from the polymerization of isobutylene. In roofing, used for membranes and flashing.

polyisocyanurate (polyiso) A polymer with a high R-value commonly used as insulation in the form of rigid, glass fiber-reinforced foam boards, usually faced with a foil paper. Increasingly, polyiso board products are also being used for sheathing. Often specified for

applications where increased fire resistance is desired.

polymer (1) The product of polymerization. Some polymers are elastomers, while others are plastics. (2) A rubber or resin consisting of large molecules formed by polymerization.

polymer-cement concrete A mixture of water, hydraulic cement, aggregate, and a monomer or polymer. The cement is polymerized in place when a monomer is used.

polymer concrete (1) Concrete in which an organic polymer serves as the binder. Also known as *resin concrete*. *See also* **concrete**. (2) Sometimes erroneously employed to designate hydraulic cement mortars or concretes in which part or all of the mixing water is replaced by an aqueous dispersion of a thermoplastic copolymer.

polymeric liner A synthetic liner used to contain liquids inside a surface berm or an excavated area.

polymerization The reaction in which two or more molecules of the same substance combine to form a compound containing the same elements, and in the same proportions, but of high molecular weight. The original substance can be generated from the compound, in some cases only with extreme difficulty.

polymethyl-methacrylate (PMMA) A transparent thermoplastic that offers good weather resistance and a high strength-to-weight ratio.

polypropylene A tough plastic with good resistance to heat and chemicals. Polypropylene is a polymer of propylene, and is found in everything from packaging to molded automobile parts.

polystyrene foam A low cost, foamed plastic weighing about 1 lb. per cu. ft., with good insulating properties and resistance to grease.

polystyrene resin Synthetic resins, varying in color from water-white to yellow, formed by the polymerization of styrene on heating, with or without catalysts. These resins may be used in paints for concrete, for making sculptured molds, or as insulation.

polysulfide coating A protective coating system prepared by polymerizing a chlorinated alkyl polyether with an inorganic polysulfide. This coating exhibits outstanding resistance to ozone, sunlight, oxidation, and weathering.

polytetrafluoroethylene (PTFE) A fluorocarbon-based polymer with high chemical and weather resistance, low friction, and electrical and thermal insulation. The most common brand name is Teflon®. PTFE's many construction applications include usage in hydraulic machinery and in plumber's joint tape.

polyurethane Reaction product of an isocyanate with any of a wide variety of other compounds containing an active hydrogen group. Polyurethane is used to formulate tough, abrasion-resistant coatings, and is also used for foam insualtion products.

polyurethane finish A synthetic varnish that is exceptionally hard, and wear-resistant.

polyurethane insulation (PUR insulation) Any of a number of insulation products made of polyurethane. Forms include rigid boards, spray foams, and pourable mixes.

polyvinyl acetate (PVA) Colorless, permanently thermoplastic resin, usually supplied as an emulsion or water-dispersible powder, which may be used in paints for concrete. Polyvinyl acetate is characterized by flexibility, stability towards light, transparency to ultraviolet rays, high electric strength, toughness, and hardness. The higher the degree of polymerization, the higher the softening temperature.

polyvinyl chloride (PVC) A thermoplastic resin derived from the polymerization of vinyl chloride. Plasticizers have been added to give it flexibility. Widely used in piping products, it is also used for siding, floor covering, window housing, and fencing. In roofing, it is used for membranes and flashing. Also used in the manufacture of nonmetallic waterstops for concrete.

pommel (1) A knob at the top of a conical or dome-like roof. (2) A rounded metal block on an end of a handle, raised and dropped by hand to compact soil.

ponded roof A flat roof designed to hold a limited amount of water as a cooling measure for a building system.

ponderosa pine (western white pine, western yellow pine) *Pinus ponderosa.* A pine species found in a wide range that reaches from British Columbia to Mexico, and from the Pacific coast to the Dakotas. The wood is widely used in general construction, most often as boards, but is more valued for its uses in millwork and in cuttings for remanufacture.

ponding (1) The process of flooding the surface of a concrete slab by using temporary dams around the perimeter in order to satisfactorily

porch

portico

cure the concrete. (2) The accumulation of water at low points in a roof. The low points may be produced or increased by structural deflection.

pond pine *Pinus serotina.* A minor species of the southern yellow pine group found along the Atlantic coast from southeast Virginia to the Florida panhandle. Lumber from this species carries a *mixed pine species* stamp.

poor pine Another name for spruce pine.

pop (blow, blister) A delaminated area in a plywood panel.

popcorn concrete No-fines concrete containing insufficient cement paste to fill voids among the coarse aggregate so that the particles are bound only at points of contact. *See also* **no-fines concrete.**

poplar A member of the willow family. Its wood is used in furniture core stock, crates, and plywood. In North America: *Populus tretnula,* aspen, *P. balsamifera,* cottonwood, *P. tacamahaca,* and *balsam poplar.*

popout The breaking away of small portions of a concrete surface due to internal pressure, leaving a shallow, typically conical, depression.

popping Shallow depressions ranging in size from pinheads to 1/4″ in diameter, immediately below the surface of a lime-putty finish coat. Popping is caused by expansion of coarse particles of unhydrated lime or of foreign substances.

pop valve A safety valve made to open immediately when the fluid pressure is greater than the design force of a spring.

porcelain A hard glazed or unglazed ceramic used for electrical, chemical, mechanical, or thermal components.

porcelain enamel A silicate glass bonded to metal by fusion at a temperature above 800°F (427 °C). Porcelain enamel is not a true porcelain.

porcelain tile A dense, usually impervious, fine-grained, smooth-surfaced, ceramic mosaic tile or paver.

porcelain tube A ceramic tube, with a slight shoulder at one end, used to carry an exposed, insulated wire where it passes through a wood joist, stud, etc.

porch A structure attached to a building, usually roofed and open-sided, and often at the entrance. Sometimes screened or glass-enclosed.

porch lattice An open lattice that closes the open side(s) of a porch below floor level.

porcupine boiler A vertical, cylindrical boiler with many projecting, closed stubs to provide an additional thermal surface.

pore water The free water present in soil.

pore water pressure The pressure of the water in a saturated soil.

porosity The ratio, usually expressed as a percentage, of the volume of voids in a material to the total volume of the material, including the voids.

porous fill *See* **pervious soil.**

porous woods Hardwoods that have pores or vessels that can be seen with the naked eye.

port In electronics, a point of entry into a network or switch.

portico (1) A covered walk consisting of a roof supported on columns. (2) A colonnaded (continuous row of columns) porch.

Portland blast-furnace slag cement *See* **cement, Portland blast-furnace slag.**

Portland cement *See* **cement, Portland.**

Portland cement concrete *See* **concrete.**

portlandite A mineral, calcium hydroxide, that occurs naturally in Ireland. Portlandite is a common product of hydration of Portland cement.

Portland-pozzolan cement *See* **cement, Portland-pozzolan.**

Portland stone A limestone, from the island of Portland off the coast of England, used as a building stone.

port of entry (POE) A port that provides all customhouse services for imported products.

Port Orford cedar *Chamaicyparis lawsoniana.* A cedar common to the coastal belt of western Oregon and extreme northern California, having limited markets, but its light-colored wood is greatly desired in Japan for exposed use in houses.

position (1) A trader's open contracts in the futures market. (2) A reference to a shipping period, as in "Feb/March position."

positioned weld A weld on a joint that has been oriented to facilitate the welding.

position indicator A device that shows the position of an elevator in its hoistway. Also called a *hall position indicator* if at a landing, or a *cab position indicator* if in the cab.

position trading An approach to futures trading in which the trader either buys or sells contracts and holds them for an extended period, as distinguished from a day trader, who will normally initiate and offset his position in a single trading day.

positive cutoff A below-ground wall that extends to an impervious lower stratum to block subsurface seepage.

positive displacement Wet-mix shotcrete delivery equipment in which the material is pushed through the material hose in a solid mass by a piston or auger.

positive moment A condition of flexure in which, for a horizontal simply supported member, the deflected shape is normally considered to be concave downward and the top fibers subjected to compression stresses. For other members and other conditions, consider positive and negative as relative terms. *See also* **negative moment**. (Note: For structural design and analysis, moments may be designated as positive or negative with satisfactory results as long as the sign convention adopted is used consistently.)

positive pressure Force in a vent or piping system that is greater than atmospheric pressure.

positive reinforcement Reinforcement for positive moment.

possum-trot plan Plan of a house with two areas separated by a breezeway, and all sections having a common roof.

post (1) A member used in a vertical position to support a beam or other structural member in a building, or as part of a fence. In lumber, 4x4s are often referred to as posts. Most grading rules define a post as having dimensions of $5'' \times 5''$ or more in width, with the width not more than $2''$ greater than the thickness. (2) Vertical formwork member used as a brace. Also called a *shore, prop,* and *jack*. (3) A secondary column located at the end of a building to support its girts.

post and lintel construction

post shore, adjustable timber

post and beam construction *See* **post and lintel construction.**

post and beam framing A structural framing system in which beams rest on posts rather than bearing walls.

post and lintel construction Construction that uses posts or columns and a horizontal beam to span an opening, as opposed to construction using arches or vaults.

post and pane A type of construction in which timber framings are filled in with brick or plaster panels, leaving the timbers exposed.

postbuckling strength The load that can be carried by a structural member after it has been subjected to buckling.

post-completion services *See* **post-construction services.**

post-construction services (1) Services rendered after the release of the final invoice for payment or over 60 days from the date of substantial completion of the project. (2) Any services necessary to allow the owner to use and/or occupy the facility.

postern (1) Any small, often inconspicuous, door. (2) A smaller door, for pedestrian passage, located next to a large door that is used by vehicles.

post pole *See* **post shore.**

post shore, adjustable timber single-post Individual timber used with a fabricated clamp to obtain adjustment and not normally manufactured as a complete unit.

post shore, fabricated single-post Type 1: Single all-metal post, with a fine-adjustment screw or device in combination with pin-and-hole adjustment or clamp. Type 2: Single or double wooden post members adjustable by a metal clamp or screw

and usually manufactured as a complete unit.

post shore, timber single-post shore Timber used as a structural member for shoring support.

posttensioned concrete Concrete that has the reinforcing tendons tensioned after the concrete has set.

posttensioning A method of prestressing reinforced concrete in which tendons are tensioned after the concrete has hardened.

potable water Water that satisfies the standards of the responsible health authorities as drinking water.

potato masher A simple hand tool used to mix joint compound. The tool has a wire mixer similar to that of the kitchen implement of the same name.

potentially responsible party (PRP) A party who may have financial liability for the cleanup of a hazardous waste site.

potentiometer An instrument for controlling electrical potential. Measures an unknown voltage by comparing it to a standard voltage.

pot floor A floor surface of structural clay tiles.

pot life Time interval, after preparation, during which a liquid or plastic mixture is usable.

pound-calorie The amount of heat required to raise one pound of water 1 °C.

pour coat (top mop) The top coating of asphalt on a built-up roof, sometimes including embedded gravel or slag.

pour point The lowest temperature at which a lubricant flows under specified conditions.

pour strip In concrete formwork, a narrow guide placed inside the form to direct the concrete.

power cable

power panelboard

power transformer

pouring box A device designed to contain spills that may occur when transferring liquids from one container to another.

pouring of concrete *See* **placement and placing**.

pouring rope *See* **asbestos joint runner**.

powder factor The amount of explosive required to dislodge and fragment one cubic yard of rock.

powder molding A method of manufacturing objects by melting polyethylene powder in a mold.

powder post A condition in which wood has decayed to powder or been eaten by borers that leave holes full of powder.

power The rate of performing work or the rate of transforming, transferring, or consuming energy. Power is usually measured in watts, Btu/hour, or horsepower.

power buggy A wheelbarrow-sized machine powered by a gasoline engine or an electric motor.

power cable A usually heavy cable, consisting of one or more conductors with insulation and jackets, for conducting electric power.

power consumption The rate at which power is consumed by a device or unit (such as a building), usually expressed in kilowatt-hours, Btu/hour, or horsepower-hours.

power drill An electric-powered, hand-held drill, activated by pressing a trigger-like switch.

power factor A calculation, expressed as a percentage, that relates the volt amperes of an AC circuit, or the apparent power, to the wattage, or the true power. In essence, it provides a measurement of how effectively electrical power is being used. A higher power factor

means a more effective use of electrical power.

power float *See* **rotary float**.

power of attorney An authorization to act as an agent for another party. *See also* **attorney-in-fact**.

power panelboard A panelboard used for circuits supplying motors and other heavy power-consuming devices, as opposed to a panelboard used for lighting circuits.

power sander An electric-powered hand tool used for smoothing and/or polishing.

power shovel A self-propelled, power-operated machine used to excavate and/or load soils or debris.

powers spacing factor *See* **spacing factor**.

power take-off On construction equipment, an attachment enabling the power from the prime mover to be used to drive an auxilliary machine or tool.

power transformer A device in an alternating-current electrical system that transfers electric energy between circuits, usually changing the voltage in the process.

power trowel *See* **mechanical trowel**.

power wrench *See* **impact wrench**.

pozzolan A siliceous, or siliceous and aluminous, material which, in itself, possesses little or no cementitious value but will, in finely divided form and in the presence of moisture, chemically react with calcium hydroxide at ordinary temperatures to form compounds possessing cementitious properties.

pozzolan cement A natural cement, used in ancient times, made by grinding pozzolan with lime.

pozzolanic Of or pertaining to pozzolan.

Pratt truss

preaction sprinkler system

pozzolanic reaction *See* **pozzolan**.

Pratt truss A type of truss with parallel chords, all vertical members in compression, and all diagonal members in tension. The diagonals slant toward the center.

preaction sprinkler system A dry pipe sprinkler system in which water is supplied to the piping when a smoke or heat detector is activated.

preassembled lock A factory-assembled lock requiring little or no alterations on installation.

preboring (1) Drilling a pilot hole. (2) Boring a hole, for a bearing pile, through a hard stratum that would damage the pile if driven.

precast (1) A concrete member that is cast and cured in other than its final position. (2) The process of placing and finishing precast concrete.

precast concrete Concrete structural components, such as piles, wall panels, beams, etc., fabricated at a location other than in-place.

precipitator *See* **electrostatic precipitator**.

precise level An instrument similar to an ordinary surveyor's level but capable of finer readings and including a prism arrangement that permits simultaneous observation of the rod and the leveling bubble.

precise leveling rod A leveling rod with fine graduations on an insert of metal under constant tension, with a low thermal expansion coefficient.

precoating *See* **tinning**.

precompressed zone The area of a flexural member that is compressed by the prestressing tendons.

precon Contraction for preconstruction meeting.

preconsolidation pressure The greatest effective pressure a soil has experienced.

precooling coil In an HVAC system, a cooling coil located at the air-entering side of the primary cooling coil.

precure The process of curing a glued joint prior to pressing or clamping.

precured period *See* **presteaming period**.

precuring In plywood manufacturing, the premature curing of an adhesive due to press temperatures being too high, a too rapid resin-curing speed, or a malfunctioning press. Precuring can result in plywood delamination or a poor quality surface in particleboard.

precut A lumber item, usually a stud, that is cut to a precise length at the time of manufacture, so that it may be used in construction without further trimming at the job site.

predesign services Services provided by the design professional which precede customary services. Predesign services include assistance of the owner in establishing the program, schedule, budget, and project limitations. *See also* **programming phase**.

predrilled Lumber, such as roof decking, that has been drilled at the mill to accommodate bolts or other hardware.

prefabricate To fabricate units or components at a mill or plant for assembly at another location.

prefabricated construction A construction method that uses standard prefabricated units that are assembled at a site along with site fabrication of some minor parts.

prefabricated flue

prefabricated tie

preformed asphalt joint filler

prefabricated flue A metal vent for fuel-fired equipment that is assembled from factory-made parts.

prefabricated joint filler A compressible material used to fill control, expansion, and contraction joints and may also be used alone, or as a backing for a joint sealant.

prefabricated masonry panel A wall panel of masonry units constructed at an assembly site and moved to a job site for erection.

prefabricated modular units Units of construction that are preassembled at the factory and shipped as a complete unit to the job site. They usually can be installed with a minimum of adjustments.

prefabricated pipe conduit system Prefabricated units consisting of insulated piping for one or more utilities, ready to be installed either above or below ground.

prefabricated tie A manufactured assembly consisting of two heavy parallel wires tied together by welded wires. The tie is laid in masonry joints to tie two wythes together.

prefabricated wall See **demountable partition**.

preferred angle (1) Any angle of inclination of a stair between a 30° pitch and a 35° pitch. (2) Any angle or pitch of a ramp 15° or less.

prefilled A particleboard panel whose surface has been made smooth by the application of a solvent-based filler before being shipped. Such panels have decorative overlays or laminates applied to them.

prefilter In an air-conditioning system, a filter placed before the main filter(s). A prefilter is coarser and is used to remove larger particles.

prefinished Lumber, plywood, molding, or other wood products with a finish coating of paint, stain, vinyl, or other material applied before it is taken to the job site.

prefinished door A standard-sized door with both faces factory-finished and cuts and recesses provided for hardware.

prefiring Raising the temperature of refractory concrete under controlled conditions prior to placing it in service.

preformed asphalt joint filler Premolded strips of asphalt, vegetable or mineral filler, and fibers for use as a joint filler.

preformed foam Foam produced in a foam generator prior to its introduction into a mixer with other ingredients to produce cellular concrete.

preformed joint sealant See **preformed sealant**.

preformed sealant A factory-shaped sealant that requires little field fabrication prior to installation.

preframed A construction term for wall, floor, or roof components assembled at a factory.

preheat coil A coil, in an air-conditioning system, used to preheat air which is below 32°F (0 °C).

preheater (1) A heat exchanger used to heat air that is to be used in the combustion chamber of a large boiler or furnace. (2) See **preheat coil**.

preheat fluorescent lamp A fluorescent lamp, the electrodes of which must be preheated before the arc can be started. The preheating can be manual or automatic.

prehung door A packaged unit consisting of a finished door on a frame with all necessary hardware and trim.

preliminary assessment The first phase in an environmental remediation operation, in which it is determined whether there is a reasonable probability that a hazardous waste exists at a site.

preliminary drawings Drawings prepared in the early phase of building design. *See also* **schematic design phase** *and* **design development phase**.

preliminary estimate A rough estimate made in an early stage of the design work, prior to receipt of firm bids. *See also* **statement of probable construction cost**.

premature stiffening *See* **false set** *and* **flash set**.

premises premium (1) In commodity futures trading, a sum above the value of the item in the cash market. (2) A product of better quality than another product.

premises wiring Strictly speaking, the external and internal wiring that runs from the service point of utility conductors into a structure and to its outlets. Also includes all associated hardware and fittings.

premium grade A general term describing the quality of one item as superior to another.

premolded asphalt panel A panel with a core of asphalt, minerals, and fibers, covered on each side with asphalt-impregnated felt or fabric and pressure-bonded. The outside is then coated with hot asphalt.

prepacked concrete *See* **concrete, preplaced-aggregate**.

prepared roofing *See* **asphalt prepared roofing**.

prepayment meter A coin-operated water or gas meter that passes a fixed amount of fluid for each coin.

preplaced-aggregate concrete *See* **concrete, preplaced aggregate** *and* **colloidal concrete**.

preposttensioning A method of fabricating prestressed concrete in which some of the tendons are pretensioned and a portion of the tendons are posttensioned.

prepreg In reinforced plastic, the reinforcing with applied resin before molding.

prequalification of bidders The investigation and subsequent approval of prospective bidders' qualifications, experience, availability, and capability regarding a project.

present value method A means of evaluating capital expenditures by converting projections of cash inflows and outflows over time to their present value, using an estimated discounting rate.

preservation The act of applying measures necessary to sustain the integrity and materials of a historic property. Preservation work, including the preliminary measures to protect and stabilize the property, generally focuses on ongoing maintenance and repair of historic materials and features, rather than extensive replacement and new construction. New exterior additions are not within the scope of this treatment. However, limited and sensitive upgrading of mechanical, electrical and plumbing systems (and other code-required work to make a property functional) is appropriate. Preservation may include use of various techniques and scientific procedures to protect old building materials from the harmful effects of natural elements (e.g., light, heat, moisture) and from exposure to people through building use.

pressed glass

pressed steel

pressure connector

pressure gauge

preservationist A term applied to one who objects to the use of natural resources because of a belief that such use will destroy basic values of the resource. The term is often used to refer to a member of various groups opposed to the expansion of industrial/commercial uses of public lands.

preservative Any substance applied to wood that helps it resist decay, rotting, or harmful insects.

preset period *See* **presteaming period**.

preshrunk (1) Concrete which has been mixed for a short period in a stationary mixer before being transferred to a transit mixer. (2) Grout, mortar, or concrete that has been mixed one to three hours before placing to reduce shrinkage during hardening.

press brake A machine used to bend and shape cold-form metal sheets and strips.

pressed brick Brick that is molded under mechanical pressure. The resulting product is sharp-edged and smooth, and is used for exposed surfaces.

pressed edge Edge of a footing along which the greatest soil pressure occurs under conditions of overturning.

pressed glass Glass units, such as pavement units or glass block, that are pressed into shape.

pressed reflector lamp *See* **parabolic aluminized reflector lamp**.

pressed steel Die-stamped building components.

pressed wood A panel wood product manufactured by compressing wood fibers and adhesive under heat. Common examples include particleboard, hardwood plywood paneling and medium density fiberboard.

pressure (1) The force per unit area exerted by a homogenous liquid or gas on the walls of a container. (2) The force per unit area transferred between surfaces.

pressure bulb The zone in a loaded soil mass that is bounded by a selected stress isobar.

pressure cell An instrument used to measure the pressure within a soil mass or the pressure of the soil against a rigid wall.

pressure connector A mechanical device which forms a conductive connection between two or more electric conductors, or between one or more conductors and a terminal, without the use of solder.

pressure creosoting The process of forcing creosote, by use of pressure chambers, into timber.

pressure differential valve A valve controlled by the pressure difference in the supply and return main to divert flow from the supply main to the return main.

pressure drop (1) The drop in pressure between two ends of a pipe or duct, between two points in a system, or across valves, fittings, etc., caused by friction losses. (2) In a water system, the drop caused by a difference in elevation.

pressure forming A thermoforming process for plastics in which pressure forces a sheet against a mold, as opposed to vacuum forming.

pressure gauge An instrument for measuring fluid pressure.

pressure gluing A method used to glue wood that places the members under high pressure until the glue sets.

pressure gun *See* **caulking gun**.

pressure-reducing valve

pressure-injected footing
A cast-in-situ concrete pile that features a steel cylindrical shaft with an enlarged base that is driven into the ground. It can be used in nearly all soil conditions and can safely withstand very high compressive and tensile forces and substantial horizontal loads.

pressure line Locus of force points within a structure, resulting from combined prestressing force and externally applied load.

pressure-locked grating Metal grating in which cross bars and bearing bars are locked together at their intersections by deforming or swaging the metal.

pressure preserved Wood that has been treated with a preservative under pressure in a closed container.

pressure process The process of treating under pressure in a closed container. Pressure is usually preceded or followed by a vacuum.

pressure-reducing valve A valve which maintains a uniform fluid pressure on its outlet side as long as pressure on the inlet side is at or above a design pressure.

pressure regulating valve A valve that automatically reduces water pressure to maintain a predetermined design pressure.

pressure-relief damper A damper which will open when pressure on the inside exceeds a design pressure.

pressure-relief device A disk or seal that is designed to open or rupture when pressure on a designated side exceeds a design value.

pressure-relief hatch A roof hatch designed to open or blow off under pressure from an explosion in a building. Some smoke and heat vents are also designed as pressure-relief hatches.

pressure-relieving joint A horizontal expansion joint in panel wall masonry, usually below supporting hangers at each floor. These joints prevent the weight of higher panels from being transmitted to the masonry below.

pressure-sensitive Capable of adhering to a surface when pressed against it.

pressure-sensitive adhesive
An adhesive material that remains tacky after the solvents evaporate and will adhere to most solid surfaces with the application of light pressure.

pressure treating A process of treating lumber or other products with various chemicals, such as preservatives and fire retardants, by forcing the chemicals into the structure of the wood using high pressure.

pressure weatherstripping
Weatherstripping designed to provide a seal by means of spring tension.

pressure wire connector Any device that maintains a mechanical connection between electrical conductors through the use of pressure.

presteaming period In the manufacture of concrete products, the time between molding of a concrete product and start of the temperature-rise period.

prestress (1) To place a hardened concrete member or an assembly of units in a state of compression prior to application of service loads. (2) The stress developed by prestressing, such as by pretensioning or posttensioning. *See also* **prestressed concrete, prestressing steel, pretensioning,** *and* **posttensioning.**

prestressed concrete

pretensioned concrete

prick punch

prestressed concrete Concrete in which internal stresses of such magnitude and distribution are introduced that the tensile stresses resulting from the service loads are counteracted to a desired degree. In reinforced concrete, the prestress is commonly introduced by tensioning the tendons.

prestressed concrete wire Steel wire with a very high tensile strength, used in prestressed concrete. The wire is initially stressed close to its tensile strength. Then some of this load is transferred to the concrete, by chemical bond or mechanical anchors, to compress the concrete.

prestressing Applying a load to a structural element to increase its effectiveness in resisting working loads. Prestressed concrete is a common example.

prestressing cable A cable or tendon made of prestressing wires.

prestressing steel High-strength steel used to prestress concrete, commonly seven-wire strands, single wires, bars, rods, or groups of wires or strands. *See also* **prestressed concrete, pretensioning,** *and* **posttensioning.**

pretensioned concrete Concrete which has its reinforcing tendons stressed before the concrete is placed. Tension on the tendons is then released to provide load transfer where concrete has achieved strength.

pretensioning A method of prestressing reinforced concrete in which the tendons are tensioned before the concrete has hardened.

pretensioning bed (or bench) The casting bed on which pretensioned members are manufactured and which resists the pretensioning force prior to release.

prevailing wage Wage set by Federal and State governments for construction work based upon wages paid for similar work in the same local area.

prevalent levels Air contamination levels measured under normal conditions.

price out (1) The activity of applying dollar values to the items in a takeoff. (2) The final estimate sheet showing all dollar values.

pricking up Scoring the first coat of plaster on lath.

pricking-up coat The first, or base, coat of plaster on lath.

prick post An intermediate post in a truss. Theoretically, no loads are placed on it.

prick punch A pointed steel hand punch used to mark metal.

primacord A detonating fuse for high explosives, consisting of an explosive core in a strong, waterproof covering.

primary air Air which is fed to a burner to be mixed with gas.

primary battery A battery of two or more primary cells.

primary blasting The blasting operation in which a natural rock formation is dislodged from its original location.

primary branch (1) A drain between the base of a soil or waste stack and a building drain. (2) The largest single branch of a water supply line or an air supply duct in a building.

primary cell A cell that generates electric current by electrochemical action. In the process, one of the electrodes is consumed and the process cannot be effectively reversed. The cell cannot be recharged from an external source of electric power.

primary member

primary consolidation Soil compaction caused by the application of sustained loads, principally due to the squeezing out of water in the voids of the affected soil.

primary crusher A heavy crusher suitable for the first stage in a process of size reduction of rock, slag, or the like.

primary distribution feeder A feeder which operates at primary voltage supplying a distribution circuit.

primary excavation Excavating undisturbed soil.

primary light source (1) A source of light in which the light is produced by a transformation of energy. (2) The most obvious source of light when several sources are present.

primary member One of the main load-carrying members of a structural system, generally columns or posts. *See also* **secondary member**.

primary nuclear vessel Interior container in a nuclear reactor designed for sustained loads and for working conditions.

primary subcontractors Subcontractors who may perform major portions of the work in a construction project, such as installation of plumbing, mechanical, or electrical systems. They may have a contract directly with the owner.

prime (1) A grade of finish lumber ranking below superior, the highest grade, and above E, the lowest grade of finish. Finish graded prime must present a fine appearance and is designed for application where finishing requirements are less exacting. (2) To supply water to a pump to enable it to start pumping. (3) In blasting, to place the detonator in a cartridge or charge of explosive. (4) The primary architect or contractor on a job that features several.

prime bid A bid presented directly to the owner or his agent, rather than a subcontractor's bid to a general contractor.

prime coat (1) An application of low-viscosity liquid asphalt to an absorbent surface. (2) The first or preparatory coat in a paint system.

prime contract An agreement formed between the owner and the contractor for a major portion of the work on a construction contract.

prime contractor Any contractor on a project having a contract directly with the owner.

prime mover The parts or pieces of construction equipment that make it possible for the equipment to do its work, such as tracks on a dozer or cables on a crane. In the case of towed equipment, such as a scraper, the whole tractor becomes a prime mover.

prime professional A firm or individual performing contractually agreed upon professional services for an owner.

prime professional service The chief among multiple professional entities (each under separate contracts with the prime professional) responsible for providing services to an owner.

primer A base, preparatory paint that is applied to an uncoated surface to improve the adhesion and durability of the finish coat. Primer can be latex or alkyd (oil-based) paint.

primer/sealer A paint product manufactured to both prime a material for future paint application while sealing it from moisture.

principal post

processed shake

priming (1) The application of a prime coat. (2) Filling a pump or siphon with fluid to enable flow. (3) The first or annual filling of a canal or reservoir with water.

Prince Albert fir Another name for west coast hemlock.

princess pine Another name for jackpine.

princess post Subsidiary verticals, between queen posts or the king post, and walls, used to stiffen a roof truss.

principal (1) The principal authority or person responsible for a business such as architecture, engineering, or construction. (2) The capital amount of a loan or other obligation as distinguished from the interest. (3) In professional practice, any person legally responsible for the activities of that practice.

principal beam The main beam in a structural frame.

principal-in-charge The professional individual within a design firm ultimately responsible for monitoring services in connection with a given project.

principal planes *See* **principal stress**.

principal post A corner post in a framed building or a door post in a framed partition.

principal rafter One of the diagonals in a roof truss which support the purlins on which rafters are laid.

principal stress Maximum and minimum normal stresses at a point in a stressed body.

print *See* **blueprint**.

prism A surveying device used as a reference target when using electronic equipment to measure distance.

prismatic beam A beam with a uniform cross section. Both of its flanges run parallel along its longitudinal axis.

prismatic glass Glass with parallel prisms rolled into one face. The prisms refract light rays and change their direction.

prismatic rustication Rusticated masonry with a diamond-shaped projection worked into the face of each stone.

prism glass *See* **prismatic glass**.

private branch exchange (PBX) A telephone system, located on a customer's premises, that is owned and operated by the customer rather than a telephone company. A PBX system switches internal calls between the customer's users on local lines while also making external lines available. Using a PBX can save a customer money because it eliminates the need for direct lines from each user to the telephone company.

private sewer A sewer that is not in the public sewer system and subject only to the provisions of the local code.

private stairway A stairway intended to serve only one tenant.

privity of contract This occurs when a party has a direct contractual relationship with another party.

privy An outhouse serving as a toilet.

probabilistic design Method of design of structures using the principles of statistics (probability) as a basis for evaluation of structural safety.

probable construction cost *See* **statement of probable construction cost**.

processed shake A sawn cedar shingle which is textured on one surface to resemble a split shingle.

Proctor compaction test A test to determine the moisture content of a soil at which maximum compaction can be obtained. The test establishes the density-moisture relationship in a soil.

Proctor penetration needle An instrument that measures the resistance of a fine-grained soil to penetration by a standard needle at a standard rate.

procure To obtain or receive, such as a construction or material contract.

producer Provider of building materials or equipment such as processor, manufacturer, or equipment rental/sales firm.

product data Information furnished by the manufacturer to illustrate a material, product, or system for some portion of the work which includes illustrations, standard schedules, performance charts, instructions, brochures, diagrams, warranties.

production Total quantity of work performed.

productivity Work performed per unit of time, or time to perform unit of work, such as square feet per hour.

products liability insurance Insurance for liability imposed for damages caused by an occurrence arising out of goods or products manufactured, sold, handled, or distributed by the insured or others trading under the insured's name. Occurrence must occur after product has been relinquished to others and away from premises of the insured. *See also* **completed operations insurance**.

product standard A published standard that establishes: (1) dimensional requirements for standard sizes and types of various products; (2) technical requirements for the product; and (3) methods of testing, grading, and marking the product. The objective of product standards is to define requirements for specific products in accordance with the principal demands of the trade. Product standards are published by the National Bureau of Standards of the U.S. Department of Commerce, as well as by private organizations of manufacturers, distributors, and users.

professional advisor A design professional employed by the owner to conduct a design competition for the selection of project designer.

professional corporation A corporation created expressly for the purpose of providing professional practice and related services which may have special requirements under the law, as opposed to requirements for corporations in general.

professional engineer A professionally qualified and duly licensed individual that performs services such as structural, mechanical, electrical, sanitary, and civil engineering.

professional fee *See* **fee.**

professional liability insurance Insurance coverage protecting against legal liability for damage claims sustained by others. Damage claims allege negligent acts, errors, or omissions in the performance of professional services. *See also* **negligence**.

professional practice The conduct and work of a design professional in which services are rendered within the framework of recognized professional ethics, standards, and applicable legal requirements. *See also* **environmental design**.

profile (1) A drawing showing a vertical section of ground, usually taken along the center line of a highway or other construction project. (2) A template used for shaping plaster. (3) A guide used in masonry work. (4) A British term for batter board.

profit sharing Provisions in special agreements or contracts for construction where the contractor, as an incentive to save money for the owner, is paid, in addition to the final contract sum, some percentage of any net savings he may achieve if he is able to deliver the finished project to the owner's satisfaction at a total cost below a specified limiting amount.

pro forma invoice An invoice sent before the order has been shipped in order to obtain payment before shipment.

program A written statement presenting design objectives, constraints, and project criteria, including space requirements and relationships, flexibility and expandability, special equipment, and systems and site requirements.

programming phase The design stage in which the owner develops and provides full information regarding requirements for the project, including a program. *See also* **predesign services**.

progress chart (1) A chart that shows various operations in a construction project, such as excavating and foundations, along with planned starting and finish dates in the form of horizontal bars. Progress is indicated by filling in the bars. (2) A similar chart for the design phase of a project. The bars usually identify specific drawings.

progressive kiln A dry kiln in which green lumber enters one end and is dried progressively as it moves to the other end where it is removed.

progressive scaling The progressive disintegration of materials, such as concrete, which first appears as surface scaling but continues in deeper layers.

progress payment A scheduled partial payment made during the work process to cover costs of work completed or materials delivered to date.

progress schedule A pictorial or written schedule (including a graph or diagram) that shows proposed and actual start and completion dates of the various work elements. *See also* **critical path method (CPM)** *and* **PERT schedule**.

project The total construction activities, usually on one site. The work performed under the contract documents may be the whole or a part of the project.

project application for payment Certified requests for payment from project contractors, requiring certification by the designer before submittal to the owner. *See also* **application for payment**.

project architect The party designated by the principal-in-charge to manage a given project for a firm. *See also* **project manager**.

project certificate for payment A statement to the owner confirming the amounts due individual contractors. Issued by the design professional where multiple contractors have separate necessary agreements with the owner. *See also* **certificate for payment**.

project cost The total project cost, which includes the cost of construction, professional compensation, land, furnishings and equipment, financing, and other charges.

projected window

projection

project designer (1) (designer's office) The person assigned by the principal-in-charge to be responsible for guiding the overall direction of a project's design. (2) (consultant's office) The individual responsible for the design of a specific portion of a project, including mechanical, structural, electrical, civil, sanitary, acoustical, etc. *See also* **project engineer**.

projected window A window with one or more sashes that swing either inward or outward.

project engineer The engineer in the architect's or consultant's office, who is responsible for the design and management of the engineering portions of a project.

project evaluation and review technique (PERT) schedule A schedule that charts the activities and events anticipated in a work process. *See also* **critical path method (CPM)**.

projecting belt course A course of masonry which projects beyond the face of the wall to form a decorative shelf.

projecting brick One of a number of bricks that project from a wall to form a pattern.

projecting scaffold A work platform which is cantilevered from the face of a building by means of brackets.

projecting sign A sign attached to the face of a building and extending outward.

projection Any component member or part which extends out from a building for a relatively short distance.

projection booth A booth, usually at the rear of a room or hall, used for the operation of still or moving projectors or spotlights.

project manager The individual designated by the principal-in-charge to manage a given project. Normally includes administrative and technical responsibilities.

project manual The document(s) prepared by the project designer such as bidding requirements, sample forms, conditions of the contract, and specifications.

projector (1) A lighting unit which concentrates light within a limited solid angle by means of lenses or mirrors. (2) A line dropped perpendicularly from a point to a plane surface.

project record documents The documents, certificates, and other information relating to the work, materials, products, assemblies, and equipment that the contractor is required to accumulate during construction and convey to the owner for use prior to final payment and project closeout.

project representative The architect's representative at the project site who assists in the administration of the construction contract.

project site *See* **site**.

project team A collection of professional entities directed and otherwise coordinated to perform work or services for a project.

project web site An Internet site created for those involved in a specific construction project with the goal of increasing efficiency by improving access to information. Such sites can make a variety of information available—from a file of project team members and their e-mail addresses, to the project manual, field reports, meeting notes, and the shop drawing log.

promenade tile *See* **quarry tile**.

promissory note A legal instrument, agreement or contract made between a lender and a borrower by which the lender conveys to the borrower a sum or other consideration known as principal for which the borrower promises repayment of the principal plus interest under conditions set forth in the agreement.

promoter *See* **catalyst**.

proof stress (1) Stress applied to materials sufficient to produce a specified permanent strain. (2) A specific stress to which some types of tendons are subjected in the manufacturing process as a means of reducing the deformation of anchorage, reducing the creep of steel, or ensuring that the tendon is sufficiently strong.

prop *See* **post and shore**.

propeller twist Twisted grain in a red cedar shake that prevents it from lying flat and causes it to take the shape roughly resembling an airplane propeller.

property damage insurance Insurance covering legal liability for claims for injury to or destruction of tangible property (including loss of use). *See also* **care, custody,** *and* **control**.

property insurance Insurance that compensates the insured for loss of property (real or personal) resulting from direct physical damage. Damages include fire, lightning, extended coverage perils, vandalism, and malicious mischief, among other damages. *See also* **builder's risk insurance, extended coverage insurance, measurable value,** *and* **special hazards insurance**.

property line A recorded boundary of a plot.

proportional control In an HVAC system, the controlled device (valve or damper) is positioned proportionally in response to slight changes in the controlled variable (temperature, pressure).

proportional dividers An instrument for enlarging or reducing lengths of lines that consists of two pivoted bars pointed at each end. The pivot is movable to adjust the relative lengths between the two pairs of points.

proportional limit The greatest stress which a material is capable of developing without any deviation from proportionality of stress to strain (Hooke's Law).

proportioning Selection of proportions of ingredients for mortar or concrete to make the most economical use of available materials to produce mortar or concrete of the required properties.

proposal (contractor's) *See* **bid**.

proposal form *See* **bid form**.

proprietary The naming of a product manufacturer as in a proprietary specification.

proprietary specification A specification that describes a product, material, assembly, or piece of equipment by trade name and/or by naming the manufacturer or manufacturers who may produce products acceptable to the owner or design professional.

prorate Distribute proportionately; divide by ratio.

proscription The acquisition of title to real property by one who openly and continuously is in adverse possession of it for a period sufficiently long that the statute of limitation bars the previous owner from reclaiming it (usually 20 years).

protected corner Corner of a slab with adequate provision for load

protected metal sheeting

transfer, so that at least 20% of the load from one slab corner to the corner of an adjacent slab is transferred by mechanical means or aggregate interlock.

protected metal sheeting Sheet metal coated with zinc, paint, and/or a thin coating of asphalt for corrosion protection.

protected noncombustible construction Noncombustible construction in which bearing walls (or bearing portions of walls), whether interior or exterior, have a minimum fire resistance rating of two hours and are stable under fire conditions. Roofs and floors, and their supports, have minimum fire resistance ratings of one hour. Stairways and other openings through floors are enclosed with partitions having minimum fire resistance ratings of one hour.

protected opening An opening, in a rated wall or partition which is fitted with a door, window, or shutter having a fire resistance rating appropriate to the use of the wall.

protected ordinary construction Construction in which roofs and floors and their supports have a minimum fire resistance rating of one hour, and stairways and other openings through floors are enclosed with partitions that have minimum fire resistance ratings of one hour. Such construction must also meet all the requirements of ordinary construction.

protected paste volume The portion of hardened cement paste that is protected from the effects of freezing by proximity to an entrained air void.

protected waste pipe A waste pipe from a fixture that is not directly connected to a drain, soil, vent, or waste pipe.

protected wood-frame construction Construction in which roofs and floors and their supports have minimum fire resistance ratings of one hour, and stairways and other openings through floors are enclosed with partitions with minimum fire resistance ratings of one hour. Such construction must also meet all the requirements of wood frame construction.

protection screen A screen woven of moderately heavy stainless steel wires and set in a steel frame, used to protect windows at a psychiatric unit.

protective covenant (1) An agreement in writing which restricts the use of real property. (2) A restriction, in the legal document conveying title to real property, that restricts the use of the property.

protective lighting Lighting that is provided to facilitate the nighttime policing of a property or area.

protocol A procedure or practice established by long or traditional usage and currently accepted by a majority of practitioners in similar professions or trades. Protocol represents the generally accepted method of action or reaction that may be expected to be followed in a transaction.

protractor A graduated drafting instrument used to lay out angles.

proving ring A device for calibrating load indicators of testing machines, consisting of a calibrated elastic ring and a mechanism or device for indicating the magnitude of deformation under load.

proximate cause The cause of an injury or of damages which, in natural and continuous sequence, unbroken by any legally recognized intervening cause, produces the injury, and without which the result would not have occurred. Existence

p-trap

of proximate cause involves both (1) causation in fact, i.e., that the wrongdoer actually produced an injury or damages, and (2) a public policy determination that the wrongdoer should be held responsible.

proximity switch A sensor which is activated by the intrusion of objects into an area.

proximo (prox) A credit term meaning next month.

prybar *See* **pinch bar**.

psychrometer An instrument for measuring water vapor in the atmosphere, utilizing both wet- and dry-bulb thermometers. A wet-bulb thermometer is kept moistened and is cooled by evaporation, giving a slightly lower reading than the dry-bulb thermometer. Because evaporation is greater in dry air, the difference between the two thermometer readings is greater in a dry atmosphere.

psychrometric Relating to the measurement of atmospheric conditions, particularly regarding the moisture mixed with air.

psychrometric chart A chart that graphically represents the interrelation of air temperature and moisture content. Commonly used by building engineers and designers.

p-trap P-shaped trap that provides a water seal in a waste or soil pipe, used mostly at sinks and lavatories.

public area An area that is open to the public.

public garage Garage for temporary parking or storage of small- to medium-size motor vehicles, usually for a fee.

public housing Low cost housing owned, maintained, and administered by a municipal or other government agency.

public liability insurance Insurance covering liability for negligent acts causing bodily injury, disease, or death of persons other than employees of the insured. Also covers liability for property damage. *See also* **comprehensive general liability insurance** *and* **contractor's liability insurance**.

public sewer A common sewer controlled completely by a public authority.

public space (1) An area within a building to which the public has free access, such as a foyer or lobby. (2) An area or piece of land legally designated for public use.

public system A water or sewer system owned and operated by a governmental authority or by a utility company that is controlled by a government authority.

public utility A service for the public such as water, sewers, telephone, electricity, or gas.

public water main A water supply pipe controlled by public authority.

public way A street, alley, or other parcel of land open to the outside air and leading to a public street. A public way is deeded or otherwise permanently appropriated for public use. A minimum width is usually specified by code.

puddle (1) To settle loose soil by flooding and turning it over. (2) To vibrate and/or work concrete to eliminate honeycomb. (3) Clay which has been worked with some water to make it homogeneous and increase its plasticity so it can be used to seal against the passage of water.

puddle weld A weld used to join two sheets of light-gauge metal. A hole is burned in the upper sheet and filled with weld metal to fasten the two together.

pulley

pulley block

puddling *See* **puddle.**

puff pipe A short vent pipe on the outlet side of a trap; used to prevent siphoning.

pug box (1) A box, with a removable cover, placed in an electric raceway to facilitate the pulling of conductors through the raceway. (2) A manual activator for a fire alarm system.

Puget Sound pine An archaic term for Douglas fir.

pugging A layer of clay, mortar, sawdust, or felt used for soundproofing purposes.

pug mill (1) A machine for mixing and tempering clay. (2) The part of an asphaltic concrete plant where the heated batch materials are mixed.

pull (1) A handle used for opening a door, drawer, etc. (2) To loosen rock at the bottom of a hole by blasting.

pull-chain operator A chain or control used to open or close a device such as a damper.

pulldown handle A handle fixed to the bottom rail of the upper sash of some double-hung windows.

pulley (pulley sheave) A wheel, with a grooved rim, that carries a rope or chain, and turns on a frame.

pulley block A frame that contains one or more pulleys.

pulley mortise *See* **chase mortise.**

pulley sheave *See* **pulley.**

pulley stile The upright in a window frame on which the sash pulleys are supported and along which the sash slides.

pull hardware A handle or grip on a door for opening the door.

pulling (1) The drag on a paintbrush caused by high paint viscosity.

(2) Installing and connecting wires in an electric system.

pulling over Smoothing a lacquer on wood by rubbing with a solvent-soaked cloth.

pulling up The softening of a coat of paint as the next coat is applied.

pull scraper A hand scraper, consisting of a steel blade at approximately right angles to the handle, that is used to remove old finishes or for smoothing wood.

pull shovel *See* **backhoe.**

pull switch *See* **chain-pull switch.**

pulpboard A solid board composed of wood pulp. *See also* **fiberboard.**

pulsed arc transfer An arc welding method that involves operating a power source between low and high current levels. The high current level, called a "pulse," forces an electrode drop to the workpiece, while the low current level, or "background," maintains the arc between pulses. Major benefits of the process include better arc characteristics and greatly reduced spatter and fume generation.

pulse tube boiler A boiler using a sealed combustion system in which residual heat from the initial cycle ignites all subsequent air-gas mixtures, and flue gas condensation takes place in the heat exchanger.

pulverized fuel ash *See* **fly ash.**

pumice A highly porous lava, usually of relatively high silica content, composed largely of glass drawn into approximately parallel or loosely entwined fibers.

pumice concrete A lightweight concrete in which pumice is used as the coarse aggregate and which has good thermal insulation value.

pumice stone A solid block of pumice used to rub or polish surfaces.

purlin

pumicite Naturally occurring finely divided pumice.

pump A machine, operated by hand or a prime mover, used to compress and/or move a fluid.

pumped concrete Concrete which is transported through hose or pipe by means of a pump.

pump head The pressure differential produced by an operating pump.

pumping (of pavements) The ejection of water, or water and solid materials, such as clay or silt, along transverse or longitudinal joints and cracks, and along pavement edges. Pumping is caused by downward slab movement activated by the passage of loads over the pavement after the accumulation of free water on or in the base course, subgrade, or subbase.

pump jack An adjustable support used to raise and lower scaffolding.

punch (1) A small pointed tool which is struck with a hammer and used for centering and starting holes. (2) A steel tool, usually cylindrical, with sharpened edges and used in a hydraulic machine to make holes through metal.

puncheon (1) Roughly dressed, heavy timber used as flooring, or as a footing for a foundation. (2) Short timbers supporting horizontal members in a cofferdam.

punching shear (1) Shear stress calculated by dividing the load on a column by the product of its perimeter and the thickness of the base or cap, or by the product of the perimeter taken at one half the slab thickness away from the column and the thickness of the base or cap. (2) Failure of a base when a heavily loaded column punches a hole through it.

punch list A list of items within a project, prepared by the owner or his representative, and confirmed by the contractor, which remain to be replaced or completed in accordance with the requirements of the contract for construction at the time of substantial completion.

punitive damages (exemplary damages) Damages are awarded by a judge to a plaintiff not merely to compensate the plaintiff for losses incurred, but to punish the defendant for wrongful conduct and to use the plight of the defendant as an example to potential wrongdoers.

punning An obsolete term designating a light form of ramming. *See also* **ramming** *and* **tamping**.

PUR insulation *See* **polyurethane insulation**.

purchase and sale agreement The written contract for the sale of real property. The statute of frauds requires that a contract for the sale of real property must be in writing.

purchase order A formal written authorization to a vendor to provide certain goods or services and to bill the buyer for them at the specified price. The purchase order becomes a contract when it is accepted by the vendor.

purchaser A person or company that buys or contracts to buy real property. *See also* **vendor**.

purge To remove unwanted air or gas from a ductline, pipeline, container, space, or furnace, often by injecting an inert gas.

purge pump A compressor that removes noncondensibles from a refrigeration system.

purge valve *See* **air purge valve**.

purlin One of several horizontal structural members that support roof loads and transfer them to roof beams.

purlin cleat

pyramidal light

pyramid roof

purlin cleat A shaped metal fastener used to secure a purlin to its support.

purlin plate A purlin, in a curb roof, located at the curb and supporting the ends of the upper rafters.

purlin post A strut which supports a purlin to reduce sag.

purlin roof A roof in which purlins are supported directly on walls rather than rafters.

push bar A heavy bar across a glazed door, screen door, or horizontally pivoted window sash, used to open or close the door or window.

push button A device in an electric circuit with a button that is pressed to activate or disconnect the circuit.

push drill A hand drill which is operated by pushing on its handle. A spiral ratchet rotates the bit.

push hardware A fixed bar or plate operated by pushing.

push plate A metal plate used to protect a door while it is pushed open.

push point A thin piece of metal used in glazing to hold glass in a wooden frame. A bent section of the point makes it easy to push the point into the wood.

push-pull rule A thin steel rule which coils into a case when not in use.

putlog Short pieces of timber that support the planks of a scaffold. One end of the timber is supported by the scaffold, the other is inserted in a temporary hole left in the masonry.

putlog hole The temporary hole in masonry that supports one end of a putlog.

puttied split A split in a wood product, such as a panel surface, that has been filled with putty, usually an epoxy, then sanded.

putty A dough-like mixture of pigment and vehicle, used to set glass in window frames and fill nail holes and cracks.

putty coat Final smooth coat of plaster.

putty knife A knife, with a broad flexible blade with a flat end, used to apply putty.

pycnometer A vessel for determining the specific gravity of liquids or solids.

pylon (1) A steel tower used to support electrical high-tension lines. (2) A movable tower for carrying lights.

pyramidal light A skylight shaped like a pyramid.

pyramid roof A roof with four slopes terminating at a peak.

pyrolyze To bring about a chemical change through the action of heat.

pyrometer An apparatus for measuring high temperatures.

pyrometric cone A small, slender, three-sided oblique pyramid made of ceramic or refractory material for use in determining the time-temperature effect of heating and in obtaining the pyrometric cone equivalent of refractory material.

pyrometric cone equivalent The number of that cone whose tip would touch the supporting plaque simultaneously with that of a cone of the refractory material being investigated, when tested in accordance with a specified procedure such as ASTM C 24.

pyrophoric Liable to ignite or burn.

Q

ABBREVIATIONS

The abbreviations listed below are those most commonly used in the construction industry. Alternative forms (usually nonstandard) are shown in parentheses.

q quart

qa quality assurance

qc quality control

qda quantity discount agreement

QF quick firing

qr quarter

QR quarter-round

qs quarter sawn

qt quart

QTR quarry-tile roof; on drawings, quarter

quad quadrant

QUAD quadrangle

QUAL quality

quar quarterly

Q DEFINITIONS

quarry-faced

quarter bend

quadrangle (quad) An open rectangular courtyard surrounded on all sides by buildings.

quadrant (1) One quarter of the circumference of a circle; an arc of 90°. (2) An angle-measuring instrument. (3) *See* **Dutch door bolt**.

quadripartite An assembly involving four parts; usually describing groined vaulting.

quad-tube lamp A compact fluorescent lamp with a double twin tube configuration.

quaking concrete A method of vibrating *mass concrete*.

qualitative analysis The analysis of a sample (solid, liquid, or gas) to identify its components.

quality A grade of Idaho white pine equivalent to D *select* in other species.

quality assurance A system of procedures for selecting the levels of quality required for a project or portion thereof in order to perform the functions intended, and for assuring that these levels are obtained.

quality control A system of procedures and standards by which a constructor, product manufacturer, materials processor, or the like, monitor the properties of the finished work.

quantitative analysis The analysis of a sample (solid, liquid or gas) to determine the proportions of its various components.

quantities Measured amounts of construction items expressed in their customary units.

quantity overrun/underrun The difference between estimated quantities and the actual quantities in the completed work.

quantity survey A detailed analysis of material and equipment required to construct a project.

quantity takeoff *See* **take-off**.

quarrel A small diamond or square-shaped tile or piece of glass, often set diagonally.

quarry An open excavation in the surface of the earth for mining stone.

quarry-faced Freshly split ashlar squared off at the joints only; used for facing a masonry wall.

quarry run Indiscriminate building stone as it comes from the pit without regard to color or structure.

quarrystone bond In masonry, a term applied to the manner in which stone is arranged in rubblework.

quarry (promenade) tile Machine-made, unglazed tile.

quarry sap (quarry water) Groundwater contained in stone that has just been quarried.

quart A liquid measure containing one-fourth of a gallon.

quarter bend A 90° bend, as in piping.

quarter closer (quarter closure) A brick cut to 1/4 of its normal length; used either as a spacer, or to complete a course.

quarter-cut *See* **quartersawn**.

quartered *See* **quartersawn**.

quartered lumber Lumber that has been quartersawn approximately radially from the log.

quarter-turn

queen closer

quartered veneer Veneer that has been sliced in a radial direction, that is, at right angles to the growth rings. The term quartered comes from the use of blocks that have been cut into quarters before slicing. Quarter slicing brings out the presence of medullary rays; quarter-sliced veneer appears striped.

quarter hollow A concave molding formed by a 90° arc; the opposite of a quarter round.

quartering (1) A method of obtaining a representative sample by dividing a circular pile of a large sample into four equal parts and discarding opposite quarters successively until the desired size of sample is obtained. (2) Process of using small timbers as studs in a framed partition. (3) Quarter sawing.

quarterpace landing Platform between flights of stairs turning at a 90° angle.

quarter round A type of molding used as a base shoe; presenting the profile of a quarter circle.

quartersawn (rift-sawn) Lumber sawn so that the annual rings form angles from 45° to 90°.

quarter-turn Descriptive of a stair that turns 90° as it progresses from top to bottom.

quartz glass (silica glass) Glass consisting of pure, or nearly pure, amorphous silica. Of all glass, quartz glass has the highest heat resistance and ultraviolet transmittance.

quartz-idiode lamp Obsolete term for a tungsten-halogen lamp.

quartzite A sandstone composition consisting primarily of quartz and a siliceous cement.

Quebec pine *Pinus resinosa.* Red pine.

Quebec spruce *Picea alba., P. glauca.* White spruce.

Queen Anne arch The arch over a Palladian window with the middle curved over the higher central section, and flat above the lower side openings.

Queen Anne style An architectural style common in Britain in the early 1700s which utilized brick exteriors, carved relief ornamentation, and often stone parapets. (2) The earlier style was reinterpreted in more exuberant fashion in the late 1800s in North America and Britain. Exteriors often incorporated turrets, dormers, hip and gable roofs, bay windows, and extensive decorative moldings or carvings. Wood, stone or stucco was used in addition to brick.

Queen Anne window A window with small lights or panes arranged in various patterns. Usually found on the top sash only.

queen bolt *See* **queen rod.**

queen closer A half brick of normal thickness, but half-normal width. Used in a course of brick masonry to prevent vertical joints from falling above one another.

queen post One of the two vertical members in a queen-post truss.

queen-post truss (queen truss) A pitched roof support using two vertical tie posts connected between the tie beam and the rafters.

queen rod (queen bolt) A metal rod used as a queen post.

quenching Immersing hot, solid items in a cool liquid. Used as a means of tempering metals.

quetta bond Vertical voids in brickwork where reinforcing rods

quoin

are installed. The voids are then filled with mortar.

quick condition Soil that is weakened by the upward flow of water. Minute channels are created that significantly reduce the bearing capacity of the soil.

quick-leveling head A ball and socket attachment under the head of a surveyor's level or transit.

quicklime Calcium oxide (CaO). *See also* **lime**.

quick-load test Compression testing of piles that applies loads of increasing weight for brief time periods.

quick response sprinkler A sprinkler very sensitive to high temperatures, that reacts quickly to a fire, helping to limit smoke damage by arresting the fire at an earlier stage.

quicksand Fine sand in a *quick condition*, having virtually no bearing capacity.

quick set *See* **flash set** *and* **false set**.

quilt insulation A thermal barrier with paper faces that are stitched or woven.

quirk (1) A narrow groove or bead located at or near the intersection of two surfaces or next to a molding, so as to reduce the possibility of uncontrolled cracking. (2) Acute angle between adjoining pieces of molding. (3) Thin groove on the bottom of a drip cap to keep water away from the joint.

quirk molding (1) Trim piece with a narrow groove. (2) Trim with both inward and outward curves.

quitclaim deed A document that transfers the sellers interest in property to another party.

quoin (coign, coin) A right angle stone in the corner of a masonry wall to strengthen and tie the corner together.

quoin bonding In masonry, the interlocking of stones in the corner of a wall with staggered stretchers and headers.

Quonset hut A prefabricated building with a semicircular cross section; usually built with corrugated steel and thermal insulation.

quotation A price for materials or services provided by a contractor, subcontractor, supplier, or vendor.

quote To make an offer at a guaranteed price.

R

R ABBREVIATIONS

The abbreviations listed below are those most commonly used in the construction industry. Alternative forms (usually nonstandard) are shown in parentheses.

r rain, range, rare, red, river, roentgen, run

R radius, right, symbol for capacity of a pile

Ra radium

RA remedial action

R.A. registered architect

rab rabbeted

RAB rabbet

rad radiator

raft. rafter

RBM reinforced brick masonry

RC, R/C reinforced concrete, red cedar

RC asphalt rapid-curing asphalt

RCP reinforced concrete pipe

RCR room cavity ratio

RCRA Resource Conservation and Recovery Act

1/4 RD quarter-round

1/2 RD half-round

rd road, rod, round

RD roof drain, round, remedial design

rdm random

REA Rural Electrification Administration

rebar reinforcing bar

recap. recapitulation

recd received

recip reciprocal

RECP receptacle

rec. room recreation room

rect rectangle, rectified

red. reduce, reduction

ref reference, refining

REF refer, reference

REFR refractory, refrigerate

refrig refrigeration

reg registered

Reg regular

REG register, regulator

rein., reinf reinforced

REINF reinforce, reinforcing

REM removable

remod remodel

rent. rental

rep, REP repair

repl, REPL replace, replacement

REPRO reproduce

reqd, REQD required

res resawn

ret retain, retainage

RET. return

rev revenue, reverse, revised

REV revise

rf roof

RF roof, radio frequency

RFA RCRA Facility Assessment

Rfg roofing

RFI radio frequency interference

RFI/CMS RCRA Facility Investigation/Corrective Measures Study. *See also* **RCRA**.

RFP request for proposal

RFQ request for quotation

rgh, Rgh rough

Rh rhodium, Rockwell hardness

RH relative humidity

RHN Rockwell hardness number

RI refractive index, remedial investigation

R.I.B.A. Royal Institute of British Architects

rib. gl. ribbed glass

RI/FS Remedial Investigation/ Feasibility Study

RIS Redwood Inspection Service

riv river

Rj road junction

RKI rotary kiln incineration

R/L, RL random lengths

rm ream, room

RM room

r. mld. raised mold

rms root mean square

ROD Record of decision

ROP record of production

ROPS roll-over protection system

rot. rotating, rotation

rpm revolutions per minute

RRGCP reinforced rubber gasket concrete pipe

RRS railroad siding

R/S resawn

RSJ rolled steel joist

RSPA Research and Special Program Administration

rt right

RT raintight

Rub., rub. Ruberoid, rubble

r.w. redwood, roadway, right-of-way

RW, R/W random widths

R/W right-of-way

R/W&L, RW/L random widths and lengths

rwy, ry railway

rabbet joint

raceway

radial grating

rab A rod or stick used to mix concrete or mortar.

rabbet (1) A cut or groove along or near the edge of a piece of wood that allows another piece to fit into it to form a joint. (2) A rabbet joint. *See also* **dado**.

rabbet bead A bead placed in the reentry corner of a rabbet.

rabbet depth The depth of a glazing rabbet.

rabbeted doorjamb A doorjamb with a rabbet to receive a door.

rabbeted lock (rebated lock) A lock which is fitted into and flush with the rabbet on a rabbeted doorjamb.

rabbeted siding *See* **drop siding**.

rabbeted stop A stop that is an integral part of a door or window frame.

rabbet joint A longitudinal edge joint formed by fitting together rabbeted boards.

rabbet plane A plane for cutting a rabbet or fillister in wood, open on one side, with the blade extending to the open side.

rabbet size The actual size of a rabbeted glass opening, equal to the glass size plus two edged clearances.

race (1) A channel intended to contain rapidly moving water. (2) A groove in a machine part in which an object moves.

raceway (1) Any furrow or channel constructed to loosely house electrical conductors. These conduits may be flexible or rigid, metallic or nonmetallic, and are designed to protect the cables they enclose. (2) A man-made channel for directing water flow as in a hydroelectric plant.

rack A framework of metal bars used to prevent waterborne trash from entering a waterway.

rack-and-pinion elevator A platform or enclosure in which linear motion is created by the use of a rotating gear pinion mated to, and revolving on, a vertical stationary rack.

racked A temporary support used to brace and prevent deformation.

racking (racking back) (1) A method entailing stepping back successive courses of masonry in an unfinished wall. (2) The movement of structural elements out of level or plumb by forces such as stress, wind, or material shrinkage or expansion. (3)The installation of roof shingles in a straight line across the roof instead of on the diagonal. This method is quick, but is not often used because it can produce shingles incorrectly nailed and color variations.

rack saw A saw with wide teeth.

radial Radiating from, or converging to, a common center.

radial arch roof A roof supported by arches that radiate out from a central point.

radial-arm saw (radial saw) A circular saw suspended above the saw table on a cantilevered arm. The material remains stationary while the saw is free to move along its projecting beam.

radial bar *See* **radius rod**.

radial brick *See* **arch brick**.

radial-curved fans Backward-curved centrifugal fans with flat blades.

radial grating Grating in which the *bearing bars* extend radially from a common center, and the *cross bars* form concentric circles.

radiator

rafter

radially cut grating Rectangular grating cut into panels shaped as segments of a circle to fit annular or circular openings.

radial sawn *See* **quartersawn**.

radial shrinkage The shrinkage of wood across its diameter or growth rings as it dries.

radial step *See* **winder**.

radian The standard metric unit for a plane angle, as compared to customary units of degree(°), minute ('), and second (").

radiant energy Energy traveling in electromagnetic waves.

radiant glass Glass with embedded heating elements.

radiant heating system A system with heating terminals that deliver heat by radiation from a hot surface, such as those heated by the flow of hot water or electric current.

radiant panel test An ASTM method using radiant heat to test the surface flammability of different materials.

radiating brick *See* **arch brick**.

radiation The transmission of energy by means of electromagnetic waves of very long wave length. The energy travels in a straight line at the speed of light and is not affected by the temperature or currents of the air through which it passes.

radiation-shielding concrete A high density concrete used primarily for enclosing nuclear installations.

radiator A visually exposed heat exchanger consisting of a series of pipes that allows the circulation of steam or hot water. The heat from the steam or hot water is given up to the air surrounding the pipes.

radio frequency (RF) curing *See* **high-frequency gluing**.

radionuclide A radioactive nuclide that can emit radiation.

radio frequency interference (RFI) Disturbance of radio frequency bands by other high frequency equipment nearby. Fluorescent lighting creates RFI.

radiological screening A soil test than can determine approximate areas of local contamination.

radius gauge (fillet gauge) A gauge that measures the radius of curvature of small concave and convex surfaces.

radius of curvature A measure of the dimensions of a curve, as in the radius of curvature of a directional wall.

radius of gyration An imaginary distance from an axis to a point such that, if an object's mass were concentrated at the point, the moment of inertia would not change.

radius rod A long arm with a marker at one end and an adjustable pointer at the other, used to draw large radius circles or curves.

radon An odorless, colorless radioactive gas given off by some soils and rock with a short half-life (less than four days).

rafter One of a series of sloping parallel beams used to support a roof covering.

rafter plate A plate used to support the lower end of rafters and to which they are fastened.

rafter table A carpenter's square with a table of values for determining the lengths and angles of cut for roof rafters.

rafter tail That part of a rafter overhanging the wall.

raft foundation A continuous slab of concrete, usually reinforced.

515

rail

Employed as a foundation laid over soft ground, or where heavy loads must be supported. *See also* **mat foundation**.

rag bolt *See* **lewis bolt**.

rag felt An asphaltic felt consisting of rags saturated with asphalt, creating a waterproof composition for use on roofs, i.e., roofing paper and asphalt shingles.

raggle (reglet, raglin) A narrow channel or furrow in building stone for which metal flashing is fitted.

rag-rolled finish A decorative paint finish made by rolling a twisted rag over a wet paint surface so that portions of the undercoat show through. The effect can be simulated with a special paint roller.

ragstone Building stone quarried in thin blocks or slabs.

ragwork Courses of irregular stone masonry laid in a random pattern without parallel surfaces. The stones are roughly shaped with non-uniform joints. *See also* **random work**.

rail (1) A horizontal member supported by vertical posts, e.g., a handrail along a stairway. (2) A horizontal piece of wood, framed into vertical stiles, such as in a panelled door. (3) Track used to direct or control the path of a vehicle or device.

rail bead A bead on a flat, continuous surface. *See* **cock bead**.

rail fence A barrier or boundary constructed of rails and their supporting posts.

rail head (1) A loading point, or the nearest point of access to a railroad. (2) The farthest point on a railroad to which rails have been laid.

railing (1) A solid wood band around one or more edges of a plywood panel. (2) A *balustrade*.

rails (1) The horizontal members that form the outside frame of a door, including pieces used as a cross bracing between the top and bottom rails. (2) The horizontal members of a fence between posts. (3) The side pieces of a ladder to which rungs or steps are attached.

rail steel reinforcement Reinforcing bars hot-rolled from standard T-section rails.

Raimann patch (football patch) A patch, elliptical in shape, used to fill voids caused by defects in the veneers of plywood panels. The Raimann patch is one of the two patch designs allowed in A-grade faces.

rain cap A protective cover installed at the top of a roof vent to prevent rain from entering. Sometimes screened to keep out birds as well.

rain leader *See* **downspout**.

rainwet (1) Lumber that has excess moisture content because of exposure to rain after it was dried. (2) Surface lumber that has been stained or weathered by exposure to rain.

raised flooring system A floor constructed of removable panels supported by stringers allowing easy access to the space below.

raised girt (flush girt, raised girth) A stiffening member, parallel to and level with the floor joists, used to strengthen and protect.

raised grain A roughened condition on the surface of dressed lumber whereby the hard summerwood is raised above the softer springwood but not torn loose from it.

raised molding A molding not on the same level or plane as the wood member or assembly to which it is applied.

rake

raked joint

random ashlar

raised panel A panel that projects outward beyond the surrounding frame or wall.

raising hammer A hammer with a long head and a rounded face that is used in sheet metal work.

raising piece A piece of timber laid on top of a brick wall, or across posts of a timber-framed house, to support a beam or beams.

raising plate A horizontal timber carrying the feet of other structural members.

rake (1) To slant or incline from the vertical or horizontal. (2) A board or molding that is placed along the sloping edge of a frame *gable* to cover the edges of the siding. (3) A tool used to remove mortar from the face of a wall.

rake angle Angle attached to purlins at rake in order to attach end walls.

rake trim Flashing used to close gap between the roof and the end walls.

rake classifier Machine for separating coarse and fine particles of granular material temporarily suspended in water. The coarse particles settle to the bottom of a vessel and are scraped up an incline by a set of blades. The fine particles remain in suspension to be carried over the edge of the classifier.

raked joint A joint in a masonry wall that has the mortar raked out to a specified depth while it is still soft.

rake-out (raking out) An action for removing mortar an even distance from the face of a wall.

raker (1) A sloping brace for a *shore head*. (2) A tool for raking out decayed mortar from the joints of brickwork.

raking bond A bricklaying pattern that is created by arranging face brick diagonally or vertically, i.e.,

herringbone, basket weave, or diagonal.

raking course A course of bricks laid diagonally across faces of a brick wall for added strength.

raking flashing A parallel flashing used at the intersection of a chimney or other projection, with a sloping roof.

raking pile *See* **batter pile.**

raking riser A riser that is not vertical, but slopes away from the *nosing* for added foot room on the lower riser.

raking stretcher bond A bond in brickwork in which the vertical joint of each brick is displaced a small, fixed distance from the vertical joint of the brick below.

ram (1) A cylinder that contains a plunger instead of a piston and rod. (2) The plunger in a hydraulic press.

rammed earth A mixture of aggregate and water that has been compressed and dried.

ramming A form of heavy tamping of concrete, grout, or the like by means of a blunt tool forcibly applied. *See also* **dry pack, punning,** *and* **tamping.**

ramp A sloping surface to provide an easy connection between floors.

rampant vault A type of barrel vault exhibiting two quarters of different radii. The quarters have a common crown but the abutments are at different levels.

randle bar A rod horizontally assembled into the walls of an open chimney to which hooks are attached for hanging cooking pots and utensils.

random ashlar (random bond) Constitutes ashlar masonry in which stones are set without

random rubble

random shingle

ratchet

continuous joints, and appear to follow a random pattern, although a large pattern may be repeated. *See also* **ashlar**.

random course An ashlar or squared stonemasonry course of irregular height.

random lengths (RL) Lumber of various lengths. A random length loading is presumed to contain a fair representation of the lengths being produced by a specific manufacturer.

random line A surveyor's reference line laid between two points which are not visible from the other.

random paneling Board paneling of varying widths of the same grade and pattern. The term refers to plywood paneling grooved to represent random width paneling.

random range ashlar *See* **random work**.

random rubble Stonemasonry, built of rubble.

random shear A style of carpet that has only the higher loops sheared.

random shingle One of a number of shingles of the same length, but varying widths.

random widths Boards, lumber, and shingles of varying widths.

random work (1) A wall built of odd-sized stones. (2) Masonry of rectangular stone laid in broken courses by use of stones of different heights and widths.

range (1) A row or course of masonry. (2) A straight line of objects such as columns. (3) The difference between prices, costs, estimates, and bids. (4) The difference between the hot water temperature entering a cooling tower and the cold water leaving a cooling tower.

range closet A multi-seated latrine.

range-in (wiggling-in) The term used by a surveyor for the trial-and-error procedure of finding a previously established line.

ranger *See* **wale**.

range lines North-south lines used as reference points in the rectangular survey system, originally created to survey land in the U.S. public domain. *See* **rectangular survey system**.

range rod (range pole) A device that consists of a pole 7' to 8' long, equipped with a metal point. It is painted alternately red and white in bands one foot wide. The pole is used by surveyors for locating points of reference.

range work In masonry, squared-off blocks of building stone laid in horizontal courses.

ranging bond Small strips of wood at the face of a masonry wall, usually laid in joints and projecting slightly; used to provide a nailing surface for furring and battens.

rapid-curing asphalt A liquid composed of asphalt, cement, and a highly volatile diluent such as naphtha or gasoline.

rapid-curing cutback *See* **rapid-curing asphalt**.

rapid-hardening cement A high-early-strength cement.

rapid-start fluorescent lamp A fluorescent lamp designed for operation with a ballast that provides a low-voltage winding to preheat the electrodes and initiate the arc without a starting switch or the application of high voltage.

rasp A file with projecting teeth for rough work.

ratchet A mechanism with a hinged catch, or pawl, that slides over and

rawl plug

locks behind sloped teeth on a gear or rod, allowing motion in one direction only.

ratchet brace A carpenter's clamp used in confined spaces where a full turn of the brace cannot be achieved. It is fitted with a pawl mechanism allowing the bit to be rotated while in the hole.

ratchet drill A hand-operated drill that works with a hinged catch engaging on a wheel or chuck.

rated lamp life The average life of a particular lamp fixture.

rated load The overall weight that a piece of machinery is designed to carry.

rated speed The speed at which a piece of machinery is designed to operate with an appropriate load.

ratio The relative size of two quantities expressed as one divided by the other.

rat patching Filling holes or voids with caulking, concrete, or other materials to prevent vermin from entering a structure.

rat stop A barrier in a masonry wall to prevent rats from burrowing down along the exterior of a masonry wall.

rat-tail file A file with a circular cross section that tapers to a small diameter at the end opposite the handle.

rattrap bond A bond in brickwork in which *headers* and *stretchers* are alternated and laid on edge on each face, creating a wall of two brick *wythes* (leaves) thick with a series of cavities between strechers.

raummeter (stere) A German term for one cubic meter of stacked wood.

raveling A term used for the progressive deterioration of asphalt pavement. The aggregate dislodges and becomes fragmented.

raw linseed oil Linseed oil that has been refined, but has not received further processing such as boiling, blowing, or bodying.

rawl plug A short fiber cylinder with a lead lining, driven into a hole in wood, masonry, glass, plaster, tile, concrete, or other materials to receive and hold a screw.

raw material A material used for the construction or manufacture of goods or products.

raw mix Blend of raw materials, ground to desired fineness, correctly proportioned, and blended ready for burning, such as that used in the manufacture of cement clinker.

raw water (1) Water that requires treatment before it can be used, such as water for steam generation. (2) Any water used in ice making except distilled water. (3) Water used strictly for cooling such as river water or sea water at a nuclear generating plant.

rays, wood The radial cells (rings) within a tree. They create a distinctive pattern in some quartersawn woods, such as oak.

raze To tear down, demolish, or level to ground.

RCRA Facility Assessment (RFA) A site investigation, regulated under RCRA, that is used to determine the nature and extent of contamination at a particular location.

RCRA Facility Investigation/ Corrective Measures Study A combined project that includes both the RFI and CMS as a single integrated activity. *See* **Resource Conservation and Recovery Act**.

RDX (Cyclotrimethylenetrinitramine) An explosive commonly encountered in unexploded ordnance sites.

reactance Opposition to alternating current (AC) by capacitance or inductance or both. It is expressed in ohms, and symbolized by X.

reaction Resistive forces acting on a structural member that serve to hold it stable.

reactivated carbon Carbon that has been used for volatile organic compound adsorption, which is then treated for reuse.

reactive aggregate Aggregate containing substances capable of reacting chemically with the products of solution or hydration of the Portland cement in concrete or mortar, under ordinary conditions of exposure, resulting in harmful expansion, cracking, or staining.

reactive silica material Several types of materials that react at high temperatures with Portland cement or lime during autoclaving, including pulverized silica, natural pozzolan, and fly ash.

reactivity The propensity of one substance to chemically react with another.

ready-mixed concrete Concrete manufactured for delivery to a purchaser in a plastic and unhardened state. *See also* **concrete, ready-mixed, central-mixed concrete, shrink-mixed concrete,** *and* **transit-mixed concrete**.

reagent A substance used in analysis and synthesis of chemical reactions.

real estate Property in the form of land and all improvements such as buildings and paving.

realignment A change in the horizontal layout of a highway, may also affect vertical alignment.

real property (real estate) Land and anything growing on the land, or constructed on it, such as buildings, stone walls, fences, driveways, garages, underground swimming pools, trees, shrubs, and gardens. Real property also includes *fixtures*, or items that are permanently affixed to real property, such as light fixtures, oil burners, fuse boxes, and plumbing. Real property does not include things that are grown on the land for the purpose of being sold, such as crops, or trees from a tree farm. Such products that are to be severed from real property and sold are treated as *goods*.

ream To enlarge or smooth a hole using a reamer.

reamer A bit with sharp, spiral, fluted, cutting edges along the shaft which may be slightly tapered. Used to enlarge drilled holes or remove burrs from the inside of pipe.

rear arch An arch forming a true opening and faced by a larger arch for decoration.

reasonable care and skill *See* **due care**.

reasonable cost A cost that would be incurred by an ordinarily prudent person in the conduct of competitive business.

rebar Short for reinforcing bar.

rebate Discount, deduction, or refund of money.

rebound Aggregate and cement or wet shotcrete that bounces away from a surface against which it is being projected.

rebound hammer An apparatus providing a rapid indication of the strength of concrete based on the distance of rebound of a spring-driven missile.

rebutted and rejointed (R&R) Shingles with edges machine-trimmed to be exactly parallel and butts retrimmed at precisely right angles for use primarily in sidewall applications.

receptacle

recessed fixture

recessed pointing

receipt of bids The official action of an owner in receiving sealed bids that have been invited or advertised in accordance with the owner's intention to award a contract for construction.

receiver A tank to hold fluids or gases, as on an air compressor.

receptacle A contact device installed in an electric outlet box for the connection of portable equipment or appliances.

receptacle outlet An electric outlet with one or more receptacles.

receptacle plug A device, usually attached to a flexible chord, that is inserted in a receptacle to connect portable equipment or appliances to an electric circuit.

receptor The shallow basin in the floor of a shower.

recessed fixture A lamp fixture the bottom edge of which is flush with the finish surface.

recessed head A specially constructed mechanical fastener that is designed to fit flush into the surface.

recessed pointing A type of joint where the mortar is kept back approximately 1/4″ from the face of the wall. This particular joint protects the mortar from peeling.

recharging (1) The replenishment of ground water through direct injection or infiltration from trenches outside the area. (2) The replenishment of electric energy in a storage battery.

reciprocal leveling A surveying technique used in leveling across streams, gullies, and other obstructions. To eliminate instrumental errors, levels are taken from two setups, one near each point.

reciprocating chiller (reciprocating compressor) Single-acting compressor using pistons that are driven by a connecting rod from a crankshaft.

reciprocating compressor An air compressor using a piston to compress the air, and employing valves for intake and discharge. *See also* **rotary compressor.**

reciprocating drill *See* **push drill.**

reciprocating engine A steam or internal-combustion engine with cylinders and pistons as opposed to a turbine.

reciprocating pump A water pump using a piston(s) for intake and discharge. Depending upon valve arrangement, the pump can be either single- or double-acting.

reciprocating saw A saw operated in a back and forth or up and down motion extending from an engine or other power source, e.g., a saber saw.

recirculated air Return air that is reconditioned and distributed once again, as opposed to makeup air.

recloser Device that protects a power system from service interruption by automatically opening and closing as overcurrents (short circuits) are detected. They detect the fault, close and reset to open the line, often more than once. It clears the fault and re-energize the distribution line.

reconditioned wood Hardwood lumber steam-dried to correct defects that occurred during the original curing, such as collapse or warp.

reconstruction The process of depicting (by means of new construction) the form, features and detailing of a non-surviving site, landscape, structure or object for the purpose of replicating its appearance at a specific period of time, and in its historic location.

record drawings Construction drawings updated to show the progress of the work, usually based on data furnished by the contractor to the designer.

record of decision (ROD) An agreement between the site owner(s) and other responsible parties and the regulators that stipulates the remedial action requirements, schedule, and cost sharing for cleanup.

record sheet A sheet or form that preserves the memory of events.

recovery peg A temporary surveying marker of known location and elevation, used to reestablish a permanent marker that is to be replaced.

rectangular survey system A land survey system using longitude and latitude geographical coordinates. Established by the U.S. government, it is also called government survey system.

rectangular tie A piece of bent heavy wire in the shape of a rectangle used as a wall tie.

rectifier An electrical device that converts alternating current(AC) to direct current (DC).

recycled concrete Hardened concrete that is crushed to be used as aggregate.

red alder *Alnus rubra*. See **alder**.

red cedar *See* **western red cedar, incense cedar,** *and* **eastern red cedar.**

red fir An archaic description of Douglas fir lumber made from smaller, younger timber principally from the coast range and southern Oregon. *See also* **California red fir.**

red knot A slang term for a knot caused by cutting through a live pine branch.

red label A grade of shingle between blue label #1 and black label #5, graded by the Red Cedar Shingle and Handsplit Shake Bureau.

red lead A compound of lead used in paints to improve the anticorrosive properties of the paint used on steel and iron.

red meranti *Shorea* species. Any of a number of tropical hardwoods, mainly used as veneers, such as lauan.

red oak *Quercus rubra* and others, such as southern red oak.

red oxide A pigment used in paints to prevent rusting and corrosion.

red pine (Norway pine) *Pinus resinosa.* This species is found in the Great Lakes states, the northeastern U.S., and eastern Canada. The wood is used for general construction and for remanufacturing into such items as sash, molding, flooring, and crating.

redress (1) Financial compensation for a loss caused by the actions of another. (2) To set right, remedy, or rectify.

red rot An early stage of decay.

redry To turn material to a dry kiln or veneer dryer for additional drying when the material is found to have a higher moisture content level than desired.

red silver fir (Pacific silver fir) *Abies amabilis.*

red spruce (eastern spruce) *Picea rubens.* This species is found in southeastern Canada, the New England states, and along the Appalachian Mountains as far south as North Carolina. In addition to general construction

reducer

reducing joint

reducing pipe fitting

reeding

applications, the wood is often used for such products as ladder rails and as a source of pulpwood.

red stripe Fungi that have entered cracks in wood and caused decay.

reducer (1) A solvent used in paints to reduce the viscosity of the paint. (2) A pipe fitting, larger at one end than at the other. A reducing coupling. (3) A substance that chemically reacts with another by removing an oxygen atom from the chemical structure of the second substance. (4) A pipe coupling with a larger size at one end than the other. The larger size is designated first. Reducers are threaded, flanged, welded, etc. Reducing couplings are available in either eccentric or concentric configurations.

reducing joint The connecting joint of unequally sized electrical conductors.

reducing pipe fitting Fitting that is constructed to facilitate the joining of unequally sized pipes.

reduct A small piece of material cut from a larger piece to make the larger piece uniform or symmetrical.

reduction of area The difference between the original cross-sectional area of a tensile specimen and the smallest area after rupture, expressed as a percentage of the original area.

redundant power An extra power source. It may be a complete second power system or a just an additional generator. Duplicate power service allows users to switch large amounts of a building's power load to another system.

redwood *Sequoia sempervirens*. This species is found only in limited areas of northern California and southern Oregon. It is resistant to decay and is used for many of the same purposes as cedar, especially siding and paneling. Another species of redwood, *Sequoia gigantea*, grows in the Sierra mountains of central California. It is protected from harvest.

Redwood Inspection Service One of seven regional grading agencies in North America that are authorized to write and publish grading rules for lumber. *See also* **grade stamp**.

reed switch Two or more highly conductive reeds inside a glass container. The reeds open or close together in response to a magnetic field.

reeding A decorative molding with several parallel half-round moldings.

reentrant angle An internal angle of usually less than 90°.

reeving (1) Threading a rope through the blocks to assemble a block and tackle. (2) Threading or placing a pulling or control line.

reference line A series of two or more points in line to serve as a reference for measurements.

reference mark A supplementary mark close to a survey station. One or more such marks are located and recorded with sufficient accuracy so that the original station can be reestablished from the references.

reference standards Professionally prepared generic specifications and technical data compiled and published by competent organizations generally recognized and accepted by the construction industry. These standards are sometimes used as criteria by which the acceptability and/or performance of a product, material, assembly, or piece of equipment can be judged.

reference standard specification
A type of nonproprietary specification that relies on accepted reference standards to describe a product, material, assembly, or piece of equipment to be incorporated into a project.

referendum A special election subdivision of municipal law that establishes public approval (e.g., for elected officials to sell general obligation bonds as a means of financing a public project).

refill tube A tube in toilets that sends water from the ballcock into an overflow tube to refill the bowl after a siphon break.

reflectance The ratio of light reflected from a surface to the light incident on the surface. Reflectances are often used for lighting calculations. The reflectance of a dark carpet is around 20%, and a clean white wall is roughly 50% to 60%.

reflected glass Glass with a special metallic coating used to repel light and radiant heat.

reflected plan A plan of an upper surface, such as a ceiling projected downward.

reflection The return from a material's surfaces of light or sound waves.

reflection cracking The occurrence of cracks in overlays and toppings that coincide with the location of cracks in the base slab.

reflective insulation A thermal material having one or both faces metallically coated to reflect the radiant energy that strikes its surface.

reflector A device used to redirect light or sound energy by the process of reflection.

reflector lamp An incandescent lamp in which a part of the bulb acts as a reflector.

reflux valve *See* **check valve**.

refraction The change in path of a light ray or energy wave as it passes obliquely from one medium to another.

refractories Materials, usually nonmetallic, used to withstand high temperatures.

refractoriness In refractories, the property of being resistant to softening or deformation at high temperatures.

refractory Resistant to high temperatures.

refractory aggregate Materials having refractory properties that form a refractory body when bound together into a conglomerate mass by a matrix.

refractory brick A brick manufactured for high temperature use.

refractory cement A high temperature bonding material used in furnaces, consisting of crushed brick and diatomaceous earth.

refractory concrete Concrete having refractory properties and suitable for use at high temperatures, generally about 315 °C to 1315 °C, in which the binding agent is a hydraulic cement.

refractory insulating concrete Refractory concrete having low thermal conductivity.

refrigerant The medium used to absorb heat in a cooling cycle.

refrigerant charge The quantity of refrigerant in a refrigeration system.

refrigerant compressor unit A unit consisting of a pump with various controls for regulating refrigerant flow.

register

reglet

regressed luminaire

reinforced blockwork

refrigeration cycle
A thermodynamic process whereby a refrigerant accepts and rejects heat in a repetitive sequence.

refrigeration system A system in which a refrigerant is compressed, condensed, and expanded as a means of removing heat from a cold reservoir. The heat is rejected elsewhere at a higher temperature.

refrigerator A container or space and the machinery for cooling it.

refusal The depth at which a pile cannot be driven any deeper.

regenerative heating The use of heat rejected from one part of the heating cycle and transfered to another part.

register An opening to a room or space for the passage of conditioned air. The register has a grill and a damper for flow regulation.

registered architect *See* **architect**.

reglet A groove in a wall to receive flashing.

reglette Surveyor's measuring device graduated down to hundredths of a foot.

regrating The cleaning of masonry by removing the outer layer, leaving a fresh stone surface.

regressed luminaire A *luminaire* mounted above a ceiling with its opening above the ceiling line.

regulated-set cement A Portland cement with admixtures for the purpose of controlling its set and early strength.

regulated unit The term for any surface impoundment, waste pile, land treatment unit, or landfill that received waste after July 26, 1982.

regulation The ability of a ballast to hold constant (or nearly constant) the output watts (light output) during fluctuations in the voltage

feeding of the ballast. Normally specified as +/– percent change in output compared to +/– percent change in input.

regulator (1) A device that maintains an appropriate rate of release of pressurized substances. (2) An electronically controlled device that regulates system voltage.

regulatory Related to provisions specified in a regulation implementing a law.

regulus metal *See* **antimonial lead**.

rehabilitation (rehab) The process of making possible a compatible use for a property through repair, alternations and additions, while preserving those portions or features which convey what have been determined to be important cultural or architectural values.

reheat coil A coil in an air supply duct, used to control the temperature of air being supplied to individual spaces or a group of spaces.

reheating The heating of return air in an air-conditioning system for reuse.

reimbursement expenses Amounts expended for, or on account of, a project that are to be reimbursed by the owner in accordance with the terms of the appropriate agreement.

reinforced bitumen felt A light roofing felt saturated with bitumen and reinforced with jute cloth.

reinforced blockwork Masonry blockwork with reinforcing steel and grout placed in the voids to resist tensile, compressive, or shear stresses.

reinforced brick masonry Brick masonry in which steel reinforcement is placed.

reinforcement

reinforcement, helical

reinforcement, hoop

reinforced cames Lead bars with a steel core for reinforcing, used in leaded lights.

reinforced concrete Concrete containing adequate reinforcement, prestressed or not prestressed, and designed on the assumption that the two materials (steel and concrete) act together in resisting forces. *See also* **plain concrete**.

reinforced concrete masonry Concrete masonry construction in which steel reinforcement is so embedded that the materials act together in resisting tensile, compressive, and/or shear stresses.

reinforced masonry Unit masonry construction in which steel reinforcement is so embedded that the materials act together in resisting tensile, compressive, and/or shear stresses. *See also* **masonry unit**.

reinforced plastic Plastic that has components added to it, such as glass fiber, to increase its strength and stiffness.

reinforced T-beam A concrete T-beam strengthened internally with steel rods to resist tensile and/or shear stresses.

reinforcement Bars, wires, strands, and other slender members embedded in concrete in such a manner that the reinforcement and the concrete act together in resisting forces.

reinforcement, cold-drawn wire Steel wire made from rods that have been hot-rolled from billets and cold-drawn through a die used for concrete reinforcement of small diameter such as in gauges not less than 2 mm nor greater than 16 mm.

reinforcement, cold-worked steel Steel bars or wires which have been rolled, twisted, or drawn at normal ambient temperatures.

reinforcement displacement Movement of reinforcing steel from its specified position in the forms.

reinforcement, distribution bar Small-diameter bars, usually at right angles to the main reinforcement, intended to spread a concentrated load on a slab and to prevent cracking.

reinforcement, dowel bar *See* **dowel**.

reinforcement, expanded metal fabric *See* **expanded metal**.

reinforcement, four-way A system of reinforcement in flat slab construction comprising bands of bars parallel to two adjacent edges and also to both diagonals of a rectangular slab.

reinforcement, helical Steel reinforcement of hot-rolled bar or cold-drawn wire fabricated into a helix, more commonly known as spiral reinforcement. Used in round columns.

reinforcement, high-strength Concrete reinforcing bars having a minimum yield of 60,000 psi or 414 MPa.

reinforcement, hoop A one-piece closed tie or continuously wound tie not less than #3 in size, the ends of which have a standard 135° bend with a 10-bar-diameter extension, that encloses the longitudinal reinforcement in a column.

reinforcement, lateral Usually applied to ties, hoops, and spirals in columns or column-like members.

reinforcement, mesh *See* **welded-wire fabric** *and* **welded-wire fabric reinforcement**.

reinforcement, principal Elements or configurations of reinforcement that provide the main resistance of reinforced concrete to tensile loads borne by structural components. *See also* **reinforcement, secondary**.

reinforcement, two-way

Main Ribs
Letter or Symbol for Producing Mill
Bar Size
Type Steel
Grade Mark
Grade Line One Line Only

H • 11 • S

• H
• 11
• S
• 60

reinforcing bar

reinforcement ratio Ratio of the effective area of the reinforcement to the effective area of the concrete at any section of a structural member. *See also* **percentage of reinforcement**.

reinforcement, secondary Reinforcement other than main reinforcement.

reinforcement, spiral *See* **spiral reinforcement**.

reinforcement, transverse Reinforcement at right angles to the longitudinal reinforcement. Transverse may be main or secondary reinforcement.

reinforcement, twin-twisted bar Two bars of the same nominal diameter twisted together.

reinforcement, two-way Reinforcement arranged in bands of bars at right angles to each other.

reinforcement, welded Reinforcement joined together by welding.

reinforcing bar A steel bar, usually with manufactured deformations, used in concrete and masonry construction to provide additional strength.

reinforcing plate An added plate used to strengthen a member or part of a member.

reinforcing rod *See* **reinforcing bar**.

reinforcing steel *See* **reinforcing bar**.

reinforcing tape A tape that is used to hide and strengthen joints between drywall sheets.

reinforcing unit A box-shaped reinforcement in a hollow metal door that houses a bored lock and that provides supports for the latch.

rejection of work The act of rejecting work that is defective, or that which does not conform to contractually agreed upon requirements.

relamping The replacement of lamps (bulbs) in light fixtures. May be done as each fails, or may be done on a schedule.

relaskop A patented instrument used by foresters to measure tree heights and/or slope gradients by trigonometric means.

related trades The different building trades required to complete a project.

relative compaction The dry density of soil expressed as a percentage of the density of the soil after a standard compaction test.

relative humidity The ratio of the quantity of water vapor actually present to the amount present in a saturated atmosphere at a given temperature, expressed as a percentage.

relative settlement *See* **differential settlement**.

relaxation of steel Decrease in stress in steel as a result of creep within the steel under prolonged strain, or as a result of decreased strain of the steel, such as results from shrinkage and creep of the concrete in a prestressed concrete unit.

relay An electromagnetic or electromechanical device using small currents and voltages to activate switches or other secondary devices.

release agent Material used to prevent bonding of concrete to a surface, such as to forms. *See also* **bond breaker**.

release of lien The act of releasing a person's or entity's mechanics lien against a property. *See also* **mechanic's lien** *and* **waiver of lien**.

release paper A protective film, coated lightly on one side with adhesive, used to protect a surface during shipment and installation.

relief valve

relief (1) Carved or embossed decoration raised above a background plane. (2) The representation of elevations of the earth's surface, usually referenced to a mean-sea-level datum plane, by means of contour lines.

relief angle Structural angle introduced to help support masonry over an opening or at specified elevations or multistory construction.

relief cut An initial cut made to keep the saw from binding when a curved section is about to be cut.

relief damper A damper in an air-conditioning system which opens automatically at a set pressure differential to balance pressures in a building.

relief holes Several holes drilled into rock in a line to aid in the fracture of the rock along that line.

relief map A map showing relief by means of contour lines, shading, tinting, or relief models.

relief valve A pressure-activated valve held closed by string tension and designed to automatically relieve pressure in excess of its setting.

relief vent An auxiliary vent that is supplementary to regular vent pipes. The primary purpose is to provide supplementary circulation of air between drainage and vent pipes.

relish In carpentry, the shoulder around or at the side of a tenon.

reluctance The opposition a material offers to magnetic force.

rem (Rad equivalent man) These are units used to measure radiation as it affects humans.

remedial action A permanent remedy taken instead of, or in addition to, a removal action that is in response to a release or threatened release of hazardous substances.

remedial design The phase of the site remediation process in which remedial technologies and processes are designed prior to installation.

Remedial Investigation/Feasibility Study (RI/FS) The phase of the site remediation process in which the nature of contaminants is determined and a remedial remedy is selected. It is a site investigation and cleanup selection process that includes activities such as project scoping, data collection, risk assessment, treatability studies, analysis of alternatives, and remedy selection.

remedies The manner in which a breach of contract is settled by a court or arbitrators.

remodeling Making alterations to an existing structure such that it will be better suited to current needs. This type of work may involve changing the use of interior space by repositioning walls, replacing bathroom or kitchen fixtures, or other such modifications. Remodeling projects generally incorporate new replacement materials, and are not concerned with maintaining historic authenticity.

remoldability The readiness with which freshly mixed concrete responds to a remolding effort such as jigging or vibration, causing it to reshape its mass around reinforcement and to conform to the shape of the form. *See also* **flow**.

remolding test A test to measure remoldability.

remote-control circuit An electrical circuit that controls another circuit by means of a relay device.

removable mullion A door mullion that can be removed from a door

rendering

repetitive member

frame to allow passage of oversized objects.

removable stop A removable molding or trim used to stop motion and permit the installation of windowpanes or doors.

removal action A short-term action in response to a release of hazardous substances that might present an imminent and substantial danger to human health or to the environment.

repeat The distance between repetitions of identical patterns on wallpaper.

render (1) To shade an architectural or machine drawing to give it a more real-life appearance. (2) To apply plaster, especially the first coat, directly to brickwork or other masonry.

rendered brickwork Brickwork that has a waterproof material applied to the face.

rendering (1) The application, by means of a trowel or float, of a coat of mortar. (2) A drawing of a project or a portion of a project that delineates materials, shades, and shadows.

renovation Modernizing the elements within a structure to meet current functional and aesthetic requirements. Renovation work may also be considered remodeling or adaptive reuse.

repeatability Variability among replicate test results obtained on the same material within a single laboratory by one operator. Repeatability is a quantity that will be exceeded in only about 5% of the repetitions by the difference, taken in absolute value, of two randomly selected test results obtained in the same laboratory on a given material. In use of the term, all variable factors should be specified.

repeater A device that can receive a weak one-way or two-way communications signal, amplify or reshape it, and retransmit it. In digital transmission, a weak pulse train of discrete signals is received, amplified, retimed, and reconstructed for delivery back to the source. In fiber optics, a low-power light signal is converted electronically and retransmitted via a light-emitting diode or laser light source.

repeating theodolite A theodolite designed so that an angle can be turned several times; and successive angle measurement accumulated, with the final reading representative of the accumulations.

repetitive member One of a series of framing or supporting members such as joists, studs, planks, or decking that are continuous, or spaced not more than 24 inches apart; and are joined by floor, roof, or other load-distributing elements. In repetitive-member framing, each member is connected to, and receives some shared support from, the others.

replacement cost coverage Type of insurance that guarantees that the insurance company will pay to replace the damaged property with new property (depreciation will not be deducted).

replacement value The estimated cost to replace an existing building based on current construction costs.

repointing *See* **pointing**.

reporting form *See* **property insurance**.

reposting *See* **reshoring**.

reproducibility Variability among replicate test results obtained on the same material in different laboratories. Variability is a quantity that will be exceeding in

residence casement

resilient channel

only about 5% of the repetitions by the difference, taken in absolute value, of two single test results made on the same material in two different, randomly selected laboratories. In use of the term, all variable factors should be specified. *See also* **repeatability**.

reproductive toxin A substance that chemically or biologically interferes with the reproductive process; a teratogen.

request for payment *See* **application for payment**.

request for proposals (RFP) Material provided to potential contractors to communicate government requirements and solicit proposals.

re-rod Steel rods used to reinforce concrete or block.

resaw (1) To saw a piece of lumber along its horizontal axis. (2) A band saw that performs such an operation.

resawn board A piece of lumber, most commonly 11/16″ thick, obtained by resawing a piece of 6/4 common. Used mostly for sheathing and industrial applications. Produced most often from ponderosa pine and white fir.

resawn lumber Lumber that has been sawn on a horizontal axis to produce two thinner pieces. *See also* **resawn board**.

resealing trap A trap connected to a plumbing fixture drainpipe so constructed as to allow the rate of flow to seal the trap without causing self-siphonage.

reservoir A tank or receptacle used for the accumulation and retention of a fluid.

reset program *See* **load reset program**.

resetting (of forms) Setting of forms separately for each successive

lift of a wall to avoid offsets at construction joints.

reshoring The construction operation whereby the original shoring or posting is removed and replaced in such a manner as to avoid deflection of the shored element or damage to partially cured concrete.

residence casement A window sash that opens outwards. Used in homes, hotels, and commercial buildings.

resident engineer An engineer retained by the owner as a representative on the construction site. Frequently used on governmental projects. *See also* **owner's inspector** *and* **clerk of the works**.

residential occupancy Occupancy of a building in which sleeping accommodations are provided for normal residential purposes. The term excludes institutional occupancy.

resident inspector *See* **owner's inspector, resident engineer,** *and* **project representative**.

residual deflection The amount of deviation that remains after an applied load has been removed.

residual soil Soil formed by the aging of the subsurface mineral material.

residual stress The stress remaining in a member after an applied force has been removed.

residual tack *See* **aftertack**.

resilience The work done per unit volume of a material in producing strain.

resilient channel A mounting device with flexible connectors used for fastening gypsum board to studs or joists. Helps reduce the transmission of vibrations.

resilient clip

resilient clip A flexible metal device for mounting gypsum board to studs or joists; used to reduce noise and vibrations.

resilient flooring A manufactured interior floor covering material, in either sheet or tile form, that is resilient.

resin (1) A natural or synthetic solid, or semisolid organic material of indefinite and often high molecular weight having a tendency to flow under stress. It usually has a softening or melting range and fractures conchoidally. (2) A natural vegetable substance occurring in various plants and trees, especially the coniferous species, used in varnishes, inks, medicines, plastic products, and adhesives.

resin chipboard A particle board which uses a resin to ensure a uniform consistency.

resin-emulsion paint Paint with a vehicle consisting of an oil, oleo-resinous varnish, or resin binder dispersed in water.

resin mortar (or concrete) *See* **polymer concrete**.

resin treated wood *See* **compregnated wood** *and* **compressed wood**.

resistance *See* **electrical resistance**.

resistance brazing A process in which coalescence is produced by the heat obtained from the resistance of the work to the flow of an electrical current.

resistance welding A process creating a metallurgical bond between metal by producing heat obtained from the resistance offered by the work to the flow of electric current, and by the application of an external pressure.

resistor A device included in an electric circuit to introduce a desired resistance.

resolve Use of a microscope to distinguish between different objects.

resonance A condition reached in an electrical or mechanical system when the applied load frequency coincides and is equal to the natural undamped frequency of the system.

resonator (1) A device that intensifies vibration and volume, usually of sound waves. (2) A hollow metal container that is utilized to create microwaves.

resorcinol adhesive A bonding material that is workable and water soluble for two to four hours. After this, it becomes insoluble and chemically resistant.

resorcinol resin adhesive A synthetic resin adhesive made with resorcinol-formaldehyde resin using a hardener, usually composed of wood flour and paraform. The adhesive provides an exterior quality glueline and will cure at room temperature. It is used in the manufacture of laminated beams or scarf joints.

Resource Conservation and Recovery Act (RCRA) The primary federal law that governs hazardous and toxic materials at operating facilities. It defines solid and hazardous waste, authorizes the EPA to set standards for facilities that generate or manage hazardous waste, and establishes a permit program for hazardous treatment, storage, and facilities.

respirator A device used to facilitate breathing in a hazardous atmosphere.

respond A support, usually a pilaster or corbel, attached to a wall and supporting one end of an arch, groin, or vault rib.

retaining walls

responsibility A bidder's ability to properly perform the contract work.

responsible bidder *See* **lowest responsible bidder**.

responsiveness The bid's conformance with the solicitation's salient requirements (price, quantity, quality, performance time).

rest bend A right-angle pipe fitting with an integral seat for mounting on a support. *See also* **base elbow**.

restitution A court-ordered money award that is intended to restore the parties to their financial position as it existed before the contract was formed.

restoration Returning an existing property to a condition that depicts its form, features and character as they appeared at a particular period of time. Restoration may involve removal of features from other periods in the property's history and reconstruction of missing features from the targeted period. (Where a building has been changed over time or additional structural elements added, the period chosen for the restoration is usually the one that reflects the highest level of aesthetics or historical significance.) Wherever possible, the materials and methods used to perform the restoration should match those originally used to build the structure. Limited and sensitive upgrading of mechanical, electrical and plumbing systems (and other code-required work) is appropriate within a restoration project.

restraint (of concrete) Restriction of free movement of fresh or hardened concrete following completion of placing in formwork or molds, or within an otherwise confined space. This restraint can be internal or external and may act in one or more directions.

restricted Relative to electrical systems, it refers to areas classifed hazardous; or a confined area.

restricted list of bidders *See* **invited bidders**.

restrictive covenant An agreement between individuals, incorporated within a deed, which stipulates how land can be used. The constraints may include: the specific use to which property may be put, setback of buildings, size of yards, locations and dimensions of fences, and type of architecture. Racial and religious restrictions on inhabitants are not legally enforceable.

resurfacing The placing of a new surface on an existing pavement to improve its conformation or increase its strength.

retainage A specific portion of the contract sum that is withheld from progress payments as specified in the owner-contractor agreement.

retained percentage *See* **retainage**.

retaining wall (1) A structure used to sustain the pressure of the earth behind it. (2) Any wall subjected to lateral pressure other than wind pressure.

retardation Reduction in the rate of hardening or setting, i.e., an increase in the time required to reach initial and final set or to develop early strength of fresh concrete, mortar, or grout. *See also* **retarder**.

retarder An admixture which delays the setting of cement paste, and hence of mixtures such as mortar- or concrete-containing cement.

retempering Addition of water and remixing of concrete or mortar that has lost its workability and become too stiff. This is not usually recommended, as some of the strength is lost. *See also* **tempering**.

return bend

return corner block

retention (1) A percentage, usually 10%, withheld from a periodic payment to a contractor, in accordance with the owner-contractor agreement, for work completed. The retention is held until all terms of the contract have been fulfilled. (2) The amount of preservative, fire-retardant treatment, or resin retained by treated or impregnated wood.

retention time The length of time a wastewater is retained in a clarification tank for settling of suspended solids.

retentivity The capacity of a material to hold magnetism.

reticulated Covered with crossing lines, netted.

reticuline bar Sinuously bent bars that interconnect adjacent bearing bars in a grating.

retort A vessel used to treat wood by applying various chemicals under pressure.

retract The mechanism on a dipper shovel bucket excavator that moves the bucket.

retrofit To modify an existing structure or system within the structure to accommodate upgrading.

return The continuation, in a different direction, of a molding or projection, usually at right angles.

return-air Air returned from a conditioned room or space for processing and recirculation.

return-air intake An opening, usually with a control damper, through which return air reenters an air-conditioning system.

return bend A 180° bend in a pipe.

return corner block A concrete masonry unit with a plane surface at one end as well as the front face; used at outside corners.

return grille The grille on a return air intake, usually employing a damper.

return mains Pipes or ducts that reroute fluid or air back to the supply source.

return pipe The drain line that returns the water from condensed heating steam to the boiler for reuse.

return system A series of ducts, pipes, or passages that returns a substance, whether it be air or water, to the source for reuse.

return wall A short wall placed perpendicular to the end of a wall to increase its stability.

revalé Stone molding that is carved after being set in place.

reveal (1) The side of an opening in a wall for a window or door. (2) Reveal is the depth of exposure of aggregate in an exposed aggregate finish. *See also* **exposed-aggregate finish**.

reveal pin (reveal tie) A screw or clamp located inside a window opening used to secure scaffolding to the opening.

revent pipe An individual vent that connects directly to a waste fixture and the main or branch vent pipe.

reverse In plastering, a template with the reverse shape of the molding it is intended to match.

reverse-acting controllers Devices that decrease control pressure as the control variable (temperature, pressure) increases.

reverse-acting diaphragm valve A valve that opens on application of pressure on a diaphragm and closes when the pressure is released.

reverse-acting thermostat A thermostat that activates a circuit when a preset high temperature is detected.

rheostat

rib

ribbed panel

reverse bevel A latch bolt that is inclined or sloped in the opposite direction of a regular bolt.

reverse board & batten A siding pattern in which the wider boards are nailed over the battens, producing a narrow inset.

reverse-trap water closet Toilet that has a siphonic trapway at the rear of the bowl and integral flushing action.

reversed door *See* **reverse-swing door**.

reverse-swing door (reversed door) A door that swings outward from a room.

reversible grating A framework of bars that can be installed with either side exposed without affecting the load capabilities or appearance.

reversible lock A lock that can be adapted to fit a door of either hand.

reversible siding Resawn board siding that may be installed with either the surfaced or sawn side exposed.

reversion (1) The tendency of a processed material to return to its original state. (2) Chemical reaction leading to deterioration of a sealant due to moisture trapped behind the sealant.

revertible flue A flue or chimney that momentarily redirects the gas flow path downward during its normal upward ascent.

revet To face a foundation or embankment with a layer of stone, concrete, or other suitable material.

revetment Facing, such as masonry, used to support an embankment.

revibration One or more applications of vibration to concrete after completion of placing and initial compaction, but preceding initial setting of the concrete.

revolving door An exterior door consisting of four leaves set at right angles to each other and revolving on a central pivot. Used to limit the passage of air through the opening and eliminate drafts.

revolving shelf *See* **lazy susan**.

revolving shovel Earthmoving equipment with the shovel able to rotate independently of its support.

rheology The science dealing with flow of materials, including studies of deformation of hardened concrete, the handling and placing of freshly mixed concrete, and the behavior of slurries, pastes, and the like.

rheostat An electric resistor, so constructed that its resistance may be varied without opening the circuit in which it is installed. Used to control the flow of electric current as in a light dimmer.

rib (1) One of a number of parallel structural members backing sheathing. (2) The portion of a T-beam which projects below the slab. (3) In deformed reinforcing bars, the deformations or the longitudinal parting ridge.

riband (ribband) *See* **ribbon strip**.

ribbed panel A panel composed of a thin slab reinforced by a system of ribs in one or two directions, usually orthogonal.

ribbed slab *See* **ribbed panel**.

ribbed vault A vault with ribs that support, or appear to support, the web of the vault.

ribbing (crimping, washboarding) A more-or-less regular corrugation of the surface of wood, caused by differential shrinkage.

ridgeboard

ridgecap

ridging

ribbing up   Circular joinery made by gluing several layers of veneer with a parallel grain structure.

ribbon   A narrow strip of wood or other material used in formwork.

ribbon board   (1) A horizontal brace used in balloon framing where the board is applied to notches in the studs. (2) A *let-in brace*.

ribbon course   A rugged roof texture that can be achieved by applying a triple thickness of asphalt shingles on alternate courses. This feature adds visual appeal and is especially suited for large roof areas of a long one-story building.

ribbon loading   Method of batching concrete whereby the solid ingredients, and sometimes the water, enter the mixer simultaneously.

ribbon strip   A horizontal board set into the studs to help support the ends of rafters or joists.

ribbon stripe   A pattern on quartered veneer that has the appearance of a ribbon.

riblath (rib lath)   Stiffened expanded metal lath with ribs that provide greater strength and allow for increased spacing between members. It is not used for curved surfaces.

rich concrete   Concrete of high cement content. *See also* **lean concrete**.

rich lime   A pure lime which, when mixed with mortar, improves the plasticity or workability of the mortar.

rich mixture   A concrete mixture containing a high proportion of cement.

rich mortar   *See* **fat mortar**.

riddle   A coarse sieve for separating and grading granular material.

rider cap   *See* **pile cap**.

ridge   The horizontal line formed by the upper edges of two sloping roof surfaces. *See also* **ridge beam**.

ridge beam   A horizontal timber to which the tops of rafters are fastened.

ridgeboard (ridgepole, roof tree)   The longitudinal board set on edge used to support the upper ends of the rafters.

ridgecap (ridge cap)   A layer of wood or metal topping the ridge of a roof.

ridge connection   *See* **moment connection**.

ridge cut   *See* **plumb cut**.

ridge fillet   The ridge between two depressions, as on a fluted column.

ridgepole   *See* **ridgeboard**.

ridge rib   A projecting structural element following the ridge of a vault.

ridge roll   (1) A round wooden strip with the underside "V" cut; used to finish the upper edges of the roof surface. (2) A flexible metal covering used to cap the ridge of a roof.

ridge roof   A roof with two slopes meeting at a central crest.

ridge stop   The flashing that forms a watertight barrier between the edge of the roofing membrane and the vertical wall or chimney rising above it.

ridge vent   A vent installed along the top ridge of a roof to permit air to pass through to the attic or the peak of a cathedral ceiling.

ridging   (1) An upward dislodgement of the roof membrane. (2) Long narrow blisters in the surface of built-up roofing.

rift   A narrow fissure in rock.

rift sawn   *See* **quartersawn**.

rigid connection

rigid frame

rig (1) To provide with equipment or gear for a special purpose. (2) To assemble in a makeshift manner. (3) An assembled piece of equipment, such as an oil-drilling rig.

rigger (1) A long-haired, slender brush used for precision painting. (2) A worker who prepares heavy equipment or loads of materials for lifting.

rigging Lines or cables used to lift heavy loads.

rigging line A line or cable used with others to lift heavy loads.

riggot A trough or gutter for draining off rainwater.

right bank The bank located on the right as one looks downstream.

right-hand door *See* **hand**.

right-hand lock A lock to be used on a right-hand door.

right-hand reverse door *See* **hand**.

right-hand rule (1) A rule for determining polarity produced by flowing electric current. (2) Rule-of-thumb to envision the orientation of nut movement on a bolt to loosen/tighten it. Right thumb points along threaded shaft; direction of fist opening shows direction of nut loosening.

right-hand stairway A stairway having the outside handrail on the right as one ascends.

right of survivorship A feature of a joint tenancy and of tenancy by the entirety. When one owner dies, the deceased owner's share of ownership is split among the surviving owners, thereby increasing the surviving owners' proportional shares. *See also* **joint tenancy**.

right-of-way A strip of land, including the surface and overhead or underground space, that is granted by deed or easement for the construction and maintenance of specific linear elements such as power and telephone lines, roadways and driveways, and gas or water lines.

right-to-know A right granted to workers by the Occupational Safety and Health Act (OSHA), by which they must be informed of the risks and hazards associated with the chemicals and substances that they are required to use in the workplace.

Right to Work Law State law providing, in general, that employees are not required to join a union as a condition of retaining or receiving a job.

rigid connection A connection between two structural members that prevents end rotation of one relative to the other.

rigid foam *See* **cellular plastic**.

rigid foam insulation Panels of polyurethane foam that are used in commercial and residential construction as roof or outside wall insulation. The panels or boards include barrier board, and structural insulation panels (SIPs). The facings on the boards include metals, foil, glass fiber, kraft paper, or oriented strand board (OSB).

rigid frame A structural framing system in which all columns and beams are rigidly connected; there are no hinged joints.

rigidized The term used for the strengthening and increased rigidity of sheet metal by embossing the steel in a rolling process.

rigid metal conduit A raceway constructed for the pulling in or withdrawing of wires or cables after the conduit is in place and made of standard weight metal pipe permitting the cutting of standard threads.

riser

riser pipe

rigid pavement Pavement that will provide high bending resistance and distribute loads to the foundation over a comparatively large area.

rime The rung of a ladder.

rim joist Perimeter joist for wood floor framing system. Usually referred to in conjunction with composite wood floor joists.

rim latch A surface-mounted latch.

rim lock A face-mounted door lock.

rimpull The friction forces, expressed in pounds, exerted by rubber tires on driving wheels and the contact surface.

Ringelmann chart A table of values used as a standard for determining the density of smoke emitted from a chimney.

ring network A type of network configuration in which each node is connected to two adjacent nodes to form a continuous ring-like pattern.

ring scratch awl A pointed tool made especially for use on sheet metal.

ring-shank nail A nail with ring-like grooves around the shank to improve its grip.

rip To saw lumber parallel to the grain.

riparian right A landowners right to the use of a body of water that borders his land.

ripper A device with protruding claws that is pulled by a tractor. Used to penetrate and disrupt the earth's surface up to 3′ in depth.

ripping *See* **ripsawing**.

ripping bar *See* **pinch bar**.

riprap Irregularly broken, large pieces of rock, used along stream banks and oceanfronts as protection against erosion.

ripsaw A coarse-toothed saw used for cutting wood in the direction of the grain.

ripsawing (ripping) Sawing lumber parallel to the grain.

rise (1) The vertical distance from the top of a tread to the top of the next higher tread. (2) The height of an arch from springing to the crown. (3) The vertical height from the supports to the ridge of a roof. (4) Height difference between the crown of a road and its lowest point. (5) *See* **travel, rise**.

rise and run The angle of inclination or slope of a member or structure, expressed as the ratio of the vertical rise to the horizontal run.

riser (1) A vertical member between two stair treads. (2) A vertical pipe extending one or more floors.

riser board The member forming the vertical face of a step.

riser height The vertical distance between the tops of two successive treads.

riser pipe A pipe that extends vertically from one floor level to the next for the purpose of conducting water, steam, or gas.

rising hinge (rising butt hinge) A door hinge fabricated with a slope on the knuckle which causes the door to rise when opened. A rising hinge is used when there are obstructions along the door's bottom edge, e.g., carpeting.

risk management An approach to management and procedure designed to prevent occurrence of culpability, potential liability, contravention of law, or other potential risk that could bring about loss in the process of building construction.

rive Splitting wood along the grain. Shingles are cut in this fashion.

rivet

riveting

rock rake

riverine profile Section through a river depicting the riverbed in relation to the flood plain and watershed drainage basin.

rivet A metal cylinder or rod with a head at one end which is inserted through holes in the materials to be fastened. The protruding end is flattened to tie the two pieces together.

riveted grating A grating assembled from straight bearing bars and bent connecting bars, which are joined at contact points by rivets.

riveting The act of fastening or securing two or more parts with rivets.

road forms Wood or steel forms set on edge to form the side of a concrete road slab, also used as screeds.

road heater A traveling machine that prepares a road surface for treatment by blowing a flame or hot air on it.

road oil A heavy petroleum oil, usually a slow-curing asphalt.

roadway The area of a highway including the surface over which vehicles travel as well as the land along the edges, such as slopes, ditches, channels, or other gradations necessary to ensure proper drainage and safe use.

rock Slang for Sheetrock®, a well-known brand name of drywall.

rock anchor Steel rod anchored in rock by grouting used to hold temporary shoring or retaining walls around an excavation.

rock cover Top cover that is sometimes used to protect underlying layers in a cap when vegetative cover is not possible.

rock drill A high-powered pneumatic or electrically-driven device for boring holes into rock.

rock elm *Ulmus racernosa*. A lighter colored and finer textured wood than common elm, used primarily for veneer.

rock-faced A type of rough finish on stone. Essentially the same face that resulted when the stone was first struck from the quarry.

rocker shovel Mechanical tunneling shovel.

rockers Slang term for drywall installers.

rock lath *See* **gypsum board**.

rock pocket A porous, mortar-deficient portion of hardened concrete, consisting primarily of coarse aggregate and open voids, caused by leakage of mortar from form, separation or segregation during placement, or insufficient consolidation. *See also* **honeycomb**.

rock rake Tractor attachment with multiple teeth that is used to clear trees and rocks.

rock saw A circular saw that removes a wide kerf on the upper surface of a log. A rock saw is used to remove stones or debris before a log enters the head rig.

Rockwell hardness A measure of the resistance of a material to indentation, expressed as an index number obtained by pressing a standard steel ball or diamond into the material under controlled conditions. A high index number indicates a hard material.

rock wool A type of mineral wool made by forming fibers from molten rock and slag. Used as insulation in walls and ceilings.

rod Sharp-edged cutting screed used to trim shotcrete to forms or ground wires. *See also* **screed**.

rod bender A power-assisted device with adjustable rollers and supports

rolled beam

roller

rolling grille door

that is used for bending steel reinforcing rods into usable shapes.

rod buster   The colloquial term for one who installs reinforcement for concrete.

rod cutter   Trench-type, hydraulically operated, wedge-like shear, used to cut steel reinforcing rods.

roddability   The susceptibility of fresh concrete or mortar to compaction by means of a tamping rod.

rodding   Compaction of concrete or the like by means of a tamping rod. *See also* **rod, tamping** *and* **roddability**.

rod dowel   *See* **dowel**.

rod level   A device used to assure a leveling rod or stadia rod is in the vertical position before taking any instrument readings.

rod man   *See* **staff man**.

rod, tamping   A round, straight, steel rod having one or both ends rounded to a hemispherical tip.

rod target (target rod)   A metal disc that slides upon a track on a leveling rod, used for taking sights in surveying.

roll   (1) A quantity of sheet material wound in cylindrical form. (2) A rounded strip of roofing fastened to and running along the ridge of a roof. (3) Any type of rounded molding. (4) Any heavy, metal cylinder used to flatten, smooth, or form material.

rolled beam (rolled steel beam)   A beam that is fabricated of steel and passed through a hot-rolling mill.

rolled glass   Glass that is manufactured with a patterned surface that partially obscures vision and light.

rolled roofing   *See* **asphalt prepared roofing**.

roller   (1) A heavy, self-propelled or towed device used to compact granular fill. (2) A small hand tool used to smooth wall covering and flooring. (3) *See* **paint roller**.

Rollerbug™ tamper   The name brand of a tool used to compact fresh concrete. It is made of steel mesh on a rotating frame, and rolled along the concrete.

rolling   The use of heavy metal or stone rollers on terrazzo topping to extract excess matrix.

rolling doors   *See* **roll-up door**.

rolling grille door   A device similar to a roll-up door, but with an open grille rather than slats; used as security protection.

roll insulation   *See* **insulation blanket**.

roll joint   A point of connection formed by rolling two edges of sheet metal together and then compressing the roll.

roll marks   Parallel scratches on glass that are created in the manufacturing process as rollers pass over the glass.

roll-up door (rolling shutters)   A device consisting of horizontal interlocking metal slats that ride along wall guides. When the door is opened the slats coil around a barrel assembly located above the door.

Roman brick   Brick that measures 4″ x 2″ x 12″.

Roman cement   A misnomer for a hydraulic cement made by calcining a natural mixture of calcium carbonate and clay, such as argillaceous limestone, to a temperature below that required to sinter the material, but high enough to decarbonate the calcium carbonate, followed by grinding. The term is so named because its

539

roof deck

roof hatch

roofing

roofing tile

brownish color resembles ancient Roman cements produced by use of lime-pozzolan mixtures.

Romanesque architecture   Style of building with massive walls, vaults and rounded arches.

Romex   The most familiar trade name for non-metallic sheathed cable.

roof   The outer cover and its supporting structures on the top of a building.

roof comb   A wall along the ridge of a roof to give the illusion of a taller building.

roof covering   The covering material installed in a building over the roof deck. The type of covering used depends on the roofing system specified to weatherproof the structure properly.

roof deck   (1) The foundation or base upon which the entire roofing system is dependent. Types of decks include steel, concrete, cement, and wood. (2) A flat open portion atop a roof, such as a terrace or sundeck.

roof decking   Prefabricated sections of lightweight insulated waterproof panels. This type of roof deck is quickly completed and consequently inexpensive. Roof decking is made of different roofing materials, such as plywood, aluminum, steel, or timber.

roof drain   A drain designed to accept rainwater on a roof and discharge it into a leader or downspout.

roofed ingle   See **chimney corner**.

roofers   Lumber used as backing for shingles or shakes on a roof, usually 1″ x 4″ size.

roof flange   A collar that fits around a pipe penetrating through the roof making the opening watertight.

roof framing   A group of members fitted or joined together to provide support for the roof covering.

roof hatch (roof scuttle)   A weather-tight assembly with a hinged cover, used to provide access to a roof.

roofing   Any material that acts as a roof covering, making it impervious to the weather, such as shingles, tile, or slate.

roofing bond   A guarantee by a surety company that a roof installed by a roofer in accordance with specifications will be repaired if it fails within a certain period of time. Failure must be due to normal weathering.

roofing bracket   A bracket used in slope roof construction, having provisions for being fastened to the roof, or supported by ropes fastened over the ridge and secured to some suitable object.

roofing felt   See **asphalt prepared roofing**.

roofing nail   A special-purpose, short-threaded nail with a large head, usually galvanized or aluminum with a neoprene or plastic washer to aid in fastening roof coverings.

roofing square   (1) A steel square used by carpenters. (2) A measure of roofing material. (3) See **square**.

roofing tile   A preformed slab of baked clay, concrete, cement, or plastic laid in rows as a roofing cover. Tiles have a variety of patterns, but fall into two classifications: roll and flat.

roof insulation   Lightweight concrete used primarily as insulating material over structural roof systems.

roof live load   Any external loads that may be applied to a roof deck,

roof purlin

such as rain, snow, construction equipment, and personnel.

roof overhang The part of a roof that extends over the side wall or end wall of a building.

roof pitch. The slope of a roof expressed as the ratio of the rise of the roof to the horizontal span. More roofing material is required to cover the increased roof area when the slope or pitch is great.

roof plate A wall plate that supports the lower end of rafters.

roof principal A roof truss.

roof purlin See **purlin**.

roof saddle See **saddle**.

roof scuttle See **roof hatch**.

roof sheathing Any sheet or board material, such as plywood or particle board, connected to the roof rafters to act as a base for shingles or other roof coverings.

roof slope The angle of a roof compared to a horizontal plane. See **roof pitch**.

roof snow load See **snowload**.

roof space The space between the roof and the ceiling of the highest room.

roof span (1) The shortest distance between the seats of opposite common rafters. (2) The distance across a roof.

roof structure Any structure on or above the roof of a building.

roof terminal The top point of the plumbing vent pipe as it exits through the roof, often 12″.

roof tree The *ridgeboard* of a roof.

roof truss A truss used in the structural system of a roof. See also **truss**.

roof valley See **valley**.

roof vent A device used to ventilate an attic or roof cavity.

room cavity ratio (RCR) A ratio of room dimensions used to quantify how light will interact with room surfaces. A factor used in illuminance calculations.

room finish schedule Information provided on design drawings specifying types of finishes to be applied to floors, walls, and ceilings for each location.

root (1) The part of a tenon that widens at the shoulders. (2) The point where the back or bottom of the weld meets the base metal.

root diameter A measurement of the major diameter on nuts and the minor diameter on screws.

rope (1) Twisted strands of fiber made into strong, flexible cord. (2) Strands of wire braided or twisted together that are used for heavy hoisting or hauling.

rope caulk A preformed, rope-like bead of caulking compound which may contain twine reinforcement to facilitate handling.

roped hydraulic elevator A car connected by cables to an operating ram. A motor-driven positive displacement pump discharges oil into the pressure cylinder which extends the ram. The ram is retracted by bleeding oil off the pressure cylinder and into a storage tank.

rope diameter The largest diameter of the cross section of a wire rope. Fiber ropes are usually measured by circumference (3.14 x diameter).

rope lay The direction in which the wires or strands are twisted during manufacture.

rope suspension equalizer A device that equalizes the tensions in hoisting cables.

rotary float

rotary hammer

rotary pump

rose (1) The metal plate or escutcheon between a doorknob and the door. (2) *See* **rosette**.

rose bit A bit for countersinking holes in wood.

rose nail A wrought nail with a cone-shaped head.

rosette (1) A round pattern with a floral motif. (2) A circular or oval, ornamental, wood plaque that is used to terminate a wood piece such as a stair rail at a wall. (3) A decorative nailhead or screwhead.

rose window (wheel window) Circular window with a radial pattern resembling a wheel with spokes and a hub.

rosewood *See* **bubinga**.

rosin *See* **resin**.

rosin paper A paper coated with resin. Rosin paper is laid between lead sheets and sheathing to allow for thermal movement in lead roofing.

rot Decay in wood caused by fungi and other microorganisms. Rot reduces the strength, hardness, and density of the wood.

rotary compressor An air compressor using a rotary impeller driving air through a curved chamber to compress the air.

rotary cutting A method of obtaining wood veneers by rotating logs against a flat knife and peeling the veneer off in a long continuous sheet. Peeling provides a greater volume and a more rapid production then does sawing or slicing.

rotary drill A machine for making holes in rock or earth by a cutting bit at the end of a metal rod, usually turned by a hydraulically- or pneumatically-driven motor.

rotary float (power float) Motor-driven revolving blades that smooth, flatten, and compact the surface of concrete slabs or floor toppings.

rotary hammer Electric boring tool that rotates with percussive action and cuts very hard materials.

rotary kiln A long steel cylinder with a refractory lining, supported on rollers so that it can rotate about its own axis, and erected with a slight inclination from the horizontal so that prepared raw materials fed into the higher end move to the lower end, where fuel is blown in by air blast. Often used to treat hazardous waste through thermal destruction. *See also* **kiln** *and* **cement**.

rotary kiln incineration (RKI) Incineration using a rotary kiln. *See* **rotary kiln.**

rotating laser A leveling and surveying instrument with a revolving head that emits a laser beam horizontally. A sensor then picks up the beam to determine an elevation.

rotary pump Any pump using gears, vaned-wheels, or a screw mechanism to displace liquid, usually delivering large volumes at low pressure.

rotary trowel *See* **rotary float.**

roto operator A mechanical device consisting of a crank-driven gear which operates a hinged lever; used to open and close jalousies, casement windows, and awning windows.

rotor The rotating armature or member within an electrical device or motor.

rottenstone A porous, lightweight, siliceous limestone used for polishing soft metals and wood.

rough floor

rough hardware

router

rotunda A circular building or hall that is round inside and out and usually domed.

rough ashlar A block of stone before dressing, as delivered from a quarry.

rough axed brick *See* **axed brick.**

roughback (1) The concealed end of bondstone in a masonry wall. (2) A slab of stone with one side rough and the other sawn, cut from a block fed through a gang saw.

rough-cut joint (flat joint, flush joint, hick joint) A mortar joint that is flush with the face of the brickwork.

rough estimate An estimate made without detailed investigation.

rough floor A base or subfloor, consisting of a layer of boards or plywood nailed to the floor joists.

rough flooring Any materials used to construct an unfinished floor.

rough grading Cutting and filling the earth for preparation of finish grading.

rough grind The initial operation in which coarse abrasives are used to cut the projecting chips in hardened terrazzo down to a level surface.

rough hardware Any fittings, such as screws, bolts, or nails that should be concealed for a finished product.

rough-in dimensions In plumbing installations, the distance from the center of a water supply, waste opening or mounting holes to the finished wall or floor.

roughing-in (1) The base coat in three-coat plasterwork. (2) Any unfinished work in a construction job. (3) Installing the concealed portion of electrical or plumbing systems to the point of connection for electrical outlets or appliances, or plumbing fixtures.

roughing-out A preliminary shaping operation in carpentry.

rough lumber Wood that has been sawn at the mill, but not trimmed. *See* **dressed.**

rough opening An opening in a wall or framework into which a door frame, window frame, subframe, or rough buck is fitted.

rough rendering Applying a coat of plaster without removing the irregularities.

rough sill A horizontal member laid across the bottom of an unfinished opening to act as a base during construction of a window frame.

rough service lamp An incandescent lamp with additional filament supports designed to withstand minor impact without failing.

rough work The framing, boxing, and sheeting for a wood-framed building.

round (1) A molding that may be semicircular to full round, as in a closet rod. (2) A turn of wire rope around a drum.

roundel (1) A semicircular panel, window, or recess. (2) A small, semicircular molding or astragal.

round molding (round) A fairly large molding with a circular or nearly circular cross section.

round timber Felled trees which have not been converted to lumber.

rout (1) To deepen and widen a crack, preparing it for patching or sealing. (2) To cut out by gouging.

router An electrically driven device with various bits for cutting grooves or channels in wood.

router gauge A carpenter's tool consisting of a guide, a bar with a scale, and a narrow chisel as a cutter; used in inlaid work to cut

rowlock course

out narrow channels in which colored strips are laid.

router patch (Davis patch) A wood patch in plywood with straight sides and rounded ends, similar to a tongue depressor; used to fill voids caused by defects. The router patch is one of two patch designs allowed in A-grade faces.

router plane (router plough, router plow) A woodworker's plane for cutting grooves or channels in wood.

rover A member that is curved, typically molding.

row house A house in a row of houses separated by party walls and covered by a continuous roof.

rowlock course (bull header) Brick pattern in which bricks are set on their face edges with the ends visible in the wall face.

row spacing The measured distance between the centers of mechanical fasteners in a row.

royals Shingles with 24″ edges and a thickness of 1/2″ at the butt.

rubbed brick Brick that has one or more smooth faces.

rubbed finish (1) On woodwork, a dull finish obtained from hand rubbing with a rag or pad saturated with water or oil and pumice. (2) A finish obtained by using an abrasive, often a carborundum stone, to remove surface irregularities from concrete. *See also* **sack rub**.

rubbed joint A process for joining two narrow boards. Both boards are planed smooth, and then coated with glue and rubbed together until all air pockets and excess glue are expelled from the joint. No clamping is necessary, and the joint is extremely strong.

rubbed work Masonry work having a rubbed finish.

rubber (1) A highly resilient natural material manufactured from the juice of rubber trees and other plants. (2) Any of various synthetically manufactured materials with properties similar to natural rubber. (3) A cushioned backing for a carpet.

rubber-emulsion paint *See* **latex paint.**

rubber set *See* **false set.**

rubber silencer (bumper) A small round rubber device that attaches to a rabbeted doorjamb which silences the noise caused by a slamming door.

rubber tile A soft and yielding floor covering that reduces the transmission of impact noises produced by walking or from other causes.

rubber-tired roller A machine for compacting and kneading soil using pneumatic-tired rollers.

rubbing brick A silicon-carbide brick used to smooth and remove irregularities from surfaces of hardened concrete.

rubble Rough stones of irregular shape and size, broken from larger masses by geological processes or by quarrying.

rubble concrete (1) Concrete similar to cyclopean concrete, except that small stones, such as one man can handle, are used. (2) Concrete made with rubble from demolished structures. *See also* **cyclopean concrete.**

rub brick *See* **rubbing brick.**

ruff sawn A designation for plywood paneling or siding that has been saw-textured to provide a decorative, rough-sawn appearance.

rung

running trap

rule (1) A straightedge with graduations used for measuring, laying out lengths, or drawing straight lines. (2) A straightedge for working plaster to a plane surface.

rule joint A pivoted joint connecting two flat strips, and allowing relative rotation around the pivot.

rule of thumb A statement or formula that is not exact but is close enough for practical work.

ruling pen A pen used by draftspersons to draw ink lines of uniform thickness.

run (1) In plumbing, a pipe or fitting that continues in the same straight line as the direction of flow. (2) In roofing, the horizontal distance between the outer face of the wall and the roof ridge. (3)In stairs, the horizontal distance from the face of the first riser to the face of the last riser. (4) Series of surveyed elevation changes in one direction. (5) To sieve plaster or putty. (6) Window sash.

runaround system A heat recovery system in which coils in an exhaust duct transfer a portion of the exhaust air heat to a fluid. The fluid is then circulated to coils that give up a portion of the fluid's heat to the air in a cold air duct.

rung A bar, usually of circular cross section, used as a step in a ladder.

run molding A formed molding of plaster or similar material formed by passing a template over the plastic material.

runner (1) The lengthwise horizontal bracing or bearing members. (2) A cold-rolled channel used to support steel studs in a partition or ceiling tile.

running (1) Descriptive of a repeating design in a band having a smooth progression. (2) Forming a cornice of plaster or similar material in place with a running mold. (3) Operating a powered hand tool, particularly a drill.

running bond *See* **stretcher bond**.

running foot A linear foot. The term is a measurement of the actual length of a piece of lumber, without regard to the thickness or width of the piece.

running ground Earth in a semi-plastic state that will not stand without support.

running inch A linear inch. The term is a measurement of the actual length of a piece of lumber. *See also* **running foot**.

running mile rate A charge that includes all miles traveled by the transporter.

running mold A template shaped to a desired cornice and mounted on a wood frame; used by plasterers to form a molding or cornice in place by applying plaster as the mold is moved along the ceiling line.

running screed A narrow strip of plaster used in place of a rule to guide a running mold.

running shoe A metal guide on a running mold to prevent wear and allow it to slide freely on a rule.

running trap A U-shaped pipe fitting installed in a drain line to prevent the backflow of sewer gases.

run-of-bank gravel *See* **bank-run gravel**.

runoff Water that is carried away from, rather than absorbed by, the area on which it falls.

runway Decking over an area of concrete placement, usually of movable panels and supports, on

rustication

which buggies of concrete travel to points of placement.

rupture disk A pressure-activated safety device consisting of a breakable disk that bursts at a predetermined pressure.

ruptured grain Breaks in veneer that have resulted from cutting or irregular grain.

rust Any of various powdery or scaly reddish-brown or reddish-yellow, hydrated, ferric oxides formed on the surface of iron or steel that is exposed to moisture and air. Rust eventually will weaken or destroy the material if allowed to progress.

rust bloom Discoloration of a surface finish indicating the early stages of rust.

rustic finish (washed finish) A type of terrazzo topping in which the matrix is recessed by washing prior to setting so as to expose the chips without destroying the bond between chip and matrix. A retarder is sometimes applied to the surface to facilitate this operation. *See also* **exposed aggregate finish.**

rusticated A formed or cut reveal in concrete masonry or stone used to highlight or conceal joints in concrete, masonry, or stone fascia.

rustication Providing a continuous groove in vertical concrete at a preferred location by applying a form strip prior to placing concrete, and removing it after concrete has set.

rustication strip A strip of wood or other material attached to a form surface to produce a groove or rustication in the concrete.

rustic brick A brick that has a rough-textured finish produced by covering it with sand, wire brushing, or impressing it with a pattern. These bricks are often in a variety of colors.

rustic joint A deeply sunk mortar joint that is accented by beveling the edges of the adjacent stone.

rustic stone Any rough, broken stone suitable for masonry with an uneven appearance, most commonly limestone or sandstone, usually set with the longest dimension horizontal.

rustic woodwork Decorative or structural woodwork made of unpeeled logs and saplings.

rust-inhibiting paint *See* **anticorrosive paint.**

rust joint A watertight pipe connection that uses iron filings as a catalyst to induce rusting in iron pipe joints.

rust pocket An area in the bottom of a ventilating pipe for the collection and removal of rust and debris.

rutile (1) A reddish-brown to black natural mineral. (2) A form of titanium dioxide used in paints and fillers.

"R" value A measure of a material's resistance to heat flow at a given thickness of material. The term is the reciprocal of the "U" value. The higher the "R" value, the more effective the particular insulation.

S

S ABBREVIATIONS

The abbreviations listed below are those most commonly used in the construction industry. Alternative forms (usually nonstandard) are shown in parentheses.

S side, south, southern, seamless, subject, sulphur

S1E surfaced one edge

S1S surfaced one side

S1S1E surfaced one side and one edge

S1S2E surfaced one side and two edges

S2E surfaced two edges

S2S surfaced two sides

S2S1E surfaced two sides and one edge

S2S&CM surfaced two sides and center matched

S2S&SL surfaced two sides and shiplapped

S4S surfaced four sides

S4S&CS surfaced four sides and caulking seam

S/A shipped assembled

SAE Society of Automotive Engineers

SAF safety

SAN sanitary

sanit sanitation

SAP sampling and analysis plan

sar supplied air respirator

sat. saturate, saturation

SB1S single bead one side

SBA Small Business Association

SBC Standard Building Code

SBS sick building syndrome

SC site closeout

scba self-contained breathing apparatus

sch school

SCH schedule

Scp spherical candlepower

SD sea-damaged, standard deviation

S/D shop drawings

SDA specific dynamic action

Sdg siding

S&E surfaced one side and edge

Se selenium

S/E square-edged

sec second

SECT section

sed sediment, sedimentation

sel select, selected

Sel select

sep, SEP separate

SERI Solar Energy Research Institute

SERV service

SE&S square edge and sound

SE Sdg, S.E. Sdg. square-edge siding

SEW. sewer

sf surface foot

SFRC steel-fiber-reinforced concrete

Sftwd. softwood

sfu supply fixture unit

S&G studs and girts

SG slash grain

SGD sliding glass door

S&H staple and hasp

SH sheet, shower, single-hung

sh shingles

shf superhigh frequency

shp shaft horsepower

SHSS site health and safety supervisor

sht sheet, sheath

Si silicon

SIC Standard Industrial Classification

sid siding

SIM similar

SJI Steel Joist Institute

SK sketch

Sk sack

sky. skylights

SL&C shipper's load and count

slid. sliding

S/L, S/LAP shiplap

SM standard matched, surface measure

S&M surfaced and matched

SMACCNA Sheet Metal and Air Conditioning Contractor's National Association.

s. mld. stuck mold

SMS sheet-metal screw

so. south

SO. seller's option

soln solution

SOV shutoff valve

sp specific, specimen, spirit, single pitch (roof)

SP soil pipe, standpipe, self-propelled, single pole

SPEC specification

sp. gr., SP GR specific gravity

sp. ht. specific heat

SPKR loudspeaker

spl spline

SPL special

spr spruce

SPT standard penetration test

sp. vol. specific volume

sq. square

sq. e. square edge

sq. E&S square edge and sound

sq. ft. square foot

sq. in. square inch

sq. yd. square yard

SR sedimentation rate

ss single strength (glass)

SS, S/S stainless steel

sst standing seam tin (roof)

SST stainless steel

st stairs, stone, street

ST steam, street

STC sound transmission class

std., STD standard

Std. M standard matched

STG storage

STK stock, select tight knot

STL steel

STP standard temperature and pressure

Stpg stepping

STR1E straight line rip one edge

str stringers

Str. structural

STR. strike

Struc. structural

st. sash. steel sash

ST W storm water

sty. story

sty. hgt. story height

SUB. substitute

sub. fl. subfloor

subpar subparagraph

subsec subsection

sup supplementary, supplement

SUP supply

supp supplement

SUPSD supersede

supt, SUPT, SUPER superintendent

SUPV supervise

supvr supervisor

sur, SUR surface

surv survey, surveying, surveyor

svc service

SVE soil vapor extraction

sw switch

SW switch, seawater, southwest

SWBD switchboard

SWG, S.W.G. standard wire gauge

sy jet syphon jet (water closet)

SYM symmetrical

SYN synthetic

SYS system

syst system

S

Definitions

saber saw

saddle

saddle joint

saber saw A hand-held power saw with a reciprocating blade extending through the base of the saw.

sabin A unit of measure used to rate the sound absorption qualities of a material or assembly. Equal to one foot of a perfectly absorptive surface.

sack *See* **bag**.

sack joint A flush masonry joint that has been wiped or rubbed with a rag or an object such as a rubber heel or a burlap sack.

sack rub (sack finish) A finish for formed concrete surfaces, designed to produce even texture and fill all pits and air holes (*See also* **bug holes**.) After dampening the surface, and before it dries, a mixture of dry cement and sand is rubbed over it with a wad of burlap or a sponge-rubber float to remove surplus mortar and fill the voids.

sacrificial protection The use of a metallic coating, such as zinc-rich paint, to protect steel. In the presence of an electrolyte, such as salt water, the metallic coating dissolves instead of the steel.

saddle (1) A fitted device used with hangers to support a pipe. (2) A series of bends in a pipe over an obstruction. (3) A short horizontal member set on top of a post as a seat for a girder. (4) Any hollow-backed structure with a shape suggesting a saddle, as a ridge connected to two higher elevations or a saddle roof. (5) *See* **threshold**. (6) *See* **cricket**.

saddleback A coping stone with its top surface sloped from a high line in the center to either edge.

saddleback board *See* **threshold**.

saddle-backed coping *See* **saddleback**.

saddleback joint *See* **saddle joint (2)**.

saddleback roof *See* **saddle roof**.

saddle bar One of the horizontal iron bars across a window opening to secure leaded lights.

saddle bead A glazing bead or channel for securing two panes of glass together.

saddle bend A bend made in a conduit to provide clearance where it crosses another conduit.

saddle block The boom swivel block through which the stick of a dipper shovel slides.

saddle board A board used to cover the joint at the ridge of a pitched roof.

saddle coping *See* **saddleback**.

saddle fitting A type of gasketed fitting clamped around the exterior of a pipe; used when a connection to a previously installed pipe is required.

saddle flange A flange that is curved to conform to the surface of the boiler or tank to which it is welded, riveted, or otherwise attached, and designed to accept a threaded pipe.

saddle flashing Flashing installed over a cricket.

saddle joint (1) A joint in sheet-metal roofing, in which one end of one sheet is folded downward over the turned-up edge of the adjacent sheet. (2) A stepped joint in a projecting masonry course to prevent the penetration of water.

saddle piece A metal cricket used in sheet-metal roofing.

safety nosing

safety switch

saddle roof A roof with two gables and one ridge.

saddle scaffold A scaffold erected so as to bridge the ridge of a roof, usually used during chimney repair.

safe (1) A built-in or portable chamber used to protect materials or documents from fire and/or theft. (2) A pan or other collector placed beneath a pipe or fixture to collect leakage or overflow.

safe-edge A strip-form detector mounted on the leading edge of an elevator door, it will reopen or close slowly if programmed to do so. The safe-edge is vertically mounted to extend from the bottom to the top of a door panel.

safe leg load The load which can safely be directly imposed on the frame leg of a scaffold. *See also* **allowable load**.

safe load The maximum load on a structure that does not produce stresses greater than those allowable.

safety belt A belt-like device worn around the waist and attached to a life-line or structure to stop a worker during a fall.

safety can An approved closed container, of not more than five gallons capacity, having a flash-arresting screen, spring-closing lid, and spout cover; so designed that it will safely relieve internal pressure when subjected to fire exposure.

safety curtain *See* **asbestos curtain**.

safety factor *See* **factor of safety**.

safety fuse A cord containing black powder or other burning medium encased in flexible wrapping and used to convey fire at a predetermined and uniform rate for firing blasting caps.

safety glass *See* **wire glass, tempered glass,** *and* **laminated glass**.

safety lintel A load-carrying lintel positioned behind a more decorative but somewhat less functional lintel, as in the aperture of a window or door.

safety nosing An abrasive, nonslip stair nosing whose surface is flush with the tread against which it is placed.

safety shoe A workman's shoe with a steel-protected toe and low-slip sole and heel.

safety shutoff device A device in a gas burner that will shut off the supply of gas if the flame is extinguished.

safety switch In an interior electric wiring system, a switch enclosed within a metal box that has a handle protruding from the box to allow switching to be accomplished from outside the box.

safety tread A tread on a stair which has a roughened surface or roughened inserts to improve traction.

safety valve *See* **pressure-reducing valve**.

safe working pressure The maximum working pressure at which a vessel, boiler, flask, or cylinder is allowed to operate, as determined by the American Society of Mechanical Engineers Boiler Code; usually so identified on each individual unit.

safflower oil An oil, obtained from safflower seeds, that has properties similar to linseed oil and is used in paints.

safing (1) Noncombustible material used as a fire barrier around the perimeter of a floor or around protrusions or penetrations. (2) In ductwork, a type of barrier

sag rod

saltbox

or similar device installed around a component to ensure that air flows through that component and not around it.

sagging (1) Subsidence of shotcrete material from a sloping, vertical, or overhead placement. (2) The condition of a horizontal structural member bending downward under load. *See also* **sloughing.** (3) A paint defect where paint runs after it has been applied.

sag member *See* **sag rod.**

sag rod A tension member used to limit the deflection of a girt or purlin in the direction of its weak axis or to limit the sag in angle bracing.

sailing course *See* **string course.**

sailor A rectangular masonry unit, such as a brick, that is set upright with its largest side facing out.

salamander A portable source of heat, customarily oil-burning, used to heat an enclosure around or over newly placed concrete to prevent the concrete from freezing.

sal ammoniac (ammonium chloride) A material used in soldering flux and iron cement.

salient Descriptive of a projecting part of an object or member, as a salient corner.

sally A projection, such as the end of a rafter beyond the notch, which has been cut to fit a plate or beam.

salmon brick (chuff brick, place brick) Comparatively soft and underburnt brick, usually because of its high placement in the kiln, and so named because of its color.

saltbox A wood-framed house, common in colonial New England, with a short, pitched roof in front and a roof which sweeps down to the ground in back.

salt-glazed brick (brown-glazed brick) Brick whose surface faces have a lustrous glazed finish resulting from the thermochemical reaction between silicates of clay and vapors of salt or other chemicals during firing.

salt-glazed tile Facing tile with a lustrous glazed finish, obtained by thermochemical reaction between silicates of clay and vapors of salt or other chemicals during firing.

salt treatment One method of preserving wood, using any of various waterborne salts to impregnate the wood. Among the more widely used systems are Wolman Salts and Osmose Salts.

salvage The remaining value of property after it has been partially damaged. Salvage can also mean the act of saving and preserving such partially damaged property, so as to prevent further loss.

salvage value The value assigned to the piece of equipment at the end of the depreciation period.

samples Examples of workmanship establishing the standards against which the rest of the work will be measured. Includes products, materials, and equipment as well.

sand (1) Granular material passing the 3/8″ sieve, almost entirely passing the No. 4 (4.75-millimeter) sieve, and predominantly retained on the No. 200 (75-micrometer) sieve, and resulting from natural disintegration and abrasion of rock or processing of completely friable sandstone. (2) That portion of an aggregate passing the No. 4 (4.75-millimeter) sieve, and resulting from natural disintegration and abrasion of rock or processing of completely friable sandstone. *See also* **fine aggregate.** *Note:* The definitions are alternatives to be

sander

sand filter trenches

applied under differing circumstances. Definition (1) is applied to an entire aggregate either in a natural condition or after processing. Definition (2) is applied to a portion of an aggregate. Requirements for properties and grading should be stated in the specifications. Fine aggregate produced by crushing rock, gravel, or slag commonly is known as manufactured sand.

sand asphalt A mixture of ungraded sand and liquid asphalt used for an economical base or wearing surface for pavements.

sandbag A canvas bag that is filled with sand and used as a counterweight or for emergency damming of water flow.

sandblast A system of cutting or abrading a surface, such as concrete, by a stream of sand ejected from a nozzle at high speed by compressed air. Sandblasting is often used for cleanup of horizontal construction joints or for exposure of aggregate in architectural concrete.

sand box (sand jack) A tight box filled with clean, dry sand, on which rests a tight-fitting timber plunger that supports the bottom of posts used in centering. A plug from a hole near the bottom of the box permits the sand to run out when it is necessary.

sand clay A naturally occurring sand that contains about 10% clay, or just enough to make the material bind tightly when compacted.

sand-coarse aggregate ratio Ratio of fine to coarse aggregate in a batch of concrete, by weight or volume.

sand cone test A test used to measure soil density that involves drilling a hole, filling it with sand, and then measuring the sand's weight and volume.

sand-dry Descriptive of a stage in the drying process of paint where sand will not adhere to the surface.

sanded Panel products that have been processed through a machine sander to provide a smooth surface on one or both sides. In sanded plywood, A- or B-grade veneers are used for one side of the panel.

sanded bituminous felt
See **asphalt-prepared roofing**.

sanded-face shingle A shingle with retrimmed edges and butts that has been sanded to remove saw marks, etc., and is to be applied to a wall as part of a decorative effect.

sanded fluxed-pitch felt A felt that is saturated with a fluxed coal tar, coated on both sides with the same material, sanded, and rolled for handling.

sanded grout *See* **sand grout**.

sand equivalent A measure of the relative proportions of detrimental fine dust or clay-like material in soils or fine aggregate.

sander A machine designed to smooth wood and remove saw or lathe marks and other imperfections. Sanders range in size from hand-held to large drums or belts capable of surfacing a full-size panel.

sand-faced brick A brick formed in a mold that has been sprinkled with sand to facilitate removal.

sand filter A bed of sand laid over graded gravel, used as a filter for a water supply.

sand filter trenches A network of sewage-effluent-filtering trenches incorporating perforated pipe or drain tiles surrounded by fine sand sandwiched between coarse aggregate, and equipped with an underdrain to remove whatever material has passed through. The

sandwich panel

trenches are used to remove solid or colloidal material that cannot be removed by sedimentation.

sand finish (1) In plastering, a textured final coat, usually containing sand, lime putty, and Keene's cement. (2) A smooth finish derived from rubbing and sanding the final coat.

sand-float finish A rough plaster finish obtained by using a wood float.

sand grout (sanded grout) Any grout in which fine aggregate is incorporated into the mixture.

sandhog A laborer who works under compressed air conditions, as in underwater tunnel construction.

sanding block A device to hold a piece of sandpaper while sanding by hand.

sanding machine A stationary machine having a moving belt, disk, or spindle with an abrasive surface, usually a sandpaper; used for smoothing surfaces.

sanding sealer A clear-coat wood sealer that fills the pores of raw wood, preventing the finish from penetrating into the grain.

sand interceptor (sand trap) A watertight device which can be directly or indirectly connected to a drainage system to intercept and prevent sand or other solids from passing into the system.

sand jack *See* **sand box**.

sand-lime brick *See* **calcium-silicate brick**.

sand, Ottawa *See* **Ottawa sand**.

sandpaper Strong, tough paper coated on one side with glue or other adhesive material, into which an abrasive such as flint, silica, or aluminum oxide has been embedded. The resulting product is used primarily for resurfacing or cutting wood, metal, plastic, or glass and is available in an extensive range of coarseness or grit.

sandpile A foundation formed by ramming sand into a hole left by a pile that was driven and removed.

sand pine *Pinus clausa*. This pine is found almost exclusively in north central Florida, where it grows in very sandy soil. The wood is used mostly for pulp.

sand plate A flat steel plate or strip welded to the legs of bar supports for use on compacted soil.

sand pocket A zone in concrete or mortar containing sand without cement.

sand seal Emulsified asphalt covered with fine aggregate applied to pavement to improve skid resistance and to prevent air and water penetration.

sandstone A cemented or otherwise compacted sedimentary rock composed predominantly of sand grains. It has been used as cut stone for carved ornament.

sand streak A streak of exposed fine aggregate in the surface of formed concrete caused by bleeding.

sand trap *See* **sand interceptor**.

sandwich beam *See* **flitch beam**.

sandwich construction Composite construction usually incorporating thin layers of a strong material bonded to a thicker, weaker, and lighter core material, such as rigid foam or paper honeycomb, to create a product which has high strength-to-weight and stiffness-to-weight ratios.

sandwich panel (1) A panel formed by bonding two thin facings to a thick, and usually lightweight, core. Typical facing materials include plywood, single veneers, hardboard,

sanitary tee

sash

sash and frame

plastics, laminates, and various metals, such as aluminum or stainless steel. Typical core materials include plastic foam sheets, rubber, and formed honeycombs of paper, metal, or cloth. (2) A prefabricated panel, which is a layered composite, formed by attaching two thin facings to a thicker core. An example is precast concrete panels, which consist of two layers of concrete separated by a nonstructural insulating core.

sanitary code Municipal regulations established to control sanitary conditions of establishments that produce and/or distribute food, serve food, or provide medical services.

sanitary cove A piece of metal used in a stair between the surface of the tread and the face of the riser to facilitate cleaning.

sanitary cross In a soil pipe system, a cross pipe, whose 90° transitions are curved to direct the flow from the branches toward the direction of the main flow.

sanitary engineering That part of civil engineering related to public health and the environment, such as water supply, sewage, and industrial waste.

sanitary sewage (domestic sewage) Sewage containing human excrement and/or household wastes which originate from sanitary conveniences of a dwelling, business, building, factory, or institution. Does not include storm water.

sanitary sewer (1) A sewer line designed to carry only liquid or waterborne waste from the structure to a central treatment plant. (2) The conduit or pipe that carries sanitary sewage.

sanitary tee A T-fitting for pipe, having a slight curve in the 90° transition so as to channel flow from a branch line toward the main flow.

sanitary ware Devices of porcelain enamel, stainless steel, or other material, such as bathtubs, sewer pipes, toilet bowls, and washbasins.

Santorin earth A volcanic *tuff* originating on the Grecian island of Santorini and used as a *pozzolan*.

sap grade (1) A grade of southern yellow pine export lumber. (2) KD saps.

sapwood The wood just beneath the bark of a tree, normally lighter in color than the rest of the wood, but usually not as strong as the rest of the wood.

sarking (sarking board) A thin board employed in sheathing applications, as under the tiles or slates of a roof.

Sarnafill A roofing manufacturer known for a product used as a substitute for copper roofing because of its lower cost and green color.

sash (window sash) The framework of a window that holds the glass.

sash adjuster *See* **casement stay**.

sash and frame A preassembled unit consisting of a cased frame and a double-hung window.

sash balance A spring-loaded device, usually a spring balance or tape balance, used as a counterbalance for a sash in a double-hung window. A sash balance replaces sash weights, cords, and pulleys.

sash bar *See* **glazing bar**.

sash block *See* **jamb block**.

sash center (sash plate) The support for a horizontally pivoting sash or transom, consisting of a socket which is secured to the jamb or frame, and a pin on which the sash or transom actually pivots.

sash pull

sash chain A metal chain used in place of a sash cord to connect a vertically hung sash with its counterweight.

sash chisel A chisel having a wide blade honed on both sides, used for deep cutting, such as cutting the mortises in pulley stiles.

sash cord A rope connecting a sash with its counterweight in a double-hung window.

sash-cord iron A metal holder used to connect a sash cord or chain to the window.

sash counterweight *See* **sash weight**.

sash door *See* **glazed door**.

sash fast (sash fastener, sash holder) Any fastening device that holds two window sashes together to prevent their opening or rattling. A sash fast is usually attached to the meeting rails of a double-hung window.

sash fillister (1) A rabbet cut in a glazing bar to receive the glass and glazing compound. (2) A special plane for cutting such rabbets. *See also* **fillister plane**.

sash hardware All accessories used to balance a vertically hung sash, including chains or cords, weights, and pulleys.

sash holder *See* **sash fast**.

sash lift *See* **window lift**.

sash lift and hook A sash lift having a locking lever that holds the window fixed by contact with a strike in the frame. Raising the sash automatically releases the strike.

sash line *See* **sash cord**.

sash lock A sash fast that is controlled by a key. *See also* **sash fast**.

sash plane A carpenter's plane having a notched cutting blade for

trimming the inside of a door frame or window frame.

sash plate (sash center) One of the pair of plates constituting the pivoting mechanism for a horizontally pivoting sash or transom.

sash pocket *See* **pocket**.

sash pull A plate, with a recess for fingers, set in a sash rail, or a handle attached to a rail to use in raising or lowering a window.

sash pulley A pulley mortised into the side of the frame of a double-hung window. The sash chord or chain passes over the pulley to the sash weight.

sash ribbon A metal tape used in place of a sash chord or chain.

sash saw (1) A small miter saw used to cut the tenons of sashes. (2) A saw fitted in a frame that moves vertically.

sash schedule Information provided on design drawings regarding the selection and installation of window sashes.

sash spring bolt *See* **window spring bolt**.

sash stop (window stop) A small strip fastened to a cased frame to hold a sash of a double-hung window in place.

sash stuff Wood cut to standard sizes and shapes for use in making window frames.

sash tool A round brush used in painting items such as window frames and glazing bars.

sash weight A weight, usually cast iron, used to balance a vertically hung window.

sash window Any window, but usually a double-hung window, having a vertically or horizontally sliding sash.

saucer dome

sauna

satin sheen   Descriptive of a paint film with a subdued gloss resembling satin.

satinwood   The hard, fine-grained, pale to golden yellow wood of the gum arabic tree, which is especially used in cabinetwork and decorative paneling.

satisfaction   The cancellation of an encumbrance on a piece of real property, most often resulting in the payment of whatever debt had been secured by it.

satisfaction piece   The document which records and acknowledges the payment of an indebtedness secured by a mortgage.

saturant   (1) A substance, usually a diluted encapsulant, added to water to increase the amount of solute that can be dissolved at a certain temperature. A wetting agent used to improve penetration. (2) A bituminous material with a low softening point, used for impregnating felt in asphalt-prepared roofing.

saturated air   Air that contains the maximum amount of water vapor it can hold at its temperature and pressure.

saturated felt   See **asphalt-prepared roofing**.

saturated surface dry   Condition of an aggregate particle or other solid when the voids between the particles are filled with water and no water is on the exposed surfaces.

saturated vapor pressure The pressure at a given temperature in a closed container that contains a liquid and the vapor from that liquid, once equilibrium conditions have been reached.

saturation line   A line used on a cross-sectional drawing to indicate the ground water level.

saturation temperature The temperature at which vapor and liquid coexist in stable equilibrium.

saucer dome   A dome that has a rise less than its radius.

sauna   A room in which a person bathes in steam produced when water is sprayed or poured over heated rocks or another heated surface.

saw   (1) To cut by means of a hand or powered tool having a thin, flat metal blade, band, or stiff plate with cutting teeth along the edge. (2) A toothed steel device used to cut construction materials.

saw, band   See **band saw**.

saw bench   A bench on which a circular saw is mounted.

sawbuck   See **sawhorse**.

saw, chain   See **chain saw**.

saw, circular   See **circular saw**.

saw cut (control joint)   A cut made in hardened concrete by diamond or silicone-carbide blades or discs.

saw, drag   See **drag saw**.

sawdust concrete   Concrete in which the aggregate consists mainly of sawdust from wood.

sawed finish   Descriptive of the surface of any stone that has been sawn.

sawed joint   A joint cut in hardened concrete by special equipment to less than the full depth of the member.

saw, gang   See **gang saw**.

sawhorse (sawbuck)   A four-legged bench, usually used in pairs, made primarily to hold wood while being sawed.

saw kerf   A slot or kerf that is cut into wood with a saw.

sawmill   A plant in which logs are converted to lumber by sawing.

scabbling hammer

scaffold

scaffolding

saw, miter *See* **tenon saw**.

sawn face *See* **sawed finish**.

sawn veneer Veneer that has been cut from a block with a saw, rather than peeled on a lathe or sliced off by a blade. Sawn veneer is sometimes said to be more solid than sliced or peeled veneer. Because of saw kerf waste, it is more costly to produce.

saw, rock *See* **rock saw**.

saw, saber *See* **saber saw**.

saw, sash *See* **sash saw**.

saw, scroll *See* **scroll saw**.

saw set (1) The angle at which the teeth of a saw are set. (2) A tool used to set the teeth of a saw at a desired angle.

saw, slasher *See* **slasher saw**.

saw, swing *See* **swing saw**.

saw table The table or platform of a power saw.

saw, tenon *See* **tenon saw**.

saw tex *See* **saw texture**.

saw texture A texture put on a piece of siding or paneling by a saw or knurled drum to give it a textured, rough, and/or resawn appearance.

saw-tooth roof (sawtooth roof) A roof with a profile similar to the teeth in a saw, composed of a series of single-pitch roofs, whose shorter or vertical side has windows for light and air. This roof shape is found primarily on industrial buildings.

saw, twin (double arbor saw) *See* **twin saw**.

sawyer In a sawmill, a worker who operates the head rig, or main saw, to make the initial cuts on a log.

Sawzall® *See* **reciprocating saw**.

scab (1) A short piece of wood fastened to two formwork members to secure a butt joint. (2) A slang term for a nonunion worker.

scabbing hammer *See* **scabbling hammer**.

scabble To dress stone with a pick, scabbling hammer, or broad chisel, leaving prominent tool marks so that a rough surface is left. Finer dressing usually follows.

scabbled rubble Rubble with only the roughest irregularities removed.

scabbling (1) A chip or fragment of stone produced during rough dressing. (2) Dressing down rough stone.

scabbling hammer (scabbing hammer) A hammer, used for rough dressing stone, with one end pointed for picking.

SCADA system *See* **supervisory control and data acquisition system**.

scaffold (1) Any temporary, elevated platform and its supporting structure used for supporting workmen and/or materials. (2) Any raised platform.

scaffold board A board used in forming a work platform on a scaffold.

scaffold height That height of a wall under construction, which necessitates the addition of another section of scaffold so that construction of the wall can continue.

scaffolding A temporary structure for the support of deck forms, cartways, and/or workers, such as an elevated platform for supporting workers, tools, and materials. Adjustable metal scaffolding is frequently adapted for shoring in concrete work.

scagliola Plasterwork in imitation of ornamental marble, consisting of ground gypsum and glue colored with marble or granite dust.

scale (1) A draftsman's tool with proportioned, graduated spaces. (2) A system of proportioned drawing in which lengths on a drawing represent larger or smaller lengths on a real object or surface. (3) The flaky material resulting from corrosion of metals, especially iron or steel. (4) A heavy oxide coating on copper or copper alloys resulting from exposure to high temperatures and an oxidizer. (5) Any device for measuring weight.

scale drawing A drawing in which all dimensions are reduced proportionately according to a predetermined scale.

scaling Local flaking or peeling away of the near-surface portion of hardened concrete or mortar, or of a layer from metal. *See also* **peeling**, **spelling**, *and* **mill scale**.

scaling hammer A hand or power hammer used in a chiseling fashion in masonry work.

scaling, light Does not expose coarse aggregate.

scaling, medium Involves loss of surface mortar to 5 to 10 mm in depth and exposure of coarse aggregate.

scaling, severe Involves loss of surface mortar to 5 to 10 mm in depth with some loss of mortar surrounding aggregate particles 10 to 20 mm in depth.

scaling, very severe Involves loss of coarse aggregate particles, as well as mortar, generally to a depth greater than 20 mm.

scallop One of a series of segments of a circle, used in decorative patterns.

scalper A sieve for removing oversized particles.

scalping The removal of particles larger than a specified size by sieving.

scalp rock The waste material from a rock-grading operation.

scant Less than standard or required size.

scantling (1) A small piece of lumber, ordinarily yard lumber, 2″ thick and less than 8″ wide, or lumber not more than 5″ square. (2) The dimensions, especially width and thickness, of construction materials such as stone or timber. (3) A stud or similar upright framing timber. (4) Any hardwood that has been squared, but is not of standard dimensions.

scarcement A ledged setback in a wall or bank of earth.

scarf The end of one of the pieces of a scarf joint.

scarf connection A connection made by precasting, beveling, halving, or notching two pieces to fit together. After overlapping, the pieces are secured by bolts or other means.

scarf joint A joint made by chamfering, or beveling, the ends of two pieces of lumber or plywood to be joined. The angled cut on each is made to correspond to the other so that the surfaces of the two pieces being joined are flush. *See also* **scarf connection**.

scarifier (1) An attachment, on a machine, having a series of long teeth which are used to tear up a pavement. (2) A plastering tool with long, wire-like teeth, used to scratch a plaster coat to form a surface for another coat.

scarify (1) To break up or scratch a surface such as earth or pavement. (2) To roughen a surface by sanding or other means to improve adhesion of paint.

scissors truss

scarp A steep slope, natural or man-made.

SC asphalt Slow-curing asphalt.

schedule A chronological itemization, often in chart form, of the sequence of project tasks. *See also* **progress schedule**.

schedule number Schedule numbers are American Standards Association designations for classifying the strength of pipe. Schedule 40 is the most common form of steel pipe used in the mechanical trades.

schedule of values (cost breakdown) A listing of elements, systems, items, or other subdivisions of the work, establishing a value for each, the total of which equals the contract sum. The schedule of values is used for establishing the cash flow of a project.

schematic design documents Documents and drawings that illustrate the relationship and scale of the components of the project.

schematic design phase (schematic drawing) The phase of design services in which the design professional consults with an owner to clarify the project requirements. The design professional prepares schematic design studies with drawings and other documents illustrating the scale and relationship of the project's components to the owner. A statement of estimated construction cost is often submitted at this phase.

schist A metamorphic rock, the constituent minerals of which have assumed roughly parallel beds, used principally for flagging.

Schmidt hammer An instrument used to measure the compressive strength of concrete. Testing involves gauging the distance of the hammer's rebound after it strikes the material.

scissor lift An electric or gas-powered platform mounted on a folding arms and used to provide elevated work areas or to raise or lower unit loads.

scissors truss A roof truss with tension members extending from the foot of each principal rafter to the upper half of its opposite member.

sconce A bracket for a candlelight or a similar electric fixture, placed on a wall.

score (1) In concrete work, to modify the top surface of one pour, as by roughening, so as to improve the mechanical bond with the succeeding pour. (2) To tool grooves in a freshly placed concrete surface to reduce cracking from shrinkage. (3) To scratch or otherwise roughen a surface to enhance the bond of plaster, mortar, or stucco which will be applied to it. (4) To groove, notch, or mark a surface for practical or decorative purposes.

scoria Vesicular volcanic ejecta of larger size, usually of basic core position and characterized by dark color. The material is relatively heavy and partly glassy, partly crystalline. The vesicles do not generally interconnect. *See also* **aggregate, lightweight**.

S corporation A corporation that has elected to be taxed like a partnership, in accordance with the provisions of subchapter S of the Internal Revenue Code.

Scotch pine *Pinus sylvestris*. An imported European conifer widely used in reforestation.

SCR brick

screed

screen door

scotia A deep, concave molding more than 1/4 round in section, especially as found in classical architecture at the base of a column.

Scots fir *See* **Scotch pine**.

Scots pine *See* **Scotch pine**.

scour (1) Erosion of a concrete surface by water movement exposing the aggregate. (2) Erosion of a river bottom by water movement.

scouring Smoothing freshly applied mortar or plaster by working it in circular motions with a cross-grained wooden float.

scragg mill An arrangement of four fixed saws used to break down logs or peeler cores of fairly uniform sizes. The scragg produces two slabs, two 2″ cants, and a 4″ cant in a single operation. These can then be reduced to 2x4s and 4x4s in a resaw.

scraper (1) A digging, hauling, and grading machine having a cutting edge, carrying bowl, a movable front wall or apron, and a dumping or ejecting mechanism. (2) A machine that is towed behind a vehicle to level the ground surface.

scratch To score or groove a coat of plaster to provide a better bonding surface for a successive coat.

scratch awl An awl used for scribing surfaces of wood, plastic, etc.

scratch-brushed finish (satin finish) A surface finish rendered by mechanical wire brushing or abrasive buffing.

scratch coat The first coat of plaster or stucco applied to a surface in three-coat work and usually cross-raked or scratched to form a mechanical key with the brown coat.

scratch tool Any hand tool for scratching a plaster surface to

increase bonding of the successive coat, such as a devil float, drag, or scarifier.

SCR brick A patented brick with nominal dimensions of 2-2/3″ x 6″ x 12″, as designated or classified by the Structural Clay Research (trademark of the Structural Clay Products Institute). It will render three courses in 8″ and will render a wall whose nominal thickness is 8″.

screed (1) To strike off concrete lying above the desired plane or shape. (2) A tool for striking off the concrete surface, sometimes referred to as a *strikeoff*.

screed coat The plaster coat made flush with the screeds.

screed guide Firmly established grade strips or side forms for unformed concrete which will guide the strikeoff in producing the desired plane or shape.

screeding The operation of forming a surface by the use of screed guides and a strikeoff. *See also* **strikeoff**.

screed rail Grade strips or side forms for concrete that will also guide the strikeoff in screeding.

screed strip One of a series of long narrow strips of plaster, carefully leveled to serve as guides for the application of plaster to a specified thickness.

screen *See* **sieve**.

screen analysis *See* **sieve analysis**.

screen door A lightweight exterior door, with a wood or aluminum frame and small mesh screening in place of panels, which permits ventilation but bars insects.

screen-door latch A light locking or latching device for use on screen doors and operated by a knob, a lever handle, or a handle and push button.

screwdriver

screw jack

scrub sink

screen façade An architectural facing used to disguise the shape or size of a building.

screenings That portion of granular material that is retained on a sieve.

screen mold A molding, originally used in the construction of screens and now used extensively in cabinetry and finished carpentry, where a clear strip is required, as on the edge of a shelf made of plywood or particle board.

screen wall *See* **perforated wall**.

screw A fastener with an external thread.

screw anchor A type of molly whose metal, plastic, or fiber shell is inserted into a hole in masonry, plaster, or concrete, and expanded when the screw is driven in.

screw clamp A woodworking tool consisting of a pair of opposing jaws that can hold pieces of wood and are adjusted by two screws.

screw conveyor A helical screw shaft turning on the concentric axis of a pipe. Conveys fine-grained or liquid material.

screw dowel A dowel pin with a straight or tapered thread.

screwdriver A hand tool with the shanks tip shaped to fit the recess in the head of a screw; used to drive or remove the screw.

screwed joint A pipe joint consisting of threaded male and female parts joined together.

screw eye A screw with a loop or eye for its head.

screw jack *See* **jackscrew**.

screwless knob A doorknob that is attached to the spindle using a special wrench, rather than the more common side screw.

screwless rose A rose with a concealed method of attachment.

screwnail *See* **drivescrew**.

scribe To mark and cut the edge of a member for an irregular cut that will allow it to fit a similarly irregular space.

scribed joint See **coped joint**.

scriber A pointed tool used to mark guide lines on wood, metal, and plastic.

scrim A coarse, meshed material, such as wire, cloth, or fiberglass, that spans and reinforces a joint over which plaster will be applied.

scroll compressor A rotary positive displacement compressor with a fixed and a rotating scroll, in which compression takes place by confining gas volume by the meshing of the scrolls.

scroll molding An ornamental molding, semicircle in cross section, with a slight overhang on the rounded surface that faces outward.

scroll saw A handsaw consisting of a thin blade in a deep U-shaped frame and a handle. A scroll saw is used for cutting thin boards, veneers or plates, and is especially good for cutting curves.

scrubboard See **baseboard**.

scrub plane A wood plane having a blade with a convex cutting edge, used in rough carpentry work.

scrub sink A plumbing fixture equipped to enable medical personnel to scrub their hands prior to a surgical procedure. The hot and cold water supply is activated by a knee-action mixing valve or by wrist or foot control.

scuba A self-contained underwater breathing apparatus utilizing an air tank connected directly to a respirator face mask.

scum (1) A deposit, sometimes formed on the surface of clay bricks, caused by soluble salts in the clay

563

scupper

seam

which accumulate on the surface during drying, or by the formation of deposits during kiln firing. (2) A mass of organic matter that floats on the surface of sewage. (3) A film of impure matter that forms on the surface of a body of water.

scumbling The process of lightly rubbing a paintbrush containing a small amount of opaque or semi-opaque color over a surface to soften and blend bright tints, or to produce a special effect. The deposited coat may be so thin as to seem semi-transparent.

scupper Any opening in a wall, parapet, bridge curb, or slab that provides an outlet through which excess water can drain.

scutch (scotch) A tool used by bricklayers to cut, trim, and dress masonry units.

scutching Dressing stone with a special hammer whose head contains several steel points.

scuttle See **roof hatch**.

s-dry A description of lumber seasoned to a moisture content of 19% or less prior to surfacing.

seal A legal term used to describe the signature or other representation of an individual agreeing to the terms and conditons of an agreement or contract.

sealant See **joint sealant, membrane curing** and **encapsulant**.

seal coat See **sealer**.

sealed bearing A conventional bearing which has been provided with seals on its sides so that the bearing can be used for longer periods without greasing.

sealed bid A bid, based on contract documents, that is submitted sealed for opening at a designated time and place.

sealed bidding A basic method of procurement that involves the solicitation of bids and the award of a contract to the responsible bidder submitting the lowest responsive bid. This type of bidding is commonly used on public works projects.

sealed double glass See **insulating glass**.

sealer (1) Any liquid applied to the surface of wood, paper, or plaster to prevent it from absorbing moisture, paint, or varnish. (2) A liquid coating applied over bitumen or creosote to restrict it from bleeding through other paints. (3) A final application of asphalt or concrete to protect against moisture. (4) Any liquid coating used to seal the pores of the surface to which it is applied.

sealing compound See **joint sealant** and **membrane curing**.

seal slab A concrete slab placed along the bottom of a trench to stabilize bedding material.

seal weld A weld used primarily to seal a joint against leakage.

seam A joint between two sheets of material, such as metal.

seamer A hand tool used in the making of seams in sheet metal.

seaming The process of joining metal sheets by bending over or doubling the edges and pinching them together.

seamless door (1) A hollow-metal door having no visible seams on its faces. (2) A door constructed from sheet-steel bonded to a solid, structural mineral core so as not to have any edge seams.

seamless flooring Fluid- or trowel-applied floor surfaces that do not contain aggregates.

seamless pipe An extruded seamless tube having certain standardized

seat angle

sizes of outside diameter and wall thickness, commonly designated by nominal pipe sizes and American National Standards Institute's schedule numbers.

seamless tubing Tubing manufactured with no visible seams.

seam weld A resistance weld made in overlapping parts.

seasonal energy efficiency ratio (SEER) A measure of cooling efficiency for air conditioning products. The higher the SEER rating, the more energy efficient the unit. The government's established minimum rating for air conditioning is 10.

season crack A crack occurring in metals that have undergone rolling or some other process that causes internal stress.

seasoned (1) Timber that is not green, having a moisture content of 19% or less, and is air- or kiln-dried. (2) Cured or hardened concrete.

seasoning (1) The process by which lumber is dried, either by air or in a kiln. (2) The curing or hardening process that occurs in concrete.

seasoning check A small split that occurs in the grain of wood when moisture is extracted too rapidly.

seat (1) The cut made at the lower end of a rafter which enables it to fit securely over the top wall plate. (2) See **valve seat**.

seat angle A short leg on a steel angle fastened to a column or girder to support the end of a beam.

seat cut The shaped cut in the end of a rafter where it rests on, and is connected to, a plate or beam.

seating pressure The pressure generated by the action of a spring and control air to close the automatic control valve plug against its seat.

sebrogation See **subrogation**.

secant modulus See **modulus of elasticity**.

second (1) A piece of secondary quality or one not meeting specified dimensions. (2) A unit measure of time.

secondary air (1) Air that is introduced into a burner above or around the flames to promote combustion, in addition to the primary air which is premixed with the fuel or forced as a blast under a stoker. (2) Air already in an air-conditioned space, in contrast to primary air which is supplied to the space.

secondary beam A flexural member that is not a portion of the principal structural frame of a building.

secondary blasting Blasting used to reduce the dimensions of oversized material to render it suitable for handling.

secondary branch In the plumbing of a building drain or water-supply main, any branch that is not the primary branch.

secondary combustion The burning of combustible gases and smoke which are not burned during primary combustion. Such combustion can be either by design to create added energy or an unintentional, undesirable event.

secondary consolidation (secondary compression, secondary time effect) The reduction in volume of a soil mass caused by the application of a sustained load to the mass and due principally to the adjustment of the internal structure of the soil mass after most of the load has been transferred from the soil water to the soil solids.

secondary reinforcement

secondary containment A chamber for the collection of oil that has leaked from a fuel oil tank.

secondary crusher An aggregate crusher used for the second stage in a process of size reduction. *See also* **primary crusher**.

secondary feeder Any electrical conductor that runs from a building's service entrance to one of its distribution centers.

secondary light source A light source that is not itself a luminaire or otherwise intrinsically light-producing or light-emitting, but which, instead, receives light from another source and simply serves to redirect it, as by reflection or transmission.

secondary member A structural member that carries a load to a primary member. Examples include purlins, headers and jambs. *See also* **primary member**.

secondary moment In statically indeterminate structures, the additional moments caused by deformation of the structure due to the applied forces. In statically indeterminate prestressed concrete structures, the additional moments caused by the use of a nonconcordant prestressing tendon.

secondary nuclear vessel Exterior container or safety container in a nuclear reactor subjected to a design load only once in its lifetime, if at all.

secondary reinforcement Reinforcing steel in reinforced concrete, such as stirrups, ties, or temperature steel. Secondary steel is any steel reinforcement other than main reinforcement.

secondary sheave A supplementary sheave or block used to enable double wrapping of hoisting ropes and increase traction and/or lifting power.

secondary subcontractor A subcontractor employed by the contractor to complete minor portions of the work, or a subcontractor other than those identified as primary subcontractors.

secondary winding The winding on the output side of a transformer.

second coat The second coat of plaster, which is the brown coat in three-coat work or the finish coat in two-coat work.

second-growth timber Wood from trees grown after a virgin forest has been cut down.

seconds A grade of lumber used in the hardwood industry and sometimes in the overseas trade, as in firsts and seconds.

secret dovetail (miter dovetail) A joint whose external appearance implies a simple miter joint, but having dovetailing concealed within it.

secret gutter A concealed gutter.

secret nailing *See* **blind nailing**.

section (1) A topographical measure of land area, equal to one mile square or 640 acres. One of the 36 divisions in a township. (2) The most desired pieces of veneer, clipped to standard widths of 54″ and 27″, because of the ease of using them in assembling a panel. The actual width may vary from 48–54″, or 24–27″. (3) A drawing of an object or construction member cut through to show the interior makeup. (4) A segment of the project specifications that cover a work item.

sectional insulation Insulation that is manufactured to be assembled in the field, such as pipe insulation molded

sectional overhead doors

security screen

in two parts to fit around a pipe in the field.

sectional overhead doors Doors made of horizontally hinged panels that roll into an overhead position on tracks, usually spring-assisted.

sectional valve In a piping system, a control valve that is used to isolate a section for repair or other reason.

section modulus A term pertaining to the cross section of a flexural member. The section modulus with respect to either principal axis is the moment of inertia with respect to that axis divided by the distance from that axis to the most remote point of the tension or compression area of the section, as required. The section modulus is used to determine the flexural stress in a beam.

sectorwood A method of wood processing, patented by Weyerhaeuser Company, in which round logs are first quartered and then cut into pie-shaped pieces called sectors. These pieces are then glued together to form wood 2″ thick and up to 3′-4′ in width. This wood can then be ripped to the desired widths. The process is designed to greatly increase the yield from small logs.

security glass *See* **bullet-resisting glass** *and* **laminated glass**.

security screen A heavy screen in a special frame used as a barrier against escapes or break-ins. *See also* **detention screen** *and* **protection screen**.

security screw A screw with a tamper-proof head design.

security window A steel window used in stores, warehouses, and similar commercial buildings to provide protection against burglary.

sediment (silt) Material that settles to the bottom of a liquid.

sedimentary rock Rock such as limestone or sandstone that is formed from deposits of sediment consolidated by cementitious material and/or the weight of overlying layers of sediment.

seedy Descriptive of a rough finish on paint caused by a dirty brush or by undispersed particles of pigment or insoluble gel particles in the paint.

seepage (1) The slow percolation of water through a soil. (2) The quantity of water which has moved slowly through a porous material.

seepage bed A trench at least a yard wide into which coarse aggregate and a system of distribution pipes are placed so as to allow the treated sewage which passes through them to seep into the surrounding soil.

seepage force The force which is transferred to soil particles by seepage.

segmental arch An arch where the curve through the length of the arch is less than a semicircle.

segmental member A structural member made up of individual elements prestressed together to act as a monolithic unit under service loads.

segment saw A large-diameter circular saw consisting of pie-shaped sections and whose narrow kerf makes it especially suitable for cutting veneer.

segregation The differential concentration of the components of mixed concrete, aggregate, or the like, resulting in nonuniform proportions in the mass. *See also* **separation**.

seismic bracing Structural reinforcement that is designed to protect against wind and earthquake.

seismic design Construction designed to withstand earthquake force.

seismic load (earthquake load) The assumed lateral load an earthquake might cause to act upon a structural system in any horizontal direction.

seizing (1) Friction damage to a metal surface by another metal surface. (2) Restriction or prevention of motion of a metal component caused by fusion or coherence with another component.

select A high-quality piece of lumber graded for appearance. Select lumber is used in interior and exterior trim, and cabinetry. It is most often sold S4S in a 4/4 thickness, but may also be produced S2S in a variety of thicknesses.

selected bidder The bidder selected by the owner to consider the award of a construction contract.

selected list of bidders See **invited bidders**.

selective bidding A process of competitive bidding for award of the contract for construction whereby the owner selects the constructors who are invited to bid to the exclusion of others, as in the process of open bidding.

selective digging Separating two or more types of soil while excavating, such as loam from sandy soil.

select material Excavated pervious soil suitable for use as a foundation for a granular base course of a road, or for bedding around pipes.

select merchantable (1) A grade of boards intended for use where knotty-type lumber of fine appearance is required.

(2) An export grade of sound wood with tight knots and close grain, suitable for high-quality construction and remanufacture.

select structural The highest grade of structural joists and planks. This grade is applied to lumber of high quality in terms of appearance, strength, and stiffness.

select tight knot (STK) A grade term frequently used for cedar lumber. Lumber designated STK is selected from mill run for the tight knots in each piece, as differentiated from lumber which may contain loose knots or knotholes.

selenite Gypsum in a transparent, foliated, crystalline state, usually used as ornamental building stone.

selenitic cement (selenitic lime) A type of lime cement that has had its hardening properties improved by the addition of 5-10% plaster of paris.

self-ballasted lamp An arc-discharge lamp with a special built-in filament coil that controls both starting and operating currents.

self-centering lath Expanded-metal rib lath used as lathing in solid plaster or pneumatic-placed concrete partitions and walls, or as formwork for concrete slabs.

self-closing device See **closing device**.

self-closing fire door A fire door equipped with a closing device.

self-contained air-conditioning See **packaged air-conditioner**.

self-contained breathing apparatus (SCBA) Personal protective equipment consisting of a mask and air supply that is used where there is a threat of toxic fumes or an oxygen-deficient atmosphere.

self-desiccation The removal of free water by chemical reaction so as to

semibasement

self-furring

semicircular arch

leave insufficient water to cover the solid surfaces and to cause a decrease in the relative humidity of the system. The term is applied to an effect occurring in sealed concretes, mortars, and pastes.

self-drilling screw A fastener that does not require a pre-drilled hole.

self-faced stone An undressed stone such as a flagstone.

self-finished roofing felt *See* **asphalt-prepared roofing**.

self-furring Metal lath or welded-wire fabric formed in the manufacturing process to include means by which the material is held away from the supporting surface, thus creating a space for *keying* of the insulating concrete, plaster, or stucco.

self-furring nail A nail with a flat head and a washer or spacer in the shank, used for fastening reinforcing wire mesh and spacing it from the nailing member.

self-ignition temperature The minimum temperature at which a material will self ignite with no external flame source.

self-leveling sealant A sealant, such as one used on concrete joints or cracks, with properties such that the simple force of gravity will level it.

self-reading leveling rod A leveling rod designed so that the instrument man sights on a target and the rodman takes the reading off the rod.

self-sealing paint A type of paint that can be applied over a surface of inconsistent porosity to seal it and still dry to a uniform color and sheen.

self-spacing tile Ceramic tile with protuberances on the sides that space the tiles for grout joints.

self-stressing concrete (chemically prestressed concrete) Expansive-cement concrete (mortar or grout) in which expansion, if restrained, induces persistent compressive stresses in the concrete.

self-supporting wall A non-load- bearing wall.

self-tapping screw A screw designed to cut its own threads in a predrilled hole.

seller's market A condition in which demand for goods is greater than supply, thereby giving sellers the upper hand in negotiations.

selvage (selvedge) (1) An edge or edging that differs from the main part of a fabric or granule-surfaced roll roofing. (2) The finished lengthwise edge of woven carpet that will not unravel or require binding.

selvage joint In roofing, a lapped joint mortised with mineral-surfaced cap sheets. A small part of the longitudinal edge of the sheet below contains no mineral surfacing so as to improve the bond between the lapped top sheet surface and the bituminous adhesive.

semiautomatic arc welding Arc welding with equipment that feeds the filler metal at a preset rate. The advance of the welding is controlled manually.

semiautomatic batcher *See* **batch mixer**.

semibasement A basement that is only partly below ground level.

semicircular arch A round arch whose *intrados* is a complete semicircle.

semicircular dome A dome constructed in the shape of a half-sphere.

semi-detached house

semiconductor (1) An electric conducting material, with resistivity in the range between metals and insulators, such as germanium or silicon. (2) Miniature electric devices manufactured from semiconductor materials.

semi-detached dwelling One of a pair of dwellings with a party wall between them.

semi-detached house One of a pair of houses with a party wall between them.

semi-direct lighting Lighting from luminaires that direct 60° to 90° of the emitted light downward and the balance upward.

semi-dome A half-dome equal to 1/4 of a hollow sphere, as might be found above a semicircular niche or apse.

semi-engineering brick Brick whose crushing strength is somewhere between that of building brick and engineering brick.

semi-flexible joint In reinforced concrete construction, a connection in which the reinforcement is arranged to permit some rotation of the joint.

semi-gloss (1) The degree of surface reflectance midway between glass and eggshell. (2) Paints and coatings displaying these properties.

semi-housed stair A stair which has a wall on one side only.

semi-hydraulic lime A type of lime categorized intermediately between high-calcium lime and eminently hydraulic limes. When run to putty it is almost as workable as nonhydraulic lime, even though its hydraulic characteristics can be substantially reduced by soaking in water for several hours.

semi-indirect lighting Lighting from luminaires that direct 60° to 90° of their emitted light upward and the balance downward.

semi-rigid frame A type of structural framework construction in which some flexibility is allowed at the joints of columns and beams.

semi-split A trade name used by the Red Cedar Shingle and Handsplit Shake Bureau for a product with a partially sawn and split face.

semi-steel Low-carbon cast iron produced by adding steel scrap to molten pig iron.

semi-trailer A trailer that has a set or sets of wheels at the rear only. The front part is supported on a towing vehicle.

sensible heat Heat that alters the temperature of a material without causing a change in state in that material.

sensitizer A substance that causes a person to become susceptible to the adverse health effects of the same or different substance to which he/she had previously not been susceptible.

sensor A device designed to detect an abnormal ambient condition, such as smoke or high temperature, and to sound an alarm or operate a device.

separate-application adhesive An adhesive consisting of two parts, each part being applied to a different surface. The surfaces are brought together to form a joint.

separate contract A prime contract which is one of several on a project. Distinguished from a subcontract.

separate contractor A contractor who has a direct contract with the owner. *See also* **separate contract**.

separated aggregate (1) A quantity of aggregate that has been separated into two or more batches based on

septic tank

service conductors

service door

size. (2) Fine and coarse aggregate considered separately before mixing.

separation (1) The tendency of coarse aggregate to separate from the concrete and accumulate at one side as concrete passes from the unconfined ends of chutes, conveyor belts, or similar arrangements. (2) The tendency of the larger aggregate to separate from the mass and accumulate at one side as processed aggregate leaves the ends of conveyor belts, chutes, or similar devices with confining sides. (3) The tendency of the solids to separate from the water by gravitational settlement. *See also* **bleeding** *and* **segregation**.

septic tank A watertight receptacle that receives the discharge from a sewage system, or part thereof. They are constructed to separate solids from the liquid, digesting organic matter during a period of detention, and discharging the clarified liquids.

sequence-stressing loss In posttensioning, the elastic loss in a stressed tendon resulting from the shortening of the member when additional tendons are stressed.

serial configuration *See* **series wiring**.

serial distribution A group of absorption trenches, seepage pits, or seepage beds arranged in a series so total effective absorption area of one is used before flow enters the next.

series circuit A circuit supplying electrical energy to a number of devices connected so that the same current passes through each device.

series wiring A wiring configuration in which electrical current travels along one conductor or wire. Unlike parallel wiring, series wiring is seldom used.

serpentine Rock largely composed of hydrous magnesium silicate and commonly occurring in greenish shades. It forms the main constituent in some marbles.

serpentine wall Garden wall that follows a curved *ogee* path resembling a serpent.

service The conducting equipment used to deliver electricity from the supply system to the wiring system of a building.

service box Within a building, a metal box located at the point where the electric service conductors enter the building.

service cable Cable composed of service conductors.

service conductors Those conductors (wires) that carry electrical current from the street mains, or transformers, to the service equipment of the building being supplied.

service dead load The dead weight supported by a member.

service door (service entrance) An exterior door in a building, intended primarily for deliveries, for removal of waste, or for the use of service personnel.

service drop The overhead conductors that connect the electrical supply or communication line to the building being served.

service elevator An elevator intended for combined passenger and freight use.

service ell (street ell) A fitting for threaded pipe with a 45° or 90° bend, a male thread on one end, and a female thread on the other.

service entrance The location where an electrical supply line enters a building.

571

service pipe

service entrance switch The circuit breaker or switch, with fuses and accessories, located near the point of entrance of supply conductors to a building and intended to be the main control and cut-off for the electrical supply to that building.

service equipment The equipment located at the point of entry of supply conductors to a building intended to control and, if necessary, cut off the electrical supply to that building. Consists of a circuit breaker or switch and fuses.

service lateral Those underground electrical service conductors (wires) between the street main, including any risers at a pole or other structure or from transformers, and the point of initial connection with the service entrance conductors in a terminal box or other enclosure either inside or outside a wall of the building being served. In the absence of such a box or enclosure, the service lateral connects the street main and the point at which the service conductors enter into the building.

service lead The electrical supply line running from a utility pole that delivers power to a customer service panel.

service live load The live load specified by the general building code or bridge specification, or the actual nonpermanent load applied in service.

service load *See* **service dead load** *and* **service live load.**

service panel The main circuit breaker panel or fuse box where the service lead ties into the building's circuits.

service period In lighting, the number of hours per day that natural daylight provides a specified amount of illumination, often expressed as a monthly average.

service pipe (1) The water or gas pipe that leads from a supply source, usually public distribution mains in the street, to the particular building(s) being served. (2) The pipe or conduit through which underground service conductors are run from the outside supply wires to the customer's property.

service refrigerator Any refrigerated display case or reach-in refrigerator from which an attendant serves a customer.

service road (1) A lesser road parallel to the main road, used primarily by local traffic. (2) A road or drive in a complex that is intended for vehicles making deliveries or collecting waste.

service systems The heating, ventilating, air-conditioning, water, and electric distribution systems in a building.

service tee A tee fitting used for threaded pipe and having one end threaded on the outside, and the other end and the branch threaded on the inside.

service temperature The highest temperature at which a material can be used without compromising its strength or other properties.

service valve In a piping system, any valve that isolates a device or apparatus from the rest of the system.

set (1) The condition reached by a cement paste, mortar, or concrete when it has lost plasticity to an arbitrary degree usually measured in terms of resistance to penetration or deformation. Initial set refers to first stiffening; final set refers to attainment of significant rigidity. *See also* **permanent set**. (2) The rehydration and consequential hardening of gypsum plaster. (3) The strain which remains in a member after the removal of the load that initially produced the deformation. (4) To transform a resin or adhesive from its initial liquid or plastic state to a hardened state by physical or chemical action, such as condensation, polymerization, oxidation, vulcanization, gelation, hydration, or the evaporation of volatile ingredients. (5) To drive a nail so far that its head is below the surface into which it has been driven. (6) To apply a finish coat of plaster. (7) The permanent distortion produced in a spring which has been stressed beyond the elastic limit of its constituent material. (8) The overhang given to the points of sawteeth resulting in a kerf slightly wider than the saw to facilitate sawing motion.

setback The minimum distance required by code or ordinance between a building and a property line or other reference.

setback buttress A buttress set slightly back from the angle or corner of a building.

set point The desired value of the controlled variable (i.e., temperature, pressure).

setscrew (1) An often headless screw used to secure two separate parts in a position relative to each other, preventing the independent motion of either part. (2) A screw used to adjust the tension of a spring.

setting bed The mortar subsurface to which *terrazzo* is applied.

setting block In glazing, a small block of wood, lead, neoprene, or other suitable material placed under the bottom edge of a light or panel to support it within the frame and prevent it from settling down onto the lower rabbet or channel.

setting shrinkage A reduction in volume of concrete prior to the final set of cement, caused by settling of the solids and by the decrease in volume due to the chemical combination of water with cement.

setting space The distance between the finished face of a veneer, such as a brick panel, and the outside of the main wall.

setting temperature The temperature to which an adhesive or resin must be subjected in order for setting to occur.

setting time *See* **initial setting time** *and* **final setting time**.

setting-up That point in the initial drying of a paint or other liquid coating at which it is no longer able to flow.

settlement (1) Sinking of solid particles in grout, mortar, or fresh concrete, after placement and before initial set. *See also* **bleeding**. (2) An agreement by which the parties consent to settle a dispute between them. (3) The total amount of money that both the insurance company and the policyholder agree on to close the claim.

settling The lowering in elevation of sections of pavement or structures due to their mass, the loads imposed on them, or shrinkage or displacement of the support.

settling basin An enlargement or basin within a water conduit which provides for the settling of suspended matter, such as sand; and is usually equipped with some means of removing the accumulated material.

sewage ejector

shaft

set up (1) The stationing of a surveying instrument, such as a transit. (2) Descriptive of concrete or similar firm material. (3) In plumbing, to bend up the edge of a sheet of lead lining material. (4) To caulk a pipe joint with lead by driving it in with a blunt chisel.

sewage Any liquid home waste containing animal or vegetable matter in suspension or solution. Sewage may include chemicals in solution; ground, surface, or storm water may be added as it is admitted to or passes through the sewers.

sewage disposal The treatment and dispersal of sewage.

sewage ejector A plumbing device used to raise sewage to a higher elevation.

sewage gas The mixture of gases, odors, and vapors, sometimes including poisonous and combustible gases, found in a sewer.

sewage treatment Any process to which sewage is subjected to remove or alter its objectionable constituents by reduction in the organic and bacterial content, rendering it less offensive and dangerous.

sewage treatment plant Structures and appurtenances that receive raw sewage and bring about a reduction in organic and bacterial content of the waste so as to render it less dangerous and less odorous.

sewer (1) Generally, an underground conduit in which waste matter is carried in a liquid medium. (2) A pipeline in which sewage is conveyed.

sewerage The entire works required to collect, treat, and dispose of sewage, including the sewer system, pumping stations, and treatment plant.

sewer appurtenances Manholes, sewer inlets, and other devices, constructions, or accessories related to a sewer system but exclusive of the actual pipe or conduit.

sewer brick Low absorption, abrasive-resistant brick intended for use in drainage structures.

sewer gas *See* **sewage gas**.

sewer pipe The piping used in a sewer.

sewer plank Timbers, mostly in the sizes of 3″ x 8″ and 3″ x 10″, 18′ and 20′ lengths, that are used to repair or construct drainageways, especially in older cities.

sewer tile Impervious clay tile pipe intended to carry water or sewage.

sewer trap *See* **building trap**.

s-green A description of lumber surfaced while at a moisture content of more than 19%.

shack *See* **shanty**.

shade The degree to which a color is mixed with black to decrease illumination, or darken it.

shade pine *See* **sugar pine**.

shading coefficient The measure of the solar heat coming through the glass of a window. A low shading coefficient means reduced air conditioning expense. *See also* **solar heat gain coefficient**.

shadow construction Refers to orientating and building a structure with true sun angles in relation to north-south axis, azimuth, and altitude angle of the sun at a desired time.

shaft (1) That portion of a column between the base and the capital. (2) An elevator well. (3) A pit dug from the ground surface to a tunnel to furnish access and ventilation. (4) Any enclosed vertical space in a building used for utilities or

shake

shape

shear connector

ventilation. (5) Any cylindrical rod connecting moving parts in a machine.

shake (1) Roofing or sidewall material produced from wood, usually cedar, with at least one surface having a grain split face. (2) A crack in lumber due to natural causes.

shale A laminated and fissile sedimentary rock, the constituent particles of which are principally clay and silt.

shank (1) The main body of a nail, screw, bolt, or similar fastener extending between the head and the point. (2) The usually metal part of a drill or other tool that connects the working head to the handle. (3) In a Doric frieze, a plain space between channels of a *triglyph*.

shank hanger Device used to attach metal gutters to a structure by fastening to sheathing or rafters.

shanty A small wooden building, usually temporary and haphazardly constructed.

shape (1) A solid section, other than flat product, rod, or wire sections, furnished in straight lengths and usually made by extrusion; but sometimes fabricated by drawing. (2) A solid section other than regular rod, bar, plate, sheet, strip, or flat wire. It may be oval, half oval, half round, triangular, pentagonal, or of any special cross section furnished in straight lengths. (3) A wrought product that is long in relation to the dimensions of its cross section, which is of a form other than that of sheet, plate, rod, bar, tube, or wire. (4) To give a profile or detail to a piece of work, such as providing a board with a head or rounded edge. (5) To work

on a piece of wood or other material to make it conform to a predetermined desired or required pattern, or to render from its surface a specific texture or degree of smoothness.

shaper (1) A woodworking machine with a vertically revolving cutter for cutting irregular outlines, moldings, etc., in wood placed on a table below the cutter. (2) A metalworking machine similar to a planer, except that the cutting tool is moved back and forth across the surface.

shaping machine *See* **shaper**.

sharp pencil A great effort to prepare a competitive bid through accuracy in estimating.

sharp sand Coarse sand made up of particles of angular shape.

shasta red fir *See* **California red fir**.

shatterproof glass *See* **laminated glass**.

shaving A very thin slice of wood removed in dressing, and used in some types of panels.

shear (1) An internal force tangential to the plane on which it acts. *See also* **shearing force**. (2) The relative displacement of adjacent planes in a single member. (3) To cut metal with two opposing passing blades or with one blade passing a fixed edge. (4) The tool used for the operation in definition 3.

shear connector (1) A welded stud, spiral bar, short length of channel, or any other similar connector that resists horizontal shear between components of a composite beam. (2) A timber connector.

shear diaphragms Members in a structure utilized to resist shear forces, such as those caused by wind load. *See also* **shear wall**.

shear plate

shear stud

sheathing

shear failure (failure by rupture) Failure in which movement caused by shearing stresses in a soil or rock mass is of sufficient magnitude to destroy or seriously endanger a structure.

shearhead Assembled unit in the top of the columns of flat slab or flat plate construction to transmit loads from slab to column.

shearing force The algebraic sum of all the tangential forces acting on either side of the section at a particular location in a flexural member.

shearing machine (1) An apparatus having a movable blade that passes a fixed cutting edge to cut metal. (2) A machine used in carpet finishing to remove stray fibers and fuzzy loop pile and produce a smooth, level surface.

shear legs A hoisting device from two or more poles fastened together near their apex, from which a pulley is hung to lift heavy loads.

shear plate (1) A shear-resisting plate used to reinforce the web of a steel beam. (2) In heavy timber construction, a round steel plate usually inserted in the face of a timber to provide shear resistance in joints between wood and nonwood.

shear-plate connector A type of timber connector employed in wood-to-wood or wood-to-steel applications.

shear reinforcement Reinforcement designed to resist shear or diagonal tension stresses.

shears A metal-cutting tool which has two opposing pivoted blades with beveled edges facing each other.

shear slide A type of landslide where a section of earth slides away from the material beneath it in a single consolidated mass.

shear splice A type of splice designed to distribute the shear between the two members that it joins.

shear strain (shearing strain) The angular displacement or deformation of a member caused by a force perpendicular to its length.

shear strength The maximum shearing stress that a material or structural member is capable of developing, based on the original area of cross section.

shear stress The shear-producing force per unit area of cross section, usually expressed in pounds per square inch.

shear stud A short unthreaded bolt welded to the top flange of a steel beam. The shear studs are embedded in a concrete slab to form a composite beam and stud.

shear wall (shearwall) A wall portion of a structural frame intended to resist lateral forces, such as earthquake, wind, and blast, acting in the plane or parallel to the plane of the wall.

sheath An enclosure in which posttensioning tendons are encased to prevent bonding during concrete placement. *See also* **duct**.

sheathed cable Electric cable protected by nonconductive covering, such as vinyl. *See also* **nonmetallic sheathed cable**.

sheathing (1) The material forming the contact face of forms. Also called *lagging* or *sheeting*. (2) Plywood, waferboard, oriented strand board, or lumber used to close up side walls, floors, or roofs preparatory to the installation of finish materials on the surface. The sheathing grades of lumber are also commonly used for pallets, crates,

she bolt

shed dormer

shed roof

sheeting

and certain industrial products. (3) The first covering of exterior studs or rafters by boards, plywood, or particle board.

sheathing felt Roofing felt that has been saturated or impregnated, usually with some type of bitumen of low softening point (100°-160°F).

sheathing paper *See* **building paper.**

sheave (1) The grooved wheel of a pulley or block. (2) The entire assembly over which a rope or cable is passed, including not only the pulley wheel but also its shaft bearings and side plates.

sheave block A pulley with a housing and bail.

she bolt A type of form tie and spreader bolt in which the end fastenings are threaded into the end of the bolt, eliminating cones and reducing the size of holes left in the concrete surface.

shed A small, usually roughly constructed shelter or storage building, sometimes having one or more open sides, and sometimes built as a lean-to.

shed dormer A dormer window having vertical framing projecting from a sloping roof, and an eave line parallel to the eave line of the principal roof. A shed dormer is designed to provide more space under a roof than a gabled dormer would provide.

shed roof A roof having a single sloping plane.

sheen On a flat paint finish, the luster or gloss that can be seen only from certain angles.

sheen uniformity An applied finish with a consistent luster across its entire surface.

sheepsfoot roller A powered or towed earth-tamping or compacting

machine consisting of a large drum with projecting studs or feet with enlarged outer ends.

sheer legs *See* **shear legs.**

sheet A thin piece of material, such as glass, veneer, plywood, or rolled metal. *See also* **panel.**

sheet asphalt A plant-mixed asphalt paving material containing sand which has passed through a 10-mesh sieve, and some type of mineral filler.

sheet glass (common window glass) Flat glass made by continuous drawing.

sheet groove *See* **reglet.**

sheeting (1) Planks used to line the sides of an excavation, such as for shoring and bracing. *See also* **sheathing.** (2) 7/8″ tongue-and-groove board. (3) Sheet piling. (4) A form of plastic in which the thickness is very small in proportion to length or width, and in which the plastic is present as a continuous phase throughout, with or without filler.

sheeting clip A metal clip designed to fasten different thicknesses of plasterboard, plywood paneling, etc.

sheeting driver An air hammer attachment that fits onto the ends of planks to allow their being driven without splintering.

sheeting jacks Push-type turnbuckles used to support sheeting in a trench.

sheet lath Heavier and stiffer than expanded-metal lath, it is fabricated by punching geometrical perforations in copper alloy steel sheet.

sheet lead Lead which has been cold-rolled into a sheet and whose designation is determined by the weight of one square foot of the finished product.

sheet metal screw

sheet pile

shelf angles

sheet metal Metal, usually galvanized steel but also aluminum, copper, and stainless steel, that has been rolled to any given thickness between 0.06″ and 0.249″ and cut into rectangular (usually 4′x8′) sections, which are then used in the fabrication of such items as ductwork, pipe, and gutters.

sheet-metal screw Usually a self-tapping screw, either round, flat, or pan-headed, threaded from tip to head, and used without a nut for fastening lapped sheet metal and some other materials. When equipped with a pointed tip, no tap hole is required.

sheet-metal work The fabrication, installation, and/or final product, such as the ductwork of a heating or cooling system, as performed or produced by a worker skilled in that trade.

sheet notch A channel formed along a foundation's outside edge to lend support and closure to wall sheathing.

sheet pile A pile in the form of a plank driven in close contact or interlocking with others to provide a tight wall to resist the lateral pressure of water, adjacent earth, or other materials. A sheet pile may be tongued and grooved if made of timber or concrete, or interlocking if made of metal.

sheetpiling A barrier or diaphragm formed of sheet piles which is used to prevent the movement of soil or keep out water during excavation and construction. Sheet piles are constructed of timber, sheet steel, or concrete.

Sheetrock® A trade name for gypsum drywall panel products.

sheetrock screwdriver A specialized power tool designed to accept the flat Phillips head of a sheetrock screw and drive the screw when the point is placed on the sheetrock and the tool is pushed toward it.

sheet-roofing nail *See* **roofing nail**.

Shelby tube A sampling device used to collect soil samples during a drilling operation.

shelf (1) Any horizontally mounted board, slab, or other flat-surfaced device upon which objects can be stored, supported, or displayed. (2) A ledge, as of rock, of a setback.

shelf angle A section of angle iron or steel which is welded or otherwise secured to an I-beam or channel section to provide support for the formwork or the hollow tiles of a concrete slab, or which, when similarly attached to a girder, carries the ends of joists.

shelf angles Structural angles with holes or slots in one leg for bolting to the structure to support brickwork, stone, or terra cotta.

shelf cleat A wood (or other) strip that supports a shelf along one edge.

shelf life Maximum duration that a material can be stored and still remain in a usable condition.

shelf nog A shelf support that consists of a piece of wood built into a wall and protruding outward from it.

shelf rest (shelf pin, shelf support) A type of angle bracket through whose vertical portion a pin is passed and inserted into one of several position-adjusting holes such as in a wall, or cabinet.

shelf strip *See* **shelf cleat**.

shelf standard A metal or wood shelf support with slots that allow adjustable placement of brackets to support shelving.

shell (1) Structural framework. (2) In stressed-skin construction, the outer skin applied over the frame members. (3) Any hollow

shielded conductor

shingle

construction when accomplished with a very thin curved plate or slab. (4) The outer portion of a hollow masonry unit when laid.

shellac A transparent coating produced by dissolving lac, a resinous secretion of the lac bug, in denatured alcohol.

shell aggregate A type of aggregate made up of fine sands and the shells of mollusks, such as clams, oysters, and scallops.

shell bracket Any structural member secured to a wall or upright, from which it also projects to support a shelf.

shell construction (1) A type of reinforced concrete construction in which thin curved slabs are primary elements. (2) Construction in which a curved exterior surface has been obtained by using shaped steel and hardboard or curved plywood panels.

shelling *See* **checking**.

shell pile A load-supporting structural element that consists of a steel shell embedded in the ground and filled with concrete.

shelly structure *See* **perlitic structure**.

sherardizing A type of galvanizing process that is mainly used for small items such as fittings and fasteners. Sherardizing is the diffusion coating of zinc on steel, and is accomplished by submerging items in hot zinc dust.

Sherman Anti-Trust Act Enacted by Congress in 1890, to prevent the unchecked growth of "big business" by preventing companies or individuals from holding a monopoly or controlling prices in certain areas of commerce.

shielded conductor An insulated electric conductor enclosed in a metal sheath or envelope.

shielded metal-arc welding An arc welding process wherein coalescence is produced by heating with an arc between a covered metal electrode and the work. Shielding is obtained from decomposition of the electrode covering. Pressure is not used, and filler metal is obtained from the electrode.

shielded pair Two insulated wires in a cable wrapped with metallic braid or foil to prevent interference caused by external electric and magnetic fields and facilitate a clean transmission.

shielding (screening) (1) The erection of an interfering barrier (usually made of metal) to prevent electric, magnetic, or electromagnetic fields from escaping or entering an enclosed area. (2) Any device that blocks, diffuses or redirects light, such as a baffle or lens.

shielding concrete Concrete used as a biological shield to attenuate or absorb nuclear radiation; usually characterized by high specific gravity or high hydrogen (water) or boron content. *See also* **biological shielding**.

shift (1) The lateral movement of a faulted seam. (2) A work period.

shim A strip of metal, wood, or other material used to set base plates or structural members at the proper level for placement of grout, or to maintain the elongation in some types of posttensioning anchorages.

shingle (1) A roof-covering unit made of asphalt, wood, slate, asbestos, cement, or other material cut into stock sizes and applied on sloping roofs in an overlapping pattern. (2) A thin piece of material, such as wood, cement, asbestos, or plastic, used as an exterior wall finish over sheathing.

shiplap

shoe

shingle backer A specially fabricated sheathing-grade structural insulating board used as a backer strip in coursed shingle construction.

shingle lap A type of lap joint whereby the thinner of two tapered surfaces is lapped over the thicker.

shingle molding An exterior molding used at the joint of roof shingles and the fascia.

shingle nail A galvanized steel, aluminum alloy, or coated steel nail, often having a threaded shank. There are two types of shingle nails: one for wood shingles and one for asphalt shingles, the latter having a larger head.

shingle ridge finish *See* **Boston hip**.

shingle stain A low-viscosity, pigmented finish that penetrates wood shingles to provide moisture protection as well as color.

shingle tile A flat clay tile used primarily for roofing and laid so as to overlap.

shinglewood Another name for western red cedar.

shingling hatchet (claw hatchet) Similar to a lath hammer, this tool consists of a hammer head, a hatchet, and a notch or nail claw.

ship decking Full-sawn, vertical-grain pieces, knot-free on the faces; used in the construction of ship decks.

shiplap (1) Lumber that has been worked to make a rabbeted joint on each edge so that pieces may be fitted together snugly for increased strength and stability. (2) A similar pattern cut into plywood or other wood panels used as siding to ensure a tight joint.

shipping position A seller's estimate of the time required after an order is placed until it can be shipped.

shivering (peeling) The splintering that critical compressive stresses can precipitate in fired glazes or other ceramic coatings.

shock *See* **thermal shock**.

shock-free head Typical bumping post used in railroad construction that will absorb shock when hit by a rail car.

shock hazard Considered to exist between an accessible part in a circuit and the ground or other accessible parts, if the potential is more than 42.4 volts peak and the current through a 1,500-ohm load is more than 5 milliamperes.

shock load The impact load of material such as aggregate or concrete as it is released or dumped during placement.

shock mount *See* **vibration isolator**.

shoddy work Any work which has been performed carelessly and/or unprofessionally.

shoe (1) Any piece of timber, metal, or stone receiving the lower end of virtually any member. Also called a *soleplate*. (2) A metal device protecting the foot, or point, of a pile. (3) A metal plate used at the base of an arch or truss to resist horizontal thrust. (4) A ground plate forming a link of a track, or bolted to a track line. (5) A support for a bulldozer blade or other digging edge to prevent cutting down. (6) A cleanup device following the buckets of a ditching machine. (7) A short section used at the base of a downspout to direct the flow of water away from a wall.

shoe molding A base shoe used at the bottom of a baseboard to cover the space between the finished flooring and the baseboard.

shore

shoring

shoring, horizontal

shoe rail The molding on the top of a stair string to support the balusters.

shoot To straighten the edge of a board with a plane.

shooting The placing of shotcrete.

shooting board A jig to hold a board while its edge is being squared or beveled.

shooting plane A light plane used to square or bevel the edge of a board with a shooting board.

shop coat A surface coating applied in a fabricating shop.

shop drawings Drawings created by a contractor, subcontractor, vendor, manufacturer, or other entity that illustrate construction, materials, dimensions, installation, and other pertinent information for the incorporation of an element or item into the construction.

shop lumber (factory lumber) Lumber graded, in a shop or factory, according to the number of pieces, of designed size and quality, into which it may be cut.

shop painting The application of paint, usually one coat, to metals in the shop before shipment to a job site.

shopping center A collection of stores, shops, and service centers, along with parking facilities.

shop rivet A rivet driven in the shop.

shop steward A union official elected to represent members of a particular trade or department. Position responsibilities include soliciting new members, collecting dues, and initial negotiations for grievances.

shopwork Work manufactured or assembled in the shop.

shore (post, prop, strut, tom) A temporary support for formwork and fresh concrete or for recently built structures that have not developed full design strength. *See also* **T-head**.

shore hardness number A number representing the relative hardness of materials. It is the height of rebound observed when a standard hammer strikes the material being tested.

shore head A wood or metal horizontal member placed on and fastened to a vertical shoring member. *See also* **raker**.

shore up To support with shores.

shoring (1) Props or posts of timber or other material in compression; used for the temporary support of excavations, formwork, or unsafe structures. (2) The process of erecting shores.

shoring, horizontal A metal or wood load-carrying strut, beam, or trussed section used to carry a shoring load from one bearing point, column, frame, post, or wall to another. Horizontal shoring may be adjustable.

shoring layout A drawing prepared prior to erection showing the arrangement of equipment for shoring.

short circuit An accidental electric connection of relatively low resistance between two points of different potential in an electric circuit, causing a high current flow between the two points.

short face (narrow face) A sales term used when describing tongue-and-groove siding that includes the tongue within the stated width.

short grain Wood in which part of the grain runs diagonally to the length of the piece and which is subject to failure under load.

shortleaf pine *Pinus echinata*. This species, one of the Southern group,

short nipple

shower bath

is found in a broad range, from Texas to as far north as Pennsylvania and New Jersey.

short-length (1) A piece of stock lumber usually less than 8' (2.44m) long. (2) A piece of sawn hardwood usually less than 6' (1.83m) long (Brit).

short nipple A pipe nipple with a short unthreaded length between the threaded ends.

short-oil varnish A varnish having a low vehicle content, containing less than 15 gallons of oil per 100 pounds of resin.

shorts Short pieces of lumber. The lengths described as shorts vary widely by species, products, and regions. Generally, a dimension of 12' or less is described as short, while boards of 6' or less are also shorts.

short ton A unit of measurement of weight in the English system equal to 2,000 pounds.

short working plaster Plaster that is difficult to work and from which the sand separates, due to its being affected by moisture over a long storage period.

shotblasting A process similar to sandblasting, except that metal shot is used.

shotcrete (1) Mortar or concrete pneumatically projected at high velocity onto a surface. Also known as air-blown mortar. (2) Pneumatically applied mortar or concrete, sprayed mortar, and gunned concrete. *See also* **dry-mix shotcrete, pneumatic feed, positive displacement,** *and* **wet-mix shotcrete**.

shotcrete gun A pneumatic device used to deliver shotcrete or to move concrete.

shot saw A power tool that shoots steel pellets to cut and finish building stone.

shot tower A tower used in the manufacture of metal shot. Molten lead is dropped from a height into water.

shoulder (1)An unintentional offset in a formed concrete surface usually caused by bulging or movement of formwork. *See also* **ear**. (2) The enlarged section of a bolt or screw shank just below the head.

shoulder bolt In construction, a fastener that attaches wall and roof paneling to framing members.

shouldering Placing mortar under the top edge of a slate so the lower edge will fit closer to the slate beneath.

shoved joint A vertical joint in brickwork made by laying the brick in a bed of mortar and shoving the brick toward the last brick laid.

shower bath (shower, shower stall) The compartment and plumbing provided for bathing by overhead spray.

shower-bath drain A floor drain in a shower bath.

shower head A nozzle used to spray water in a shower bath.

shower mixer A valve in a shower bath used to mix hot and cold water supplies to obtain a desired water temperature.

shower pan A pan of concrete, terrazzo, concrete and tile, or metal used as a floor in a shower bath.

shower partition A partition used around a shower bath for privacy.

shower room Part of the worker decontamination enclosure system. Usually located between the equipment room and the clean room, acts an as airlock between

shower stall door

shutter

siamese connection

contaminated and noncontaminated areas. Contains hot and cold tap water suitable for showering during decontamination.

shower stall door A door in a shower partition.

show rafter A rafter, often ornamental, that is visible below a cornice.

show window A window used to display merchandise.

shrinkage Volume decrease caused by drying and/or chemical changes, such as of concrete or wood.

shrinkage-compensating A characteristic of grout, mortar, or concrete made using an expansive cement in which volume increase, if restrained, induces compressive stresses intended to approximately offset the tendency of drying shrinkage to induce tensile stresses. *See also* **expansive cement**.

shrinkage crack A crack due to restraint of shrinkage.

shrinkage cracking The cracking of a structure or member due to failure in tension caused by external or internal restraints from carbonation and/or reduction in moisture content.

shrinkage, drying *See* **drying shrinkage** *and* **shrinkage**.

shrinkage joint *See* **contraction joint**.

shrinkage limit The water content at which a reduction in water content will not cause a decrease in volume of the soil mass but an increase in water will increase the volume. *See also* **Atterberg limits**.

shrinkage loss Reduction of stress in prestressing steel resulting from shrinkage of concrete.

shrinkage reinforcement Reinforcement designed to resist shrinkage stresses in concrete.

shrink-mixed concrete Ready-mixed concrete mixed partially in a stationary mixer and then mixed in a truck mixer. *See also* **preshrunk**.

shrunk joint A joint made by placing a piece of heated pipe over the ends of two cool pipes and allowing it to contract.

shunt An electrical device with a low resistance or impedance connected in parallel across another electrical device to divert current from the second device.

shutter A movable cover or screen used to cover an opening, especially a window opening.

shutter bar A hinged bar used to fasten a pair of shutters together in the closed position.

shutter blind An exterior adjustable louver used at a window.

shutter butt A narrow hinge used on shutters and small doors.

shuttering (1) British term for concrete formwork. (2) Closures for windows or vents.

shutting shoe A receptacle of metal or stone set in the paving or ground beneath a gate with two leaves to receive the vertical bolt.

siamese connection A wye connection on the outside of a building with two inlet connections, used by the fire department to supply water to a sprinkler and/or standpipe system.

sick building syndrome (SBS) A condition where a significant proportion of the occupants of a building experience symptoms that are not related to a specific disease and that usually disappear when they leave the building. These

sidewalk door

siding (weatherboarding)

symptoms are usually caused by indoor pollutants such as volatile organic compounds. *See also* **indoor air quality** *and* **building-related illness.**

sidecast During the construction of a logging road, the pushing of waste soil and debris over the downhill side.

sidecasting Piling soil beside the excavation.

side-construction tile Tile designed to be used with the cells set horizontally.

side cut *See* **cheek cut.**

side-cutting pliers General purpose pliers to snip light gauge wire. Its jaws have both a gripping and a cutting section.

side-dump loader An earth loader with its bucket mounted on a pivot so it can be dumped to either side as well as in front.

side-entrance manhole A deep manhole with the access shaft built into the side of the inspection chamber.

side gutter A small gutter along a side of a chimney or dormer.

sidehill A slope crossing the line of work.

sidehill cut An excavation for a highway through a sidehill, leaving a bank on one side only.

side hook *See* **bench hook.**

side-hung window *See* **casement window.**

side jamb A vertical member forming a side of a door opening.

side knob screw A setscrew used to secure a doorknob to a spindle.

side lap The distance that a piece of material, such as steel roof deck, overlaps an adjacent piece.

side light A fixed frame of glass beside a window or door.

side mounting Typical mounting detail for posts and rails to a fascia when floor mounting is not an option.

side outlet An ell or tee fitting with an outlet at right angles to the line of run.

side post One of a pair of posts in a roof truss, each set at an equal distance from the center of the truss.

side vent A vent connected to the drain pipe at an angle of 45° or less from vertical.

sidewalk door A cellar door opening directly onto a sidewalk. The door is flush with the sidewalk when closed.

sidewalk elevator (1) An elevator opening onto a sidewalk. (2) An elevator platform without a cab that rises to a level flush with a sidewalk.

sidewall The exterior wall of a building.

side yard The open space between a side of a dwelling and the property line.

siding (weatherboarding) Lumber or panel products intended for use as the exterior wall covering on a house or other building.

siding gauge *See* **clapboard gauge siding.**

sieve A metallic plate or sheet, a woven wire cloth, or other similar device, with regularly spaced apertures of uniform size, mounted in a suitable frame or holder, for use in separating material according to size. In mechanical analysis, an apparatus with square openings is a sieve; one with circular apertures is a screen.

sieve analysis The determination of the proportions of particles within certain size ranges in a granular material by separation on sieves of different size openings. *See also* **grading**.

sieve correction Correction of a sieve analysis to adjust for deviation of sieve performance from that of standard calibrated sieves.

sieve number A number used to designate the size of a sieve, usually the approximate number of openings per inch. The number is applied to sieves with openings smaller than 1/4″ (6.3mm).

sieve size The nominal size of openings, usually between cross wires of a testing sieve.

sight draft An instrument of payment negotiated through banks. Negotiable documents are attached, such as an order bill of lading, thus ensuring payment by the consignee to the negotiating bank in exchange for the documents and prior to the delivery of goods.

sight glass A glass tube used to indicate the liquid level in boilers, tanks, etc.

sighting rod *See* **leveling rod** *and* **range rod**.

sight rail A series of rails set with a surveying instrument, and used to check the vertical alignment of a pipe in a trench.

sight rod *See* **leveling rod** *and* **range rod**.

sign (signboard) (1) A board or surface displaying directions, instructions, identification, or advertising. (2) A warning of hazard, temporarily or permanently affixed, or placed at a location where a hazard exists.

signal Aggregate waves that are transmitted or received.

signal sash fastener A sash fastener beyond reach of a person. The fastener consists of a catch operated by a ring moved by a fitting on a long pole.

silencer *See* **rubber silencer**.

silica Silicon dioxide (SiO_2).

silica brick A refractory brick made from quartzite containing approximately 96% silica with alumina and lime.

silica flour (silica powder) Very finely divided silica; a siliceous binder cement that reacts with lime under autoclave curing conditions. The flour is prepared by grinding silica, such as quartz, to a fine powder.

silica gel (synthetic silica) A drying agent made from a form of silica.

silica powder *See* **silica flour**.

silicate Salt of a silicic acid.

silicate paint A paint utilizing sodium silicate as the binding agent.

silicon A metallic element used mainly as an alloying agent but used in pure form in electrical rectifiers.

silicon bronze A copper alloy used in hardware and other applications where a high resistance to oxidation is desirable.

silicon carbide An artificial product (SiC), granules of which may be embedded in concrete surfaces to increase resistance to wear or as a means of reducing skidding or slipping on stair treads or pavement. Silicon carbide is also used as an abrasive in saws and drills for cutting concrete and masonry.

silicone A resin, characterized by water-repellent properties, in which the main polymer chain consists of alternating silicon and oxygen atoms, with carbon-containing side

sill

sill anchor

sill course

simple span

groups (free radicals). Silicones may be used in caulking or coating compounds or admixtures for concrete.

silicone-carbide paper A tough, black, water-resistant sandpaper used in wet sanding and finishing.

silicone paint A heat- and chemical-resistant paint used on chimneys, stoves, and heaters, that requires heat to cure.

sill (1) The horizontal member of the bottom of a window or exterior door frame. (2) As applied to general construction, the lowest member of the frame of the structure, resting on the foundation and supporting the frame. *See also* **mudsill**.

sill anchor An anchor bolt used to fasten a sill to its foundation.

sill block A solid concrete masonry unit used as a sill for an opening.

sill cock A water faucet located on the exterior of a building roughly at the top of the sill. A sill cock is usually threaded to provide a connection for a hose.

sill course A course of brickwork at a windowsill, usually projected to shed water.

sill high (1) Located at the height of a sill above the floor. (2) Located at the height of a sill above ground level.

sill, lug A sill with ends that project into the masonry. Lug sills must be installed as the structure is built.

silo (1) A tower-like structure, usually cylindrical, used to store items such as grain, coal, or minerals. (2) A structure built in the ground to house a military missile.

silt (inorganic silt, rock flour) (1) A granular material resulting from the disintegration of rock, with grains largely passing a No. 200 (75-micrometer) sieve. (2) Such particles in the range from 2 to 50 micrometers in diameter.

siltation test A test to measure the impurities present in a sand sample.

silt box A steel box in a catch basin that can be removed to clean out the silt.

silt grade Descriptive of sediment having particles of silt size.

silt trap A trap that catches waterborne soil before it can enter a drainage system and obstruct flow.

silver fir *See* **Pacific silver fir**.

silver-lock bond Brickwork consisting of courses of alternating headers and stretchers laid on edge.

silver solder A solder containing silver and having a high melting point, used for high-strength solder joints.

silver spruce *See* **Sitka spruce**.

silver white (1) Any white pigment used in paints. (2) A very pure white lead.

simple beam A beam without restraint or continuity at its supports.

simple span The support-to-support distance of a simple beam.

simplex casement A swing-out window with no mechanical device for opening and closing.

single-acting door Any door mounted so that it swings in only one direction.

single-acting hammer A pile-driving hammer using compressed air or steam to raise the ram to the height from which it is dropped.

single bridging Single pieces of wood fixed between joists, as opposed to diagonal bridging.

single-hubpipe

single-ply roofing

single-cleat ladder A ladder made of two side rails with single treads between them. *See also* **double-cleat ladder**.

single contract A construction contract arrangement under which a prime contractor is accountable for all of the work.

single-cut file A file having serrations cut in one direction only.

single-duct system An air-conditioning system using one duct to serve a number of different areas.

single Flemish bond A bond in a brick wall using Flemish bond for the facework and English bond for the body.

single floor A floor of joists and flooring only, without intermediate support.

single-framed roof A roof-framing system in which the rafters are tied together by boards or by the framing of the floor or ceiling below.

single-hubpipe A pipe with a hub at one end only.

single-hung window A window with a movable and a fixed sash that is vertically hung.

single-lap tile A curved roofing tile laid so as to overlap only the tile directly below it.

single-package refrigeration system A factory-assembled and tested refrigeration system shipped in one section. No refrigerant-containing parts are connected in the field.

single-ply roofing A membrane roofing system that uses polymer-based synthetic material in flexible sheet or liquid form as an alternative to traditional built-up roofing. Made from a variety of bitumens, polymers, fillers, plasticizers, stabilizers and other additives, single-ply roofing products are commonly applied over an insulating material and secured with ballast, mechanical fasteners or an adhesive.

single-point adjustable suspension scaffold A manually or power-operated platform supported by a single wire attached to its frame; used for light work only.

single-pole scaffold A platform resting on putlogs or crossbeams supported on ledger beams and posts on the outer side and by the wall on the inner side.

single-pole switch An electric switch with one movable and one fixed contact.

single prime contractor A constructor acting alone to fulfill the contractor's responsibility under the contract for construction.

single-roller catch A catch consisting of a spring-loaded roller on the door and a strike plate on the jamb. The door catches automatically and is opened by pushing or pulling.

single roof A roof supported only by common rafters.

single-sized aggregate Aggregate in which a major portion of the particles are of sizes between narrow limits.

single span Any structure without intermediate support.

single-stage absorption In an HVAC system, absorption chillers with one generator to evaporate refrigerant (water) from the solution.

single-stage curing An autoclave curing process in which precast concrete products are put on metal pallets for autoclaving and remain there until stacked for delivery or yard storage.

single wythe wall

sink

siphon trap

single-swing frame A frame in which one swinging door is mounted.

single-throw switch An electric switch opened or closed by the operation of a single pair of contacts.

single wythe wall A stone, brick, or concrete wall that is one masonry unit thick.

sink A plumbing fixture consisting of a water supply, a basin, and a drain connection.

sinker nail A wire nail with a small, slightly depressed head, driven below the surface of a wood member as a hidden fastener.

sinking (1) A shallow depression in an object. (2) The process of removing wood in a jamb so that the hinges can be installed flush.

sinking in The penetration of a paint binder into an unprimed, porous surface resulting in a finish coat with low gloss.

sinter The process of forming a material by heating powder to a temperature just below its melting point so that it fuses together.

sintering grate A grate on which material is sintered.

siphonage The removal of fluid from a device, such as a trap, caused by suction produced by fluid flow.

siphon break (1) During a toilet flush, the point when air is re-introduced into the trapway, ending the siphoning or pulling action that empties the bowl. (2) A small groove in a surface that breaks capillary action and diverts water.

siphon trap An S-shaped plumbing trap containing water as a gas seal.

S-iron A retaining plate at each end of a tie rod used with a turnbuckle to tie two masonry walls together.

sisal A fiber from the leaves of the sisal plant; used in making rope and cord, and as reinforcing in plaster.

sissing *See* **cissing**.

sistering The reinforcement of a structural member by nailing or attaching a stronger piece to a weaker one.

sit-down strike A strike in which the workers stay on the site or in the plant but refuse to work.

site The location of the project geographically, usually defined by legal boundaries.

site analysis services Services, as described in a schedule of designated services, that are necessary to determine limitations of the site and the corresponding project requirements.

site audit A review of activities at a construction site to identify inappropriate material and wasteful management practices.

site built The construction of a structure at the site where it is to remain.

site characterization In an environmental remediation operation, the process of defining and analyzing the contaminants and media of a site to determine the nature and extent of contaminants present.

site closeout The final phase in an environmental remediation effort that occurs after it is determined that site poses no future significant health risk.

site drainage (1) An underground system of piping carrying rainwater or other wastes to a public sewer. (2) The water so drained.

site exploration *See* **site investigation**.

skewed

site-foamed insulation Thermal insulation foamed in place.

site investigation A complete examination, investigation, and testing of surface and subsurface soil and conditions. The report resulting from the investigation is used in design of the structure.

site plan A plan of the area of a proposed construction operation, including the building outline, parking, work areas, and/or property lines.

site safety officer The person responsible for establishing the appropriate health and safety equipment to be used by workers at a hazardous waste site.

Sitka spruce *Picea sitchemis.* A lightweight, but particularly strong species still used in aircraft construction and for other special uses. The range of Sitka spruce is a narrow belt extending along the Pacific coast from Alaska to northern California.

sitzbath A bathtub, designed to support a person in the sitting position, used for therapeutic treatment.

size (1) To bring a piece to specified dimensions. (2) *See* **sizing**.

sized dry Surfaced or sawn to a specific size after being dried.

sized green Surfaced or sawn to a specific size while still green and subject to further shrinkage. The National Grading Rule for dimension lumber sets slightly larger sizes for green lumber than for dry to reflect shrinkage.

sized lumber Lumber uniformly manufactured to net surfaced sizes. Sized lumber may be rough, surfaced, or partly surfaced on one or more faces.

sizing (size) The application of diluted glue or adhesive to hardwood veneer to prepare the wood for application of a standard concentration of glue. Sizing reduces the amount of standard glue that will be absorbed. Sizing is often used when woods of different densities are glued together.

sizing saw A saw that trims large timbers to the desired dimensions.

skeleton construction A type of construction in which loads are carried on frames made of beams and columns. Walls of upper floors are supported on the frames.

skeleton steps A simple stairway consisting of treads and a support carriage, but no risers.

skew back (skewback) A sloping surface against which the end of an arch rests, such as a concrete thrust block supporting the thrust of an arch bridge. *See also* **chamfer strip**.

skew chisel A woodworking chisel with a sharp cutting edge of oblique angle and beveled sides.

skew corbel A specially shaped stone at the bottom of a stone gable forming an abutment for the coping, eave gutters, or wall cornices.

skewed Forming an oblique angle with a main center line.

skew fillet A fillet-shaped piece nailed along the gable coping under the slate to divert water from the edge.

skew nailing *See* **toenailing**.

skew plane A woodworking plane with the blade at an oblique angle across the face.

skid resistance A measure of the frictional characteristics of a surface.

skylight

slab floor

slab on grade

skim coat A thin coat of plaster, usually either the finish coat or the leveling coat.

skin (1) The materials, such as steel, aluminum and/or glass that make up a curtain wall. (2) The outer veneer or ply of a lamination or built-up piece. (3) The thin face of a hollow-core door. (4) A tough layer formed on the surface of paint in a container. (5) A dense layer on the surface of a cellular material.

skin drying The rapid drying of the surface of a paint film while the material underneath remains wet.

skin friction The friction between soil and a structure, such as a retaining wall, or between soil and a pile.

skinner saw A saw that trims and sizes the 8' side of a plywood panel as it leaves the press. The 4' side is trimmed by a cut-off saw.

skintled brickwork Brickwork laid so the resulting face is irregular.

skirt (apron) The border or section of molding under a window stool.

skirting block (1) A corner block where a base and vertical framing meet. (2) A concealed block to which a baseboard is attached.

skylight A glazed opening in a roof to admit light.

slab (1) A flat, horizontal (or nearly horizontal) molded layer of plain or reinforced concrete, usually of uniform but sometimes of variable thickness, positioned either on the ground or supported by beams, columns, walls, or other framework. (2) The outside, lengthwise cut on a log. *See also* **flat slab** *and* **flat plate**.

slab bar bolster A wire form used to support reinforcing while placing concrete.

slab board A rough board cut from the side of a log with bark and sapwood intact.

slab bolster *See* **bolster, slab**.

slab floor A floor of reinforced concrete.

slab form The formwork used in placing a concrete slab.

slabjacking A process used to correct concrete slabs that have sunk. Holes are drilled through the slab and materials are forced through the holes to raise the slab.

slab on grade A concrete slab placed on grade, sometimes having insulation board or an impervious membrane beneath it.

slab-on-grade construction A type of construction in which the floor is a concrete slab poured after plumbing and other equipment is installed.

slab spacer Bar support and spacer for slab reinforcement, similar to slab bolster but without corrugations in top wire, no longer in general use. *See also* **bolster, slab**.

slab strip *See* **middle strip**.

slack The amount allowed for contingency in an estimate. *See also* **loose estimate.**

slack-rope switch A safety device that shuts off electric power to the drive of an elevator if the supporting cables become slack.

slag *See* **blast-furnace slag**.

slag block A concrete masonry unit with blast furnace slag as the coarse aggregate.

slag concrete Portland cement concrete with blast furnace slag as the coarse aggregate.

slag sand A sandlike material made by crushing and grading blast furnace slag.

slating

slake (1) To add water to quicklime to make putty. (2) To crumble or disintegrate on exposure to moist air.

slaked lime *See* **hydrated lime**.

slaking box A wooden box used to hold materials while slaking lime.

slamming strip An inlay along the edge of the lockstile of a flush wood door.

slant A sewer pipe connecting a house sewer to a common sewer.

slasher saw A set of circular saws operated in combination for quick cross-cutting of lengths of wood before chipping or grinding into pulp fibers, or as fuel.

slash pine *Pinus elliottii*. One of several pine species grouped under the designation of southern yellow pine (SYP). Slash pine is native to the Southeastern and Gulf Coast states. It is fast-growing and matures early. Its wood closely resembles that of the longleaf pine, another of the SYP group.

slat A thin, narrow strip of wood, metal, or plastic.

slate A fine-grained metamorphic rock possessing a well-developed fissility (slaty cleavage) usually not parallel to the bedding planes of the rock.

slate-and-a-half slate Slate 1-1/2 times as wide as other slates on a roof but of the same length.

slate batten A batten fastened across rafters in order to support slates on a roof.

slate boarding Close boarding used to support slates or tiles.

slate powder A powder made from slate, used as an extender in paint.

slate roll (slate ridge) A cylindrical rod formed from slate, having a V-shaped notch cut on its underside, and used to form the ridge on a roof.

slating (1) The installation of slates on a roof or wall. (2) The slate shingles on a roof or wall, taken collectively.

slave A mechanism under the control of a similar mechanism. A point that responds to a trigger. In fire safety systems, for example, if a fire alarm causes a siren to go off, the siren is the slave.

slave unit A device or machine controlled or activated through another unit.

sledgehammer (sledge) A heavy hammer of up to 100 lbs. (45kg), having two striking faces, and swung with both hands.

sled runner A hand tool with a curved or right-angled blade that is used to create uniform masonry joints.

sleeper (1) One of many strips of wood fastened to the top of a concrete slab to support a wood floor. (2) Any horizontal timber laid on the ground to distribute load from a post.

sleeper clip A metal clip used to fasten sleepers to a concrete subfloor.

sleeper joist A joist supported on sleepers.

sleeper wall Any short wall that supports floor joists.

sleepiness A film defect consisting of an area of lower gloss in a high-gloss film.

sleeve *See* **pipe sleeve**.

sleeve fence A short, decorative fence extending out from a dwelling.

slender beam A beam that if loaded to failure without lateral bracing of

sliding sash

slip-joint conduit

the compression flange would fail by buckling rather than in flexure.

slenderness ratio The ratio of effective length or height of a wall, column, or pier to the radius of gyration. The ratio is used as a means of assessing the stability of the element.

slewing Rotating the jib of a crane so the load moves through a horizontal arc.

sliced veneer Veneer sliced from a face of a squared-off log.

slicker *See* **darby**.

slick line The end section of a pipe-line used in placing concrete by pump which is immersed in the placed concrete and moved as the work progresses.

slide rule A device used to make certain calculations rapidly, consisting of a base of wood, metal, plastic, or cardboard with various scales and a scaled sliding insert. The calculations are made by offsetting appropriate scales.

sliding bearing A support for a structure that slides relative to a base structure.

sliding fire door A fire door hung from an overhead track. The track may be sloped for direct gravity operation or horizontal with operation by weights, cables and pulleys.

sliding form *See* **slipform**.

sliding sash Any window that moves horizontally in grooves.

sliding T-level A hand tool with an adjustable blade that is used to locate, transfer and lay out angles from 0 to 360 degrees.

sliding window *See* **sliding sash**.

slimline lamp A type of instant-starting fluorescent lamp with a single pin base.

slip Movement occurring between steel reinforcement and concrete in stressed, reinforced concrete indicating anchorage breakdown.

slip form (slipform, sliding form) A form that is pulled or raised as concrete is placed. The form may move in a generally horizontal direction to lay concrete evenly for highway paving or on slopes and inverts of canals, tunnels, and siphons; or vertically to form walls, bins, or silos.

slip joint (1) A vertical joint between an old and a new brick wall, made by cutting a slot in the old wall and filling it with brick projecting from the new wall. (2) A joint in plumbing in which one pipe slips within another and the seal is made by a pressure device fitting over the joint, often threaded to the larger pipe.

slip-joint conduit Electric conduit connected by short couplings that slip over the ends of the conduit.

slip-joint pliers Pliers having jaws connected by a rivet through a slot in one part, allowing two settings for the jaws.

slip match A veneer pattern that creates a repeat effect by laying similarly grained wood sheets alongside each other.

slip mortise *See* **slot mortise**.

slip newel A newel that either has a hollowed base to slip over a peg, or is grooved to fit a wall.

slip-on flange A flange slipped over the end of a pipe, and welded in place.

slippage The lateral movement of adjacent roofing plies.

slip-resistant tile Ceramic tiles with abrasive particles or grooves in the surface.

slop sink

slip sheet Protective paper placed over the faces of prefinished plywood paneling to protect them during transport.

slip sill A sill cut to fit between jambs and installed after the walls are in place.

slip stone A handheld, coarse sharpening stone used to hone cutting and woodworking tools.

slip tongue *See* **spline**.

slogging chisel A heavy chisel used to cut off the heads of bolts.

slope (1) The angle of repose at which a soil material will stand without moving. (2) The slope of a roof expressed as one unit of rise to one unit of run. *See also* **oracle, pitch, incline,** *and* **grain slope**.

slope correction *See* **grade correction**.

sloped footing A footing having a sloping top or sloping side faces.

slope map A map displaying the topography of an area, along with a discussion of topographic features.

slope ratio Relation of the horizontal projection of a surface to its rise. For example, 2′ horizontal to 1′ rise is shown as 2:1 or 2 to 1.

slop sink A deep sink set low on a wall, used to clean mops and to empty and clean pails.

sloshed joint A vertical joint made by sloshing mortar into the joint after the unit is laid.

slot mortise (open mortise, slip mortise) A mortise that does not extend the full length of the member in which it is cut.

slot outlet An air supply outlet with a length-to-width ratio greater than 10:1.

slot weld A weld between two members made by welding within a slot in one of the members.

sloughing Subsidence of shotcrete, due generally to excessive water in mixture. *See also* **sagging**.

slow-burning A misleading term implying that a material is fire-safe. The term must be related to a particular test for interpretation.

slow-burning construction Heavy timber construction with large flat surfaces, as opposed to joisted construction.

slow-burning insulation Insulation that burns or chars without a flame. *See also* **slow-burning**.

slow-curing asphalt Liquid asphalt made of asphalt cement and oils of low volatility.

slow down An organized effort by workers by which production is slowed in an effort to pressure management for better terms or conditions for working.

slow-evaporating solvent A solvent with a high boiling point, used to lengthen, and thus improve, the drying time of paint.

sludge (1) The semi-liquid, settled solids from treated sewage. (2) Waste material composed of wet fines produced from grinding a terrazzo floor. (3) Accumulated solids in the wash water reservoir of paint spray booths.

slugging The pulsating and intermittent flow of shotcrete material due to improper use of delivery equipment and materials.

sluice A steep, narrow passage for water. *See also* **sluicing**.

sluicing Moving soil by use of rapidly flowing water, for excavation or particle grading.

slump A measure of consistency of freshly mixed concrete, mortar, or stucco equal to the subsidence measured to the nearest 1/4″ (6 mm)

slump block

slump cone

smoke chamber

of the molded specimen immediately after removal of the slump cone.

slump block A concrete masonry unit intentionally removed early from a mold so that it slumps slightly.

slump cone A mold in the form of the lateral surface of the *frustum* of a cone with a base diameter of 8″ (203 mm), top diameter 4″ (102 mm), and height 12″ (305 mm), used to fabricate a specimen of freshly mixed concrete for the slump test. A cone 6″ (152 mm) high is used for tests of freshly mixed mortar and stucco.

slump loss The amount by which the slump of freshly mixed concrete changes during a period of time after an initial slump test was made on a sample or samples thereof.

slump test The procedure for measuring slump. *See also* **concrete slump test**.

slurry A mixture of water and any finely divided insoluble material, such as Portland cement, slag, or clay in suspension.

slurry seal machine A self-propelled machine used for delivering a mixture such as an asphalt emulsion slurry seal.

slurry wall A vertical trench used to contain, capture or redirect groundwater flow in the vicinity of a environmental remediation site.

slush grouting Distribution of a grout with or without fine aggregate, as required, over a rock or concrete surface that is subsequently to be covered with concrete. The grouting is usually accomplished by brooming it into place to fill surface voids and fissures.

smart building *See* **intelligent building**.

smart window Any window that uses removable coatings or a light-sensitive suspended particle device to allow for greater control of solar gain.

smelting The process of melting a metal, typically in a blast furnace, or fusing it to separate it from impurities.

smoke (1) A suspension in air of particles that are usually solid. (2) Carbon or soot particles less than 0.1 micron in size, resulting from incomplete combustion, such as of oil, wood, or coal.

smoke and fire vent A vent cover, installed on a roof, that opens automatically when activated by a heat-sensitive device, such as a fusible link.

smoke chamber The transition portion of a chimney between the fireplace and the flue.

smoke damper A damper arranged to close and stop flow automatically when smoke is detected.

smoke-developed rating A relative number indicating the smoke produced when the surface of a material burns, as measured during an ASTM E-1 19 flame spread test.

smoke door A smoke and fire vent over a stage that opens either automatically or manually by cutting a line.

smoke-dried lumber Lumber seasoned by exposing the material to the heat and smoke from a fire.

smoke hatch *See* **smoke door**.

smoke shelf A concave shelf at the back of a smoke chamber to redirect downdrafts up the chimney.

smokestop A partition intended to retard the spread of smoke. Any opening in a smokestop should be protected by a door with an automatic closer.

smooth-surfaced roofing

snap cutter

smoke test A test using a nontoxic, visible smoke to determine the routes taken by air currents and/or to detect leaks.

smooth ashlar A rectangular stone block with smooth faces used in masonry construction.

smoother bar A heavy, rod-like attachment to excavation equipment that breaks up clumps of soil disturbed during excavation operations.

smoothing iron A hand-held, hot iron with a long handle used for smoothing asphaltic pavement joints.

smoothing plane A small, fine carpenter's plane used for finishing.

smooth-surfaced roofing A built-up roofing membrane, the top surface of which is either hot-mopped asphalt, an asphalt emulsion of a cutback coating, or an inorganic top felt.

smudge (1) An accidental mark or smear on a surface. (2) A paint primer made from the scraping of paint pots. (3) A mixture of glue and lamp black spread on a surface to prevent adhesion of solder.

snake (1) A long, resilient wire used by electricians in running wires through conduit. The snake is pushed through and then used to pull the wires. (2) A flexible metal wire used to clear clogged plumbing fixtures.

snake hole A hole driven into rock at an angle.

snakeholing Drilling blast holes under a rock or surface.

snap cutter One of a variety of hand tools used to cut tile, cast iron pipe and fittings.

snap head *See* **button head**.

snap header A **half bat**.

snap line *See* **snapping line**.

snapped work Masonry laid using more snap headers than full headers.

snapping line A layout line made by stretching a chalked line across a surface and snapping the line.

snap switch A manually operated switch used to control low-power indoor circuits.

snap tie A proprietary concrete wall-form tie, the end of which can be twisted or snapped off after the forms have been removed.

snatch block A pulley or block with a side that can be opened to receive a rope or line.

snifter valve A valve that allows air into a tank or piping system automatically through the use of a mechanical device or by other external means.

snips *See* **tin snips**.

snow fence A fence of wood strips connected by wire and used to catch drifting snow.

snow load The live load allowed by local code, used to design roofs in areas subject to snowfall.

snub gable *See* **Dutch hip roof**.

soakaway An excavated pit designed to receive excess surface water for gradual draining.

soaker A piece of flashing used on a slate roof at a hip or valley, or at the intersection of a roof and a vertical wall.

soaking period In high-pressure and low-pressure steam curing, the time during which the live steam supply to the kiln or autoclave is shut off and the concrete products are exposed to the residual heat and moisture.

socket wrench

soffit

soffit bracket

soap A brick or tile of normal face dimensions but with a nominal thickness of 2″.

soapstone A soft rock containing a high proportion of talc; used for such items as sinks, bench tops, and carved ornaments.

socket (1) British term for the enlarged end of bell-and-spigot pipe. (2) A mechanical device for supporting a lamp or plug fuse and completing the electric circuit. (3) *See* **coupling**.

socket fuse *See* **plug fuse**.

socketing A connection of two timber pieces by fitting one into a mating cavity in the other.

socket plug A plug for the end of an interior-threaded pipe fitting consisting of a threaded piece with a recess into which a tool is placed to turn it.

socket weld A pipe joint made by use of a socket weld fitting which has a female end or socket for insertion of the pipe to be welded.

socket wrench A box wrench with a recessed socket at the end of a shank that fits over the head of a nut or bolt for tightening or removing the nut or bolt.

sod (1) The upper layer of soil containing grass roots. (2) High quality grass grown commercially for use in landscaping. Laid as a finished lawn.

soda-acid fire extinguisher A fire extinguisher that discharges water under pressure. The pressure is produced by mixing soda and acid to generate carbon dioxide.

sod house A house with walls made of layers of sod. The roof is usually logs covered with earth and sod.

sodium light The orange-yellow light from a low-pressure sodium-vapor lamp.

sodium silicate adhesive A non-combustible, inorganic, high-strength adhesive with unsatisfactory weather resistance.

sodium vapor lamp An electric discharge lamp that produces light when sodium vapor is activated by current passing between two electrodes. Commonly used in street lights, they can take three to four minutes to warm up to full light output.

soffit The underside of a part or member of a structure, such as a beam, stairway, or arch.

soffit block A special concrete masonry unit used under a beam and slab concrete floor to conceal the beam soffits and provide a flat ceiling.

soffit board A board that forms the soffit of a cornice.

soffit bracket A bracket used to mount an exposed exterior door closer to a door frame head or transom bar.

softening point The temperature at which bitumen softens or melts; used as an index of fluidity.

soft-face hammer A hammer with an absorbent striking surface, such as one made with plastic or rubber.

soft solder A solder used to join metals in welding and brazing applications. It is typically a mixture of tin and lead, although soft solder of pure lead is used in some industries to join copper.

soft water Water with a low mineral content. *See also* **hard water**.

softwood (1) A general term referring to any of a variety of trees having narrow, needle-like or scale-like leaves, usually coniferous. (2) The wood from such trees. The term has nothing to do with the actual

softness of the wood; some
softwoods are harder than
certain of the hardwood species.

soft glass Glass susceptible to
thermal shock because it has a high
coefficient of thermal expansion
and a low softening point.

soft light Dispersed light producing
soft shadows.

soft maple *Acer rubrum, A. sccarinum.*
Red maple and river maple, softer
than rock or sugar maple.

soft-mud brick Brick produced by
molding, often by hand, relatively
wet clay (20% to 30% moisture).
When the inside of the mold is
sanded to prevent sticking of the
clay, the product is sand-struck
brick. When the molds are wetted
to prevent sticking, the product is
water-struck brick.

soft particle An aggregate particle
possessing less than an established
degree of hardness or strength as
determined by a specific testing
procedure.

soft rot Decay in wood, where
the residue is chiefly cellulose.

soil A generic term for
unconsolidated natural surface
material above bedrock.

soil absorption system A disposal
system, such as an absorption
trench, seepage bog, or seepage pit,
that utilizes the soil for subsequent
absorption of treated sewage.

soil analysis *See* **mechanical
analysis**.

soil binder Soil that just passes
through a No. 40 (40 squares per
inch) sieve.

soil branch A branch line of a soil
pipe.

soil-cement Soil, Portland cement,
and water mixed and compacted in
place to make a hard surface for
sidewalks, pool linings, and
reservoirs, or for a base course
for roads.

soil class A classification of soil
by particle size, used by the U.S.
Department of Agriculture:
(1) gravel, (2) sand, (3) clay, (4)
loam, (5) loam with some sand,
(6) silt-loam, and (7) clay-loam.

soil classification test A series
of tests combined with sensory
observations used to classify a soil.
The tests may include such aspects
as grain size, distribution, plasticity
index, liquid limit, and density.

soil cover *See* **ground cover**.

soil creep The slow movement of a
mass of soil down a slope, caused by
gravity and aggravated by pore
water.

soil drain A horizontal soil pipe.

soil flushing A process that removes
soil contaminants from a site by
flushing organic and/or inorganic
constituents from in-situ soils for
treatment.

soil hydraulic conductivity
A measure of the rate at which
water will flow through a soil
matrix.

soil mechanics The application
of the laws and principles of
mechanics and hydraulics to
engineering problems dealing
with soil as a building material.

soil pipe A pipe that conveys the
discharge from water closets or
similar fixtures to the sanitary
sewer system.

soil pressure *See* **contact pressure**.

soil profile A vertical section
through a site showing the nature
and sequence of layers of soil.

soil sample A representative sample
of soil from a specific location or
elevation of a construction site,

solar flat plate collector

solar heating system

solarium

usually extracted to determine bearing capacity.

soil stabilizer (1) A machine that mixes in-place soil and an added stabilizer, such as cement or lime, in order to stiffen the soil. (2) A chemical added to soil to stiffen it and increase the stability of a soil mass.

soil stack A vertical soil pipe that carries the discharge from water closet fixtures.

soil structure The pattern in which the soil particles are arranged in the aggregate.

soil survey *See* **subsurface investigation**.

soil test *See* **soil classification test**.

soil vapor extraction A process that removes volatile organic compounds from a soil matrix through vacuum extraction of the air in the soil.

solar collector Any device intended to collect solar radiation and convert it to energy.

solar constant The average rate at which radiation energy from the sun is received at the surface of the earth, equal to 430 Btus per hour per square foot (1.94 cal. per min. per sq. cm.).

solar dryer A wood dryer that uses solar energy to raise the dry-bulb temperature of the air being circulated through the wood.

solar energy The radiant energy from the sun.

solar flat plate collector A solar collector in the shape of a flat plate, consisting either of a series of photovoltaic cells or a sandwich panel made up of a black surface, a film of circulating water or air, and a transparent cover.

solar fraction The percentage of the seasonal heating requirement of a building that is provided by a solar heating system.

solar gain Heat that enters a building through windows as solar energy. Considered a "passive" heat source, as opposed to those sources that artificially generate heat.

solar heat Heat supplied by radiation from the sun.

solar heat exchanger A means of transferring the heat in storage in a solar heating system to the area to be heated.

solar heat gain coefficient (SHGC) The measure of the solar radiation admitted through a window, including radiation directly transmitted and that absorbed and subsequently released inward. *See also* **shading coefficient**.

solar heating system An assembly of components, including collectors, heat exchangers, piping, storage system, controls, and supplemental heat source, used to provide heat and/or hot water to a building, with the sun as the main source of energy.

solar house A house designed and located so as to use the sun's rays to maximum advantage in heating the house.

solar insolation The amount of solar energy available at a given time in a given area.

solarium A room or porch with a great deal of glass and located for maximum exposure to the sun.

solar orientation The alignment of a building relative to the sun, initially set either for maximum or minimum heat gain, depending on the local climate.

soldier course

solar photovoltaic system
A system that converts solar energy into electrical energy.

solar pin That part of a building's heat load produced by solar radiation striking the building or passing through windows.

solar screen (1) An openwork or louvered panel of a building positioned to act as a sun shade. (2) A perforated wall used as a sun shade.

solar storage Fluid and/or rocks used to hold some of the heat energy collected by a solar heat collector.

solder (1) An alloy, usually lead-tin, with a melting point below 800°F (427 °C), used to join metals or seal joints. (2) The process of joining metals or sealing joints using solder and heat.

soldered joint A gas-tight pipe joint made by applying solder to a heated joint.

soldering gun A tool with a pistol grip and a small electrically heated bit that reaches operating temperatures rapidly, used to solder electrical components.

soldering nipple A nipple with one end threaded and the other plain. The plain end is used for a soldered joint and the threaded end for a mechanical joint.

solderless connector See **pressure connector**.

soldier (1) A vertical wale used to strengthen or align formwork or excavations. (2) A masonry unit set on end so its long, narrow face is vertical on the face of the wall.

soldier arch A flat, brick arch in which the stretchers are set vertically.

soldier beam A rolled-steel section driven into the ground to support a horizontally sheeted earth bank.

soldier course A course of brick units set on end with the long, narrow face vertical on the wall face.

soldier pile (1) In an excavation, a vertical member that supports horizontal sheeting and is supported by struts across the excavation and by embedment below the excavation. (2) A vertical member used to support formwork and held in place by struts, bolts, or wires. See also **soldier**.

sole (1) See **solepiece (1)**. (2) See **soleplate (2)**.

solenoid An electromagnetic coil used to activate a mechanical device or switch.

solenoid valve A valve opened by a plunger in which movement is controlled by an electromagnet.

solepiece (1) Any horizontal member used to distribute the loads from one or more uprights or struts. (2) A member that supports the foot of a raking shore.

soleplate (1) A solepiece or shoe that serves as a base for studs in a core of solid wood or mineral composition, as opposed to a partition. (2) A plate welded or bolted to the underside of a plate girder that bears on a pad. (3) A *sill*.

sole proprietorship A business that is owned and controlled by one person called a *proprietor*. A proprietorship may or may not have employees.

solid brick A brick meeting the specifications for a solid masonry unit.

solid bridging See **block bridging**.

solid core (1) The inner layers of a plywood panel that contain no open irregularities, such as gaps or open knotholes, and in which the grain runs perpendicular to the outer plies. Solid core is primarily used

solid masonry unit

solid masonry wall

as underlayment for resilient floor covering. (2) A flush door, used in entries and as fire-resistant doors in which particle board or wood blocks completely fill the area between the door skins.

solid-core door A door having a core of solid wood or mineral composition.

solid cross (X) band A cross band in plywood consisting of plugged veneer allowing limited open defects or splits. The term is no longer used by softwood plywood manufacturers, who have substituted plugged innerplies or plugged crossbands as a more accurate description.

solid door *See* **solid-core door**.

solid frame The frame of a door or window having jambs, head, and sill made of solid pieces of timber rather than parts.

solid glass door A door in which the glass essentially provides all the structural strength.

solid loading Filling a drill hole with explosive, except for a stemming space at the top.

solid masonry unit (1) A masonry unit whose minimum net cross-sectional area parallel to its bearing surface is 75% or more of its gross cross-sectional area. (2) A masonry unit having holes less than 3/4″ (2 cm) wide or less than 0.75 sq. in. (5 sq cm) passing through, or having frogs that do not exceed 20% of its volume. In either type, up to three handling holes, not exceeding 5 sq. in. (32.5 sq cm) each, are allowed. The total area of all through holes may not exceed 25% of the gross area.

solid masonry wall A wall built of solid masonry units with all joints filled with mortar and no hollow wythes.

solid modeling The most complete type of geometric modeling used in computer aided design. Solid models are three-dimensional and can include far more engineering data than two-dimensional drawings. *See also* **wireframe modeling**.

solid molding A molding produced from a single piece of wood, as distinguished from finger-jointed moldings produced from two or more pieces of wood joined together end to end.

solid mopping The application of hot asphalt over an entire roof surface.

solid panel A solid slab, usually of constant thickness.

solid partition A partition with no cavity.

solid plasterwork Solid core plaster formed in place.

solid punch A steel rod used to drive bolts out of holes.

solid rock Rock that can not be moved or processed without being blasted.

solids That part of paint, varnish, or lacquer that does not evaporate but stays on the surface to form the film.

solids content (1) The portion of a protective coating material that remains on the surface after drying. Sometimes referred to as non-volatiles. (2) In an adhesive, the percentage of weight of the nonvolatile matter.

solid-state welding A welding process in which coalescence takes place at temperatures below the melting point of the metals being joined and without use of a brazing filler metal. Sometimes this is accomplished through the use of pressure.

solid-web steel joist

Sonotube®

sound insulation

solid wall A wall of solid concrete. *See also* **solid masonry wall**.

Solid Waste Disposal Act A predecessor law to the federal Resource Conservation and Recovery Act.

solid-web steel joist A steel truss or light beam having a solid web; usually cold-formed from sheet steel and having a channel shape.

solution A liquid solvent in which one or more substances are dissolved.

solvent A liquid in which another substance may be dissolved.

solvent adhesive An adhesive having a volatile organic liquid as a vehicle.

solvent extraction An ex-situ remediation process in which contaminated sediment, soil or sludge is mixed with a solvent to separate the contaminant from its existing matrix.

solvent welding A process where a chemical liquid solvent is used to soften and join together two or more thermoplastic materials.

sonic modulus *See* **dynamic modulus of elasticity**.

sonic pile driver (1) A vibrating pile-driving hammer. Puts a pile into its resonant vibration range, causing it to slide down into the soil. (2) A machine used to drive piles or sheet piling into soil using a head vibrated at a high frequency, usually less than 6,000 times per minute.

Sonotube® A product consisting of a preformed casing made of laminated, waxed paper; used to form cylindrical piers or columns.

soot door An access door to a flue for cleaning or repairing the flue.

soot pocket A place at the foot of a chimney where soot collects; usually fitted with a door so the soot can be removed easily.

sound (1) A vibratory disturbance, with the frequency in the approximate range between 20 to 20,000 cycles per second, capable of being detected by a human ear. (2) Wave motion in the air.

sound absorption (1) The process of dissipating sound energy. (2) The measure of the absorptive ability of a material or object, expressed in sabins or metric sabins.

sound attenuating door *See* **sound-rated door**.

sound attenuator An assembly installed in a duct system to absorb sound.

sound deadening board A board with good sound absorption qualities; used in sound-control.

sound door *See* **sound-rated door**.

sounding well A vertical conduit used to determine the elevation of grout being placed in preplaced aggregate concrete.

sound-insulating glass A glazing unit consisting of two or more lights fixed in resilient mountings and sealed to provide one or more dead air spaces.

sound insulation (acoustic insulation) (1) The use of materials and assemblies to reduce sound transmission from one area to another or within an area. (2) The degree to which sound transmission is reduced.

sound isolation *See* **sound insulation**.

sound-rated door

space heater

sound knot A dead knot in wood which is undecayed, at least as hard as the surrounding wood, and held firmly in place.

sound level The reading of a sound level meter, expressed in decibels and based on one of three weighting networks: A, B, or C.

soundness The freedom of a solid from cracks, flaws, fissures, or variations from an accepted standard. In the case of a cement, soundness is freedom from excessive volume change after setting. In the case of aggregate, soundness is the ability to withstand the aggressive action to which concrete containing it might be exposed, particularly that action due to weather.

soundproofing (1) The design and construction of a building or unit to reduce sound transmission. (2) The materials and assemblies used in a building or unit to reduce sound transmission.

sound-rated door A door constructed to provide greater sound attenuation than that provided by a normal door; usually carrying a rating in terms of its sound transmission class (STC).

sound reduction factor The effectiveness, measured in decibels, that a building assembly exhibits at lessening the intensity of sound.

sound transmission The passage of sound from one point to another, as from one room to another, or from a street to a room within a building.

sound transmission class (STC) A single number indicating the sound insulation value of a partition, floor-ceiling assembly, door, or window, as derived from a curve of insulation value as a function of frequency. The higher the number is, the greater the insulation value.

sound transmission loss The reduction in sound when it passes through a partition, wall or ceiling.

sound trap *See* **sound attenuator**.

southern balsam fir *See* **balsam fir**.

southern pine *See* **southern yellow pine**.

southern red cedar *Juniperus silicicola*. A species very similar to eastern red cedar and found in wet lowlands and swampy areas along the southern Atlantic and Gulf coasts.

southern yellow pine A species group composed primarily of loblolly, longleaf, shortleaf, and slash pines. Various subspecies also are included in the group. The southern yellow pine region refers to the southeastern United States, from Texas to Virginia.

space frame Any three-dimensional structural frame capable of transmitting loads in the three dimensions to supports. A space frame is usually an interconnected system of trusses or rigid frames.

space heater A small heating unit, usually equipped with a fan, intended to supply heat to a room or portion of a room. The source of heat energy may be electricity or a fluid fuel.

spacer (1) A device that maintains reinforcement in proper position, or keeps wall forms a given distance apart before and during concreting. (2) A small block of wood or other material placed during installation on the edges of a pane of glass to center it in the channel and maintain uniform width of sealant beads to prevent excessive sealant distortion. *See also* **spreader**.

spacing criterion The maximum distance between interior light fixtures that will ensure a uniform illumination on a work plane.

spandrel glass

spacing factor (power spacing factor) An index related to the maximum distance of any point in a cement paste or in the cement paste fraction of mortar or concrete from the periphery of an air void.

spackle (speckling, sparkling) A paste, or a dry mixture blended with water to form a paste; used to fill holes and cracks in plaster, wallboard, or wood.

spade A sturdy digging tool having a thick handle and a flat blade that can be pressed into the ground with a foot.

spading Consolidating mortar or concrete by repeatedly inserting and withdrawing a flat, spade-like tool.

spall A fragment usually in the shape of a flake, detached from a larger mass by a *blow* through the action of weather, by pressure, or by expansion within the larger mass. A small spall involves a roughly circular depression not greater than 20 mm in depth nor 150 mm in any dimension; a large spall may be roughly circular or oval or, in some cases, elongated.

spalling The development of spalls.

span The horizontal distance between supports.

spandrel (spandril) That part of a wall between the head of a window and the sill of the window above it.

spandrel beam A beam in the perimeter of a building spanning columns, and usually supporting floor or roof loads.

spandrel frame A triangular-shaped frame.

spandrel glass Opaque glass used in curtain wall construction to conceal structural elements.

spandrel wall The area of a curtain wall between the sill of one

window and the top of a window one story below.

Spanish tile *See* **mission tile**.

span length *See* **effective span**.

spanner (1) A horizontal cross brace. (2) A collar beam.

span roof A pitched roof with the same slope on either side.

spar (1) A common rafter. (2) A heavy, round timber. (3) A bar used as a gate latch. *See also* **common rafter**.

sparge pipe A perforated pipe used to distribute flushing water for a urinal.

spark arrester (bonnet) A device at the top of a chimney or stack to catch sparks, embers, or other ignited material over a given size. *See also* **arrester**.

sparrow peck (1) A texture given to finish plaster by dabbing it with a stiff brush. (2) A texture given to stone by pitting it with a pick.

spar varnish A varnish with superior weather-resisting qualities; used on exterior wood.

spat A protective sheet, usually stainless steel, installed at the bottom of a door frame.

spatter dash (spatterdash) A rich mixture of Portland cement and coarse sand, thrown onto a background by a trowel, scoop, or other appliance so as to form a thin, coarse-textured, continuous coating. As a preliminary treatment, before rendering, it assists bonding of the undercoat to the background, improves resistance to rain penetration, and evens out the suction of variable backgrounds. *See also* **parge** *and* **dash-bond coat**.

SpecData® sheet A copyrighted name, owned by the Construction Specifications Institute (CSI). For a document written or approved and published by CSI, this sheet presents all pertinent properties and technical data related to a particular product. Useful to contractors and specifiers in the preparation of specifications for the construction process.

special assessment A charge imposed by a government on a particular class of properties to defray the cost of a specific improvement or service; presumably of benefit to the public but of special benefit to the owners of the charged properties.

special conditions An additional governmentally imposed charge designed to pay for a specific improvement or service.

special hazards insurance Insurance coverage for damage such as sprinkler leakage, water damage, collapse, and coverage for materials in transit (or off-site). The damage must be caused by additional perils and risks not covered in standard property insurance. *See also* **property insurance**.

special matrix terrazzo A finish flooring consisting of colored aggregate and organic matrix.

special-purpose industrial occupancy Industrial occupancy for particular operations characterized by a relatively low density of employee population, with much of the area occupied by machinery or equipment. Hazardous usage is excluded.

special-quality brick A brick that is durable when used under conditions of exposure.

special use permit Permission granted to a landowner to use property in a way that would not normally be allowed in a zoning district.

species A category of biological classification. A species is a class of individuals having common attributes and designated by a common name. *Species* is always properly used with the "s" when referring to trees or other biological classifications; *specie* refers only to money in coin.

specific adhesion A bond created by chemical means, rather than mechanical.

specification A detailed and exact statement of particulars, especially a statement prescribing materials, dimensions, and workmanship for something to be built or installed.

specifications Documents that define the qualitative requirements for products, materials, and workmanship upon which the contract for construction is based.

specific gravity (1) The ratio of the mass of a unit volume of a material at a stated temperature to the mass of the same volume of gas-free distilled water at a stated temperature. (2) The ratio of the density of one substance to another when used as the standard. Water is the standard for determining specific gravity of solids and liquids; hydrogen is used for gases.

specific gravity, apparent The ratio of the mass in air of a unit volume of a material at a stated temperature to the mass in air of equal density of an equal volume of gas-free distilled water at a stated temperature. If the material is a solid, the volume is that of the impermeable portion.

specific gravity, bulk The ratio of the mass in air of a unit volume of a permeable material, including both permeable and impermeable voids normal to the material, at a stated temperature to the mass in air of equal density of an equal volume of gas-free distilled water at a stated temperature. Saturated-surface-dry basis bulk specific gravity is the same as bulk specific gravity except that the mass includes the water in the permeable voids.

specific gravity factor The ratio of the weight of aggregates, including all moisture, as introduced into the mixer to the effective volume displaced by the aggregates.

specific heat A quantity that describes the ability of a body to absorb heat and increase its temperature. The specific heat of a substance is the ratio of the amount of heat that must be added to a unit mass to raise its temperature through one degree to the amount of heat that is required to raise the temperature of an equal mass of water one degree.

specific retention The ratio of the volume of water retained by rock or soil to the gross volume of rock or soil, after the sample has been saturated and drip-drained.

specific surface The surface area of the contained particles in a unit weight of material.

specific volume The volume of a given weight of a material, typically a gas, expressed as cubic feet per pound at specific conditions. Simply put, the reciprocal of density.

specific yield The ratio of the volume of water obtained by draining a sample of saturated rock or soil to the gross volume of the sample.

specifier One who writes or prepares specifications.

specs Contraction of specifications.

spectral power distribution The distribution of radiant power, usually expressed in watts per nanometer, with respect to wavelength.

spectrophotometer An instrument for measuring the intensity of radiant energy of desired frequencies absorbed by atoms of molecules. Substances are analyzed by converting the absorbed energy to electrical signals, proportional to the intensity of radiation.

speculative builder A contractor who develops, constructs, and then sells (or leases) a property.

speed square A triangular-shaped tool used to mark perpendicular and angled lines.

spigot (1) The end of a pipe that fits into the bell, or upset, end of another pipe to form a joint after caulking. (2) A faucet.

spigot joint *See* **bell-and-spigot joint**.

spike A heavy nail, sometimes having a square cross section, and 3″ to 12″ (7.6 to 30.5 cm) long.

spike-and-ferrule insulation A type of gutter installation in which the gutter is secured by long nails in metal sleeves.

spiked-and-linked chain An iron chain consisting of spikes linked with a length of chain and attached to posts to enclose a planted area.

spiked grill fastener A multi-tooth connector made of steel that is used to fasten heavy timbers. Commonly used in roof truss and flooring construction.

spile (1) A peg or plug of wood. (2) A spout for directing the flow of sap from sugar maples. (3) A heavy wooden stake.

spillway A passage to convey overflow water from a dam or similar structure.

spiral reinforcement

spiral stair

splashboard

splice

spindle (1) A small axle on which an object turns. (2) The bar in a lock that connects the knob(s) or handle(s) with the latching mechanism. (3) A short, turned-wood part, such as a baluster.

spiral A continuously wound length of reinforcing steel in the form of a cylindrical helix.

spirally reinforced column A column in which the vertical bars are enveloped by spiral reinforcement, (i.e., closely spaced, continuous hooping).

spiral ratchet screwdriver A screwdriver with a ratchet stem and a spring-loaded handle that permits a screw to be driven or withdrawn by pushing on the handle.

spiral reinforcement Continuously wound reinforcement in the form of a cylindrical helix.

spiral spacer Reinforcement that keeps spirals a uniform distance apart.

spiral stair A flight of stairs whose treads wind around a central newel in a spiral or helix shape. *See also* **circular stair**.

spire Any long, slender, pointed construction on top of a building. A spire is often a narrow, octagonal pyramid set on a short, square tower.

spirit level A device used to set an instrument to true horizontal or true vertical, consisting of a glass tube nearly filled with liquid so a traveling air bubble is formed. Cheap levels are bent concave; better levels are ground internally to an overall concave shape.

spirit stain An alcohol-soluble dye with good penetrating properties; used to stain wood.

spirit varnish A varnish with a highly volatile liquid as the solvent for the oil or resin.

spit The depth of one hand-shovel blade.

splash block A small masonry block set in the ground beneath a rain gutter to receive roof drainage and prevent puddling or soil erosion.

splashboard (1) A board placed on a wall at a sink to protect the wall. (2) A weather molding placed on the bottom of an outside door. (3) A board set against a wall at a scaffold to protect the wall.

splash brush A brush used to apply water to a finish coat of plaster while it is being troweled smooth.

splash lap That part of the overlap of a seam in sheet-metal roofing that extends onto the flat surface of the next sheet.

splash shield A metal shield placed between a fire pump and the electric motor drive to prevent water drainage during operation.

splay (1) To form with an oblique angle, or to bevel. (2) To spread out or extend.

splay brick (cant brick) A brick with one side beveled at about 45°.

splayed edge A bevel across the full thickness of a piece of wood.

splayed heading joint A joint between the ends of two adjacent floor boards. Their ends are cut at an angle of 45°, rather than 90° in a butt joint.

splayed joint A joint between the ends of two adjacent members in which the ends of each are beveled to form an overlap.

splayed window Any window set in a wall at an irregular angle.

splice Connection of two similar materials to another by lapping,

split astragal

split face

split-level

welding, gluing, mechanical couplers, or other means.

splice plate A plate laid over a joint and fastened to the pieces being joined to provide stiffness.

spline (false tongue, feather, slip feather, slip tongue) A piece of metal or wood used to join two pieces of wood, such as decking, together.

spline joint A joint formed by inserting a spline into slots formed in the two pieces to be joined.

splinter (1) A small, thin, sharp piece of wood broken from a larger piece. (2) To split or break something into splinters.

split (1) A crack extending completely through a piece of wood or veneer. (2) A tear in a built-up membrane resulting from tensile stresses. (3) A masonry unit one-half the height of a standard unit.

split astragal Two pieces of molding attached to the meeting edges of two leaves of a pair of swinging doors, allowing both leaves to be active.

split-batch charging A method of charging a mixer in which the solid ingredients do not all enter the mixer together. Cement or different sizes of aggregate may be added separately.

split block *See* **split-face block**.

split-bolt connector A device that holds electrical wires in close contact with a simple assembly. Wires are fed through the device and held in place by a nut tightened on a threaded shaft.

split-conductor cable A cable in which each conductor consists of two or more insulated wires normally in parallel.

split course A course made of bricks cut so they are of less than normal thickness.

split face An exposed, rough face of a masonry unit or stone created by splitting rather than forming or sawing the face.

split-face block Concrete masonry units with one or more faces produced by purposeful fracturing of the unit to provide architectural effects in masonry wall construction.

split-face finish A rough-faced, building stone cut from stratified rock so that the split face exposes the bedding. Usually the stone is cut so the bedding is set horizontally, but sometimes the cut is made to set the bedding vertically.

split fitting A section of electric conduit that is split longitudinally. After conductors have been placed in one half, the unit is assembled and secured with screws.

split frame (split jamb) A door frame with the jambs split in two or more pieces to allow the use of a pocket-type sliding door.

split hanger A two-piece pipe hanger that is tightened around a pipe.

split jamb A two-piece doorjamb that can be adjusted to accommodate varying wall thicknesses.

split level A type of house in which the floor levels on one side of the house are one-half story above or below those on the other side.

split phase motor An induction motor that typically has two windings, a main and an auxiliary. While noisier, more expensive and harder to start than three-phase motors, single-phase motors are

split-ring connector

spray bar

excellent for medium duty applications and where stops and starts are somewhat frequent.

split pin A pin or spike that spreads during insertion, or that can be split after insertion.

split ribbed block Concrete masonry units featuring a ribbed face with ribs that have been slit off, providing a rough texture.

split-ring connector A timber connector consisting of a metal ring set in circular grooves in two pieces; the assembly being held by bolts.

split-spoon sampler A sampling device used to collect soil samples during well drilling.

splitter damper A single blade damper hinged at one end, installed to divert air from a main duct into a branch duct.

splitting tensile strength Tensile strength of concrete determined by a splitting tensile test.

splitting tensile test (diametral compression test) A test for tensile strength in which a cylindrical specimen is loaded to failure in diametral compression applied along the entire length.

spoil Dirt or rock excavated and removed from its original location but not used for embankment or fill.

spoil area A site where excavated material is to be dumped.

spokeshave A carpenter's tool for shaping curved edges, consisting of two handles and used as a drawing knife or planing tool.

sponge rubber Expanded rubber having interconnected cells, used as a resilient padding and as thermal insulation.

sponsor Any person or institution representing the owner. *See also* **owner**.

spoon (1) A small, steel plasterer's tool used in finishing moldings. (2) A recovery tool used in soil sampling.

spoon bit *See* **dowel bit**.

spot board *See* **mortarboard**.

spot elevation A point on a map or plan with its existing or proposed elevation noted.

spot ground A piece of wood attached to a plaster base and used as a gauge for thickness of applied plaster.

spotter (1) The person who directs a truck driver into a loading or unloading position. (2) The horizontal framework between the machinery deck of a pile driver and the leads.

spotting (1) Directing trucks for loading or unloading. (2) Spots of adhesive material used to fasten a veneer to its backing. (3) A defect in a painted surface consisting of spots of a different color, shade, or gloss than the rest.

spot-weld A small circular weld between two metal pieces made by applying heat and pressure.

spout A short tube used to direct water from gutters, balconies, etc., so the water will run down the building wall.

spray bar A pipe with ports used to apply liquid asphalt to a road surface.

spray booth An enclosed or partly enclosed area used for the spray-painting of objects, usually equipped with a waterfall system to catch overspray and/or a filtered air supply and exhaust system.

spray drying A method of evaporating the liquid from a solution by spraying it into a heated gas.

sprayed fireproofing

spreader

spread footing

sprayed acoustical plaster
An acoustical plaster applied with a special spray gun. The plaster usually has a rough surface and may be perforated with hand tools before hardening.

sprayed asbestos A fire-resistive and sound-absorbing coating of asbestos fibers and an adhesive, applied to surfaces with a spray gun. Sprayed asbestos is no longer used in the U.S.A.

sprayed fireproofing An insulating material sprayed directly onto structural members with or without wire mesh reinforcing to provide a fire endurance rating.

spray-in-place insulation An insulation material applied with a gun or sprayer to surfaces or cavities. Examples include loose cellulose fiber fill and polyurethane foam.

sprayed insulation *See* **spray-on insulation**.

sprayed mortar *See* **shotcrete**.

spray-on insulation Any of a number of lightweight concretes or mineral fibers and adhesives applied to surfaces and/or structural members for fire resistance, thermal insulation, or acoustic absorption.

spray painting Applying paint, lacquer, or a similar material with a special tool activated by air pressure.

spray pond A component of a cooling system that cools water for use by forcing it upward through spray nozzles and collecting it in a pool.

spread (1) The mobile power equipment, such as a paving spread or earth-moving spread, under the direction of a spread superintendent. (2) Same as range; the difference between prices or bids.

spreader (1) A piece of wood or metal used to hold the sides of a form apart until the concrete is placed. (2) A brace between two wales. (3) A device for spreading gravel or crushed stone for a pavement base course. (4) A stiffening member used to keep door or window frames in proper alignment during shipment and installation. (5) An additive that increases the surface area over which a given volume of liquid will spread when poured on a solid or other liquid.

spreader bar A temporary member at the base of a preassembled door frame to maintain alignment during shipment and installation.

spreader box A piece of heavy construction equipment that connects to the back of a vehicle and spreads rock, asphalt, concrete, or other materials.

spread footing A generally rectangular prism of concrete, larger in lateral dimensions than the column or wall it supports; used to distribute the load of a column or wall to the subgrade.

spreading rate (1) The number of square yards of surface covered by a gallon of paint. (2) The rate at which bitumen or other material is applied to the surface of a roof.

spread-of-flame test A fire test for roof coverings in which a specified flame source is applied to a sample while a specified air stream is directed at the sample. The sample may be mounted horizontally or at an angle, depending on the intended end use of the product.

spreadsheet Large, wide sheet with many columns that is used to tabulate all estimates and sub-bids when putting a bid together. *See also* **bid assembly**.

spring hinge

sprinklered

sprinkler head

spring (1) An elastic body or shape, such as a spirally wound metal coil, that stores energy by distorting and imparts that energy when it returns to its original shape. (2) The line or surface from which an arch rises.

spring-bolt (cabinet lock) A spring-loaded, beveled bolt that self-latches when a door or drawer is closed.

spring brace Temporary brace used to adjust wood frame walls for straightness and plumb.

spring buffer An assembly containing a spring that is designed to absorb and dissipate kinetic energy, such as that from a descending elevator car or counterweight.

spring clamp Any clamp with pressure exerted by a spring. One variety is used to hold parts during gluing; another is used as a temporary electric connection.

springer (skewback, summer) (1) The stone from which an arch springs. (2) The bottom stone of the coping of a gable. (3) The rib of a groined vault.

spring hinge A hinge with one or more springs mounted in its barrel to return a door to the closed position. The hinge may be single-acting or double-acting for a swing door.

springing (spring) (1) The support point from which an arch rises. (2) The initial angle of rise of an arch.

springing line The horizontal line connecting the points from which an arch or arches rise.

spring washer *See* **lock washer**.

springwood Wood that grows during the early part of a tree's annual growth period. Its thin, large cells make it weaker than summerwood.

sprinklered Said of an area of a building that is protected from fire by an automatic sprinkler system.

sprinkler head A distribution nozzle used in a fire-protection sprinkler system. The head may be closed by a plug held in place by a heat-sensitive device.

sprinkler system *See* **fire-protection sprinkler system**.

sprocked eaves Eaves having been raised by a sprocket.

sprocket (cocking piece, sprocket) A wedge-shaped piece of wood attached to the upper side of a rafter at the eave to form a break in the roof line.

spruce *Picea species*. Yellow to reddish-white wood, usually straight-grained, light, and soft.

spruce fir *See* **red spruce**.

spruce pine *Pinus guba*. A minor pine species found in the South bearing a close resemblance to spruce. The wood is considerably weaker than the major southern yellow pine species. Lumber from this species must be stamped *spruce pine*.

spruce-pine-fir (SPF) Canadian woods of similar characteristics that have been grouped for production and marketing. The SPF species have moderate strength, are worked easily, take paint readily, and hold nails well. They are white to pale yellow. The largest volume comes from western Canada (British Columbia and Alberta), where the principal species in the group are white spruce, Engelmann spruce, lodgepole pine, and alpine fir. The principal species in the group originating in eastern Canada are white spruce, black spruce, jack pine, and balsam fir. Some lumber production in the New England

spud vibrator

squared rubble

squeezed joint

states also is marketed as spruce-pine-fir and includes these species.

sprung molding A molding that has its interior corner beveled off to better fit a right-angle joint.

spud (1) A hand tool used to strip bark from logs. (2) A sharp, narrow bar or spade used for removing gravel and roofing from a built-up roof.

spud vibrator A vibrator used for consolidating concrete, having a vibrating casing or head that is inserted into freshly placed concrete.

spud wrench A tool, used by ironworkers to align holes and tighten bolts, that has a long, tapering steel handle with an open-end wrench on one end.

spun concrete Concrete compacted by centrifugal action, such as in the manufacture of pipes and utility poles.

spun lining The smooth bituminous lining in a corrugated metal pipe formed by spinning the pipe around its axis.

spur (1) An appendage to a supporting member such as a buttress, shore, or prop. (2) A decorative stone base that makes the transition from a round column to a square or polygonal plinth. (3) A carpenter's tool with a sharp point used for cutting veneer. (4) A rock ridge left projecting from a side wall after a blast. (5) A short length of railroad track; usually parallel to a main track and used for loading, unloading, or storage.

square (1) A quantity of shingles, shakes, or other roofing or siding materials sufficient to cover 100 square feet when applied in a standard manner; the basic sales

units of shingles and shakes. (2) *See* **carpenter's square**.

square bolt A door bolt with a square cross section.

squared rubble Wall construction using various-sized, square stones to make patterns.

square-framed Joinery framing with all angles of stiles, rails, and mountings cut square.

square-headed Being cut off at right angles at the top, such as a doorway with a horizontal lintel as opposed to an arched opening.

square roof A roof with two sloping surfaces, each at an angle of 45° from the horizontal.

square staff A narrow wood strip used as an angle bead for plastering.

square up To trim a timber or piece of wood, using a plane, so that its cross section is rectangular.

squaring Aligning or constructing an item or assembly so that all angles are 90°.

squatter's right The right to acquire the ownership of land through long-continued occupancy.

squeezed joint A joint formed by coating surfaces of two pieces with cement and squeezing them together.

squinch A small arch built across an interior corner of a room to support a superimposed load, such as a dome or the spire of a tower.

squint A small oblique opening in an interior wall of a medieval church to allow a view of the high altar from the aisles.

stab To roughen bricks in preparation for a plaster coat.

stability A measure of the ability of a structure to withstand overturning, sliding, buckling, or collapsing.

stack bond

staging

stabilizer A substance that makes a solution or suspension more stable, usually keeping particles from precipitating.

stack (1) A chimney. (2) A vertical structure containing one or more flues for the discharge of hot gas. (3) A vertical supply duct in a warm, air-heating system. (4) Any vertical plumbing pipe, such as soil pipe, waste pipe, vent, or leader pipe. (5) A collection of vertical plumbing pipes. (6) A tier of shelves for books.

stack bond (stacked bond) A masonry pattern bond in which all vertical and horizontal joints are continuous and aligned.

stack cap *See* **chimney cap**.

stack effect *See* **chimney effect**.

stackhead A vertical duct that discharges exhaust air into the atmosphere at high velocity.

stack vent (1) The extension of a soil or waste stack above the highest horizontal drain or fixture connected to the stack. (2) A device installed through a built-up roof covering to allow entrapped water vapor to escape from the insulation.

stack venting A method of venting a single fixture connected directly into a soil or waste stack. The term is applicable only to the top fixture or fixtures of a stack.

stadia rod (stadia) A graduated surveyor's rod used with a transit or similar instrument to determine distances. An observed intercept on the rod, as defined by two lines in the reticle of a telescope, is converted into the distance between the instrument and the rod by use of *similar triangles*.

staff angle *See* **angle bead**.

staff bead A thick exterior molding placed between a door or window and a masonry wall.

staff man (rodman) A person who sets the leveling rod for a surveyor in leveling or stadia work.

stage grouting Sequential grouting of a hole in separate steps or stages, in lieu of grouting the entire length at once.

staggered Descriptive of fasteners, joints, or members arranged in two or more rows so that the beginning of each row is offset from the adjacent one.

staggered course A course, of shingles or tiles for instance, where the butts do not form a continuous horizontal line.

staggered riveting Rows of rivets installed in a staggered pattern.

staggered-stud partition A partition made of two rows of studs with alternating studs supporting opposite faces of the partition and each stud making contact with only one wall. Staggered-stud partitions often have an interwoven fiberglass blanket to improve the sound-insulation value of a partition.

staging (scaffolding) (1) A temporary working platform against or within a building for construction, repairs, or demolition. (2) A temporary working platform supported by the temporary timbers in a trench.

stain (1) Color in a dissolving vehicle. When spread on wood or similar material, the stain penetrates and gives color to the material. (2) A discoloration in the surface of a material, such as wood or plastic.

stained glass Glass given a desired color by use of an additive to the molten material, or by firing a stain

staircase

stairwell

stanchion

into the surface of the formed glass. Stained glass is used for decorative windows or mosaics.

stainless steel Any of a number of steels alloyed with chromium and nickel. Depending on the alloy, the metal may possess good corrosion resistance, high heat tolerance, or high strength.

stair (1) A single step. (2) A series of steps or flights of steps connected by landings, used for passage from one level to another.

stair bolt *See* **handrail bolt**.

stair bracket A stiffener, often decorative, fixed under the nosing of a tread on an open-string stair.

stairbuilder's truss Crossed beams used to stiffen a landing of a stair.

staircase (1) A single flight or multiple flights of stairs including supports, frameworks, and handrails. (2) The structure containing one or more flights of stairs.

stairhead The first stair at the top of a flight of stairs.

stair headroom The least clear vertical distance measured from a nosing of a tread to an overhead obstruction.

stair rod A metal rod used under a stair nosing to hold a carpet in place.

stair turret (1) A structure containing only a winding stair. (2) A housing projecting above a roof and containing a stair.

stairwell A vertical shaft enclosing a stair.

stake (1) A short, pointed piece of wood or metal driven into the ground as a marker or an anchor. (2) The process of marking a work or survey site with stakes. (3) A small anvil, used in working

sheet metal, supported by a sharp vertical leg inserted into a hole in a work surface.

staking out The process of driving stakes for batter boards to locate the limits of an excavation, or to identify the boundaries of a parcel of land.

stalactite A downward-pointing deposit formed as an accretion of mineral matter produced by evaporation of dripping water from the surface of rock or of concrete; commonly shaped like an icicle. *See also* **stalagmite**.

stalagmite An upward-pointing deposit formed as an accretion of mineral matter produced by evaporation of dripping water, projecting from the surface of rock or concrete, commonly conical in shape. *See also* **stalactite**.

stamp A seal required on drawings for commercial projects that contains the architect's or engineer's name and registration number. The individual's signature is usually required over the stamp.

stanchion (1) A vertical post or prop supporting a roof, window, etc. (2) An upright bar or post, as in a window, screen, or railing.

standard (1) A grade of lumber suitable for general construction and characterized by generally good strength and serviceability. In light framing rules, the standard grade applies to lumber that is 2-4″ thick and 2-4″ wide. It falls between the construction and utility grades. (2) A grade of Idaho white pine boards equivalent to #3 common in other species. (3) In the British timber trade, a quantity of lumber that equals 1,980 board feet. (4) General recognition and conformity to established practice.

standard absorption trench
An absorption trench 12″ to 36″ (30-90 cm) wide, containing 12″ (30 cm) of clean, coarse aggregate and a distribution pipe covered with a minimum of 12″ (30 cm) of earth.

standard air Air with a density of 0.075 lb. per cu. ft. (0.0012 gm per cc) which is close to air at 68°F (20 °C) dry bulb and 50% relative humidity at a barometric pressure of 29.9″ (76 cm) of mercury.

standard and better A mix of lumber grades suitable for general construction. The *and better* signifies that a portion of the lumber is actually of a higher grade than standard (but not necessarily of the highest grade). The proportion of higher grades included is a factor in determining market value.

standard atmosphere A pressure equal to 14.7 lb. per sq. in. (1.01 x 10 dynes per sq. cm).

standard brick Brick with the dimensions 2¼″ x 3¾″ x 8″. Standard modular brick measures 2 2/3″ x 4″ x 8″.

standard curing Exposure of test specimens of concrete to specified conditions of moisture, humidity, and temperature. *See also* **fog curing**.

standard deduction Fixed deduction from taxable income used when a taxpayer does not itemize deductions.

standard deviation A statistic, used as a measure of dispersion in a distribution, that is equal to the square root of the arithmetic average of the squares of the deviations from the mean.

standard hook A hook at the end of a reinforcing bar made in accordance with a standard.

standard knot Any knot in wood 1-1/2″ (3.8 cm) or less in diameter.

standard matched
Tongue-and-groove lumber with the tongue and groove offset, rather than centered as in center-matched lumber. *See also* **center matched**.

standard net assignable area
The area of a project that can be rented to an occupant.

standard penetration resistance (Proctor penetration resistance)
The load required to produce a standard penetration of a standard needle into a soil sample at a standard rate.

standard penetration test A test to estimate the degree of compactness of soil in place by counting the number of blows required to drive a standard sampling spoon 1′ (0.3 meter) using a 140 pound (64 kilogram) weight falling 30″ (0.8 meter).

standard pile *See* **guide pile**.

standard pressure *See* **standard atmosphere**.

standard sand Ottawa sand accurately graded to pass a U.S. Standard No. 20 (850-micrometer) sieve and be retained on a U.S. Standard No. 30 (600-micrometer) sieve, for use in the testing of cements. *See also* **Ottawa sand** *and* **graded standard sand**.

standard source A (light source A)
A tungsten filament lamp operating at a color temperature of 2856°K (2583 °C).

standard source B (light source B)
A light source having a correlated color temperature of 4874°K (4601 °C), approximating sunlight at noontime.

standard source C (light source C)
A light source having a correlated color temperature of 6774°K

standing seam

standpipe system

(6501 °C), approximating a combination of direct sunlight and a clear sky.

standard temperature and pressure (STP) The standard conditions used to measure properties of matter. Standard temperature is 32°F, 0 ° or 273° Kelvin—the freezing point of water. Standard pressure is the pressure exerted by a column of mercury 760 milimeters high, referred to as 1% atmosphere.

standard tolerance A generally accepted tolerance for a specific product.

standard wire gauge The legal standard wire gauge in Great Britain and Canada.

standby lighting Lighting provided to supply illumination in the event of failure of the lighting system so that normal activities can continue.

standing bevel A bevel that forms an obtuse angle.

standing finish Those items of interior finish that are permanent and fixed, as distinguished from such items as doors and movable windows.

standing leaf An inactive leaf of a double-door bolted in the closed position.

standing panel A panel with the longer dimension vertical.

standing seam A seam, in sheet metal and roofing, made by turning up two adjacent edges and folding the upstanding parts over on themselves.

standing timber Trees that have not been cut, but are of merchantable size.

standing waste A vertical overflow pipe connected to piping at the bottom of a water tank to control the height of storage.

standpipe (1) A pipe or tank connected to a water system and used to absorb surges that can occur. (2) A pipe or tank used to store water for emergency use, such as for fire fighting.

standpipe system A system of tanks, pumps, fire department connections, piping, hose connections, connections to an automatic sprinkler system, and an adequate supply of water used in fire protection.

St. Andrew's cross bond *See* **English cross bond**.

staple A double-pointed, U-shaped piece of metal used to attach wire mesh, insulation batts, building paper, etc.; usually driven with a staple gun.

staple gun (stapler) A spring-driven gun used to drive staples used for fastening materials such as building paper and batt insulation.

staple hammer A hand tool that holds a magazine of staples and drives a staple when the face strikes a surface.

stapler *See* **staple gun**.

stapling flange A flange on the edges of a faced insulation batt or blanket that is used to staple the insulation to studwork.

star drill *See* **plugging chisel**.

star expansion bolt A fastener used in concrete, consisting of two semicircular shields that are forced apart, to bear on the walls of a hole, as a bolt is driven into the shields.

starter (1) A device used with a ballast to start an electric-discharge lamp. (2) An electric controller used to accelerate a motor from rest to running speed and to stop the motor.

starter board A 6″ or 8″ board used at the eave of a roof to provide a solid nailing surface for the first courses. A starter board is also used in reroofing to replace the old shingles at the eaves.

starter frame Shallow formwork projecting above floor level used to locate a column or wall.

starter piece The piece of pipe that *starts* the branch line. It extends from the cross main or riser nipple to the first head for a fire protection system.

starter strip (starting strip) A strip of composition roofing material applied along the eaves before the first row of shingles is laid.

starting board The first board nailed in place at the base of a form for concrete.

starting course The first course of shingles applied along the eaves.

starting newel The first support post for a handrail at the bottom of a stairway.

starting strip The first row of composition roofing laid along the eaves.

starved joint A poorly bonded glue joint resulting from the use of too little glue.

statement of probable construction cost A cost estimate prepared by the design professional during each of the design phases for the owner's use.

statements of ethical principles Guidelines for professional conduct distributed by professional societies.

static head The static pressure of a fluid expressed as the height of a column of the fluid that the pressure could support.

static load The weight of a single stationary body or the combined weights of all stationary bodies in a structure, such as the load of a stationary vehicle on a roadway. During construction, the static load of the combined weight of forms, stringers, joists, reinforcing bars, and the actual concrete to be placed. *See also* **dead load**.

static modulus of elasticity The value of Young's modulus of elasticity obtained by arbitrary criteria from measured stress-strain relationships derived from other than dynamic loading. *See also* **modulus of elasticity**.

static pressure (1) The pressure exerted by a fluid on a surface at rest with respect to the fluid. (2) The pressure a fan must supply to overcome resistance to airflow in an air distribution system.

statics That branch of mechanics dealing with forces acting on bodies at rest. Statics is the basis of structural engineering.

static test (1) A test that subjects a curtain wall to a pressure differential equal to a specified wind pressure. (2) A test that simulates the flow of water over a curtain wall during a hurricane. (3) A test to determine the pressure exerted by a fluid while the system is at rest.

station (1) A point on the earth's surface that can be determined by surveying. (2) On a survey traverse, particularly a roadway, every 100′ interval is called a station.

stationary hopper A container used to receive and temporarily store freshly mixed concrete.

station roof (1) A roof shaped like an umbrella and supported by a single column. (2) A long roof supported on a row of columns and cantilevering off one or both sides of the column line.

stay

station yards of haul The product of the number of cubic yards in a haul and the number of 100' (30.48-meter) stations through which it is hauled.

statute A law or enactment of the various federal, state, and local rule-making bodies such as Congress, state legislatures, and local planning and zoning boards.

statute of frauds A statute specifying that certain kinds of contracts, such as for the sale or lease of real property, are unenforceable unless signed and in writing, or unless there is a written memorandum of terms signed by the party to be charged. Statute varies by state.

statute of limitations Provision of law establishing a certain time limit from an occurrence during which a judgment may be sought from a court of law.

statute of repose A legislative enactment that bars a claim against a party unless the claim is brought within a specified period of time following an event described in the statute, regardless of whether or not the statute of limitations period for that claim has expired.

statutory Related to provisions specified in a law.

statutory bond A bond of which the content and form are established by statute.

statutory requirements Requirements that are embodied in the law.

staunching piece A gap left between adjacent concrete bays until the concrete has cured and shrunk, when it is then filled with more concrete.

stave (1) A narrow strip of curved wood used in the construction of barrels, buckets, or tanks. (2) A ladder rung.

stay Anything that stiffens a frame or stabilizes some structural component.

stay bolt A long, metal rod with a threaded end and used as a stay.

stay rod Any rod-shaped tie used temporarily or permanently to prevent spreading of the parts it connects.

Steading's compound Dicalcium aluminate monosilicate-8-hydrate, a compound that has been found in reacted lime-pozzolan and cement-pozzolan mixtures.

steam box An enclosure for steam-curing concrete products. *See also* **steam-curing room**.

steam chest A container in which wood is steamed for bending or forming.

steam cleaner A machine that provides pressurized steam to a nozzle for the purpose of cleaning grease or dirt from a surface. Detergents or chemicals are sometimes added.

steam curing Curing of concrete or mortar in water vapor at atmospheric or higher pressures and at temperatures between about 100° and 420° F (40° and 215 °C).

steam-curing cycle (1) The time interval between the start of the temperature-rise period and the end of the soaking period or the cooling-off period. (2) A schedule of the time and temperature of periods that make up the cycle.

steam-curing room A chamber for steam curing of concrete products at atmospheric pressure.

steamed wood Wood that has been softened in preparation for bending or for producing veneer.

steel-frame construction

steel sheet piling

steam grid humidifier An air duct humidifier that introduces steam into the air through perforated pipes.

steam hammer A pile hammer activated by steam pressure.

steam heating system A heating system in which heat is transferred from a boiler or other source, through pipes, to a heat exchanger. The steam can be above, at, or below atmospheric pressure.

steaming A process in which logs are heated with steam or hot water in special vats prior to peeling them into veneer. Steaming results in smoother veneer and improved recovery from the log. A similar process is used to prepare wood for bending or shaping.

steam injection In an environmental remediation operation, the process of injecting steam into soil to aid in the extraction of soil vapor or groundwater.

steam kiln See **steam-curing room**.

steam pipe Any pipe for the conveyance of steam.

steam shovel A power shovel operated by steam from an integral boiler. Steam shovels have largely been replaced by diesel-powered shovels.

steam stripping (1) A process of removing volatile contaminants from soil or water by passing steam through the soil or water. (2) A method of removing wallpaper.

steam table A table or section of counter equipped with removable food containers, the contents of which are kept warm by steam, hot water, or hot air circulating beneath the containers.

steam traps A device that discharges condensate air and prevents the passage of steam.

steam vat (steam chest) A container used in steaming to soften logs or flitches before peeling or slicing veneers.

steel Any of a number of alloys of iron and carbon, with small amounts of other metals added to achieve special properties. The alloys are generally hard, strong, durable, and malleable.

steel casement A casement generally made from hot-rolled steel sections and classified as a residence, intermediate, or heavy-intermediate steel casement.

steel domes 19″ x 19″ or 30″ x 30″ metal forms used in two-way joist construction of cast-in-place concrete slabs.

steel erector A contractor who undertakes to place, plumb, and secure a steel structure.

steel-frame construction Construction in which steel columns, girders, and beams comprise the structural supporting elements.

steel sheet Cold-formed sheet or strip steel shaped as a structural member for the purpose of carrying the live and dead loads in lightweight concrete roof construction.

steel sheet piling Interlocking rolled-steel sections driven vertically into the ground to serve as sheeting in an excavation or to cut off the flow of ground water.

steel square A steel carpenter's square.

steel stair fill Concrete that is poured into metal pans to form stair treads and landings.

steel stud anchor A steel clip fastened to a door frame and used to secure the frame to a steel stud.

steel trowel

stem bars

stepped foundation

steel trowel A smooth concrete finish obtained with a steel trowel. *See also* **trowel**.

steel troweling A steel hand tool or machine used to create a dense, smooth finish on a concrete surface.

steel wool A matted mass of fine steel fibers, used principally for cleaning and polishing wood or metal surfaces.

steelworker (ironworker) A craftsman skilled in assembling structural steel or concrete reinforcing steel.

steening Brickwork laid without mortar.

steeplejack A craftsman who builds and/or repairs steeples, chimneys, and other tall masonry structures.

steering brake A brake to slow or stop one side of a tractor.

steering clutch A clutch that can disconnect power from one side of a tractor.

stem bars Bars used in the wall section of a cantilevered retaining wall or in the webs of a box. When a cantilevered retaining wall and its footing are considered as an integral unit, the wall is often referred to as the stem of the unit.

stemming A suitable inert, incombustible material or device used to confine or separate explosives in a drill hole, or to cover explosives in mudcapping.

step brazing A method of brazing in which filler metals of successively lower brazing temperatures are used to prevent softening of previously brazed joints.

step down transformer An electric transformer with a lower voltage at the secondary winding terminals than at the primary winding terminals.

step joint (1) A notched joint used to connect two wood members meeting at an angle, such as a tie beam and a rafter. (2) A joint between two rails with different heights and/or cross sections.

stepladder A ladder with an integral supporting frame and narrow treads instead of rungs, usually built in the form of an inverted "V".

stepped flashing Flashing at the intersection of a sloped roof and a wall or chimney. The upper edge of each sheet is stepped with relation to adjacent sheets to maintain a safe distance from the sloped roof surface.

stepped floor A floor on a stage or platform that rises in steps, as opposed to a ramped floor.

stepped footing (1) A wall footing with horizontal steps to accommodate a sloping grade or bearing stratum. (2) A column or wall footing composed of two or more steps on top of one another to distribute the load.

stepped foundation A foundation constructed in a series of steps that approximate the slope of the bearing stratum. The purpose is to avoid horizontal force vectors that might cause sliding.

stepping Lumber designed to be used for stair treads. Stepping is vertical-grained and is customarily shipped kiln-dried, surfaced three sides, and bull-nosed on one edge. Besides the "C & Better" and "D" grades of solid wood, stepping is also made from particle board for use where it will be covered.

stepping off Laying off the required length of a rafter by use of a carpenter's square.

step-plank Any hardwood lumber used to make steps, usually 1-1/4″ to 2″ (3.2 to 5.1 cm) thick.

stick built

stile

step soldering A method of soldering in which solders with successively lower application temperatures are used to prevent the disturbing of previously soldered joints.

step-taper pile A pile formed of straight-sided, thin-walled segments of spirally corrugated steel that, once driven into the ground, are filled with concrete.

step-up transformer An electric device that used to convert a power supply to a higher voltage circuit.

stereobate The foundation, substructure, or platform upon which a building is constructed.

stereo photogrammetry The science of measuring from two photographs taken from known positions in relation to the building or structure. Using known dimensions of parts of the structure, other dimensions can then be determined by scaling.

stereotomy The practice of cutting stone to specified forms and then placing it.

sterling A grade of Idaho white pine boards, equivalent to #2 common in other species.

stick (1) Any long, slender piece of wood. (2) A waxed paper cartridge containing an explosive, usually 1-1/8″ x 8″ (3 x 20 cm). (3) A rigid bar fastened to the bucket and hinged at the boom of a power shovel or a backhoe.

stick built A term describing frame houses assembled piece-by-piece from lumber delivered to the site with little or no previous assembly into components. The more typical type of residential construction is stick built.

sticker An additive that increases the strength with which water-soluble materials attach to solid surfaces.

sticky cement Finished cement that develops low or zero flowability during or after storage in silos, or after transportation in bulk containers, hopper-bottom cars, etc. Sticky cement may be caused by: (a) interlocking of particles, (b) mechanical compaction, (c) electrostatic attraction between particles, or (d) moisture. *See also* **warehouse set**.

stiffback *See* **strongback**.

stiffened compression element A compression element that has been stiffened on its weak axis in order to resist buckling on that axis.

stiffener (1) A bar, angle, channel, or other shape attached to a metal plate or sheet to increase its resistance to buckling. (2) Internal reinforcement, usually light-gauge channels, for a hollow metal door.

stiff frame *See* **rigid frame**.

stiff leg derrick An erection derrick with a vertical mast shorter than its boom. The mast is tied from its peak to a triangular structural frame at its base by rigid steel members.

stiff-mud brick Brick produced by extruding a stiff but plastic clay (12% to 15% moisture) through a die and cutting the extruded material to length with wires.

stiffness Resistance to deformation.

stiffness factor A measure of the stiffness of a structural member. For a prismatic member, the stiffness factor is equal to the ratio of the product of the moment of inertia of the cross section and the modulus of elasticity for the material to the length of the member.

stile (1) The vertical members forming the outside framework of a door or window. (2) A set of steps crossing over a fence or wall.

(3) A roofing tile with an S-shaped cross section.

stilt (1) A post used to raise a structure above ground or water level. (2) A compression member placed above or below a similar member to gain additional height.

stinger A slang term for a welding rod.

stipple To make dots or short dashes on a surface as a decorative effect.

stippled finish A dotted or pebbly-textured finish on the surface coat of paint, plaster, or porcelain enamel, induced by punching the unset surface with a stiff brush.

stipulated sum agreement A contractual agreement in which a fixed amount is established for performance of the work.

stirrup (1) A reinforcement used to resist shear and diagonal tension stresses in a concrete structural member. (2) A steel bar bent into a "U" or box shape and installed perpendicular to, or at an angle to the longitudinal reinforcement, and properly anchored. (3) Lateral reinforcement formed of individual units, open or closed, or of continuously wound reinforcement. The term *stirrups* is usually applied to lateral reinforcement in flexural members and the term *ties* to lateral reinforcement in vertical compression members. *See also* **tie**.

stitched veneer Veneer sheets composed of random width pieces of veneer sewn together with heavy thread. Several stitch lines run across the width of each piece of stitched veneer. In veneer production, the random width pieces are run through a large sewing machine and reclipped in desired (usually standard 48″-54″) sizes. Stitched veneer is usually used in the core plies of plywood.

stitch rivet One of a number of rivets installed at regular intervals and in a straight line to connect two parts and provide lateral stiffness.

stitch welding The union of two or more parts with a line of short equally-spaced welds.

St. John's spruce Canadian spruce.

stock (1) Material or devices readily available from suppliers. (2) The body or handle of a tool. (3) A frame to hold a die when cutting external threads on a pipe. (4) The total value of the equity in a corporation.

stock, 1244 In the event that a corporation's stock becomes worthless, it may offset up to $50,000 of loss against ordinary income in each taxable year, provided the corporation meets the requirements of Section 1244 of the Internal Revenue Code.

stock brush A brush used to apply water to base coat or finish coat plaster to improve workability.

stock companies In defining insurance companies, those owned by a group of stockholders for the purpose of selling insurance. *See also* **mutual companies**.

stockhouse set *See* **sticky cement** *and* **warehouse set**.

stock lumber Lumber cut to standard sizes and readily available from suppliers.

stock millwork Millwork manufactured in standard shapes and sizes and readily available from suppliers.

stockpile Material stored for later use, such as topsoil.

stone

stonework

stool

stock size A standard size of an item that is readily available from suppliers.

stoichiometric combustion A controlled combustion where fuel is reacted with the exact amount of oxygen required to oxidize all carbon, hydrogen, and sulfur in the fuel to carbon dioxide, water, and sulfur dioxide.

stone (1) Individual blocks of rock processed by shaping, cutting, or sizing. For use in masonry work. (2) Fragments of rock excavated, usually by blasting, from natural deposits and further processed by recrushing and sizing. For use as aggregate. (3) A carborundum or other natural or artificial hone used to sharpen cutting edges of tools.

stone bolt A bolt cemented in a hole of a masonry unit for connection to another object.

stone chip A small, angular chip of stone that has been washed of dust.

stone dust Pulverized stone used in the construction of walkways or other stable surfaces. The dust is mixed with soil and compacted or used with gravel to fill spaces between irregular stones. Stone dust is a by-product of stone crushing operations.

stonemason A craftsman skilled in constructing stonemasonry, including any preparation at the site.

stone sand Fine aggregate resulting from the mechanical crushing and processing of rock. *See also* **sand** *and* **fine aggregate**.

stone seal An asphaltic wearing surface made by rolling aggregate into a heavy application of bituminous material. Application is usually repeated several times.

stone-setter's adjustable multiple-point suspension scaffold A swinging-type scaffold having a platform suspended at the four corners by hoisting devices to permit lowering or raising the platform to any desired working level.

stone slate Slate-like slabbing or flashing obtained from limestone or sandstone that has been separated along its bedding. Used as rough shingling on a roof.

stone veneer, thin Stone cut 2″ thick or less and applied to an interior or exterior building surface in a non-load-bearing manner. Granite, marble, limestone, slate and travertine are most commonly used.

stonework (1) Masonry construction using stone. (2) The preparation or setting of stone for building or paving.

stool (1) A narrow interior shelf, across the lower part of a window opening, that butts against the sill. (2) A framed support. (3) A commode.

stool cap The molding that sits on the windowsill and extends into a room to form a kind of shelf.

stoop A small platform at the entrance to a house, often consisting of several wide steps.

stop (1) On doors, the molding on the inside of the doorjamb that causes the door to stop in its closed position, preventing it from swinging through. On windows, the molding that covers the inside face of the jamb. (2) A type of molding nailed to the face of a door frame to prevent the door from swinging through. A stop is also used to hold the bottom sash of a double-hung window in place.

stop-and-check valve *See* **nonreturn valve**.

storefront sash

storm drain

stop-and-waste cock A stopcock with a drain plug in the valve. When the valve is closed, water in the downstream piping can be drained through the plug. A stop-and-waste cock is often used at connections to outdoor faucets so the exterior piping can be drained for the winter.

stopcock A valve to shut off the flow of fluid in a branch of a distribution system in a building.

stope An excavating operation carried out in a series of steps.

stop glazing Either the lip at the back of a rabbet or the molding applied at the front. These serve to hold a light in a sash or frame with the help of spacers.

stopped dado A dado that ends before the front edge of the receiving board.

stopped miter A miter joint used with members of different thickness.

stop valve Any valve in a piping distribution system that is used to stop flow.

stopwork A mechanism on a lock to hold the bolt in the latched position so the lock cannot be opened from the outside. A stopwork can usually be set by a sliding or push button.

stop work order An order issued by the owner's representative to stop work on a project. Reasons for the order include failure to conform to specifications, unsatisfied liens, labor disputes, and inclement weather.

storage hopper *See* **stationary hopper**.

storage life (shelf life) The length of time that a product, such as a package adhesive or sealant, can be stored at a specified temperature range and remain usable.

storage tank Any tank that receives a fluid and holds it for later distribution.

storefront sash An assembly of light metal members that form a frame for a fixed-glass storefront.

storey rod *See* **story rod**.

storm clip A clip on the exterior of a glazing bar that holds the pane in place.

storm door (weather door) A door, usually fully glazed, fitted to the outside of the frame of an exterior door to provide additional protection against cold and wind.

storm drain A drain used to convey rain water, subsurface water, condensate, or similar discharge, but not sewage or industrial waste.

storm porch A porch, or portion thereof, intended to protect an entrance to a house from the weather.

storm sash *See* **storm window**.

storm sewage That material flowing in combined sewers or storm sewers as a result of rainfall.

storm sewer A sewer used for conveying rainwater and/or similar discharges, but not sewage or industrial waste, to a point of disposal.

storm-sewer system A sewer system consisting of only storm sewers.

storm sheet A sheet of roofing curved down over an eave to protect the eave from rain.

storm water That portion of rainfall or other precipitation that runs over the ground surface for the short period after a storm as the flow exceeds the normal runoff.

storm window

story-and-a-half

storm window (storm sash)
An exterior window placed over an existing window to provide additional protection against the weather.

story (1) That part of a building between the upper surface of a floor and the upper surface of the floor above. Building codes differ in designations applied when a part of a story is below grade. (2) A major division in the height of a building even when created by architectural features, such as windows, rather than horizontal divisions. For example, an area may be two stories high.

story-and-a-half The designation of a building in which the second story rooms have low headroom at the eaves.

story height See **floor height**.

story pole A pole used to gauge height (in stories) during masonry construction.

story post An upright post that helps support a beam on which a floor rests.

story rod A wooden rod of a length equal to one story height, sometimes divided in parts each equal to one riser in a stair, for use in stair construction.

stove bolt A common bolt with a round or flat head and a slot for a screwdriver.

straddle pole One of two poles laid along a roof line from an upright at the eaves and connected to the other pole at the ridge. Used in a saddle scaffold.

straddle scaffold See **saddle scaffold**.

straight claw hammer A hammer with a claw well-suited for nail pulling and a striking face with a better-centered mass than a traditional curved claw hammer.

straightedge (rod) A rigid, straight piece of wood or metal used to strike off or screed a concrete surface to proper grade, or to check the flatness of a finished grade. See also **rod**, **screed**, and **strikeoff**.

straight grain A piece of wood in which the principal grains run parallel to its length.

straight jacket A stiff timber attached to a wall to reinforce and increase the wall's rigidity.

straight joint (1) A continuous joint in a wood floor formed by the butt ends of parallel boards. (2) An edge joint between two parallel timbers. (3) Vertical joints in masonry that form a continuous straight line.

straight-joint tile A term describing single-lap tiles designed to be laid so that the edges of each course run in a straight line from eave to ridge.

straight-line edger (straight-line rip saw) A mechanically fed saw used to dress and straighten edges of lumber or veneer.

straight-line theory An assumption in reinforced-concrete analysis according to which the strains and stresses in a member under flexure vary in proportion to the distance from the neutral axis.

straight lock A lock mounted on the inside face of a door. The only preparation is cutting a keyhole.

straight tee A pipe fitting that has a side port at right angles to the run, with all openings the same size.

strain Deformation of a material resulting from external loading. The measurement for strain is the change in length per unit of length.

strain gauge A sensitive electrical or mechanical instrument used to measure strain in loaded members or objects, usually for research or development.

stranded wire

S-trap

street lighting luminaire

street lighting unit

straining beam (straining piece, strutting piece) (1) A horizontal strut in a truss, placed above the tie beam or the bottom of the rafters, usually mid-height. (2) The chord between the upper ends of the posts in a queen post truss.

strake A single row of clapboard siding.

strand A prestressing tendon composed of a number of wires twisted about a center wire or core.

stranded wire A group of fine wires used as a single electric conductor.

strand grip A device used to anchor a prestressing tendon.

S-trap An S-shaped trap that provides a water seal in a waste or soil pipe. Used most commonly at sinks and lavatories.

strap (1) A metal plate fastened across the intersection of two or more timbers. (2) See **pipe strap**.

strap bolt A bolt in which the middle portion of its shank is flattened, so the unit can be bent in a U-shape. See also **lug bolt**.

straphanger A hanger made from a thin, narrow strip of material.

strap joint A butt joint between two pieces secured by a strap, or straps, and fasteners.

strapping (tuffing) Flexible metal bands used to bind units for ease of handling and storage.

strap wrench A hand tool with a flexible, adjustable strap that is used to tighten or remove irregularly shaped connectors, pipes or fittings.

stratification (1) The separation of overwet or overvibrated concrete into horizontal layers with increasingly lighter material toward the top. Water, laitance, mortar, and coarse aggregate will tend to occupy successively lower positions in that order. (2) A layered structure in concrete resulting from placing of successive batches that differ in appearance. (3) The occurrence in aggregate stockpiles of layers of differing grading or composition. (4) A layered structure in a rock formation. (5) The flow at the junction of two airstreams in layers that prevent the proper mixing of the two airstreams.

stratified rock Rock that has been formed by compaction, cementation, or crystallization of successive beds of deposited material.

stratum A bed or layer of rock or soil.

streamline flow Fluid flow in which the velocity at every point is equal in magnitude and direction.

streamlined specification A shortened, often preliminary version of a specification that includes vital technical information.

stream shingle Flat pieces of thin rock having a sloped, overlapping pattern resembling shingling; usually found in small, fast streams.

street elbow (service ell, street ell) A pipe elbow with male threads on one end and female threads on the other.

street ell See **street elbow**.

street floor That floor of a building nearest to street level. According to some building codes, the street floor is a floor level not more than 21″ above or 12″ below grade level at the main entrance.

street lighting luminaire A complete lighting unit intended to be set on a pole or post with a bracket.

street lighting unit An assembly consisting of a pole or post, bracket, and luminaire.

stressing end

stretcher bond

street line (1) A line dividing a lot or other area from a street. (2) A side boundary of a street, as legally defined.

strength *See* **compressive strength, fatigue strength, flexural strength, shear strength, splitting tensile strength, tensile strength, ultimate strength,** *and* **yield strength**.

strength design method (ultimate strength method) A design method in which service loads are increased sufficiently by factors, often referred to as *load factors*, to obtain the ultimate design load. The structure or structural element is then proportioned to provide the desired ultimate strength.

stress Intensity of internal force (i.e., force per unit area) exerted by either of two adjacent parts of a body on the other across an imagined plane of separation. When the forces are parallel to the plane, the stress is called *shear stress*; when the forces are normal to the plane, the stress is called *normal stress*; when the normal stress is directed toward the part on which it acts it is called *compressive stress*; when it is directed away from the part on which it acts it is called *tensile stress*.

stress corrosion Corrosion of a metal accelerated by stress.

stress corrosion cracking Cracking of metal that occurs under the combined influence of certain corrosive environments and applied or residual stresses.

stress crack An external or internal crack in a plastic as a result of applied tensile stresses.

stress diagram *See* **stress-strain diagram**.

stressed-skin construction Construction in which a thin material on the surface of a building is used to carry loads.

stressed-skin panel A panel assembled by fastening plywood or similar sheets over a frame or core, on both sides. The result is a composite structural member.

stress-graded lumber Lumber graded for strength according to the rate of growth, slope of grain, and the number of knots, shakes, and other defects.

stressing end In prestressed concrete, the end of the tendon from which the load is applied when tendons are stressed from one end only.

stress relaxation Stress loss developed from strain when a constant length is maintained under stress.

stress-relief heat treatment A process used to relieve residual stresses that involves the uniform heating of a material or structure to a high temperature.

stress-strain diagram A diagram for a particular material with values of stress plotted against corresponding values of strain, usually with stress plotted as the ordinate.

stress wave timing A technique used on-site to locate and measure areas of decay in wood support members. A compression stress is induced in a member, and the speed in which it spreads is measured.

stretcher A masonry unit laid with its length parallel with the face of the wall. *See also* **header**.

stretcher block A concrete masonry unit used as a stretcher.

stretcher bond (running bond, stretching bond) A masonry bond with all courses laid as stretchers and

striated face

strike plate

with the vertical joint of one course falling midway between the joints of the courses above and below.

stretcher leveling A method of straightening sheet metal.

striated Having parallel grooves in the face, as in a fluted column.

striated face The face of a plywood panel that has been given closely spaced, shallow grooves to provide a vertical pattern.

strike (1) In masonry, to cut off the excess mortar at the face of a joint with a trowel stroke. (2) To remove formwork. (3) A work stoppage by a body of workers.

strike breaker One who takes the place of a workman who has gone on strike. *See also* **scab**.

strike edge *See* **leading edge**.

strike jamb The jamb on which the strike plate is mounted.

strike off (strikeoff) (1) To remove concrete in excess of that which is required to fill the form evenly or bring the surface to grade, performed with a straightedged piece of wood or metal by means of a forward sawing movement or by a power-operated tool appropriate for this purpose. (2) The name applied to the tool. *See also* **screed** *and* **screeding**.

strike plate (strike, striking plate) A plate or box, mounted in a jamb, with a hole or recess shaped to receive and hold a bolt or latch from a lock on the door.

striker A slightly beveled metal plate attached to a strike plate to guide a door latch to its socket.

strike reinforcement A metal piece welded inside a hollow metal frame to which the strike plate is attached and which also serves to strengthen the frame.

strike stile *See* **strike plate**.

striking The removal of temporary supports from a structure.

striking plate *See* **strike plate**.

striking stile *See* **lock stile**.

stringcourse (belt course) A horizontal band of masonry, usually narrower than the other courses, which may be flush or projecting, and plain or ornamented.

stringer (1) A secondary flexural member parallel to the longitudinal axis of a bridge or other structure. *See also* **beam**. (2) A horizontal timber used to support joists or other cross members.

stringer bead A continuous bead of weld metal made by moving the electrode in a direction parallel to the bead without much transverse oscillation.

stringing mortar Spreading a long enough mortar bed to lay several masonry units at one time.

strip (1) Board lumber 1″ in nominal thickness and less than 4″ in width, frequently the product of ripping a wider piece of lumber. The most common sizes are 1″ x 2″ and 1″ x 3″. *See also* **furring**. (2) To remove formwork or molds. (3) To remove an old finish with paint removers. (4) To damage the threads on a nut or bolt.

strip core (blackboard) A composite board whose core is made of strips of wood, laid loose or glued together. Veneer is glued to both sides of the core with its grain at right angles to the grain of the core pieces.

strip flooring Flooring made of wood strips that are pieced together in a tongue-and-groove assembly.

strip footing *See* **continuous footing**.

strongback

structural clay tile

strip foundation A continuous foundation of which the length considerably exceeds the breadth.

striplight A lighting assembly used to flood all or part of a stage, consisting of a row of lamps mounted in a trough with a reflecting hood and color frames.

strip mopping A method of applying hot bitumen to a roof deck in parallel strips.

stripper (1) A liquid compound formulated to remove coatings by chemical and/or solvent action. (2) A drywall tool with a serrated wheel for cutting wallboard.

stripping *See* **strip**.

stripping agent *See* **release agent**.

stripping felt A narrow strip of roofing felt used to cover a flange of metal flashing.

stripping piece A splayed narrow member used to facilitate removal of formwork in a confined space.

stripping shovel A mobile power shovel with a long boom for ditching and removal of bulk material.

strip pouring A quick and economical way to place concrete slabs, allowing for a continuous pour with control points cut after the concrete has set.

strip slates *See* **asphalt shingles**.

strip taping *See* **taping strip**.

stroke (1) A run of clapboard on the side of a house. (2) A row of steel plates in a steel chimney.

strongback A frame attached to the back of a form to stiffen or reinforce it during concrete placing or handling operations.

strop A smooth-surfaced hand tool, often made of leather, that is used for final polishing or smoothing of the honed edge of a wood-cutting tool.

struck joint A masonry joint in which excess mortar is removed by a stroke of a trowel.

struck tools Tools that perform work by placing the sharp end (called the *working* end) of the tool on a surface and striking the other end (the *struck* end) with a hammer. The working end of a struck tool must be kept sharp. The face on the struck end must be kept smooth and even to prevent off-center blows. Examples of struck tools include chisels, punches, and wedges.

structural A term applied to those members in a structure that carry an imposed load in addition to their own weight.

structural analysis The determination of stresses in members in a structure due to imposed loads from gravity, wind, earthquake, thermal effects, etc.

structural-borne sound Sound that has traveled through a structure as vibration in solid material.

structural clay facing tile A structural clay tile with a finished ceramic face.

structural clay tile A hollow masonry unit molded from clay, shale, fireclay, or a mixture of such materials.

structural engineering That branch of engineering concerned with the design of the load-supporting members of a proposed structure, and also with the investigation of existing structures which are suspect.

structural failure (1) The inability of a structure or structural member to perform its intended function, perhaps caused by collapse or excessive deformation. (2) A marked increase in strain without an increase in load.

structural glued-laminated
timber

structural steel

structural frame All the members of a building or other structure used to transfer imposed loads to the ground.

structural glass Rectangular tiles or panels of glass used as finish for walls.

structural glued-laminated timber A wooden structural member made from selected boards strongly glued together.

structural insulation board A rigid panel, often constructed of polyurethane foam insulation between a facing material such as foil or oriented strand board, that exhibits both strength and thermal insulating properties. Many such products are suitable for use as wall or roof sheathing.

structural joists and planks Lumber 2″, 3″, or 4″ thick and 6″ or wider, graded for its strength properties. Such planks are used primarily for joists in residential construction and graded, in descending order, select structural, #1, #2, and #3. The #1 and #2 grades are usually marketed in combination as #2 & Better.

structural light framing A category of dimension lumber up to 4″ in width which provides higher bending strength ratios for use in engineered applications, such as roof trusses. The lumber is often referred to by its fiber strength class, such as 175f for #1 & Better Douglas Fir, or as stress-rated stock.

structural lumber Any lumber with nominal dimensions of 2″ or more in thickness and 4″ or more in width and which is intended for use where working stresses are required. The working stress is based on the strength of the piece and the use for which it is intended, such as beams,

stringers, joists, planks, posts, and girders.

structural plate With reference to drainage structures, heavily corrugated steel plate, usually curved, that are bolted together to form large pipes, arches, and other drainage structures.

structural shape A hot-rolled or cold-formed member of standardized cross section and strength, generally used in a structural frame. Common structural shapes are angle irons, channels, tees, H-sections, and wide flange beams.

structural steel Steel rolled in a variety of shapes and manufactured for use as load-bearing structural members.

structural steel fastener Any fastener used to connect structural steel members to each other, or to supporting elements, or with concrete to make a composite section.

structural tee (1) A structural shape made by cutting a wide-flange beam or I-beam in half. (2) A hot-rolled steel member shaped like the letter "T."

structural timber Structural lumber with a nominal dimension of 5″ or more on each side, used mainly as posts or columns.

structural timber connector See **timber connector**.

structural veneer Veneers used in the construction of structural plywood panels, as opposed to decorative veneers.

structure A combination of units fabricated and interconnected in accordance with a design and intended to support vertical and horizontal loads.

stucco

stud partition

structure height The vertical distance from grade to the top of the structure.

strut *See* **shore**.

stub A short projecting element.

stub mortise A mortise that does not project entirely through the piece in which it is cut. *See also* **blind mortise**.

stub mortise and tenon *See* **blind mortise and tenon**.

stub pile A short pile.

stub tenon A short tenon cut to fit a stub mortise.

stub wall A low wall, usually 4″ to 8″ (100 mm to 200 mm) high, placed monolithically with a concrete floor or other members to provide for control and attachment of wall forms.

stucco A cement plaster used to cover exterior wall surfaces; usually applied over a wood or metal lath base.

stud (1) A vertical member of appropriate size (2″ x 4″ to 4″ x 10″) (or 50 mm x 100 mm to 100 mm x 250 mm) and spacing (16″ to 30″) (or 400 mm to 750 mm) to support sheathing or concrete forms. (2) A framing member, usually cut to a precise length at the mill, designed to be used in framing building walls with little or no trimming before it is set in place. Studs are most often 2″ x 4″, but 2″ x 3″, 2″ x 6″ and other sizes are also included in the stud category. Studs may be of wood, steel, or composite material. (3) A bolt having one end firmly anchored. *See also* **shear stud**.

stud anchor A floor anchor for studs in a wall.

stud bolt A bolt firmly anchored in, and projecting from, a structure, such as a concrete pad; used to

secure another member, as in bolting a sill plate to concrete.

stud crimper A hand tool used to speed metal stud construction. The crimper joins vertical studs to horizontal runners with a piercing action.

studding (1) The material from which studs are cut. (2) *See* **stud** (2).

stud driver A device for driving a hardened steel fastener into concrete or other hard material, consisting of a hand-held driver that positions the fastener. A blow on the head of the driver forces the fastener into the material.

stud grade A grade of framing lumber under the National Grading Rule established by the American Lumber Standards Committee. Lumber of this grade has strength and stiffness values that make it suitable for use as a vertical member of a wall, including use in load-bearing walls.

stud gun A stud driver in which the impact is from a contained blank cartridge.

stud opening A rough opening in wood framing.

stud partition A partition in which studs are used as the structural base. A wallboard is usually applied over the studs.

stud shooting Installing fasteners with a stud gun.

stud welding Attaching a special metal shear stud into a steel member by resistance welding. A special gun is used to hold the stud and provide electric current for the welding process. Shear studs are used for composite construction in which steel and concrete form a composite beam.

studwork Brick masonry interspaced with studs.

stuffing box

subbase

study (1) A prefatory sketch composed to develop a design. (2) A room in a dwelling dedicated to the purpose of reading, writing, and studying.

stuff Sawn timber.

stuffing box A packing gland surrounding a shaft to prevent leakage, usually filled with soft packing to prevent fluids or gases from leaking.

stump veneer Veneer that has been produced from the roots of a tree, used in hardwood plywood manufacturing because of its grain configurations.

Sturd-i-floor® A trade name registered by the American Plywood Association for a panel designed specifically for use as combined subfloor/underlayment in residential floor applications. It is available in several thicknesses, each keyed to a recommended spacing of floor joists from 16″-48″.

Sturd-i-wall® APA 303 siding panels intended to be attached directly to studs, as combined sheathing/siding, or over nonstructural wall sheathing. The name is a registered grade-trademark of the American Plywood Association.

styrene butadiene rubber (SBR) A general-purpose synthetic rubber with good abrasion resistance. Widely used, its applications include automobile tires and wiring insulation.

Styrofoam® The brand name of a lightweight extruded polystyrene product noted for its excellent thermal insulation performance.

sub Contraction of subcontractor.

subalpine fir *Abies iasiocarpa*. One of the true firs, this species is grouped for commercial purposes under the White Woods designation.

subbase (1) A layer in a pavement system between the subgrade and base course or between the subgrade and the concrete pavement. (2) The bottom front strip or molding of a baseboard.

subbasement (1) A level, or levels, of a building below the basement. (2) A story immediately below a basement.

sub-bid A bid offered by a subcontractor.

sub-bidder (subbidder) A person or entity who has a direct contract with the contractor for a portion of the work at the site.

subcasing *See* **blind casing**.

subcontract An agreement between a prime contractor and a contractor (specializing in a particular trade) for the completion of a portion of the work for which the prime contractor is responsible.

subcontractor One under contract to a prime contractor by subcontract for completion of a portion of the work for which the prime contractor is responsible. *See also* **supplier** *and* **vendor**.

subcooling Cooling a refrigerant below its saturated condensing temperature.

subdivided truss A truss with additional framing members in the panels to shorten the effective length of the panels.

subdivision regulations Local municipal ordinances specifying the conditions under which a tract of land can be subdivided. The ordinances may include layout and construction, street lighting and signs, sidewalks, sewage and storm water systems, water supply systems, and dedication of land for schools, parks, etc.

subfloor

subgrade finisher

submersible pump

subdrain A pipe with perforations or open joints that has been buried in a trench backfilled with pervious soil for the purpose of intercepting groundwater or seepage.

subfeeder An electric feeder that originates at a distribution center other than the main distribution centers and supplies one or more branch-circuit distribution centers.

subfloor (blind floor, counterfloor) A rough floor laid on floor joists and serving as a base for the finish floor. A subfloor may also be used as a structural diaphragm to resist lateral loads.

subflooring Plywood sheets or construction grade lumber used to construct a subfloor.

subflorescence Salt crystallization inside masonry units, which can cause damage to the units' internal structure. It may occur when the mortar surrounding the masonry units has a lower rate of permeability than the units themselves.

subframe (rough buck, subbuck) (1) A structural frame of wood members or channel-shaped metal members that support the finish frame of a door or window. (2) A framework supporting wall siding or panels.

subgrade (1) The soil prepared and compacted to support a structure or a pavement system. (2) The elevation of the bottom of a trench in which a sewer or pipeline is laid.

subgrade finisher A highway fine grading machine with tracks or wheels both behind and in front of a helical rotating cutting device that spreads the excess material to either side of the cut.

subgrade reaction *See* **contact pressure**.

subgrade soil The soil that lies below ground level and extends to such depth as may affect the support of the pavement.

subheading A subdivision of a heading used in an organizational system.

subject to mortgage A legal subjection of a property to an existing mortgage if the purchaser has actual or constructive notice of the mortgage. For example, if a mortgage of real property has been recorded, the new owner is not liable for mortgage payments unless he has agreed to that liability. However, the mortgagee may foreclose if there is a default in payments.

sublease A lease by a tenant of part or all of leased premises, for part or all of the term of the original lease.

sublet To issue a contract to a subcontractor.

submerged arc welding A type of arc welding in which the arc and weld are shielded by a blanket of powdered metal called flux.

submersible pump A water pump with an electric motor in the same housing with the pump, designed to operate while submerged in water. Eliminates suction lift limitations, loss of prime, need for suction hose, and the noise and fumes of an internal combustion engine.

submittal A sample, manufacturer's data, shop drawing, or other such item submitted to the owner or the design professional by the contractor for the purpose of approval or other action, usually a requirement of the contract documents.

submit the bid Deliver a bid to a sponsor. *See also* **tender**.

subordinate lien Any mortgage lien subsequent to the first. In event of foreclosure, holders of such liens

sub-purlin

substructure

may resort to the property for payment only if there is any surplus after prior liens have been paid, with priority usually determined by the chronological sequence in which the mortgages were initiated.

subparagraph The first subdivision of a paragraph in construction specifications and contracts. May be subdivided into several clauses.

sub-purlin (subpurlin) A light structural section used as a secondary structural member, and used in lightweight concrete roof construction to support the formboards over which the lightweight concrete is placed.

subrail A component of a stair rail system that runs down the stairs from the top of the string and upon which the balusters are mounted.

subrogation The assumption by a third party of the legal rights of another to collect debts and damage. An insurance carrier may, for example, step into the shoes of the insured and file a claim or lawsuit against any party when the insured could have sued.

subsealing The placing of a waterproofing material under an existing pavement to waterproof the pavement and to fill voids in the subsoil.

subsidence Settlement over a large area as opposed to settlement of a single structure.

subsill (1) An additional sill fitted to the outside of a window as a stop for screens and to increase the shedding distance. (2) A rough doorsill fixed to the groundsill.

subsoil The bed or stratum of soil lying immediately below the surface soil and which is usually devoid of humus or organic matter.

subsoil drain A drain installed to collect subsurface or seepage water and convey it to a point of disposal.

substantial completion The condition of the work when the project is substantially complete, and ready for owner acceptance and occupancy. Any items remaining to be completed should, at this point, be duly noted or stipulated in writing.

substantial performance A party's performance of most of its contractual obligations, which entitles it to payment of at least a portion of the contract price and precludes a termination for default.

substation An assembly of equipment, including switches, circuit breakers, buses, and transformers, for switching power from one voltage or system to another.

substitution A product, material, or piece of equipment offered in place of that specified.

substrate An underlying material that supports or is bonded to another material on its surface.

substrate failure A surface failure in a concrete wall at a joint, caused by a sealant of high tensile strength that tears weak concrete or mortar from the face of the joint.

substructure The foundation of a building that supports the superstructure.

sub-subcontractor One under contract to a subcontractor for completion of a portion of the work for which the subcontractor is responsible.

subsurface contamination The presence of hazardous materials in the soil or groundwater under a site.

subsurface investigation (geotechnical investigation) The sampling and laboratory testing process (including soil borings) to establish subsurface profiles, relative strengths, compressibility, and other characteristics of strata deep enough to affect project design.

subsurface rights The exclusive right of real property owners to use the ground beneath the surface of their land.

subsurface sand filter A sewage filtering system consisting of a number of lines of perforated pipe or drain tile surrounded by coarse aggregate, an intermediate layer of sand as filtering material, and a system of underdrains to carry off the filtered liquid.

subsurface sewage disposal system A system for treating and disposing of domestic sewage, usually from a single residence, by means of a septic tank and a soil absorption system.

successful bid A bid that is accepted by a sponsor for award of contract; a low bid (assuming that there will be an award of contract).

successful bidder The contractor chosen by the project owner to receive award of the contract for construction. *See also* **selected bidder**.

sucker A shoot rising from an underground root or stem.

suction (1) The absorption of water from a plaster finish coat by the base coat, gypsum block, or gypsum lath, functioning to increase bond and promote better adhesion to the base. (2) The adhesion of mortar to brick. (3) A vacuum effect created when wind load on a building creates a load in an outward direction.

suction dredge A barge with a closed pipe attached to a boom, a centifugal pump for suction, and a pipeline to the point of deposit. The excavated solids suspended in water are transported and deposited.

suction pump A pump that draws water from a reservoir at a level lower than the pump, or from a pipe operating at a lower hydraulic gradient than the pump.

sugar pine *Pinus lambertiana*. A pine species from northern California and southern Oregon. Light, smooth, and easily worked; widely used in millwork, patternwork, and various interior applications. Its name is derived from the sugary, sweet tasting deposits of resin exuded from its bark after injury to the tree.

sulfate attack A chemical and/or physical reaction between sulfates usually in soil or ground water and concrete or mortar, primarily with calcium aluminate hydrates in the cement-paste matrix, often causing deterioration.

sulfate resistance The ability of concrete or mortar to withstand sulfate attack. *See also* **sulfate attack**.

sulfur cement A cement of clay or a similar substance, usually with additives such as sulfur, metallic oxides, silica, or carbon used for sealing joints and coatings in high-temperature areas such as furnace fire boxes.

sullage (1) Drainage, sewage, or other waterborne waste. (2) Sediment or silt transported by flowing water.

summary judgment An award of a court by a judge without taking a matter to a formal trial because both the facts in the court record and the law clearly indicate that one party is entitled to a particular verdict.

sun deck

summer (1) A horizontal beam supporting floor joists or a wall of a superstructure. (2) Any heavy timber that serves as a bearing surface. (3) A lintel of a door or window. (4) A stone set on a column as a support for construction above, such as a base for a column-supported arch.

summertree *See* **summer**.

summerwood Wood that grows at the height of a tree's annual growth period. Its thick cells make it stronger than springwood.

sump (1) A pit, tank, or basin that receives sewage, liquid waste, seepage, or overflow water and is located below the normal grade of the disposal system. A sump must be emptied by mechanical means. (2) A depression in a roof deck at a drain.

sump pump A small pump used to remove accumulated waste or liquid from a sump. *See also* **sump**.

sun deck A deck or flat roof intended for sunbathing.

sunken joint A small, narrow depression on the face of a piece of plywood. Sunken joints occur over joint gaps in the core plies of plywood.

sunk face A building stone with material removed from a portion of the face to give the appearance of a sunken panel.

sunk fillet A fillet formed by a groove in a flat surface.

sunk molding A molding that is slightly depressed below the surface it frames.

sunk panel A panel carved into solid masonry or timber, or recessed below the surrounding molding.

super Contraction of superintendent. *See also* **superintendent**.

superfund The Comprehensive Environmental Response, Compensation and Liability Act.

superheated steam Steam at a temperature higher than the saturation temperature corresponding to the pressure.

superheaters Devices that add heat to saturated fluids.

superimposed drainage (1) A natural drainage system developed by erosion and having little relation to the area's geological structure. (2) A man-made drainage system developed against the existing geological structure.

superintendent The contractor's representative who is responsible for field supervision, coordination, completion of the work, and sometimes is also responsible for the prevention of accidents.

superstructure (1) The part of a building or other structure above the foundation. (2) The part of a bridge above the beam seats or the spring line of an arch.

supervision Direction of work performed by the contractor's (or others) workers on site, as specifically defined by the contract.

supervisory control and data acquisition (SCADA system) A computer system used in industry to monitor and control facility operations and status. The automation capabilities of a SCADA system provide early detection of developing problems and improve efficiency in acquiring data and generating reports.

supplemental agreement A change to an existing contract accomplished by the mutual action of the parties.

supplemental authorization A written agreement that authorizes a modification to a service contract.

supply grille

supply system

supplemental conditions
See **supplementary conditions**.

supplemental general conditions
Written modifications to the general conditions that become part of the contract documents.

supplemental instructions to bidders
Written modifications to the instructions to bidders that become part of the bidding requirements.

supplemental services
Services described in the *schedule of designated services* which are outside the normal range of services, including renderings, energy studies, value analyses, project promotion, and expert testimony.

supplementary conditions (supplemental conditions)
A portion of the contract documents which supplements, modifies, changes, adds to, or deletes from provisions stated in the general conditions.

supplied air respirator (SAR)
A breathing apparatus, connected by a long air hose either to a source of compressed air or to an air pump.

supplier A person or entity who supplies materials or equipment from off the site for the work, including specially fabricated work. *See also* **vendor**.

supply air The conditioned air delivered to a space or spaces.

supply air outlets Air terminals (such as grilles and diffusers) for the discharge of supply air.

supply fixture unit A measure of the probable demand on a water supply by a particular type of plumbing fixture. The value depends on the volume of water supplied, the average duration of a single use, and the number of uses per unit time.

supply grille A grille through which conditioned air is delivered to a space.

supply line In a hot water heating system, the pipe that carries water from the water heater to individual heating units.

supply mains (1) The pipes that bring water, gas, or other elements into a building. (2) The pipes through which the heating or cooling fluid flows from the source of heating or cooling to the laterals or risers leading to heating or cooling units.

supply system The connected ducts, plenums, and fittings through which conditioned air is transferred from a heat exchanger to the space or spaces to be conditioned.

suppressed pine (blackjack pine, bull pine) Small ponderosa pine that has grown under adverse conditions. It usually has dark bark, as opposed to the reddish bark found on most mature ponderosa pine.

supreme A grade in Idaho white pine equivalent to B & Better 1&2 clear, the highest grade of select lumber.

surbase A decorative molding at the top of a baseboard molding or pedestal base.

surcharge load A force or combination of charges acting on the upper level of a retaining wall.

surety An individual or company that provides a bond or pledge to guarantee that another individual or company will perform in accordance with the terms of an agreement or contract.

surety bond A bond or pledge made by an individual or company that guarantees another individual's or company's performance according to a contract's terms.

surface hinge

surface metal raceway

surface active Having the ability to modify surface energy and to facilitate wetting, penetrating, emulsifying, dispersing, solubilizing, foaming, and frothing of other substances.

surface-active agent An additive to a concrete mix to reduce the surface tension of the mixing water and facilitate wetting, penetrating, emulsifying, dispersing, solubilizing, foaming, and frothing of other additives.

surface area *See* **specific surface**.

surface bonding A method of bonding masonry that involves first laying masonry units with no mortar or cement between the blocks, and then coating the surface with a fiber-reinforced mortar.

surface course The top course of asphalt pavement–the wearing course.

surfaced sizes Sized lumber may be rough, surfaced, or partly surfaced on one or more faces.

surface gauge A metalworker's hand tool with a rod and a pivoting arm that can be raised or lowered to make measurements or to scribe a level line around an object.

surface hardware preparation The reinforcement of a hollow-metal door or frame to receive surface hardware.

surface hinge A hinge, often ornamental, mounted on a face of a door rather than the edge.

surface impoundment A lagoon or pond designed to hold waste materials and prevent their escape to the environment.

surface latch A latch mounted on a face of a door rather than inset.

surface metal raceway Any surface-mounted furrow or channel constructed of metal to house and protect electrical conductors.

surface moisture (free water, surface water) Free water retained on surfaces of aggregate particles and considered to be part of the mixing water in concrete, as distinguished from absorbed moisture.

surface planer A machine used to plane and smooth the surface of materials such as wood, stone, or metal.

surface retarder A retarder applied to a form, or to the surface of freshly mixed concrete to delay setting of the cement in order to facilitate construction joint cleanup or to facilitate production of exposed aggregate finish.

surface, specific *See* **specific surface**.

surface tension That property, due to molecular forces, in the surface film of all liquids that tends to prevent the liquid from spreading.

surface texture Degree of roughness or irregularity of aggregate particles or of the exterior surfaces of hardened concrete.

surface vibrator A vibrator used for consolidating concrete by application to the top surface of a mass of freshly mixed concrete.

surface voids Cavities visible on the surface of a solid. *See also* **bug holes**.

surface water *See* **surface moisture**.

surface wiring switch An electric switch intended for mounting on a surface, such as a wall post, with most of the body of the switch exposed.

suspended acoustical
ceiling

suspended ceiling

suspended formwork

surfacing (1) The upper wearing or protective layer of materials, such as on a roof or road. *See also* **surfacing weld**.

surfacing weld A deposit of weld metal on the surface of a material to provide desired dimensions or properties.

surfactant Chemicals that change the properties of surfaces with which they come in contact. In construction, surfactants are used as wetting or spreading agents and to facilitate the mixture of normally incompatible substances. They also affect the emulsification characteristics and alter the behavior (the dispersion, suspension, or precipitation) of pesticides in water. In environmental remediation, a surfactant is used to solubilize contaminants and mobilize the highly contaminated fines material. *See also* **anionic surfactant** *and* **non-ionic surfactant**.

surform tool A hard tool similar to a file with a surface of sharp cutting teeth pitched at an angle of about 45° which removes surface wood like a plane.

surge A transient voltage effect that causes a sudden, undesirable rise or fall in current.

surge arrester A protective electrical device used to absorb overvoltage surges so that circuitry and equipment are not damaged.

surge drum *See* **accumulator**.

surge header *See* **accumulator**.

surge tank A tank in a water supply system used to absorb water during a sharp pressure rise or to supply water in a sudden pressure drop.

survey (1) A topographic or boundary mapping of a job site. (2) Taking measurements of an existing building. (3) A building

use-of-space analysis. (4) The process of identifying the owner's requirements. (5) The investigation and reporting of necessary project data. (6) The examination of the physical or chemical characteristics of the site.

surveying The measurement of distances, elevations, or angles of the earth's surface, including natural and man-made features; usually for the preparation of a plan or map.

surveyor An engineer or technician skilled in surveying.

surveyor's arrow *See* **chaining pin**.

surveyor's level *See* **level (1)**.

survey stakes Small pieces of wood, usually 1″ x 2″ or 2″ x 2″, that have been cut and pointed for driving into the ground to mark a survey line or some boundary of construction.

survey traverse A sequence of lengths and angles between points on the earth established and measured by a surveyor. A survey traverse is used as a reference in making a detailed survey.

suspended absorber A sound-absorbing assembly designed for overhead suspension in an area.

suspended acoustical ceiling A ceiling designed to be sound absorbent and to be hung from the structural slab or beams in an area.

suspended ceiling (dropped ceiling) A finished ceiling suspended from a framework below the structural framework.

suspended formwork Formwork suspended by hangers from a structural system.

suspended metal lath A system in which metal lath is attached to a light framing system that, in turn, is hung from a structural slab or beam.

suspension bridge

swage

sweep fitting

suspended span A span supported by two cantilevers or a cantilever and a column or pier, used mainly in bridges and some roofs.

suspended-type furnace A unit furnace designed to be suspended from a floor or roof and to supply heated air through ducts to areas other than that in which the furnace is located.

suspension bridge A bridge with a deck suspended from cables that are typically raised on towers.

suspension of work A situation in which the contractor must stop performance of the contract work.

suspension roof A roof system supported by cables attached to a frame.

sustainable design Design that seeks to create spaces where materials, energy and water are used efficiently and where the impact on the natural environment is minimized. The goal of sustainable design is to sensibly meet the needs of the present without exhausting resources that are critical to future generations.

swage (1) A tool or die used to bend or form cold metal. (2) A tool used to set the teeth of a saw by bending each one to the proper transverse angle.

swale (1) A shallow depression, in a flat area of land, that may be artificial and used in a storm water drainage system. (2) A low tract of land, usually marshy.

swan-neck (1) The connector between a gutter outlet and the downspout. (2) The curved portion of the handrail of a stair connecting the rail to a newel post.

swaybrace A diagonal brace used to resist wind or other lateral forces. *See also* **bracing** *and* **X-brace**.

sweating (1) A soldering technique for joining metal parts. (2) A gloss that develops on a dull, or matte, paint or varnish film and is caused by rubbing the dry film. (3) A collection of condensation moisture on a surface that is below the dew point of the air.

sweat joints In plumbing, the union of two copper pipes made by coating the pipes with a tin-based solder, fitting them together, and applying heat to the joint, fusing the pipes together.

sweat-out A defective condition in gypsum plaster, characterized by a soft damp area surrounded by dry plaster, and usually caused by poor air circulation.

swedge bolt An anchor bolt used in concrete or mortar.

sweep (1) The curvature or bend in a log, pole, or piling; classified as a defect. (2) A bend in an electrical conduit.

sweep fitting Any plumbing fitting with a large radius curve.

sweep lock A device used to secure two sections of sash. One part is a flat lever attached to the upper sash; the other is a receiving catch attached to the lower sash.

sweep strip A flexible weather-stripping used on the top and bottom edges of a revolving door.

sweetheart deal A contract between an employer and a union which grants concessions to one party or the other in order to prevent a rival union from working on the site.

swell factor The ratio of the weight or volume of loose excavation material to the weight or volume of the same material in place.

swelling A volume increase caused by wetting and/or chemical changes.

swing check valve

swinging scaffold

switchboard

switchgear

swift A reel or turntable on which prestressing tendons are placed to facilitate handling and placing.

swing (1) The movement of a door on hinges on a pivot. (2) The rotation of a power shovel on its base.

swing check valve A check valve with a hinged gate to permit fluid to flow in one direction only; used mostly where fluid velocities are low.

swinging door *See* **double-acting door**.

swinging joint A type of joint in threaded pipe that allows for expansion and contraction without stressing the piping.

swinging latch bolt A latch bolt hinged to a lock or door and operated by swinging rather than sliding.

swinging scaffold A scaffold suspended from a roof by hooks, and a block and tackle.

swing joint An arrangement of screwed fittings to allow for movement in a pipeline. Commonly used for setting correct elevations in pop-up sprinkler head irrigation systems.

swing leaf (1) The active leaf in a double door. (2) A hinged sash in a casement window.

swing offset In surveying, a method of referencing a point by swinging bisecting arcs, with a tape, from established points nearby.

swing saw (pendulum saw) A power saw for ripping, deep cutting or cross cutting that is mounted on a frame and pushed down into the material to be cut.

swing scaffold *See* **swinging scaffold**.

swing-up garage door A rigid overhead door that opens as one unit.

swirl The irregular, curving pattern in wood at knots or crotches.

swirl finish (sweat finish) A nonskid texture imparted to a concrete surface during final troweling by keeping the trowel flat and using a rotary motion.

Swiss hammer *See* **rebound hammer**.

switch A device used to open, close, or change the connection of an electric circuit.

switchboard A large panel, frame, or assembly with switches, overcurrent and other protective devices, fuses, and instruments mounted on the face and/or back. Switchboards are usually accessible from front or rear and are not intended to be mounted in cabinets.

switchgear Any switching and interrupting devices combined with associated control, regulating, metering, and protective devices, used primarily in connection with the generation, transmission, distribution, and conversion of electric power.

switch plate A flush plate used to cover an electric switch.

switch-start fluorescent lamp *See* **preheat fluorescent lamp**.

swivel joint A special pipe fitting designed to be pressure-tight under continuous or intermittent movement of the equipment to which it is connected.

swivel spindle A spindle in a door latch unit with a joint in the middle of its length to allow one knob to be fixed by a stop; works while the other knob operates the latch.

sycamore A tough, yellowish wood with a close, firm texture, that takes a fine polish and is used for flooring and veneer.

symmetrical construction (balanced construction) A plywood panel in which the plies on one side of the center ply are balanced in thickness with those on the other side.

synchronous motor A constant-speed electric motor, usually direct current. The operational speed is equal to the frequency of supply voltage divided by one-half the number of cycles or windings on the machine.

syneresis The contraction of a gel, usually evidenced by the separation from the gel of small amounts of liquid; a process possibly significant in the bleeding and cracking of fresh Portland cement mixtures.

synthetic resin Any of a large number of products similar to natural resins and made either by polymerization or condensation or modifying a natural material.

synthetic rubber A chemically manufactured elastomer, rubber-like in its degree of elasticity.

system effect factor A pressure loss factor that recognizes the effect of fan inlet and outlet restrictions that influence fan performance.

systems A process of combining prefabricated assemblies, components, and parts into single assembled units utilizing industrialized production, assembly, and other methods.

T ABBREVIATIONS

The abbreviations listed below are those most commonly used in the construction industry. Alternative forms (usually nonstandard) are shown in parentheses.

t temperature, time, ton

T tee, township, true, thermostat

Ta tantalum

TAD thoroughly air dried

TAT turnaround time

t.b. turnbuckle

TB through-bolt

TBE threaded both ends

TBR timber

TC terra-cotta

TCE Trichloroethylene

TCLP Toxicity Characteristic Leaching Procedure

T&C threaded and coupled

TDD (TTY) Telecommunications Devices For The Deaf (teletypewriter)

Te tellurium

TE table of equipment, trailing edge

tech technical

TEL telephone

T.E.M. Total Energy Management

temp temperature, temporary

TEMP temperature

TER terrazzo

TEU technical escort unit

t.f. tar felt

T&G, T and G tongue-and-groove

TG&B tongued, grooved, and beaded

t.g.&d. tongued, grooved, and dressed

TH true heading

therm thermometer

THERMO thermostat

thou thousand

THK thick

thp thrust horsepower

THRU through

Ti titanium

TL transmission loss

tlr trailer

TM technical manual

tn ton, town, train

TN true north

tnpk, tpk turnpike

TNT Trinitrotoluene

t.o. take-off (estimate)

TOC total organic carbon

TOE thread one end

TOL tolerance

T-O-L Thread-O-Let

tonn tonnage

topog, topo topography

TOT. total

tp tar paper

TPH total petroleum hydrocarbon

tps townships

tr tread

trans transom

TRANS transformer

transp transportation

trf tuned radio frequency

trib tributary

trib. ar tributary area

ts tensile strength

TSCA Toxic Substance Control Act

TSD treatment, storage, and disposal

TSDF treatment, storage, and disposal facility

TSS total suspended solids

T&T truck and trailer

TTY text telephone (teletypewriter)

TU trade union, transmission unit

TUB. tubing

TV terminal velocity

twp township

TYP typical

T DEFINITIONS

table saw

tabby A type of concrete consisting of a mixture of lime and water, with shells, gravel, or stones used to make blocks for masonry.

tabia Compacted soil mixed together with lime and small stones.

tabled joint A joint in stonemasonry in which a projection cut into a stone fits into a channel cut into the stone below.

table joint Any of various joints in which the fitted surfaces are parallel to the edges of the pieces being joined, with a vertical break in the middle. This break is termed the table. Such joints are used in lengthening structural members.

table-mountain pine *Pinus pungens*. This pine is found primarily in the Appalachian states. It is not a commercial species.

table saw A power saw, with a circular blade, set below a table. The blade projects above the table through a slot, with the projection height adjustable to suit the work.

tachometer A device for measuring rotation speed. Usually refers to revolutions per minute (RPM) of a revolving shaft.

tachymeter An instrument used by surveyors that determines distance, direction and elevation variation with one observation.

tack (1) A short, sharp-pointed nail with a large head used in laying linoleum and carpets. (2) A strip of metal, usually lead or copper, used to secure edges of sheet metal in roofing. (3) The property of an adhesive that allows it to form a strong bond as soon as the parts and adhesive are placed in contact.

(4) To glue, weld, or otherwise fasten in spots.

tack coat A coat of emulsion that enhances the bonding of two layers of asphalt.

tack cloth *See* **tack rag**.

tack dry The state of an adhesive at which it will adhere to itself although it seems dry to the touch.

tack-free dry The point where paint or varnish is no longer sticky.

tack hammer A lightweight hammer used to attach small fasteners to finish work.

tackless strip A metal or wood strip, with many small upstanding hooks, fastened to a floor or stair. A carpet is stretched beyond the strip. Hooks engage the backing and hold the carpet in place.

tack rag A rag treated with slow-drying or nondrying varnish or resin, and used to clean dirt and foreign matter from the surfaces of articles before they are painted.

tack weld (1) A temporary weld to position parts. (2) One of a series of short welds used where a continuous weld is unnecessary.

Taft-Hartley Act An act of the Congress of the United States of 1947, introduced by Senator Taft and Representative Hartley, and titled the Labor Management Relations Act. This legislation lessened the power of management over labor and provided that labor participate in some management decisions.

tag A strip of sheet metal folded on itself and used as a wedge to hold metal flashing in a masonry joint.

tail

tagline (1) A line that runs from a crane boom to a clamshell bucket and keeps the bucket firmly in position during operations. (2) A safety line used by workers performing a job at high elevations or in other dangerous locations where a fall could be injurious. (3) Rope attached to a heavy member, such as a truss or beam, or a piece of equipment being lifted. The rope is used by a worker on the ground to control the item as it swings up.

tail (1) The bottom part of a slate shingle. (2) The part of the roof rafter that extends beyond the wall line. (3) The section of a stone step that extends into a wall.

tail bay (1) The area between a wall and the nearest column line. (2) In a framed floor or roof, the area between an end wall and the nearest girder.

tail beam A short beam or joist with one end set in a wall and the other supported by a header.

tailgate The hinged, rear wall of a dump truck through which materials are dumped.

tail in (1) To secure or fasten one end of a timber, such as a floor joist, at a wall. (2) To secure one end or edge of a projecting unit of masonry, such as a cornice.

tailing iron A steel member, built into a wall, to take the upward thrust of a cantilevered member which projects from the wall.

tailings (1) Stones left on a screen used to grade material, as in a crushing operation. (2) The waste material or residue of a product.

tailpiece (1) A subordinate joist, rafter, or the like supported by a header joist at one end and a wall or sill at the other. (2) A handle

on the bar end of a two-man power saw.

tail pipe The outlet pipe from an evaporator.

tailwater Water that flows downstream from a building site or structure.

take-off (takeoff, quantity takeoff) (1) The process in which detailed lists are compiled, based on drawings and specifications, of all the material and equipment necessary to construct a project. The cost estimator uses this list to calculate how much it will cost to build the project. (2) The activity of determining quantities from drawings and specifications. *See also* **quantity survey**. (3) The actual quantity lists.

take-up block A pulley block rigged so that its weight or a spring will prevent slack in the lines passing through it.

talc A mineral with a greasy or soapy feel. It is very soft, having the composition $Mg_3Si_4O_{10}(OH)_2$. *See also* **masonry cement**.

talus (1) A slope formed of rock debris at the bottom of a steep slope. (2) The slope of a wall.

tamarack (eastern tamarack) *Larix laricina*. This species is common in the northeastern states. However, its range extends as far as southern Alaska. As a member of the larch family, it is one of the few conifers that sheds its needles in the fall.

tambour door A sliding door made of thin folding panels on a flexible backing.

tamp To press a loose material such as soil or fresh concrete into a firm, compact mass by pounding repeatedly on it.

tamper (1) An implement used to consolidate concrete or mortar in

647

tandem roller

tap

tape

molds or forms. (2) A hand-operated device for compacting flooring topping or other unformed concrete by impact from the dropped device in preparation for strikeoff and finishing. Contact surface often consists of a screen or a grid of bars to force coarse aggregates below the surface which prevents interference with floating or trowelling. *See also* **jitterbug.**

tamping The operation of compacting freshly placed concrete by repeated blows or penetrations with a tamping device.

tamping rod *See* **rod, tamping.**

tandem (1) A pair of moving parts in which one part follows the action of the other, such as tandem rollers. (2) A vehicle made up of two units attached to one another, as the cab and trailer of a truck.

tandem drive A vehicle with three axles, two of which are driving axles.

tandem roller A unit of two rollers of equal diameter set one behind the other on the same track.

tandem wiring (master-slave wiring) A method of wiring two or more luminaires with one ballast. It saves on installation costs, and electricity.

tang The narrow extending tongue or prong on an object by which it is affixed to another piece, such as the tongue that secures a chisel to a handle.

tangent A straight line or curve that touches another curve at a single point without crossing the curve.

tangent modulus *See* **modulus of elasticity.**

tangential In reference to lumber, it refers to sawing the truck or branch in a longitudinal fashion, perpendicular to the growth rings.

Flat-grained lumber is produced by this method.

tank farm One contiguous site that may contain multiple tank fields, typically used for defining and classifying underground storage tanks and aboveground storage tanks.

tank field One continuous cluster of tanks.

tank group One or more tanks within a tank field.

tankless water heater (instantaneous heater) A water heater system that relys on instantaneous increases of power to heat water as it is demanded. It has only a mini-assembly of heater coils 36″ high or less, and provides an endless amount of hot water. It stores only the water within the coils, and is consequently energy efficient.

tannin A soluble compound found in all woods that can cause staining.

tap (1) A connection to a water supply. (2) A faucet. (3) A tool used to cut internal threads. (4) To cut internal threads in a nut or hole.

tap bolt A machine bolt that screws into a hole in material without requiring a nut or internal threads. A fully threaded bolt.

tap borer A hand tool used to bore tapered holes, as in a lead pipe for a connection.

tape (1) A flexible measuring strip of fabric or steel marked off with lines similar to the scale of a carpenter's rule, usually contained in a case to allow rewinding or retracting after use. (2) One of a number of adhesive-backed fabric or paper strips of assorted width used for various purposes within construction systems.

tape balance A balancing device on a sash that counterbalances the

tapered insulation

tapped fitting

weight of the sash by force of a metal tape coiled around a spring-loaded reel.

tape correction A correction that is figured into a distance measured by a tape in order to compensate for errors resulting from the condition of the tape or the manner in which it was handled.

tape measure (tapeline) A steel strip used by builders and surveyors to measure distances, usually graded in feet, tenths, and hundredths of a foot for use in surveying and engineering. Or, graded in feet, inches, and fractions of an inch for use in the building trades.

taper A gradual diminution of thickness, diameter, or width in an object.

tapered insulation Preformed rigid insulation used on roofs at drains or roof intersections requiring a slight change in elevations at the surface.

tapered tenon A tenon decreasing in width from the root to the projecting end.

taper file A triangular file equipped with fine teeth, used to sharpen saws.

tapersawn A trade name used by the Red Cedar Shingle and Handsplit Shake Bureau for shakes fully sawn on both faces.

tapershank The tapered end of a tool that fits into a socket.

tapersplit Shakes produced by using a mallet and froe, a sharp steel blade, to obtain split faces on both sides. The taper of the shake is a result of reversing the block and splitting the shake from a different end after each split.

taper thread A screw thread developed on a frustum of a cone, used in piping systems to ensure a tight joint, also used on some

fasteners such as a screw or plug for a hole with worn threads.

taper tie A tapered steel rod used to hold concrete forms in place. When the forms are being stripped, the tie is removed by hitting the small diameter end and forcing it out through the hole created by the larger end.

taping The process of measuring the distance across ground with a chain or tape.

taping knives Drywall finishing knives that range in width from 4″ to 24″. The smaller knives (4″-6″) are utilized for taping, spotting fasteners, taping angles and finishing. The wider blade knives are used in finishing. All have square corners.

taping pin *See* **chaining pin**.

taping strip (1) A strip of roofing felt laid over the joint between adjacent precast concrete units before roofing operations. (2) A strip of tape used to cover the joint between adjacent roof insulation boards.

tapped fitting Any fitting which has one or more tapped internal threads to receive threaded pipe.

tapped tee A cast-iron soil pipe tee with a tapped outlet.

tapping machine A machine producing a series of uniform impacts on a floor surface, used to measure sound transmission of a floor ceiling assembly.

tapping screw *See* **sheet-metal screw**.

tap screw *See* **tap bolt**.

tar A dark, glutinous oil distilled from coal, peat, shale, and resinous woods, used as surface binder in road construction and as a coating in roof installation. *See also* **coal-tar pitch**.

tar-and-gravel roofing

T-bar

T-beam

tar-and-gravel roofing Built-up roofing made up of gravel or sand, poured over a heavy coating of coal-tar pitch applied to an underlayer of felt.

tar cement Heavier grades of tar for use in construction and maintenance of bituminous concrete pavements.

tare The weight of a rail car, truck, or other conveyance when empty. The tare is deducted from the gross weight of the vehicle and its contents to determine the weight of the freight in figuring freight rates.

target A red-and-white target mounted on a surveyor's leveling rod; used to facilitate the sighting of the markings on the rod by the transit man.

target leveling rod A leveling rod fitted with a target to facilitate setting or reading.

target rod *See* **leveling rod**.

tarmac (tarmacadam) *See* **macadam**.

tar paper *See* **asphalt prepared roofing**.

tarpaulin A waterproof cloth, generally used in large sheets to cover and protect construction materials or other goods stored outdoors.

tarred felt *See* **asphalt felt**.

tax abatement A reduction in taxes on real property, usually accomplished by reducing the assessed value.

T-bar A light-gauge, T-shaped member used to support panels in a suspended acoustical ceiling.

TBE Threaded both ends. Term used when specifying or ordering cut measures of pipe.

T-beam A beam composed of a stem and a flange in the form of a "T";

usually of reinforced concrete or rolled metal.

T&C Threaded and coupled; an ordering designation for threaded pipe.

teak Wood from trees in southeastern Asia, India, and Burma that is dark, heavy, and particularly resistant to attack of insects; used for exterior construction, plywood, flooring, and decorative paneling.

teamster A member of the Teamster's Union.

tearoff (ripoff) The stripping off of all roof coverings down to the wood.

teazel An angle post used in the construction of a timber-frame building.

technical trader A futures trader who bases his buying and selling decisions primarily on conditions that develop within the futures market rather than on developments in the market for the physical commodity.

tee (1) An elaborately turned finial in the shape of an umbrella; used as finishing ornamental on pagodas, stupas, and topes. (2) *See* **pipe tee**. (3) A metal structural member with a T-shaped cross section. (4) A pipe fitting that has a side port at right angles to the run.

tee beam *See* **T-beam**.

tee bevel *See* **bevel square**.

tee handle A T-shaped handle used in place of a doorknob to operate the bolt on a door lock.

tee head *See* **T-head**.

tee hinge *See* **T-hinge**.

tee iron (1) A piece of flat, heavy sheet metal, shaped into a "T" and equipped with drilled, countersunk holes; used to reinforce joints in wood construction. (2) A steel T-beam section.

telescope

temperature reinforcement

tee joint A joint between two members that intersect at right angles to form a T-shaped joint.

tee nut A fastening device that consists of an internally threaded cylinder and a disk with prongs around the perimeter of the bottom. The prongs are driven into wood to hold the nut steady while a bolt is inserted.

tee square *See* **T-square**.

telegraphing Grain or other defects showing through on a smooth plywood panel.

telephone exchange The switching center for interconnecting telephone lines that terminate at the central station switch.

telescope To insert or slide one piece inside another.

telescoping boom A boom that can be extended as a telescope from within itself, eliminating the need to manually add sections to lengthen its reach.

telltale Any device designed to indicate movement of formwork or a point along the length of a pile under load.

tellurometer An electronic instrument that measures distance by transmitting microwaves to an object and determining how fast they bounce back. The time measurement is then converted to feet and inches.

temper (1)To bring clay mortar or plaster to the proper consistency by moistening and mixing. (2) To make stronger through processes of heating and cooling. In metals, stress is relieved without affecting hardness by heating to a temperature of 500°F. Other processes use 1000°F to heat materials and which are then allowed to cool naturally in order to

soften them and reduce brittleness. (3) The process of treating a wood surface with liquids resins or oils to increase resistance to water damage.

tempera A fast-drying, water soluble paint composed of eggs, gum, pigment, and water, used chiefly for painting murals.

temperature, curing
The temperature to which an assembly with adhesives is subjected in order to cure the adhesive.

temperature reinforcement
Reinforcement designed to carry stresses resulting from temperature changes.

temperature rise The increase of temperature caused by absorption of heat or internal generation of heat, as by hydration of cement in concrete.

temperature rise period
The time interval during which the temperature of a concrete product rises at a controlled rate to the desired maximum in autoclave or atmospheric-pressure steam curing.

temperature steel A steel reinforcement used within concrete slabs and other units of masonry to reduce the chances of cracking caused by temperature changes.

temperature stress Stress in a structure or a member due to changes or differentials in temperature in the structure or member.

temperature stress rod Concrete reinforcing that is provided to control cracks that are caused by shrinkage and temperature stresses.

tempered air Air that is warmed before being distributed.

tempered board A strong, durable composition board such as wood fiber that has been impregnated with drying oil or an oxidizing resin,

template

temporary shoring

and then cured with heat to improve its hardness and moisture resistance.

tempered glass Glass that is prestressed by heating and then rapidly cooled, a process that makes it two to four times stronger than ordinary glass. It shatters into pebbles instead of slivers.

tempered hardboard *See* **tempered board.**

tempered water Warm water between 85° and 110°F.

tempering The addition of water and mixing of concrete or mortar as necessary to bring it to the desired consistency during the prescribed mixing period. For mixed concrete, this will include any addition of water as may be necessary to bring the load to the correct slump on arrival at the work site, but not after a period of waiting to discharge the concrete.

template (templet) (1) A thin plate or board frame used as a guide in positioning or spacing form parts, reinforcement, or anchors. (2) A full-size mold, pattern, or frame shaped to serve as a guide in forming or testing contour or shape. (3) A member of stone, metal or wood that is embedded in a wall in order to support a horizontal member or beam to distribute the load.

template hardware Hardware that is an exact match for a master template drawing, conforming to the spacing of air holes and dimensions.

temporary shoring Shoring installed to support a structure while it is being built, and removed when construction is finished.

temporary stress A stress which may be produced in a precast concrete member or a precast concrete

component during fabrication or erection, or in cast-in-place concrete structures due to construction or test loadings.

tenancy Occupation of property by one who has less than a fee interest, whether a life tenancy arranged by agreement with the owner or heirs, or a tenancy created by lease for a stated term of years.

tenancy at will A tenancy that is established not by written agreement (a lease), but by oral agreement between the parties. Typically, the tenancy is for an unspecified amount of time. Either party may end the tenancy at any time. Rent is often paid weekly or monthly, and such a pattern may imply a minimum term for the tenancy. If so, the tenancy can normally only be terminated at the end of an established interval (for instance, at the end of the week or month).

tenancy by the entirety A special form of ownership that can only be formed between a husband and wife. When a married couple owns real property as tenants by the entirety, their interests in the property are equal, and each has a right to occupy and use the entire property. Neither spouse, acting alone, may sell his/her share of the property as long as the other spouse is alive. A tenancy of the entirety carries the right of survivorship; when one spouse dies, the deceased spouse's share of the property passes to the surviving spouse.

tenancy in common A form of ownership among two or more people, each with equal rights to occupy and use all of the real property owned in common. Although the owners may all fully occupy and use the property, they do not necessarily have equal shares

tendon

of ownership. A major distinguishing feature of a tenancy in common is that when one owner dies, his or her share does not pass to the surviving owner(s) but, instead, passes to those named in the deceased's will or to the deceased's heirs under the law.

tenant In the broadest sense, one who possesses real property, under any kind of right or title, for any period of time. This broad meaning is used with respect to the different forms of multiple ownership. *See also* **tenancy in common, joint tenancy,** *and* **tenancy by the entirety**.

tenant's improvements Improvements made to a house or parcel of land by a tenant at his own expense that commonly become a part of the property and cannot be removed by a departing tenant unless the owner gives his consent.

tender (1) An offer showing a willingness to buy or sell at a specific price and under specific conditions. (2) In futures, the act on the part of a seller of a contract of giving notice to the clearinghouse that he intends to deliver the physical commodity in satisfaction of a futures contract. (3) A hooktender. (4) A railroad car attached to a steam locomotive for carrying fuel and water, or a ship providing similar services in a fleet. (5) A formal offer of a bid. *See also* **submit the bid**.

tendon A steel element such as a wire, cable, bar, rod, or strand used to impart prestress to concrete when the element is tensioned.

tendon profile The path or trajectory of the prestressing tendon.

tenement (tenement house) Any dwelling, but usually an apartment house, that is situated in a poorer section of a city and has fallen into disrepair.

Tennessee red cedar (eastern red cedar) *Juniperus virginiana*. A pioneer species of wood found in most of the eastern U.S.

tenon A projecting, tongue-like part of a wood member designed to be inserted into a slot or mortise of another member to form a mortise and tenon joint.

tenon-and-slot mortise A glued wood joint formed by a tenon and mortise. Usually the two pieces join at a right angle to each other.

tenoner A machine used to form tenons.

tenon saw (mitre saw) A small backsaw used for cutting tenons.

tenpenny A particular size of nail, generally 3″ long with 69 of them to a pound. The term is believed to have originated in England, where nails of the same size once sold for ten pence per hundred.

tensile strain Elongation of a material that has been subjected to tension by pulling or stretching.

tensile strength Maximum unit stress which a material is capable of resisting under axial tensile loading, based on the cross sectional area of the specimen before loading. Tensile strength is often used as a measure of fastener strength; it is the load required to pull open the fastener.

tensile stress Stress resulting from tension.

tension The state or condition imposed on a material or structural member by pulling or stretching.

terminal

tension member A tie or other structural member subjected to tension.

tension reinforcement Reinforcement designed to carry tensile stresses such as those in the bottom of a simple beam.

tension wood Defective wood usually cut from the upper side of hardwood branches or leaning trunks. The processed lumber exhibits high longitudinal shrinkage, causing warping and splitting.

ten wheeler A tandem truck having ten wheels, commonly called a bogie. In construction, the term refers to a tandem dump truck.

teratogen A term used in labeling hazardous construction or other materials that adversely affect the human reproductive system.

teredo A marine worm that damages untreated wood by boring holes in it.

terminal (1) An element attached to the end of a conductor or to a piece of electric equipment to serve as a connection for an external conductor. (2) A decorative element forming the end of an item of construction. (3) A point of departure or arrival such as a railway or airport terminal.

terminal box A box, on a piece of electrical equipment, that contains leads from the equipment, ready for connection to a power source. The box is usually provided with a removable cover.

terminal element The fixture that delivers the element, such as water faucet, light fixture, or heat register.

terminal expense An expense incurred by one or both parties to a contract at the time of its termination.

terminal unit (1) A unit, at the end of a duct in an air-conditioning system, through which air is delivered to the conditioned space. (2) Devices located near the conditioned space that regulate the temperature and/or volume of supply air to the space.

terminal velocity The average speed of an airstream in an air-conditioning system as it reaches the end of its throw, used as an indicator of comfort level and degree of draftiness.

termination expenses Costs that can be directly connected with the termination of a professional service agreement. Termination expenses may include any compensation earned until the termination occurred.

termination for convenience The unilateral right of the government to terminate contracts at will.

termination for default A sanction which the government may impose for a contractor's unexcused failure to perform.

termites Insects that destroy wood by eating the wood fiber. Termites are social insects that exist in most parts of the U.S., but they are most destructive in the coastal states and in the Southwest. Termites can enter wood through the ground or above the ground, although the subterranean type is most common in the U.S. They eat the softer springwood first and prefer sapwood over heartwood.

termite shield A sheet of metal used on a foundation wall or pier as a projecting shield to prevent the passage of termites from the ground to a structure.

terne metal An alloy of lead, composed of up to 20% tin.

terrace

terrazzo

texture

terneplate Sheet steel coated with an alloy of lead and tin, used chiefly in roofing.

terrace (1) An embankment with a level top surface and stabilized side slopes. It may be used for agriculture or paved and/or planted for recreational use. (2) A platform or paved embankment adjoining a building and used for recreational purposes.

terra-cotta Units of hard, unglazed fired clay, used for ornamental masonry.

terrazzo A type of flooring material made from marble or other stone chips set in Portland cement and polished when dry.

tertiary beam A beam that transfers its load to a secondary beam.

tertiary treatment An advanced stage of the wastewater treatment process, employing methods such as ion exchange, carbon absorption, reverse osmosis, and demineralization of residual solids.

tessera A small square of glass, stone, tile, or marble used in geometric and figurative mosaic work in pavements or floors.

test A trial, examination, observation, or evaluation used as a means of measuring a physical or chemical characteristic of a material, or a physical characteristic of a structural element or a structure.

test case A term used by legal practitioners to refer to a trial whose pleadings and merits have, or possess the potential to form, precedence for future judgments in similar cases.

test cylinder A sample of a concrete mix, cast in a standard cylindrical shape, cured under controlled or job conditions and used to determine the compressive strength of the mix after a specified time interval.

testing Action whereby a portion or sample of a material is subjected to procedures designed to prove performance characteristics.

testing machine A device for applying test conditions and accurately measuring results.

test piling A foundation piling that is installed on the site of a proposed construction project and used to conduct load tests to determine the size and quantity of pilings needed for the actual structures.

test pit An excavation made to examine the subsurface conditions on a potential construction site. Samples are taken at specified elevations for lab analysis. *See also* **testing**.

test plug A device that contains water test pressure in drainage pipes as part of a process to check plumbing systems for leakage.

test pressure Air pressure or water pressure used in plumbing to test pipes and fittings for strength and water-tightness.

test tee A pipe tee that is inserted into a drainage system to test it for leaks by subjecting it to water pressure.

tetracalcium aluminoferrite A compound in the calcium aluminoferrite series, having the composition $4CaOAl_2O_3 \bullet Fe_2O_3$, abbreviated C_4AF, which is usually assumed to be the aluminoferrite present when compound calculations are made from the results of chemical analysis of Portland cement. *See also* **brown-millerite**.

texture (1) The pattern or configuration apparent in an exposed surface, as of concrete or

Texture 1-11

thermal break

mortar, including roughness, streaking, striation, or departure from flatness. (2) In referring to lumber, it is the grain of the wood.

texture brick A rough, fired clay brick, often multicolored, commonly used for facing work. *See also* **rustic brick**.

texture cracking Cracking tensile failure, caused by temperature drop in members subjected to external restraints, or temperature differential in members subjected to internal restraints.

texture float A tool used to give texture to a plaster surface.

texturing The process of producing a special texture on unhardened or hardened concrete.

Texture 1-11 A registered trade name of the American Plywood Association for siding panels with special surface treatments, such as saw-textured, and having grooves spaced regularly across the face.

T&G joint *See* **tongue-and-groove joint**.

thatch A roof covering made of straw, red palm leaves, or similar material fastened together to shed water and provide thermal insulation.

T-head (1) In precast framing, a segment of girder crossing the top of an interior column. (2) The top of a shore formed with a braced horizontal member projecting on two sides and forming a T-shaped assembly.

theodolite An instrument used in precise surveying consisting of an alidade which is equipped with a telescope, a leveling device, and an accurately graduated horizontal circle. A theodolite may also have an accurately graduated vertical circle.

therm A quantity of heat equal to 100,000 Btus.

thermal break (thermal barrier) An element of low conductivity placed between two conductive materials to limit heat flow; for use in metal windows or curtain walls which are to be used in cold climates.

thermal conductance The rate at which heat flows from one surface of a material to the other, usually measured or specified at the rate over a unit area and under a unit temperature differential.

thermal conduction The process of heat transfer through a material by internal molecular action.

thermal conductivity A property of a homogeneous body measured by the ratio of the steady state heat flux, time rate of heat flow per unit area, to the temperature gradient, temperature difference per unit length of heat flow path, in the direction perpendicular to the area.

thermal coefficient of expansion A measure of the expected amount of expansion of a material when heated.

thermal cutout An overcurrent protective device containing a heater element and a renewable fusible member which opens the circuit. The thermal cutout is not designed to interrupt short-circuit currents.

thermal diffusivity Thermal conductivity divided by the product of specific heat and unit weight. The term is an index of the facility with which a material undergoes temperature change.

thermal desorption A process that removes organic contaminants (as vapors or condensed liquids) from soils, sludges, and other solid media, which may then be destroyed in a permitted incinerator or used as supplemental fuel.

thermal expansion The change in length or volume experienced by a material or mass when subjected to a change in temperature.

thermal factor A factor applied in doing lighting calculations that compensates for changes in the light given off by a fluorescent lamp when the ballast/lamp configuration varies from that used in photometric tests.

thermal insulating cement A dry mixture of cement and granular, flaky, fibrous, or powdery materials of low conductivity. When mixed with water and applied to a surface, it dries to provide an insulating covering.

thermal insulation (heat insulation) A material that provides a high resistance to heat flow. Examples are foamed plastics, mineral or glass fibers, cork, and foamed glass. The material is used in the form of blankets, boards, blocks, and poured or granular fill.

thermal interference A naturally occurring process in which temperature differentials can interfere with the operation of injection wells.

thermal lag The time required to add or remove heat from a mass before it reaches the design set point temperature.

thermal limit switch Automatically disconnects the electric supply if air flow through a heater is reduced below a safe level.

thermal oxidation A process that heats a gas stream to a sufficiently high temperature with adequate residence time to oxidize the hydrocarbons to carbon dioxide and water.

thermal process (hot-and-cold-bath treatment) A type of wood preservation treatment whereby the wood is heated in the preservative for several hours and then submerged in cold preservative for several more hours. Creosote or penta are the preservatives most commonly used with this treatment method.

thermally protected A label appearing on the nameplate of a motor or motor-compressor that identifies it as being provided with a thermal protector. *See also* **thermal protector**.

thermal protector A protective device consisting of one or more sensing elements and an external control device to guard against overheating which can result from overload or failure to start.

thermal radiation The transmission of heat through electromagnetic waves from a warm surface to a cooler one.

thermal regenerator A device within a heating duct that is used to recover excess heat and send it to other areas.

thermal resistance (R Value) The resistance of a material to the transmission of heat.

thermal shock The subjection of a material or body, such as partially hardened concrete, to a rapid change in temperature which may be expected to have a potentially deleterious effect.

thermal stress (temperature stress) Stress induced in an object or structural member by restraint against movement required to accommodate temperature changes.

thermal transmittance (U-value) The measure of the rate of heat flow per unit area under steady conditions from the fluid on the

Thermopane

thermostat

warm side of a barrier to the fluid on the cold side, per unit temperature difference between the fluids.

thermal unit   A unit of heat energy, usually the British thermal unit (Btu) in the English system or the calorie in the metric system.

thermal valve   A valve with an activating element that responds to temperature or rate of temperature change.

thermocouple   A device for measuring temperature that has two junctions of two dissimilar metals. When the two junctions are at different temperatures, the junction connected to an instrument, such as a voltmeter, generates voltage.

thermoelectric   Conversion of electricity to heat or heat to electricity.

thermography   Process used to photograph heat being emitted from a structure. The photographs are in color, and the rate of heat loss related to particular colors.

thermomechanical pulping (TMP)   A process in which wood chips are heated and softened by steam before being ground into fibers.

thermometer well   A specially-designed enclosure connected into the piping system and into which a thermometer can be placed to measure the temperature of a fluid in the piping.

Thermopane   Trade name of a double-glazed panel for doors or windows, used for thermal insulation.

thermopiles   A support system used in permafrost that relies on temperature differences and natural convection for removing heat from the ground to keep it frozen or refrozen.

thermoplastic   Becoming soft when heated and hard when cooled.

thermosetting   Becoming rigid by chemical reaction and not re-meltable.

thermostat   An electric switch controlled by an element that responds to temperature; used in heating and/or cooling systems.

thermostatic expansion valve   A valve regulating the flow of volatile refrigerant to a cooling unit, activated by changes in cooling unit pressure and superheat of the refrigerant leaving the cooling unit.

thermostatic trap   A steam trap using a thermally actuated element to expand and close a discharge port when a designed amount of steam flows through it, and to contract and allow condensate to flow through as the temperature drops; usually used on steam radiators.

thick-lift asphalt pavement   A paving process in which the asphalt course is placed in one or more lifts of 4″ or more compacted thickness.

thickness gauge   *See* **feeler gauge**.

thick panels   Plywood panels 5/8″ and thicker.

thimble   (1) A protective sleeve in a part intended to hold an item supported by, or passing through, the part. (2) A protective sleeve of metal in the wall of a chimney used to hold the end of a stovepipe or smoke pipe.

thin butt   A defect in western red cedar shakes in which the butt end of the shake fails to meet minimum thickness requirements.

thin edge   A defect in shakes in which the thickness of 24″ shakes, within 10″ of the butt, is less than half the minimum specified thickness.

T-hinge (tee-hinge) A T-shaped, surface-mounted hinge. The crossarm of the T is fixed to a door frame or post while the length of the T supports a door or gate.

thinner Any volatile liquid used to lower the viscosity of a paint, adhesive, or other like material.

thin-set Descriptive of bonding materials for tile which are applied in a layer approximately 1/8″ (3mm) thick.

thin-shell concrete Reinforced or prestressed concrete used to form a large shell. The thickness of the concrete is small relative to the span of the shell.

thin-shell precast Precast concrete characterized by thin slabs and web sections. *See also* **shell construction**.

thin-wall conduit Electric conduit with a wall thickness that will not support threads. Sections are joined by couplings held in place by setscrews.

third clear (Factory Select, #3 clear) The highest grade of shop lumber. This grade will yield a high percentage of cuttings, but represents a small portion of a mill's total shop production.

thixotropy The property of a material that enables it to stiffen quickly while standing, but acquire lower viscosity with mechanical agitation, such as certain gels. Material having this property is called thixotropic. *See also* **rheology**.

thoroughly air-dried (TAD) Lumber that is air-dried sufficiently to meet the grading rule requirements for dry lumber.

thread A ridge, of uniform cross section, following a helix on the external or internal surface of a cylinder.

thread-cutting screw Screw that cuts threads in metal and joins metal sections.

threaded insert A device forced into a pre-drilled hole to form screw threads.

threaded stud A fastening device with one pointed end driven into a material, such as concrete, and the other end is threaded and extends above the surface for the attachment of structural members.

threads, classes Loose tolerance threads are Class 1. Threads with Class 2 listing are usually stainless steel with normal commercial tolerances. Class 3 are made to stricter tolerances and fit much more tightly. When letter "A" is added to a class, it indicates external threads, or screws. Letter "B" means internal threads or nuts.

threads, coarse Deep threads with fewer threads per inch that provide better protection against stripping and metal fatigue.

threaded anchorage An anchoring device that is provided with threads to facilitate attaching the jacking device and to effect the anchorage.

three-coat work The application of three coats of plaster: scratch coat, brown coat, and finish coat.

three-hinged arch An arch designed in two parts that are pin-connected, or hinged, to each other and to their supports. Such arches are designed for convenience of transportation and erection.

three-phase line A conductor installation that is able to carry heavy loads of electricity.

three-phase motor Induction motor in which the voltage varies from phase to phase by 120°.

three-quarter brick

three-wire system

threshold

through lintel

three-point lock An assembly that latches the active leaf or a pair of doors at three points.

three-quarter bat *See* **three-quarter brick**.

three-quarter brick A brick that has a length equal to approximately three-quarters that of a normal brick.

three-quarter closer *See* **king-closer**.

three-quarter header A header of approximately three-quarters the length of a normal brick.

three-quarter turn Descriptive of a stair that turns through 270° in its progress from top to bottom.

three-quarter view A view of an object which is midway between a front view and a side view.

three-way strap A metal strap used to tie three members of a wood truss together at a joint.

three-way switch An electric switch used to control lights from two different points, as from two different ends of a hallway.

three-way valve A valve with two outlets and one inlet or two inlets and one outlet.

three-wire system A system of electric power supply consisting of three conductors, one of which, the neutral wire, is maintained at a potential midway between the other two.

threshold (1) A shaped strip on the floor between the jambs of a door; used to separate different types of flooring, or to provide weather protection at an exterior door. (2) The level of lighting or volume of illumination that permits an object to be seen a specified percentage of the time with specified accuracy.

threshold limit value (TLV) The concentration of a hazardous substance to which a person may be exposed continuously without adverse health effects.

thriebeam Often used as bridge railing, it is steel plate (usually galvanized) with lengthwise raised areas or corrugations.

throat (1) A groove cut in the underside of an exterior projecting piece, such as a sill or coping, to prevent water running back across the underside to a wall. *See also* **chimney throat**. (2) The thinnest part supporting a stair stringer. (3) The thinnest area of concrete stairs—between the intersection of the back of the tread and bottom of the riser and the underside of the soffit. (4) The thinnest part of a weld. (5) The opening in a wood plane hand tool where the shavings pass through.

thrombe wall A dark-colored 8"-16" masonry wall used in passive solar systems to store heat from the sun. A glass wall is placed approximately 4" from the sunny side of the wall.

through bolt A bolt that passes completely through the members it connects.

through bond The transverse bond formed by masonry units extending through a wall.

through lintel A lintel having thickness equal to that of the wall in which it is placed.

through shake A shake extending through the thickness of the timber.

through stone A bond stone that extends through the full thickness of a wall.

through tenon A tenon extending completely through the part in which the mortise is cut.

tie

tieback

through-wall flashing A flashing that extends completely through a wall, as at a parapet.

throw (1) The distance a latch bolt extends. (2) The horizontal or vertical distance an airstream travels after leaving an outlet until its velocity is reduced to a specific value. (3) The effective distance between a fixture and the area being illuminated. (4) The scattering of fragments from a blast. (5) The longest straight distance traveled in a complete stroke of a rotary part.

throwout bearing A bearing which rides on the clutch jackshaft, that carries the engage-and-disengage mechanism.

thrust (1) The amount of force or push exerted by or on a structure. Sometimes the horizontal component of that force. (2) In an arch, the resultant force normal to any cross section of the arch.

thrust bearing A support for a shaft which is designed to resist its end thrust.

thrust block Additional support introduced at the point of intersection between a brace and its support.

thrust washer A washer that holds a rotating part in place and keeps it from moving sideways relative to its bearings.

thumb knob *See* **turn knob**.

thumb latch *See* **latch**.

thumb nail bead Refers to quarter round molding commonly found on the inside edge of rails and stiles on glazed or raised panel doors.

thumb nut *See* **wing nut**.

thumb piece A small pivoted part above a door handle. Pressure on this part by a thumb operates the latch.

thumbscrew A screw which has a head that is either curled or flattened so it can be turned with a thumb and fingers.

thumbturn A small lever attached to a bolt lock that operates the lock much like a key by turning it.

tideland spruce Sitka spruce.

tidewater red cypress Bald cypress.

tie (1) A member or device that keeps two separate parts together, ie, tie beam. (2) Loop of reinforcing bars encircling the longitudinal steel in columns. (3) A tensile unit adapted to holding concrete forms secure against the lateral pressure of unhardened concrete, with or without provision for spacing the forms a definite distance apart, and with or without provision for removal of metal to a specified distance from the finished concrete surface. *See also* **cross tie**.

tieback A rod fastened to a deadman, a rigid foundation, or a rock or soil anchor to prevent lateral movement of formwork, sheet pile walls, retaining walls, or bulkheads.

tie bar (1) Bar at right angles to, and tied to, minimum reinforcement to keep it in place. (2) Bar extending across a construction joint.

tie beam (1) A concrete beam that connects individual pile caps or spread footings. (2) A horizontal timber that connects the lower end of two opposite rafters to prevent spreading.

tied column A column, laterally reinforced with ties.

tie iron *See* **wall tie**.

tier *See* **lift**.

Tier I or Tier II Form required under SARA Title III for reporting inventory of hazardous substances.

661

tile field

tilting mixer

tilt-up

tie rod *See* **form tie** and **tieback**.

tie wall A wall built perpendicular to a spandrel wall for lateral stability.

tie wire (1) A wire used to hold forms together so they will not spread when filled with concrete. (2) A single-strand wire used to tie reinforcing in place or metal lath to a column.

tight An estimate that does not allow for contingencies and that has no slack.

tight knot A knot in a piece of lumber that is sound and poses no detriment to the proper use of the wood member.

tight sheathing (1) Tongue-and-groove or matched boards nailed to rafters or studs which may run at an angle to provide stiffness to the roof or wall. (2) Excavation sheathing with the vertical planks interlocked for use in saturated soils. *See also* **closed sheeting**.

tile A thin rectangular unit used as a finish for walls, floors or roofs, such as ceramic tile, structural clay tile, asphalt tile, cork tile, resilient tile, and roofing tile.

tile-and-a-half tile A roof tile that is the same length as the other tiles on a roof, but 1-1/2 times as wide.

tileboard (1) A wallboard with a factory-applied facing which is hard, glossy, and decorated to simulate tile. (2) A square or rectangular board of compressed wood or vegetable fibers, used for ceiling or wall facings.

tile creasing A water-shedding barrier at the top of a brick wall consisting of two courses of tile which project beyond both faces of the wall.

tile field A system of distribution tile normally associated with a septic tank and leaching field system.

tile hammer A small brick hammer used to strike glazed tiles and bricks, and sometimes face brick.

till (glacial till, boulder clay) An unstratified glacial deposit consisting of compacted pockets of clay, silt, sand, gravel, and boulders, usually having good bearing capacity.

tilt controls Devices that change the angle of a heat pipe tube to allow gravity to vary the velocity of the liquid refrigerant flowing down the tube.

tilting concrete mixer *See* **tilting mixer**.

tilting drum mixer *See* **tilting mixer**.

tilting fillet (cant strip, doubling piece) A thin wedge placed under the eave course of shingles or tiles to shed water more effectively.

tilting level A surveyor's level with a bubble mounted on the telescope and a provision for slight tilting of the telescope and level. The upright axis of the unit does not need to be vertical, but the level and telescope must be precisely aligned.

tilting mixer A small mixer for concrete or mortar that is emptied by tilting the mixer about a horizontal pivot.

tilt-up (tilt-up construction) A method of concrete construction in which members are cast horizontally at a location adjacent to their eventual position and tilted into place after removal of forms.

timber (1) Uncut trees or logs suitable for cutting into lumber. (2) Wood sawn into balks and planks, suitable for use in carpentry

timber connector

timber pile

or construction. (3) Square-sawn lumber having a minimum nominal dimension of 5″ in U.S., or approximately equal cross dimension greater than 4″ x 4-1/2″ or 10 cm x 11 cm in Britain. (4) Any heavy wood beam used for shoring or bracing.

timber connector One of a variety of metal connectors used in conjunction with bolts to form connections of timbers. Usually the bolt holds the timbers together while the connector prevents slippage.

timber-framed building A building that has timbers for above-ground structural elements (except foundations).

timber pile A large, debarked, pressure-treated straight log that is driven into the ground as foundation support.

time Term used in construction contracts to refer to limits or periods by or during which certain activities will take place. The statement, "time is of the essence of the contract" is used to indicate that the parties consider timely performance an essential element in the performance of the work.

time-based program A program which starts and stops equipment as a function of preprogrammed time.

time-delay fuse A fuse in an electric circuit that takes more than twelve seconds to open at 200% load.

time-dependent deformation Combined effects of autogenous volume change, contraction, creep, expansion, shrinkage, and swelling occurring during an appreciable period of time, not synonymous with inelastic behavior or volume change.

time division multiplexing Splitting a channel into a series of time slots and allotting them for certain sources so that messages from a number of devices are received at sufficiently spaced intervals.

timekeeper A representative of the contractor who keeps records of hours worked by employees of the contractor and allocates the hours to various parts of the work.

timely completion Completion of the specified work, or an agreed upon portion of the work, within the required time limits.

time of completion A specific date stated in the construction contract for substantial completion of the work. *See also* **date of substantial completion**.

time of haul In production of ready-mixed concrete, the period from first contact between mixing water and cement until completion of discharge of the freshly mixed concrete.

time of set *See* **initial setting time** and **final setting time**.

time of setting *See* **initial setting time** and **final setting time**.

timesharing A sequential method of computer operation in which a number of computer operators at remote locations simultaneously use a single multiple-access computer.

time system A system of clocks and control devices, with or without a master timepiece, that will display current time at various locations and may include devices to program other systems, such as bells.

time weighted average (TWA) The average exposure of a person during eight hours to an airborne chemical hazard.

tin-clad fire door

tin roofing

tin (1) A lustrous, white, malleable metal with a low melting point, highly resistant to corrosion; used to make alloys and solder, and to coat sheet metal. When it is added to brass alloys, it provides greater strength and hardness, and also provides corrosion resistance from salt water. (2) To coat with a thin layer of tin or other protective metal. (3) Trade slang for aluminum siding.

tin-canning *See* **oil-canning**.

tin-cap A small, flat metal washer used under roofing nails.

tin-clad fire door A door of two or three plywood planks, core covered with metal sheets and constructed in accordance with specifications of labeling authorities.

tingle A flexible metal clip designed to hold a sheet of metal or glass.

tinker's dam Small dam of sand or other non-combustible material that contains the spread of molten solder.

tin knocker (tin bender) A sheet metal worker.

tinning Coating metal with a tin alloy for corrosion protection or as a presoldering procedure.

tinplate Sheet steel or iron that has been coated with tin as protection against corrosion.

tin roofing A roof covering of tinplate or terneplate.

tin snips Strong shears with a blunt nose, used to cut sheet metal.

tint A light color made by diluting a color with white.

T-iron *See* **tee iron**.

titanium A light-weight, silver-grey metal that is strong and quite expensive. It is often added to other metals. Its properties include corrosion resistance against chlorides, acids and salt water.

title (1) The right of ownership in real property. (2) Legal documents which indicate right of ownership of real property.

title insurance Insurance policy that a title to property is clear or that it can be cleared by resolving certain defects.

title search A search into the historical ownership record of a property to establish its true ownership and check the existence of liens or easements which might affect the sale of the property.

title sheet The first page of a set of blueprints that usually includes location, name, a plot or sketch of the project, designer's name, and a list of the prints.

Title VII of the Civil Rights Act of 1964 A federal law that prohibits employers from discriminating against employees. Under Title VII, discrimination is defined as treating employees differently with respect to compensation, promotion, job conditions, hiring, or discharge on the basis of race, color, religion, sex, or national origin.

T-joint *See* **tee joint**.

tobermorite (1) A mineral found in northern Ireland and elsewhere, having the formula $5CaO \bullet 6SiO_2 \bullet 5H_2O$. (2) Ca:4H O, the artificial product tobermorite, G, of Brunauer, a hydrated calcium silicate having CaO/SiO ratio in the range 1.39 to 1.75. It forms minute layered crystals that constitute the principal cementing medium in Portland cement concrete, a mineral with 5 mols of lime to 6 mols of silica, usually occurring in plate-like crystals which are easily synthesized at steam pressures of

toe

toggle bolt

toilet enclosure

about 100 psi and higher. Tobermorite is the binder in several properly autoclaved products.

tobacco juicing Term given to the brown residue that comes out of asphalt products during weathering. Typically, it is seen on asphalt roofing shingles after periods of sun and rain in the first year exposed to the weather. It often disappears after that time.

tobermorite gel The binder of concrete cured moist or in atmospheric-pressure steam. A lime-rich gel-like solid containing 1.5 to 2.0 mols of lime per mol of silica.

toe (1) Any projection from the base of a construction or object to give it increased bearing and stability. (2) That part of the base of a retaining wall that projects beyond the face away from the retained material. (3) The lower portion of the lock stile. (4) The junction between the base metal and the face of a filled weld. (5) To drive a nail at an oblique angle. (6) That portion of sheeting below the excavated material. (7) The part of a blasting hole furthest from the face.

toeboard A vertical barrier at floor level erected along exposed edges of a floor opening, wall opening, platform, runway, or ramp to prevent falls of materials.

toed Descriptive of a board or strut that has its ends secured by nailing at an oblique angle.

toehold A batten or board temporarily nailed to a sloping roof as a footing for workers.

toe joint A joint between a horizontal timber and another angle from the horizontal, as between a rafter and a plate.

toenail (1) To drive a nail at an angle. (2) A nail driven diagonally from a stud into another framing member.

toenailing Fastening a piece of lumber by driving nails obliquely to the surface. Alternate nails may be opposing to increase holding power.

toeplate A metal bar fastened to an outer edge of grating or the rear of a tread, and projecting above the surface to form a lip. *See also* **kickplate**.

toe wall A low wall built at the bottom of an embankment for greater stability.

toggle bolt A bolt and nut assembly used to fasten objects to a hollow wall or a wall accessible from only one side. The nut has pivoted wings that close against a spring when the nut end of the assembly is pushed through a hole and is open on the other side.

toggle switch A lever-actuated snap switch.

toilet The room housing one or more water closets.

toilet enclosure A compartment placed around a water closet for privacy.

toilet partition One of the panels forming a toilet enclosure.

tolerance (1) The permitted variation from a given dimension or quantity. (2) The range of variation permitted in maintaining a specified dimension. (3) A permitted variation from location or alignment.

tom *See* **shore**.

ton (1) A measure of weight equal to 2,000 lbs. or 907.2 kg. (2) In cooling systems, a measurement of chiller size equal to 12,000 Btus of heat removal per hour.

tongue and groove

top car clearance

Tonawanda pine *Pinus strobus.* *See* **eastern SPF**.

tone The quality of color; a tint or shade.

tongue One edge of a piece of lumber that has been rabbeted from opposite faces, leaving a projection intended to fit into a groove cut into another board.

tongue and groove (1) Lumber machined to have a groove on one side and a protruding tongue on the other, so that pieces will fit snugly together, with the tongue of one fitting into the groove of the other. (2) A type of lumber or precast concrete pile having mated projecting and grooved edges to provide a tight fit, abbreviated "T&G".

tongue-and-groove joint (T&G joint) A joint made by fitting a structural, cast-in-place surface for metal. The joint may also be welded. For plastic or wood pieces, the joint may be glued.

tongue-and-groove material *See* **dressed and matched boards**.

tongue-and-groove pliers Self-locking, adjustable pliers with serrated teeth.

tongue-and-lip joint (tongue joint) A type of tongue-and-groove joint, except the tongue is wedge-shaped and the groove is tapered to receive it.

tongued miter A miter joint incorporating a tongue.

ton of refrigeration A measure of refrigerating effect equal to 12,000 Btu per hour.

tooled ashlar Ashlar masonry with a tooled finish.

tooled finish (tooled surface) A stone finish with the surface having 2 to 12 concave grooves per inch, or 5 to 30 grooves per centimeter.

tooled joint A masonry joint in which the mortar has been shaped or worked before it sets.

tooling (1) Shaping and compacting a mortar joint. (2) The work involved in making a tooled finish.

tool pad A tool consisting of a handle and a chuck for holding small tool bits, such as awls or screwdriver blades. The handle may be hollow for storage of a collection of bits.

tooth A fine texture in a paint film provided by pigments or by abrasives used in sanding, providing a base for adhesion of a second coat.

toothed plate (bulldog plate, toothed gusset) A punched metal plate in which the punched metal protrudes from one side, forming teeth. Toothed plates are used for timber connections.

toothed ring A toothed ring that serves as a timber connector, generally used in the manufacture of large member wood trusses. *See also* **toothed plate**.

toothing Cutting or chipping out courses in old work as a bond for new work.

toothing plane A plane with a serrated blade mounted nearly vertically, used to roughen a surface prior to application of a veneer.

top-and-bottom cap One of the metal channels attached, on the job site, to the top or bottom of a hollow metal door that is not so finished at the factory.

top beam A collar beam.

top car clearance The clearance between the top of an elevator car, or crosshead if provided, and the lowest overhead obstruction when the car is level with the top terminal landing.

topping

top plate

top coat The final coat in a paint system.

top cut The vertical cut at the top of a rafter.

top dressing A thin layer of manure, humus, or loam applied to improve soil conditions in planted areas.

top form Form required on the upper or outer surface of a sloping slab or thin shell.

top hung-in window An awning window that pivots at the top, and the bottom swings in.

topiary Trees pruned or trimmed in a geometric pattern, or sculptural shapes resembling flowers or animals.

topographic survey A review process and record of information regarding the surface conditions of a proposed construction site. The resulting drawing normally uses contour lines to convey the surface height or depth relative to a given level.

topology In telecommunications, the physical layout of the network.

top out To install the highest structural member or complete the highest course in a construction.

topping (1) A layer of concrete or mortar placed to form a floor surface on a concrete base. (2) A structural, cast-in-place surface for precast floor and roof systems. (3) The mixture of marble chips and matrix which, when properly processed, produces a terrazzo surface.

topping joint A joint in a topping layer that is directly over a joint in the base material.

top plate A member on top of a stud wall on which joists rest to support an additional floor or to form a ceiling.

topsoil The surface layer of soil, usually containing organic matter, a mixture of particle sizes, and some animal life. *See also* **loam**.

torch brazing A brazing process in which the heat is supplied by a torch.

torchere A floor lamp that directs almost all, if not all, of its light upwards.

torching The application of a lime mortar under the up-slope edges of roof tiles or slates. In full torching, the exposed underside of slates between battens is mortared.

torch soldering Soldering, with a gas flame supplying the required heat.

torn grain Part of the wood torn out in surfacing. Torn grain is classified for grading purposes as slight, medium, heavy, or deep.

torpedo level Hand level, which may have a laser, that is used to level and plumb short members.

torque (1) The force used to rotate something. (2) Turning or twisting energy measured as the product of a force and a lever arm. (3) That which tends to produce rotation.

torque converter A hydraulic coupling that introduces slippage to increase torque.

torque viscometer An apparatus used for measuring the consistency of slurries in which the energy required to rotate a device suspended in a rotating cup is proportional to viscosity.

torque wrench A tool used to turn nuts, bolts, and other similarly threaded fasteners. Unlike other types of wrenches, torque wrenches have a built-in device that measures the amount of torque (the turning or twisting force) applied to a nut or bolt. The device may be an audible signal, a scale built into the handle,

total float

tower crane

or a dial, calibrated scale, or light. Torque wrenches limit the maximum amount of force that can be used, thereby preventing damage to the fastener and the material to which it is fastened.

torsel A piece of timber, steel, or stone placed under one end of a beam or joist to distribute its load.

torsion The twisting of a structural member by two equal and opposite torques.

torsion strength The measure of resistance of a material to twisting about an axis. For example, the amount of force needed to twist a fastener apart.

torus roll A joint in sheet metal or lead roofing at the intersection of two surfaces with different slopes. The joint is formed to allow for differential movement.

total float In CPM terminology, the difference between the time available to accomplish an activity and the estimated time required.

total harmonic distortion (THD) A measure of the distortion of sinusoidal waves by harmonics. Fluorescent fixtures reflect harmonics back into the electrical supply system.

total heat The sum of both latent and sensible heat.

total pressure (impact pressure) The sum of velocity pressure and static pressure in a moving liquid. Measurement is expressed in inches of water.

total rise of a roof The vertical distance between the plate and the ridge of a roof.

total run The distance covered by a rafter including any overhang.

total suspended solids (TTS) A measure of the solid or particulate content of a liquid.

touch sanding A light surface sanding.

tough ash (European white ash) *Fraxinus excelsior.* Widely used in bentwood products.

toughness The property of matter which resists fracture by impact or shock.

tower A composite structure of frames, braces, and accessories.

tower crane A crane with a fixed vertical mast that is topped by a rotating boom and equipped with a winch for hoisting and lowering loads. The winch can be moved along the boom so that any location within the diameter of the boom can be reached.

tower equalizing lines Pipes installed to directly connect adjacent cooling tower basins to maintain a common basin water level.

town planning *See* **city planning**.

toxic Causing an adverse health effect.

toxic agent A substance that causes an adverse health effect in humans.

TPH test A test used to determine the total quantity of petroleum hydrocarbons in a sample of soil or water.

T-plate A flat metal plate in the shape of a T, used to join or strengthen a right angle joint made between two timbers.

trabeated system A system of building construction using beams or lintels supported by columns.

trabeation (entablature) A type of construction utilizing horizontal members supported by columns. Trabeation is a common method of construction in Japan.

tracing cloth A smooth linen fabric impregnated and coated with sizing to make it transparent, used for tracing.

track

track roller

track (1) A light gauge U-shaped metal member attached to a floor and used to anchor studs for a partition. (2) A U-shaped member attached to a floor, ceiling, door or window header; used as a guide for a sliding or folding partition, door, or curtain. (3) A pair of special structural shapes with fastenings or ties for a craneway, movable wall, or railroad. (4)An electrical raceway that allows the placement and use of a variety of types of luminaires along it.

track lighting A series of movable lights arranged in a line and located on a strip on the ceiling or mounted flush. Typically used for accent or spot lighting.

track roller In a crawler machine, the small wheels that are under the track frame and which rest on the track.

traction The friction developed between a body and a surface on which it moves relative to the total amount of driving force exerted.

traction steel Steel with strength of 180,000 to 190,000 pounds per square inch that is used to manufacture wire rope.

tractor A vehicle on tracks or wheels used for towing or operating equipment.

trade (craft) (1) The business or work in which one engages regularly and which may require manual skill. (2) A group representing a particular occupation or craft.

trade discount A dealer discount offered to the contractor by the supplier representing the difference between list price and the actual charge for goods or services.

trade price list The published price sheet issued to contractors by manufacturers.

trade secrets Chemical formulae or manufacturing processes that enable a particular business entity to gain a competitive edge in the marketplace, the disclosure of which would cause the business to lose that advantage.

trade stacking Having more subcontractor or prime contractor work crews performing different types of construction work in the same area than is efficient for the flow of the work.

traffic (1) The total number of messages handled by a communications channel in a given period, expressed in hundred call seconds (CCS) or other units. (2) Number of vehicles within a specific space and time.

traffic cone A pliable and highly visible cone used as a temporary marker to direct traffic away from a work area.

traffic paint Paint formulated to withstand vehicular traffic, and to be highly visible at night; used to mark traffic lanes and pedestrian crossings.

trailer on flat car (TOFC) A truck trailer carried on a flat car, piggyback.

train A string of connected or unconnected vehicles or mobile equipment, such as a paving train, which consists of mobile machines to lay the various courses of a pavement.

trajectory of prestressing force The pith along which the prestress is effective in a structure or member. It is coincident with the center of gravity of the tendons for simple flexural members and statically indeterminate members that are prestressed with concordant tendons; but, it is not coincident with the center of gravity of the

transformer

transit

tendons of a statically indeterminate structure which is prestressed with nonconcordant tendons.

transducer A substance or device that converts input energy into output energy of a different form, such as a photoelectric cell.

transfer The act of transferring the stress in prestressing tendons from the jacks or pretensioning bed to the concrete member.

transfer bond In pretensioning, the bond stress resulting from the transfer of stress from the tendon to the concrete.

transfer case A transmission or gear set in an all-wheel drive vehicle that provides drive to the front shaft.

transfer column A column in a multistory framed building that is not continuous to the building foundation. At some floors the column is supported by a girder or girders, and its load transferred to adjacent columns.

transfer girder A girder that supports a transfer column.

transfer grille A grille or pair of grilles that allow air to move from one space to another, installed in locations such as a wall or door.

transfer length *See* **transmission length**.

transfer medium The material that carries heat from a solar collector to a living area or storage medium.

transfer molding An injection molding using a thermosetting material.

transfer strength In prestressed concrete, the concrete strength required before stress is transferred from the stressing mechanism to the concrete.

transformed section A hypothetical section of one material arranged so as to have the same elastic properties as a section of two materials.

transformer An electric device with two or more coupled windings, with and without a magnetic core, for introducing mutual coupling between circuits; generally used to convert a power supply at one voltage to another voltage.

transient adaptation The expansion and contraction of the pupil of the eye as light levels change.

transistor A semiconductor device with three terminals that amplifies electrical power.

transit A surveyor's instrument used to measure or lay out horizontal or vertical angles, or measure distance or difference in elevation.

transit-and-stadia survey A type of survey in which angles are measured with a transit and distances are measured with a transit and a stadia rod.

Transite® A well-known brand name of high-strength cement made from Portland cement and non-asbestos fibers. It is sold in panels and as pre-formed items and pipe. Formerly made of asbestos-reinforced cement.

transit line Any line of a survey traverse projected by use of a transit or similar instrument.

transit mix (transit-mixed concrete) Concrete that is wholly or mainly mixed in a truck mixer, usually while in transit to the job site.

transit-mix truck *See* **truck mixer**.

translucent Descriptive of a material that transmits light, but diffuses it sufficiently that an object cannot be seen clearly through the material.

transom

trap

trapdoor

transmission (1) A gear set or similar device that permits changes in the speed/power ratio and/or direction of rotation. (2) The process by which incident light leaves an object or surface from a side other than that which receives the light. (3) The transportation of bulk electricty from the generator to the substation.

transmission length (transfer length) The distance at the end of a pretensioned tendon necessary for the bond stress to develop the maximum tendon stress.

transmission line Any electric line operating at 69,000 or more volts.

transmittal A form or letter conveying the action to be taken on an item being transmitted from one party to another.

transmittance The capacity of glass to transmit solar energy—in visible light, as well as ultraviolet and infrared ranges. Transmittance in measured of percentages of each type of light.

transom A glazed or solid panel over a door or window, usually hinged and used for ventilation. The transom and bar may be removable for passage of large objects.

transom bar (1) A horizontal member separating a transom from the door or window. (2) Any intermediate horizontal member of the frame of a door or window.

transom bracket A bracket that supports an all-glass transom over an all-glass door.

transom catch A lock, used on a transom, with the latch bolt operated by a ring-shaped part. It may be opened using a pole with a hook on its end.

transom lift A linkage system attached to a door frame and used to open a transom.

transom light A glazed light above the transom bar of a door.

transponder A radio or radar device that responds to a certain received signal by emitting a radio signal itself.

transverse cracks Cracks that develop at right angles to the long direction of the member.

transverse joint A joint parallel to the intermediate dimension of a structure.

transverse load A load applied at right angles to the longitudinal axis of a structural member, such as a wind load.

transverse prestress Prestress that is applied at right angles to the principal axis of a member.

transverse reinforcement Reinforcement at right angles to the principal axis of a member.

transverse rib A rib in vaulting that spans the nave, cross aisle, or aisle, at right angles to the longitudinal axis of the area spanned.

transverse section A section of a building taken at right angles to its longest dimension.

transverse shear A shearing action or force perpendicular to the main axis of a member.

transverse strength *See* **flexural strength** and **modulus of rupture.**

trap (1) A plumbing fixture so constructed that, when installed in a system, a water seal will form and prevent backflow of air or gas, but permit free flow of liquids. (2) A removable section of stage floor. *See also* **traprock.**

trap coil A coil used in the electromagnet that activates a trip.

trapdoor A door set in a floor, ceiling, or roof.

travel (rise)

traprock (trap) Any of various fine-grained, dense, dark-colored igneous rocks, typically basalt or diabase.

trap seal (deep seal) The head (vertical distance between the crown weir and the dip of a trap fixture), expressed linearly resisting back pressure. The height of the water in a toilet bowl, it prevents sewer gases from entering the building.

trapway (passageway) The channel in a toilet that connects the bowl to the waste outlet. The trapway is where siphonic action occurs, and its size is measured in terms of the largest ball that can pass through it.

trash chute (1) A smooth, open shaft in a multistory building, used to convey trash from upper floors to a collection room. (2) A temporary chute used for trash removal during the construction of a multistory building.

trash rack A grid of metal bars placed in front of a water inlet to collect larger solids transported by the water.

trass A natural pozzolan of volcanic origin found in Germany.

T-rated switch A switch rated in accordance with the national electric code for use in circuits containing tungsten filament lamps.

trave (1) A beam or timber crossing a building. (2) A panel in a ceiling delineated by beams or timbers.

travel (rise) The vertical distance between the bottom landing of an elevator or escalator and the top landing.

traveler An inverted, U-shaped structure usually mounted on tracks that permit it to move from one location to another to facilitate the construction of an arch, bridge, or building.

travelers Electrical wires between three-way and/or four-way switches.

traveling cable A cable made of electric conductors, that connects an elevator or dumbwaiter car with a fixed electric outlet in the hoistway.

traveling crane A tower crane mounted on tires, crawlers, or rails.

traveling form *See* **slip form**.

travel time Wages paid to workers under certain union contracts and/or under certain job conditions for time spent traveling between their home and the work site.

traverse (1) To plane across the grain of wood. (2) A structural crosspiece, such as a transom bar. (3) A gallery or loft crossing a building. (4) A barrier to allow passage by an official or dignitary, but discouraging unauthorized passage. *See also* **survey traverse**.

traverse closure The calculated line that closes a traverse; the resultant error of measurements, sometimes referred to as "linear error of closure".

travertine A variety of limestone deposited by running water, usually stratified; used for interior walls and for floors.

tray ceiling A horizontal ceiling constructed part way up the slope of a gabled roof.

tread (1) The horizontal part of a stair. Historically, treads have been made from 5/4″ x 12″ vertical-grain lumber called stepping. In recent years, however, most stepping has been made from particle board that is given a bullnosed edge. (2) High-friction coating on a pulley for the purpose of reducing slippage of the belt.

tread width

tree grate

trench brace

trench duct

tread length The length of a tread measured perpendicular to the travel line of the stair.

tread plate A fabricated metal tread with a slip-resistant surface.

tread return The projection of a tread beyond the stringer of an open stair.

tread run The horizontal distance between nosings of stair treads.

tread width The horizontal distance from the nosing of a stair tread to the riser above the tread. The tread run plus nosing.

treated Wood products infused or coated with any of a variety of stains or chemicals designed to retard fire, decay, insect damage, or deterioration due to weather.

treated wood Wood that has been treated with a wood preservative. *See also* **fire-retardant wood**.

treatment train A collection of independent remedial technologies that meet the requirements of particular contaminants affecting the site.

treble damages (punitive damages) An award of three times the actual loss to the plaintiff as a means of punishing a defendant for a serious wrongful action or bad faith conduct.

tree belt A strip of soil between a sidewalk and a street, planted with grass, and sometimes, trees.

tree-dozer An attachment for a tractor or bulldozer consisting of metal bars and a cutting blade, used to clear bushes and small trees.

tree grate A metal grating set around a tree and flush with a pavement.

treenail A hardwood pin formerly used as a wood fastener.

trellis A latticework of wood or metal, usually used to support vines.

tremie A pipe or tube through which concrete is deposited under water, having at its upper end a hopper for filling and a bail for moving the assemblage.

tremie concrete Subaqueous concrete placed by means of a tremie.

tremie seal The depth to which the discharge end of the pipe is kept embedded in the fresh concrete that is being placed. The seal is a layer of concrete placed in a cofferdam for the purpose of preventing the intrusion of water when the cofferdam is dewatered.

trenail *See* **tree nail**.

trench box (trench shield) Box-shaped sheathing made of wood or steel, permanently braced across a trench for excavation and pipe laying. The trench-box unit is pulled along the trench as excavation and pipe laying proceed. It prevents sidewall cave-in during trenching.

trench brace A normally adjustable device, used as crossbracing to support sheeting in a trench.

trench drain A cast-in-place or preformed concrete trench usually covered with a grate that serves as both a drain and a collection point for run-off water or other liquid.

trench duct A trough with removable covers through which electric power and control cables are run. It can be a metal unit that is set in concrete or formed in a concrete slab. The top of the covers are level with the floor.

trenched footing (neat excavation) A type of footing in which a trench has been excavated to the exact dimensions of the desired footing, and the concrete poured directly into the trench. This type of footing requires no formwork.

673

trench excavator

trimmer

trencher *See* **trench excavator.**

trench excavator A self-propelled machine with a side-mounted shovel or chain of buckets, used to excavate trenches.

trench header duct A preformed duct laid in concrete slabs to provide raceways for wiring and communication lines.

trenching machine *See* **trench excavator.**

trench jack A hydraulic or screw jack used as a cross brace in a trench bracing system.

trench shield *See* **trench box.**

trestle A framework used to support a bridge. *See also* **sawhorse.**

trial Term commonly applied to an action in a court of law.

trial batch A batch of concrete prepared to establish or check proportions of the constituents.

trial pit A small pit dug to investigate the soil, sometimes dug to bedrock or other dense material.

triangular scale A drafting instrument that is triangular in cross section and has a different scale on each edge. Some edges have two opposing scales, one two times the other, such as 1/8″ and 1/4″ equals 1′.

triangular truss A light wood roof truss used for short spans.

triangulation A method of surveying over long distances by establishing a network of triangles. Most sides in the network are computed from a known side that may be calculated, and two measured angles. Lengths are measured periodically as a check.

triaxial compression test A test whereby a specimen is subjected to a confining hydrostatic pressure, and then loaded axially to failure.

triaxial test A test whereby a specimen is subjected simultaneously to lateral and axial loads.

tricalcium aluminate A compound having the composition $3CaO \bullet Al_2O_3$, abbreviated C_3A. Its mineral phase name is *celite.*

tricalcium silicate A compound having the composition $3CaO \bullet SiO_2$ abbreviated $C3S$. An impure form of it (alite or celite) is a main constituent of Portland cement. *See also* **alite.**

trig (1) Bricks laid in the center of a wall to prevent sagging and keep it plumb. (2) Metal clip used to hold a mason's line.

trigger The condition or event that initiates or causes an interlocking process to occur.

trigger start The ballast usually used with 15-watt and 20-watt straight fluorescent lamps.

trilateration A method of surveying similar to triangulation, except that distances are measured by electronic instruments, and the two angles are calculated. Quadrilaterals are used in addition to triangles.

trim Millwork, primarily moldings and/or trim to finish off and cover joints around window and door openings.

trim band A metal strip used as a closing band on sides or ends of grating panels.

trim hardware Decorative finish hardware that is functional or used to operate functional hardware.

trimmed opening *See* **cased opening.**

trimmer (header) (1) A short beam that supports one or more joists or beams at an opening in the floor. (2) A beam or joist inserted in a floor on the long side of a stair

trowel

truck crane

opening and supporting a header. (3) Shaped ceramic tile used as bases, caps, corners, moldings, and angles.

trimming joist A joist parallel to the common joists, but of larger cross section, possibly two pieces nailed together, that support a trimmer.

trimming rafter A rafter supporting the end of a header. *See also* **trimming joist.**

trimstone (trim) Decorative masonry members on a structure built or faced largely with other masonry; includes sills, jambs, lintels, coping, cornices, and quoins.

trip (release catch) A device that releases a mechanism, such as a pawl.

trip blank In environmental testing, it is a sample prepared with deionized water and shipped with other samples taken at a site to establish a baseline for follow-on analysis.

trip coil A control device that utilizes a solenoid to open a circuit breaker.

triple glazing Energy-saving windows composed of three panes of glass sandwiched together with air in between. Gases such as argon or others may be used to increase efficiency.

triple-phase motor *See* **three-phase motor.**

triplex cable Electrical cable compose of three conductor cables twisted together.

triple window A group of three windows with square tops. They give an effect similar to Palladian windows, but are less expensive.

tripod A three-legged, adjustable stand for an instrument.

trivet A low support for a surveying instrument used where a tripod can not be accommodated.

troffer A long recessed lighting unit that is usually installed flush with the ceiling.

trolley beam An exposed steel beam on the underside of a structure, used to support a trolley crane.

trolley hoist Lifting apparatus that features a hoist that moves along an I-beam that is supported above the work area.

trough A channel used to contain electric power or control cables.

trough gutter *See* **box gutter.**

trough mixer *See* **open-top mixer.**

trough roof *See* **M-roof.**

trowel (1) A flat, broad-blade, steel hand tool used in the final stages of finishing operations to impart a relatively smooth surface to concrete floors and other unformed concrete surfaces. (2) Also a flat, triangular-blade tool used for applying mortar to masonry.

trowel finish The smooth finish surface produced by troweling.

troweling Smoothing and compacting the unformed surface of fresh concrete by strokes of a trowel.

truck crane A crane mounted on a wheeled vehicle.

truck-mixed concrete *See* **transit-mixed concrete.**

truck mixer A concrete mixer suitable for mounting on a truck chassis and capable of mixing concrete in transit. *See also* **inclined axis mixer, open-top mixer,** *and* **agitator.**

true bearing The clockwise angle between a direction line and a meridian line that is referenced to the geographic North Pole.

truss

trussed joist

trussed purlin

true cedar (Lebanon cedar)
Cedrus libanotica.

true firs A collective term for a group of firs of the genus *Abies*, including white fir and grand fir.

true wood Heartwood.

trunk (1) The main wood shaft of a tree. (2) The shaft portion of a column. (3) Descriptive of the main body of a system, as a sewer trunk line. (4) Transmission channel that runs between two central office or switching devices, connecting exchanges to the main telephone network.

trunk sewer A main sewer that receives flow from many tributaries, covering a large area.

trunnion A pivot consisting of two cylinders or pins projecting from the body of the pivoted object.

truscan order One of the five classical orders featuring columns in which the bottom one-third is straight and the top two-thirds are tapered.

truss A structural component composed of a combination of members, usually in a triangular arrangement, to form a rigid framework; often used to support a roof.

truss beam *See* **trussed beam**.

trussed beam A beam, usually composed of timber that is reinforced by a center post beneath the beam and two rods running from the bottom of the post to the ends of the beam.

trussed joist (open web joist) A joist in the form of a truss. *See also* **bar joist**.

trussed partition A framed partition that is freestanding and does not depend on intersecting panels for support.

trussed purlin A lightweight trussed beam used as a purlin.

trussed rafter roof A roof system in which the cross framing members are some form of light wood truss.

trussed ridge roof A pitched roof in which the upper support for the rafters is a truss.

trussed-wall opening Any opening in a framed structure with a truss system used to span the opening.

truss rod (1) A metal rod used as a tension member in a truss. (2) A metal rod used as a diagonal tie.

try cock Valve used as a backup system of determining water level in a boiler.

try square A normally graduated square, the legs of which are at 90°.

T-shore A shore with a T-head.

T-square (tee square) A guide, in the shape of a T, used in engineering and architectural drawing. The short arm slides along the edge of a drawing board, keeping the long arm in a parallel state.

tube-and-coupler scaffold A scaffold system using tubes for posts, bearers, braces, and ties. Special couplers connect the parts.

tube-and-coupler shoring A load-carrying assembly of tubing or pipe that serves as posts, braces, and ties. A base supports the posts, and special couplers connect the uprights and join the various members.

tube axial fans Single-width airfoil wheel fans arranged in a cylinder to discharge air radially against the inside of the cylinder.

tubing Any material in the form of a tube.

tub mixer *See* **open-top mixer**.

tubular-welded-frame scaffold

tubular fiber form Long tubes of compressed paper used as concrete forms. Often used to pour footings.

tubular saw *See* **crown saw.**

tubular scaffolding Scaffolding manufactured from galvanized steel or aluminum tube and connected by clamps.

tubular-welded-frame scaffold A scaffold system using prefabricated welded sections that serve as posts and horizontal bearers. The prefabricated sections are braced laterally with tubes and bars.

tuck A recess in a horizontal masonry joint formed by raking out mortar in preparation for tuck pointing.

tuck and pat pointing *See* **tuck pointing.**

tuck-in That part of a counterflashing, skirting, or roofing felt that is inserted in a reglet.

tuck pointing A method of refinishing old mortar joints. The loose mortar is dug out and the tuck is filled with fine mortar which is left projecting slightly or with a fillet of putty or lime.

Tudor architecture English architectural style characterized by steep roofs, small windows, tall chimneys, and shallow trim moldings.

tulipwood A close-textured wood, yellowish or rose-colored; used for veneers, inlay, and millwork.

tumbler The mechanism in a lock holding the bolt until operated by a key.

tumbler switch A lever-operated electric snap switch.

tumbling course A sloping course of brickwork that intersects a horizontal course.

tung oil An oil that dries to a clear finish and resists water, it is often used as a wood finish.

tungsten-halogen lamp (quartz lamp) An incandescent lamp that consists of a tungsten filament, a gas containing halogens, and an envelope of a high-temperature resistant material, such as quartz. The lamp is small compared with lamps of similar wattage.

tungsten steel A very hard, heat-resistant carbon steel containing tungsten.

tupelo *Nyssa aquatica, water tupelo, and Nyssa sylvatica, black tupelo.* Light, tough hardwoods largely of the southern and southeastern United States, used for paneling and turnings.

turbidimeter A device for measuring the particle-size distribution of a finely divided material by taking successive measurements of a suspension in a fluid.

turbidimeter fineness The fineness of a material such as soil or Portland cement, usually expressed as total surface area in square centimeters per gram, as determined with a turbidimeter. *See also* **Wagner fineness.**

turbidity The clarity of water, measured by light transmission through a water sample.

turbine Any of various machines that convert the kinetic energy of a moving fluid to mechanical energy. The turbine is often used for driving an electric generator.

turbine mixer *See* **open-top mixer.**

turf The uppermost layer of soil containing roots of propagated grass.

turnaround time (TAT) The amount of time required to complete a process. In reference

turnbuckle

turned bolt

turn tread

to environmental testing, it refers to the time required to process an analysis of a sample.

turnbuckle A device for adjusting the length of a rod or cable, consisting of a right screw and a left screw coupled by a link.

turned bolt A machine bolt, usually with a hexagonal head, the shank of which is finished to a close tolerance.

turned work Pieces of stone or woodwork having a circular cross section, such as posts and balusters. Turned work is usually cut on a lathe.

turning Shaping objects by use of cutting tools while the piece to be shaped is rotated on a lathe.

turning angles The process of measuring angles between lines with a transit or similar instrument.

turning gouge Hand tool used to rough cut wood on a lathe.

turning piece A wood template used by a mason to form a small arch which does not require centering.

turning point Surveying bench mark.

turning vane One of several curved fins that are placed inside ductwork at a change in direction in order to promote better better airflow.

turnkey contract A contract similar to design/construct except the contractor is responsible for all financing, and owns the work until the project is complete and turned over to the owner.

turnkey job A project constructed under a turnkey contract.

turnkey system A system in which the hardware and software, as well as assembly and installation, is sold as a complete package by the vendor.

turn knob A small knob on the inside of a door, used to control the bolt.

turn-of-the-nut method A method used to pre-tension high-strength bolts. The nut is turned from the snug-tight position by either a man using his full strength on a wrench, or a few hits with an impact wrench.

turn piece A small knob used to control a deadbolt from the inside of a door, usually crescent- or oval-shaped for gripping with thumb or fingers.

turnstile A barrier rotating on a vertical axis, usually allowing movement in one direction only and admitting one person at a time. A turnstile is sometimes coin- or token-operated.

turn tread A wedge-shaped tread used where a stair changes direction.

turnup That edge of roofing material turned up along a vertical surface.

turpentine A thin, volatile oil obtained by steam distillation from the wood or exuded resin of certain pine trees. Turpentine was once widely used as a paint thinner and solvent, but now is replaced by solvents derived from petroleum.

tusk Rocks or masonry protruding from the face of a wall.

tusk tenon A tenon with stepped reinforcing at the lower side.

twin brick A double-sized brick.

twin cable A cable consisting of two parallel, insulated conductors fastened side-by-side through the insulation, or by common wrapping.

twin-filament lamp An incandescent lamp with two filaments that are wired independently, used as double-function lamps as in automobile stop lights or as three-level wattage lamps.

twisted pair

two-core block

two-way joist construction

two-way reinforced footing

twin pug (pugmill) A mill with two blade-supporting shafts running in opposite directions.

twin saw, twin (double arbor saw) Two circular saws mounted one above the other to cut in the same plane.

twin tenons *See* **double tenons**.

twist The distortion from a flat plane caused by the turning or winding of the edges of a board.

twist drill A drill with one or more helical cutting grooves, used to drill holes in metal, wood, and plastic.

twisted pair Two single, insulated wires that have been twisted together to reduce the likelihood of interference to and from other wire pairs.

two-by-four A commonly used piece of timber with nominal dimensions 2″ thick by 4″ wide, i.e., 5 cm thick by 4 cm wide.

two-coat work The application of two coats of plaster: a base coat followed by a finish coat.

two-core block A concrete masonry unit with two hollow cells.

two-four-one (2-4-1) Structural wood panels, at least 1-1/8″ thick, designed for single-floor applications over joists spaced 48″ apart and also used as roof sheathing in heavy timber construction. The term is synonymous with APA-Rated Sturd-I-Floor and is a registered trade name of the American Plywood Association.

two-handed saw A large saw with two handles intended to be worked by two people; used for felling trees or cross cutting logs, largely replaced by chain saws.

two-light window A window which is two panes high or wide. *See also* **gemel window**.

two-man riprap Stones suitable for riprap but of a size that can only be handled by two people.

two-part line A single strand, rope, or cable that is doubled back around a sheave to double the capacity.

two-point suspension scaffold *See* **swinging scaffold**.

two-stage absorption A refrigeration system in which the hot refrigerant (water) vapor travels to a second generator. There, upon condensing, it supplies heat for further refrigerant vaporization from the absorbant of intermediate concentration that flows from the first generator.

two-stage curing A process whereby concrete products are cured in low-pressure steam, stacked, and then autoclaved.

two-step sealed bidding A procurement procedure whereby contractors submit technical proposals in response to government performance specifications. Each contractor whose technical proposal is acceptable then submits a sealed bid in accordance with normal bidding procedures.

two-way footing *See* **two-way reinforced footing**.

two-way joist construction Floor or roof construction in which the floor or roof is supported on two mutually perpendicular systems of parallel joists.

two-way reinforced footing A footing having reinforcement in two directions, generally perpendicular to each other.

two-way reinforcement (two-way system) A system of reinforcement. Bars, rods, or wires are placed at right angles to each other in a slab, and are intended to resist stresses due to bending of the slab in two directions.

two-way slab A reinforced concrete slab in which the main reinforcing runs in two directions, parallel to the length and width of the panel.

two-way system *See* **two-way reinforcement**.

Type I & IA Duty Rating Safety ratings for ladders based on load limits. Type I is rated for 250 lbs. Type IA is rated for 300 lbs.

Type X A fire-resistant type of gypsum wallboard.

Tyvek® house wrap Brand name for a weather protector building wrap. In addition to adding insulation, it works to keep moisture from penetrating walls while also allowing the building to "breathe."

U

U ABBREVIATIONS

The abbreviations listed below are those most commonly used in the construction industry. Alternative forms (usually nonstandard) are shown in parentheses.

u unit

U uranium

UBC Uniform Building Code

UCS unconfined compressive strength

UDC universal decimal classification

U/E unedged

UHF ultrahigh frequency

UL Underwriters' Laboratories, Inc.

ult ultimate

unins. uninsurable

uns unsymmetrical

up upper

ur, UR urinal

USG United States gauge

UST underground storage tank

UV ultraviolet

U-bolt

U-bolt A bolt formed in the shape of the letter U, with threads on the ends to accommodate nuts.

UL Label A seal of certification attached by Underwriters' Laboratories, Inc. to building materials, electrical wiring and components, storage vessels, and other devices, attesting that the item has been rated according to performance tests on such products, is from a production lot that made use of materials and processes identical to those of comparable items that have passed fire, electrical hazard, and other safety tests, and is subject to the UL reexamination service.

ultimate design resisting moment The theoretical, applied bending moment which will cause failure in a reinforced concrete member through yield in the tensile reinforcing steel or crushing of concrete.

ultimate load (1) The maximum load a structure can bear before its failure due to buckling of column members or failure of a component. (2) The load at which a unit or structure fails.

ultimate set The final degree of firmness obtained by a plastic compound after curing.

ultimate shear stress The stress at a section loaded to its maximum in shear. *See also* **shear strength**.

ultimate strength The maximum resistance to load that a member or structure is capable of developing before failure occurs. With reference to cross sections of members, the largest moment, axial force, torsion, or shear a material can sustain without failure.

ultimate strength design *See* **strength design method**.

ultimate wiring capacity The average load per unit of area required to cause the rupture and subsequent failure of a supporting mass.

ultrasonic soldering A soldering process, usually performed without a flux, wherein unwanted surface films are removed from the base metal by transmitting high frequency sounds through molten solder, resulting in a more effective welding of the base metal with the solder.

ultrasonic testing A non-destructive method used to test the structural integrity of a pile or a metal element.

ultrasonic welding A process in solid-state welding wherein the metal parts are held together under pressure and joined by applying high frequency sound waves to their surface.

ultraviolet Literally beyond violet in the color spectrum. A minor component of the sun's radiation, it is also produced artificially in arc lamps.

umbrella liability insurance Insurance that provides direct coverage for losses that are not covered by other policies (such as employer's liability, general liability, etc.) *See also* **liability insurance**.

unbalanced bid A contractor's bid based on increased unit costs for tasks to be performed early and decreased unit costs for later tasks. The unbalanced bid is used in an attempt to get money early to finance later parts of a job.

unbraced frame

uncoursed

unbalanced partition A wall built with two layers of drywall on one side and a single layer on the other. Such an imbalance occurs when fire or sound insulation is just needed on one side.

unbonded member A posttensioned, prestressed concrete element in which tensioning force is applied against end anchorages only, with tendons free to move within the elements.

unbonded posttensioning Posttensioning in which the tendons are not grouted after stressing.

unbonded tendon A tendon not bonded to the concrete section.

unbraced frame A structural frame, resistant to the lateral load carried, due to the ability of its members and connections to withstand bending and shear stresses without additional diagonal bracing, K-bracing, or other extra supporting devices.

unbraced length The greatest length between points on a compression member not restrained against lateral movement by beams, slabs, or bracing.

unbraced length of column Distance between adequate lateral supports.

unbuttoning Unfastening rivet steel connections by breaking off the heads of rivets.

uncased pile An unlined concrete pile, often reinforced, that has been poured directly into a bored hole in the ground.

unclassified excavation An excavation priced with a single unit cost, regardless of whether the excavator finds loose fill or embedded rock. Bidders on an unclassified excavation assume the risk for whatever appears.

unconscionability With respect to contracts, where one party takes advantage of another party's inexperience, or does not give a fair explanation of the contract terms. A contract that is unfair or unconscionable is not enforceable.

uncoursed Descriptive of irregularly placed masonry, which is not laid in courses with continuous horizontal joints, but in a seemingly random pattern.

underbed In terrazzo floor construction, the base mortar, usually horizontal, into which strips are embedded and on which terrazzo topping is applied.

undercloak (1) The part of a lower sheet in sheet metal roofing that serves as a seam. (2) A course of tiles or slate used in roofing to provide an underlayer for the first course installed at the eaves.

undercoat (1) A coat of paint that improves the seal of wood or of a previous coat of paint, and provides a superior adhesive base for the top coat. (2) A paint used as a base for enamel. (3) A colored primer paint.

unconfined compressive strength (UCS) A measure of soil bearing capacity, determined by a variety of tests.

undercourse Low-grade, usually #4, shingles used as the initial layer of material at the eaves of a roof. *See also* **undercloak**.

undercured Descriptive of concrete, paint, sealant, or other substances applied in wet or elastic form which have not had time to harden properly because of unsuitable environmental conditions.

undercut To cut away a lower portion of architectural stonework, creating a projection above it that functions as a drip.

underfloor raceway

underground piping

undercut door A door with greater than normal clearance at the floor to give more ventilation to an area.

underdrain A drain installed in porous fill under a slab to drain off ground water.

underfloor heating A heating system that uses embedded pipes or electric heating cables beneath a finished floor so that heat radiates steadily from floor level.

underfloor raceway A raceway installed beneath a finished floor to distribute electric conductors and communications wiring. Suitable for use in a concrete floor.

underground Items or installations that are below grade or ground level.

underground feeder (UF) cable Cable rated for external, underground use.

underground piping Piping which has been or will be laid beneath the surface of the ground.

underground storage tank (UST) A tank system that has at least 10% of its volume underground.

underlay A material, such as asphaltic felt, which isolates a roof covering from the deck. *See also* **underlayment** *and* **carpet underlayment**.

underlayment Structural wood panels designed to be used under finished flooring to provide a smooth surface for the finish material.

underlining felt The material, usually a Number 15 felt, applied to a wood roof deck before shingles are laid.

underpass A roadway that crosses under another roadway.

underpinning The construction of new substructure support beneath a column or a wall, without removing the superstructure, in order to increase the load capacity or return it to its former design limits.

underrun (1) Opposite of overrun; same as pickup; the (lesser) difference between the actual cost and the estimate. (2) Decrease in estimated quantity.

undersanded With respect to concrete, containing an insufficient proportion of fine aggregate to produce optimum properties in the fresh mixture, especially workability and finishing characteristics.

underslung car frame The car frame of an elevator with fastening sheaves for hoisting cables attached at or below its platform.

underwriter An insurance company or an employee of the insurance company who is responsible for approving the issue of policies. Underwriters approve of the amounts, the terms, and the conditions of the policies.

Underwriters' Laboratories, Inc. (UL) A private, nonprofit organization that tests, inspects, classifies, and rates devices and components to ensure that manufacturers comply with various UL standards.

Underwriters' loop *See* **Hartford loop**.

undisturbed sample A sample taken from soil in such a manner that the soil structure is deformed as little as possible.

undressed Descriptive of lumber products that have not been surfaced.

uneven grain Wood grain showing a distinct difference in appearance between springwood and summerwood. Examples are ring-porous hardwoods such as oak,

union

union elbow

and softwoods such as yellow pine that have soft springwood and hard, dense summerwood.

unfaced insulation Board, batt or blanket insulation without a vapor barrier.

unglazed tile A hard ceramic tile of homogeneous composition throughout, deriving its color or texture from the materials used and the method of manufacture. The unglazed tile is used for floors or walls.

uniform angle sander A drywall finishing tool with a right-angled sanding device that can be adjusted to fit corner angles. The tool enables a worker to sand both sides of a corner simultaneously.

Uniform Building Code (UBC) One of several national building codes used to promote building safety, health and public welfare. Published by the International Conference of Building Officials (ICBO), it is used throughout the western U.S. states.

Uniform Commercial Code (UCC) A model law developed to govern commercial transactions.

Uniform Construction Index The forerunner of the MasterFormat adopted by the Construction Specifications Institute in 1978. This system divides technical data and all related accounting, specifying, and tracking functions into 16 divisions.

Uniform Fire Code A model law devoted to ensuring practices consistent with protecting life and property from fire, explosion, and hazardous materials and conditions.

uniform grading A particle-size distribution of aggregate in which pan fractions are approximately

uniform with no one size or group of sizes dominating.

uniformity coefficient A coefficient related to the size distribution of a granular material, obtained by dividing the size of the sieve of which 60% of the sample weight passes by the size of the sieve of which 10% of the sample weight passes.

uniform load A load distributed uniformly over a structure or a portion of a structure.

uniform system A coordinated system developed by the AIA whereby construction specifications, product literature, technical data and cost accounting are organized into several divisions based on an interrelationship of place, trade, function, or material.

unilateral modification A change in the contract requirements unilaterally directed by the owner.

uninterruptible power supply An electrical supply system that will continue to provide current during a power outage.

union (1) A confederation of individuals who share the same trade or similar trades and who have joined together for a common purpose. (2) A pipe fitting used to join two pipes without turning either pipe, consisting of a collar piece which is slipped on one pipe, and a shoulder which is threaded or soldered on that pipe and against which the collar piece bears. Unions allow dismantling a fitting without disturbing the pipe.

union bend *See* **union elbow**.

union clip A fitting used to connect two rainwater gutters into one functioning unit.

union elbow A pipe elbow outfitted with a union coupling at one end

unit heater

unit-type vent

that makes it possible for the coupling end to connect with the end of a pipe without turning or disturbing the pipe.

union fitting *See* **union elbow** *or* **union tee**.

union joint A pipe joint made using a union.

union tee A pipe tee with a union-type joint on one end.

union vent *See* **dual vent**.

unit air-conditioner *See* **packaged air-conditioner**.

unitary air-conditioner A fabricated assembly of equipment to move, clean, cool, dehumidify, and sometimes heat the air, consisting of a fan, cooling coil, compressor, and condenser.

unit construction *See* **modular construction**.

unit cooler *See* **packaged air-conditioner**.

unit cost The cost per unit of measurement.

unit cost contract A contract for construction with a stipulated cost per unit of measure for the volume of work produced.

unit costs The actual costs of items or materials when work has been completed.

united inches The sum of the length and width of a piece of rectangular glass, each in inches.

unit heater A factory-assembled heating unit consisting of a housing, a heating element, a fan and motor, and a directional outlet.

unitized Wood products securely gathered into large standard packages or units, usually fastened with steel straps and often covered by tough paper or plastic.

unit lock A preassembled lock.

unit masonry *See* **masonry unit**.

unit price (1) Current and accurate cost of materials, equipment, and labor used to develop a unit price estimate. (2) The sum stated in a project bid representing the price per unit for materials and/or services.

unit price contract A construction contract in which payment is based on the work done and an agreed on unit price. The unit price contract is usually used only where quantities can be accurately measured.

unit rise In a stairway, the distance from the top of one tread to the top of the next. May be calculated by dividing the total rise by the total number of risers.

unit run In a stairway, the distance between the face of one riser to the face of the next. May be calculated by dividing the total run by the number of treads.

unit-type vent One of several relatively small openings on the roof of a structure, equipped with a metal frame and housing as well as manual or automatic hinged dampers which are opened in case of fire.

unit vent *See* **dual vent**.

unit ventilator A unit with operable air inlets, and often with heating and/or cooling coils, that conveys outdoor air into an interior room.

unit water content (1) The quantity of water per unit volume of freshly mixed concrete, often expressed as pounds or gallons per cubic yard. (2) The quantity of water on which the water-cement ratio is based, not including water absorbed by the aggregate.

unit weight *See* **bulk density** *and* **specific gravity**.

universal joint

upright

universal Descriptive of a door lock, door closer, or similar piece of hardware which can be used on either a left-hand or right-hand swing door.

universal drill A power drill with a drill head that can be rotated or swiveled for special applications.

universal joint A coupling between two shafts set at an angle that allows them to rotate and swivel.

universal motor A motor that can operate on either alternating or direct current and is usually less than one horsepower.

unloader A control for an electric-motor-driven compressor. The unloader controls the pressure head of the compressor and allows the motor to be started at low torque by disconnecting one or more cylinders during the initial period of operation.

unmerchantable Logs or products that are faulty and not saleable.

UN number A classification code assigned to a particular material by the Department of Transportation.

unprotected corner Corner of a slab with no adequate provision for load transfer, so that the corner must carry over 80% of the load. *See also* **protected corner**.

unreinforced concrete *See* **plain concrete**.

unrestrained member A structural member which is allowed to rotate freely about its supports.

unseasoned Lumber that has not been dried to a specified moisture content before surfacing. The American Softwood Lumber Standard defines unseasoned lumber as having a moisture content above 19%.

unsound Not firmly made, placed, or fixed, and thus subject to deterioration or disintegration during service exposure.

unsound plaster Hydrated lime, plaster, or mortar which contains particles that are unhydrated and may expand later, causing popping or pitting.

unstable soil Earth material, other than running, that because of its nature or the influence of related conditions, cannot be depended upon to remain in place without extra support, such as would be furnished by a system of shoring.

unstiffened member A structural member or portion thereof that must withstand compressive force, but is not reinforced in the direction perpendicular to that in which it bends most readily.

unsupported wall height Masonry wall construction limit for wall height set by local codes determined by ratio of wall thickness to height of wall.

upcharge An additional charge for performing some extra service or providing special processing.

uplift The upward load that wind or water pressure can create on a building.

upright A vertical length of stone or timber. Also any vertical structural member, such as a stanchion.

upset (1) To make an object or part of an object shorter and thicker by hammering on its end. (2) A flaw in timber caused by a heavy blow or impact that splits fibers across the grain. (3) In welding, an increase in volume at the point of the weld caused by applied pressure.

upset price *See* **guaranteed maximum cost**.

upset welding A process of resistance-welding making use of both the pressure and heat

upstand (upturn)

urinal

generated by the flow of current as it passes through the resistance provided at the contact point of the surfaces being welded.

upstairs The floors of a house located above the ground or main floor.

upstand (upturn) That portion of a flashing or roof covering that is run up a wall without being tucked in, and which is usually covered with stepped flashing.

upstanding beam A beam projecting above a concrete floor rather than concealed beneath it.

upturned beam A concrete beam that extends above the slab it is designed to support.

urban area An area within the city limits or closely linked to the city by use of common services or utilities.

urban planning *See* **city planning**.

urban renewal The improvement of deteriorated and underused portions of a city. Urban renewal usually implies improvement through city, state, and federal programs, including demolition of slums and sales of properties to others, rehabilitation of relatively sound structures, and control measures to prevent further deterioration.

urea resin adhesive A powder which is mixed with water before use and has high early strength and good heat resistance. Urea resin adhesive is not recommended for exposure to moisture or use in poorly fitted joints.

urea resin glue Urea-formaldehyde resin, an adhesive used in the manufacture of hardwood plywood and interior particle-board panel products. Urea is a soluble, crystalline material found in the urine of mammals, but it is also produced synthetically for the manufacture of plastics and adhesives.

urinal A plumbing fixture designed for the collection of urine and equipped with a water supply for flushing.

usable life *See* **pot life**.

U-stirrup A rod shaped like a "U"; used in reinforced concrete construction.

U-strap Column anchorage to a concrete base using a steel U-shaped anchor bolt embedded in concrete.

usury laws Laws that limit the amount of interest that can be charged on a loan. These limits vary from state to state. In some states, the limits are applied only to certain types of loans. Other states have no usury laws.

U-tie A wall form tie made of heavy wire bent into a U-shape.

utility (1) A grade of softwood lumber used when a combination of strength and economy is desired. Utility grade is suitable for many uses in construction, but lacks the strength of Standard, the next highest grade in light framing, and is not allowed in some applications. (2) A grade of Idaho white pine boards, equivalent to #4 Common in other species. (3) A grade of fir veneer that allows white speck and more defects than are allowed in D grade. Utility grade veneer is not permitted in panels manufactured under Product Standard PS-1-83.

utility and better (Util&Btr) A mixture of light framing lumber grades, the lowest being utility. The "and better" signifies that some percentage of the mixture is of a higher grade than utility, but not necessarily of the highest grade.

U-trap

In joist and plank grades, the corresponding term is "#3&Btr."

utility knife *See* **board knife**.

utility pole An outdoor pole installed by a utility company for the support of telephone, electric, and other cables.

utility sheet Metal sheeting that is mill-finished and cut into numerous widths and lengths for general use within the building construction industry.

utility survey A map depicting the site utilities existing on a piece of property.

utility tractor A tractor of low to moderate horsepower used in construction to tow auxiliary equipment and for other site preparation work.

utility transformer A transformer of primary and secondary wire coils that reduces voltage supplied by a utility to a facility.

utility vent A pipe that helps provide an air supply within a drainage system or fixture to prevent siphonage. The vent rises above the highest water level of the fixture, and turns downward before connecting to the main vent.

utility window A hot-rolled steel window, generally inexpensive, equipped with a hopper light and a fixed light and used principally in garages, shops, and basements.

utilization equipment Equipment powered by electric energy and used in heating, lighting, and numerous mechanical operations.

U-trap A running trap, built in the shape of a U, that forms a seal against the passage of gasses in a pipe, while allowing liquid to flow freely.

U-tube (manometer) A U-shaped glass tube filled with water or mercury and used to measure pressure by liquid displacement.

U-type concrete stairs Cast-in-place concrete stairs, usually enclosed in a stairwell in which the stair makes a 180° turn at a landing.

U-value (thermal transmittance) The time rate of heat flow per unit area between fluids on the warm side and cold side of a barrier, calculated in accordance with the difference in unit temperature between the two test fluids.

V

ABBREVIATIONS

The abbreviations listed below are those most commonly used in the construction industry. Alternative forms (usually nonstandard) are shown in parentheses.

V volt, valve, vacuum, V-groove

val value, valuation

van vanity

VAP vapor

var variation, varnished

VAR visual-aural range, volt-ampere reactive

VAT vinyl-asbestos tile

VCP visual comfort probability

VD vapor density

vel velocity

ven veneer

vent., VENT. ventilator, ventilate

vert, VERT vertical

VF video frequency

VG vertical grain

vhf very high frequency

VHO very high output

vic vicinity

VIF verify in field

vil village

vis visibility, visual

VIT vitreous

vit. ch. vitreous china

v.j. V-joint

vlf very low frequency

VLR very long range

voc volatile organic compound

vol, VOL volume

vou voussoirs

VP vent pipe

VS versus, vent stack, vapor seal

VT vacuum tube, variable time

VU volume unit

V1S vee one side

V

DEFINITIONS

vacuum breaker

valance lighting

valley

vacuum (1) A space that contains no matter. (2) A space with reduced air pressure.

vacuum breaker A pipe or fixture element in a water supply system that prevents siphon or suction action and the backflow that can result.

vacuum circuit breaker An electrical circuit breaker with its surge protection components housed in a vacuum.

vacuum concrete Concrete from which water and entrapped air are extracted by a vacuum process before hardening occurs.

vacuum pump A pump that removes air or steam from a space or system by producing a partial vacuum in the area treated.

vacuum saturation A process for increasing the amount of filling of the pores in a porous material, such as lightweight aggregate, with a fluid, such as water, by subjecting the porous material to reduced pressure in the presence of the fluid.

vacuum tank In a hot water heating system, a container that holds condensate drawn into the boiler by a vacuum pump.

vadose zone The layer of unsaturated soil above the groundwater level.

valance (1) A board at the top of a window, used to conceal the hanging mechanism for draperies. (2) A short drapery hung across the top of a window.

valance lighting Lighting from sources that are concealed and shielded by a board or panel at the wall-ceiling intersection.

This lighting may be directed either upward or downward.

valley The place where two planes of a roof meet at a downward, or "V," angle.

valley board The board nailed to the valley rafter of a roof to accommodate the metal gutter.

valley flashing Sheet metal with which the valley of a roof is lined.

valley gutter The exposed open gutter in the valley of a roof, constructed with sloping sides.

valley jack A rafter in a roof system that is cut shorter than a common rafter and connects the ridge and a valley rafter.

valley rafter In a roof frame, the rafter that follows the line of the valley and connects the ridge to the wall plate along the line where the two inclined, perpendicular sides of the roof meet.

valley roof A pitched roof having one or more valleys.

valley shingle A specially cut shingle, designated for placement next to a valley, with grains that run parallel to the valley.

valley tile A trough-shaped roofing tile used at a roof valley to create a channel for water runoff.

value (1) The utility of an object or service or its worth consisting of the power of purchasing other objects or services. (2) The relative lightness or darkness of a color.

valued policy laws State laws governing the amount insurance companies must pay relative to the value of the loss. Practically all Standard Fire Policies limit claim payments to the "actual cash value"

valve seat

vaneaxial fan

vapor barrier

of the property at the time of loss, even though the full amount of insurance might be more. (If a house is insured for $100,000 but is really worth only $80,000, the insurance company would only have to pay $80,000 if the house burned to the ground.) However, in some states there are valued policy laws which require the insurance company to pay the full amount of insurance. (In those states, the homeowner would get the full $100,000.)

value engineering A science that studies the relative value of various materials and construction techniques. Value engineering considers the initial cost of construction, coupled with the estimated cost of maintenance, energy use, life expectancy, and replacement cost.

valve bag Paper bag for cement or other material, either glued or sewn, made of four or five plies of kraft paper and completely closed except for a self-sealing paper through which the contents are introduced.

valve flutter Any undesirable movement of a compressor valve during operation.

valve motor An electric or pneumatic control that operates a valve within an air-conditioning system, regulating it at a location remote from the unit.

valve plug A valve component that moves against a stationary seat to control steam pressure or flow of a fluid.

valve seat The stationary portion of the valve which, when in contact with the movable portion, stops the flow.

valve stem A threaded, spindle-like valve component that connects the

valve plug to an external handle, gearset or actuator.

vandalism and malicious mischief insurance Insurance protection against loss or damage to a property, specifically caused by willful and malicious damage or destruction.

vaneaxial fan A fan with a disk-type wheel within a cylinder and a set of air-guided vanes on the wheel. The fan is either belt-driven or connected directly to a motor.

vaned elbow A square 90° duct elbow with turning vanes to uniformly direct the airflow.

vane test A test used to evaluate soil strength and consistency. After a hole is drilled into the earth, a spinning four-bladed shaft is inserted and the soil's resistance to the shaft's vanes is measured.

vanishing point A point on a perspective drawing towards which a series of normally parallel lines converge.

vanity A cabinet and lavatory combination for a bathroom.

van stone A type of joint made by using loose flanges on lengths of pipe whose ends are lapped over to give a bearing surface for the flange.

vapor barrier Material used to prevent the passage of vapor or moisture into a structure or another material, thus preventing condensation within them. *See also* **perm.**

vapor heating system A system of steam heating functioning at or near atmospheric pressure, wherein the condensed liquid is returned to the boiler by gravity.

vapor lock The formation of vapor in a pipe carrying liquids, thereby preventing normal flow.

vapor migration Penetration of vapor through walls or roofs, caused

variable air volume unit

by the vapor pressure differential between the inside and the outside of a structure.

vapor pressure A component of atmospheric pressure caused by the presence of vapor. Vapor pressure is expressed in inches, centimeters, or millimeters of height of a column of mercury or water.

vapor retarder (1) A layer of material used to protect roof insulation and moisture sensitive roofing membranes from the damaging effects of internal humidity. (2) *See* **vapor barrier**.

vapor seal *See* **vapor barrier**.

variable air volume (VAV) An air distribution system capable of automatically delivering a reduced volume of constant temperature cool air to satisfy the reduced cooling load of individual zones.

variable costs Variable costs change directly in proportion to changes in volume.

variable inlet vanes (VIV) Vaned dampers installed at the inlet to a fan to produce a spin to the air entering the fan which reduces the fan performance.

variable-volume air system An air-conditioning system that automatically regulates the quantity of air supplied to each controlled area according to the needs of the different zones, with preset minimum and maximum values based on the load in each area.

variance (1) Permission granted to a landowner to depart from the specific requirements of a zoning ordinance. A variance allows a landowner to use his or her land differently than specified in the ordinance. (2) A written authorization from the responsible agency permitting construction in a

manner which is not allowed by a code or ordinance.

variegated Descriptive of a material or surface having streak-marks, or patches of a different color or colors.

varnish A clear, colorless substance used chiefly on wood to provide a hard, glossy, protective film. Varnish is manufactured from resinous products dissolved in oil, alcohol, or a number of volatile liquids.

varnish stain A colored transparent varnish with a lesser power of penetration than a true stain.

varved clay Sedimentary soil with alternating layers of clay and silt or fine sand that display contrasting colors as they dry, formed during the differing sedimentation conditions in various seasons of the year.

vats In the timber industry, large containers used for steaming logs or submerging them in hot water prior to peeling, slicing them into veneer, or cutting them into wafers. The steaming or heating of logs makes them easier to process. Vats were first widely used in hardwood veneer manufacturing, but are now frequently used in the manufacture of softwood plywood panels, waferboard, and oriented strand board.

vault (1) An enclosure built above or below ground, large enough to accommodate human entry. Vaults are used to install, operate, and maintain electrical cables and equipment. (2) A masonry structure with an arched ceiling. (3) A room used for storage of valuable records and/or computer tapes that is of fire-resistant construction, has safe electric

veneer

components, and has a controlled atmosphere.

V-bank filter box   An air-handling unit section in which the filters are arranged in a "V" configuration in order to provide a greater filter surface.

V-beam sheeting   Corrugated sheeting formed with flat, V-angled surfaces instead of a rippled or curved surface.

V-brick   Brick that is vertically perforated.

V-cut   (1) Descriptive of a style of lettering carved into stone in acute, triangular cuts. (2) A V-shaped saw cut or incision in wood.

vehicle   (1) In painting, a substance, such as oil, in which pigments are mixed for application. (2) Any device for conveyance.

vein   A thin layer or deposit of one material in another, usually in an approximate plane.

velocity head   A measurement of the velocity of fluid through a pipe or watercourse. The velocity head is equal to the height that the fluid must fall to achieve that same velocity.

velocity riser   A vertical pipe with a smaller diameter than adjacent piping that is used to increase the flow velocity of the material conveyed in the pipeline.

vendor   An entity that provides standard materials or equipment for a project. *See also* **supplier**.

veneer   (1) A masonry facing attached to the backup, but not so bonded as to act with it under load. (2) Wood peeled, sawn, or sliced into sheets of a given constant thickness and combined with glue to produce plywood. Veneers laid up with the grain direction of adjoining sheets at right angles

produce plywood of great stiffness and strength, while those laid up with grains running parallel produce flexible plywood most often used in furniture and cabinetry construction. *See also* **laminated wood**.

veneer adhesives   Several basic substances are used in the gluing of veneers to produce plywood. These include blood, soybean, and phenolic resins. Other adhesives made from urea, resorcinol, polyvinyl, and melamine are sometimes used in edge gluing, patching, and scarfing. Among the principal adhesives are: (1) soybean glue, a protein-type adhesive made from soybean meal and usually blended with blood and used in certain panels for interior use; (2) blood glue made from animal blood from slaughterhouses, dried and supplied in powder form, and intended for interior uses; and (3) phenolic resin produced from synthetic phenol and formaldehyde. Phenolic resin is cured only under heat and undergoes chemical changes, which makes it impervious to attack by micro-organisms. It is used in undiluted form for the production of exterior plywood. However, it may be extended by the addition of other substances in the production of interior plywood.

veneer base   Gypsum lath sheeting, ordinarily cut in widths of four feet and in varying lengths and thicknesses, with a core of gypsum and a special paper facing that is receptive to veneer plaster.

veneered construction   Construction of wood, reinforced concrete, or steel, faced with a thin layer of another material such as structural glass or marble.

veneered door   A hollow or solid core door with veneer faces.

veneer wall

venetian window

vent sash

veneered plywood Plywood faced with a decorative veneer, usually wood or plastic.

veneer holddown The part of a veneer clipper that holds down the veneer to ensure proper alignment with the clipper blade.

veneer plaster A mill-mixed gypsum plaster made up of one or two components and desired for its bond, strength, and ease of installation.

veneer saw A hand or power saw with a fine-toothed blade used to cut wood veneers.

veneer tie A wall tie designed to hold a veneer to a wall.

veneer wall A wall with a facing which is attached to, but not bonded to, the wall.

veneer wall tie *See* **veneer tie.**

venetian blind (1) A blind made of thin slats mounted so as to overlap when closed and provide spaces for admitting light and/or air when open. The mounting usually consists of strips of webbing. The unit is operated by cords. (2) Adjustable exterior slatted shutters.

venetian mosaic A type of terrazzo topping in which large chips of stone are incorporated.

Venetian plaster A wall plaster applied with a trowel in several layers and often coated with a polished waxed finish.

venetian window *See* **palladian window.**

vent (1) A pipe built into a drainage system to provide air circulation, thus preventing siphonage and back pressure from affecting the function of the trap seals. (2) A stack through which smoke, ashes, vapors, and other airborne impurities are discharged from an enclosed space to the outside atmosphere. (3) Any opening serving as an outlet or inlet for air.

vent connector A metal pipe connecting the exhaust of a burner to a chimney.

vented form A concrete form that retains the solid constituents of concrete and permits the escape of water and air.

vent flue *See* **vent.**

ventilating bead *See* **draft bead.**

ventilating brick A brick with holes in it for the passage of air.

ventilating eyebrow *See* **eyebrow.**

ventilating jack A sheet metal hood over the inlet to a vent pipe to direct flow into the pipe.

ventilation A natural or mechanical process by which air is introduced to or removed from a space, with or without heating, cooling, or purification treatment.

ventilator (1) A device or opening in a room or building through which fresh air enters the enclosure and stale air is expelled. (2) A pivoted sash or framework, outfitted with hinged panes of glass that may be opened without opening the sash.

ventilator frame An assembly designed to accommodate a pivoted sash, with two rails and two stiles into which the operable panes are set.

vent pipe A small-diameter pipe used in concrete construction to permit the escape of air in a structure being concreted or grouted.

vent sash A small, operable light (usually hinged on its upper edge) in a window, which may be swung open to allow some ventilation without opening the entire sash.

vent stack (main vent) A vertical vent pipe whose functions are to provide air circulation to or from any part of a building drainage system and to protect its trap seals from siphonage.

vent system (1) Piping that provides a flow of air to or from a drainage system to protect trap seals from siphonage or back pressure. (2) A chimney or vent combined with a vent connector to form a clear passageway for expulsion of vent gases from gas-burning equipment to the outside air.

venturi (1) A short tube with a constriction used to measure fluid or gas velocity by the differential pressure as the fluid or gas flows. (2) A constricted throat in an air passage of a carburetor used to mix fuel and air.

veranda A covered porch or balcony along the outside of a building, intended for leisure.

verdigris A bluish green patina that naturally forms on copper, bronze or brass over time as it is exposed to atmospheric conditions.

verge (1) The edge that projects over the gable of a roof. (2) A small shaft of a column employed for ornamental effect. (3) The unpaved section of a road right-of-way.

vergeboard *See* **bargeboard**.

verge fillet A strip of wood that is fastened to the roof battens of a gable to cover the upper edges of the gable wall.

vermiculated work A form of incised masonry surface with ornamental track-like grooves, frets, or knots, employed architecturally on wall surfaces and pavements.

vermiculite A group name for certain clay minerals, hydrous silicates or aluminum, magnesium, and iron that have been expanded by heat. Vermiculite is used for lightweight aggregate in concrete and as a loose fill for thermal insulating applications.

vermiculite concrete Concrete in which the aggregate consists of exfoliated vermiculite.

vermiculite plaster A fire-retardant plaster covering for steel beams, concrete slabs, and other heavy construction materials, constituted with an aggregate of very fine exfoliated vermiculite.

vernier An auxiliary scale that slides along a larger scale and allows more accurate interpretation of subdivisions.

vertical angle An angle in a vertical plane.

vertical bar An upright muntin.

vertical bond Masonry bond with one brick or block placed directly on top of the next. *See also* **stack bond**.

vertical circle A graduated circle mounted on an instrument so that the plane of the circle will be in a true vertical plane when the instrument is leveled.

vertical curve A parabolic curve in the vertical plane used to connect two highway grades in order to form a smooth transition.

vertical exit A stairway, ramp, fire escape, escalator, or any other route of movement that serves as an exit from the floors of a building above or below street level.

vertical-fiber brick A paving brick cut with wire during the manufacturing process, and laid on pavement with the wire-cut side exposed to view.

vertical firing Mechanical arrangement of gas, oil, or coal

vertical siding

vertical sliding window

burners in a furnace so that fuel is vertically discharged up from burners below or down from burners on top.

vertically pivoted window A window having a sash that pivots on a vertical axis near its center so the outside of the glass can be conveniently cleaned.

vertical photograph A photograph taken from an airplane looking straight down. The vertical photograph is used in aerial surveying.

vertical pipe Any pipe or fitting that makes an angle of 45° or less with the vertical.

vertical sand drain A boring through clay or silt filled with sand or gravel to allow soil to drain. Most effective when bored to permeable soil below.

vertical sash *See* **vertical sliding window**.

vertical section An illustration of an object as it would appear if a vertical plane were cut through it. An example of a vertical section is a drawing of sedimentary soil layers or of the wood layers on a sheet of plywood.

vertical siding A type of exterior wall cladding consisting of wide matched boards.

vertical sliding window A window with one or more sashes that move only in a vertical direction and make use of friction or a ratchet device to remain in an open position.

vertical slip form A form which is jacked vertically during construction of a concrete structure. Movement may be continuous with placing or intermittent with horizontal joints.

vertical spring-pivot hinge A spring hinge that is mortised into the heel of a door, which in turn is fastened with pivots to its door head and the floor.

vertical tiling Tile that is hung on the surface of a wall in a vertical arrangement and protects the wall against moisture.

vertical tray conveyors A vertical conveying system designed to carry trays or boxes.

vertical-vision-light door *See* **narrow-light door**.

very high output fluorescent lamp (VHO lamp) A rapid-start fluorescent lamp designed to operate on a very high current, providing a light flux per unit length of lamp higher than that obtained from a high output fluorescent lamp.

vestibule An anteroom or foyer leading to a larger space.

V-groove Any of several longitudinal cuts made on the faces of pieces of lumber or plywood. The face veneer of plywood paneling is V-grooved to relieve the flat appearance of the surface. The grooving usually creates a pattern resembling random width boards placed side by side. Usually, V-grooves in paneling are stained darker than the surface. In lumber, edges are sometimes chamfered to create a "V" where pieces are placed edge to edge. A "V" may also be machined the length of the piece to provide decoration. A "V" pattern also may be used to form tongue and groove connections on hardwood or plywood.

V-gutter *See* **valley gutter**.

viaduct A bridge constructed in the form of several towers or piers that support arches. Usually made of steel or concrete.

vibration isolator

vibrator

vibrated concrete Concrete compacted by vibration during and after placing.

vibrating pile driver See **sonic pile driver**.

vibrating roller A towed or self-propelled roller with a motor-driven vibrating mechanism.

vibrating screed A machine designed to act as a vibrator while leveling freshly placed concrete.

vibration Energetic agitation of freshly mixed concrete during placement by mechanical devices, either pneumatic or electric, that create vibratory impulses of moderately high frequency that assist in evenly distributing and consolidating the concrete in the formwork.

vibration, external Employs vibrating devices attached at strategic positions on the forms and is particularly applicable to the manufacture of precast items and for vibration of tunnel-lining forms. In the manufacture of concrete products, external vibration or impact may be applied to a casting table.

vibration, internal Employs one or more vibrating elements to be inserted into the concrete at selected locations, and is more generally applicable to cast-in-place construction.

vibration isolator A flexible support for any form of vibrating or reverberating machinery, piping, or ductwork, serving to reduce the vibrations that are carried to the remainder of the building structure.

vibration limit That time at which fresh concrete has hardened sufficiently to prevent its becoming mobile when subjected to vibration.

vibration meter Any instrument that measures the displacement, velocity, or acceleration of a vibrating body.

vibration, surface Employs a portable horizontal platform on which a vibrating element is mounted.

vibrator An oscillating machine used to agitate fresh concrete so as to eliminate gross voids, including entrapped air, but not entrained air, and to produce intimate contact with form surfaces and between embedded materials.

vibratory hammer A pile-driving hammer, normally weighing from three to five tons, that with rapid vibrations causes the soil around the pile to change to a liquid state. The weight of the hammer then slips the pile down through the soil.

vibratory plate A piece construction machinery that is used to compact soil, pavement underlayment materials, or pavement.

vibroflotation A process used to stabilize and otherwise improve soil for building by compacting loose granular soils.

vicat apparatus A penetration device used in the testing of hydraulic cements and similar materials.

vicat needle A weighted needle for determining the setting time of hydraulic cements.

vice See **vis**.

victaulic pipe Pipe with fittings that allow for movement along joints while remaining watertight.

view sash A picture window with panes of glass divided by muntins.

vinyl A thermoplastic compound made from polymerized vinyl chloride, vinylide chloride, or vinyl acetate. Vinyl is typically tough, flexible, and shiny.

vinyl composition tile

vise

vision panel

vinyl-asbestos tile A resilient, semiflexible floor tile, composed of ground limestone, plasticizers, pigments, polyvinyl chloride binder, and asbestos fiber reinforcing. This product has been replaced by vinyl composition tile.

vinyl-clad Doors and windows that have a vinyl covering applied over all exposed surfaces that make up the frame and jamb.

vinyl composition tile A floor tile similar to vinyl-asbestos floor tile except the asbestos has been replaced by glass fiber reinforcing.

vinyl overlay An overlay applied to panel products and moldings and usually printed with a color and grain, needing no further finishing.

vinyl tile A floor tile similar to vinyl-asbestos floor tile, but which does not contain mineral or other fibers.

Virginia pine *Pinus virginiana.* This is another minor member of the southern yellow pine group. It is grouped for grading purposes with "pond pine," under the stamp "mixed pine species."

vis (vice, vise) (1) A spiral staircase, generally of stone, with steps winding around a central shaft. (2) A screw stair.

viscometer Instrument for determining viscosity of slurries, mortars, or concretes.

viscosity The degree to which a fluid resists flow under an applied force.

viscous filter An air-cleaning filter that employs a surface covered with viscous oil or fluid, to which dirt particles and other airborne impurities cling as the air passes through.

vise (1) A gripping tool with adjustable jaws controlled by a lever or screw, used to clamp an object firmly in place while work is being done on it. (2) A *vis*.

Vise Grips® *See* **locking pliers**.

visible light transmission The percentage of total visible light that passes through a window or similar glazed opening.

vision panel Glazed opening installed in a door as specified by plans and specifications.

visual comfort probability (VCP) A system that evaluates the visual comfort of a lighting system by rating its direct discomfort glare.

visual concrete *See* **exposed aggregate**.

visual inspection An inspection made without the use of instruments.

visual task The plane at which work is done, and all associated details and objects. Used to measure and specify illuminance.

vitreous In describing glazed products, a degree of impermeability in a material characterized by low water absorption. Vitreous is less than 3% absorbtion in floor and wall tile and low voltage electrical porcelain, and less than 0.3% absorption in other materials.

vitrification (1) A process of melting soil or wastes to a liquid form, and then cooling the liquid to a hard, glass-like material. (2) The fusion of grains in clay products under high kiln temperatures, resulting in closure of pores and an impervious material. (3) A process that transforms the chemical and physical characteristics of hazardous waste so that the treated residues contain hazardous material immobilized in a vitreous mass.

vitrified brick Glazed brick that is impervious to moisture and highly resistant to chemical corrosion.

virtified-clay pipe

vitrified-clay pipe Glazed earthenware pipe favored for use in sewage and drainage systems because it is impervious to water and resistant to chemical corrosion.

V-joint *See* **V-shaped joint**.

void-cement ratio Volumetric ratio of air plus net mixing water to cement in a concrete or mortar mixture.

void ratio In a mass of granular material, the ratio of the volume of voids to the volume of solid particles.

voids The air spaces between particles in granular material such as sand, or a paste such as mortar.

void-solid ratio The ratio of the sum of the areas of window and door openings to the gross area of an exterior wall of a building.

volatile material (1) Material that is subject to release as a gas or vapor. (2) Liquids that evaporate readily.

volatile organic compounds Regulated unstable compounds that lead to the formation of ozone and smog and may be hazardous to humans. VOCs contain carbon molecules and are volatile enough to evaporate from material surfaces into indoor air at normal temperatures. They are emitted on a large scale from automotive and industrial sources.

volatility The tendency of a substance to vaporize, or "escape," from the liquid phase or from the surface of a solid to the vapor phase.

volt The unit of voltage or potential difference equal to the voltage between two points of a conducting wire carrying a constant current of one ampere, when the power dissipated between the points is one watt.

voltage The greatest root-mean-square potential difference between any two points in an electric circuit.

voltage drop The difference in voltage between any two points in an electric circuit.

voltage, nominal A value assigned to a circuit or system for classification purposes. Operation may actually be possible within a range, and the nominal voltage is often the midpoint of that range.

voltage regulator A control device within an electrical system that automatically keeps the voltage supply constant despite variable line voltage at the point of input.

voltage relay A voltage monitoring device that detects changes in levels of current and controls the flow of electricity accordingly.

voltage-to-ground (1) The voltage between a conductor in a grounded electric circuit and the point of the circuit that is grounded. (2) The maximum voltage between a conductor in an ungrounded electric circuit and another conductor.

volt-ampere The product obtained by multiplying one volt times one ampere, equivalent to one watt in direct-current circuits and to one unit of apparent power in alternating current circuits.

voltmeter An instrument used to measure the voltage drop between any two points in an electric circuit.

volume batching The measuring of the constituent materials for mortar or concrete by volume.

volume change An increase or decrease in volume. *See also* **deformation**.

volume damper Device installed in a duct system circuit to add resistance to the circuit for air volume balancing.

voussoir

V-shaped joint

volume method (of estimating cost) A cost estimating method determined by multiplying an estimated cost per unit of volume by the volume of the building. *See also* **architectural volume, architectural area of buildings,** *and* **area method.**

volumetric test (1) A test to determine the integrity of an underground storage tank through review and comparison of tank volume. (2) A test to determine the air content of fresh concrete.

volute (1) The spiral-turned handrail detail at the first tread on some stairs. (2) The spiral treatment that appears at the top of a column (usually Ionic).

vomitory An opening dividing a bank of seats to provide access to and egress from an aisle.

voussoir A wedge-shaped masonry unit in an arch or vault, the converging sides of which are cut along radii of the vault or arch.

voussoir brick *See* **arch brick.**

V-shaped joint (V-joint, V-tooled joint) (1) A V-shaped horizontal joint in mortar, formed with a steel jointing tool, that serves to resist rainwater penetration. (2) Two adjacent wood boards, with beveled or chamfered edges, that form a joint in the same plane.

V-tool A gauge with a V-shaped cutting edge. *See also* **parting tool.**

V-tooled joint *See* **V-shaped joint.**

vulcanization A chemical process in which a rubber compound becomes less plastic, more resistant to swelling by organic liquids, and more elastic, and its elastic properties are extended over a greater temperature range.

ABBREVIATIONS

The abbreviations listed below are those most commonly used in the construction industry. Alternative forms (usually nonstandard) are shown in parentheses.

w water, watt, weight, wicket, wide, width, work, with

W watt, west, western, width

w/ with

WA with average

WAF wiring around frame

WB welded base, water ballast, waybill

WBT wet-bulb temperature

WC, W.C. water closet

WCLIB West Coast Lumber Inspection Bureau

wd wood, window

Wdr wider

WF wide flange, white fir

wfl waffle

wg wing, wire gauge

wh watt-hour

WH water heater

WHP water horsepower

whr watt-hour

whse, WHSE warehouse

WI wrought iron

WK week, work

wm wattmeter

W/M weight or measurement

WM wire mesh

w/o water-in-oil, without

WP waterproof, weatherproof, white phosphorus

wpc watts per candle

w proof waterproofing

wrc western red cedar

wrt wrought

WS weather strip

wsct/wains wainscoting

wt., Wt. weight

WT water table, watertight

ww white wash, white woods

WWM welded wire mesh

WWPA Western Wood Products Association

waffle slab

wale

wall anchor

waferboard A panel product made of discrete wafers of wood bound together by resin, heat, and pressure. Waferboard can be made of timber species, such as aspen, that are not suitable for lumber or plywood manufacture.

waffle *See* **dome**.

waffle floor *See* **waffle slab**.

waffle slab A reinforced concrete slab with equally spaced ribs parallel to the sides, having a waffle appearance from below.

Wagner fineness The fineness of Portland cement, expressed as total surface area in square centimeters per gram, determined by the Wagner turbidimeter apparatus and procedure.

wagon drill A movable rig for positioning and holding a pneumatic drill, consisting of a mast with a carrier for the drill and a supporting wheeled carriage.

wagon-head dormer A dormer with a semicircular roof.

wainscot The lower portion of an interior wall whose surface differs from that of the upper wall.

wainscot cap The finish molding at the top of wainscot.

wainscot oak Selected oak planks used in wainscoting.

waist The narrowest section of a column or similar building element.

waiver of lien An instrument by which a person or organization, who has or may have a right of mechanic's lien against the property of another, relinquishes such a right. *See also* **mechanic's lien** *and* **release of lien**.

wale (waler, whaler) (1) Timber placed horizontally across a structure to strengthen it. (2) Horizontal bracing used to stiffen concrete form construction and to hold studs in place.

walk A paved or planked path for foot traffic.

walk-in box A refrigerator or freezer large enough for one or more persons to enter to deposit or retrieve food.

walking edger A concrete finishing tool mounted on a long handle and used to produce a radius at the edge of a concrete slab.

wall A vertical element used primarily to enclose or separate spaces.

wall anchor A steel strap used to attach a back-up surface to the masonry fascia.

wall arcade A blind arcade used as an ornamental dressing to a wall.

wall base *See* **base**.

wall beam (1) A special form of reinforced concrete framing, used for some apartment buildings, in which walls between apartments are used as deep, transverse beams supporting one edge of a floor slab below and one above. The deep beams alternate between floors and between columns. (2) A header bolted to a wall and used to support joists or beams.

wall-bearing construction A structural system where the weight of the floors and roof are carried directly by the masonry walls rather than the structural framing system.

wall-bearing partition *See* **load-bearing partition**.

wall bracket

wall form

wall-hung water closet

wallboard A manufactured sheet material used to cover large areas. Wallboards are made from many items, including wood fibers and gypsum. In North America, the most common is *Sheetrock®*, a gypsum-based panel bound by sheets of heavy paper. It is used to cover interior walls and ceilings in place of wet plaster.

wall box (beam box, wall frame) (1) A bracket fixed to a wall to support a structural member. (2) A metal box set in a wall to house an electric switch or receptacle.

wall bracket A bracket fastened to a wall and used to support a structural member, pipe, an electric insulator, an electric fixture, or a section of scaffolding.

wall chase *See* **chase**.

wall clamp A brace or tie used to connect two parallel walls to each other.

wall column A steel or concrete column fully or partly embedded in a wall. *See also* **pilaster**.

wall coping *See* **coping**.

wall covering Any material or assembly used as a wall finish and not an integral part of the wall.

wall crane A crane with a horizontal arm supported from a wall or columns of a building. The arm may support a trolley.

wall expansion A break designed into a wall to allow room for building materials to expand and contract with thermal conditions.

wall fabric Any wall covering used to finish a wall, whether wallpaper or an actual fabric.

wall footing A strip of reinforced concrete that is wider than the wall it supports and thus distributes the wall load over a wider area.

wall form A retainer or mold erected to give the necessary shape, support, and finish to a concrete wall.

wall furring Strips of wood or shaped sheet metal attached to a rough wall to provide a plane on which lath and plaster, paneling, or wainscoting may be installed.

wall grille A perforated plate, casting, punched sheet, or frame used to conceal an opening, radiator, or the like, while allowing a passage for air.

wall guard A protective, resilient strip attached to a wall to protect the surface from carts, transporters, or other movable conveyors.

wall handrail A rail attached to a wall at a flight of stairs and running parallel with the slope of the stairs for use as a handrail.

wall hanger A stirrup or bracket fixed to a wall and used to support one end of a horizontal member.

wall height The vertical distance from the top of a wall to its support, such as a foundation or support beam.

wall hook (1) A special large nail or hook used as a beam anchor or used on a beam plate. (2) A hook or bracket fixed in a masonry wall to hold downspouts, lightning rods, etc.

wall-hung water closet A water closet mounted on a wall so the area beneath is clear for cleaning.

wall opening An opening at least 30″ high and 18″ wide in any wall or partition through which persons may fall, such as a chute opening.

wall outlet An electric outlet mounted in a wall with a decorative cover.

wall plate The top plate in construction, placed on top of studs

wall spacer

warm-air heating system

and bearing the joists of the next floor above.

wall plug *See* **plug** *and* **wall outlet**.

wall post A post next to, and often fastened to, a wall.

wall puller A simple hand tool used to help position a stud wall or similar construction.

wall rib A longitudinal rib against an exterior wall of a vaulting compartment.

wall shaft A small column, supported on a corbel or bracket, which appears to support a rib of a vault.

wall sign (1) A sign mounted on, or fastened to, a wall. (2) A sign attached to the exterior wall of a building and projecting not more than a code-defined distance.

wall socket *See* **wall outlet**.

wall spacer A metal tie used to hold forms in position until concrete has set.

wall tie A metal strip or wire used to tie masonary wythes together, or tie a masonry veneer to a wood or concrete frame or wall. *See also* **wythe**.

wall tile A glazed tile used in a wall facing.

wall-wash luminaire A luminaire located adjacent to or on a wall with most of its light directed onto the wall.

walnut (English walnut, black walnut, butternut) *Juglans regia, J. nigria,* and *J. cinerea* respectively. The last two, native to North America, are used for veneer and furniture stock, in addition to their edible nuts.

Walter pine *See* **spruce pine**.

wane A defective edge of a board due to remaining bark or a beveled end.

A wane is usually caused by sawing too near the surface of the log.

ward (1) A baffle in a lock to prevent use of an unauthorized key. (2) A division of a hospital or jail.

warehouse set The partial hydration of cement stored for a time and exposed to atmospheric moisture, or mechanical compaction occurring during storage. A partially hardened, unopened bag of cement.

warm-air furnace A furnace that generates warm air for a heating system.

warm-air heating system A heating system in which warm air is distributed through a single register or series of ducts. Circulation may be by convection (gravity system) or by a fan in the ductwork (forced system).

warm-in-winter side The side of a wall that faces the living area of a structure. When installing insulation with a vapor barrier, the barrier should face the warm-in-winter side.

warning pipe An overflow pipe with an outlet located so that discharge can be readily observed.

warp Distortion in the shape of a plane surface, such as that in lumber as a result of a change in moisture content.

warping A deviation of a slab or wall surface from its original shape, caused by temperature and/or moisture differentials within the slab or wall. *See also* **curling**.

warping joint A longitudinal or transverse joint, with bonded steel or tie bars passing through it, with the sole function of permitting warping of pavement slabs when moisture and temperature differentials occur in the pavement.

warren truss

washer

waste and overflow fitting

warranty A promise made by a seller or contractor responsible for work performed under a contract that the work performed is fit for the purpose intended and is free from structural, electrical, mechanical, and other defects.

warranty deed A deed conveying real property, in which the grantor makes binding representations concerning the quality of his title and its freedom from encumbrances.

warren truss (warren girder) A truss consisting of horizontal top and bottom chords, separated by sloping members, and without vertical pieces.

wash (1) The top surface of a building element, such as a coping or sill, intended to shed water. (2) A manner of applying water colors to a rendering.

washable Descriptive of a material that may be washed repeatedly without a noticeable deterioration in appearance or function.

wash boring A boring made in the earth by a rotary drill that uses water to stabilize the sides of the hole.

wash coat A thin, almost transparent coat of paint applied to a surface as a sealer or stain.

wash cut A beveled cut in a stone windowsill that diverts water away from the window and the structure.

washer (1) A flat ring of rubber, plastic, or fibrous material, used as a seal in a faucet or valve or to minimize leakage, as in a threaded connection. (2) A flat ring of steel that may be split, toothed, or embossed; used in threaded connections to distribute loads, span large openings, relieve friction, or prevent loosening.

Washington fir *See* **Douglas fir**.

wash primer Any thin paint that promotes adhesion of the subsequent coat.

wash water (flush water) Water carried on a truck mixer in a special tank for flushing the interior of the mixer after discharge of the concrete.

waste and overflow fitting A common bathtub fixture that provides one outlet for a tub drain and another in case water rises above a safe level.

waste-disposal unit An electrically operated device for grinding waste food and disposing of it through the plumbing drainage pipes.

waste heat boiler A boiler that is fired by the hot exhaust gases of incinerators, engines, or industrial processes.

waste heat recovery An economical measure that involves capturing the heat produced by a process in a cyclic process to serve another need, such as pre-heating combustion air.

waste management Activities undertaken to minimize, contain, control, store, transport, treat, or dispose of waste material.

waste oil Lubricants, typically automotive lubricants, that are no longer usable for their intended purpose.

waste pile An accumulation of solid waste materials at a specific location.

waste pipe A pipe to convey discharge from plumbing pipes.

waste plug A tapered, rubber-like object used to close the drain of a wash basin or tub.

waster A slang term for a brick with surface imperfections that leave it suitable to be used only as a backing brick.

water closet

water main

waste stream A continuously or regularly generated quantity of waste materials from a particular facility, process, or activity.

wastewater Water that has been used in a process and contains contaminants.

wasting (dabbing) Splitting of excess stone with a hand tool so that the resulting surfaces of block are nearly flat.

water analysis Chemical and bacteriological analysis of water.

water bar (weather bar) A wood or metal strip fixed to the exterior sill of a window or door to resist the penetration of water.

waterborne preservative Preservative salts dissolved in water and transferred to the wood during the treating process.

water-cement ratio The ratio of the amount of water, exclusive only of that absorbed by the aggregates, to the amount of cement in a concrete or mortar mixture. The ratio is preferably stated as a decimal by weight.

water closet (W.C., flushable closet) (1) A plumbing fixture used to receive human wastes and flush them to a waste pipe. (2) A room that contains a water closet.

water content *See* **moisture content**.

water cooling tower *See* **cooling tower**.

water crack A fine crack in a coat of plaster, caused by applying a coat over a previous coat that had not dried sufficiently or by using plaster with a water content that is too high.

water gain *See* **bleeding**.

water gauge A manometer filled with water.

water-gel explosive A wide variety of explosives, all containing water and ammonium nitrate, used for blasting. The explosives are sensitized with an explosive such as TNT or smokeless powder, with metals such as aluminum, or with other fuels. They may be premixed at a plant or site-mixed immediately prior to loading in a blast hole.

water hammer (1) A loud thumping noise in a water service line due to the surge of suddenly checked water. (2) A banging in steam lines occurring at the time of steam flow. The steam, traveling at high velocity picks up drops of condensed water and slams them against the piping at a bend.

water joint *See* **saddle joint (2)**.

water level A simple device used to see that surfaces are level. Most often a long (up to 50-foot), thin plastic tube filled with water.

water-level control A control on a boiler used to maintain the water at a safe level.

water lime A hydraulic lime or cement that will set under water.

waterline The highest water level in a cistern or flush tank to which the shut-off should be adjusted.

water main A main supply pipe in a water system providing water for public or community use.

water outlet (1) Any opening or end of pipe used to discharge water to a plumbing fixture, boiler, or other device. (2) An opening through which water is discharged to the atmosphere.

waterproof Any material, treatment, or construction that resists flow or penetration of water.

waterproof adhesive An adhesive that, when properly cured, is not affected by water.

waterproofing

waterstop

water-supply system

water tap

"waterproofed" cement Cement interground with a water-repellent material such as calcium stearate. *See also* **hydraulic cement**.

waterproofing Any of a number of materials applied to various surfaces, e.g. a building foundation, to prevent the infiltration of water.

waterproof paper A paper made water-impervious by adding a resin during the manufacturing process.

water reactive A substance that generates heat or gas in the presence of water.

water-reducing agent A material that either increases workability of freshly mixed mortar or concrete without increasing water content, or maintains workability with a reduced amount of water; the effect being due to factors other than air entrainment.

water-repellent cement A hydraulic cement having a water-repellent agent added during the process of manufacture, with the intention of resisting the absorption of water by the concrete or mortar.

water retentivity The property of mortar that prevents rapid loss of mix water by absorption.

water rights (1) The right of real property owners to make reasonable changes in the flow of water that is flooding their land. (2) A legal right to use water of a natural stream or body of water for a general or specific purpose.

water ring A perforated manifold in the nozzle of dry-mix shotcrete equipment through which water is added to the materials.

water-saving toilet A toilet that uses between 1.6 and 3.5 gallons per flush.

water seal The water in a trap acting as a seal against the passage of gases.

water seasoning The seasoning of lumber by soaking it in water for a period, usually two weeks, and air drying it.

water-service pipe The part of a water-service main owned by the water department.

watershed The area of land that drains naturally into a stream or complex of streams. The management of watersheds in the national forests is a principal function of the Forest Service.

water softener A device to remove calcium and magnesium salts from a water supply, usually by ion exchange.

water stone A synthetic sharpening stone used with water to hone tool blades. Water keeps the accumulation of metal residue from the blades to a minimum.

waterstop A thin sheet of metal, rubber, plastic, or other material inserted across a joint to obstruct the seeping of water through the joint.

water-supply stub A vertical supply pipe that supplies fixtures and that reaches less than one story in height.

water-supply system (1) The system that supplies water throughout a building, including the service pipe(s), distribution and connecting pipes, fittings, and control valves. (2) The system that supplies water to units in a community, including reservoirs, tunnels, and pipelines.

water table (1) The top surface of groundwater. (2) A horizontal, sloped ledge on an exterior wall with a drip molding to prevent water from running down the outside of the wall below.

water tap (faucet) An outlet valve for water.

watertight A joint, enclosure, or assembly that is designed to prohibit the entry of water.

water tube boiler A boiler in which water circulates through the tubes, while combustion gases surround the tubes.

water vapor diffusion
The movement of water vapor through permeable materials to areas of different water vapor pressure.

watt A unit of power equal to the power dissipated in an electric circuit in which a potential difference of 1 volt causes a current flow of 1 ampere. The power required to do work at the rate of 1 joule per second.

watt-hour A unit of work equivalent to the power of 1 watt operating for 1 hour, which is equal to 3600 joules.

wattle A framework consisting of interwoven rods, poles, branches, etc.

wattmeter A calibrated instrument that measures electric power in watts.

wavelength The distance between two successive points in a sound or light wave that are characterized by the same phase of oscillation.

wax A material obtained from vegetable, mineral, and animal matter that is soluble in organic solvents, and solid at room temperature. Wax is applied in a liquid or paste form on wood and metal surfaces to provide gloss, and to protect the surface.

waxing The filling of cavities in a finished piece of marble with materials to match the stone in color and texture.

weakened-plane joint *See* **groove joint**.

wearing course A topping or surface treatment to increase the resistance of a concrete pavement or slab to abrasion.

weather (1) The length of shingle or tile that is exposed, as measured along the slope of a roof. (2) To deteriorate or discolor when exposed to the weather. (3) To slope a surface for the purpose of shedding rainwater.

weatherability The ability of a masonry joint to resist deteriorating in relationship to how it is jointed-off.

weatherboard (1) Boards or siding lapped to shed water. (2) A projecting member attached to the bottom rail of an external door to divert water from the sill or threshold.

weathered (1) Descriptive of a surface exposed long enough that distinct weathering has taken place. (2) Having an upper surface that is sloped to shed water.

weathered joint *See* **weather-struck joint**.

weathering (1) Changes in color, texture, strength, chemical composition, or other properties of a natural or artificial material due to the action of the weather. (2) The mechanical or chemical disintegration and discoloration of the surface of wood, caused by exposure to light, the action of dust and sand carried by the wind, and the alternate shrinking and swelling of the surface fibers due to continual variation in temperature and moisture content brought on by changes in the weather.

weathering steel Any of several high-strength, low-carbon steel alloys that, when exposed to normal atmospheric conditions, form a thin, protective orange or brown patina that is four to eight times more corrosion-resistant than plain,

weather-struck joint

web

web reinforcement

low-carbon steels. Weathering steel is not appropriate in environments where it would be exposed to extreme wetness.

weatherometer A device that uses accelerated weathering techniques to analyze durability, weather-resistance, and other properties of a building material or coating.

weather resistance The ability of a material or coating to resist weathering. *See also* **weathering (1)**.

weatherseal channel A channel installed, flanges downward, on the top of an exterior door.

weatherstrip A strip of wood, metal, felt, plastic, or other material applied at an exterior door or window to seal or cover the joint made by the door or window with the sill, casings, or threshold.

weather-struck joint (weathered joint) A horizontal masonry joint sloped from a point inside the face of the wall to the face of the wall so the joint will shed water.

weaving (1) The alternate lapping of shingles on opposite surfaces when two adjacent roofs intersect. (2) The process of making a rug by interlacing surface and backing yarns.

web (1) That part of a beam or truss between the flanges or chords, used mainly in resisting shear stresses. (2) The walls connecting the face shells of a hollow concrete masonry unit.

web bar *See* **web reinforcement**.

web clamp A device consisting of a fabric tape with a fastener that is secured with a wrench or screwdriver, used to hold carpentry work while gluing.

web crippling Local failure of the web of a structural member caused by a concentrated load.

web member In a truss, a secondary structural member that joins the top and bottom chords.

web plate A steel plate forming the web of a built-up girder truss, or beam.

web reinforcement Reinforcement placed in a concrete member to resist shear and diagonal tension.

web splice A splice joining two web plates.

web stiffener (1) A vertical steel shape attached to the web of a structural member and used to prevent web buckling. (2) Blocking added to the web of a composite wood structural member to prevent web buckling.

wedge A piece of wood or metal tapering to a thin edge, used to adjust elevation or tighten formwork.

wedge anchor A wedging device used in the anchorage of a tendon in posttensioned, prestressed concrete.

weep cut A groove cut in the underside of a horizontal board or masonry unit that extends from an exterior wall to keep water from moving back toward the wall.

weep hole (weeps) (1) A small hole in a wall or window member to allow accumulated water to drain. The water may be from condensation and/or surface penetration. (2) A small hole in a retaining wall located near the lower ground surface. The hole drains the soil behind the wall and prevents build-up of water pressure on the wall.

weeping pine (Himalayan pine) *Pinus exelsa*. A species of pine with long, drooping needles.

welded-wire fabric

welding fitting

weight batching Measuring the constituent materials for mortar or concrete by weight.

weight box The channel in a window frame housing the sash weights.

weighted average An average in which certain entries, usually at the extremes of the range of values, are manipulated so a number is obtained that is believed to be more representative of the true mean than that obtained by straight averaging.

weir A structure across a ditch or stream used for measuring, or for diverting the flow of water.

weir head The depth of water above the top of a flat weir, or above the bottom of a notch in a notched weir.

weld (1) To build up or fasten together, as with cements or solvents. (2) To fasten two pieces of metal together by heating them until there is a fusing of material, either with or without a filler metal.

weld decay Local corrosion at or adjacent to a weld.

welded butt splice A reinforcing bar splice made by welding the butted ends.

welded cover plate A cover plate welded to the flange of a structural member, usually to increase strength in the middle length of a span.

welded joint A joint connecting two metal parts by welding.

welded reinforcement Concrete-reinforcing steel joined by welding, and most often used in columns to extend vertical bars.

welded truss A truss of metal members in which the joints are made by welding.

welded-wire fabric (welded-wire mesh) A series of longitudinal and transverse wires of various gauges, arranged at right angles to each other and welded at all points of intersection; used for concrete slab reinforcement.

welded-wire fabric reinforcement Welded-wire fabric in either sheets or rolls, used to reinforce concrete.

welded wire lath *See* wire lath.

welding cables The pair of cables supplying electric energy for use in welding. One lead connects a welding machine with an electrode; the other lead connects the machine with the work.

welding fittings Wrought steel elbows, tees, reducers, saddles, and the like, beveled for butt welding to pipe. Forged fittings with hubs or with ends counter-bored for fillet welding to pipe; they are used for small pipe sizes and high pressures.

welding neck flange A flange with a long neck that is beveled for butt-welding to pipe.

welding nozzle A stub-pipe that is shop-welded to a vessel to facilitate welding a connecting pipe in the field.

welding rectifier Equipment used in arc welding to convert AC power to DC power.

welding rod Filler metal in the form of wire or rod used in gas welding and brazing and in some arc welding processes.

welding screw A screw with lugs or weld projections on the top or underside of the head to facilitate attaching the screw to a metal part by resistance welding.

weldment Any assembly made by welding parts together.

weld metal That part of a weld that was melted while welding.

weld nut A nut designed to be attached to a part by resistance welding.

well-point system

welt

well (wellhole) (1) Any enclosed space of considerable height, such as an air shaft or the space around which a stair winds. (2) A correction device for ground water. (3) A wall around a tree trunk to hold back soil. (4) A slot in a machine or device into which a part fits.

well drill A rotary drill mounted on a truck and used to drill for water.

well-graded aggregate Aggregate with a particle-size distribution producing maximum density, or minimum void space.

wellhold See well (1).

well point A perforated pipe surrounded by pervious soil to permit the pumping of ground water.

well-point system A series of well points connected to a header and used to drain an area or to control ground water seepage into an excavation.

welt (1) A seam in sheet metal, formed by folding over the edges of two sheets, interlocking the folded portions, and flattening the formed seam. (2) A strip of wood fastened over a seam, joint, or shaped piece fastened over an angle for reinforcing.

welting strip A strip of sheet metal at the intersection of the roof and a vertical surface. One edge of the strip is fastened to the roof, and the other edge is bent to lock with the lower edge of a vertical sheet.

West Coast hemlock See hemlock.

West Coast Lumber Inspection Bureau (WCLIB) One of seven regional grading agencies in North America that are authorized to write and publish grading rules for lumber. See also grade stamp.

western balsam See grand fir.

western framing See platform framing.

western jackpine See lodgepole pine.

western larch See larch.

western pine Any of several pines growing in the western United States or Canada, including ponderosa, sugar, and western (Idaho) white pine.

western red cedar Thuia plicam. This species is found principally along the western edges of British Columbia, Washington, and Oregon. The wood is soft, straight-grained, and extremely resistant to decay and insect damage. It is used extensively in roof coverings, exterior sidings, fences, decks, and other outdoor applications.

western S-P-F Lumber of the spruce-pine-fir group produced in British Columbia or Alberta. See also spruce-pine-fir.

western spruce (Sitka spruce) See spruce.

western tamarack See larch.

western white pine (Idaho white pine) Pinus monticola. A species of pine found in a wide range throughout the western U.S. and British Columbia. It is easily worked, and is favored for shelving, cabinets, and a variety of specialized uses.

Western Wood Products Association One of seven regional grading agencies in North America that are authorized to write and publish grading rules for lumber. See also grade stamp.

western yellow pine See ponderosa pine.

westside (1) An unofficial division of the southern yellow pine-producing region, located west

wet standpipe system

of the Mississippi-Alabama state line, and including southwestern Alabama. Products from this region are most often marketed in the central southern states and the midwest. (2) The area west of the Cascade Mountains in Oregon and Washington, as contrasted with the east side or pine country.

West Virginia spruce *See* **red spruce**.

wet bulb A thermometer utilizing evaporation of moisture from a water-saturated cloth on its bulb to measure temperature.

wet-bulb depression The difference between the dry-bulb and the wet-bulb temperatures.

wet-bulb temperature (1) The reading on a thermometer whose bulb is enclosed in a layer of wet fabric. (2) The ambient temperature of an object cooled by evaporation.

wet-bulb thermometer A thermometer in which the bulb is enclosed in a layer of wet fabric.

wet cleaning The use of water-dampened cloths, mops, and other tools to eliminate asbestos contamination from an area or an object. The asbestos-contaminated cloths and mops are then either decontaminated, or disposed of properly.

wet construction Any construction using materials that are placed or applied in other than a dry condition, as in concreting or plastering.

wet galvanizing The practice of galvanizing steel for protection by immersing it in molten zinc.

wet glazing Sealing glass in a frame using a glazing compound or sealant applied with a blade or gun.

wet mix Concrete containing too much water, immediately evidenced by a runny consistency.

wet-mix shotcrete Shotcrete in which all ingredients, including mixing water, are mixed before introduction into the delivery hose. The shotcrete may be pneumatically conveyed or moved by displacement. *See also* **pneumatic feed** *and* **positive displacement**.

wet-on-wet painting A procedure of spraying a coat of paint over a first coat that is not completely dry.

wet process In the manufacture of cement, the process in which the raw materials are ground, blended, mixed, and pumped while mixed with water. The wet process is chosen where raw materials are extremely wet and sticky, making drying before crushing and grinding difficult. *See also* **dry process**.

wet process hardboard Hardboard manufactured by a process in which a wood slurry is combined with a resin binder; and is then dried, first on a screen and later under pressure. The pressure imparts high density to the board and also sets the binder.

wet rot Decay of wood, in the presence of moisture and warmth, as a result of attack by fungi.

wet sanding Applying an abrasive to a surface while one or both are wet. Wet finishing reduces dust and keeps sanding machinery cleaner.

wet screeds Concrete strips placed beforehand at the proper elevation to act as height guides when pouring a concrete slab.

wet screening Screening to remove from fresh concrete any aggregate particles larger than a certain size.

wet sieving Use of water during sieving of a material on a No. 200 or (even finer) No. 325 sieve.

wet standpipe system A standpipe system filled with water at design pressure, ready for immediate use.

wheel excavator

wet strength The measured strength of an adhesive joint after it has been submerged in a liquid.

wettability The degree to which a surface will absorb a liquid poured upon it.

wettest stable consistency The condition of maximum water content at which cement grout or mortar will adhere to a vertical surface without sloughing.

wetting (1) The soaking of asbestos materials to diminish the level of air contamination they give off when disturbed. The water is mixed with saturants and surfactants before it is applied to the asbestos. (2) Coating a base metal with filler metal prior to soldering or brazing. *See also* **tinning**.

wetting agent A substance capable of lowering the surface tension of liquids, facilitating the wetting of solid surfaces and permitting the penetration of liquids into the capillaries.

wet-use adhesive Adhesives used in glue-laminated timber that will perform satisfactorily under a wide variety of uses, as well as exposure to weather and dry atmosphere.

wet vent A vent that receives the discharge of wastes other than those from water closets.

wet wall A plaster or stucco wall that sets up as the material dries.

whaler *See* **wale**.

wheelabration The application of steel abrasives in the form of grit or shot to clean a surface.

wheelbarrow A hand cart with one wheel in front plus two legs and two handles in back; used to move materials short distances.

wheel ditcher A trench digger consisting of a vehicle equipped with a large wheel on which buckets are mounted.

wheel dresser A hand tool used to clean or reshape the surface of a grinding wheel.

wheel excavator (continuous excavator) (1) A self-propelled unit for excavating a bank with buckets mounted on wheels. The earth is deposited on a conveyor belt for loading up hauling units. (2) Any power-driven machine used in excavation that moves on wheels, rather than crawlers.

wheel load The portion of the gross weight of a loaded vehicle transferred to a supporting structure under a given wheel of the vehicle.

wheel loader *See* **wheel excavator (1)**.

wheel trencher A trencher using a rotating wheel made of two ring plates with buckets every 20° to 30° around the circumference.

whetstone A piece of natural or manufactured abrasive stone used to sharpen cutting tools.

whip A slang term that describes the vertical movement of improperly secured underlayment.

white balsam *See* **white fir**.

white cedar *See* **Port Orford cedar**.

white coat (finish coat) A lime-putty plaster coat with a troweled finish.

white fir (inland hemlock-fir) *Abies concolor*. The most important of the true firs, this species is found in a wide range in the western U.S. Northern California accounts for the majority of white fir lumber produced in the U.S. The wood is fine-textured and relatively light. It is used in general construction and for such special uses as moldings and doors.

whole-brick wall

wide-flange beam

wide-throw hinge

white hemlock *See* **eastern hemlock**.

white lauan *See* **Philippine mahogany**.

white lead Basic lead carbonate, white in color; used as a pigment in exterior paints, ceramics, and putty.

white mahogany *See* **avodire**.

white oak Any of several species of American oaks, principally *Quercus alba*, whose wood is more white than red.

white pine (northern white pine, Idaho white pine, sugar pine) *Pinus strobus*, *P. monticola*, and *P. lambertiana*, respectively.

white Portland cement Portland cement made from materials with low iron content, used to produce concrete or mortar that is white in color.

whiteprint A reproduction of a drawing or other document that is a positive image of the original; a reproduction produced by the exposure of light to paper treated with a diazo compound developed in ammonia fumes.

white rot A type of decay in wood caused by a fungus that leaves a white deposit.

white spruce *Picea glauca*. A species of spruce found predominantly in British Columbia and Alberta. It is marketed as part of the spruce-pine-fir group and is an important source of general construction lumber. It is also used extensively in pulp production.

white walnut *See* **butternut**.

whitewash Water added to quicklime or slaked lime, whiting, and glue and applied like paint, leaving a white coating.

whitewood *See* **tulipwood**.

whiting Calcium carbonate pigment, used as an extender in paint, putty, and whitewash.

Whitney® punch One of a number of hand or power tools used to punch holes in metal.

Whitney strain diagram The assumed strain distribution of a reinforced concrete member in the yield state which is used in ultimate strength design.

whole-brick wall A brick wall having a thickness equal to the length of one brick.

wholesale Selling to retailers rather than directly to consumers.

wicket A small door or gate, especially one that is mounted as part of a larger one.

wicking The tendency of water or any liquid to rise above an established level to saturate a porous solid.

wide-flange beam A hot-rolled steel beam having a cross section resembling an "H" and having wider flanges than an I-beam.

wide-throw hinge A rectangular hinge having extra-wide leaves.

widow's walk A narrow walkway on the roof of a house.

wiggle nail *See* **corrupted fastener**.

wigwam A sheet metal structure in the shape of a conical pyramid, used as a large incinerator.

wigwam burner A metal structure, shaped roughly like an Indian wigwam or tepee, in which mill wastes are burned. Although still used in some areas, such burners are being phased-out, partly because mill wastes are being utilized to a greater degree, and partly because the burners can be a major source of air pollution.

winch

window

window frame

wildcat strike Strike called without authorization from the union or in spite of a no-strike clause in a collective bargaining agreement.

Williot diagram A graphical method used to determine deflections of trusses.

winch A stationary hoisting machine having a rotating drum around which a cable, rope, or chain is wrapped.

windage loss Water removed by circulating air, as in a cooling tower.

wind-brace A brace provided in a frame to support the frame against wind loads.

windbreak A dense growth of trees, a fence, wall, etc., provided as protection against the wind.

wind column A vertical support to a wall system that is designed to help the system withstand wind loads.

wind drift The horizontal deflection of a structure as a result of wind.

winder A tread that is used where a stair turns a horizontal angle, or in a spiral stair; shaped like a wedge or truncated wedge.

winding stair A stair constructed mostly of winders.

windlass A device for lifting heavy objects, usually consisting of a horizontal drum turned by a lever or crank. A cable runs from the object over a pulley to the drum where a cable is wound or unwound to move the object.

wind load The horizontal load used in the design of a structure to account for the effects of wind.

window (1) A normally glazed opening in an external wall to admit light and, in buildings without central air-conditioning, air. (2) An assembly consisting of a window frame, glazing, and necessary appurtenances. (3) A small opening in a wall, partition, or enclosure for transactions, such as a ticket window or information window.

window bead *See* **inside stop**, **draft bead**.

window board *See* **window stool**.

window box *See* **weight box**.

window catch A fastening device fixed to a window sash to secure it in the closed position.

window cleaner's anchor An anchor, fastened near a window on an outside wall of a multistory building, to which a person washing the window from the outside can attach a safety belt.

window cleaner's platform A platform suspended from a trolley on the roof of a multistory building used for outside window-washing and maintenance. The entire assembly is custom-made and may be either manually or mechanically operated.

window frame The fixed part of a window assembly attached to the wall and receiving the sash or casement and necessary hardware.

window glass (sheet glass) A soda-lime-silica glass made in continuous sheets of varying thickness and cut to size as required. *See also* **float glass**.

window glazing bar *See* **muntin**.

window hardware All the devices, fittings, or assemblies necessary to operate a window as intended. Window hardware may include catches, cords, fasteners, hinges, handles, locks, pivots, pulls, pulleys, and sash weights.

window jack scaffold A scaffold, the platform of which is supported by a bracket or jack projecting through a window opening.

window stool

window wall

window lead A slender lead rod with grooves used to hold glass in a window, usually in a decorative window.

window lift (sash lift) A handle fastened to the lower sash of a sliding window for use in moving the sash up or down.

window lock *See* **sash lock**.

window of time analysis A method of measuring labor productivity losses on a specific project by comparing labor productivity achieved during a period of time when work activities are subject to disruptive events and conditions, versus productivity during a period of time without disruption.

windowpane A segment of glass in a window.

window pull *See* **sash pull**.

window sash *See* **sash**.

window schedule A tabulation, usually on a drawing, listing all windows on a project; and indicating sizes, number of lights, type of sash and frame, and hardware required.

window screen (1) An ornamental grille or lattice set in a window opening. (2) *See* **insect screen**.

window seat A built-in seat at a window.

windowsill *See* **sill**.

window spring bolt A spring bolt, used on a sash that is not counter-balanced, that holds the sash in a desired position.

window stool A horizontal board or plate at the windowsill on the inside of the window, fitted against the bottom rail of the lower sash to form a base for the casing.

window stop *See* **sash stop**.

window trim The finished casing around a window.

window wall An exterior curtain wall using a frame containing windows that may be fixed or operable. The glazing may be clear, tinted, and/or opaque.

window weight *See* **sash weight**.

window well A well dug outside of a below-grade window, commonly a basement window, to allow it to operate.

wind pressure The pressure produced when wind blows against a surface.

windrow (1) A ridge of loose soil, such as that produced by the spill off of a grader blade. (2) A row of leaves or snow heaped up by the wind.

wind sock A bright-colored cloth tube, used to indicate wind direction.

wind stop (1) A weatherstrip used around a door or window. (2) A strip of wood or metal which covers the joint where a sash or casement meets a stile. (3) Any wood or metal strip used to cover a crack in an exterior wall of a building.

windtight Construction terminology to indicate that all openings and cracks in exterior walls have been sealed.

wind tunnel A structure through which a controlled stream of wind is directed at a model in order to study the probable effects of wind on a structure.

wind uplift The upward component of the force produced as wind blows around or across a structure or an object.

wine cellar (wine vault) A storage room for wine, usually located underground to maintain constant temperature and humidity.

wing

wing wall

wire lath

wing (1) A section or addition extending out from the main part of a building. (2) The offstage space at a side of a stage. (3) One of the four leaves of a revolving door.

wing compass A compass with an arc-shaped piece permanently fastened to one leg and damped at the other by a screw. The arc is usually graduated.

wing dividers Dividers made similar to a wing compass.

wing nut A nut provided with wing-like projections to facilitate turning by fingers and thumb.

wing pile A bearing pile (post), usually of concrete, widened at the upper portion to form part of a sheet pile wall.

wing screw A screw provided with wing-like projections to facilitate turning by fingers and thumb. A wing screw is often used to secure windows against unauthorized entry.

wing wall (1) A short section of wall at an angle to a bridge abutment, used as a retaining wall and to stabilize the abutment. (2) A short section of wall used to guide a stream into an opening, such as at a culvert or bridge.

wiped joint A wiped lead joint connecting two lead pipes.

wire A drawn metal strand or filament.

wire brad See **brad**.

wire cloth A stiff fabric of woven wire, usually having a larger mesh than insect screen material, and used as reinforcing in plaster, in sieves, and as a leaf catcher in gutters. The number of openings per square inch designates the fineness of the mesh.

wire, cold-drawn Wire made from the rods hot-rolled from billets and then cold-drawn through dies. *See also* **reinforcement, cold-drawn wire**.

wire comb A tool with long wire teeth, used to scratch a coat of wet plaster to increase the bond of a subsequent coat.

wire-cut brick Brick that has been extruded to shape and then cut to length with wire before firing.

wired glass *See* **wire glass**.

wireframe modeling In computer-aided design, the representation of an object in either a two-dimensional or three-dimensional form, using lines, circles, arcs, and other similar entities to create an outline of the part.

wire gauge (1) The diameter of a wire as defined by several different systems. Ordinarily, the thicker the wire is, the smaller the gauge number is. (2) A device for measuring the thickness of a wire; usually consists of a metal sheet with standard-sized notches on one or more edges.

wire glass Sheet glass with wire mesh embedded in the glass to prevent shattering.

wire holder An electrical insulator having a screw or bolt for fastening the insulator to a support.

wire lath A welded-wire mesh used as a base for plaster.

wire mesh *See* **welded-wire fabric**.

wire nail A very thin nail with a small head, often used as a finishing nail.

wire nut A connector for two or more electric conductors, made in the form of a plastic cap with an internal spring-thread. It is turned over the parallel or twisted ends of the conductor wires.

wiring box

wood-cement concrete

wood chisel

wire rope A rope made of twisted steel strands laid around a central core.

wire saw A machine for sawing stone using a rapidly moving continuous wire carrying a slurry of sand or other abrasive material.

wire stripper A hand tool with notched jaws that can grip and cut wire or remove insulation.

wireway A raceway with a removable cover for access to wires inside.

wire winding Application of high tensile wire, wound under tension by machines, around concrete circular or dome structures to provide tension reinforcing.

wire wrapping *See* **wire winding**.

wiring box A box used in interior electric wiring at each junction point, outlet, or switch, which serves as protection for electric connections and as a mounting for fixtures or switches.

withe (wythe) A partition used to separate two flues in a chimney stack. *See also* **wythe**.

witness corner A marker set on a property line near to, but not at, a corner. Its relation to the corner is recorded.

wobble coefficient A coefficient used in determining the friction loss occurring in posttensioning which is assumed to account for the secondary curvature of the tendons.

wobble friction In prestressed concrete, the friction caused by the unintended deviation of the prestressing sheath or duct from its specified profile.

wobble saw *See* **drunken saw**.

wobble-wheel roller A pneumatic compactor consisting of a weighted bed mounted on a series of wheels that are loosely assembled, and allowed to work the surface of a soil.

wood block floor A finished floor consisting of rectangular blocks of a tough wood such as oak, set in mastic with the end grain exposed, usually over concrete slab. A wood block floor is used where very heavy traffic and heavy loads are expected.

wood brick (fixing brick, nailing block) A block of wood, the same size as a brick, inserted into brickwork as a base for attaching nailed or screwed objects.

wood-cement concrete A Portland cement concrete using sawdust and wood chips as aggregate.

wood-cement particle (WCP) board A high-density board manufactured in Europe for use on exteriors, or where fire resistance is needed. Wood particles are combined with Portland cement, or another mineral, as a binder.

wood chipboard *See* **particle board**.

wood chisel Any of a number of firmer chisels used in carpentry and woodworking.

wood dough A synthetic putty containing wood fibers; used as a filler.

wood-fibered plaster A plaster mix containing wood fibers.

wood-fiber emulation Thermal insulation using wood fibers and an asphalt binder.

wood filler A liquid or paste compound used to fill pores or checks in wood before finishing.

wood finishing The final finishing of a wood surface, including planing, sanding, staining, varnishing, waxing and/or painting.

wood gutter

wood molding

wood screw

woodwork

wood fire-retardant treatment
The impregnation of wood or wood products with special solutions to reduce the flame spread of the finished product.

wood firestop Wood pieces that are placed between framing members in a wall to slow the spread of fire.

wood flooring Flooring consisting of dressed and matched boards.

wood flour A finely ground, dried, wood powder that is used in plastic wood as an extender. It is also employed in some glues, and in the molding of plastics.

wood-frame construction A type of construction where floors and roofs, as well as exterior and other bearing walls are of wood, rather than masonry.

wood-grain print A simulated wood-grain pattern used on plastic veneer, hardboard, and low-grade plywood.

wood gutter A gutter, under the eaves of a roof, made from a solid piece of wood or built-up boards.

wood lath Narrow strips of wood used as a base for plaster.

wood molding Wood strips that are factory-shaped to commercially available patterns.

wood oil (1) Tung oil used in the manufacture of varnish, putty, etc. (2) An oleoresin used for caulking and waterproofing.

wood preservative Any chemical preservative for wood, applied by washing-on or pressure impregnating. Products used include creosote, sodium fluoride, copper sulfate, and tar or pitch.

wood rasp *See* **rasp**.

wood screw A threaded fastener that cuts its way into wood when turned under axial pressure.

wood sill *See* **sill**.

wood slip A wooden nailing strip fixed in a masonry or concrete wall as a means of attaching wood trim or furring strips.

wood stud anchor (nailing anchor) A metal clip attached to the inside of a door frame and used to secure the frame to a wood stud partition.

wood treatment Treatment of wood with a preservative to prevent or retard its decay. *See also* **fire-retardant wood**.

wood veneer *See* **veneer**.

wood wool *See* **excelsior**.

woodwork Work produced by carpenters and woodworkers, especially the finished work.

woodworker's vise Any of a number of tools consisting of two jaws and a mechanism to hold a piece of wood while it is being worked on.

work (1) All labor and materials required to complete a project in accordance with the contract documents. (2) The product of a force times the distance traveled.

workability That property of freshly mixed concrete or mortar that determines the ease and homogeneity with which it can be mixed, placed, compacted, and finished.

work capacity The greatest volume in number and/or size of construction projects that a contractor can manage efficiently without increasing the overhead costs.

workers' compensation insurance *See* **insurance, workers' compensation**.

working (movement) The alternate swelling and shrinking of wood caused by changes in its moisture content induced by variations in the humidity of its environment.

working capital The excess of current assets over current liabilities. Cash and other liquid assets.

working drawings *See* **drawings**.

working life The length of time a liquid resin or adhesive remains useful after the ingredients have been mixed.

working load Forces normally imposed on a member in service.

working point A point designated on construction drawings as a reference for other points.

working stage A section of an assembly room or auditorium partially cut off from the audience section by a proscenium wall. It is equipped with some or all of the following: scenery loft, gridiron, fly gallery, and lighting equipment.

working stress Maximum permissible design stress using working stress design methods.

working stress design A method of proportioning structures or members for prescribed working loads at stresses well below the ultimate, and assuming linear distribution of flexural stresses.

work-in-process The inventory of partly finished projects in various stages of completion at any given time.

work life *See* **working life**.

work light (1) A light in a theater used to provide illumination for rehearsing, scene shifting, or other work onstage or backstage. (2) A lamp in a protective cage, and having a long, heavy, flexible cord; used to provide temporary illumination in work areas.

workmanship The quality of work performed.

work order *See* **notice to proceed**.

work plane In lighting, the plane at which work is usually done and at which the level of illumination is specified and measured.

work product exclusion In a liability insurance policy, a provision that excludes coverage for business risks, including damages to work performed by or on behalf of the insured.

worksheet The paper on which the calculations supporting the final estimate are recorded.

works made for hire A rule applied to works produced within the scope of a job whereby employers are considered creators and owners of their employees' works.

worm-drive saw A circular power saw turned by a worm-gear drive. It is heavier and produces more torque on the blasé than a standard circular saw.

woven valley A roof valley where shingles or other roofing materials from both sides of the valley are woven together as they are applied by overlapping alternate courses.

woven-wire fabric A prefabricated steel reinforcement for concrete composed of cold-drawn steel wires mechanically twisted together to form hexagonally shaped openings.

woven-wire reinforcement *See* **woven-wire fabric**.

wrap-around hinge An offset hinge attached to the rabbeted rail of a door or window, providing increased surface area for mounting.

wrapping A method of applying narrow strips of veneer around a curved surface, such as a piece of furniture.

wreath A short, curved portion of a stair handrail that joins the newel post to the rail.

wrench

wye

wythe

wrecking The process of demolishing a structure.

wrecking ball A heavy steel ball or concrete mass on a heavy chain or cable swung by a crane to demolish parts of a structure.

wrecking bar *See* **pinch bar**.

wrecking strip A small piece or panel fitted into a formwork assembly in such a way that it can be easily removed ahead of main panels or forms, making it easier to strip those major form components.

wrench A hand tool consisting of a handle and a jaw at one end; used to turn or hold a bolt, nut, pipe, or fitting. The jaw may be shaped for a specific-sized object or may be adjustable.

wrinkling (crinkling, reveling) (1) The distortion in a paint film that appears as ripples and may be deliberately induced as a decorative effect or accidentally caused by drying conditions or paint applied too thickly. (2) The rippling or crinkling of the surface of an adhesive, usually not affecting performance. (3) The rippling of an area of veneer, caused by lack of contact with the adhesive.

wrought Descriptive of metals or metalwork shaped by hammering with tools.

wrought iron (1) Nearly pure ductile iron with a very small percentage of silica throughout. Once the surface iron decomposes, the silica surfacing prevents further oxidation. Wrought iron is no longer commercially available. (2) A number of easily welded or wrought irons with low impurity content used for water pipes, tank plates, or forged work.

wrought nail A nail wrought by hand, often having a head with a decorative pattern.

wrought timber Wood that has been planed on one or more surfaces.

W-truss A wood roof truss with the web members in the shape of a "W."

wye A pipe fitting with a side outlet that is any angle other than 90° to the main run or axis.

wye branch *See* **Y-branch**.

wye fitting *See* **Y-fitting**.

wye level *See* **Y-level**.

wythe (leaf) Each continuous vertical section of a wall one masonry unit in thickness.

X

X ABBREVIATIONS

The abbreviations listed below are those most commonly used in the construction industry. Alternative forms (usually nonstandard) are shown in parentheses.

X experimental

XBAR crossbar

XEPS extruded expanded polystyrene

XH, X HVY extra heavy

XL extra large

xr without rights

X STR extra strong

xw without warrants

XXH double extra heavy

X Definitions

X-brace

X-brace (cross brace)
A paired set of sway braces.

XCU (insurance terminology)
Reference to letters that represent items excluded from property damage coverage that result from: (1) blasting or explosion (designated by X), (2) structural damage to or collapse of a structure (designated by C), and damage caused during excavation by mechanical equipment.

xonolite Calcium silicate monohydrate (C_3S_5H), a natural mineral that is readily synthesized at 150°-350 °C under saturated steam pressure. Xonolite is a constituent of sand-lime masonry units.

x-ray diffraction (1) The diffraction of x-rays by substances having a regular arrangement of atoms. (2) A phenomenon used to identify substances having such structure.

x-ray fluorescence Characteristic secondary radiation emitted by an element as a result of excitation by x-rays, used to yield a chemical analysis of a sample.

x-ray protection Lead encased in sheetrock or plaster to prevent the escape of radiation from the encased room.

xylol An aromatic hydrocarbon distilled from coal tar, used as a solvent for paints and varnishes.

xyst (1) A tree-shaded walk or promenade. (2) A roofed colonnade for exercise in bad weather.

Y

ABBREVIATIONS

The abbreviations listed below are those most commonly used in the construction industry. Alternative forms (usually nonstandard) are shown in parentheses.

y yard

Y yttrium, wye, Y-branch

yd yard

y.p. yellow pine

YP yield paint

YR year

YS yield strength

Y
DEFINITIONS

Y-fitting

yoke

yakima pine *See* **ponderosa pine.**

Yankee screwdriver *See* **spiral ratchet screwdriver.**

yard (1) A unit of length in the English system equal to 3′. (2) A term applied to that part of a plot not occupied by the building or driveway.

yardage (1) An amount of excavated material equal to the volume in cubic yards. (2) An area of surface (two dimensions) measured in square yards.

yard drain A drain in a pavement or earth surface, used to drain surface water.

yard lumber (general building construction lumber) Lumber graded according to its size, length, and intended use, stockpiled in a lumber yard.

Y-branch (wye branch) A plumbing system branch, in the shape of a "Y."

yellowing Development of yellow color or cast in white or clear coatings, after aging.

yellow pine The hard resinous wood from this long-leafed pine tree is used as flooring and in general construction.

yellow poplar (poplar) A moderately low-density, even-textured hardwood from central and southern United States, used for veneer, plywood, and cabinet work.

yelm A bundle of reeds or straw used as thatching material for a roof.

Y-fitting (wye fitting) A pipe fitting in the shape of a "Y." One arm is usually at 45° to the main fitting and may be of reduced size.

Y-highway Expressway intersection at a grade that steers traffic in three directions.

yield (1) The volume of freshly mixed concrete produced from a known quantity of ingredients. (2) The total weight of ingredients divided by the unit weight of the freshly mixed concrete. (3) The number of product units, such as block, produced per bag of cement or per batch of concrete.

yield point (1) The point at which a stressed material begins to exhibit plastic properties. (2) The point beyond which the material will not return to its original length.

yield strength The stress, less than the maximum attainable stress, at which the ratio of stress to strain has dropped well below its value at low stresses, or at which a material exhibits a specified limiting deviation from the usual proportionality of stress to strain.

Y-level A surveyor's level with the telescope and level supported by Y-shaped fittings. The telescope can be removed and reversed in order to average out internal sources of error.

yoke (1) A tie or clamping device around column forms or over wall or footing forms to keep them from spreading as a result of lateral pressure of fresh concrete. (2) Part of a structural assembly for slipforming that keeps the forms from spreading and transfers form loads to the jacks. (3) A collar for supporting lead pipe. (4) A soil pipe fitting in the shape of a "Y".

yoke vent (1) A pipe connecting upward from a soil or waste stack

to a vent stack for venting.
(2) A vertical or 45° relief vent
of the continuous waste and vent
type formed by the extension of
an upright wye-branch inlet of
the horizontal branch to the stack.
A yoke vent is called a *dual yoke
vent* when two horizontal branches
are thus vented by the same relief
vent.

Young's modulus *See* **modulus of
elasticity**.

Z

Z ABBREVIATIONS

The abbreviations listed below are those most commonly used in the construction industry. Alternative forms (usually nonstandard) are shown in parentheses.

z zero, zone

Z modulus of section

ZI zone of interior

Zn azimuth, zinc

Z

Definitions

zee

Z-bar A Z-shaped member that is used as a main runner in some types of acoustical ceiling.

zebrawood *Connarus guianensis*. A tropical hardwood with strikingly marked grain, used for decorative purposes in cabinetry and paneling.

zee A light-gauge member with a Z-like cross section. The flanges of the Z are approximately at right angles to the web.

zeolite A group of hydrous aluminum silicate minerals or similar synthetic compounds used in water-softening equipment.

zero-slump concrete Concrete of stiff or extremely dry consistency showing no measurable slump after removal of the slump cone. *See also* **slump** *and* **no-slump concrete**.

zeta (1) A small closed room. (2) Originally a room over the porch of a Christian church, used as living quarters for a porter or sexton and for storage of documents.

z flashing Z-shaped metal flashing applied between panels of plywood siding to shed water.

z-furring channel A z-shaped, galvanized steel track used to mechanically attach blanket or rigid plastic foam insulation to interiors of exterior walls. Also used to attach drywall to concrete, brick, concrete block, and tile.

zigzag bond Similar to herringbone bond.

zigzag rule A folding ruler made of pieces connected by a pivot.

zinc A metallic element used for galvanizing steel sheet and steel or iron castings, as an alloy in various metals, as an oxide for white paint pigment, and as a sacrificial element in a cathodic protection system. Characterized by its brittleness in ordinary temperatures.

zinc chromate A bright yellow pigment, used in paints, which has good rust-inhibiting properties.

zinc coating *See* **galvanize**.

zinc dust Zinc ground to a fine powder and used as a pigment in priming paints, especially those for use on galvanized surfaces.

zinc oxide (zinc white) A pigment used in paints to provide durability, color retention, and hardness, and to improve sag resistance.

zinc white *See* **zinc oxide**.

zinc yellow Bright yellow pigments of zinc chromates used in primers and paints as a rust inhibitor.

zone (1) A space or group of spaces in a building with common control of heating and cooling. (2) A form of public control over land use.

zoning (1) The reservation of certain specified areas within a community or city for buildings and structures, for use of land, or purposes with limitations (such as height, lot coverage, and other stipulated requirements). (2) Dividing a building into sections for heating and cooling purposes.

zoning envelope See **envelope**.

zoning permit A permit issued by municipal or local government officials authorizing the use of a piece of land for a stated purpose.

REFERENCE SECTION

Standard Weights and Measures

Linear Measure		Square Measure	
1000 mils =	1 inch	144 square inches =	1 square foot
12 inches =	1 foot	9 square feet =	1 square yard
3 feet =	1 yard		
2 yards =	{ 1 fathom { 6 feet	30-1/4 square yds. =	{ 1 square rod { 272-1/4 square feet
5-1/2 yards =	{ 1 rod { 16-1/2 feet	160 square rods =	{ 1 acre { 43,560 square feet
40 rods =	{ 1 furlong { 660 feet	640 acres =	{ 1 square mile { 27,878,400 { square feet
8 furlongs =	{ 1 mile { 5280 feet	A circular mil is the area of a circle 1 mil, or 0.001 inch in diameter.	
1.15156 miles =	{ 1 nautical mile, { or knot { 6080.26 feet	1 square inch =	1,273,239 circular mils
3 nautical miles =	{ 1 league { 18,240.78 feet	A circular inch is the area of a circle 1 inch in diameter	0.7854 square inches.
		1 square inch =	1.2732 circular inches
Dry Measure		**Weight—Avoirdupois or Commercial**	
2 pints =	1 quart	437.5 grains =	1 ounce
8 quarts =	1 peck	16 ounces =	1 pound
4 pecks =	{ 1 bushel { 2150.42 cubic in. { 1.2445 cubic feet	112 pounds =	1 hundredweight
		20 hundredweight =	{ 1 gross, or long ton { 2240 pounds
		2000 pounds =	1 net, or short ton
		2204.6 pounds =	1 metric ton
		1 lb. of water (39.1°F) =	27.681217 cu. in.
		=	0.016019 cu. ft.
		=	0.119832 U.S. gallon
		=	0.453617 liter

Decimals of a Foot for Each 32nd of an Inch

Inch	0	1	2	3	4	5	6	7	8	9	10	11
0	0	.0833	.1667	.2500	.3333	.4167	.5000	.5833	.6667	.7500	.8333	.9167
1/32	.0026	.0859	.1693	.2526	.3359	.4193	.5026	.5859	.6693	.7526	.8359	.9193
1/16	.0052	.0885	.1719	.2552	.3385	.4219	.5052	.5885	.6719	.7552	.8385	.9219
3/32	.0078	.0911	.1745	.2578	.3411	.4245	.5078	.5911	.6745	.7578	.8411	.9245
1/8	.0104	.0938	.1771	.2604	.3438	.4271	.5104	.5938	.6771	.7604	.8438	.9271
5/32	.0130	.0964	.1797	.2630	.3464	.4297	.5130	.5964	.6797	.7630	.8464	.9297
3/16	.0156	.0990	.1823	.2656	.3490	.4323	.5156	.5990	.6823	.7656	.8490	.9323
7/32	.0182	.1016	.1849	.2682	.3516	.4349	.5182	.6016	.6849	.7682	.8516	.9349
1/4	.0208	.1042	.1875	.2708	.3542	.4375	.5208	.6042	.6875	.7708	.8542	.9375
9/32	.0234	.1068	.1901	.2734	.3568	.4401	.5234	.6068	.6901	.7734	.8568	.9401
5/16	.0260	.1094	.1927	.2760	.3594	.4427	.5260	.6094	.6927	.7760	.8594	.9427
11/32	.0286	.1120	.1953	.2786	.3620	.4453	.5286	.6120	.6953	.7786	.8620	.9453
3/8	.0313	.1146	.1979	.2812	.3646	.4479	.5313	.6146	.6979	.7813	.8646	.9479
13/32	.0339	.1172	.2005	.2839	.3672	.4505	.5339	.6172	.7005	.7839	.8672	.9505
7/16	.0365	.1198	.2031	.2865	.3698	.4531	.5365	.6198	.7031	.7865	.8698	.9531
15/32	.0391	.1224	.2057	.2891	.3724	.4557	.5391	.6224	.7057	.7891	.8724	.9557
1/2	.0417	.1250	.2083	.2917	.3750	.4583	.5417	.6250	.7083	.7917	.8750	.9583
17/32	.0443	.1276	.2109	.2943	.3776	.4609	.5443	.6276	.7109	.7943	.8776	.9609
9/16	.0469	.1302	.2135	.2969	.3802	.4635	.5469	.6302	.7135	.7969	.8802	.9635
19/32	.0495	.1328	.2161	.2995	.3828	.4661	.5495	.6328	.7161	.7995	.8828	.9661
5/8	.0521	.1354	.2188	.3021	.3854	.4688	.5521	.6354	.7188	.8021	.8854	.9688
21/32	.0547	.1380	.2214	.3047	.3880	.4714	.5547	.6380	.7214	.8047	.8880	.9714
11/16	.0573	.1406	.2240	.3073	.3906	.4740	.5573	.6406	.7240	.8073	.8906	.9740
23/32	.0599	.1432	.2266	.3099	.3932	.4766	.5599	.6432	.7266	.8099	.8932	.9766
3/4	.0625	.1458	.2292	.3125	.3958	.4792	.5625	.6458	.7292	.8125	.8958	.9792
25/32	.0651	.1484	.2318	.3151	.3984	.4818	.5651	.6484	.7318	.8151	.8984	.9818
13/16	.0677	.1510	.2344	.3177	.4010	.4844	.5677	.6510	.7344	.8177	.9010	.9844
27/32	.0703	.1536	.2370	.3203	.4036	.4870	.5703	.6536	.7370	.8203	.9036	.9870
7/8	.0729	.1563	.2396	.3229	.4063	.4896	.5729	.6563	.7396	.8229	.9063	.9896
29/32	.0755	.1589	.2422	.3255	.4089	.4922	.5755	.6589	.7422	.8255	.9089	.9922
15/16	.0781	.1615	.2448	.3281	.4115	.4948	.5781	.6615	.7448	.8281	.9115	.9948
31/32	.0807	.1641	.2474	.3307	.4141	.4974	.5807	.6641	.7474	.8307	.9141	.9974

Water: Various Pressure and Flow Units

Comparison of Heads of Water in Feet with Pressures in Various Units
One foot of water at 39.1° F = 62.425 pounds per square foot (psf)
= 0.4335 pounds per square inch
= 0.0295 atmosphere
= 0.8826 inches of mercury at 30° F
= 773.3 feet of air at 32° F and atmospheric pressure
One foot of water at 62° F = 62.355 pounds per square foot
= 0.43302 pounds per square inch
One pound of water on the square inch at 62° F = 2.3094 feet of water
One ounce of water on the square inch at 62° F = 1.732 inches of water
1 atmosphere at sea level (32° F) = 14.697 lbs. per sq. in.
= 29.921 in. of mercury
1 inch of mercury (32° F) = 0.49119 lbs. per sq. in.
Flowing Water
cfs = cubic feet per second, or second feet
gpm = gallons per minute
1 cfs = 60 cu. ft. per min.
= 86,400 cu. ft. per 24 hrs.
= 448.83 U.S. gals. per min.
= 646,317 U.S. gals. per 24 hrs.
= 1.9835 acre-foot per 24 hrs. (usually taken as 2)
= 1 acre-inch per hour (approximate)
= .028317 cu. meter per second
1 U.S. gpm = 1440 U.S. gals per 24 hrs.
= 0.00442 acre-foot per 24 hrs.
= 0.0891 Miners inches, Ariz., Calif.
1 million U.S. gal. per day = 1.5472 cfs
= 3.07 acre-feet
= 2.629 cu. meters per min.

Volume and Capacity

Units and Equivalents	
1 cu. ft. of water at 39.1° F	= 62.425 lbs.
1 United States gallon	= 231 cu. in.
1 imperial gallon	= 277.274 cu. in.
1 cubic foot of water	= 1728 cu. in.
	= 7.480519 U.S. gallons
	= 6.232103 imperial gallons
1 cubic yard	= 27 cu. ft. = 46.656 cu. in.
1 quart	= 2 pints
1 gallon	= 4 quarts
1 U.S. gallon	= 231 cu. in.
	= 0.133681 cu. ft.
	= 0.83311 imperial gallons
	= 8.345 lbs.
1 barrel	= 31.5 gallons = 4.21 cu. ft.
1 U.S. bushel	= 1.2445 cu. ft.
1 fluid ounce	= 1.8047 cu. in.
1 acre-foot	= 43,560 cu. ft.
	= 1,613.3 cu. yds.
1 acre-inch	= 3,630 cu. ft.
1 million U.S. gallons	= 133,681 cu. ft.
	= 3.0689 acre-ft.
1 ft. depth on 1 sq. mi.	= 27,878,400 cu. ft.
	= 640 acre-ft.
1 cord	= 128 cu. ft.

Mechanical-Electrical Equivalents

Power

1 horsepower (hp)	=	550 foot-pounds (ft.-lbs.) per second (sec.)
	=	33,000 ft.-lbs. per minute (min.)
	=	1,980,000 ft.-lbs. per hour (hr.)
	=	.275 ft.-tons per sec.
	=	16.5 ft.-tons per min.
	=	990 ft.-tons per hr.
1 horsepower-second (hp-sec.)	=	550 ft.-lbs.
	=	.275 ft.-tons.
1 horsepower-minute (hp-min.)	=	33,000 ft.-lbs.
	=	16.5 ft.-tons.
1 horsepower-hour (hp-hr.)	=	1,980,000 ft.-lbs.
	=	990 ft.-tons
1 horsepower (hp)	=	746 watts (w)
	=	.746 kilowatts (kw)

Energy

1 horsepower-hour	=	2544 BTU
	=	.746 kw-hr.
1 kilowatt-hour	=	3413 BTU

Pressure

1 lb. per sq. in.	=	2.0360" of mercury at 32° F
	=	27.71" of water at 32° F
	=	2.3091 ft. of water at 60° F
	=	144 lbs. per sq. ft.
1 in. of mercury	=	.491 lbs. per sq. in.
1 in. of water	=	5.2 lbs. per sq. ft. = .0361 PSI

Average Weights for Various Materials

Substance	Weight Lbs. per C.F.	Substance	Weight Lbs. per C.F.
Ashlar Masonry		Excavations in Water	
Granite, syenite, gneiss	165	Sand or gravel	60
Limestone, marble	160	Sand or gravel and clay	65
Sandstone, bluestone	140	Clay	80
Mortar Rubble Masonry		River mud	90
Granite, syenite, gneiss	155	Soil	70
Limestone, marble	150	Stone riprap	65
Sandstone, bluestone	130	Minerals	
Dry Rubble Masonry		Asbestos	153
Granite, syenite, gneiss	130	Barytes	281
Limestone, marble	125	Basalt	184
Sandstone, bluestone	110	Bauxite	159
Brick Masonry		Borax	109
Pressed brick	140	Chalk	137
Common brick	120	Clay, marl	137
Soft brick	100	Dolomite	181
Concrete Masonry		Feldspar, orthoclase	159
Cement, stone, sand	144	Gneiss, serpentine	159
Cement, slag, etc.	130	Granite, syenite	175
Cement, cinder, etc.	100	Greenstone, trap	187
Expanded slag aggregate	100	Gypsum, alabaster	159
Haydite (burned clay agg.)	90	Hornblende	187
Vermiculite/perlite, load bearing	70–105	Limestone, marble	165
Vermiculite and perlite, non-load bearing	25–50	Magnesite	187
		Phosphate rock, apatite	200
Concrete Masonry Reinforced		Porphyry	172
Stone aggregate	150	Pumice, natural	40
Slag aggregate	138	Quartz, flint	165
Lightweight aggregates	30–106	Sandstone, bluestone	147
Various Building Materials		Shale, slate	175
Ashes, cinders	40–45	Soapstone, talc	169
Cement, Portland, loose	90	Stone, Quarried, Piled	
Cement, Portland, set	183	Basalt, granite, gneiss	96
Lime, gypsum, loose	53–64	Limestone, marble, quartz	95
Mortar, set	103	Sandstone	82
Slags, bank slag	67–72	Shale	92
Slags, bank screenings		Greenstone, hornblende	107
Slags, machine slag	96	Bituminous Substances	
Slags, slag sand	49–55	Asphaltum	81
Earth, Etc., Excavated	98–117	Coal, anthracite	97
Clay, dry	63	Coal, bituminous	84
Clay, damp, plastic	110	Coal, lignite	78
Clay and gravel, dry	100	Coal, peat, turf, dry	47
Earth, dry, loose	76	Coal, charcoal, pine	23
Earth, dry, packed	95	Coal, charcoal, oak	33
Earth, moist, loose	78	Coal, coke	75
Earth, moist, packed	96	Graphite	131
Earth, mud, flowing	108	Paraffine	56
Earth, mud, packed	115	Petroleum	54
Riprap, limestone	80–85	Petroleum, refined	50
Riprap, sandstone	90	Petroleum, benzine	46
Riprap, shale	105	Petroleum, gasoline	42
Sand, gravel, dry, loose	90–105	Pitch	69
Sand, gravel, dry, packed	100–120	Tar, bituminous	75
Sand, gravel, wet	118–120		

Average Weights for Various Materials (continued)

Substance	Weight Lbs. per C.F.	Substance	Weight Lbs. per C.F.
Coal and Coke, Piled		Rubber goods	94
Coal, anthracite	47–58	Salt, granulated, piled	48
Coal, bituminous, lignite	40–54	Saltpeter	67
Coal, peat, turf	20–26	Starch	96
Coal, charcoal	10–14	Sulphur	125
Coal, coke	23–32	Wool	82
Metals, Alloys, Ores		Timber, U.S. Seasoned	
Aluminum, cast, hammered	165	Moisture Content by Weight:	
Brass, cast, rolled	534	Seasoned timber 15 to 20%	
Bronze, 7.9 to 14% Sn	509	Green timber up to 50%	
Bronze, aluminum	481	Ash, white, red	40
Copper, cast, rolled	556	Cedar, white, red	22
Copper ore, pyrites	262	Chestnut	41
Gold, cast, hammered	1205	Cypress	30
Iron, cast, pig	450	Fir, Douglas spruce	32
Iron, wrought	485	Fir, eastern	25
Iron, spiegel-eisen	468	Elm, white	45
Iron, ferro-silicon	437	Hemlock	29
Iron ore, hematite	325	Hickory	49
Iron ore, hematite in bank	160–180	Locust	46
Iron ore, hematite loose	130–160	Maple, hard	43
Iron ore, limonite	237	Maple, white	33
Iron ore, magnetite	315	Oak, chestnut	54
Iron slag	172	Oak, live	59
Lead	710	Oak, red, black	41
Lead ore, galena	465	Oak, white	46
Magnesium, alloys	112	Pine, Oregon	32
Manganese	475	Pine, red	30
Manganese ore, pyrolusite	259	Pine, white	26
Mercury	849	Pine, yellow, long-leaf	44
Monel Metal	565	Pine, yellow, short-leaf	38
Nickel	565	Poplar	30
Platinum, cast, hammered	1330	Redwood, California	26
Silver, cast, hammered	565	Spruce, white, black	27
Steel, rolled	490	Walnut, black	38
Tin, cast, hammered	459	Walnut, white	26
Tin ore, cassiterite	418	Various Liquids	
Zinc, cast, rolled	440	Alcohol, 100%	49
Zinc ore, blende	253	Acids, muriatic 40%	75
Various Solids		Acids, nitric 91%	94
Cereals, oats, bulk	32	Acids, sulphuric 87%	112
Cereals, barley, bulk	39	Lye, soda 66%	106
Cereals, corn, rye, bulk	48	Oils, vegetable	58
Cereals, wheat, bulk	48	Oils, mineral, lubricants	57
Hay and straw, bales	20	Water, 4°C. max. density	62.428
Cotton, flax, hemp	93	Water, 100°C.	59.830
Fats	58	Water, ice	56
Flour, loose	28	Water, snow, fresh fallen	8
Flour, pressed	47	Water, sea water	64
Glass, common	156	Gases	
Glass, plate or crown	161	Air, 0°C. 760 mm	.08071
Glass, crystal	184	Ammonia	.0478
Leather	59	Carbon dioxide	.1234
Paper	58	Carbon monoxide	.0781
Potatoes, piled	42	Gas, illuminating	.028–.036
Rubber, caoutchouc	59	Gas, natural	.038–.039

Average Weights for Various Materials (continued)

Material	Weight Lbs. per S.F.	Material	Weight Lbs. per S.F.
Gases (cont.)		Partitions	
Hydrogen	.00559	Clay Tile	
Nitrogen	.0784	3 in.	17
Oxygen	.0892	4 in.	18
Ceilings		6 in.	28
Channel suspended system	1	8 in.	34
Lathing and plastering	See Partitions	10 in.	40
Acoustical fiber tile	1	Gypsum Block	
		2 in.	9-1/2
Floors		3 in.	10-1/2
Steel Deck	See Mfg.	4 in.	12-1/2
		5 in.	14
Concrete–Reinforced 1 in.		6 in.	18-1/2
Stone	12-1/2	Wood Studs 2 x 4	
Slag	11-1/2	12–16 in. o.c.	2
Lightweight	6 to 10	Steel partitions	4
Concrete–Plain 1 in.		Plaster 1 inch	
Stone	12	Cement	10
Slag	11	Gypsum	5
Lightweight	3 to 9	Lathing	
		Metal	1/2
Fills 1 in.		Gypsum Board 1/2 in.	2
Gypsum	6		
Sand	8	Walls	
Cinders	4	Brick	
		4 in.	40
Finishes		8 in.	80
Terrazzo 1 in.	13	12 in.	120
Ceramic or Quarry Tile 3/4 in.	10	Hollow Concrete Block	
Linoleum 1/4 in.	1	(Heavy Aggregate)	
Mastic 3/4 in.	9	4 in.	30
Hardwood 7/8 in.	4	6 in.	43
Softwood 3/4 in.	2-1/2	8 in.	55
		12-1/2 in.	80
Roofs		Hollow Concrete Block	
Copper or tin	1	(Light Aggregate)	
3-ply ready roofing	1	4 in.	21
3-ply felt and gravel	5-1/2	6 in.	30
5-ply felt and gravel	6	8 in.	38
		12 in.	55
Shingles		Clay Tile	
Wood	2	(Load Bearing)	
Asphalt	3	4 in.	25
Clay tile	9 to 14	6 in.	30
Slate 1/4 in.	10	8 in.	33
		12 in.	45
Sheathing		Stone 4 in.	55
Wood 3/4 in.	3	Glass Block 4 in.	18
Gypsum 1 in.	4	Windows, Glass, Frame & Sash	8
		Curtain Walls	See Mfg.
Insulation 1 in.		Structural Glass 1 in.	15
Loose	1/2	Corrugated Cement	
Poured in place	2	Asbestos 1/4 in.	3
Rigid	1-1/2		

Basic Metric Units and Prefixes

Basic Metric Units		Prefixes for Metric Units		
Quantity	Unit	Multiple and Submultiple	Prefix	Symbol
length	meter (m)	$1{,}000{,}000{,}000{,}000 = 10^{12}$	tera	T
mass	kilogram (kg)	$1{,}000{,}000{,}000 = 10^{9}$	giga	G
time	second (s)	$1{,}000{,}000 = 10^{6}$	mega	M
electric current	ampere (A)	$1{,}000 = 10^{3}$	kilo	k
temperature (thermodynamic)	kelvin (K)	$100 = 10^{2}$	hecto	h
amount of substance	mole (mol)	$10 = 10$	deka	da
luminous intensity	candela (cd)	$0.1 = 10^{-1}$	deci	d
		$0.01 = 10^{-2}$	centi	c
		$0.001 = 10^{-3}$	milli	m
		$0.000\,001 = 10^{-6}$	micro	μ
		$0.000\,000\,001 = 10^{-9}$	nano	n
		$0.000\,000\,000\,001 = 10^{-12}$	pico	p
		$0.000\,000\,000\,000\,001 = 10^{-15}$	femto	f
		$0.000\,000\,000\,000\,000\,001 = 10^{-18}$	atto	a

Metric Equivalents

Length	
CM. = 0.3937 in.	In. = 2.5400 cm.
Meter = 3.2808 ft.	Ft. = 0.3048 m.
Meter = 1.0936 yd.	Yd. = 0.9144 m.
Km. = 0.6214 mile	Mile = 1.6093 km.

Area	
Sq. cm. = 0.1550 sq. in.	Sq. in. = 6.4516 sq. cm.
Sq. m. = 10.7639 sq. ft.	Sq. ft. = 0.0929 sq. m.
Sq. m. = 1.1960 sq. yd.	Sq. yd. = 0.8361 sq. m.
Hectare = 2.4710 acres	Acre = 0.4047 hectare
Sq. km. = 0.3861 sq. mile	Sq. mile = 2.5900 sq. km.

Volume	
Cu. cm. = 0.0610 cu. in.	Cu. in. = 16.3872 cu. cm.
Cu. m. = 35.3145 cu. ft.	Cu. ft. = 0.0283 cu. cm.
Cu. m. = 1.3079 cu. yd.	Cu. yd. = 0.7646 cu. m.

Capacity	
Liter = 61.0250 cu. in.	Cu. in. = 0.0164 liters
Liter = 0.0353 cu. ft.	Cu. ft. = 28.3162 liters
Liter = 0.2642 gal. (U.S.)	Gal. = 3.7853 liters
Liter = 0.0284 bu. (U.S.)	Bu. = 35.2383 liters

$$
\text{Liter} = \begin{cases} 1000.027 \text{ cu. cm.} \\ 1.0567 \text{ qt. (liquid) or } 0.9081 \text{ qt. (dry)} \\ 2.2046 \text{ lbs. of pure water at } 4°C + 1 \text{ kg.} \end{cases}
$$

Weight	
Gram = 15.4324 grains	Grain = 0.0648 g.
Gram = 0.0353 oz.	Oz. = 28.3495 g.
Kg. = 2.2046 lbs.	Lb. = 0.4536 kg.
Kg. = 0.0011 ton (short)	Ton (short) = 907.1848 kg.
Ton (met.) = 1.1023 ton (short)	Ton (short) = 0.9072 ton (met.)
Ton (met.) = 0.9842 ton (large)	Ton (large) = 1.0160 ton (met.)

Pressure
1 kg. per sq. cm. = 14.223 lbs. per sq. in.
1 lb. per sq. in. = 0.0703 kg. per sq. cm.
1 kg. per sq. m. = 0.2048 lbs. per sq. ft.
1 lb. per sq. ft. = 4.8824 kg. per sq. m.
1 kg. per sq. cm. = 0.9678 normal atmosphere

$$
1 \text{ normal atmosphere} = \begin{cases} 1.0332 \text{ kg. per sq. cm.} \\ 1.0133 \text{ bars} \\ 14.696 \text{ lbs. per sq. in.} \end{cases}
$$

Metric Conversion Table

Conversion Formulas: Inches x 2.54 = Centimeters
Feet x .3048 = Meters
Pounds x .4536 = Kilograms

	Inches to Centimeters	Feet to Meters	Pounds to Kilograms		Inches to Centimeters	Feet to Meters	Pounds to Kilograms
1	2.54	.3048	.4536	51	129.54	15.5448	23.1336
2	5.08	.6096	.9072	52	132.08	15.8496	23.5872
3	7.62	.9144	1.3608	53	134.62	16.1544	24.0408
4	10.16	1.2192	1.8144	54	137.16	16.4592	24.4944
5	12.7	1.524	2.268	55	139.7	16.764	24.948
6	15.24	1.8288	2.7216	56	142.24	17.0688	25.4016
7	17.78	2.1336	3.1752	57	144.78	17.3736	25.8552
8	20.32	2.4384	3.6288	58	147.32	17.6784	26.3088
9	22.86	2.7432	4.0824	59	149.86	17.9832	26.7624
10	25.4	3.048	4.536	60	152.4	18.288	27.216
11	27.94	3.3528	4.9896	61	154.94	18.5928	27.6696
12	30.48	3.6576	5.4432	62	157.48	18.8976	28.1232
13	33.02	3.9624	5.8968	63	160.02	19.2024	28.5768
14	35.56	4.2672	6.3504	64	162.56	19.5072	29.0304
15	38.1	4.572	6.804	65	165.1	19.812	29.488
16	40.64	4.8768	7.2576	66	167.64	20.1168	29.9376
17	43.18	5.1816	7.7112	67	170.18	20.4216	30.3912
18	45.72	5.4864	8.1648	68	172.72	20.7264	30.8448
19	48.26	5.7912	8.6184	69	175.26	21.0312	31.2984
20	50.8	6.096	9.072	70	177.8	21.336	31.752
21	53.34	6.4008	9.5256	71	180.34	21.6408	32.2056
22	55.88	6.7056	9.9792	72	182.88	21.9456	32.6592
23	58.42	7.0104	10.4328	73	185.42	22.2504	33.1128
24	60.96	7.3152	10.8864	74	187.96	22.5552	33.5664
25	63.5	7.62	11.34	75	190.5	22.86	34.02
26	66.04	7.9248	11.7936	76	193.04	23.1648	34.4736
27	68.58	8.2296	12.2472	77	195.58	23.4696	34.9272
28	71.12	8.5344	12.7008	78	198.12	23.7744	35.3808
29	73.66	8.8392	13.1544	79	200.66	24.0792	35.8344
30	76.2	9.144	13.608	80	203.2	24.384	36.288
31	78.74	9.4488	14.0616	81	205.74	24.6888	36.7416
32	81.28	9.7536	14.5152	82	208.28	24.9936	37.1952
33	83.82	10.0584	14.9680	83	210.82	25.2984	37.6488
34	86.36	10.3632	15.4224	84	213.36	25.6032	38.1024
35	88.9	10.668	15.876	85	215.9	25.908	38.556
36	91.44	10.9728	16.3296	86	218.44	26.2128	39.0096
37	93.98	11.2776	16.7832	87	220.98	26.5176	39.4632
38	96.52	11.5824	17.2368	88	223.52	26.8224	39.9168
39	99.06	11.8872	17.6904	89	226.06	27.1272	40.3704
40	101.6	12.192	18.144	90	228.6	27.432	40.824
41	104.14	12.4968	18.5976	91	231.14	27.7368	41.2776
42	106.68	12.8016	19.0512	92	233.68	28.0416	41.7312
43	109.22	13.1064	19.5048	93	236.22	28.3464	42.1848
44	111.76	13.4112	19.9584	94	238.76	28.6512	42.6384
45	114.3	13.716	20.412	95	241.3	28.956	43.092
46	116.84	14.0208	20.8656	96	243.84	29.2608	43.5456
47	119.38	14.3256	21.3192	97	246.38	29.5656	43.9992
48	121.92	14.6304	21.7728	98	248.92	29.8704	44.4528
49	124.46	14.9352	22.2264	99	252.46	30.1752	44.9064
50	127	15.24	22.68	100	254	30.48	45.36

Standard and Metric Linear and Area Conversion Tables

Linear Conversions							
Inches	Feet	Yards	Rods	Miles	Centi-meters	Meters	Kilo-meters
1	0.083	0.028	0.005	—	2.540	0.0254	—
12	1	0.333	0.061	0.0002	30.480	0.305	0.0003
36	3	1	0.182	0.0006	91.440	0.914	0.0009
0.3937	0.033	0.011	—	—	1	0.01	—
39.37	3.281	1.094	0.199	0.0006	100	1	0.001
					Furlongs		
198	16.5	5.5	1	0.003	0.025	5.029	0.005
	5,280	1,760	320	1	8	1,609,347	1.609
	660	220	40	0.125	1	201.168	0.201
	3,280.83	1,093.61	198.838	0.621	4.971	1,000	1
Area Conversions							
Square Inches	Square Feet	Square Yards	Acres	Square Centi-meters	Square Meters	Hectares	Square Kilo-meters
1	0.007	—	—	6.452	0.0006	—	—
144	1	0.111	0.00002	929.034	0.093	—	—
1,296	9	1	0.0002	8,361.31	0.836	—	—
0.155	0.001	—	—	1	0.0001	—	—
1,549.997	10.764	1.196	0.0002	10,000	1	0.0001	—
				Square Miles			
	43,560	4,840	1	0.002	4,046.87	0.405	0.004
	27,878,400	3,097,600	640	1	2,589,998	258.999	2.590
	107,638.7	11,959.9	2.471	0.004	10,000	1	0.01
	10,763,867	1,195,985	247.104	0.386	1,000,000	100	1

General Conversion Factors

Multiply	By	To Obtain
acres	43,560	square feet
acres	4047	square meters
acres	1.562×10^{-3}	square miles
acres	5645.8	square varas
acres	4840	square yards
amperes	1/10	abamperes
amperes	3×10^9	statamperes
atmospheres	76.0	cms. of mercury
atmospheres	29.92	inches of mercury
atmospheres	33.90	feet of water
atmospheres	10.333	kgs. per sq. meter
atmospheres	14.70	pounds per sq. inch
atmospheres	1.058	tons per sq. foot
British thermal units	0.2520	kilogram-calories
British thermal units	777.5	foot-pounds
British thermal units	3.927×10^{-4}	horse-power-hours
British thermal units	1054	joules
British thermal units	107.5	kilogram-meters
British thermal units	2.928×10^{-4}	kilowatt-hours
B.t.u. per min.	12.96	foot-pounds per sec.
B.t.u. per min.	0.02356	horse-power
B.t.u. per min.	0.01757	kilowatts
B.t.u. per min.	17.57	watts
B.t.u. per sq. ft. per min.	0.1220	watts per sq. inch
bushels	1.244	cubic feet
bushels	2150	cubic inches
bushels	0.03524	cubic meters
bushels	4	pecks
bushels	64	pints (dry)
bushels	32	quarts (dry)
centimeters	0.3937	inches
centimeters	0.01	meters
centimeters	393.7	mils
centimeters	10	millimeters
centimeter-grams	980.7	centimeter-dynes
centimeter-grams	10^{-5}	meter-kilograms
centimeter-grams	7.233×10^{-5}	pound-feet
centimeters of mercury	0.01316	atmospheres
centimeters of mercury	0.4461	feet of water
centimeters of mercury	136.0	kgs. per sq. meter
centimeters of mercury	27.85	pounds per sq. foot
centimeters of mercury	0.1934	pounds per sq. inch
centimeters per second	1.969	feet per minute
centimeters per second	0.03281	feet per second
centimeters per second	0.036	kilometers per hour
centimeters per second	0.6	meters per minute
centimeters per second	0.02237	miles per hour
centimeters per second	3.728×10^{-4}	miles per minute
cubic centimeters	3.531×10^{-5}	cubic feet
cubic centimeters	6.102×10^{-2}	cubic inches
cubic centimeters	10^{-6}	cubic meters
cubic centimeters	1.308×10^{-6}	cubic yards
cubic centimeters	2.642×10^{-4}	gallons
cubic centimeters	10^{-3}	liters

General Conversion Factors (continued)

Multiply	By	To Obtain
cubic centimeters	2.113×10^{-3}	pints (liquid)
cubic centimeters	1.057×10^{-3}	quarts (liquid)
cubic feet	62.43	pounds of water
cubic feet	2.832×10^{4}	cubic cms.
cubic feet	1728	cubic inches
cubic feet	0.02832	cubic meters
cubic feet	0.03704	cubic yards
cubic feet	7.481	gallons
cubic feet	28.32	liters
cubic feet	59.84	pints (liquid)
cubic feet	29.92	quarts (liquid)
cubic feet per minute	472.0	cubic cms. per sec.
cubic feet per minute	0.1247	gallons per sec.
cubic feet per minute	0.4720	liters per second
cubic feet per minute	62.4	lbs. of water per min.
cubic inches	16.39	cubic centimeters
cubic inches	5.787×10^{-4}	cubic feet
cubic inches	1.639×10^{-5}	cubic meters
cubic inches	2.143×10^{-5}	cubic yards
cubic inches	4.329×10^{-3}	gallons
cubic inches	1.639×10^{-2}	liters
cubic inches	0.03463	pints (liquid)
cubic inches	0.01732	quarts (liquid)
cubic yards	7.646×10^{5}	cubic centimeters
cubic yards	27	cubic feet
cubic yards	46,656	cubic inches
cubic yards	0.7646	cubic meters
cubic yards	202.0	gallons
cubic yards	764.6	liters
cubic yards	1616	pints (liquid)
cubic yards	807.9	quarts (liquid)
cubic yards per minute	0.45	cubic feet per sec.
cubic yards per minute	3.367	gallons per second
cubic yards per minute	12.74	liters per second
degrees (angle)	60	minutes
degrees (angle)	0.01745	radians
degrees (angle)	3600	seconds
dynes	1.020×10^{-3}	grams
dynes	7.233×10^{-5}	poundals
dynes	2.248×10^{-6}	pounds
ergs	9.486×10^{-11}	British thermal units
ergs	1	dyne-centimeters
ergs	7.376×10^{-8}	foot-pounds
ergs	1.020×10^{-3}	gram-centimeters
ergs	10^{-7}	joules
ergs	2.390×10^{-11}	kilogram-calories
ergs	1.020×10^{-8}	kilogram-meters
feet	30.48	centimeters
feet	12	inches
feet	0.3048	meters
feet	.36	varas
feet	1/3	yards
feet of water	0.02950	atmospheres
feet of water	0.8826	inches of mercury

General Conversion Factors (continued)

Multiply	By	To Obtain
feet of water	304.8	kgs. per sq. meter
feet of water	62.43	pounds per sq. ft.
feet of water	0.4335	pounds per sq. inch
feet per second	30.48	centimeters per second
feet per sec. per sec.	0.3048	meters per sec. per sec.
foot-pounds	1.286×10^{-3}	British thermal units
foot-pounds	1.356×10^{7}	ergs
foot-pounds	5.050×10^{-7}	horse-power hours
foot-pounds	1.356	joules
foot-pounds	3.241×10^{-4}	kilogram-calories
foot-pounds	0.1383	kilogram-meters
foot-pounds	3.766×10^{-7}	kilowatt-hours
foot-pounds per min.	1.286×10^{-3}	B.t. units per minute
foot-pounds per min.	0.01667	foot-pounds per sec.
foot-pounds per min.	3.030×10^{-5}	horse-power
foot-pounds per min.	3.241×10^{-4}	kg.-calories per min.
foot-pounds per min.	2.260×10^{-5}	kilowatts
foot-pounds per sec.	7.717×10^{-2}	B.t. units per minute
foot-pounds per sec.	1.818×10^{-3}	horse-power
foot-pounds per sec.	1.945×10^{-2}	kg.-calories per min.
foot-pounds per sec.	1.356×10^{-3}	kilowatts
gallons	8.345	pounds of water
gallons	3785	cubic centimeters
gallons	0.1337	cubic feet
gallons	231	cubic inches
gallons	3.785×10^{-3}	cubic meters
gallons	4.951×10^{-3}	cubic yards
gallons	3.785	liters
gallons	8	pints (liquid)
gallons	4	quarts (liquid)
gallons per minute	2.228×10^{-3}	cubic ft. per second
gallons per minute	0.06308	liters per second
grains (troy)	1	grains (av.)
grains (troy)	0.06480	grams
grains (troy)	0.04167	pennyweights (troy)
grams	980.7	dynes
grams	15.43	grains (troy)
grams	10^{-3}	kilograms
grams	10^{3}	milligrams
grams	0.03527	ounces
grams	0.03215	ounces (troy)
grams	0.07093	poundals
grams	2.205×10^{-3}	pounds
horse-power	42.44	B.t. units per min.
horse-power	33,000	foot-pounds per min.
horse-power	550	foot-pounds per sec.
horse-power	1.014	horse-power (metric)
horse-power	10.70	kg.-calories per min.
horse-power	0.7457	kilowatts
horse-power	745.7	watts
horse-power (boiler)	33,520	B.t.u. per hour
horse-power (boiler)	9.804	kilowatts
horse-power-hours	2547	British thermal units
horse-power-hours	1.98×10^{6}	foot-pounds

General Conversion Factors (continued)

Multiply	By	To Obtain
horse-power-hours	2.684×10^6	joules
horse-power-hours	641.7	kilogram-calories
horse-power-hours	2.737×10^5	kilogram-meters
horse-power-hours	0.7457	kilowatt-hours
inches	2.540	centimeters
inches	10^3	mils
inches	.03	varas
inches of mercury	0.03342	atmospheres
inches of mercury	1.133	feet of water
inches of mercury	345.3	kgs. per sq. meter
inches of mercury	70.73	pounds per sq. ft.
inches of mercury	0.4912	pounds per sq. in.
inches of water	0.002458	atmospheres
inches of water	0.07355	inches of mercury
inches of water	25.40	kgs. per sq. meter
inches of water	0.5781	ounces per sq. in.
inches of water	5.204	pounds per sq. ft.
inches of water	0.03613	pounds per sq. in.
kilograms	980,665	dynes
kilograms	10^3	grams
kilograms	70.93	poundals
kilograms	2.2046	pounds
kilograms	1.102×10^{-3}	tons (short)
kilogram-calories	3.968	British thermal units
kilogram-calories	3086	foot-pounds
kilogram-calories	1.558×10^{-3}	horse-power-hours
kilogram-calories	4183	joules
kilogram-calories	426.6	kilogram-meters
kilogram-calories	1.162×10^{-3}	kilowatt-hours
kg.-calories per min.	51.43	foot-pounds per sec.
kg.-calories per min.	0.09351	horse-power
kg.-calories per min.	0.06972	kilowatts
kilometers	10^5	centimeters
kilometers	3281	feet
kilometers	10^3	meters
kilometers	0.6214	miles
kilometers	1093.6	yards
kilowatts	56.92	B.t. units per min.
kilowatts	4.425×10^4	foot-pounds per min.
kilowatts	737.6	foot-pounds per sec.
kilowatts	1.341	horse-power
kilowatts	14.34	kg.-calories per min.
kilowatts	10^3	watts
kilowatt-hours	3415	British thermal units
kilowatt-hours	2.655×10^6	foot-pounds
kilowatt-hours	1.341	horse-power-hours
kilowatt-hours	3.6×10^6	joules
kilowatt-hours	860.5	kilogram-calories
kilowatt-hours	3.671×10^5	kilogram-meters
$\log^{10} N$	2.303	$\log_\epsilon N$ or $\ln N$
$\log^\epsilon N$ or $\ln N$	0.4343	$\log_{10} N$
meters	100	centimeters
meters	3.2808	feet
meters	39.37	inches

General Conversion Factors (continued)

Multiply	By	To Obtain
meters	10^{-3}	kilometers
meters	10^3	millimeters
meters	1.0936	yards
miles	1.609×10^5	centimeters
miles	5280	feet
miles	1.6093	kilometers
miles	1760	yards
miles	1900.8	varas
miles per hour	44.70	centimeters per sec.
miles per hour	88	feet per minute
miles per hour	1.467	feet per second
miles per hour	1.6093	kilometers per hour
miles per hour	0.8684	knots per hour
miles per hour	26.82	meters per minute
miles per hour per sec.	44.70	cms. per sec. per sec.
miles per hour per sec.	1.467	ft. per sec. per sec.
miles per hour per sec.	1.6093	kms. per hr. per sec.
miles per hour per sec.	0.4470	M. per sec. per sec.
months	30.42	days
months	730	hours
months	43,800	minutes
months	2.628×10^6	seconds
ounces	8	drams
ounces	437.5	grains
ounces	28.35	grams
ounces	.0625	pounds
ounces per square inch.	0.0625	pounds per sq. inch
pints (dry)	33.60	cubic inches
pints (liquid)	28.87	cubic inches
pounds	444,823	dynes
pounds	7000	grains
pounds	453.6	grams
pounds	16	ounces
pounds	32.17	poundals
pounds of water	0.01602	cubic feet
pounds of water	27.68	cubic inches
pounds of water	0.1198	gallons
pounds of water per min.	2.669×10^{-4}	cubic feet per sec.
pounds per cubic foot	0.01602	grams per cubic cm.
pounds per cubic foot	16.02	kgs. per cubic meter
pounds per cubic foot	5.787×10^{-4}	pounds per cubic in.
pounds per cubic foot	5.456×10^{-9}	pounds per mil foot
pounds per square foot	0.01602	feet of water
pounds per square foot	4.882	kgs. per sq. meter
pounds per square foot	6.944×10^{-3}	pounds per sq. inch
pounds per square inch	0.06804	atmospheres
pounds per square inch	2.307	feet of water
pounds per square inch	2.036	inches of mercury
pounds per square inch	703.1	kgs. per sq. meter
pounds per square inch	144	pounds per sq. foot
quarts	32	fluid ounces
quarts (dry)	67.20	cubic inches
quarts (liquid)	57.75	cubic inches
rods	16.5	feet

General Conversion Factors (continued)

Multiply	By	To Obtain
square centimeters	1.973×10^5	circular mils
square centimeters	1.076×10^{-3}	square feet
square centimeters	0.1550	square inches
square centimeters	10^{-6}	square meters
square centimeters	100	square millimeters
square feet	2.296×10^{-5}	acres
square feet	929.0	square centimeters
square feet	144	square inches
square feet	0.09290	square meters
square feet	3.587×10^{-8}	square miles
square feet	.1296	square varas
square feet	1/9	square yards
square inches	1.273×10^6	circular mils
square inches	6.452	square centimeters
square inches	6.944×10^{-3}	square feet
square inches	10^6	square mils
square inches	645.2	square millimeters
square miles	640	acres
square miles	27.88×10^6	square feet
square miles	2.590	square kilometers
square miles	3,613,040.45	square varas
square miles	3.098×10^6	square yards
square yards	2.066×10^{-4}	acres
square yards	9	square feet
square yards	0.8361	square meters
square yards	3.228×10^{-7}	square miles
square yards	1.1664	square varas
temp. (degs. C.) + 17.8	1.8	temp. (degs. Fahr.)
temp. (degs. F.) – 32	5/9	temp. (degs. Cent.)
tons (long)	2240	pounds
tons (short)	2000	pounds
yards	.9144	meters

Approximate Comparison of Drawing Scales

Metric			Approximate English Equivalent			Usage
1:1500	(means 1 cm	= 15 m)	1 in.	=	100 ft.	Location plans
1:1000	(means 1 cm	= 10 m)	1 in.	=	80 ft.	Site plans
1:500	(means 1 cm	= 5 m)	1 in.	=	40 ft.	Plot plans
1:200	(means 0.5 cm	= 1 m)	1/16 in.	=	1 ft.	Small scale plans
1:100	(means 1 cm	= 1 m)	1/8 in.	=	1 ft.	Normal scale plans
1:50	(means 2 cm	= 1 m)	1/4 in.	=	1 ft.	Large scale plans
1:20	(means 5 cm	= 1 m)	1/2 in.	=	1 ft.	Sections and details
1:10	(means 10 cm	= 1 m)	1 in.	=	1 ft.	Details
1:8	(means 12.5 cm	= 1 m)	1-1/2 in.	=	1 ft.	Details
1:1	(means 1 m	= 1 m)	Full size			Large details

Preliminary Building Size Determination

The following tables are helpful when estimating conceptually.

With basic information such as type of occupancy and number of people intended to occupy the structure, and/or rough dimensions, it is possible to calculate other needed information.

Example:
A potential client wants to know how big a building he will need and how much it will cost. All he knows at this time is that there will be approximately 75 people working in the building. To begin a conceptual estimate, some size information is needed.

Step 1: *Determine the net area.* Consult the "Occupancy Determinations—Net Areas" table. The table states that for each occupant, 100 S.F. (net) of office space is required. (Note that in this case all codes have the same requirements. Check your area for the code used.)

Step 2: *Determine the gross area.* (Net area does not include common areas, stairwells, toilet area, mechanical areas, etc.) To obtain the gross area, consult the "Floor Area Requirements" table. The *gross to net ratio* for offices is 135%. Therefore, 100 S.F. (net) x 1.35 (gross/net), or 135 square feet per person, is needed for this office building. Since we expect an occupancy of 75 persons, the total office space will be 10,125 square feet.

(Note: In some cases, such as in apartment buildings, schools, hospitals, etc., the basic information will be in unit form, such as "I want an apartment building with 50 units," or "a hospital with 200 beds," etc. In these cases, use the "Unit Gross Area" table provided. To use this table, it is necessary to know a little about the quality of the structure. If the quality is to be "above average," then the units will be larger; if they are to be of "economy" construction, then you can assume the units will be smaller. If, in the case of an apartment building, the client wants 50 units of average quality, to obtain the overall size, multiply the number of units by the median gross square footage—in this case 50 units x 860 square feet per unit or 43,000 square feet *gross area.*)

Step 3: *Determine the size.* A 10,000+ square foot building lends itself nicely to a 100' x 100' economical square building. If the land available does not allow for this design, adjust the dimensions to fit. You now have the basic building size and shape to start the estimate.

Occupancy Determinations - Net Areas

	Description	S.F. Required Per Person*			
		BBC	BOCA	SBC	UBC
Assembly Areas	Fixed Seats	6	**	6	7
	Movable Seats	15		15	15
	Concentrated		7		
	Unconcentrated		15		
	Standing Space		3		
Educational	Unclassified	40			
	Classrooms		20	40	20
	Shop Areas		50	100	50
Institutional	Unclassified	150		125	
	In-Patient Areas		240		
	Sleeping Areas		120		
Mercantile	Basement	30	30	30	20
	Ground Floor	30	30	30	30
	Upper Floors	60	60	60	50
Office		100	100	100	100

* BBC=Basic Building Code
  BOCA=Building Officials & Code Administrators
  SBC-Southern Building Code
  UBC=Uniform Building Code
**The occupancy load for assembly area with fixed seats shall be determined by the number of fixed seats installed.

Unit Gross Area Requirements

The figures in the table below indicate typical ranges in square feet as a function of the "occupant" unit. This table is best used in the preliminary design stages to help determine the probable size requirement for the total project. The "1/4" means that of all buildings of this type built, 1/4 will be smaller in unit size and 3/4 will be larger; "median" means that 50% of the units will be smaller and 50% will be larger; the "3/4" indicates that 3/4 of the building units will be smaller and 1/4 will be larger.

Building Type	Unit	Gross Area in S.F.		
		1/4	Median	3/4
Apartments	Unit	660	860	1,100
Auditorium & Play Theaters	Seat	18	25	38
Bowling Alleys	Lane		940	
Churches & Synagogues	Seat	20	28	39
Dormitories	Bed	200	230	275
Fraternity & Sorority Houses	Bed	220	315	370
Garages, Parking	Car	325	355	385
Hospitals	Bed	685	850	1,075
Hotels	Rental Unit	475	600	710
Housing for the Elderly	Unit	515	635	755
Housing, Public	Unit	700	875	1,030
Ice Skating Rinks	Total	27,000	30,000	36,000
Motels	Rental Unit	360	465	620
Nursing Homes	Bed	290	350	450
Restaurants	Seat	23	29	39
Schools, Elementary	Pupil	65	77	90
Junior High & Middle		85	110	129
Senior High		102	130	145
Vocational		110	135	195
Shooting Ranges	Point		450	
Theaters & Movies	Seat		15	

Floor Area Ratios: Commonly Used Gross-to-Net and Net-to-Gross Area Ratios Expressed in % for Various Building Types

Building Type	Gross-to-Net Ratio	Net-to-Gross Ratio	Building Type	Gross-to-Net Ratio	Net-to-Gross Ratio
Apartment	156	64	School Buildings (campus type)		
Bank	140	72	Administrative	150	67
Church	142	70	Auditorium	142	70
Courthouse	162	61	Biology	161	62
Department Store	123	81	Chemistry	170	59
Garage	118	85	Classroom	152	66
Hospital	183	55	Dining Hall	138	72
Hotel	158	63	Dormitory	154	65
Laboratory	171	58	Engineering	164	61
Library	132	76	Fraternity	160	63
Office	135	75	Gymnasium	142	70
Restaurant	141	70	Science	167	60
Warehouse	108	93	Service	120	83
			Student Union	172	59

The gross area of a building is the total floor area based on outside dimensions.

The net area of a building is the usable floor area for the function intended and excludes such items as stairways, corridors and mechanical rooms. In the case of a commercial building, it might be considered as the "leasable area."

Definitions of Abbreviations Used in Formulas

F = Future amount; the amount of money you will end up with or want to end up with at the end of the time period specified.

P = Present value; the amount of money you have or need to have at the beginning of the time period specified.

n = Number of time periods being calculated (coordinate with i).

i = Interest rate per time period. (Note: if n, the number of time periods, is in days, weeks, months or years, i must also be in that time period.)

Formulas for Compound Interest

A) $F = P(1 + i)^n$

Use: To find the value of funds at the end of the number of time periods (n) if the interest rate is i per time period. A time period is the time the interest rate is compounded. For example, if you wish to know how much you will have in an account at the end of five years and the bank compounds their rate monthly at 5% interest, then **F** is what you are looking for, **n** would equal 5 years x 4 quarters per year = 20, and i = 5% per year divided by 4 quarters per year = 1.25.

B) $P = F \left[\dfrac{1}{(1 + i)^n} \right] = F(1 + i)^{-n}$

Use: To find the amount needed today (present value) to end up with the desired amount **F** (future value) at the end of time period **n**, at the interest rate of i per time period.

C) Annuity Compound Amount

$F = A \left[\dfrac{(1 + i)^n - 1}{i} \right]$

Use: To find the future value of an annuity if amount **A** is added (or paid) to an account at regular intervals for the time period of **n** intervals, at interest rate of i per interval. This formula can also be used to determine what the total of all payments (principle and interest) of a loan will be.

D) Sinking Fund

$A = F \left[\dfrac{i}{(1 + i)^n - 1} \right]$

Use: To find the amount **A** needed to add to an account at regular intervals, to end up with a future amount **F** after a time period of **n** intervals at an interest rate of i per interval.

E) Capital Recovery (Loan Repayment)

$A = P \left[\dfrac{i (1 + i)^n}{(1 + i)^n - 1} \right] = P \left[\dfrac{i}{1 - (1 + i)^{-n}} \right]$

Use: To find what payments are necessary per time interval to pay back a loan **R** over the number of time intervals **n** at an interest rate of i per time interval. For example, if you wanted to find your *monthly* payment for a loan of $100,000 spread over 30 years at a fixed rate of 10% per year, then P = $100,000, n = 30 years x 12 months per year = 360, and i = 10%/year/12 months/year = 0.833.

F) Present Value of a Loan

$P = A \left[\dfrac{((1 + i)^n) - 1}{(i(1 + i)^n)} \right] = A \left[\dfrac{1 - (1 + i)^{-n}}{i} \right]$

Use: To find the present value of payments, if you are making payments **A** over a number of time intervals **n** at the interest rate i per time interval

Lighting Outlets

○   Ceiling Surface Incandescent Fixture

⊢○   Wall Surface Incandescent Fixture

Ⓡ   Ceiling Recess Incandescent Fixture

⊢Ⓡ   Wall Recess Incandescent Fixture

^{A}○$_{3b}$ Standard Designation for All Lighting Fixtures – A = Fixture Type, 3 = Circuit Number, b = Switch Control

Ⓑ   Ceiling Blanked Outlet

⊢Ⓑ   Wall Blanked Outlet

Ⓔ   Ceiling Electrical Outlet

⊢Ⓔ   Wall Electrical Outlet

Ⓙ   Ceiling Junction Box

⊢Ⓙ   Wall Junction Box

Ⓛ$_{PS}$ Ceiling Lamp Holder with Pull Switch

⊢Ⓛ$_{PS}$ Wall Lamp Holder with Pull Switch

Ⓛ   Ceiling Outlet Controlled by Low Voltage Switching when Relay is Installed in Outlet Box

⊢Ⓛ   Wall Outlet – Same as Above

◇   Outlet Box with Extension Ring

[EX]→   Exit Sign with Arrow as Indicated

[○]   Surface Fluorescent Fixture

[○] P   Pendant Fluorescent Fixture

[OR]   Recessed Fluorescent Fixture

[○]   Wall Surface Fluorescent Fixture

⊢[==]   Channel Mounted Fluorescent Fixture

[○][ ][ ]   Surface or Pendant Continous Row Fluorescent Fixtures

[○R][ ]   Recessed Continuous Row Fluorescent Fixtures

●   Incandescent Fixture on Emergency Circuit

[●]   Fluorescent Fixture on Emergency Circuit

Receptacle Outlets

⊢⊖   Single Receptacle Outlet

⊢⊖   Duplex Receptacle Outlet

⊢^{x}⊖   Duplex Receptacle Outlet "X" Indicates above Counter Max. Height = 42" or above Counter

⊢⊖$_{WP}$ Weatherproof Receptacle Outlet

⊢⊕   Triplex Receptacle Outlet

⊢⊕   Quadruplex Receptacle Outlet

⊢⊖   Duplex Receptacle Outlet – Split Wired

⊢⊕   Triplex Receptacle Outlet – Split Wired

⊢⬠   Single Special Purpose Receptacle Outlet

⊢⬠   Duplex Special Purpose Receptacle Outlet

⊢⊖$_R$ Range Outlet

⊢⬟$_{DW}$ Special Purpose Connection – Dishwasher

⊢⊖$_{XP}$ Explosion-proof Receptacle Outlet Max. Height = 36" to ℄

⊢⊖$_x$ Multi-outlet Assembly

Ⓒ   Clock Hanger Receptacle

Ⓕ   Fan Hanger Receptacle

⊟   Floor Single Receptacle Outlet

Receptacle Outlets (Cont).

Floor Duplex Receptacle Outlet

Floor Special Purpose Outlet

Floor Telephone Outlet – Public

Floor Telephone Outlet – Private

Underfloor Duct and Junction Box for Triple, Double, or Single Duct System as Indicated by Number of Parallel Lines

Cellular Floor Header Duct

Switch Outlets

S Single Pole Switch
Max. Height = 42″ to ℄

S_2 Double Pole Switch

S_3 Three-way Switch

S_4 Four-way Switch

S_D Automatic Door Switch

S_K Key Operated Switch

S_P Switch & Pilot Lamp

S_{CB} Circuit Breaker

S_{WCB} Weatherproof Circuit Breaker

S_{MC} Momentary Contact Switch

S_{RC} Remote Control Switch (Receiver)

S_{WP} Weatherproof Switch

S_F Fused Switch

S_L Switch for Low Voltage Switching System

S_{LM} Master Switch for Low Voltage Switching System

S_T Time Switch

S_{TH} Thermal Rated Motor Switch

S_{DM} Incandescent Dimmer Swtich

S_{FDM} Fluorescent Dimmer Switch

Switch & Single Receptacle

Switch & Double Receptacle

Special Outlet Circuits
S_A

Institutional, Commercial, & Industrial System Outlets

Nurses Call System Devices – any Type

Paging System Devices – any Type

Fire Alarm System Devices – any Type

Fire Alarm Manual Station – Max. Height = 48″ to ℄

Fire Alarm Horn with Integral Warning Light

Fire Alarm Thermodetector, Fixed Temperature

Smoke Detector

Fire Alarm Thermodetector, Rate of Rise

Fire Alarm Master Box – Max. Height per Fire Department

Magnetic Door Holder

Fire Alarm Annunciator

Staff Register System – any Type

Electrical Clock System Devices – any Type

Public Telephone System Devices

Institutional, Commercial, & Industrial System Outlets (Cont).

$+\triangleleft$ Private Telephone System Devices

$+\triangle$ Watchman System Devices

$+\boxed{L}$ Sound System, L = Speaker, V = Volume Control

$+\bigcirc$ Other Signal System Devices – CTV = Television Antenna, DP = Data Processing

$\boxed{\text{SC}}$ Signal Central Station

Telephone Interconnection Box

(PE) Pneumatic/Electric Switch

(EP) Electric/Pneumatic Switch

$\boxed{\text{GP}}$ Operating Room Grounding Plate

$\boxed{P}_6$ Patient Ground Point – 6 = Number of Jacks

Panelboards

Flush Mounted Panelboard & Cabinet

Surface Mounted Panelboard & Cabinet

Lighting Panel

Power Panel

Heating Panel

$\boxtimes$ Controller (Starter)

Externally Operated Disconnect Switch

Busducts & Wireways

Trolley Duct

Busway (Service, Feeder, or Plug-in)

Cable through Ladder or Channel

Wireway

$\boxed{J}$ Bus Duct Junction Box

Electrical Distribution or Lighting System, Aerial, Lightning Protection

$\bigcirc$ Pole

$\bigcirc\!\!-$ Street Light & Bracket

$\triangle$ Transformer

—— Primary Circuit

– – – – Secondary Circuit

— – — Auxiliary System Circuits

$\longrightarrow$ Down Guy

$\bullet\!\!-$ Head Guy

$\circ\!\!-\!\!\longrightarrow$ Sidewalk Guy

$\mathsf{C}\!\!-$ Service Weather Head

$\oplus$ Lightning Rod

—L— Lightning Protection System Conductor

Residential Signaling System Outlets

$\boxed{\bullet}$ Push Botton

$\boxed{}$ Buzzer

$\triangleleft$ Bell

Bell and Buzzer Combination

$-\!\diamondsuit$ Annunciator

Outside Telephone

$\triangleleft$ Interconnecting Telephone

Telephone Switchboard

$\boxed{\text{BT}}$ Bell Ringing Transformer

Residential Signaling System Outlets (Cont).

[D]	Electric Door Opener
[M]	Maid's Signal Plug
[R]	Radio Antenna Outlet
[CH]	Chime
[TV]	Television Antenna Outlet
(T)	Thermostat

Underground Electrical Distribution or Lighting System

[M]	Manhole
[H]	Handhole
[TM]	Transformer – Manhole or Vault
[TP]	Transformer Pad
– – –	Underground Direct Burial Cable
	Underground Duct Line
	Street Light Standard Fed from Underground Circuit

Panel Circuits & Miscellaneous

– – – –	Conduit Concealed in Floor or Walls
– – – – –	Wiring Exposed
	Home Run to Panelboard – Number of Arrows Indicate Number of Circuits
	Home Run to Panelboard – Two-Wire Circuit
–///–	Home Run to Panelboard – Number of Slashes Indicate Number of Wires (When more than Two)
L5-L1,3,5	Home Run to Panelboard – 'LS' Indicates Panel Designation; LI, 3, 5, Indicates Circuit Breaker No.

—C—	Clock Circuit, Conduit and Wire
—E—	Emergency Conduit and Wiring
—T—	Telephone Conduit and Wiring
—	Feeders
—o	Conduit Turned Up
—●	Conduit Turned Down
(G)	Generator
(M)	Motor
(5)	Motor – Numeral Indicates Horsepower
(I)	Instrument (Specify)
[T]	Transformer
[8]	Remote Start-Stop Push Button Station
[8]	Remote Start-Stop Push Button Station w/Pilot Light
[HTR]	Electric Heater Wall Unit

Common Abbreviations on Drawings

EWC	Electric Water Cooler
EDH	Electric Duct Heater
AFF	Above Finished Floor
UH	Unit Heater
GFI	Ground Fault Interrupter
GFP	Ground Fault Protector
GFCB	Ground Fault Circuit Breaker
EC	Empty Conduit
WP	Weatherproof
VP	Vaporproof

HVAC Ductwork Symbols

Supply Duct

Return/Exhaust Duct

Duct-First Number is Side Shown — 10 x 20

Direction of Flow

Lined Ductwork

Inclined Drop in Direction of Air Flow — D

Inclined Rise in Direction of Air Flow — R

Canvas Connection

Access Door

Intake Louver & Screen

Exhaust Louver — 20 x 10-L ↑650 CPM

Splitter Damper

Round Elbow Turning Vanes

Automatic Damper

Fire Damper — FD

Volume Damper — VD

Smoke Damper — SD

24" Dia. CD 1250 CFM — Supply Outlet Ceiling Diffuser

20 x 10 CD 500 CFM — Supply Outlet Ceiling Diffuser

84 x 6-LD 375 CFM — Linear Diffuser

Round Elbow

Square Elbow

Square Elbow Turning Vanes

Double Duct Air System

OA — RA — F — PH — CC — FAN — HP — RH — HOT — MP — HP — CC — COLD — MP — LP

Mixing Boxes (VV or CV) or Induction Units

OA = Outside Air	CC = Cooling Coil	LP = Low Pressure Duct
RA = Return Air	RH = Reheat Coil	VV = Variable Volume
F = Filter	HP = High Pressure Duct	CV = Constant Volume
PH = Preheat Coil	MP = Medium Pressure Duct	

HVAC

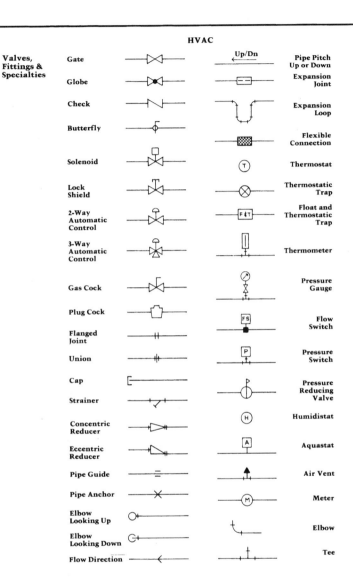

Valves, Fittings & Specialties		
Gate		Pipe Pitch Up or Down
Globe		Expansion Joint
Check		Expansion Loop
Butterfly		Flexible Connection
Solenoid		Thermostat
Lock Shield		Thermostatic Trap
2-Way Automatic Control		Float and Thermostatic Trap
3-Way Automatic Control		Thermometer
Gas Cock		Pressure Gauge
Plug Cock		Flow Switch
Flanged Joint		
Union		Pressure Switch
Cap		Pressure Reducing Valve
Strainer		
Concentric Reducer		Humidistat
Eccentric Reducer		Aquastat
Pipe Guide		Air Vent
Pipe Anchor		Meter
Elbow Looking Up		
Elbow Looking Down		Elbow
Flow Direction		Tee

HVAC

Hot Water Heating Supply	—— HWS ——	
Hot Water Heating Return	—— HWR ——	
Chilled Water Supply	—— CHWS ——	
Chilled Water Return	—— CHWR ——	
Drain Line	—— D ——	
City Water	—— CW ——	
Fuel Oil Supply	—— FOS ——	
Fuel Oil Return	—— FOR ——	
Fuel Oil Vent	—— FOV ——	

HVAC

—— FOG ——	Fuel Oil Gauge Line
—○— PD —○—	Pump Discharge
— — — — — —	Low Pressure Condensate Return
—— LPS ——	Low Pressure Steam
—— MPS ——	Medium Pressure Steam
—— HPS ——	High Pressure Steam
—— BD ——	Boiler Blow-Down

HVAC (Cont.)

Piping Symbols

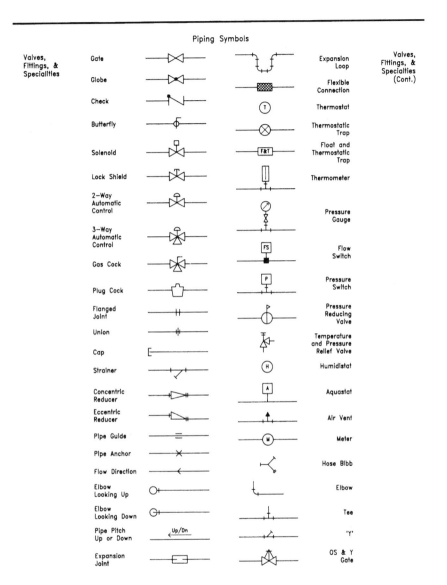

Gate	Expansion Loop
Globe	Flexible Connection
Check	Thermostat
Butterfly	Thermostatic Trap
Solenoid	Float and Thermostatic Trap
Lock Shield	Thermometer
2—Way Automatic Control	Pressure Gauge
3—Way Automatic Control	Flow Switch
Gas Cock	Pressure Switch
Plug Cock	Pressure Reducing Valve
Flanged Joint	Temperature and Pressure Relief Valve
Union	Humidistat
Cap	Aquastat
Strainer	Air Vent
Concentric Reducer	Meter
Eccentric Reducer	Hose Bibb
Pipe Guide	Elbow
Pipe Anchor	Tee
Flow Direction	'Y'
Elbow Looking Up	OS & Y Gate
Elbow Looking Down	
Pipe Pitch Up or Down	
Expansion Joint	

771

Piping Symbols (Cont.)

Valves,
Fittings, &
Specialties
(Cont.)

Valves,
Fittings, &
Specialties
(Cont.)

Shock Absorber	
House Trap	
'P' Trap	
Floor Drain	
Indirect Waste	IW
Sanitary Below Grade	S
Sanitary Above Grade	S
Storm Below Grade	ST
Storm Above Grade	ST
Vent	
Combination Waste & Vent	CWV
Acid Waste Below Grade	AW
Acid Waste Above Grade	AW
Acid Vent	AV

CW	Cold Water
HW	Hot Water
HWC	Hot Water Circulation
DWS	Drinking Water Supply
DWR	Drinking Water Return
G	Gas—Low Pressure
MG	Gas—Medium Pressure
HG	Gas—High Pressure
CA	Compressed Air
V	Vacuum
VC	Vacuum Cleaning
N	Nitrogen
N2O	Nitrous Oxide
O	Oxygen
LOX	Liquid Oxygen
LPG	Liquid Petroleum Gas

Fire Protection Piping Symbols

Fire Protection Water Supply	F	
Wet Standpipe	WSP	
Dry Standpipe	DSP	
Combination Standpipe	CSP	
Automatic Fire Sprinkler	SP	
Upright Fire Sprinkler Heads		
Pendent Fire Sprinkler Heads		

	Fire Hydrant
	Wall Fire Dept. Connection
	Sidewalk Fire Dept. Connection
FHR	Fire Hose Rack
FHC	Surface Mounted Fire Hose Cabinet
FHC	Recessed Fire Hose Cabinet

Plumbing Fixture Symbols

Baths	Corner		Single Basin	Kitchen Sinks
	Recessed		Twin Basin	
	Angle		Single Drainboard	
	Whirlpool		Double Drainboard	
	Institutional or Island			Dishwasher
Showers	Stall	DF	Floor or Wall	Drinking Fountains or Electric Water Coolers
	Corner Stall	DF	Recessed	
	Wall Gang	DF	Semi-Recessed	
Water Closets	Tank	LT	Single	Laundry Trays
	Flush Valve	L T	Double	
Bidet		SS	Wall	Service Sinks
Urinals	Wall	SS	Floor	
	Stall	WF	Circular	Wash Fountains
	Trough	WF	Semi-Circular	
Lavatories	Vanity	WH	Heater	Hot Water
	Wall	HWT	Tank	
	Counter	G	Gas	Separators
	Pedestal	O	Oil	

Material Indication Symbols

MATERIAL INDICATION SYMBOLS			
MATERIAL	PLAN	ELEVATION	SECTION
EARTH	NONE	NONE	
POROUS FILL	NONE	NONE	
CONCRETE			SAME AS PLAN
BRICK			SAME AS PLAN
CONCRETE BLOCK			SAME AS PLAN
STONE	CUT STONE / RUBBLE	CUT STONE / RUBBLE	SAME AS PLAN
STEEL	OR / OR	NONE	
FRAMING WOOD	WALL OR PARTITION	SIDING / FINISH WOOD	BLOCKING / FRAMING
PLYWOOD	INDICATED BY NOTE	INDICATED BY NOTE	
SHEET METAL FLASHING	INDICATED BY NOTE		SHAPED HEAVY LINE

MATERIAL INDICATION SYMBOLS			
MATERIAL	PLAN	ELEVATION	SECTION
BATT INSULATION		NONE	SAME AS PLAN
RIGID INSULATION		NONE	SAME AS PLAN
GLASS			SMALL SCALE / LARGE SCALE
GYPSUM WALLBOARD			SAME AS PLAN
ACOUSTICAL TILE		NONE	
CERAMIC WALL TILE			SAME AS PLAN
FLOOR TILE		NONE	

WINDOW AND DOOR SYMBOLS

TYPE	PLAN	ELEVATION
DOUBLE HUNG WINDOWS		
CASEMENT WINDOW		INDICATES WINDOW HINGE
SLIDER		
EXTERIOR DOOR		
INTERIOR DOOR		
BIFOLD DOOR		

ASC: Adhesive and Sealant Council

7979 Old Georgetown Road,
Suite 500
Bethesda, MD 20814
(301) 986–9700
www.ASCouncil.org

ADSC: The International Association of Foundation Drilling

9696 Skillman Street, Suite 280
Dallas, TX 75243
(214) 343–2091
www.adsc-iafd.com

ACHP: Advisory Council on Historic Preservation

1100 Pennsylvania Avenue, NW
Suite 809
Washington, DC 20004
(202) 606–8503
www.achp.gov

A & WMA: Air and Waste Management Association

One Gateway Center, Third Floor
Pittsburgh, PA 15222
(412) 232–3444
www.awma.org

ARI: Air Conditioning and Refrigeration Institute

1501 Wilson Boulevard, Sixth Floor
Arlington, VA 22209
(703) 524–8800
www.ari.org

ACCA: Air Conditioning Contractors of America

1712 New Hampshire Avenue, NW
Washington, DC 20009–2502
(202) 483–9370
www.acca.org

API: Alliance for the Polyurethanes Industry

1300 Wilson Boulevard, Suite 800
Arlington, VA 22209
(202) 947–5325
www.polyurethane.org

ASE: Alliance to Save Energy

1200 18th Street, NW, Suite 900
Washington, DC 20036
(202) 857–0666
www.ase.org

AA: Aluminum Association

900 19th Street, NW, Suite 300
Washington, DC 20006
(202) 862–5100
www.aluminum.org

AAMA: American Architectural Manufacturers Association

1827 Walden Office Square, Suite 104
Schaumburg, IL 60173–4628
(847) 303–5664
www.aamanet.org

AASHTO: American Association of State Hwy. & Trans. Officials

444 North Capitol Street, NW
Suite 249
Washington, DC 20001
(202) 624–5800
www.aashto.org

ACS: American Ceramics Society

P.O. Box 6136
Westerville, OH 43086–6136
(614) 890–4700
www.acers.org

ACI: American Concrete Institute International

P.O. Box 9094
Farmington Hills, MI 48333
(248) 848–3700
www.aci-int.org

ACPA: American Concrete Pavement Association

5420 Old Orchard Road, Suite A-100
Box W499
Skokie, IL 60077
(847) 966–2272
www.pavement.com

ACPA: American Concrete Pipe Association

222 W. Las Colinas Boulevard
Suite 641
Irving, TX 75039–5423
(972) 506–7216
www.concrete-pipe.org

ACEC: American Consulting Engineers Council

1015 15th Street, NW, #802
Washington, DC 20005
(202) 347–7474
www.acec.org

ACEEE: American Council for an Energy-Efficient Economy

1001 Connecticut Avenue, NW
Suite 801
Washington, DC 20036
(202) 429–8873
www.aceee.org

ADDA: American Design & Drafting Association

P.O. Box 11937
Columbia, SC 29211
(803) 771–0008
www.adda.org

AFSA: American Fire Sprinkler Association

12959 Jupiter Road, Suite 142
Dallas, TX 75238–3200
(214) 349–5965
www.sprinklernet.org

AHMA: American Hardware Manufacturers Association

801 North Plaza Drive
Schaumburg, IL 60173–4977
(847) 605–1025
www.ahma.org

AIA: The American Institute of Architects

1735 New York Avenue, NW
Washington, DC 20005
(202) 626–7460
www.aiaonline.com

AIBD: American Institute of Building Design

991 Post Road East
Westport, CT 06880
(800) 366–2423
www.aibd.org

AISC: American Institute of Steel Construction

One East Wacker Drive, Suite 3100
Chicago, IL 60601–2001
(312) 670–2400
www.aisc.org

AITC: American Institute of Timber Construction

7012 S. Revere Parkway, Suite 140
Englewood, CO 80112
(303) 792–9559
www.aitc-glulam.org

AISI: American Iron and Steel Institute

1101 17th Street, NW, Suite 1300
Washington, DC 20036
(202)452–7100
www.steel.org

ALSC: American Lumber Standards Committee

P.O. Box 210
Germantown, MD 20875
(301) 972–1700

ANSI: American National Standards Institute

11 West 42nd Street
New York, NY 10036
(212) 642–4900
www.ansi.org

APA: American Planning Association

1776 Massachusetts Avenue, NW
Washington, DC 20036
(202) 872–0611
www.planning.org

ARTBA: American Road and Transportation Builders Association

1010 Massachusetts Avenue, NW
Washington, DC 20001–5402
(202) 289–4434
www.artba-hq.org

ASNT: American Society for Nondestructive Testing

P.O. Box 28518, 1711 Arlingate Lane
Columbus, OH 43228–0518
(800) 222–2768
www.asnt.org

ASTM: American Society for Testing and Materials

100 Barr Harbor Drive
West Conshohocken, PA 19428–2959
(610) 832–9585
www.astm.org

ASCE: American Society of Civil Engineers

1015 15th Street, NW, Suite 600
Washington, DC 20005
(800) 548–2723
www.asce.org

ASHRAE: American Society of Heating Refrigerating and Air Engineers

1791 Tullie Circle, NE
Atlanta, GA 30329
(800) 527–4723
www.ashrae.org

ASID: American Society of Interior Designers

608 Massachusetts Avenue, NE
Washington, DC 20002–6006
(202) 546–3480
www.asid.org

ASME: American Society of Mechanical Engineers

Three Park Avenue
New York, NY 10016–5990
(800) 843–2763
www.asme.org

ASPE: American Society of Plumbing Engineers

3617 E. Thousand Oaks Boulevard,
Suite 210
Westlake Village, CA
(805) 495–4861
www.aspe.org

ASPE: American Society of Professional Estimators

11141 Georgia Avenue, Suite 412
Wheaton, MD 20902
(301) 929–8848
www.aspenational.com

ASSE: American Society of Sanitary Engineering

28901 Clemens Road Suite 100
Westlake, OH 44145
(440) 835–3040
www.asse-plumbing.org

ASA: American Subcontractors Association

1004 Duke Street
Alexandria, VA 22314
(703) 684–3450
www.asaonline.com

AWS: American Welding Society

550 NW LeJeune Road
Miami, FL 33126
Phone (800) 443–9353
www.aws.org

AWC: American Wood Council

1111 Nineteenth Street, NW
Suite 800
Washington, DC 20036
(202) 463–2766
www.awc.org

AWPI: American Wood Preservers Institute

2750 Prosperity Avenue, Suite 550
Fairfax, VA 22031–4312
(800) 356–2974
www.awpi.org

AHM: Appalachian Hardwood Manufacturers

P.O. Box 427
High Point, NC 27261
(336) 885–8315
www.appalachianwood.org

AWI: Architectural Woodwork Institute

1952 Isaac Newton Square West
Reston, VA 20190
(703) 733–0600
www.awinet.org

AIA: Asbestos Information Association

1745 Jefferson Davis Highway,
Suite 406
Arlington, VA 22202
(703) 412–1150

AI: Asphalt Institute

P.O. Box 14052, Research Park Drive
Lexington, KY 40512–4052
(606) 288–4960
www.asphaltinstitute.org

ARMA: Asphalt Roofing Manufacturers Association

4041 Power Mill Road, Suite 404
Calverton, MD 20705
(888) 256–2732
www.asphaltroofing.org

ABC: Associated Builders & Contractors

1300 N. Seventeenth Street, Suite 800
Rosslyn, VA 22209
(703) 812–2000
www.abc.org

AACE: Association for the Advancement of Cost Engineering

209 Prairie Avenue, Suite 100
Morgantown, WV 26501
(800) 858–2678
www.aacei.org

AFE: Association for Facilities Engineering

8180 Corporate Park Drive, Suite 305
Cincinnati, OH 45242
(888) 222–0155
www.afe.org

AEE: Association of Energy Engineers

4025 Pleasantdale Road, Suite 420
Atlanta, GA 30340
(770) 447–5083
www.aeecenter.org

APPA: The Association of Higher Education Facilities Officers

1643 Prince Street
Alexandria, VA 22314
(703) 684–1446
www.appa.org

AISE: Association of Iron & Steel Engineers

3 Gateway Center, Suite 1900
Pittsburgh, PA 15222–1004
(800) 966–6323
www.aise.org

AWCI: Association of the Wall & Ceiling Industry-International

803 West Broad Street, Suite 600
Falls Church, VA 22046
(703) 534–8300
www.awci.org

BIA: Brick Industry Association

11490 Commerce Park Drive
Reston, VA 20191
(703) 620–0010
www.bia.org

BOCA: Building Officials and Code Administrators International, Inc.

4051 W. Flossmoor Road
Country Club Hills, IL 60478
(800) 214–4321
www.bocai.org

BOMA: Building Owners and Managers Association International

1201 New York Avenue, NW
Suite 300
Washington, DC 20005
(202) 408–2662
www.boma.org

BSCAI: Building Service Contractors Association International

10201 Lee Highway, Suite 225
Fairfax, VA 22030
(800) 368–3414
www.bscai.org

CRA: California Redwood Association

405 Enfrente Drive, Suite 200
Novato, CA 94949
(888) 225–7339
www.calredwood.org

CSA: Canadian Standards Association

178 Rexdale Boulevard
Etobicoke (Toronto), Ontario M9W 1R3
(800) 463–6727
www.csa.ca

CSI: Cast Stone Institute

10 West Kimball Street
Winder, GA 30680
(770) 868–5909
www.caststone.org

CSSB: Cedar Shake & Shingle Bureau

P.O. Box 1178
Sumas, WA 98295
(604) 462–8961
www.cedarbureau.org

CISCA: Ceilings & Interior Systems Construction Association

1500 Lincoln Highway, Suite 202
St. Charles, IL 60174
(630) 584–1919
www.cisca.org

CIMA: Cellulose Insulation Manufacturers Association

136 South Keowee Street
Dayton, OH 45402
(937) 222–2462
www.cellulose.org

COT: Center for Office Technology

301 N. Fairfax Street, Suite 102
Alexandria, VA 22314
(703) 684–7760
www.cot.org

CRSI: Concrete Reinforcing Steel Institute

933 North Plum Grove Road
Schaumburg, IL 60173–4758
(847) 517–1200
www.crsi.org

CSDA: Concrete Sawing & Drilling Association

6089 Frantz Road, Suite 101
Dublin, OH 43017
(614) 798–2252
www.csda.org

CFMA: Construction Financial Management Association

29 Emmons Drive, Suite F-50
Princeton, NJ 08540
(609) 452–8000
www.cfma.org

CSC: Construction Specifications Canada

100 Lombard Street, Suite 200
Toronto, Ontario M5C 1M3
(800) 668–5684
www.csc-dcc.ca

CSI: Construction Specifications Institute

99 Canal Center Plaza, Suite 300
Alexandria, VA 22314
(800) 689–2900
www.csinet.org

DBIA: Design-Build Institute of America

1010 Massachusetts Avenue, NW
Suite 350
Washington, DC 20001
(202) 682–0110
www.dbia.org

DHI: Door and Hardware Institute

14150 Newbrook Drive, Suite 200
Chantilly, VA 20151
(703) 222–2010
www.dhi.org

APA: The Engineered Wood Association

P.O. Box 11700
Tacoma, WA 98411–0700
(253) 565–6600
www.apawood.org

EPA: Environmental Protection Agency

401 M Street, SW
Washington, DC 20460
(202) 260–2090
www.epa.gov

FPS: Forest Products Society

2801 Marshall Court
Madison, WI 53705–2295
(608) 231–1361
www.forestprod.org

FIA: Forging Industry Association

25 W. Prospect Avenue, Suite 300
Cleveland, OH 44115
(216) 781–6260
www.forging.org

GA: Gypsum Association

810 First Street, NE, #510
Washington DC, 20002
(202) 289–5440
www.gypsum.org

HPVA: Hardwood Plywood & Veneer Association

P.O. Box 2789
Reston, VA 20195
(703) 435–2900
www.hpva.org

IESNA: Illuminating Engineering Society of North America

120 Wall Street, 17th Floor
New York, NY 10005
(212) 248–5000
www.iesna.org

IFI: Industrial Fasteners Institute

1717 East Ninth Street, Suite 1105
Cleveland, OH 44114–2879
(216) 241–1482
www.industrial-fasteners.org

IEEE: Institute of Electrical & Electronics Engineers

3 Park Avenue, 17th Floor
New York, NY 10016–5997
(800) 678–4333
www.ieee.org

INCE: Institute of Noise Control Engineering

P.O. Box 3206 Arlington Branch
Poughkeepsie, NY 12603
(914) 462–4006
www.ince.org

ITE: Institute of Transportation Engineers

525 School Street, SW, Suite 410
Washington, DC 20024
(202) 554–8050
www.ite.org

ICEA: Insulated Cable Engineers Association

P.O. Box 440
South Yarmouth, MA 02664
(508) 394–4424
www.icea.net

ISDI: Insulated Steel Door Institute

30200 Detroit Road
Cleveland, OH 44145–1967
(440) 899–0010
www.isdi.org

ICAA: Insulation Contractors Association of America

1321 Duke Street, Suite 303
Alexandria, VA 22314
(703) 739–0356
www.insulate.org

IAPMO: International Association of Plumbing and Mechanical Officials

20001 East Walnut Drive South
Walnut, CA 91789
(909) 595–8449
www.iapmo.org

ICPA: International Cast Polymer Association

8201 Greensboro Drive, Suite 300
McLean, VA 22102
(800) 414–4272
www.icpa-hq.org

CABO: International Code Council

5203 Leesburg Pike, Suite 708
Falls Church, VA 22041
(703) 931–4533
www.intlcode.org

ICBO: International Conference of Building Officials

5360 Workman Mill Road
Whittier, CA 90601–2298
(800) 423–6587
www.icbo.org

IFMA: International Facility Management Association

One E. Greenway Plaza, Suite 1100
Houston, TX 77046–0194
(713) 623–4362
www.ifma.org

IIDA: International Interior Design Association

341 Merchandise Mart
Chicago, IL 60654
(888) 799–4432
www.iida.org

IMI: International Masonry Institute

823 Fifteenth Street, NW, Suite 1000
Washington, DC 20005
(800) 464–0988
www.imiweb.org

ISO: International Organization for Standardization

1, Rue de Varembe
Case Postale 56
CH–1211 Geneva 20, Switzerland
www.iso.ch

KCMA: Kitchen Cabinet Manufacturers Association

1899 Preston White Drive
Reston, VA 20191–5435
(703) 264–1690
www.kcma.org

MFMA: Maple Flooring Manufacturers Association

60 Revere Drive, Suite 500
Northbrook, IL 60062
(847) 480–9138
www.maplefloor.org

MIA: Marble Institute of America

30 Eden Alley, Suite 301
Columbus, OH 43215
(614) 228–6194
www.marble-institute.com

TMS: The Masonry Society

3970 Broadway, Suite 201–D
Boulder, CO 80304–1135
(303) 939–9700
www.masonrysociety.org

MCAA: Mechanical Contractors Association of America

1385 Piccard Drive
Rockville, MD 20850
(800) 556–3653
www.mcaa.org

NAPA: National Asphalt Pavement Association

5100 Forbes Boulevard
Lanham, MD 20706–4413
(888) 468–6499
www.hotmix.org

NAAMM: National Association of Architectural Metal Manufacturers

8 South Michigan Avenue, Suite 1000
Chicago, IL 60603
(312) 332–0405
www.naamm.org

NADC: National Association of Demolition Contractors

16 N. Franklin Street, Suite 200B
Doylestown, PA 18901–3536
(800) 541–2412
www.demolitionassn.com

NAHB: National Association of Home Builders

1201 15th Street, NW
Washington, DC 20005
(800) 368–5242
www.nahb.com

NAHRO: National Association of Housing & Redevelopment Officials

630 Eye Street, NW
Washington, DC 20001
(202) 289–3500
www.nahro.org

PHCC: National Association of Plumbing Heating Cooling Contractors

180 S. Washington Street
P.O. Box 6808
Falls Church, VA 22040
(800) 533–7694
www.naphcc.org

NAWIC: National Association of Women in Construction

327 S. Adams Street
Fort Worth, TX, 76104
(800) 552–3506
www.nawic.org

NBGQA: National Building Granite Quarries Association

1220 L. Street, NW, Suite 100–167
Washington, DC 20005
(800) 557-2848
www.nbgqa.com

NCPI: National Clay Pipe Institute

P.O. Box 759
Lake Geneva, WI 53147
(414) 248-9094
www.ncpi.org

NCMA: National Concrete Masonry Association

2302 Horse Pen Road
Herndon, VA 20171–3499
(703) 713-1900
www.ncma.org

NECA: National Electrical Contractors Association

Three Bethesda Metro Center
Suite 1100
Bethesda, MD 20814
(301) 657-3110
www.necanet.org

NEMA: National Electrical Manufacturers Association

1300 North 17th Street, Suite 1847
Rosslyn, VA 22209
(703) 841-3200
www.nema.org

NFRC: National Fenestration Rating Council

1300 Spring Street, Suite 500
Silver Spring, MD 20910
(301) 589-6372
www.nfrc.org

NFPA: National Fire Protection Association

11 Tracy Drive
Avon, MA 02322–1145
(800) 344-3555
www.nfpa.org

NFSA: National Fire Sprinkler Association

P.O. Box 1000, 40 Jon Barrett Road
Patterson, NY 12563
(914) 878-4200
www.nfsa.org

NGA: National Glass Association

8200 Greensboro Drive
McLean, VA 22102
(703) 442-4890
www.glass.org

NHLA: National Hardwood Lumber Association

P.O. Box 34518
Memphis, TN 38184–0518
(800) 933-0318
www.natlhardwood.org

NIBS: National Institute of Building Sciences

1090 Vermont Avenue, NW, Suite 700
Washington, DC 20005–4905
(202) 289-7800
www.nibs.org

NIST: National Institute of Standards and Technology

100 Bureau Drive
Gaithersburg, MD 20899–0001
(301) 975-3058
www.nist.gov

NIA: National Insulation Association

99 Canal Center Plaza, Suite 222
Alexandria, VA 22314
(703) 683-6422
www.insulation.org

NKBA: National Kitchen and Bath Association

687 Willow Grove Street
Hackettstown, NJ 07840–9988
(908) 852-1695
www.nkba.org

NOFMA: National Oak Flooring Manufacturers Association

P.O. Box 3009
Memphis, TN 38173–0009
(901) 526–5016
www.nofma.org

NPCA: National Paint & Coatings Association

1500 Rhode Island Avenue, NW
Washington, DC 20005
(202) 462–6272
www.paint.org

NPCA: National Precast Concrete Association

10333 North Meridian Street
Suite 272
Indianapolis, IN 46290
(800) 366–7731
www.precast.org

NRMCA: National Ready Mixed Concrete Association

900 Spring Street
Silver Spring, MD 20910
(888) 846–7622
www.nrmca.org

NRCA: National Roofing Contractors Association

10255 W. Higgins Road, Suite 600
Rosemont, IL 60018
(800) 323–9545
www.nrca.net

NSC: National Safety Council

1121 Spring Lake Drive
Itasca, IL 60143–3201
(800) 621–7615
www.nsc.org

NSDJA: National Sash & Door Jobbers Association

10047 Robert Trent Parkway
New Port Richey, FL 34655–4649
(800) 786–7274
www.nsdja.com

NSPE: National Society of Professional Engineers

1420 King Street
Alexandria, VA 22314–2794
(888) 285–6773
www.nspe.org

NSA: National Stone Association

1415 Elliot Place, NW
Washington, DC 20007
(800) 342–1415
www.aggregates.org

NTMA: National Terrazzo & Mosaic Association

110 East Market Street, Suite 200A
Leesburg, VA 20176
(800) 323–9736
www.ntma.com

NTHP: National Trust for Historic Preservation

1785 Massachusetts Ave, NW
Washington, DC 20036
(800) 944–6847
www.nthp.org

WDMA: National Wood Window and Door Association

1400 East Touhy Avenue, Suite 470
Des Plaines, IL 60018
(847) 299–5200
www.nwwda.org

NAIMA: North American Insulation Manufacturers Association

44 Canal Center Plaza, Suite 310
Alexandria, VA 22314
(703) 684–0084
www.naima.org

NELMA: Northeastern Lumber Manufacturers Association

P.O. Box 87A, 272 Tuttle Road
Cumberland Center, ME 04021
(207) 829–6901
www.nelma.org

PLIB: Pacific Lumber Inspection Bureau

P.O. Box 7235
Bellevue, WA 98008–1235
(425) 746–6542

PPFA: Plastic Pipe & Fittings Association

800 Roosevelt Road, Building C
Suite 20
Glen Ellyn, IL 60137–5833
(630) 858–6540

PDI: Plumbing and Drainage Institute

45 Bristol Drive
South Easton, MA 02375
(800) 589–8956
www.pdionline.org

PHCC: Plumbing Heating Cooling Contractors

180 S. Washington Street
Falls Church, VA 22040
(800) 533–7694
www.naphcc.org

PIMA: Polyisocyanurate Insulation Manufacturers Association

1331 F Street, NW, Suite 975
Washington, DC 20004
(202) 628–6558
www.pima.org

PCA: Portland Cement Association

5420 Old Orchard Road
Skokie, IL 60077
(847) 966–6200
www.portcement.org

PTI: Post Tensioning Institute

1717 W. Northern Avenue, Suite 114
Phoenix, AZ 85021
(602) 870–7540
www.post-tensioning.org

PCI: Precast/Prestressed Concrete Institute

175 W. Jackson Boulevard, Suite 1859
Chicago, IL 60604
(312) 786–0300
www.pci.org

PCEA: Professional Construction Estimators Association of America

P.O. Box 11626,
Charlotte, NC 28220–1626
(704) 522–6376
www.pcea.org

PWC: Professional Women in Construction

342 Madison Avenue, Suite 451
New York, NY 10173
(212) 687–0610

PMA: Property Management Association of America

7900 Wisconsin Avenue, Suite 204
Bethesda, MD 20814
(301) 657–9200
www.pma-dc.org

RPA: Radiant Panel Association

P.O. Box 717
Loveland, CO 80539–0717
(800) 660–7187
www.rpa-info.com

RIS: The Redwood Inspection Service

405 Enfrente Drive, Suite 200
Novato, CA 94949
(888) 225–7339
www.calredwood.org

RFCI: Resilient Floor Covering Institute

966 Hungerford Drive, Suite 12-B
Rockville, MD 20850
(301) 340–8580

RIEI: Roofing Industry Educational Institute

14 Inverness Drive East, H-110
Englewood, CO 80112–5608
(303) 790–7200
www.riei.org

RMA: Rubber Manufacturers Association

1400 K Street, NW
Washington, DC 20005
(800) 220–7622
www.rma.org

SWRI: Sealant, Waterproofing & Restoration Institute

3101 Broadway, Suite 585
Kansas City, MO 64111
(816) 472–7974
www.swrionline.org

SMACNA: Sheet Metal & Air Conditioning Contractors National Association

4201 Lafayette Center Drive
Chantilly, VA 20151–1209
(703) 803–2980
www.smacna.org

SPRI: Single Ply Roofing Institute

200 Reservoir Street, Suite 309A
Needham, MA 02494
(781) 444–0242
www.spri.org

SFPE: Society of Fire Protection Engineers

7315 Wisconsin Avenue, Suite 1225W
Bethesda, MD 20814
(301) 718–2910
www.sfpe.org

SPE: Society of Plastics Engineers

P.O. Box 403
Brookfield, CT 06804–0403
(203) 775–0471
www.4spe.org

SPI: Society of The Plastics Industry

1801 K Street, NW, Suite 600K
Washington, DC 20006
(202) 974–5200
www.plasticsindustry.org

SWE: Society of Women Engineers

120 Wall Street, Eleventh Floor
New York, NY 10005–3902
(212) 509–9577
www.swe.org

SSSA: Soil Science Society of America

677 South Segoe Road
Madison, WI 53711
(608) 273–8080
www.soils.org

SEIA: Solar Energy Industries Association

1111 North 19th Street, Suite 260
Arlington, VA 22209
(202) 383–2600
www.seia.org

SBCCI: Southern Building Code Congress International

900 Montclair Road
Birmingham, AL 35213–1206
(800) 877–2224
www.sbcci.org

SCMA: Southern Cypress Manufacturers Association

400 Penn Center Boulevard, Suite 530
Pittsburgh, PA 15235
(412) 829–0770

SFPA: Southern Forest Products Association

P.O. Box 641700
Kenner, LA 70064–1700
(504) 443–4464
www.southernpine.com

SPIB: Southern Pine Inspection Bureau

4709 Scenic Highway
Pensacola, FL 32504–9094
(850) 434–2611
www.spib.org

SSINA: Specialty Steel Industry of North America

3050 K Street, NW
Washington, DC 20007
(800) 982–0355
www.ssina.com

SES: Standards Engineering Society

13340 SW 96th Avenue
Miami, FL 33176
(305) 971–4798
www.ses-standards.org

SDI: Steel Deck Institute

P.O. Box 25
Fox River Grove, IL 60021–0025
(847) 462–1930
www.sdi.org

SJI: Steel Joist Institute

3127 10th Avenue North Extension
Myrtle Beach, SC 29577–6760
(843) 626–1995
www.steeljoist.org

SPFA: Steel Plate Fabricators Association

11315 Reed Hartman Highway
Suite 104
Cincinnati, OH 45241
(513) 469–0500
www.spfa.org

SWI: Steel Window Institute

1300 Sumner Avenue
Cleveland, OH 44115–2851
(216) 241–7333
www.steelwindows.com

SBA: Systems Builders Association

28 Lowry Drive, P.O. Box 117
West Milton, OH 45383–0117
(800) 866–6722
www.systemsbuilders.org

TCAA: The Tile Contractors Association of America

11501 Georgia Avenue, Suite 203
Wheaton, MD 20902
(800) 655–8453
www.tcaainc.org

TCA: Tile Council of America

100 Clemson Research Boulevard
Anderson, SC 29625
(864) 646–8453
www.tileusa.com

UL: Underwriters Laboratories

333 Pfingsten Road
Northbrook, IL 60062–2096
(847) 272–8800
www.ul.com

OSHA: U.S. Department of Labor (OSHA)

Office of Public Affairs, Room N3647
200 Constitution Avenue
Washington, DC 20210
(202) 219–8148
www.osha.gov

VMAA: Valve Manufacturers Association of America

1050 17th Street, NW, Suite 280
Washington, DC 20036–5503
(202) 331–8105
www.vma.org

VSI: Vinyl Siding Institute

1801 K Street NW, Suite 600K
Washington, DC 20006
(202) 974–5200
www.vinylsiding.org

WRC: Welding Research Council

3 Park Avenue, 27th Floor
New York, NY 10016–5902
(212) 591–7956
www.forengineers.org/wrc

WCLIB: West Coast Lumber Inspection Bureau

P.O. Box 23145
Portland, OR 97281–3145
(503) 639–0651
www.wclib.org

WRCLA: Western Red Cedar Lumber Association

1200–555 Burrard Street
Vancouver, BC V7X 1S7
(604) 684–0266
www.wrcla.org

WWPA: Western Wood Products Association

522 SW Fifth Avenue, Suite 500
Portland, OR 97204–2122
(503) 224–3930
www.wwpa.org

WAI: Wire Association International

1570 Boston Post Road, P.O. Box 578
Guilford, CT 06437–0578
(203) 453–2777
www.wirenet.org